OXFORD HISTORY OF
General Editor

The history of eastern European is dominated by the story of the rise of the Russian empire, yet Russia only emerged as a major power after 1700. For 300 years the greatest power in Eastern Europe was the union between the kingdom of Poland and the grand duchy of Lithuania, one of the longest-lasting political unions in European history. Yet because it ended in the late-eighteenth century in what are misleadingly termed the Partitions of Poland, it barely features in standard accounts of European history.

The Making of the Polish-Lithuanian Union 1385–1569 tells the story of the formation of a consensual, decentralised, multinational, and religiously plural state built from below as much as above, that was founded by peaceful negotiation, not war and conquest. From its inception in 1385–6, a vision of political union was developed that proved attractive to Poles, Lithuanians, Ruthenians, and Germans, a union which was extended to include Prussia in the 1450s and Livonia in the 1560s. Despite the often bitter disagreements over the nature of the union, these were nevertheless overcome by a republican vision of a union of peoples in one political community of citizens under an elected monarch. Robert Frost challenges interpretations of the union informed by the idea that the emergence of the sovereign nation state represents the essence of political modernity, and presents the Polish-Lithuanian union as a case study of a composite state.

The modern history of Poland, Lithuania, Ukraine, and Belarus cannot be understood without an understanding of the legacy of the Polish-Lithuanian union. This volume, now issued in a paperback edition with minor revisions and corrections, is the first detailed study of the making of that union ever published in English.

Robert Frost was educated at the universities of St Andrews, Cracow, and London. After teaching for eighteen years at King's College London, he moved in 2004 to the University of Aberdeen, where he currently holds the Burnett Fletcher Chair in History. He is interested in the history of eastern and northern Europe from the fourteenth to the nineteenth centuries. His principal research interests are in the history of Poland-Lithuania, and in the history of warfare in the early modern period.

'Robert Frost has written an outstanding book, as good as it is big—a major contribution to the history of the polity linked by the hyphen in its title, and to the history of early modern Europe. The book is a major benchmark in Frost's distinguished output addressing specific aspects of the Polish-Lithuanian Commonwealth's history, situated in the broad context of its contemporary Europe . . . Robert Frost's great achievement is to situate the Commonwealth of Lithuania and Poland at the highest level of thematic inquiry, analysis, and expository prose, fully in the company of the best work concerning comparable questions elsewhere in Europe.'

Piotr Gorecki, *The Medieval Review*

'[Frost] gives us the opportunity to re-think many concepts of the union and its definition, and to overcome the narrow image created by national historiographies, reviving discussions of the union's assessment at a new level . . . [it] arouses creative scientific thought and discussion, and provides a great impulse to search for new sources and continue research on the topic of the union.'

Jurate Kiaupiene, *Lithuanian Historical Studies*

'Such meticulous attention to the historiography of his subject is one of the great merits of Frost's work, in which he is nothing if not colorful and unflinching in his judgment of the often conflicting, confused, or biased interpretations of earlier historians . . . By limiting his attention in this first volume to just the years from Krevo to Lublin, Frost manages a far more focused, nuanced, and richly detailed treatment of political currents in this crucial formative period than Davies and earlier historians have been able to offer . . . Professor Frost's work is poised to be the definitive treatment of Poland-Lithuania within the temporal and topical limitations that he has set for himself.'

Jay Atkinson, *The Sixteenth Century Journal*

The Oxford History of Poland-Lithuania

Volume I: The Making of the Polish-Lithuanian Union, 1385–1569

ROBERT FROST

OXFORD
UNIVERSITY PRESS

Great Clarendon Street, Oxford, OX2 6DP,
United Kingdom

Oxford University Press is a department of the University of Oxford.
It furthers the University's objective of excellence in research, scholarship,
and education by publishing worldwide. Oxford is a registered trade mark of
Oxford University Press in the UK and in certain other countries

© Robert Frost 2015

The moral rights of the author have been asserted

First published 2015
First published in paperback 2018

All rights reserved. No part of this publication may be reproduced, stored in
a retrieval system, or transmitted, in any form or by any means, without the
prior permission in writing of Oxford University Press, or as expressly permitted
by law, by licence or under terms agreed with the appropriate reprographics
rights organization. Enquiries concerning reproduction outside the scope of the
above should be sent to the Rights Department, Oxford University Press, at the
address above

You must not circulate this work in any other form
and you must impose this same condition on any acquirer

Published in the United States of America by Oxford University Press
198 Madison Avenue, New York, NY 10016, United States of America

British Library Cataloguing in Publication Data
Data available

Library of Congress Cataloging in Publication Data
Data available

ISBN 978–0–19–820869–3 (Hbk.)
ISBN 978–0–19–880020–0 (Pbk.)

Links to third party websites are provided by Oxford in good faith and
for information only. Oxford disclaims any responsibility for the materials
contained in any third party website referenced in this work.

In Memoriam
Oskar Halecki (1891–1973)
Adolfas Šapoka (1906–1961)
Mykhailo Hrushevsky (1866–1934)
Matvei K. Liubavskii (1860–1936)

Preface

This is not the history of a state, or a nation, the usual concepts that frame the writing of political history, but of a political relationship: a political union that grew and changed over time, and expanded to include more peoples and cultures than the Poles and Lithuanians who established it in its original form in 1386. Historians often write of state- and nation-building; they rarely write of the formation of unions, and if they do, they usually do so from the point of view of one or other of the states or nations that form the union. After the process usually—and erroneously—referred to as the 'partitions of Poland' removed Poland-Lithuania from the map between 1772 and 1795, the complex historical development of the lands that once formed Poland-Lithuania has resulted for much of the time since 1795 in the union being presented in a negative light: it is seen as a failure, and above all an episode in Polish history, in which the Poles extended political control over the territories of what now constitute the modern states of Lithuania, Belarus, Ukraine, Latvia, and parts of what became Estonia, Russia, and (until 1945) Germany. This approach has led many non-Polish historians to portray the Polish-Lithuanian union as an exercise in Polish imperialism that stunted their own national development, while there is a strong tradition in Polish historiography, dating back to Michał Bobrzyński and beyond, that blames the union for the partitions. Yet the union was no empire. In its origin it was a classic late-medieval composite state, in which the various realms that came together under the rule of the Jagiellonian dynasty between 1386 and 1569 gradually formed a strong political union through negotiation and consent, despite some spectacular disagreements as to its nature and form. Its disappearance in 1795, just as revolutionaries in France were proclaiming the doctrine of the sovereign nation, one and indivisible, means that the history of east central Europe has been written largely through the eyes of the partitioning powers and their successors—above all Russia and Germany—or by historians of the individual nation states that fought for the independence that was only secured after 1918 or 1990. Yet the largely negative assessments of the union fail to explain why it came to be, and why it lasted so long. This book attempts to answer the first of those questions.

When, more years ago than I care to admit, Robert Evans invited me on behalf of Oxford University Press to write a history of the Polish-Lithuanian commonwealth from 1569 until 1795, I had originally intended the story of the making of this union between 1386 and 1569 to be a brief introductory section. I soon realized, however, that it is impossible to understand the political dynamics of such a complex political construct as the Polish-Lithuanian commonwealth without a clear grasp of how it was formed. There is no detailed study in English of the making of this union; indeed there is very little on it in English at all, since the Anglo-Saxon scholarly world has for far too long been largely content with the versions of the history of eastern Europe written by Russianists and Germanists.

With this in mind, and aware that there has been no comprehensive re-evaluation of the making of the union since Oskar Halecki's classic two-volume *Dzieje unii jagiellońskiej*, published in 1919, I suggested to OUP that I might publish a two-volume study of the union from its formation in 1386 to its dissolution, against the will of its citizens, in 1795. This book is the result. It takes the story from the origins of the union in the late fourteenth century up to its consummation at Lublin in 1569. Halecki's great work was written as the partitioning powers imploded in the maelstrom of the First World War, and published as Poles and Lithuanians began a war over Vilnius, the former capital of the grand duchy of Lithuania. While it is sympathetic to the Lithuanian and Ruthenian inhabitants of the former grand duchy, and is frequently critical of Polish policy towards them, it is written from a Polish perspective. This book is an attempt to provide a history of the making of the union that eschews any national perspective, and which suggests that the non-Polish peoples within the union state played as great a part in its formation as the Poles. It therefore tells the story from multiple viewpoints in order to explain the success of the union, which remains, despite its inglorious end, one of the longest-lasting political unions in European history, whose cultural legacy is evident to this day. It is the first part of a two-volume attempt to study the union on its own terms, and not to judge it for failing to be what it did not try to be. Above all, it seeks to restore the history of the largest state in late medieval and early modern Europe to the general story of European development after years of historiographical neglect outside eastern Europe.

This first volume is not and cannot be an *histoire totale* of the vast geographical area that constituted the union state. It is conceived as a political history that tells the story of the union's making; it is therefore largely a *histoire événementielle*, and only deals with economic, social, and cultural factors of direct relevance to the making of the union, such as the political role played by religion, and the development of the rural economy, which was of crucial importance to the nobility that formed—although never exclusively—the union's citizen body. There will be a fuller, thematic treatment of important issues such as religion, the Renaissance and the influence of humanism, and the union's unique urban world in volume two.

The book is dedicated to the memory of four great scholars of the Polish-Lithuanian union: a Pole, a Lithuanian, a Ukrainian, and a Russian. They had very different attitudes towards it, and one of them—Mykhailo Hrushevsky—loathed it and all it stood for. All of them lived through the traumas of the twentieth century in eastern Europe, and suffered for their fearless and uncompromising attitude towards their scholarship. Two of them—Oskar Halecki and Adolfas Šapoka—ended their lives in exile, without access to the sources that nourished and sustained their scholarship; two of them—Matvei Liubavskii and Mykhailo Hrushevsky—ended theirs in Soviet detention, as their works were denigrated or suppressed by the communist regime. None of them ever abandoned their integrity as historians: this work owes much to all of them. Its shortcomings are entirely the responsibility of its author, who has had the good fortune to live in an age when the difficulties they faced have largely evaporated, and the peoples of the successor states of the Polish-Lithuanian union have mostly—although alas not yet entirely—had the freedom to explore its history on their own terms. I hope that they will accept this view from an outsider in the spirit in which it was written.

Robert Frost

Warsaw, January 2014

Acknowledgements

I owe a great deal to the many people who have helped me in the writing of this book, and to the institutions which have provided support. My greatest debt is to the British Academy and the Wolfson Foundation, who appointed me to a three-year research professorship in 2009; without the precious time that this afforded me, I could neither have conceived the book, nor completed it. I owe much to everyone at Oxford University Press, who have shown great belief in the project: to Professor Robert Evans, who invited me to undertake it, who has given me unstinting support and advice, and who read the text, making many invaluable suggestions that have improved it considerably; to Christopher Wheeler, Stephanie Ireland, and Cathryn Steele, who waited patiently for me to produce it, and were extremely understanding and helpful when I asked whether they would allow me to write a work double the length that they had expected; and to Emily Brand, who proved a most helpful and constructive editor. I would also like to thank my copy editor, Miranda Bethell, and my proofreader, Ela Kotkowska, whose sharp eyes saved me from many infelicities. I owe a considerable debt to my employers during the work's long gestation: King's College London and the University of Aberdeen, both of which granted me research leave and funding. I am grateful to the Archiwum i Biblioteka Krakowskiej Kapituły Katedralnej, the Archiwum Główne Akt Dawnych in Warsaw, the Zamek Królewski in Warsaw, the Muzeum Historii Polskiej in Warsaw, the Zamek Królewski na Wawelu in Cracow, and the Muzeum Lubelskie in Lublin for permission to publish illustrations of materials in their collections.

Many individuals provided inspiration, help, support, and advice. Geoffrey Parker first introduced me to the problems of composite states in St Andrews three decades ago, while Norman Davies guided my first steps in Polish history; I have learnt much from both of them. Hamish Scott has proven an invaluable source of wisdom over the years; his ability tactfully to save an author from the consequences of his own folly is unrivalled. I am particularly grateful to Igor Kąkolewski, who helped enormously with regard to the illustrations, and to the historians and librarians of the Nicholas Copernicus University in Toruń, who have supported and helped me since my first visit in 1992, in particular Krzysztof Mikulski, Jarosław Poraziński, Janusz Małłek, Roman Czaja, Tomasz Kempa, Adam Szweda, the late Jacek Staszewski, the late Stefan Czaja, and Urszula Zahorska. Chester Dunning read the first draft with characteristic care and thoughtfulness, and made numerous perceptive suggestions. I owe much to Andrei Ianushkevich, who invited me to Minsk, and took me to Kreva, where it all began, and to Olenka Pevny, who was a splendid guide to the churches of Kyiv and Chernihiv, who read parts of the typescript, and whose scepticism about the value of unions was always bracing. Marek Ferenc kindly sent me his splendid biography of Mikołaj Radziwiłł Rudy long after it had disappeared from the shops. I have benefited greatly from the practical help of, and discussions with, many other scholars, including Hans-Jürgen Bömelburg, Michael Brown, Paul Bushkovitch, Jola Choińska-Mika, Jim Collins, Iaroslav Fedoruk, David Frick, Natalya Iakovenko, Andrzej Kamiński, Jūrate Kiaupienė, Colin Kidd, Val Kivelson, Paul Knoll, Krzysztof Link-Lenczowski; Henryk Litwin, Henryk Lulewicz, Allan Macinnes, Karol Mazur, Michael Müller, Natalia Nowakowska, Micheál Ó Siochrú, Rimvydas Petrauskas, Serhii Plokhy, Andrzej Rachuba, Martyn Rady, John Robertson, Stephen Rowell, Henadz Sahanovich, Mindaugas Šapoka, Alex Storożyński, Frank Sysyn, Artūras Vasiliauskas, Michelle Viise, Thomas Wünsch, and Andrzej Zakrzewski. My greatest personal debt, as ever, is to my wife, Karin Friedrich, who taught me the importance of Royal Prussia, and much else besides. This book could not have been written without her. The complete indifference of our children, Tommy and Anna, to the whole project has helped me keep it in perspective.

Contents

List of Maps and Tables	xv
List of Illustrations	xvi
List of Abbreviations	xvii
A Note on Personal and Place Names	xx
A Note on Currency	xxii
A Note on the Genealogies	xxiii

I. TOWARDS UNION

1. Krėva, Крэва, Krewo	3
2. Poland	5
3. Lithuania	18
4. On Unions	36
5. The Krewo Act	47

II. ESTABLISHING THE UNION

6. Structures	61
7. Baptism	71
8. Cousins	74
9. Vilnius-Radom	91
10. Fruits of Union	99
11. Horodło	109
12. Defending the Union	122

III. CRISIS, 1422–47

13. The Coronation Tempest	131
14. Švitrigaila	151
15. Rus′	158
16. After Jagiełło	177
17. Resolution	182

IV. CONSOLIDATION AND CHANGE

18. Defining the Union	199
19. Prussia	209
20. The Thirteen Years War	222
21. Nieszawa	231
22. Peasants	242

V. DYNASTY AND CITIZENSHIP

23. New Monarchs	265
24. Jagiellonian Europe	277
25. From Sejmiks to Sejm	286
26. *Shliakhta*	291
27. Litva	309

VI. REFORM

28. Mielnik	327
29. *Nihil Novi*	344
30. Parliamentary Government	354
31. Mazovia	374
32. Prussia and the Union	381

VII. UNION ACCOMPLISHED

33. *Æque Principaliter*	405
34. Transformation	424
35. Execution Proposed	433
36. Execution Achieved	446
37. Failure	456
38. Interlude	469
39. Lublin	477

Bibliography	495
Glossary	524
Gazetteer	527
Index	531

List of Maps and Tables

MAPS

1. The Kingdom of Poland in the fourteenth century	9
2. The Grand Duchy of Lithuania in 1385	19
3. The Polish-Lithuanian Union in the early fifteenth century	62
4. The Prussian lands, 1454–1525	229
5. The Polish-Lithuanian Union in the early sixteenth century	284
6. The Commonwealth of Poland-Lithuania in 1569	490

TABLE

1. The Lithuanian reforms of 1565–6	474

List of Illustrations

1. Genealogy 1. The Gediminids	22
2. Genealogy 2. The descendants of Algirdas	23
3. Genealogy 3. The Kęstutids	32
4. The Krewo Act (1385)	48
5. The Union of Horodło (1413)	112
6. Genealogy 4. The Piasts, the Angevins, and the Jagiellons	133
7. Portrait of Władysław II Jagiełło. Fresco from the Chapel of the Holy Trinity, Lublin	161
8. Portrait of Władysław II Jagiełło on horseback. Fresco from the Chapel of the Holy Trinity, Lublin	162
9. Genealogy 5. The decendants of Casimir IV	279
10. View of Vilnius in the sixteenth century	310
11. View of Hrodna in the sixteenth century	328
12. The estates of the Sejm. Frontispiece, *Statute of Jan Łaski*, 1506	362
13. Arms of the Kingdom of Poland and the Grand Duchy of Lithuania, from the tapestries of King Sigismund August	437
14. View of Cracow from the north-west by Abraham Hogenberg, *c.*1603–5	478
15. View of Lublin in the sixteenth century	478
16. The Union of Lublin (1569)	493

List of Abbreviations

AA	*Akta Aleksandra króla polskiego, wielkiego księcia litewskiego itd. (1501–1506)*, ed. Fryderyk Papée (Cracow, 1927)
AF	*Altpreussische Forschungen*
AHR	*American Historical Review*
Annales	Johannes Dlugossius (Jan Długosz), *Annales seu cronicae incliti Regni Poloniae*
APH	*Acta Poloniae Historica*
ASP	*Acten der Ständetage Preussens unter der Herrschaft des Deutschen Ordens*
ASPK	*Acta Stanów Prus Królewskich*
AT	*Acta Tomiciana*
AU	*Akta Unji Polski z Litwą 1385–1791*, ed. Stanisław Kutrzeba and Władysław Semkowicz (Cracow, 1932)
AUNC	*Acta Universitatis Nicolai Copernici*
AW	*Ateneum Wileńskie*
AZR	Акты относящіеся къ исторіи Западной Россіи [Akty otnosiashchiiesia k istorii Zapadnoi Rossii]
BCzart.	Biblioteka Książąt Czartoryskich, Cracow
BPGdańsk	Biblioteka Gdańska Polskiej Akademii Nauk
BHA	*Беларускі Гістарычны Агляд*
BZH	*Białoruskie Zeszyty Historyczne*
CDMP	*Codex diplomaticus Majoris Poloniae*
CDP	*Codex diplomaticus Poloniae*
CDPr	*Codex diplomaticus Prussicus*
CESXV	*Codex epistolaris saeculi decimi quinti*
CEV	*Codex epistolaris Vitoldi magni ducis Lithuaniae 1376–1430*, ed. Antoni Prochaska (Cracow, 1882).
CIP	*Corpus iuris polonici, Sectionis primae: Privilegia statuta constitutiones edicta decreta mandata regnum Poloniae spectantia comprehendentis*, iii: *Annos 1506–1522 continens*, ed. Oswald Balzer (Cracow, 1906)
CPH	*Czasopismo Prawno-Historyczne*
Dnevnik	Дневник Люблинского сейма 1569 года: Соединнение Великаго Княжества Литовского с Королеством Польским, изд. М. Коялович (St Petersburg, 1869)
dod.	dodatek (appendix)
EcHR	*Economic History Review*
HUS	*Harvard Ukrainian Studies*
Ius Polonicum	*Ius Polonicum: Codicibus veteribus manuscriptis et editionibus quibusque collatis*, ed. Wincenty Bandtkie Stężyński (Warsaw, 1831)

JGO	*Jahrbücher für Geschichte Osteuropas*
JMH	*Journal of Modern History*
KA	*1385 m. rugpjūčio Krėvos Aktas*, ed. Jūratė Kiaupienė (Vilnius, 2002)
KH	*Kwartalnik Historyczny*
KHKM	*Kwartalnik Historyczny Kultury Materialnej*
LHS	*Lithuanian Historical Studies*
Liublino Unija	Glemža, Liudas and Šmigelskytė-Stukienė, Ramunė (eds), *Liublino unija: idėja ir jos tęstinumas* (Vilnius, 2011)
LIM	*Lietuvos Istorijos Metraštis*
LIS	*Lietuvos Istorijos Studijos*
LSP	*Lituano-Slavica Posnaniensia: Studia Historica*
LTSRMAD	*Lietuvos TSR Mokslų Akademijos darbai*
MPH	*Monumenta Poloniae Historica*
NP	*Nasza Przeszłość*
ORP	*Odrodzenie i Reformacja w Polsce*
OSP	*Oxford Slavonic Papers*
PER	*Parliaments, Estates and Representation*
PH	*Przegląd Historyczny*
P&P	*Past and Present*
PSB	*Polski Słownik Biograficzny*, 49 vols (1935 to date)
PSRL	Полное Собрание Русских Летописей (*Polnoe Sobranie Russkikh Letopisei*)
PW	*Przegląd Wschodni*
PZ	*Przegląd Zachodni*
RAU	*Roczniki Akademii Umiejętności*
RAUWHF	*Rozprawy Akademii Umiejętności: Wydział Historyczno-Filozoficzny*
RDSG	*Roczniki Dziejów Społecznych i Gospodarczych*
RG	*Rocznik Gdański*
RH	*Roczniki Historyczne*
RIB	Русская Историческая Библиотека (*Russkaia Istoricheskaia Biblioteka*)
Roczniki	Jan Długosz, *Roczniki czyli kroniki sławnego Królestwa Polskiego*
RSAU	*Rozprawy i Sprawozdania z posiedzeń Wydziału Historyczno-Filozoficznego Akademii Umiejętności*
SEER	*The Slavonic and East European Review*
SH	*Studia Historyczne*
Skarbiec	*Skarbiec dyplomatów papieżkich, cesarskich, królewskich, książęcych, uchwał narodowych, postanowień różnych władz i urzędów posługujących do krytycznego wyjaśnienia dziejów Litwy, Rusi Litewskiej i ościennych im krajów*, ed. Ignacy Daniłowicz, 2 vols (Wilno, 1860–62)
SMHW	*Studia i Materiały do Historii Wojskowości*
SR	*Slavic Review*

List of Abbreviations

SPS	*Społeczeństwo Polski Średniowiecznej*
SRP	*Scriptores Rerum Polonicarum*
SRPr	*Scriptores Rerum Prussicarum*
SŹ	*Studia Źródłoznawcze*
TK	*Teki Krakowskie*
UAM	*Uniwersytet im. Adama Mickiewicza, Poznań*
UIZh	*Український Історичний Журнал*
UPK	*Urzędnicy Prus Królewskich*
UWXL	*Urzędnicy centralni i dostojnicy Wielkiego Księstwa Litewskiego*
VC	*Volumina Constitutionum*
VL	*Volumina Legum*
ŹDU	*Źródłopisma do dziejów unii Korony Polskiej i W. X. Litewskiego*, ed. A. T. Działyński (Poznań, 1861)
ZH	*Zapiski Historyczne*
ZNUJPH	*Zeszyty Naukowe Uniwersytetu Jagiellońskiego: Prace Historyczne*
ZO	*Zeitschrift für Ostforschung*
ZOF	*Zeitschrift für Ostmitteleuropa-Forschung*
ZPL	*Zbiór praw litewskich*, ed. A.T. Działyński (Poznań, 1841)

A Note on Personal and Place Names

There is no completely satisfactory solution to the problems, both practical and political, of rendering the personal and geographical names of eastern Europe in a text written in English. A balance has to be struck between scholarly exactitude and readability for those who do not know Slavic or Baltic languages. I have tried to strike such a balance. With regard to personal names, I have generally used English equivalents for the names of ruling princes and their families: thus Casimir, not Kazimierz; Sigismund, not Zygmunt; and Catherine, not Katarzyna. Where there is no exact English equivalent, I have preferred the native version over archaic anglicizations: thus Władysław and László, not Ladislas; Vasilii, not Basil, although I have preferred the German forms of Slavic names for the Germanized Slavic families who ruled in Silesia and Pomerania: thus Wladislaus and Bogislaw. I have preferred Louis of Anjou to Ludwig, Ludwik, or Lewis. For the man who instituted the union, I use the Lithuanian form Jogaila until his conversion to Catholicism, from which point I use the Polish form Jagiełło, since this is mostly how he is known in the English-language literature. I have used the Lithuanian form of Vytautas rather than the Polish Witold or the transliterated Russian form Vitovt, and Žygimantas for his brother, rather than Sigismund, to distinguish him from Sigismund of Luxembourg, Sigismund I, and Sigismund August. In order to help readers without Slavic and Baltic languages to discriminate between the different backgrounds of the individuals and families I have discussed, I have adopted a scheme in which Polish forms are used for Poles, and Lithuanian forms for Lithuanians until the mid sixteenth century, when Polish spread rapidly among the Lithuanian and Ruthenian elites. I have signalled the gradual switch to Polish in the sixteenth century by using Polish forms for Lithuanian names for the generation politically active in the lead-up to the Lublin union. This is the point at which the Radvila become the Radziwiłł, though the fact that Polish was the first language of Mikołaj Radziwiłł the Black (Czarny) and Mikołaj Radziwiłł the Red (Rudy) says nothing about their national identity.

The situation is even more complex with regard to names of Ruthenians, a term used to denote the inhabitants of what was known as Rus'. Modern Slavic languages distinguish between Rus' and Russia, a distinction that was unknown in the period covered by this book. Modern nationalist battles, however, make it important to distinguish between Russian (*rosyjski* in Polish) and Rus'ian (*ruski* in Polish). In order to avoid the awkward form Rus'ian in English, I have followed convention by using the English form Ruthenian, derived from the contemporary Latin. The Ruthenians in this book are the ancestors of modern Belarus'ians and Ukrainians, although Ruthenians in this period did not know any such distinction. Since Ruthenians spoke a number of different dialects of eastern Slavic, and orthography was by no means fixed, I have transliterated largely from modern forms of the names, using Ukrainian forms for Ruthenians from the southern lands,

A Note on Personal and Place Names xxi

Belarusian forms for Ruthenians from the lands of modern Belarus, and Russian forms for Muscovites. I have simplified the transliterations, omitting soft signs and diacritics to make the text more readable for non-Slavic specialists; thus I use Hrushevsky, not Hrushevs'kyi; Ostrozky, not Ostroz'kyi. For families of Lithuanian origin who became Ruthenianized and Orthodox, I have used the Ruthenian version of their names: thus the Holshansky, not the Alšeniškiai.

Similar principles are used with regard to geographical names. Where there is a standard English form, I have used it: thus Warsaw, Cracow, Moscow, Vienna. My general principle is to use the language in which places appear most often in the sources, and which is used by the dominant elites in a city or province. Thus I prefer the German forms Danzig, Thorn, and Elbing to the Polish forms Gdańsk, Toruń, and Elbląg. Matters are more complex in the lands of the grand duchy of Lithuania, where the linguistic map has altered considerably since the period covered by this book. On the whole, I have therefore used Lithuanian forms for places within the territory of modern Lithuania (Vilnius, not Wilno or Vilna; Trakai, not Troki), and Ruthenian forms for territories with a largely Ruthenian population. Rather than adopt one of the numerous variant spellings that appear in the sources, I have preferred to use the modern place names in Belarusian, Ukrainian, and Russian. Thus I use Kyiv, not Kiev—although I do refer to Kievan Rus'; Navahrudak, not Nowogródek; Hrodna, not Grodno. The exception is for Red Ruthenia, most of which is now in Ukraine, but which was part of the Polish kingdom from the 1340s until 1795, and where Polish was the dominant language among most of the elites by the late fifteenth century. Thus I prefer Lwów to L'viv, although I use Kamianets (Podilsky) not Kamieniec Podolski, since this territory was disputed between Poland and Lithuania.

Transliterations from Cyrillic are based on a modified form of the Library of Congress system, omitting diacritics. It has long been standard for bibliographic information in footnotes to be transliterated, but computerization has made it easier and less expensive to print different alphabets. I have therefore left titles in the bibliography and footnotes in the Cyrillic alphabet. Those who read east Slavic languages do not need them to be transliterated; for those who do not, it may be useful to be able to tell at a glance whether a source is in Russian, Belarusian, or Ukrainian, rather than Polish. I have provided a gazetteer with equivalents for place names in the various languages of the region. All translations are my own, unless otherwise indicated.

A Note on Currency

Until 1569 Poland and Lithuania had different currencies, as did Mazovia until 1529 and the Prussian lands, until the currency union with Poland established between 1526 and 1530. Polish monarchs also maintained a separate system of coinage in Red Ruthenia in the fourteenth and fifteenth centuries.

The Polish monetary system in the fourteenth century was heavily influenced by the currency reforms carried out in 1300 by Václav II of Bohemia, king of Poland 1300–5, and the introduction of a gold coinage in Bohemia in 1325. The silver Prague *grosz*—the name derives from the Latin *denarius grossus*, or large penny—circulated freely in Poland, as did the gold Bohemian florin in this period, at a rate of roughly twelve groszy to the florin. Władysław Łokietek's 1315 currency reform owed much to the Bohemian example. From 1315, 48 groszy were minted from one mark of silver—*grzywna* in Polish—which weighed half a pound; this was worth 576 pennies (*denary*). In 1315, one grosz contained 3.6 grams of silver, equivalent to the Prague grosz. By 1384–86, there were 16 pennies to the grosz, and 768 were struck from one mark.

The silver content of the grosz declined steadily between 1300 and 1530, and the Polish grosz devalued substantially against its Bohemian equivalent: if in 1300–10 they both contained 3.6 grams of silver, in 1400–10 the Polish grosz contained 1.38 grams compared with 1.75 grams contained by the Prague grosz; by 1530 the figures were 0.77 grams and 1.18 grams. The mark remained a money of account.

Łokietek and his son Casimir III (1333–70) minted gold ducats, probably largely for representational reasons, and Bohemian and Hungarian ducats long remained the main gold coins circulating in Poland. Under John I Albert (1492–1501) the problems caused by fluctuations in the value of silver and gold led to a half-hearted currency reform whose major achievement was the introduction of a new gold coin, the Polish złoty (*florenus polonicus*; *aureus polonicus*), as the equivalent of the ducat, whose value was established at 30 groszy, although this was raised to 32 groszy in 1505. In 1528 Sigismund I's currency reform laid the foundations of the bimetallic system for the rest of the early modern period. It established a new ducat or red złoty (*czerwony złoty*). Henceforth, the złoty became a money of account; in 1528, one ducat or red złoty was worth $1^1/_2$ złoties. In 1558 Sigismund August raised the weight of the mark from 198 to 202 grams. Between 1547 and 1571 one ducat or red złoty was worth 54 Polish groszy.

Lithuania in the fifteenth century adopted the Culm mark (*hryvna*) from the Teutonic Knights at a weight of 191.29 grams. In 1500, 100 Lithuanian groszy were worth just over 136 Polish groszy; after the reforms of Sigismund I, the figure was 100:125. Monetary calculations in Lithuania and Ruthenia were often carried out in kop groszy, in which a *kopa* was a unit of measurement denoting 60 pieces. Thus 100 kop groszy was worth 6,000 Lithuanian groszy.

A Note on the Genealogies

The genealogies in Figures 1–3 are based on Darius Baronas, Artūras Dubonis, Rimvydas Petrauskas, *Lietuvos Istorija*, iii: *XIII a.–1385 m.* (Vilnius, 2011), 338–9, 356–9; Stephen Rowell, *Lithuania Ascending* (Cambridge, 1994), genealogical tables 1–4; Леонтій Войтович, *Княжа доба на Русі: Портрети еліти* (Біла Церква, 2006) and *Удільні князівства Рюриковичів і Гедиміновичів у XII–XIV ст.* (Львів, 1996); and Jan Tęgowski, *Pierwsze pokolenia Giedyminowiczów* (Poznań and Wrocław, 1999), table 1, 304–5. The exact order and number of the children of Gediminas, Algirdas, and Kęstutis is a matter of some controversy. With regard to Algirdas's children, I have accepted the traditional view of Andrei of Polatsk as the eldest son of Algirdas's first marriage, and Jogaila/Jagiełło as the eldest son of the second. This is the view of Rowell and Nikodem. Tęgowski and *Lietuvos Istorija*, iii: 356–7 take a different view. The order and birth dates of Algirdas's children are based largely on Jarosław Nikodem, 'Data urodzenia Jagiełły: Uwagi o starszeństwie synów Olgierda i Julianny', *Genealogia*, 12 (2000), 23–49. For a full discussion of the problem, see Chapter 8, 74–5.

PART I
TOWARDS UNION

1
Krėva, Крэва, Krewo

The small, sleepy town of Kreva is little more than a straggling village, hard to distinguish from the rolling wooded countryside in which it lies. Rundown wooden houses with hens running free in their vegetable gardens cluster haphazardly round a large, whitewashed Catholic church. There is a small café with parking for the odd bus-party of tourists visiting the ruins of an imposing fourteenth-century fortress. The scaffolding erected at some point to effect repairs has mostly collapsed. A sign declares the castle to be a valuable historical and cultural monument of the republic of Belarus, and that anyone damaging the ruins will be prosecuted. One is tempted to ask whom the authorities intend to prosecute for neglect.[1]

Little about Kreva today suggests that it was ever of any great importance. In the fourteenth century, however, it was Krėva, a power-centre of the Gediminid dynasty. In 1338 it was given by Gediminas, grand duke of Lithuania (1317–41), to his son Algirdas (c.1300–77). Long after Algirdas became grand duke in 1345, he in turn bestowed it upon his chosen heir, Jogaila. It was here that Jogaila was imprisoned in 1381 after being deposed by his father's brother and co-ruler Kęstutis. It was here that Kęstutis was imprisoned a year later after Jogaila overthrew him. Five days later Kęstutis was found dead in mysterious circumstances. Besieged and sacked by the Perekop Tatars between 1503 and 1506, the castle was visited by the imperial ambassador Sigismund Herberstein en route to Moscow in 1518. It was at Krėva that Andrei Kurbskii took refuge after 1564 from the blood-spattered rule of Ivan the Terrible. Thereafter, Krėva lost its military and political significance. When Napoleon Orda sketched it in the mid nineteenth century in his classic survey of the historic monuments of the former Polish-Lithuanian commonwealth, the castle had long been an abandoned ruin. It suffered further damage during the First World War, when for three years Krėva lay on the front line. Abandoned by its inhabitants, who were evacuated deep into Russia, it was heavily bombarded in 1916, and was at the centre of a major battle in 1917 as the Germans pounded the Russian line.

It is for other reasons that Kreva has gone down in history. It was here, on 14 August 1385, that Europe's political geography was transformed by a document of a mere 26 lines and 560 words. It was written in Latin, on a parchment to which were attached the seals of Jogaila, his brothers Skirgaila, Kaributas, and Lengvenis, and his cousin, Kęstutis's son Vytautas. The seals disappeared during the nineteenth century, but the document is preserved in the chapter archive of Cracow

---

[1] Kreva's population in 2004 was 726, down from a peak of 2,300 in 1909, <http://krevo.by/readarticle.php?article_id=17> accessed 2 July 2010.

cathedral. It marked Jogaila's acceptance of terms agreed in Cracow the previous January for his marriage to Jadwiga, elected queen regnant of Poland in 1384, two years after the death of her father, Louis of Anjou, king of Hungary and Poland. Since Jadwiga was a minor, Skirgaila travelled to Buda to secure the consent of her mother, Elizabeth of Bosnia, who sent a delegation to Krėva where the document known as the Krewo Act was agreed.[2]

It took five months to consummate the relationship. In December Duke Siemowit IV of Mazovia, from a cadet branch of the Piast dynasty that had ruled Poland until 1370, was persuaded to resign his claims to the throne. On 11 January 1386 a Polish delegation met Jogaila in Vaukavysk, between Vilnius and Brest, presenting him with a document in which his safety was guaranteed and the Poles confirmed their promise to elect him as their king.[3] The election—or rather pre-election, since Jogaila would not be crowned until he had fulfilled his promises—took place in Lublin on 2 February, whence Jogaila travelled to Cracow, where he was baptized on 15 February, adopting the Christian name Władysław in homage to Jadwiga's great-grandfather, Władysław Łokietek, who had refounded the Polish kingdom in 1320. Vytautas and Jogaila's pagan brothers Vygantas, Karigaila, and Švitrigaila were baptized alongside him. Three days later Jogaila married Jadwiga; on 4 March he was crowned by the Polish primate, Bodzęta, archbishop of Gniezno.[4]

Thus did the pagan grand duke Jogaila metamorphose into the Christian king Władysław II Jagiełło (1386–1434) and two very different realms were united in an association that was to last 409 years. Why the Krewo Act should have laid the foundations for what remains one of the longest political unions in European history is hard to glean from the brief documents agreed at Krėva and Vaukavysk, which left a great deal unsaid and contained much that was unclear. There was nothing inevitable about the momentous decision that Jogaila took in committing Lithuania to a political relationship with the Poles and their western, Catholic, culture, and much to suggest that this association would prove as short-lived as the Polish unions with Bohemia (1300–6) and Hungary (1370–82).

---

[2] *AU*, no. 1, 1–3; *KA*, 17–20.   [3] *AU*, no. 2, 4.
[4] Grzegorz Błaszczyk, *Dzieje stosunków polsko-litewskich od czasów najdawniejszych do współczesności*, i: *Trudne początki* (Poznań, 1998), 206–8; Jadwiga Krzyżaniakowa and Jerzy Ochmański, *Władysław II Jagiełło* (Wrocław, 2006), 94–7. For a translation of the Vaukavysk document, see Stephen Rowell, '1386: The marriage of Jogaila and Jadwiga embodies the union of Poland and Lithuania', *LHS*, 11 (2006), 137–44.

2
Poland

The Krewo Act was the result of contingency rather than any long-term process. The immediate cause was Louis's failure to produce a male heir. On his death in 1382, his Polish and Hungarian subjects had the opportunity to reconsider the personal union that had begun on Louis's accession to the Polish throne in 1370. For the Poles, the relationship had been difficult. Hungary was the senior partner: the crown of St Stephen was long established, and its bearers ruled a populous, dynamic, and wealthy realm. The Polish monarchy rested on fragile foundations. Since the establishment of the Polish state, first mentioned in written sources in the 960s, only four of its rulers, Bolesław I (992–1025), his son Mieszko II (1025–34), Mieszko's grandson Bolesław II (1058–79), and Przemysł II (1295–6) had been crowned. Only Mieszko enjoyed royal status for long: Bolesław I was crowned around Easter 1025, shortly before his death in June. Bolesław II only received papal permission for his coronation in 1076, eighteen years after succeeding his father, and was driven from his throne in 1079 after ordering the murder of Stanisław, bishop of Cracow; he died in exile in 1081. Przemysł II claimed the title of king of Poland, but only controlled Pomerania and his own duchy of Wielkopolska. He did not long enjoy his status: crowned in 1295, he was kidnapped and murdered in 1296 on the orders of the margraves of Brandenburg. Other Polish rulers bore the title *książę*, rendered in Latin as *dux* or *princeps*, whether they ruled over all, or only part, of the Polish lands.

The Piasts were bedevilled by dynastic rivalries. These were exacerbated by the attempt of Bolesław Krzywousty (the Wrymouth) (1107–1138), to provide for his five surviving sons and to systematize the opaque principles of succession among the burgeoning numbers of Piast dukes. Patrilineal inheritance and male primogeniture were not Slavic customs. Collateral succession was the norm. Brothers took precedence over sons, and rulers nominated their successor.[1] Wrymouth's testament divided the kingdom among his sons, establishing a complex system in which the senior member of the dynasty held Cracow and exerted supreme authority over other family members. He does not deserve his popular reputation as the man who wilfully smashed the unity of the Polish state: he tried to solve an increasingly intractable problem, prevent the worsening of the position through his own fecundity—altogether he fathered seventeen children—and to protect the position of his four sons born of his second wife Salomea. Nevertheless, while a

---

[1] Marek Barański, *Dynastia Piastów w Polsce* (Warsaw, 2005), 218. For Polish succession law see Oswald Balzer, *Królestwo Polskie 1295–1370*, 2nd edn (Cracow, 2005), 515–86.

common dynastic sense lingered after 1138, Wrymouth's testament undermined the hereditary principle by establishing non-hereditary duchies for his sons. The failure of the principle of seniority, by which the duke of Cracow was to preside over the rest, brought nothing but confusion. The once-proud kingdom disintegrated over the generations into a mess of petty, squabbling duchies, whose rulers grew in assertiveness as their territories declined in size: if there were still only five duchies in 1202, there were nine by 1250, and seventeen by 1288.[2] It was not until 1320 that Louis of Anjou's maternal grandfather Władysław Łokietek (the Short) secured the permission of Pope John XXII for his coronation and revived Poland's status as an independent monarchy.

His achievement was made possible by a reaction to the dark days following Przemysł II's assassination, when the Bohemian Přemyslid dynasty briefly sustained its claim to the Polish throne. Łokietek's own claims, as the third son of Casimir I of Cujavia, were weak. Yet he managed to unite the core provinces of Wielkopolska and Małopolska, though he lost control of Pomerelia and with it access to the Baltic Sea to the Teutonic Order in 1308–9, and was unable to recover Silesia or Mazovia. Rejecting Łokietek's advances, the Silesian dukes swore homage in the 1320s to John of Luxembourg, king of Bohemia, who sustained the Přemyslid claim to the Polish throne. The Mazovian dukes were fiercely protective of their independence. One of them, Konrad I, invited the Teutonic Order into Prussia in 1226 to aid Mazovia against attacks by the pagan Prussian tribes to his north. Wary of Łokietek, the Mazovian Piasts swore homage to John of Luxembourg in 1329. For them, as for the Silesian Piasts, the resurrection of a Polish monarchy was unwelcome. As so often in dynastic politics, blood proved thinner than water.

Łokietek's son Casimir III (1333–70) built impressively on the foundations laid by his father, but his major successes lay in the east, not the west, where he had to accept the status quo. He exploited the deaths without issue of Bolesław III of Płock in 1351 and Casimir I of Czersk in 1355 to secure oaths of homage to him personally, but not to the Polish kingdom: the vassal status of both duchies lapsed on his death, and the Mazovian dukes, like their Silesian cousins, were to be thorns in the side of Polish monarchs for generations to come.[3] For all his achievements, Casimir faced daunting rivals. Apart from the Order, he had to deal with the fundamental shift in political gravity following the extinction of the Árpáds in Hungary (1301) and the Přemyslids in Bohemia (1306). The flourishing economies of these established kingdoms drew the attention of more powerful dynasties, with roots in western Europe and tendrils that snaked across the continent: the Neapolitan branch of the Angevins, which claimed the Hungarian crown, and the Luxembourgs, who succeeded the Přemyslids in Bohemia. The contrast between the dingy Piast capital of Cracow and the glittering courts of Buda and Prague was

---

[2] Benedykt Zientara, 'Społeczeństwo polskie XIII–XV wieku', in Ireniusz Ihnatowicz et al. (eds), *Społeczeństwo polskie od X do XX wieku* (Warsaw, 1988), 96.
[3] *Historia Śląska*, ed. Marek Czapliński (Wrocław, 2002), 70–1; *Dzieje Mazowsza*, i, ed. Henryk Samsonowicz (Pułtusk, 2006), 251–4, 266–7. For the reigns of Łokietek and Casimir, see Jan Baszkiewicz, *Odnowienie królestwa polskiego 1295–1320* (Poznań, 2008) and Paul Knoll, *The Rise of the Polish Monarchy: Piast Poland in East Central Europe, 1320–1370* (Chicago, 1972).

all too evident; the more so after the election of the glamorous cosmopolitan king of Bohemia, Charles IV of Luxembourg, as Emperor in 1347.

Casimir was a pragmatist. He abandoned thoughts of recovering eastern Pomerania, ceding it to the Order at Kalisz in 1343, thereby surrendering Poland's direct access to the Baltic. His major problem, however, was his lack of a male heir. He therefore turned to the Angevin king of Hungary, Charles Robert, husband of his sister Elizabeth. In March 1338 Charles Robert agreed with the Luxembourgs that the Polish throne should be inherited by the Angevins in return for a promise that Charles Robert would do all he could to persuade Casimir to renounce his claims to Silesia, something that Casimir, aware he had little chance of recovering it, duly did in February 1339. He agreed that, should he die without a male heir, Elizabeth would succeed him and, through her, Charles Robert or one of his three sons; the agreement was probably sealed at Vyšegrád following the death of Casimir's beloved Lithuanian wife Aldona in May 1339, although its existence is only known indirectly.[4]

In 1339 Casimir was only 29 and had fathered two daughters with Aldona. His prospects of a male heir were ruined by his disastrous second marriage to Adelheid of Hesse who, after a brief period of spectacular conjugal disharmony, was despatched to a remote castle where she stubbornly refused an annulment, only leaving Poland in 1357. By 1355 Casimir was ready to sign away his daughters' rights, putting flesh on the bones of the 1339 treaty by agreeing a succession pact with his nephew Louis, Charles Robert's only surviving son, who was to succeed him should he die without male heirs. Casimir did not help Poland's prospects of avoiding an Angevin succession by bigamously marrying his mistress, the widowed Krystyna Rokičana, daughter of a Prague burgher, in 1357 and then, in 1364 or 1365, after declaring himself divorced from her, Hedwig, daughter of the Piast duke Henry of Sagan, on the basis of a falsified papal dispensation purporting to deal with the issue of consanguinity, but not the more awkward one of bigamy. Hedwig bore him three daughters, all of them eventually legitimized by Urban V and—after Casimir's death—Gregory XI. Polish law did not recognize succession in the female line, however, and Casimir confirmed his arrangement with Louis in a treaty signed in Buda in February 1369.

In 1370, just before his death, Casimir reconsidered. He negotiated with Charles IV for a marriage between Charles's son and one of his daughters, and legitimized his favourite grandson, Casimir (Kaźko) of Stolp, son of Bogislaw V of Pomerania, whose sister Elizabeth had married Charles IV in 1363. Casimir probably did not intend to challenge Louis's accession, for all the pro-Luxembourg sentiments of his chancellor, Janusz Suchywilk, and vice-chancellor, Janko of Czarnków. Louis's lack of a male heir, however, meant that the succession was not secure, and it is likely that Casimir's intention was to make Kaźko the heir presumptive should Louis die without a male heir. After Casimir's unexpected death Louis duly

---

[4] Paul Knoll, 'Louis the Great and Casimir of Poland', in S.B. Vardy, Géza Goldschmidt, and Leslie S. Domonkos (eds), *Louis the Great, King of Hungary and Poland* (New York, 1986), 108–9; Stanisław Szczur, 'W sprawie sukcesji andegaweńskiej w Polsce', *RH*, 75 (2009), 64–71, 101–2.

succeeded him under the terms of the 1355 and 1369 agreements, although his rapid arrival in Poland in 1370 and hasty coronation in Cracow suggest he was nervous of his prospects (see Map 1).[5]

The brief personal union of Poland and Hungary was not a happy one. Louis may have earned the title 'Great' in Hungary, but he did not in Poland, which he barely visited during his reign, feebly claiming that the climate was disagreeable.[6] He appointed as governor his formidable mother, Elizabeth Łokietkówna, who proved unpopular, partly because of the Hungarians who thronged her court. In 1376 resentment boiled over in a rising in which some of her Hungarian entourage were massacred. Elizabeth fled to Hungary; she was replaced by Wladislaus duke of Oppeln, a Silesian Piast, until her return in 1378.[7]

It was not so much Elizabeth's unpopularity, however, as uncertainty about the succession that lay behind the political instability. Since Krzywousty's testament dealt only with males, the fact that Polish customary law did not recognize succession through the female line gave the kingdom's powerful elites considerable room for manoeuvre, not least because Louis's tenure of the throne was based on their acceptance of Casimir's disinheritance of the Piast cadet lines. In order to secure an agreement that on his death one of his three daughters would succeed him, in 1374 Louis granted a set of privileges at Kassa in the kingdom of Hungary—Košice in modern Slovakia; Koszyce in Polish—the foundation stone of the liberty of the Polish szlachta.[8]

The Koszyce agreement allowed Louis to choose which of his daughters should inherit the Polish throne. Several magnates swore oaths of loyalty to Catherine on behalf of the kingdom, but her death, aged eight, in 1378 threw Louis's plans into disarray. Between 1373 and 1375 he negotiated the betrothal of Catherine's younger sister, Mary, born in 1371, to Sigismund of Luxembourg, second son of Charles IV and great-grandson of Casimir III, who was three years her senior.[9] Jadwiga, his youngest daughter, underwent a ceremony of *sponsalia de futuro*—a form of betrothal—with William, son of Leopold III von Habsburg, in 1378, when Jadwiga was four and William eight. After Catherine's death Louis anointed Mary as his choice for the Polish throne, with Jadwiga intended for Hungary, as her nuptial agreement with William stipulated. At Kassa in August 1379 representatives of the leading Polish lords were invited to swear homage to Mary as their future queen. To overcome their evident reluctance, Louis shut the city gates, preventing them from leaving until the oath was sworn.[10] In February 1380 he confirmed the arrangements

---

[5] Knoll, *Rise*, 229–30; Wanda Moszczeńska, 'Rola polityczna rycerstwa wielkopolskiego w czasie bezkrólewia po Ludwiku Wielkim', *PH*, 25 (1925), 88–91.

[6] Jarosław Nikodem, *Jadwiga, król Polski* (Wrocław, 2009), 64–5. Polish historians generally reject Dąbrowski's claim that Louis was also a great king of Poland: Jan Dąbrowski, *Ostatnie lata Ludwika Wielkiego 1370–1382*, 2nd edn (Cracow, 2009).

[7] Jerzy Wyrozumski, *Królowa Jadwiga*, 2nd edn (Cracow, 2006), 44; Dąbrowski, *Ostatnie*, 318–20.

[8] See Chapter 6.

[9] Dąbrowski, *Ostatnie* 18–23. Hoensch mistakenly suggests she was eight, confusing her with another Mary, born in 1365, who died soon after her birth: Jörg Hoensch, *Kaiser Sigismund: Herrscher an der Schwelle der Neuzeit 1368–1437* (Munich, 1996), 45.

[10] Johannes de Czarnkow, *Chronicon Polonorum*, ed. Jan Szlachtowski, *MPH*, ii (Lwów, 1872), 711.

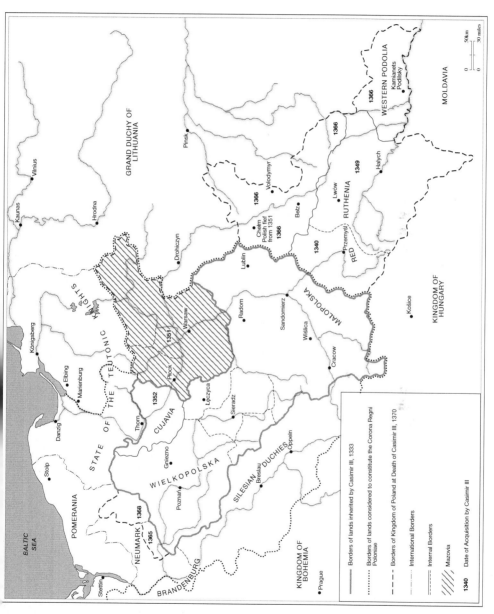

Map 1. The Kingdom of Poland in the fourteenth century.

for Jadwiga and William's marriage, stipulating that it should take place as soon as Jadwiga reached the canonical age in 1386, and secured Hungarian recognition of these arrangements.[11] In July 1382 he extracted another oath of loyalty to the fourteen-year-old Sigismund from representatives of the Polish nobility at Zólyom.

Whatever Louis's intentions, after his death on the night of 10/11 September 1382, the vultures circling the Angevin inheritance discovered that the elites of his kingdoms had their own ideas and were as ready to break their promises as their royal masters. Five days later the Hungarians declared Mary, not Jadwiga, to be their queen, leaving the regency council appointed in 1381 after Elizabeth Łokietkówna's death with an interesting dilemma and an enticing opportunity.[12] Sigismund entitled himself *Herr des Kunygreiches zu Polen* despite not being married yet, and secured oaths of loyalty from several Wielkopolskan towns and some members of the clergy. He met significant resistance, however, from the province's nobility, who sought a commitment that after his coronation Sigismund would reside permanently in Poland.[13]

The Poles had had their fill of absentee monarchy, but this was an undertaking to which Sigismund, who knew of Mary's election, was unwilling to agree. Whatever Louis's intentions, Sigismund had always been more interested in Hungary than Poland. He refused to enter into any commitments in Poland that might compromise his position in Hungary. Encouraged by Konrad Zöllner von Rottenstein, the Order's grand master, Sigismund returned to Hungary to secure his throne; no easy task as it transpired. His candidature was by no means dead, but his refusal to accept their terms left the Poles with a dilemma. They could remain loyal to Louis's broad intentions—if not his last wishes—and the oaths they had sworn since 1374, and seek to avoid another absentee monarch by supporting Jadwiga's accession. Yet Jadwiga was eight years old.[14] She had never visited Poland, had been raised in expectation of the Hungarian throne, and was the ward of her mother, Elizabeth of Bosnia. She was betrothed to a German princeling largely unknown in Poland who was no match for the mighty Luxembourgs. There were other candidates, not least Siemowit IV of Mazovia, who attracted supporters, especially in Wielkopolska; Wladislaus of Oppeln; and the last surviving male in the royal Piast line, Władysław the White, who had already mounted a claim to the throne in 1370, when he had unexpectedly stirred himself from his Benedictine monastery in Dijon. He only reached Poland after Louis's accession; although he had some support in Cujavia and Wielkopolska, having failed to persuade the pro-Angevin pope, Gregory XI, to release him from his vows, he could do little more than seize Gniewkowo, his hereditary duchy. In 1373 and 1375–6 he laid siege to several Wielkopolskan and Cujavian towns, before his final defeat after the siege of Złotoria in 1377, at which

---

[11] Nikodem, *Jadwiga*, 72–6.
[12] Jacek Gzella, *Małopolska elita władzy w okresie rządów Ludwika Węgierskiego w latach 1370–1382* (Toruń, 1994), 146.
[13] Hoensch, 'König/Kaiser Sigismund, der Deutsche Orden und Polen-Litauen', *ZOF* NF 46 (1997), 3–4; Wyrozumski, *Jadwiga*, 76.
[14] She was probably born on 18 February 1374: Nikodem, *Jadwiga*, 80.

Kaźko of Stolp, who had joined his cause, was fatally wounded. Louis bought Władysław out of Gniewkowo and granted him an abbacy in Hungary. Clement VII, who was hostile to the Angevins, issued a bull in September 1382 releasing Władysław from his vows, but Władysław showed no inclination to leave his abbey. Wielkopolskan resentment at Angevin rule was channelled into support for Siemowit IV, an experienced politician who had many links to Wielkopolska, not least with the archbishopric of Gniezno, which had substantial estates around Łowicz in Siemowit's lands.[15]

Whatever the merits of the various candidates, none was in a position to dictate to the Poles who should rule over them. By 1382 they had developed an ideology that justified their right to decide, and the institutional means to effect that decision. Both rested on the concept of the *corona regni Poloniae*—the crown of the Polish kingdom—formed during the fourteenth century, influenced by contemporary developments in Bohemia and Hungary.[16] The concept of the *corona regni* in east central Europe embodied the idea that, as Susan Reynolds puts it in her study of western Europe:

> A kingdom was never thought of merely as the territory which happened to be ruled by a king. It comprised and corresponded to a 'people' (*gens, natio, populus*), which was assumed to be a natural, inherited community of tradition, custom, law, and descent.[17]

Reynolds argues that this concept, which she terms 'the community of the realm', was deeply embedded in medieval political consciousness. The idea of a political community distinct from the person of the ruler was familiar across Europe, although its expressions varied according to local conditions. Whereas in Bohemia it was used by Charles IV to give institutional coherence to the eclectic collection of realms he had gathered under his rule, in Scotland it provided a theoretical basis for setting limits to the power of the crown: the 1320 declaration of Arbroath, which claimed the right to depose Robert I should he recognize English claims to suzerainty over Scotland, was drawn up in its name.[18]

The Polish concept of *corona regni* was influenced by contemporary Hungarian and Bohemian examples, but developed somewhat differently. As in Bohemia, it was originally nurtured from above by Łokietek and Casimir, for whom it served

---

[15] Dąbrowski, *Ostatnie*, 210–15; Józef Śliwiński, *Powiązania dynastyczne Kazimierza Wielkiego a sukcesja tronu w Polsce* (Olsztyn, 2000), 122–42; Oswald Balzer, *Genealogia Piastów*, 2nd edn (Cracow, 2005), 640–7.

[16] The classic account is Jan Dąbrowski, *Korona Królestwa Polskiego* (Wrocław, 1956; repr. 2010), abridged, tr. Ch. Woesler, as: 'Die Krone des polnischen Königtums im 14. Jahrhundert', in Manfred Hellmann (ed.), *Corona Regni: Studien über die Krone als Symbol des Staates im späteren Mittelalter* (Darmstadt, 1961), 399–548. Cf. Balzer, *Królestwo*, 586–649; Knoll, *Rise*, 40–1, 170.

[17] Susan Reynolds, *Kingdoms and Communities in Western Europe 900–1300*, 2nd edn (Oxford 1997), 250.

[18] Josef Karpat, 'Zur Geschichte des Begriffes *Corona Regni* in Frankreich und England', in Hellmann (ed.), *Corona Regni*, 70–155; Fritz Hartung, 'Die Krone als Symbol der monarchischen Herrschaft im ausgehenden Mittelalter', in Hellmann (ed.), *Corona Regni*, 1–69; Edward Cowan, *For Freedom Alone: The Declaration of Arbroath, 1320*, 2nd edn (Edinburgh, 2008). For a full discussion of her views, see Reynolds, *Kingdoms*, 250–331.

the purposes of strengthening royal authority and asserting the essential unity of the Polish lands. Although Casimir was forced to accept the de facto loss of eastern Pomerania and Silesia, the concept of the *corona regni* allowed him to claim that although control over these territories had been lost, they still formed an integral part of the regnum: the Silesian dukes were referred to in Poland throughout the fourteenth century as *duces Poloniae* despite paying homage to the Bohemian crown.[19] Initially the monarch's right to alienate parts of his realm was not questioned: as Janisław, archbishop of Gniezno put it in 1339: 'the king of Poland is lord of all lands that constitute the kingdom of Poland, and can grant them to whomsoever he wishes'.[20] Yet when Casimir bequeathed Łęczyca, Sieradz, and Dobrzyń to Kaźko of Stolp in his testament, the concept of *corona regni* was invoked to block the move. Louis was inclined to respect Casimir's wishes, but strong opposition persuaded him to refer the matter to a tribunal, which decided that no monarch had the right to treat the territory of the *corona regni* as his patrimony, a verdict that Louis accepted.[21]

The triumph of the concept was apparent at Louis's coronation, when he became the first Polish monarch to swear to maintain the kingdom's territorial integrity: not only was he not to reduce it, but he swore to augment it through recovering lost provinces, a pledge he renewed at Koszyce in 1374.[22] Under Casimir and Louis, the central government asserted its authority against the local and provincial institutions established before 1320. The chancellor and vice-chancellor were no longer referred to as 'of Cracow' or 'of the court': Jan Radlica, chancellor from 1381 to 1382, styled himself '*regni Poloniae supremus cancellarius*'. The separate chancellors for the various provinces disappeared, and central control was asserted by starostas appointed by the king, who acted on his orders; of particular importance were the starostas general, who had responsibility for a whole province.[23] The influence of these officials, and of a small group of leading lords, particularly in Małopolska, grew during the unpopular governorships of Elizabeth Łokietkówna and Wladislaus of Oppeln. Louis's decision to appoint a regency council after Elizabeth's death placed substantial powers in the hands of this overwhelmingly Małopolskan group. Since Jadwiga was ten years old when she was crowned in October 1384, it was not until Jagiełło's coronation in February 1386 that royal authority was restored.

For all the powers vested in the regents, they struggled to dictate the course of events. There was some unrest, notably in Wielkopolska, where, in 1377, the powerful position of the Grzymalita family was sealed by the appointment as starosta general of Domarat of Pierzchna, a dedicated Angevin loyalist and the province's only member of the regency council. Wielkopolska, the main centre of power under the early Piasts, had long resented its loss of political influence to Małopolska. Przemysł II's murder in 1296 deprived it of its duke, while Łokietek and Casimir based their power in Cracow and openly favoured the Małopolskan

---

[19] Dąbrowski, *Korona*, 72.   [20] Quoted in Dąbrowski, *Korona*, 77.
[21] Dąbrowski, *Ostatnie*, 145–6, 150–3 and *Korona*, 83.   [22] Dąbrowski, *Korona*, 85.
[23] Dąbrowski, *Korona*, 87.

elite. Louis ignored Wielkopolskan demands and chose to be crowned in Cracow rather than—as was traditional—in Gniezno, a decision that provoked resentment, especially when he broke a promise to attend a ceremonial welcome in his coronation robes in Gniezno cathedral.[24]

There were good reasons for choosing Jadwiga. One of Casimir's greatest achievements had been his acquisition of the Ruthenian principality of Halych-Volhynia after the murder of its young ruler Bolesław/Iurii, a Mazovian Piast, in 1340. Halych-Volhynia had emerged relatively intact from the destruction of Kievan Rus' by the Mongols, despite its subjection to Mongol power in 1246. Stretching from Lwów and Przemyśl in the north-west, it had originally included Volhynia, Black Ruthenia, and the cities of Halych, Volodymyr, Bełz, and Chełm. Orthodox in religion, its economy blossomed in the fourteenth century as the Mongol grip slackened, the Ottoman stranglehold on the Bosphorus tightened, and eastern trade sought alternative overland routes.

The murder of Bolesław/Iurii, who had claimed the throne after the death of its last Rurikid prince in 1323, saw Poland, Lithuania, and Hungary advance claims to this strategically vital territory. Hungary had included the claim to be *rex Galiciae et Lodomeriae* in the titles of the crown of St Stephen since the early thirteenth century, while Casimir's claim rested on the fact that Bolesław/Iurii had designated him his successor.[25] During the 1340s Casimir occupied much of Red Ruthenia; concerned at possible conflict with the Angevins, he signed an agreement with Louis in April 1350 in which both sides gambled: Louis signed away his rights to the territory for Casimir's lifetime; if Casimir had a male heir, it would be sold to Hungary for the knockdown price of 100,000 florins. If, however, Louis or another Angevin should inherit the Polish throne, it would remain Polish. Louis thereafter supported Casimir's military campaigns against the Lithaunians, and in 1366 they agreed to divide the principality between Poland and Hungary.[26] On his accession Louis ignored these agreements, treating Halych-Volhynia as a Hungarian possession. By his death in 1382 he had recovered lands seized by the Lithuanians after 1370 and had put Hungarian garrisons into its major cities.

Louis's Ruthenian policy drove a wedge between him and the Małopolskan lords, who had long supported Casimir's Ruthenian ambitions, foreseeing rich pickings for themselves. They had, however, a powerful incentive to support the candidacy of one of Louis's daughters: according to the 1350 treaty, under an Angevin ruler Ruthenia would legally belong to Poland. As the Hungarian garrisons streamed home in 1382 to fight in the bitter struggles over the Hungarian throne, Jadwiga's claim as Louis's heir was asserted. Following her coronation Polish control was gradually re-established.

Whatever the arguments in favour of Jadwiga, it was the way in which the succession was settled that was to have the greatest significance for the future. In the

---

[24] Moszczeńska, 'Rola', 71–2, 98.   [25] Wyrozumski, *Jadwiga*, 70.
[26] Knoll, 'Louis', 110; Wyrozumski, *Jadwiga*, 70–1; Матвей Любавский, *Областное деление и местное управление Литовско-Русского государства ко времени издания первого Литовского статута* (Moscow, 1892), 38–9.

name of the *corona regni*, decisions over the vacant throne were taken at substantial assemblies of—to use Reynolds's term—the 'community of the realm'. The most important were at Radomsko (25 November 1382), Wiślica (6 December 1382), and Sieradz (27 February and 22 March 1383).[27] These assemblies marked an important stage in the development of the Polish political system. The setting aside of Casimir's testament marked the end of patrimonial dynasticism in Poland. Memory of the fragmentation of the realm between 1138 and 1320 was still fresh, while under Louis the principle that the monarch must consult with the community of the realm over the succession had been firmly established. What is remarkable, given the experience of other European states facing disputed successions, is the relative lack of bloodshed, despite the existence of several potential candidates in both 1370 and 1382–4. In part this was due to the fact that Polish succession law did not privilege male primogeniture. As in other Slavic societies, Polish custom allowed considerable latitude to the ruler to decide his successor, but Casimir's promise of the succession to the Angevins had required the consent of leading figures in the realm. Louis was a Piast on the distaff side, but given the lack of support for succession in the female line in Polish customary law he was already in a weak position before his lack of a male heir ensured that he had to make further concessions to secure the throne for one of his daughters. In 1384 those agreements were honoured, at least in spirit. Despite strong support in Wielkopolska for a Piast, which led to a short-lived armed conflict that never quite degenerated into full-scale civil war, general opinion, particularly in Małopolska, was in favour of remaining true to the oaths sworn to Louis. The fact that it was the community of the realm, not the dynasty that would ultimately decide helped contain the violence and established an important precedent.

In his classic history of the institution of confederation in Poland, Rembowski singles out the assemblies of 1382 as being of particular significance for the development of what became a distinctively Polish form of political organization.[28] While they were not the first Polish assemblies to use the concept of confederation, they were the first with such broad aims, and which so manifestly acted in the name of the whole political community: the *regnicolae regni Poloniae*. The concern for legality was underlined by a strong attachment to procedure throughout the interregnum, and a determination to reach decisions collectively. After the initial rejection by the Wielkopolskans of Sigismund's candidature, a general assembly for Wielkopolska and Małopolska was summoned to Radomsk on 25 November 1382. It formally confederated itself to provide a legal basis for its actions, before deciding 'unanimously' to honour the promises concerning the accession of one of Louis's daughters. There was initial opposition from Bodzęta and Domarat of Pierzchna, yet two of the most powerful political figures in the kingdom could not shake the consensus. The community of the realm had taken charge of the

---

[27] Wyrozumski, *Jadwiga*, 76–7.
[28] Aleksander Rembowski, *Konfederacja i rokosz*, ed. Jola Choińska-Mika, 2nd edn (Cracow, 2010), 264.

interregnum; if there were to be an Angevin succession, it would have to be on terms negotiated with that community.[29]

The phrases used in these accounts encapsulate the way in which the community of the realm was conceptualized. The Radomsk declaration of 27 November 1382 was made on behalf of the 'lords and the whole community' of Wielkopolska, represented by the barons and the '*nobiles*' and '*milites*', who were individually named, and representatives of the communities of Małopolska, Sieradz, and Łęczyca.[30] The documents talk of 'inhabitants of the kingdom' (*regnicolae*), or 'the whole community of lords and citizens' (*toti communiti dominorum et civitatum*).[31] In these assemblies, the participants stressed that the community of the whole realm of Poland was formally uniting its constituent parts to form an alliance (*foedus*) to provide a legal basis for its actions. This represented far more than simply the coming together of separate political units for a common aim: the documents express clearly the concept of a political community that transcended the local communities from which it was formed, using phrases such as 'the community of this land' (*communitas ipsius terre*) to denote the local communities which, taken together, formed the 'the whole community' (*tota communitas*) or 'the whole kingdom of Poland' (*universitas regni Poloniae*).[32]

Thus by 1382 there was a strong conception of the *corona regni* as a political community that transcended the various *terrae* of which it was composed. Although it was not until 1420 that the term was rendered in Polish as *wszystkie korony pospólstwo* (the whole commonality of the crown), the concept had taken root by the 1380s. While the monarch was seen as part of the community of the realm, and as necessary for the smooth functioning of the kingdom, the community of the realm was perfectly capable of running its affairs without a monarch, as it demonstrated between 1382 and 1386: even after Jadwiga's 1384 coronation, her status as a minor meant that she was in office but not in power.

Jadwiga's coronation represented an important victory for the community of the realm over her mother, who fought tenaciously to dictate the course of events. Although Elizabeth probably realized that Mary's claim was unsustainable by the time her envoys attended the Sieradz assembly in February 1383, she did not give up, even if her envoys had to promise to send Jadwiga to Poland after Easter. Jadwiga had not arrived when the assembly reconvened. Bodzęta asked whether the community of the realm wished Siemowit IV to be king. Although this proposal—which may have been merely a demonstration to Elizabeth that she

---

[29] 'convenit universa multitudo procerum et primatum regni Poloniae in Radomsko..., ubi mature de statu suo et Poloniae regni salubriter pertractantes, unanimi voluntate conglobati et mutuo foedere uniti, fide praestita, promiserunt invicem sibi auxiliari fidemque factam et homagium praestitum duabus filiabus: Mariae et Hedvigi Lodvici regis praemortui firmiter tenere et observare...' Johannes de Czarnkow, *Chronicon*, 723.

[30] The document lists the principal Wielkopolskan office-holders and dignitaries present, then adds '*ceterique nobiles, milites totaque communitas Maioris Polonie*'; similar formulae are used for Małopolska and the other territories. *CDMP*, iii, no. 1804.

[31] 'Conclusiones per dominos regni de unione regni et quomodo regi debetur usque ad regis novi electionem et coronationem', *CESXV*, i, no. 2, 3; Dąbrowski, *Korona*, 93.

[32] Dąbrowski, *Korona*, 93.

risked losing everything—was rejected on the grounds that there was significant dissent from Małopolska, Elizabeth missed several deadlines for Jadwiga's arrival in Poland during 1383, and even mounted a clumsy attempt to send Sigismund into Poland at the head of a small army, ostensibly to help put down unrest.[33]

At Sieradz, legalism and *Realpolitik* triumphed over sentiment. Siemowit would have brought little benefit to the realm. While his accession would have reunited his lands to the Polish crown, he did not even rule over the whole of Mazovia, which he shared with his elder brother Janusz I.[34] He had few resources to offer, and could not have challenged the Luxembourgs, who, if Sigismund were to secure the Hungarian throne, would rule Hungary, Brandenburg, and Bohemia; with the dynasty's close links to the Order, Poland would be all but surrounded. Under Siemowit, the tender young Polish monarchy was likely to wither in their shadow.

Most Poles did not want Sigismund either. He was politely turned back at the border, and when Elizabeth missed a further deadline in November, the community of the realm took steps to ensure that it had a proper institutional basis for running its affairs should a rapid resolution of the succession prove impossible. On 2 March 1384 it was stated that until a king was crowned, authority in the realm would lie with the 'community of lords and citizens', and would be exercised by the starostas, the main royal officials in each locality, together with the local lords and representatives of the cities, who were 'joined' to him. The starosta was to take decisions with the unanimous agreement of two consuls selected from the local community. In naming them, attention was paid to the need for representation of different regions, and of the cities. Oaths of loyalty were to be taken to this collective leadership; in return, the authorities swore that they would act for the good of the 'community and crown of this realm'.[35]

Those who depict authority in this period as 'feudal', based on lordship and a hierarchy of vertical allegiance to an ultimate suzerain, would do well to study the documents of the Polish interregnum of 1382–4. They do much to substantiate Reynolds's assault on the idea that medieval politics can be understood in such terms, and to demonstrate that, while the early modern debate on the nature of sovereignty lay far in the future, political communities had sophisticated ideas about the nature of political authority and the relationship between the monarch, the dynasty, and the community of the realm.[36] In the struggle between the Angevins and the Polish community of the realm, it was the dynasty that lost. The Poles stressed their wish to honour their commitments to Louis's daughters, who alone possessed hereditary rights to the kingdom. Yet these natural rights were limited: the claims of Louis's daughters ultimately depended upon the oaths taken by the community of the realm since 1374 to recognize those rights, and set aside Piast claims. These oaths were taken in good faith, but it was stressed after Louis's

---

[33] Wyrozumski, *Jadwiga*, 77–80; Nikodem, *Jadwiga*, 101–10.
[34] Siemowit was duke of Płock, Rawa, Sochaczew, Gostyń, and Płońsk; Janusz was duke of Warsaw, Wyszogród, Ciechanów, Zakroczym, and Liw. Following agreements with their father, Siemowit III, the duchies of Czersk and Wizna were transferred from Siemowit to Janusz between 1379 and 1381: Balzer, *Genealogia*, 819–20, table x.
[35] *CESXV*, i/i, no. 2, 2; Dąbrowski, *Korona*, 92.   [36] Reynolds, *Kingdoms*, xi–lxvi.

death that while the Poles would honour them, they would do so only if the dynasty fulfilled its obligations: the community of the realm reserved the right to set aside natural rights to the throne, as it had with regard to the Silesian Piasts who, by swearing loyalty to the crown of Bohemia, were deemed to have broken with the *corona regni* and thereby released the community of the realm from its obligation to respect their natural rights.[37] The community of the realm reserved the right to decide which of Louis's daughters it wished to elevate to the throne. It was no longer to be the exclusive preserve of the dynasty to decide which of its members was most fitted to rule.

Thus although Jadwiga formally exercised royal power from the moment that she was crowned *in regem Poloniae* in October 1384, that power could only be exercised in concert with the community of the realm and after she reached her majority.[38] The dynasty's reduced authority was revealed by the annulment of Jadwiga's 1378 betrothal. Despite its formal nature—which constituted the basis of a Habsburg challenge in the Papal curia—by 1384, Poland's political leaders were considering other options. William, born in 1370, was young and inexperienced; he was from a junior branch of the Habsburgs; and he would bring little with him to the throne. If the Polish crown was to stand firm alongside the Luxembourg realms of Bohemia and Hungary, it would need a different kind of monarch.

By October 1384, there was an alternative. It is unclear just when Jogaila became a serious candidate. He was not an obvious choice. Poland's relations with Lithuania had recently been tense on account of the struggle over Halych-Volhynia. The fourteenth century had seen a decline in the frequency of Lithuanian raids, but Jogaila himself participated in a devastating attack on Sandomierz in 1376 that resulted allegedly—if implausibly—in the capture of 23,000 prisoners.[39] Yet circumstances were changing, and there was much to recommend a rapprochement with Lithuania and its pagan grand duke.

---

[37] Dąbrowski, *Korona*, 72.

[38] Rowell questions the common assertion that Jadwiga was crowned king, not queen, of Poland in 1384, suggesting that, although some sources do use '*rex*' or '*ad regem*', they are outnumbered by those that state '*ad regnum*', '*regina*', or '*in reginam*'. His suggestion that the occasional use of '*rex*' merely acknowledged that Jadwiga was queen regnant, not queen consort, is sensible: Rowell, '1386', 139–40.

[39] Simas Sužiedėlis, 'Lietuva ir Gediminaičiai sėdant Jogailai į didžiojo kunigaikščio sostą', in Adolfas Šapoka (ed.), *Jogaila* (Kaunas, 1935; repr. 1991), 36–7; Błaszczyk, *Dzieje*, i, 67.

3

Lithuania

The grand duchy of Lithuania was a remarkable creation. After 1200 its rulers, in little over a century, welded a cacophony of feuding Baltic tribes into a powerful, sophisticated realm that gradually extended its authority over the mixed Baltic and Slavic populations to its south by means that remain controversial. From their remote and isolated fastnesses among the network of lakes, rivers, and marshes that pierced the great forests of north-eastern Europe, the Lithuanians harassed and raided their neighbours, extending their sway in an astonishingly short period after 1240 over much of the vast territory that had been Kievan Rus' before it was shattered by the Mongols.

The Lithuanian heartland was remote indeed: travelling fifteen leagues from Dyneburg to Vilnius in 1414, the diplomat Ghillebert de Lannoy entered a vast forest in which he travelled for forty-eight hours without seeing a trace of habitation.[1] Unlike related Baltic peoples—the Prussians, the Livs, and the Curonians—who succumbed to the far from tender rule of the Teutonic Order, their inaccessibility helped the Lithuanians not just to repel their enemies and survive in a hostile Christian world, but to establish their rule over one of the largest territorial agglomerations in European history, about 1 million km^2 at its peak around 1430 (see Map 2).[2]

The grand duchy was a sophisticated power system, under a princely dynasty that only entered the written record in the thirteenth century. Since Lithuanian—a member of the Baltic branch of the Indo-European family along with Latvian and several extinct languages, including Prussian—was not a written language until the sixteenth century, the names of Lithuania's rulers—apart from one reference to a *rex* Netimer in 1009—are unknown before the semi-legendary Ringaudas, who died around 1219. Ringaudas's son Mindaugas (1238–63) launched the spectacular expansion that—after an interruption following his 1263 assassination—

---

[1] *Oeuvres de Ghillebert de Lannoy, Voyageur, Diplomate et Moraliste*, ed. Charles Potvin (Louvain, 1878), 38.
[2] Matthias Niendorf, 'Die Beziehungen zwischen Polen und Litauen im historischen Wandel: Rechtliche und politische Aspekte in Mittelalter und Früher Neuzeit', in Dietmar Willoweit and Hans Lemberg (eds), *Reiche und Territorien in Ostmitteleuropa: Historische Beziehungen und politische Herrschaftslegitimation* (Munich, 2006), 129. The best account in English is Stephen Rowell, *Lithuania Ascending: A Pagan Empire within East Central Europe, 1295–1345* (Cambridge, 1994). For a warning against believing that the forests and lakes of the region were impenetrable, see Henryk Paszkiewicz, *O genezie i wartości Krewa* (Warsaw, 1938), 130.

Map 2. The Grand Duchy of Lithuania in 1385.

continued in the reigns of Vytenis (*c.*1295–1315) and his brother Gediminas (1315/16–1341/2).

What is striking is not so much the extent of that expansion—which was remarkable enough—but its lasting nature. Initially, the Lithuanians terrorized their neighbours. Between 1200 and 1236 they mounted regular destructive raids: twenty-three against the Curonians and Livonians to their north, fifteen against Ruthenian territories to their south and east, and four into the Polish lands to their west. In 1219, the Lithuanian political elite appeared in a written document for the first time, when one duchess and twenty dukes, including five recognized as seniors, witnessed peace with Halych-Volhynia.[3] By 1238 Mindaugas had established himself as overall ruler, although the term grand duke (*didysis kunigaikštis* in Lithuanian; *великий князь* in Ruthenian) was not common until its institutionalization by Gediminas's son Algirdas after 1345. It is sensible, however, to follow tradition in using one name for the prince instead of the varied forms found in the sources.[4]

The Lithuanians pushed south into lands where the devastating Mongol attacks that followed their first assault on Riazan in December 1237 exposed the incapacity of the squabbling Ruthenian principalities to defend themselves. Kievan Rus', united for periods under strong rulers such as Volodymyr the Great (980–1015), Iaroslav the Wise (1019–54), and Volodymyr Monomakh (1113–25), followed the Slavic system of collateral succession, in which the prince of Kyiv was recognized as supreme ruler over the numerous Ruthenian principalities. As in Poland after 1138, this proved more pious wish than practical politics. In the period of disintegration that began in 1132, three main power-centres emerged in Halych-Volhynia, Vladimir-Suzdal', and Novhorod-Siversky.[5] After the razing of Kyiv in 1240 and the extension of Mongol overlordship over the Rus'ian principalities, any vestigial political unity was destroyed, leaving Rus' open for infiltration by a more dynamic and less traumatized political culture.

Lithuania's extension of power southwards was a complex process. It was not based on force alone. Lithuania deployed forces well suited to warfare in the sparsely populated terrain of eastern Europe; they were by no means solely Lithuanian, rapidly incorporating Ruthenians into their ranks, which indicates the nature of Gediminid rule. Although military force was undoubtedly important, it is insufficient to explain the speed of expansion, or its consolidation: by 1385 Gediminid rule over much of the former lands of Kievan Rus' had lasted well over a century. Black Ruthenia—the lands along the upper reaches of the Niemen—already contained a mixed population. It had been settled by Baltic tribes before Slavic expansion into the region in the sixth and seventh centuries. Baltic and Slavic populations had mingled and assimilated ever since. Lithuanian grand dukes successfully extended their power in part because they faced few serious rivals. The Lithuanian and northern Ruthenian lands, protected by their great forests, in which the Mongol armies could not operate, had escaped the Mongol tsunami. Under Mindaugas, the cities of Black Ruthenia, including

---

[3] Rowell, *Lithuania*, 50; Błaszczyk, *Dzieje*, i, 34.   [4] Rowell, *Lithuania*, 50, 64–5.
[5] Nancy Shields Kollmann, 'Collateral succession in Kievan Rus'', *HUS*, 14/3–4 (1990), 377–87.

Hrodna, Navahrudak, Vaukavysk, and Slonim, were absorbed gradually without any reference in the sources to their being taken by force.[6] The Lithuanian grand dukes emerged over the next half a century as the most effective force for resistance to Mongol domination, as they did not, like the shattered remnants of the already splintered Rurikid dynasty, have to bend their knee to the Mongol khan.[7] Where force was used, as in the wars over Halych-Volhynia after 1340, or in the capture of Kyiv in the 1360s, it was directed primarily against rivals for control: the kings of Poland and Hungary. This was not a conquest by a foreign national group—the 'Lithuanian occupation' as Hrushevsky terms it—but a complex process in which force, accommodation, and assimilation all played their part.

Lithuanians and Ruthenians already traded with one another; penetration of the trade routes of White Ruthenia and other more easterly territories soon followed. By 1307 the grand dukes controlled Polatsk, while Vitsebsk—intermittently under their control—was secured when Algirdas, Gediminas's son, married the heiress of its last Ruthenian prince. Kyiv was first occupied by the Lithuanians in 1323; in 1332 there is evidence of a Lithuanian prince ruling there in a Lithuanian-Tatar condominium, although it was not until after the great Lithuanian victory at the Blue Waters in 1362 that it came under unchallenged Lithuanian control.[8]

The expanding dynasty was central to the extension of Lithuanian power. In contrast to Poland and Kievan Rus', where collateral inheritance promoted political fragmentation, the Gediminids largely contained and channelled the potential for disintegration posed by their staggering fecundity. Despite a system of succession similar to the Slavic communities surrounding them, in Lithuania the dynasty's rapid growth proved a spur to expansion, not fragmentation. Even ignoring the children of his brothers and cousins, Gediminas himself had eight sons and five or six daughters (see Fig. 1. Genealogy 1).[9]

Several of his sons were just as fertile, none more copiously than Algirdas, who, together with his younger brother Kęstutis, ousted their brother Jaunutis as grand duke in a coup in 1345. Although the details of the order and the number of his offspring are unclear, with his two wives Algirdas produced twelve or thirteen sons and nine or ten daughters (see Fig. 2. Genealogy 2).[10]

---

[6] Генадзь Сагановіч, *Нарыс гісторыі Беларусі ад старажытнасці да канца XVIII стагоддзя* (Minsk, 2001), 60–1; Michał Giedroyć, 'The arrival of Christianity in Lithuania: Early contacts (thirteenth century)', *OSP*, 18 (1985), 15–16.

[7] Jaroslaw Pelenski, 'The contest between Lithuania and the Golden Horde in the fourteenth century for supremacy over eastern Europe', in *The Contest for the Legacy of Kievan Rus'* (Boulder, CO, 1998), 131–50.

[8] Rowell, *Lithuania*, 83–4; Pelenski, 'Contest', 134.

[9] Błaszczyk, *Dzieje*, i, 110. Tęgowski suggests eight sons and six daughters: Jan Tęgowski *Pierwsze pokolenia Giedyminowiczów* (Poznań, 1999), table 1, 304–5; Rowell has seven sons and six daughters: *Lithuania*, genealogical table 2.

[10] This is based on Darius Baronas, Artūras Dubonis, and Rimvydas Petrauskas, *Lietuvos Istorija*, iii: *XIII a.–1385 m.* (Vilnius, 2011), 338–9, 356–9; Rowell, *Lithuania*, genealogical tables 1–4, Tęgowski, *Pierwsze pokolenia*, table 1, 304–5; and Tadeusz Wasilewski, 'Daty urodzin Jagiełły i Witolda: Przyczynek do genealogii Giedyminowiczów', *PW*, 1 (1991), 15–34. It is largely, informed, however, by Nikodem, 'Data urodzenia Jagiełły: Uwagi o starszeństwie synów Olgierda i Julianny', *Genealogia*, 12 (2000), 23–49, the most convincing analysis: see Ch. 8, 74–5.

Gediminas c.1275–1341 × 1342, Grand Duke 1315–41 × 1342													
Narimantas (Hleb), d. of Hrodna, Polatsk, Pinsk † 1348	Danutė/Elžbieta = (1316) Wacław, d. of Płock † 1364	Vytautas (?), d. of Trakai † 1336	**Algirdas** Grand Duke 1344/5–1377 † 1377	Marija = (1320) Dmitrii, d. of Tver † 1349	Karijotas (Mykhailo), d. of Novaharodak † 1365	Jaunutis Grand Duke 1342–1344 d. of Zaslavl 1346–1366 † 1366	**Kęstutis** Grand duke 1381–1382 d. of Trakai = (c. 1344) Birutė	Aldona (Anna) = (1325) Casimir III, king of Poland † 1339	Liubartas (Dmitrii) d. of Lutsk & Volodymyr 1340–1384 † 1384	Manvydas d. of Kernavė & Slonim † 1343	Eufemija = (1331) Bolesław/Iurii, d. of Halych-Volhynia † 1341	Aigustė (Anastasia) = (1333) Semen Ivanovich, duke of Muscovy † 1345	Unnamed daughter = Andrei Mstislavich of Kozelsk
1. Semen † after 1386 2. Patryk = Helena of Starodub † 1383 × 1387 3. Alexander † after 1386 3. Iurii, d. of Betz † 1392 4. Nikolai d. of Pinsk			**For children see Fig. 2.**		1. Iurii, d. of Podolia † 1374/5 2. Dmitrii = (1356) Anna, dtr of Ivan Ivanovich, d. of Muscovy † 1399 3. Alexander Duke of Volodymyr (1366) & Podolia (1374) † 1386 × 1388 4. Kostiantyn d. of Podolia † 1388 × 1392 5. Fedor, d. of Podolia, † 1409 × 1416 6. Vasyl, d. of Podolia (1390) 7. Anastasia = (c.1370) Roman I of Moldavia † 1408	1. Mikhail, d. of Zaslavl, † 1399 2. Hryhory 3. Semen	**For children see Fig. 3. Genealogy 3**		1. Fëdor d. of Lutsk (1383–c.1392); d. of Volodymyr (c.1392–1431); d. of Novhorod-Sevirsk (1393–5), † 1431 2. Lazar 3. Semen 4. Anna = (pre 1394), Přemek, d. of Opava † 1404 × 1406				

Fig. 1. Genealogy 1. The Gediminids.

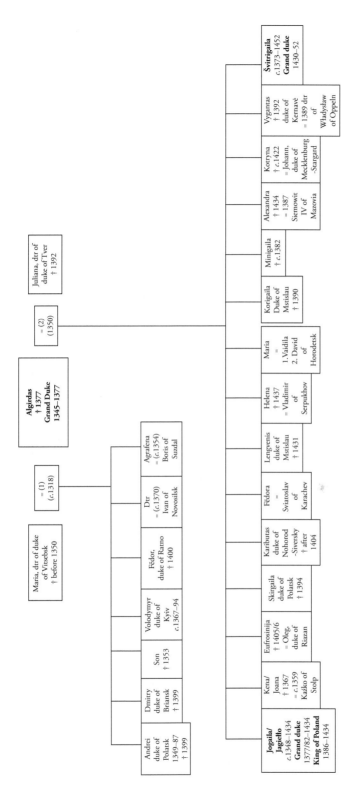

Fig. 2. Genealogy 2. The descendants of Algirdas.

Notes: Tęgowski and *Lietuvos Istorijos* regard Fëdor of Ratno as the eldest son of Algirdas's first marriage. For a discussion of the problem of the order and birthdates of Algirdas's children, see Ch. 8, 74–5.

Unlike Poland, hemmed in by the Holy Roman Empire to its west and Hungary to its south, Lithuania could expand to satisfy—for the most part—the ambitions of Gediminas's progeny. Daughters were married to Ruthenian princes, giving the Gediminids claims to Ruthenian territory when local dynasties died out.[11] Algirdas's first marriage to Maria/Anna of Vitsebsk opened the way to the absorption of a vital centre on the trade routes of northern Eurasia, while the marriage of his brother Liubartas to a Volhynian princess provided the basis of the Lithuanian claim to part of the kingdom of Halych-Volhynia.[12] Yet if dynastic manoeuvres played a significant role, it was the Gediminids' successful resistance to Mongol domination that ensured the loyalty of many Ruthenians.[13]

The results were impressive. By Algirdas's death in 1377 his sons ruled duchies across the Ruthenian lands. Of the sons of his first marriage, Andrei held Polatsk, Dmitry was established in Briansk, Fëdor held Ratno, and Volodymyr ruled Kyiv. Gediminas's other sons and their descendants were not neglected. Narimantas was duke of Pinsk and Polatsk, and governor of Novgorod for the brief period after 1333 when it swore allegiance to Lithuania. Four of Narimantas's five sons acquired Ruthenian duchies, while the sons of Karijotas, duke of Navahrudak, ruled Podolia.

Gediminid retention of Ruthenian duchies depended on the dynasty's rapid acculturation based on its adoption of Ruthenian as the language of government. A sophisticated written language, it was ideal for the purpose of building Gediminid authority, while its use meant that Ruthenians could integrate successfully into the Gediminid system. The Gediminids who held Ruthenian principalities, and the daughters who married into Ruthenian princely families, were baptized into the Orthodox faith and took Ruthenian names: Narimantas became Hleb and Karijotas was baptized Mykhailo; their children bore Slavic names.

The Gediminids fused Lithuanian and Ruthenian elements into a composite, dynastic system. The long argument between nationalist historians of Lithuania, Belarus, and Ukraine over whether this process produced a Lithuanian state, or a Ruthenian-Lithuanian state, in which the leading role was played by the more advanced culture of the Ruthenians, rather misses the point by concentrating on state power and projecting back an image of statehood that owes more to the nineteenth than the fourteenth century. The grand duchy was not a unitary modern state, but a successful dynastic condominium built on family loyalty. Its decentralized, composite nature explains its expansion and survival. Long before 1386 the Lithuanians and Ruthenians developed a system that allowed pagan and Orthodox cultures to survive and prosper alongside each other. Ultimate control lay with the pagan grand duke in the Lithuanian heartland, but paganism was no

---

[11] Stephen C. Rowell, 'Pious princesses or the daughters of Belial: Pagan Lithuanian dynastic diplomacy 1279–1423', *Medieval Prosopography*, 15/1 (1994), 3–75.

[12] Rowell, *Lithuania*, 88; Любавский, *Областное*, 38–40.

[13] Alvydas Nikžentaitis, 'Litauen unter den Grossfürsten Gedimin (1316–1341) und Olgerd (1345–1377)', in Marc Löwener (ed.), *Die 'Blüte' der Staaten des östlichen Europa im 14. Jahrhundert* (Wiesbaden, 2004), 66–8.

missionary faith, and the dynastic system held together well under the powerful rule of Gediminas, and then Algirdas and Kęstutis.

Lithuania was a formidable construct, suited to its environment. By Algirdas's death in 1377 it stretched from the shores of the Baltic virtually to the Black Sea. Yet if the Gediminids held the upper hand for much of the fourteenth century, they had important rivals in the Orthodox grand dukes of Muscovy, who were more attractive to successive patriarchs of Constantinople than the pagan Gediminids. Muscovy's first great success was the transfer of the Orthodox metropolitanate of all Rus' from Vladimir-Suzdal' to Moscow in 1325. Algirdas brought Smolensk precariously into the Lithuanian orbit, but despite his second marriage to Juliana of Tver, Tver and Novgorod preserved their independence by playing Lithuania off against Muscovy, and could not be absorbed. Algirdas led three attacks on Moscow: in 1368 he turned back after three days; in 1370 he stayed little longer, while in 1372 he refused battle although both armies were drawn up ready. Once intimidation failed, Algirdas was unwilling to risk all-out war against an Orthodox enemy who might use religion to subvert the loyalty of his Ruthenian subjects.[14] It was a dilemma that faced all his successors, and Lithuanian-Muscovite rivalry was to shape the history of eastern Europe for centuries to come.

By 1377 the very factors that had enabled Lithuania's rapid expansion were causing the problems that are inevitable once territorial accumulation reaches its natural limits. Orthodox Ruthenians now considerably outnumbered pagan Lithuanians in the Gediminid realms. Given the rapid cultural assimilation of so many Gediminids, the possibility that the whole dynasty would be absorbed into the Slavic world was starkly apparent: all the children of Algirdas's first marriage accepted Orthodox baptism, and Algirdas's second wife, Juliana, noted for her piety, brought Orthodox influences to the heart of the Gediminid system. Algirdas and Kęstutis were strongly attached to their pagan faith, and too much trust should not be placed in later Ruthenian chronicles that suggest Algirdas converted to Orthodoxy on his deathbed and was buried, instead of undergoing the spectacular traditional pagan funeral by immolation attested by other sources.[15]

There were good reasons for remaining pagan. Lithuania straddled the great cultural faultline dividing the Orthodox east from the Catholic west. Its rulers were adept at playing off west against east and manoeuvring effectively between the Orthodox and Catholic worlds while avoiding long-term commitment to either. The dangers of opting for one side were demonstrated by Mindaugas. In 1251, in order to win the Livonian Order's support for a campaign against the Samogitians, he accepted baptism in the Latin rite, for which, in 1253 he was sent a royal crown by Innocent IV. Mindaugas was thus the first—and last—Lithuanian ruler before 1386 whose title of *rex* was recognized beyond its borders: Gediminas might style himself Gedeminne (*Dei Gratia*) *Letwinorum et* (*multorum*) *Ruthenorum Rex* or *Koningh van Lettowen*, but if popes might occasionally

---

[14] Paszkiewicz, *O genezie*, 126.
[15] *PSRL*, xvii, col. 416. For the evidence see Sužiedėlis, 'Lietuva', 38–9.

use the title for politeness' sake they, like other Catholic rulers, did not recognize his royal status.[16]

The perils of conversion rapidly became apparent. The Lithuanian boyars and non-princely dukes were fiercely wedded to paganism, while Mindaugas's acceptance of sponsorship from the Livonian Order, which was busily subduing the pagan Baltic tribes, provoked opposition from those who saw it as Lithuania's deadliest enemy. Civil strife soon followed. In 1261 Mindaugas returned to paganism and expelled Catholics from Lithuania, although it was not enough to save him from assassination by Daumantas of Nalšia, acting on behalf of Mindaugas's nephew Treniota, who succeeded him, only to be assassinated in his turn, as were his two immediate successors, one of whom, Mindaugas's son Vaišvilkas, murdered in 1267, was a proselytizing Orthodox Christian.[17]

Order was only restored in the reigns of Vytenis and Gediminas. The resistance to Mindaugas's apostasy gives a tantalizing glimpse of the role of the *bajorai* (boyars), a word that entered Lithuanian from Ruthenian and that can—if with reservations—be translated as 'nobles'.[18] Fleeting references in the sources—all of them foreign—make it clear that although under Vytenis and Gediminas the dynasty had firmly established its control, it did consult with its boyars, especially before mounting military campaigns. The nature of this consultation is unclear, and too much should not be read into Peter of Dusburg's reference to one such assembly in 1308 as *parlamentum*.[19] Gediminid Lithuania was a patrimonial system, but the dynasty's authority was in practice limited by custom, not least because of Lithuania's rudimentary institutional structure. Authority depended on the charisma of the grand duke and his relationship with his brothers, sons, and boyars. Mindaugas's assassination was a warning that there were limits to charismatic power.

Gediminas learnt from Mindaugas's fate. He sought to diminish the significance of the metropolitan of Kyiv's relocation to Moscow by following the lead of Iurii I, prince of Halych-Volhynia, who successfully lobbied in Constantinople for the establishment of a separate metropolitanate in 1303. It only lasted five years, but a separate Lithuanian metropolitanate was established in Navahrudak at some point between 1315 and 1317. Thus Orthodoxy was more than simply tolerated. It was actively promoted by the dynasty, partly to ensure the loyalty of its Ruthenian subjects, and partly to advance Gediminid ambitions to rule all Rus'. Orthodox clerics contributed substantially to Lithuanian government and its relations with the Orthodox world.[20] Yet neither Gediminas nor Algirdas was willing to convert. The dangers of assimilation and the obliteration of Lithuanian culture were clear, paganism was deep-rooted and well organized, and resistance to any such move among the Lithuanian boyars was fierce.

---

[16] Catholic sources described Gediminas as *rex sive dux*: Rowell, *Lithuania*, 63–4.
[17] Rowell, *Lithuania*, 51–2; Giedroyć, 'Arrival', 16–20, 22–6.   [18] See Ch. 26, 298.
[19] Peter von Dusburg, *Chronica terrae Prussiae*, in *SRPr*, i, 171–2; Rowell, *Lithuania*, 61–2.
[20] See Rowell, *Lithuania*, 149–88.

Lithuania's relations with western Europe were equally complex. Its acquisition of Ruthenian lands coincided with rising pressure from the Order, whose conquest of the pagan Prussians was complete by the 1280s. The decayed Livonian Knights of the Sword were placed under the control of the Teutonic Order in 1237, giving the Order a great incentive to seize control of Samogitia, which divided Livonia from Prussia. The Samogitians occupied a unique position. The heartland of the Lithuanian state lay in Aukštaitija, which contained the principal power-centres of Vilnius and Trakai. The Samogitian clans were closely related to the Aukštaitijans, but jealously guarded their separate identity, distinctive culture, and political autonomy. Samogitia was but loosely integrated into the Gediminid system and remained strongly pagan: Samogitians had been prominent in the opposition to Mindaugas's conversion.

In the fourteenth century, the revitalized Order increased the pressure. The fall of Acre in 1291 ended its long commitment to Palestine, while the destruction of the Templars after 1307 implicitly threatened all the military orders. A new role was required. In 1309 grand master Siegfried von Feuchtwangen prudently moved the Order's headquarters from Venice to the Marienburg in Prussia, which was reconstructed as a massive fortress-monastery at the centre of a vast network of subsidiary houses across the Empire. The Order channelled its considerable resources into the crusade against the remaining pagans of northern Europe. Its call for support met an enthusiastic response from across Europe, encouraged by John of Luxembourg. From the 1320s, foreign knights swelled the ranks of the north Germans who formed the core of the Order's recruits. As they came, raids became more frequent and more devastating.

To contain this growing threat, the Lithuanians turned west. Gediminas proved as adept an operator in the murky labyrinth of Latin diplomacy as he was in the Orthodox world. He flirted with the papacy, writing to John XXII in 1322 expressing his desire for peace with his Catholic enemies and hinting at possible conversion. Peace was signed in Vilnius in 1323 and ratified in Rome, but when John's envoys arrived in Vilnius in 1324 Gediminas refused baptism or support for their missionary activities. He allowed the construction of a church for foreign merchants in Vilnius dedicated to St Nicholas; and the Franciscans were permitted to build a hospital: they were to remain, ministering to the sick and providing Latin secretaries for the dynasty's increasingly frequent contacts with western Europe, although they had to be careful not to cross the line into missionary activity. When they did, they suffered: Franciscans were executed in 1341 and 1369 for publicly challenging paganism.[21]

As pressure from the Order grew, the number of Lithuanian raids on Poland declined: of fifty-two mounted between 1210 and 1376, thirty-four took place before 1300.[22] As raiding declined in intensity, the Gediminids played off the numerous competing powers to their west, including the Order. In 1229 Konrad I, duke of Mazovia, hired Lithuanian troops during his struggle with Władysław Laskonogi for

---

[21] Rowell, *Lithuania*, 189, 274–5. [22] Błaszczyk, *Dzieje*, i, 77, table 1.

the Cracow throne. Mazovia was ravaged by Lithuanian raids, but in 1279, in an attempt to prevent them, Bolesław II married Gaudemantė, daughter of grand duke Traidenis; she was baptized into the Catholic church, taking the name Sophia. Thereafter the Mazovians sustained largely friendly relations until the Lithuanian occupation of Podlasie in 1323–4.

Gediminas used Lithuanian princesses as bargaining counters in the west as in the east. At some point between 1316 and 1318, his daughter Danutė or Danmila married Wacław, Bolesław II's son by his second marriage, taking the Christian name Elizabeth. In 1331, another, Eufemia, married Bolesław, Bolesław II's grandson, who took the name Iurii when he converted to Orthodoxy on becoming prince of Halych-Volhynia. The most significant marriage, however, was that of another daughter Aldona, christened Anna, who in 1325 married Łokietek's sixteen-year-old son, the future Casimir III. Historians have claimed that this was the centrepiece of the first formal Polish-Lithuanian alliance, seen by some as an important step on the road to Krewo. No treaty survives, but it is clear that there was some kind of agreement, though whether it took the form of a defensive-offensive alliance, a more limited pact, or a simple contract to hire Lithuanian troops is impossible to establish. There were Lithuanian troops in the army with which Łokietek attacked Brandenburg in 1326. The Poles and Lithuanians co-operated in campaigns against the Order until 1331, when a refusal by Łokietek's Hungarian allies to fight alongside pagans may have been the reason behind his failure to turn up for a joint campaign in which Gediminas—unusually, for he was no soldier—was to take part.[23] The rapprochement did not last long. It was destroyed by Casimir's decision to make peace with the Order in 1343, and the contest for control of Halych-Volhynia. Relations over the next three decades were hostile, with major Lithuanian raids on Poland in 1341, 1350 (twice), 1353, 1370, and 1376. Lithuania now stood alone against the Order, which flourished under Winrich von Kniprode (1351–82), raiding ever deeper into Lithuanian territory and threatening Samogitia.

By Algirdas's death in 1377, the Gediminid system was under strain. The emergence of Muscovy from the Golden Horde's shadow following Dmitrii Donskoi's 1380 victory at Kulikovo Field created a new and dangerous rival for the heritage of Kievan Rus'. The failure to subdue Muscovy meant that the days of easy territorial acquisitions to the east and south were over, while the Polish-Hungarian alliance under Louis of Anjou secured most of Halych-Volhynia. There would be no easy pickings for the next generation of Gediminids and no fat new duchies to distribute to ambitious princelings. By 1377 pagans were outnumbered by the Orthodox within the dynasty itself. This fact, as much as the extraordinary number of Gediminas's descendants—in 1377, three sons, at least thirty-five grandsons, and some thirteen great-grandsons were alive in the male line alone—threatened to undermine the remarkable dynastic cohesion that had sustained Lithuania's explosive expansion.[24]

---

[23] Stanisław Zajączkowski, 'Przymierze polsko-litewskie 1325 r.', *KH*, 40 (1926), 567–617; Błaszczyk, *Dzieje*, i, 130–49; Rowell, *Lithuania*, 232–7.

[24] See Figs 1 and 2. Genealogies 1 and 2, pp. 22, 23.

Dynastic strife was contained after Gediminas's death by Algirdas and Kęstutis, but it now threatened to break out in a new and more dangerous form. The successful collaboration of Algirdas and Kęstutis depended upon a division of labour: Algirdas controlled Vilnius and the grand duchy's eastern and southern Ruthenian lands, while Kęstutis, from his base in Trakai, ruled over much of the ethnic Lithuanian heartland, and Samogitia, where he enjoyed particular influence after his marriage to Birutė of Palanga, daughter of a powerful Samogitian boyar. It seems that Algirdas and Kęstutis intended this arrangement to continue after their deaths through their favourite sons and chosen heirs, Jogaila and Vytautas, who, according to chronicle accounts, were childhood friends and companions, born within a couple of years of each other.[25] According to Algirdas's wishes, Jogaila inherited Algirdas's grand ducal title, but Kęstutis was now the dynastic patriarch. The delicate balance established by Algirdas and Kęstutis was about to be severely tested.

It was a difficult balance to maintain against the ambitions of Algirdas's other sons. The eldest, Andrei, had ruled Polatsk since 1349; Dmitry was duke of Briansk; Volodymyr, duke of Vitsebsk, had been granted Kyiv in 1367; while Fëdor was duke of Ratno. The loyalty of these Orthodox princes to the pagan establishment was open to question now that Muscovy was a growing pole of attraction. Algirdas's testament raised potential problems for the pagan sons of his second wife, Juliana. For if Jogaila was bequeathed all of his father's extensive patrimony, his pagan brothers—Skirgaila, Lengvenis, Karigaila, Vygantas, Kaributas, and Švitrigaila—received little or nothing. Given that Kęstutis held much of pagan Lithuania as duke of Trakai and would undoubtedly expect to pass these lands on to his own sons, there was almost nothing that could be granted to them in the Lithuanian heartlands, and Kaributas converted to Orthodoxy in 1380 when granted Novhorod-Siversky.[26]

The favourable circumstances that had sheltered Lithuanian paganism in the fault line between the Latin and Orthodox worlds were coming to an end. The issues were laid bare after Algirdas's death, as Lithuania faced simultaneous threats from west and east. In July 1377 Louis of Anjou attacked areas of Halych-Volhynia in Lithuanian hands with a joint Polish-Hungarian force. Only duke Iury Narymuntovich of Belts offered any resistance. Fëdor, duke of Ratno and Algirdas's brother Liubartas, duke of Lutsk, swore loyalty to Louis, as did the three sons of Karijotas, who had accepted Catholic baptism, in Podolia.[27]

In the east, disorder was the result of Jogaila's first attempt to unravel the dynastic conundrum left by his father. Jogaila, aware of Andrei of Polatsk's resentment at being overlooked in Algirdas's testament, stripped him of his duchy in the winter of 1377–8, granting it to Skirgaila, his younger brother and right-hand man, who, like the other sons of Juliana, had received nothing from

---

[25] Henryk Łowmiański, *Polityka Jagiellonów* (Poznań, 1999), 128; Zenonas Ivinskis, 'Jogailos santykiai su Kęstučiu ir Vytautu iki 1392 metų', in Šapoka (ed.), *Jogaila*, 47–8.
[26] Ludwik Kolankowski, *Dzieje Wielkiego Księstwa Litewskiego za Jagiellonów*, i (Warsaw, 1930), 12.
[27] Krzyżaniakowa and Ochmański, *Jagiełło*, 58.

Algirdas.[28] Andrei fled, first to Pskov, and then to Moscow; within a year, he returned with Dmitrii Donskoi to ravage Sevirsk, as Skirgaila was chased from Polatsk by its inhabitants, reluctant to accept a pagan governor. Skirgaila converted to Orthodoxy, but failed to retake the city despite a thirteen-week siege.

Jogaila's deposition of Andrei was risky, but it confirms that the dynastic condominium was breaking down. Algirdas and Kęstutis had cooperated successfully, but although some historians talk of a system of diarchic rule, there was no formalized structure, and the system of Algirdas and Kęstutis rested on their personal relationship.[29] Relations between uncle and nephew soon deteriorated. In 1380 Jogaila allied himself with Mamai, khan of the Blue Horde, against Dmitrii Donskoi, only to arrive too late—probably deliberately—for the decisive battle of Kulikovo. Between 1377 and 1379 the Order plundered Samogitia and Podlasie and threatened Vilnius. Kęstutis could not mount any serious raids in response. Fearing that the Order might support Andrei, Jogaila persuaded Kęstutis to sign a ten-year truce in September 1379, although it did not cover Samogitia.[30] The Order, keen to drive a wedge between uncle and nephew, insinuated that Kęstutis was planning a coup. In February 1380 the Livonian Order signed a secret treaty with Jogaila alone, in which it agreed not to attack his lands. As mistrust grew, Jogaila signed another secret treaty in May 1380, promising not to aid Kęstutis if the Order attacked Trakai.

In 1381 the pot boiled over. The Order hinted to Kęstutis of its treaties with Jogaila. While Jogaila's forces were besieging Polatsk after Skirgaila's expulsion, Kęstutis marched into Vilnius where he caught Jogaila unprepared. He found the secret treaty with the Order, declared Jogaila deposed, and adopted the title of supreme duke, forcing Jogaila to renounce his powers in writing, and to swear an oath of loyalty.[31] Jogaila was deprived of his patrimony and granted the duchies of Krėva and Vitsebsk. If Kęstutis calculated that Jogaila would follow the example of Jaunutis, who had accepted his 1345 deposition with relatively good grace, he miscalculated badly.

Jogaila's brother Kaributas, encouraged by Jogaila, led the counterattack. As Kęstutis hastened south-east to confront him, Jogaila struck. The Vilnius merchants, fearing that Kęstutis's hostility to the Order might adversely affect trade, handed the city over to Jogaila. He formed an alliance with the Order, which besieged Trakai. When asked whether they wished to surrender to the Order or to Jogaila, the inhabitants chose Jogaila. Vytautas, hurrying to his father's aid, was routed in a bloody encounter beneath the walls of Vilnius. When Kęstutis and Vytautas deployed their forces outside Trakai opposite Jogaila's much larger army on 3 August 1382, Jogaila suggested that to avoid further bloodshed they should talk peace. Despite giving assurances of their personal safety, Jogaila arrested them,

---

[28] For the problems of Gediminid genealogy, see Ch. 8, 74–5.

[29] Jonė Deveikė, 'The Lithuanian diarchies', *SEER*, 28 (1950), 392–405; the revival of the idea by Gudevičius and Nikžentaitis is criticized by Nikodem: 'Jedynowładztwo czy diarchia? Przyczynek do dziejów ustroju W. Ks. Litewskiego do końca XIV w.', *ZH*, 68 (2003), 7–30.

[30] Krzyżaniakowa and Ochmański, *Jagiełło*, 61.   [31] Kolankowski, *Dzieje*, i, 21.

sending Kęstutis in chains to Krėva, where he died in mysterious circumstances five days later, suffocated or strangled according to Vytautas and other sources favourable to him, although there is no independent confirmation of the allegation, and suicide has also been suggested. Jogaila did not execute Vytautas, who escaped dressed as one of his wife's female attendants, possibly because Jogaila deliberately ensured he was loosely guarded.[32] Kęstutis's duchy of Trakai was given to Skirgaila. There was to be no return to ducal rule, and apparently no place for the Kęstutids in Jogaila's Lithuania (see Fig. 3. Genealogy 3).

Jogaila had overthrown Kęstutis with the Order's support, but the Order had little interest in sustaining him. It sought to destabilize the Gediminid dynastic state, hoping to sever the pagan Lithuanian core from its Orthodox hinterland. Having supported Jogaila against Kęstutis, it kept the pot bubbling by offering a safe haven to Vytautas, despite signing peace with Jogaila on 31 October/ 1 November on the Dubissa river, where it exploited the political turbulence to inflict harsh terms. Jogaila agreed to support the Order against all its enemies, not to declare war without the Order's permission, to accept baptism for himself and all Lithuania, and, in the most painful clause, to cede Samogitia up to the Dubissa. The terms were so harsh that Jogaila refused to ratify them, and grand master Konrad Zöllner von Rottenstein declared war on 30 July 1383.[33]

If Jogaila was to feel secure on his throne, he would have to find a solution to the grand duchy's structural problems, exposed by Andrei's rebellion and Kęstutis's coup. By 1382 the days of paganism were numbered. Should more Orthodox Gediminids follow Andrei and Dmitry of Briansk in defecting to Moscow, control over the grand duchy's Ruthenian lands would be fundamentally threatened. An obvious solution would be for Jogaila to accept Orthodox baptism. Events to the east produced an apparently favourable conjuncture: in August 1382 Tokhtamysh (Tohtamış), khan of the Golden Horde, razed Moscow to avenge Kulikovo. Although Jogaila allowed his mother to negotiate a peace treaty with Dmitrii at some point in 1383–4, its terms constituted a Faustian pact. In return for the hand of one of Dmitrii's daughters, Jogaila promised to accept Orthodox baptism, but it was clear that Dmitrii expected him to recognize, if not his outright suzerainty, then at least his superiority. Should the Gediminids abandon paganism, the Lithuanians would be dominated or completely swallowed up by east Slavic culture, if Dmitrii did not serve them up to the Order.[34]

---

[32] *SRPr*, ii, 712–13; Krzyżaniakowa and Ochmański, *Jagiełło*, 65–73. Nikodem suggests that Kęstutis died of natural causes, and that Skirgaila was not responsible for his murder, as rumour maintained: Jarosław Nikodem, *Witold Wielki Książę Litewski (1354 lub 1355–27 października 1430)* (Cracow, 2013), 68–9, and 'Rola Skirgiełły na Litwie do r. 1394', *Scripta Minora* 2 (1998), 99–100. For the fullest chronicle account, which claims Kęstutis was throttled by Jogaila's servants, see *PSRL*, xxxv, col. 64.

[33] Mečislovas Jučas, *Lietuvos ir Lenkijos unija (XIV a. vid.–XIX a. pr.)* (Vilnius, 2000), 104–6; Paszkiewicz, *O genezie*, 143–50.

[34] Krzyżaniakowa and Ochmański, *Jagiełło*, 79–81; Oskar Halecki, *Dzieje unii jagiellońskiej*, i (Cracow, 1919), 83–4; Jučas, *Unija*, 106.

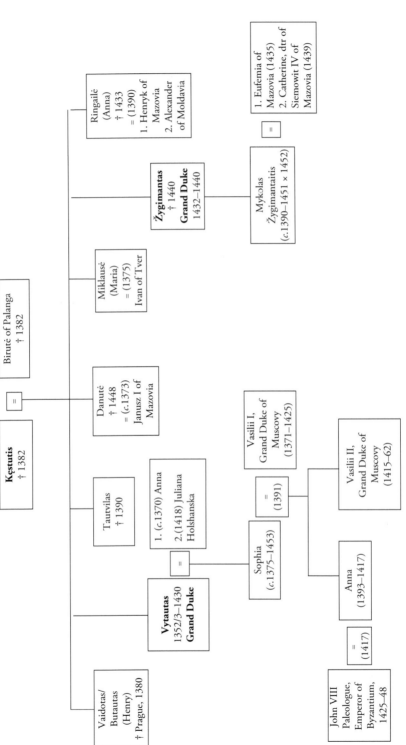

Fig. 3. Genealogy 3. The Kęstutids.

Notes: This is a simplified table. It follows Rowell, *Lithuania Ascending*, genealogical table 2b in only giving the seven children of Kęstutis known from verifiable sources. Rowell regards Vaidotas and Butautas as dialect variations of the same name, unlike Tęgowski and *Lietuvos Istorija*, iii.

Jogaila had another iron in the fire. Historians have long argued about which side initiated the negotiations that led to the Krewo Act, with many Polish scholars following Halecki, whose classic 1919 account claimed that it was the Poles who first suggested a marriage between Jadwiga and Jogaila.[35] It is impossible to determine who made the first move: attempts to do so depend on intuition and creative reading of the scanty sources. Despite the unresolved conflict over Halych-Volhynia, where a *de facto* partition had embedded itself by the 1380s, several unconnected developments opened the way to a rapprochement. For the Poles, a political relationship with Lithuania was enticing. Although they had crowned Jadwiga *in regem* in 1384, it was vital to find her a husband to sustain the dynasty. Jogaila was an attractive candidate. A union with Lithuania would strengthen Poland after the severing of the link with Hungary. This was necessary given the prospect of Luxembourg control of Brandenburg, Hungary, Bohemia, and the Empire, where Sigismund's elder brother Wenzel (Václav) was elected King of the Romans in 1376. Union would end the Lithuanian raids that had caused so much damage to Poland's eastern palatinates and open the way to a settlement over Halych-Volhynia, while Jogaila's baptism and the conversion of his pagan subjects to Catholicism would strengthen Poland's position within the Catholic world and embarrass the Order. Yet it would be wrong to see hostility to the Order as the fundamental factor bringing the two realms together: Poland had been at peace with it since 1343, and although Krewo contained a clause in which Jogaila swore to regain lands lost by the *corona regni*, the Poles were reluctant to end the long peace. For the Małopolskan lords who played such a prominent role in the negotiations with Jogaila, Prussia was of little concern; they were far more interested in the south and east.

The Lithuanians, however, needed help against the Order. Not counting numerous minor border incursions, the Order mounted 96 raids on Lithuanian territory between 1345 and 1382: 66 from Prussia and 30 from Livonia. The Lithuanians managed 42 in reply: 31 on Prussia and 11 on Livonia.[36] By the 1370s the Order could strike deep into the Lithuanian heartlands, using the rivers as highways into the dense forests that were Lithuania's defensive barrier. It devastated the Trakai region in 1374, 1376, and 1377; Kaunas in 1362 and 1368; and attacked Vilnius itself in 1365 and 1377.[37] The cession of much of Samogitia in 1382, however temporary Jogaila regarded it, demonstrated all too plainly the dangers of dynastic strife. If Kaunas and the line of the Niemen fell, the Lithuanian heartlands would be dangerously exposed.

Conversion to Catholicism would have two advantages. Unlike conversion to Orthodoxy with its risks of cultural assimilation, it might allow Lithuanians to retain their separate identity within the grand duchy, while removing at a stroke the

---

[35] Halecki, *Dzieje*, i, 83–112, and *Jadwiga of Anjou and the Rise of East Central Europe* (Boulder, CO, 1991), 118. Paszkiewicz, *O genezę*, 201–2. For the debate, see Błaszczyk, *Dzieje*, i, 198–232.
[36] Zenonas Ivinskis, 'Litwa w dobie chrztu i unii z Polską', in Jerzy Kłoczowski (ed.), *Chrystianizacja Litwy* (Cracow, 1987), 24, 25.
[37] Jučas, *Unija*, 99.

Order's justification for its attacks, and securing the support of Poland, an important Catholic power with good links to the papacy. While conversion would undoubtedly complicate relations with Lithuania's Ruthenian territories and with the Orthodox Gediminids, for Jogaila union held out the prospect of strengthening grand ducal power by utilizing the sophisticated instruments of government developed in the Latin west. As Halecki put it, Jogaila would rather be king of Poland than a Muscovite vassal. His flirtation with Dmitrii was probably designed to put pressure on the Poles as the interregnum followed its tortuous course. Orthodox baptism would bring nothing to the table that was not already there, while the acquisition of a royal crown would strengthen Jogaila's position within the dynasty.[38]

Negotiations began in earnest after Jadwiga's coronation. In January 1385 a Lithuanian delegation led by Skirgaila arrived in Cracow with a formal request for Jadwiga's hand. There were many obstacles to the marriage, not least the attitude of Elizabeth of Bosnia, who in July 1385 expressed her readiness to fulfil the obligations entered into with Leopold von Habsburg for Jadwiga's marriage to his son William. Given that Jadwiga was soon to reach the canonical age for marriage, that William set out for Cracow to claim his bride, and that Jadwiga was nervous at the prospect of marrying a man three times her age rather than her childhood companion, supporters of the Lithuanian marriage had to move quickly: the Krewo Act was signed within a month of Elizabeth's declaration. The betrothal was a potentially serious obstacle but, although the Habsburgs asserted in a case they pursued in the papal curia that William had consummated his marriage with Jadwiga in Cracow, the young Queen was under the control of the Cracow lords who had committed themselves to the Lithuanian marriage; it is inconceivable that they would have allowed the youngsters to share a bed. Jan Długosz, who relished a good scandal, denies and then supports the rumours in his contradictory account, which relates the tale, almost certainly apocryphal, that Jadwiga was so determined to reach William she used an axe to break down the door of the apartment in Wawel castle to which she had been confined after his arrival. William slunk back to Austria, muttering about the 'Lithuanian Saracen'. He always considered himself Jadwiga's rightful husband, refused the 200,000 florins compensation negotiated by Elizabeth of Bosnia at Kréva, and did not marry until after Jadwiga's death.[39]

Jogaila now sought to heal the breach with Vytautas, to prevent the Order from disrupting the negotiations by exploiting dynastic divisions. After the breakdown of the Dubissa peace, the Order mounted a powerful raid in May 1384. Kaunas was

---

[38] For Paszkiewicz, this was the most important motive: *O genezie*, 162–3, 256–7; cf. Gotthold Rhode, *Die Ostgrenze Polens: Politische Entwicklung, kulterelle Bedeutung und geistige Auswirkung*, i (Cologne, 1955), 297. Halecki, *Jadwiga*, 121.

[39] *The Annals of Jan Długosz: A History of Eastern Europe from A.D. 965 to A.D. 1480*, tr. Maurice Michael (Chichester, 1997), 346. This is an abridged translation from the modern Polish, not the original Latin version. While it gives a good flavour of Długosz's rich work, it is frequently unreliable and occasionally misleading. All future references are to the modern Latin edn. Nikodem, *Jadwiga*, 122–56 and 'Gniewosz-Jadwiga-Wilhelm: Krytyka przekazu "Annales" Jana Długosza', *PH*, 98 (2007), 175–96; Tęgowski, 'Wprowadzenie w życiu postanowień aktu krewskiego w l. 1385–1399', *Studia z dziejów państwa i prawa polskiego*, 9 (2006), 79, 83.

captured and razed, and the Order constructed a castle there that they called Neu-Marienwerder as a launching-pad for further conquests. Fearing a new civil war, Jogaila secretly contacted Vytautas in his Prussian exile. In July 1384 Vytautas accepted his offer, returned to Lithuania, and appended his seal to the Krewo Act. With William eliminated and Vytautas back in the fold the way was open to consummate the union.

4

On Unions

Historians of late medieval and early modern Europe have shown a remarkable lack of interest in political unions. This is not to say that there has been no study of them; there has been a great deal, but it has overwhelmingly been conducted within the framework of individual national histories, or of the history of individual dynasties. With some distinguished exceptions, there have been few comprehensive attempts to define the nature of political unions in this period, or to study them in a comparative framework. The domination of political history by interest in the rise of the modern state means that historians have traditionally concentrated on state power, concerning themselves with the rationalization and extension of that power at the expense of particularism and provincial diversity. This domination was first established in the nineteenth century by the siren call of nationalism and the idea, given powerful sanction by the American and French revolutions, that the nation-state was the natural and highest form of political organization, to the extent that Alter has claimed that: 'Since ... 1789, the nation-state has become the sole legitimating principle of the order of states.'[1]

Whether or not this is true, the stories of nation- and state-building have been linked by generations of historians. Although the establishment and growth of the European Union has revived interest in the issue of non-unitary states and political federations, this revival is of questionable value for the study of unions before 1789, since faith in the sovereign nation-state as the basic component of what Steiger termed '*Überstaatlichkeit*', has remained largely unruffled, and studies of political union usually focus on the relations of sovereign states entering into federal arrangements.[2] Thus Forsyth, who entitles his 1981 study *Unions of States*, adds the significant subtitle *The Theory and Practice of Confederation*, stressing that he is interested in: 'the process by which states form themselves into federal unions or confederations'.[3] Insofar as he is interested in the historical background, Forsyth, like many others, considers only those pre-modern states deemed to have been proto-federalist, such as the Ancient Greek leagues of city states, the Swiss confederation, and the Dutch republic. He excludes unions that saw 'a complete fusion or incorporation in which one or all the members lose their identity as states', is

---

[1] Peter Alter, *Nationalism* (London, 1989), 93.
[2] Heinhard Steiger, *Staatlichkeit und Überstaatlichkeit: Eine Untersuchung zur rechtlichen und politischen Stellung der Europäischen Gemeinschaften*, Schriften zum Öffentlichen Recht, Bd 31 (Berlin, 1966).
[3] Murray Forsyth, *Unions of States. The Theory and Practice of Confederation* (New York, 1981), ix.

uninterested in 'so-called "real" unions', and spurns unions that were monarchical rather than republican in form.[4] He is not interested in the United Kingdom, which embodies one of the longest-lasting political unions in modern history. This is not uncommon among political scientists, since the United Kingdom, as Elazar observes, 'is assiduous in its rejection of federalist terminology'.[5] Davis states, with a hint of disapproval, that 'texts on "federal governments", having distinguished the "federal" form by a process of positive and negative differentiation, proceed to gather all "the rest" into an undifferentiated pile—confederal, devolutionary, unitary, federal unitary, etc.', suggesting that 'there is a treatise to be written on the "non-federal system of government"', but showing no interest in providing one.[6]

This obsession with federal unions leaves scant room for the many non-federal forms of union so common before 1789. One has to go back to 1882 for a comprehensive attempt to provide a framework for the study of all types of political union. In that year Georg Jellinek began his *Lehre von den Staatenverbindungen* with a characteristically pungent condemnation of current scholarship:

> In few areas of public law does such a lack of clarity reign supreme as in the study of unions of states. The essence of leagues of states and of union states, the nature of real unions, the juridical character of protectorates and of sovereignty, and so on, are so far from scholarly clarity that with regard to some of these ideas... no dominant interpretation has been constructed, and the academic legitimacy of the whole field can even be called into question.[7]

Jellinek cannot be accused of a lack of clarity. With forensic skill he formulated his views on the nature of unions, examining colonies and dependent territories; unions by incorporation and personal and dynastic unions; communities of states (*Staatengemeinschaften*) and systems of states, which he defined as unorganized juridical associations; the *Staatenstaat*, in which sovereign authority was not centralized to create a unitary state; what he called '*organisierten Verwaltungsbündnisse*', by which he meant arrangements established between states to facilitate international postal services and the like; confederal unions (*Staatenbunde*); real unions; and, finally, properly federal unions (*Bundesstaaten*).

As Jellinek observed, despite the concentration on the unitary state (*Einheitsstaat*) in classical political theory, such states were, in 1882, very much the exception. Yet scholarship on pre-1789 unions was then, as it is now, dominated by a teleological concern with the origins of unitary states. Jellinek's rigorously conceived ideas were informed and illustrated by examples drawn from history; yet

---

[4] Forsyth, *Unions*, 1. For similar approaches see: S. Rufus Davis, *The Federal Principle: A Journey through Time in Quest of a Meaning* (Berkeley, CA, 1978); Ernst Deuerlein, *Die historischen und philosophischen Grundlagen des föderativen Prinzips* (Munich, 1972); Daniel Elazar, *Exploring Federalism* (Tuscaloosa, 1987); Carl Joachim Friedrich, *Trends of Federalism in Theory and Practice* (London, 1968); David Lassere, *Étapes du féderalisme* (Lausanne, 1954); G.F. Sawyer, *Modern Federalism* (London, 1969).
[5] Elazar, *Federalism*, 48. [6] Davis, *Federal Principle*, 61, n. 33.
[7] Georg Jellinek, *Die Lehre von den Staatenverbindung* (Berlin, 1882), 3.

despite his critique of abstraction, his training in jurisprudence formed his account of unions, which was based on two principles: the indivisibility of sovereignty, and the state as a legal personality (*Staatspersönlichkeit*) in which that sovereignty resides. He dismissed the idea, central to much early modern political discourse, that sovereignty could reside in more than one part of the polity, be it the prince, the people, or some external or abstract principle, such as God, the law, or justice; or that it could be shared between different elements. Sovereignty, according to Jellinek, lies with the state alone and is embodied in its organs.[8]

Jellinek distinguished between political-historical and juridical unions. By the former he meant relationships that arose through contingency, such as personal unions, based on the vagaries of dynastic inheritance, in which states remained united only in the person of the ruler, and the union could dissolve at any time—as happened to the union of Britain with Hanover through the operation of the Salic Law in Hanover in 1837.[9] His principal interest, however, was in juridical unions, which rested on a legal basis, usually in the form of a foundation treaty or treaties, and which he categorized as unorganized or organized. By unorganized juridical unions he meant communities and leagues or alliances of states, and what he termed the 'state of estates' (*Staatenstaat*), by which he meant polities that formed political unions on a legal basis, but whose feudal roots and legal interpretation of lordship and authority were incompatible with modern ideas of sovereignty, which meant that they cannot be seen as true federations. Thus he contested the common view that the Holy Roman Empire after 1648 was a federation in which *Landeshoheit* was a form of sovereignty.[10]

In the second category, organized juridical unions, Jellinek analyses confederal unions, real unions, and federal unions. Although much of his treatment of the issues is similar to that of modern scholars, it is striking that he insists that federal unions, rather than constituting more mature forms of confederal unions, are a form of real union. They are juridical unions because, as with the 1707 Anglo-Scottish union, or the federal union of the United States of America established in 1789, they are legal creations and, as states brought into existence by the law, possessed the legal personality necessary to embody Jellinek's idea of sovereignty, while confederal unions fall short of the fusion of sovereignty required for a unitary state.

Jellinek's distinction between confederal and federal unions was strongly influenced by the debates among the founding fathers of the United States over whether sovereignty was vested in the states of the union or in the union itself. The great merit of his work is that, unlike most modern political scientists and historians, he endeavoured to provide a comprehensive taxonomy of political union that looked beyond federal unions. There are problems with his approach, however, not least in his jurist's insistence on what Hughes once called 'a false politico-legal doctrine, the analytical theory of sovereignty', a view echoed by Franklin, who accused Bodin of

---

[8] Jellinek, *Lehre*, 24–6.   [9] Jellinek, *Lehre*, 82–8.   [10] Jellinek, *Lehre*, 137–57.

primary responsibility for 'the seductive but erroneous notion that sovereignty is indivisible'.[11]

Yet even if most of his examples were drawn from the nineteenth century, Jellinek had a sense of history, arguing that judging historical unions within a framework based on theories of the modern state is of dubious value. Thus in talking—with an uncharacteristic note of humour—of what he termed the scholastic distinctions made by medieval and early modern writers between incorporating unions, *unio per suppressionem, per confusionem, per novationem*, of *unio realis aequali jure, inaequali jure*, and of *incorporativa, incorporatio plena* and *minus plena*, he recognized that before the development of the modern state, based as he saw it on the principle of indivisible sovereignty, it was perfectly legitimate for scholars to conceptualize unions differently, borrowing their ideas from private and canon law, rather than public law, or a law of nations that did not yet exist.[12]

It is important to recognize, as Jellinek did, that medieval and early modern unions should be understood on their own terms, a task for which the tools of modern political scientists are not always useful. As Jellinek observes, it is by no means only federal unions that are formed by a *foedus* or treaty; this was equally true of real unions such as the British union of 1707 or the British-Irish union of 1801. Yet modern political scientists may be forgiven their uncertainty regarding the classification of pre-modern unions. For historians have not been as helpful as they might in providing the necessary raw material upon which comparative work might be based. That is not to say that they have ignored pre-modern unions; far from it. There is a considerable body of work devoted to them, but almost all of it has been written within the framework of national history, with little attempt at comparison.[13] Although Pocock's appeal for a new British history that abandons the anglocentric history of the British unitary state has stimulated impressive attempts to replace the writing of separate histories of England, Scotland, Wales, and Ireland with a more integrated vision of the political unions of the British Isles, the new British history has neither killed off the writing of separate national histories, nor has it, as Robertson observes, brought any particular interest in locating the British unions in a comparative context.[14] Robertson's own work is a distinguished exception to this trend; much of the recent work on the British unions, however,

---

[11] Christopher Hughes, *Confederacies: An Inaugural Lecture delivered in the University of Leicester 8 November 1962* (Leicester, 1963), 10; Julian Franklin, 'Introduction', in Jean Bodin, *On Sovereignty*, ed. and tr. Franklin (Cambridge, 1992), xiii.

[12] Jellinek, *Lehre*, 68–9.

[13] Notable exceptions are Thomas Fröschl (ed.), *Föderationsmodelle und Unionsstrukturen: Über Staatenverbindungen in der frühen Neuzeit vom 15. zum 18. Jahrhundert* (Vienna, 1994); Joachim Bahlcke, 'Unionsstrukturen und Föderationsmodelle im Osten des ständischen Europa: Anmerkungen zu vergleichenden Ansätzen über das frühneuzeitliche Ostmitteleuropa', *Comparativ* (1998), 5, 57–73; Balázs Trencsényi and Márton Zászkaliczky (eds), *Whose Love of Which Country? Composite States, National Histories and Patriotic Discourses in Early Modern East-Central Europe* (Leiden, 2010).

[14] J.G.A. Pocock, 'British History: A plea for a new subject', *JMH*, 47 (1975), 601–21; J.G.A. Pocock, 'The limits and divisions of British History: In search of the unknown subject', *AHR*, 97 (1982), 311–36; John Robertson, *A Union for Empire: Political Thought and the British Union of 1707* (Cambridge, 1995), 3–4, 16.

shows little interest in contemporary comparisons, preferring to locate the problem within an Atlantic framework.[15]

Much study has recently been devoted to the idea of composite or multiple monarchy in late medieval and early modern Europe. This paradigm did not develop out of an interest in unions per se, but stemmed from unease about standard accounts of the development of the modern state before 1789. When Koenigsberger observed in 1975 that: 'most states in the early modern period were composite states, including more than one country under the sovereignty of one ruler', he was merely erecting one section of the conceptual framework within which he wished to discuss his main concern, the history of early modern representative assemblies and their relation to state formation.[16] Elliott, who was interested in monarchical unions, pointed out just how common the phenomenon of what he termed 'composite monarchy' was in early modern Europe.[17] By applying Koenigsberger's term 'composite state' to what were conventionally termed 'unions of the crowns' or 'personal unions', Elliott introduced a possible source of confusion into the debate. For Koenigsberger was explicitly referring to what Joseph Strayer had termed 'mosaic states', made up of many different provinces and regions with different characteristics, which, so Strayer argued, was true of most European states in this period.[18] Russell recognized this tension and preferred to use the term 'multiple' rather than 'composite' for monarchies of this type, arguing that since England did not have the single system of law characteristic of the unitary state it was therefore a composite monarchy, whereas after 1603, the Stuart realms of England and Wales, Scotland, and Ireland constituted a multiple kingdom. He concluded that: 'All multiple kingdoms are composite monarchies, but not all composite monarchies are multiple kingdoms'.[19]

The distinction is important, although it might have been clearer had Russell used the term 'composite state' instead of 'composite monarchy'. For the debate on composite monarchies is still overwhelmingly concerned with the development of the modern sovereign state, rather than the process of political union. Strayer, who argued that by 1300 'it was evident that the dominant political form in western Europe was going to be the sovereign state', was not interested in unions, but in states and the ways in which state-builders, usually—although not necessarily—

---

[15] For example Linda Colley, *Britons: Forging the Nation 1707–1837*, 2nd edn (New Haven, CT, 2005). For attempts to redress the balance, see Micheál Ó Siochrú and Andrew Mackillop (eds), *Forging the State: European State Formation and the Anglo-Scottish Union of 1707* (Dundee, 2009) and D.W. Hayton et al. (eds), *The Eighteenth Century Composite State: Representative Institutions in Ireland and Europe, 1689–1800* (Basingstoke, 2010).

[16] H.G. Koenigsberger, '*Dominium Regale* or *Dominium Politicum et Regale*: Monarchies and parliaments in early modern Europe', *Politicians and Virtuosi. Essays in Early Modern History* (London, 1986), 1–25.

[17] J.H. Elliott, 'A Europe of composite monarchies,' *P & P*, 137 (1992), 48–9, and 'Introduction', in Jon Arieta and J.H. Elliott (eds), *Forms of Union: The British and Spanish Monarchies in the Seventeenth and Eighteenth Centuries* (Donostia, 2009), 14.

[18] Joseph Strayer, *On the Medieval Origins of the Modern State* (Princeton, NJ, 1970), 53.

[19] Conrad Russell, 'Composite monarchies in early modern Europe: The British and Irish example', in Alexander Grant and Keith Stringer (eds), *Uniting the Kingdom: The Making of British History* (London, 1995), 133.

monarchs, overcame provincialism and regional resistance to central authority to produce the unitary states that embodied their claims to undivided sovereignty.[20] Rulers of multiple monarchies might seek to integrate their different realms more closely and treat them as provinces of a single state, but—as James I discovered after 1603—such a project was easier to conceive than to realize. Addressing the English parliament in 1607 he claimed that it was as impossible:

> for one King to governe two Contreys *Contiguous* . . . then for one head to governe two bodies, or one man to be husband of two wives, whereof Christ himselfe said, *Ab initio non fuit*.[21]

Parliament was unmoved, despite the analogies James drew between the union of the Picts and Scots that had created the kingdom of Scotland, and of the Anglo-Saxon heptarchy out of which the medieval English kingdom had emerged.[22] In practice, as Elliott shows, rulers of multiple kingdoms were more likely to respect the institutions, laws, and privileges of their separate realms and govern them separately:

> In return for a degree of benign neglect, local élites enjoyed a measure of self-government which left them without any urgent need to challenge the status quo. In other words, composite monarchies were built on a mutual compact between the crown and the ruling class of their different provinces which gave even the most arbitrary and artificial of unions a certain stability and resilience.[23]

When monarchs sought to impose a greater unity on their subjects, as in the British Isles under Charles I, or in Olivares's Spain, the result was often resistance, rebellion or civil war.[24]

Not all unions were arbitrary or artificial, however, and although historians have tended to view personal unions from above, from the point of view of monarchs and dynasties, the political communities of their various realms often took a close interest in the relationship between the constituent parts of political unions, and on occasion played a full part in the construction of that relationship. Elliott stresses the importance of examining the terms and concepts used by contemporaries when talking of political union, observing that they thought much about such issues as contiguity and conformity in institutions and political culture, both of which were regarded as important—if not sufficient—factors for the establishment of successful unions. He drew attention to the work of the seventeenth-century Spanish jurist Juan de Pereira Solórzano, who distinguished, as many did, between what Elliott termed 'accessory unions'—in which 'a kingdom or province, on union with another, was regarded juridically as part and parcel of it, with its inhabitants

---

[20] Strayer, *Origins*, 57.
[21] James I, 'A speech to both the Houses of Parliament, delivered in the Great Chamber at White-Hall, the last day of March 1607', in *The Political Works of James I*, ed. Charles Howard McIlwain (Cambridge, MA, 1918), 292.
[22] James I, 'A speech, as it was delivered in the upper house of the Parliament . . . Munday the XIX day of March 1603', in *The Political Works of James I*, 272–3.
[23] Elliott, 'Europe', 57.   [24] Elliott, 'Europe', 63–4.

possessing the same rights and subject to the same laws'—and unions *aeque principaliter*, in which a union's constituent parts retained their separate identities, retaining their own laws and privileges.[25]

Elliott's recognition that contemporaries devoted considerable attention to the problems of political union, and his suggestion that early modern unions should be judged on their own terms and not according to the state-building paradigm are very welcome. For, as Duchhardt observes in his preface to one of the rare attempts at a comparative approach to dynastic and personal unions, historians as yet lack any convincing typology of what was such a common phenomenon before 1789.[26] The structure of the collection in which it appears, however, indicates the problem, with parallel essays on monarchs from the national perspectives of individual components of the unions which show little interest in the problems of typology. The distinctions between different kinds of monarchical union matter, however. Europe was formed largely by composite states and multiple monarchies. Yet these multiple monarchies and unions differed greatly, both internally and in comparison with one another. France may well have been, as Strayer argued, a mosaic or composite state; it was not, however, a multiple monarchy.[27] The relationship between England and Scotland within the United Kingdom was very different to the relationship of either with Wales or Ireland, just as the relationship of the United Kingdom with Hanover was of another nature entirely. Some dynastic or personal unions proved highly durable; others faltered after a few years. In some personal unions, such as Poland-Lithuania's brief unions with Hungary (1370–82 and 1440–4) and Sweden (1592–9), and its rather longer union with Saxony (1697–1763), the component parts of the union remained very separate. As Jellinek recognized, however, in personal unions, long coexistence, institutional fusion, and attempts by monarchs to rule previously separate parts of their inheritance as one state, could lead to a growing together of the political communities in a process that could result in a real union, as in Britain between 1603 and 1707.

For such a process to occur needed the engagement of those political communities in the various parts of the union, and required sufficient support among them for fusion to take place. Yet political unions are usually studied and categorized on the basis of the treaties that founded them, rather than on the messy reality of these unificatory processes, and historians are often cavalier in their use of terms. As Jellinek observed:

> Scholarship concerning so-called unions in a closer sense, i.e. the uniting of several states under one and the same ruler, has been obscured by vague and unstable terminology, in which historical and legal aspects are partly confused, and partly mixed up.[28]

---

[25] Elliott, 'Europe', 52–3.
[26] Heinz Duchhardt, 'Vorwort', in Heinz Duchhardt (ed.), *Der Herrscher in der Doppelpflicht: Europäische Fürsten und ihre beiden Throne* (Mainz, 1997), 3.
[27] Strayer, *Origins*, 53.   [28] Jellinek, *Lehre*, 82.

He pointed out that for some, a real union meant the formation of a unitary state, while the term 'personal union' simply denoted the sharing of a common ruler. For Jellinek, a real union was founded on a statute (*Gesetz*) agreed by the parties to the union, which integrated some—if not necessarily all—state institutions. Such a union of independent states could only come about with the full agreement of both parties.[29]

It is worth bearing these distinctions in mind. The term real union is often used—especially by historians of the United Kingdom—as a synonym for parliamentary union. Yet for Jellinek, the union of Sweden and Norway, confirmed by the parliaments of both states in 1815, was a real union of states that remained sovereign, each with its own parliament and without a common government erected over them, since they conducted a common foreign policy through the common ruler; likewise, he regarded the Austro-Hungarian monarchy as a real union, although the Austrian and Hungarian parts of the monarchy retained separate parliaments after the 1867 *Ausgleich*.[30]

As Jellinek maintained, there is a distinction to be drawn between legal definitions and historical and political reality. There was a spectrum of relationships between the constituent parties to personal and real unions that can blur the lines between the neat jurist's categories: it is for this reason that Jellinek insisted upon the necessity of a formal statutory basis for a relationship to be considered a real union.[31] Yet although he recognized that personal unions could develop into real unions, he does not consider how this occurs, as this is properly the territory of the historian rather than the jurist. Regardless of whether a union is a personal or a real union from the jurist's point of view, however, it is also a relationship between two polities that changes over time, often substantially. Although historians understandably devote considerable attention to the treaties that define the legal basis of unions, these treaties reflected long processes in which the relationship between the partners to the treaty changed and developed. As in the case of Scotland and England, the development towards closer union was not necessarily the result of friendly feelings. Relations between the two countries in the seventeenth century were characterized more by hostility than harmony, with invasion, conquest, and the forced—albeit brief—Cromwellian incorporating union of 1652 more prominent than any growth of mutual affection.

Yet neighbours could have common interests. There were strong unionist currents of thought in both England and Scotland. English unionism might have rested on the hegemonic and tactless assertion that Scotland was a fief of the English crown; nevertheless, a considerable body of Scottish unionist thought existed long before 1603, some of it pragmatic, some idealistic.[32] As Kidd argues,

---

[29] Jellinek, *Lehre*, 82–4, 197–9. [30] Jellinek, *Lehre*, 223–53.
[31] As he drily observed, the Swedish-Norwegian union of 1815 was variously categorized as a real union, a *Bundesstaat*, a personal union, and a personal union that could also be called a real union: Jellinek, *Lehre*, 225 n. 27.
[32] Arthur Williamson, *Scottish National Consciousness in the Age of James VI* (Edinburgh, 1979), 97–107; Roger Mason, 'Scotching the Brut: Politics, history and national myth in sixteenth-century Britain', in Mason (ed.), *Scotland and England 1286–1815* (Edinburgh, 1987), 60–83; Roger Mason,

such pro-unionist sentiments have not been given the attention they deserve, since historians of Scotland tend to focus on the distinctiveness of Scotland and Scottish historical and cultural trends, and have generally 'paid vastly greater attention to nationalism than to unionism'.[33]

Historians of Scotland are by no means the only ones. The development of modern political nationalism after 1789 created a climate hostile to the concept of political union. The doctrine of the sovereign nation, one and indivisible, exported on the bayonets of the French revolutionary armies, roused powerful forces across Europe, as nations—or at least their elites—sought to define themselves and express their claim to sovereign independence according to Bodin's seductive concept of indivisible sovereignty, in order to take their place in the post-1648 international system, which treated all sovereign states as legally equal regardless of their size and importance. Multinational polities faced demands for independence and came under increasing pressure to recognize claims to national autonomy within their borders long before Woodrow Wilson pulled the stopper from the genie's bottle with his endorsement of the right of self-determination in 1918.

This hostile climate affected the writing of the history of the Polish-Lithuanian union; it was exacerbated by the unexpected return of political independence for Poland and Lithuania in 1918 following the collapse of the partitioning powers. Among the Polish-speaking elites of the former Polish-Lithuanian state, there had long been support for its reconstitution within the borders of 1772 as a multi-national federation. In the nineteenth century, however, the rise of national consciousness among Lithuanians, Ukrainians, and Belarusians brought competing demands for the establishment of new nation-states on the basis of these national groups, all of which developed traditions of history-writing in the nineteenth century hostile to the idea of union, and to the old union state. By the 1830s Narbutt's Polish-language history of Lithuania was already marked by a strong commitment to Lithuanian independence.[34] As the philologists Kristijonas Donelaitis and Liudvikas Rėza studied the origins of the Lithuanian language, historians writing in Lithuanian began constructing an alternative account of the Lithuanian past. The partitioning powers fostered the publication of historical works presenting the union as a Polish imperialist project. In Ukraine, where nationalist historians had the dual problem of extricating the story of the Ukrainian past from its entanglement with Russia as well as Poland, Hrushevsky, whose great history of Ukraine-Rus' was published between 1898 and 1936, and who in March 1917 was head of the Ukrainian government that declared independence from Russia, used his formidable erudition to give a highly negative portrayal of the union and its effects on the Ukrainian nation. In what is now Belarus, Mikhail Koialovich fostered the development of 'western Ruthenianism', which preached the unity of

---

'Imagining Scotland: Scottish political thought and the problem of Britain 1560–1660', in Mason (ed.), *Scots and Britons: Scottish Political Thought and the Union of 1603* (Cambridge, 1994), 3–13; and Colin Kidd, *Unions and Unionism: Political Thought in Scotland, 1500–2000* (Cambridge, 2008), 39–80.

[33] Kidd, *Unions*, 1, 2.
[34] Teodor Narbutt, *Dzieje starożytne narodu litewskiego*, 10 vols (Vilnius, 1835–41).

western Ruthenians, and trumpeted the negative effects upon them of all contacts with Poland.[35]

The territorial and national struggle after 1918 created a climate even more hostile to objective study of the common Polish-Lithuanian past, as Polish-speakers in the lands of the former grand duchy of Lithuania who had regarded themselves as Lithuanians or Ruthenians faced growing hostility from nationalist movements among Lithuanian, Ukrainian, and Belarus'ian nationalists, who simply regarded them as Poles unless they renounced all traces of their Polish identity in a process that divided families and communities.[36] The problems were exacerbated by the terrible fate of these lands between 1939 and 1945, where people suffered genocide, ethnic cleansing, and the complete breakdown of political order. Quite apart from the Holocaust visited upon the Jews, in the bloodlands of eastern Europe,[37] Poles, Lithuanians, Ukrainians, Belarusians, and others were subject to—and sometimes perpetrators of—the massacres and ethnic cleansing that changed eastern Europe forever. Between 1945 and 1990, historical study in the Soviet Union, with its Russian nationalist foundations, encouraged negative portrayals of the union.

The twentieth century created deep wounds, not all of which have healed. Polish historians, apart from those who saw the union as an unmitigated disaster ultimately responsible for the failure of the Polish state, tended to portray it in broadly positive terms, even in communist Poland, where historians after 1956 were allowed more latitude than elsewhere in the Soviet bloc. Lithuanian, Ukrainian, and Belarusian historians were far less willing to see anything of value in the union. Hrushevsky depicted the Ukrainian people as the victims of adverse historical circumstances, which 'bedimmed its manifestations of vitality and its creative energy, and abandoned it for long centuries at the crossroads of political life as a defenceless and vulnerable prey to the avaricious appetites of its neighbours'.[38] Lithuanian attitudes were broadly similar in the interwar period, when historians concentrated on the medieval origins of Lithuania and its achievements until 1385, when Jogaila set Lithuania on what Sužiedėlis, writing in 1935, termed the 'fatal path' to union.[39]

During the debates over the formation of the United States of America, Alexander Hamilton quoted Mably's observation that neighbours were naturally enemies

---

[35] Rimvydas Petrauskas, 'Der litauische Blick auf den polnisch-litauischen Staatsverband–"Verlust der Staatlichkeit" oder Bewahrung der Parität', *ZOF*, 53 (2004), 363–72; Robert Frost, 'Unmaking the Polish-Lithuanian Commonwealth: Mykhailo Hrushev'skyi and the making of the Cossacks', *HUS*, 27 (2004–5), 313–33; Henadź Sahanowicz, 'Źródła pamięci historycznej współczesnej Białorusi: Powrót zachodniorusizmu', in Jerzy Kłoczowski and Andrzej Gil (eds), *Analizy Instytutu Europy Środkowo-Wschodniej*, 14 (Lublin, 2006), 6–7.

[36] See Robert Frost, 'Ordering the Kaleidoscope: Nation and State Power in the lands of Poland-Lithuania since 1569', in Oliver Zimmer and Len Scales (eds), *Power and the Nation in History* (Cambridge, 2005), 212–31.

[37] For the bloodlands, see Timothy Snyder, *Bloodlands: Europe between Hitler and Stalin* (Philadelphia, PA, 2010).

[38] Mykhailo Hrushevsky, *History of Ukraine-Rus'*, i, ed. Andrzej Poppe and Frank Sysyn (Edmonton, Alberta, 1997), 2.

[39] Sužiedėlis, 'Lietuva', 14; cf. Zenonas Ivinskis, 'Vytauto jaunystė ir jo veikimas iki 1392 m.', in Paulius Šležas (ed.), *Vytautas Didysis, 1350–1430* (Kaunas, 1930; repr. Vilnius, 1988), 28.

unless common weakness forced them to join together to form a confederative republic.[40] Relations between neighbours in European history have frequently been characterized by hostility, war, and mutual loathing. If an important factor in the construction of the sense of identity that today is so often seen as central to the nation-building process, is using the 'other' to define what one is not, then neighbours are the most readily available other against which this definition can be established, even if those neighbours speak a related—or the same—language. Yet the obsession with the 'other' in recent literature on identity-formation and its relation to the state has produced a distorting emphasis on polarization, when attitudes to other peoples in practice spread across a broad spectrum in which outright hostility was by no means necessarily dominant. The formation of unions—often despite long traditions of mutual hostility—showed that neighbours could and did recognize that relations need not be characterized by violence, however difficult the necessary hatchet-burying might be, and that political union had much to recommend it. This study focuses on one such union, in which a long process of unification, driven from below as much as from above, established a framework within which mutual hostility was contained and channelled, and in which a powerful political fusion gradually developed, forming a unique political culture, yet one that was also truly European.

[40] Davis, *Federal Principle*, 101.

5

The Krewo Act

The Krewo Act has long been controversial. There were not many conditions. In return for Jadwiga's hand, Jogaila agreed to pay 200,000 florins to William von Habsburg as compensation for the breach of his betrothal agreement, and to accept Catholic baptism for himself, unbaptized members of his family, and his pagan subjects.[1] He agreed to release noble Polish prisoners captured in raids and to recover lands lost by Lithuania and Poland at his own expense. Finally, he promised that he would unite in perpetuity his Lithuanian and Ruthenian lands to the Polish crown: *'demum eciam Jagalo dux sepe dictus promittit Terras suas Litvanie et Rusie Corone Regni Polonie perpetuo aplicare'* (see Fig. 4).[2]

That little word, *'applicare'* has exercised generations of historians. What, precisely, did it mean? In the 1890s Koneczny and Lewicki argued that *'applicare'* was a synonym for *'incorporare'*; therefore what came to be known as the 'union of Krewo' was believed to have effected the incorporation of Lithuania into Poland and the liquidation of the Lithuanian state. This incorporation thesis, also accepted by Liubavskii, became dominant among Polish historians by 1918, when the contest for the old Polish-Lithuanian lands lent a considerable edge to historical research.[3] The legal historians Balzer and Kutrzeba endorsed it, if with reservations, as did Halecki, author of the first comprehensive history of the making of the union, which he saw as the expression of what he called 'the Jagiellonian idea', a federalist conception that, to Halecki, offered a model for peaceful coexistence in post-1918 eastern Europe.[4]

Lithuanian historians, keen to assert Lithuania's historic claims to statehood, rejected the incorporationist thesis and Halecki's rose-tinted Jagiellonian idea. Although professional historians largely shunned the populist vision that attacked

---

[1] *AU*, no. 1, 1–2.

[2] *AU*, no. 1, 2; the editors published the document in classical Latin spelling; here the original spelling is given, based on the versions in *KA*, 19 and Maria Koczerska, 'Autentyczność dokumentu unii krewskiej 1385 roku' *KH*, 99 (1992), 77.

[3] Feliks Koneczny, *Jagiełło i Witold* (Lwów, 1893), 33; Anatol Lewicki, 'Über das staatsrechtliche Verhältnis Littauens zu Polen unter Jagiełło und Witold', *Altpreussische Monatsschrift*, 31 (1894), 7; Матвей Любавский, *Очерк историй литовско-русского государства до Люблинской унии включительно* (1910; 2nd edn, St Petersburg, 2004), 74. For comprehensive surveys of the historiography, see Błaszczyk, *Dzieje* i, 195–267 and Jučas, *Unija*, 11–85, 110–16.

[4] Stanisław Kutrzeba, 'Unia Polski z Litwą', in *Polska i Litwa w dziejowym stosunku* (Cracow, 1914), 447–658; Oswald Balzer, *Tradycja dziejowa unii polsko-litewskiej* (Lwów, 1919); Oskar Halecki, *Dzieje unii Jagiellońskiej*, 2 vols (Cracow, 1919–20); and Oskar Halecki, 'Wcielenie i wznowienie państwa litewskiego przez Polskę (1386–1401)', *PH*, 21 (1917–1918), 1–77.

Fig. 4. The Krewo Act (14 August 1385). Jogaila, Grand Duke of Lithuania together with his brothers swears to enact certain obligations if he should marry Jadwiga, Queen of Poland. Latin, parchment, 330 mm × 220 mm. Traces of lost seals. Archiwum i Biblioteka Krakowskiej Kapituły Metropolitalnej, Cracow, D. perg. 188. By kind permission of the Archive and Library of the Metropolitan Chapter of Cracow Cathedral.

Jogaila as a traitor who betrayed Lithuania in 1386, they had little liking for the union. Ivinskis argued that Jogaila's baptism and coronation instituted a personal union, in which he ruled Lithuania separately as grand duke, although he had to institute new mechanisms for governing it since he spent most of his time in Poland after 1386.[5] Šapoka translated 'applicare' as 'prijungti', meaning 'to attach' or 'to connect', arguing that although Jogaila joined Lithuania to Poland, and not the other way round, on account of the greater status of the royal title in Poland, Polish historians had too narrow an understanding of Krewo and the relationship it instituted. Lithuania was not incorporated and remained a separate state.[6] Under Soviet rule from 1940 to 1990 negative views of the union were institutionalized in

---

[5] Ivinskis, 'Jogailos santykiai', 72–3. For popular views of Jogaila, see Alvydas Nikžentaitis, *Witold i Jagiełło: Polacy i Litwini we wzajemnym stereotypie* (Poznań, 2000).
[6] Šapoka, 'Valstybiniai Lietuvos Lenkijos santykiai Jogailos laikais', in Šapoka (ed.), *Jogaila*, 190–3.

Lithuania, while nationalist historians in exile were virulently hostile to the union, a trend that climaxed in 1989 with the hysterical accusation that Jogaila was guilty of instituting the genocide of the Lithuanian people.[7]

More significant was the 1975 claim by Dainauskas, another American Lithuanian, that the Krewo Act was a forgery, fabricated at some point between the sixteenth and the nineteenth century—he was not precise—by Poles wishing to prove Lithuania's subordination to Poland.[8] Dainauskas's article remained largely unknown until published in Polish in 1987, when it provoked a storm: the journal's editors made it clear that they regarded the article as more of a curio than a serious piece of scholarship. It was subjected to withering critiques by Korczak and Koczerska, who demolished its claims. A Lithuanian team subjected the document to close analysis, reaching broadly similar conclusions.[9] Agreement over Krewo's authenticity has brought no consensus as to its meaning.[10] While many Polish historians still argue—with reservations—that Lithuania was incorporated into Poland in 1386, albeit for a relatively short period, others deny that incorporation ever took place.[11] Błaszczyk argues first that it should no longer be a matter for discussion that Krewo was 'an act of incorporation of Lithuania into Poland', then admits that it was, as Lithuanian historians maintain, a *promise* of incorporation that was only realized 'to a small extent', and from which the Lithuanians rapidly withdrew, thus making it a 'brief episode', lasting from 1386 until 1392 or 1398, before he reaches the contradictory conclusion that 'the Lithuanian state did not cease to exist in 1386'.[12]

So what was the nature of the relationship instituted in 1385–6? Krewo was not an act of union, but a prenuptial agreement in which Jogaila and his closest male pagan relations gave undertakings as to what would happen should Jogaila's marriage to Jadwiga take place; it was reciprocated in the obligations confirmed at Vaukavysk in January 1386 by representatives of the Polish community of the realm, who formally offered Jadwiga's hand and accepted Jogaila as their lord in what was a pre-election, subject to confirmation at a wider assembly of the community of the realm at Lublin, and conditional upon Jogaila's marrying Jadwiga.[13]

---

[7] V.P. Uluntaitis, *Lenkų įvykdytas lietuvių tautos genocidas* (Chicago, 1989).

[8] Jonas Dainauskas, 'Kriavo akto autentiškumas', *Lituanistikos instituto 1975 metų suvažiavimo darbai* (1976), 51–71.

[9] Jonas Dainauskas, 'Autentyczność aktu krewskiego', *LSP*, 2 (1987), 125–42; Lidia Korczak, 'O akcie krewskim raz jeszcze (na marginesie rozprawy J. Dainauskasa)', *SH*, 34 (1991), 473–9; Koczerska, 'Autentyczność', 59–78; Jūratė Kiaupienė, '1385 m. rugpjūčio 14 d. aktas Lietuvos-Lenkijos unijų istoriografiojoje (problemos formulavimas)', in Zigimantas Kiaupa and Arturas Mickevičius (eds), *Lietuvos valstybė XII–XVIII a.* (Vilnius, 1997), 39–68.

[10] See the sharp exchanges between Błaszczyk and Kiaupienė: Błaszczyk, *Dzieje*, i, 265–7, and 'Czy była unia krewska?' *KH*, 110/4 (2003), 83–96; Jūratė, Kiaupienė, 'Akt krewski z 14 sierpnia 1385 r.: gdzie kryje się problem—w dokumencie czy w jego interpretacjach?' *KH*, 108/4 (2001), 47–61; and Jūratė Kiaupienė, 'W związku z polemiką Grzegorza Błaszczyka w sprawie unii krewskiej', *KH*, 110/3 (2003), 97–8.

[11] Błaszczyk, *Dzieje*, i, 233–52; Nikodem, *Jadwiga*, 157–200; Kolankowski, *Dzieje*, i, 33.

[12] Błaszczyk, *Dzieje*, i, 250–1.

[13] 'pro domino ac rege regni eiusdem, videlicet Poloniae, domino nostro praeelegimus et assumpsimus': *AU*, no. 2. Rowell translates this as 'we have chosen him in preference and assumed him as lord and king of the said realm, namely Poland, as our lord', though in the explanatory text he

Although some of the promises made at Krėva and Vaukavysk were immediately fulfilled—Jogaila, his pagan brothers, and Vytautas were duly baptized; the evangelization of Lithuania began shortly thereafter; and Jogaila was married to Jadwiga and crowned king—others were not, or subsequently become irrelevant, such as William's compensation, which he refused. Thus even if '*applicare*' really did mean 'to incorporate'—and Łowmiański demonstrates that the term was so used in both private and public law by citing a range of contemporary documents—it remained a promise.[14] No incorporation document survives, and no other sources give any indication that incorporation formally took place in 1386, beyond assertions made in the 1413 Horodło union. Łowmiański argued on scraps of circumstantial evidence that such a document did exist, and later disappeared, but his arguments are unpersuasive, and in his posthumously published history of the Jagiellons he was more cautious, talking of '*przyłączenie*' (joining) not '*wcielenie*' or '*włączenie*' (incorporation).[15]

Research into contemporary usage of '*applicare*' led Adamus to assert that what occurred in 1386 was the direct incorporation only of Jogaila's own patrimony—that is the duchy of Vilnius—and the indirect incorporation of the duchies held by other members of the Gediminid dynasty as fiefs, in a relationship of *feudum oblatum*.[16] The main evidence for such a claim, Adamus argued, lies in the documents in which members of the Gediminid dynasty swore oaths of homage to Jogaila, Jadwiga, and the *corona regni Poloniae*.[17]

The problem with such formulations is the tendency to assume that Krewo was a treaty between two sovereign states in the modern sense. It was not. Formally, it was an agreement between three parties: Jogaila, his pagan brothers, and Vytautas on the Lithuanian side; Elizabeth of Bosnia representing the Angevin dynasty; and envoys acting on behalf of the *corona regni Poloniae*, the community of the Polish realm. Krewo's wording suggests that the relationship forged in 1386 was intended to be far more than a personal or dynastic union: a multiple monarchy or dynastic agglomeration united solely in the person of the ruler. Its very existence demonstrates that the Polish-Lithuanian union did not begin as personal or dynastic unions usually began, through simple inheritance, as was the case at the institution of the Anglo-Scottish personal union in 1603, when James VI's accession by hereditary right was accepted by the English political elite, and he simply crossed

---

refers to 'pre-election', which better captures the important point that this assumption of Jogaila was only provisional, subject to the confirmation of the Lublin assembly, his marriage, and the fulfilment of the promises made at Krėva: Rowell, '1386', 137, 139.

[14] Henryk Łowmiański, *Studia nad dziejami Wielkiego Księstwa Litewskiego* (Poznań, 1983), 353–5.

[15] Henryk Łowmiański, 'Wcielenie Litwy do Polski w 1386 r.', in *Prusy—Litwa—Krzyżacy*, ed. Marceli Kosman (Warsaw, 1989), 294–402, and *Polityka*, 45, 57.

[16] Jan Adamus, 'Państwo litewskie w latach 1386–1398', in Stefan Ehrenkreutz (ed.), *Księga pamiątkowa ku uczczenia 400. rocznicy wydania I Statutu Litewskiego* (Wilno, 1935), 15–48.

[17] Documents have survived for Skirgaila (1386), Vytautas (1386), Žygimantas Kęstutaitis (1386), Karijotas (1386, 1388), Vasyl of Pinsk (1386), Vygantas (1388), Volodymyr of Kyiv (1388), and Lingvenis (1389): *AU*, nos 7–9.

the border to claim his throne. If, as Jellinek argues, one of the defining features of a real union is a formal, legal foundation treaty, then the relationship launched by Krewo fulfils this condition, not least because of the involvement of the community of the Polish realm as one of the parties.

If the Polish-Lithuanian union began largely as a result of the failure of the Piast and Angevin dynasties in the male line, the involvement of the Polish community of the realm in deciding who was to rule over it distinguishes it from most personal unions. Most began as the Anglo-Scottish union began in 1603, when the failure to produce heirs, accidents of mortality, or, in the case of England, Elizabeth I's refusal to marry, disrupted the normal course of the hereditary succession that was usual in western Europe. Too often it is assumed by scholars of unions that this pattern was universal, and it is for this reason that 'personal unions' are barely discussed in the theoretical literature on unions: they are seen as accidents of history that might, as in the case of England and Scotland, develop into a real union, but more usually were brief episodes in which, beyond the common monarch, the parties to union shared little or nothing. Yet hereditary succession by was by no means the European norm. In eastern and northern Europe, when native dynasties died out, as they did in Denmark, Sweden, Hungary, Bohemia, and Poland in the fourteenth century, the community of the realm asserted its right to involvement in the determination of the succession, as in Hungary and Poland in 1382. In Scandinavia, after the wars sparked by the deaths without male heirs of Valdemar Atterdag in Denmark and Magnus Eriksson in Sweden, the 1397 Kalmar assembly elected Erik of Pomerania, the adopted son of Valdemar's daughter Margaret, as king of a Nordic union, despite the existence of other candidates with hereditary claims to one or other of the three thrones.

The institution of the Spanish union of the crowns was rather different. It stemmed from the decision taken in January 1469 by Isabella, just named heir to the throne of Castile by her half-brother Henry IV, to marry Ferdinand, heir to the Aragonese throne, as opposed to Charles Valois, son of Charles VII of France, or Afonso V of Portugal, Henry's favoured candidate. Although there was a strong pro-Aragonese party at court, led by the archbishop of Toledo, this was Isabella's decision, and the marriage contract, signed at Cervera on 5 March 1469, indicated the strength of her position as the legitimate and recognized heir. It was, as Elliott writes, 'humiliating' for Ferdinand, since it dictated that he should live in Castile, where he was to be subordinate to Isabella. Henry died in 1474; it was only after a five-year civil war against supporters of his daughter Joanna—whose paternity was widely doubted—that this dynastic decision could be implemented. Without the direct involvement of the community of the realm, the personal nature of the Castilian-Aragonese union was encapsulated by the terms of Isabella's will: after her death in 1504 Ferdinand was rudely stripped of the title of king of Castile that he had assumed under the Segovia agreement of 1475, although he was allowed to retain the governorship of Castile until Joanna—their mentally unstable daughter—returned from the Netherlands to take up her crown, or until her son Charles should reach his majority. Only after the premature death of Joanna's husband, Philip the Fair of Burgundy, tipped his widow over the edge into insanity was Ferdinand left as effective ruler of Castile until his death in 1516.[18]

Even if Krewo was but a prenuptial agreement, the involvement of the Polish community of the realm meant that it was very different from the Cervera treaty, which established the arrangements by which Ferdinand and Isabella would rule in Castile. The agreement was necessary because neither Jogaila nor Jadwiga possessed a clear hereditary right to the Polish throne in Polish law or custom. Jadwiga, for all that the Poles recognized her natural rights, had only acquired the Polish crown by election, while Elizabeth of Bosnia had to accept that Jadwiga's marriage would be determined by the Polish community of the realm. Jogaila, although he had some Piast blood in his veins, had no claim to the throne, and could only be elected to it by the Polish political community, the third party to the Krewo Act.

The Polish lords who represented their fellow citizens were well aware of the distinction between the community of the realm and the state. It was expressed in the documents through different uses of the terms *corona regni*, referring to the community of the realm, and the kingdom of Poland, the *regnum*. The term 'kingdom of Poland' is used three times in the Krewo Act: twice to refer to the barons of the kingdom (*baronibus regni Poloniae*); its only other use came in the promise Jogaila made to recover the lost territories of the kingdom: '*universas occupantes et defectus regni Poloniae perquorumvis manus distractas et occupata*'. Significantly, it was to the *corona regni Poloniae*, not the *regnum*, that Jogaila swore to join his Lithuanian and Russian dominions.[19] If he fulfilled his obligations Jogaila was to become, in the words of the Vaukavysk document, 'lord and king' of the kingdom of Poland.[20] Before his coronation, he was referred to as '*tutor et dominus regni Poloniae*'; it was, however, to Jogaila and Jadwiga, as king and queen of Poland, and to the *corona regni Poloniae*, not the *regnum*, that Lithuanian princes and boyars swore loyalty.[21]

The Poles were perfectly capable of distinguishing between the political community and an abstract 'state', which they termed the kingdom, and of separating the person of the ruler from that state, distinctions which some scholars have deemed medieval politicians incapable of making:

> Growing out of feudalism and harking back to Roman imperial times, the system of government that appeared in Europe during the years 1337–1648 was still, in most respects, entirely personal. The state as an abstract organization with its own persona separate from that of the ruler did not exist.[22]

According to van Creveld, 'with the exception of the classical city states and their magistrates, none of the political communities which existed until 1648 distinguished between the person of the ruler and his rule', an idea that was, he suggested, invented by Hobbes, and was only instituted between 1648 and 1789.[23] The

---

[18] Elliott, *Imperial Spain* (London, 1963), 9–10, 127.
[19] *AU*, no. 1, 1–3.   [20] *AU*, no. 2, 4.   [21] *AU*, nos 6, 16.
[22] Martin van Creveld, *The Rise and Decline of the State* (Cambridge, 1999), 126.
[23] van Creveld, *Rise and Decline*, 53, 57, 170, 179.

examples of Bohemia, Hungary, and Poland show that this is simply untrue: as Reynolds argues, the concepts of transpersonal kingship or a transpersonal state existed from at least the eleventh century in Germany and even earlier in England.[24]

By 1385, Poles not only had well-developed ideas of the political community, and of an abstract state separate from the person of the ruler; they also had a sophisticated state structure, with institutions of government that had developed significantly since 1320. During the long interregnum after 1382, in an age in which, according to Creveld, authority was 'entirely personal', the community of the realm ran affairs tolerably peacefully and nipped incipient civil war in the bud. It assembled to resolve contentious matters, the most important of which was the determination of the succession, on pragmatic political principles. While at Jogaila's coronation in March 1386 the community of the realm accorded their new king the respect and obedience owed to a monarch, it was made clear that this obedience was conditional.

The Polish monarch did not own his kingdom, whatever might be the case in Lithuania, where the limitations on princely power were practical, rather than legal or theoretical. Lithuania in 1385 was certainly a state: it had survived for nearly two centuries in a hostile environment; it had an effective military structure that had enabled it to expand prodigiously. Yet it was a composite, patrimonial state, in which the power of the dynasty was paramount and government was conducted through the households of the various members of a loose dynastic conglomerate under the ultimate suzerainty of the grand duke. There was little meaningful distinction between the public and private spheres, and although much was regulated by custom, there was no body of written law to protect the property of individuals from the grand duke or his Gediminid relatives. While the integrative force of that dynastic authority was considerable, the tribal origins of Lithuanian power were still apparent in the core Lithuanian territories, and the links with the Ruthenian territories—which possessed a sophisticated legal heritage from Kievan Rus′—were fragile, as the power-struggle after Algirdas's death demonstrated.

This is not to say that the non-princely Lithuanian—as distinct from Ruthenian— elites were politically insignificant. The resistance to Mindaugas's conversion, his assassination, and the bitter power-struggle that followed, are ample demonstration that Lithuania's boyars were not simply the obedient tools of their grand dukes. Some families—most notably the Alšėniškai—had married into the dynasty and played a substantial part in internal politics.[25] Łowmiański argued that although there was no mention of the Lithuanian boyars in the Krewo Act apart from as objects of Jogaila's promises concerning conversion, other contemporary documents make it clear that they were an important political force, suggesting that Krewo was the work not just of Jogaila, but of the whole military-social elite at whose head he stood.[26]

---

[24] Reynolds, *Kingdoms*, xxxv.   [25] Rowell, 'Pious', 66.
[26] Łowmiański, *Studia*, 365–454.

It is clear from the work of Petrauskas that the Lithuanian boyars constituted an important political force, and that if it can certainly be seen as a patrimonial system, the claim that the grand dukes enjoyed unlimited authority is unsustainable.[27] Yet if the Lithuanian boyars were undoubtedly informed of Jogaila's plans, they were not a party to Krewo, as the Polish community of the realm undoubtedly was, and Paszkiewicz and Błaszczyk are right to criticize Łowmiański for reading too much into certain formulae in the documents which talk of consultation and consent. Lithuanian boyars travelled in large numbers in Jogaila's entourage to Lublin and Cracow in 1386, but it was not to negotiate with the Polish nobility, and the Lublin assembly was in no way the counterpart of the 1397 Kalmar assembly, in which representatives of Denmark, Sweden, and Norway jointly elected Erik of Pomerania king.[28] The Lithuanian boyars were informed of what transpired, and in that sense consulted, but it was Jogaila and his closest relatives who put their seals to the Krewo Act. The boyars then swore loyalty to their prince in his new capacity.

Thus Krewo, and the union that followed, was not, and could not be, the result of a tidy political arrangement between equal sovereign states according to the neat definitions of modern scholars. While Polish law and legal thought had a relatively sophisticated conception of the political community and of the nature of the abstract state, the power-system in the grand duchy was still largely, if not entirely, patrimonial in nature. This imbalance between the partners to the union in terms of political development and political culture lies at the basis of much of the uncertainty about what Krewo signified. Yet if one should be properly sceptical about the extent to which the Lithuanian boyars were involved in forging the union, one should not read too much into the pious phrases concerning 'the whole community of the Polish realm' and its involvement in the negotiations, which were clearly carried out in practice by a narrow group of lords, most of them from Małopolska. Nevertheless, the fact that it was felt necessary to consult the community of the realm while acting in its name is significant, and that consultation was no formality, as was the case in Lithuania.

Although Krewo was the product of negotiations between three separate parties, its most striking feature is its brevity. It was far shorter than the document signed by Louis of Anjou in 1355 when he was recognized as Casimir's heir, which regulated relations between his Polish and Hungarian kingdoms should the personal union reach fruition.[29] It was also shorter than either of the documents produced by the Kalmar assembly: the coronation letter (*kroningsbrevet*), drawn up on 13 July 1397 and the union letter (*unionsbrevet*). The former, witnessed by sixty-seven individuals from all three realms, established the basis on which Erik ruled the union states as one entity from Copenhagen.[30] The *unionsbrev* was much longer, drafted on paper instead of the parchment on which all official documents were prepared. It

---

[27] Rimvydas Petrauskas, *Lietuvos diduomenė XIV a. pabaigoje–XV a.* (Vilnius, 2003), 31–2, 153–76.
[28] Paszkiewicz, *O genezie*, 196–8; Błaszczyk, *Dzieje*, i, 221–3.
[29] Paszkiewicz, *O genezie*, 226–7.
[30] 'Kroningsbrevet', in Aksel Christensen, *Kalmarunionen og nordisk politik 1319–1439* (Copenhagen, 1980), Bilag 1, 301.

sought to curtail royal power on behalf of the community of the realm. It seems that it was never accepted by Erik or Margaret, who remained the power behind the throne until her death in 1412. The programme laid out in the *unionsbrev* remained influential, but it was never enacted, and Erik governed through one council for all his realms, until growing aristocratic opposition after 1436, which drew on the *unionsbrev*, led to his 1439 deposition and the elections of his nephew Christopher of Bavaria as king of Denmark (1440), Sweden (1441), and Norway (1442).[31]

The Kalmar Union was very different to the Polish-Lithuanian union instituted nine years earlier.[32] The Nordic kingdoms had closely related languages that were to a significant extent mutually comprehensible; their political cultures were at a similar stage of development and had much in common. Norway and Sweden had recently been in a personal union under Magnus Eriksson (1319–43), and there were numerous family links between the elites of all three realms. The contrast with Poland and Lithuania is striking, but there was one interesting parallel. Despite a strong aristocratic programme that sought to limit the powers of the crown, as expressed in the *unionsbrev*, it was drawn up after Erik's coronation. Margaret and Erik were able to ignore it and govern on the basis of the coronation letter, which marked the limits of the concessions they were prepared to make. Similarly, once Jogaila was crowned, and his Polish subjects had sworn loyalty to him, they were no longer in a position to extract from him any definition of what Krewo's vague terms signified. The lack of any equivalent of the *unionsbrev*, in which a vision of what the union might in practice look like was drafted but not agreed, suggests that neither party cared to define more closely what '*applicare*' actually meant. The complete silence in other sources suggests, as Łowmiański's critics have argued, that no document of incorporation was ever drafted, and no formal incorporation took place.[33]

The Krewo Act was a perfectly normal diplomatic document for the time.[34] Yet if, as Rowell argues, in form it was similar to the 1469 Cervera treaty, there were differences, not least because this was not a purely dynastic marriage treaty, since the Polish community of the realm was a party to the negotiations, and—in stark contrast to Cervera, which seriously limited Ferdinand's powers in Castile—it contained no practical guidance as to how government of the united realms was

---

[31] Jens Olesen, 'Erik af Pommern og Kalmarunionen: Regeringssystemets udformning, 1389–1439', in Per Ingesman and Jens Villiam Jensen (eds), *Danmark i senmiddelalderen* (Aarhus, 1994), 143–65; Erik Lönnroth, *Sverige och Kalmarunionen 1397–1457* (Göteborg, 1969), 40–51; Christensen, *Kalmarunionen*, 131–261; Poul Enemark, 'Motiver for nordisk aristokratisk unionspolitik: Overvejeler omkring kildegrundlag og tilgangsvinkler i unionsforskningen', in Ingesman and Jensen (eds), *Danmark*, 166–81.

[32] For comparisons see Stephen C. Rowell, 'Forging a union? Some reflections on the early Jagiellonian monarchy', *LHS* 1 (1996), 19; Halecki, 'Unia Polski z Litwą a unia kalmarska', in *Studia historyczne ku czci Stanisława Kutrzeby*, i (Cracow, 1938), 217–32; Zenon Nowak, 'Krewo i Kalmar: Dwie unie późnego średniowiecza', in Nowak (ed.), *W kręgu stanowych i kulturowych przeobrażeń Europy Północnej w XIV–XVIII w.* (Toruń, 1988), 57–75; and Zenon Nowak, *Współpraca polityczna państw unii polsko-litewskiej i unii kalmarskiej w latach 1411–1425* (Toruń, 1996), 5–20.

[33] Adamus, 'Państwo', 28.

[34] Stephen C. Rowell, 'Krėvos aktas: Diplomatijos ir diplomatikos apžvalga', in *KA*, 69–78.

to be conducted, or what *applicare* signified. Rowell suggests that it was a neutral and broad word, whose meaning was not narrowly tied to the sense of incorporation, but was similar to the term *adhaerere*, which appeared in the various acts of homage sworn to by Lithuanian princes and nobles after 1386.[35]

Yet Rowell goes too far in suggesting that historians have created a problem for themselves over the meaning of '*applicare*', and that Krewo lost its significance once the marriage between Jadwiga and Jogaila had taken place. For although the marriage was a necessary part of the process that turned Jogaila into Jagiełło, his crown depended crucially on the election at Lublin that preceded it. By the time he was crowned he had fulfilled what was in many respects the most important promise made at Krėva: to undergo baptism for himself and the remaining pagan Gediminid princes. His coronation, and the oaths he swore, took place after the marriage, by which time both sides had fully committed themselves. It is unlikely that either side, in the circumstances, wished to jeopardize the fragile new relationship by attempting to define too closely the way in which the union would operate. Jadwiga had reached the canonical age of marriage; had the Poles pulled out of the Krewo arrangements they would have thrown the initiative back to Elizabeth, who might again have attempted to force Sigismund of Luxembourg upon them.

Jagiełło was therefore in a strong position, and he had no need to define more closely what '*applicare*' meant. Yet it is unlikely that either he or the Polish lords regarded it as an entirely neutral term. Rowell is right to say that the term '*perpetuo*' should not be taken entirely seriously: it was a common feature of contemporary peace treaties that were broken almost as soon as they were drawn up. Nevertheless, in the Krewo Act the parties stated that, in some undefined form, Lithuania was to be joined to the *corona regni Poloniae* in perpetuity. It is all but certain that for the Poles '*applicare*' did mean 'incorporate'; this was to be made abundantly clear in the 1413 Horodło union—as Rowell admits—and the claim that Lithuania had been incorporated *de iure* in 1386 was asserted regularly thereafter. Yet that incorporation was not, according to the words used in the act, into the kingdom of Poland, but into the *corona regni Poloniae*.[36] That there was a difference is abundantly clear from contemporary sources, and Dąbrowski long ago argued that Krewo marked an important step in the development of the concept of the *corona regni*. The extension of Polish control over Red Ruthenia from the 1340s had already brought non-Polish lands into the *corona regni*; now, Dąbrowski argues, the Polish negotiators utilized the idea of the *corona regni* to indicate that they were thinking of a relationship that was more than a personal union that might easily be broken, as the personal union with Hungary was broken in 1382.[37]

It seems reasonable to suppose that for the Poles, the joining to, or inclusion of, Lithuania into the *corona regni* was an important aim; this may have been the

---

[35] Rowell, 'Krėvos', 76–7.

[36] This point was stressed by Pfitzner in the 1930s, and has recently been endorsed by Andrzej Rachuba: 'Historia Litwy', in Rachuba et al., *Historia Litwy: Dwugłos polsko-litewski* (Warsaw, 2009), 34.

[37] Dąbrowski, *Korona*, 96.

expression of a genuine belief in the benefits of the developing concept of the community of the realm, although the baser motives of opening up Lithuania to Polish influence and colonization, should not be overlooked. For all that, Jagiełło may not have grasped the full significance of the concept of *corona regni*; as Rowell suggests, he was undoubtedly interested in something more than a mere personal union.[38] Without a firmer link than the person of the ruler, there was no guarantee that he would be able to pass on the throne to his heir, or even that he would remain king should Jadwiga predecease him.

As Uruszczak has demonstrated, the concept of 'union' as a legal act, was unkown in Roman law, feudal law, or in German or Polish law; it was a concept unique to canon law, and it was canon lawyers who drafted the Krewo Act. '*Applicare*' was therefore a canon law concept. It was applied in legal acts concerning the union of benefices and churches, on a basis of the equality of both parties (*unio aeque principalis*).[39] The Krewo Act therefore did not sanction the legal incorporation into the Polish state as so many Polish historians have presented it, but envisaged a different kind of union altogether. Nevertheless, for a century and more, Polish politicians were happy to ignore the principle of equality, claiming simply that Lithuania had been incorporated into Poland. Yet Poland was in no position to annex Lithuania or absorb it into the Polish *regnum* in 1386, not least because Lithuania's political and institutional culture was so different from that of Poland. Krewo should therefore be seen more as a starting-point in a process in which both the Polish negotiators and Jagiełło were careful not to commit themselves too far. The Poles wished to end their long interregnum and install an adult king on the throne; Jagiełło sought a new throne that might give him the resources to end Lithuania's political and dynastic crisis by restoring his control and strengthening his hand against the threat posed by the Order. Each side clearly intended this to be a lasting relationship; sensibly, in 1385–6, neither side committed itself to a detailed programme of union. At Jagiełło's coronation on 4 March 1386 the two polities were formally joined together. Yet the very brevity of the Krewo Act, and the fact that so much about the future relationship was undefined meant that if it were to survive, the issues of lordship, dominion, and the respective status of the two parties to the union had to be clarified. That process brought conflict and upheaval, in which the ambiguity surrounding the relationship between the *corona regni Poloniae* and the *regnum Poloniae* was to be of critical importance.

---

[38] Rowell, 'Krėvos', 72.
[39] Wacław Uruszczak, *Unio regnorum sub una corona non causat eorum unitatem. Unia Polski i Litwy w Krewie w 1385 r. Studium Historyczno-Prawne.* (Cracow, 2017), 42–3. http://www.khpp.wpia.uj.edu.pl/publikacje.

PART II

ESTABLISHING THE UNION

6

Structures

The disputes over the nature of Krewo demonstrate the problems inherent in attempts to classify unions on the basis of foundation treaties alone. Unions—even the loosest—are relationships that change and grow over time. Many falter and fail; some develop and deepen. Although foundation treaties establish the framework for the relationship, a union is a process, not a moment, and political reality tempers the broad aspirations they express. If the Polish lords who negotiated Krewo intended that Lithuania should be incorporated into the *corona regni*, it rapidly became clear that this was not Jagiełło's understanding of the matter; that the Polish state—the *regnum* rather than the *corona regni*—was in no position to absorb the grand duchy; and that Lithuania's elites still saw the grand duchy as a separate realm. Krewo was far from the equivalent of the 1536 Act of the English parliament by which the principality of Wales, annexed as one of the dominions of the English crown in the late thirteenth century, was incorporated into England. That Act, welcomed by most among the Welsh elites—to the consternation of not a few modern historians of Wales—was the culmination of a long process in which the principality and the other conquered Welsh territories experienced the gradual extension of English institutions and English law. The establishment of shires on the English pattern after 1284 demonstrated the benefits of English-style local government; thus there were many in the turbulent marcher lordships that had remained under the crown but which were ruled by an amalgam of local custom and feudal law, who saw the benefits of full incorporation. The 1536 Act of Union shired the rest of Wales and introduced English common law. It marked the end, not the beginning, of a process of union, albeit one inaugurated not by treaty but by conquest, while acceptance of incorporation came at the end of a long period of cultural, legal, and political assimilation.[1]

In stark contrast, the relationship between Poland and Lithuania was only beginning in 1386, and the two realms were at very different stages of social, political, legal, and institutional development. The process of union, therefore, was initially slow (see Map 3).[2] The kingdom of Poland, itself only recently reunited,

---

[1] Peter Roberts, 'The English Crown, the Principality of Wales and the Council of the Marches, 1534–1641', in Brendan Bradshaw and John Morrill (eds), *The British Problem, c.1534–1707: State Formation in the Atlantic Archipelago* (Basingstoke, 1996), 118–47; Brendan Bradshaw, 'The Tudor Reformation and Revolution in Wales and Ireland: The origins of the British problem', in Bradshaw and Morrill (eds), *The British Problem*, 39–65.

[2] Halecki, 'Wcielenie', 4.

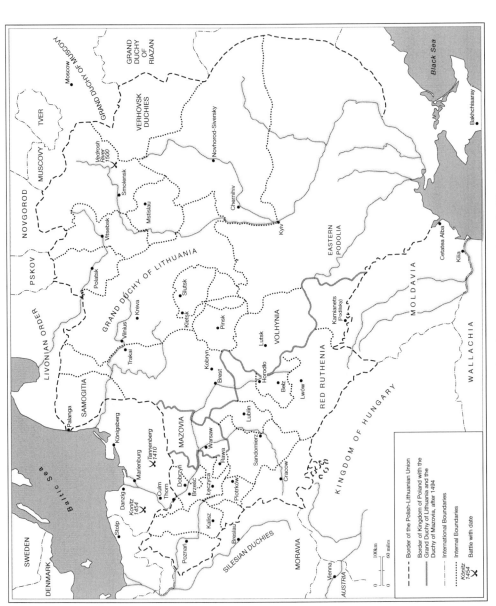

Map 3. The Polish-Lithuanian Union in the early fifteenth century.

had developed rapidly since Łokietek's coronation in 1320, but the long period of political disintegration after 1138 had left its mark. While a common sense of Polish identity survived the fragmentation, at least among the elites, Poland's division into an ever-shifting constellation of principalities established different trajectories of social, political, and legal development across the Polish lands.[3] These differences diminished after 1320, but strong local identities and attachment to local and provincial institutions as the basic building blocks of the socio-political order survived, and shaped future development.

This period saw the consolidation of the Polish szlachta (nobility), which was emerging as the dominant political force. The szlachta's roots lay deep in the tribal era. It emerged from the kinship groups or clans (*rody*) that formed the basis of the Polish social elite from the twelfth century to the fourteenth century. Although the details are obscure, it is clear that many clans provided a form of local organization, led by starostas (elders). Important decisions were taken at clan assemblies (*wiece*). Landed property belonged to the clan, and was shared out among its male members.[4]

By 1320 the passing of the generations had undermined the integrity of the clans, not least because the landed class grew substantially, as princes recruited warriors for their retinues, granting land under *ius militari* to sustain them. Princes offered generous terms and privileges to attract them, especially in Mazovia, whose dukes were desperate to defend their duchy against pagan tribes to the north and east. Initially newcomers were adopted by individual clans, intent on strengthening their position through the extension of membership beyond the core kinship group. The idea of the clan survived long after clans had ceased to have any real social or political significance, not least in the notion that membership of the szlachta—a term derived from the German *Geschlecht* (family)—depended primarily on noble descent. Clans lived on in their names, as the basis of the heraldic clans that survived as an important badge of noble identity; literally so, since the heraldic device of the clan, its *herb*, from the German *Erbe*, was adopted by its members and their descendants.

The clan ethos lingered in the tradition of regarding landed property as the common inheritance of the extended kinship group. Partible inheritance shaped the szlachta's development over the next four centuries, working over the longer term against the consolidation of powerful magnate dynasties and a narrow oligarchy. While individual magnate families used their positions to secure their status and wealth over several generations, the nobility's steadily increasing size and the recurrent need to divide family lands among all children ensured that the position even of the most powerful families was never secure: there were always ambitious and hungry challengers for office, honour, and status. Grants of land on military tenure were made directly by individual princes, and usually—initially at least—for life. These were not feudal grants on the western European pattern. Problems of monitoring the status of land meant that over time they tended to be folded into a

---

[3] Stanisław Kutrzeba, *Historia ustroju Polski: Korona* (updated repr. based on 8th edn, Poznań, 2001), 27.
[4] Kutrzeba, *Korona*, 34–40.

family's allodial holdings. The szlachta gradually secured full allodial rights to their lands, outside frontier areas such as Red Ruthenia, where defence needs ensured that a tighter grip was kept on military tenures. Thus if western concepts of vassalage and feudal hierarchy did spread through the influence of German law, the western European system did not take root on Polish soil.[5] In consequence, although deep into the fifteenth century bishops and dignitaries issued fiefs to their retainers, no feudal hierarchy emerged. In Małopolska, the status of Cracow as the senior principality and the fact that the province was not subdivided ensured that a handful of powerful families dominated political and social life in the palatinates of Cracow and Sandomierz. In contrast, extensive subdivision in Wielkopolska gave fewer opportunities for the consolidation of power and wealth. Wielkopolska was to remain the heartland of the middling nobility, those holding one—or at best a few—villages, for generations to come.[6]

In the fourteenth century the legal position of the *szlachta* was consolidated. Casimir III's statutes declared that nobility was an inherited status, giving legal form to what was already the dominant conception of *szlachectwo* (nobility). In Wielkopolska, descent from three noble families was demanded, usually one's father, mother, and paternal grandmother, to secure recognition of noble status; in Małopolska, descent from one noble family was sufficient until the fifteenth century. Attestation by six family members on the paternal side was all that was required. In Wielkopolska, four members of two different noble families were needed in addition to two blood relations. This public attestation of noble status by witnesses decided whether or not an individual was regarded as a noble; but even as the noble estate defined itself and attempted to shut itself off to outsiders, its most remarkable feature was how broadly it defined nobility. Nobility was closely associated with landowning, but ownership of land was neither sufficient to secure recognition as a noble, nor was it considered essential. Thus the szlachta contained not just wealthy landowners, the *possessionati*, but also those who worked their land themselves without dependent peasants—the *szlachta zagrodowa*—those who leased their land, and even those without land—the *impossessionati*—were not excluded if they could demonstrate noble descent. By the fifteenth century the Małopolskan nobility contained great magnates like Jan Głowacz Oleśnicki, grand marshal of Poland and palatine of Sandomierz, who owned one town and fifty-nine villages, alongside the forty-seven nobles who owned slithers of the village of Krzyszkowice in Proszowska county.[7]

Mazovia, which was not gathered into the Polish realm in 1320, was exceptional for the size and poverty of its nobility, which may have constituted an astonishing twenty per cent or more of the population by 1400.[8] Despite the huge differences in wealth between the Małopolskan magnates and the hordes of impoverished *impossessionati*, and despite the extensive clientage relations that to an extent replaced the old clans, the szlachta rejected hierarchical internal structures in favour

---

[5] Zientara, 'Społeczeństwo', 59.   [6] Zientara, 'Społeczeństwo', 146.
[7] Kutrzeba, *Korona*, 87–8; Zientara, 'Społeczeństwo', 148–9.
[8] *Dzieje Mazowsza*, i, ed. Henryk Samsonowicz (Pułtusk, 2006), 375.

of a broad presumption of equality of status, at least in legal and, gradually, in political terms. The phenomenon of *scartabellat*, which emerged in Mazovia and Małopolska—though not in Wielkopolska—in the thirteenth century as a form of semi-noble status for those serving the knights who constituted the princely retinues, disappeared in the fourteenth century as these squires (*włodycy, ścierałscy,* or, in Latin, *scartabelli*) either sank back into the commonality, or slipped into full noble status.[9] The most important causes of this development were the reunification of the kingdom, which encouraged belief in the nature of the szlachta as a national elite transcending the divisions within the *corona regni*, and the privileges that the nobility obtained as a result of the succession problems faced by Casimir and Louis of Anjou.

Of particular importance were the 1374 Koszyce privileges. They constituted the first set of privileges issued to the szlachta as a whole, thus consolidating its position as a legally defined estate across the kingdom. Louis confirmed all privileges issued to nobles by his predecessors and granted new ones, in what has traditionally been depicted as a needlessly generous grant of rights. It is still sometimes inaccurately asserted that he exempted the szlachta from all taxes except for the land tax (*poradlne*), henceforth levied at what is often referred to as the 'symbolic' or 'nominal' sum of 2 groszy per hide (*łan*) of land worked by their peasants.[10] Nobles were only obliged to provide military service within the kingdom's borders, and the king would henceforth pay them for service abroad. Local offices could only be filled by the king from among the local nobility, and Louis affirmed that the territory of the *corona regni* was inviolate, and could not be divided or alienated.[11]

The Koszyce privileges eloquently expressed the new sense of unity, based round the idea of the *corona regni*, among the szlachta of Małopolska and Wielkopolska. With hindsight, they have often been presented as the founding charter of the noble irresponsibility and selfishness that, so it is frequently argued, destroyed the Polish-Lithuanian state at the end of the eighteenth century. While their significance is undeniable, they should be viewed in context and not as part of the corrosive teleology of failure that rots so much historical writing on Poland-Lithuania. Louis was a clear-headed, expert negotiator, and the privileges represented a compromise between king and nobility rather than an outright victory for the szlachta, as is often assumed, based on the false claim that the rate of 2 groszy per hide represented a substantial drop in the rate of the *poradlne*, which had supposedly been levied at 12 groszy prior to 1374.[12] In fact, as Matuszewski's careful analysis of land-tenure documents reveals, there was no permanent land tax before 1374; what concerned the szlachta was the arbitrary way in which monarchs levied the *poradlne*.

---

[9] Kutrzeba, *Korona*, 40.

[10] The size of a hide varied. Two systems were in operation in Poland from the fourteenth to the eighteenth century: the Flemish hide (16.7 to 17.5 hectares), and the Franconian hide (22.6 to 25.36 hectares).

[11] *VL*, i, 24–5.

[12] For example, Jerzy Lukowski and Hubert Zawadzki, *A Concise History of Poland* (Cambridge, 2001), 31; Norman Davies, *God's Playground: A History of Poland*, i, 2nd edn (Oxford, 2005), 90.

While it is true that it had occasionally been raised at rates of 12 or even 24 groszy, collection had been intermittent and unpredictable. Since the *poradlne* was not raised every year, on average it yielded the equivalent of 2 groszy per annum before 1374. At Koszyce Louis secured a principle that suited both parties: the *poradlne* was to become permanent, allowing the royal treasury to budget properly, and ensuring that landowners faced a steady and predictable burden.[13]

Far from being a foolish concession that demonstrated the monarchy's weakness, this measure attained recognition for a principle that many late medieval monarchs failed to secure: the right to tax their nobility on a permanent basis. In 1381 it was complemented by a similar agreement with the church, in which the lands of the secular clergy were taxed at the same rate, while monastic lands paid 4 groszy per hide. It was not Louis's fault that, over the next two centuries, inflation gradually eroded the tax's value. It was the failure to increase the rate at which it was levied, not the Koszyce privileges, that eventually reduced the *poradlne* to a symbolic gesture. That problem was by no means unique to Poland, and the compromise worked well initially: treasury revenues, while not lavish, were sufficient to ensure that monarchs only had to raise extraordinary taxes on two occasions—1404 and 1440—in the next seventy years.[14] In 1374 two groszy per hide was by no means insignificant, constituting around fifteen per cent of the average lord's income from his lands, and possibly more, since revenues from noble estates seem to have dipped slightly after 1374, before recovering later in the century.[15]

The Koszyce privileges were nevertheless an important milestone. While they did not exempt the nobility from taxation in perpetuity, they established the important principle that the monarchy could only levy extraordinary taxation with szlachta consent. This principle was the cornerstone of the consensual Polish political system whose foundations were laid in Louis' reign, and during the interregnum after his death. Between 1374 and 1386, the szlachta came of age as a political community, establishing a system that profoundly influenced the elites of neighbouring lands, above all in the grand duchy of Lithuania.

Lithuania in 1386 was a composite, not a unitary polity. As a dynastic agglomeration it was not ruled in a uniform manner, and its component parts were marked by substantial differences in law, institutions, and political practice, although to judge it a disorderly mess, as does Pietkiewicz with reference to the late fifteenth century, is to apply the anachronistic standards of a later age.[16] Composite states were by definition irregular in their composition, and the grand duchy was no more a mess than France, the Empire, or the composite monarchy of Castile and Aragon. It is true that it is difficult to establish the exact relationship of the various parts to each other. The use of the terms 'Lithuania' and 'Ruthenia' have proven confusing to those who choose to see in them a clear division along national lines. For the

---

[13] Jacek Matuszewski, *Przywileje i polityka podatkowa Ludwika Węgierskiego w Polsce* (Łódź, 1983), 130–9, 173–83, 245–50.
[14] Matuszewski, *Przywileje*, 182.   [15] Matuszewski, *Przywileje*, 170–1, 248.
[16] Krzysztof Pietkiewicz, *Wielkie Księstwo Litewskie pod rządami Aleksandra Jagiellończyka* (Poznań, 1995), 66, 202.

term 'Lithuania' did not refer to an ethnic Lithuanian state in 1386, but to the heartlands of the Gediminid realm: the duchies of Vilnius and Trakai, which Liubavskii, reflecting contemporary usage, christened 'Lithuania proper' (*собственная Литовская земля, Litwa ścisła, Lithuania propria*). Despite Kutrzeba's attempt to add Samogitia to Lithuania proper, in order to include all the territories that nineteenth-century Lithuanian nationalists—though by no means all Samogitians—regarded as forming 'ethnic Lithuania', the concept as reflected in contemporary sources was much as Liubavskii suggested. Lithuania proper excluded Samogitia, and comprised the core territories of the grand duchy, including Black Ruthenia—the territories round Hrodna, Vaukavysk, and Navahrudak, and extending as far east as Minsk and Mahiliou. While Lithuanian settlements survived—some heavily Ruthenianized, others maintaining Lithuanian culture and the Lithuanian language—large areas of 'Lithuania proper' were Ruthenian in culture and Orthodox in religion.[17] Contemporaries, including Długosz—who put the border between 'Lithuania' and 'Ruthenia' on the river Berezina—and even the Muscovites, referred to these lands as Lithuania.[18]

The other territories under grand ducal authority were treated differently. Throughout the fifteenth century they received separate grants of privileges and were administered differently. Liubavskii presents the grand duchy as a federation comprising twelve parts: Lithuania proper and the 'annexed territories' or '*cetera dominia*' (other lordships) to use the contemporary term: Samogitia, Polesie, Podlasie, and the five Ruthenian territories of Polatsk, Vitsebsk, Smolensk, Volhynia, and Kyiv, plus Lithuanian Podolia and the principalities of Chernihiv-Siversky.[19] To call it a federation, however, as Gudavičius also does, is anachronistic. There was no federal treaty to regulate relations, each of the 'annexed' territories had a different relation to the centre, and the relationship between the various parts of the realm was conceived in terms of personal lordship: Jagiełło, as his titles make clear, saw his realms as separate entities, and the term 'grand duchy' referring to the whole does not appear in the sources until 1430.[20] Yet the relationship between the grand duke and the appanage dukes was not a feudal one in the western European sense: the workings of the Gediminid and east Slavic dynastic system were different, and Niendorf's characterization of it as quasi-feudal (*lehnsähnlich*) seems fair: the annexed territories were—for the most part—no longer fiefs whose princes were vassals of the grand duke, but territories which, despite being largely left in charge of their own affairs, were considered part of the

---

[17] Oskar Halecki, 'Litwa, Ruś i Żmudź jako części składowe wielkiego księstwa litewskiego', *RAUWHF*, serya ii, 34 (1916), 214–54; Matthias Niendorf, *Das Großfürstentum Litauen: Studien zur Nationsbildung in der Frühen Neuzeit (1569–1795)* (Wiesbaden, 2006), 24.

[18] Любавский, *Областное*, 2–5; Stanisław Kutrzeba, *Historia ustroju Polski*, ii: *Litwa*, 2nd edn (Lwów, 1921), 6; Jerzy Ochmański, *Litewska granica etniczna na wschodzie od epoki plemiennej do XVI wieku* (Poznań, 1981), 69–73. Other historians accept Liubavskii's general argument but postulate different territorial divisions: Pietkiewicz regards Polesie and Podlasie as part of Trakai, and treats Smolensk and Chernihiv-Siversky, and Podolia and Volhynia as single units: Pietkiewicz, *Wielkie księstwo*, 48–66.

[19] Любавский, *Областное*, 1–62; Niendorf, *Großfürstentum*, 24.

[20] Edvardas Gudavičius, *Lietuvos Istorija*, i (Vilnius, 2001), 383–97; Niendorf, *Großfürstentum*, 25.

grand duke's patrimony.[21] The grand duchy was neither a unitary state nor a modern federation. It was a classic composite state.

At Krewo, Jagiełło promised to join his Lithuanian and Ruthenian territories to Poland. While he showed little inclination to effect the incorporation that was the Polish understanding of '*applicare*', it was not long before he looked to Polish models to promote social change within the grand duchy. On 20 February 1387, back in Vilnius to convert his pagan subjects, he issued privileges to all pagan nobles (*armigeris sive boyaris*) who accepted Catholic baptism. They were to receive the same rights as their Polish counterparts: this meant that for the first time they were explicitly granted full property rights at law, including hereditary title to allodial noble land and the freedom to decide on the marriage of daughters and other female family members without asking the grand duke's permission. All labour services for the grand duke from their allodial lands, except for the duty to construct and repair fortifications, were abolished.[22]

It was to be some time before the full effects of this act became apparent, since Lithuania as yet lacked the legal and political institutions to give it force, but its symbolic importance was considerable. As Halecki observes, it was more the declaration of a programme than the instant transformation of a social group: although it hinted at the establishment of a system of local noble courts on the Polish model, no practical steps were taken to establish one.[23] The explicit mention of the rights of the Polish nobility in the documents demonstrates that despite his lack of enthusiasm for incorporation, Jagiełło was from the outset thinking of a relationship between his two realms that was more than a simple personal union: he wished to bring them into closer harmony. For the Lithuanian boyars the wording highlighted the extensive rights and privileges enjoyed by their Polish counterparts. It was the first step on what was to prove a long journey.

The grand duchy's noble elites were at a very different stage of social, legal, and political development: if there was contiguity between the two realms, there was little conformity. The paucity of sources—and the fact that most of those that have survived are the chronicles of Lithuania's enemies, the Teutonic Knights—make it difficult to be precise about the nature of the Lithuanian—as opposed to the Ruthenian—nobility before 1386. In origin it was a military class, serving first the local tribal leaders, and then the grand ducal dynasty after the consolidation of central power under Mindaugas and Gediminas. By 1350 the semi-independent class of dukes (*kunigai, kunigaikščiai*) had largely been eclipsed by the power of the dynasty, except in Samogitia, whose connections to the centre remained loose.[24]

The view, common in older Polish historiography, that the 1387 privileges sparked a revolutionary transformation of the Lithuanian elites can no longer be sustained. It depended upon two key assumptions: that Lithuania was a despotic, patrimonial state in which the absolute power of the grand duke meant that there were no private rights in land until the 1387 privileges; and that landholdings

---

[21] Niendorf, *Großfürstentum*, 24. [22] ZPL, 1–2. [23] Halecki, *Dzieje*, i, 251–2.
[24] Rowell, *Lithuania*, 49–50; Konstantinas Avižonis, *Die Entstehung und Entwicklung des Litauischen Adels bis zur litauisch-polnischen Union 1385* (Berlin, 1932), 92, 97.

remained small, for most boyars consisting of one village, with only the most important servants of the prince holding two or at most three.[25] The concentration on individuals and agnatic lineages has distorted the picture, however. The landholding system in Lithuania proper—as in the annexed territories—was based on the tradition of collective ownership of the land by the cognatic kinship group. It was the extended horizontal kinship group—common generations of brothers and cousins—that was most important.[26]

While in theory all land ultimately belonged to the grand duke, Lithuania already knew allodial landholding in 1387—as the wording of the privilege makes clear—and there are indications that expropriation of allodial—as opposed to military-service—land by the grand duke was regarded as illegal.[27] Landholding, however, was a collective, not an individual matter, in which an inherited patrimony—as with the ruling dynasty—belonged to the extended cognatic family; thus its free disposal could only be made with the agreement of brothers, uncles, and cousins. Although the oldest documentary record of this practice dates from 1437, it clearly reflects earlier custom.[28] Landholding was complex and dispersed; if one looks at families rather than individuals, there were already complexes of estates and the small elite of families that were to dominate Lithuanian politics after 1386 was largely in place already. It was not the creation of the union.

Yet the union was to exercise a significant influence over the development of the Lithuanian nobility, in particular for the large group of middling and lesser boyars. While private landholding certainly existed, the extent of legal protection for the customary arrangements for its disposal and inheritance is unclear. The grand duke's patrimony was vast, and a considerable amount of land held by individuals took the form of temporary assignations of land granted during the performance of military service. Estates might be granted for life, or even in perpetuity as allodial holdings, although this was rare.[29] Although in practice—as in most military service systems—holdings were often passed on to the sons of boyars, there was no legal guarantee providing for such bequests, and they could be revoked at the grand duke's pleasure. Although few new men—or new families—penetrated the small group at the apex of Lithuanian landed society, the mass of the *boiarstvo* was not yet closed, and recruitment into it from the large class of free peasants, was still common. Boyar estates were traditionally worked by their families and by slaves, captured in raids: it was only in the fourteenth century that the old tribal practice of killing the menfolk and taking only women and children to provide domestic

---

[25] The first was asserted most strongly by Kamieniecki; the second by Łowmiański: Witold Kamieniecki, *Społeczeństwo litewskie w XV wieku* (Warsaw, 1947), 27–30; Łowmiański, *Studia*, 142–50.
[26] Petrauskas, *Diduomenė*, 103–17.
[27] Nikžentaitis, 'Litauen', 70–1; Petrauskas, *Diduomenė*, 131; Gudavičius, 'Baltų alodo pavbeldėjimas ir disponavimas juo', in Gudavičius (ed.), *Lietuvos Europėjimo keliais*, 100–11; and Gudavičius, 'Baltų alodo raida', in Gudavičius (ed.), *Lietuvos Europėjimo keliais*, 87–99.
[28] Petrauskas, *Diduomenė*, 117–25.
[29] Avižonas, *Entstehung*, 116–18.

labour died out, as did the custom of burning slaves alive on the funeral pyres of their master along with the rest of his moveable property.[30]

The agricultural economy, while increasingly sophisticated, was not as developed as its largely rent-based counterpart in Poland, and Lithuanian boyars did not yet have the economic or intellectual resources on which to build the sophisticated challenge to untrammelled royal authority mounted by their Polish counterparts after 1370. Challenges to grand ducal power tended to come from within the dynasty itself, rather than from below, although the civil war after 1377 enabled the more important boyars to increase their political influence, as Jogaila and Kęstutis sought support. Jogaila's power-base lay to a considerable extent among Ruthenian and Orthodox nobles, while Kęstutis drew substantial support from Aukštaitija and Samogitia.[31] Yet for all that the boyars were by no means passive before 1386, it was the union that shaped the Lithuanian nobility's political development more than any other factor.

---

[30] Łowmiański, *Studia*, 151, 160–3.   [31] Avižonis, *Entstehung*, 104.

7

Baptism

On 20 February, four days after issuing his privilege for boyars who converted to Catholicism, Jagiełło launched the baptism of Lithuania, or at least of Aukštaitija. The details remain murky. Długosz gives the most comprehensive account, but he is often misleading. The process was not easy. At an assembly in Vilnius Jagiełło faced resistance even before he ordered the destruction of the Vilnius temple and its eternal flame. According to Długosz, Jagiełło's personal intervention won the day, since he spoke Lithuanian, unlike the Polish priests accompanying him. While boyars were christened individually, the common people were baptized in groups of six, who all received the same Christian name. The white woollen clothes, brought from Poland and given to all who accepted baptism, were particularly popular, as people preferred them to their normal linen attire.[1]

How much of this is true is unclear. The conversion was a substantial undertaking. Pagan temples were destroyed and the sacred groves felled across Aukštaitija, as the institutional basis for the new church was established. On 17 February 1387 Jagiełło founded the diocese of Vilnius, endowing it richly to ensure that the bishop and chapter would have the means to lead the Christianization. A new cathedral, dedicated jointly to Poland's patron saint Stanisław and Jagiełło's own patron, the Hungarian saint László (Władysław), was built on the site of the pagan high temple. The bishopric was granted 50–60 villages, with some 600 hearths, not counting the 50 or so it held in Vilnius. At a stroke, Jagiełło created Lithuania's first latifundium, by far the greatest complex of landed property after the holdings of the grand duke himself.[2]

The Catholic Church was granted wide privileges on 22 February. Its lands were to be held on the same basis as those of the grand duke. It was to enjoy complete fiscal and juridical immunity: the church was to pay no taxes or dues to the state, and was to have full authority over those living on its lands.[3] Jagiełło toured Lithuania, founding new parishes as he went. Seven were established in the initial phase: in Krėva, Ukmergė, Maišiagala, Nemenčinė, Medininkai, and two that Jagiełło did not visit in Oboltsy and Haina. Three were founded in Vilnius, apart from the cathedral; others followed in Bystrytsa (1392), Lida (1397), and Ašmena (1398). Two of them—Haina, near Minsk, and Oboltsy, near Orsha, south of

---

[1] *Annales*, x, 159–62.
[2] Jerzy Ochmański, *Powstanie i rozwój latyfundium biskupstwa wileńskiego (1387–1550)* (Poznań, 1963), 1–40.
[3] Krzyżaniakowa and Ochmański, *Jagiełło*, 119.

Vitsebsk—were in largely Ruthenian territory, but had substantial Lithuanian populations: some ten per cent in Oboltsy.[4]

Despite early difficulties, the conversion succeeded, even if popular pagan beliefs proved harder to eradicate. Jagiełło's grip was sufficient to ensure there was little noble resistance of the sort that had led to the assassination of Mindaugas 120 years earlier, at least in Aukštaitija; in Samogitia, where paganism was strongly rooted, it was different: in 1382 the Samogitians had warned that if Jagiełło ordered their baptism, they would resist.[5] Although it was to be three decades before he sought to break that resistance, the process ran relatively smoothly in Aukštatija.

That it did owed much to Polish assistance. Lithuania's conversion laid the foundations of the closer relationship between Poles and Lithuanians that grew gradually over the next two centuries. Polish influence over the early development of the Lithuanian church was substantial. Jagiełło turned to the Poles to provide him with the necessary priests and missionaries. It is unlikely that Jagiełło personally translated the Paternoster and other prayers into Lithuanian, as was maintained by Długosz and Mikołaj Kozłowski in his 1434 funeral address, and since he left Lithuania in July 1387, it was others who were responsible for completing the conversion.[6] Essential to the success was a small group of Polish clerics who already had experience of Lithuania, and who spoke the language, including the first two bishops of Vilnius: Andrzej Jastrzębiec (1388–98), who had undertaken missionary work in Lithuania, and Jakub Plichta (1398–1407), a Franciscan resident in Lithuania; thanks to the phrase in his document of election '*vicarium Lythuanie, eiusdem nacionis et lingue*', he has been claimed as a Lithuanian. Even if he was— and his Slavic name makes it doubtful—he had lived in Poland, and it is likely that his long residence in Lithuania explains his designation as a Lithuanian.[7]

Before 1386 the Franciscan mission was run by the Saxon province. Responsibility now passed to the Bohemian-Polish province, and Polish Franciscans flooded into Lithuania. The parish network long remained rudimentary, but the well-organized Franciscans, who already possessed two houses in Vilnius, built monasteries in Ašmena, Lida—although here they were only present from 1397 to *c*.1402—Kaunas, and Drohichyn, establishing a separate Lithuanian vicariate in 1398. Other orders played a lesser role, with only individual Dominicans mentioned in this period, but the Benedictines founded a monastery in Trakai in 1405, a filial house of Tyniec near Cracow. Also important were the regular canons of the Atonement, known as Markists, from the church of St Mark in Cracow, who arrived in 1390–1391, founding a house in Bystrytsa with a filial in Medininkai.[8]

The context for Jagiełło's conversion was very different to that of Mindaugas. The ground had been prepared by years of missionary effort, and the Polish church had the institutional structures capable of supplying clergy and religious institutions

---

[4] Błaszczyk, *Dzieje*, 213–14; Jučas, *Unija*, 121; Marceli Kosman, *Drogi zaniku pogaństwa u Bałtów* (Wrocław, 1976), 36, 39; Ochmański, *Granica*, 58–65.
[5] *Die Chronik Wigands von Marburg*, SRPr, ii, 619; Jučas, *Unija*, 128.
[6] Błaszczyk, *Dzieje*, ii/i, 207–10; Antoni Gąsiorowski, *Itinerarium króla Władysława Jagiełły 1386–1434* (Warsaw, 1972), 30.
[7] Błaszczyk, *Dzieje*, ii/i, 200–2. [8] Błaszczyk, *Dzieje*, ii/i, 201, 204–7.

to sustain the new faith. The Lithuanian church took time to develop a native clergy, and Poles largely filled the breach. The Polish religious orders brought organization and intellectual traditions that rapidly penetrated Lithuanian culture. While Polish clerics did learn Lithuanian in order to preach, much of the intellectual life of the Lithuanian church took place in Latin or Polish: since Lithuanian was not yet a written language, it was in no position to compete. The use of Polish made Catholicism more accessible to Ruthenian speakers, while the dynamism and missionary ethos of Catholic orders, especially the Franciscans, contrasted sharply with the more inward-looking world of Orthodox monasticism and offered competition to the Orthodox Church.

By choosing Catholicism Jagiełło introduced a new cultural and political divide within the grand duchy. This was made explicit in the privileges granted to the Lithuanian church in February 1387, when marriages between Catholics and Orthodox were banned; henceforth, only the conversion of the Orthodox partner to Catholicism would allow the marriage to take place. This was a cultural barrier that was more significant than that between paganism and Orthodoxy, given the tensions between the Latin and Greek branches of Christendom. While the decentralized, composite nature of the Gediminid system meant that there was initially no challenge to Orthodoxy in the annexed territories, as grand dukes sought to consolidate their central authority, tensions inevitably emerged.

8

Cousins

The union's first four decades were dominated by Jagiełło and Vytautas, the most politically talented of Jagiełło's Gediminid relations. Much remains obscure about their relationship. Born within a couple of years of each other, they were—according to chronicle accounts—the favourite sons of their respective fathers, raised on the understanding that they would succeed to their fathers' patrimonies and political positions.[1] Their exact birthdates are unknown: traditionally Jagiełło's was given as 1348, Vytautas's as 1350.[2] In 1991 Wasilewski claimed that Jagiełło was not the eldest of Algirdas's sons by his second wife Juliana, as was commonly accepted, but was born in 1362 or 1363.[3] His views have been influential.[4] Yet Wasilewski's thesis fails to convince. The case rests on later redactions of the chronicle of Metropolitan Cyprian, compiled in 1408, the original of which has disappeared, and the oldest copy of which, the Troitskii chronicle, was burnt in Moscow in 1812, leaving historians dependent upon notes taken by Karamzin.[5] Wasilewski dismisses the evidence of German chroniclers as unreliable, yet is prepared to take evidence from the Ruthenian chronicles more seriously than it deserves: they contain numerous errors and disagree wildly as to the number, order, and even the names of the children of Algirdas and Kęstutis. He argues that Vytautas was ten years older than Jagiełło, discounting the testimony of Bitschin's chronicle, which states that Jogaila was twenty-two and Vytautas twenty when they fought at Rudau in 1370, and of Długosz, who depicts Jagiełło as decrepit by the 1420s—if Wasilewski is right he would have been in his sixties—and remarks when discussing the 1428 Novgorod campaign that Vytautas was over eighty, which would place his birth around 1348.[6] Wasilewski makes much of sources that claim that Jagiełło was 'young' when he succeeded his father, without defining what this might mean, and is overly keen to dismiss sources stressing his advanced age towards the end of his life: Waynknecht's chronicle states that he was old at Tannenberg in 1410, suggesting a man approaching his sixties rather than one not yet fifty, but Wasilewski prefers to claim that a younger Jagiełło makes a more plausible victor in the battle.[7]

[1] *PSRL*, xxxv, col. 62.   [2] Sužiedėlis, 'Lietuva', 28–31; Ivinskis, 'Vytauto', 3–6.
[3] Wasilewski, 'Daty', 15–34.
[4] Tęgowski endorses many of Wasilewski's findings in *Pierwsze pokolonia*, although he moves Jagiełło's birth slightly earlier, to 1361 or 1362. They have also been influential in Lithuania: see Baronas, Dubonis, and Petrauskas (eds), *Lietuvos Istorija*, iii, table 95, 356–7.
[5] Wasilewski, 'Daty', 20–1.   [6] *SRPr.*, iii, 479–80; *Annales*, xi, 245.
[7] *SRPr.*, iii, 432.

Wasilewski's dating is implausible. In the 1430s Bitschin worked closely with the Order's hierarchy, many of whom knew Jagiełło and Vytautas personally; while Długosz may have rounded up Vytautas's age by a couple of years, he is unlikely to have been too wide of the mark: he gleaned his knowledge of Jagiełło and Vytautas from his mentor, Zbigniew Oleśnicki, whose service he entered three years before Jagiełło's death, which makes it likely that he had opportunities to observe or meet Jagiełło.

Ochmański plausibly argues that Algirdas's marriage to Juliana could only have taken place in 1350 or 1351, suggesting that Jagiełło could not have been born earlier than 1351. Nikodem agrees, arguing that Jagiełło was the eldest son of Algirdas's second marriage, born between 1351 and 1353, probably earlier rather than later; and accepts the traditional line—confirmed by Długosz—that Vytautas was younger, being born in 1354 or 1355.[8] Nevertheless, this would mean that Długosz's testimony regarding Vytautas's age in 1428 was out by seven or eight years, a substantial rounding-up. Given that it is impossible to be accurate about dates, and the difficulties involved in moving Jagiełło's date of birth forward to 1353, there is much to be said for accepting the earliest date proposed by Ochmański, which would put Jagiełło's birth in 1351, with Vytautas's in 1352 or 1353.

Whatever the truth, the nature of the relationship between the cousins is controversial, partly because of the detailed picture provided by Długosz, who was no objective observer. Born in 1415, he received his political education from Oleśnicki, who clashed repeatedly with Jagiełło after 1420 and ended his life in sour opposition to Jagiełło's son, Casimir IV. Długosz disliked Lithuanians in general and the Jagiellons in particular, despite long service to Casimir. While he admired Vytautas, his portrait of Jagiełło, if recognizing positive traits such as his sense of honour, depicted him as 'uneducated and simple; more suited to hunting than to government'.[9]

Jagiełło, if he spurned pomp, show, and alcohol, was no naïve, uneducated barbarian. His handling of Vytautas suggests that he had considerable political skill. Vytautas was short of stature and slight in build, but his energy and force of character were palpable. Długosz testified that Jagiełło realized 'there was nobody better able to govern Lithuania and rebuild it out of the ruin and destruction of recent wars', thereby recognizing Jagiełło's shrewdness in inviting him to do so.[10] Vytautas could be cruel: 'the Poles fear him more than they do [Jagiełło], because [he] tends to demand instant revenge for crimes committed, and his ability to achieve his ends is twice that of the king'. Abstemious—he did not touch alcohol—

---

[8] Tęgowski, *Pierwsze pokolenia*, table iii, 308–11; Jan Tęgowski, 'Kilka uwag do genealogii Gediminowiczów', *SŹ*, 36 (1997), 113–16; Nikodem, 'Data urodzenia Jagiełły: Uwagi o starszeństwie synów Olgierda i Julianny', *Genealogia*, 12 (2000), 23–49; and Nikodem, *Witold*, 33–41. Tęgowski supports Wasilewski against Nikodem: 'Data urodzenia Jagiełły oraz data chrztu prawosławnego jego starszych braci', *Genealogia*, 15 (2003), 137–44; as Nikodem observes, however, he concedes the unreliability of the chronicle evidence, without which Wasilewski has no case: Nikodem, 'Ponownie o dacie urodzenia Jagiełły', *Genealogia*, 16 (2004), 143–58. Cf. Леонтій Войтович, *Княжа доба на Русі: Портрети еліти* (Біла Церква, 2006), 630–42; Rowell, *Lithuania*, 87–8; Krzyżaniakowa and Ochmański, *Jagiełło*, 54–5, 310.

[9] *Annales*, x, 144.   [10] *Annales*, x, 197.

and an uxorious lover of domesticity, he was nevertheless, according to Długosz's contradictory portrait, a womanizer with a strong sex-drive capable of abandoning a battle at its height to rush to the bed of his wife or mistress.[11]

If the two were childhood companions, events following Algirdas's death stretched their friendship past breaking-point. After Vytautas's dramatic 1382 flight to Prussia, while several associates, including Ivan Holshansky, followed him into exile, many Kęstutid supporters remained in Lithuania.[12] Jagiełło, an eminently practical politician, could not afford to have an unreconciled Vytautas scheming in Marienburg and stirring up Kęstutid supporters to oppose the momentous changes he was planning. In 1384, therefore, he reached out to his childhood companion.

He did not reach out very far. The details of his offer, which Vytautas accepted in July 1384, are unknown.[13] Vytautas returned, but although his seal on the Krewo Act bore the legend 'duke of Trakai', Skirgaila still held Kęstutis's duchy, which he had been granted in 1382. Jagiełło did not confirm this until April 1387, suggesting that he deliberately kept Vytautas's hopes of securing his patrimony alive until he felt secure on the Polish throne.[14] Instead, Vytautas received parts of Kęstutis's Ruthenian lands, including Hrodna, Podlasie, Brest, Drohichyn, Mielnik, and Vaukavysk, which were no compensation. Vytautas later claimed that Jagiełło had promised him Trakai, although it is likely that this is how Vytautas interpreted hints about the restoration of his patrimony. His testimony on other points is dubious: he claimed that Jagiełło forced him to undergo Orthodox baptism, but this was probably an attempt to explain to the Order why he had renounced the Catholic baptism he had undergone during his first Prussian exile. It was Vytautas himself, angered at Jagiełło's failure to return his patrimony, who decided on this step, in the hope of securing support from Jagiełło's mother for his claim to Lutsk.[15] Vytautas had burnt his bridges, however; Jagiełło could stand firm on Trakai. Yet although Vytautas publicly endorsed Krewo, he demonstrated his political shrewdness by renouncing his freshly minted Orthodoxy and accepting Catholic baptism in Cracow along with Jagiełło's pagan brothers, retaining the Christian name of Alexander which he had adopted on his Orthodox baptism, instead of Wigand, the name bestowed on him at his first baptism in 1383.[16]

Vytautas refused to allow Jagiełło to consign him to the Ruthenian margins; his third baptism put him in an excellent position to influence the creation of the new Catholic establishment once Jagiełło returned to Poland in July 1387. Jagiełło was going to be largely an absentee monarch: he was not to return to Lithuania until early 1390, staying from February to May before heading back to Poland. He spent a couple of months in Lithuania in the spring of 1391, but was then absent for six years, until a brief visit to Lida in May 1397. He did not return until January 1400, leaving again in March.[17]

---

[11] *Annales*, xi, 228, 245–6; 303.   [12] Krzyżaniakowa and Ochmański, *Jagiełło*, 82.
[13] Halecki, *Dzieje*, i, 106–7. Cf. Ivinskis, 'Vytauto', 26.
[14] Paszkiewicz, *O genezie*, 178; Błaszczyk, *Dzieje*, ii/i, 128.   [15] Nikodem, *Witold*, 94–6.
[16] Krzyżaniakowa and Ochmański, *Jagiełło*, 81–4, 96–7; Nikodem, *Witold*, 102–3.
[17] Gąsiorowski, *Itinerarium*, 30–41.

These were uncharted waters. Gediminid Lithuania had been ruled by the extended dynasty under the control of powerful grand dukes. Important decisions were taken by meetings of leading members of the dynasty; there were no mechanisms to deal with the grand duke's long-term absence, and no proper chancery to handle routine government business: the secretaries who prepared Latin documents were sought on an ad hoc basis among the Polish or German clergy resident in Vilnius. Treaties were often drafted by the other party: in 1322, Rigan envoys brought a draft treaty from Livonia; the Polish chancery prepared the Ruthenian texts of Algirdas's 1366 treaty with Casimir III; and the text of the 1371 treaty with Dmitrii Donskoi was drafted by the Muscovites.[18]

At first Jagiełło used the Polish chancery for matters concerning the grand duchy; since it was perfectly capable of preparing documents in Ruthenian there was no need to bring secretaries from Vilnius. He initially issued documents under his Lithuanian seal; once a new one was ready it was attached to documents concerning Lithuania even though it only bore his Polish title. This practice and the symbolism of the seal have been presented as evidence of incorporation, although Kosman rightly warns against such a conclusion.[19] It is neither surprising that Jagiełło approved a seal proclaiming his most prestigious title, nor that he—for eminently practical reasons—utilized the services of a properly institutionalized chancery that far surpassed anything he had known in Vilnius. In the conduct of foreign relations, his royal title raised him to a different level among the crowned heads of Europe, while the chancery was careful to list his Lithuanian and Ruthenian titles in all documents that it issued. The organization of a separate chancery for Jadwiga dealing solely with Poland indicates that the distinction between Poland and the rest of Jagiełło's domains was maintained.

For all the practised routines of the Polish chancery, Jagiełło could not run Lithuania from Cracow. This was made clear by the first challenge to the new order from Jagiełło's Orthodox half-brothers Andrei, who still held Polatsk after Skirgaila's failure to recapture it in 1381, and Dmitry of Briansk. In close contact with Moscow, Andrei swore homage to the Livonian Order for his duchy and allied with Sviatoslav Ivanovich, duke of Smolensk. In February 1386 the Livonians declared war, raiding deep into Lithuania. Sviatoslav struck towards Vitsebsk and besieged Mstislau.

Jagiełło hurried back to Vilnius after his coronation but, aware he would have to return to Cracow, he appointed Skirgaila governor on 13 March 1386, explicitly granting him powers over Lithuania. These powers, it was stressed, derived not just from Jagiełło but, in the spirit of Krewo, also from Jadwiga and the Polish community of the realm, whose consent to the appointment was noted.[20] Skirgaila dealt efficiently with the immediate problem, winning a battle at Mstislau on 29

---

[18] Marceli Kosman, 'Kancelaria Wielkiego Księcia Witolda', in Kosman, *Orzeł i pogoń: Z dziejów polsko-litewskich XIV–XV w.* (Warsaw, 1992), 109–10.

[19] Krzyżaniakowa and Ochmański, *Jagiełło*, 112; Łowmiański, 'Wcielenie', 118; Kosman, 'Kancelaria', 111.

[20] *CESXV*, i/i, no. 4, 5–6.

April in which Sviatoslav was killed, then persuading Sviatoslav's son Iurii to abandon Andrei and return Smolensk to Lithuanian control. He led two expeditions against Polatsk: unsuccessfully in October 1386 and successfully in March 1387, when he captured Andrei, whose son Semën was killed in the fighting. Andrei was brought in chains to Poland and imprisoned for seven years. In 1388 Dmitry returned from Moscow, ending the rebellion.

In April 1387 Skirgaila was formally invested with Polatsk; on 18 June he renewed his oath of loyalty to Jagiełło, Jadwiga, and the *corona regni Poloniae*, promising that should he die without issue, his lands would pass to them.[21] As duke of Trakai and Polatsk and governor of Minsk and Krėva, he controlled substantial territories in the most densely populated part of the grand duchy and ran the duchy of Vilnius on his brother's behalf. Whatever Jagiełło's original intentions concerning Vytautas, Skirgaila's deft handling of the crisis ensured it would be difficult to deprive him of Trakai. Vytautas's exclusion was highlighted in Jagiełło's privilege of 20 February 1387, which raised Skirgaila above the other Gediminid princes and stressed that his authority extended over the annexed Ruthenian territories.[22]

Much was being placed upon Skirgaila's shoulders. Historians are divided as to his character. Some follow Długosz's dismissive portrait of an audacious, defiant man with considerable manual dexterity and a ready tongue, prone to drunken bouts of temper in which he could wound friends and servants. He was feared for his cruelty, having executed or maimed many who fell foul of him.[23] Despite this fearsome reputation, he is often dismissed as incompetent and unworthy of the role Jagiełło assigned him.[24] Yet there was good reason for the trust Jagiełło placed in him. As Długosz acknowledged, Skirgaila was able. He probably led the Lithuanian delegation at Jadwiga's 1384 coronation, and was responsible for the 1385 negotiations over Jagiełło's marriage. It was not just Skirgaila's loyalty that commended him to Jagiełło: Długosz was clearly not misinformed about the effectiveness of his tongue, and he observes that Vytautas was afraid of him, not least because of his popularity among Ruthenians after his conversion to Orthodoxy.[25]

Skirgaila's Orthodoxy, however, limited his effectiveness as governor. According to Długosz, Jagiełło urged him to convert, but Skirgaila's conscience was less flexible than Vytautas's: he replied that he would only do so in Rome.[26] Vytautas, fuming on the margins to which Jagiełło had consigned him, was therefore well placed to build up support among the new Catholic elite. By 1389 his relations with Skirgaila were poisonous, and Jagiełło was forced to intervene. At a joint

---

[21] *CESXV*, i/i, no. 9, 9–11; *AU*, no. 18, 15; Wanda Maciejewska, 'Dzieje ziemi połockiej (1385–1430)', *AW*, 8 (1931–1932), 3–13; Rhode, *Ostgrenze* (Cologne, 1955), 342–3.
[22] *ZPL*, 1; Błaszczyk, *Dzieje*, ii/i, 42; Šapoka, 'Valstybiniai', 197.
[23] *Annales*, x, 174, 206.
[24] For example Paszkiewicz, *O genezę*, 183; Šapoka, 'Valstybiniai', 199.
[25] *Annales*, x, 174. For a generally persuasive reassessment of Skirgaila see Nikodem, 'Rola', 83–129; Jarosław Nikodem, 'Charakter rządów Skiergiełły i Witolda na Litwie w latach 1392–1394', *LSP*, 11 (2005), 153–63. Błaszczyk tends towards the older view: *Dzieje*, ii/i, 83, 155.
[26] *Annales*, x, 206.

Polish-Lithuanian council—the only one held in this period—in Lublin in May 1389, Vytautas had to swear not to believe malicious rumours concerning Skirgaila, to maintain loyalty and brotherly affection towards him, and to support him against everyone except Jagiełło.[27]

Jagiełło conceded nothing, however, and the ink was barely dry on the agreement before Vytautas was plotting to seize Vilnius while Skirgaila was in Polatsk preparing to support a siege of Pskov led by Lengvenis. His plans were betrayed to Kaributas, who had been left in charge by Skirgaila.[28] Vytautas had no choice but to throw himself once more on the Order's mercy. Rottenstein was suspicious of the man who had fled Prussia five years earlier, destroying three castles as he left; nevertheless, after insisting that Vytautas send his wife Anna, his sister Ryngailė, his brother Žygimantas, and his nephew Mykolas as hostages, he agreed to shelter him again. Vytautas might be unreliable, but Rottenstein could not spurn an opportunity to sow dissent between Poland and Lithuania. In a treaty dated 19 January 1390 Vytautas agreed to surrender Hrodna to the Order; in May, a treaty of mutual support was signed with the pagan Samogitians.[29]

Vytautas poured his bile into his *Sache*, a bitter justification of his actions, claiming that Jagiełło had destroyed the harmony that had existed between their fathers, who divided Lithuania between them and ruled together amicably. In contrast Jagiełło, on succeeding Algirdas, had conspired with the Order behind Kęstutis's back. This provoked Kęstutis into mounting his coup, after which he treated Jagiełło with consideration. Jagiełło, however, had acted treacherously, first offering Kęstutis and Vytautas safe conduct, and then seizing them, before murdering Kęstutis and his wife. He had also reneged on his promise to restore Vytautas's patrimony.[30]

Vytautas's *Sache* is a powerful, if tendentious, indictment. Despite the support he attracted from Kęstutid supporters—one source claimed 2,000 followed him into exile—and despite the Order's military backing, he was not powerful enough to overthrow his cousin.[31] Jagiełło acted decisively. In May 1390 he travelled to Lithuania, where he replaced Andrius Goštautas as starosta of Vilnius with the Polish vice-chancellor, Klemens of Moskorzew in a move that has frequently been presented as evidence of Lithuania's incorporation, since Klemens was accorded the title of starosta general, and the equivalent offices in Małopolska and Wielkopolska enjoyed considerable authority.

Too much should not be read into this title, or Klemens's appointment, almost certainly made in May 1390, not late 1389, as was once believed. Skirgaila was neither dismissed, nor were his powers limited to Trakai, as Halecki argued.[32] The appointment was occasioned by the political crisis, not by any desire on Jagiełło's part to effect Lithuania's incorporation. Klemens was to command the Vilnius

---

[27] *CEV*, no. 53, 18. [28] Błaszczyk, *Dzieje*, ii/i, 136, 141.
[29] *CEV*, nos 63–4, 20–1; Nikodem, *Witold*, 127–33.
[30] 'Dis ist Witold's sache wedir Jagalu und Skargalu', *SRPr*, ii, 711–14.
[31] *Skarbiec*, i, no. 607, 289.
[32] Halecki, *Dzieje*, i, 133; Šapoka, 'Valstybiniai', 199; Błaszczyk, *Dzieje*, ii/i, 140.

garrison, and Jagiełło did not confer any wider powers upon him. Even in Vilnius control was divided, with Klemens controlling the lower, and Skirgaila the upper castle. It would have been uncharacteristically rash of Jagiełło to dismiss Skirgaila at the height of a major political crisis. With Vytautas commanding considerable support among the Lithuanian boyars, Jagiełło clearly felt he could not rely on Goštautas, while the Polish garrison brought important expertise in siege warfare.

It was a sensible precaution. In September the Order's large international force—the earl of Derby, the future Henry IV of England, brought 300 archers—joined Vytautas and his followers to attack Vilnius. The besieging army took the crooked castle, the third fortress guarding the city, when its defenders betrayed its commandant, Jagiełło's brother Karigaila, who was killed, as was Vytautas's brother Tautvilas.[33] The other two castles held out, however, and the siege was lifted on 7 October. Klemens promptly resigned following disputes with Skirgaila, neatly demonstrating where real power lay. Jagiełło struggled to find another Pole willing to replace him, before eventually persuading Jaśko of Oleśnica. The war was not over, however. Vytautas still had considerable support.[34] It was marked by cruelty on both sides: according to Długosz, when the Gediminid prince Narimantas was captured at the siege of Vilnius he was strung up by the legs and used as target practice by the Prussian gunners; Długosz also mentions the impalement of children, while fifteen Poles were executed after Vytautas's recapture of Hrodna in 1391.[35]

These may be tall stories: Długosz is the only source to mention Narimantas, by whom he probably meant Tautvilas: Gediminas's brother Narimantas had died in 1348, and Długosz claims that he was married to Juliana, who was Tautvilas's wife. There is no reason to doubt the cruelty of the conflict, however. It was a critical moment for the union. The vultures were circling: in early 1392 Sigismund of Luxembourg opened talks with the Order, his brother Wenzel, and Wladislaus of Oppeln—who attempted to seize Cracow in Jagiełło's absence in 1389—over a partition of Jagiełło's dominions.[36] Sigismund encouraged the Order to accept Wladislaus's offer to pawn the strategic territory of Dobrzyń, which he had been granted by Louis of Anjou in return for surrendering Podolia. In May Sigismund proposed selling the Neumark to the Order, which, if it had happened, would have greatly increased the threat to Poland's western borders.[37] Finally, the marriage in January 1391 of Vytautas's only daughter, Sophia, to Vasilii I, who succeeded Dmitrii Donskoi on the Muscovite throne in 1389, showed the breadth of Vytautas's vision and demonstrated that despite his freshly reminted Catholicism he was seeking allies and influence on another front. Drastic action was required. Jagiełło therefore took a momentous and ruthless decision. Once again he reached out to Vytautas.

---

[33] Błaszczyk, *Dzieje*, ii/i, 148–9.

[34] *PSRL*, xvii, cols 200–1; Błaszczyk, *Dzieje*, ii/i, 136–42; Nikodem, 'Rola', 113, 118; Halecki, *Dzieje*, i, 134; Łowmiański, *Polityka*, 65.

[35] *Annales*, x, 187; Błaszczyk, *Dzieje*, ii/i, 153.   [36] Błaszczyk, *Dzieje*, ii/i, 136.

[37] Marian Biskup and Gerard Labuda, *Dzieje Zakonu Krzyżackiego w Prusach* (Gdańsk, 1986), 360; Krzyżaniakowa and Ochmański, *Jagiełło*, 137, 168–9.

This time he had to reach much further. Contact was established in late 1391 through Henryk, bishop-elect of Płock and son of Siemowit III of Mazovia, who on arrival in Prussia fell for Vytautas's sister Ryngailė, for whom he was to renounce his religious career, marrying her in June 1392. He cannot have been entirely distracted, for the secret talks succeeded. At Astrava on 4–5 August 1392 Vytautas again swore loyalty to Jagiełło, Jadwiga, and the *corona regni Poloniae* in return for the restoration of his patrimony, including Trakai and Lutsk, which had remained loyal to Jagiełło. Skirgaila was to receive Kyiv in compensation, although it would first have to be taken away from Volodymyr, Jagiełło's half-brother, who had held it since 1364. There was no apology from Vytautas for his actions: responsibility for the disputes between the two cousins was ascribed to the poisonous machinations of a conveniently abstract serpent.[38]

Astrava marked the end of Vytautas's direct challenge to Jagiełło's authority. Its significance is a matter of controversy. The chronicle account states that Vytautas was placed on the grand ducal throne to rule over all the Lithuanian and Ruthenian land, as does Długosz, who gives a touching account of a tearful Vytautas begging Jagiełło's forgiveness, stating that not only was Vytautas's patrimony restored, but that he was given authority over all the land.[39] These accounts have led historians to make some grand claims, suggesting that Astrava marked the end of incorporation, that it demonstrated conclusively that Lithuania had preserved its character as an independent, sovereign state, and even that it suspended the union for Vytautas's lifetime, marking 'the end of Jagiełło's rule' in Lithuania.[40] Łowmiański, while arguing that Astrava changed nothing in the legal relations between Poland and Lithuania, accepts that Vytautas was granted power over the whole grand duchy as governor, a view shared by Nikodem.[41]

Yet the chronicle account—which Długosz knew—was influenced by Vytautas, and none of this emerges from the Astrava documents. They were neither acts of union, as Koneczny and Ivinskis maintained, nor were they, as Błaszczyk asserts, 'the first revision of Krewo'. They neither appointed Vytautas governor, nor conferred upon him 'partial sovereignty', as Gudavičius avers. Nikodem, who regularly attacks other historians for exercising historical intuition beyond the documents, asserts that Jagiełło granted Vytautas the governorship orally, although the evidence he cites is circumstantial at best, and his conclusion owes much to his intuition concerning the relationship between Jagiełło and Vytautas.[42] Halecki

---

[38] *AU*, nos 29–31, 26–9.

[39] 'поидет оу Литву, и сядет на великом кнжени Литовском на Вилни, і были ради оуся земля Литовская і Руская': *PSRL*, xvii, col. 275; *Annales*, x, 197.

[40] Zigimantas Kiaupa, *Lietuvos valstybės istorija* (Vilnius, 2006), 56; Krzyżaniakowa and Ochmański, *Jagiełło*, 139; Dėdinas cites Liubavskii in support of his contention that Astrava restored Lithuanian independence and sovereignty, although Liubavskii is more cautious, talking of 'a certain autonomy': V. Dėdinas, 'Vytauto vidaus ir užsienio politika ligi Žalgirio mūsio', in Šležas (ed.), *Vytautas*, 45–68; Матвей Любавский, *Литовско-Русскій Сеймъ: Опытъ по исторіи учрежденія въ связи съ внутреннимъ строемъ и внешнею государства* (Moscow, 1900), 19.

[41] Łowmiański, *Polityka*, 65; Nikodem, 'Rola', 119; Nikodem, *Witold*, 147–57.

[42] Koneczny, *Jagiełło i Witold*, 212; Ivinskis, 'Vytauto', 44; Błaszczyk, *Dzieje*, ii/i, 49; Gudavičius (ed.), *Istorija*, i, 178; Nikodem, *Witold*, 149–51.

considers that Posilge's chronicle confirms Długosz's assertion, but it does no such thing, accurately stating that Vytautas was granted his patrimony, with no mention of wider powers.[43] The documents deal only with the conferment upon Vytautas of the duchies of Trakai and Lutsk. Vytautas swore loyalty on behalf of himself and his supporters not just to Jagiełło, but also to Jadwiga and the *corona regni Poloniae*, which suggests that the Krewo framework remained intact. Significantly, it was stated that he received his authority from Jagiełło alone.[44]

How extensive was that authority? The Astrava documents do not specify: they were the equivalent of the acts of homage sworn by the Gediminids in 1387, whose form and wording they echo. Astrava was not concerned with the union, but with the complex dynastic dispute over the legacy of Algirdas and Kęstutis. Vytautas's outrage, expressed in his *Sache*, concerned the duchy of Trakai, his patrimony, which had been stripped from him. Jagiełło was taking a substantial risk in restoring it to him, not least because he had to take it from Skirgaila, who was to be compensated with Kyiv, a city whose name and glorious past did not match its current importance, and which would have to be prised from Volodymyr's grasp. It is implausible that Jagiełło, given Vytautas's record, would grant him control not only of his own patrimony of Vilnius, but of the whole grand duchy while reducing Skirgaila, to whom he owed much, to a subordinate position. There is no document similar to that which had raised Skirgaila above all the other Gediminid dukes in 1387 to suggest that Vytautas was granted this role. The grand master's chronicle, a well-informed source, suggests that Jagiełło floated the idea of granting Vilnius to Vytautas, but that Skirgaila vigorously and successfully opposed the idea, as Jagiełło must have known he would.[45] It seems that—as Posilge suggests—Jagiełło secured Skirgaila's agreement to the restoration of Trakai, but left him in control of Vilnius, to act, with Kaributas, as a counterweight to Vytautas. As for Vytautas, while Nikodem is right to reject Halecki's optimistic view that Astrava marked the start of close cooperation between the cousins, during his second exile Vytautas was—as Nikodem recognizes—in a weak position.[46] Jagiełło, recognizing his earlier misjudgement, was happy to restore Trakai, but there was no need for him to concede more, which would risk alienating Skirgaila. Astrava sought to establish dynastic peace, not Lithuanian statehood.

Dynastic peace proved elusive. Vytautas accepted the deal, but he had no intention of accepting subordination to Skirgaila. Relations broke down immediately, and meetings with Jagiełło in December 1392 in Bełz, in October 1393 in

---

[43] 'sy welden im alle dy lant yngebin, dy sinem vatir Kinstottin vor hettin gehort': Johann von Posilge, *Chronik des Landes Preussen*, in SRPr, iii, 179; Halecki, *Dzieje*, i, 138.

[44] *AU*, no. 29, 27.

[45] 'Umb disze vorretthnisses willen hatte Jagel Wytolde globet dy Wille mit allem zcugehore. Das wolde Schirgal nicht gestaten, szunder her besasz sy selber': SRPr, iii, 622; Halecki nevertheless concluded that Skirgaila accepted Vytautas's supremacy: *Dzieje*, i, 138, n.2. Nikodem initially dismissed Posilge's evidence; he later modified his views, finding the suggestion that Skirgaila was left in charge of Vilnius 'tremendously suggestive': 'Rola', 119–20; 'Jednowładztwo', 11, n. 19. His latest account, however, maintains that Jagiełło did make Vytautas governor: *Witold*, 151.

[46] Nikodem, *Witold*, 133, 149.

Lwów, and in February 1394 in Dołatycze brought no relief from the endless quarrels.⁴⁷ Skirgaila proved an ineffective counterweight. He was in Poland from 1393 to the autumn of 1394 urging Jagiełło to order Vytautas to assist him in seizing Kyiv from Volodymyr to secure his compensation for surrendering Trakai. Vytautas was in no hurry, while Jagiełło could offer little more than sympathy: the Poles were uninterested in internal Lithuanian politics, while to ask them to help would raise questions about the grand duchy's position. Although the siege of Kyiv began in late 1394, Skirgaila did not live to see its fall, dying, reputedly poisoned, on 23 December.⁴⁸ The sources merely note this, without attributing blame; whether or not anyone wielded the bottle, the death of his only real rival was highly convenient for Vytautas.

Skirgaila was the most competent of Jagiełło's brothers: the others, according to Długosz, were too fond of hunting and drinking, and were incapable of ruling.⁴⁹ Of his younger brothers only Lengvenis, Kaributas, and Švitrigaila were still alive, and only Švitrigaila was Catholic. In 1392 Jagiełło committed himself to bringing Vytautas back into the fold. Even if he was initially cautious, Skirgaila's Orthodoxy made it difficult for him to establish himself at the head of the new, Catholic system to which Jagiełło had committed himself. Vytautas, after his return to Catholicism, was far better placed to build up support among the newly Catholic boyar elite, not least because he already had a considerable political following, which Skirgaila lacked. Jagiełło had committed himself to Catholicism. If it were to survive and flourish in a polity in which most nobles and the overwhelming majority of the population was Orthodox, it would require strong Catholic leadership which Jagiełło, in distant Cracow, could not directly provide. Like it or not, with Skirgaila dead, he had little option but to entrust Vilnius and the effective governorship of the grand duchy to Vytautas, who had the drive, energy, and political skills to establish the new system.

It was a considerable risk, and Vytautas's actions over the next seven years seem to provide much evidence for those historians who see him as the champion of Lithuanian independence and sovereignty, and for Nikodem who, while careful to stress that Vytautas did not directly challenge the union, argues that throughout his career he pursued a dynastic policy in favour of the Kęstutids, consistently seeking to undermine the Algirdaičiai—the descendants of Algirdas—in general, and Jagiełło in particular. Such views challenge the idea, most fully developed by Halecki, and endorsed by many Polish historians, that in the 1390s Jagiełło and Vytautas established the close cooperation that henceforth supposedly characterized their relationship: as Błaszczyk put it, their collaboration in the 1390s 'is, perhaps, an obvious fact'.⁵⁰

---

⁴⁷ *CESXV*, i/i, no. 20, 17.
⁴⁸ Tęgowski, 'Zagadnienie', 7–18; Nikodem, 'Charakter', 153–63; Nikodem, *Jadwiga*, 306–7, 312, 314, 317.
⁴⁹ *Annales*, x, 196.
⁵⁰ Błaszczyk, *Dzieje*, ii/i. 63; cf. Halecki: *Dzieje*, i, 146, 154; Nikodem, *Witold*, 156–7.

It is not, perhaps, quite that obvious. Vytautas first turned his attention to the dynasty. The harrying of Skirgaila launched a campaign against the appanage duchies that sapped the crumbling foundations of the Gediminid condominium. The appanage princes were not consulted over Astrava, and several refused to pay Vytautas dues they had previously rendered to Jagiełło.[51] In 1393, Fëdor Lubartovych, removed from Lutsk a year earlier to make room for Vytautas, was deprived of Volodymyr; as compensation he was granted the sparsely populated marchland duchy of Siversk, later receiving the small territory of Zhydachiv in Red Ruthenia. Fëdor, son of Algirdas's younger brother Liubartas, was a relatively easy target, and Volhynia had been promised to Vytautas at Astrava. Fëdor was not granted all of Siversk, and did not long retain control of what he received: by 1398 he was in exile in Hungary. Other victims were more prominent. In 1392 Siversk was held by Kaributas. Long loyal to Jagiełło, he rebelled after Astrava. He was defeated at Dokudov, captured and stripped of his duchy. Later released, he was granted Bratslav and Vinnitsa and ceased to play a significant role.[52]

Next in line was Jagiełło's youngest brother Švitrigaila. After their mother's death in 1392 Švitrigaila, displaying the brutal impetuosity that marked his whole career, seized Vitsebsk from its governor, Fëdor Vesna, whom he executed. Švitrigaila was captured by Vytautas and Skirgaila in a rare cooperative moment, and despatched to Cracow, where he kicked his heels for several years, before heading to Silesia and then Hungary. In 1393 Fëdor Koriatovych, duke of Podolia, was forcibly deprived of his duchy; uncompensated, he fled to Hungary.[53] The removal of Volodymyr from Kyiv, which he had ruled for thirty years, highlighted the inability of the appanage dukes to defend themselves: Volodymyr's appeal for help to Vasilii I fell on deaf ears, and he was shunted off to the tiny duchy of Kopyl, where he died four years later.[54] Of the substantial appanages, Polatsk, Vitsebsk, Novhorod-Siversky, and Kyiv were now in Vytautas's hands; only Dmitry of Briansk was left alone. The leading Gediminid princes now held insignificant duchies: Volodymyr (Kopyl), Fëdor (Ratno), and Mikhail Javnutovich (Zaslav).[55]

The age of the princes was drawing to a close; the age of the boyars was dawning. Vytautas turned his back on the dynasty, appointing Lithuanians to act as governors of the vacant duchies, rewarding those who had supported him during the civil wars. Most were Catholics, but Vytautas assigned the greatest prize of Kyiv to his Orthodox brother-in-law Ivan Holshansky, son of one of Algirdas's followers from the Ruthenianized Alšėniškai family of Lithuanian *kunigaikščiai*.[56] The appointment of Catholic governors significantly increased Vytautas's personal authority.

---

[51] Любавский, *Сеймъ*, 19–20.

[52] Любавский, *Областное*, 45; Олена Русина, *Україна під Татарами і Литвою* (Kyiv, 1998), 79; Błaszczyk, *Dzieje*, ii/i, 61.

[53] Любавский, *Областное*, 57; Русина, *Україна*, 79.

[54] *PSRL*, xxxv, col. 66; Михайло Грушевський, *Історія України-Руси, XIV–XVI віки— відносини політичні* (repr. Kyiv, 1993), 166–7; Błaszczyk, *Dzieje*, ii/i, 61–2; Русина, *Україна*, 80–1. According to Liubavskii, the expulsion took place in 1395: Любавский, *Областное*, 37.

[55] Rhode, *Ostgrenze*, i, 350–1; Błaszczyk, *Dzieje* ii/i, 61–2.

[56] Avižonis, *Entstehung*, 113–14; Józef Wolff, *Kniaziowie litewsko-ruscy* (Warsaw, 1895), 94–5; *PSB*, ix, 587–8.

Since the appanage duchies were subsumed into the grand ducal estate, his revenues and his ability to provide patronage increased significantly. He now had the means to institute a new system, controlled through a small group of largely Catholic Lithuanian boyars, who came to be known as lords: the term, *pany*, was borrowed from Polish. They formed Vytautas's growing clientele, but there was a price to be paid. In order to secure their support, Vytautas had to reward his protégés with generous grants of land and office.[57]

It was now that the significance of the 1387 privilege became apparent, as Vytautas's associates began to establish the great complexes of estates that were to become such a prominent feature of the Lithuanian social structure. The eclipse of the Algirdaičiai worked to their benefit. Where previously the dynasty had played the central role in the administration of grand ducal lands, leading boyars were now granted substantial service holdings, in various forms. What had been largely, if not entirely, a military-service class, bound tightly to the prince, began to evolve into a primarily landed class.[58]

The consolidation of Vytautas's authority was accompanied by an ambitious foreign policy. Initially he had to deal with the backlash to his second defection from the Order, which mounted six raids on Lithuania between 1392 and 1394, penetrating as far as Navahrudak and Lida, and laying siege to Vilnius.[59] Vytautas was looking in another direction, however. Sensing Muscovy's weakness under Vasilii I, his inexperienced son-in-law, he sought to establish himself as the most powerful prince in the eastern Slavic lands. In 1395 he secured Smolensk, which won him recognition from the petty Ruthenian princes along the upper Oka river, and cast his eye towards the wealthy cities of Novgorod and Tver.

It was a good moment, thanks to internecine squabbles among the Tatars. In 1381 Tokhtamysh defeated Mamai to unite both halves of the Golden Horde; in 1391 he lost control of the eastern half to his former patron Timur (Tamurlane); in April 1395 Timur defeated him on the Terek river, deposed him and installed Temür Kutlugh as khan of the Golden Horde. Tokhtamysh threw himself on Vytautas's mercy. In 1397 Vytautas led a joint force to secure the Black Sea coast to the south of the Ukrainian steppe, building forts at Chorny Horod on the Dniester estuary, and on the site of what later became Odessa, returning with large numbers of captives. In 1398 an expedition reached the Don. In 1399 Vytautas and Tokhtamysh ventured south in a grand campaign in which Vytautas sought to break the Horde's grip once and for all.

As Vytautas turned east he needed to secure his rear. Peace with the Order did not come cheap, however. In terms agreed at Hrodna in April and confirmed on Salin island in the river Niemen on 12 October 1398, Vytautas ceded Samogitia to the Order. The sacrifice was in vain. His eastern ambitions were rudely halted by a

---

[57] Jerzy Suchocki, 'Formowanie się i skład narodu politycznego w Wielkim Księstwie Litewskim późnego średniowiecza', *ZH*, 48/1–2 (1983), 48–9; Błaszczyk, *Dzieje*, ii/i, 62.
[58] Avižonis, *Entstehung*, 13–15, 116–17.
[59] Jerzy Ochmański, *Historia Litwy*, 3rd edn (Wrocław, 1990), 77.

shattering defeat on the Vorskla river on 12 August 1399. Temür Kutlugh lured Vytautas out of his fortified camp, and the Lithuanian army was surrounded and massacred by another force led by Emir Edigü that had lurked unseen. Vytautas escaped; seventy-four princes, including Andrei of Polatsk and Dmitry of Briansk, and several prominent Poles, including Spytek of Melsztyn, were not so lucky.[60]

The Vorskla debacle ended Vytautas's expansive ambitions for the moment. The effects of the humiliating defeat are a matter for controversy. For those who see Vytautas as the great defender of Lithuanian independence and sovereignty, the Salin treaty was the keystone of an independent foreign policy designed to destroy the union: the cession of Samogitia to the Order was the act of a 'sovereign, not a governor'.[61] It was only the Vorskla catastrophe that forced him to draw back and restore relations with Jagiełło.[62] Much of the evidence can certainly be read in this way. Vytautas gradually inflated the titles he accorded himself. At Astrava he was referred to simply as *dux Lituaniae*; he soon began using the title *magnus dux*, however, which is how he appeared in the Hrodna agreement in April 1398; by the time of its ratification at Salin he was styling himself *supremus dux Lithuaniae*. This was the prelude to an incident reported by Posilge at the banquet celebrating the Salin treaty, in which Vytautas was hailed as king of Lithuania by the Lithuanian and Ruthenian boyars present.[63]

The suggestion that in 1392 Jagiełło and Vytautas slipped easily from the hostility that characterized their relations since 1381, so viscerally exposed in Vytautas's *Sache*, into a harmonious collaboration based on trust and the pursuit of common goals is inherently implausible. Nevertheless, despite plenty of evidence from the 1390s of Vytautas's headstrong independence, there is still much to suggest that the political interests of the cousins were not as divergent as might be assumed, and that it was the Polish council, rather than Jagiełło himself, that was most strongly opposed to Vytautas's assertive foreign policy, although it cared little about internal Lithuanian politics. While Jagiełło was undoubtedly perturbed at some of his cousin's actions, it seems that he and Vytautas recognized the usefulness of cooperation; and that they gradually established a *modus vivendi* which characterized their whole relationship thereafter, finding considerable common ground with regard to the grand duchy's government and its relationship to Poland. To understand why, it is necessary to abandon anachronistic ideas of national sovereignty and independence in favour of a perspective rooted firmly in contemporary ideas of lordship and composite monarchy. For although both men challenged the traditional Gediminid dynastic system, they had grown up within it, and still thought broadly in terms not of unitary state-building, but of personal government, of lordship, of the tradition of dynastic consultation that had marked the joint rule

---

[60] *PSRL*, xxxv, col. 53; Rusyna questions the figure, but the toll was undoubtedly high: Русина, *Україна*, 84–94.

[61] Kiaupa, *Lietuvos valstybės*, 57; cf. Грушевський, *Історія*, iv, 143, n. 1; Łowmiański, *Polityka*, 66, 68. For Lithuanian, Polish, and Ukrainian scholars sharing this view, see Błaszczyk, *Dzieje*, ii/i, 84.

[62] Šležas, 'Vytauto', 153; Dėdinas, 'Vytauto', 45–68; Nikodem, *Witold*, 192–4.

[63] 'Und uf die cziit worfin die Littowin und Russin Wytowten eynen koning uf czu Littowen und czu Russin, da vor ny gehort was': Posilge, *Chronik*, 224.

of their fathers, and of the flexible arrangements possible within the composite polities of late medieval east central Europe.

Jagiełło was perfectly willing to challenge the Gediminid system. While the sacrifice of Skirgaila was personally difficult, there is no reason to suppose that brotherly love had much influence over Jagiełło's relationship with his male siblings, several of whom had rebelled against him, some more than once. There is nothing to indicate that he opposed the destruction of the appanages; indeed, Jagiełło himself began the process by ruthlessly stripping Skirgaila of Trakai and Fëdor Lubartovich of Lutsk, while Volodymyr's loyalty did not prevent Jagiełło approving his ousting from Kyiv at Astrava. Skirgaila himself was involved in defeating and capturing Švitrigaila after his seizure of Vitsebsk, while the fact that Vytautas sent Kaributas in chains to Jagiełło after his capture suggests that Jagiełło approved.[64] The dispossession of the Gediminids was the inevitable and accepted consequence of Astrava, and Jagiełło was closely involved in it, although he did not always indulge Vytautas, as his 1395 grant of Podolia to his Polish favourite, Spytek of Melsztyn, '*cum pleno iure ducale*', demonstrated.[65]

Such actions were a subtle demonstration that whatever titles Vytautas claimed, Jagiełło remained ultimately in control as he condoned actions that transformed the grand duchy's politics and destroyed a system that had served the Gediminids well, but whose deficiencies had long been apparent. By 1400 all of Jagiełło's older brothers from his father's first marriage were dead: Volodymyr (1398), Andrei and Dmitry (1399), and Fëdor of Ratno (1400). The Gediminids had largely been broken. There were no significant rivals to Vytautas from within the dynasty, owing to the principles of cognatic, collateral succession, in which sons could not succeed to an office their father had not held.[66] Both Vytautas and Jagiełło had invested considerable political capital in the transformation of Lithuania into a Catholic polity; the breaking of the Orthodox Gediminids removed one of the most significant obstacles to the realization of the Krewo plan.

For all his political acumen, Vytautas was by no means unassailable. His power rested firmly on the newly Catholic Lithuanian boyars who had benefited from the 1387 privileges: the Ruthenian boyars had largely supported Jagiełło in 1390–1391.[67] Removing or neutralizing the influence of the Orthodox Gediminids, who had provided leadership to the Ruthenian boyars, and centralizing authority in his own hands was a risk, however. It remained to be seen how the annexed Ruthenian territories would react to their new governors. Vytautas was aware of the problem, and the extent to which the old order was disrupted should

---

[64] Błaszczyk, *Dzieje*, ii/i, 60–1; Rhode, *Ostgrenze*, i, 347–8; Dėdinas, 'Vytauto', 46. Nikodem's account of Kaributas's rebellion is marred by his desire to fit the evidence—or ignore it if inconvenient—to his assumptions concerning the relationship between Jagiełło and Vytautas: 'Kaributo maištas', *LIM* (2007/1), 5–20.

[65] Русина, *Україна*, 79.

[66] Nancy Shields Kollmann, *Kinship and Politics: The Making of the Muscovite Political System, 1345–1547* (Stanford, CA, 1987), 59–70; Jan Tęgowski, 'O następstwie tronu na Litwie po śmierci Olgierda', *PH*, 84 (1993), 127–34.

[67] Łowmiański, 'Wcielenie', 114.

not be exaggerated: the grand duchy was neither turned into a single political unit as Dėdinas claims, nor did Vytautas's policy see 'a rapid acceleration of the development of a centralized unitary state' as Rhode asserts.[68] Lithuania was still very much a composite polity, and Vytautas was careful not to alienate the Ruthenian boyars by challenging their laws, privileges, and customs. He stressed his respect for the old ways, the *starina*, and did not challenge the large number of more minor princely clans in the annexed territories, especially in the princely heartland of Volhynia. Brothers were dangerous; distant cousins were not.

There was another consideration. Jagiełło faced a complex and increasingly difficult political situation in Poland after 1392. Jadwiga was now eighteen. Without an heir to seal the Krewo deal, Jagiełło's position with regard to the Polish throne was unclear. His right to it depended on election and the fulfilment of the promises he had made at Krewo. If Jadwiga should predecease him without producing an heir, his very possession of the throne might come into question, as was made clear in 1395 when, as Długosz noted with some relish, on her sister Mary's death the Hungarian lords assembled to consider the possibility of electing a new monarch 'as if Sigismund had ceased to be king'.[69] Although Sigismund retained his throne he by no means sat securely upon it; the lesson was not lost on Jagiełło. The group of 'Cracow lords', as they are usually called, who had masterminded the union in 1385–6, and who still dominated politics, made it clear that they did not consider that he had fulfilled his promise to join Lithuania to Poland in their incorporationist understanding of Krewo. Jagiełło was forming his own clientele in an attempt to free himself from the shackles imposed by this narrow group, but this took time, and provoked opposition: if his 1395 donation of Podolia to Spytek turned one of the Cracow lords into a mainstay of the embryonic royal party, the grant provoked outrage, not least from Jadwiga, because Jagiełło made it as grand duke of Lithuania, and Podolia was claimed by Poland.[70]

Jadwiga was emerging as a powerful figure in her own right. Her court, which was Polish-speaking, in contrast to Jagiełło's whose core was formed by Lithuanians and Ruthenians, became a magnet for those who wished to execute and institutionalize the incorporationist interpretation of Krewo.[71] Thus it was very much in Jagiełło's interests to support Vytautas's consolidation of power in Vilnius and to form a common front with him in defence of his patrimony and of the grand duchy's separate status within what Jagiełło refused to regard as an accessory union. Vytautas had no desire to see Jagiełło forced off the Polish throne, since this would bring his return to Vilnius. He had every reason to cooperate.

---

[68] Dėdinas, 'Vytauto', 49; Rhode, *Ostgrenze*, i, 350–1. [69] *Annales*, x, 212.
[70] Jerzy Sperka, 'Faworyci Władysława Jagiełły', in Mariusz Markiewicz and Ryszard Skowron (eds), *Faworyci a opozycjoniści: Król a elity polityczne w Rzeczypospolitej XV–XVIII wieku* (Cracow, 2006), 41–2; Sperka, 'Biskup krakowski Zbigniew Oleśnicki a ugrupowanie dworskie w okresie panowania Władysława Jagiełły i w pierwszych latach Władysława III', in Feliks Kiryk and Zdzisław Noga (eds), *Zbigniew Oleśnicki książę kościoła i mąż stanu* (Cracow, 2006), 107–8.
[71] Janusz Kurtyka, *Tęczyńscy: Studium z dziejów polskiej elity możnowładczej w średniowieczu* (Cracow, 1997), 212–13.

Matters came to a head in February 1398, when a breakdown in relations between Jagiełło and Jadwiga was reported by the Order.[72] The cause was a letter from Jadwiga to Vytautas demanding that he pay an annual rent in respect of the dower granted to her by Jagiełło which, according to Posilge—the only source—comprised 'the land of Rus' and Lithuania'.[73] There has been much debate about what this meant. Łowmiański and Bardach conclude that it simply referred to estates that formed part of Jadwiga's dower settlement, whose terms are unknown.[74] Vytautas's reaction, however, suggests that the letter was far more provocative, suggesting that Jadwiga's dower consisted of the whole grand duchy, which was one possible interpretation of Krewo.[75] He assembled leading Lithuanian and Ruthenian boyars and asked them if they felt themselves to be Polish subjects, required to pay a yearly tribute. They replied that they were free, as their ancestors had been free; that they had never paid rent to the Poles; and that they wished to remain in their original state of liberty.[76] While there is no corroboration of Posilge's account, it would explain the independently reported breakdown of relations between Jagiełło and Jadwiga. Vytautas, of course, may have deliberately misrepresented the terms of the letter to the boyars, but the episode as related by Posilge fits with other indications that the Cracow lords, concerned at Jagiełło's failure to take any steps to incorporate Lithuania, were pushing Jadwiga to resolve the dispute in Poland's favour.

The quarrel provides a plausible explanation for Jagiełło's apparent support for Vytautas's policy towards the Order. For the proclamation of Vytautas as king at the Salin banquet did not fall suddenly out of a clear blue sky. It was neither a misunderstanding in which the term 'king' did not mean an anointed monarch in the general European sense, nor a simple case of drunken revelry. Raising Vytautas to royal status was not the Order's idea: the previous February it reported that Jagiełło and Vytautas had written to Boniface IX requesting that he authorize Vytautas's coronation as king of Lithuania and the Ruthenian lands.[77]

The approach was a reaction to the refusal of Jadwiga and the Cracow lords to sanction Polish support for Lithuania's war against the Order. Jadwiga and her supporters stood by the 1343 Kalisz peace, demonstrating that they only supported an incorporationist vision of the union when it suited them. Jagiełło responded by dismissing several opponents of the war from their positions as starostas in the Ruthenian lands in dispute between Poland and Lithuania, replacing them with Orthodox Ruthenians.[78] Błaszczyk sees this as the reason for Jadwiga's letter to

---

[72] 'die konigynne in grosen ungnaden ist des koniges un ouch etliche dy besten syner houbtluten': *CDPr*, vi, no. 50, 64.

[73] *SRP*, iii, 219.

[74] Łowmiański, 'Wcielenie', 71–2; Juliusz Bardach, 'Krewo i Lublin: Z problemów unii polsko-litewskiej', in Bardach, *Studia z ustroju i prawa Wielkiego Księstwa Litewskiego XIV–XVII w.* (Warsaw, 1970), 29.

[75] Halecki, 'Wcielenie', 48–9.

[76] *SRP*, iii, 219.

[77] 'das der konig von Polan dornach stee und Wytawte, das sie die crone obir Littowerland und Ruscheland von unserm heyligen vater dem Pabiste dirwerben wellen, daz her die geruche czu lehenen und czu eym konige bestetigen Wytawten obir die egeschreben lande' *CDPr*, vi, no. 61, 66.

[78] *CDPr*, vi, no. 65–6.

Vytautas, suggesting that the approach to Boniface was a response to it. This is plausible, but although Błaszczyk accepts Jagiełło's support for the conferment of a crown on Vytautas, he finds it puzzling, arguing that the plan's success would affect Jagiełło's own rights to Lithuania, and undermine the union. He suggests that Jagiełło, despite the evidence of his involvement in the plan, opposed his cousin's rapprochement with the Order, and the Hrodna and Salin treaties.[79]

Yet Jagiełło undoubtedly understood the implications of the coronation scheme when the letter to Boniface was written, and Błaszczyk does not explain why he should abandon his support for Vytautas beyond suggesting he had little room for manoeuvre, since opposition to war in Cracow was so strong. The Hrodna treaty, however, contained a clause allowing for its confirmation by Jagiełło if Vytautas felt it necessary.[80] This was omitted from the Salin text, but if this may have been because Vytautas did not feel it necessary, or had broken with Jagiełło, the omission probably had more to do with Vytautas's cession of Samogitia: as Vytautas well knew he did not have the authority to cede part of Jagiełło's patrimony. It left the way open for Jagiełło to challenge the treaty's legality.

If Jagiełło and Vytautas really did fall out, and Vytautas was pursuing Lithuania's independence with the Order's backing, it is hard to explain subsequent events. For the remarkable thing about the Salin incident is that it was not followed up. Posilge testifies that there were Poles present; the lack of any Polish protest suggests either that they did not regard it as important—an unlikely scenario—or that they were Jagiełło's agents.[81] Far from proclaiming Lithuania independent or lobbying the pope for confirmation of his royal status, Vytautas visited Cracow in early 1399 to discuss his eastern campaign with Jagiełło and Jadwiga. According to Długosz, both advised him against undertaking it, despite Boniface's declaring the war to be a crusade.[82] Yet the claim that Jagiełło opposed the expedition on the grounds that, had Vytautas succeeded, it would have rendered him unassailable is dubious.[83] In August, grand master Konrad von Jungingen expressed his pleasure at the friendly relations between Jagiełło and Vytautas, which suggests there was no disagreement between the cousins over relations with the Order.[84] Since the Order supported the campaign, and a contingent of 100 knights fought in Vytautas's army, it is likely that Jungingen would have mentioned any opposition to the expedition on Jagiełło's part. Finally, if there was no official Polish support for the campaign, the fact that the 400 Polish volunteers who did fight on the Vorskla—many of whom lost their lives—were led by Jagiełło's favourite Spytek of Melsztyn, suggests that even if he felt the campaign was unwise, he privately backed Vytautas.

---

[79] Błaszczyk, *Dzieje*, ii/i, 75–6, 85. Nikodem dismisses the approach as 'rumour' since it does not fit his understanding of the relationship between Vytautas and Jagiełło: *Witold*, 185–6.

[80] *CEV*, no. 179, 51–4.

[81] Nikodem dismisses them as 'private individuals', though he provides no evidence for his supposition: *Witold*, 186.

[82] *Annales*, x, 226.   [83] Nikodem, *Jadwiga*, 344–5.

[84] *CEV*, no. 201, 59; Rhode, *Ostgrenze*, i, 357.

9

Vilnius-Radom

Vytautas's failure to push his coronation suggests that the episode was a deliberate ploy by the cousins to fend off incorporationist pressure: Halecki's suggestion that the plan was hatched during Jagiełło's visit to Lithuania in May 1397 is plausible.[1] Vytautas—possibly with Jagiełło's support—may have engineered the Salin banquet incident to show the Cracow lords that Vytautas, as his response to Jadwiga's letter demonstrated, was eminently capable of appealing to his boyars to defend Lithuania's status.

Jagiełło's support was important, even if he necessarily had to be more circumspect than Vytautas. The cousins had a common interest in opposing the idea that '*applicare*' signified incorporation. For Jagiełło, in the absence of an heir, the uncertainty over his position should Jadwiga die was a central consideration; for Vytautas it was just as important, since he would be seriously affected should Jagiełło be forced to return to Lithuania on Jadwiga's death. The solidarity between the two cousins seems to have worked: the lack of any echo of the Salin incident in Cracow during Vytautas's visit in early 1399 suggests that the point had been taken.[2]

By now, however, Jadwiga was pregnant. A daughter was born on 22 or 23 June, but died on 13 July. Jadwiga followed her into the grave four days later. Within a month, Vytautas had suffered his great reverse on the Vorskla. Taken together, these two very different tragedies brought a sudden end to the crisis, as all parties faced up to the failure of the main element in the Krewo plan. Jadwiga's death without an heir exposed the frailty of the Krewo arrangements in the light of the cousins' defence of Lithuania's autonomy and the traditional patrimonial view of the grand duchy, while the Vorskla catastrophe exposed the gulf between Vytautas's ambition and his resources.

On 20 August, six days after Jadwiga's lavish funeral, Jagiełło left for Ruthenia, declaring that he was returning to Lithuania since it was unseemly to remain in another's kingdom after she who had inherited it had died. He reached Lwów on 1 October, but did not need to travel any further. His Polish councillors hurriedly swore new oaths of loyalty to him, confirming his status, and assuring him that his position was secure.[3] There is no confirmation of Długosz's account,

---

[1] Halecki, *Dzieje*, i, 154.
[2] Halecki, *Dzieje*, i, 155–6. Nikodem does not mention the visit.
[3] *Annales*, x, 235–6; Gąsiorowski, *Itinerarium*, 41.

although in the light of the battles over the nature of the union and the Salin incident, it is entirely plausible that Jagiełło should have sought reassurances as to his position.

The ploy was only partially successful. The Poles swore new oaths of loyalty to their king, but if Jagiełło had hoped to secure recognition that following Jadwiga's death he held the Polish throne with all the rights of his predecessors, including hereditary title for his heirs, he was to be disappointed. Subsequent developments cast doubt on Kurtyka's suggestion that after negotiations at the Cistercian monastery in Koprzywnica Jagiełło returned to Cracow for a new election to the throne, this time with hereditary rights. The insistence of the Cracow lords that he marry Anna of Celje, a granddaughter of Casimir III, implies that any heirs would enjoy a natural right to the throne only through their mother. Jagiełło finally agreed—tradition holds that Jadwiga urged this course on her deathbed—marrying Anna in 1401, after stalling, according to Długosz, because she was unattractive.[4]

Jagiełło was meanwhile quietly negotiating the first major attempt to define the nature of the relationship between the union partners. He thrashed out terms with Vytautas at Hrodna in December. Although Jagiełło's document is lost, Vytautas's acceptance of it, sealed in Vilnius on 18 January 1401, survives, as do a document bearing the same date in which the bishop of Vilnius, three princes and 58 Lithuanian boyars and their sons accepted its terms; the formal acceptances drawn up for several Lithuanian princes; and its ratification by 52 Polish nobles at Radom on 11 March.[5] Great claims have been made for what is known as the Vilnius-Radom treaty. For Rhode, it was the most important of the alterations to Krewo, which established a completely new relationship between the parties to the union.[6] For Błaszczyk it marked the recognition by Poland of Lithuania's separate statehood; others, aware that Krewo was a prenuptial agreement, have argued that it was the first true treaty of union, since it made formal provisions on practical matters of governance.[7]

Vilnius-Radom was not a treaty of union, but a comprehensive amplification of Astrava, concerned with internal arrangements for Lithuania's government. Nevertheless, it had considerable implications for the union. Jagiełło delegated to Vytautas his regalian rights in Lithuania, but only for his lifetime, without rights of succession. Jagiełło retained the title *supremus dux Lithuaniae ac heres Russiae*, and Vytautas swore that on his death the grand duchy would revert to Jagiełło and his

---

[4] *Annales*, x, 237–8; Kurtyka, *Tęczyńscy*, 229–32. Kurtyka's view is accepted by Jerzy Sperka, *Szafrańcowie herbu stary koń: Z dziejów kariery i awansu w późnośredniowiecznej Polsce* (Katowice, 2001), 72. Nikodem's playing down of the problem is unconvincing: 'Problem legitymizacji władcy Władysława Jagiełły w 1399 r.', in *Nihil superfluum esse: Prace z dziejów średniowiecza ofiarowane profesor Jadwidze Krzyżaniakowej* (Poznań, 2000), 393–401. Cf. Franciszek Piekosiński, 'Czy Władysław Jagiełło był za życia królowej Jadwigi królem Polski czy tylko mężem królowej?', *RAUWHF*, ser. ii, 35 (1897), 287–9; Franciszek Sikora, 'W sprawie małżeństwa Władysława Jagiełły z Anną Cylejską', in Janusz Bieniak, Ryszard Kabaciński, Jan Pakulski, and Stanisław Trawkowski (eds), *Personae—Colligationes—Facta* (Toruń, 1991), 93–103; Tadeusz Silnicki, *Prawo elekcji królów w dobie jagiellońskiej* (Cracow, 1919), 158–9; Wojciech Fałkowski, 'Idea monarchii w Polsce za pierwszych Jagiellonów' in Fałkowski (ed.), *Polska około roku 1400* (Warsaw, 2001), 210–11.

[5] *AU*, nos 38–44, 34–47.
[6] Rhode, *Ostgrenze*, i, 317–18.   [7] Błaszczyk, *Dzieje*, ii/i, 259.

heirs in perpetuity. Claims that Lithuanian statehood was thereby restored or confirmed are anachronistic: Vilnius-Radom was a personal, dynastic arrangement, concerned with lordship—*dominium*—not sovereignty in the modern sense: Skurvydaitė's claim that it established Vytautas as sovereign grand duke in Lithuania under Jagiełło's nominal suzerainty, and that his entire policy thereafter was dedicated to establishing Lithuania as a separate monarchy is unconvincing.[8] The language of the documents makes the position clear. They were drafted by men who knew their canon law: the phrase used to define the relationship between Jagiełło and Vytautas was '*nos in partem sollicitudinis assumpsit supremumque principatum suarum Littwuaniae et caeterorum dominiorum suorum de manu sua nobis dedit et contulit ad tempora vitae nostrae*'.[9] Thus the powers granted to Vytautas over Jagiełło's Lithuanian and other dominions came from Jagiełło personally (*de manu sua*): there was no mention of Poland or the *corona regni*. Vytautas's position was clear. '*In partem sollicitudinis*' was the phrase used in canon law to denote the status of bishops in relation to the pope: they were *vocati in partem sollicitudinis, non in plenitudinem potestatis* (called to a share of responsibility, not in the fullness of power).[10] For all the huffing and puffing about 'statehood', 'sovereignty', and 'independence' from modern scholars, Vytautas recognized that his power was legally circumscribed, and that Jagiełło remained supreme duke: Vytautas was entitled '*dux Lithuaniae*'. He was already using the title grand duke (*magnus dux*) in official correspondence, except with Poland, although it was not recognized by Jagiełło until 1411.[11] The fact that Vytautas exercised the full panoply of regalian powers, and that Jagiełło largely ceased to do so in practice for the grand duchy, did not, therefore, signify, as Balzer suggests, that Vytautas's powers were equal to those of Jagiełło, or that Jagiełło was excluded from the government of Lithuania. Future events would demonstrate that this was not the case.[12]

Vilnius-Radom was, nevertheless, far more than just a private dynastic arrangement. It was a confirmation of the union that represented the first real attempt to define how it might work in practice, which took account of Jagiełło's establishment of Vytautas as his deputy in Lithuania. Vytautas renewed his vows not just to Jagiełło, but also to the crown, kingdom, and inhabitants of Poland (*corona ac regnum et regnicolas regni Poloniae*), and swore to provide assistance to them when required. On his death, the territories he held were to revert not just to Jagiełło, but also to the crown and kingdom of Poland.[13] Vytautas's dynastic interests were recognized through provision for his brother Žygimantas, who was to receive lands from the patrimony of their deceased brothers Vaidotas and Tautvilas, while

---

[8] Loreta Skurvydaitė, 'Lietuvos valdovo titulas ir valdžia XIV a. pab.–XV a. viduryje', *LIS*, 7 (1999), 18–27; Loreta Skurvydaitė, 'Lietuvos valdovo titulatūra: Kada Vytautas ima tituluotis Didžiuoju kunigaikščiu?' *LIS*, 8 (2000), 9–19.
[9] *AU*, no. 38, 35.
[10] Stanisław Kutrzeba, 'Charakter prawny zwiazku Litwy z Polską 1385–1569', in *Pamiętnik VI Zjazdu Powszechnego Historyków Polskich*, i (Lwów, 1935), 168.
[11] Halecki, *Dzieje*, i, 180.c
[12] Balzer, 'Unia horodelska', *RAU* (1912/1913), 153–4.   [13] *AU*, no. 38, 35–6.

Vytautas's wife Anna was to enjoy the lands she had been granted by Vytautas for her lifetime should he predecease her. The document sworn to by the Lithuanians followed this text closely, recognizing Jagiełło as '*supremus principatus terrarum Litwaniae*', and referring to him as '*dominus noster*'. They recognized that on Vytautas's death the lands granted to him would revert to Jagiełło and to the crown and kingdom of Poland, after which they promised to 'adhere, submit, and yield to' the crown and kingdom of Poland, and to serve it faithfully thereafter.[14]

The language of the documents demonstrates why the Poles were happy to accept these arrangements during Vytautas's lifetime. For the Polish conception of the union had not been challenged. In 1401, as in 1386, the Lithuanian elites swore loyalty not just to Jagiełło as supreme duke of Lithuania, but also to the crown and kingdom of Poland, and agreed to maintain the union in perpetuity and irrevocably.[15] The Vilnius-Radom documents reveal more about the nature of that Polish idea of union than the Krewo Act. The Poles were happy to compromise on technical arrangements for the governance of Lithuania, and to recognize that Jagiełło, as supreme duke, had the right to rule his Lithuanian patrimony as he saw fit, in return for an acknowledgement of where supreme authority ultimately lay. The Lithuanians swore that they would remain united with the Poles in perpetuity: '*adhaerere*', '*subici*', '*obsequi*', and '*servire*' were all unambiguous in their connotations.

Nevertheless, although these terms indicate that the Poles felt that the kingdom of Poland was the superior partner in the union, the canon law concepts in the Vilnius-Radom treaty suggest that it is more useful to consider what '*applicare*' might have meant in practice to the Poles than simply to assert—or deny—that Lithuanian was incorporated in 1386. The distinction made throughout the documents between the '*corona*' and the '*regnum*' of Poland is significant. While the appeal to the concept of the *regnum* indicates that the idea of Polish statehood did exist for the Polish elites, it was the concept of the *corona regni* as the embodiment of the community of the realm that was of greater significance. Despite the institutionalization of royal government after 1320, Poland was no centralized unitary state, and the decisive role of the *communitas regni* in determining the succession in the 1380s indicated not only that much power effectively lay in the provinces of Wielkopolska and Małopolska, but also that the community of the realm, while it included the monarch, was viewed as an entity built from the bottom up. It was embodied in the assemblies of citizens that had—in each province—gathered to discuss the succession after 1382, before reaching a national agreement. It formed a union of provinces, in which decisions affecting the whole *regnum*, such as the succession, could only be taken in an assembly of all the provinces of the realm. Government was still very much the business of the king;

---

[14] 'Et nos etiam cum nostris posteris atque successoribus, post decessum domini ducis Wytowdi, ut praemittitur, praedicto domino Wladislao regi, coronae et regno Poloniae adhaerere, subici, obsequi et servire sine dolo et fraude toto posse et viribus tenebimur': *AU*, no. 39, 40.

[15] *AU*, no. 41.

the community of the realm was increasingly concerned with defining the limits of his powers.

It was the incorporation of Lithuania into this concept of the *corona regni* as a political community that was more important than any sense that Lithuania had been incorporated into, or annexed by, the Polish state, although the issue of Lithuania's relations with the Order crystallized Polish desires for the *regnum* to conduct a common foreign policy. Błaszczyk argues that the Poles did not abandon the idea of incorporation in 1401, suggesting that they merely recognized that, for the moment, it could not be implemented; it might be better to suggest that they regarded the *regnum* as a composite, not a unitary state.[16] They made no move to govern Lithuania directly and accepted Jagiełło's arrangements for the government of Lithuania in Vytautas's lifetime. As in canon law, the exercise of considerable power by a legally subordinate authority threatened neither the monarch's legal superiority, nor the rights of the *communitas regni* to constrain the royal prerogative, just as the considerable autonomy of bishops in their dioceses did not call into question the superiority of pope or the *communitas ecclesiae*, the community of the church. The terms of Vilnius-Radom suggest that the Polish negotiators, while maintaining the idea of incorporation, recognized that this was not a full accessory union: it was what was later to be known as an *incorporatio minus plena*, in which the two parties were not merged into a unitary structure.

These aspects of the 1401 arrangements call into question the widely accepted idea that Vilnius-Radom instituted a purely personal union.[17] It was endorsed by the elites of both parties to the union. The Lithuanian boyars for the first time explicitly stated that they did so with the knowledge of, and in the name of, the Lithuanian and Ruthenian political communities.[18] Even if this was an empty formula—as the Lithuanian boyars were later to claim on the grounds that in those days they simply did what their grand dukes told them—it indicates the importance to the Poles of the consent of the community of the realm within the union.

There was one new element to the treaty whose significance has not been given the prominence it deserves. It was agreed that should Jagiełło die without an heir, the Poles would not elect a new monarch without consulting Vytautas and the Lithuanian elites.[19] This clause indicates that this was more than just a personal union. The succession was not clear in either Poland or Lithuania in 1401. Had Jadwiga lived, the fact that she was regarded as the natural heir and inheritor of the Polish kingdom meant that any child of her marriage to Jagiełło had a strong claim to succeed by hereditary right. Yet even if she had given birth to a son, there was no guarantee that he would have succeeded automatically: Jadwiga's claim rested on

---

[16] Błaszczyk, *Dzieje*, ii/i, 261.
[17] Kutrzeba struggles to fit Vilnius-Radom into his legal-historical categories, but suggests that 'the best analogy is the idea of a personal union': 'Charakter', 7.
[18] 'cum cognationibus et genoloys [= genelogiis] suis necnon tota universitas omnium et singulorum nobilium et terrigenarum praedictarum Litwaniae et Russiae terrarum.' *AU*, no. 39, 38.
[19] *AU*, no. 39, 40–1; no. 44, 47.

the choice made by the Polish community of the realm in 1382, and the claims of her older sister and a welter of Piasts had been set aside in her favour. Once she was dead, even if Jagiełło's right to the throne was confirmed, there was no guarantee that his children would be regarded as natural heirs to the kingdom, as the demand that he marry Anna of Celje demonstrated.

Historians have spilt much ink worrying about whether Vilnius-Radom inaugurated a feudal relationship between Poland and Lithuania, as if the law of the Île-de-France operated on the Vistula and Niemen, without appreciating the significance of the concession of this right of consultation over any future Polish monarch.[20] The Polish negotiators effectively recognized that the inclusion of Lithuania into the community of the realm conferred certain rights upon it, including the most important of all: the right exercised by Wielkopolska and Małopolska in 1382 to determine the succession. Vilnius-Radom gives the first concrete sign that the Poles did regard the Lithuanians—or at least the Catholic Lithuanian boyars—as part of the wider *corona regni*. As the future was to show, the question of the succession was to drive the process of union more than any other factor. While the arrangements for future royal elections, and the exact role of the Lithuanians within them, were opaque to say the least, Vilnius-Radom proposed the first truly common institutional link between the two parties to union beyond the person of the monarch: the concept of consultation over the succession was the first step on the road to a common election. It was an idea that was to develop and flourish, even if its realization was to prove challenging.

The clause sheds light on another matter that has exercised historians: who gained most from the compromise. Answers to this question depend upon assumptions concerning the motivations of the actors that are usually deduced from preconceptions about the nature of the relationship between Poland and Lithuania, or the aims and objectives of Jagiełło and Vytautas. For those who see Jagiełło and the Poles as proponents of the incorporation of Lithuania into the Polish state, 1401 marked a defeat, in which Lithuania's separate statehood was supposedly recognized, if only for Vytautas's lifetime; for those who see him as the champion of Lithuanian independence, Vilnius-Radom represented a defeat for Vytautas, who was forced to acknowledge the superiority not just of Jagiełło, but of the *corona regni Poloniae*.[21]

---

[20] Nikodem supports the idea of feudal dependency, as does Adamus. Halecki hedges his bets by arguing that the relationship between Lithuania and Poland 'was close to' that of a feudal relationship, allowing for local particularities; Łowmiański argues that Vilnius-Radom represented a 'concealed' example of *feudum oblatum*: Nikodem, *Witold*, 206; Jan Adamus, 'O prawno-państwowym stosunku Litwy do Polski', in *Pamiętnik VI Zjazdu Powszechnego Historyków Polskich w Wilnie 17–20 września 1935 r*, i: *Referaty* (Lwów, 1935), 178; Halecki, *Dzieje*, i, 160–1, 162–6; Łowmiański, 'Wcielenie', 331. Hrushevsky sensibly warns against applying western concepts of feudal relations, despite apparent similarities in aspects of land tenure, though he is prepared to use the term 'feudal' with reservations: Грушевський, *Історія*, v, 6, n. 1.

[21] Kutrzeba argues that Vilnius-Radom was a defeat for Jagiełło, who had to recognize the practical impossibility of incorporation: 'Unia', 483.

Nikodem, who rightly asserts the importance of dynastic considerations for both Jagiełło and Vytautas, ignores this clause, arguing, on the dubious basis that Salin represented the high-point of Vytautas's supposed programme to establish Lithuania as an independent monarchy, that Vilnius-Radom marked a clear defeat for him, even if he was granted much of the practical power he sought.[22] Yet the clause on the succession in the event of Jagiełło's death without an heir was very much in Vytautas's interests. In 1401 Jagiełło was fifty. He had no heir; even after his second marriage it would be at least a decade and a half before any son would enter his majority, and a few years more before his heir would be capable of governing. At Vilnius-Radom the Poles agreed to consult the Lithuanians over the succession, pledging not to elect a king without Lithuanian consent. This placed Vytautas in a strong position. He was younger than Jagiełło, and already had a child, albeit a daughter. By 1401 he had established a powerful political position among the Lithuanian elites and good relations with leading Polish politicians that would stand him in excellent stead should Jagiełło die without issue. Vytautas's most dangerous rival was the unstable Švitrigaila, who had no patrimonial holdings in the grand duchy, although he had been granted western Podolia by Jagiełło following Spytek of Melsztyn's death on the Vorskla. Should Jagiełło die before Vytautas, Vilnius-Radom opened up the enticing prospect that Vytautas himself would be the obvious candidate to succeed him on the Polish throne, especially since he would be able to count on the support of the leading Lithuanian boyars. Even if Jagiełło produced an heir, the likelihood was that he would designate Vytautas as guardian or regent during any minority. Union, not separation, was very much in Vytautas's interests.

Švitrigaila recognized the way the wind was blowing. Shortly after Vilnius-Radom he followed the time-honoured path of disgruntled Gediminids by scuttling into the Order's welcoming arms. Far from retreating to run some Lithuanian satrapy, or to plot an independence campaign, Vytautas, who was fascinated by western culture, cultivated his links with Poland. He well knew, as the Vorskla debacle confirmed, that Polish military support was vital if his broader goals were to be realized. Lithuania lacked the resources to fight a long war of conquest on any of its frontiers alone, and the Order had ravaged its territory with increasing impunity. He was surrounded in Vilnius by Polish secretaries and officials who had the technical skills he needed. Gradually he established a significant clientele in Poland, which eventually reached far into ministerial circles, including Wojciech Jastrzębiec, appointed bishop of Poznań in 1399, who rose to be grand chancellor and bishop of Cracow before ending his career as archbishop of Gniezno.[23]

Vilnius-Radom suited all the parties to it. After quarter of a century of upheaval, Lithuanian domestic politics settled down, while Jagiełło and Vytautas, though by no means always agreeing, established a working relationship that introduced much-needed stability into the politics of the union. Jagiełło made regular visits to Lithuania to consult with Vytautas that became annual after 1409. While it is

---

[22] Jarosław Nikodem, *Polska i Litwa wobec husyckich Czech w latach 1420–1433* (Poznań, 2004), 90–4.
[23] Łowmiański, *Polityka*, 79.

not credible to suppose, as some have supposed, that after 1401 these two powerful characters worked in constant harmony, their collaboration was successful. Over the next twenty-five years its benefits became apparent both at home, as the new union stabilized itself internally, and abroad, as both parties harvested the fruits of union and the union state established itself internationally as a major power.

10
Fruits of Union

After his humiliation on the Vorskla Vytautas settled with Muscovy in 1401 and turned his attention to relations with the Order. The price he had paid for its support was high, and the meagre benefits had not been worth the sacrifice of Samogitia. Moreover, if opinion among the Polish elites still favoured peace with the Order, attitudes were changing. Jagiełło had long pushed for a more hostile stance, while the issue of Dobrzyń had soured relations considerably since 1391, when Wladislaus of Oppeln, who held Gniewkowo and Dobrzyń as Polish fiefs, pawned Złotorija castle in Dobrzyń to the Order without Jagiełło's permission. Jagiełło took swift military action to reclaim this vital fortress on the Vistula upstream from Thorn, one of the Order's principal strongholds. Encouraged by Sigismund of Luxembourg, the Order occupied the territory of Dobrzyń, which Wladislaus had pawned to them in July 1392 for 50,000 florins.[1] The seizure of Dobrzyń aroused great anger in Poland. Although most Małopolskan lords were more interested in the east, Jagiełło's gradual construction of his own clientele had reduced his dependence on them, and there was a growing party that shared his concern at the Order's actions.

These concerns were magnified when war broke out between Lithuania and the Order in March 1401. The cause was Vytautas's refusal to return Samogitian refugees who had fled to Lithuania, as he was required to under the Salin treaty, claiming that they were not serfs but freemen who were not covered by the agreement.[2] Discontent in Samogitia ran high as the Order imposed labour service on its previously free peasantry. In March 1401 resentment boiled over. The rebels turned to Vytautas, who almost certainly had encouraged them, and who offered support. The war was not intensive; an affair of raids and counter-raids, it peaked in 1402 when the Order's army, with Švitrigaila in tow, attacked Vilnius, but with Vytautas easily suppressing the few pro-Order elements in his capital it sputtered out in inconsequential raiding. The rebels sacked Memel and harried the Order's garrisons across Samogitia. Little substantial was achieved by either side; in May 1404 the peace of Raciążek restored the status quo. The Order returned Złotorija and Dobrzyń for a considerably lower price than it had paid. In exchange for

---

[1] Sławomir Jóźwiak et al., *Wojna Polski i Litwy z Zakonem Krzyżackim w latach 1409–1411* (Malbork, 2010), 76; Maryan Goyski, 'Sprawa zastawu ziemi dobrzyńskiej przez Władysława Opolczyka i pierwsze lata sporu (1391–1399)', *PH*, 3 (1906), 22–51, 174–98, 333–50.
[2] Błaszczyk, *Dzieje*, ii/i, 283–4.

keeping Samogitia it abandoned Švitrigaila, agreeing not to support rebellions by Jagiełło's relatives.³

The war was of no great consequence, but revealed changing attitudes in Poland, and an embryonic sense of common Polish-Lithuanian purpose that worried the Order enough for it to return Dobrzyń. This was expressed more in diplomatic than military terms: Jagiełło sent 1,000 knights to support Vytautas, but majority opinion in Poland was wary of breaking the 1343 peace, and Polish diplomatic support was more important. It came at a price, however. An indication of the new climate was a document of 19 June 1403, in which Vytautas publicly swore his loyalty to Jagiełło, promising not to ally with the Order without his knowledge and agreement.⁴ Jagiełło, under pressure from the Polish council, was attempting to curb Vytautas—in public at least—and ensure that his independent foreign policy was consigned to the past.

The importance of Polish support was apparent in 1401, when Iurii Sviatoslavich, exploiting Lithuania's distraction, seized Smolensk with the support of local princes, beating off a four-week siege led by Vytautas in the autumn. While Lithuania's eastern borders were ably defended thereafter by Lengvenis and loyal Ruthenian princes, the blow to Vytautas's prestige was significant. Another siege by Lengvenis failed to retake Smolensk, as did a seven-week attempt by Vytautas during the 1404 truce preceding the Raciążek treaty.⁵

Jagiełło's support for Vytautas's eastern adventures was limited. Taking advantage of the clauses in Raciążek dividing the east into spheres of influence between the Order and Lithuania, Vytautas turned again to the Order. Although he retook Smolensk in June 1404, Iurii asked Vasilii I for protection, and Lithuania faced full-scale war on its eastern frontier. At Kaunas in August 1404 Vytautas—ignoring the promises made to Jagiełło in Lublin the previous year—signed a new treaty with the Order establishing an alliance against all enemies except the Catholic Church, the Empire, and Jagiełło.⁶ Jagiełło reacted swiftly to rein him in, summoning him to Kamianets in distant Podolia where, on 19 September—a bare month after the Kaunas treaty—Vytautas had to swear a new oath of loyalty to Jagiełło and the *corona regni*, and to buttress his 1403 promises by abrogating all treaties contrary to the interests of Jagiełło and the *corona regni*.⁷ While the Kaunas treaty was not directly mentioned, it did not have to be. Jagiełło had given Vytautas a public warning that he could not repeat his adventurous policies of the 1390s.

The point had been made. Vytautas subsequently received Polish support for his eastern escapades, in which he enjoyed reasonable success. With Smolensk back under Lithuanian control, both Pskov and Novgorod accepted Lithuanian governors: Iury of Pinsk for Pskov and Lengvenis for Novgorod. Vasilii entered the war in 1406 in support of Pskov, but hostilities did not amount to much: Vytautas led an expedition against Moscow in 1408 with considerable military support from the

---

³ Przemysław Nowak, 'Dokumenty pokoju w Raciążku z 1404 r.', *SŹ*, 40 (2002), 57–77.
⁴ *AU*, no. 45, 47–8; Błaszczyk, *Dzieje*, ii/i, 287–8.   ⁵ Jóźwiak et al., *Wojna*, 36–7.
⁶ Błaszczyk, *Dzieje*, ii/i, 294.   ⁷ *AU*, no. 46, 47–50.

Order and Poland, but he avoided open battle and signed a treaty on 14 September 1408 that proved remarkably durable, demonstrating that, with military support from Poland, and with realistic plans that avoided the hubris of the 1390s, Lithuania could sustain its position as the dominant power in the east.[8]

Vytautas again turned his gaze westwards. The extension of his authority over Pskov broke the Salin and Raciążek agreements over spheres of influence and indicates a subtle shift in the balance of power. He was aware of his need for Polish military support—several garrisons in the east largely comprised Polish troops— and of Jagiełło's increased watchfulness. Yet the gains Vytautas stood to make from the Salin agreement made Raciążek bearable. Raciążek granted him little, but its failure to halt the deterioration in relations between Poland and the Order opened new prospects for Lithuania.

The Order was well aware of how the union had weakened it. In the 1390s, Vytautas's headstrong ambition had provided considerable opportunities to sow the seeds of dissension, but for all that Vytautas displayed flashes of his old impulsiveness after 1401, Jagiełło's increased watchfulness meant that his freedom of manoeuvre was considerably reduced, while the Order's attempt to exploit Švitrigaila failed: unlike Vytautas, Švitrigaila had no political following and he was rapidly abandoned to tout his grievances to Muscovy—to which he fled in 1408—and to the Tatars.

The most important change, however, was the successful Christianization of Lithuania. By 1409 it was apparent that the Catholic Church had established firm institutional foundations and was successfully spreading the faith, undermining the Order's claims that the conversion was opportunistic and cosmetic. Although the education of the masses was a slow process, there was negligible resistance among the elites. The advance of Catholicism in Lithuania was in stark contrast to the situation in Samogitia, where little progress had been made by the Order: in 1405 it twice had to ask for Vytautas's help in putting down the unruly Samogitians under the terms of the Raciążek peace, which he duly provided.[9] This failure contrasted with the successful Christianization of Aukštaitija and challenged the Order's very *raison d'être*. The Polish church's close involvement in the Christianization drew it into the controversy with the Order, in which Cracow University, refounded in 1400, provided intellectual ballast.[10] The sense of engagement increased as Jagiełło promoted loyal churchmen of middling szlachta backgrounds who had served in the royal chancery to important ecclesiastical posts: Mikołaj Kurowski, successively bishop of Poznań (1395–99) and Cujavia (1399–1402), then archbishop of Gniezno (1402–11); the vice-chancellor, Mikołaj Trąba (1403–12), raised to the archbishopric of Halych in 1410; and Wojciech Jastrzębiec. While some bishops, including Piotr Wysz (Cracow), Jan Kropidło (Cujavia), and Jakub of Korzkiew (Płock), initially opposed war, they later changed their minds.[11]

---

[8] Jóźwiak et al., *Wojna*, 40–1.   [9] Błaszczyk, *Dzieje*, ii/i, 295.
[10] Tomasz Graff, *Kościół w Polsce wobec konfliktu z zakonem krzyżackim w XV wieku* (Cracow, 2010), 20.
[11] Krzyżaniakowa and Ochmański, *Jagiełło*, 194–5; Jóźwiak et al., *Wojna*, 72.

Jagiełło's ecclesiastical advisers conducted the propaganda battle against the Order, and Poland's intricate diplomatic relations with it. The Polish church had long been less favourably inclined towards the Order than lay politicians, not least because of the perennial issue of ecclesiastical jurisdiction: considerable parts of the diocese of Cujavia lay within the *Ordensstaat*, while the bishopric of Culm, within the lands conquered by the Order in 1308–9, remained under Gniezno's jurisdiction. Inevitably these arrangements brought friction. As relations with the Order worsened after 1386, the many ecclesiastics among Jagiełło's closest political advisors helped form the more hostile policy he adopted after 1401.

It was not just churchmen who were concerned. The union provoked the Order into a new assertiveness. The acquisition of Dobrzyń—like the seizure of Samogitia—showed a desire to buttress its defences through territorial acquisition, as did its 1402 purchase of the Neumark from Sigismund of Luxembourg, which secured control of the routes from the Empire into its territory, cut off Wielkopolska from Pomerelia, and triggered disputes over the border strongpoints of Santok and Drezdenko on the Warta and Noteć rivers. In the increasingly tense atmosphere these disputes took on greater significance, as did the Order's 1409 seizure at Ragnit of twenty ships containing Polish grain en route to Lithuania on the pretext that they contained arms for the Samogitian rebels.[12] Yet the outbreak of war in 1409 had more to do with a conscious decision taken by Jagiełło and his Polish supporters that the time was ripe. The need to raise money for the purchase of Dobrzyń meant that for the first time since 1374 the king had to raise an extraordinary tax from the nobility, at a rate of 12 groszy per hide in addition to the *poradlne*. It was collected without difficulty; a total of 100,000 marks was raised, more than the 50,000 florins required. In June 1405 Dobrzyń was returned to Polish rule, but the episode turned many Poles against the Order.[13] Times were changing. The death in 1405 of Jan Tęczynski, castellan of Cracow and a leader of Jadwiga's party, symbolized the passing of the generation that had masterminded Krewo and dominated politics in its aftermath. Jagiełło's careful use of his powers of appointment meant that the major offices of state and many of the most vital provincial offices, in particular the general starosties, were now held by royal supporters.[14] He was in a position to move.

In December 1408 Jagiełło and Vytautas met in Navahrudak. The only source concerning this meeting is a report by Michael Küchmeister, governor of Samogitia, which says nothing about its outcome, although historians have traditionally assumed that a decision was taken to foment a new Samogitian uprising.[15] This is a plausible inference: it was important to move quickly, since the Order was tightening its grip on Samogitia, having defeated the 1405 risings with the aid of

---

[12] Błaszczyk, *Dzieje*, ii/i, 300. Nadolski suggests that the Order's claim was justified: Andrzej Nadolski, *Grunwald 1410* (Warsaw, 2010), 31.
[13] Jóźwiak et al., *Wojna*, 80.
[14] Kurtyka, *Tęczyńscy*, 197–250; Sperka, 'Oleśnicki', 107.
[15] *CEV*, i, no. 388, 165. Krzyżaniakowa and Ochmański, *Jagiełło*, 194, wrongly date the meeting in the 'late autumn': Błaszczyk, *Dzieje*, ii/i, 301.

Vytautas himself.[16] There is no direct evidence confirming that Jagiełło supported this decision.[17] Given the closer watch he had kept over Vytautas since 1401, however, and the fact that the Polish stance in negotiations with the Order hardened rapidly once the rebellion erupted in May 1409, it seems reasonable to suppose that Jagiełło approved Vytautas's action in provoking it, and that his Polish advisors agreed.

When war broke out in the summer of 1409 residual Polish attachment to peace evaporated. The Samogitian uprising erupted in late May. It took Küchmeister completely by surprise: there was no hint that a rebellion was brewing in a letter he wrote to the Order's marshal, Friedrich von Wallenrode, on 20 May.[18] Jagiełło and Vytautas, in contrast, were well prepared, outmanoeuvring the Order in masterly fashion. Although Vytautas's support for the rebels was known from an early date, until late July the Order's leaders were not sure whether Poland was actively supporting the rising: one report suggested that Vytautas and Jagiełło had never had so many disagreements, which may indicate that the Poles were spreading disinformation.[19] Meanwhile Jagiełło made sure that he had domestic backing for his aggressive stance. A general assembly in Łęczyca in July agreed to despatch an embassy to the Order; although no account of its other decisions survives, it seems that Jagiełło persuaded it to support Vytautas.[20]

When negotiations opened in Marienburg in late July, Polish support for Lithuania held firm. The Polish delegation, led by Kurowski, agreed to ask Vytautas to withdraw the administrators he had sent to Samogitia, but refused to give any guarantee of neutrality if the Order used force.[21] According to Długosz, annoyed by the Order's threats, Kurowski incautiously blurted out that if it declared war, Poland would support Lithuania, adding that: 'Lithuania's enemies are our enemies; if you attack them, we shall turn our arms against you'.[22] Historians have doubted this claim, suggesting that it may have been invented for literary effect since it is not corroborated by other sources. Długosz states that it was unknown whether Kurowski said this on his own initiative, or whether he had been instructed to do so. Given Długosz's close links to Oleśnicki, then a royal secretary, it is likely that he derived his knowledge of what was said from an informed source. If the tale is true, it is interesting that Oleśnicki was unsure as to whether Jagiełło was behind the outburst.

Whatever Kurowski said, the Order could only conclude from the uncompromising Polish stance that Polish support for Lithuania was likely. The outcome was Jagiełło's first victory of the campaign. On 6 August 1409 grand master Ulrich von Jungingen informed him that, unable to secure any assurance from the Poles despite numerous requests not to support the Lithuanians, the Order had no choice but to declare war on Poland. Jagiełło had outmanoeuvred him. That the Order

---

[16] Kolankowski, *Dzieje*, i, 88.   [17] Jóźwiak et al., *Wojna*, 55.
[18] *CEV*, i, no. 397, 174–5. Jóźwiak et al., *Wojna*, 55.
[19] *CEV*, i, no. 402, 179; no. 404, 179–80; no. 409, 181.
[20] Jóźwiak et al., *Wojna*, 89–90, Błaszczyk, *Dzieje*, ii/i, 305.
[21] Jóźwiak et al., *Wojna*, 113–14.   [22] *Annales*, x/xi, 30.

was the aggressor, through its declaration of war and invasion of Poland, in which it retook Dobrzyń and captured Bydgoszcz, was of great importance for rallying Polish support.[23] Its breaking of a peace that had held for nearly seven decades gave the Poles an important advantage in the battle to influence opinion across Catholic Europe.

For Jagiełło and Vytautas faced serious challenges in convincing Catholic opinion of the justice of their war against the Order, which could claim not only that they were openly supporting a pagan revolt in breach of their treaty obligations, but also that they enlisted Orthodox 'schismatics' and Muslim 'infidels' in their armies. The Order could rely on Sigismund of Luxembourg, with whom it signed a preliminary alliance in October 1409, in which it agreed to pay him 300,000 florins and support the 10,000 troops he promised to raise to strike against southern Poland at a rate of 24 florins per lance should the Poles and Lithuanians deploy pagans against the Order.[24] Sigismund's brother Wenzel, king of Bohemia, was also favourably inclined towards the Order, as he demonstrated after mediating a truce signed on 8 October 1409 following the Polish recapture of Bydgoszcz. The truce was to last until 24 June 1410; Wenzel was to issue a judgement in February on the causes of the war as a basis for a peace settlement.

His judgement proved so favourable to the Order that the Polish delegation refused even to listen to it, on the grounds that it was to be read in German, a language they claimed not to understand. Their rejection of mediation ensured that hostilities would resume in the summer of 1410. When they did, the Order gained little from the Luxembourgs. The death of Rupert I, king of the Romans, in May 1410 ensured that the dynasty was dragged into the complex politics of the Empire: Sigismund's election by a minority of the electors was challenged, before his cousin Jobst I, margrave of Moravia—supported by Wenzel—was elected in October.[25]

With the German princes distracted, Jagiełło and Vytautas quietly built support and neutralized the Order's potential allies. While the Silesian Piasts favoured it, the Poles had more success among the Pomeranians. Swantibor III of Stettin, Bogislaw VIII of Stolp, and Wartislaw VIII of Wolgast all signed treaties promising to support the Order in 1409, but only Swantibor honoured their terms: Wartislaw remained neutral, while Bogislaw, in a major success for Polish diplomacy, joined the war against the Order. Janusz I of Mazovia opted early for the Polish-Lithuanian camp; if his brother Siemowit IV was reluctant, he eventually came out in somewhat grudging support, despatching his son Siemowit to command the troops he sent to fulfil his obligations as a Polish vassal. The greatest diplomatic coup was achieved by Vytautas, who negotiated a three-month truce with the Livonian Order in August 1409, which meant that Jungingen could not rely on a diversionary attack on Lithuania; it only expired after the start of the October truce. This did not extend to the Lithuanians, but although the Prussians raided Lithuania in early 1410, the Livonians showed no inclination to support them, and Vytautas was able to extend the Livonian truce from May 1410.[26] Jagiełło and Vytautas had

---

[23] Jóźwiak et al., *Wojna*, 116–17.   [24] Jóźwiak et al., *Wojna*, 201–3.
[25] Jóźwiak et al., *Wojna*, 210.   [26] Jóźwiak et al., *Wojna*, 201, 210–11, 225.

Fruits of Union 105

neutralized the Order's diplomatic advantages. Denied Livonian support, it faced a war on two fronts without the ability to mount diversionary attacks on Lithuania from Livonia, or upon southern Poland, since Sigismund's absorption in the politics of the Empire meant that the invasion on which the Order had counted came to naught.

The Order's rule over the Prussian lands was based on a tiny core of several hundred full brothers and some 3,000 half-brothers. In the past it had relied on volunteers from across Europe to man its armies inspired by the crusading ideal that had brought Derby to the walls of Vilnius in 1390. Between 1409 and 1411, however, despite copious propaganda attacking Jagiełło's dependence on pagans, schismatics, and infidels, the fact that the Order was waging war on a Catholic power meant that the flow of volunteers was far smaller than in previous years. It was able to raise troops from its traditional recruiting-grounds in the Empire, but most were mercenaries, who had to be paid. Its resources were stretched as never before.

The Order had nevertheless prepared well: if the Marienburg foundries produced cannon to the value of 60 marks between 1401 and 1403, by 1408–9, they were churning them out to the value of $1,475^{1}/_{2}$ marks, with other preparations on a similar scale.[27] As a military organization with well-oiled mechanisms for putting armies in the field, it was able to deploy its forces rapidly in August 1409, seizing the initiative by capturing Dobrzyń and Bydgoszcz. The Poles were slow to respond, but the recapture of Bydgoszcz checked the advance and led directly to the October truce, which gave Jagiełło and Vytautas time to assemble a large army and agree a strategy long before its expiry. When its size became apparent Jungingen considered breaking the truce with a surprise attack on Poland in early June 1410. When this had to be aborted, he used Hungarian mediators to secure an extension of the truce until 4 July.[28]

Jagiełło now took the initiative according to plans agreed in his discussions with Vytautas, and the vice-chancellor, Mikołaj Trąba, at Brest in late November and early December 1409.[29] The Polish-Lithuanian army gathered at Czerwińsk, northwest of Warsaw, after the Poles crossed the Vistula on a pontoon bridge. On the truce's expiry they moved north, crossing the border on 9 July, intending to strike at Marienburg through Kauernik. The army was well supplied and well equipped. When it found its way blocked at Kauernik, Jagiełło turned east, taking Gilgenburg and then, on the morning of 15 July, found the Order's army deployed in rolling countryside near the villages of Grünfelde (today the Polish village of Grunwald) and Tannenberg (today the Polish village of Stębark) that were to lend their names to the campaign's decisive battle in Polish and German respectively.

---

[27] Andrzej Nadolski, *Grunwald 1410* (Warsaw, 2010), 29.
[28] Sven Ekdahl, 'Die Söldnerwerbungen des Deutschen Ordens für einen geplanten Angriff auf Polen am 1. Juni 1410: Ein Beitrag zur Vorgeschichte der Schlacht bei Tannenberg', in Bernhart Jähnig (ed.), *Beiträge zur Militärgeschichte des Preussenlandes von der Ordenszeit bis zum Zeitalter der Weltkriege* (Marburg, 2010), 89–102; Nadolski, *Grunwald*, 34.
[29] Jóźwiak et al., *Wojna*, 211, 239.

Jagiełło enjoyed a considerable numerical advantage. The size of the armies that fought at Tannenberg has long been a matter of dispute, with historians forced to make educated guesses to reach estimates more realistic than the fantastic numbers given in contemporary chronicles. The most reliable, based on the number of banners (companies) deployed, depend on the application of factors of multiplication to the number of lances—armed knights with their retinues—that banners were, in theory, meant to contain.[30] Nadolski estimates that the Order's force was around 15,000 strong, opposed by 20,000 Poles and 10,000 Lithuanians, a number that is considerably lower than Kuczyński's regularly quoted estimate of 21,000 cavalry and 11,000 infantry in the Order's army, and 29,000 cavalry, 10,000 infantry, and 10,000 camp followers in the Polish-Lithuanian force, based on the questionable methodology of comparing the general mobilization capacity of fifteenth-century states.[31] These figures are optimistic. Ekdahl suggests 12,000–15,000 in the Order's army and 20,000–25,000 in the Polish-Lithuanian force.[32] Given that scholars seem not to allow for wastage rates, it might be prudent to accept the lower figures of Heveker and Kujot, who estimated the Order's force at 11,000, and the Polish-Lithuanian force at 16,500, with Kujot suggesting 10,500 Poles and 6,000 Lithuanians.[33]

Whatever the truth, Tannenberg was a large battle by fifteenth-century standards. Both armies were armed and equipped in the latest western style: the core of each force comprised armoured knights, with the Order deploying field artillery. The Lithuanian army, containing Lithuanians, Ruthenians, and a Tatar unit, was largely light cavalry in the eastern style. The battle's outcome demonstrated the old military truth that, on the whole, larger armies defeat smaller forces. In its initial phase the Lithuanians on the union army's right engaged first. After fierce fighting they withdrew from the battlefield; whether this was a planned manoeuvre or a flight, is disputed. Although there is good cause for scepticism concerning the ability of such a large force to accomplish such a complex tactic after an hour of hard fighting, one contemporary source suggests that some units—possibly the Tatars—may indeed have deliberately retreated.[34] Whatever the reality, Vytautas rallied some of his Lithuanians and returned to the battlefield, where the Polish army, together with three Ruthenian banners from Smolensk, still enjoyed a sufficient numerical advantage to give it the upper hand. After several hours of fighting, the Order's army was shattered. Jungingen, grand marshal Wallenrode, and virtually all the Order's senior officers were killed, as were between 203 and

---

[30] For sensible surveys see Sven Ekdahl, *Die Schlacht bei Tannenberg 1410: Quellenkritische Untersuchungen*, i: *Einführung und Quellenlage* (Berlin, 1982), 69–73; 144–55; Jóźwiak et al., *Wojna*, 263–4.

[31] Marian Biskup, *Wojny polskie z zakonem krzyżackim 1308–1521* (Gdańsk, 1993), 57–8; Błaszczyk, *Dzieje*, ii/i, 318–19; Stefan Kuczyński, *Wielka wojna z zakonem krzyżackim w latach 1409–1411* (Warsaw, 1955), 177–202, 259.

[32] Sven Ekdahl, 'Žalgirio mūsis ir jo reikšmė Ordino gyvenimui', in Rūta Čapaitė and Alvydas Nikžentaitis (eds), *Žalgirio laikų: Lietuva ir jos kaimynai* (Vilnius, 1993), 3–33.

[33] Nadolski, *Grunwald*, 82; Sven Ekdahl, *Die »Banderia Prutenorum« des Jan Długosz: Eine Quelle zur Schlacht bei Tannenberg 1410* (Göttingen, 1976), 146.

[34] Sven Ekdahl, 'Die Flucht der Litauer in der Schlacht bei Tannenberg 1410', *ZO*, 12 (1963), 11–19.

211 out of the 270 brothers of the Order who fought, out of a total of some 570 then active in Prussia.³⁵

Tannenberg sent shock waves round Europe. The outcome was wholly unexpected; taken in conjunction with Vytautas's advantageous peace with Muscovy the year before, it marked the arrival of a new power in north-eastern Europe and demonstrated to both domestic and international audiences the fruits of union. Such is clear with hindsight at least, although at the time Jagiełło was criticized for not securing a greater advantage from the stunning victory. Długosz attacked him for dawdling on the battlefield for three days instead of heading straight for Marienburg, where he would, so Długosz argued, have been able to capture the Order's headquarters without resistance. By the time the army reached Marienburg on 22 July, Heinrich von Plauen, the energetic komtur of Schwetz, had organized its defences sufficiently for it to survive a three-month siege.³⁶

The fighting at Tannenberg had been hard, however, and it was as unrealistic to expect the exhausted army to march 120 kilometres to Marienburg immediately after the battle, as it was to suppose that a force substantially composed of cavalry could impose Polish rule over the Order's lands. The Poles had siege artillery, but the army that triumphed at Tannenberg was a force assembled to win on the battlefield, and was not suited to conducting sieges or garrisoning castles.³⁷ Nevertheless, although Marienburg was stoutly defended, many towns and fortresses across the Order's lands, impressed by the shattering of its army, opened their gates to the victors. In the Elbing *Altstadt* burghers expelled the Order's garrison on 18 or 19 July and provided arms and ammunition for the siege of Marienburg, while Thorn and the Culm lands came over to Jagiełło in August, with Danzig following.³⁸ Relations between the Order and the local Catholic hierarchy were cool. The bishops, of Ermland, Pomezania, and Culm all swore homage to Jagiełło. Heinrich von Vogelsang of Ermland offered him considerable support, later being accused of treason by the Order, and was specifically excluded from the clause in the 1411 peace of Thorn that allowed refugees from the fighting to return to their possessions.³⁹

Despite these defections, in the months after Tannenberg the very completeness of the Polish-Lithuanian victory helped rally support behind the Order. In August the Livonians abandoned their passive stance, sending a 3,000-strong force to Königsberg. The November election of Plauen as grand master completed the process of rebuilding the Order's hierarchy. The military situation gradually altered in its favour, as hired troops began arriving in larger numbers from the Empire, where Tannenberg had made a great impression. Fighting continued into the autumn. While the Poles won a skirmish at Koronowo on 10 October, they proved unable to hold more than a handful of the castles and towns they had occupied in July and August, although they did retain some important fortresses, including Thorn castle. The Lithuanians left Prussia after the battle, thereby reducing

---

³⁵ Nadolski, *Grunwald*, 82; Jóźwiak et al., *Wojna*, 437.   ³⁶ *Annales*, x/xi, 117, 119–20.
³⁷ Błaszczyk, *Dzieje*, ii/i, 351.   ³⁸ Jóźwiak et al., *Wojna*, 479, 502, 511.
³⁹ Jóźwiak et al., *Wojna*, 494–5, 512–13; Błaszczyk, *Dzieje*, ii/i, 364.

considerably the numerical superiority enjoyed by the union forces. By November the Polish army was deteriorating. Many had gone home, and the Bohemian mercenaries were demanding their pay.[40] It was not clear that Jagiełło would enjoy such a clear advantage in the following year. Peace was, for the moment, the sensible choice.

Długosz's criticisms reflect his disappointment at the minor gains made at the peace of Thorn (1 February 1411), which ended the war, although it by no means settled the issues between the two parties. Samogitia was returned to Lithuania, but only for the lifetimes of Jagiełło and Vytautas, after which it would revert to the Order. Apart from this concession and the substantial payment of 100,000 kop groszy by the Order as compensation for the return of prisoners, the terms largely restored the status quo. Długosz argued that Poland, as distinct from Lithuania, gained very little from Tannenberg. He wrote bitterly of the failure to recover Culm and Pomerelia and claimed that the sum paid for the return of prisoners was derisory, waspishly concluding that Jagiełło and Vytautas were content that Lithuania be restored while Poland remained in its mutilated condition.[41] His running gripe that Jagiełło always favoured Lithuania over Poland is aired, but his assessment is unrealistic, if not downright misleading: Poland recovered Dobrzyń unconditionally, while Samogitia had only temporarily been restored to Lithuania. Even if the terms were not generous, Tannenberg had altered the balance of power. The reaction in Europe, however, suggested that the struggle would continue on another front.

---

[40] Jóźwiak et al., *Wojna*, 633. [41] *Annales*, x/xi, 177–8; Błaszczyk, *Dzieje*, ii/i, 363–4.

11
Horodło

Tannenberg vindicated the union in spectacular fashion. Lithuania had for years fought a rearguard action against the Order. Raids had become frequent and dangerous, while the Order's exploitation of divisions among the Gediminids had prolonged the political disunity endemic since 1377. Only Polish aid could break the vicious circle; Tannenberg and the return of Samogitia, albeit only temporarily, demonstrated what might be achieved. For the Poles, accustomed to peace with the Order at the price of accepting the loss of Pomerelia, Tannenberg encouraged hopes that, in due course, it might be recovered.

The anticlimactic campaign that followed, and the deflating peace of Thorn demonstrated that the Order was far from broken, and that hopes for the recovery of Pomerelia and Samogitia's permanent return were premature, given the Order's standing within the Catholic world. Subject to both pope and emperor, it was unlikely that it would regard the peace as final.[1] Plauen was determined on revenge. He urged the pope to declare a crusade against Vytautas, claiming that Lithuania was still pagan, that Jagiełło's conversion was cosmetic, and attacking him for deploying pagans, schismatics, and infidels at Tannenberg.[2]

The diplomatic context worked, however, to Poland-Lithuania's advantage. Sigismund of Luxembourg had favoured the Order since his humiliating rejection by the Poles in 1382. Now, however, he was promoting the idea of a general council of the church in Constance as a means of ending the papal schism. Sigismund needed the support of as many Catholic powers as possible; he therefore had an interest in tempering his hostility to Poland, whose support was also important for the realization of his vision of a Catholic Europe united against the Ottoman threat. This opportunity was too good to miss. The Order's defeat had weakened it considerably as a political partner, while war against a resurgent Poland was not in Sigismund's interests. He was distracted by the turbulent politics of the Empire following his failure to be elected king of the Romans in 1410, and concerned at Jagiełło's construction of an anti-Luxembourg front with Moldavia, Venice, and Leopold IV of Further Austria, younger brother of Jadwiga's ill-starred fiancé William von Habsburg. Sigismund was forced to backtrack, offering a tentative rapprochement to the Poles, which brought Jagiełło to Lubovňa in the spring of 1412 where a Polish-Hungarian alliance, known in Poland as the treaty of Lubowla, was signed on 15 March. The terms were not particularly favourable to

[1] Nikodem, *Witold*, 296.   [2] Halecki, *Dzieje*, i, 206.

Poland, not least because they raised the spectre of Hungarian claims to Red Ruthenia, which was to remain a Polish possession until five years after the death of one of the two monarchs, at which point a commission of representatives from both nations would decide its ultimate fate.³

Jagiełło also accepted Sigismund's offer of mediation with the Order, as bitter wrangling demonstrated that the Thorn treaty had done little to advance the cause of permanent peace. Mediation began in Buda in the summer, and continued in Kaunas in January 1413. It soon became clear that a final settlement was unlikely. The Order presented a carefully prepared case to support its permanent possession of Samogitia, claiming that the continuing attachment of the Samogitians to paganism gave it the right to rule over them, and cited the Salin and Raciążek treaties, producing the ratifications signed by Jagiełło and Vytautas. The union negotiators took a radical approach. They argued that no prince had ruled over the Samogitians until they had voluntarily accepted the cousins' joint overlordship. As a free people, they would recognize their rule as long as they chose, but Jagiełło and Vytautas did not have the right to alienate Samogitian land without consent. If the Samogitians did not wish to continue under their rule, they were free to choose another prince.⁴

This was radical indeed; that this line of argument was clearly sanctioned by Jagiełło and Vytautas indicates not only the importance they accorded Samogitia, but also that they were thinking deeply about the nature of the composite system over which they presided. They were already consulting over a major restatement of the nature of the union that reached fruition in a treaty formally promulgated on 2 October 1413 at Horodło on the river Bug in southeast Poland. That the deteriorating relations with the Order and the failure of mediation played a large part in the preparation of this new union treaty is clear. The talks merely sharpened mutual antagonisms and the propaganda war. Although mediation dragged on into 1414, both sides talked openly of war. Plauen's replacement by the less bellicose Küchmeister in October 1413 made no difference.⁵ It was imperative that the new unity that had brought the great victory at Tannenberg was sustained and deepened as both sides prepared to present their case before the whole of Latin Christendom at Constance.

This motive was explicitly acknowledged in the first article of the Horodło Union of 2 October 1413, which expressed the desire that:

> the . . . lands of Lithuania, ravaged by the hostile and insidious acts of the Order and its allies . . . who wish to destroy these lands of Lithuania and . . . Poland, . . . be brought into safety, security, and protection, and that their prosperity be established in perpetuity.⁶

---

³ Krzyżaniakowa and Ochmański, *Jagiełło*, 212–13; Żydrūnas Mačiukas, 'Zigmanto Liuksemburgiečio veiksnys Lietuvos santykiuose su Vokiečių ordinu 1411–1418 m.', in Alfredas Bumblauskas and Rimvydas Petrauskas (eds), *Tarp istorijos ir būtovės* (Vilnius, 1999), 159–76.
⁴ Jadwiga Krzyżaniakowa, 'Rok 1413', in Karol Olejnik (ed.), *Pax et bellum* (Poznań, 1993), 78–9.
⁵ Błaszczyk, *Dzieje*, ii/i, 372; Krzyżaniakowa and Ochmański, *Jagiełło*, 212–19.
⁶ *AU*, no. 51, 63–4; *VL*, i, 30; *1413 m. Horodlės aktai*, eds Jūratė Kiaupienė and Lidia Korczak (Vilnius and Cracow, 2013), 19–21; 29–31; 37–42 (henceforth *Horodlės Aktai*).

There was, however, far more behind Horodło than the desire to present a united front. It comprised three documents.[7] The most important was issued jointly by Jagiełło and Vytautas. Vytautas was officially accorded the title 'grand duke of Lithuania', and, on a par with Jagiełło, that of 'lord and inheritor of the Ruthenian lands'.[8] Vytautas had first used the title 'grand duke' in 1392 in Ruthenian documents; from 1395 he used it in German.[9] Jagiełło did not recognize it at Vilnius-Radom, but allowed its use at Thorn in 1411. The formal raising of Vytautas's status was not just a message to the outside world; it reflected the close cooperation of the cousins since 1408, and their role in the preparation of the Horodło documents, which were discussed at a long meeting at Hrubieszów in September 1412, at a Polish assembly at Niepołomice in November, and in a long consultation with Vytautas in Lithuania.[10] This careful preparation was necessary for the new approach to the relationship between Poland and Lithuania that was outlined in what has been called the union's 'first full constitution' (see Fig. 5).[11]

Its preamble stressed the union's achievement in bringing Lithuania into the Catholic fold and freeing it from the 'yoke of servitude'. The first article stressed the benefits of Lithuania's conversion to Christianity, 'through the breath of the Holy Spirit', and explained the meaning of Krewo, amplifying the controversial term *applicare* with a string of synonyms, firstly in the perfect tense, to stress that Jagiełło's Lithuanian and Ruthenian lands had indeed been incorporated, and then in the present tense to indicate that they were being reincorporated:

> Et primo, quamvis eo tempore quo almo Spiritu inspirante fidei catholicae recepta et cognita claritate, coronam regni Poloniae assumpsimus pro Christianae religionis incremento, et bono statu et commodo terrarum nostrarum Lyttwaniae praedictarum ipsas et cum terris ac dominiis ipsis subiectis et connexis praefato regno nostro Poloniae *appropriavimus, incorporavimus, coniunximus, univimus, adiunximus, confoederavimus* de consensu unanimi nostro et aliorum fratrum nostrorum et omnium baronum, nobilium, procerum et boyarorum eiusdem terrae Lyttwaniae voluntate accedente et assensu... easdem terras, quas semper cum pleno dominio ac iure mero et mixto hactenus habuimus et habemus usquemodo a progenitoribus nostris et ordine geniturae tamquam domini legitimi, baronum, nobilium, boyarorum voluntate, ratihabitione et consensu adhibitis, praedicto regno Poloniae iterum et de novo *incorporamus, invisceramus, appropriamus, coniungimus, adiungimus, confoederamus et perpetue anectimus*, decernentes ipsas cum omnibus earum dominiis, terris, ducatibus, principatibus, districtibus, proprietatibus omnique iure mero et mixto coronae regni Poloniae perpetuis temporibus irrevocabiliter et irrefregabiliter semper esse unitas.[12]

---

[7] For a recent critical analysis see Piotr Rabiej, 'Dokumenty unii horodelskiej', in *Horodlės Aktai*, 83–110.

[8] 'Allexander alias Vytowdus magnus dux Lyttwaniae necnon terrarum Russiae dominus et haeres etc.' *AU*, no. 51, 62.

[9] Skurvydaitė, 'Lietuvos', 14–15.

[10] Krzyżaniakowa, 'Rok 1413', 81.

[11] Jerzy Wyrozumski, 'Formowanie się politycznej i ustrojowej wspólnoty polsko-litewskiej w latach 1385–1501', *CPH*, 45 (1993), 450.

[12] *AU*, no. 51, 63–4; my emphasis. 'Nonetheless, at that time whereby, having accepted and recognized the clarity of the Catholic faith thanks to the inspiration of the nourishing Holy Spirit, we assumed the crown of the Kingdom of Poland for the augmentation of the Christian religion, and for

Fig. 5. The Union of Horodło (1413). Władysław Jagiełło, King of Poland and Supreme Duke of Lithuania, together with Vytautas, Grand Duke of Lithuania, establish the character of the union between the Kingdom of Poland and the Grand Duchy of Lithuania, Horodło, 2 October 1413. Latin, parchment, 650 mm × 370 mm. Biblioteka Książąt Czartoryskich, Cracow, perg. 301. By kind permission of the Fundacja Książąt Czartoryskich.

Despite this impressive concatenation of synonyms, historians have denied that Horodło sealed Lithuania's incorporation, on account of subsequent clauses which, they claim, render this clause meaningless. Most importantly, in a startling departure from Vilnius-Radom, provision was made for the election of a new grand duke

the sake of the good order and welfare of our aforesaid lands of Lithuania, we *appropriated, incorporated, conjoined, united, adjoined, and confederated* these lands, which up to the present we have always held and hold now as legitimate lord from our ancestors by the order of our birth with full dominium, and every right, pure and impure, together with the lands and lordships subjected and joined to them, to our aforesaid Kingdom of Poland, with our unanimous consent, and that of our other brothers, and of all the barons, nobles, dignitaries, and boyars of these same Lithuanian lands, who voluntarily approved and assented, desiring that these same lands [be secured against their enemies] ... and by the wish, approval and consent of the barons, nobles, and boyars here summoned, we once again *incorporate, inviscerate, appropriate, conjoin, adjoin, confederate, and perpetually annexe* these same lands to the aforementioned Kingdom of Poland, decreeing that they, together with all their lordships, territories, duchies, principalities, districts, and domains, by every right, pure and impure, shall in perpetuity always be irrevocably and inviolably united with the Crown of the Polish Kingdom.'

following Vytautas's death, although it was stipulated that should such an election take place, the Lithuanian 'barons and nobles' would only choose a candidate 'elected, designated, and agreed' by Jagiełło or his successors, and the 'prelates and barons' of the kingdom of Poland. In return it was promised that, should Jagiełło die without a legitimate heir, Poland would not elect a successor without the knowledge and consent of Vytautas and the Lithuanian 'barons and nobles'.[13]

It is striking that Jagiełło permitted Vytautas to be designated 'grand prince and lord' (*magnus princeps et dominus*). Yet the document's real significance was that the government of Lithuania was no longer conceived simply in terms of the dynasty and the grand duke. Clause ten instituted new offices of palatine and castellan on the Polish model for Vilnius and Trakai, with provision made for their establishment elsewhere should the need arise.[14] The creation of a new governing structure based on the devolved local offices that enjoyed considerable powers in Poland, together with the institutionalization of the office of grand duke, has seemed to many historians to have confirmed the existence of a separate Lithuanian state and to have rendered irrelevant the first clause's incorporationist rhetoric.[15]

Historians have therefore tended to dismiss Horodło's first clause, suggesting that, as Jagiełło prepared to defend the war against the Order at Constance, it was directed at an international audience and was intended merely as a public statement of unity in the face of the Order's attempts to deny the reality of the union and to drive a wedge between Poland and Lithuania. Its purpose was to depict Poland and Lithuania 'as one state', even though this did not accord with reality.[16] Łowmiański claimed that the clause hid Horodło's true meaning; Kutrzeba, who believed that Lithuania *had* been incorporated in 1386, but that the incorporation had been reversed in 1392 and 1401, argued that Horodło did not effect incorporation, since throughout the rest of the document Lithuania was treated as a separate state, not as a province incorporated into Poland, adding that under Vytautas Lithuania was a great power that conducted an independent foreign policy. Only Kolankowski, the most determined adherent of the incorporation thesis, took clause one seriously, regarding it as the heart of the document.[17] Lithuanian historians emphasize Lithuania's independent statehood after 1413, as do Liubavskii—although he stresses Jagiełło's ultimate suzerainty—Hrushevsky, and other historians of the Ruthenian lands.[18] Rowell suggests that the incorporation was a 'clever dynastic ploy' aimed at undermining the Order's claims, adding that Horodło was more like

---

[13] *AU*, no. 51, 67–8. [14] *AU*, no. 51, 66–7.
[15] For the debate, see Błaszczyk, *Dzieje*, ii/i, 368–426.
[16] Krzyżaniakowa and Ochmański, *Jagiełło*, 229–30.
[17] Łowmiański, *Polityka*, 75–6; Kutrzeba, 'Unia', 498–503; Kolankowski, *Dzieje*, i, 117; Kolankowski, *Polska Jagiellonów* (Lwów, 1936), 46.
[18] Šapoka, 'Valstybiniai', 231–40; Jučas, *Unija*, 143–6; Gudavičius, *Istorija*, i, 220–4; Bronius Dundulis, *Lietuvos kova dėl valstybinio savarankiškumo XV amžiuje*, 2nd edn (Vilnius, 1993), 46; Любавский, *Очерк*, 80–1; Грушевський, *Історія*, iv, 151; Сагановіч, *Нарыс*, 90.

an agreement between states in its form, a view shared by Rabiej and Kiaupienė.[19] Błaszczyk holds to the consensus that the apparent contradiction between the incorporation stressed so pedantically in article one and the rest of the document lies only on the surface, since clause one was intended exclusively for external consumption. Although he maintains that Horodło was the most significant union treaty between 1386 and 1569, he concludes that its importance should not be exaggerated.[20]

As the frequent citation of Horodło in subsequent disputes between Poles and Lithuanians demonstrates, contemporaries did not share the belief of these historians that article one had no significance for the union's internal politics. Długosz, reflecting widespread Polish opinion, had no doubts, stating baldly that Lithuania and Samogitia had been incorporated, annexed, and invisiverated.[21] His phraseology is significant. He talks of incorporation into the kingdom, but stresses that the union was one not of states, but of peoples: '*populos Polonicos cum Lithuanicis et Samagiticis*'.[22] Yet historians continue overwhelmingly to follow Balzer, who in 1913 concluded: 'to use modern terms, one can state that the Horodło union embodied the constitutional confirmation of Lithuania's independent statehood'.[23]

Balzer's phrasing suggests that he was aware that modern terms might not be appropriate, but most historians express no such reservations, concluding that Horodło's most important feature was its affirmation of an independent Lithuanian state, and that therefore, to use terms even less carefully, 'Lithuania' could not have been incorporated into 'Poland'.[24] Such language reflects the concerns of the twentieth century, not the fifteenth. Horodło is significant because of the light it sheds on the thinking of those involved in forming and defining the nature of the union, and because it, for the first time, asserted a vision of what the union might become that was to influence the whole process of union down to 1569. Looked at on its own terms, not only can it be seen as internally consistent, but also as broadly consistent with Krewo and Vilnius-Radom. Horodło represented a stage in the evolution of a complex political relationship, and the first comprehensive attempt to define what union signified. It was neither a new beginning, nor a radical revision of the original union, nor the complete change of direction as which it is conventionally portrayed.

Długosz's evaluation and the position maintained by Polish statesmen after 1413 call fundamentally into question the consensus that Horodło embodied a simple personal or dynastic union that was, moreover, looser than other personal unions in

---

[19] Stephen C. Rowell, 'Dynastic bluff? The road to Mielnik, 1385–1501', *LHS*, 6 (2001), 9–10; Rabiej, 'Dokumenty', 85; Kiaupienė, '1413 m. Horodlės dokumentų "gyvenimai"', in *Horodlės aktai*, 255.

[20] Błaszczyk, *Dzieje*, ii/i, 426.

[21] 'terrarum et principatuum suorum rectores optimi, Lithuanie Samogicieque terras dudum Polonie Regno *incorporatas, annexas, invisceratas et unitas*, geminato funiculo difficile solvendo eidem Polonie Regno arccius solidiusque conglutinare et populos Polonicos cum Lithuanicis et Samagiticis federe iungere sempiterno'. *Annales*, xi, 14; my emphasis.

[22] The Polish translation renders 'populos' as *narody* (nations); it is better translated as 'peoples', in the classical sense of a body of citizens: *Roczniki*, xi, 10.

[23] Balzer, 'Unia', 157.   [24] Błaszczyk, *Dzieje*, ii/i, 426.

contemporary Europe because of its institutionalization of the office of a separate grand duke.[25] It was far more than simply a dynastic arrangement agreed between Jagiełło and Vytautas, or a mere extension of Vilnius-Radom. In conception and in form it reflected the interests of the two political communities it sought to bring together, and with whom it was discussed, at Niepołomice in November 1412, in Lithuania in December, and at Horodło itself, where the Polish and Lithuanian nobles present debated its terms in separate assemblies, before agreeing to separate documents in which the two political communities formally endorsed the act presented by Jagiełło and Vytautas.[26]

The documents devoted considerable attention to those political communities and their future relationship. Clauses 2–7 of the principal document amplified and defined the general liberties of the Lithuanian church and the Catholic Lithuanian lords and boyars. Henceforth, the Lithuanian church and nobility were to enjoy the ancient rights and liberties of their Polish partners (*iuxta consuetudinem regni Poloniae ab antiquo observatum*). These clauses established the right to bequeath allodial estates, security of tenure for hereditary lands, and the rights of wives and daughters to a portion of the family's estates. Finally, Catholic nobles were exempted from labour service for the construction and repair of fortresses.[27]

After clauses demanding that Polish and Lithuanian nobles swore oaths to Jagiełło and Vytautas, and stipulating that those who enjoyed these privileges were obliged to show them loyalty, provision was made in clause 15 for future assemblies (*conventiones et parlamenta*) of the Polish and Lithuanian nobilities in the border cities of Lublin or Parczew—or another appropriate location—to discuss matters of common interest.[28] Then, in the most remarkable clause in the document, provision was made for forty-seven families of Catholic Lithuanian lords and boyars, selected by Vytautas, to be adopted by forty-seven Polish szlachta families. They were thereby admitted to the heraldic clans of these families, who were henceforth to regard them as brothers and relations:

> We Alexander, alias Vytautas, with the consent of his most serene highness Władysław king of Poland... elect to the arms and honours of the nobility of the kingdom of Poland the nobles herein listed of our lands of Lithuania, whom, together with all those who derive their origin from the same lineage, the nobles of this kingdom of Poland welcome into the fellowship of brotherhood and consanguinity.[29]

This clause, sworn to and attested separately by the Poles and Lithuanians, marked a watershed in the formation of the Lithuanian nobility as an estate.[30] All forty-seven Lithuanian nobles and forty-five of the Polish families involved are known through their seals.[31] The adoption has occasioned much debate. Some

---

[25] e.g. Šležas, 'Vytauto', 183; Kutrzeba, 'Charakter', 170–2.   [26] *AU*, no. 49; no. 50, 50–9.
[27] *AU*, no. 51, 64–6.   [28] *AU*, no. 51, 66–8.   [29] *AU*, no. 51, 69.
[30] Władysław Semkowicz, 'Braterstwo szlachty polskiej z boyarstwem litewskim w unii horodolskiej 1413 roku', in *Polska i Litwa w dziejowym stosunku* (Cracow, 1914), 393–446; Władysław Semkowicz, 'O litewskich rodach bojarskich zbratanych ze szlachtą polską w Horodle w 1413, r.', *LSP*, 3, repr. (1989), 3–139; Suchocki, 'Formowanie', 50–5.
[31] See the table in Błaszczyk, *Dzieje*, ii/i, 396–7.

Lithuanian scholars have presented it as a subtle change of strategy by the Poles: unable to effect incorporation, they deviously sought to achieve it by indirect means, through the gradual assimilation and polonization of the Lithuanian ruling classes.[32] Others have dismissed it on the grounds that it was hastily put together, and had little practical effect: the adoption did not lead to any close contact between the Polish and Lithuanian families listed, beyond the adoption of Polish coats-of-arms, which some Lithuanian families later abandoned.[33]

While the practical impact of the clause was slight, at least in the short term, it is the thinking behind it that is significant. For if Horodło was undoubtedly drafted with one eye on the propaganda war with the Order, its main motivation was domestic. After twenty-seven years much had been learned about how in practice union might work, not least through the success of Vilnius-Radom, which, through providing a clear framework for Vytautas's rule in Lithuania, laid the foundations for the closer cooperation that had led to Tannenberg. Confident that the exercise of power by a separate grand duke did not necessarily weaken the union, Jagiełło agreed to the possible continuation of the arrangement after Vytautas's death. Yet the core of the Horodło union was not concerned with practical arrangements for governing Lithuania, but constituted a vision of what the union was, or at least what it might become: a relationship of two political communities, rather than the annexation of one 'state' by another.

Understood in this way, the first clause concerning Lithuania's incorporation is entirely consistent with the rest of the document. It was not a piece of legerdemain directed at the Order, but a serious attempt to define the nature of the union. In this article we hear Jagiełło's voice, for although the document was issued jointly with Vytautas, it is Jagiełło who speaks here, as the use of the term 'our Polish kingdom' makes clear. The clause opens with Jagiełło describing how, with the inspiration of the Holy Spirit, he accepted the Polish crown. He states that he had 'appropriated, incorporated, conjoined, united, adjoined, and confederated' his Lithuanian territories and dominions with 'our Polish kingdom'.[34] There is, in this sentence, a significant difference to Krewo, in which the term *applicare* is used with reference not to the Polish kingdom but to the *corona regni*. Since the *regnum* and the *corona regni* were carefully distinguished in contemporary documents, the use of the term '*regnum Poloniae*' at Horodło was clearly deliberate. Here the international context is indeed relevant: on the eve of Constance it was necessary for Jagiełło, and Vytautas to present Poland and Lithuania as one united *regnum*, capable of acting as one body under its king and supreme duke on the international stage; as such, Horodło was consistent with Vilnius-Radom and the agreements in which Vytautas had sworn not to act independently of Jagiełło and the Poles in the conduct of foreign affairs. This was certainly the position maintained at Constance.

---

[32] Dundulis, *Lietuvos kova*, 46–7.
[33] Egidijus Banionis, 'Lietuvos bajorai 1413 m. Horodlėje', in Čapaitė and Nikžentaitis (eds), *Žalgirio*, 189–206.
[34] *AU*, no. 51, 63.

In the words of Paweł Włodkowic (Paulus Vladimiri), rector of Cracow University and the most effective defender of the Polish-Lithuanian cause:

> [The princes of Poland and Lithuania] after they arranged that Lithuania with all its lands, lordships, and everything that belonged to it, with the consent of the people and the said princes, should be united, joined, and incorporated into the kingdom of Poland in perpetuity, in such a way that the whole peoples of Lithuania and Poland should remain together with the said kingdom, as if they formed one body and one complete dominion, or kingdom.[35]

Włodkowic had a clear idea of the *regnum* as a sovereign political entity and legal persona, with defined borders and its own government. His position was entirely consistent with the text of Horodło and with the canon-law concept of Vytautas as governing *in partem sollicitudinis* as set out in Vilnius-Radom.

What, in practice, did incorporation mean? As Rowell observes, the Horodło document functions on many levels.[36] In the first clause, the two great lists of synonyms are not, in fact, synonyms at all, or at least each list readily falls into two separate lists of synonyms with different connotations. For if '*appropriavimus*' and '*incorporavimus*' from the first list, and '*incorporamus*', '*invisceramus*', '*appropriamus*', and '*anectimus*' from the second, can certainly be seen as synonymous, the words in the second group express a different vision: '*univimus*', '*adiunximus*', and '*confoederavimus*' from the first section, and '*coniungamus*', '*adiungamus*', and '*confoederamus*' from the second, cannot be regarded as synonyms for the first list. Moreover, at the end of the clause, there is a brief explanation of what this 'incorporation' might mean in practice, in which the concept of the *corona regni*, not the *regnum* is invoked. Here, the emphasis is on union and unity, not incorporation; on the perpetual nature of that union; and on the enjoyment of all the laws operating in the *corona regni*.[37]

This article works on three levels. On the first, it is indeed intended to demonstrate the unity of Poland and Lithuania to the international Catholic community, hence the emphasis on the inspiration of the Holy Spirit as lying behind the original consummation of the union, and the stress that it was agreed with the unanimous consent of the Gediminid dynasty and the Lithuanian elites.[38] On another level, it was directed at the Poles: Jagiełło formally and in public stated that he had fulfilled the promise he had made at Krėva in 1385, and that—in case there was any vestige of doubt—he was once more incorporating Lithuania into the *regnum Poloniae*, thus ensuring that Poland and Lithuania acted as one on the international stage. Finally, he was renewing that act, and, in so doing, he, together with Vytautas, was

---

[35] Paulus Vladimirus, quoted by Stanislaus Belch, *Paulus Vladimiri and his Doctrine concerning International Law and Politics* (The Hague, 1965), i, 281 n. 20; cf. 287 n. 63.

[36] Rowell, 'Forging', 16.

[37] 'decernentes ipsas cum omnibus earum dominiis, terris, ducatibus, principatibus, districtibus, proprietatibus omnique iure mero et mixto coronae regni Poloniae perpetuis temporibus irrevocabiliter et irrefregabiliter semper esse unitas': *AU*, no. 51, 64.

[38] 'de consensu unanimi nostro et aliorum fratrum nostrorum et omnium baronum, nobilium, procerum et boyarorum eiusdem terrae Lyttwaniae voluntate accedente et assensu': *AU*, no. 51, 64.

explaining more fully what, in practice, union meant for Lithuania. Hence the second list of synonyms provide a vision of union, not incorporation: the use of *confoederamus* was particularly significant given the resonance of the term in Polish political dialogue since the great confederations of Wielkopolska and Małopolska that had decided the succession in 1382.[39] Confederation in Polish political discourse indicated the formal constitution of the political community in a *foedus* to enact decisions in common, at the local, provincial, or national level; its use at Hordło was another indication to the Lithuanians of the nature of the union of which they were now a part. The emphasis on the extension of law indicated that this was to be a political community bound together by law, and not solely by the person of the ruler, or on the basis of ad hoc arrangements between Jagiełło and Vytautas.

In this clause Jagiełło performed a subtle balancing act, which he brought off with considerable aplomb. To assess it in terms of the concepts of statehood that were of such burning significance in the nineteenth and twentieth centuries is to misunderstand it. For it is the medieval concepts of lordship (*dominium*) and of the community of the realm, not the modern idea of statehood—except in the context of the conduct of international relations—that primarily inform Horodło. In this clause, Jagiełło repeated what he had made clear in his various agreements with Vytautas since 1392: that he, as king of Poland and supreme duke of Lithuania, possessed regal authority across the union. While Horodło introduced the principle of election for the grand duke—to whom regal authority was delegated—Jagiełło's hereditary rights as supreme duke were not affected, and he had an unchallenged right to dispose of his patrimony as he saw fit. As supreme duke he had therefore incorporated, and was incorporating anew, the grand duchy into the Polish *regnum*; the clause reminded Vytautas and the world that Vytautas had accepted this in 1385, 1392, 1401, and 1403. Jagiełło was stressing that he, as king and supreme duke, spoke for the *regnum* and the union on the international stage where, especially in 1413, it was vital that it spoke with one voice. Thus, for all that it was issued jointly, the document was, at least in part, the latest of a series of acts by which Jagiełło publicly reined in Vytautas and reminded him that he was not to conduct his own foreign policy.

Yet this was Vytautas's treaty as much as it was Jagiełło's. Vytautas could accept Horodło because in it the Poles conceded not only the establishment of a proper localized structure on the decentralized Polish pattern with the creation of the palatinates of Vilnius and Trakai, which extended over most of Lithuania proper, but also provision for the possible continuation of the grand ducal office after Vytautas's death. This was perfectly consistent with the idea that, in domestic terms Lithuania had been incorporated into the *corona regni*; a political community, not a kingdom or state. Clarification was necessary, for the situation with regard to the

---

[39] Wiskont, while anachronistically emphasizing that Vytautas sought to defend the independence of the Lithuanian state, is one of the few historians to stress that Horodło was a union not with Poland, but with the *corona regni Poloniae*: Antoni Wiskont, 'Wielki książę litewski Witold a unia horodelska', *AW*, 7 (1930), 488.

succession had changed since 1401. Jagiełło now had a five-year-old daughter, Jadwiga, by Anna of Celje, who was formally recognized as heir to the Polish throne by an assembly at Jedlnia in early 1413.[40] Jadwiga's birth reduced Vytautas's prospects of becoming king of Poland after Jagiełło's death, although by no means eliminated them, and the clauses in Horodło concerning the election of a king of Poland if Jagiełło were to die without a male heir—still a very real prospect given his age—should be seen in this light: Lithuanian custom did not embrace female succession, thus Jagiełło's death might threaten the union. The institutionalization of the office of grand duke gave Vytautas the prospect of securing the succession in Lithuania for his preferred candidate after his own death through the elective principle introduced at Horodło: in any election the forty-seven families who owed their dominant position to the Horodło adoption masterminded by Vytautas would play a significant role.

The rest of the document spells out the nature of the union as conceived for domestic purposes. Despite the separate provisions for the government of Lithuania, the union was not to be joined simply by the person of its supreme ruler, and the institutionalization of the office of grand duke did not mean it was to be a loose relationship. Neither, despite the talk of incorporation, was it to be based on the annexation of the grand duchy, but on a partnership of the dynasty with a joint community of the realm, in which Lithuania—or at least its Catholic noble elites—would occupy a privileged position, since they, unlike their counterparts in Wielkopolska or Małopolska, would have their own grand duke: thus if Lithuania was incorporated, this was not a full accessory union, but an *incorporatio minus plena*. Moreover, since Vytautas nominated the Lithuanian families to be included in the incorporation, Horodło enabled him to strengthen his political position in Lithuania by rewarding his supporters.[41] It was a price worth paying for the limiting of his independence on the international stage. For the Lithuanian Catholic elites, on the other hand, Horodło established the legal basis for their political liberties, a fact they were never to forget.

Ivinskis, who believed that Krewo instituted a purely dynastic union, argued that it was Horodło that set Lithuania and Poland on the path to real union.[42] It might be better to suggest that the path to real union began at Krewo, but the direction and nature of that process was established at Horodło. While the dynasty undoubtedly played a central role, as the elaborate demonstrations of public consent from the communities of the two realms on 2 October 1413 indicate, this was equally envisaged as a union of peoples, as Długosz suggests. Thus the union was to be driven as much from below as from above; moreover, Horodło's carefully constructed phraseology ensured that two interpretations of its meaning were possible: the Polish view that the grand duchy had been fully incorporated into Poland, and the Lithuanian view, based on the canon law concept of *aeque principaliter*, in which the union was seen as a composite polity that encompassed two realms and a different political structure within the grand duchy.

---

[40] Błaszczyk, *Dzieje*, ii/i, 389.   [41] *AU*, no. 51, 69.
[42] Zenonas Ivinskis, 'Jogaila valstybininkas ir žmogus', in Šapoka (ed.), *Jogaila*, 316.

The different interpretations of the nature of the union state, however, were obscured in the two documents of acceptance by the concept of a community of peoples, an idea that was to develop powerfully over the next 150 years. Thus the Polish version begins by stressing the importance of love and concord, 'by which laws are made, kingdoms ruled, cities established, and the condition of the republic perfected'.[43] The use of 'republic' indicates the direction in which Polish thinking on the nature of the community of the realm was tending. When it came to welcoming Lithuanian boyars into their heraldic clans, the language was that of union, not of annexation or incorporation: '*coniunximus, univimus, et tenore praesentium coniungimus, conponimus, coadunamus et conformamus . . . in vim verae caritatis et fraternae unionis valeant utifrui, gaudere et potiri*'.[44] In their document, the Lithuanian boyars swore not to elect a successor to Vytautas without consulting the Poles, and that they would not desert them in time of need.[45]

Horodło set both the tone and direction of the process of union in a way that had not been achieved in any of the treaties agreed since 1385. It was undoubtedly a compromise between the parties involved—Jagiełło, Vytautas, and the Polish and Catholic Lithuanian elites—and if it is therefore full of the ambiguities that inevitably arise from such compromises, it gives a more coherent picture of how the union was conceived than most historians have allowed. It was a genuine union treaty, and not testimony to a simple annexation of a supposed Lithuanian state by its Polish counterpart; to that extent, the historians who have insisted that it saw no effective incorporation of the grand duchy are right. It nonetheless instituted far more than a simple dynastic union of otherwise separate 'states'. To depict it, as some have, as a defeat for either Jagiełło or Vytautas—both points of view have been advanced—is to misunderstand the nature of the compromise. Apart from the practical measures for the government of Lithuania—the establishment of the palatinates of Vilnius and Trakai—Horodło was more a blueprint for a particular kind of union than an effective treaty of union. While there were occasional joint assemblies of the Poles and Lithuanians as provided for under the treaty, these had occurred before 1413—Horodło itself was one such meeting—the provision was rarely used; it was not, however, forgotten.

Horodło, however, had two serious shortcomings that were to have significant consequences. Firstly, despite the potential institutionalization of the office of a separate grand duke, the stipulations concerning the means by which the succession in each part of the union was to be decided were ambiguous and unclear.[46] Secondly, the benefits of Horodło were only extended to Catholic boyars, who were overwhelmingly of ethnic Lithuanian descent. The success of Gediminid Lithuania was built on its open-handed treatment of the Orthodox Ruthenian population and of its elites, most of whom identified with the Gediminid condominium and defended it, although there were undoubtedly differing levels of integration and loyalty: there were many Ruthenians living within the Lithuanian heartlands, but attachment to the Gediminid realm weakened in direct proportion

---

[43] *AU*, no. 49, 53.   [44] *AU*, no. 49, 53.   [45] *AU*, no. 50, 59.
[46] *AU*, no. 51, 67–8; no. 50, 59; no. 49, 53–4. See Ch. 14, 152, 156.

to the distance of Ruthenian communities from Vilnius. Jagiełło's baptism, when he stressed the difference between the Ruthenians and 'the whole Lithuanian nation' (*omnes nacione Lithvanos*) had introduced a new sense of privilege for those who converted to Catholicism that was only reinforced at Horodło.[47]

Nevertheless, despite these problems, Horodło's attempt to define incorporation marked a notable change of direction that has not received enough attention. The debate about incorporation has revolved around the issue of whether or not a Lithuanian 'state' was incorporated into the Polish state in 1413. Yet Horodło treated the grand duchy as a composite polity, not a unitary state. Whereas in the Krewo Act Jogaila promised to join both his Lithuanian and his Ruthenian territories to Poland, Horodło omitted any mention of the Ruthenian lands, except in the titles of Jagiełło and Vytautas. The incorporation clause referred only to '*terrarum nostrarum Lyttwaniae*', with no mention of the Ruthenian lands, although incorporation included all Lithuania's 'dominions, territories, duchies, principalities, districts and lordships'.[48] Thus the *regnum* was writ large, but the political community was to exclude the Orthodox and the benefits of Horodło were intended to affect only Lithuania proper: the territories included in the two new palatinates of Vilnius and Trakai. Although they contained many Ruthenians, both noble and non-noble, the majority of the grand duchy's Ruthenian territories were excluded and office in the central government and the new palatinates was specifically restricted to Catholics. Despite Horodło's location on the river Bug, in an area of the Polish kingdom with a considerable Ruthenian population, the great Ruthenian lords did not attend, and the Ruthenian princes were not required to swear to Horodło, as they had sworn to Krewo.[49]

Horodło's silence concerning the status of the annexed Ruthenian lands was to have significant consequences. At the international level, however, the concentration on Lithuanian Catholics was sensible in the context of the bitter propaganda war against the Order, which, from 1414, was fought out at Constance on the greatest public stage possible, before the pope and the elites of the Latin church. The Order's attacks on Jagiełło's deployment of pagans, infidels, and schismatics could be countered or at least neutralized by Horodło's emphasis on the union of two Catholic polities and the establishment of a common, Catholic ruling elite.

---

[47] Paszkiewicz, *O genezie*, 161, 168.   [48] *AU*, no. 51, 62, 63.
[49] Halecki, *Dzieje*, i, 214; Halecki, 'Litwa, Ruś', 229. Maksimeiko, polemicizing with Liubavskii, agreed that Horodło only applied to Lithuania proper: Николай Максимейко, *Сеймы литовско-русскаго государства до люблинской уній 1569 г.* (Kharkov, 1902), 62–4; cf. Kazimierz Chodynicki, *Kościół prawosławny a Rzeczpospolita polska 1370–1632* (Warsaw, 1932), 84–7.

12

Defending the Union

The propaganda war began immediately. It was conducted by the Polish-Lithuanian side in terms that reveal much about the nature of the union, based on the developing concept of the *corona regni* which—as Rowell observes—was 'not an anti-royal concept per se, but one representing 'the bond uniting the monarch and the community of the realm'.[1] Horodło demonstrated to all Europe that Lithuania had been admitted to that community in a perpetual union established with the consent of both political communities; it asserted that the union state spoke with one voice, which it did in practice, at least for the moment.

Although Jagiełło and Vytautas always stressed their personal and dynastic authority, it was very much to their advantage to emphasize that the union was based on the consent of the community of the realm. Aware that the Order could produce documents testifying to the surrender of Samogitia in perpetuity, they based their arguments for its return to Lithuania upon the proposition that, according to *ius gentium* and natural law, princes did not have the authority to alienate any part of their principality without the consent of those affected, which meant both their heirs and the political community of the affected territory. This argument was applied not only to Samogitia, but also to Pomerelia, ceded to the Order in perpetuity in 1343. These arguments were put during the mediation talks, but they were in the interests of the dynasty as well as the communities of the realm, and were supported by Mikołaj Wiśliczka, representing Jagiełło's daughter Jadwiga, and Mikołaj Cebulka, a Pole in Vytautas's service, representing Vytautas's daughter Sophia.

Błaszczyk argues that Cebulka's submission on Sophia's behalf was in breach of Vilnius-Radom, which envisaged the return of the whole grand duchy to Poland on Vytautas's death.[2] Yet this is to misunderstand the situation, as the fact that Wiśliczka also made a submission on Samogitia on behalf of Jadwiga demonstrates. Samogitia, like Trakai, had been part of Kęstutis's patrimony; as such Vytautas had a legitimate claim to it. The significance of Wiśliczka's submission is rather that, having secured the agreement of the Poles that Jadwiga was the natural heir to the Polish throne, Jagiełło was now publicly putting her forward as heir to the position of supreme prince in the grand duchy which, given the lack of any precedent in Lithuania for female succession was bold indeed. These arguments were partly for domestic consumption, an attempt to use the need to preserve the union to assert

---

[1] Rowell, 'Dynastic bluff?', 9. [2] Błaszczyk, *Dzieje*, ii/i, 372–3.

the natural rights of Jagiełło and his heirs in Poland as well as in Lithuania, and the rights of Vytautas and his heirs to the Kęstutid patrimony.

The major battles were fought at Constance, however, which marked the start of a long engagement with conciliarist ideas that was to play a significant role in the development of Polish-Lithuanian political thought, and was to have a substantial effect on the union's development. From the start of the schism in 1378 Poland had remained loyal to the Roman popes Urban VI, Boniface IX, Innocent VII, and Gregory XII. In 1409, however, it sent delegates to the council of Pisa, a risky step, for Jagiełło's good relations with the papacy had persuaded Boniface to condemn the Order's anti-Polish policies and ban it from waging war on Lithuania in 1403. The election of Alexander V at Pisa gave the Poles hope that they might secure more effective support from him: Alexander had visited Lithuania and Ruthenia, had met Jagiełło and Vytautas, and had seen the effects of the Order's depredations in Lithuania. In December 1409 Jagiełło swore loyalty to him, and to his successor, John XXIII, after Alexander's death in May 1410. John repaid this loyalty with a bull annulling all the Order's papal and imperial privileges for the conversion of Lithuania and the Orthodox east.[3]

Polish support for John evaporated after his deposition at Constance in March 1415. Although the Polish delegation, in Constance from 20 January 1415 until 17 May 1418, took a full part in the council, it concentrated on the conflict with the Order, which was debated in two dramatic set-piece confrontations in July 1415 and February 1416.[4] The ground was prepared well, and the delegation was intellectually of very high quality. It was led by Mikołaj Trąba, archbishop of Gniezno since 1412, who, as vice-chancellor from 1403 until 1412, had been one of Jagiełło's most reliable ministers. He was accompanied by his associate Andrzej Łaskarz, bishop-elect of Poznań, who had led the mediation negotiations, Jakub of Korzkiew, bishop of Płock, and Jan Kropidło, a Silesian Piast and bishop of Cujavia. They were accompanied by several lay representatives, and by Włodkowic, Jagiełło's personal envoy. The canon lawyer Peter Wolfram, procurator of the bishop of Cracow, Wojciech Jastrzębiec, represented his master who, as chancellor, was unable to attend.

Włodkowic was a canon lawyer. Like his friend Łaskarzyc, Kropidło, Wolfram, and several other delegates, he had studied at Prague University in the flourishing intellectual climate that nourished Jan Hus, and then in Padua. Although there is no evidence that Trąba had studied at any university, Jakub of Korzkiew held doctorates in canon law from Rome and Bologna.[5] These were sophisticated men, in tune with the intellectual currents of the day. The case against the Order was carefully prepared in Cracow University, whose faculty had largely been educated

---

[3] Tomasz Graff, *Episkopat monarchii jagiellońskiej w dobie soborów powszechnych XV wieku* (Cracow, 2008); Thomas Wünsch, *Konziliarismus und Polen* (Paderborn, 1998), 32; Jan Fijałek, 'Kościół rzymskokatolicki na Litwie: Uchrześcijanienie Litwy przez Polskę i zachowanie w niej języka ludu po koniec Rzeczypospolitej', in Kłoczowski (ed.), *Chrystianizacja*, 152.
[4] Graff, *Episkopat*, 202.
[5] Karol Górski, *Z dziejów walki o pokój i sprawiedliwość międzynarodową: Ostatnie słowo Pawła Włodkowica o Zakonie Krzyżackim* (Toruń, 1964), 8–9; Wünsch, *Konziliarismus*, 54–7.

in Prague: twenty-five of the thirty-one professors listed in 1404 had studied there, as had nine out of eleven of the university's earliest rectors.[6] The intellectual foundations were laid by its first rector, Stanisław of Skarbimierz, who had taken his doctorate in Prague and who, as one of Cracow's first professors of law, probably helped draft Vilnius-Radom.[7] In 1410 he published a sermon entitled *On Just Wars*, in which he drew on canon and natural law to argue that pagans had the right to their own state, and to defend it; furthermore, if their state were attacked without good reason by Christians, other Christians were permitted to aid them.[8] These ideas underpinned the Polish-Lithuanian case at Constance. Their fullest expression came in Włodkowic's *Treatise on the power of pope and emperor with regard to infidels*; he also delivered fifty-two theses at a session of the German nation—which included Poland-Lithuania—in June 1416.[9]

In his treatise Włodkowicz mounted a radical attack not just on the Order, but on the tradition of evangelization that it represented. After a brief introduction outlining the Order's history and the atrocities it had perpetrated upon pagan Prussians and Lithuanians, Włodkowic turned to the legal basis for such actions, setting himself the bold task of demolishing the claims of popes and emperors concerning pagans and infidels.[10] He first considered the legal position of Jews and Muslims living in Christian states, citing the Bible and a range of authorities and legal precedents to support his argument that Christian princes were not permitted to molest or expel infidels if they were peaceable and accepted the laws of the Christian community among whom they lived.[11] Since infidels were rational beings created by God himself, a prince could not despoil them of their possessions or expel them from his dominions without good cause.[12] Pagans had the right to their own state and the Emperor and other secular powers did not have a natural right to use violence against pagan states that did not recognize their authority unless there was good cause: the annexation of a pagan state could only take place by the will of God, or with the consent of its inhabitants. Thus the Order's attacks on the peaceful pagans of Lithuania and Samogitia contravened divine and natural law, although Włodkowic was happy to allow that the wars of the Spanish monarchies against the Saracens were just, since they were to recover territories once held by Christians. Pagans who were unjustly attacked had a right to defend themselves despite their ignorance of divine and natural law. Similarly, it was wrong to use force to compel infidels to convert to Christianity: created as rational beings by God, they had freedom of conscience, and the right to choose.[13]

---

[6] Wünsch, *Konziliarismus*, 34.   [7] Krzyżaniakowa and Ochmański, *Jagiełło*, 182.
[8] Stanisław from Skarbimierz, 'De bellis justis', in Ludwik Ehrlich (ed.), *Polski wykład prawa wojny* (Warsaw, 1955), 90–144.
[9] Hartmut Boockmann, *Johannes Falkenberg, der Deutsche Orden und die polnische Politik* (Göttingen, 1975), 209–10; Paweł Włodkowic, *Tractatus de potestate papae et imperatoris respectu infidelium* in *Rerum publicarum scientiae quae saeculo XV in Polonia viguit monumenta litteraria*, ed. Michał Bobrzyński (Cracow, 1878), 161–94.
[10] Włodkowic, *Tractatus de potestate*, 161–2.   [11] Włodkowic, *Tractatus de potestate*, 164–5.
[12] Włodkowic, *Tractatus de potestate*, 165–6; 188.
[13] Włodkowic, *Tractatus de potestate*, 173–4; 175; 178; 188.

Włodkowic was no modern liberal, and his arguments were skilfully selected to cause the maximum damage to the Order's case. Nevertheless, his treatise is a remarkable document. Although in impeccable medieval fashion he drew on past authorities, few had attempted such a comprehensive defence of the rights of non-Christians to freedom from unjustified aggression, and if his treatise remained largely forgotten after Constance, it anticipated many of the themes that became familiar in early modern discourses on international law.[14] It did much to secure its immediate aims. In February 1416 its contention that Samogitia was naturally part of Lithuania, and that peaceful methods of conversion were more desirable and more effective than the Order's violent approach, were bolstered by the sensational arrival in Constance of a sixty-strong Samogitian delegation, which bore witness to the rapid success of the evangelization of the province that Jagiełło and Vytautas had begun in October 1413, when they sailed down the Niemen and Dubissa rivers into the Samogitian heartlands, where they repeated the tactics that had worked so successfully in Lithuania twenty-six years earlier, gathering the leading Samogitians at an assembly which Jagiełło addressed personally.[15]

The Samogitian delegation was formally welcomed in Constance cathedral on 4 December 1415. At a plenary session on 13 February 1416, the *Propositio Samaytarum*, possibly drafted by Włodkowic, was presented. It contained forty points in which the Order's violent attempts to convert Samogitia were contrasted vividly with the peaceful means adopted by Jagiełło and Vytautas.[16] This public relations exercise exaggerated the success of the conversion: Jagiełło and Vytautas spent only a week in Samogitia, and Długosz's account, with its affecting picture of Jagiełło addressing the Samogitians in their own language, is overdrawn. More effective were the deliberate destruction of the sacred groves and temples, and the efforts of Vytautas and a legion of Polish priests, accompanied by local translators over the following years. The process of conversion was much slower than the Constance delegation implied, and met with considerable resistance, which forced a relaunch in 1417. Nevertheless, the delegation successfully won over the majority of the Constance delegates: they could point to the considerable success of Jagiełło's peaceful methods in Lithuania and the failure of the Order's long campaign of violence and oppression. In 1417 the council agreed to the establishment of a new bishopric at Medininkai; as in Aukštaitija the establishment of the Church's institutional structure, with the creation of a network of parishes and the training of Lithuanian priests at Cracow University, slowly laid the foundations for ultimate success.[17]

The campaign achieved much, but not outright victory. Włodkowic's pamphlet challenging the Emperor's powers, and the refusal of the Polish delegation to

---

[14] Frederick Russell, 'Paulus Vladimiri's attack on the Just War. A case study in legal polemics', in Brian Tierney, and Peter Linehan (eds), *Studies on Medieval Law and Government presented to Walter Ullmann* (Cambridge, 1980), 243–4, 253–4.

[15] Ivinskas, 'Litwa', 121.

[16] Błaszczyk, *Dzieje*, ii/i, 458; Ivinskis, 'Litwa', 122–3.

[17] Fijałek, 'Kościół', 152–4, 183–263; Ivinskis, 'Litwa', 121–6; Marian Banaszak, 'Chrzest Żmudzi i jego reperkusje w Konstancji', in Marek Zahajkiewicz (ed.), *Chrzest Litwy* (Lublin, 1990), 57–76.

recognize imperial authority over the kingdom of Poland in the session of 5 July 1415 displeased Sigismund, who began defending the Order. Yet if no conclusive outcome to the dispute was reached at Constance, there was no doubt that the Poles won the propaganda battle. They were helped by the Dominican Johannes Falkenberg, who followed up an attack on Włodkowic's treatise—effectively rebutted—with an inflammatory satirical pamphlet whose intemperate tone was counterproductive. As is frequently the case with satire, it was taken seriously, and its call for what amounted to genocide against the Poles was so extreme that Falkenberg was disowned and imprisoned by the Order, which realized the damage he had done, even if the Poles failed to secure his outright condemnation from Martin V, despite a dramatic appeal at the plenary session closing the council on 9 May 1418, which they refused to withdraw despite papal threats.[18]

The Polish-Lithuanian campaign at Constance did much to ensure that the Order did not receive any substantial military support when the Thorn treaty proved incapable of preserving peace. Poland-Lithuania emerged victorious from three brief wars with the Order after 1413—the 'hunger war' of 1414, when a large army devastated the Order's lands, only retreating when it could no longer feed itself; the 1419 'war of retreat', when the Order hastily sued for peace before another large army had even crossed the frontier; and the 'Golub war' in the same year, when the allies besieged and captured Golub and cut a swathe of devastation across Prussia. Military superiority, backed by the diplomatic offensive at Constance, finally produced the desired result. In the 1422 treaty of Melno, Samogitia was recognized unconditionally and in perpetuity as a Lithuanian possession; Lithuania also received the port of Palanga and a narrow strip of land fifteen kilometres across that provided access to the Baltic Sea, separating the lands of the Order's two branches. Poland secured relatively little—the castle of Nieszawa near Thorn and a handful of Cujavian villages—but the Polish-Lithuanian triumph was decisive: the Lithuanian-Prussian border fixed at Melno was to remain unchanged until 1919. Two years later Falkenberg formally renounced his theses, and the Poles withdrew their appeal.[19]

The Order was by no means finished, but the tide had turned decisively. The striking feature of the Polish-Lithuanian campaign at Constance is the extent to which it was rooted in Polish views about the nature of politics, and the Polish conception of the nature of the union with Lithuania. The case presented was selective and designed to win over an international audience, but it rested on propositions about the nature of the political community that drew extensively on currents in Catholic political thought. Włodkowic, who had studied in Padua, drew on the works of Marsiglio of Padua in his *Treatises*.[20] Echoes of Marsiglio's

---

[18] Johann Falkenberg, *Liber de doctrina potestatis papae et imperatoris editus contra Paulum Vladimiri Polonum in Sacro Constantiensi Consilio*, in *Rerum publicarum*, 196–232; Paweł Włodkowic, *Tractatus de Ordine Cruciferorum et de bello Polonorum contra dictos fratres ad confutanda scripta Johaniiis de Bamberga (Johannis Fal[k]enberg) in sacro Constantiensi Generali Concilio*, in *Rerum publicarum*, 233–96. Falkenberg's satire is printed in Boockmann, *Falkenberg*, 312–53.

[19] Błaszczyk, *Dzieje*, ii/i, 438; Boockmann, *Falkenberg*, 297–305.

[20] e.g. Włodkowic, *Tractatus de potestate*, 170.

view that 'the legislator, or the primary and proper efficient cause of law, is the people or whole body of citizens, or the weightier part thereof, through its election or will expressed by words in the general assembly of the citizens' are clearly evident in his writings, informing the argument that territory could only be ceded with the consent of its inhabitants.[21] These ideas underpinned the whole development of the Polish political system after 1382. They informed the practice of confederation, and they ran like a golden thread through all the union treaties. The consent of the citizens was central to the process of union, and it was this concept, embodied in ideas about the *corona regni* as the community of the realm, that underlay that process, not ideas about statehood. The Polish-Lithuanian interventions at Constance demonstrate how deeply such ideas had penetrated Polish Catholicism, upon which Jagiełło's government rested so firmly.

Horodło demonstrates the extent to which Jagiełło and Vytautas accepted and propagated—up to a point—this vision of the political community. For Vytautas, the support of the Catholic Lithuanian boyars was essential to buttress his position as grand duke. He was an enthusiastic supporter of the extension to them of the rights and privileges of their Polish counterparts. Nevertheless, for all the apparent vindication of the union that Tannenberg and Melno provided, it was still a fragile creation, as is demonstrated by the number of adjustments that had been made to it since 1386. That it had worked so effectively reflected the working relationship thrashed out between Jagiełło and Vytautas between 1392 and 1413. Horodło's provisions concerning Lithuania's government indicate that both Jagiełło and Vytautas were looking to the future: the union had to be secured after their deaths if the gains of Melno were not to be squandered. Yet if Horodło sought to provide a mechanism for deciding the succession, there was no guarantee that it would be accepted, either by surviving members of the Gediminid dynasty, or by the political communities of Poland and Lithuania. In the years after 1422, as both Jagiełło and Vytautas lived on and on, the strains became increasingly apparent, until a fullblown crisis of union erupted in their last years, a crisis that exposed the ambiguities in Horodło and all but destroyed the union.

---

[21] Marsilius [Marsiglio] of Padua, *Defensor pacis*, tr. Alan Gewirth (Toronto, 1956; 2nd edn 1980), 45.

PART III

CRISIS, 1422–47

13

The Coronation Tempest

On Sunday 5 March 1424 Jagiełło's fourth wife, Sophia (Sonka) Holshanska, was crowned and anointed queen of Poland by primate Wojciech Jastrzębiec in St Stanisław's Cathedral in Cracow. It was a magnificent occasion that bore eloquent testimony to the prestige enjoyed by Jagiełło and his united realms. The guests included Sigismund of Luxembourg and Erik of Pomerania, King of Denmark, Norway, and Sweden. Ludwig of Bavaria, brother of Isabeau, the dowager queen of France, turned up uninvited, attracted by rumours of the magnificence of the planned ceremony. Cardinal Placenta Branda de Castiglione, representing Martin V, and the auditor of the Holy See, Julian Cesarini were there, as was an ambassador from the Byzantine co-emperor John VIII Palaeologus, whose wife was Vytautas's granddaughter. There was a swarm of Piast princes: the Mazovian dukes Siemowit V, Władysław I, Casimir II, and Trojden II; and the Silesians: Bernard of Oppeln; Boleslaus of Teschen; Johann of Ratibor; Casimir of Oświęcim; Wenzel of Troppau; Konrad IX, 'the Black', of Oels-Kosel; Konrad VII, 'the White', of Beuthen-Kosel; and Wenzel of Sagan. Paul von Rusdorf, the Order's grand master, was represented by the komturs of Elbing and Thorn. The horde of Polish nobles was augmented by an impressive array of Lithuanian and Ruthenian princes. At the sumptuous coronation banquet guests feasted on mountains of game slaughtered by Jagiełło during his Christmas sojourn in Lithuania. Sigismund presided as King of the Romans, with Jagiełło on his right, and Erik of Pomerania on his left. Feasting, tournaments, and dancing lasted three days until the start of Lent initiated a no doubt necessary period of sobriety.[1]

There was one notable absentee. Vytautas declined his invitation. This was odd, for Długosz states that it was his idea that Jagiełło marry Sonka, granddaughter of his half-brother Dmitry and of Vytautas's brother-in-law Ivan Holshansky.[2] Between the wedding, celebrated in Navahrudak in February 1422, and the coronation, however, Vytautas fell out with Sonka. Długosz gives no reason, although he made his own feelings clear, sneering at the 'decrepit' Jagiełło marrying such a young girl and observing that she brought no dowry, that she had been raised Orthodox, that she was related to Jagiełło in the third and fourth degree, and that

---

[1] *Annales* xi, 194–8; Franciszek Sikora, 'Uroczystości koronacyjne królowej Zofii w 1424 r.', in Stanisław Bylina et al. (eds), *Kościół—Kultura—Społeczeństwo* (Warsaw, 2000), 161–79.
[2] *Annales*, xi, 151–2. Jagiełło stressed Vytautas's consent to the match: *CEV* no. 1128, 619. Maleczyńska questions Vytautas's matchmaking role: *Rola polityczna królowej Zofii Holszańskiej na tle walki stronnictw w Polsce w latach 1422–1434* (Lwów, 1936), 25–6; Sonka's latest biographer has no such doubts: Bożena Czwojdrak, *Zofia Holszańska* (Warsaw, 2012), 19.

her appearance was more beautiful than her manners. Presumably Vytautas knew all of this when he suggested her; he may have taken umbrage at the spirited Sonka's refusal to act as his obedient tool.[3]

Długosz's uncharitable view reflects the marriage's unpopularity. It was not the first time Jagiełło had upset people with his choice of bride. After Anna of Celje's death in 1416 he spurned suggestions for a diplomatically advantageous marriage to wed Elizabeth Pilecka-Granowska, widow of Wincenty Granowski, castellan of Nakło, in what was a love match. The thrice-married Elizabeth had a racy past. Famed for her wealth and beauty, she was over forty when Jagiełło proposed in 1417. Her first husband, Višel Čambor, a Bohemian-Moravian nobleman had abducted her, only to be promptly murdered by Jenčik of Hičina, a Moravian rival for her hand, who married her, but died shortly thereafter. Following Wincenty's death in 1410 she ran her estates in southern Poland with consummate shrewdness on behalf of her five children by him, before Jagiełło, who had known her for years, pressed his suit during a visit to Sanok in a matchmaking exercise engineered by his favourite sister Alexandra, duchess of Mazovia.[4]

This was Jagiełło's happiest marriage, although it lasted barely three years until Elizabeth's unexpected death in 1420. It came at a price. It was opposed by the Polish council and Vytautas, outraged that he had not been consulted. Jagiełło dashed off to mollify him in a meeting at Dobrotwór on the Bug. Vytautas accepted his decision, but observed that the marriage shamed the Gediminids, since Jagiełło could have secured a more advantageous and seemly match. Resistance to Elizabeth's coronation was widespread, and it was only when Jagiełło threatened to return to Lithuania that permission was grudgingly given. She was crowned in Cracow on 19 September 1417 not by Trąba, the primate, but by Jan of Rzeszów, archbishop of Lwów. Only three Wielkopolskan dignitaries turned up, begging Jagiełło to postpone the ceremony. When Elizabeth died, Długosz maliciously observed that the court rejoiced along with the whole country: 'the ovation at her funeral was greater than at her coronation'.[5]

Although Sonka was to prove a more adept political operator than Elizabeth, Jagiełło's choice upset many. She was not only his subject, as Elizabeth had been; she was also of Lithuanian-Ruthenian descent, only converting to Catholicism on the eve of the wedding. Most of Jagiełło's Polish advisers favoured a marriage to another Sophia (Ofka), widow of Sigismund of Luxembourg's brother Wenzel. Jagiełło refused. Ofka was past childbearing age, and he yearned for an heir. A suggestion that he marry Sigismund's eleven-year-old daughter Elizabeth held no appeal for a seventy-year-old who had already wed one child bride. Jagiełło took Vytautas's advice and settled upon Sonka, who was seventeen when he married her. It proved an inspired choice. To the consternation of those who thought him decrepit, Sonka gave birth on 31 October 1424 to a healthy son, named Władysław

---

[3] *Annales*, xi, 157–8; 194–5; Halecki, *Dzieje*, i, 236–7.
[4] *Annales*, xi, 69–73; Krzyżaniakowa and Ochmański, *Jagiełło*, 248–9.
[5] *Annales*, xi, 74, 131; Halecki, *Dzieje*, i, 236, 238; Wioletta Zawitkowska, *W służbie pierwszych Jagiellonów: Życie i działalność kanclerza Jana Taszki Koniecpolskiego* (Cracow, 2005), 91.

after his father. Another son, Casimir, did not long survive, but in 1427 Sonka bore Jagiełło another, also christened Casimir, who did. All that winter hunting was clearly invigorating (see Fig. 6. Genealogy 4).

The birth of the first male heirs to the Polish throne in over a century constituted a minor political earthquake, and Sonka had to endure suspicion that her sons were not Jagiełło's: in 1427 seven alleged lovers, including the royal marshal, Wawrzyniec of Kalinowa, and Piotr Kurowski, brother of Mikołaj, archbishop of Gniezno, were accused on the basis of evidence obtained by torture from two of Sonka's attendants. Four were arrested; three fled to Hungary, and it took strenuous denials on Sonka's part and the public support of Zbigniew Oleśnicki, bishop of Cracow, to clear her name. Długosz blamed Vytautas for

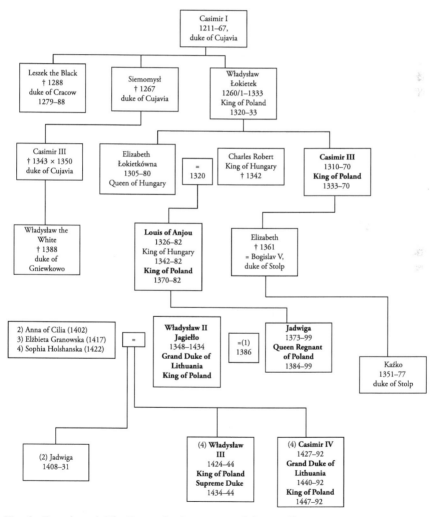

Fig. 6. Genealogy 4: The Piasts, the Angevins, and the Jagiellons.

the accusations, although it was to Vytautas that Sonka appealed, and he wrote a letter defending her honour. The interventions of two such prominent individuals proved decisive, and the charges were dropped. Although accusations resurfaced in 1431, several of the accused, including Jan Koniecpolski and Jan Hincza of Rogów went on to enjoy distinguished careers in royal service.[6]

Vytautas's absence from Sonka's coronation and Długosz's allegation that he was behind the 1427 accusations have been presented as evidence that his relationship with Jagiełło was cooling around the time of the 1422 Melno treaty.[7] Yet Melno was the expression of a new sense of unity. Vytautas's commitment to the war had occasionally been lukewarm, but Sigismund of Luxembourg's arbitration verdict, delivered in Breslau on 6 January 1420, which stipulated that Samogitia should return to the Order on Vytautas's death in accordance with the 1411 Thorn peace, restored his ardour.[8] The verdict was a shock: Jagiełło had urged Sigismund to act as arbiter, and expected a favourable outcome. According to Długosz when the cousins learned of it in Lithuania their weeping and angry cries were audible outside the room.[9] Vytautas regained his enthusiasm for war, participating energetically in the 1422 campaign.

Nikodem nevertheless argues that the Breslau verdict marked the end of close cooperation between the cousins, suggesting that thereafter Vytautas, motivated primarily by his dynastic interests, consistently sought to undermine Jagiełło with greater subtlety than in the 1390s, directing his intrigues not so much against the Poles, or the union which—so Nikodem argues—Vytautas never challenged, but directly against Jagiełło, with a view to establishing his unrivalled control over an autonomous Lithuania, and the succession to it for the Kęstutids. Thus, when Vytautas's first wife Anna died in July 1418, he took a second wife, the widowed Juliana, granddaughter of Anna's sister, who was young enough to bear him an heir. Although the marriage remained childless, Nikodem argues that Vytautas still pursued his vision, intending that he should be succeeded by his brother Žygimantas.[10]

Nikodem's attack on the traditional Polish view that from the 1390s Jagiełło and Vytautas worked closely together with common aims and largely in harmony is robust, and his close attention to the sources clearly demonstrates the extent to which historians have allowed this assumption to colour their interpretations of the evidence. In many instances his criticisms are justified. Yet his attack on received wisdom goes too far, and his view on the nature of the relationship colours his

---

[6] *Annales*, xi, 226–8; *Liber cancellariae Stanislai Ciołek*, ed. Jacob Caro (Vienna, 1874), no, 83; Krzyżaniakowa and Ochmański, *Jagiełło*, 292–3; Zawitkowska, *W służbie*, 123–4; Czwojdrak, *Zofia*, 30–2.

[7] Błaszczyk, *Dzieje*, ii/i, 507–9; Dundulis, *Kova*, 53–7; Gudevičius, 'Vytautas kaip Europos dinastas', in *Vytautas Didysis ir Lietuva*, ed. Brigita Balčtienė (Vilnius, 1996), 66–71; Carl Lückerath, *Paul von Rusdorf, Hochmeister des Deutschen Ordens 1422–1441* (Bad Godesberg, 1969), 57–60.

[8] Zenon Nowak, 'Materiały źródłowe do sprawy wyroku wrocławskiego Zygmunta Luksemburskiego w procesie polsko-krzyżackim z 1420 r.', *ZH*, 41/3 (1976), 149–65.

[9] *Annales*, xi, 117.

[10] For the latest summary of his case, see Nikodem, *Witold*, 423–49.

approach to the sources: he is as guilty as those whom he attacks of reading the sources according to his assumptions, and of dismissing or overlooking evidence that does not suit his case.[11]

The simple truth is that Melno's recognition of Lithuanian rule over Samogitia in perpetuity removed the common purpose that had bound the cousins and their realms since 1409. In its aftermath Polish and Lithuanian interests diverged, and differences of opinion with regard to political strategy and aims emerged; heightened tension was the inevitable result. Yet if one discards the assumption that all Vytautas's actions were driven by a burning commitment to Kęstudid domination, the evidence suggests not that Vytautas embarked on a Machiavellian campaign to undermine Jagiełło while pretending to cooperate with him, but that a common purpose and willingness to compromise survived for much of the decade, until the spectacular conflagration that flared up in 1429.

The problem was that Vytautas and Lithuania secured far more from Melno than the Poles, to whom Samogitia meant little.[12] They received scant reward for abandoning the stable peace they had enjoyed with the Order since 1343, despite considerable investment in thirteen years of warfare. Melno left numerous minor issues unresolved, most of them concerning the border between Poland and the *Ordensstaat*, and the treaty was not ratified until June 1424. Border disputes still festered on, however, in particular over the fortified mill at Lübitsch near Thorn, on the Order's side of the river Drwęca, the border agreed at Melno. The mill had caused friction since 1292. Destroyed and rebuilt on several occasions, its demolition was ordered in the only clause of the Breslau verdict favourable to Poland. It was rebuilt, but Melno again decreed its destruction, although Vytautas unexpectedly supported the Order over the issue during the negotiations. In 1423–4 he backed it over the border between Poland and the Neumark, and in November 1425 he raised the matter following intensive lobbying from Rusdorf. In 1426 he even suggested that if the Poles insisted on the mill's demolition he would return Palanga to the Order.[13]

Melno did not so much drive a wedge between Vytautas and Jagiełło as indicate that Polish and Lithuanian interests were diverging. Vytautas supported the Order over its border with Poland not out of spite, but because he needed peace in the west to pursue his ambitions in the east, where the opportunity afforded by Vasilii I's death in 1425 and the succession of Vytautas's grandson and ward, the infant Vasilii II, was too good to miss. With Muscovy neutralized, he launched campaigns to subdue Pskov (1426) and Novgorod (1428).[14] Far from indicating a Machiavellian policy to undermine Jagiełło, the Lübitsch dispute reflected Vytautas's impatience at Polish wrangles over the border, which delayed Melno's ratification and threatened stable relations with the Order. It was Polish politicians, not

---

[11] See the critical review by Sperka and Kurtyka of *Polska i Litwa wobec husyckich Czech*, and their reply to Nikodem's objections to it: *RH*, 70 (2004), 245–50; 71 (2005), 309–19.
[12] Halecki, *Dzieje*, i, 222–4.
[13] Lückerath, *Rusdorf*, 58–67; Błaszczyk, *Dzieje*, ii/i, 467–70.
[14] Błaszczyk, *Dzieje*, ii/i, 494–502.

Jagiełło, who proved obstinate; far from being obstructive, Jagiełło supported the Pskov and Novgorod campaigns, in which many Poles fought.

Vytautas and Jagiełło cooperated on another front. Sigismund faced a serious challenge to Luxembourg authority in Bohemia after the 1415 execution of Jan Hus following his condemnation for heresy at Constance. In August 1419 Wenzel, King of Bohemia, died with characteristic bad timing at the height of a rebellion that erupted in Prague in July. Although Sigismund's rights to the throne were not initially questioned despite the fact that Hus had travelled to Constance under a safe-conduct he had issued, his aggressive response united moderate and radical Hussites. Sigismund managed to have himself crowned in July but was already losing control. Outmanoeuvred and defeated in battle, on 7 July 1421 he was deposed by the Bohemian estates. The throne remained vacant until 1436, which stimulated intrigue and instability across central Europe.

The Hussite challenge enabled Jagiełło and Vytautas to force Sigismund to abandon his support for the Order during the last years of the war. They had to tread carefully, however. Support for Hussitism after the declaration of a crusade against it by Martin V in January 1420 risked squandering the political capital amassed at Constance. Yet there was considerable sympathy for Hussitism in Poland: many Poles had studied in Prague, and knew Hus and his circle, while Hussite resistance to the dominance of German culture struck a chord. The danger that Hussitism would seep into Poland worried authorities in church and state alike.[15]

Jagiełło's dilemma was exposed in May 1420 when the Hussites offered him the Bohemian crown. He played for time, replying that he could not accept without consulting his advisors. An assembly in Łęczyca in July rejected the idea, although it allowed Jagiełło to give an equivocal answer to put pressure on Sigismund.[16] A second Bohemian delegation informed Jagiełło of Sigismund's misdeeds; it was told he could not respond without consulting Vytautas and an assembly was called to Niepołomice in November, which again rejected the offer.[17] The Bohemians, however, received hints from Jagiełło and the anti-Luxembourg Szafraniec brothers that they should persevere. Another embassy travelled to Lithuania, where Jagiełło was wintering. When the Bohemians arrived in February, Jagiełło refused to accept the crown; they responded by offering it to Vytautas.

It was difficult for Jagiełło to accept the offer given the hostility to Hussitism of most of his councillors. For Vytautas to explore the possibility was another matter, and his envoys travelled to Bohemia in the autumn. Sigismund, aware of the danger, suggested that Jagiełło marry his daughter or sister-in-law, with Silesia as the dowry. The Polish council, keen to recover Silesia, accepted the offer, and Zawisza the Black was despatched to negotiate arrangements. If Jagiełło was to

---

[15] Stanisław Bylina, 'Oddźwięki husytyzmu w królestwie polskim', in Bylina, *Hussitica: Studia* (Warsaw, 2007), 163–79.
[16] *Annales*, xi, 133–6; Sperka, *Szafrańcowie*, 132–3; Krzyżaniakowa and Ochmański, *Jagiełło*, 273–6.
[17] *Annales*, xi, 142. Długosz confuses the timing of the embassies: Jerzy Grygiel, *Życie i działalność Zygmunta Korybutowicza* (Cracow, 1988); 16–21.

avoid a marriage he did not desire, he needed Vytautas's support. At their annual meeting, following a papal declaration of neutrality, they seized the opportunity afforded by the Hussite victory at Kutná Hora (21–22 December 1421), where Zawisza was captured. They agreed that Jagiełło should marry Sonka, and that Vytautas should accept the Hussite offer. Vytautas sensibly refused to go to Prague himself; Jagiełło's nephew Sigismund Korybutovych, duke of Novhorod-Siversky, was despatched to secure Bohemia in his name.[18]

Thus for all the subsequent cooling of Vytautas's relationship with Sonka, the marriage resulted from the cousins working in their common dynastic interest against a powerful group on the Polish council. There is no reason to doubt Długosz's view that Korybutovich's mission had Jagiełło's approval. Nikodem's attempt to demonstrate that Vytautas's acceptance of the Bohemian offer was intended to undermine Jagiełło and stress Vytautas's position as an independent prince is convoluted and as unconvincing as Halecki's suggestion that his acceptance was due not to ambition, but an attachment to the idea of union as a general political principle, or Jučas's view that his main aim was to assert Lithuanian sovereignty.[19] Although the expedition was officially Lithuanian, and Jagiełło repeatedly denied that he had sanctioned it to the German electors and the Polish episcopate, the majority of Korybutovich's 2,500 troops were Poles recruited from the Cracow palatinate. It is implausible to suppose that Jagiełło did not know or approve.[20]

Although Prague gave Korybutovich a hero's welcome in May 1422, his expedition failed. His force was too small; in early 1423, as the Hussite radicals under Jan Žižka seized control, the perils of Polish-Lithuanian involvement became evident. Korybutovich navigated the rough waters of Bohemian politics skilfully enough, but if the intention was to force Sigismund of Luxembourg to settle, as seems likely, the ploy was successful. In March 1423 the 1412 Lubowla treaty was renewed at Kežmarok, where Sigismund promised not to aid the Order.[21] Jagiełło and Vytautas officially turned against the Hussites, and Korybutovich was forced to withdraw, although he returned to Bohemia between 1424 and 1427 on his own account, probably with tacit support from Jagiełło and Vytautas: the pro-Hussite Szafraniec brothers, the cornerstones of the court party, assisted his preparations.[22] Despite Kežmarok, the crushing of the Hussites was not necessarily in the Gediminid interest.

Until 1424 the relationship between Jagiełło and Vytautas functioned much as before. They by no means agreed on everything, and their winter meetings could be stormy, but they used them to thrash out a common position on important matters. It was Władysław's birth, not geopolitics, that radically changed the assumptions upon which relations between the cousins, and between Poland and

---

[18] *Annales*, xi, 164–5. Długosz's account is confused: Sperka, *Szafrańcowie*, 141–2; Grygiel, *Życie*, 25–31, 39–53.
[19] Nikodem, *Polska*, 218–39, 265–73; Nikodem, *Witold*, 333–9; Halecki, *Dzieje*, i, 225–6; Jučas, 'Vytautas ir Čeku husitai', in *Vytautas Didysis ir Lietuva*, 43–53.
[20] Grygiel, *Życie*, 56–8.   [21] Grygiel, *Życie*, 113–14; Sperka, *Szafrańcowie*, 145.
[22] Błaszczyk *Dzieje*, ii/i, 492–3; Grygiel, *Życie*, 77–104. Nikodem has problems explaining Vytautas's volte-face: *Witold*, 349–51.

Lithuania, had been based since 1413. For the rest of his life, Jagiełło fought to secure his sons' hereditary rights in both Poland and Lithuania. His campaign had serious implications for Vytautas and for Jadwiga, recognized as Jagiełło's natural heir in 1413. Yet despite Nikodem's assumption of a natural clash of interests between the new Jagiellon dynasty and the interests of the Kęstutids, there is no indication that 1424 changed much.

There is plenty of evidence that Jagiełło still trusted Vytautas. When Jadwiga reached marriageable age in 1420, Jagiełło approached Frederick von Hohenzollern, margrave of Brandenburg, supporter of the Order, and Sigismund's ally. In April 1421, in return for signing an alliance against the Order, Frederick secured the betrothal of his infant son Frederick to Jadwiga. Vytautas was to be his guardian, with every prospect of dominating the union after Jagiełło's death. Nothing changed on Jagiełło's side after the birth of his sons. Given his advanced age, Jagiełło needed Vytautas to protect their interests after his death, which was bound to occur before they reached their majority. Sonka was energetic and capable, but she lacked Vytautas's experience and the respect he enjoyed among Polish politicians. There was no compelling dynastic reason for Vytautas to scheme against Jagiełło's sons: he had no son of his own, and, despite Nikodem's assertions to the contrary, there is no evidence that he showed any interest in the claims of his brother and nephew: they were not mentioned in Horodło, and he subsequently gave no indication that he was grooming them to succeed him. His dynastic hopes were invested in his grandson, whose position in Moscow was precarious. Vytautas's campaigns against Pskov and Novgorod were expensive failures, however. Several Ruthenian princes paid him homage, but such acts were cheap, and Muscovy energetically resisted his bid for control of Pskov and Novgorod.

To pursue his eastern ambitions Vytautas needed Jagiełło's support, while Jagiełło needed Vytautas's backing to secure recognition of his sons' rights to the Polish throne ahead of Jadwiga. For if Horodło stipulated that an election would only be held if Jagiełło lacked heirs, it was agreed when Anna of Celje was still alive. The position of sons born of a commoner he had married against council advice was unclear. Jagiełło used a lavish christening in February 1425, to assert Władysław's hereditary right to the throne, but it was by no means obvious that his birth eclipsed Jadwiga's claim.[23] As in 1370 and 1382, it was likely that the community of the realm would insist on having its say. Far from falling out over the succession, Jagiełło and Vytautas appear to have worked closely together, and Jagiełło was well aware of the importance of keeping Vytautas's trust: on hearing of Władysław's birth, instead of rushing to Sonka's side, he headed for Lithuania to consult with his cousin. It was not until early 1425 that he returned to Poland to see his son.[24]

Jagiełło now seized the initiative. He began collecting oaths of loyalty from towns across Poland to Władysław as *verus dominus et heres*, who would inherit the

---

[23] Wojciech Fałkowski, 'Król i biskup: Spór o rację stanu Królestwa Polskiego w latach 1424–1426', in Kiryk and Noga (eds), *Oleśnicki*, 126–7; Stanisław Roman, 'Konflikt prawno-polityczny 1425–1430 r. a przywilej brzeski', *CPH*, 14/2 (1962), 64–5.

[24] Fałkowski, 'Król', 124–7.

throne ahead of Jadwiga. Starting in Cracow on 28 February, he travelled to Wielkopolska gathering declarations; twenty-five have survived. Initially, Sonka was made protector of her sons' interests, but with the agreement of the Polish council, Vytautas was appointed their guardian in the event of Jagiełło's death. He would thus play a central role in maintaining their natural rights to the throne. Given his dominance in Lithuania and Polish support for the union, his position on Jagiełło's death would be powerful indeed.[25]

Jagiełło certainly needed Vytautas's support. The success of his oath-gathering in the cities encouraged him to extend it to the nobility, with leaseholders on royal estates targeted first.[26] Yet if most starostas promised to surrender royal castles under their control to Władysław on Jagiełło's death, resistance soon flared. Jagiełło therefore summoned a general assembly in Brześć, hoping to secure an agreement. It proved willing to recognize Władysław as Jagiełło's heir, but there was a price to pay. On 30 April it presented its terms. Władysław was to be accepted as hereditary successor to the Polish throne, but the provisional nature of that acceptance was stressed. Before being crowned he was to swear to uphold all rights and privileges conferred by previous monarchs, and to a new set of privileges. If he did not, the community of the realm would consider itself free of any commitment to him.[27] A general privilege giving Jagiełło's consent was prepared by the royal chancery and sealed on 1 May.[28] Yet it was not issued, and was retained in the royal archive. Without Jagiełło's formal ratification, the assembly declared that its own document, sealed by all who publicly assented to it, should be consigned for safekeeping to Zbigniew Oleśnicki, to be presented to Jagiełło when he issued his formal consent.[29]

Why did Jagiełło not ratify the privilege? It was traditionally argued that he had second thoughts, and wished to consider the matter at greater length before committing himself.[30] His reluctance to accept the offer, however, is evident in the privilege's text, which differs from the document presented to him the day before. While some differences were minor, those concerning the throne were not. Władysław had been designated the 'true and legitimate successor', whereas the assembly's document omitted the term '*legitimus*', and distinguished between the hereditary princes of the Piast line, and 'natural and elected' rulers. Finally, Jagiełło's privilege did not contain the crucial clause requiring his heirs to confirm the rights and privileges granted by his predecessors before their coronation.[31] The assembly's formulation reminded Jagiełło that he held the throne not by hereditary right, but by his 1386 election, which had been reconfirmed on Jadwiga's death. Jagiełło countered by inserting '*legittimus*', thereby suggesting that Władysław had a

---

[25] Halecki, *Dzieje*, i, 238–9; Šležas, 'Vytauto', 192–3. Nikodem's suggestion that Jagiełło, having appointed Vytautas as guardian, suddenly lost faith in him and attempted to appoint Rusdorf in his place rests on a slender source-base and several questionable assumptions: *Witold*, 375–6.
[26] Fałkowski, 'Król', 127–9.   [27] *Liber*, no. 51, 118–19; Fałkowski, 'Król', 133–6.
[28] *CESXV*, ii, no. 149, 187–92.   [29] Roman, 'Konflikt', 64–91.
[30] For example Halecki, *Dzieje*, i, 238.
[31] *CESXV*, ii, no. 149, 187. 'quas a predicto patre suo et aliis regibus principibus ducibus heredibus et dominis regni Polonie tam naturalibus quam electis': *Liber*, 119; Fałkowski, 'Król', 134–5.

natural right to succeed his father, and denying that Polish kings held their thrones conditionally by election.

The stakes were high. A victory for Jagiełło would secure his dynasty's hereditary right to the Polish throne; to accept the assembly's demands would constitute a public concession of the right of the community of the realm to select its rulers from within the dynasty, a principle that Jagiełło had never publicly accepted. Thus the suggestion that it was Jagiełło who, after reaching agreement with the assembly, had second thoughts is wide of the mark. It is more likely that the privilege was drafted to indicate the limits of what he was willing to concede, and was rejected by the assembly: Długosz observes that the reason for Oleśnicki retaining the assembly's document was to hold it until Jagiełło issued a document identical in its wording.[32] The privilege languishing in the royal archive was not, and Jagiełło left to ponder and consult with Vytautas.

There was much to ponder. The consequences of accepting the conditional basis of royal authority had been demonstrated in 1422, when, at the climax of the war against the Order, the noble levy refused to leave its Czerwińsk camp unless Jagiełło confirmed the szlachta's existing privileges and granted new ones. Most were economic in nature, but several clauses placed new restrictions on the monarch. The most significant stipulated that he would no longer have the power to confiscate noble estates without previously securing a judgement in a court of law. Court verdicts were to be based on written law, and the king himself was to be subject to the law in boundary disputes with nobles. He was no longer to mint coins without council permission. Even more damaging was the stipulation that the office of starosta, the monarch's main official at the local level, could no longer be held together with that of land judge. Equally worrying was the 1423 Warta statute, agreed at an assembly held there in Jagiełło's absence, which adjusted Polish land law in the light of the new privileges.[33]

Jagiełło ratified the Warta statute, but after Władysław's birth he was unwilling to accept further limitations on the authority he hoped to bequeath him. He did not intend to leave his heirs open to the sort of blackmail he had faced at Czerwińsk. He responded immediately, issuing an edict in Wieluń in 1424 which decreed that any Poles fighting for the Hussites who did not obey the call to return from Bohemia by Ascension Sunday would have their moveable and immoveable property confiscated in a direct challenge to a central clause in the Czerwińsk privileges.[34]

Jagiełło's backbone was stiffened by Vytautas and Sigismund of Luxembourg. Sigismund advised him to hold firm, maintaining that his subjects were required to accept Władysław by divine law, and urged him to gather oaths individually from office-holders. Jagiełło decided to make a stand. On 19 May 1426 at an assembly in Łęczyca he hurled down the gauntlet by formally refusing his consent to the Brześć

---

[32] *Annales*, xi, 211.
[33] *VL*, i, 36–8; Stanisław Roman, 'Zagadnienie prawomocności przywileju czerwińskiego z 1422 r.', *CPH*, 11/2 (1959), 73–93; Krzyżaniakowa and Ochmański, *Jagiełło*, 338.
[34] *VL*, i, 38.

terms. It was adroitly picked up by Oleśnicki, who took the document entrusted to him in 1425 and, with an exquisite sense of political theatre, returned it to the floor of the house, declaring that Jagiełło had failed to keep his promise. Outraged nobles slashed it to pieces with their sabres before Jagiełło's eyes.[35]

Oleśnicki was a formidable opponent. He knew Jagiełło well and had an insider's knowledge of the workings of his government. Born in 1389 into a middling noble family—his father was land judge of Cracow from 1405—he had studied in Cracow and Breslau, where he had learned German and obtained a perspective on life and politics outside Poland that served him well. Family connections brought him to court; while serving as a royal secretary he performed the feat that earned him fame and favour: as part of Jagiełło's entourage at Tannenberg he shattered the lance of the Meissen knight Dypold von Kökeritz, who had penetrated the royal bodyguard and was bearing down on the king.[36]

Saving Jagiełło's life was a useful career move, but it was Oleśnicki's intelligence and talent that propelled him up the ladder. In 1411 he was among the envoys sent to John XXIII and began the work in the royal chancery that engaged him until his unexpected elevation in 1423 to the bishopric of Cracow, the wealthiest and most powerful Polish see, a remarkable advance for a man of only thirty-four who, although a canon of Cracow, had not previously held any church office higher than the—admittedly prestigious—provostry of St Florian granted as compensation when Jan Szafraniec was preferred to him for the vice-chancellorship in 1418. This suggests that Oleśnicki, who opposed Jagiełło's third marriage, was already seen as less tractable than Szafraniec, who became a pillar of the court party.

Oleśnicki's revenge came in 1423, when Jastrzębiec was unceremoniously and unwillingly shunted out of Cracow to become archbishop of Gniezno after taking the blame for the 1420 Breslau fiasco. Jagiełło intended to replace him with Szafraniec, but the intervention of a group of Małopolskan lords led by Jan Tarnowski, palatine of Cracow, whose influence had waned, and who had family links with Jastrzębiec, caused a last-minute change of heart. Szafraniec had to content himself with the chancellorship, while Oleśnicki was unexpectedly elevated to a see that was, because of its proximity to the royal court, more politically influential than Gniezno.[37]

Assessment of Oleśnicki as a politician is difficult because of the influence of Długosz's *Annals*. Długosz worked for Oleśnicki for nearly twenty-five years; it was Oleśnicki who suggested that he write his great work; and it was from Oleśnicki that Długosz derived first-hand knowledge of recent political events and a substantial cache of documents, the foundations on which his great history rested, although he did not begin writing it until after Oleśnicki's death in 1455.[38] While Długosz placed a high value on historical accuracy, his presentation of Oleśnicki's life and

---

[35] *Annales*, xi, 216–17.
[36] *PSB*, 23, 776; *Annales*, x/xi, 111.
[37] Sperka, 'Zmiany na arcybiskupstwie gnieźnieńskim, biskupstwie krakowskim i urzędach kancelaryjnych na przełomie lat 1422 i 1423', *TK*, 5 (1997), 139–46.
[38] Stanisław Gawęda, 'Ocena niektórych problemów historii ojczystej w "Rocznikach" Jana Długosza', in Gawęda (ed.), *Długossiana: Studia historyczne w pięćsetlecie śmierci Jana Długosza*

career served a different end. It is not that he simply acted as Oleśnicki's mouthpiece, as many have assumed, but the way in which his account is arranged round Oleśnicki that distorts. Although Długosz treated Oleśnicki as a historical figure, he also symbolized Długosz's conception of Polish patriotism, spearheaded by the church, and was represented as the modern equivalent of St Stanisław, bishop of Cracow, who died a martyr's death on the orders of Bolesław the Bold in 1079.[39]

Oleśnicki's dramatic gesture at Łęczyca in 1426 ensured deadlock in the dispute over the succession, but it was his commitment to the union that put him at the heart of the crisis in Polish-Lithuanian relations that blew up out of a seemingly clear blue sky in 1429, and which has gone down in history as the *burza koronacyjna*: the coronation tempest. It erupted during a meeting of Jagiełło, Vytautas, and Sigismund of Luxembourg at Lutsk in January 1429. Vytautas's grandson, Vasilii II, was present, as was Boris, Grand Duke of Tver, the papal legate, Andrea de Palatio, one of the Mazovian dukes—probably Janusz I—several Silesian, Lithuanian, and Ruthenian princes, and a host of Polish and Hungarian nobles. Ambassadors from John VIII Palaeologus, Erik of Pomerania, Alexander, the hospodar of Moldavia, the Teutonic and Livonian grand masters, and the Tatar khan of Perekop also attended.[40] The summit's ostensible purpose was to settle various disputes between Jagiełło and Sigismund, in particular over Jagiełło's failure to aid Sigismund against the Ottomans, who had crushed the Hungarians at Golubac in Serbia in June 1428.[41] Vytautas mediated, and the assembly discussed Polish-Lithuanian relations with the Order and the Hussite challenge, while Sigismund floated a bold plan to relocate the Order to the Danube to spearhead resistance to the Ottomans.[42]

After days of inconclusive talks Sigismund lobbed a carefully prepared grenade into the proceedings by reviving a suggestion he had first made in 1410, that Vytautas should be crowned king of Lithuania. According to Długosz, when Sigismund raised the matter privately, Vytautas replied that he could not agree without first receiving Jagiełło's consent. Sigismund said that this should not be a problem, promising to take care of the matter. Early the next morning Sigismund, accompanied by Vytautas and Sigismund's wife Barbara, burst into Jagiełło's bedchamber. Chasing out the royal secretaries, Sigismund presented the plan to Jagiełło, who replied that he considered his cousin worthy not just of a royal, but of an imperial crown, scoring a neat point against Sigismund, who had as yet failed to be elected Emperor. He added that he could not agree to such an important proposal without consulting his council. When Sigismund said this was unnecessary, Długosz recounts that Jagiełło, beguiled by Sigismund and welcoming any

---

(Warsaw, 1980), 187–8; Agnieszka Nalewajek, *Dokument w* Rocznikach *Jana Długosza* (Lublin, 2006), 14.

[39] Nikodem, *Zbigniew Oleśnicki w historiografii polskiej* (Cracow, 2001), 14–23.

[40] *Skarbiec*, no. 1465, 99; *Annales*, xi, 240–1, 260–1; *PSRL* xxxv, cols 35, 59; Nikodem, 'Spory o koronację Wielkiego Księcia Litwy Witolda w latach 1429–1430, i: '"Burza koronacyjna" w relacji Jana Długosza', *LSP*, 6 (1994), 60.

[41] Błaszczyk, *Burza koronacyjna: Polska-Litwa 1429–1430* (Poznań, 1998), 44.

[42] Jučas, *Unija*, 155; Krzyżaniakowa and Ochmański, *Jagiełło*, 295.

increase in the power of his Lithuanian fatherland, 'apparently and unexpectedly gave his secret agreement, or rather he neither resisted nor rejected that which was requested'. Vytautas, encouraged by Sigismund, by his friends, 'and even by ... [Jagiełło] himself, who did not appreciate the danger threatening him and his kingdom', informed the Lithuanian council, which welcomed the plan. Vytautas then took the fatal step of sending his secretary, Mikołaj Sepieński, to address the Polish council. Sepieński outlined the proposal, stating that Jagiełło had agreed, but thought it appropriate to consult before announcing it. Vytautas now entered the chamber with his 'prelates and boyars, in the conviction that the Poles, surprised by his presence, could be persuaded to agree'.[43]

If Vytautas believed this, he was swiftly disappointed. Although Jastrzębiec gave no firm opinion on the matter despite rambling on at length, Oleśnicki was brutally dismissive. Observing that a quick decision could not be expected on such a complex matter, he immediately mentioned the union, stating that on marrying Jadwiga, Jagiełło had promised that Lithuania would convert to Catholicism, and would be 'incorporated into Poland and subjected to it'.[44] He stressed that Jagiełło, Vytautas, and other Lithuanian princes had sworn to respect this agreement, which had been renewed at Horodło, where, on Sigismund's advice, Lithuanian nobles had been welcomed into Polish clans. Now, however, Sigismund wished to tear this union apart, and foment war between Poles and Lithuanians.[45] Oleśnicki was supported by Tarnowski and most of the Polish council. After a turbulent discussion in which Jagiełło agreed to withdraw his consent, they returned to Poland, probably leaving Lutsk on 25 January; Jagiełło followed shortly afterwards. Although, according to Vytautas, the cousins spoke before he left, with Jagiełło again expressing his support for the coronation, back in Poland, he was forced to oppose the plan.[46]

The origins and significance of the coronation tempest are controversial, as the sources contain much that is unclear. Although most Polish historians accept Długosz's testimony that Sigismund was the plan's author, Kolankowski maintained that it was Jagiełło's idea: frustrated in his desire to secure recognition for Władysław's unconditional hereditary claim to the Polish throne, Jagiełło saw Lithuania's elevation to the status of a kingdom as a means to put pressure on the Poles over the succession. Since Vytautas had no sons, he would be succeeded by Władysław, who would, by inheriting Lithuania, be well placed to secure the Polish throne, assuming that the Poles wished to continue the union.[47] This interpretation is certainly plausible: Jagiełło had supported a similar plan in 1392, and there had been rumours before, notably in 1398, that he intended to pursue the matter.[48] It is not, however, confirmed in contemporary sources, resting on a passage in the Bychowiec chronicle, compiled in Lithuania in the early

---

[43] *Annales*, xi, 252.   [44] Błaszczyk, *Burza*, 50–1, 54–5.   [45] *Annales*, xi, 253.
[46] Vytautas to Jagiełło, Trakai (?), 17 February 1429, *CEV* no. 1345, 816; Błaszczyk, *Burza*, 56. Nikodem airily dismisses Długosz's testimony, arguing on specious grounds that Oleśnicki 'could not' have spoken so sharply: *Witold*, 403.
[47] Kolankowski, 'O litewską koronę', *KH*, 40 (1926), 386–99; Kolankowski, *Dzieje*, i, 150–3.
[48] Любавский, *Сеймъ*, 24. See Ch. 8, 89–90.

sixteenth century and now largely dismissed as a reliable source for earlier periods.[49] The older chronicles suggest that it was Vytautas, not Jagiełło, who instigated the affair.[50] Lithuanian historians have tended to accept this view. Jučas cites in support an unpublished letter to the Order of 5 December 1428 and summarized by the nineteenth-century historian of Prussia Johannes Voigt, in which Vytautas stated that he intended to strike at his dependence on Poland, which grew day by day, completely break Lithuania's 'increasingly loose' ties to Poland, and found his own realm (*Reich*) so that in the twilight of his days he might set a royal crown on his head.[51] Błaszczyk has demolished this claim: Voigt, not known for Prussian exactitude, was not summarizing an unknown letter, but adding his own interpretation of Vytautas's behaviour after citing Vytautas's letter of the same date, which has been published and which merely provided credentials for one of his envoys.[52] Jučas attempts to brush aside Błaszczyk's objections, but does not engage with his critique. Without this letter, however, there is no corroboration for the much later Bychowiec account, while there is considerable support for Długosz's version: a letter from Rusdorf indicates that the Poles were convinced—and implies that the Order itself believed—that Sigismund was responsible, while if Vytautas had offered Lutsk as a venue, the meeting was Sigismund's idea.[53] Sigismund had form: he had attempted to interest Vytautas in a crown in 1410, but Vytautas had rebuffed the approach.[54] Długosz had no doubts. He entered Oleśnicki's service a mere two years later, and was the bishop's chancellor by 1433, so it is likely he heard his mentor's version of the affair at first hand shortly after the event.

Nikodem, who dismisses much of Długosz's account, since it does not fit his interpretation of the relationship between Jagiełło and Vytautas, accepts that Sigismund was the plan's instigator, but argues that Vytautas must have known of the idea before the Lutsk summit. He dismisses Vytautas's denials as disingenuous, but can produce no evidence that he did know, arguing that Sigismund must have told him because it would have been stupid of him not to.[55] Yet if one looks at the evidence that does exist, such speculation seems wide of the mark. When Sigismund proposed in Lutsk that he meet with Vytautas alone, Vytautas insisted

---

[49] *PSRL* xxxii, col. 153. For the Bychowiec chronicle, see Ch. 33, 413–17.

[50] *PSRL* xxxv, cols. 58, 141; cf. *PSRL* xxxii, col. 64.

[51] Jučas, 'Nejvykęs Vytauto vainikavimas', in *Vytautas Didysis ir Lietuva*, 54–65; Johannes Voigt, *Geschichte Preussens von den ältesten Zeiten bis zum Untergange der Herrschaft des Deutschen Ordens*, vii (Königsberg, 1836), 511. The impression that Voigt was summarizing the letter's content was strengthened when Daniłowicz translated the passage into Polish in his register of diplomatic correspondence: *Skarbiec*, ii, no. 1458, 98.

[52] Błaszczyk, *Burza*, 29–30. Voigt 'war kein kritischer und ordnender Geist': Kurt Forstreuter, *Das Preußische Staatsarchiv in Königsberg: Ein geschichtlicher Rückblick mit einer Übersicht über seine Bestände* (Göttingen, 1955), 55. For Vytautas's letter of 5 December 1428 see *CEV* no. 1335, 805–6 and *Regesta historico-diplomatica Ordinis S. Mariae Theutonicorum* i: *Regesten zum Ordensbriefarchiv*, ed. Walther Hubatsch (Göttingen, 1948–1950) no. 5013, 313.

[53] Jučas, *Unija*, 149–52; *Skarbiec*, ii, no. 1481, 103; Nikodem, 'Spory', ii, 157, 164. Vytautas to Sigismund, November 1428, *CEV* no. 1333, 804.

[54] Любавский, *Сеймъ*, 32.

[55] 'de qua deo teste ante nihil scivimus nec cogitavimus, neque aliquod verbum premisimus': Vytautas to Jagiełło, Troki (?), 17.II.1429, *CEV* no. 1358, 815; cf. Vytautas to the Polish lords, June 1429, *CEV* no. 1358, 836–9; Nikodem, *Witold*, 386–7. Cf. Halecki, *Dzieje*, i, 240.

on Jagiełło's presence.⁵⁶ This demand fits with the way events developed, which suggest that Vytautas genuinely wished to secure Jagiełło's backing.

Although Kolankowski was undoubtedly wrong to see Jagiełło as the plan's initiator, his contention that Jagiełło's attitude to it was formed by the dispute over the Polish succession is plausible. Vytautas's insistence on Jagiełło's presence at his meeting with Sigismund, however, suggests that it may have been he who first saw its potential to break the sour stalemate following the dramatic events at Łęczyca in 1426. Vytautas had shown no inclination since 1424 to challenge the rights of Jagiełło's sons in either Poland or Lithuania, and had been closely consulted at all stages by Jagiełło over the succession. In the context of the failure of his campaigns against Pskov and Novgorod it would have been strange suddenly to alienate Jagiełło, who had supported them, while the Order was unable in its weakened state to provide effective military aid. Support for his ambitious eastern policy from Jagiełło or Władysław, for whom Vytautas would be guardian, was far more likely if the Polish monarchy strengthened its position and therefore its ability to act decisively.

Whether or not Vytautas saw the plan in this light, Jagiełło's initial response was favourable. The picture given by Długosz of a startled, naive, and inept monarch torn rudely from his slumbers and giving his consent without realizing its consequences is unconvincing.⁵⁷ According to Vytautas's account, written shortly after the events—which on this point there is no reason to question—Sigismund, having discussed the plan with Vytautas, then spoke with Jagiełło alone—a circumstance omitted by Długosz—and secured Jagiełło's provisional consent. The following morning Sigismund staged the dramatic scene in Jagiełło's bedchamber, which was not designed to catch him unawares, but to persuade him to repeat his agreement before Vytautas. According to Vytautas—and again there is no reason to doubt him, since Jagiełło, the recipient of the letter, must have known it was true—Vytautas then spoke to his cousin in Lithuanian, which Sigismund did not understand—discussions were being conducted in Ruthenian, which he did—suggesting that he consult with the Polish council before giving his assent. Jagiełło, however, ignored the warning, reiterating his support for the idea.⁵⁸

Thus Jagiełło knew of the plan, and had slept on it. Yet if he calculated that he could thereby put pressure on the Poles, Oleśnicki's intervention and the council's dismissal of the idea disabused him of any such notion. If Vytautas hoped that Jagiełło's support would be enough to persuade the Poles to accept the plan, he was rudely and publicly disappointed. It was the public nature of that humiliation that is the key to understanding the subsequent course of events. For it was Vytautas's precipitate actions in telling the Lithuanians of Jagiełło's consent, and sending Siepieński to address the Polish council, that unleashed the tempest. Perhaps he

---

⁵⁶ Błaszczyk, *Burza*, 42.   ⁵⁷ Halecki, *Dzieje*, i, 242.
⁵⁸ 'Nos vero in lithwanico diximus ad vos: domine rex, non festinetis in isto facto, consiliamur prius desuper cum prelatis et baronibus vestris, et nos similiter facturi sumus. Ad quod vos iterum dixistis: quomodo vobis placeret et gauderetis, immo ad hoc nimium essetis affecti': *CEV* no. 1345, 816. Nikodem, typically, dismisses Vytautas's account, though he fails to explain why he would lie to Jagiełło, to whom he had spoken: *Witold*, 387.

hoped that he could bounce the Poles into accepting the plan, but once the idea had been rejected in his presence and before the Lithuanian council, the matter became one of honour. He could not back down without loss of face.

Whatever the true story—and the surviving accounts paint an all-too-plausible picture of misunderstandings, hasty decisions, and injured pride—a vicious cat had escaped from the capacious bag in which it had long been confined. As Jagiełło wrote to Sigismund in January, the plan raised fundamental questions about the nature of the relationship between Poland and Lithuania. He asked Sigismund to abandon it, since it risked bringing conflict and even war between Poles and Lithuanians, and threatened to dissolve or break the 'agreements, unions and alliances' they had made. The raising of Vytautas to royal status would call into question the hereditary rights of Jagiełło's sons in Lithuania: he pointed out that Vytautas possessed 'many of our lands' only for his lifetime, and that if he were crowned, these lands could be lost to Jagiełło and his heirs.[59]

This letter suggests that Jagiełło's support for the plan had indeed been a ploy to put pressure on the Poles, but a tactic that had worked well in 1398 had backfired badly, and he had no choice but to withdraw his support at the risk of destroying his patiently nurtured relationship with Vytautas. Sigismund, stirring the pot with conspicuous enthusiasm, promptly sent a copy to Vytautas, who complained to Jagiełło that he had internationalized the matter without attempting to settle it privately, as the cousins had always done.[60] Jagiełło squirmed, implausibly claiming that the letter had been sent without his permission by Vytautas's *bête noire*, the vice-chancellor, Oporowski.[61] Whether or not this was true, it did not help. The problem could no longer be resolved by a cosy chat. Vytautas had already turned to the Lithuanian boyars. On 13 February, four days before he wrote his blistering response to Jagiełło, the letter to Sigismund was read out at an assembly in Eišiškės. Vytautas asked the Lithuanians if they wished to be subjects of the Poles and pay them tribute. They replied that they and their forebears had always been free; that they had never paid tribute to the Poles; that they did not wish to; and that they wished to preserve their ancient liberty.[62]

The involvement of the Polish and Lithuanian elites in the quarrel was more significant than the breakdown of relations between the cousins, although the collapse of trust was spectacular enough. The problem was not one of Polish incorporationism confronting Lithuanian separatism, as which it is frequently portrayed.[63] As Oleśnicki recognized, the key issue was the status of Lithuania within the union. Vytautas's testimony demonstrates that what he and the Lithuanians challenged was the idea that Lithuania was subordinate to Poland. Nowhere did Vytautas assert a claim to independent statehood; the coronation plan was more

---

[59] *CEV* no. 1341, 810–11.
[60] Vytautas to Jagiełło, Trakai (?), 17 February 1429, *CEV* no. 1345, 816.
[61] Historians previously accepted Jagiełło's claim, but Nikodem's cogent reasons for rejecting it are accepted by Błaszczyk: Nikodem, 'Spory', ii, 165; Błaszczyk, *Dzieje*, ii/i, 523.
[62] Vytautas to Sigismund, Eišiškės, 13 February 1429, *CEV* no. 1344, 815.
[63] For example Błaszczyk, *Dzieje*, ii/i, 526–30.

to establish that Lithuania was Poland's equal than a separatist demand for the destruction of the union.

The problem was the ambiguous formulation of the union treaties. The Lithuanian claim to equal status was a perfectly valid interpretation of the union as set out in the various agreements from Krewo to Horodło. The use of terms such as *unire* and *confoedere* implied a relationship of equals within an association of peoples or of political communities. Yet it was possible to read the treaties in a different way, for they were equally concerned with the question of lordship—rather than sovereignty, the anachronistic term that dominates much of the historiography—and therefore with royal and dynastic power and the locus of authority within the kingdom and the political community: the *regnum* and the *corona regni*. With regard to lordship, as the Poles made clear during the coronation tempest, Jagiełło held supreme power in his capacity as the head of the Polish *regnum*, into which the grand duchy had been incorporated, although within Lithuania he had, in his capacity as *supremus princeps*, delegated practical authority to his cousin.

The controversy reveals much about the Polish interpretation of the union treaties. In April 1429, the Poles circumvented Sigismund and addressed the Nuremberg Reichstag directly in a document drawn up in the royal chancery, almost certainly by Oporowski. It appealed to the community of a different realm, arguing that Sigismund, as elected king of the Romans, who had no hereditary right to his position, and who was not yet Emperor, did not have the authority to create new kingdoms. In stark contrast, the ruler of Lithuania by hereditary right was Jagiełło.[64] At first sight, this document is relentlessly incorporationist. The grand duchy's Lithuanian and Ruthenian territories, it declared, belonged to the kingdom and *corona regni Poloniae* by agreement, and had been joined to Poland in perpetuity. Vytautas, who was termed a 'lesser prince' (*ducem Lithwanie minus principalem*) had been granted them for his lifetime as a governor. His relationship to Jagiełło was defined in the same canon law terms used in Vilnius-Radom: '*in partem solicitudinis assumpsit*'.[65] His authority was thus contingent, limited, and only granted for his lifetime.

This interpretation was also entirely consistent with the union treaties. As the appeal stressed, Vytautas and the Lithuanians had accepted these terms on several occasions.[66] Yet the Poles also stressed to an international audience that they fully upheld the absolute and unconditional hereditary rights in Lithuania for Jagiełło and his successors that they had denied them in Poland in 1425.[67] This recognition rather undermined the idea that Lithuania had been incorporated in 1386 into an accessory union. For if the Poles did not believe that Jagiełło or his sons possessed natural rights to the Polish throne—as was made crystal clear in 1425—how could

---

[64] *CESXV*, ii, no. 179, 237; no. 239, 240.   [65] *CESXV*, ii, no. 238.
[66] *CESXV*, ii, no. 239.
[67] 'quod, licet prefata terra Lithwanie cum dominiis ipsius necnon suppremus ducatus Lithwanie terrarum ad ipsum dominum Wladyslaum regem Polonie ex successione paterna pleno iure et totali dominio pertineant et pertinent ac pertinere debent, ad ipsum dominum Wladislaum regem eiusque successores et heredes legittimos': *CESXV*, ii, no. 237.

they possess those rights in Lithuania, which, so they maintained, had been incorporated into the Polish *regnum*, and was, therefore, presumably subject to Polish succession law?

This public recognition of Jagiełło's hereditary rights to Lithuania reflected the realization by the Poles that the coronation tempest was threatening to blow the union apart. Should Vytautas die before Jagiełło, there was nothing to stop Jagiełło returning to Lithuania, as he had in 1399 and had threatened to in 1417, to secure the throne for his son. Should Jagiełło die before Vytautas, there was nothing to stop Vytautas accepting Sigismund's offer and crowning himself king, which would constitute the clearest possible demonstration that the 'incorporation' of Lithuania depended on nothing more substantial than a particular interpretation of certain phrases in elegant lawyers' Latin. The success of the working relationship between Jagiełło and Vytautas had been based on Jagiełło's restraint and willingness not to assert his superior position in public. His willingness to seek Vytautas's views on matters of state ensured the success not only of the personal relationship, but of the union itself: Jagiełło would routinely say with regard to substantive matters that he could not decide without consulting Vytautas; he used this excuse to buy time over difficult decisions, and to circumvent opposition among his councillors. As for Lithuania, he largely left Vytautas to his own devices. The partnership worked; it was the breach of these principles that Vytautas complained about over Jagiełło's marriage to Elizabeth Granowska, and, much more vociferously, after the Lutsk assembly. It was the public trumpeting of Lithuania's subordinate status that unleashed his rage.

He stubbornly sought to bring the coronation plan to fruition. The Poles sent three embassies to Vilnius in an attempt to secure an agreement; in one of them they even proposed—clearly with Jagiełło's approval—that Jagiełło should abdicate, and Vytautas should be crowned king not of Lithuania, but of Poland. This attempt to allow Vytautas to save face by granting him the status he craved without conceding on the central issue failed. Vytautas had staked too much on maintaining Lithuania's status; acceptance would have betrayed the Lithuanian elites he had whipped up to support him. Otherwise the Poles remained implacable.

Sigismund was better at launching intrigues than seeing them through. The Poles neatly outflanked him by securing papal support. In such circumstances, Vytautas had little chance of succeeding. He invited a glittering array of guests to Vilnius for the coronation, planned for August 1430, but it turned into a humiliating fiasco. Some came, but despite Vytautas's frantic appeals, Sigismund did not send the crown he had promised, and the Poles ensured that the coronation would have to be postponed by holding Sigismund's embassy to Vytautas at the Polish border in August. Contrary to the claims of some Lithuanian historians, it was not carrying a crown: the Poles merely confiscated documents sent by Sigismund. They made it abundantly clear, however, that they would do everything in their power to prevent the crown reaching Vilnius.

The documents were compromising enough. They revealed that Sigismund intended that Vytautas's heirs should have hereditary rights to his new kingdom, thus guaranteeing Jagiełło's opposition. There was a proposal for a perpetual alliance between Sigismund, both branches of the Order, and Lithuania that would surround Poland. Finally, Sigismund sent a judgement from legal experts at the University of Vienna seeking to allay Vytautas's doubts about the legality of any coronation: his specific concern was over the potential lack of anointment and therefore consecration. Since the Lithuanian church was subject to the archbishopric of Gniezno, it was not clear that the bishop of Vilnius had the right to perform the ritual of anointment. The Vienna professors argued that examples including Sicily, Castile, and Scotland indicated that consecration was not necessary to render a coronation legal.[68]

Sigismund was challenging the whole system of power in eastern Europe established since Krewo, a system that Vytautas himself had done much to construct. For all the political capital that he had invested in the coronation plan, it is clear that Vytautas's approach was not essentially anti-Polish; nor does it seem that—unlike Sigismund—he wished to destroy the links with Poland that had transformed Lithuania since 1386. For all that, one should not take his protestations at face value; there is much truth in his letter to the Polish lords of June 1430, in which he assured them that he had never undertaken any actions detrimental to Poland, and emphasized that he had taken his stance on the coronation because Jagiełło had broken his promise to support the idea, and on account of the harm done to Lithuania's honour.[69] When Jagiełło led another Polish delegation to Vilnius in October 1430, Vytautas, by this time gravely ill with a malignant growth between his shoulder blades, accepted defeat following the failure of one last attempt to bribe and bully Oleśnicki into changing his mind. Vytautas, facing the implacable opposition of the Polish council, reached a compromise with Jagiełło that would have allowed both him and the Lithuanians to preserve their honour. The details are not known, and suggestions that it involved Vytautas being crowned king of Lithuania with a papal, not an imperial crown, which would then be inherited by Jagiełło's sons to create a true union of the crowns, are speculative. Meanwhile Vytautas wrote to Sigismund, swearing that he would never renounce the coronation idea, and complaining that Sigismund had broken his promise to send a crown.[70] The worsening of his condition en route to Trakai on 16 October brought a final resolution. The next day, with Vytautas's health ebbing fast, Jagiełło sent home several Polish councillors, including Oleśnicki and Oporowski, ostensibly to secure council agreement to the proposed compromise, although in all probability it was to remove them from the scene while Jagiełło spoke directly to Vytautas. Whatever the truth, in the days before Vytautas's death on 27 October, the two cousins were reconciled, with Vytautas renouncing his plans, even if the touching picture painted by Długosz owes much to literary imagination.[71]

---

[68] Błaszczyk, *Dzieje*, ii/i, 556, 560.
[69] Vytautas to the Polish lords, Maladzechna, June 1430, *CEV* no. 1358, 837. The published version is erroneously dated 1429.
[70] Vytautas to Sigismund, Trakai, 13 October 1430, *CEV* no. 1456, 944–6.
[71] *Annales*, xi, 300–3; Błaszczyk, *Dzieje*, ii/i, 572–6.

Although the coronation tempest blew itself out on Vytautas's death, the underlying problems were far from resolved. The crisis forced Jagiełło reluctantly to reach agreement over the Polish succession. At an assembly in Jedlnia in March 1430, a new document was sealed to replace the one sabre-shredded at Łęczyca, on which it was closely based. Jagiełło accepted most of the conditions for the recognition of his heirs presented in Brześć in 1425, with the significant omission of the clause in which the community of the realm claimed the right to withdraw its obedience from the monarch if he did not keep his promises: the principle that in the future would be known as *de non praestanda oboedientia*.[72] Jagiełło did not achieve the unconditional recognition of the natural, hereditary rights of his heirs to the Polish throne that he had sought, but the birth of a second son opened the way to a compromise: the assembly emphasized that the community of the realm retained the right to decide which of his sons should succeed him.[73] Thus there would be an election after his death, and the new king would only be crowned, once he had sworn to uphold the privileges granted by his father and all his predecessors.[74] Nevertheless, Jagiełło had not conceded over the issue of the natural, hereditary rights of his heirs, and it was promised that Vytautas would be consulted over the election, demonstrating that even at the height of the coronation tempest, the Poles were adhering to the Horodło agreement: the privileges stressed that on Vytautas's death, the lands that Jagiełło had granted him for his lifetime would return to Jagiełło, his sons, and the *corona regni* with full hereditary rights.[75] While minor amendments were made to the Jedlnia documents in Cracow in 1433 to reflect changed circumstances following Vytautas's death, they did not affect the main agreement.[76]

The Jedlnia privileges failed to avert a crisis over the succession to Vytautas in Lithuania. For the new Lithuanian assertiveness had revealed fundamental problems with the incorporationist model of union that they upheld. Oleśnicki and the Polish council had displayed considerable flexibility in their attempt to give Vytautas a dignified route out of the coronation imbroglio, but if Jedlnia settled the question of the Polish succession, it was by no means clear what would replace the system maintained so effectively in the grand duchy by Jagiełło and Vytautas from 1401 to 1429. The union's future depended upon the successful resolution of that problem.

---

[72] Fałkowski, 'Król', 134–5, 138; Roman 'Konflikt', 78–80.
[73] *CESXV*, ii, no. 178, 234; Roman, 'Konflikt', 82–90.
[74] *CESXV*, ii, no. 178, 234–5.
[75] *CESXV*, ii, no. 177, 229; Anatol Lewicki, *Powstanie Świdrygiełły* (Cracow, 1892), 67.
[76] *CESXV*, ii, no. 212, 308–13; *VL*, i, 40–2.

14
Švitrigaila

The coronation tempest was not driven, as is often supposed, by a desire to establish Lithuanian independence and sovereignty.[1] In a Europe of composite monarchies there were many unions of kingdoms; the raising of Lithuania to a monarchy would have secured its equal status within the union, not its independent statehood. Vytautas defended his position and Lithuania's autonomy with gusto; what he opposed—as did Jagiełło—was the Polish conception of an accessory union: the cousins had a common interest in defending the grand duchy as a Gediminid patrimony within a union of equals: *aeque principaliter*. From 1401, and certainly from 1413, when he helped draft Horodło, Vytautas worked with the grain of the union to encourage the development of a genuine political community along Polish lines among the Lithuanian boyars, through opening up the Lithuanian elites to Polish influences, through the extension to Catholic nobles of the rights and privileges enjoyed by their Polish counterparts, through the Horodło adoption, and through his challenge to the extended Gediminid dynasty. He realized that Lithuania could not establish itself as an equal partner within the union unless its political elite developed into a genuine political community. His Lithuanian protégés, by acting as envoys negotiating with Poles—and with other European powers alongside Poles—and by attending assemblies with Poles, as at Horodło in 1413—became acquainted with a new political reality, a new political language, and a new politics: Błaszczyk identifies fifty examples of Polish-Lithuanian cooperation in foreign relations between 1389 and 1427, many involving Lithuanian participation in joint missions.[2] This did not mean that Lithuanians meekly accepted the Polish view of the union: far from it. The years after Vytautas's death, however, showed how much they had absorbed. By 1430 the clock could not be turned back. While the Lithuanian boyars had by no means been passive tools of their prince before 1386, Vytautas established institutional structures that gave them an increasingly influential voice. They were now ready to take a more active role in shaping the union. This change owed much to Vytautas; it was his most important legacy.

Vytautas was not even buried before conflict erupted over Lithuania's government. Jagiełło faced a dilemma which he discussed with the dying Vytautas.

---

[1] Dundulis, *Kova*, 57–80; Żydrūnas Mačiukas, 'Teisinis Vytauto karūnacijos ginčas', in Kiaupa and Mickevičius (eds), *Lietuvos valstybė*, 272; Jučas, *Unija*, 150; Gudavičius, *Istorija*, i, 273.
[2] Błaszczyk, *Dzieje*, ii/i, table 3, 484–5.

Horodło allowed for the election of a new grand duke after Vytautas's death; it did not require it—a point that is often overlooked.³ The office of grand duke was not made permanent as is often assumed: Horodło stated that *if* the Lithuanians elected a grand duke, they should not do so without consultation, although the form this should take was left vague. The Lithuanian boyars promised to elect as grand duke a candidate nominated by Jagiełło or his successors and the Polish council.⁴ Yet the wording of the main document issued by Jagiełło and Vytautas was subtly different: if the Lithuanian version suggested that the Lithuanians could only choose a candidate presented to them by the Poles, the main document stipulated that the selection of the candidate required consultation between Poles and Lithuanians: the phrase 'and of the lands of Lithuania' was inserted immediately after the formula referring to the Polish council.⁵ Likewise, if in the Lithuanian document it was promised that if Jagiełło were to die without heirs, no successor would be elected in Poland without Vytautas's consent, in the main document the phrase '*baronumque et nobilium terrarum Littwanie*' was inserted.⁶

Yet if Horodło created an expectation that the Lithuanian community of the realm would have its say in the election of Vytautas's successor, there was no requirement for Jagiełło to permit such an election. This was convenient for him, since there was no obvious candidate with whom it would be easy to establish the close working relationship that he had enjoyed with Vytautas. The prospects were not enticing. If Vytautas really did spend the last decade of his life working to ensure that Žygimantas succeeded him, as Nikodem argues, there was no sign that Jagiełło had listened, or evidence that Žygimantas had showed any interest in becoming grand duke on his brother's death. Only two of Jagiełło's brothers were still alive. The elderly Lengvenis was Orthodox and rarely left Mstislau, where he was soon to die. The volatile Švitrigaila, however, was not yet sixty. He had long nursed his smouldering resentment over his treatment. He was bequeathed nothing by Algirdas and received no reward for his 1386 baptism. He developed a profound hatred for Vytautas after being sent to Cracow in chains in 1393. Jagiełło granted him Novhorod-Siversky and western Podolia in 1400, but he lost it in 1402 after rebelling in protest at Vilnius-Radom.⁷ Following a brief Prussian exile, when he took part in raids on Lithuania, he returned in 1404, served in Vytautas's 1404 Smolensk expedition, and was granted lands on the Dnieper. In

---

³ Though not by Halecki: *Dzieje*, i, 295.

⁴ 'promittimus... quod defuncto prefato domino Vitowdo, magno duce Littwanie nullum eligemus, assumemus et recipiemus in magnum ducem Littwanie vel dominum, nisi quem prefatus dominus Wladislaus rex... vel eius successores et prelati, barones, nobiles et proceres regni Polonie duxerint eligendum, statuendum et locandum.' *Horodlės aktai* 30; *AU*, no. 50, 59.

⁵ 'quod predicti barones et nobiles etc. Littwanie post mortem Allexandri alias Witowdi magni ducis moderni nullum habebunt aut eligent pro magno principe et domino Litwanie, nisi quem rex Polonie vel ipsius successores cum consilio prelatorum et baronum Polonie et terrarum Litwanie duxerint eligendos, statuendos et locandos.' *Horodlės aktai* 40; *AU*, no. 51, 67.

⁶ *Horodlės aktai*. 30, 40; *AU*, no. 50, 59; no. 51, 68.

⁷ *PSRL* xxxv, col. 72; Lewicki, *Powstanie*, 68; Jonas Matusas, *Švitrigaila Lietuvos didysis kunigaikštis*, 2nd edn (Vilnius, 1991), 17–20; Любавский, *Областное*, 57–8. Some suggest that Švitrigaila was older, but he was probably born around 1373: Błaszczyk, *Dzieje*, ii/i, 720.

1408 he rebelled again, fleeing to Moscow, then to the Tatars. By September 1409 he was back at Vytautas's court, where he was treated with contempt: Vytautas refused to let him dine at his table, keeping him under house arrest after uncovering his contacts with the Order. Švitrigaila fled in 1418, and was reconciled with Jagiełło in 1419. He struck an uneasy peace with Vytautas in 1420, when he was granted Chernihiv, Briansk, Trubchevsk, and Novhorod-Siversky.[8]

Thereafter Švitrigaila waited as Jagiełło and Vytautas aged. The birth of Jagiełło's sons affected his prospects more than it affected Vytautas, and his support for Vytautas during the coronation tempest after years of rancid hostility indicated that he was capable of subordinating his feelings to his ambition. Immediately after the storm broke, he wrote to Sigismund offering his support; he turned up for the coronation; and as Vytautas lay dying, he pestered him to support his elevation to the grand ducal throne.[9] When Vytautas died, he was ready.

Švitrigaila had more to offer than frustrated ambition. Długosz dismisses him as weak, unstable, and prone to bouts of rage, but as Hrushevsky observes, the only surviving characterizations of him are from hostile Polish sources.[10] Švitrigaila had charisma. He was capable of attracting followers among the disaffected; this cannot entirely have been due to the fondness for drunken revelry to which Długosz attributes his popularity. Długosz grudgingly admits that he had military skills, but condemns his love of intrigue.[11] His political ability was demonstrated in 1430, as he adeptly positioned himself to lead those dissatisfied with the status quo.

After Vytautas's death events moved quickly. According to Długosz, because of his love for his brother Jagiełło decided that Švitrigaila should succeed Vytautas. There is reason to doubt this version of events: Długosz's mentor Oleśnicki left for Poland before Vytautas died, and did not observe events at first hand. Długosz claims this was a deliberate ploy by Jagiełło to prevent opposition to Švitrigaila's elevation.[12] It is more likely that Jagiełło wished to remove individuals who might complicate negotiations with the Lithuanians: Oleśnicki's incorporationist stance during the coronation tempest had been unhelpful, and twelve Polish councillors remained in Vilnius.[13] Jagiełło faced an acute dilemma. Oleśnicki urged him to honour the promise he made at Jedlnia in 1430, and to announce Lithuania's incorporation into Poland. He demanded that Podolia should return to Polish rule now that Vytautas was dead, in accordance with the agreements of 1401 and 1413. Jagiełło refused, however, to endorse the Polish view of an accessory union, which might call into question the hereditary rights of his sons to Lithuania. Yet to grant Švitrigaila the powers exercised by Vytautas was an unenticing prospect. Jagiełło had trusted Vytautas to look after his sons after his death; Švitrigaila was still young

---

[8] Matusas, *Švitrigaila*, 32; Halecki, *Dzieje*, i, 220; Błaszczyk, *Dzieje*, ii/i, 604; Łowmiański, *Polityka*, 137; Любавский, *Областное*, 64.
[9] Nikodem, 'Wyniesienie Świdrygiełły na Wielkie Księstwo Litewskie', *BZH*, 19 (2003), 17–18; Любавский, *Сеймъ*, 63.
[10] *Annales*, xi/xii, 14; Грушевський, *Історія*, iv, 186–7.
[11] *Annales*, xi/xii, 15; Русина, *Україна*, 112.
[12] *Annales*, xi, 303–4.   [13] Błaszczyk, *Dzieje*, ii/i, 617–18.

enough to marry and have sons of his own. To leave his infant sons in Švitrigaila's care would be risky indeed.

Jagiełło was no fool, whatever Długosz affected to believe. A natural prevaricator, he made no immediate announcement, playing for time by transporting Vytautas's body from Trakai to Vilnius and insisting that the funerary ceremonies should last several days. Far from rushing to elevate Švitrigaila as Długosz maintains, other sources suggest that Jagiełło decided to govern Lithuania himself. A 1432 memorial prepared by the Order for Erik of Pomerania stated that Jagiełło did not wish Švitrigaila to succeed Vytautas; three other sources—a bull from Eugene IV, a letter from Rusdorf, and one from Jagiełło to Rusdorf—confirm his reluctance.[14] In his 1431 letter to Rusdorf Jagiełło stressed that he was Lithuania's legitimate, natural, and hereditary ruler, having been nominated by his father with the unanimous consent of the Lithuanian boyars. He had appointed Vytautas grand duke for life on account of his zeal and loyalty. He recounted how Vytautas had returned his lands and the grand duchy to him on his deathbed in accordance with their agreements, apart from his second wife Juliana's dower. He made no mention of any arrangement with Švitrigaila, merely stressing the favours and lands he had granted him and his anger at Švitrigaila's ingratitude.[15] For Švitrigaila, with his burning sense of entitlement, refused to accept Jagiełło's decision. While Jagiełło was organizing Vytautas's funeral Švitrigaila's supporters occupied vital strongpoints, including Vilnius and Trakai castles. At some point—it is not clear when—he was elected grand duke by a substantial number of Lithuanian and Ruthenian boyars and placed Jagiełło under house arrest.[16]

Švitrigaila's bid for power was far more than the act of a disgruntled Gediminid with a corrosive sense of resentment. He was dangerous because, as his election revealed, he enjoyed substantial support. For the first time since 1386, after being whipped up by Vytautas during the coronation tempest, the boyar elites—both Lithuanian and Ruthenian—played a decisive political role. According to the Order's memorial for Erik, when Jagiełło announced his intention of ruling Lithuania himself, the Lithuanian and Ruthenian lords told him that they no longer wished to have him as their ruler, as he had neglected them since becoming king of Poland.[17] Annoyed by Oleśnicki tactlessly dusting off the old documents of union as Vytautas lay dying, they sought to shape their own political future.

How did they envisage that future? Rusdorf reported that feelings were running so high after the coronation tempest that the Poles and Lithuanians wanted to separate from each other.[18] That the union had reached a critical point is not in

---

[14] *CESXV*, ii, no. 208, 300–1; Nikodem, 'Wyniesienie', 8–10; 19.
[15] *CESXV*, ii, no. 191, 257–9; Nikodem, 'Wyniesienie', 17; Lewicki, *Powstanie*, 69–71; Любавский, *Сеймъ*, 65.
[16] Nikodem, 'Wyniesienie', 11–13, 19; Błaszczyk, *Dzieje*, ii/i, 617–21; Matusas, *Švitrigaila*, 41. Cf Lidia Korczak, *Monarchia i poddani* (Cracow, 2008), 22; Любавский, *Сеймъ*, 65; Грушевський, *Історія*, iv, 184.
[17] *CESXV*, ii, no. 208, 300–1.
[18] 'In eyme sulchen wandel unde abeschacht so ist nu etczwas herte czweytracht czwuschen den Polan unde den Lytawen entstanden, so das sye sich von enander meynten zu scheyden.' *ASP*, i, no. 403, 539.

doubt. Yet it should not be assumed that it was on the verge of collapse, even if Halecki's claim that neither Švitrigaila nor his supporters wished to break the union pushes optimism to its limits.[19] Sources produced by the Order need to be used with care: since Tannenberg it had desired the collapse of the union more fervently than ever. Its agents, always on the lookout for sparks of separatist feeling, sought to fan any they found into flames. Rusdorf reported that feeling was running high among both Poles and Lithuanians, and that *both* sides wished to separate. While his testimony reveals the heightened emotions after the coronation tempest, whatever individuals said in anger, the Poles did not want to end the union. As for Švitrigaila, he trod carefully. He stressed to the Order that separation could only be achieved with its help. If this was not forthcoming, he would have no choice but to remain bound to the Poles.

As events were to demonstrate, what Švitrigaila could achieve depended crucially on the Lithuanian elites, who were by no means united. Resentment of haughty Polish demands for Lithuania's reincorporation on Vytautas's death was widespread, and the desire to uphold Lithuanian territorial and political integrity was strong. This should not necessarily be taken as evidence of support for destruction of the union. Jagiełło was detained by Švitrigaila but he was neither deposed—as Jaunutis had been deposed and as Jagiełło himself had been deposed by Kęstutis—nor was he murdered, as Mindaugas and, probably, Kęstutis had been murdered. This suggests that his position as supreme duke and his hereditary rights were not challenged; when the Lithuanians said they no longer wished to be ruled by him, what they meant was that they did not wish to be ruled directly, but preferred the Vytautan system of a separate grand duke governing in Vilnius, as allowed for in the Horodło treaty. Švitrigaila seemed to many to be a better option than rule from Cracow by a supreme duke whose health was visibly failing. When Jagiełło died, Lithuanians had no intention of being governed from afar by the Polish council.

Švitrigaila's election is frequently presented as a breach of Horodło, or even a declaration of independence and the establishment of a sovereign Lithuanian state.[20] Błaszczyk argues that for Jagiełło to recognize Švitrigaila, as grand duke would entail his resignation from his hereditary rights, and the claims of his sons to Lithuania, stressing that Švitrigaila 'stood on the platform of his hereditary and natural rights in justifying his rule, thus rejecting the Horodło model'.[21] Yet if Švitrigaila had a claim, as a son of Algirdas, to succeed Vytautas and—since the succession in Lithuania was not governed by primogeniture—to succeed Jagiełło himself, he owed his position as grand duke to an election that challenged the traditional Gediminid practice of dynastic nomination: Švitrigaila had publicly challenged Jagiełło's right to dispose of the grand duchy as he saw fit. Horodło reaffirmed the supreme duke's right to nominate his successor, but crucially limited it by stressing the need for consultation with the Polish and Lithuanian elites. Thus

---

[19] Halecki, *Dzieje*, i, 274.
[20] e.g. Kiaupienė, '1413 m. Horodlės dokumentų "gyvenimai"', in *Horodlės aktai*, 257.
[21] Błaszczyk, *Dzieje*, ii/i, 620–1; Łowmiański, *Studia*, 418.

regardless of Švitrigaila's motives his election did not constitute a direct challenge to Horodło, but an affirmation of it. For it was from Horodło that the Lithuanians derived their right to participate in the election of their grand duke. In 1413 the Poles had planted a seed; they should not have been surprised at the flower that blossomed seventeen years later. The Lithuanians thoroughly understood the idea of election; what they objected to was Jagiełło's decision to decide the future form of Lithuania's government without consulting them, in breach of his promise at Horodło. Faced with the threat that there might be no election at all, the Lithuanians chose for themselves, just as the Poles had rejected the candidate selected for them in 1382 by Louis of Anjou. While Hrushevsky and Błaszczyk go too far in asserting that Švitrigaila's election was 'completely legal'—it was not under the terms of Horodło owing to the lack of Polish consent—the confusion in the Horodło documents produced deadlock, which the boyars broke by their election of Švitrigaila.[22]

The election challenged Oleśnicki's incorporationist view of union and Jagiełło's decision to govern Lithuania directly; it did not challenge Jagiełło's position as supreme duke, or his hereditary rights and those of his sons; it cannot therefore be seen as an affirmation of Lithuania's sovereign, independent statehood. Jagiełło's response suggests that he grasped this fact, and understood the importance of affirming his suzerainty before the situation ran out of control. He acted quickly to contain the damage by recognizing the election. Having sent Švitrigaila a ring as a symbol of his elevation, on 7 November he formally agreed to keep the peace between Poland and Lithuania and summoned a joint assembly for 15 August 1431 to discuss disputed matters. The document enshrining this agreement stressed his status as supreme prince while addressing Švitrigaila as grand duke. Halecki cites it as evidence that Švitrigaila did not wish to break the union, since the phraseology suggests that the assembly would discuss 'all the articles necessary and useful for the establishment of friendship, unity and concord' between the brothers and their realms, taking this to mean the negotiation of a new union, but that is to read too much into conventional diplomatic courtesies. It is probable that Švitrigaila did not wish to burn his bridges until he had sufficient foreign support to mount a real challenge to the status quo.[23] He seems not to have paid much attention to the wording: the phrase recognizing him as grand duke states that he would 'govern in peace and tranquillity [these] lands of our kingdom of Poland', which neatly emphasized both his subordinate status and the incorporationist Polish position.[24] This suggests he did not intend to keep his promises, and too much weight should not be placed on this document, or another agreement on 29 November between Jagiełło, Švitrigaila, and several Lithuanian lords, in which Jagiełło agreed to hand over four castles in western Podolia seized by Poles after Vytautas's death, which Švitrigaila would return to him and his heirs if the Poles did not recognize the

---

[22] Грушевський, *Історія*, iv, 188; Błaszczyk, *Dzieje*, ii/i, 693.
[23] Halecki, *Dzieje*, i, 276; Nikodem, 'Wyniesienie', 25.   [24] *CEV*, no. 1461, 950.

7 November agreement, if the Poles and Lithuanians failed to reach an agreement, or if Jagiełło should die.²⁵

Conflict was inevitable. On 6 December the Polish council deplored Jagiełło's detention and declared his confirmation of Švitrigaila's election illegal. While radical solutions were discussed and provision was made to use force to free Jagiełło if necessary, moderate influences prevailed: an embassy led by Oleśnicki was despatched to negotiate.²⁶ It never reached Lithuania, for Švitrigaila released Jagiełło, although he was briefly detained again when Švitrigaila learned that the Poles had refused to return the Podolian castles, and Jagiełło did not return to Poland until February, where, at a council meeting in Sandomierz, he was attacked for recognizing Švitrigaila without Polish consent.²⁷

It was not just Jagiełło who was playing for time. Immediately after settling with Jagiełło, Švitrigaila wrote to Sigismund of Luxembourg and Rusdorf proposing an alliance. He suggested that Jagiełło be included in the pact, offering to act as mediator in the disputes between Jagiełło and Sigismund, but the proposal was not serious: Švitrigaila asked Sigismund to send him the crown intended for Vytautas, while Sigismund, who agreed with alacrity, brusquely rejected negotiations with Jagiełło.²⁸

Švitrigaila's approach to the Order was crowned with a defensive alliance signed at Christmemel on 19 June 1431, guaranteeing him military support in the event of a Polish attack.²⁹ Later that year he gave a clear indication of his intentions by marrying Anna of Tver, who bore him a son in December 1432.³⁰ Although it is unclear how long he lived—the fact that his name is unknown suggests it was not long—the fact that Anna was fertile was significant. Švitrigaila intended to found his own dynasty; the threat to Jagiełło's sons was evident.

---

²⁵ *Skarbiec*, ii, no. 1521; no. 1522, 112; Halecki, *Dzieje*, i, 279; Błaszczyk, *Dzieje*, ii/i, 627. Vytautas had accepted Polish garrisons in several Podolian castles, on condition that this did not predetermine the dispute over the status of western Podolia: Любавский, *Областное*, 58.
²⁶ Nikodem, 'Zbigniew Oleśnicki wobec unii polsko-litewskiej, i: Do śmierci Jagiełły', *NP*, 91 (1999), 130–2.
²⁷ Błaszczyk, *Dzieje*, ii/i, 630.
²⁸ *CEV*, no. 1464, 953–5; *Skarbiec*, ii, no. 1519, 112.
²⁹ *Die Staatsverträge des Deutschen Ordens in Preussen im 15. Jh.*, ed. E. Weise (Marburg, 1970), no. 171, 183–5.
³⁰ Błaszczyk, *Dzieje*, ii/i, 622.

15
Rus′

There is no reason to doubt that Švitrigaila was seeking the means to effect a complete break with Poland. It does not follow, however, that those who elected him shared this aim. His prospects depended not on the foreign aid he could muster, but on his ability to sustain his support. He had been elected not by a united political nation demanding its independence from Poland, but by a coalition of the disaffected, and from the outset there were tensions among his followers. His survival depended upon him securing backing from Vytautas's supporters, who had flourished since 1413. Yet their support was not guaranteed. For there was one way in which Švitrigaila's election did breach Horodło. He had been elected by both Lithuanian and Ruthenian nobles, whereas Horodło had extended the privileges of the Polish szlachta only to Catholics. Although Švitrigaila was Catholic, he drew considerable support from the Ruthenian territories, where he had been granted estates by Jagiełło and Vytautas when not rebelling against them. He had long cultivated Ruthenian support and it was Ruthenian lords, led by Prince Dashko [Fedorovych Ostrozky] of Ostrih, who sprang him from captivity in March 1418.[1]

If Švitrigaila's Ruthenian support made him dangerous, it also rendered him vulnerable. The breaking of the union would not see the establishment of anything corresponding to the modern nation state of Lithuania, but a composite realm whose viability would be in serious doubt. The union had fundamentally altered the relations between its Lithuanian and Ruthenian elites, and between Lithuania proper and the annexed territories. If the adoption of Catholicism was a deliberate attempt to preserve a separate Lithuanian identity from the threat of absorption by Ruthenian culture and the Ruthenianization of the dynasty, the creation of a new, privileged Catholic elite raised questions about the grand duchy's internal coherence: the privilege of 20 February 1387 was extended only to those professing the Christian faith—which meant Catholics. It excluded all those who, having accepted Catholic baptism, subsequently abandoned the faith, or those who refused to convert. In another privilege of 22 February Lithuanians were banned from marrying Ruthenians who did not convert. Orthodox exclusion was institutionalized

---

[1] The Russian chronicles stress his Catholicism, while Długosz criticizes him for the favour he showed the Orthodox: *Annales*, xi, 303; Horst Jablonowski, *Westrußland zwischen Wilna und Moskau* (Leiden, 1961), 115; Błaszczyk, *Dzieje*, ii/i, 722; Lewicki, *Powstanie*, 51; Mikhail Krom, 'Die Konstituierung der Szlachta als Stand und das Problem staatlicher Einheit im Großfürstentum Litauens (15./16. Jahrhundert)', *JGO*, 42 (1994), 487.

at Horodło: privileges were extended to: '*predicti nobiles, proceres et boyari terrarum Littwanie*'. The absence of the term '*ac Russie*' was no accident.²

Lithuania had expanded as rapidly as it had and had sustained itself as effectively as it did because of its ability to encompass and satisfy the Orthodox elites at the head of a substantial majority of its population. Just how substantial is unclear. Plokhy accepts a ratio of one to twelve for 'Lithuanian ethnic territories to those settled by eastern Slavs' for the mid fifteenth century, but this begs the question of what constituted Lithuanian ethnic territory.³ Given that the area of Lithuanian settlement was much broader than the boundaries of the present-day Lithuanian state, and was more densely populated than the Ruthenian territories, this estimate is dubious. Błaszczyk calculates that Lithuanian territory constituted ten per cent of the grand duchy under Vytautas, while Łowmiański claims that circa 1400 the Lithuanians constituted up to twenty per cent of the population. Whatever the true figure, which probably lay within this range, the balance was more even among its noble elites, with Błaszczyk suggesting a fifty–fifty split for the late fifteenth century.⁴ The disparity between the estimates stems partially from differing definitions of who belonged to which ethnic group in a society in which Lithuanian nobles increasingly spoke Ruthenian, noble intermarriage was not uncommon, and many families had a hazy view of their forebears once they slipped from living memory.

Before 1386 the disparity in population was not particularly significant in political terms on account of the grand duchy's composite structure which, as Hrushevsky observes, was very similar to that known by its Ruthenian subjects before they came under Gediminid rule.⁵ The establishment of Gediminid princes in Ruthenian duchies, where they converted to Orthodoxy and rapidly assimilated, meant that the absorption of large areas of what had been Kievan Rus' made little practical difference to the local population. Grand dukes guaranteed that Ruthenian laws, privileges, and customs would be respected, encapsulated in the concept of *starina* (the old ways). Grand dukes regularly reassured their Ruthenian subjects with the phrase 'we shall neither disturb the old, nor shall we introduce the new' (старини не рушаем, а новини не вводим).⁶ Ruthenian influence on the formation of the Gediminid composite state was considerable. Kievan Rus' was a sophisticated political culture long before the unification of the Lithuanian tribes

---

² *Horodlės aktai*, 41; *AU*, no. 51, 70; *ZPL*, 1–2; Wiktor Czermak, 'Sprawa równouprawnienia katolików i schizmatyków na Litwie (1432–1563)', *RAUWHF*, serya ii, 19 (1903), 353–5.

³ Serhii Plokhy, *The Origins of the Slavic Nations* (Cambridge, 2006), 85; Jablonowski, *Westrußland*, 21–2. Shabul'do accepts the standard Soviet claim that eastern Slavic territories constituted 90% of the grand duchy: Феликс Шабульдо, *Земли юго-западной Руси в составе Великого княжества Литовского* (Kyiv, 1987), 92.

⁴ Błaszczyk, *Litwa na przełomie średniowiecza i nowożytności 1492–1569* (Poznań, 2002), 8; Łowmiański, *Studia*, 390–2.

⁵ Грушевський, *Історія*, iv, 159.

⁶ Наталя Яковенко, *Українська шляхта з кінця XIV до середини XVII ст.*, 2nd edn (Kyiv, 2008), 19; Михаил Кром, '"Старина" как категория средневекового менталитета (по материалам Великого княжества Литовського XIV–начала XVII вв.)', *Mediaevalia Ucrainica*, 3 (1994), 68–85.

into a recognizable polity, and its political structures, political culture, and legal norms greatly influenced Lithuania's development. Since Lithuanian was not a written language, Ruthenian became the language of government, of much diplomatic contact, and of the law, while even pagan Gediminids sustained courts where Ruthenian cultural influence was powerful. The Ruthenian contribution to Lithuania's development should not be exaggerated, yet if Rowell is right to signal that it did not really begin until the end of the thirteenth century, his downplaying of Ruthenian influence after 1300 is questionable.[7] Vytautas's mother was pagan, but he himself married two Ruthenian wives; both of Algirdas's wives were Orthodox princesses, and Jagiełło's mother Juliana lived in Vilnius for thirty years, giving her husband's court a powerful Ruthenian ambience (see Figs 7 and 8).[8] Thus if Jagiełło was bilingual, Ruthenian was his mother tongue, although that did not make him Ruthenian: in 1387 he indicated where his loyalties lay by stressing the differences between the Ruthenians and *'omnes nacione Lithvanos'*.[9]

The reality of Ruthenian influence upon the grand duchy's development long ago ignited a controversy about whether it was in origin and nature a 'Lithuanian' or a 'Russian', or, indeed, a Belarusian state—Ukrainians, who derive their historic claims to statehood more directly from Kievan Rus' and the seventeenth-century Cossack hetmanate, were never quite so bothered. The grand duchy was from the outset a composite polity formed by a cosmopolitan fusion of influences.[10] Yet the choices made by Jagiełło and his supporters in 1385 and 1413 transformed its nature. While the Ruthenian language retained its status, and Ruthenian culture was still influential, the establishment of Catholicism as a new focus for Lithuanian identity marked a radical new departure: there is much to suggest that Jagiełło and Vytautas favoured union in order to preserve the Lithuanians as a distinct people.[11] The assault on the Gediminid dynastic conglomerate and its replacement by a more centralized, authoritarian system signalled a significant change: the dynasty could no longer play the key unifying role that had resulted in the dilution of its Lithuanian nature.[12]

In 1413, Vytautas and Jagiełło took a deliberate decision to treat Lithuania proper differently from the annexed Ruthenian territories and Samogitia: there were no Samogitian boyars among the forty-seven families adopted by the Polish heraldic clans and Samogitia was excluded from the administrative structures established by the treaty. Horodło created a two-tier polity, while Vytautas reduced the considerable degree of autonomy that the southern and eastern Ruthenian lands had enjoyed through the appanage duchies. Even if Horodło applied only to Lithuania proper, and the ban on non-Catholics holding office did not cover the annexed Ruthenian territories, it stated that only Catholics were permitted to counsel the grand duke and consider the public good. Only Catholics could be appointed to major office in the new palatinates of Vilnius and Trakai, which

---

[7] Rowell, *Lithuania*, 295.
[8] Sužiedėlis, 'Lietuva', 32.
[9] Paszkiewicz, *O genezę*, 168.
[10] For the debate see Błaszczyk, *Litwa*, 6–8.
[11] Paszkiewicz, *O genezę*, 170.
[12] Грушевський, *Історія*, iv, 159.

Fig. 7. King Władysław Jagiełło and the Virgin Mary. Fresco from the Holy Trinity Chapel, Lublin Castle, c.1418. The frescoes of the Catholic Holy Trinity Chapel in Lublin were commissioned by Władysław II Jagiełło c.1407, and were painted by Ruthenian artists trained in the Orthodox tradition. They indicate the extent of Ruthenian cultural influence on Jagiełło's court. By kind permission of the Muzeum Lubelskie w Lublinie (Lublin Province Museum). Photograph by Piotr Maciuk.

included many large, preponderantly Orthodox territories.[13] Yet Vytautas also sought to consolidate his lordship and his control of the large number of royal estates scattered across the grand duchy; to this end he rewarded his servants and trusted agents with control over them, spreading Catholic noble administrators across the Ruthenian lands. Nevertheless, it is important not to overemphasize the extent of centralization, or to portray Vytautas anachronistically as a visionary builder of a unitary state.[14] Horodło created a highly complex structure, in which the political relations between the various parts of the composite Gediminid realm

[13] *Horodlės aktai*, 40; *AU*, no 51, 66–7.   [14] Korczak, *Monarchia*, 56.

Fig. 8. King Władysław Jagiełło on horseback. Fresco from the Holy Trinity Chapel, Lublin Castle, *c.*1418. By kind permission of the Muzeum Lubelskie w Lublinie (Lublin Province Museum). Photograph by Piotr Maciuk.

were ambiguous and unclear. This lack of clarity was to cause serious problems after 1430, in Samogitia as well as in the Ruthenian lands.

For all that Vytautas insisted on his respect for *starina* in the annexed territories, and his appointment of Catholic governors and administrators of royal estates did not herald a major challenge to the control of the local elites within them, Krewo and Horodło raised important questions concerning the position of Orthodox nobles. The privileges granted to Lithuanian Catholics in 1387 and 1413 mattered, particularly since, after his assault on the Gediminid appanages, Vytautas's generosity in rewarding his supporters meant that prominent Catholic nobles began amassing holdings of land across the grand duchy's Ruthenian territories, over which they acquired rights after 1387 not granted to the Orthodox. These land grants gradually began to undermine the principle of *starina*, and brought legal problems on account of the different treatment of lands held by Catholic and Orthodox nobles.

Moreover, for all the broad toleration afforded to the Orthodox Church by Jagiełło and Vytautas in a continuation of the pagan tradition, their adoption of Catholicism radically altered the grand duchy's political dynamic. As pagans, Gedimin, Algirdas, and Kęstutis could stand as neutrals between the Latin west and the Orthodox east; as Catholics, Jagiełło and Vytautas could not: paganism had been replaced by adherence to a powerful church that regarded the Orthodox as schismatics. Promotion of Catholicism was not limited to Lithuania proper. The original grant of land made by Jagiełło when he established the diocese of Vilnius in 1387 contained estates round Lida and Bakshty, areas of ancient Lithuanian settlement, but by then largely Ruthenian.[15] The Catholic Church had long sustained small outposts across the Ruthenian lands—the Dominicans and Benedictines were present in Kyiv from the thirteenth century, and Henry, a Dominican friar, was appointed Catholic bishop of Kyiv in 1321, although the diocese failed to establish itself. While the majority of the forty-two parishes in the Catholic diocese of Vilnius by 1430 lay in Aukštaitija and Black Ruthenia, which had a substantial Lithuanian population, Jagiełło and Vytautas granted the Catholic Church estates across the grand duchy: Jagiełło's donation of Streshevska (1391) was followed by Vytautas's grants of Uborch (1412), Kamianets (1415), and Ihumen (1430); this gave the Vilnius diocese a cluster of estates in the middle Dnieper region, with around sixty villages and vast tracts of forest.[16]

Jagiełło and Vytautas were aware of all these problems; they sought to address them through the promotion of a union of the western and the eastern churches, or at least a union of the Catholic and Orthodox Churches within the grand duchy. It was a good moment. Byzantium's retreat in the face of Ottoman expansion had reduced the prestige of the Constantinople patriarchate, while the emergence of Lithuania as the dominant state in eastern Europe provoked a power struggle within the Ruthenian church. Kyiv ceased to be the seat of the metropolitanate of all Rus' in 1299 or 1300, when Metropolitan Maximos abandoned it for Vladimir in the wake of the Mongol devastation of the southern Ruthenian lands. Maximos's successor Peter moved to Moscow in 1325. The separate metropolitanate of Halych-Volhynia founded in 1303, was formally dissolved in 1331 after a successful protest by Teognost, metropolitan of Kyiv and all Rus', then resident in Moscow, against Patriarch Isiaih's recognition of the metropolitan title of Fëdor, bishop of Halych, in 1328. After a failed attempt to revive it between 1345 and 1347, it was re-established in 1371 following a request by Casimir III.[17]

---

[15] Ochmański, *Powstanie*, 20.
[16] Tadeusz Trajdos, *Kościół katolicki na ziemiach ruskich Korony i Litwy za panowania Władysława II Jagiełły (1386–1434)*, i (Wrocław, 1985), 27–38.
[17] Ігор Скочиляс, *Галицька (Львівська) єпархія XII–XVIII ст.* (L'viv, 2010), 195–209.

Tension grew between Moscow-based metropolitans and the grand duchy's Orthodox bishops, who complained that their Church was neglected. In 1375 Patriarch Philotheos agreed to consecrate Cyprian, a Bulgarian monk, as metropolitan of Kyiv, Rus', and Lithuania, although Metropolitan Alexius was still alive, sparking a power struggle in which Constantinople's vacillations saw Lithuanian and Muscovite candidates claiming the title of metropolitan of all Rus', with Muscovy winning a significant propaganda victory when Cyprian moved to Moscow in 1390.[18]

The divisions within the Ruthenian church and Constantinople's declining cultural and political influence thus created a favourable climate for church union. For Jagiełło and Vytautas, church union would provide a neat solution to the grand duchy's major political problem: if Orthodox Ruthenians could be welcomed in some form into the arms of the Catholic Church, then the privileges granted to Catholics could be extended to their elites, thereby securing their loyalty and reducing Muscovy's attraction.[19] In 1396 a meeting with Cyprian, who was visiting Lithuania, led to a proposal for a Ruthenian council to discuss union that was rejected by patriarch Antonius IV, who expressed support but thought the time was not right. Further discussions during Cyprian's next visit in 1405 led nowhere; after his death in 1406 church union disappeared from view.[20]

Jagiełło and Vytautas, absorbed in the wars against the Order, only returned to the idea a decade later, but with a different approach. Cyprian might have moved to Moscow, but he had originally been based in Lithuania and he was willing to listen to and—to an extent—work with Jagiełło and Vytautas. His successor, Fotius, was cut from a different cloth, loyal to Muscovy and its rulers. By 1415 Jagiełło and Vytautas had seen enough. On 15 November a synod of Lithuania's Orthodox bishops in Navahrudak elected Cyprian's nephew Grigorii Tsamblak metropolitan of Kyiv and all Rus' in a direct challenge to both Moscow and Constantinople. In a sharply worded justification of the election sent to Constantinople, Vytautas and the bishops complained at the neglect of the Lithuanian church by its Moscow-based metropolitans, arguing that they were appointed not by synods, but by Muscovite grand dukes, in breach of canon law. Vytautas decried the stripping of the wealth of the Kyivan church when the metropolitanate moved to Moscow, complaining that the patriarch had ignored his request that Feodosius, Orthodox bishop of Polatsk, be appointed metropolitan of all Rus' after Cyprian's death, and that he be based in Kyiv. He played on the Ruthenian sense of tradition by arguing that the return of the metropolitanate to Kyiv would restore the situation to what it had been in the past (*по давному*).[21]

Hrushevsky presents proposals for church union in this period as emanating from Rome for entirely political reasons, suggesting that they lacked support among the Orthodox clergy and Ruthenian society.[22] He offers no evidence in support of

---

[18] Borys Gudziak, *Crisis and Reform: The Kyivan Metropolitanate, the Patriarch of Constantinople, and the Genesis of the Union of Brest* (Cambridge, MA, 1998), 1–6.
[19] Lewicki, 'Sprawa unii kościelnej za Jagiełły', *KH*, 11 (1897), 312.
[20] Chodynicki, *Kościół*, 43; Lewicki, 'Sprawa', 322, 326; Грушевський, *Історія*, v, 509–11.
[21] *AZR*, i, no. 24, 33–5; no, 26, 35–7; Gudziak, *Crisis*, 5–6.
[22] Грушевський, *Історія*, v, 508–9.

this contention. The discontent of Orthodox bishops with Fotius was palpable. Tsamblak's election marked a decision to explore union with Rome on the part of the Lithuanian Orthodox Church alone and not, as in the initiative launched in the 1390s by Jagiełło and Cyprian, on behalf of the whole Orthodox Church. When Tsamblak made a spectacular ceremonial entrance to the council of Constance on 19 February 1418, his entourage contained Ruthenian, Tatar, and Moldavian princes, sixteen Basilian monks, and representatives of Ruthenian communities across Jagiełło's realms.[23] They did not attend on Rome's orders: Tsamblak had an audience with Martin V, whose polite refusal to pursue the matter casts doubt on Hrushevsky's interpretation. Although Tsamblak stayed to the end of the council, no substantive negotiations took place. His magnificent entrance impressed the assembled delegates, but Constance was concerned with ending the schism within the Latin Church; it was unrealistic to suppose it would be willing or able to heal the older and deeper schism with the Orthodox. On Tsamblak's death around 1419 church union and the Ruthenian issue disappeared from sight for a decade and more.

The problems of knowing what the Ruthenian elites thought of these changes are all but insurmountable, as there are few contemporary sources that give access to their ideas. The Ruthenian and Lithuanian chronicles are problematic sources, partly on account of their provenance, partly on account of the fact that many of them were compiled substantially after the events they relate, and partly on account of their particular approach to historical narrative. When they discuss events known from other sources, they frequently turn out to be unreliable. They have been used tendentiously to support various sides in the debate over the formation of the modern Russian, Belarusian, and Ukrainian nations. Despite the importance of the idea of Rus′ to the grand duchy's Ruthenian elites, caution is necessary before ascribing to them the national sentiments of a later age: the fourteenth-century Halych chronicle makes it clear that religion, while important, was not a necessary factor in provoking loyalty to individual princes, with the Black Ruthenians along the river Niemen preferring pagan Lithuanian rule to that of the Orthodox Halych Rurikids.[24] The Ruthenian chronicles—compiled by Orthodox clerics—sought to instil a general Ruthenian consciousness that they were constructing in their own time, rather than reflecting the conditions of the age they purported to describe. Kievan Rus′ was a decentralized polity, whose fragmentation had been exacerbated by the Mongol conquest and the coming of Lithuanian overlordship. There were substantial differences within the Ruthenian lands: Ruthenians living in Lithuania proper, where Ruthenian and Lithuanian populations lived side by side, interacting socially and economically, often intermarrying and assimilating, were in a different position to those living in distant Kyiv or Chernihiv. To postulate the existence of a strong pan-Ruthenian identity and a common set of political demands is to read history backwards. Loyalty was a complex matter, in which ethnic and religious identity undoubtedly played a role, but in which lordship,

---

[23] Lewicki, 'Sprawa', 332.   [24] Plokhy, *Origins*, 1–48, 85–115.

personal ties, and local traditions were equally significant: particularism was usually of more consequence than supposed national loyalties.[25] While the Ruthenian language played a central role in Ruthenian consciousness, it was a double-edged sword since it was also the language of the law and of government in Lithuania proper, where religion, not language excluded Ruthenians from power after 1413.

If the Lithuanian Catholic elites broke the union, they would have to solve the Ruthenian question. Would they seek to maintain their privileged position within an independent grand duchy? If so, the Ruthenians might well compare Lithuanian policies towards them with those of the Poles towards the significant Ruthenian population in the kingdom of Poland. Could the small Lithuanian Catholic elite maintain its control over the annexed territories outside the union, which had let the powerful genie of noble privilege out of its jewelled bottle? There is no indication that Švitrigaila or his Catholic supporters had even broached these questions, let alone developed a political programme to take account of them before the quarrel between Poles and Lithuanians flared into the open warfare that had threatened since 1429. The war was not, however, caused by the quarrel over the nature of the union, but broke out in the annexed Ruthenian territories where Vytautas's death unleashed a bitter dispute over Podolia and Volhynia, which Poles and Lithuanians had contested since 1340. Conflict sharpened after 1392, when Vytautas removed Fëdor Koriatovych as duke of Podolia. Although the Poles claimed that Podolia and Volhynia were integral parts of their kingdom, the situation on the ground was complex and constantly shifting. In 1395 Jagiełło divided Podolia: Vytautas was granted the eastern half, while Jagiełło's Polish favourite Spytek of Melsztyn received the western half with full ducal rights for a substantial payment, of which Vytautas received 20,000 groszy.

When Spytek was killed at the Vorskla in 1399, Jagiełło purchased western Podolia from his widow for 5,000 Prague groszy in order to grant it to Švitrigaila, while Vytautas paid the considerable sum of 40,000 Lithuanian kop groszy for it in 1410.[26] In 1411 Jagiełło postponed the day of reckoning for a generation by granting Podolia to Vytautas for life, although its western half was to remain within the kingdom of Poland. On his death all Podolia was to revert to Poland. Vytautas introduced Lithuanian administration across both halves, although Poles in western Podolia resisted swearing oaths of loyalty to him; only Jagiełło's intervention in 1418, when he stressed that their oaths to himself as king of Poland and to the *corona regni* would not thereby be invalidated, resolved the matter. The Poles still maintained their claims to Volhynia as part of the principality of Halych-Volhynia.[27]

The subordinate position of Orthodox nobles in both Poland and Lithuania was highlighted after 1413. As Poles settled in Red Ruthenia, the contrast between

---

[25] Oskar Halecki, *Ostatnie lata Świdrygiełły i sprawa wołyńska za Kazimierza Jagiellończyka* (Cracow, 1915), 2.
[26] 40,000 *kop groszych*. Nikodem, *Jadwiga*, 345; Любавский, *Областное*, 57–8.
[27] Błaszczyk, *Dzieje*, ii/i, 51–61, 625–6; Janusz Kurtyka, 'Wierność i zdrada na pograniczu: Walki o Bracław w latach 1430–1437' in Kurtyka, *Podole w czasach jagiellońskich* (Cracow, 2011), 219–20, 225–6.

Polish nobles, protected by the 1374 Koszyce privileges, and Ruthenian boyars, who were not, and who were, under Ruthenian law, subject to various burdens imposed upon them by princes or the local starosta, became ever starker, especially after the 1422 Czerwińsk privileges. Ruthenian boyars, unlike Polish nobles, were not entitled to the five marks per spear payable to Polish noblemen for fighting beyond their borders, while they were subject, in addition to the *poradlne*, to tax payments in kind, in oats and rye; others, holding land on service tenures from the king or from great landowners, had to reside on their estates and perform military service according to the terms of the grant.[28]

The contrast between the privileged position of the Polish nobility and their Ruthenian counterparts brought increasing pressure from Ruthenian boyars for the extension of Polish privileges to the Ruthenian territories. Such an extension was promised in a clause of the 1425 Brest privilege to the kingdom's Ruthenian nobles, but the privilege's destruction at Łęczyca meant it did not take effect. The problems were highlighted in 1426 when, at Sigismund of Luxembourg's request, Jagiełło summoned the Red Ruthenian boyars for a campaign against the Ottomans. Sigismund failed to show up, and the 5,000 or so Ruthenians who did kicked their heels for two months in a camp on the Danube in Bessarabia before dispersing. Many stayed at home, demanding their five marks per spear. Jagiełło arrested the ringleaders and confiscated their estates, but his harsh reaction provoked widespread demands for the extension of Polish privileges. Jagiełło was forced to release the prisoners and restore their lands, although he reaped a reward for his magnanimity when some 400 middling and lower Ruthenian boyars swore acts of homage in Halych in June 1427 agreeing to accept the succession of his sons.[29]

The Poles recognized the attractive force of noble privilege during the struggle over Podolia and Volhynia. The 1430 Jedlnia confirmation of the Brześć privileges repeated the clause concerning the extension of privileges to Red Ruthenia; one of the three surviving original copies—drafted for the Sandomierz nobility—qualified it by stating that Ruthenian nobles would still be subject to their traditional burdens, but in their reconfirmation at Cracow in 1433, this phrase was omitted.[30] It was therefore not a surprise when members of the local Polish and Ruthenian nobility in Podolia, led by Vytautas's former chaplain, Paweł of Bojańczyce, the Catholic bishop of Kamianets, took matters into their own hands. On hearing of Vytautas's death they seized several local castles, including Kamianets, and declared their loyalty to the *corona regni Poloniae*. Švitrigaila was outraged, and secured the 29 November agreement over the future of Podolia with Jagiełło, then under house arrest, although the Polish council undermined it by sending secret instructions

---

[28] Janusz Kurtyka, 'Z dziejów walki szlachty ruskiej o równouprawnienie: represje lat 1426–1427 i sejmiki roku 1439', in Kurtyka, *Podole*, 32–3.
[29] Kurtyka, 'Z dziejów', 31–47.
[30] 'eciam terram Russie includendo': *CESXV*, ii, no. 177, 232; Kutrzeba, 'Przywilej jedlneński z 1430 r. i nadanie prawa polskiego Rusi', in *Księga pamiątkowa ku czci Bolesława Ulanowskiego* (Cracow, 1911), 5–6, 16–19; Kurtyka, 'Z dziejów', 47–8.

that Jagiełło's order to implement it should be ignored.³¹ The dispute rapidly escalated into open war. In February 1431 the Sandomierz assembly, outraged by the siege of Smotrych and Lithuanian raids across Podolia, sent an embassy to demand that Švitrigaila apologize for his actions, that he recognize Horodło, and that Volhynia as well as Podolia be handed over to Poland. This amounted to a declaration of war.³² Polish and Lithuanian delegations did meet at Biecz in April, with the Order mediating. The Lithuanians rejected the Polish demands and asked for the restoration of the Podolian fortresses. War was now inevitable. A few days after Švitrigaila signed the Christmemel treaty, the Poles began military action, although war was not formally declared until early July.³³ With a grim sense of irony the first town they attacked was Horodło.

The coming of war by no means indicated that the two sides were irreconcilable. The fighting was not intensive. Jagiełło's forces took Lutsk in August, but a storm of the castle failed, and the two sides began talking. A two-year truce signed at Chartorysk on 26 August 1431 was confirmed by Švitrigaila in early September. Historians have been baffled by Švitrigaila's decision, since three days earlier the Order had fulfilled its obligations by attacking Poland. Newly secure on their south-eastern frontier, the Poles concentrated their forces and again demonstrated that the Order—horrified to learn of the truce—was a shadow of its former self by crushing its army at Nakło on 13 September and driving it back across the border.

It has been suggested that Švitrigaila signed the truce because he had not received Rusdorf's 12 August letter telling him of the invasion. The Order had been preparing for war since Christmemel, however, and it is likely that Švitrigaila knew it, even if he was unaware of the intended invasion date. Hrushevsky, who believed he did know, concluded that even if he did not, the truce demonstrated that he was an imbecile with little military or political talent.³⁴ Yet there were other factors that lay behind the truce. For the Lutsk war demonstrated the fragility of Švitrigaila's support. There was little appetite for war, which suggests that feelings on the issue did not run as high among fifteenth-century Lithuanian or Ruthenian nobles as they did among nineteenth- and twentieth-century nationalist historians.

There was little appetite for war on the Polish side either. Jagiełło's passive conduct of the 1431 campaign is only partially explained by his age. The Poles, as they demonstrated after Švitrigaila's election, were inclined to negotiation, not war. They were well aware that the union could not be sustained by force. After the truce they despatched embassies to Švitrigaila seeking to restore good relations. Lithuanian prisoners were released, and it was even suggested that Švitrigaila be appointed regent after Jagiełło's death, although Jagiełło rejected the idea.³⁵ Nevertheless, at an assembly in Sieradz in late April and early May 1432, the Poles recognized

---

³¹ *Annales*, xi, 311–13; Janusz Kurtyka, 'Podole w średniowieczu', in Kurtyka, Podole, 128–9; Błaszczyk, *Dzieje*, ii/i, 626–7; Любавский, *Областное*, 58–9.
³² *Annales*, xi, 13–14. Грушевський, *Історія*, iv, 195.
³³ Błaszczyk, *Dzieje*, ii/i, 638.
³⁴ Грушевський, *Історія*, iv, 198–9.   ³⁵ Błaszczyk, *Dzieje*, ii/i, 652–3.

Švitrigaila as grand duke of Lithuania on the same basis as Vytautas—a remarkable concession given events since the latter's death.

Švitrigaila would have done well to accept. He did not. The Lutsk war demonstrated the superiority of the Polish armies over his own forces and those of the Order, yet he renewed his alliance with the Order at Christmemel on 15 August. His position was much weaker than it had been in 1431 as Lithuanians abandoned him *en masse* when the extent of his reliance on Ruthenian support became apparent. Loyalty to Jagiełło remained strong, and the conflict rapidly turned into a civil war. As the struggle for Podolia and Volhynia demonstrated, the Lithuanians and Ruthenians had fundamentally different interests: the Lithuanians wanted to assert their rights to lands they regarded as integral parts of the grand duchy, while local Ruthenians, already divided between Poland and Lithuania, were keen to defend their local traditions against centralizing forces from Vilnius and some appreciated the possible benefits of accepting Polish rule over Podolia and Volhynia.

For the Lithuanians, the dangers were all too apparent. All the witnesses to Švitrigaila's first surviving document as grand duke, dated 5 November 1430, were Ruthenians. Although Lithuanian names generally dominate in other documents from the early period of his rule—the first Christmemel treaty was witnessed by one Ruthenian boyar, Khodko Iurevich, alongside eight Lithuanians—the number of Ruthenians grew steadily: among the fifty witnesses to the second Christmemel treaty were over a dozen Ruthenians, and representatives of thirteen Ruthenian towns compared to only three in Lithuania. Švitrigaila acted cautiously, and the rise in Ruthenian influence was gradual: Łowmiański exaggerates when he claims that he sought a complete equalization of the rights of the Orthodox Ruthenians and the admission of Ruthenians to the grand ducal council and all high offices: despite scaremongering by Oleśnicki, who claimed in 1432 that the Orthodox now counted for more in Lithuania than Catholics, Švitrigaila made no appointments that breached Horodło. The only major offices he granted to Orthodox nobles were the governorship of Vitsebsk awarded to Vasyl Drutsky-Krasny, and the starosty of Lutsk, given to Iursha Ivanovich, who had defended it in 1431. Neither appointment was in Lithuania proper. Nevertheless, if Oleśnicki's lurid picture was overdrawn, Švitrigaila did not make a single donation to the Catholic Church in his two years in power, a striking contrast with Vytautas's reign.[36] Whatever Švitrigaila's aims, his policies provoked discontent among Lithuanian nobles, in particular those who had been closely associated with Vytautas. By 1431 opposition, in which the Catholic bishops played a leading role, was growing. Anti-Polish feelings whipped up during the coronation tempest slowly abated. If any Lithuanians had truly sought to break the union, the growth of Ruthenian influence provoked second thoughts.

It was now that the relatively restrained Polish response to Švitrigaila's rebellion paid dividends. After the breakdown of Polish-Lithuanian talks concerning the

---

[36] Lewicki, *Powstanie*, 78–9, 90; Łowmiański, *Polityka*, 143, 150; Błaszczyk, *Dzieje*, ii/1, 669–71.

extension of the truce in February 1432, the Poles adopted a different approach. The offer of the Sieradz assembly to restore the Vytautan system, with Švitrigaila as grand duke and effective autonomy for Lithuania, sent a signal to Lithuanians disturbed by Švitrigaila's policies, and marked a retreat from the tactless insistence on incorporation during the coronation tempest. When Švitrigaila rejected the offer and opted for war, Lithuanian resistance crystallized.[37]

According to Halecki, the subsequent plot to overthrow Švitrigaila was a Polish initiative, yet Długosz's claim that it was planned by his Lithuanian opponents, encouraged by Jagiełło and the Poles, is entirely plausible.[38] Although the Poles gave assistance, in particular during the diplomatic missions of Wawrzyniec Zaremba, castellan of Sieradz, in May and July, a group of Lithuanian lords who had been closely associated with Vytautas hatched the plot.[39] The leader was prince Semën Holshansky, Sonka's uncle and former guardian. Other prominent supporters were Olelko and Ivan, the sons of Volodymyr, the former duke of Kyiv, and Prince Fëdor Korybutovich, another of Algirdas's grandsons, which suggests that not all Ruthenians and not all Gediminids were enamoured with Švitrigaila. The princes resented his usurpation of lands and titles they felt to be rightly theirs: dynastic and personal loyalties were far more important than the national patriotism that so many historians emphasize.[40] The bulk of their fellow plotters were Lithuanians, including Vytautas's close associates Petras Mantigirdaitis, Jonas Goštautas, Mykolas Kęsgaila and his brother Rumbaudas Volimuntaitis; Kristinas Astikas, castellan of Vilnius, and his son Radvila Astikaitis, all leading figures in Vytautas's new Lithuanian establishment.[41] That so many were plotting to overthrow Švitrigaila barely eighteen months after his election calls into question the idea that separatism was the dominant motivation for their actions. Without Polish support, the Catholic Lithuanian establishment could not sustain itself. The coalition of the disaffected had fallen apart. The result was eight years of civil war and political upheaval.

The plotters struck on the night of 31 August–1 September 1432. Švitrigaila was in Ašmena, on his way to Brest to meet Jagiełło. His pregnant wife and some members of his entourage were arrested, but Švitrigaila escaped with several supporters, including two leading Lithuanians, Jurgis Gedgaudas, palatine of Vilnius, Ivaško Monvidaitis, who had warned him of the plot, and possibly Jonas Sungaila, castellan of Trakai.[42] The plotters and their Polish supporters had a candidate to replace Švitrigaila: Vytautas's brother Žygimantas, who led the attempt to seize Švitrigaila, and was immediately proclaimed grand duke; the extent of support for the coup meant that he rapidly secured Lithuania proper. Švitrigaila,

---

[37] Lowmiański, *Polityka*, 144; Błaszczyk, *Dzieje* ii/i, 654–5.
[38] *Annales*, xi/xii, 64–5; Halecki, *Dzieje*, i, 288–9. Lewicki sees the plot originating in Lithuania: *Powstanie*, 147.
[39] Nikodem, 'Oleśnicki wobec unii', i, 139–40; Błaszczyk, *Dzieje*, ii/i, 668.
[40] Грушевский, *Історія*, iv, 204; Rowell, '1446 and all that', in Irena Valikonytė (ed.), *Lietuva ir jos kaimyna* (Vilnius, 2001), 195–6.
[41] Błaszczyk, *Dzieje*, ii/i, 671–2.   [42] *Dzieje*, ii/i, 694.

however, retained control over most of the annexed territories, including Polatsk, Vitsebsk, Smolensk and Kyiv.[43]

While the civil war that followed was bitter enough, despite the predominance of Lithuanians supporting Žygimantas and Švitrigaila's reputation as the spokesman of Ruthenia there were Lithuanians who supported Švitrigaila and Ruthenians in Žygimantas's camp. Hrushevsky, true to his populist inclinations, saw Švitrigaila as the spokesman for the Ruthenian aristocracy; there is something in this assertion, although Volodymyr's sons resented his control of Kyiv, which they regarded as their patrimony, while if lesser nobles were not tied by clientage or kinship to his aristocratic supporters they were as likely to look to Žygimantas, whose policy of wooing the Ruthenians through political concessions soon bore fruit.[44] Žygimantas and his supporters, who were essentially Vytautas's men, returned to the tried and tested. An embassy to Jagiełło requested that Žygimantas be confirmed as grand duke; a high-level embassy led by Oleśnicki and Oporowski was immediately sent to Vilnius.[45] On its arrival in Hrodna, according to Długosz, it was met by the new grand duke and his supporters 'respectfully and cheerfully'.[46] On 15 October, after a week of talks, Oleśnicki issued a document widely known as the union of Hrodna, though it was not a treaty of union but an agreement over how Žygimantas was to rule the grand duchy; it did not come into force until its confirmation by Jagiełło in Cracow on 3 January 1433, and its reconfirmation by Žygimantas's son Mykolas in Vilnius on 18 October 1432, and by Žygimantas himself in Trakai on 20 January 1433.[47]

According to Krzyżaniakowa, the Hrodna treaty was a victory for the Poles; according to Lewicki, the Lithuanians secured what they desired: their right to statehood, albeit in continued subordination to Poland.[48] Both judgements rest on anachronistic assumptions. Hrodna did not replace Horodło; it marked little more than a return to the arrangements established in 1401, adjusted to take account of changed circumstances.[49] There is no indication that its negotiation was particularly difficult; it was a compromise acceptable to both sides. Strikingly, this was achieved by a Polish delegation led by Oleśnicki. His selection by Jagiełło suggests that Nikodem is justified in his view that Oleśnicki's approach to the union was realistic and practical, and that he appreciated the unfortunate consequences of his incorporationist posturing during the coronation tempest.[50]

Hrodna demonstrates that Švitrigaila's election and the two years of upheaval that followed had introduced an air of sober realism in Poland. It contained none of Horodło's incorporationist rhetoric. Jagiełło's instructions to Oleśnicki stressed a desire to restore peaceful alliance, a fraternal league, union, and perpetual concord

---

[43] *Annales*, xi/xii, 64–5; Lewicki, *Powstanie*, 147–8; Matusas, *Švitrigaila*, 75–5; Błaszczyk, *Dzieje*, ii/i, 675.
[44] Грушевський, *Історія*, iv, 202, 206.   [45] Błaszczyk, *Dzieje*, ii/i, 678.
[46] 'honeste et hilariter': *Annales*, xi/xii, 66–7.   [47] *AU*, nos 55–9, 77–94.
[48] Krzyżaniakowa and Ochmański, *Jagiełło*, 307; Lewicki, *Powstanie*, 155.
[49] Halecki, *Dzieje*, i, 294–8; Łowmiański, *Polityka*, 147.
[50] Although Nikodem, who believes Oleśnicki did not behave in 1429 as Długosz testifies, does not use the last of these arguments: 'Oleśnicki', i, 140–1.

between Poland and Lithuania.[51] They talked of restoring the various agreements and pacts made between the two realms, and Jagiełło empowered his ambassadors to make certain changes to those agreements.[52] The outcome was a text that satisfied the supporters of Vytautas who negotiated it, and was acceptable to the Poles. Žygimantas was recognized as grand duke, subject to the limitations placed on Vytautas's power; the canon law phrase '*in partem sollicitudinis*' was again deployed to emphasize his subordinate status. It was stressed that Žygimantas held his position from Jagiełło, and after deliberation and election by the 'princes, prelates, barons, and nobility of both realms'. Thus were the forms established at Horodło preserved. As had Vytautas, Žygimantas was to hold these territories for life. It was emphasized that they included Vilnius and other lands belonging to Jagiełło's patrimony; they were conferred by Jagiełło not in his capacity as king of Poland, but as supreme duke of Lithuania, in an acknowledgement of Lithuanian sensitivities.[53] On Žygimantas's death they were to revert by hereditary right to Jagiełło and his heirs, and to the crown and kingdom of Poland, the only overt reference in the document to the broader framework of union as established by Krewo and Horodło. Trakai was explicitly granted to Žygimantas as his patrimony; after his death it would pass to Mykolas, although it was stressed that he would have to obey Jagiełło, his successors, the crown and kingdom of Poland, and whoever was elected grand duke after his father. Kęstutis's patrimony was preserved for the Kęstutids, but their place in the political structure was carefully defined.[54]

Hrodna confronted two of the issues that had bedevilled Polish-Lithuanian relations. It stipulated that the grand duke would neither seek nor aspire to a royal crown, nor accept any offer of one from another power without the consent of Jagiełło, his successors, and the crown and kingdom of Poland. With regard to Podolia and Volhynia, the negotiators compromised, postponing a final decision. All Podolia was to return to Polish control, while Žygimantas was to be granted Volhynia—except for several towns to be handed over to the Poles—for his lifetime, in a similar arrangement to that which Vytautas had enjoyed with regard to Podolia. Volhynia was to revert to Poland on Žygimantas's death.[55]

Błaszczyk contends that Hrodna was a weak treaty that had to be reconfirmed more than once and only lasted eight years.[56] That, however, was more to do with Žygimantas's subsequent actions than the treaty's shortcomings. In many ways Hrodna showed the robustness of the idea of union. It demonstrated the pragmatism of both sides, and in particular of the Poles, as they faced up to the imminent reality of Jagiełło's demise: in December 1431 Piotr Szafraniec wrote to Švitrigaila of the effects of ageing that had left the king 'nearer to death than life'. Jagiełło was to live another two and a half years, but by 1433 he was almost blind and his energy was fading.[57] Błaszczyk expresses mild surprise at the absence of any mention of

---

[51] *AU*, no. 54, 76.   [52] *AU*, no. 54, 76.
[53] *AU*, no. 58, 87.   [54] *AU*, no. 58, 87.
[55] *AU*, no 58, 87–8. Švitrigaila still controlled eastern Podolia, which meant that the treaty resolved little in the short term: Любавский, *Областное*, 59.
[56] Błaszczyk, *Dzieje*, ii/i, 699.
[57] *CESXV*, ii, no. 203, 286; *Annales*, xi/xii, 81, 86; Matusas, *Švitrigaila*, 83.

incorporation in the text of the treaty, but does not consider the reasons.[58] It is unlikely that the Poles had abandoned their incorporationist position; indeed hints of it did appear in the treaty in the passages concerning Žygimantas's relationship to the crown and kingdom of Poland, and in the clause concerning the possibility— but no more than that—of the election of a new grand duke following Žygimantas's death, the one major echo of Horodło in the text that demonstrates that Hrodna was not simply a restatement of Vilnius-Radom.

Now was not the time, however, to stress incorporation. Jagiełło's imminent death promised to open a new period of uncertainty, with a royal minority inevitable, and it was imperative to protect the union. Events since 1429 had brought it close to collapse. Švitrigaila's volatile reign, however, had revealed the divisions among the grand duchy's elites and opened the way to a deal that might save it and preserve the position that the united realms had achieved in European politics since 1386. Hrodna was more a temporary measure to buy time than a reconceptualization of the union. The Poles realized that the bathos of the coronation tempest had to be avoided if it were to survive: it was agreed that all future disputes must be resolved peaceably, on the basis of old documents.[59]

As the future was to show, it was not easy to secure that agreement, but the Poles were aware that Hrodna was a temporary solution to a real problem. With Švitrigaila still controlling most of the annexed territories after the botched coup, it was essential first to win the civil war; renegotiation of the union—if such were to prove necessary—could wait, although the Hrodna treaty was redrawn in December 1437, to take account of the changed circumstances since Jagiełło's death on 1 June 1434, and again in October 1439 and January 1440 as the Poles became concerned at Žygimantas's increasingly independent foreign policy.[60]

The Poles and Žygimantas's supporters proved more than a match for Švitrigaila and his Livonian allies, who were defeated in December 1432 at Ašmena. Although Švitrigaila captured Brest in the spring of 1433 and, supported by the Livonian Order, took Kaunas in July, the military balance favoured his opponents. Švitrigaila, realizing this, tried to negotiate, but overtures to Jagiełło failed. A new round of betrayals by leading Ruthenian lords after Jagiełło's death delivered much of Volhynia to his enemies and extended Žygimantas's reach into the annexed territories. In 1435 the Prussian Order, alarmed at the summoning of the Polish noble levy, mobilized despite the twelve-year truce agreed at Łęczyca in December 1433, but did not enter the war. On 1 September 1435 Žygimantas crushed Švitrigaila and the Livonians on the river Šventoji near Ukmergė. The Polish council had summoned the noble levy, and Poles comprised nearly half Žygimantas's 9,500-strong army. Švitrigaila's force was larger—some 11,000—but over half of it comprised light Ruthenian and Tatar cavalry, which was no match for the heavily armed Polish knights. Švitrigaila's army was driven into the river, and many were killed or drowned; its commanders, Zygmunt Korybutovych, his son Mykhailo, and the Livonian master Frank von Kersdorf, were killed, together with

---

[58] Błaszczyk, *Dzieje*, ii/i, 695.   [59] Błaszczyk, *Dzieje*, ii/i, 695.
[60] *AU*, no. 63, 106–8; no. 64, 108–110; no. 65, 110–14; no. 66, 113–14; no. 67, 114–15; Błaszczyk, *Dzieje*, ii/i, 699–700.

six Order officials and thirteen Ruthenian princes.[61] The Livonians withdrew from the war, signing the peace of Brześć on 1 December 1435, which lasted nearly twenty years. Švitrigaila, though he still had the support of Tver, now talked peace. A temporary agreement was reached at Lwów on 4 September 1436, although its status was never clear, and it was only after Hrodna's renewal in December 1437 that Švitrigaila's defeat was sealed. He was granted land in south-eastern Poland, but went into exile in Wallachia to pasture sheep, as one of the chronicles put it.[62]

Švitrigaila's eclipse was not simply due to Žygimantas's military superiority. The support he enjoyed among Ruthenians forced Poles and Lithuanians to seek a solution to the Ruthenian question, which threatened not just the union, but the viability of the grand duchy itself: the exclusion of Orthodox nobles from the benefits of union. It was clear that a new approach was necessary. Following the extension at Jedlnia in March 1430 of Polish noble privilege to Orthodox boyars in Red Ruthenia, a similar approach was adopted in Lithuania after the coup against Švitrigaila. In a document issued on 30 September 1432 by Oleśnicki after negotiations with Žygimantas and his supporters, Orthodox nobles were granted the same privileges as their Catholic counterparts and, on the Horodło model, were to be welcomed into Polish heraldic clans.[63]

Lewicki termed this act 'the most noble adjustment of the Polish-Lithuanian union', arguing that no other contemporary Catholic power would have been capable of it.[64] It was not quite as remarkable as he thought, however. Although the document opened by talking of the need to restore harmony to the Lithuanian and Ruthenian lands, the extension of privileges was explicitly made to Ruthenian princes, boyars, nobles, and inhabitants 'subject to Lithuania'. This form of words suggests that the extension of privileges only applied to Lithuania proper, and not to the annexed territories; moreover, as Hrushevsky observes, there was no mention of the Orthodox religion in the document, with the privileges only extended to Ruthenian nobles, probably reflecting Oleśnicki's reluctance, as a Catholic bishop, explicitly to sanction political consessions to the Orthodox.[65] Despite having given his negotiators full plenipotentiary powers, Jagiełło never ratified the agreement.[66] He did, however, issue a similar privilege in Lwów on 30 October 1432 for the Ruthenian nobility of Lutsk and Volhynia that explicitly extended privileges to Orthodox nobles and made important concessions to Orthodox believers. The document granted all the princes, prelates, boyars, knights, and nobles of Volhynia

---

[61] *PSRL*, xxxv, col. 36; Stanisław Zakrzewski, 'W pięćsetną rocznicę: bitwa nad Świętą inaczej pod Wiłkomierzem 1 września 1435 r.', in *Pamiętnik VI Powszechnego Zjazdu* (Lwów, 1935), 551–8; Marek Plewczyński, *Wojny Jagiellonów z wschodnimi i południowymi sąsiadami królestwa polskiego w XV wieku* (Siedlce, 2002), 39–44.

[62] Kolankowski, *Dzieje*, 214. [63] *CESXV*, iii, dod. 17, 523–4.

[64] Lewicki, *Powstanie*, 155, 157.

[65] 'Et quia eo tempore, quo eosdem gracias privilegia et libertates terris predictis et earum incolis concessimus principes boiari nobiles et incole Rutheni, terre Lithvanie subditi': *CESXV*, iii, dod. 17, 523; Грушевський, *Історія*, iv, 209.

[66] Czermak, 'Sprawa', 352–71. Although the document was drafted in Hrodna, it gave Lwów as the place of issue, since that is where Jagiełło was currently residing. For the plenipotentiary powers see *AU*, no. 54, 76–7.

the full rights, liberties, and privileges enjoyed by their Polish counterparts and promised that Orthodox believers 'of whatever sex or status' would not be subject to forced conversion.[67]

Jagiełło's generous concessions to Ruthenian nobles in Volhynia, after refusing to confirm similar privileges for Lithuania proper demonstrated that age had not dimmed his political skills, despite Długosz's sneers about his senility and incapacity. The generosity of the Lwów privileges demonstrates that Jagiełło was not opposed to toleration in itself.[68] The granting of privileges only within Lithuania proper, however, would not solve the problem of the annexed territories, where Orthodoxy was strong and Catholicism weak. Instead he sought to confront Švitrigaila in his heartlands, and to resolve a long-running problem for the union by settling the vexed question of Podolia and Volhynia by giving the Volhynian elites a reason to support the incorporation of their province into the Polish kingdom. The extension of privileges was made conditional on their acceptance of that incorporation.[69]

If not quite as remarkable as Lewicki thought, these acts were still of major significance. Even if the Hrodna privileges were limited to Lithuania proper, were not confirmed by Jagiełło, and therefore did not receive legal force, it is nevertheless striking that a Catholic prelate of Oleśnicki's stature should seek to save the union by offering such extensive concessions to the Orthodox, even if he did not name them directly. They demonstrate that for all his doctrinaire insistence that Lithuania had already been incorporated into Poland, Oleśnicki was a pragmatist. Both documents reflect intellectual currents that were powerful in contemporary Polish Catholicism: the provision guaranteeing no forced conversions in the Volhynian privileges was entirely consistent with the elegant arguments of Włodkowic at Constance. At Hrodna, Oleśnicki demonstrated that the Polish Catholic Church was prepared to practise as well as preach.

Jagiełło's ploy was risky. In seeking to solve the Volhynian question in favour of the Poles he allowed Žygimantas to adopt the role of liberator of the Lithuanian Orthodox Church and defender of Lithuania's claim to Volhynia and Podolia. In Trakai on 6 May 1434 Žygimantas issued a general privilege to the grand duchy's Ruthenian elites that did have legal force, as is demonstrated by its inclusion in the general reconfirmation of privileges by king Sigismund August in 1551.[70] It was witnessed by Radvila Astikaitis, Jurgis Gedgaudas, and Khodko Iurevich. All were former supporters of Švitrigaila, and Iurevich was a prominent Ruthenian.[71] It closely followed the Hrodna document. Žygimantas granted the elites of his 'Lithuanian and Ruthenian lands', both Catholic and Orthodox, extensive privileges.[72] Although Žygimantas—like Oleśnicki but unlike Jagiełło—did not explicitly mention the Orthodox religion, the preamble made it clear that these

---

[67] *CESXV*, i/i, no. 82, 78.   [68] Czermak, 'Sprawa', 363.
[69] 'Promittimus...quod praefatam terram Lucensem et ipsius incolas non alienabimus a corona nostra regni Poloniae': *CESXV*, i/i, no. 82, 78.
[70] Czermak, 'Sprawa', 374. The original survives.
[71] *CESXV*, iii, dod. 22, 531; Halecki, *Dzieje*, i, 313.   [72] *CESXV, iii*, dod. 22, 530.

privileges were being extended to the Ruthenian as well as the Lithuanian nobility, and that the intention was to restore unity and end the disharmony of recent years. Ruthenian nobles were granted the same rights and liberties with regard to their estates and taxation already enjoyed by Catholic boyars, and the Horodło model of adoption into Polish heraldic clans was extended to them.[73]

This document, along with Jagiełło's privilege to the Volhynian nobility, marked an important watershed. Taken together, they removed almost all the limitations on the rights, liberties, and privileges enjoyed by Orthodox nobles as compared with their Catholic counterparts. Almost, but not all. There was no clause in either document concerning the right of Orthodox Ruthenians to hold office, and although the Polish system of district courts run by the local nobility, and of local office-holders was extended to the Ruthenian lands within Poland on Jagiełło's death, no such step was taken in Lithuania. Thus the Horodło ban on Ruthenians holding office in Lithuania proper survived, although there were no such restrictions in the annexed lands, which were still covered by their own privileges.[74]

The concessions were controversial enough: Długosz condemned them, testifying that many complained about the grant of privileges which the Poles had fought for so long 'without any conditions'.[75] His hostility highlights the remarkable nature of the concession of religious toleration by a contemporary Catholic state. The civil war after Švitrigaila's election had demonstrated to both the Poles and the Lithuanian Catholic elites the chronic political instability that threatened the grand duchy as a result of the exclusion of the Orthodox nobility from the benefits of citizenship. Although the principal motivation was undoubtedly practical and political, rather than any philosophical attachment to the legitimacy of religious toleration, the intellectual tradition established by Włodkowic and others in the context of the war against the Order should not be lightly dismissed. Orthodox nobles might remain second-class citizens on account of the Horodło provisions on office; they were nevertheless recognized as having most of the rights, liberties, and privileges of citizens. They could, and did, participate in politics. Whatever the motivation behind them, the privileges of 1432 and 1434 helped restore peace to the grand duchy and opened the way to the coming together of its Lithuanian and Ruthenian elites in a process that, while never complete, was crucial to the future of the union.

---

[73] *CESXV, iii*, dod. 22, 530. [74] Halecki, *Dzieje*, i, 314–15; Chodynicki, *Kościół*, 85–6.
[75] *Annales*, xi/xii, 139.

16

After Jagiełło

Although the new privileges encouraged many Ruthenians to abandon Švitrigaila, they did not end the civil war. Švitrigaila still enjoyed considerable support in Kyiv and Volhynia, and it was not until 1437 that the tide decisively turned.[1] The situation was complicated by Jagiełło's death on 1 June 1434. Oleśnicki was in Poznań en route to the Council of Basle when he heard the news. Recognizing the dangers of another long interregnum he acted decisively. He summoned an assembly of the Wielkopolska nobility to Poznań and threw his weight behind the immediate election of Władysław, Jagiełło's elder son, who had been acclaimed as the preferred successor at the 1432 Sieradz assembly.[2] Oleśnicki skilfully secured Wielkopolska's agreement to a swift election and coronation, playing on Wielkopolskan resentment of the dominance of the Małopolskan lords, a group of whom, led by Spytek of Melsztyn the younger, wished to reject Jagiełło's sons and turn to Siemowit V of Mazovia instead. He formed an alliance with Sonka and the court party to outmanoeuvre Spytek at Małopolskan assemblies in Opatów and Cracow to secure Władysław's election. The coronation took place on 25 July.[3]

The succession of the nine-year-old Władysław strengthened Oleśnicki's position considerably. Co-operation with Sonka did not long survive the election. Denied the regency, Sonka gathered round her a growing number of malcontents opposed to Oleśnicki's strengthening grip on power. The royal council, on which Oleśnicki played a leading role, took over the government and agreement was reached over a division of offices: the chancellorship remained with Jan Taszka Koniecpolski, Sonka's protégé, while Oporowski, a court supporter, resigned as vice-chancellor. Raised to the bishopric of Cujavia he was replaced by Wincenty Kot, a neutral figure who had served as tutor to Jagiełło's sons, but who was acceptable to Oleśnicki. Although Nikodem questions Oleśnicki's opposition to Jagiełło in the last decade of his reign, there is no reason to doubt Długosz's claim that in their last meeting he delivered a sharply critical speech in which he accused Jagiełło of spending his nights in drunken revelry and sleeping the day through, neglecting affairs of state and church, and complained that the country had been reduced to chaos and disorder. His diatribe was probably a reaction to Jagiełło's contacts with the Hussites, and in particular his meeting with a Hussite delegation in Cracow in 1431, to which Oleśnicki strongly objected.[4]

---

[1] Halecki, *Dzieje*, i, 317, 322.   [2] *Annales*, xi/xii, 55.
[3] Karol Olejnik, *Władysław III Warneńczyk (1424–1444)*, 2nd edn (Cracow, 2007), 42–5.
[4] *Annales*, xi/xii, 110–13; Jagiełło was a late riser: *Annales*, xi/xii, 124–5.

The years after Jagiełło's death saw the highpoint of Oleśnicki's political influence, but he was by no means as powerful as he was portrayed by the admiring Długosz. Government authority was weakened during Władysław's long minority. The council remained divided. Oleśnicki depended on the support of a group of Małopolskan families led by the Tęczyńskis and the Tarnowskis, and of his brother Jan Głowacz Oleśnicki, starosta of Cracow and grand marshal since 1430. Apart from smouldering Wielkopolskan resentment at Oleśnicki's failure to reward their support for Władysław's election, he faced considerable opposition from the Szafraniec, who had enjoyed Jagiełło's favour in his last years. Chancellor Jan Szafraniec died in 1433, but Jagiełło replaced him with Koniecpolski, who had emerged as a key member of the court party despite his marriage to Oleśnicki's relative, Dorota Oleśnicka and the fact that he had been one of those accused of inappropriate behaviour with Sonka in 1427.[5] Despite not being regent, Sonka played a significant role after her husband's death as guardian of her sons' interests. She cultivated a large group of nobles of a new generation—called the *iuniores* by Długosz—who felt excluded from power, including Spytek of Melsztyn, Jan Hincza of Rogów, and Dziersław Rytwiański. These ambitious young men from wealthy families resented the domination of the ageing politicians who had served Jagiełło.[6]

Jagiełło's death was a serious test of the union, and the Hrodna treaty. Little changed immediately. As long as Žygimantas needed Polish help in his struggle with Švitrigaila Hrodna held. After his victory on the Šventoji river and the 1435 peace of Brześć, however, as Žygimantas extended his authority across the grand duchy, he no longer had such need of Polish support, and the Hrodna compromise over Podolia and Volhynia came under strain. This development persuaded the Polish council to cultivate Švitrigaila. Talks began in early 1436 and a one-year truce was agreed in November. In August 1437 Švitrigaila buried his pride and came to Cracow seeking to return to Władysław's favour.[7] He requested Polish aid against Žygimantas, promising that Kyiv and his other southern Ruthenian lands would pass to Poland on his death. The Poles negotiated a deal in which Švitrigaila was granted Volhynia and eastern Podolia as fiefs for his lifetime; on his death they were to revert to Poland.[8] A showdown over Podolia and Volhynia was again postponed.

The council's caution was prudent. Whatever the Polish view of the nature of the union, it had been sustained for nearly sixty years thanks to the personal loyalty felt by many Lithuanian nobles to Jagiełło. Between 1409 and 1429 Jagiełło visited Lithuania every year and consulted with Vytautas to demonstrate publicly that as supreme duke he was closely involved in its government. Władysław had none of

---

[5] Zawitkowska, *W służbie*, 142–3.
[6] Bożena Czwojdrak, 'Kilka uwag o konfederacji Spytka z Melsztyna z 1439 roku', in Idzi Panic and Jerzy Sperka (eds), *Średniowiecze polskie i powszechne* (Katowice, 2002), 204 and Bożena Czwojdrak, 'Królowa Zofia Holszańska a biskup krakowski Zbigniew 'Oleśnicki—konflikt, współpraca czy rywalizacja?', in Kiryk and Noga (eds), *Oleśnicki*, 147; Sperka, 'Oleśnicki', 118.
[7] Błaszczyk, *Dzieje*, ii/i, 686, 730.
[8] Nikodem, 'Zbigniew Oleśnicki wobec unii polsko-litewskiej, ii: W latach 1434–1455', *NP*, 92 (1999), 90; Любавский, *Областное*, 59–60.

his father's advantages. He grew up in Poland and he was in no position to enforce his personal authority over Žygimantas, then in his seventies. Despite the Polish recognition of Władysław's hereditary rights to the grand duchy, the fact that Žygimantas had an adult son, Mykolas, for whom he clearly had expectations, represented an obvious danger. It remained to be seen if the undertakings he made at Hrodna in 1432 and renewed in February 1434, were of any value. The Polish flirtation with Švitrigaila showed Žygimantas that continued support was not guaranteed. He took the hint. An embassy led by Oleśnicki persuaded him to reconfirm Hrodna on 6 December 1437 with minor changes necessary following Władysław's accession. The key clause stressing that after Žygimantas's death Mykolas would only be entitled to his father's patrimony and would have no claim on the grand duchy as a whole, was left unchanged.[9]

Žygimantas could look elsewhere for support. In July 1436 Sigismund of Luxembourg, who had finally been crowned Emperor in 1433, made his peace with the Bohemians and at last secured the Bohemian throne. He was not to enjoy it long, dying in December 1437, leaving only a daughter, Elizabeth, who was married to Albert V von Habsburg. Albert was unanimously elected king of Hungary on Sigismund's death, and king of the Romans in March 1438, assuming the title of Albert II. Although he was acclaimed king of Bohemia by a coalition of Catholics and moderate Hussites, the radical Hussites, still strongly anti-German, sought an alternative. Their eyes soon alighted on Jagiełło's second son, Casimir.

Oleśnicki was initially hostile, but he was persuaded by Sonka to turn a blind eye when some of her supporters, including Spytek of Melsztyn and Dziersław Rytwiański led troops into Silesia and Bohemia in June 1438 to rally support.[10] Oleśnicki's concerns were justified. Despite his reconfirmation of Hrodna, Žygimantas was seeking allies against Poland. He proposed an anti-Polish alliance to the Order in 1437 and 1438, while supporting the Polish expedition to Bohemia in the hope that it would bring war with Albert.[11] In 1439 he approached Albert, claiming to be an independent ruler who had inherited his throne from his brother.[12]

Such an alliance was attractive to Albert after the Polish force entered Bohemia in June 1438. Yet the idea, whoever first proposed it—a matter of some controversy—came to nothing. Rusdorf, smarting from his experiences with Švitrigaila, refused to consider it, while the Polish force was too small to secure victory for Casimir. By 1439 Albert had defeated his opponents and talks with the Poles began in Breslau. Žygimantas wrote to Albert expressing openly separatist views, denying that Lithuania was subject to Polish rule, and falsely claiming that he had inherited the grand duchy from Vytautas.[13] Albert's embassy to Žygimantas in early 1439

---

[9] Nikodem, 'Oleśnicki wobec unii', ii, 91.   [10] Czwojdrak, 'Zofia', 148–9.
[11] Nikodem argues that Žigimantas did not initiate the plan, but his alternative proposal, that it was the brainchild of an anonymous canon of Cracow, is unconvincing: Jarosław Nikodem, 'Uwagi o genezie niedoszłego przymierza Zygmunta Kiejstutowicza z Albertem II', *Docendo discimus* (Poznań, 2000), 335–56. Cf. Błaszczyk, *Dzieje*, ii/i, 733–74.
[12] Gudavičius, *Istorija*, i, 284.
[13] *CESXV*, ii, no. 261, 402–3. It is wrongly dated 27 October.

turned back when Rusdorf refused to join an anti-Polish coalition, but a second embassy later in the year proposed an alliance. Now Žygimantas was less enthusiastic; when Rusdorf again refused to join the coalition he changed tack, reconfirming Hrodna on 31 October 1439, four days after Albert's unexpected death.[14]

Suspicion was endemic. The Poles showed no inclination to hand over Lutsk, promised to Žygimantas in 1437. Losing patience, he seized it in early 1439.[15] It was becoming obvious that the model of a separate Lithuanian grand duke was problematic, since it depended upon mutual trust and the establishment of the close working relationship that Jagiełło and Vytautas had enjoyed until 1429. Such a relationship was dependent upon the contingent factors of personality and circumstance, and could not be reduced to a legal formula. Yet for all the problems, Žygimantas's efforts to construct an anti-Polish coalition failed, and they failed most clearly in Lithuania itself, where they met strong opposition.[16]

Žygimantas, who owed his throne to the Poles, could not unite the grand duchy's elites behind him, and there is no evidence that they shared his view that he had inherited his position, which was simply untrue: he had been elected by those very elites, whose subsequent behaviour suggests they had not forgotten. Žygimantas had little to offer beyond his personal ambition, while his cruelty to those who opposed him alienated many. On Palm Sunday (20 March) 1440 he was assassinated in Trakai castle by conspirators led by Prince Ivan Chortorysky, who slipped into his apartments with concealed daggers under their cloaks. Mykolas and Žygimantas's servants were attending mass in the castle chapel but Žygimantas had chosen to hear mass in his bedchamber.[17] He died under a hail of blows and his body was conveyed on a cart to Vilnius, where he was interred with due honours in Vytautas's grave.[18]

Led by a Ruthenianized Gediminid, the assassins included both Ruthenians and Lithuanians. Among them were Chortorysky's brother Oleksander, Jonas Daugirdas, palatine of Vilnius, and Petras Lėlius, palatine of Trakai. There is no reason to doubt Długosz's assertion that the triggers of the assassination were Žygimantas's cruelty and the fear that he was about to strike against his enemies. The Chortorysky brothers had long been loyal to Švitrigaila, only abandoning his cause after 1438.[19] Nikodem's attempt to prove that Žygimantas's reputation as a cruel tyrant was propaganda is unconvincing. The civil war was brutal, and Žygimantas showed little mercy to his enemies: among the victims were Vytautas's favourites Rumbaudas Valimantaitis and his brother Jaunutis, executed in 1432; Žygimantas even executed his own envoys when they returned empty-handed from a mission to Švitrigaila.[20] There is ample evidence of Žygimantas's

---

[14] *AU*, no. 66, 113–14; Błaszczyk, *Dzieje*, ii/i, 750–5.
[15] Nikodem, 'Oleśnicki wobec unii', ii, 90–1.   [16] Nikodem, 'Uwagi', 346.
[17] *PSRL*, xxxv, col. 157.   [18] *Annales*, xi/xii, 216–17; Русина, *Україна*, 118.
[19] Błaszczyk, *Dzieje*, ii/i, 756.
[20] Nikodem, 'Przyczyny zamordowania Zygmunta Kiejstutowicza', *BZH*, 17 (2002), 5–33; Błaszczyk, *Dzieje*, ii/i, 772.

unsympathetic and psychotic character to suggest that the plotters had good reason to fear that their lives were in danger; his assassination was provoked by rumours that he intended to strike against his opponents during the Easter festivities. He had no obvious successor, and his death posed a real problem for the union.

17

Resolution

Žygimantas's murder caught the Poles by surprise. Apart from the problem of who—if anyone—was to succeed him as grand duke, Poland was itself experiencing a crisis of government. Albert's death opened up an enticing prospect for the Jagiellonian dynasty. Two years earlier a significant body of opinion in Hungary, mindful of the historic links with Poland, favoured offering the crown of St Stephen to Władysław. It was not substantial enough to prevent Albert's election, but when Albert died without a male heir, Władysław, who celebrated his fifteenth birthday four days later, again attracted attention. Albert's widow Elizabeth was pregnant; although she tenaciously defended the rights of the unborn child she claimed was unquestionably a son, the Ottoman threat ensured that the Hungarians did not want a long minority. Albert's humiliating defeat by the Ottomans shortly before his death reminded them that neither he nor Sigismund, distracted by events in Bohemia and the Empire, had effectively countered the threat. When the Hungarian diet assembled on 1 January 1440, only two candidates were discussed: Lazar, son of Durad Branković, despot of Serbia, and Władysław.[1]

The proposal did not fall on stony ground in a Poland riven with dissent. The failure of the 1438 Bohemian adventure compromised the pro-Hussite opposition, which attracted much support among the szlachta during a bitter dispute with the church over tithes.[2] A challenge to the council from the *iuniores* came to grief when the impetuous Spytek of Melsztyn tried to seize and possibly to assassinate Oleśnicki and other dignitaries during an assembly in Korczyn in May 1439. On 3 May a confederation was formed, signed by 168 knights; the next day Spytek failed in an attempt to seize the city. Two days later, the royal army won a brief skirmish at Grotniki in which Spytek was killed.[3]

According to Długosz, Sonka was behind the plot; whatever the truth, its aftermath brought a rapprochement between her supporters and Oleśnicki.[4] Oleśnicki's position was strengthened, but he had been reminded of the power of szlachta opinion, and the dangers of divisions among the narrow elite that dominated Polish politics. The rapprochement with Sonka opened the way to an

---

[1] Jan Dąbrowski, *Władysław I Jagiellończyk na Węgrzech (1440–1444)* (Warsaw, 1922), 14–18; Olejnik, *Władysław III*, 90–1.

[2] Łowmiański, *Polityka*, 191–4.

[3] *Annales*, xi/xii, 202–6; Anna Sochacka, 'Konfederacja Spytka z Melsztyna z 1439 r. Rozgrywka polityczna czy ruch ideologiczny?', *Rocznik Lubelski*, 16 (1973), 41–65; Czwojdrak, 'Kilka uwag', 197–211; Zawitkowska, *W służbie*, 171–2.

[4] Czwojdrak, 'Zofia', 149–50.

understanding over the Hungarian throne. The Hungarian offer was fiercely debated by the council. Władysław expressed concern at the prospect, and the proposal that he should marry Albert's widow Elizabeth, who was twice his age. Nevertheless, according to Długosz 'the greater and more sensible part' of the council won and the offer was accepted.[5]

Długosz's approval suggests that Oleśnicki supported the 'more sensible part' of the council, and Oleśnicki was later to pray for the successful union of Poland and Hungary. He was probably not the architect of the plan, however, or even its most powerful advocate, as was once supposed.[6] Długosz considered that the union would be difficult because of the king's long absences, and the problems of ruling two kingdoms.[7] Hungary was still the richer and more powerful kingdom. Poland's union with Lithuania and the relentless Ottoman pressure on Hungary's exposed southern frontier had altered the balance of power; nevertheless it was inevitable that Władysław would spend more time in Hungary, where his new subjects expected him to wage vigorous war on the Ottomans.

The plot thickened in February 1440 when Elizabeth gave birth to a son, László, known as the Posthumous. She had already launched a campaign for recognition of his hereditary right to the throne: two days before the birth the crown of St Stephen was spirited away into her keeping. The Hungarian envoys in Cracow, however, had plenipotentiary powers to negotiate in the event that Elizabeth's child was male; after an agreement in principle was reached, Władysław formally accepted the Hungarian throne in a ceremony on 8 March in the cathedral of St Stanisław. The congregation sang a *Te Deum*, and the *Bogu Rodzica*, the Marian hymn sung by the Polish army before Tannenberg.[8] They had, after all, effectively decided to go to war against the might of the Ottoman empire.

The price was high. Władysław had to confirm all privileges granted by his predecessors on the Hungarian throne and promise to defend Hungary against the Ottomans. Spisz, pawned to Poland by Sigismund of Luxembourg in 1412, was to be returned to Hungary without compensation. In a clause that had implications for Lithuania, ownership of Red Ruthenia and Podolia, contested by Hungary, was to be determined by a Hungarian-Polish court of mediation. Władysław was to marry Elizabeth before the coronation; he also promised to help László secure his inheritance outside Hungary: the kingdom of Bohemia and his father's Austrian lands.[9] The treaty was never implemented, but its terms make an interesting contrast with the Krewo act agreed by Jagiełło with another Elizabeth, queen of Hungary, fifty-five years earlier. There was no talk of '*applicare*': the two realms were to remain separate, united only in the person of their king.

---

[5] *Annales*, xi/xii, 212–13.
[6] Krzysztof Baczkowski, 'Zbigniew Oleśnicki wobec II unii polsko-węgierskiej 1440–1444', in Kiryk and Noga (eds), *Oleśnicki*, 53–71; Tomasz Graff, 'Zbigniew Oleśnicki i polski episkopat wobec unii personalnej z królestwem Węgier w latach 1440–1444', in Janusz Smołucha et al. (eds), *Historia vero testis temporum* (Cracow, 2008), 349–64.
[7] *Annales* xi/xii, 212.   [8] Dąbrowski, *Władysław*, 21–3; Olejnik, *Władysław III*, 94–5.
[9] Olejnik, *Władysław III*, 23–4.

The swift Polish response brought Władysław his prize. Elizabeth was supported initially by the primate, Dénes Szésci, who crowned László with the crown of St Stephen in Székesfehérvár on 15 May 1440. The rest of the royal regalia was missing, however, and the coronation had not been approved by the Hungarian diet. Władysław entered Hungary with a magnificent entourage on 23 April, and secured Buda, beating off an attempt by Elizabeth's uncle to seize it. In June the diet declared László's coronation invalid and confirmed the elective nature of the Hungarian crown. On 17 July, two months after he had crowned László, the unabashed Szésci, assisted by Oleśnicki and nine Hungarian bishops, crowned Władysław in Székesfehérvár cathedral. Although the crown had not been recovered, a replacement was taken from St Stephen's reliquary, and the rest of the royal regalia was used to indicate divine approval. It was made clear, however, that Władysław's elevation was dependent on the consent of the community of his new realm.[10] In Hungary, as in Poland, the citizens, not God, decided who their king should be.

The eclipse of the Luxembourgs and the Hungarian union could have established the Jagiellons as the dominant dynasty in east central Europe. The obstacles they faced, however, were formidable. Elizabeth did not give up easily, and Władysław had to fight a two-year civil war before his new throne was secure. Thereafter he had to fulfil his promise to defend Hungary against the Ottoman threat. Two attacks were beaten off in 1442; in 1443 he led a successful campaign, although its actual commander was János Hunyadi, who took Sofia and won a spectacular victory at Kustinitza in November. Despite signing a ten-year peace with the Ottomans, who surrendered Bosnia and Serbia, Władysław was encouraged by papal diplomats against his councillors' inclinations to mount a new Balkan campaign in 1444 in support of a joint Venetian, Genoan, and Burgundian fleet that was to strike at Constantinople through the Dardanelles. The reluctant Hunyadi was persuaded to lead it. This time there was no glorious outcome. Despite papal encouragement, other powers showed no inclination to rescue the pitiful remnants of the Byzantine empire, and Władysław's army numbered barely 16,000. On 10 November, at Varna on the Black Sea coast, it was destroyed by a considerably larger Ottoman force. The impetuous Władysław, leading a rash charge of a few hundred knights, was cut down at a point when his army under Hunyadi's skilful leadership was giving a good account of itself. Demoralized by the king's death, it disintegrated.[11] The Hungarian intermezzo ended with László the Posthumous's election to his father's throne.

Poland's second Hungarian union may have been even briefer than the first, but its effects on the Polish-Lithuanian union were considerable. Władysław's long absence in Hungary left the government of Poland in the hands of the council; but without the monarch's presence, its authority was weakened. Although only a few hundred Polish volunteers fought in Władysław's Hungarian campaigns, his constant need of money to finance his military adventures drained his resources in both

---

[10] Olejnik, *Władysław III*, 24–39.
[11] Edward Potkowski, *Warna 1444* (Warsaw, 1990), 141, 185–204.

Poland and Hungary. By the time of his death Polish complaints were becoming ever louder at the increasing burdens, and at the growing chaos and anarchy that all remarked upon.

The Hungarian tragedy had a profound effect on Polish-Lithuanian relations, not least because Władysław's absence and Poland's internal problems weakened it in relation to Lithuania at the very moment that Žygimantas's assassination, twelve days after Władysław formally accepted the Hungarian crown, destroyed the Hrodna system. Władysław had already crossed his Rubicon, and it is idle to speculate whether the Polish council would have decided differently had Žygimantas been assassinated earlier. Władysław's acceptance of the Hungarian throne meant that for the first time the Lithuanians were in a position to define the relationship with Poland on terms that suited them.

As Władysław prepared to depart for Hungary, he faced a dilemma. Although Žygimantas had been abruptly removed from the scene, Švitrigaila was very much alive. Some of the plotters backed his return to power: the Chortoryskys had long supported him, having only recently gone over to Žygimantas.[12] Švitrigaila enjoyed some support among Ruthenians, though he had alienated many by his cruel execution of Herasym, appointed metropolitan of Kyiv and all Rus′ in 1433 on Švitrigaila's recommendation, but burned in Vitsebsk in July 1435 for allegedly plotting against him.[13] The palatines of Vilnius and Trakai, Jonas Daugirdas and Petras Lėlius, initially backed Švitrigaila but former supporters such as Jonas Manvydaitis, his starosta of Podolia, opposed his return: as Łowmiański put it, the Lithuanians had not rid themselves of one aged despot to welcome back another whose caprices they remembered well enough.[14] Švitrigaila had identified himself too closely with the Ruthenians, and memories of the cruelty shown by his forces on their raids into Lithuania remained vivid.[15] There were few alternatives. Žygimantas's son Mykolas had some adherents in Samogitia and his grandfather's patrimony of Trakai, but Žygimantas's assassins, fearing revenge, opposed his elevation.[16]

Instead, several Lithuanian dignitaries, including Motiejus, bishop of Vilnius, Kristinas Astikas, Jonas Goštautas, and Petras Mantigirdaitis, turned to Władysław. Długosz suggests that they wanted him to rule directly, but later writes that they merely wished him to come to Lithuania to sort out the mess.[17] This was probably simple courtesy: they also suggested that Władysław send his brother, the thirteen-year-old Casimir, to Vilnius to be raised to the grand ducal throne.[18] There is no reason to doubt Długosz's testimony that Władysław hesitated before deciding that he could not breach the undertakings he had just given to the Hungarians. Instead he and his Polish advisers took a bold step, deciding that they would adopt a modified version of the Vytautan model, by sending Casimir to

---

[12] Halecki, *Ostatnie lata*, 6.
[13] *PSRL*, xxxv, col. 36; Lidia Korczak, 'Wielki książę litewski Świdrygiełło wobec soboru bazylejskiego i papieża Eugeniusza IV', in Smołucha et al. (eds), *Historia*, 347.
[14] Halecki, *Ostatnie lata*, 8; Łowmiański, *Polityka*, 162.   [15] *PSRL*, xxxv, cols. 142, 166.
[16] Łowmiański, *Polityka*, 162.   [17] *Annales*, xi/xii, 217–18, 219.
[18] Любавский, *Сеймъ*, 95.

Vilnius not as grand duke, but as Władysław's deputy and governor.[19] As Władysław left for Hungary, Casimir set off for Vilnius with an entourage led by the Mazovian dukes Casimir and Bolesław and including Jan of Czyżów, castellan and starosta of Cracow, Dobiesław Oleśnicki, palatine of Sandomierz, Jan Głowacz Oleśnicki, castellan of Sandomierz, and Jan Hryćko Kierdej, palatine of Podolia.

If the Poles hoped that this magnificent retinue would mollify the Lithuanians they were to be disappointed. To treat Lithuania as a mere province to be ruled by a governor was insensitive after the coronation tempest, when the issue of Lithuania's status had almost destroyed the union, and ignored Hrodna, which confirmed Horodło by permitting the election of a grand duke on Žygimantas's death.[20] The Poles again disregarded the spirit and the letter of the union treaties, which stressed the need for discussion and consensus over the succession. It was hardly surprising that after Casimir's arrival in Vilnius the Lithuanians took matters into their own hands, as they had in 1430. Ignoring Władysław's wishes, they elected Casimir grand duke of Lithuania on 29 June 1440.[21] They were not to be fobbed off with a mere governor.

Lithuanian historians have tended to see Casimir's election as an expression of Lithuanian sovereignty and a unilateral declaration of independence.[22] Polish historians have tended to agree. Błaszczyk suggests it marked the 'formal' breaking of the union; a couple of pages later, he drops the reservation, writing that 'one can simply state that the Polish-Lithuanian union was broken in 1440'. Łowmiański is more cautious, claiming that although Casimir became a 'sovereign monarch', all links to Poland were not broken.[23]

The truth is rather more complex. Although Žygimantas's assassins were led by the Ruthenian Chortoryskys, who favoured Švitrigaila's return, the Lithuanians among them had been closely associated with Vytautas. For those who see Vytautas as the champion of Lithuanian independence and sovereignty, Žygimantas was murdered because he was too pro-Polish. This view, advanced by Matusas and Nikodem, depends on an assumption that Žygimantas was not the instigator of an anti-Polish alliance with Albert II and the Order in 1438–1439, which was, so it is argued, the work of Lithuanian 'separatists', who supported his assassination because of his overtly pro-Polish policies, supposedly confirmed by the 1439 reconfirmation of Hrodna.[24]

Łowmiański criticized Halecki's suggestion that the group of Vytautas's former supporters, who were among the asassins, formed a 'pro-Polish' faction. Nikodem cites Łowmiański in support of his case, yet Łowmiański's view is more nuanced: these men were not 'pro-Polish', but pro-Jagiellonian, favouring cooperation with the Poles and the continuation of the union, because they feared Ruthenian

---

[19] *Annales*, xi/xii, 219.   [20] Любавский, *Сеймъ*, 95.
[21] *Annales*, xi/xii, 251–3; *PSRL*, xxxv, col. 110.
[22] Zigimantas Kiaupa, *The History of Lithuania* (Vilnius, 2002), 103; Dundulis, *Kova*, 175–8. For a more nuanced view see Gudavičius, *Istorija*, i, 290–1.
[23] Błaszczyk, *Dzieje*, ii/i, 775, 780; Nikodem, 'Oleśnicki wobec unii', ii, 105; cf. Kutrzeba, 'Charakter', 172; Łowmiański, *Polityka*, 163; Любавский, *Сеймъ*, 137.
[24] Matusas, *Švitrigaila*, 149–52; Nikodem, 'Uwagi', 346–56; Nikodem, 'Przyczyny', 24–7.

irredentism led by Švitrigaila.²⁵ This is far more likely. Supporters of the coup were numerous: apart from Motiejus, bishop of Vilnius, Kristinas Astikas, Jonas Goštautas, and Petras Mantigirdaitis, they included the influential Valimuntaitis clan, led by Kęsgaila, whose brothers had been executed by Žygimantas.²⁶ They were either men who had long supported Vytautas—such as Astikas and Kęsgaila—or who had risen to prominence in the 1430s, many of them associated with Sonka's court.²⁷

They were not 'pro-Polish' or 'subservient to Poland'. They looked to the dynasty and the union that had brought stability to Lithuania between 1401 and 1429 and had transformed the position of the leading boyar families. As Długosz observes, their first inclination in 1440 was to turn to their supreme duke, Władysław, whom they would 'take as their lord in accordance with the union treaties and their oaths'.²⁸ This invitation to Władysław and the emphasis on 'written agreements and oaths' is overlooked by historians anxious to present Casimir's subsequent election as evidence of a desire to break the union. This group represented those families who had played a part in negotiating the agreements on which that union was based, and who had, as they stated, sworn oaths of loyalty to Jagiełło and his heirs.

If in 1440 anyone was acting in breach of those agreements it was Władysław. There was nothing in the treaties about the appointment of a governor, a step which baldly asserted the disputed Polish position that Lithuania had been incorporated. Even if Władysław and the Polish council wished simply to play for time as he secured his Hungarian throne, and Casimir's appointment was only a stopgap until they could make more permanent arrangements, the decision was taken without consultation with the Lithuanians, who had every right to feel that—as in 1430—the agreements on which the Poles placed so much stress had simply been ignored.²⁹

Despite the magnificence of Casimir's entourage, it had no powers to negotiate. Casimir was to be governor and that was that. It is hardly surprising that the Lithuanians should react badly. Horodło and Hrodna emphasized the need for bilateral assemblies to discuss matters of joint concern, yet the Poles had not offered one to discuss the single most important issue in Lithuanian political life: by whom, and how, they were to be governed. The Lithuanians therefore appealed to the union treaties: Długosz attests that they made every effort to persuade Casimir's retinue that they should be allowed to elect him grand duke in accordance with Horodło. It was only the abrupt rejection of these approaches that persuaded them to take matters into their own hands. Early on the morning of 29 June 1440, while the Poles were still snoring in their beds, Casimir was elected grand duke.³⁰ He was not elected supreme duke; thus Władysław's rights to Lithuania were respected.

---

[25] Łowmiański, *Polityka*, 159–60, 162; Halecki, *Ostatnie lata*, 6; Halecki, *Dzieje*, i, 335.
[26] Halecki, *Dzieje*, i, 333.
[27] Rowell, 'Bears and traitors, or political tensions in the Grand Duchy ca. 1440–1481', *LHS*, 2 (1997), 30–1.
[28] *Annales*, xi/xii, 217–18.   [29] *Annales*, xi/xii, 219.   [30] *Annales*, xi/xii, 253–4.

This was no challenge to the union, let alone an assertion of independence. It was the Poles, not the Lithuanians, who had shown scant respect for the spirit of union; they now paid the price. As the Lithuanians observed, it was shameful for them to be deprived of their grand duke, and for Casimir's title to depend on negotiations that were bound to take a long time since Władysław was far away in Hungary.[31]

The Lithuanians were challenging the Poles to live up to the rhetorical assertions of fraternity that pervaded the acts of union. In 1413 and 1432 they had been given to understand that they would have a say in who was to rule over them. Casimir's election as grand duke was not at all comparable—as Halecki and Nikodem suggest—to the drunken acclamation of Vytautas at Salin in 1398, and there is no evidence to back Halecki's assertion that it conferred on Casimir 'full royal power', or that the Lithuanians thought that it did: as he admits, Casimir immediately sent ambassadors to Hungary to ask Władysław to confirm his election, which suggests that neither he nor his Lithuanian advisors believed that he was an independent monarch.[32] There was no talk of a crown. The Lithuanians had learned the lesson of the coronation tempest, even if the Poles had not.

If the union was to survive, it had to be based on negotiation and consent, not arbitrary decisions by one party to it. Jagiełło's greatness lay in his recognition of this fact. Władysław was understandably nervous about his own authority, yet his decision did little to bolster it. In 1440 the Lithuanians were in a strong position. There was no appetite for reigniting the civil war. Mykolas Žygimantaitis's exiguous support soon evaporated, and Casimir's election was accepted by the Ruthenians.[33] Švitrigaila swore loyalty to Władysław on 6 June 1440, recognizing that he had no chance of reclaiming his throne. He had learned his lesson while tending sheep in his Moldavian exile and eventually received his reward: the Chortoryskys and other leading Ruthenians invited him to become governor of Lutsk in early 1442; in 1443 Casimir granted him an appanage duchy in two of Volhynia's three districts, with Lithuania retaining direct rule over the other.[34] The deal ensured a common front over the future of Volhynia, where Švitrigaila peacefully lived out his days until his death in 1453.

By 1443 Casimir had ended the long civil war, demonstrating that he had inherited much of Jagiełło's hard-headed political pragmatism. Initially his power was limited largely to Lithuania proper once he had secured the surrender of the upper castle in Trakai by a promise not to punish Ivan Chortorysky for Žygimantas's murder. He did not control Smolensk, which had rebelled before his election, recognizing Algirdas's grandson Iury Lengvinevich as its duke, or Samogitia, long a Kęstutid powerbase, which also rebelled in 1441, electing the pagan Daumuntas as its starosta. In 1440 Bolesław IV of Mazovia occupied the Podlasian territories of Drohichyn and Mielnik on the basis of Jagiełło's 1390 grant of the former to Janusz I; Władysław approved the annexation just before his departure

---

[31] *Annales*, xi/xii, 253. Kiaupienė's claim that the Lithuanians elected Casimir without asking Władysław and the Poles is simply wrong: *Horodlės aktai*, 291–2.
[32] Halecki, *Dzieje*, i, 339; Nikodem, 'Oleśnicki wobec unii', ii, 94.
[33] Rowell, 'Dynastic bluff', 10.   [34] *CESXV* i/i, no. 113, 122–3; Halecki, *Ostatnie lata*, 10.

for Hungary in another move that outraged Lithuanian opinion and sparked a war with Mazovia.[35]

Casimir quickly established his authority, albeit at a price. Iury Lengvinevich's attempt to extend his control of Smolensk and Mstislau to Polatsk and Vitsebsk was defeated. After two sieges Smolensk was retaken and Iury escaped to Moscow. In Samogitia, where the Kęsgaila were among Casimir's strongest supporters, a negotiated settlement was reached in 1442 when Casimir issued a privilege, known from its 1492 confirmation, that formed the basis for Samogitia's special status until the end of the union.[36] In the annexed Ruthenian territories a different approach was adopted: Švitrigaila's recognition as duke of Volhynia was matched by the return in 1441 of Kyiv to Olelko, son of Volodymyr, who had been stripped of it in 1394. Although he was granted it not as duke but as governor, Olelko remained loyal to Casimir.[37]

These developments are often presented as a step backwards; a move away from Vytautas's supposed system of strong centralized rule.[38] Yet they were pragmatic politics. Vytautas's reforms brought many benefits to the grand duchy, but left it seriously divided on his death, and without a clear programme to maintain its unity. In rallying behind Casimir, Lithuanians and Ruthenians took an important step towards establishing their own community of the realm. The restoration of Švitrigaila to his Volhynian appanage and the appointment of a governor of Kyiv did not herald a return to the Gediminid dynastic condominium. Lithuania had all but fallen apart in the 1430s, and there were some in the annexed Ruthenian territories who felt that they might be better off joining their brethren in Red Ruthenia under the authority of the Polish crown. Here the ideal of the community of the realm had a different resonance, stirred by historical memories of the glories of Kievan Rus': the Nikiforovskaia chronicle, one of the redactions of what is known as the first Lithuanian chronicle, compiled in the mid fifteenth century, claimed that Švitrigaila was elected grand duke of Rus' and depicts the war as one in which Lithuanians and Poles fought against Ruthenians.[39] The danger that the grand duchy might splinter into two halves was clear.[40] Casimir's grant of considerable autonomy under their own leaders to Volhynia and Kyiv recognized that for all Vytautas's reforms, the grand duchy was still very much a composite polity. Švitrigaila was over seventy and had no heir; his rule over Volhynia gave Lithuania a breathing space to prepare for the inevitable Polish challenge to Lithuanian control when he died, while the restoration of limited autonomy to Kyiv under a Gediminid prince loyal to Casimir had considerable symbolic force. The extension

---

[35] Błaszczyk, *Dzieje*, ii/i, 782–5.

[36] *ZPL*, 67–72; *Žemaitijos žemės privilegijos XV–XVII a*, eds Darius Antanavičius and Eugenijus Saviščevas (Vilnius, 2010), nos. 3–8, 33–9; Stephen C. Rowell, 'Rusena karas žemaičiouse: Keletas pastabų apie 1442 m. privilegijos genezės', *Žemaičių Praetitis*, 8 (1998), 9–10.

[37] Karol Górski, 'Młodość Kazimierza i rządy na Litwie (1440–1454)', in Biskup and Górski (eds), *Kazimierz Jagiellończyk* (Warsaw, 1987), 11.

[38] For example Błaszczyk, *Dzieje*, ii/i, 782.

[39] *PSRL*, xxxv, col. 35; 'На ту же осень князь великыи Жигимонт собра силу многу литовьскую и ляхы, и приде на Руськую землю': *PSRL*, xxxv, col. 36; cf. *PSRL*, xxxv, col. 59.

[40] Русина, *Україна*, 111–12.

of privileges to the Ruthenian nobility had changed their legal and political position, and confronted the major threat to the grand duchy's political and social coherence. It had by no means solved the problem, but it had shown a way forward and provided a basis upon which Ruthenian loyalty to the grand duchy could develop. The consensual Polish model of decentralized elective monarchy, in which citizens of individual provinces had considerable responsibility for their own affairs was spreading its influence in the Ruthenian lands as well as in the core Lithuanian territories. It was an attractive model, regardless of attitudes towards the Poles themselves.

The balance of union had tilted. The Poles were now experiencing absentee monarchy and royal decisions were becoming harder to secure.[41] With Poland likely to be dragged into war against the Ottomans, they had little appetite for enforcing their will on Lithuania. Władysław and the Polish council obstinately refused to recognize Casimir's election or use his new title, but there was little they could do.[42] When a joint Polish-Lithuanian assembly met at Parczew in November 1441 the Lithuanians stood firm, blithely rebuffing appeals from Mykolas Žygimantaitis, who had fled to Mazovia, for possession of the Kęstutid patrimony he had been promised. They blocked Polish attempts to mediate a settlement with Bolesław IV, duke of Mazovia, and their war with Mazovia over Podlasie continued until another assembly at Piotrków in August 1444, when Lithuanian military superiority persuaded the Poles to ignore Władysław's orders and broker a settlement in which Lithuanian rule over Podlasie was recognized by the Mazovians in return for a modest payment. Significantly, Casimir sought to win over the Podlasians by granting them—with certain minor exceptions—Polish law, which was now used as a means of asserting Lithuanian authority.[43]

Długosz claims that after the November 1441 Parczew assembly the Poles blustered about carving the grand duchy up into several principalities to curb Lithuanian pride, and it seems that Władysław and his councillors made overtures to Švitrigaila.[44] The assembly demonstrated that such gestures were empty. Despite Władysław's order that it should offer Mazovia armed support, the assembly refused to countenance war with Lithuania.[45] For all the haughty insistence on Lithuania's inferior status, the Polish programme of union was built round the conceit that the Lithuanian boyars had consented to it at all stages of its development. Now that Lithuanian consent could no longer be secured through princely authority, the Poles found themselves hoist with the petard they had themselves packed with gunpowder. Polish political culture was based on consent and

---

[41] *Annales*, xi/xii, 253.
[42] *Annales*, xi/xii, 245–5. Rowell argues that Władysław eventually recognized his brother's elevation: he cites Władysław's use of the title of supreme duke in 1441, but Długosz states that neither the Poles nor Władysław ever recognized Casimir's title, while he used the title of supreme duke before as well as after 1440; its use in 1441 proves nothing: Rowell, 'Bears', 32; Rowell, 'Rusena karas', 6; *Annales*, xi/xii, 254. Cf. Błaszczyk, *Dzieje*, ii/i, 780–1; Halecki, *Dzieje*, i, 340.
[43] Błaszczyk, *Dzieje*, ii/i, 785–7; Halecki, *Dzieje*, i, 350.
[44] *Annales*, xi/xii, 267–8; Halecki, *Dzieje*, i, 339–40.
[45] Halecki, *Dzieje*, i, 347–9; Błaszczyk, *Dzieje*, ii/i, 787–8; Nikodem, 'Oleśnicki wobec unii', ii, 103.

negotiation; the Lithuanians were beginning to demonstrate an understanding of how it worked, and were using the union agreements to their own advantage. The union would never be the same again.

The extent to which the balance had shifted was revealed in the aftermath of Władysław's heroic death at Varna. The fact that Casimir had by far the best claim to the Polish throne put both him and the Lithuanians in a powerful bargaining position; their exploitation of it launched a new stage in the union process. The strength of Casimir's claim was recognized by Oleśnicki. He persuaded an assembly in Sieradz on 23 April 1445 that despite the lack of firm confirmation of Władysław's death—his body had not been recovered, and many hoped that he was concealing himself somewhere in the Balkans—Casimir should be elected without delay. Another assembly was summoned to Piotrków for 24 August; Casimir was invited to attend to have his election confirmed.[46]

It was a sensible decision. The Hungarians, in electing László, recognized that Władysław was dead, as did Sonka, who thanked Oleśnicki for his efforts.[47] In urging his election, Oleśnicki recognized the obligations the community of the realm had taken upon itself in the agreements made with Jagiełło before his death.[48] Casimir's response surprised everyone. He refused to come to Piotrków, informing the startled Poles that, disturbed and dispirited by his brother's misfortune, he lacked the strength to undertake any new public responsibilities. He stressed that he was by no means rejecting the offer, but considered that the time was not right to accept it.[49] He suggested that everyone should wait until firmer news of Władysław's fate emerged, but this excuse, trotted out regularly in the months that followed, could not disguise his true intention: if the Poles wished him to accept what he regarded as his birthright they would have to negotiate. He did not intend to have terms dictated to him.[50]

It seems that this was as much Casimir's strategy as that of the Lithuanian council. He was nineteen days short of his seventeenth birthday when his brother was killed, but was already showing that he had inherited his father's shrewd political instincts. It seems that by 1445 he was not dominated by the Lithuanian council, although it is unlikely that there was much disagreement with it over how to approach the matter.[51] He was in a strong position. The Lithuanians and Ruthenians had demonstrated their respect for hereditary right; they already had their grand duke, even if his title was not recognized by the Poles, who had challenged the hereditary claims of Jagiełło's sons and were now paying the price:

---

[46] *Annales*, xii/i, 14–16; Nikodem, 'Oleśnicki wobec unii', ii, 104. Lewicki's classic account of the interregnum, 'Wstąpienie na tron polski Kazimierza Jagiellończyka', *RSAU*, 20 (1887), 1–40 is still valuable, but the best analysis is Rowell, 'Casimir Jagiellończyk and the Polish gamble', *LHS*, 4 (1999), 7–39; cf. Rowell '1446', 188–277.

[47] *Annales*, xii/i, 15.   [48] Rowell, 'Casimir', 15.   [49] *Annales*, xii/i, 18–19.

[50] Rumours of Władysław's miraculous survival were rife, and a cult soon emerged: Rowell, 'Pomirtinis Vladislovo Varniečio gyvenimas—vidurio Europos Karalius Artūras iš Lietuvos', *LIM*, 2 (2006), 5–30.

[51] Rowell, 'Casimir', 29; Rowell, '1446', 191.

given the shortage of plausible alternatives they had few cards in their hand. Time was on Casimir's side.

Lewicki's claim that the Poles were powerless is an exaggeration, but the long interregnum was frustrating after four years of absentee rule.[52] In August 1445 an assembly in Sieradz appointed a high-level embassy led by primate Wincenty Kot and including Oleśnicki. It met Casimir in October in Hrodna, where he flatly rejected the Polish suggestion that he accept the throne in return for confirmation of the union treaties.[53] This offer, and the embassy's lengthy, incorporationist account of the union in an audience with Casimir on 15 October, was neither tactful nor conducive to securing Lithuanian consent, especially since it ended with a polite threat: if Casimir failed to turn up to be crowned on December 5, the Poles would look elsewhere.[54] Sonka, afraid her son might throw away his Polish throne, travelled to Hrodna to mediate. Her efforts were in vain. According to Długosz, Casimir wished to accept, but after discussion with his Lithuanian advisors, rejected the terms: the Lithuanians argued that if Casimir departed for Poland, the terrible days of Vytautas and Žygimantas might return, while Mykolas Žygimantaitis would seize power and exact a dreadful revenge for his father's murder.[55]

The stress on the bad old days of Vytautas's rule suggests that the Lithuanians—if not being downright mischievous—were displaying good tactical sense. Whatever Casimir's personal views, it was clear that they were not going to accept any deal that saw him leave for Cracow without a settlement that took account of their grievances, and their conception of the union. The Poles could only suggest three options: that Casimir become king of Poland and that, on the Horodło model, a new grand duke acceptable to the Lithuanians be elected; that Casimir remain in control in Lithuania and someone else be elected king of Poland; or that Casimir should rule over both Poland and Lithuania. Neither Casimir nor the Lithuanians were inclined to accept any of them for the moment; only the intervention of Sonka, who travelled to Hrodna on her own initiative, persuaded the Poles to allow the Lithuanians more time. She secured a promise that the Lithuanians would consider the matter at an assembly of the Lithuanian, Samogitian, and Ruthenian lands, and would reply to the Polish assembly called to Piotrków for 6 January.[56]

The Lithuanians had played their hand skilfully. The Poles had thought they could simply summon Casimir from Vilnius to rule over them; they discovered that they needed to persuade the Lithuanians to allow their grand duke to become king.[57] The Lithuanians were using Horodło against them: the insistence on securing the agreement of the Lithuanian community of the realm was shrewd. The Poles could scarcely complain at such an explicit appeal to the basic principles of their own political system. The Lithuanians assembled in Vilnius at the end of November; their gathering was pure political theatre, designed to put pressure on

---

[52] Lewicki, 'Wstąpienie', 4.   [53] Błaszczyk, *Dzieje*, ii/i, 799.
[54] *Annales*, xii/i, 19–22; Rowell, 'Casimir', 19; Lewicki, 'Wstąpienie', 5–6.
[55] *Annales*, xii/i, 22–4; Lewicki, 'Wstąpienie', 6.
[56] *Annales*, xii/i, 23; Lewicki, 'Wstąpienie', 6; Błaszczyk, *Dzieje*, ii/i, 800.
[57] Lewicki, 'Wstąpienie', 7–8.

the Poles. It was well attended by both Lithuanians and Ruthenians. Olelko Volodymyrovych came with his brothers, and Švitrigaila dragged his aching bones up from Lutsk to swear homage to his nephew. The grand duchy's elites rallied around the grand duke they had chosen, and Casimir's hand was strengthened. The embassy it appointed contained two Ruthenian princes and four Lithuanian boyars, a subtle indication of the new unity of the political elites, and it was a Ruthenian, Vasily Krasny Ostrozky, who disabused the Poles of the notion that they could send Casimir to Lithuania then recall him at their own convenience. He maintained that Casimir ruled over Lithuania by hereditary right, as his forefathers had, and, like them, enjoyed full powers over it.[58] The Lithuanian position was entirely consistent with Horodło: Casimir had been elected grand duke in accordance with its terms—allowing for the lack of Polish consent—but Władysław's death made him supreme duke by hereditary right. Since Władysław's death was unconfirmed, Casimir could not yet ascend the Polish throne, but he asserted that he would allow nobody else to be chosen in his place.[59] The Polish bluff had been called.

For another eighteen months the Poles blustered and fumed, but they were stymied. Another assembly in Piotrków in March sought to seize the initiative by electing another candidate. The cupboard, however, was bare. Jadwiga, Jagiełło's daughter, had died childless in 1431; Oleśnicki and Kot proposed Frederick von Hohenzollern, her one-time fiancé, who had spent part of his childhood in Poland. Despite the support of two other bishops there was considerable hostility to the prospect of a German king, even one who spoke Polish. Paweł Giżycki, bishop of Płock, suggested Bolesław IV of Mazovia, who carried the day. He was declared king-elect, though he would only ascend the throne if Casimir failed to accept the Polish offer by 26 June.[60] The election was half-hearted. Few believed that the elevation of an impoverished Mazovian duke and the sundering of the union would bring Poland much benefit. Like his great-uncle Siemowit IV in the 1380s, Bolesław only ruled part of Mazovia, and he had just been defeated by Casimir in the Podlasian war. Half of Mazovia would be scant recompense for all of Lithuania and the hostility of a Jagiellon who claimed to be the natural heir to the Polish throne.

The Poles knew it and the Lithuanians knew it. In the end, attachment to the Jagiellonian dynasty, to which both Poles and Lithuanians had sworn oaths of allegiance, and to the union was too strong. In Lithuania, Bolesław's election concentrated minds, while Casimir worried about Mykolas.[61] In Poland, Sonka gathered support for Casimir. Oleśnicki's Małopolskan opponents met in April 1446 at Bełżyce, which belonged to Jan Pilecki, Jagiełło's stepson. Most were from the younger generation excluded from power by the council oligarchs; through Sonka they were in contact with Casimir. It was their envoy, Piotr Kurowski, rather

---

[58] *Annales*, xii/i, 24; Lewicki, 'Wstąpienie', 8.
[59] Halecki, *Ostatne lata*, 76; Halecki, *Dzieje*, i, 356.
[60] Błaszczyk, *Dzieje*, ii/i, 803–4; Rowell, 'Casimir', 25–6; Lewicki, 'Wstąpienie', 11–14.
[61] Rowell, 'Casimir', 8, 27, 39; Łowmiański, *Polityka*, 215.

than the official embassy sent by another Piotrków assembly, who obtained a private promise from Casimir to accept the throne.[62]

The stalemate was broken. When Oleśnicki proposed at a Małopolskan assembly in Cracow on 8 May that Bolesław's election be confirmed, he was trumped by Kurowski, who produced Casimir's promise. With no agreement possible, Oleśnicki proposed that a final decision should not be taken before an assembly of the Wielkopolskans in Koło in June. The envoy chosen by the Małopolskans to attend this assembly, however, was Jan Pilecki. On 13 June the Wielkopolskans chose Casimir, and proposed another embassy to meet him in Parczew in September, a decision accepted by the Małopolskans in August.[63]

The terms still needed thrashing out. It was no easy matter. The Poles assembled in Parczew, but Casimir and the Lithuanians won an important symbolic victory by staying in Brest, just across the border in Lithuania. They refused to come to Parczew, insisting that the talks take place in Lithuania, a condition to which the Poles reluctantly agreed. According to Długosz, Casimir denied that he had agreed to accept the Polish crown or that he had promised Kurowski that he would come, saying he had only accepted Sonka's pleas.[64] The Poles had few cards left to play. When Casimir said he would refuse the throne if the Lithuanian terms were not accepted, the Poles capitulated, though not without bitter complaints. Casimir finally agreed to accept the offer of the throne; his coronation was fixed for 24 June 1447.

Casimir and the Lithuanians had won. In his promise to uphold the union and to come to Cracow for his coronation, drawn up on 17 September, and the document issued two days later by the Polish envoys on behalf of the Polish community of the realm, Casimir was entitled: '*Dei gratia electus rex regni Poloniae et magnus dux Lythwaniae*'.[65] Thus the Poles were forced publicly to accept the legitimacy of Casimir's 1440 election as grand duke; he had been previously been described in Polish documents merely as '*dux Lithuaniae*', a title accorded to all Gediminid princes. Casimir promised to maintain Poland and Lithuania *in unione caritatis*, as his predecessors had done. In this renewal of the union, he stated that, with unanimous consent, he had joined the two polities together; the language was of consent and fraternal union, with none of Horodło's incorporationist language.[66]

The Poles had to swallow several bitter pills. They agreed that Casimir was free to maintain at his court individuals of 'any language' he chose, and to reside in either of his realms as and when he saw fit.[67] Thus the Lithuanians secured a right to a permanent presence at Casimir's side, and therefore the possibility of influencing

---

[62] Błaszczyk, *Dzieje*, ii/i, 805–6; Rowell, 'Casimir, 27.   [63] Błaszczyk, *Dzieje*, ii/i, 806.
[64] *Annales*, xii/i, 38–41; Wojciech Fałkowski, 'Polsko-litewskie negocjacje w 1446 roku', in Kras et al. (eds), *Ecclesia Cultura Potestas* (Cracow, 2006), 470.
[65] *AU*, no. 68, 116, no. 69, 117.
[66] 'ipsum regnum Poloniae et magnum ducatum Lythwaniae utriusque dominii consilio, voluntate unanimi et assensu in unam fraternam unionem iunximus, copulavimus et annexuimus, volentes ipsorum esse dominus et rector divina disponente clementia': *AU*, no. 68, 116.
[67] *AU*, no. 68, 116–17.

him and playing a role in decision-making. The documents were silent on the dispute over Volhynia and Podolia; resolution of the problem was postponed until Švitrigaila should die. Casimir had gained much. There was good reason for the clause concerning his freedom to have Lithuanians present at court: the Vytautan model, which the Lithuanians had defended for so long, had been quietly abandoned. There was to be no separate grand duke in Vilnius; Casimir was to rule both his realms himself.

The crisis was over and the union had been saved. Casimir's coronation symbolized the reconciliation of the parties that had squabbled, fought, and disputed the nature of the union for nearly two decades. He was crowned by Kot in the presence of several Piasts, including both dukes of Mazovia and the Silesian dukes of Teschen, Ratibor, and Oświęcim. Representatives of the Order, which had studiously avoided interfering, also attended. Most telling was the presence of Švitrigaila, Algirdas's only surviving son. He completed his public reconciliation with Casimir, who allowed him to retain the title of grand duke. The old man was no longer a threat. The peoples of the union were entering a new era.

PART IV

CONSOLIDATION AND CHANGE

18
Defining the Union

What was the nature of the union after 1447? Most historians have concluded that the events of 1440–7 buried the Polish vision of an accessory union: if the Poles never forgot the contents and spirit—as they saw it—of the union treaties, and revived incorporationist sentiments after Casimir's death in 1492, from 1447 until 1569 the Polish-Lithuanian union was purely personal and, between 1492 and 1501, when there were again separate rulers in Cracow and Vilnius, it constituted a mere dynastic union. Błaszczyk considers that the union was broken in 1440; 1447 therefore saw the establishment of a personal union between two sovereign states. Bardach maintains that since this personal union was not based on a treaty it was contingent in nature. For Halecki, it was not the union that was broken in 1440 but the agreements on which it was based; after 1440 it constituted a dynastic relationship between two equal states, although he suggested that this was only recognized in 1499. Lithuanian historians keen to emphasize the preservation of Lithuanian sovereignty and independence and the looseness of the link with Poland agree that this was a loose relationship between two sovereign states.[1]

Yet this was no ordinary personal union and there was much more to it than a common ruler. The Brest documents of September 1446 may not have constituted a formal treaty of union and may have lacked Horodło's incorporationist rhetoric, but they spoke the language of fraternal union, and provided a framework, however rudimentary, for relations between the two realms. The definitive establishment of the elective nature of the Polish monarchy with the election of Władysław III in 1430—albeit with continued respect for the dynasty's natural rights—and the elections of Švitrigaila, Žygimantas, and Casimir in Lithuania demonstrated the extent to which the two communities of the realm had established their right to be consulted with regard to who ruled over them. The union depended upon collective acts of will, not the vagaries of hereditary succession.

The institution of royal election, defined in Poland between 1382 and 1430 and extended to Lithuania in 1413 for the position of grand duke, meant that it was not so easy to end the union. It was not broken in 1440: the Lithuanians elected Casimir under the terms of Horodło and never challenged Władysław's hereditary rights as supreme duke. The complex legal position with regard to elections was defined in the union treaties, none of which were repealed. While some, such as Hrodna, lost their relevance when circumstances changed, the Poles never forgot

---

[1] Kutrzeba, 'Charakter', 172; Błaszczyk, *Dzieje*, ii/i, 812; Bardach, 'Krewo', 605; Halecki, *Dzieje*, i, 331; Dundulis, *Kova*, 188; Gudavičius, *Istorija*, 299; Petrauskas, 'Blick', 363.

them and—whatever historians have argued—believed them still to be in force. The Poles may have toned down their rhetoric after 1446, but they still believed that Lithuania had been incorporated, even if they were unclear as to what incorporation signified. The elective principle quickly took root in Lithuania: although the Jagiellons claimed hereditary rights to the grand duchy, Władysław and John Albert were the only Lithuanian supreme dukes between 1413 and 1569 who were not first elected grand duke.

It was not just the Poles, therefore, who remembered the treaties: the Lithuanians were perfectly capable of appealing to them when it suited them, as in 1446, when Casimir and the Lithuanians told the Order that Bolesław IV's provisional election breached Horodło, which required the Poles to consult the Lithuanians when electing their king.[2] They rejected the Polish interpretation of the treaties, but those treaties established limits to grand ducal power which the Lithuanians were loath to surrender. Horodło introduced the Polish system of provincial government in the palatinates of Vilnius and Trakai, which meant that Lithuania proper was exposed to the culture of consultation that had flourished in Poland since 1370, albeit in a limited form, since neither sejmiks—as the local and provincial dietines were called—nor elective Polish courts were introduced. Nevertheless, the new system of local administration, which drew in more of the local nobility, and increasingly frequent assemblies on the Polish pattern, meant that leading Lithuanian boyars gained a political voice. Finally, Horodło, by limiting government office to Catholics, ensured that despite the extension of rights and privileges to Ruthenian nobles in 1434, Catholic Lithuanians remained in charge.

Horodło's provision for joint assemblies was not forgotten. Between 1447 and 1453 three such assemblies were held at the venues designated by Horodło: Lublin (1448) and Parczew (1451 and 1453); another was held at Brest in 1454. The first, at Lublin in May 1448, was attended on the Polish side by two archbishops and four bishops, including Oleśnicki and Kot. Jan of Czyżów, castellan of Cracow, and Jan Tęczyński, palatine of Cracow, led a significant number of lay dignitaries. The Lithuanian delegation, led by Motiejus, bishop of Vilnius, included Iury Lengvinovich and the men who had masterminded Casimir's election: Jonas Goštautas, palatine of Vilnius; Jonas Manvydaitis, palatine of Trakai; Marshal Petras Mantigirdaitis, and Iury Holshansky. Ruthenians from both the kingdom and the grand duchy, including Vasyl Krasny, Prince Ostrozky, came to discuss Podolia and Volhynia.[3]

The attendance of so many dignitaries suggests that the assembly intended to discuss more than Polish support for Lithuania's forthcoming Muscovite campaign, its ostensible purpose, but reflected the desire of moderates on both sides to reach agreement over the union's nature following the years of crisis.[4] This was no easy task. Emboldened by their recent success, the Lithuanians returned to the issue that had provoked the coronation tempest, demanding the removal from the union

---

[2] *CESXV*, iii, no. 3, 5.
[3] *Annales*, xii/i, 60; Halecki, *Dzieje*, i, 366; Dundulis, *Kova*, 191.
[4] Łowmiański, *Polityka*, 221–2.

treaties of all clauses implying that Lithuania had been incorporated into Poland, on the grounds that they implied that Lithuanians were of inferior status. The Poles countered by suggesting that the office of grand duke be abolished in perpetuity, thus rejecting a key clause in Horodło, but conceding that the union treaties could be altered. They stressed that if the Lithuanians accepted incorporation it would render irrelevant the dispute over Podolia and Volhynia. The Lithuanians rejected these proposals. They were happy to be ruled by a common prince, but refused to accept that Lithuania was a Polish province. They were determined to retain the separate title of grand duke and the possibility that they might elect another after Casimir's death. The Poles vainly rehearsed their mantra that the Lithuanians had agreed to the terms of union in 1386 and 1413, and that the grand duchy had already been incorporated. Agreement was impossible, and the Lithuanians withdrew, refusing to discuss Podolia and Volhynia.[5]

It was three years before they reassembled in Parczew in late September 1451. As Švitrigaila's long life drew to a close it was necessary to discuss Podolia and Volhynia. The prospects for agreement were poor. Casimir initially spent most of his time after 1447 in Lithuania, and first held an assembly in Vilnius with Lithuanians and Ruthenians from both parts of the union, at which the Lithuanian position was carefully prepared. Długosz, a member of the delegation that discussed the matter with Casimir, castigated him for favouring Lithuania.[6] Jonas Goštautas, leader of the Lithuanian hardliners, returned to Vilnius when the Poles refused to issue safe-conducts. Casimir had to travel to the border to persuade the other Lithuanians to come to Parczew.[7]

No progress was made. Oleśnicki bored everyone with lengthy lectures on the history of the union, waving around the 1432 Hrodna treaty, which stipulated that Podolia and Volhynia would revert to Poland on Žygimantas's death. The Lithuanians, led by Motiejus, bishop of Vilnius, were well acquainted with the treaties. Motiejus condemned Horodło's incorporationist clauses, which were 'onerous and highly insulting', claiming that they cast the yoke of slavery upon the Lithuanians. He demanded that Lithuanian rule over Podolia and Volhynia be confirmed and requested a new union treaty, arguing that the Lithuanians had only agreed to Horodło because they had been ordered to by Vytautas, not knowing what it contained.[8]

None of this was acceptable to the Poles, and the assembly achieved nothing. Yet the Lithuanians showed that they had learned much. Motiejus's claim that they had not known what they were agreeing to in 1413 was cunning. It appealed directly to the Polish principle that ultimate authority lay with a community of the realm that refused to bow to the prince's arbitrary will, and neatly countered the standard Polish claim that the Lithuanians had consented to the union treaties. It reduced

---

[5] *Annales*, xii/i, 60–4; Halecki, *Dzieje*, i, 367–8; Любавский, *Сеймъ*, 117.
[6] *Annales*, xii/i, 98, 108–10; Halecki, *Ostatnie lata*, 156–8; Halecki, *Dzieje*, i, 373–4.
[7] *Annales*, xii/i, 114; Błaszczyk, *Dzieje*, ii/i, 822–3, 825–6; Halecki, *Dzieje*, i, 374; Любавский, *Сеймъ*, 117–18.
[8] *Annales*, xii/i, 114; Любавский, *Сеймъ*, 118; Dundulis, *Kova*, 192–3.

Oleśnicki to blustering that the treaties should be honoured for they had been drafted by 'such wise princes' as Jagiełło and Vytautas; his discomfort at this line of argument is hinted at by Długosz, who wrote that he presented it not with his usual forceful, confident air, but 'with a strange modesty and courtesy'.[9] Motiejus had turned the great champion of the *communitas regni* into a flatterer of princes, albeit ones who were safely dead.

Motiejus claimed that Lithuania was neither incorporated into Poland nor subject to it; he spoke of the relationship as an association or league.[10] These were the terms used in a document Lewicki dates September 1446, and presents as a Lithuanian project of union submitted to the Parczew-Brest assembly before Casimir's coronation in Cracow. A fuller version was discovered by Ulanowski and published by Kutrzeba. Fałkowski argues that it was drafted as the basis for negotiation over the terms of Casimir's accession to the Polish throne in 1446, although, as Rowell observes, the fact that Casimir is referred to as king suggests it was presented at one of the Parczew assemblies in 1451 or 1453.[11] Whenever it was drafted, the suggestion that it was a project for a new union depends on the assumption that a new union was necessary. Thus it, together with Motiejus's 1451 speech, have been used to suggest that the Lithuanians were separatists, who proposed nothing more than a mere alliance of two independent, sovereign states.[12]

Fałkowski is right, however, to reject the idea that the document constituted a proposal for a new union.[13] It contains no indication that the Lithuanians regarded the union as broken: quite the contrary. It was a statement of how the Lithuanians understood the nature of the voluntary relationship they had entered into with Poland that stressed the consent of the citizens of both parties to the union, who had joined together in 'fraternal equality' and friendship, before supplying a list of synonyms that echoed those used at Horodło to denote fraternal union, rather than incorporation: '*sinceritate confederavimus, complicavimus, composuimus, colligavimus et presentibus confederamus, complicamus, componimus et liga perpetua colligamus*'.[14]

While the document stressed that Poland and Lithuania were separate realms, the use of the perfect tense in the list of synonyms demonstrates that the union had been formed; the use of the present tense suggests that the Lithuanians wished to renew it, as at Horodło, through mutual agreement over what it signified. Throughout, the stress is on the equality of the two realms (*dominia*) joined in union, whose honour and status should be respected. Neither should be subject to the other, or incorporated, or appropriated, and each should remain a free realm.[15]

---

[9] *Annales*, xii/i, 114–15.

[10] 'non incorporacionem aut subieccionem terrarum Lithuaniae et Russiae, sed societatem et ligam cum Regno Poloniae contineant': *Annales*, xii/i, 114.

[11] *CESXV*, iii, no. 5, 7; Lewicki, 'Wstąpienie', 23–5; 'Projekt unji polsko-litewskiej z r. 1446', ed. Bolesław Ulanowski, *Archiwum Komisji Prawniczej*, 6 (1926), 235–9; Fałkowski, 'Negocjacje', 469; Rowell, 'Casimir', 31. Prochaska, who did not know of Ulanowski's discovery, rejects the 1446 dating: Prochaska, 'O rzekomej unii z 1446', *KH*, 18 (1904), 24–31.

[12] For example Грушевський, *Історія*, iv, 238.   [13] Fałkowski, 'Negocjacje', 469.

[14] 'Projekt', 237.

[15] 'quod unumquodque dominiorum predictorum et incole eorundem in suo honore permaneant, nec unum alteri sit subiectum aut incorporatum sive appropriatum, sed prout alias liberum et speciale extitit dominium, ita modo et peramplius debet permanere.' 'Projekt', 237; Fałkowski, 'Negocjacje', 468.

The document ends by directly citing Horodło's stipulation on the vital issue of the succession, reminding the Poles that the union treaties decreed that the Poles should not elect their king without Lithuanian participation, and that Lithuanians should not elect a grand duke without consulting the Poles.[16]

In the sense that the Lithuanians envisaged the union as a relationship between two separate realms, this document is separatist, but the term is best avoided, as historians tend to use it to signify support for the breaking of the union and establishment of Lithuania as a fully independent sovereign state in the modern sense. By stressing the possible future election of a grand duke they reminded the Poles that it was they who had forgotten the Horodło provisions in 1430 and 1440. The Lithuanians demonstrated their awareness of the terms of the union treaties, proposing a different vision of the relationship. They did not see it as a purely personal union, for to do so would be to deprive them of the possibility of electing their grand dukes.

The document encapsulates the Lithuanian vision of a fraternal union entered into by two separate and equal realms: the term '*equalitate*' is used to characterize the formation of the union. Its emphasis on the union treaties that had institutionalized their right to elect their grand duke suggests that, if Jellinek is right to insist that a true personal union is not a juridical but a historical-political relationship, which from the legal point of view constitutes an accidental political community (*Gemeinschaft*) united only in the person of the ruler and possessing as many separate legal personalities as there were polities united under the one sceptre, then the Polish-Lithuanian union was far more than a personal union.[17]

So what was it? Jellinek suggests that a personal union in a modern constitutional monarchy can be formed through election, and not just dynastic inheritance, but he does not discuss personal unions in elective monarchies.[18] His back-projection, however, of his rigid concepts of the indivisibility of sovereignty and of the unitary state as a legal personality is unhelpful. Neither the Poles nor the Lithuanians thought in these terms in the fifteenth century. The debates centred around dynastic patrimony, its nature, its basis, and its legitimate claims, and the role of the community of the realm, rather than concepts of statehood or sovereignty.[19] Jellinek, in discussing incorporation, argues that there are two forms: one in which the sovereignty of one state is completely subjected to that of the state into which it is incorporated; in the second, the sovereignty of both states is dissolved, and a wholly new entity is created.[20] He recognizes, however, that in pre-modern *Staatsrecht* matters were different, and that theorists were influenced by what he terms the 'scholastic distinctions' of canon law, grudgingly conceding that for the pre-modern period to talk, as contemporaries did, of unions by partial incorporation in which legal systems remained separate and unequal, has a 'certain validity'.[21]

The Polish conception of incorporation was not based on the modern idea of the unitary, sovereign state. It was informed by canon law ideas that recognized various

---

[16] 'Projekt', 239. [17] Jellinek, *Lehre*, 85. [18] Jellinek, *Lehre*, 87.
[19] Rowell, 'Casimir', 7–8, 38–9; Rowell, '1446', 203. [20] Jellinek, *Lehre*, 68.
[21] Jellinek, *Lehre*, 68–9.

types of union, of which complete incorporation, in which the laws of the incorporated realm were dissolved—*unio per suppressionem*—was but one type. Incorporation could be complete—*incorporatio plena*—but also partial—*minus plena*. Other forms of union allowed for the dissolution of both bodies and their reformation or fusion into a new entity—*unio per novationem* or *per confusionem*. Real unions could be formed without the necessity for incorporation, in which the laws of both realms were preserved on an equal basis—*unio realis aequali jure*—or in which the laws of one party were regarded in the final instance as superior, in a union *inaequali jure*.[22]

Jellinek, with his tidy jurist's mind, disliked such messy arrangements.[23] Most historians of the union have interpreted it in Jellinek's terms, conceiving it as a relationship between two sovereign, unitary states. Yet many of those who discussed it between 1429 and 1453 were steeped in canon law and the concepts that Jellinek dismisses. In rejecting the idea of *incorporatio plena*, the Lithuanians were not defending a unitary, sovereign, modern state, but a vision of a union *aequali iure*, or *aeque principaliter*, in which the grand duchy was equal in status to Poland. The Poles clung to the incorporationist clause in Horodło, but the lack of clarity in both Krewo and Horodło as to the nature of that incorporation meant that they themselves were unclear as to what it might in practice mean.

While the Poles continued to believe Lithuania had been incorporated, they could neither persuade the Lithuanians to accept their interpretation, nor agree to the amendment of the union treaties. In practice, therefore, they had to accept that the incorporation was *minus plena* after a third assembly at Parczew in June 1453 ended in deadlock. It marked the last attempt to reach agreement over the nature of the union during Casimir's long reign.[24] Yet it is not that failure that should be emphasized, but the spirit of compromise that ultimately prevailed. The Poles and Lithuanians agreed to differ, and the issue was buried for a generation. This did not mean, however, that the relationship between the two polities was that of two independent states joined merely by the person of the ruler. After 1454 there was much contact and cooperation, as well as the rancorous disputes stemming from the defence of local interests that are common to all unions. During Casimir's forty-five year reign the process of union, the quiet growing together of the two separate polities that formed it, meant that by the time of his death, the political landscape had been transformed.

This was possible in part because the absence of any serious dynastic challengers to Casimir reduced the temperature considerably, and enabled him to establish himself securely on the thrones of both his realms. By 1447 Švitrigaila and Iury Lengvinevich were old men, neither of them inclined to challenge Casimir. He secured their loyalty by restoring their patrimonies, on which they quietly lived out their days. Švitrigaila had no heir, while Iury's descendants joined the mass of minor Gediminid princes whose status diminished generation by generation.[25] No such generosity was shown to Mykolas Žygimantaitis, whose claim to Trakai was

---

[22] Jellinek, *Lehre*, 68. [23] Jellinek, *Lehre*, 68. [24] Halecki, *Dzieje*, i, 384–5.
[25] Rowell, 'Casimir', 32, 38; Tęgowski, *Pierwsze*, 121–3.

not upheld. Although some early Lithuanian support for his election as grand duke soon withered, his cause was taken up by Polish malcontents: Oleśnicki urged Casimir to restore his patrimony at Parczew in 1451. Mykolas paid the price, however, for taking up arms against Casimir. Rebuffed by the Order and the Mazovians, he participated in a Tatar raid on Lithuania in 1448, and led a more devastating one in 1449 which briefly captured Kyiv, Briansk, Starodub, and Novhorod-Siversky.[26] The attacks alienated any Lithuanian supporters he had left, and he ceased to be a threat. Following the well-beaten path of aggrieved Gediminids to Moscow, he was neutralized by an agreement between Casimir and Vasilii II in August 1449, and poisoned at some point before 10 February 1452.[27] The Kęstutids were no more, while the childless Švitrigaila's death in 1453 removed the last of Algirdas's sons from the scene. The way was open for the Jagiellons to establish themselves as one of Europe's great dynasties, eclipsing the Luxembourgs and proving powerful rivals to the Habsburgs for over a century.

Casimir's acceptance of the Polish throne ended the long, bitter Lithuanian dynastic struggle that had begun in 1377, and which had done much to shape the process of union. It is better to see the fifteenth-century relationship between Poland and the grand duchy in terms of patrimony, suzerainty, and lordship, than to squeeze it into the anachronistic procrustean bed of sovereign national statehood. The loyalties of those that formed it were directed towards princes, however the basis of their authority was conceived. The force of tradition, and a fundamental attachment to the hereditary transmission of authority—whether or not it was subject to the principle of election—was powerful. The language was of lordship—*dominium, gosudarstvo, panowanie, Herrschaft*—not of sovereignty. Although there were undoubtedly strong elements of feudal law in the way in which the early Jagiellons conceived their lordship, most notably in the relationship between Poland and its vassal duchies, and in the patrimonial dispositions made to individual members of the dynasty, the relationship between Poland and Lithuania, as opposed to the personal relationship between Jagiełło and Vytautas, or Jagiełło and Žygimantas, was never one of feudal dependency, and was not conceived in this way.

In textbook accounts, the Polish-Lithuanian union is usually described as moving from a personal union after 1386 to a real union in 1569. Yet in many respects the Polish-Lithuanian union from 1386, and in particular from 1413, meets Jellinek's definition of a real, rather than a personal union, making allowances for the fact that Jellinek's view of unions between states depends on a modern definition of sovereignty and legal personality.[28] For Jellinek, monarchical unions were peculiarly well suited to the formation of real unions, since sovereignty in monarchical states lay firmly in one place, in the person of the monarch.[29] This would certainly accord with Jagiełło's—if not Vytautas's—view of the union, but it is the other features of Jellinek's definition of real union that are significant in this

---

[26] Błaszczyk, *Dzieje*, ii/i, 814–15.
[27] *Annales*, xii/i, 105–6; Błaszczyk, *Dzieje*, ii/i, 813–16; Rowell, 'Casimir', 38.
[28] Jellinek, *Lehre*, 197–222.   [29] Jellinek, *Lehre*, 211.

context. For him, a real union had to have a juridical unity (*rechtliche Einheit*) that could be embodied in the person of the common monarch, if that monarch embodied a unitary state in the modern sense.[30] While the Polish-Lithuanian union after 1386 was a composite, not a unitary state of the modern kind, nevertheless, the union treaties certainly expressed—at least in the incorporationist Polish interpretation of them—a sense that the grand duchy was being attached to the Polish *regnum*; this may have been for tactical reasons in the Horodło treaty, to demonstrate the unity of the Polish-Lithuanian union as a single actor on the international stage, but it certainly means that there was a sense of unity transcending the person of the king.

Whatever the contested nature of the union, it fulfils Jellinek's next criterion for a real union: namely that—again in contrast to personal unions, which arose without the consent of the polities involved—real unions are the result of an act of will of the parties in the form of an agreement embodied in one or more foundation treaties.[31] Despite the objection raised by Motiejus at Parczew in 1451 concerning the obedience of the Lithuanian elites to the commands of their princes, the emphasis in all the union treaties was on the agreement of the Polish and Lithuanian communities of the realm. For Jellinek, the necessity for a foundation treaty meant that a real union could only take place between two polities with strongly developed estates systems.[32] While it would be premature to claim that the grand duchy had a developed estates system, the emergence of the concept of the community of the realm in Poland and its increasing direct involvement in politics through regular assemblies at the local and national level certainly meets this criterion, while—as political developments in Lithuania after 1429 demonstrate—the culture of consensus and debate soon spread into the grand duchy, as a direct result of the union.

Moreover, Jellinek saw real unions—in stark contrast to personal unions—as difficult to dissolve, since they were based on treaties, and, from the legal standpoint, dissolution required the consent of both parties.[33] That this was true of the Polish-Lithuanian union is neatly demonstrated by the joint assemblies held at Lublin and Parczew between 1448 and 1453. The Lithuanians sought not to break the union, but to secure Polish acceptance of their view of the union as a relationship *aeque principaliter*. They had good reason not to wish to break the union, for their political liberties and the principle that they should have a say in who was to rule over them as grand duke depended upon Horodło. If the treaties of union were repealed it would be difficult to contest the patrimonial view of their own authority held by their grand dukes. It was not just that the reigns of Švitrigaila and Žygimantas had given them good reason for concern at such a prospect; the exposure for six decades to Polish notions of citizenship and consensual politics had transformed Lithuanian views of their own polity and how it should operate. Motiejus's observation that the Lithuanians no longer wished simply to do what their princes commanded indicates that the Lithuanian political elite had travelled a long way by 1451.

---

[30] Jellinek, *Lehre*, 212. [31] Jellinek, *Lehre*, 212.
[32] Jellinek, *Lehre*, 213, 216. [33] Jellinek, *Lehre*, 218.

The Lithuanians failed to secure Polish agreement for the redrafting of the union treaties after 1447. Yet despite all the rancour and the complete failure to agree on its nature, the union remained in force. While the Poles never forgot their incorporationist interpretation, and would reassert it, they had failed to give it any real form between 1385 and 1453. The Lithuanians defended their view that they were of equal, not subordinate status, and they had done so using terms and ideas drawn from the conceptual arsenal assembled in Poland during the fourteenth century and deployed in the union treaties: as they pointed out in Parczew in 1451, union treaties issued by the grand dukes were not binding upon them, for they had been issued without the participation of the estates of the Grand Duchy.[34] They did not specify which treaties they had in mind, but their point was clear: if the union were to survive it had to be a consensual relationship sealed by the parliamentary institutions the Poles held so dear. It helped that after 1453 the temperature diminished somewhat. With no plausible alternatives to him after Mykolas's poisoning, Casimir rapidly established himself as a shrewd ruler whose early identification with Lithuania and whose frequent presence in the grand duchy—though the length of his stays diminished substantially after 1454—demonstrated that he did not regard it as inferior in status. This shrewdness was manifested in his handling of the issue of Podolia and Volhynia. The Lithuanians, with Casimir's encouragement—he was in Lithuania at the time, which hindered any effective Polish response—prepared carefully for Švitrigaila's death. In early 1452 Casimir made grants of land to Volhynian nobles to secure their support for Lithuanian rule, and Švitrigaila expressed his wish that control should pass to Lithuania on his death. When he died on 10 February the Lithuanians moved swiftly, garrisoning Lutsk, and, concerned at preparations by Red Ruthenian nobles to mount an armed expedition to seize it back, partially burned Volodymyr castle to prevent them using it as an operational base. Casimir issued a new Volhynian privilege in which he promised to maintain Lithuania's borders as they had been under Vytautas. The Poles were outraged, but although a Małopolskan assembly at Sandomierz in March talked war, few were prepared to fight, and Casimir secured support from Wielkopolska, where resentment at the Małopolskan lords was considerable and interest in Podolia and Volhynia minimal.[35] Despite several assemblies in which sabres were loudly rattled and Casimir was castigated for favouring Lithuania, and furious confrontations over the matter at Parczew in 1453, a compromise was negotiated. A Polish delegation from which Oleśnicki was conspicuously absent attended a Lithuanian assembly in Brest in early April 1454 where a deal was struck on the basis of the status quo: the Poles retained control of western Podolia with Kamianets and the Volhynian towns of Olesko and Ratno, and agreed not to challenge Lithuanian rule over eastern Podolia and Volhynia.[36]

---

[34] Грушевський, *Історія*, iv, 241.
[35] Halecki, *Ostatnie lata*, 176–7, 186–7, 190–3, 200–1.
[36] Halecki, *Dzieje*, i, 388; Halecki, *Ostatnie lata*, 234–5; Górski, 'Młodość', 14.

Attitudes softened. From 1454 the Poles looked north as the Order's Prussian subjects rebelled against its rule. While the Lithuanians had little interest in supporting Polish intervention, the Poles, haunted by memories of Salin and Christmemel, needed to ensure Lithuanian neutrality. The Lithuanians had to reckon with the revival of discontent in Volhynia where the Chortoryskys and Sangushkos led a group of Ruthenian nobles with links to Red Ruthenia who were unreconciled to Lithuanian rule, and who plotted with Ruthenians under Polish rule to seize Lutsk and hand it over to the Poles.[37] Compromise suited both sides, and the issue largely disappeared until its dramatic re-emergence in 1569.

[37] Halecki, *Ostatnie lata*, 161, 164, 227; Halecki, *Dzieje*, i, 382–3; Błaszczyk, *Dzieje*, ii/i, 818–42.

19

Prussia

As the Poles and Lithuanians wrangled at Brest in April 1454, events to the north launched a process that was to transform the union. By 1435 the Order's glory days were over. The conversion of Lithuania, Tannenberg, and the challenge mounted at Constance posed serious questions about its role. While the Livonian Order could still claim some legitimacy for its struggle against the Orthodox of Pskov, Novgorod, and Muscovy, their Prussian superiors were swept from the moral heights at Constance.[1] As the supply of western volunteers dried up and mercenaries were hired to fight in their place, the Order turned to its subjects to meet its rising costs. It had encouraged settlers from Germany and Poland by offering land tenure with few obligations beyond military service, and by issuing generous privileges, including exemptions from tax and customs dues. For 150 years, and in particular during the six decades of peace with Poland after 1343, the Order flourished. Advanced techniques of government, carried out by its elite of several hundred brothers bound by the strict discipline of its rule, brought prosperity. Good roads encouraged trade; magnificent brick churches and municipal buildings turned towns across the *Ordensstaat* into beacons of sophisticated civilization among the largely wooden settlements of northeastern Europe.

Before Tannenberg the Order's rule was broadly accepted. Military service was mostly undertaken abroad; volunteers were paid, and benefited from the booty they seized on raids into neighbouring lands. After Tannenberg conditions changed dramatically. Most of the fighting now took place within the *Ordensstaat* itself. The enemy regularly laid waste to the Prussian lands. The devastation made local elites increasingly unwilling or unable to fulfil their obligation to defend the realm, for which they were not paid. The Order faced a recruitment crisis, partly due to social change among the knightly class in north-west Germany that was starkly evident after the losses sustained at Tannenberg: the number of brothers declined from around 700 before 1409 to some 400 thereafter, while accusations of moral decline from the secular clergy, and even from within the Order's own ranks, began to grow.[2] Prussia was no longer attractive for young Germans on the make.

The willingness of so many cities across the *Ordensstaat* to swear loyalty to Jagiełło in 1410 demonstrated that all was not well in relations between the Order and its subjects. After 1343 its brothers turned to trade despite their oaths to

---

[1] Biskup and Labuda, *Dzieje*, 379–80. [2] Biskup and Labuda, *Dzieje*, 380–1.

renounce worldly pursuits.³ In the harsher economic climate after the Black Death towns resented the competition. Complaints multiplied after 1400 as the Order, forced to raise money to sustain its military campaigns, developed what Burleigh terms a 'grasping fiscality'. Even if the economic damage to the towns was not as great as the volume of complaints might suggest, the perception that competition from the Order was undermining trade soured relations: trade by Order officials was one of the nine reasons given by Danzig in 1453 to justify joining the Prussian Bund in 1440.⁴ Grasping fiscality was symbolized by the *Pfundzoll*, a Hanseatic levy first raised in 1361. In 1389 the Prussian estates, which owed the Order money, collected it without Hanse sanction, but with the grand master's permission; from 1395 it was raised permanently. The cities used it for their own purposes, but in 1403 the Order began syphoning off one-third of the proceeds. Opposition flared, and the Order defeated an attempt to abolish it in 1407. Tension grew after 1409, when the Order raised its share to two-thirds despite fierce resistance.⁵

The Order's exemption from taxation gave bite to urban complaints about unfair competition. It was no better in the countryside. Nobles were told to forget their military obligations and remain on their estates in wartime, while the Order taxed them to support mercenary armies. Grants of land on Culm law became infrequent; instead they were made on Magdeburg—or even Polish—law, since these were less favourable to landholders: the Order could secure control of estates without a male heir in the direct line, which was resented since it prevented local families from consolidating their holdings through inheritance from collateral lines, or through marrying heiresses. Burdens on the peasantry increased, and restrictions on their freedom of movement provoked a spate of peasant flight.⁶

That the Order was an alien, non-hereditary elite bound by oaths of chastity and in need of constant refreshment from outside had not mattered in the prosperous years before 1400. The sharp change in its fortunes meant that its diminishing core of knights was detached from the native and settler families that constituted the local elites, who resented the grip of southern German families on the Order's hierarchy.⁷ As discontent grew, the Prussian estates, comprising prelates and representatives of the nobility and the cities, which had been called occasionally before 1409, began to matter. At an assembly in Osterode in 1411 Heinrich von

---

³ Karol Górski, *Państwo krzyżackie w Prusach* (Gdańsk/Bydgoszcz, 1946), 120–6. The best account of the Order's economic activity is Jürgen Sarnowsky, *Die Wirtschaftsführung des Deutschen Ordens in Preußen (1382–1454)* (Cologne, 1993).

⁴ Michael Burleigh, *Prussian Society and the German Order* (Cambridge, 1984), 141; Sarnowsky, *Wirtschaftsführung*, 294; Roman Czaja, 'Związki gospodarcze wielkich szafarzy zakonu krzyżackiego z miastami pruskimi na początku XV wieku', in Zenon Nowak (ed.), *Zakon krzyżacki a społeczeństwo państwa w Prusach*, Roczniki Towarzystwa Naukowego w Toruniu, 86/3 (Toruń, 1995), 29–31; Roman Czaja, 'Der Handel des Deutschen Ordens und der preußischen Städte—Wirtschaft zwischen Zusammenarbeit und Rivalität', in Zenon Nowak (ed.), *Ritterorden und Region: Politische, soziale und wirtschaftliche Verbindungen im Mittelalter* (Toruń, 1995), 118–19; Josef Lienz, 'Die Ursachen des Abfalls Danzigs vom Deutschen Orden: Unter Besonderer Berücksichtigung der Nationalen Frage', *Jahrbuch der Geschichte Ost- und Mitteldeutschlands*, 13–14 (1965), 2.

⁵ Jürgen Sarnowsky, 'Zölle und Steuern im Ordensland Preußen (1403–1454)', in Nowak (ed.), *Ritterorden*, 68–72; Burleigh, *Prussian Society*, 106.

⁶ Burleigh, *Prussian Society*, 94–6; Biskup and Labuda, *Dzieje*, 390, 384–6.

⁷ Burleigh, *Prussian Society*, 141.

Plauen forced through taxes against fierce opposition to pay the reparations decreed by the Thorn peace.[8] When his brother, the komtur of Danzig—also Heinrich—met opposition from the city council, he executed the mayor, Konrad Letzkau, and two councillors without trial, along with five Culm nobles; their bodies were thrown into the castle ditch to rot.[9]

This was shocking to elites accustomed to the rule of law and possessing extensive privileges granted by the Order itself, including a form of *habeas corpus* conceded to the Culm nobility as recently as 1409.[10] The first concerted opposition came in 1397 with the formation of the *Eidechsengesellschaft* (Lizard League) in the Culm lands, where there was a substantial petty nobility of Polish descent. Its charter contained no overt political demands, calling instead for mutual support and assistance to members in trouble, but despite the innocuous phrasing its formation had strong political overtones.[11] It was tolerated by the Order, but was treated with suspicion after its founder, Nikolaus von Rynes, paid homage to Jagiełło on the battlefield after Tannenberg, and later sought refuge in Poland. Another member, Johann von Pulkau, occupied Schönsee on behalf of the Poles in 1410.[12]

The Order had to call the estates regularly after 1411. Between 1414 and 1422, grand master Küchmeister was careful to secure their agreement for his foreign policy, but his successors were less accommodating, and the estates protested at a lack of consultation. Their overriding desire was to keep the peace. They were outraged at Rusdorf's support of Švitrigaila in 1432 and the three years of war that followed, during which Polish armies devastated the Prussian lands: in some areas surveys claimed that abandoned farms constituted 70–80 per cent of the cultivated land.[13] In 1432 the estates sought a written guarantee of their participation in decisions over taxation and internal affairs; in 1434 they demanded that the Order should not mount raids, declare war, or make alliances without their agreement. The commonality of Thorn declared its neutrality in any war against Poland.[14]

Defeat shifted the balance between the Order and the estates. Following lobbying from the estates, clauses were inserted into the peace treaties of Melno (1422) and Brześć (1435) allowing the Order's subjects to withdraw their obedience should it break their terms.[15] Although the 1435 treaty was not particularly

---

[8] Górski, *Państwo*, 147.   [9] *Annales*, x/xi, 188, 287; Leinz, 'Ursachen', 2–4.

[10] Henryk Samsonowicz, 'Der Deutsche Orden in seinem Verhältniss zur Gesellschaft Polens unter kultur- und verwaltungsgeschichtlichen Aspekten', in Nowak (ed.), *Ritterorden*, 102.

[11] For the founding charter, see Karol Górski (ed.), *Związek pruski a poddanie się Prus Polsce: Zbiór tekstów źródłowych* (Poznań, 1949), no. 1, 117–18.

[12] Biskup and Labuda, *Dzieje*, 340–1; Górski, *Państwo*, 150.

[13] Biskup and Labuda, *Dzieje*, 383; Burleigh, *Prussian Society*, 87–8. For war damage, see Burleigh's appendix 2, 181–5.

[14] Biskup and Labuda, *Dzieje*, 395; Klaus Neitmann, 'Die preussischen Stände und die Aussenpolitik des Deutschen Ordens vom I. Thorner Frieden bis zum Abfall des Preussischen Bundes (1411–1454)', in Klaus Conrad et al. (eds), *Ordensherrschaft Stände und Stadtpolitik: Zur Entwicklung des Preußenlandes im 14. und 15. Jahrhundert* (Lüneburg, 1985), 35, 37; Burleigh, *Prussian Society*, 144.

[15] Neitmann, 'Stände', 34–5; Edith Lüdecke, 'Der Rechtskampf des Deutschen Ordens gegen dem Bund der preussischen Stände, 1440–1453', *AF*, 12 (1935), 3; Biskup, 'Do genezy inkorporacji Prus', *PZ*, 7/8 (1954), 294; Górski, *Państwo*, 164, 168.

harsh considering the abject performance of the Order's armies during the war, the Order's grand master in the Empire attempted to depose Rusdorf for accepting it. Albert II refused to recognize it, and in 1438 tried to persuade the Order to declare war following the Polish intervention in Bohemia. In February 1440 divisions within the Order provoked an attempted coup. Rusdorf was forced to accept the elevation of one of the plotters, Konrad von Erlichshausen, to the position of grand marshal. Discontent simmered as the Order ratcheted up its demands to pay reparations imposed at Brześć, and continued its assault on the rights of nobles under Culm law. Its rejection of demands for a high court containing members of the estates gave little hope that cases involving it would be favourably judged. Resistance spread after demands for the abolition of the *Pfundzoll* were rejected in March 1439. In Elbing on 21 February 1440 a meeting of nobles and urban representatives from Culm, Elbing, Osterode, Christburg, Pomerelia and Ermland agreed to form a Prussian union (*Preussischer Bund*) to secure internal peace and justice. The Bund was formally established at a meeting of fifty-three nobles and representatives of nineteen towns on 14 March in Marienwerder, where the Order had no castle and therefore no garrison to interfere.[16]

A Bund delegation assured Rusdorf of its loyalty and requested that he uphold the privileges of the estates.[17] Its charter, however, was a blunt warning of the possible consequences if he did not. It began with a statement of its desire to serve the common good, and of loyalty to the Order and the ecclesiastical lords under whose jurisdiction the signatories lived. That loyalty, however, was conditional: the signatories pledged to fulfil their obligations so long as they accorded with their privileges, liberties, and rights. Their overlords were warned that they must respect their agreements with the Prussians and their ancestors, and not seek to lay new obligations upon them. If these agreements were breached, and if the injured party secured no redress—the document rhetorically, dutifully, and implausibly stated that the signatories believed this to be unlikely—then the matter should be put before a court, which was to meet annually to consider such cases. If the court did not dispense justice, then the knights and cities of Culm and Thorn would summon the Bund to judge the matter. If after a formal hearing the Bund decided that the complaint was justified, they would demand the plaintiff's restoration to his honour and rights, and use their best efforts to secure such an outcome.[18]

Quite what these best efforts might entail was not spelt out. For all its careful language of obedience the message was clear. The Order understood, as its strenuous efforts to suppress the Bund demonstrate. Over the next decade, however, the Bund made little progress in its attempts to persuade the Order to institute more acceptable forms of governance, including a court with the power to judge abuses by Order officials, which was rejected on the grounds that canon law did not permit hybrid institutions.[19] Erlichshausen, who succeeded Rusdorf in 1441, proved an able politician, restoring a measure of calm with minor concessions,

---

[16] Górski, *Państwo*, 169–76; Biskup and Labuda, *Dzieje*, 398; Burleigh, *Prussian Society*, 147–57.
[17] Górski, *Państwo*, 174–5.   [18] Górski (ed.), *Związek*, ii, 119–26.
[19] Górski, *Państwo*, 177.

and a strategy of dividing the towns from the nobles; he was helped by Władysław III's lack of interest in Prussia.[20]

Erlichshausen's conciliatory approach was undermined by the Prussian bishops, who attacked the Bund, claiming that it breached canon law. Franz Kuhschmalz, bishop of Ermland, defended the liberties of the church, arguing that no subject could bind his ruler through statute.[21] A measure of calm held until Erlichshausen's death in September 1449. He was succeeded in March 1450 by his nephew, Ludwik von Erlichshausen, a choleric, tactless man dominated by his hard-line uncle, Heinrich Reuss von Plauen.[22] He summoned only representatives of the great cities and a handful of nobles to his inauguration, demanding that they swear oaths of homage to whose wording the estates took exception. As discontent grew, Erlichshausen asked that a papal legate be sent to Prussia to adjudicate.

The arrival of the Portuguese Louis Perez, bishop of Silves, in November 1450 merely heightened the tension. With his encouragement the Order argued that the Bund was illegal and should be dissolved, threatening excommunication if it refused.[23] In autumn 1452 Nicholas V agreed to a hearing in Rome in response to Bund embassies requesting adjudication from him and from Emperor Frederick III. The Bund buttressed its arguments with copious biblical citations concerning the right to resist tyrants, but it became obvious that it could not expect favourable verdicts from pope or emperor.[24] As the church closed ranks, Frederick delivered a damning verdict on 5 December 1453. The Bund was to be dissolved forthwith, and swingeing fines were levied on its leaders. Three hundred of its members were condemned to death. This was annihilation, not arbitration.[25]

Both sides prepared for war. The Bund's secret council, led by Hans von Baysen, a former member of the grand master's council, sat in permanent session in its headquarters in the Thorn Altstadt. In February 1453 the Order's representatives met envoys from Brandenburg and Saxony in Marburg, where they were promised troops, but at a significant cost. After Frederick's verdict Wilhelm Jordan, Danzig's envoy in Vienna, hitherto a supporter of compromise, asked whether he should recruit troops in Bohemia. The Bund was already recruiting in the Empire, while volunteers began arriving in Thorn of their own accord. The Order reinforced its castles and Erik of Pomerania sent 1,000 men.[26]

Aware that the Order wished to delay hostilities until after the harvest, the Bund struck. An act withdrawing obedience was handed to Erlichshausen in the Marienburg on the evening of 6 February, the day that simultaneous attacks were launched on many of the Order's castles. Most garrisons, lacking the will or means to fight, capitulated. Thorn fell on 8 February; Elbing and Danzig soon followed. Within

---

[20] Górski, *Państwo*, 178; Burleigh, *Prussian Society*, 152–7.
[21] Górski, *Państwo*, 188; Lüdicke, 'Rechtskampf', 15–22.
[22] Górski, *Państwo*, 194; Burleigh, *Prussian Society*, 158.
[23] Burleigh, *Prussian Society*, 162–3; Lüdicke, 'Rechtskampf', 178.
[24] Lüdicke, 'Rechtskampf', 187–92.
[25] Górski, *Państwo*, 214–15; Lüdicke, 'Rechtskampf', 183; Biskup and Labuda, *Dzieje*, 400–1.
[26] Biskup, *Trzynastoletnia wojna z Zakonem Krzyżackim 1454–1466* (Warsaw, 1967), 99–104; Górski (ed.), *Związek*, 256 n. 11.

three weeks all important castles and major cities were in rebel hands except the elaborately fortified Marienburg, and Stuhm, which resisted until 8 August. Thorn and Elbing castles were destroyed by the burghers, determined never to allow the Order to dominate them again.[27] The Ermland chapter joined the rebellion in Kuhschmalz's absence, showing that attitudes within the church were divided. Both sides sought foreign aid. The Bohemian noble Mikulas Skalski of Valdštejn and Johann IV the duke of Oświęcim blocked the Order's attempts to raise 3,000 men, recruiting 12,000 themselves for the Bund.[28] Yet as its leaders knew, they could not stand alone. From the moment Frederick delivered his verdict, they sought Polish support.

It was not an easy step to take. Despite strong economic links between the Prussian lands and their vast Polish hinterland, there were economic rivalries as well as economic cooperation. Although there were cultural and family links, in particular between the Culm nobility and their counterparts—and frequently relatives—across the border in Wielkopolska and Cujavia, relations had been scarred by war. Yet by 1454 there were few realistic options open to the Bund. It had already contacted leading Wielkopolskan and Cujavian families, including the Górkas, the Oporowskis, and the Szarlejskis. In 1452–3 Mikołaj Szarlejski, palatine of Brześć, acted as an intermediary between the Bund and Sonka's party, led by Koniecpolski. The Małopolskan opposition, led by the disaffected Oleśnicki and still licking its Volhynian wounds, was uninterested in Prussia. Oleśnicki had an expert knowledge of relations with the Order gleaned while serving in the royal chancery. Although in favour of reclaiming the lands lost in 1308–9, he opposed any offer of military support to the Bund, which, he argued, would contravene the Brześć treaty.[29]

A considerable party, led by Oleśnicki's rival Oporowski and including Sonka, Koniecpolski, and bishop Jan Gruszczyński of Cujavia, favoured intervention. Casimir was nevertheless cautious; his meetings with Erlichshausen in Nieszawa and Thorn in July 1452 were cordial enough, but his mediation offer in July 1453 was rejected.[30] In the autumn, as it became clear that Frederick's verdict was likely to be negative, Baysen tried again, negotiating discreetly with Szarlejski and the Polish treasurer, Hincza of Rogów, who held the border starosties of Inowrocław and Nieszawa.[31] Events moved swiftly after Frederick's verdict. On 19 January 1454 an embassy led by Rutger von Birken and Baysen's brother Gabriel arrived in Sandomierz, where Casimir was staying, and offered to place the Prussian lands under the Polish crown. It is unclear whether they received encouragement or promises of assistance, but on 21 February Hans von Baysen arrived in Cracow. He invited Casimir to accept the inhabitants of Prussia and Pomerelia as his subjects in

---

[27] Tadeusz Nowak, 'Walki obronne z agresją Brandenburgii i Zakonu Krzyżackiego w latach 1308–1521', in Janusz Sikorski (ed.), *Polskie tradycje wojskowe*, i (Warsaw, 1990), 109–11.
[28] Biskup and Labuda, *Dzieje*, 404; Górski, *Państwo*, 216–19.
[29] Dariusz Wróbel, 'Zbigniew Oleśnicki a kwestia pruska i krzyżacka', in Kiryk and Noga (eds), *Oleśnicki*, 85–101.
[30] Zawitkowska, *W służbie*, 236, 240–1.   [31] Biskup and Labuda, *Dzieje*, 403.

perpetuity, and to restore to the Polish crown the lands torn away in 1308–9. The next day Casimir formally accepted the offer; on 6 March the Prussians declared that they were incorporating their lands into the kingdom of Poland and the chancery issued a ceremonial act embodying that incorporation. Three days later Hans von Baysen was named governor of Prussia; on 15 April, the Prussian estates ratified the agreement in Thorn.[32]

On 4 February 1454 the claim to a right of resistance was embodied in the Bund's formal withdrawal of obedience to the Order. It was a short document. After observing that they had willingly sworn oaths of obedience, the signatories stated that obedience was conditional upon respect for the privileges, rights, and liberties outlined in the charter. It listed 65 breaches of those privileges since 1410 that constituted the justification for its action.[33] This was a revolutionary act which drew on Polish political thought. The Bund's leaders were aware of the controversy over the limits of obedience that had dominated Polish politics in the 1420s, when Jagiełło fought to exclude the right *de non praestando obœdientiae* from the privileges he was forced to grant after 1422. The Bund knew it could not resist the Order alone. It might, however, find a more acceptable home within a decentralized, multinational union state with a political culture that venerated consensus, respect for the law, and resistance to tyrannical authority. Since independence was not a realistic option, union with such a polity was preferable to continuing under the Order's theocratic rule, in which canon law was used to justify arbitrary actions by an elite detached from the political community over which it ruled.

The Prussians bargained fiercely. Unlike the Lithuanian boyars in 1386, they walked into union with their eyes wide open. The negotiations in Cracow in February and March 1454 were complex.[34] It is difficult to gauge exactly what was discussed, since Długosz, the most detailed source, opposed the union, and lets it show. The plenipotentiary powers given to the Bund's envoys have not survived, although two different versions of a speech delivered by Hans von Baysen during the ceremonial welcoming of the delegation, probably on 21 February 1454, were published by Długosz and, in 1592, by Caspar Schütz.[35]

Górski suggests that the latter was composed by Schütz, not von Baysen. Vetulani argues more convincingly that the texts are of two different speeches given at different stages of the negotiations, although the circumstantial evidence he produces to suggest that the texts, at least that of the Schütz version, was prepared with the help of the royal chancery is not so persuasive.[36] There is no reason to

---

[32] Biskup, *Trzynastoletnia Wojna*, 105, 110, 171; Biskup, 'Geneza', 304; Wojciech Hejnosz, 'Prawnopaństwowy stosunek Prus do korony w świetle aktu inkorporacyjnego z r. 1454', *PZ*, 10 (1954), 312.
[33] Górski (ed.), *Związek*, no. v, 131–44; no. vi, 145–6.
[34] The best account is Adam Vetulani, 'Rokowanie krakowskie z r. 1454 i zjednoczenie ziem pruskich z Polską', *PH*, 45 (1954), 188–236.
[35] *Annales*, xii/i, 180–3; Kasper Schütz, *Historia rerum prussicarum* (Leipzig, 1599), 198–200; Górski, *Związek*, nos vii–viii, 147–58.
[36] Górski, *Związek*, nos lxi; Vetulani, 'Rokowanie', 202–11.

suppose that the speeches were not Baysen's own work, although he may drafted them following discussions with Poles favourable to the Bund.

Both begin by stressing that much of the territory under the Order's rule was once part of the kingdom of Poland, and had been illegally occupied.[37] In the Długosz version the stress is on how these lands were torn away from Poland (*'a Regno Poloniae abstraxerunt'*), while in the Schütz version it is stated that they belonged to the forebears of Casimir, who is named as their hereditary lord (*Erbherr*). This may indicate that the speeches were given to different audiences, with the second delivered before Casimir. Both speeches—with different emphases—catalogue the Order's sins: the Długosz version concentrates on the international context, condemning the Order's support for Švitrigaila, while the Schütz version stresses its domestic crimes, accusing it of rapine, whoring, and ignoring the privileges, liberties, and rights of its subjects. Both justify the Bund's formation as the only way to protect and preserve these rights, with the Długosz version complaining at the 'perpetual servitude' imposed by the Order.[38]

That the Schütz version was delivered later is plausible. Casimir was told that he should uphold local law codes, whether Culm law, Lübeck law, or Prussian law, and respect local privileges, liberties, and rights. He was not to rebuild any ruined castles, and he was respectfully reminded that it was the Bund, not the Poles, that had seized control of the *Ordensstaat*.[39] Only part of it—Pomerelia, Culm, and Michelow—had formerly been under Polish rule; if all of Prussia were to come under the Polish crown, it was made clear that loyalty was to be conditional. Baysen invited Casimir to take the *Ordensstaat* under his protection in the language of union: he spoke of 'annexing' (*'annectere'*) and 'uniting' (*'unire'*) them to the Polish crown.[40] The Danzig envoys, led by Wilhelm Jordan, were particularly hard-headed; it was not until 3 March that they finally agreed terms. Later that day conciliatory proposals arrived from Erlichshausen. Jordan expressed his regret that they had not arrived earlier, as he might not have agreed to submit to Poland.[41] Three days later two documents were issued by the royal chancery: an act of submission by the Bund, and an incorporation privilege issued by Casimir. The envoys swore an oath of loyalty that was ratified by the Prussian estates in Thorn on 15 April.[42] A new union had been born.

What was its nature? As with the Polish-Lithuanian union, hindsight has influenced interpretations. In his 1722 history of Royal Prussia, Gottfried Lengnich argued that the link was purely personal: from 1454 the Prussian lands shared

---

[37] *Annales*, xii/i, 180; Górski, *Związek*, no. vii, 152. [38] *Annales*, xii/i, 181.
[39] Górski, *Związek*, no. viii, 156, 157; Vetulani, 'Rokowanie', 222–3.
[40] Górski, *Związek*, no. viii, 157; *Annales*, xii/i, 183. [41] Górski, *Państwo*, 220.
[42] *Conpactatio et incorporatio terrarum Prussie etc. Regno Polonie et corone eius temporibus perpetuis incorporatarum etc.*: Górski, *Związek*, no. x, 163–71; *Incorporation terrarum Prusie*, in Górski, *Związek*, no. x, 172–82; Górski prints the 6 March oath and the oath of the Culm nobility and cities (28 May), but not the ratification: Górski, *Związek*, no. xiii, 189–93. The incorporation and ratification documents are printed in *VL*, i, 78–3, from which the citations are taken; apart from minor differences in spelling and punctuation, the incorporation privilege matches the version in Hejnosz, 'Stosunek', dodatek, 325–30, based on a photographic reproduction of the original, which disappeared during World War II. Górski's version contains transcription errors: Górski, *Związek*, 314 n. 26.

'nothing more in common than the [person of] the king', and were only joined to the kingdom of Poland 'by a form of alliance; otherwise, however, they formed a separate state'.[43] This interpretation was repeated by Caro, while Bobrzyński argued that it was a 'dynastic' union. German scholarship before 1945 enthusiastically concurred.[44] This interpretation is unpersuasive. Lengnich was advancing a position that suited the purposes of certain circles in Danzig after the Great Northern War, during which the city was occupied by enemy armies, at a time when Poland-Lithuania was suffering economic decline, was struggling to recover from the devastation of war, and appeared to be subsiding into political anarchy. To argue that the relationship constituted a purely personal union takes no account of the documents on which it was based, which, according to Górski, are 'clear... and unambiguous'.[45]

They are certainly clear, if not entirely unambiguous. The act of incorporation, after summarizing the reasons for withdrawing obedience to the Order, addressed Casimir as 'King of Poland, Grand Duke of Lithuania, and hereditary ruler of the lands of Ruthenia and Pomerania', designating him the true heir and patron—in the sense of legal protector—and lord of all the Prussian lands. The Prussians took Casimir as their lord, hereditary ruler, defender, and king of all the aforesaid lands in perpetuity, though this was made subject to certain conditions.[46]

It explicitly stated that the Prussian lands were to be incorporated into the kingdom of Poland, using several synonyms. As in the Horodło treaty both the perfect and present tenses were used:

> assumpsimus et terras nostras et nos ipsos regno Polonie invisceravimus imperpetuum, univimus, integravimus et incorporavimus ac presentibus unimus, integramus, incorporamus et invisceramus coniunctim et indivisum,[47]

The use of the perfect tense here bears a rather different message. At Horodło, it was Jagiełło and Vytautas who had employed it to clarify the consequences of Krewo. Here it was used by the Prussian envoys to declare that the Prussian lands had originally been incorporated into the kingdom of Poland as the result of an act of will on the part of their inhabitants, who were now publicly reincorporating them, after a period in which they had freely given their loyalty to a different suzerain. They, not Casimir or the Polish kingdom, were the subjects of the sentence. After rehearsing the Order's crimes and the path that had led to the withdrawal of obedience, they declared that the Prussians were submitting to

---

[43] Gottfried Lengnich, *Geschichte der Preussischen Lande: Königlich-Polnischen Antheils seit dem Jahr 1526 biß auf dem Todt Königes Sigismundi I* (Danzig, 1722), 5.
[44] For example Ernst Turowski, *Die innenpolitische Entwicklung Polnisch-Preußens und seine staatsrechtliche Stellung zu Polen vom 2. Thorner Frieden bis zum Reichstag von Lublin (1466–1569)* (Berlin, 1937), 36. Cf. Hejnosz, 'Stosunek', 307–8 and Janusz Małłek, 'Stany Prus Królewskich a Rzeczpospolita Polska w latach 1526–1660', in Małłek, *Dwie części Prus: Studia z dziejów Prus Książęcych i Prus Królewskich w XVI i XVII wieku* (Olsztyn, 1987), 72.
[45] Karol Górski, 'The Royal Prussia estates in the second half of the 15th century and their relation to the Crown of Poland', in Górski, *Communitas, princeps, corona regni* (Warsaw, 1976), 42.
[46] Górski, *Związek*, no. x, 164.   [47] Górski, *Związek*, no. x, 164.

Casimir of their own free will and in perpetuity as their only legal and legitimate ruler, and reintegrating their lands into the crown of Poland.[48]

This was not the language of personal union. Although the Prussians were to retain their own laws, customs, privileges, and rights, the negotiators stressed that they expected to share fully in the privileges, rights, and liberties of citizens of the Polish crown, including the right to participate in royal elections, a concession confirmed in the incorporation privilege.[49] This was a real, not a personal union. Prussia was to be part of the Polish kingdom, not a separate realm subject to its own ruling council under the king. If Polish rights, liberties, and privileges were to be extended to the Prussian elites, then they would have to be defended in Prussian as well as Polish courts. In participating in royal elections, the Prussian elites would publicly join with the Polish community of the realm in performing the most important act that it collectively undertook. Otherwise the Prussians would have deprived themselves of a say in who was to rule over them.

There are other indications in the document that this was no simple personal union. Casimir incorporated the Prussian territories into his titles in a formulation that was different from that used in the submission:

> Nos, Casimirus Dei gratia Rex Poloniae, necnon Cracoviae, Sandomiriae, Siradiae, Lanciciae, Cujaviae, M.D.Lithv., Russiae, Prussiaeque, Culmensis, Kynsburgensis, Elbingensis et Pomeraniae Terrarum Dominus et Haeres.[50]

Hejnosz claims that this iteration of all the individual territories was redundant, yet it was necessary to make it clear that Casimir was claiming lordship over all the Prussian lands, not just those taken from Poland in 1308–1309; to this end, the constituent territories of the crown of Poland were also listed, although this was unusual.[51] The titles were not in the traditional form—Michelow was omitted—instead the document lists what, by a later decree, were to become four new palatinates on the Polish pattern: Culm, Pomerelia, Elbing, and Königsberg. Prussia's administrative structure was to be reorganized on Polish lines more completely than had been the case in Lithuania. It was necessary to replace the Order's system of government, but the Prussians were not to be left to their own devices. As in Lithuania, this extension of Polish structures ensured that Polish political, administrative, and judicial culture would penetrate the Prussian lands.

In the incorporation document Casimir presented himself and the kingdom of Poland as providing a refuge for those suffering from calamity, oppression, and tyranny. He stressed that it was the whole Prussian community of the realm that had approached him with a request to help them preserve its privileges, rights, and

---

[48] 'dedimus et subiiecimus et presentibus voluntarie et spontanee perpetue damus et subiicimus ipsumque dominum Kazimirum regem Polonie pro unico, iusto et legittimo domino et herede suscipimus, recipimus et acceptamus ac nos et terras predictas in ius, sortem, proprietatem et titulem corone Polonie reintegramus, reunimus, incorporamus et invisceramus': Górski, *Związek*, 169.

[49] 'omnium privilegiorum, libertatum et prerogativarum regni Polonie usum et participacionem et signanter comunem cum aliis regnicolis futurorum regum eleccionem et coronacionem habituri': Górski, *Związek*, 169; *VL*, i, 80.

[50] *VL*, i, 78.   [51] Hejnosz, 'Stosunek', 317.

liberties, and to support the Bund, formed to protect them.[52] After rehearsing the history of the Order's oppression of their subjects, the document described how, in the light of the Order's disdain for their privileges, rights, and immunities, the Prussians had been deprived of hope and realized that bound as they were by divine and human law, their rulers could no longer expect obedience.[53]

Casimir stressed that the Prussians, having asked him to protect the Bund, had invited him to take them under his protection as their legitimate and hereditary lord. After further consideration of the Order's perfidy and tyranny, he stated that, with his council's agreement, he had agreed. The terms reflected the language of the Bund's submission. It was stated that the Prussians accepted their reintegration into the Polish crown 'not by error or recklessly, but with our certain knowledge and according to our will, in God's name'. The synonyms were again stacked high: *reintegramus, reunimus, invisceramus et incorporamus*.[54]

Although Casimir was very much the subject of this sentence, after pledging that the Prussian elites would share in the privileges, liberties, and rights enjoyed by the Polish nobility, the rest of the document, by specifying in great detail the privileges, rights, and liberties that Casimir and the Polish kingdom swore to uphold, indicated that whatever else the Prussians were invisceratiung themselves into, it was not a unitary state. This was an incorporating union *minus plena*. The Prussian lands were granted considerable autonomy within the union. Their law codes—Culm law, Magdeburg law, Prussian law, and Polish law as instituted before 1454—were to be respected. The *ius indigenatus*, by which only natives could be appointed to public office, was confirmed. The *Pfundzoll* was abolished and Prussia was freed from all tolls on land and sea levied by 'old or new custom'. No decisions were to be taken concerning the Prussian lands without consultation with the Prussian council. Prussia's 1454 borders were to be maintained intact. Danzig, Elbing, Thorn, and Königsberg were to retain the right to mint coins, although these were to bear the image of Casimir and his successors. Assurances were given to merchants plying their wares across the kingdom concerning their security and freedom from tolls.[55]

Baysen's speeches and the incorporation documents reveal a common conceptualization of politics that underpinned the new union. As in the Horodło treaty, careful distinctions were made between the *regnum* and the *corona regni*, or the *corpus regni*. Thus Baysen stressed that Pomerelia had been torn away from the Polish *regnum* by the Order's treacherous actions; describing its violent removal from the 'body of the kingdom'; he asked that Casimir accept the Prussians back under his rule, returning them to 'the body of the kingdom' (*ad corpus Regni*).[56] Thus he was aware of the subtle political distinctions between the *regnum* as a legal subject and political actor on the international stage, and the *corpus regni* or *corona regni*—the body or crown of the kingdom. As he stressed, the Bund had, through its own actions, liberated the Prussian lands from the Order's rule, and was asking for this reunification—unification for those lands not previously part of the Polish

---

[52] *VL*, i, 78.   [53] *VL*, i, 79.   [54] *VL*, i, 80.
[55] *VL*, i, 80–1.   [56] *Annales*, xii/i, 183.

kingdom—of its own free will. Thus it was appropriate to stress that, despite the wide-ranging autonomy they demanded and were granted in the incorporation privilege, and despite their realization that the legal basis of this act in terms of the international Christian community was precisely that the 'Pomeranian' lands had once formed part of the Polish kingdom they were also joining the community of the Polish realm. It was for this reason that they asked for—and received—the assurances that they would partake of all the privileges of other members of that realm, including the right to participate in royal elections.

In appealing to the concept of the *corona regni* the Bund recognized that Prussia would form one of the several lands of the Polish crown.[57] Yet the term *corona* also embodied a sense of political community, the *communitas regni*; it was the idea that political authority was rooted in, and depended upon, the consent of the citizens that had animated resistance to the Order, and it was that idea that the Bund saw embodied by the Polish system. These formulations recur in the ratification and oath of homage sworn by the Prussian estates on 15 April 1454, the *Reciproca sponsio*, whose text was substantially based on the 6 March submission.[58] The key phrases were similar: it protested at the violation of the territory of the Polish *regnum* by the Order, and talked of how the Bund in taking its case to the Emperor deplored the Order's wars against the 'king and kingdom of Poland.[59] It reiterated that the Prussian lands were to be reintegrated into, and reunited with, the *corona*, and were to enjoy all the privileges, rights, and liberties enjoyed by inhabitants of the Polish kingdom.[60]

The Prussian envoys knew what they wanted, and they secured their essential demands. Their position within the union was buttressed by the rights, privileges, and liberties recognized by Casimir and the Poles. With their own estates body, whose structure and composition was institutionalized several decades before the establishment of the bicameral Polish sejm in the 1490s, the Prussians were able to keep their political distance, refusing to participate in Polish assemblies—except for royal elections—and to claim that they were only subject to the king's personal authority. Yet if the Prussian estates after 1466 maintained a similar position to the Lithuanians who fought so pugnaciously against the idea that the grand duchy had been incorporated into Poland, in practice the ground on which they stood was not as firm. Lithuania had its grand dukes, and even when—as under Casimir after 1447—the grand duke and the king of Poland were the same person, the Lithuanians could legitimately maintain that the union was personal in nature. There had been no independent Prussian principality before 1454, however, and therefore no king or prince of Prussia to form a personal union with Poland: the 1454 act was based on the idea that the bulk of the Prussian lands had been part of the Polish kingdom, from which they had been illegally torn away. Thus if the Prussians emphasized that they were not Polish subjects, they had no qualms about being considered citizens of the wider Polish community of the

---

[57] Erich Weise, 'Zur Kritik des Vertrages zwischen dem Preußischen Bund und dem König von Polen vom 6. März 1454', *AF*, 18 (1941), 251.
[58] *VL*, i, 81–3.   [59] *VL*, i, 82.   [60] *VL*, i, 83.

realm, albeit ones with substantial legal and political autonomy, and they did not contest declarations such as that made by Casimir in 1485 that they had become 'together with us inhabitants of the kingdom, one crown, and one dominion.[61] The Prussian lands were inhabited by a mixed population: in the early fifteenth century it is estimated that the balance was roughly 140,000 native Prussians—related to the Lithuanians—about the same number of Poles, and some 200,000 Germans.[62] Although a common Prussian identity formed after 1454, it could not call upon a tradition of independent statehood. Although, as in the case of Lithuania, the Poles respected, on the whole, Prussian autonomy, and although the Prussians possessed in their estates far more developed political institutions to defend that autonomy, they were in a weaker position than the Lithuanians when demands for closer integration with Poland emerged in the sixteenth century.

---

[61] 'ir mit yn geworden seyt eyne crone und hirschaft'. Quoted by Górski, 'Prussian estates', 42. I have preferred 'dominion' to Górski's rendering of 'Herrschaft' as 'state'.

[62] Janusz Małłek, 'Powstanie poczucia krajowej odrębności w Prusach i jej rozwój w XV I XVI wieku', in Małłek, *Dwie części Prus*, 10.

20

The Thirteen Years War

For now Poland and the Bund had to concentrate on winning the war, declared on the day of incorporation but backdated to 22 February.[1] This proved to be no easy matter. Despite the blows inflicted upon the Order in the initial phases of the rebellion, it proved more resilient than the Poles or the Bund expected. The war lasted thirteen years, and victory in 1466 was only partial.[2] The political and military context had changed substantially since 1435. Although the end of the civil war in Lithuania and the establishment of Casimir on the Lithuanian throne without a serious rival meant that the days of Gediminid intrigues with the Order were over, the fact that Lithuania had secured what it wanted from the Order by 1422 meant that it had no interest in joining the fray. Although some Lithuanians fought in the war, the grand duchy made no substantial contribution to it. The Mazovians, who had played a generally supportive role—if sometimes reluctantly—between 1409 and 1422, now favoured the Order, afraid that its defeat would expose them to Polish domination. Poland stood alone, while the Order received more effective support from the Empire than had been the case under the mercurial Sigismund of Luxemburg.

European warfare was changing. Faced by the diminishing effectiveness of the armoured knight, warlords deployed infantry in greater numbers through the recruitment of professional soldiers who had mastered the increasingly complex disciplines of infantry warfare. Poland's military superiority over the Order had owed much to its ability to dominate the battlefield through the deployment of armoured knights in greater numbers and of greater quality, than its opponents. Lighter cavalry units, many raised in the Lithuanian and Ruthenian lands, had, through a policy of deliberate destruction, helped bring the Order to the negotiating table. Poland's forces were not suited, however, to the capture and defence of castles and fortified towns, as the failure to take Marienburg in 1410 demonstrated.

Thus the Order was not in such a desperate position as the dramatic losses in 1454 might suggest, even allowing for the fact that it would normally have expected to raise up to 20,000 men from the Prussian lands. Although the Regensburg Reichstag in April failed to agree aid, goodwill towards the Order within the Empire created favourable conditions for recruitment if it could raise the necessary funds, while—in contrast to the situation between 1409 and 1422—it enjoyed full

---

[1] Górski, *Związek*, no. xii, 183–8.
[2] Convention suggests that a war that began in 1454 and ended in 1466 should be called the Twelve, not the Thirteen Years War, but it is universally referred to under the latter name.

papal support until 1463. Calixtus III excommunicated the Bund and all its allies in September 1455. Enea Sylvio Piccolomini, who succeeded him as Pius II in 1458, knew Poland well, but was friendly with Oleśnicki and had been provocatively nominated bishop of Ermland by Calixtus in 1457. He was disinclined to soften his predecessor's line.[3] With papal backing the Order strengthened its position. In 1454–5 it pawned the Neumark to Frederick II of Brandenburg—Jadwiga's former fiancé—for the knock-down price of 40,000 Rhenish guilders. The move was initially resisted by the Neumark estates, where a strong party supported the Bund. Casimir promised them extensive privileges if they accepted Polish overlordship, but Frederick won majority support in March.[4]

This injection of capital turned the tide. A professional force of 9,000 horse and 6,000 foot was raised, led by Rudolf, duke of Sagan, a Silesian Piast, and Bernard von Zinnenberg, a talented Moravian soldier of fortune. Facing them were a mere 2,000 professional troops, raised by the Bund and led by Mikołaj Szarlejski, an inexperienced soldier who refused to listen to advice from his professional officers. Five hundred Pomerelian knights were unsuccessfully besieging Konitz, which the Order had recaptured at the end of March, and which they were to hold until the end of the war, protecting their communication lines with the Neumark.

Casimir summoned the Wielkopolskan levy in August. It was harvest time, the call to arms was unpopular, and Casimir failed to seek approval from the provincial sejmik. A generation had passed since Tannenberg. Economic and social change in the largely peaceful years since 1422 had changed the outlook of the petty and middling nobility. Up to 18,000 szlachta turned up grumblingly reluctant to meet their obligations and largely untouched by experience of war. They assembled at Cerekwica, eighteen kilometres from Konitz, and promptly went on strike, demanding new privileges, as their predecessors had in 1422. Casimir arrived on 12 September, and was forced to make substantial concessions before the army would move.[5]

Persuading amateur soldiers to take the field did not solve the military problem. Casimir advanced on Konitz, taking up a strong position on 18 September with 16,000 men, hoping to lure the Order's army over a small stream running through boggy ground. The Order's professionals—9,000 horse and 2,000 foot—arrived in mid afternoon, and promptly established a tabor—a fortified camp protected by waggons linked together with chains—refusing to fight on the advantageous ground the Poles had selected. The Poles decided to cross the stream and mount their own attack. Although initially successful in a cavalry action in which Sagan was killed and much of the Order's horse chased from the battlefield, the Polish

---

[3] Karol Górski, 'Rządy wewnętrzne Kazimierza Jagiellończyka w Koronie', in Biskup and Górski (eds), *Kazimierz*, 107; Marian Biskup, 'Dyplomacja polska w czasach Casimira Jagiellończyka, i: W kręgu wielkiego konfliktu zobrojnego z Zakonem Krzyżackim (1454–1466)', in Biskup and Górski (eds), *Kazimierz*, 200–3; Jan Friedberg, 'Zatarg Polski z Rzymem podczas wojny 13-letniej', *KH*, 24 (1910), 422–67.
[4] Biskup, *Dzieje*, 407–8; Biskup, *Trzynastoletnia Wojna*, 146–7; 224–8.
[5] Biskup, *Dzieje*, 410; Biskup, *Trzynastoletnia Wojna*, 251–2; Nowak, 'Walki', 111–12. For the political concessions see Ch. 21.

army contained a mere 1,000 infantry, and was incapable of storming the tabor, manned by professionals. When the Order's cavalry rallied and returned to the field, and the Polish force besieging Konitz moved to aid the main army, the garrison under Heinrich Reuss von Plauen attacked the Poles unexpectedly in the flank. The szlachta broke and panic set in. Some 3,000 Poles were killed, including 60 knights and vice-chancellor Piotr Woda of Szczekocin; 330 were captured, including Szarlejski, Łukasz Górka, palatine of Poznań, and the new palatine of Pomerelia, Johann von Jane. The Polish baggage train fell into the Order's hands; as did the royal standard, five other standards, the great and lesser seal, and chancery documents. Długosz moaned at the levy's ill discipline, blamed Koniecpolski for urging Casimir to fight against Oleśnicki's advice, and grumbled at the errors of the inexperienced commanders.[6]

Konitz has earned none of the retrospective renown of Tannenberg. It does not appear in lists of 'decisive battles of the Western World' and offers little to the student of military science, but in terms of its results, its influence on the future course of European history makes it at least as significant as Tannenberg. If the Order had lost, the war would effectively have been over. Although there was much sympathy for its cause in the Empire, and Frederick placed the Bund under an imperial ban in March 1455, the fall of Constantinople in 1453 ensured that both he and Calixtus were far more concerned with the Ottoman threat.[7] The Order had nothing left to pawn, and lacked the resources to raise a new army—they could not even pay the one they had raised by pawning the Neumark. If Casimir had won at Konitz the union of all Prussia with Poland would have been completed, and European history might have looked rather different.

Yet the Order won the battle. The military structures that had served the Poles well enough for half a century were no longer adequate. The ill-disciplined amateurs of the noble levy could no longer overwhelm smaller professional forces through sheer numbers and were incapable of undertaking protracted sieges.[8] The aftermath of the battle was equally decisive. The maintenance of small professional garrisons across the Prussian lands placed considerable strain upon Bund finances. Much of the burden fell upon Danzig, but its capacious coffers were emptying fast: the 3,200 professionals besieging Konitz and Marienburg were costing it 400 marks per day in pay alone.[9] After Konitz the Order retook Stuhm, Christburg, Osterode, Dirschau, and Marienwerder. Casimir summoned the Małopolskan levy, which assembled at Nieszawa, across the Vistula from Thorn, and promptly demanded similar privileges to those granted to the Wielkopolska szlachta at Cerekwica. It was only in late November that the army advanced on Marienburg. It spent most of its time gathering fodder for the mass of horses accompanying it. When nobles began dying from the cold, the levy lost what little martial fervour it possessed, and

---

[6] *Annales*, xii/i, 209–16; Biskup, *Trzynastoletnia Wojna*, 261–9; Nowak, 'Walki' 112–13.
[7] Biskup, *Dzieje*, 411; Biskup, *Trzynastoletnia Wojna*, 384–6.
[8] Biskup, 'Z zagadnień wojskowiści polskiej okresu wojny trzynastoletniej', in Biskup and Górski (eds), *Kazimierz*, 141–72.
[9] Biskup, *Trzynastoletnia Wojna*, 186.

dispersed without achieving anything.[10] In February 1455, as the szlachta streamed home, the Order mounted a new offensive. An attempt to capture Thorn Neustadt was foiled by the Bund's professional forces, but when it decreed new taxes in March to pay for them, opposition began to stir. The Altstadt and Löbenicht, two of Königsberg's three cities, defected to the Order, which also took Allenstein and other strongpoints in Lower Prussia and Ermland. Kneiphof, Königsberg's third city, held out for the Bund until its capitulation in July, despite reinforcements sent by Hans von Baysen.[11]

Both sides now consolidated. The Lithuanians remained aloof, although they did close the Samogitian border to embassies and reinforcements from Livonia. Without aid, the Poles struggled. In the summer of 1455 Casimir summoned the Wielkopolskan and Małopolskan levies, but the large force—claimed to be up to 40,000 though it was undoubtedly smaller—again proved inadequate: it could not even take the small town of Lessen, garrisoned by a mere 350 men.[12] The Order now had a firm base in Königsberg and Lower Prussia, while its possession of Dirschau and Mewe on the Vistula, and of Konitz to the southwest, ensured that communications to the Empire remained open for the recruitment of fresh troops. Despite its financial problems, it kept the initiative on land until 1461, and while the Bund was too powerful in the west and south for it to contemplate winning back what it had lost, as the war dragged on, it became clear that the Poles and the Bund were unlikely to reverse its military gains of 1454–5.

Much of the burden of raising the money to hire professional troops fell upon the Prussian estates, and in particular on Danzig, Thorn, and Elbing. It was only Königsberg that resisted the taxes necessary to prosecute the war sufficiently for it to return to loyalty to the Order; for the majority of the Prussian elites the prize won in 1454 was too great to sacrifice. Loyalty to Casimir and the union with Poland remained largely firm, although Danzig negotiated an extensive set of new privileges, including the acquisition of territory, granted on 16 June 1454.[13] It was only gradually that the Poles were able to rebuild their military capacity, and to provide the decisive military aid that the Bund had hoped for in 1454.

The problem was financial. Under Jagiełło, the monarchy, although not rich by contemporary standards, mobilized considerable resources from royal land. Władysław, however, had alienated, mortgaged, or donated royal estates on a massive scale during his brief reign to fund his Hungarian adventure, and Casimir could not hope to raise enough money from his own possessions to fund the professional army necessary to win the war. Gradually, a new system of recruitment was established, based on letters of commission issued by the king to officers who

---

[10] Tadeusz Nowak and Jan Wimmer, *Dzieje oręża polskiego, 963–1795* (Warsaw, 1981) 246–7.
[11] Nowak, 'Walki', 117–20.
[12] Nowak and Wimmer, *Dzieje*, 252. Biskup claims that the levy numbered 25,000–30,000 men, but Wimmer suggests caution: Biskup, *Trzynastoletnia Wojna*, 304; Wimmer, *Historia piechoty polskiej do roku 1864* (Warsaw, 1978), 77.
[13] Ernst Manfred Wermter, 'Die Bildung des Danziger Stadtterritoriums in den politischen Zielvorstellungen des Rates der Stadt Danzig im späten Mittelalter und in der frühen Neuzeit', in Conrad et al. (eds), *Ordensherrschaft*, 94–5.

recruited units as specified in the commission, which were paid quarterly; the funds for these units, which could be kept together over the winter after the noble levy had dispersed, were cobbled together from loans, to be covered by taxes agreed by the szlachta and the clergy, and the minting of new money, which merely fuelled inflation.[14]

Gradually, the ability to raise taxation from Poland's embryonic parliamentary institutions, even if that money was grudgingly given and came at a heavy price to the monarchy, gave the Poles the advantage in what became a war of attrition between two toothless adversaries. The decisive move came off the battlefield, as the Poles won the financial war. Even in the immediate aftermath of Konitz the Order could not pay its troops. In October 1454, in a desperate move to keep the mercenaries in service, Erlichshausen handed over several fortresses, including Marienburg, Dirschau, and Ehlau as security. The income derived from these castles was nowhere near enough to cover the arrears, which by April 1455 had reached the enormous sum of 500,000 Hungarian ducats.[15] The problem was not that the mercenaries might strike or simply abandon their service, as frequently happened with unpaid hired troops, but that they might exploit their new assets.

This is precisely what several mercenary leaders, led by the Bohemian Oldřich Červonka did, as the Poles sought to purchase what they could not take by force. Thus began the phoniest of phony wars. From late 1455 until the summer of 1457 there was little fighting, as both sides conducted a bidding war. The mercenaries sat back, content to seek the best deal, although the seventeen-month contract they suggested to the Poles in December 1454 at a rate of 200 Hungarian ducats per horse was pitching it high: in February the Poles and the Bund offered 55, plus ten ducats compensation for a lost horse, although in secret talks with the Bohemians without the knowledge of the Prussians—who would in practice have footed much of the bill—the Poles offered 70. At least the Poles had some hope of raising these sums, whereas the Order in Germany had to report the complete failure of its fundraising efforts, which produced the miserly figure of 10,000 Rhenish guilders.[16] The Poles won the bidding war. In July 1456 they agreed that twenty-one Prussian castles would be handed over for 436,000 Hungarian ducats, 100,000 of which were paid in cloth, beer, and other goods. Divisions among the mercenaries and the fact that the Order came in with counter-offers, blew the deal off course. The Poles reached an agreement on 15 August with around a third of the mercenaries, a group of seventy-four, led by Červonka's Bohemians, but it was much less ambitious, involving the surrender of only six fortresses, though these included Marienburg, Dirschau, Konitz, and Ehlau. The cost was considerably lower, but the Poles struggled even to raise this sum. An assembly at Piotrków in early 1457 voted some of the funds, while the financial muscle of the Prussian cities was again called upon, though the renewed demands provoked revolts in Thorn and Danzig from a commonality weary of ever higher taxes, which were repressed

---

[14] Nowak, 'Walki', 115, 117.
[15] Biskup, *Trzynastoletnia Wojna*, 283–5; Nowak, 'Walki', 123.
[16] Biskup, *Trzynastoletnia Wojna*, 427–32.

with some severity. Another Piotrków assembly in the autumn criticized the deal for being too generous but finally agreed to relatively high taxes, although the clergy dragged its feet as usual; in the event, half the money, some 190,000 Hungarian ducats, was paid by the Poles; half by the Bund.[17]

The first instalment was ready by the summer of 1457. On 6 June the once-proud Order suffered the ignominy of seeing the city and fortress of Marienburg, its headquarters for two centuries, sold out from under its control. The humiliated Erlichshausen slunk out of the Marienburg with tears in his eyes, vowing revenge on the treacherous mercenaries just before the jubilant Poles marched in to give Casimir, who made the most of his ceremonial entry, a priceless propaganda victory.[18] Zinnenberg, who had led a group of mercenaries resisting the deal, soon returned at the head of a force that managed to recover the city. Although the castle remained in Polish hands it was not until August 1460 that the city was recaptured. Dirschau and Ehlau were also handed over, though the Order held on to Konitz.[19]

It was a peculiar way to wage war. The deal delivered far less than had been hoped, but it marked an important turning point. Gradually, with the Bund's support, the Poles consolidated their advantage. Danzig and Elbing established a powerful fleet of 33 privateers that harried the Order by sea, interfering with the Königsberg trade, and keeping at bay the Danes, who had entered the war on the Order's side in 1454.[20] On land, another disastrous showing by the levy summoned to Konitz in 1461 convinced Casimir that there was no point in summoning it at all: few Małopolskans bothered to turn up. In September 1461, gathered reluctantly once more, the szlachta formed what was known as a 'horseback sejm', and agreed to a one-off tax of five per cent on their annual income in return for release from their military obligations. This only allowed the recruitment initially of 2,000 soldiers, but it represented a political breakthrough. Gradually enough money flowed into the royal exchequer to support a professional force, commanded by the capable Piotr Dunin, sizable enough to make a difference. Further taxes were voted in December and the army grew steadily: by the end of 1466 it comprised 46 companies.[21]

The force may have been small, but the Order could no longer put large armies into the field, and it was far more effective than the large, unwieldy levy, which no longer knew what it was supposed to be doing, and did not wish to do it. Dunin, reinforced with troops raised by Danzig, led 1,000 horse and 1,000 foot into Pomerelia to winkle out the Order's garrisons and to bring much-needed relief to towns loyal to the Bund, which the Order had been picking off at its leisure. This army, with its high percentage of infantry, was more suited to the kind of warfare necessary for victory. On 16–17 September 1462, Dunin, basing his tactics on the

---

[17] Biskup, *Trzynastoletnia Wojna*, 440–73; Karol Górski, 'Wojna trzynastoletnia (1454–1466)', *PZ*, 10 (1954), 343.
[18] Nowak, 'Walki', 123; Maria Bogucka, *Kazimierz Jagiellończyk i jego czasy* (Warsaw, 1981), 84.
[19] Biskup, *Trzynastoletnia Wojna*, 487.
[20] Nowak, 'Walki', 125–6; Nowak and Wimmer, *Dzieje*, 256–7.
[21] Biskup, *Trzynastoletnia Wojna*, 589–94, 612, 735–9; Nowak, 'Walki', 126.

tabor, won a hard-fought victory over a larger force at Schwetzin; Długosz, whose nephew Janusz fought in the campaign, claimed improbably that 2,000 of the Order's army were killed and 600 taken prisoner for the cost of only 100 Polish dead; the true figure for the Order's casualties was perhaps half that number, with many of the infantry drowning as they sought to escape across a lake after the Poles, who had won the cavalry battle, stormed the tabor.[22] In the summer of 1463, the Poles sought to retake Mewe and regain control of the lower Vistula. The Order sent a large relief force of 3,500, supported by a fleet that sailed into the Vistula delta. On 15 September the Danzig privateers won a crushing victory over it, in which they boarded every one of the Order's vessels. The Order's army withdrew, and Dirschau surrendered on 1 January.[23] Gradually the Order's forces were cleared out of Pomerelia. In September 1464, Danzig forces took Putzig after a five-month siege; Konitz fell in September 1466.[24] The Order's allies were melting away and its resources dwindling. After the failure of its siege of Frauenburg in the summer of 1462, broken off when Dunin led his forces into Pomerelia, the new bishop of Ermland, Paul Legendorf, abandoned the Order, signing a treaty in Elbing in March 1464 that placed Ermland under the protection of the Polish crown.[25] Appeals for money to the Livonians and the German grand master were in vain; both urged Erlichshausen to settle.[26] As their last footholds to the west and south of Ermland fell, the Order sued for peace, signing a treaty at Thorn on 19 October 1466 that preserved what they still held (see Map 4).

Despite the failure to secure control of all of the *Ordensstaat*, the second peace of Thorn was a victory for Poland and the Bund. Although they were not strong enough to defeat the Order completely, it had again been humbled. The treaty instituted a perpetual peace and an inviolable alliance between the two parties, defined as the king, the dukes Konrad, Casimir, Bolesław, and Janusz of Mazovia, Duke Erik II of Stolp, Bishop Paul Legendorf and the Ermland chapter, Stefan III, hospodar of Moldavia, and the Polish kingdom and all its territories on the one hand, and the grand master, the Order, and its lands in 'part of Prussia' on the other.[27] The treaty restored to the king and the kingdom of Poland the lands of Culm, Pomerelia, and Michelow, lost in 1308–9, and the Order renounced all claims to them. The eastern Prussian lands, no longer subject to the incorporation of March 1454, were made a fief of the Polish crown. Future grand masters were to pay homage in person, swearing an oath of loyalty to the king of Poland, his successors, and the kingdom of Poland.[28] The bishopric of Culm was to return to Polish control and revert to the archdiocese of Gniezno with a secularized chapter; the Order also

---

[22] *Annales*, xii/ii, 42–6; Biskup, *Trzynastoletnia Wojna*, 622–9; Nowak and Wimmer, *Dzieje*, 260–1.
[23] Józef Dyskant, *Zatoka Świeża 1463* (Warsaw, 1987) 137–68; Nowak and Wimmer, *Dzieje*, 264; Biskup, *Trzynastoletnia Wojna*, 645–9.
[24] Nowak and Wimmer, *Dzieje*, 265.
[25] Górski, *Związek*, lxxxii; Biskup, *Trzynastoletnia Wojna*, 653–4.
[26] Dyskant, *Zatoka*, 170.   [27] Górski, *Związek*, no. xvii, 204, 205.
[28] Górski, *Związek*, no. xvii, 215–16; Adam Vetulani, *Lenno pruskie od traktatu krakowskiego do śmierci księcia Albrechta 1525–1568* (Cracow, 1930), 18–19.

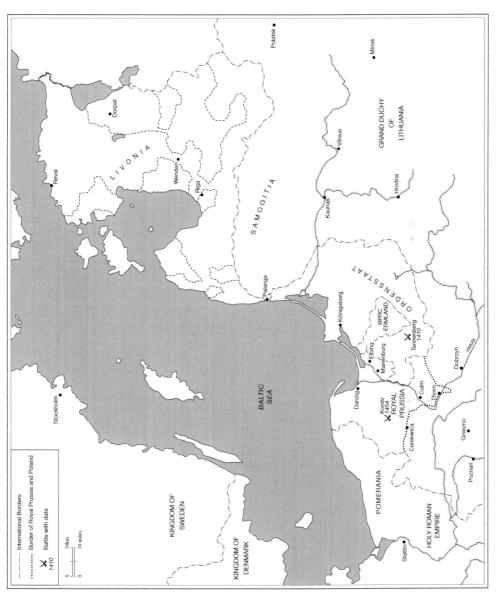

Map 4. The Prussian lands, 1454–1525.

renounced its overlordship of the bishopric of Ermland, which was to be an ecclesiastical principality—thus not subject to Gniezno's jurisdiction—under the protection of the Polish crown. Only the bishopric of Pomezania, whose chapter was also secularized, was to remain within the Order's orbit, though for the moment it was placed under the administration of Wincenty Kiełbasa, the bishop of Culm; only on his death would it revert to the Order.[29]

Długosz, who participated in the Thorn negotiations, claimed that many in Lithuania and Poland were unhappy at the treaty, not because of the division of the Prussian lands, or any sense that it made too many concessions to the Order, but because the Lithuanians saw that it had strengthened Poland, and that therefore Podolia's recovery would be more difficult in the future, while the Poles felt it would enrich the king and strengthen his position.[30] Yet for all the carping, the second peace of Thorn was a success, establishing the political framework for the southern Baltic shore for over three centuries. It never received the papal confirmation both sides agreed to seek; on this basis the Order, after allying with Matthias Corvinus, king of Hungary, briefly and unsuccessfully challenged its legality in 1477; this led to a short war in which it was decisively defeated. The lands restored to the Polish crown, now known as Royal Prussia, were to remain loyal, though fiercely protective of the autonomy under the union secured in 1454. Those Prussians still under the Order's direct rule did not forget the rights and liberties promised to them through the incorporation into Poland, and down to 1657 appealed regularly to their feudal overlord, the king of Poland, for protection of their rights, liberties, and privileges against challenges from the Order and its successors.

---

[29] Vetulani, *Lenno pruskie*, 217–18.   [30] *Annales*, xii/ii, 167–8.

21

Nieszawa

The terms that the Poles had granted to the Prussians were generous, but the rewards were substantial. The incorporation of Royal Prussia transformed the union state by securing control over a substantial swathe of the southern Baltic coast. Possession of Danzig and Elbing was later to galvanize the Polish economy by providing access for Polish grain to the markets of western Europe, which from the early sixteenth century experienced population growth, the development of new financial mechanisms, and, after 1550, stimulation from the influx of silver from the New World. In 1466, however, Poland was mired in economic stagnation. Although the relatively sparsely peopled lands of east central Europe did not suffer as badly as western and southern Europe from the Black Death, Poland was not entirely untouched. Population growth slowed, but its upward trajectory was not reversed, and by the mid fifteenth century the disparity between the density of settlement in Poland and western Europe had eased. There are problems in calculating that population, for the figures vary depending upon the borders used by historians, who have not always escaped the shadow of the anachronistic criteria adopted in Communist Poland, which included Mazovia, Prussia, and even Silesia according to the borders of 1945, and, less anachronistically, Red Ruthenia, although it was no longer part of Poland after 1945. One estimate suggests that the population in the reign of Casimir III (1333–70) reached two million at a density of 8.3 per square kilometre, but it includes Mazovia, whose princes recognized Casimir's overlordship, but not that of the Polish kingdom, or of Louis of Anjou.[1] Kuklo excludes Silesia, but includes Mazovia and Prussia: the result is an estimated population of 1.25 million in 1000, with a density of five per square kilometre, growing to 2 million (eight per square kilometre) in 1370, and 3.4 million in 1500 at a density of 13, or 6.5 million including the grand duchy, which brings the density of the union state down to 6.[2]

The population rise before 1350 depended substantially on inward migration, particularly of German settlers, who were offered generous terms and who brought German law—largely Magdeburg or Culm law—with them. German law, with its strong village communities based round the village headman or *sołtys*—from the German *Schulz* or *Schultheis*—was a useful tool for nobles wishing to attract the labour without which their lands were worthless. New settlements of Polish peasants were established on German law, which was also introduced to many—

---

[1] Zientara, 'Społeczeństwo', 95.
[2] Cezary Kuklo, *Demografia Rzeczypospolitej przedrozbiorowej* (Warsaw, 2009), table 29, 211.

though by no means all—existing villages. By 1333, 300 villages had been established on German law in Wielkopolska, and 280 in Małopolska; over the thirteenth and fourteenth centuries, 250,000 German migrants settled in Poland.[3]

The stream was abruptly halted by the Black Death, whose catastrophic effects elsewhere meant that demand for the products of the Polish economy collapsed after 1350. It was not just the supply of migrants that dried up: capital flows were just as abruptly halted, and the Polish economy suffered from a shortage of specie. Population stagnation meant that the internal market could not compensate. These unpromising economic circumstances affected the development of socio-economic structures within Poland, and lay behind the political challenges faced by Jagiełło at Czerwińsk in 1422, and by Casimir at Cerekwica and Nieszawa in 1454. For if a narrow group of magnates—particularly from Małopolska—prospered in the early decades of Jagiellon rule, they did so through the generosity of the needy Jagiellon monarchs, who had pawned, mortgaged, alienated, or donated royal lands to the great lords—mostly from Małopolska—who dominated Polish politics, in return for political support or cash in hand. The practice accelerated in the last years of Jagiełło's reign, as he alienated villages and estates in an attempt to secure recognition of his sons' hereditary rights to the throne—one third of all mortgages he issued in Poland were granted between 1424 and 1434—and during the reign of Władysław, who sought to raise money for his crusading ventures through alienations on a massive scale.[4]

Royal supporters benefited substantially. Families such as the Koniecpolskis, Odrowąż, and Kurozwęckis built up huge complexes of royal estates effectively under their control until the unlikely day when the king could redeem his debts. Their control of the key local office of starosta—which was remunerated by the royal estates attached to the post—enabled them to dominate local politics: a glaring example was the tight grip of the Odrowąż over Red Ruthenia. According to Długosz, the fear that Bolesław of Mazovia would not be so generous, and, not feeling bound by the agreements of his predecessors, would seek to reclaim royal lands, ensured that Małopolskan magnates were lukewarm or hostile to the prospect of his becoming king.[5] Casimir represented less of a threat, but his strong position after his coronation meant that he was able to reverse the trend in the early years of his reign. The outbreak of war in 1454 saw the problem return, however: if between 1447 and 1455 there were 243 alienations, there were 324 in the four years between 1456 and 1460. Over a quarter (27.7 per cent) of entries in the crown *metryka*, the chancery archive, between 1447 and 1492 were mortgages on crown estates.[6]

---

[3] Christoph Schmidt, *Leibeigenschaft im Ostseeraum: Versuch einer Typologie* (Cologne, 1997), 41; Zientara, 'Społeczeństwo' 91, 107; Benedykt Zientara, '*Melioratio terrae*: The thirteenth-century breakthrough in Polish history', in J.K. Federowicz (ed.), *A Republic of Nobles* (Cambridge, 1982), 37–42.

[4] Jerzy Luciński, *Rozwój królewszczyzn w Koronie od schyłku XIV wieku do XVII wieku* (Poznań, 1970), 33–5; Anna Sucheni-Grabowska, *Odbudowa domeny królewskiej w Polsce 1504–1548*, 2nd edn (Warsaw, 2007), 40–2, 45–6.

[5] *Annales*, xii/i, 33–4; Sucheni-Grabowska, *Odbudowa*, 46–7.

[6] Kazimierz Tymieniecki, 'Wpływy ustroju feudalnego w Polsce średniowiecznej', *RDSG*, 3 (1934), 107.

For the recipients, royal land became a vital part of their property holdings and a means of avoiding the worst effects of the partible inheritance normal under Polish law. Wealthier, politically influential families were better able to weather economic stagnation after 1386; the first half of the fifteenth century therefore saw a marked diversification of the noble estate, as the small group of families at the top—particularly from Małopolska—grew richer, while the fortunes of middling and lesser landowners declined as the effects of partible inheritance spread through the generations. By 1450 population growth was strong enough to affect the size of landholdings among the middling and lesser nobility negatively, but not strong enough to offset the effects of the collapse of migration from western and central Europe. The shortage of labour and the stagnant economy meant that it was difficult for nobles without access to royal lands to mitigate the effects of partible inheritance through the capital-intensive means of founding new villages, as their forebears had done in the age of expansion before 1350.[7]

For the elite, while times were also hard, access to royal land was crucial for maintaining a family's position. Jagiełło's outright donation of the town of Nowa Góra in the district of Cracow to Jan Tęczyński, castellan of Cracow, at some point between 1398 and 1402—the transaction is known through its 1512 confirmation—did much to preserve Tęczyński fortunes after Jan's death in 1405, when his lands were divided among the three sons of his first marriage. He made provisions in his 1402 will against the need to provide dowries for his three daughters and any daughters of his second marriage; in the event the second marriage produced only sons, who played no role in the bitter disputes over the Tęczyński inheritance that followed. Nowa Góra, apart from the town itself, possessed five villages and lucrative lead mines that helped sustain the family fortunes until its final extinction in 1637.[8]

The funds generated enabled Tęczyński's grandson, also Jan (1408–70), successively palatine of Sandomierz, palatine of Cracow, and castellan of Cracow, to reconstitute his grandfather's holdings, dispersed in a 1414 family agreement. He was helped by the death of his uncles without male heirs, but his efforts were complicated by the provisions made for his own brothers in 1414, and for the widow of his uncle, Nawój, who died—deeply indebted—in 1422, which enabled Jan to administer all the family domains until a new division in 1438 with his brother Andrzej established two main Tęczyński lines.[9]

The struggles of the Tęczyńskis were repeated across the spectrum of Polish noble society from rich to poor. As family holdings fractured, the shortage of specie meant that it was increasingly difficult for middling and lesser nobles to raise money through credit, mortgage, pawning, or sale to pay debts and consolidate holdings. Landowners could gather complexes of estates into blocs, but consolidation

---

[7] Krzysztof Mikulski and Jan Wroniszewski, 'Folwark i zmiany koniunktury gospodarczej w Polsce XIV–XVII wieku', *Klio*, 4 (2003), 27–8.
[8] Janusz Kurtyka, *Latyfundium tęczyńskie: Dobra i właściciele (XIV–XVII wiek)* (Cracow, 1999), 35–62.
[9] Kurtyka, *Latyfundium tęczyńskie*, 90–1.

complicated provisions for children, and even contiguous villages and estates were often treated as separate entities, which gave more flexibility to debt-ridden nobles whose immovable property was their chief asset. Without access to royal grants or leaseholds, most families struggled to maintain their holdings, and were often unable, unlike Jan Tęczyński the younger, to buy back from family members or creditors estates that had formed part of the protoplast's patrimony. A widening gap developed between the ordinary nobility and the wealthy magnates at the top of the system: the ratio of dowries offered by the two groups in the palatinate of Sieradz grew from 1:5 in 1400 to 1:10 by 1450, and 1:65 by 1500.[10]

These developments had serious implications for a military system based on the obligation of noble landowners to serve and equip themselves in time of war. Moralists might decry the declining martial qualities of the szlachta, but economic stagnation had not so much sapped the szlachta's military vitality or its attachment to the ideal of the nobility as a warrior class, as rendered it incapable of sustaining its obligations. The division of the Polish kingdom after 1138 into appanage duchies helped prevent the spread of feudal law on the western European pattern: the increasing number of petty Piast dukes preferred to keep direct control over their nobles, rather than allowing the construction of hierarchies of vassalage. Their policies stimulated the development of the noble heraldic clans, with their emphasis on kinship and horizontal links, and prevented the downgrading of the legal rights of collateral lines that elsewhere accompanied the strengthening of vertical ties of vassalage. Since noble status was inherited by all children of nobles, the szlachta—already large in 1370 by European standards—continued to grow. The entrenching of allodial rights to land held technically under 'knightly law' (*prawo rycerskie*) with the obligation to serve the prince directly prevented the spread of feudalism on the western European pattern, with its emphasis on obligations to serve one's superior in the feudal hierarchy. This deprived the royal government of the intermediate vassals who helped to mobilize the armies of western Europe, although it also meant that Poland did not suffer from the problem of bastard feudalism. In Poland, the challenge to royal power came more through collective resistance.[11] The strike of the noble levy at Czerwińsk in 1422 established a pattern: its success in securing the extension of privileges was a lesson for the ordinary nobles who shouldered the burden of warfare, but saw the rewards go to a small group of wealthy lords.

The lesson was not forgotten by those summoned to fulfil their military obligations in 1454. It was no accident that the challenge came from the Wielkopolska levy that assembled at Cerekwica in September. For if Małopolskan politics had been dominated for generations by a small group of wealthy magnates, there were few magnates in Wielkopolska, where it was the middling szlachta, most of whom owned but one village, that predominated; apart from church lands, most properties were considerably smaller than in Małopolska, something that was also true of royal estates, which meant that they were not as lucrative for the Wielkopolskan

---

[10] Jan Wroniszewski, *Szlachta ziemi sandomierskiej w średniowieczu* (Poznań, 2001), 82.
[11] Sławomir Gawlas, 'Dlaczego nie było w Polsce feudalizmu lennego?', *RDSG*, 58 (1998), 101–23; Zientara, 'Społeczeństwo', 146.

elite as they were for their Małopolskan counterparts.[12] Anticlericalism was growing among the Wielkopolskan nobility, resentful of the wealth of the church, especially of the large estates accumulated by the ecclesiastical hierarchy, and of their tax privileges. Jagiełło did not challenge Małopolska's political domination: although he was a peripatetic king, he usually visited Wielkopolska only once a year to hear legal cases and to hunt. Władysław III, before leaving for Hungary, appointed Wojciech Malski as governor of Wielkopolska and outraged many by replacing the popular native starosta general, Stanisław of Ostroróg, with Krzesław Kurozwęcki, a Małopolskan magnate, but was forced to reverse his decision in 1443. The Wielkopolskans did not share Małopolskan enthusiasm for Władysław's Hungarian adventure, even if many served on his crusade in search of profit or place.[13]

Matters improved somewhat at the start of Casimir's reign, as he challenged the power of Oleśnicki and the Cracow lords. In 1451 Casimir outraged Oleśnicki by granting precedence on the royal council to Oporowski, the Wielkopolskan primate, despite Oleśnicki's status as a cardinal; two years later he blocked Oleśnicki's candidate to replace Oporowski in favour of Jan Sprowski, a Wielkopolskan.[14] Despite these favourable signs, and although the Wielkopolskan nobility had always been more favourably disposed towards war against the Order, resentment built up over a generation and more, and the problems of fulfilling their military obligations ensured that the szlachta gathering in Cerekwica were in militant mood.

The origins of the political standoff in the autumn of 1454 lay in Casimir's refusal, following his accession, to confirm the grants of privileges made by his predecessors despite the promises he had made before his coronation. He declined to do so at the Piotrków assembly of August 1447, where he merely confirmed several individual points and stressed his judicial powers.[15] By 1453, with Casimir still refusing a general confirmation of privileges, feelings were running high. Those who gathered at Piotrków for another general assembly were in militant mood, determined to counter what many saw as the king's willingness to use his support among the highest government dignitaries to ignore the law. Casimir might have neutralized the ageing Oleśnicki, but now he faced a new challenge. Although the most militant muttered about dethronement, and there were calls for confederation and the formal withdrawal of obedience, Casimir, who displayed an 'iron will' according to Długosz, managed to disarm the opposition. He had to confirm the privileges granted by his predecessors, but he did so in very general terms, without the detailed reaffirmation and extension of privileges that Jagiełło had been forced to concede in 1430.[16]

The general nature of the confirmation did not appease noble discontent. Yet there was little hope that ordinary nobles could secure their aims at a general

---

[12] *Dzieje Wielkopolski*, i, ed. Jerzy Topolski (Poznań, 1969), 322; Zientara, 'Społeczeństwo', 146.
[13] *Dzieje Wielkopolski*, i, 316–19. [14] *Dzieje Wielkopolski*, i, 319.
[15] *Annales*, xii/i, 52–3; Abdon Kłodziński, 'W sprawie przywilejów nieszawskich z r. 1454', in *Studya historyczne wydane ku czci prof. Wincentego Zakrzewskiego* (Cracow, 1908), 247; Górski, 'Młodość', 14.
[16] *Annales*, xii/i, 162–4; Kłodziński, 'W sprawie', 247–8.

assembly. Such assemblies had met increasingly frequently since 1386, but they lacked any institutionalized procedure or form. Although ordinary nobles turned up in varying numbers, the magnates dominated proceedings, and the ordinary nobility took little direct part. Decisions were taken by a narrow group of office-holders and dignitaries, and communicated to the general assembly.[17] If there was political division among the magnates, the ordinary nobility could play a role, if only the negative one of howling down unpopular proposals or raucously acclaiming popular ones. Although historians routinely speak of the 'ordinary nobility' as if it were a cohesive force with a common interest, the szlachta was riven with local rivalries, and individuals often had links, whether of clientage or other forms of obligation, to wealthier nobles. It was difficult, therefore, for it collectively to seize the political initiative.

By 1453, however, ordinary nobles across the kingdom were resentful of the way in which the governing elite of office-holders—and the principal beneficiaries of royal largesse—closed ranks around the king at moments of crisis to block szlachta demands. The coming of war in 1454 gave ordinary nobles the opportunity to voice their concerns. When the Wielkopolskan levy gathered in September at Cerekwica its mood was mutinous. The szlachta had been called away at harvest time, a circumstance that highlighted the extent to which the obligation to serve had become oppressive. One issue encapsulated the wider problems. For all that the concept of the *corona regni* suggested that the Prussian lands, whose incorporation the levy was to defend, had remained part of the realm after their illegal annexation in 1308–9, for those gathered at Cerekwica the war was to be fought outside Poland's borders; they therefore demanded payment of five marks per lance for their military service as stipulated in the Koszyce privileges. The failure to make such payments in the wars against the Order highlighted the more general problem of enforcing compliance upon rulers who conceded privileges under pressure but failed to honour them. The general confirmation of privileges in 1453 did not allay these fears.

The course of events leading to the promulgation of the so-called privileges of Nieszawa, the last great set of general privileges granted to the szlachta, was complex. The normally garrulous Długosz relates the Cerekwica events in a couple of lines. Having criticized the levy for its lack of discipline, and for burning and looting church property, he merely states that Casimir pacified the szlachta by confirming old privileges, without even hinting that new privileges were issued; he passes over in silence subsequent events in the camps of the Małopolskan levy at Opoki and Nieszawa.[18] Textbooks routinely refer to the 'privileges of Nieszawa', since historians long believed that the privileges issued for Wielkopolska at Cerekwica were subsequently replaced by a general privilege issued for the whole kingdom at Nieszawa. The original of this general privilege had disappeared, although it was apparently confirmed by John Albert in 1496, and was incorporated into Jan Łaski's 1506 digest of Polish law.

---

[17] Juliusz Bardach, 'Początki sejmu', in *Historia sejmu polskiego*, i: *Do schyłku szlacheckiego Rzeczypospolitej*, ed. Jerzy Michalski (Warsaw, 1984), 17.
[18] *Annales*, xii/i, 209–11, 223.

Bobrzyński realized that no general privilege was issued in 1454, but a series of privileges for individual provinces and territories: it was only in 1496 that John Albert consolidated them into one general privilege, which he then confirmed.[19] Bobrzyński's thesis was contested, but was confirmed in 1957 by Roman, whose painstaking reconstruction of the 1454 events revealed a much more complex reality. The crisis indeed began at Cerekwica, where Casimir, having declared war on the Order, had no room for manoeuvre: if the Wielkopolskans refused to fight, he would be unable to aid the Bund, and his credibility would be destroyed. Casimir therefore consented to a radical set of privileges, whose pointed language— in places bordering on the offensive—revealed the extent of Wielkopolskan anger at the cosy cartel of largely Małopolskan magnates that ran Polish politics. Royal judges were bluntly told to base their verdicts on the law, and not dream them up out of their own heads. Casimir was obliquely criticized, being told to rule wisely, with the implication that he had not yet learned how.[20]

The anti-magnate tenor was encapsulated in two key passages. The first clause stipulated that palatines, castellans, dignitaries, and high local officials were henceforth barred from serving as starostas in a measure that sought to ensure that the principal royal officers at the local level were more accountable to the local political community. It was clause 18, however, that formed the document's centrepiece. In it Casimir promised that:

> in order that in future the republic might be more soundly governed, we desire and... decree that henceforth no new measures should be decided through private counsel, nor any [military] campaign be undertaken in whatever way without the consent of assemblies of the local landed community, but that all new matters should first be decided and approved by assemblies of the local communities.[21]

This clause had momentous implications. It was a direct response to events at the 1452 general assembly in Sieradz, where Casimir demonstrated his willingness to ignore szlachta opinion. After he again refused to confirm noble privileges, the 'noble representatives of the community' (*nobiles ex comunitate*), as Długosz put it, rejected his request for an extra year to determine the fate of Podolia and Volhynia following Švitrygaila's death, demanding that he definitively attached them to Poland. Facing deadlock, Casimir suspended the assembly, summoning eight of his closest advisors, who promptly agreed to his proposal.[22] Such actions suggested that he was willing to ride roughshod over the consensual norms of Polish political life. It was difficult for a general assembly, even one in which the szlachta deliberated separately from the lords—as in 1453—to impose its views upon the

---

[19] Michał Bobrzyński, *O ustawodawstwie nieszawskim Kazimierza Jagiellończyka*, 2nd edn (Cracow, 1973); Stanisław Roman, *Przywileje nieszawskie* (Wrocław, 1957), 12.

[20] Roman, *Przywileje*, 154.

[21] 'Ut igitur respublica in posterum sanius dirigatur, volumus et... statuimus, ne aliquae novae institutiones privatis consiliis statuantur, neque expeditio aliqua absque communi terrestri conventione in posterum suscitetur quovismodo, sed omnes res de novo inveniendae in conventionibus, communitatibus terrestribus prius practicatae, statuantur et laudentur.' Quoted by Roman, *Przywileje*, 156. '*communi terrestri*' is usually translated as 'szlachta': cf. Bardach, 'Początki', 32.

[22] *Annales*, xii/i, 136; Bardach, 'Początki', 17, 33.

king. Only if local sejmiks needed to give their explicit consent to new measures could the ordinary nobility establish control over important decisions.

For all his bravado, it was difficult in 1454 for Casimir to resist these demands. He needed professional troops, yet he could not raise the necessary money from his own resources. The only possible means of securing the funds was through taxation, but his hands were tied by the Koszyce privileges, which limited his ability to collect taxation from the nobility to the *poradlne*, levied at 2 groszy per hide. This had hitherto proven sufficient, and his predecessors had been forced to seek consent for extra taxation from general and local assemblies on only two occasions since 1374: in 1404, to raise money to purchase Dobrzyń from the Order, and in 1441.[23] If the king wished to levy further taxes on the szlachta he could only do so with the consent of local assemblies, although he still had the power to impose customs duties from which the nobility was not exempt, a major point of grievance. It was such considerations that lay behind clause 18 of the Cerekwica document, whose significance lay in its stress on the need for the consent not of a general assembly (*conventio generalis*), but of assemblies of the local nobility, the *communi terrestris*: the community of landholders.

The origins of these assemblies lay in the period before the reunification of the kingdom in 1320, when, in the duchies and territories of the Polish lands, judicial bodies known as 'general assemblies' (*colloquia generalia*) of local lay and ecclesiastical dignitaries and office-holders met regularly: seventy such assemblies are known from the thirteenth century.[24] After 1320, and the transformation of ducal into local and provincial officials, a distinction arose between assemblies with a judicial function—*colloquia* in Latin, *wiece* in Polish—and meetings of officials to settle matters of local law and administration, termed *consilia*, or *conventiones dominorum terrae*. As the economic and political power of the lesser and middling szlachta grew, assemblies of all the local nobility, the *communitas nobilium*, or *omnes terrigenae* became common. While ordinary nobles had always attended in the retinues of the dignitaries, they soon demanded an independent role. Such *consilia generalia*, which in Polish came to be known as *sejmiki* spread throughout the Polish lands after 1382, fostered by the interregnum of 1382–6, when competing magnates appealed for support to the broader nobility.[25]

By the 1420s, sejmiks met regularly in Wielkopolska, where they were established at the district and county level beneath the provincial sejmik, which met in Środa. In Małopolska, however, there was only a provincial sejmik, and local sejmiks were not established until the 1490s. This more decentralized structure lent an edge to politics in Wielkopolska, where the division between central dignitaries and office-holders and the ordinary nobility was explicit, as is demonstrated in the laws passed by the Łęczyca sejmik in 1418, which stated that they were passed by 'all their lordships the dignitaries, with the agreement of the whole community'.[26] At the local level where the king played no part in the deliberations

---

[23] Bardach, 'Początki', 29, 30.   [24] Roman, *Przywileje*, 109.
[25] Bardach, 'Początki', 28–9; Kutrzeba, *Korona*, 64–7; Roman, *Przywileje*, 108–13.
[26] 'Cum consensu totius communitatis': Bardach, 'Początki', 29.

of these assemblies, for the most part it was easier for the local nobility to hold their office-holders to account than in the general assemblies, where royal officials and the council dominated: Długosz usually only mentions the lesser nobles at general assemblies if they turned up in significant numbers.[27]

It is unlikely that the nobles gathered at Cerekwica thought they were instituting the constitutional revolution that many historians have discerned in the events of 1454. Although there was no formal requirement for the king to consult before he called out the noble levy, consultation was customary, as in other matters affecting the local szlachta.[28] It was precisely because Casimir had not consulted them before calling out the levy in 1454 that the Wielkopolska nobles were so determined to assert themselves: the 1452 general assembly demonstrated his willingness to take important decisions with the support of a narrow group of dignitaries in the teeth of szlachta opposition. It was this challenge to what ordinary nobles regarded as customary law, not any desire to innovate, that lay behind clause 18.

The radical formulation of this principle in the Cerekwica document openly challenged Casimir and the council elite in whose hands effective power lay at national and provincial level. Although Casimir—who had little choice—agreed to the Cerekwica privileges on 15 September, the levy's crushing defeat at Konitz three days later strengthened his hand. When the Małopolskan levy, which gathered at Opoki in November, demanded similar privileges, he was better able to resist. There were more dignitaries present, who put pressure on their clients and mediated between the szlachta and the king. Thus the demands set out at Opoki in the form of instructions, though based on the Cerekwica document, included several new points but were less radical, as were the privileges issued at Nieszawa on 10 November for the core Małopolskan lands of Cracow, Sandomierz, Lublin, Radom, and Wiślica. In these, the first clause of the Cerekwica privileges, which barred office-holders and dignitaries from being appointed as starostas—except for the starosty of Cracow—was considerably watered down: it was only to apply to palatines. Most significantly, the Małopolskan redaction omitted the vital clause 18.[29]

Not a single dignitary put themselves forward as a guarantor of the Cerekwica privileges, and it is clear that there was opposition to them among Wielkopolskan dignitaries. This enabled Casimir to renegotiate the Wielkopolskan terms with the participation of provincial dignitaries and magnates. At Nieszawa a new set of privileges for Wielkopolska was drawn up, which were influenced by the Małopolskan redaction, although they differed on several points.[30] The Nieszawa redaction, though retaining much of the Cerekwica blueprint, substantially modified the controversial elements: clause one concerning the accumulation of offices was based on the Małopolskan redaction, although it added the office of castellan to that of palatine, while clause 18—clause 33 in the new redaction—abandoned the critical tone of Cerekwica and was considerably reduced in bite:

---

[27] Roman, *Przywileje*, 114–15.
[28] Roman, *Przywileje*, 115–16.
[29] Roman, *Przywileje*, 150–4.
[30] Roman, *Przywileje*, 90–1, 145.

We promise neither to make new statutes nor to call out the nobility to war without having first called an assembly of the nobility to Środa.[31]

This was a significant change, not so much in terms of the basic principle, but in the fact that Casimir only consented to call a provincial sejmik, where office-holders and dignitaries exercised greater influence than in the local sejmiks. Cerekwica's stress on the prior consent of the ordinary szlachta was omitted.[32]

The process was completed in December, as the Wielkopolskan and Małopolskan redactions formed the basis for local versions compiled for the districts of the two provinces, and the issuing of privileges for Sieradz, which was not formally part of Wielkopolska, and for Poland's Ruthenian provinces that were not formally part of Małopolska: one for Chełm, and a common one for Sanok and Przemyśl, issued in Radzyń on 11 December. No such privileges were issued for the territories of Lwów and Halych, which—unlike the other Red Ruthenian lands—did not summon the levy to fight in the Prussian war.[33] Nevertheless, two years later, at a provincial sejmik in Korczyn, both Małopolska and the Ruthenian territories were granted a version of clause 33 in the Wielkopolskan redaction, in a new set of privileges, although it only specified that the sejmiks should be consulted before the king called out the Małopolskan, Ruthenian, or Podolian levies to fight in the Prussian war.[34] There was no mention of consent to 'new measures', as in the Wielkopolskan redaction, and it was not until John Albert issued his consolidated privilege in 1496 that clause 33 in the Nieszawan redaction was applied to the whole kingdom. It was strengthened with the stipulation that consultation had to take place at the level of the district, not the provincial sejmiks, but it did not repeat the stronger wording of clause 18 in the Cerekwica redaction.[35]

Thus the common claim that the Nieszawa privileges constituted a fundamental watershed in Polish political history through the establishment of the principle that no new laws could be enacted without the prior consent of the sejmiki is misleading, as is the contention that Casimir, despite the challenge to royal power implicit in the privileges, allied with the szlachta, seizing an opportunity to appeal to them over the heads of the magnates.[36] Roman's claim that, far from representing a radical innovation, the Nieszawa privileges merely recognized that sejmiks already possessed the right to consultation that the privileges, in the traditional view,

---

[31] 'Item pollicemur, quod nullas novas constituciones faciemus, neque terrigenas ad bellum moveri mandabimus absque conventione communi terrestri in Srzoda instituenda': Roman, *Przywileje*, 156.

[32] Roman, *Przywileje*, 157.

[33] Wojciech Hejnosz, 'Przywileje nieszawsko-radzyńskie dla ziem ruskich', in *Studia historyczne ku czci Stanisława Kutrzeby*, 238, 242.

[34] 'Insuper expeditionem generalem versus terras Prussiae movere non debemus, nisi prius habita conventione desuper terrarum Cracoviensis, Sandomiriensis, Russiae et Podoliae': *Ius Polonicum*, 299.

[35] *VC*, i, 66.

[36] Davies, *God's Playground*, i, 164; Lukowski and Zawadzki, *Concise History*, 49; Daniel Stone, *The Polish-Lithuanian State, 1386–1795* (Seattle, 2001), 28, all suggest that the Nieszawa privileges were general, and that they prevented the king from levying new taxation without the consent of the sejmiks, of which there was no mention in any of the redactions. Davies erroneously implies that it was only after Nieszawa that sejmiks began to meet: *God's Playground*, i, 247, 250.

granted them, is broadly convincing.[37] Wielkopolskan outrage at the summoning of the levy without consultation suggests that there was an expectation that the sejmiks were normally informed of royal intentions. Roman explains the omission of this vital clause from the Małopolskan redaction by arguing that they had no need to insert such a clause because they were confident that the Małopolskan provincial sejmik already possessed these rights.[38] This suggestion is less persuasive, however. As he recognizes, the political structure of Małopolska was different. Without local sejmiks, the provincial sejmik was much more open to domination by the office-holding elite, which undoubtedly explains the less radical position adopted by Małopolska in 1454.

The Nieszawa privileges were nevertheless a significant milestone in the development of the Polish political system and Polish political culture, and substantially influenced the process of union. The Wielkopolska szlachta may indeed have considered consultation to be enshrined in customary law, but the monarch still had substantial prerogative powers. Casimir's stubborn refusal to confirm the privileges granted by his predecessors—and the vague wording when eventually he did—represented a clear threat to the culture of consultation and consensus that had become embedded in Wielkopolska in particular since 1382. By raising the requirement to consult from the status of customary law to that of written law, the Nieszawa privileges laid the cornerstone of the consensual system, based ultimately on the local political communities at district level, that subsequently spread throughout the union. In 1454 Casimir was forced to accept that the monarchy had to work within the political framework provided by the sejmiks, even if the issuing of several privileges, rather than one general privilege left him considerable room for manoeuvre.

The Nieszawa privileges are often presented as a crucial stage in the process by which the Polish parliamentary system, in contrast to estates bodies elsewhere, became not just dominated by the nobility, but exclusively reserved to it. It is doubtful, however, if any such intention lay behind them. The main concern in the various redactions at Nieszawa was military, and specifically the issue of the levy, which was an obligation only for nobles. The necessity of securing consent to military expeditions was the sole focus of the clauses in the 1456 Korczyn privileges for Małopolska and the Ruthenian lands. Even in the Cerekwica text, and in the final Wielkopolskan redaction, the clause is a simple reflection of the szlachta's desire to be consulted on matters that affected it, rather than any wish to exclude other social groups from a parliament that did not yet exist.

---

[37] Roman, *Przywileje*, 108–37.   [38] Roman, *Przywileje*, 119–21.

22

Peasants

The establishment of a noble monopoly over the legislative process was traditionally seen as the key element that enabled the szlachta to shape the Polish rural economy in its own interest. Noble domination of the legislature and a progressive weakening of royal power have been widely blamed for the establishment of a manorial system of agriculture in which the szlachta farmed its own demesne or manor—*folwark* in Polish, from the German *Vorwerk*—with free labour-service provided by serfs tied to the land, unable to appeal to the royal courts for protection, and burdened with ever higher demands from their rapacious lords. Although the system influentially categorized in 1882 by Engels as 'the second serfdom' and known to German scholarship as *Gutsherrschaft*, spread across Europe to the east of the Elbe from the fifteenth century, it has been widely presented as peculiarly oppressive in Poland-Lithuania on account of the szlachta's domination of the legislative system.[1]

This emphasis on the nobility as the driving force behind the creation of an oppressive serf-based economy was encouraged in Communist Poland. Publications by Polish historians in western European languages gave sufficient material to scholars outside Poland to integrate it into attempts to explain the apparently divergent paths of western Europe, in which serfdom was largely abandoned after 1350, and eastern Europe, where, so it was argued, it had not been known before the fourteenth century, but where it became the basis of the rural economy after 1500. The work of the distinguished economic historian Marian Małowist in the 1950s and 1960s provided much evidence for those who argued that the key feature was the economic expansion experienced by western Europe from the late fifteenth century, where a growing population created demand for cheap Polish grain produced without significant labour costs.[2] Particularly influential was Witold Kula's *An Economic Theory of the Feudal System*, published in 1962 and translated into several languages with a laudatory preface by Fernand Braudel. Kula, using his

---

[1] For example, Robert Brenner, 'The agrarian roots of European capitalism', in T.H. Aston and C.H.E. Philpin (eds), *The Brenner Debate: Agrarian Class Structure and Economic Development in Pre-Industrial Europe* (Cambridge, 1985), 282–3. For an excellent analysis of the problems see Markus Cerman, *Villagers and Lords in Eastern Europe, 1300–1800* (Basingstoke, 2012).

[2] Marian Małowist, 'Poland, Russia and western trade in the 15th and 16th centuries', *P&P*, 13 (1958), 26–39; Marian Małowist, 'The economic and social development of the Baltic countries from the 15th to the 17th centuries', *EcHR*, 2nd ser. 12/2 (1959), 177–89; and Marian Małowist, 'The problem of the inequality of economic development in Europe in the latter Middle Ages', *EcHR*, 2nd ser., 19/1 (1966), 15–28.

own research into eighteenth-century magnate latifundia, constructed a theoretical model of the Polish manorial economy which concluded that since it lacked endogamous forces leading to capitalism, it was economically regressive.[3]

Thus, it was argued, as western economies expanded and diversified, the Polish economy entered a classical colonial relationship, supplying cheap raw materials—primarily grain, but also timber, hemp, flax, and other primary products—to burgeoning western markets. In order to maximize their profits, the szlachta increasingly adopted the monoculture of grain on their manors and, exploiting their domination of the legislature, stripped the peasantry of its rights and enserfed it to provide the necessary labour force. In the standard timetable, freedom to depart one's native village was removed in 1496; access to the royal courts was denied to peasants from 1518; and labour service was fixed at a minimum of one day per week in legislation passed in 1520 and 1521. The divergence of the economies of east and west condemned eastern Europe in general and Poland in particular to a system that was more onerous and exploitative than the 'first' serfdom of the medieval west:

> The serfdom of modern Eastern Europe was more cut and dried... Rather than spreading gradually through the ranks of the peasantry in the typically western way, as a result of the policies of estate or territorial management that lords adopted, in the modern East it was established... by government decrees which simply defined the inhabitants of private estates as the subjects of their landlord, with no right to leave and with limited access to public authority.[4]

Although in Poland serfdom was instituted by parliamentary statute rather than government decree, the results were, so it is suggested, similar; indeed, in Poland, where royal power was too weak to curb the excesses of noble power: 'for the most part, [kings] had to give free rein to a nobility that had become virtually omnipotent, thanks to the growing grain trade and the expansion of the landed estate'.[5] In Wallerstein's 'European World System', Poland was reduced to a colonial adjunct of western Europe; with its vast grain-growing latifundia served by what he termed 'coerced cash-crop labour', which he presented as the equivalent of New World slave plantations.[6]

These grand theories have come under increasing fire. In Communist Poland, which inherited a strong tradition of research on the early modern rural economy,

---

[3] Witold Kula, *Teoria ekonomiczna ustroju feudalnego*, 2nd edn (Warsaw, 1983); English version, *An Economic Theory of the Feudal System* (London, 1976), tr. Lawrence Garner from the Italian edn.
[4] Michael Bush, 'Serfdom in medieval and modern Europe. A comparison', in Bush (ed.), *Serfdom and Slavery* (Harlow, 1996), 205; Jerome Blum, 'The rise of serfdom in eastern Europe', *AHR*, 62/4 (1957), 807–36. For recent works that stress the role of the state and of legislation, see Schmidt, *Leibeigenschaft*, 126–44; Paul Freedman and Monique Bourin, 'Introduction', in Paul Freedman and Monique Bourin (eds), *Forms of Servitude in Northern and Central Europe* (Turnhout, 2005), 6, 16.
[5] Werner Rösener, *The Peasantry of Europe* (Oxford, 1994), 108.
[6] Immanuel Wallerstein, *The Modern World System*, i: *Capitalist Agriculture and the Origins of the European World-Economy in the Sixteenth Century* (New York, 1974), 67–129. For a demolition of Wallerstein's account of the Polish rural economy, see Jerzy Topolski, *Przełom gospodarczy w Polsce XVI wieku i jego następstwa* (Poznań, 2000), 41–5, 52–7.

historians quietly assembled a mass of data that enabled them to challenge many aspects of this picture well before Communism fell. They realized that a major problem with research on the Polish rural economy in this period is that the vast majority of detailed studies have been of royal and ecclesiastical estates, or great magnate latifundia. Yet these estates were untypical: the small estates of the ordinary nobility comprised eighty per cent of the land in private noble ownership, and their production was much less geared to supplying the international grain trade, owing to the logistical problems and costs involved in transporting grain to the Prussian ports.[7] Care needs to be taken in drawing general conclusions from data gathered on royal estates, which have been extensively studied by historians owing to the copious records generated by inventories and periodic audits after 1563. Royal estates, leased out for set periods, were very different from private or ecclesiastical properties; even after 1500, when leases were often for life, leaseholders treated them differently from their allodial possessions, and had an interest in giving a falsely low picture of their productivity to auditors.[8]

The grand theories of Małowist and Kula were based on data from estates that were not representative of the rural economy as a whole. Study of the estates of ordinary nobles was made easier by the compilation of the *kartoteka wiejska*, a card-file index to the records of the local castle and land courts that was prepared in every Polish state archive between 1951 and 1953, and enabled scholars to retrieve inventories, testaments, and other materials relating to smaller estates from the mass of local court records across Poland. It became clear that all manors were not 'everywhere identical to each other', as had been assumed on theoretical grounds.[9] As early as 1960, when the icy dogma of Stalinism had barely begun to thaw, Wyczański published a pioneering study of the manorial estates of the middle nobility in twelve palatinates, based on records uncovered through use of the *kartoteka*. Boldly asserting that since scholars knew next to nothing about the peasantry's economic position, Wyczański stated that he would concentrate on an economic analysis and avoid the many aspects of relations between lords and peasants which were not relevant to such an objective.[10] Although, in deference to Marxist orthodoxy, he paid lip-service to the concept of class-struggle, he claimed it lay outside the scope of his study, and in the five pages of observations he made on the subject he gently challenged the standard view of a grossly oppressive system characterized by rapacious lords and entrenched peasant resistance. He criticized scholars for failing to consider the economic basis of that

---

[7] Andrzej Kamiński, 'Neo-serfdom in Poland-Lithuania', *SR*, 34 (1975), 256. Polish historians tend to use the contemporary term '*możnowładca*' for the medieval period, and '*magnat*' for the early modern period. I use 'magnate' for both. As Kurtyka observes, the Polish terms are synonyms: 'Posiadłość, dziedziczność i prestiż: Badania nad późnośredniowieczną i wczesnonowożytną wielką własnością możnowładczą w Polsce XIV–XVII wieku', *RH*, 65 (1999), 163.

[8] For this reason Żytkowicz omits data from royal estates when calculating his figures for yield ratios: Leonid Żytkowicz, 'Grain yields in Poland, Bohemia, Hungary and Slovakia in the 16th to 18th centuries' *APH*, 24 (1971), 60.

[9] Stefan Inglot, *Z dziejów wsi polskiej i rolnictwa*, 2nd edn (Warsaw, 1986), 174.

[10] Andrzej Wyczański, *Studia nad folwarkiem szlacheckim w Polsce w latach 1500–1800* (Warsaw, 1960), 5–6.

resistance, observing that it had largely been studied on the basis of materials from royal, ecclesiastical, and a handful of magnate estates.[11] By 1978 the climate had liberalized sufficiently for him to pose the provocative question 'Was life so bad for peasants in the sixteenth century?', and to argue that the picture was not nearly as black as historians had assumed, even after the construction of the legal framework of subjection from the late fifteenth century. He concluded that Polish peasants were vigorous economic subjects in their own right rather than simple victims of szlachta oppression, and that they were perfectly capable of reacting to market stimuli, despite Kula's theoretically driven conclusion that peasant farms were 'no more' than subsistence units isolated from market forces.[12] Wyczański posed the vital question of whether fifteenth-century governments with limited means of enforcing their will could transform a vast rural economy simply by willing it, while a growing number of detailed empirical studies led scholars to question the formative role of statute law in the development of the manorial economy.

These conclusions have been confirmed by a new generation of scholars, released in 1990 from any requirement to toe the Marxist line. In reality, across east central Europe the trend towards labour rent—as opposed to labour-service—and manorial farming preceded the subjection of peasants to their lords, often by a considerable period. It is therefore difficult to argue that the decrees and statutes of governments and parliaments were the main cause of the spread of the manorial system. Although some still emphasize the role of legislation, others have increasingly drawn a distinction, using the German terms, between *Gutswirtschaft*—an economy based on demesne farming—and *Gutsherrschaft*—the system by which lords exercised a greater or lesser degree of authority over their rural 'subjects' (*Untertanen* in German; *poddani* in Polish). Subjection was, however, not the equivalent of full serfdom, since it was tenurial, based on plots of land, rather than the hereditary bondage that lay at the heart of true serfdom.[13] Hagen argues that the term 'peasant', with its negative connotations, should be abandoned, since the German word *Bauer* denotes a farmer, not a peasant; there is a similar debate among Polish scholars over the use of the term *chłop* (peasant), which was pejorative in origin, and was not used in official sources, where the term *kmieć* (plural: *kmiecie*; Latinized as *kmethonis, kmethones*), the equivalent of the German *Bauer*, was used for the tenant farmers who formed the backbone of the system.[14] The use of 'peasant' to cover the whole of the non-noble rural population lumps it together into one amorphous category and obscures the distinctions between groups of vastly different economic condition and social status: the relatively wealthy tenant

---

[11] Wyczański, *Studia*, 115–16.
[12] Andrzej Wyczański, 'Czy chłopu było źle w Polsce XVI wieku?', *KH*, 85 (1978), 627–41; Kula, *Theory*, 17, 49, 62; Topolski, *Przełom*, 18–19.
[13] Cerman, *Villagers*, 11–13; Cerman, 'Social structure and land markets in late medieval central and east-central Europe', *Continuity and Change*, 23/1 (2008), 77–8; Tom Scott, 'Economic landscapes' in Robert Scribner (ed.), *Germany: A New Social and Economic History*, i (London, 1996), 10.
[14] William Hagen, 'Subject farmers in Brandenburg-Prussia and Poland: Village life and fortunes under manorialism in early modern central Europe', in Bush (ed.), *Serfdom*, 309; Jerzy Wyrozumski, 'Kmieć czy chłop w Polsce średniowiecznej?', in Halina Manikowska et al. (eds), *Aetas media, aetas moderna* (Warsaw, 2000), 356–62.

farmers (*kmiecie*) at the top, the *zagrodnicy*, who farmed smaller plots in the middle, and the impoverished, smallholder-cottagers (*chałupnicy*) and landless labourers (*komornicy*)—at the bottom of a complex system.[15]

It is important to bear these distinctions in mind when considering the fifteenth-century origins of the early modern Polish rural economy, which owed less to noble domination of the political system than to economic conditions. The legal framework of subjection had not yet been constructed, and the dominant trend was the development of *Gutswirtschaft*, not *Gutsherrschaft*.[16] To understand this phenomenon, it is necessary to consider the interests and actions of the rural population as a whole: historians have criticized traditional accounts which survey the problem from the perspective of the lords and analyse the condition of the peasantry on the basis of *a priori* assumptions derived from the Marxist concept of class struggle. The rural population—and in particular the *kmiecie*—were as much economic actors as their landlords, and Hagen's advocacy of studying 'the view from the village' has been widely adopted, with historians using empirical evidence to undermine traditional claims, in which the pre-manorial village was often idealized in order to sharpen the contrast with what followed.[17]

The system's origins lay in the period after 1350, although it was not really until after 1400 that labour rents—'*pańszczyzna*' in Polish, literally 'that which is owed to the lord (*pan*)'—began to grow at the expense of rents paid in cash or kind. Labour rent was nothing new in a rural economy in which the balance between different forms of rent had always fluctuated in response to changing economic conditions. The Polish economy had always been sensitive to the market for agricultural products, and had adjusted in response to market forces.[18] While the fifteenth century did mark a watershed, as labour rent spread across Poland, and the number and acreage of demesne farms grew, in the period of economic expansion before 1350 the trend had been in the opposite direction, as the emphasis shifted in favour of rents payable in cash or kind, and the use of unfree labour, previously substantial, declined significantly. The notion that bondage had been unknown in Poland before the fifteenth century, and that a free peasantry lived in some prelapsarian paradise with strong communes successfully defending their rights until noble domination of the political system expelled them into a dark, cold world of misery and oppression, is fundamentally misguided. There had been a considerable unfree population in the twelfth and thirteenth centuries, many of them slaves captured on raids; they were known as *naroczniki*, or, in Latin, *decimi* or

---

[15] For the sake of brevity, however, I shall use the terms 'peasant' and 'peasantry' when referring to the non-noble rural population as a whole, translating '*kmieć*' as 'tenant farmer'.

[16] Wroniszewski criticizes Topolski for using the term '*poddaństwo*' for this period, 'when it did not yet exist': *Szlachta*, 53.

[17] Hagen, 'Subject farmers', 297. For a richly detailed study of the rural population as economic subjects in Brandenburg see William Hagen, *Ordinary Prussians: Brandenburg, Junkers and Villagers, 1500–1840* (Cambridge, 2002).

[18] For a trenchant attack on the concept of eastern European backwardness see Piotr Górecki, *Economy, Society and Lordship in Medieval Poland, 1100–1250* (New York, 1992), 1–44. Górecki provides much evidence of the complex involvement of Polish villages with the market; for the structure of rent: Górecki, *Economy*, 85, 87.

ascriptitii, with various degrees of unfreedom determined by custom or charter. The trend in the twelfth and thirteenth centuries was for the distinctions in charters between free [*liberi*] and unfree to be eroded, with the free increasingly subjected to seigneurial authority on the same basis as the unfree, as the Piast dukes excluded the rural population from the ducal courts for almost all cases, reserving jurisdiction to seigneurial courts.[19]

By 1350 the spread of German law, and its influence beyond settlements founded upon it, meant that most peasants were legally free, while rents in cash or kind dominated. Change came after 1400, as the rural economy stagnated: prices for wheat and rye showed no significant rise between 1389 and 1498.[20] Noble landholders struggled with the effects of partible inheritance in a rural economy in which labour was in short supply, tenant farmers struggled to pay their rents and taxes in a system starved of specie, while princes exacerbated the problems by manipulating the currency to cover their growing obligations: between 1300 and 1480 the amount of silver in the Prague grosz, which circulated widely in Poland, fell from 3.65 to 1.26 grams; the fall in the Polish grosz was even greater, from 3.65 to 0.67 grams. The most important cause of the trend towards labour rent was the response of tenant farmers to these changes. As demand shrank, the prices of agricultural products rose only gradually before 1440, and then fell: by 1490, they had reverted to the levels of 1380; they then doubled between 1480 and 1530.[21] As price incentives diminished, so did the area of land under cultivation. Farmers took the initiative, reducing the size of their holdings to what was necessary for feeding their family, and paying rents that were forced downwards in real terms. This development was in part stimulated by the deal on the land tax, the *poradlne*, agreed in the 1374 Koszyce privileges. Reducing their landholdings to what was required to support their household and to reflect reduced market demand was rational economic behaviour designed to cut rent and tax obligations.[22]

The number of 'vacant hides' (*łany puste*) on land designated by settlement charters as 'farmland' (literally 'farmer hides'—*łany kmiecie*) grew rapidly as farmers drew their own conclusions from the miserable economic climate. In the Lublin district the proportion of tenant holdings of one hide on noble estates fell from 93.5 per cent before 1450 to 43.8 per cent in the 1490s; by 1517 the average holding was just under three-quarters of a hide.[23] In the gradual economic revival after 1490 some vacant hides were reoccupied by tenants, but the return of better economic conditions was offset by the rising rural population, and consequent rising demand for good farmland. Thus the average tenant farm remained smaller than it had been a century earlier. Three-quarters of the holdings in the starosty of Sochaczew in Mazovia between 1496 and 1510 measured half a hide (8.4 hectares), while in 12 villages on the royal estate of Osieck in Mazovia in 1571, of 303 tenant farmers 45

---

[19] Górecki, *Economy*, 78, 80–1; 91, 112–13; 164, 168, 171–8.
[20] Wyrozumski, 'Czy późnośredniowieczny kryzys feudalizmu dotknął Polskę?', in Tomasz Jasiński et al. (eds), *Homines et societas* (Poznań, 1997), 110.
[21] Wroniszewski, *Szlachta*, 63.   [22] Zientara, 'Społeczeństwo', 154.
[23] Wroniszewski, *Szlachta*, 77–9; Grzegorz Jawor, *Ludność chłopska i społeczności wiejskie w województwie lubelskim w późnym średniowieczu (schyłek XI–początek XVI wieku)* (Lublin, 1991), 20.

held a full hide (known as a *włóka* in Mazovia), 8 held three quarters of a hide, 172 held half a hide, and 78 held a quarter of a hide.[24] Actual holdings may have been larger, since the hide was a fiscal unit, and in practice was an approximate measure: lords and their tenants had a common interest in under-declaring the size of holdings for tax purposes.[25] Nevertheless, the general trend is clear.

Stagnant market conditions encouraged a widespread if gradual move towards labour rents in a development that seems to have suited both lords and tenant farmers. Labour rent was nothing new, and had been common in the twelfth and thirteenth centuries. Settlement charters under German law, while largely based on rents paid in cash or kind, often specified labour service as part of the overall dues owed to the lord, in the form of specified annual obligations during harvest time and other periods of high demand for labour, or a practice known as *jutrzyny, jugery*, or *morgi*, in which a certain amount of land was set aside for tenant farmers to plant and harvest for the lord.[26] What was new was the introduction of labour rent in the form of a weekly obligation. The earliest accounts of weekly labour rents come from the late fourteenth century, from ecclesiastical estates. At this stage they were not extensive, with one day per week from a holding of one hide being the norm.

Although demesne farming developed steadily after 1400 it by no means became universal. Decisions to introduce it or to retain a rent-based system depended on local conditions, and, crucially, on the nature of the estate. The larger, wealthier estates pioneered the introduction of weekly labour rents, with the church leading the way: by the 1470s, the evidence of the *Liber beneficiorum* drawn up by Długosz for the Cracow diocese between the 1440s and the 1470s, shows that weekly labour service was performed in 83 per cent of 275 villages surveyed.[27] Yet if the classic manorial system began to develop in royal, ecclesiastical, and some magnate estates it never came to dominate: wealthy landlords practised a mixed economy, maintaining manors or rents in cash or kind depending upon local circumstances and economic fluctuations over time. Initially, ordinary nobles proved less willing to introduce labour rent, and there is little evidence of their doing so before 1450: at the time of the Nieszawa privileges, rents in cash or in kind still formed the basis of the income of ordinary nobles in the Sandomierz palatinate.[28] Once the ordinary nobility began to establish manors it was rare for them to depend entirely on labour rent, which was more common in Małopolska than in Wielkopolska, where as late as 1511–12, it was levied in only 36 villages owned by the archbishopric of Gniezno. Of 1,940 royal estates across the kingdom surveyed in 1563–4, only 591—less than a third—were organized into manors.[29]

---

[24] Alina Wawrzyńczyk, *Gospodarstwo chłopskie na Mazowszu w XVI w.* (Warsaw, 1962), 20, 41.

[25] Alina Czapiuk, 'O plonach zbóż w Polsce i w Wielkim Księstwie Litewskim w XVI i XVII wieku', in Cezary Kuklo (ed.), *Między polityką a kulturą* (Białystok, 1999), 236.

[26] Wroniszewski, *Szlachta*, 50–1.   [27] Wroniszewski, *Szlachta*, 59.

[28] Wroniszewski, *Szlachta*, 64, 66.

[29] Mikulski and Wroniszewski, 'Folwark', 31–2; Andrzej Wyczański, 'O folwarku szlacheckim w Polsce XVI stulecia', *KH*, 61/4 (1954), 182–3; Wroniszewski, *Szlachta*, 59, 67; Davies, *God's Playground*, i, 218.

The creation or extension of manors was not achieved through the expropriation of tenant farmers—which was rare—but through absorbing farmland abandoned since 1350 into the manor, or through new settlements.[30] Vacant hides of farmland dropped from 15.1 per cent in Małopolska between 1500 and 1550 to 4.7 per cent between 1551 and 1580, and from 33.9 per cent to 8.1 per cent in western Wielkopolska. The largest rise in manors came in eastern Wielkopolska, though vacant hides only dropped from 11.6 per cent to 10.7 per cent.[31] Where expropriation of farmers took place, it was mostly the result of action by poor nobles who, often because of subdivision of their own holdings through partible inheritance, ended up with too few tenants to provide enough labour to make the estate viable. Since they often could not afford to hire labour, many farmed their tiny estates themselves.[32] Thus emerged a social group that was to become increasingly numerous: the impoverished nobleman clinging to his status despite being poorer than many among the supposedly oppressed 'peasantry'. It was by no means uncommon for tenant holdings to exceed those of poor noblemen.[33]

Where manorial farms were introduced, although tenant farmers paid labour rent, they did not, on the whole, undertake labour service themselves, either sending their children—if they were not required to work the family farm—or hiring cottagers or day labourers. This rural proletariat did not simply serve the manor. Rising prosperity meant that it became common for tenant farmers to hire labour to work their own plots: half of tenant farms in Małopolska in 1590 used hired labour.[34] The bulk of the labour for the manor was provided by the new class of *zagrodnicy* (or *ogrodnicy* in Mazovia), who held a plot of land known as a *zagroda* or *ogród*. Literally this meant a 'garden', but the term's true significance was functional. Some of these 'gardens' were relatively large: up to half a hide in extent, although a quarter of a hide was more usual. Some *zagrodnicy* therefore held plots that were as large as those of the *kmiecie*, but they were typically settled on land that was not as fertile, and was not designated as farmland. They had less time to work their plots, for it was from among the *zagrodnicy* that the manor's basic labour-force was drawn: where villages were not attached to manors, there were no *zagrodnicy*. They generally formed a minority within the village community: of the twelve villages attached to the Osieck estate in Mazovia, eight had *ogrodnicy* in 1564; altogether there were twenty-five, an average of 3.1 per village.[35] They paid only a symbolic cash rent—if any at all—and the form of labour rent they paid was different to that of the tenant farmers: they served 'on foot' (*pieszo*), providing the manual labour necessary for agricultural production, while the tenant farmers largely performed '*pańszczyzna ciągła*' or '*wołowa*'—the latter literally means 'oxen service', providing

---

[30] Cf. Cerman, *Villagers*, 58–61.
[31] Wyczański, *Studia*, 51. For an attack on the view that manors were established through the expropriation of the peasantry, see Wyczański, 'O folwarku', 176–9.
[32] Wroniszewski, *Szlachta*, 75.   [33] Wyrozumski, 'Kryzys' 113.
[34] Anna Izydorczyk-Kamler, 'Praca najemna na wsi małopolskiej w XVI i pierwszej połowie XVII wieku', *KH*, 97/1–2 (1990), 11; Anna Kamler, *Chłopi jako pracownicy najemni na wsi małopolskiej w XVI i pierwszej połowie XVII wieku* (Warsaw, 2005).
[35] Wawrzyńczyk, *Gospodarstwo*, 20, 41.

draught animals to plough and drag carts in the service of the manor, which therefore did not have to bear the costs of maintaining its own. Various artisans lived in the village, including millers and innkeepers, who also held plots that were not usually designated 'farmland', since the rent and obligations were different.[36]

The pattern of labour service varied. Most estates of the middle and lower nobility were relatively small, as were their manors. By the sixteenth century the average size of manors in Małopolska was 3.5 hides (58.8 hectares); in western Wielkopolska and Mazovia it was 3.3 hides (55.44 hectares); in eastern Wielkopolska it was 2.4 hides (40.32 hectares). The average size of manors across all four regions was 3.1 hides (52.08 hectares).[37] Szlachta manors were usually based on one village; this pattern differed from that of the larger magnate latifundia and royal estates—the manor of the royal estate at Medyka near Przemyśl in the sixteenth century was served by no fewer than ten villages—or ecclesiastical estates, where tithe obligations continued to be paid in kind and it was common to have one large demesne served by three to five villages.[38]

The balance in terms of landholding following the move to demesne farming shifted slightly in favour of the landowner, but by 1500, it had largely settled down. Although manors grew in size in the sixteenth century by an average of 18 per cent across the four regions, this figure is distorted by a 44 per cent rise in eastern Wielkopolska, with the figures for Małopolska and western Wielkopolska being 14 and 6 per cent respectively. Proportions varied across the kingdom. Wyczański calculated on the basis of tax assessments from the palatinate of Sieradz that by the sixteenth century, discounting years in which no new tax assessment was made and allowing for under-declaration, the average amount of land held by tenant farmers in the 202 villages for which he had data ranged between 6.27 hides (105.34 hectares) in 1496 and 5.12 hides (86.02 hectares) in 1576.[39] By the second half of the sixteenth century, the average noble landowner held 8.1 hides (136.08 hectares), of which tenant plots constituted 4.5 hides (75.6 hectares) or 55.6 per cent and the demesne farm constituted 3.6 hides (60.48 hectares), or 44.4 per cent.[40] The actual amount of land in peasant hands was greater than this, since the assessments only included holdings classified as farmland, and did not take account of common land, or plots held by *zagrodnicy* and cottagers. The typical nobleman was no absentee; he lived close to his tenants in a village that was smaller than those that serviced the great royal, ecclesiastical, and magnate latifundia. The extent to which he was able to impose his will upon his tenants was rather less than that of

---

[36] Wroniszewski, *Szlachta*, 69–72; Wawrzyńczyk, *Gospodarstwo*, 12–16.
[37] Wyczański, *Studia*, 84–5.
[38] Wyczański, 'O folwarku', 181; Wroniszewski, *Szlachta*, 66–7. For ecclesiastical estates see Zbyszko Górczak, *Podstawy gospodarcze działalności Zbigniewa Oleśnickiego biskupa krakowskiego* (Cracow, 1999) and Jerzy Topolski, *Gospodarstwo wiejskie w dobrach arcybiskupstwa gnieźnieńskiego od XVI do XVIII wieku* (Poznań, 1958).
[39] Wyczański, *Studia*, 44–6. Given that tax assessment was controlled by nobles, it is probable that under-declaration remained a problem even in years when formal assessments were made by local collectors.
[40] Piotr Guzowski, *Chłopi i pieniądz na przełomie średniowiecza i czasów nowożytnych* (Cracow, 2008), 155.

great landlords controlling their estates from afar through a network of administrators.

The trend towards demesne farming was already well established by 1454, and long before the legislation of the late fifteenth and early sixteenth centuries that was previously seen as crucial to its formation. Wyczański found very few new manors established after 1500, although in some areas consolidation of land into existing manors did continue.[41] The legislation did not call the system into being; it sought to regulate a system that already existed.[42] A 1426 decree aimed to protect peasants by limiting annual labour service to a maximum of fourteen days in succession to ensure that lords could not simply demand unlimited service 'on demand' (*kiedy każą*).[43] Acts of the sejmiks of Chełm (1477), Podlasie (1501), and Wieluń (1518), and of the sejms in Thorn (1519) and Bydgoszcz (1520) indeed allowed nobles to fix labour service at a minimum of one day per week per hide, but not as an extra burden. The legislation sought to establish an equivalent between labour rent at this rate and rents in cash or kind. It was designed to regularize the burdens of the rural population, and thereby to hinder the widespread practice of encouraging tenant farmers to move through offering low rents, or exemptions from dues for a set period, both popular means of persuading tenants to change their lords.[44] While the 1519 act left it up to nobles to decide which form of rent to demand, with no mention of any need for reaching agreement with their tenants, it is unlikely that it had any major impact on actual practice. As Kutrzeba observes, it probably worsened the position of very few among the rural population.[45]

Despite the common assertion that Polish peasants were deprived of access to the royal courts in 1518, there was no statutory stripping of rights from the rural population; all that happened was that Sigismund I stated in that year that he would no longer interfere in cases between peasants and their noble landlords. If the binding nature of this declaration on Sigismund's successors is open to question, a reluctance on the part of rulers to involve themselves in such disputes was nothing new: Poland's princes in the twelfth and thirteenth centuries delegated judicial authority to the seigneurial courts in all but a few reserved matters. The removal of peasants from the jurisdiction of non-seigneurial courts was not always contrary to their interests: the 1496 act which stipulated that *kmiecie* could no longer be pursued for debt in city courts is often presented as part of the supposed stripping of legal rights from the peasantry; in a rural economy in which tenant farmers were actively engaged in a market economy that was beginning its long upturn, however, this measure was probably welcome to them, although it doubtless affected their ability to raise credit from the towns.[46]

---

[41] Wyczański, *Studia*, 28–9.   [42] Wroniszewski, *Szlachta*, 61.

[43] This decree may only have applied to royal estates; even if its scope was wider, the extent to which it was obeyed is unclear: Wroniszewski, *Szlachta*, 62.

[44] *VC*, i/i, 328, 351; Wroniszewski, *Szlachta*, 62–3; Wyczański, *Studia*, 101. For the traditional view see Zdzisław Kaczmarczyk and Bogusław Leśnodorski, *Historia państwa i prawa Polski*, ii: *Od połowy XV wieku do r. 1795* (Warsaw, 1966), 44.

[45] *VC*, i/i, 328; Kutrzeba, *Korona*, 100.   [46] *VC*, i/i, 71.

It would be naïve to suppose that the royal courts offered any great protection to peasants before 1518, or that Sigismund's decision made it easier for nobles to force their tenants to accept labour rent against their wishes. Changes to the structure of rent on individual estates, far from being a unilateral decision of the lord, were usually effected on the basis of a formal contract, as in 1387, when Bodzęta, archbishop of Gniezno, introduced labour rent at the level of one day per week in Modrzew alongside payments in cash and oats. The tenants made a shrewd decision: evidence from 1512 suggests that there was no significant change in their obligations over the intervening 120 years. In Turo, a property of the provostry of St Michael, the labour rent demanded per hide between 1388 and the 1470s was two days, alongside similar payments in cash and a different set of obligations in kind; when compared with the widely varying rental agreements in other villages owned by the provostry it is clear that labour rent was not imposed on the farmers as an extra burden, but was an equivalent for rents payable in cash and kind, and that burdens were calibrated according to the circumstances of individual villages, and usually instituted in agreement with them.[47] That is not to say that the power of landlords was insufficient to ensure that the agreement favoured their interests to a greater or lesser extent, but the general picture is nonetheless one of consent and negotiation towards agreements that suited the interests of both farmers and landlords. Older customary arrangements often survived. Despite the 1477 law passed by the Chełm sejmik allowing lords to impose labour rent of one day per week, the system known as *dworzyszcza*, in which the amount of land held by individual tenant farmers was not specified according to the usual norms based on hides, survived in many Ruthenian villages. Tenants' rental obligations remained relatively low, and they sometimes farmed considerable plots. In 1600 this form of tenure survived in 76 villages out of 280 (27 per cent) studied in the regions where it was customary.[48]

The balance of advantage did not always lie with the lord. Scholars who exaggerated the independence of the village commune and peasant wealth before the introduction of the manorial system often gave the impression that rents in cash and kind could not be raised under the terms of settlement charters. If the nobility was so powerful, however, why was it unable to force rises in such rents, yet was apparently able to impose a complete revolution based on labour-service and the curtailing of peasant freedom? In reality, settlement agreements were generally respected where they continued to reflect economic realities; if they were to be altered, the balance and the nature of obligations was a matter for negotiation between the lord and his tenants.[49] The fifteenth-century economic slump, the shortage of specie, and the devaluation of the currency meant that changes in tenant obligations were unavoidable; indeed they were necessary for all parties. Although tenant farmers often welcomed a move to labour rent, in order to secure acceptance

---

[47] Wroniszewski, *Szlachta*, 54.
[48] Małgorzata Kołacz, 'Powinności chłopskie w ziemi chełmskiej w XV–XVI wieku', in Wijaczka (ed.), *Między zachodem a wschodem*, iv: *Życie gospodarcze Rzeczypospolitej w XVI–XVIII wieku* (Toruń, 1997), 44.
[49] Wroniszewski, *Szlachta*, 45, n.145, 56, 60.

of changes to settlement charters or to long-established customary arrangements, lords frequently had to introduce labour rents at a level below that of the rents in cash and kind they were replacing.

The growth of the manorial economy was a more consensual process than was once supposed, and while there were indeed cases of resistance, they were usually provoked by discontent over terms of agreements, and not by opposition to the principle of labour rent: there was no hint of the *Bauernkrieg* that ravaged south-western Germany in the 1520s and 1530s, or, indeed, the revolts seen across the border in what became Ducal Prussia on the secularization of the *Ordensstaat* in 1525.[50] Resistance, it was traditionally argued, largely took the form of peasant flight, with peasants supposedly expressing their opposition to the imposition of serfdom by running away. Yet as the economy recovered from the late fifteenth century, the szlachta faced increasing competition for labour from magnate and ecclesiastical estates, the pioneers in introducing demesne farming, whose lords enticed farmers to move in return for accepting favourable labour rents rather than rents in cash or in kind.[51] Inevitably, the middling and lesser nobility had to offer similar conditions to persuade their peasants to stay, but as owners of small estates they did not have the flexibility of landowners who controlled large latifundia.

The problem of peasant mobility lay behind the legislation attempting to standardize labour rents across the kingdom, and other measures that sought to control the phenomenon. The term 'peasant flight' is something of a misnomer. Although some peasants undoubtedly left their native villages to escape conditions they found oppressive, the emphasis on flight as a manifestation of resistance to the imposition of the manorial system obscures the extent to which it was motivated by economic considerations, and the extent to which the farmers leaving their home village were not fleeing the system, but merely changing their lord within it.[52] The relative shortage of labour meant that *kmiecie*—and, indeed, *zagrodnicy*—enjoyed in practice substantial security of tenure.[53] Good tenants were highly valued. Their rights to bequeath their plots to their children, or to sell them, were rarely challenged, and plots could even be subdivided for such purposes, subject to the lord's consent.[54] Sale of land by tenants was common, although it required the consent of lords; the substantial land market demonstrates the extent to which peasant plots were in practice treated as private property. Customary tenant rights were usually respected: landlords were not, as was traditionally supposed, hostile to a dynamic peasant market in land, since the only reason they could, under customary law, deprive a tenant farmer of his holding was if he was not meeting his rental obligations or was farming his plot poorly.[55] A lively peasant land-market was in the lord's interest. It meant that he was not obliged to seek a new tenant

---

[50] Topolski, *Przełom*, 79–80.   [51] Mikulski and Wroniszewski, 'Folwark', 31, 32–3.
[52] For the view that flight was a protest against oppression, see Inglot, *Z dziejówwsi*, 274.
[53] Inglot, *Z dziejówwsi*, 287.
[54] See Guzowski, 'System dziedziczenia chłopów na przełomie średniowiecza i czasów nowożytnych w świetle sądowych ksiąg wiejskich', in Cezary Kuklo (ed.), *Rodzina i gospodarstwo domowe na ziemiach polskich w XV–XX wieku* (Warsaw, 2008), 29–48.
[55] Cerman, 'Social structure', 59–60, 63.

personally when, for whatever reason—advancing age, a lack of heirs, or a desire to leave—individual peasants wished to surrender their plot.

The differing levels at which rent—whether labour rent or rents in cash and kind—were levied in royal, ecclesiastical, and noble estates encouraged peasants—and in particular the highly prized *kmiecie*—to move to estates where rents were lower. The problem for lords was that while it had been relatively difficult for peasants to leave under traditional Polish law, which demanded large exit fines to compensate the lord for his capital investment, the spread of German law made it easier for peasants to leave, and many did so. Casimir III's statutes sought to limit departures without the consent of the lord to two per village per year, to ensure that village economies remained viable, but lords were free to allow more to leave.[56] Nevertheless, a sense of a tenant farmer's rights to his plot remained strong: under the 1423 Warta statute, passed by a noble assembly at which Jagiełło was not present, a landlord had to issue no fewer than four summonses to a tenant farmer who had left the village before he could settle a new tenant on his plot.[57] Ordinary nobles, who could ill afford to lose their precious labour force, were increasingly hard hit, while ecclesiastical landlords were concerned at the way in which the relatively low rents levied on royal estates tempted their tenants to up sticks and move. With even royal estates sometimes unable to absorb the influx, and their holders concerned to stop the drift from their allodial estates, there was broad support for an attempt to regulate the situation through the standardization of labour rent.[58]

The legislation establishing a minimum of one day per week labour service meant very little in practice, given the complexity of rental structures across Poland. Yet the attempt to regulate rental levels reveals an important truth about peasant mobility: the legislation was not so much directed against peasants themselves, as the landlords to whom they fled. For peasants did not take flight to escape an abstract, oppressive 'system'; they did so for many reasons, most often in the hope of bettering their condition. Individual lords could indeed be oppressive and cruel, but flight was as likely to be motivated by disputes within the village between tenant farmers, or because other landlords were offering better land to farm, or lower rents, or attractive inducements to move, such as exemption from rents—or artificially reduced rents—for a set period.

Study of the mobility of the Polish rural population was long distorted by an overemphasis on class conflict and the conceptualization of a countryside divided into implacably hostile camps of lords and 'serfs'. In reality, peasants were generally happy to remain in one place, so long as the conditions of their tenure remained relatively stable, and they could pass on their plots to their heirs. Peasants were indeed required to pursue those who fled their villages, and could be fined for assisting fugitives, or for failing to report on those intending to flee.[59] Yet

---

[56] Wyrozumski, 'Kryzys', 112–13.
[57] Stanisław Śreniowski, *Zbiegostwo chłopów w dawnej Polsce jako zagadnienie ustroju społecznego*, 2nd edn (Łódz, 1997), 123.
[58] Wyczański, *Studia*, 105–6.   [59] Inglot, *Z dziejówwsi*, 274–5.

peasants—or at least the wealthier tenant farmers—were not necessarily opposed to the tying of members of the village community to the land. Farming was a collaborative enterprise in which even relatively well-to-do farmers did not necessarily own all the draught animals or equipment required for much of the business of agriculture, especially ploughing—which required a team of eight oxen—or harvesting. The economy of a village, with its carefully balanced network of intersecting and dependent interests, was disrupted if its members could leave too easily. Labour rent and taxes were communal obligations: if peasants fled the village and were not replaced, the burdens on individual villagers increased, giving peasants, as much as their lords, an incentive to prevent flight. Thus peasants were frequently reluctant to aid those leaving, often collaborated in the pursuit and apprehension of those who did, and sometimes sought to prevent their fellow-villagers leaving on their own initiative.[60] The departure of tenant farmers from their home village was usually carefully planned, and frequently exercised with the connivance of the landlord to whose village they were moving; sometimes they were assisted by villagers from the community in which they were to settle.[61] In most cases, *kmiecie* departed with their whole household, complete with moveable possessions and livestock, thus inflicting a considerable loss upon their former landlord.

During the fifteenth-century slump, the problem of peasant mobility was not as great as the problem of the shrinking peasant economy, as farmers cut the size of their plots and curtailed their involvement with the market. As conditions improved at the end of the century, there were renewed incentives for lords—and, indeed, their tenants—to attract new productive forces into their communities. There had always been laws attempting to limit the mobility of the poorest villagers, many of whom in the twelfth and thirteenth centuries were unfree. There was a renewed concern with what were known as 'loose people' (*ludzie luźni*) from the around 1500, as landlords and *kmiecie* alike sought to ensure that their villages had enough of the casual labour necessary to perform labour service, and to assist at times of high demand, such as harvest.[62] In an agricultural economy in which the demand for labour varied substantially across the year, however, it was very hard to prevent considerable mobility among those not tied to villages by property, and in practice, as elsewhere in Europe, the rural economy depended to a considerable degree on a mobile labour force. Thus laws seeking to curb peasant mobility—whose frequency suggests their ineffectiveness—might better be seen in the light of general attempts across Europe to regulate the mobility of the rural poor, and to return them to their own parishes to receive poor relief. It was by no means only Poles who sought to tie individuals to the village of their birth.

The 1496 statute, widely represented as the crucial watershed in the 'enserfment of the Polish peasantry', was not directed at the rural proletariat, but at tenant-farmers. It did not seek to tie them to the land, but to establish rules for the conduct of cases over those wishing to leave their home village. Far from banning departures, the legislation sought simply to limit them to one member of a tenant

---

[60] Wyczański, *Studia*, 119; Śreniowski, *Zbiegostwo*, 85, 90–1.
[61] Śreniowski, *Zbiegostwo*, 110.   [62] Śreniowski, *Zbiegostwo*, 62.

farmer's family, who was allowed—with the lord's permission—to leave in order to take up service elsewhere, or to be educated in 'literary or manual pursuits'; other sons were to remain to ensure the viability of the village economy.[63] Customary inheritance law among the *kmiecie*, which the szlachta showed no interest in regulating apart from one 1588 statute, sought to keep the basic holding together, to be inherited by one son, usually the eldest, who had to buy out his siblings, with cash sums to be paid to his brothers and smaller sums to his sisters in compensation.[64] The 1496 legislation sought to ensure that there was some control over the number of those permitted to leave the village; if there was no plot available for them, and an adequate supply of labour for the demesne, they were generally allowed to leave. Sons of *kmiecie* did leave to study, some of them at university; others entered the church. There is nothing to indicate that the 1496 statute was effective in tying peasants to the land—which it did not explicitly try to do—and much evidence to suggest it was not.

Thus the many disputes over peasant flight clogging up the courts from the late fifteenth century were not criminal cases, but civil actions in which nobles sued other nobles for the return of—or compensation for—absconded tenant farmers, and the welter of legislation concerning peasant flight was more to do with establishing the procedure and norms for such cases than with the supposed aim of tying peasants to the land. In these cases, peasants acted as witnesses; occasionally *kmiecie* were given the opportunity of choosing between the lords who were litigating over them.[65] Much of the legislation was passed by local sejmiks, and there was a particular concern to prevent flight across jurisdictional boundaries, which—given Poland's decentralized court system—made it difficult to secure redress.[66]

The level of mobility among the rural population, together with the lively land market, indicates that peasants were hard-headed economic actors and not passive victims of noble oppression. By the mid sixteenth century, the Polish rural economy was highly complex. Where rents were high, it reflected market conditions: landlords could demand more from villages in fertile areas where tenant farms were profitable, and local estimates of the value of labour rent differed: in the Sandomierz palatinate in the second half of the fifteenth century, one day's labour service per week was the equivalent of half a mark (24 groszy) in rent when it was performed by a *zagrodnik*, whereas on the estate of Opatów, two days labour rent per week from a tenant farmer, which was more highly valued, was worth four times this figure at 2 marks 10 *skojcy*. In the villages noted in Długosz's *Liber beneficiorum*, where labour service was performed, it was levied at one day per week in 50 per cent of cases, two days per week in 23 per cent, and at three to five days in 10 per cent. Levels of rent were higher in the Cracow palatinate, not because the local nobility was more powerful or rapacious, but because agriculture was more profitable: rents tended to be higher near cities or markets. Rents varied within

---

[63] *VC*, i, 70.   [64] Guzowski, 'System', 29–35.
[65] Guzowski, 'System', 91, 121–2.   [66] Guzowski, 'System', 50, 53–4.

villages, depending on the productivity and fertility of the land held by individual tenants.[67] On royal estates in Mazovia in the mid sixteenth century rents varied substantially, depending on a range of factors, including the fertility of the soil, privileges granted to individual villages, or customary arrangements. Some villages were free of all rental obligations; less fertile villages tended not to pay rent in kind; elsewhere, the balance between cash rents, rents in kind, and labour rent varied substantially, from as low as one day per week to as high as four days per week—occasionally even more—though two days per week was the norm, and rents in cash or kind varied from the equivalent of under 10 groszy to as much as 48 groszy; most commonly they were in the range 20–30 groszy.[68] The increase in rents between 1500 and 1550 is not surprising in a period when prices for agricultural produce rose substantially. The wide range of rental levels, and the variation in the balance between labour rents and rents in cash and kind shows that they took account of local conditions, including custom, settlement charters, and the fertility of the land, and that the balance between the various types of rent was usually agreed in negotiations between lords and peasants. In such a complex, calibrated system, historians have to be careful about treating rental levels in terms of days of labour service required as a simple index of oppression: in a period of rising prices for agricultural produce, peasants preferred to see a rise in their labour rent, rather than in their rents in cash or in kind, if the profits to be gained from selling their produce on the market were greater than the costs of providing labour rent on the manor.

For the shift to labour rent and the spread of demesne farming did not adversely affect the ability of the tenant farmers to respond to market forces. As economic conditions improved, so did the productivity and profitability of the peasant economy. The *kmiecie* were well placed to benefit. The view of Poland as increasingly dominated by the monoculture of grain in response to west European demand could not be more misleading. While manors tended overwhelmingly to concentrate on grain production, tenant farmers conducted a much more mixed economy. In addition to producing grain, they raised cattle, sheep, pigs, and poultry, and possessed vegetable gardens and small orchards, much of whose output was for the market. In the mid sixteenth century the *average* holding of livestock per tenant farmer in Słabomierz, owned by the Gniezno chapter, was 24 head of cattle, 11 horses, 36 sheep, and 12 pigs.[69] The overall picture was not quite so impressive, even in other estates of the Gniezno archbishopric, where the average one-hide tenant farmer possessed 4 horses, 6 head of cattle, 34 pigs, and 11 sheep.[70] It has been estimated that the average livestock holding of a one-hide holding across Poland was 2 horses, 8 head of cattle, 5 sheep, and 3 goats.[71] Using the standard measure of one horse or two oxen as one draught unit, in the sixteenth century, on average 22.8 per cent of half-hide tenant farms possessed from 1 to 1.5 draught

---

[67] Wroniszewski, *Szlachta*, 56–9.   [68] Wawrzyńczyk, *Gospodarstwo*, 98.
[69] Topolski, *Przełom*, 73.   [70] Topolski, *Gospodarstwo*, 247.
[71] Guzowski, 'Sytuacja ekonomiczna chłopów polskich w XV i XVI w. na tle europejskim', in Wijaczka (ed.), *Między zachodem a wschodem*, 13–14.

units, 58.3 per cent possessed 2–3, and 18.9 per cent possessed three or more.[72] It was for this reason that lords retained a proportion of rent in kind, to ensure their household was provided with eggs, meat, and other products of the pastoral farming they did not pursue on their manors.

How productive was this system? The supposedly low yield ratios on manorial farms have been used as evidence of the low productivity and primitive nature of Polish agriculture, and of the negative effects of the introduction of demesne farming: western scholars usually suggest a figure of 1:4 for Poland around 1600, generally calculated as enough to feed a peasant household and provide a small surplus for sale.[73] Yet yield ratios rose over the period in which demesne farming spread. The scanty data make it hard to be definitive, but an average yield-ratio of 1:3 is generally estimated for royal and ecclesiastical estates in the late fourteenth century, which was not substantially out of line with the rest of Europe.[74] An exhaustive study of audits of royal estates carried out in 1564–5 and 1569–70 demonstrates that these ratios had risen substantially. Considering that the audits took place in years of poor harvest, the figures suggest a much less primitive economy than was traditionally assumed. The top quartile of manors surveyed had ratios of 1:6 and higher for rye, the staple grain; when the figures for wheat, barley and oats are included, the figure rises to 1:6.76, with a small minority of manors attaining ratios of 1:11 and 1:12.[75] Considering that these audits were controversial, and that leaseholders and their administrators had an interest in obscuring the full productive capacity of the manors they held, these figures are impressive; they bear comparison to contemporary figures for the Netherlands and England, at 1:6, though scholars, more cautiously, have proposed an average figure across Poland and over the four main grains harvested, of 1:5 for demesne farms.[76]

The productive capacity of the Polish rural economy was, however, higher than this. Peasant farms constituted some 75 per cent of the cultivated land, and it is generally agreed that they were more productive than demesne farms. There were good reasons why this should be so. Although some attention was given to manuring demesne farms, it was tenant farms that held the bulk of the village's livestock. Thus their plots were better manured, and therefore more fertile. On account of the higher level of manuring, they did not need to fallow such a high proportion of their holdings as was the case on manors.[77] Problems with sources mean it is difficult to say how much more productive they were. Wawrzyńczyk estimates yield ratios of 1:8.75 for rye, 1:10.5 for wheat, 1:12 for barley, and 1:8.1 for oats, with an average for the four grains of 1:9.1 from tenant farms on royal estates in Mazovia in the mid sixteenth century, but these figures have been

---

[72] Guzowski, *Chłopi*, 119.
[73] Jan de Vries, *The Economy of Europe in an Age of Crisis, 1600–1750* (Cambridge, 1976), 35.
[74] Guzowski, 'Sytuacja', 9, 28.
[75] Alina Wawrzyńczyk, *Studia nad wydajnością produkcji rolnej dóbr królewskich w drugiej połowie XVI w.* (Wrocław, 1974), 173–6.
[76] Wawrzyńczyk, *Studia*, 7, 50, 114–15; De Vries, *Economy*, 36; Guzowski, *Chłopi*, 113–16.
[77] Guzowski, 'Sytuacja', 10; Żytkowicz, 'Ze studiów nad wysokością plonów w Polsce od XVI do XVIII w.', *KHKM* 14/3 (1966), 475.

criticized as too optimistic.⁷⁸ They may indeed be too high: her study is based on a relatively small number of villages and partly relies on a source containing peasant claims for attainable yields following the destruction of their crops by poor weather and insect damage, which were probably inflated; she subsequently gave more realistic figures for royal lands across the kingdom. The figures for Wielkopolska are low, at 1:3.1 (1564–5) and 1:3.7 (1569–70) for rye, but are better for Małopolska (4.9 in 1564–5 and 4.8 in 1569–70) and impressive in Mazovia (5.8 in 1564–5 and 5.4 in 1569–70). Figures for oats are in a similar range, but for the valuable crops of wheat and barley, they are higher, with ratios of 1:5.1 (Małopolska 1564–5), 1:6.6 (Mazovia, 1564–5), and 1:7.6 (Royal Prussia, 1564–5) for wheat, and 1:5.9 (Wielkopolska, 1564–5), 1:6.4 (Małopolska, 1564–5), 1:7.5 (Mazovia, 1569–70), and 1:8.0 (Mazovia, 1564–5) for barley.⁷⁹ Wawrzyńczyk is aware of the problem of peasant exaggeration of the productivity of their plots, and is cautious in her extrapolations, emphasizing that these were attainable ratios in good years when weather and soil conditions were favourable. While some of the figures for the 1560s audits are relatively low, these were poor years for weather, and the overall picture is suggestive. Wawrzyńczyk was interested in what was obtainable in good years and in favourable conditions, and her work indicates what peasant farms were capable of achieving. Peasants undoubtedly put more effort into farming their own land than they did into working the lord's demesne, manured it better, and were seen as having a better understanding of agriculture than their lords. Her general conclusions can be accepted, especially since the audits suggest that some manors, albeit a minority, were themselves capable of achieving such ratios: auditors testified in the 1560s in Mazovia that yields on peasant farms were fifty per cent greater than on the manors surveyed.⁸⁰

There is good evidence that tenant farmers produced marketable surpluses, sometimes substantial ones, suggesting that these yield ratios are plausible. As prices rose, stimulated by rising internal demand more than by external markets, which were serviced overwhelmingly by the great latifundia, tenant farmers were in a good position to benefit. If in the fifteenth century they only involved themselves in the market to meet rent and tax obligations, and had very little reason to produce more than necessary to feed their family, the situation changed substantially after 1500.⁸¹ Guzowski's detailed modelling of the average half- and one-hide peasant holdings for the first half of the fifteenth century and the second half of the sixteenth demonstrates that in the first period a one-hide holding produced a surplus of about 31.5 per cent of grain (after deduction of the tithe, rent in kind,

---

⁷⁸ Wawrzyńczyk, *Gospodarstwo*, 84; Leonid Żytkowicz, 'Badania nad gospodarką chłopską w królewszczynach mazowieckich XVI i początkach XVII w.', *ZH*, 29/4 (1964), 28–37; Guzowski, 'Sytuacja', 9–11.

⁷⁹ Wawrzyńczyk, *Gospodarstwo*, 76–7, 79, 81; Guzowski, *Chłopi*, 114–15.

⁸⁰ Three and more *kopy* per *korzec* of seed compared with two on the manor. Wawrzyńczek reduced this to 2.5 for the purpose of her estimates: Alina Wawrzyńczyk, 'W sprawie gospodarstwa chłopskiego na Mazowszu w XVI w.', *ZH*, 29/4 (1964), 41; Inglot, *Z dziejów wsi*, 178.

⁸¹ Andrzej Wyczański, 'Uwagi o utowarowieniu gospodarki chłopskiej w dawnej Polski', in Stefan Kuczyński and Stanisław Suchodolski (eds), *Nummus et historia: Pieniądz Europy średniowiecznej* (Warsaw, 1985), 303–4.

and seed for sowing) to sell on the market, which, except in bad years, was enough to cover the farmer's tax and rental obligations. The surplus was much lower for a half-hide holding, at twelve per cent, and was barely enough to cover the obligations.[82] Thus at this stage the picture of a largely subsistence peasant economy is reasonable. After 1550, however, the large-scale move to a system of labour rent, improved yield-ratios, and the return of a buoyant market for agricultural produce had changed the picture substantially. The average one-hide tenant farm now produced a surplus of 45 per cent of grain for the market, while the surplus for a half-hide holding had risen to 20 per cent.[83] While taxes had risen from an average level of 14–16 groszy per annum for a one-hide holding (7–9 groszy for a half-hide holding) before 1450 to 17–24 groszy (12–17 groszy) after 1550, with average nominal rents doubling from 24–48 groszy for a one-hide holding and 12–24 groszy for a half-hide holding in the same period, the growth in production, rising prices and the switch to labour rent left tenant farmers with larger surpluses to sell, and larger disposable incomes: the rise in rent and taxes lagged far behind the fourfold increase in grain prices.[84] While farmers were, as elsewhere in Europe, vulnerable to fluctuations of climate and external factors such as warfare, the long period of peace after 1435 meant that in a good year, disposable incomes rose from 1–2 marks in the early fifteenth century to 10–20 złoties in the second half of the sixteenth century, a considerable rise in real terms.[85]

This disposable income was put to various uses. Apart from investing in land, tenant farmers needed cash to buy out their siblings on inheritance of their plots, or they might use it to purchase mills, inns, or the position of village headman. Payment for such purchases was usually made in instalments, without interest, over periods of up to twenty years—1.44 per cent of the transactions were for repayment over even longer periods—which indicates stable economic expectations, and a village legal system that could be trusted. Seventy per cent of transactions were of five marks and under.[86] The average value of transactions, and of instalments, began to rise noticeably from the mid sixteenth century as grain prices rose sharply after a long period of steady growth. The number of transactions grew substantially, although the average value fell, which suggests a general extension of the practice beyond the wealthiest farmers.[87] Farmers needed money to pay for hired labour—although part of the cost was usually paid in kind, often through board and lodging—and for purchases in local markets and inns. *Kmiecie* often held considerable sums in cash, the value of their plots was rated highly by their lords, and it was not unknown for them to lend money to their lords.[88] They lived in a real economic world, not in Kula's theoretical universe, bereft of contact with markets.

Far from undermining and destroying the peasant economy, the move to labour rent accompanied a substantial growth in the living standards of tenant farmers at

---

[82] Guzowski, *Chłopi*, 127–31.   [83] Guzowski, *Chłopi*, 131–3.
[84] Guzowski, *Chłopi*, 154.   [85] Guzowski, *Chłopi*, 123, 125, 134–5.
[86] Guzowski, *Chłopi*, 44–62.   [87] Guzowski, *Chłopi*, 65.
[88] Wyrozumski, 'Kryzys', 113; Wawrzyńczyk, *Gospodarstwo*, 189–91.

least, although it is difficult to say how far—if at all—the living standards of the growing rural proletariat improved. It would be pressing revisionism too far to suggest that the move to labour-rent had caused this change, but the rise in prosperity cannot simply be explained by rising prices, and the fact that rises in rent and taxes lagged behind the rise in grain prices calls into question the assumption that this was a period of increasing oppression. The growing prosperity confirms that tenant farmers, as well as their lords, had a real interest in the changes to rental arrangements, and explains why the change could be made with so little opposition.

By 1550 conditions were, as Wyczański suggested, by no means unfavourable for peasants in Poland—or at least for the tenant farmers at the heart of the system. Noble domination of the legislature, far from acting against peasant interests, benefited them. Noble control over taxation meant that the overall burdens on the Polish peasantry compare favourably with those levied on their counterparts in western Europe. Tax levels rose in the sixteenth century, with levies of up to 30 groszy per hide in individual years.[89] Taxation at this level did not constitute a particularly high burden in European terms. Estimates of the percentage of grain production an average peasant farm paid in rent and taxes in the fifteenth century suggest that a Polish one-hide holding (16.8 hectares) paid 12 per cent of its grain output in rent and taxes after payment of tithe, while a half-hide holding paid 9 per cent—another indication that it was worthwhile for tenant farmers to shift to farming half-hide plots. This was about the same as England where the figure was 10 per cent for a 7.28 hectare holding, but far more favourable than in Languedoc (20 per cent on a 6 hectare holding), Normandy (20 per cent on a 9 hectare holding), and the Île-de-France (25 per cent on a 6 hectare holding). Expressed in terms of the amount of grain a peasant holding had to produce to cover its obligations, a Polish holding of one hide had to produce 650 kilograms of grain, while one of half a hide had to produce 250 kilograms. This was considerably better than other areas where *Gutswirtschaft* was practised: the figure for Brandenburg was 1,000 kilograms (16 hectares) and 1,800 kilograms (16 hectares) for the duchy of Breslau. It was better than much of western Europe: the figure for England was 350 kilograms (7.28 hectares); for Languedoc 400 kilograms (6 hectares); for Normandy 800 kilograms (9 hectares); and for the Île-de-France 1,200 kilograms (6 hectares).[90] The comparison looks even more favourable for the sixteenth century. Although the demands on the average Polish peasant had risen to 700 kilograms (20 per cent of production) on a one-hide holding, and to 350 kilograms (10 per cent) on a half-hide holding, the equivalent figures were 700 kilograms (23.5 per cent, 16 hectares) in Brandenburg, and 1,800 kilograms (40 per cent, 16.5 hectares) in Muscovy. In western Europe, the figures were 850 kilograms (15 per cent, 16 hectares) for England; 850 kilograms (25 per cent, 6 hectares) for Languedoc; and 1,250 kilograms (40 per cent, 6 hectares) for the Île-de-France.[91] There were more efficient means of oppressing peasants than labour rent.

---

[89] Wawrzyńczyk, *Gospodarstwo*, 138–9; Guzowski, *Chłopi*, 149.
[90] Guzowski, 'Sytuacja', 29–30. [91] Guzowski, 'Sytuacja', 34.

PART V

DYNASTY AND CITIZENSHIP

23

New Monarchs

Casimir IV, and his sons John Albert (king of Poland, 1492–1501) and Alexander (grand duke of Lithuania, 1492–1506; king of Poland, 1501–6) have never enjoyed a high reputation. While Jagiełło is seen as the union's founder and the victor of Tannenberg, and while the reigns of Sigismund I (1506–48), the third of Casimir's sons to succeed him, and Sigismund's son Sigismund August (1548–72) are associated with the flowering of the Polish Renaissance, the period in between seemed less glamorous; its only major accomplishment the incorporation of Royal Prussia. While some have praised the Nieszawa privileges as laying the foundation stone of the Polish parliamentary system, others have seen them as the first step on the road towards political anarchy. Casimir is often presented in an unappealing light, as an instinctively authoritarian yet dithering monarch, who was cold, aloof, and intellectually undistinguished. John Albert and Alexander are usually depicted as bumbling incompetents at best and downright pernicious at worst.[1]

Part of the problem lies with the sources. Długosz died in 1480, and his account of Casimir's reign must be treated with caution. He began his great history after Oleśnicki's death in 1455, and it constitutes a powerful defence of his mentor, who dominated the political scene between 1434 and 1447, but was frozen out by Casimir after conducting a determined campaign of opposition. Długosz himself fell spectacularly foul of Casimir in the 1460s in a rancorous dispute over the appointment of a new bishop of Cracow; and although Casimir proved characteristically magnanimous in victory, appointing him as tutor to his sons in 1467, it was not until the last year of Długosz's life that he was rewarded with high office, when he was appointed archbishop of Lwów. The waspish chronicler proved less generous, threading his revenge through the pages of his history in the most unflattering of portraits. Although his chronicle remained unpublished until long after his death, its influence was profound.[2]

For if Długosz is a problematic source for Casimir's reign, he is nevertheless a rich one. His negative portrayal of Casimir's character and abilities is, however, open to question from its outset, when he avidly writes of the doubts cast on

---

[1] For a more positive view see Almut Bues, *Die Jagiellonen* (Stuttgart, 2010), 82.
[2] *Annales*, xii, 374; Biskup and Górski, *Kazimierz*, 5–6; Maria Bogucka, *Kazimierz Jagiellończyk i jego czasy* (Warsaw, 1981), 118–21; Wojciech Fałkowski, *Elita władzy w Polsce za panowania Kazimierza Jagiellończyka (1447–1492)* (Warsaw, 1992), 167; Jadwiga Krzyżaniakowa, 'Portret niedokończony: Kazimierz Jagiellończyk w *Annales* Jana Długosza', in Kras et al. (eds), *Ecclesia*, 465–76.

Casimir's paternity, depicting him as an ill-starred king. He presents Casimir as an uneducated illiterate, alleging that councillors were annoyed when Jagiełło appointed tutors to teach his sons to read, preferring that they remained ignorant, in order that they might be easily manipulated.[3] Some historians, observing that Casimir's signature does not appear on any document, have taken this passage at face value.[4] It is unlikely that Jagiełło would have allowed Casimir, seen as a possible king of Bohemia as well as a potential ruler of Lithuania, to have been poorly educated, and one document bearing his signature has emerged. Since it was only from the 1460s that signatures appear on chancery documents, the absence of a royal signature cannot be taken as evidence of illiteracy.[5] Casimir probably knew no Latin, but spoke Polish, Ruthenian, and Lithuanian; it is likely that Ruthenian was his first language.[6] Długosz presented him as a slothful monarch whose anxious dithering caused his advisors serious problems. He hinted darkly at dissolution, blaming the massive fire that destroyed much of Poznań in 1447 on the sodomitical practices he claimed were rife at court. If Miechowita—another hostile source—claims Casimir had a roving eye, he was known more for uxoriousness—he fathered thirteen children by his wife, Elizabeth Habsburg—than debauchery. A taciturn man, he was austerely abstemious: like his father he dressed modestly, shunned display—not a single contemporary portrait has survived apart from his funeral monument—and was an obsessive huntsman and a rigid teetotaller, finding even the smell of alcohol repellent.[7] The charge of dithering may stem from his refusal to listen to Oleśnicki; in reality Casimir was astute and eminently capable of decisive action.

John Albert and Alexander fare little better at the bar of history. Although they were spared Długosz's malevolent carping, they suffered at the hands of Miechowita, who had access to Długosz's chronicle and the sources on which it was based, and who inherited his dyspeptic view of the Jagiellons. Miechowita's portrait was so negative that the 1519 first edition of his chronicle was suppressed; only two copies survive. Reissued with the offending passages removed or toned down it remained far from positive, and exercised a profound influence on later accounts.[8] Thanks in part to Miechowita, the powerfully built John Albert, who enjoyed a certain reputation as a soldier and was famed for his intellectual accomplishments—it was said he spoke the Latin of a professional rhetorician—is usually presented as a maladroit politician unable to build consensus, whose choleric outbursts 'spoiled what he achieved through his personal qualities'.[9] For Papée, his virtues and

---

[3] *Annales*, xi, 228–9; xii/i, 360.   [4] Górski, 'Młodość', 10; Łowmiański, *Polityka*, 215.

[5] Urszula Borkowska, 'Edukacja Jagiellonów', *RH*, 71 (2005), 101; Bogucka, *Kazimierz*, 30–1; *PSB*, xii, 269; Irena Sułkowska-Kurasiowa, *Polska kancelaria królewska w l. 1447–1506* (Wrocław, 1967), 16, 70.

[6] Łowmiański, *Polityka*, 215; Bogucka, *Kazimierz*, 226.

[7] *Annales*, xii, 27, 50, 359, 366; Górski, 'Młodość', 11–12.

[8] Maciej Miechowita, *Chronica Polonorum* (Cracow, 1519; 2nd edn, 1521, refs to facs. of 2nd edn, 1986); Hans-Jürgen Bömelburg, *Frühneuzeitliche Nationen im östlichen Europa: Das polnische Geschichtsdenken und die Reichweite einer humanistischen Nationalgeschichte (1500–1700)* (Wiesbaden, 2006), 74–6. For the changes see Ferdynand Bostel, 'Zakaz Miechowity', *Przewodnik Naukowy i Literacki*, xii (1884), 438–51, 540–62, 637–52.

[9] *PSB*, x, 409.

accomplishments—personal courage and a capacity for hard work, a good education, and a good practical training in government—were vitiated by his overweening ambition, his refusal to consider whether he had the means to fulfil it, poor judgement of people, and a willingness to place personal interests above those of dynasty and nation.[10] Alexander was ridiculed by Miechowita for his modest intellect and peasant Latin; Papée's verdict that he was a Jagiellon 'of a weaker cut', unblessed with the physical appearance, wit, or talent necessary for kingship, has not been widely challenged, although Pietkiewicz has defended his political skills.[11] The bowdlerizing of Miechowita's chronicle did not spare the Jagiellons: the excisions were more concerned with removing passages offensive to the primate, Jan Łaski, who carried them out, and his associates. Accusations of poor government and hints that John Albert, and his brother Frederick died of syphilis remained: the passage concerning the coming of the 'French disease' to Poland came immediately after an account of the arrival of Frederick's cardinal's hat from Rome and the dissolute lives led by the brothers.[12] In this at least, they were seemingly true Renaissance princes.

Despite all the sneering, this period saw profound change, and the consolidation of the union state after a long period of crisis. Although Casimir struggled with problems of resources throughout his long reign, he did much to assert the monarchy's authority, and to devise ways of exercising royal power in a system in which political fragmentation and decentralization had survived long after the restoration of the kingdom in 1320. In doing so, he demonstrated that he was a consummate politician.

He needed to be. His cool handling of the long interregnum had put him in a strong position when he eventually accepted the Polish throne in 1447, but he inherited a difficult legacy from his vanished brother. The treasury was empty. Władysław had mortgaged 240 royal properties, including 14 castles, 36 towns and their attached villages, 4 starosties, 305 villages, 2 lakes, 3 wildernesses, and 2 taverns, signing away the income from 2 municipal courts, 2 village courts, 1 Ruthenian salt mine, and the fabulously lucrative salt works at Wieliczka, not to mention numerous customs duties and the Wielkopolskan *poradlne*.[13]

Oleśnicki and his supporters dominated the council. Angry at Casimir's long delay in accepting the throne, they suspected him of favouring Lithuania, and opposed many of his initiatives. Yet Oleśnicki's grip on power was more precarious than it looked. The political paralysis that had seeped across Poland since 1434 ensured that many were dissatisfied with the status quo. Grumbling increased as the

---

[10] Fryderyk Papée, *Jan Olbracht*, 2nd edn (Cracow, 1999), 26–7.
[11] Miechowita, *Chronica*, 372; *PSB*, i, 61; Łowmiański, *Polityka*, 329–30, 333; Błaszczyk, *Litwa*, 13–14, 24; Krzysztof Pietkiewicz, 'Spór wokół Aleksandra Jagiellończyka (1461–1506)', in Rimvydas Petrauskas (ed.), *Aleksandras* (Vilnius, 2007), 16–34.
[12] Miechowita, *Chronica*, 355, 356–7, 373. More direct accusations were levied by Maciej Grodziski and Łaski himself in their updatings of Długosz's unpublished *Catologum Episcoporum Cracoviensium*: Natalia Nowakowska, *Church, State and Dynasty in Renaissance Poland* (Aldershot, 2007), 156–62.
[13] Marcin Sepiał, 'Zastaw na dobrach ziemskich i dochodach królewskich w okresie panowania Władysława III Warneńczyka na Węgrzech (1440–1444)', *ZNUJPH*, 125 (1998), 46.

capacity of Oleśnicki's cronies to line their pockets became evident: when Jan Głowacz Oleśnicki died in 1460 he was one of the richest magnates in Poland, owning the town and castle of Pińczów, fifty villages in the Sandomierz land, six villages in the Cracow land, and three in the Lublin district.[14] Although the group is referred to as Oleśnicki's faction, it had no unifying political ideology. Oleśnicki had made his name with his defence of elective monarchy, but he, like many of his allies, had risen through royal favour. While these magnates were keen to control the succession and secure royal recognition of the rights and privileges granted to the szlachta, they opposed measures that might challenge their position.

Casimir proved adept at utilizing the powers he had, which were considerable. His most potent prerogative was the right to appoint to office and honour, which gave him the means gradually to secure control of government and council. The years of minority, absentee kingship, and interregnum brought bitter disputes over appointments, which Władysław had largely devolved to the council on his departure for Hungary.[15] As Oleśnicki's grip on power strengthened, opponents clustered round Sonka, and Długosz's *iuniores*, whose resentment at their exclusion from power survived long after the 1439 debacle.[16] After his coronation, Casimir returned to Lithuania, staying for eight months. Until the Prussian war began in 1454, he was more often resident in Lithuania, far from a Polish council still dominated by Oleśnicki, Tęczyński, and Jan of Czyżów, with the chancellor, Koniecpolski, marginalized and keeping a low profile in Sieradz.[17] Casimir gradually built up support round Koniecpolski and other opponents of Oleśnicki, including the vice-chancellor, Piotr Woda—until his untimely death at Konitz in 1454—Hincza of Rogów, and Koniecpolski's brother Przedbór, castellan of Sandomierz. Jan of Czyżów maintained reasonable relations with Oleśnicki, from whom, as castellan of Cracow, he had borrowed money to pay for Casimir's coronation. Nevertheless, he mostly supported Casimir: as one who had enjoyed good relations with Vytautas, he adopted a moderate position with regard to relations with Lithuania. Happy to recognize the continuation of a separate grand duchy, he mediated between the court party and Oleśnicki during the 1452–3 confrontation, when he was not prepared to go as far as Oleśnicki in defending Polish rights to Podolia and Volhynia.[18]

Casimir acted swiftly to establish his authority in the provinces. In Wielkopolska he replaced the starosta general Wojciech Malski with Łukasz Górka, who emerged from a middling szlachta background to become palatine of Poznań in 1441, and promoted a string of new men. In Małopolska Casimir proceeded more cautiously, but Oleśnicki was by no means all-powerful and there were many prepared to support the king. Casimir took his time. He looked to the 1439 confederates, now no longer young. Dziersław Rytwiański, grandson of Wojciech Jastrzębski, who

---

[14] *PSB*, xxiii, 765; Zawitkowska, *W służbie*, 191.
[15] Zawitkowska, *W służbie*, 161, 210–11; Górski, 'Rządy', 82–6.
[16] Czwojdrak, 'Kilka', 204; Zawitkowska, *W służbie*, 171; Górski, 'Rządy', 85–6.
[17] Zawitkowska, *W służbie*, 222–4; Nowakowska, *Church*, 23.
[18] Anna Sochacka, *Jan z Czyżowa, namiestnik Władysława Warneńczyka* (Lublin, 1993), 159–70; Zawitkowska, *W służbie*, 218–19; Fałkowski, *Elita*, 58–9.

showed his mettle as starosta of Sandomierz by backing Casimir against Oleśnicki in a dispute over the Sandomierz archdeaconry in 1450, was appointed castellan of Rozprza in 1452, and palatine of Sandomierz in 1455. Hincza of Rogów was another 1439 confederate linked to Sonka—he had been one of those accused of inappropriate relations with her in the 1420s—from whom he had received several lucrative starosties. Appointed crown treasurer, he loyally supported the king, although—like Jan of Czyżów—he was willing to work with Oleśnicki for the common good. Casimir could also count on the loyalty of Koniecpolski and his brother Przedbór, who began his career as Sonka's chamberlain.[19]

Deprived of influence over patronage, Oleśnicki was edged into political irrelevance. The chancery, virtually moribund in 1447, sprang into life under Koniecpolski and Woda. Woda accompanied Casimir to Vilnius, whence he conducted Polish chancery business. The first battle was fought over Oleśnicki's status. Having turned down one cardinal's hat and accepted another from antipope Felix V— something he did not make public—Oleśnicki lobbied Nicholas V in 1447 to confirm Eugene IV's nomination, despite the fact that he had rejected it. Nicholas assented but delayed sending Oleśnicki his insignia for two years following opposition from Casimir, who attempted to remove Oleśnicki from Cracow by offering him the primacy on Kot's death in 1448. If Oleśnicki accepted, Casimir would accept his elevation. Oleśnicki, however, had no intention of giving up his lucrative see with its proximity to the centre of power. When he appeared in his cardinal's robes at the Piotrków assembly in December 1449 he sparked a volcanic row by claiming precedence in the council over the new primate, the royalist Oporowski. At Piotrków in June 1451, after two years of rancorous controversy, Casimir imposed a settlement. While recognizing Oleśnicki's elevation, he upheld Oporowski's status and banned prelates from seeking or accepting a cardinal's hat without his blessing. He decreed that he would decide which of the two prelates he would summon to council meetings or assemblies; the other would be left to cool his heels in the royal antechamber if he did not wish to cede precedence.[20]

Długosz used all his talents to present the 1451 assembly as a triumph for Oleśnicki, quoting a speech by Jan of Czyżów which stressed the magnitude of the honour done to Poland by the pope, giving the impression that Casimir had recognized Oleśnicki's claims, and suggesting that if Oporowski felt that the elevation had damaged his prestige, he should simply stay away, only turning up if he were willing to recognize his inferior status: 'let nobody have any doubts that he is lower than a cardinal'.[21] Yet Długosz's blustering account was a travesty. As he himself observed, the assembly was well attended, and there was considerable resentment from Wielkopolskans at another attack on their province's honour. The mood was with Casimir: even Długosz noted the support of 'all the most prominent prelates and dignitaries' for his resolution to the problem. Oleśnicki and

---

[19] Fałkowski, *Elita*, 51–6; 60–3.
[20] Maria Koczerska, 'Zbigniew Oleśnicki wśród ludzi i idei swojej epoki', in Kiryk and Noga (eds), *Oleśnicki*, 30–3.
[21] *Annales*, xii, 100.

Oporowski thereafter alternated in their attendance at councils and assemblies; Casimir was no doubt pleased that his most formidable opponent chose to absent himself so frequently.[22] Membership of the council and the right to attend its meetings were not enshrined in either custom or statute, a situation that Casimir exploited in other ways. In June 1452, returning from Lithuania, he summoned a narrow group of councillors to a meeting in Sandomierz. Jan Głowacz Oleśnicki turned up but was refused entry. Casimir used this tactic of summoning only hand-picked advisors to council meetings at the three general assemblies he held in 1459.[23]

He fought another important battle over Oleśnicki's demand that he publicly confirm the rights and privileges granted by his predecessors. Although this had been one of the conditions of his election Casimir refused on the grounds that to do so would break the oath he had sworn to the Lithuanians in 1447 by implying that Lithuania had been incorporated into Poland, and that he recognized Polish rule over Podolia and Volhynia.[24] It was not until 1453 that Casimir finally swore the necessary oath, but in the most general manner and in a form that raised doubts about the legal status of the document, to which the great seal seems not to have been attached. He conceded no ground over Lithuania's status and imposed his own solution with regard to Podolia and Volhynia.[25]

Although Długosz muttered darkly that Casimir favoured Lithuania over Poland, it was not an issue that resonated widely. Control of Podolia and Volhynia was of interest to Oleśnicki and a small group of Małopolskan magnates, but not for Wielkopolska or the szlachta masses. Casimir received substantial support for royal policy: his first general assembly at Piotrków in August 1447 agreed to levy the land tax at a rate of 12 groszy per hide.[26] His general confirmation of privileges in 1453 was sufficient to satisfy most of the szlachta, and by 1454 Casimir had enough support to ignore Olesnicki's opposition to the incorporation of Prussia.

Oleśnicki died on 1 April 1455. Despite one last public proclamation of his status at his funeral through the suspension of his three cardinals hats over his coffin, and despite Długosz's best efforts, his isolation and political impotence at the time of his death cannot be overlooked. The last years of his career bear testimony to the limits of aristocratic power in fifteenth-century Poland, and to the existence of a political basis for effective royal rule. For all the close family and political links Oleśnicki enjoyed with powerful Małopolskan families, and despite his triumph over the succession, he was only able to exercise true political authority between 1434 and 1447. It is important not to exaggerate the coherence of aristocratic factions based on kinship ties: Koniecpolski, who died six days before Oleśnicki, may have been related to him through his wife, Dorota Oleśnicka, but it did not prevent him offering, on the whole, loyal support to Casimir, while

---

[22] Koczerska, 'Oleśnicki', 33–4; Bogucka, *Kazimierz*, 58; Kurtyka, *Tęczyńscy*, 345. Fałkowski accepts Długosz's assessment: *Elita*, 65–6, 70.
[23] *Annales*, xii, 127; Wojciech Fałkowski, 'Rok trzech sejmów', in Manikowska et al. (eds), *Aetas media*, 425–38.
[24] Halecki, *Dzieje*, i, 373–4.   [25] Zawitkowska, *W służbie*, 295; Halecki, *Dzieje*, i, 380–1.
[26] Zawitkowska, *W służbie*, 222.

Oleśnicki's own cousins from the Krzyżanowski family waged a long and violent campaign against him in the 1440s in the sort of property dispute that often split families.[27]

The deaths of Oleśnicki and Koniecpolski, and of Jan of Czyżów in 1458, marked the passing of the generation that had served Jagiełło. In the three years from 1458, eight out of the thirteen Małopolskan palatines and castellans died, giving Casimir a unique opportunity to shape the political scene according to his own taste. He began at the top. Jan Tęczyński, palatine of Cracow, formerly Oleśnicki's ally, was promoted to the castellany of Cracow in early 1459, as was customary. In appointing his successor Casimir broke radically with tradition by nominating his stepbrother Jan Pilecki, son of Elizabeth, Jagiełło's third wife. Pilecki had held no previous office, apart from a three-month stint as starosta of Cracow in 1440; his promotion was a dramatic assertion of royal authority made possible by the rapprochement with Tęczyński, who—in contrast to Oleśnicki—supported the Prussian war and backed Casimir during the Nieszawa crisis, for which he was generously rewarded.[28]

The fortuitous freeing up of positions enabled Casimir to consolidate his support in the difficult years after Nieszawa. His magnanimity and refusal to bear grudges paid dividends, as he won over several figures previously critical of royal policy. The Małopolskan lords Jan Amor Tarnowski and Jan Rytwiański attacked Casimir at the stormy autumn general assembly in 1459, but the former was made castellan of Sącz later that year, while the latter was appointed crown marshal in 1462; thereafter both served loyally. The situation in Małopolska was still difficult and Casimir waited two years after Tęczyński's death in 1470 before controversially promoting Pilecki to the castellany of Cracow. In 1473 the Małopolskans and Ruthenians, who were unhappy at the domination of local politics by the rapacious Odrowąż family, boycotted the general assembly in Piotrków in protest at nominations to office. It was not until the late 1470s that Casimir's authority over Małopolska was secure.[29]

Control of appointments to bishoprics was central to the establishment of royal authority. Koniecpolski was replaced as chancellor by the bishop of Cujavia, Jan Gruszczyński, a royalist who had previously worked in the chancery.[30] Gruszczyński's nomination set the trend for Casimir's reign. Koniecpolski had been a layman, and the years between 1438 and Woda's death at Konitz in 1454, were the only period in Polish history when neither chancellor was a cleric.[31] Thereafter, with the exception of Jakub of Dębno, chancellor from 1469 to 1473, all Casimir's chancellors and vice-chancellors were clerics, usually bishops. There were good reasons for this policy. Apart from the educational qualifications of clergymen in an age when Latin was the language of government, appointing them enabled Casimir to avoid individuals from the great council families, instead choosing ambitious scions of middling szlachta background. It was therefore vital for Casimir, as for other

---

[27] Górczak, *Podstawy*, 171; Nowakowska, *Church*, 22.   [28] Fałkowski, *Elita*, 83–5.
[29] Fałkowski, *Elita*, 92, 118–20.   [30] Fałkowski, *Elita*, 85.
[31] Zawitkowska, *W służbie*, 311.

contemporary European monarchs, to control appointments to ecclesiastical office, and in particular to bishoprics. Jagiełło had enjoyed a reasonable degree of control, but the end of the schism and Poland's conciliarist tradition—which re-emerged during the Council of Basle—ensured that after 1447, and especially during the Prussian war, a newly combative papacy was suspicious of Casimir and jealous of its own authority.[32] There were relatively few Polish bishoprics, and therefore considerable rivalry among churchmen to fill them.[33] Nicholas V did grant Casimir the right to fill twenty benefices in gratitude for Casimir's recognition of his rights to the papacy, enabling Casimir to raise Oporowski to the primacy. Once he felt secure, Nicholas proved less accommodating. When Casimir nominated Gruszczyński to Cujavia in 1449, Nicholas supported Oleśnicki's candidate, Mikołaj Lasocki; it was not until Lasocki's death in 1450 that Gruszczyński was consecrated. A similar battle occurred after the death of Piotr Chrząstowski, bishop of Przemyśl, in January 1452, when Casimir, without consulting the Małopolskan lords, nominated his Silesian secretary, Mikołaj of Blaschewitz, ignoring the custom by which the local chapter elected its bishops.[34]

This nomination was directed more against Oleśnicki than the papacy, as was Casimir's nomination of Mikołaj Łabuński to the bishopric of Kamianets in 1453, and, in the same year, of another of his secretaries, Jan Sprowski, as primate over Tomasz Strzempiński, who was preferred by most canons; all of these nominations were confirmed by the pope. Strzempiński, a professor at the university, had succeeded Oleśnicki as bishop of Cracow. As Oleśnicki had demonstrated, the Cracow diocese afforded its incumbent unrivalled opportunities to frustrate the royal government if he were so inclined. When Strzempiński died in September 1460, conflict loomed. The new pope was Pius II who, as Enea Silvio Piccolomini, had been a correspondent of Oleśnicki, imbibing much of his hostility to the Jagiellons. He took the opportunity of asserting his authority. The Cracow canons—including Długosz—begged Casimir not to nominate anyone, but to allow the chapter, still packed with Oleśnicki's protégés, to elect Strzempiński's successor. Casimir ignored the plea, nominating Gruszczyński. When the chapter defiantly elected vice-chancellor Jan Lutkowic, who refused the nomination during a stormy assembly at Piotrków, Pius saw his opportunity, appointing Jakub of Sienno, Oleśnicki's nephew and administrator of the diocese, who had impressed him during a diplomatic mission to Rome in 1459. Casimir, then in Lithuania, issued decrees confiscating the property of Jakub and his supporters and banishing them. In his absence Jakub was consecrated bishop by the suffragan and took up his office. When Casimir returned in early 1461 he vented his fury: the houses of several canons, including Długosz, were looted by a mob under the king's approving eyes,

---

[32] For appointments before 1447 see Tomasz Graff, *Episkopat* (Cracow, 2008), 159–86.
[33] The archbishoprics of Gniezno and Lwów, and the bishoprics of Cracow, Cujavia, Poznań, Przemyśl, Chełm, and Kamianets in the kingdom of Poland, the bishoprics of Vilnius, Miedininkai (Samogitia), Lutsk, and Kyiv in the grand duchy, and of Płock in Mazovia, and Culm in Pomerelia. It was not until the end of the century that the Polish monarchy established its influence over the Prussian bishopric of Ermland (Warmia).
[34] Bogucka, *Kazimierz*, 117; Błaszczyk, *Dzieje*, ii, 830, 837; Fałkowski, *Elita*, 73–4.

and the recalcitrant canons were stripped of their income from the tithe. Jakub fled to Pińczów; his suffragan headed for Silesia. Pius appointed archdeacon Jan Pniewski as diocesan administrator but Casimir won the day. At an assembly in Piotrków in January 1463, support for Casimir's position was overwhelming and Gruszczyński was duly installed. Casimir was magnanimous in victory, restoring the canons' incomes, nominating Lutkowic to the vacant bishopric of Płock, and even sparing Jakub of Sienno his wrath, appointing him in 1465 to the bishopric of Cujavia. Jakub remained loyal thereafter, and was ultimately rewarded with the archbishopric of Gniezno in 1474.[35]

Casimir had won a significant victory, which did much to secure the principle of royal control of episcopal nominations. He was helped by the strength of conciliarist feeling in the Polish church, with influential clerics happy to look to the monarchy to protect them against papal encroachments. Casimir was able to ban appeals to Rome, and the implementation in Poland of judgements by the papal courts or summonses before them without a squeak of protest from his bishops.[36] Lay politicians also backed him: Jan Ostroróg, in his significant undated treatise on political reform, eloquently defended the king's right to appoint bishops in a powerful attack on papal pretensions.[37] Casimir was increasingly well served by loyalist bishops such as Andrzej Bniński, bishop of Poznań (1439–79), Władysław Oporowski, archbishop of Gniezno (1449–53), and Mateusz Łomżyński, bishop of Kamianets (1479–90), and then Chełm (1490–1505).[38]

Casimir's campaign to control the church climaxed with the nomination of his sixth and youngest son, Frederick (1468–1503) to the bishopric of Cracow in April 1488. That Oleśnicki's old chapter should have confirmed the nomination '*per inspirationem*'—that is without a formal election—shows that this triumph was no unexpected coup, but had been carefully prepared, as is demonstrated by its rapid confirmation by Innocent VIII in May, accompanied by a dispensation allowing Frederick to hold the see in administration until he reached the canonical age of 25. The appointment was testimony to the success of Casimir's ecclesiastical policy; its symbolic importance was immediately apparent as Oleśnicki's nephew Zbigniew, now archbishop of Gniezno and already at loggerheads with Casimir despite a long period of faithful service in the chancery, contested Frederick's claims, as a royal prince, to take precedence over him at council meetings. By January 1489, Oleśnicki had been frozen out; like his uncle, he boycotted council meetings, thereby entering the political wilderness as the other bishops, led by the royalist archbishop of Lwów, Andrzej Boryszewski, accepted Frederick's precedence.[39]

Frederick's elevation was a masterstroke. He played a key role in the interregnum following Casimir's death on 7 June 1492, moving swiftly to ensure the election of John Albert against his older brother Władysław, and Janusz II of Mazovia,

---

[35] Bogucka, *Kazimierz*, 118–21; *PSB*, x, 366.   [36] Górski, 'Rządy', 107.
[37] Jan Ostroróg, *Monumentum pro comitiis generalibus regni sub rege Casimiro pro Reipublicae ordinatione* (undated); Bobrzyński, *Jan Ostroróg* (Cracow, 1884), 4.
[38] Witold Knoppek, 'Zmiany w układzie sił politycznych w Polsce w drugiej połowie XV w. i ich związek z genezą dwuizbowego sejmu', *CPH*, 7/2 (1955), 72–3.
[39] Nowakowska, *Church*, 39–41.

Oleśnicki's favoured candidate. Borrowing money from Cracow council to hire 600 troops, Frederick hurried to Piotrków, where the election was to take place. He garrisoned the castle, leaving Oleśnicki fuming outside the town wall. Frederick's quick thinking ensured that it was he rather than Oleśnicki who presided; he was therefore able to secure John Albert's election.[40] The extent of Jagiellon authority over the Polish church was revealed after Oleśnicki's death in 1493: in March, Frederick was elected—again *per inspirationem*—by the Gniezno chapter after John Albert's intervention. Since he remained bishop of Cracow, Frederick now attained an unprecedented position of authority within the Polish church. His status was underlined when Alexander VI made him a cardinal in September 1493.[41]

Frederick served the dynasty well before his premature death in 1503 at the age of thirty-five. He proved an able politician, administering the kingdom capably when John Albert was absent on military campaign and playing an important—if not quite so dramatic—role in the 1501 election of Alexander after John Albert's unexpected death. Despite his posthumous reputation for fecklessness and immorality, he proved an effective and dedicated ecclesiastical administrator, taking a close interest in the affairs of his sees, and presiding with notably more enthusiasm over the ecclesiastical courts than most bishops; in this, as in his political ambition, he was more similar to Zbigniew Oleśnicki the elder than he might have cared to admit. The extent of his influence should not be exaggerated, however: the browbeating of the Cracow and Gniezno chapters into accepting him as bishop was resented by many canons, and his unsympathetic portrayal by Miechowita and others indicated the extent of the backlash against such a clear royal attempt to subdue the church. Under the primacy of Jan Łaski (1510–31) the pendulum swung away from Frederick's royalist agenda. Although Sigismund I secured the appointment of his illegitimate son Jan in 1519 as bishop of Vilnius, it was not until the 1630s that Poland was again to see a royal cardinal.

While domination of the council was important, control of the chancery was vital. Government had long since moved out of the household in Poland, in part because of the interregna of 1382–4 and 1444–7, and the long minority and absentee monarchy of Władysław III. Although it was not until 1504 that a statutory duty was laid upon chancellors to refuse to issue documents that were contrary to the law, this measure merely gave legal force to existing practice: as early as 1420 Wojciech Jastrzębiec refused to attach the great seal to a document in which Jagiełło sought to confer the title of count upon his stepson, Jan Pilecki.[42] By the 1460s only the chancellor or vice-chancellor could authorize the drafting of official documents, although in exceptional circumstances the chief secretary occasionally did so. From 1466, when Zbigniew Oleśnicki the younger was grand secretary, his signature or that of the chancellor, Jakub of Dębno, began to appear on documents as a sign of their authenticity; the practice was regularized after

---

[40] Miechowita, *Chronica*, 347; Nowakowska, *Church*, 43.   [41] Nowakowska, *Church*, 44–5.
[42] *VC*, i/i, 129; *Annales*, xi, 129–31; Stanisław Kętrzyński, *Zarys nauki o dokumencie polskim wieków średnich*, 2nd edn (Poznań, 2008), 182.

Oleśnicki became vice-chancellor in 1472.[43] From 1447, the keeping of chancery record books in three series—of the chancellor, vice-chancellor, and secretary—began systematically.[44] From the 1470s Casimir began issuing documents under his signet, drawn up by the grand secretary or another of their secretaries under the formula '*dominus rex per se*'.[45] Such expedients were viewed with great suspicion, however: the key to effective royal government remained the relationship between the king and his chancellors. There was no substitute for an effective appointments policy.

By the late 1470s, Casimir's authority was considerable, and he was increasingly able to ignore the legal constraints on his power embedded in the privileges he had sworn to respect. He began to ignore the ban on multiple office-holding and the conventions that had grown up around the developing hierarchy of prestige. When Pilecki died in 1476 Casimir promoted, as was normal, Dziersław Rytwiański, the palatine of Cracow, to the castellany of Cracow. In filling the vacant palatinate, however, he overlooked the claims of the faithful Jakub of Dębno who, as palatine of Sandomierz, by custom had a strong expectation of promotion, instead appointing Dziersław's brother Jan to the position. Jan remained crown marshal and castellan of Sandomierz. Since the brothers had jointly held the starosty of Sandomierz since 1442, this meant that four of the top positions in Małopolska and one of the leading offices of state were held by two individuals from the same family.[46]

Protests at this breach of customary and statute law were sharp, not least from loyal members of the younger generation, whose expectations had been rudely shattered: the failure to free up offices at the top led to congestion further down the system. In the event, Dziersław diplomatically died in January 1478, just before the opening of a general assembly at which protests were inevitable; Casimir prudently advanced Jakub of Dębno rather than Jan Rytwiański to the castellany of Cracow. Rytwiański himself soon died; it may be that in promoting two elderly men Casimir was deliberately testing the waters to gauge the reaction. Lower down the system he was more able to ignore the legal and customary constraints on his authority to build up a strong group of loyal office-holders across Wielkopolska and Małopolska.[47] Through his nomination of loyalists to the key post of judicial starosta, in particular the starosta generals of Wielkopolska, Małopolska, Ruthenia, and Prussia, Casimir projected royal power deep into the provinces: from the appearance of the office from the turn of the thirteenth century, judicial starostas were in charge of the castle courts, the main criminal tribunals in lands and districts; they were responsible for the execution of royal judgements and decrees, for the administration of royal taxation at the local level, and for jurisdiction over nobles who did not possess

---

[43] Waldemar Chorążyczewski, *Przemiany organizacyjne polskiej kancelarii królewskiej u progu czasów nowożytnych* (Toruń, 2007), 62.
[44] Knoppek, 'Zmiany', 74–5.
[45] Waldemar Chorążyczewski, 'Początki kancelarii pokojowej za Jagiellonów', in Chorążyczewski and Wojciech Krawczyk (eds), *Polska kancelaria królewska między władzą a społeczeństwem*, iii (Warsaw, 2008), 37–46.
[46] Fałkowski, *Elita*, 131–2.   [47] Fałkowski, *Elita*, 137–9.

estates in the district, and therefore were not subject to the elected land courts. Originally he had full military authority at the local level, although the decline of the importance of the noble levy in favour of professional troops meant that his military significance faded. He retained, however, considerable administrative and judicial authority. He was responsible for the administration of the royal estates attached to the royal castle (*gród*) in his district, from which he drew substantial revenues. Since, following Wielkopolskan practice, a growing number of castle courts deemed the acts they registered to be eternally valid, the castle court was the preferred institution for local nobles to register documents of all kinds from testaments to property transactions. As the reach of the castle court grew, so the power of the starosta expanded; concern at this growth led to the clauses in the 1454 privileges decreeing that judicial starosties could no longer be held by palatines, castellans, or land judges—elected by sejmiks from the fifteenth century—who presided over the land courts.[48]

Casimir took great care over whom he appointed to judicial starosties. The post was still at the king's pleasure, although Casimir was happy to leave trusted associates in post for long periods: while the starosty of Cracow was held by individuals for very short periods in the late 1430s and 1450s, under Casimir, Jan of Czyżów held it from 1440 until 1457, and Jakub of Dębno from 1463 until his death in 1490. Maciej Mosiński of Bnin, appointed palatine of Poznań in 1477, remained starosta general of Wielkopolska in breach of Nieszawa.[49] This consolidation of royal authority at the central and the local level after 1466 was a substantial achievement.

---

[48] The term starosty was also used to denote complexes of royal estates leased out or mortgaged to individual nobles, but without judicial or administrative powers. Their holders were known as 'non-judicial starostas' [*starostowie niegrodowi*]. The Nieszawa privileges forbade the mortgaging of judicial starosties, a practice that had spread since 1400: Juliusz Bardach, *Historia państwa i prawa Polski*, i: *Do połowy XV wieku* (Warsaw, 1964), 256–7, 457–60, 475–81; Wacław Uruszczak, *Historia państwa i prawa polskiego*, i: *966–1795* (Warsaw, 2010) 174–6.

[49] Fałkowski, *Elita*, 136–8, 165.

24
Jagiellonian Europe

The restoration of domestic order ran parallel to one of Casimir's most spectacular—if short-lived—achievements: the creation of 'Jagiellonian Europe'. His career as a dynastic politician began with his marriage in February 1454 to Elizabeth Habsburg, daughter of Albert II, king of the Romans, which marked the definitive acceptance of the Jagiellons into the charmed—if not always charming—circle of European monarchs. Jagiełło, after his first marriage to an Angevin, was forced to accept a relatively minor Italian princess—albeit of Polish royal blood—as his second wife, and subsequently married two of his own subjects. Władysław III died in battle before he could marry. Casimir's bride, however, was the daughter of one Emperor and the granddaughter of another—Sigismund of Luxembourg—on her mother's side.

The origins of the match lay in the complex politics of central and southeastern Europe after the Ottoman conquest of much of the Balkans; the failure of Sigismund of Luxembourg to produce a male heir; and the premature deaths of Albert in 1439 and Władysław in 1444. Varna ended the brief Jagiellon sojourn on the Hungarian throne, but did little to restore political stability to the region. Albert's Habsburg cousin was elected as Emperor Frederick III in 1440, but his grip on the Empire was feeble after the failure of a half-hearted attempt at imperial reform in 1444. Frederick's assertion of the Habsburg claim to the thrones of Bohemia and Hungary faced considerable opposition from the native nobilities, who fiercely defended their tradition of elective monarchy. Elizabeth was removed from Frederick's care during the rebellion that broke out in Austria after he left for the last coronation of an emperor in Rome in 1452. Her protector was her uncle Ulrich of Celje, who led the rebellion. After the death of her fiancé, Frederick of Saxony, the idea of a Polish marriage emerged, since Ulrich was keen to secure Polish support.[1]

Jagiellonian power in central Europe was founded on this marriage. In personal terms it was successful by the undemanding standards of royal marriages: even Miechowita admitted that the couple were bound by ties of love.[2] Elizabeth proved a devoted wife, writing warmly of her husband in her testament, and identifying herself entirely with her new realm: after Casimir's death she stayed in Poland until her own death in 1505. Most importantly, she bore him six sons and seven

---

[1] *PSB*, vi, 251. [2] Miechowita, *Chronica*, 327.

daughters, of whom all but two daughters survived into adulthood.[3] Of her six sons, four became kings; one became a bishop, archbishop, and cardinal; and one—albeit after her death—was canonized. All her daughters married German princes; in consequence she was the Queen Victoria of her day: every monarch in modern Europe is descended from her (see Fig. 9. Genealogy 5).

Casimir's marriage proved a dynastic triumph not just because of Elizabeth's capacity for bearing healthy children, but for the simple reason that László the Posthumous died without issue in 1457. Elizabeth had already produced a son, Władysław, born in 1456, and was pregnant with her daughter Jadwiga; within two years she bore another two sons. With no clear successor to the Bohemian and Hungarian thrones, Elizabeth advanced her claims as Albert's daughter on behalf of her sons against Frederick III, who was proclaimed king by a group of Hungarian magnates in February 1459, but failed to secure the throne against the 15-year-old Matthias Corvinus, son of János Hunyadi, who was elected by the Hungarian diet in January 1458 in the expectation—soon rudely shattered—that he would prove a pliant tool in its hands. Since their children were infants, Casimir and Elizabeth declined to press their claims. The Bohemians also chose a native monarch in George Podiebrad (1458–71), the moderate Hussite leader who brokered an uneasy peace between the Catholic and Hussite parties.

The Jagiellons' day was dawning, however. The fall of Constantinople increased Ottoman pressure on Hungary and stimulated the papacy's interest in uniting the crowns of Bohemia, Hungary, and Poland to stiffen resistance. The memory of Władysław III's heroic death at Varna survived in Rome and Buda, while civil strife continued to ravage Bohemia and Hungary. As Casimir's sons matured, a Jagiellonian candidature became viable. George Podiebrad lost the support of many Catholics, and Corvinus, with papal encouragement, joined a Catholic insurgency based in Moravia, where he was crowned king of Bohemia in May 1469. Podiebrad looked to the Jagiellons for assistance, recognizing Casimir's eldest son Władysław as his heir, despite having legitimate sons of his own. When Podiebrad died in March 1471, his supporters elected Władysław to succeed him. A bitter war against Corvinus lasted until 1479, when Władysław surrendered Moravia, Silesia, and Lusatia to Corvinus to secure his throne.

Corvinus's victories, his glittering monarchy and the intellectual accomplishment of his magnificent Renaissance court could not disguise the shaky foundations of his rule. In Hungary he faced considerable—if frequently silent—opposition from many who had engineered his election, but who were dismayed at his autocratic ways. In the south he faced growing Ottoman pressure, while his failure to produce a legitimate male heir threatened his legacy. His desire to secure the succession for his illegitimate son, János, alienated his second wife Beatrice of Aragon, who loathed her stepson, and encouraged his opponents to look elsewhere.

---

[3] Bogucka, *Kazimierz*, 136; *Materiały do dziejów dyplomacji polskiej z lat 1486–1516 (kodeks zagrzebski)*, ed. Józef Garbacik (Wrocław, 1966), no. 45, 141–8.

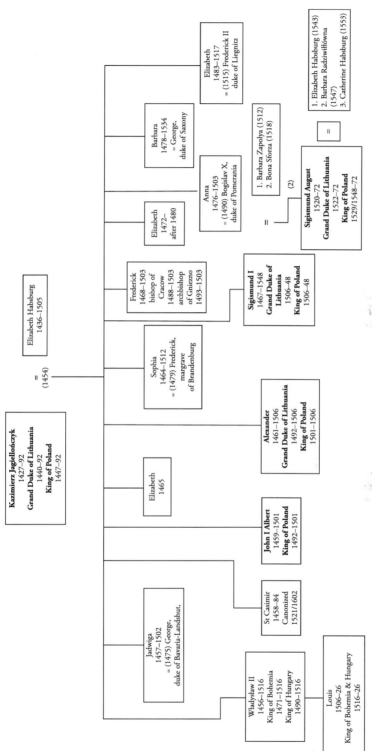

Fig. 9. Genealogy 5. The descendants of Casimir IV.

Corvinus had many enemies. The peace he signed with Frederick in 1463 broke down in 1485. Corvinus seized Lower Austria and Vienna, Styria, and parts of Carinthia, assuming the title of duke of Austria and chasing Frederick out of the Habsburg heartlands, which Corvinus held until his death in Vienna on 6 April 1490.[4] His aggression and lack of a legitimate heir left central Europe in turmoil, and the Jagiellons emerged to seize the prize, if at some cost to dynastic harmony. Casimir had prepared his sons carefully for government, giving them responsibility and practical experience. Władysław, despatched in 1471 at fifteen to secure the Bohemian throne, was an indolent sybarite, and Casimir's hopes were invested in his second son, also Casimir, born in 1458 and, like his younger brothers, given an excellent education by Długosz and the Italian humanist Filippo Buonaccorsi (1437–96), known in Poland as Kallimach. Famed for the piety that would later bring his canonization, Casimir was personable, popular, and able.[5] Aged thirteen he was despatched to Hungary in 1471 to stake a claim to the Hungarian throne as the figurehead of a magnate party plotting to overthrow Corvinus. Three years of inconsequential fighting followed, before failure was admitted. From 1481, when his father spent five years—with one small interruption—in Lithuania, Casimir governed Poland on his behalf. His death from tuberculosis in 1484 left his parents grief-stricken, and his mantle as Casimir's designated successor passed to the third son, John Albert, Elizabeth's favourite.[6]

John Albert was given considerable responsibility. In 1485 he accompanied Casimir on campaign in Moldavia, where the growing Ottoman threat to a principality over which Poland had long claimed suzerainty had been made grimly apparent with the seizure of the former Genoese colonies of Kilia and Cetatea Alba, which threatened trade down the Danube and Dniester into the Black Sea. The ending of the Lithuanian civil wars and the compromise settlement over Podolia and Volhynia stimulated trade through Kyiv, Kamianets, Lwów, and Lutsk. As the great caravans wound their way across Ruthenia with their rich cargoes of silk, velvet, damask, pepper, saffron, and spices from the east, wax and honey from Ruthenia, and cloth and manufactured goods from the west, Poland and Lithuania faced increasing competition from rival powers.[7] The days when Vytautas built castles on the Black Sea coast were long gone. As the Ottomans extended their influence northwards, the Crimean Tatars began their devastating raids into the southern Ruthenian lands. John Albert defended this southern border, winning several victories against Tatar forces.[8]

Corvinus's death in April 1490 demonstrated that fecundity can be as great a problem for a dynasty as the failure to produce an heir. Casimir now advanced John

---

[4] Krzysztof Baczkowski, *Walka o Węgry w latach 1490–1492* (Cracow, 1995), 12–14.

[5] Casimir was canonized by Leo X in 1521; the bull was lost after the Polish envoy, Erazm Ciołek, died of the plague in Rome in 1522. The bull of canonization was reissued by Clement VIII on the request of Sigismund III in 1602.

[6] *PSB*, xii, 286–8.

[7] For Ruthenian trade see Mikhailo Hrushevsky, *History of Ukraine-Rus'*, vi: *Economic, Cultural, and National Life in the 14th to 17th Centuries*, ed. Myron Kapral and Frank Sysyn (Edmonton, 2012), 1–83.

[8] Papée, *Jan Olbracht*, 18–19.

Albert's claims to the Hungarian crown. His elder brother Władysław, whose Bohemian kingdom had been truncated by the rapacious Corvinus, had different ideas, moving with uncharacteristic alacrity to challenge his younger brother and Corvinus's illegitimate son János. It took two years of civil war before the matter was settled in Władysław's favour. Casimir switched his support to Władysław, but John Albert was elected by a party among the Hungarian nobles and stubbornly refused to renounce his claim, spending two years fighting his brother before Casimir negotiated an agreement in which John Albert was granted the duchy of Głogau and half of Silesia with the title *supremus Silesiae dux*, and the promise of the Hungarian succession should Władysław die without heirs.

Jagiellons now sat on the thrones of Poland, Lithuania, Bohemia, and Hungary. By Casimir's death in June 1492, however, the favourable conjuncture that had brought this dynastic triumph had passed. Papal hopes for an anti-Ottoman league foundered as the dynasty showed a distinct lack of brotherly affection. Despite a cautious rapprochement between Władysław and John Albert, cobbled together in several meetings after the end of the Hungarian civil war, rivalry over Moldavia and Silesia soured relations. In 1497 after protracted squabbling, John Albert led a large Polish army into Moldavia at the invitation of his vassal, Stefan III, seeking to retake Kilia and Cetatea Alba. The expedition was a disaster. When the Hungarians, who also claimed suzerainty over Moldavia, failed to support it, Stefan promptly changed sides, accepting Ottoman overlordship and turning on the Poles. John Albert's army, dubiously claimed to have been 40,000 strong, mostly comprised the noble levies of Małopolska, Wielkopolska, Mazovia, and Ruthenia. It never came near its objectives and was ravaged by disease, which laid the king low and forced a withdrawal. Harried by Moldavian forces it was ambushed in a long ravine at the battle of Koźmin in Bukovina (25–26 October 1497), and was only saved from disaster through a charge of the royal bodyguard. Some 5,000 died, including many leading nobles, and the army streamed back to Poland in disorder. John Albert drowned his sorrows in an extended period of debauchery in Cracow that earned him an admonition from Cardinal Frederick, himself no model of moral rectitude.[9]

The disaster dissipated John Albert's crusading spirit and undermined his health. Its aftermath demonstrated the dangers of taking on the Ottomans alone. In 1498 a punitive revenge attack reached Przeworsk and Jarosław; a second in November 1499 approached Sambor. Two devastating raids by the Tatars in June and August 1500 were even more of a shock, crossing the Vistula and striking into Mazovia and Podlasie. Poland was in no position to contemplate an Ottoman war, and a five-year truce was negotiated in October 1502 that set the pattern for the rest of the century. Although Tatar raids continued, Poland sought to avoid war. The truce was extended in 1507, 1509, 1510, 1511, 1514, and 1519. In 1510 and 1517, papal proposals for a Polish-Hungarian campaign were politely rebuffed. When the Ottomans attacked Hungary in 1521, Sigismund I did send aid, which resulted in a brief war that was deeply unpopular in Poland. Another truce was signed in 1525.

[9] Papée, *Jan Olbracht*, 125–46, 149–50.

Thus, although up to 1,500 Poles volunteered to join the army of Sigismund's nephew Louis, who succeeded Władysław as king of Hungary and Bohemia in 1516, he was effectively abandoned to his fate, becoming the second Jagiellon to die fighting the Ottomans when he drowned in the chaotic flight after the disastrous battle of Mohács (29 August 1526). The fragile Jagiellonian dynastic edifice collapsed along with the medieval kingdom of St Stephen. The Habsburgs reaped the benefit. Ferdinand I, younger brother of Emperor Charles V, who had married Louis's sister, secured the crowns of Bohemia and the small northern strip of Hungarian territory that the Ottomans had failed to occupy, laying the foundations of a dynastic conglomeration that reaped its reward when the Ottoman tide began to ebb in the 1680s.[10]

Polish reluctance to fight the Ottomans was largely due to developments in the east. During the century after 1386 Lithuania dominated the marches of eastern Europe. Yet Vytautas's ambitious plan to secure hegemony over the eastern Ruthenian principalities foundered. Lithuania may at times have exercised its influence over the principalities of Novgorod and Pskov, but Muscovy proved more resilient despite being plagued by political conflict and a succession of weak rulers after the death of Dmitrii Donskoi in 1389. The cautious and unassertive Vasilii I (1389–1425) was easily eclipsed by the vigorous Vytautas; his son, Vytautas's grandson Vasilii II (1425–62), was only ten years old when he succeeded his father, and was immediately exposed to the rampant ambitions of his uncle, Iurii of Galich, after Vytautas's death. From 1431 civil war raged in Muscovy. Although Vasilii II fought off the challenge from Iurii, who died in June 1434, and then defeated and blinded Iurii's son, Vasilii Kosoi, in 1436, he himself was defeated in the battle of Suzdal in 1445 and captured by Ulug-Mehmet, khan of the Golden Horde. Vasili II's release on payment of a huge ransom prompted a bid for the throne by Kosoi's younger brother Dmitrii Shemiaka, who seized and blinded Vasilii in Muscovy's own revenge tragedy. Although most boyars failed to recognize Shemiaka's legitimacy, it was not until his death in 1453 that Vasilii was secure on his throne.[11]

Despite the civil war, Vasilii repelled the half-hearted attacks of the young Casimir on Muscovy in the 1440s. After his acceptance of the Polish throne in 1447 Casimir abandoned his eastern ambitions, settling with Vasilii in 1449, when he conceded that Novgorod and Pskov lay within Muscovy's sphere of influence and agreed that both should maintain friendly relations with Tver. After 1447 there was no grand duke in Vilnius capable of pursuing Vytautas's eastern ambitions. Vytautas's policy of keeping Muscovy in check through friendly relations with the Tatars was no longer possible once the khanates of the Crimea (Perekop), Kazan, Astrakhan, and Siberia began competing viciously for the Golden Horde's legacy with the Great Horde, which sought to keep alive the nomadic Mongol tradition.

---

[10] Andrzej Dziubiński, *Stosunki dyplomatyczne polsko-tureckie w latach 1500–1572 w kontekście międzynarodowym* (Wrocław, 2005), 11–57; Dariusz Kołodziejczyk, *Ottoman-Polish Diplomatic Relations (15th–18th century)* (Leiden, 2000), 110–16.

[11] Robert Crummey, *The Formation of Muscovy 1304–1613* (London, 1987), 68–75; Charles Halperin, *Russia and the Golden Horde* (Bloomington, 1987), 58.

Poland-Lithuania was drawn into the bewildering world of steppe politics, in which it competed with Muscovy and the Ottomans for influence among the splintered remnants of the Golden Horde. The Islamic faith of these khanates meant that the Ottomans possessed an advantage. Although modern scholars have demolished the view that they extended their suzerainty over the Crimean horde in 1478, none of the Crimean khans from the Giray dynasty could ignore or defy Istanbul for long. Lithuania's control of most of the lands immediately to the north of the Crimea, and the common hostility of Muscovy and the Crimean Tatars to the Great Horde meant that from the late fifteenth century, the Crimean khans broadly favoured Muscovy over Lithuania, a development that owed much to the pursuit of Jagiellon ambitions in Hungary, Bohemia, and Moldavia and the consequent deterioration of Polish-Ottoman relations.[12] Union had its price.

By his death in 1462 Vasilii II had extended his authority across Muscovy, bringing to heel the various Rurikid appanage princes and subduing the boyar conflicts that had fuelled the civil wars. In 1448 after his blinding, he made his eldest son, the eight-year-old Ivan, co-ruler without seeking the permission of any of the successors to the Golden Horde. Vasilii built well; his son, Ivan III (1462–1505) and grandson Vasilii III (1505–33) were to reap the rewards. Ivan set Muscovy on a very different political path from its Lithuanian neighbour and rival. By marrying Sophia Palaelogus, niece of the last Byzantine emperor, he enabled Muscovy—now the only independent Orthodox power—to lay claim to the heritage of the eastern Roman Empire. As Casimir looked on, largely passive, Ivan extended his control westwards. In 1478, after a long campaign of political and military pressure, he annexed Novgorod; Tver fell to him seven years later. These annexations were followed by a massive redistribution of lands that enabled Ivan to establish the *pomest'e* system of military service, which underpinned the Muscovite army until deep into the seventeenth century.

Ivan challenged Lithuanian control over the vast borderlands between the two grand duchies. He looked for support among the Rurikid and Gediminid princes scattered along the upper reaches of the river Oka, and its tributary, the Ugra, where Lithuania's borders extended to within 150 kilometres of Moscow. These lands were inhabited by princes whose main aim was the defence of their small appanage duchies against the twin threats of subdivision and the assertion of central authority from Vilnius. In the long period of Moscow's weakness they had remained loyal to the Jagiellons, but as Ivan actively sought their support, discontented individuals seeking to recover what they regarded as their rightful patrimony, or chafing at the increasing assertiveness of the Lithuanian government, began to defect to Muscovy, a trend begun in 1481–82, when Algirdas's great-grandson Fëdor Belsky fled to Moscow after the exposure of a plot to assassinate Casimir by a group of eastern Ruthenian princes. Casimir spent most of the next five years in Lithuania, leaving the government of Poland in the hands of his sons, first Casimir and then, after his death, John Albert. While his presence dampened discontent,

---

[12] Dariusz Kołodziejczyk, *The Crimean Khanate and Poland-Lithuania* (Leiden, 2011), 9–11, 21–2; Halperin, *Russia*, 59.

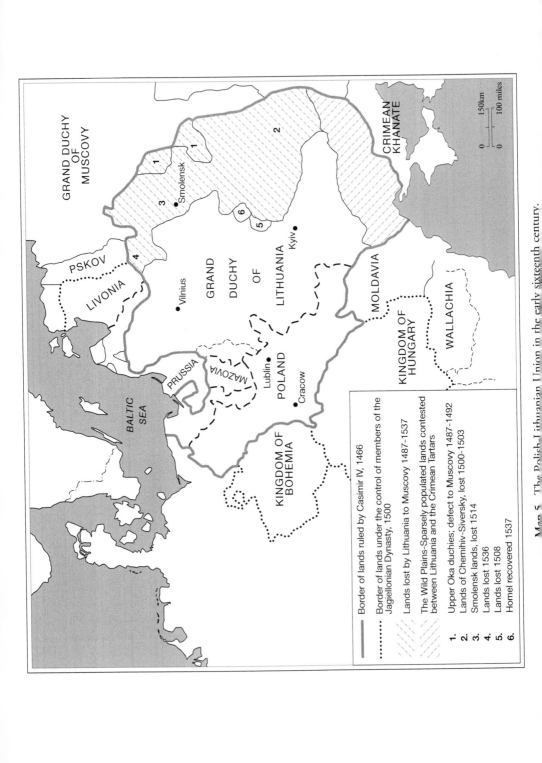

Map 5. The Polish-Lithuanian Union in the early sixteenth century.

there was another high-profile defection in 1487 when Ivan Vorotynsky recognized Ivan's suzerainty over his duchy of Peremyshl. Others followed: by Casimir's death in 1492, he had lost control of the duchies of Bely, Kozelsk, Vorotynsk, Seren, and Odoev (see Map 5).[13]

Ivan was ready. In the summer of 1492 he launched the first of a series of five wars (1492–94; 1500–3; 1507–8; 1512–22; 1534–7) that deprived Lithuania of one third of its territory. In January 1493 he used the title of lord of all Rus′ (*государъ всея Руси*) for the first time in diplomatic correspondence with Lithuania, thereby asserting that the Orthodox Rurikids, not the Catholic Jagiellons, were the true inheritors of the political tradition of Kievan Rus′. It was peremptorily dismissed by the Lithuanian council, but the claim symbolized a new era in the struggle for control of the Ruthenian lands.

The long cycle of wars against Muscovy altered the context of the Polish-Lithuanian union. Their impact on the process of union was profound. The end of the long period of peace which, for Lithuania—apart from the skirmishes with Muscovy in the 1440s—had lasted since the end of the Lithuanian civil war in 1437, and the darkening international context, stimulated profound political change. Poland-Lithuania's response of to the challenge demonstrated that the union rested on far firmer foundations than the flimsy dynastic system of 'Jagiellonian Europe', which proved to be no system at all. Dynastic ties were no basis for an effective political relationship, and despite the claims that Poland and Lithuania were united by no more than a dynastic union after the separate elections in 1492 of Alexander as grand duke of Lithuania and John Albert as king of Poland, events were to demonstrate that the Poles and Lithuanians were bound by far more than dynastic ties, and that the majority among the Ruthenian elites were more attracted by the political liberties they had secured in the 1430s than by the prospect of rule by the Orthodox princes of Muscovy. The process of union was still very much alive.

---

[13] Łowmiański, *Poliytka*, 401–2; Błaszczyk, *Litwa*, 21–3.

25

From Sejmiks to Sejm

Casimir was a shrewd politician who governed with considerable authority after subduing early opposition in Poland and extending control over the royal council. Yet if he demonstrated that government could be conducted in a highly effective manner in peacetime, the reigns of his immediate two successors showed that his system was inadequate in time of war. After 1492, the Ottoman empire, the Crimean Tatars, and a revitalized Muscovy provided far greater challenges than the impoverished and declining Order had been capable of mounting between 1454 and 1466. The challenges faced after 1492 were of a different order of magnitude. In Poland they stimulated the emergence of parliamentary monarchy; in Lithuania they unleashed a series of developments that culminated in the radical reshaping of the union between 1499 and 1569.

In Poland, the most radical change was the emergence of the sejm (diet) as the cornerstone of the political system as a consequence of the problems posed by the Nieszawa privileges, and the need to mobilize resources for war. Although 1493 was traditionally seen as the date at which the Polish sejm was established in the form that survived to the partitions, general assemblies had been a feature of Polish political life since the fourteenth century, when they were used by Łokietek and Casimir III to confirm important council decisions, although Casimir viewed them with distaste and rarely called them.[1] Two key moments embedded general assemblies in Polish political culture: the 1374 Koszyce privileges, which ensured that the monarchy would have to seek noble consent for taxes beyond the annual *poradlne*, and the 1382–4 interregnum, when general assemblies representing the citizen body—the community of the realm—determined the succession. The increased frequency of general assemblies, however, did not eclipse the provincial and local assemblies that had played a considerable role in political life during the fragmentation of the Polish kingdom between 1138 and 1320. The nature of the relationship between local, provincial, and general assemblies is unclear. Some scholars favour an evolutionary position, arguing that the sejm developed organically out of these local assemblies; others follow Kutrzeba in dating the sejm's definitive establishment to its 1493 institutionalization as a bicameral body comprising an upper chamber formed by the council, which came to be known

---

[1] Łokietek called assemblies in 1306, 1318, 1330, and 1331: Bardach, *Historia*, i, 442–3.

as the senate, and the chamber of envoys, composed of delegates (*posłowie* in Polish, *nuntii* in Latin) from the sejmiks.[2]

That the practice of calling general assemblies was embedded in Polish political culture by 1493 is clear, but there was no standard format or procedure laid down, and although historians—and the sources—use the term 'sejm' when referring to them, to avoid confusion there is much to be said for Kutrzeba's insistence on only applying the term to the institution that developed after 1493.[3] To do otherwise leads to confusion, as the term 'sejm' was previously applied to very different types of assembly. There was no fixed membership of what were called general assemblies (*conventiones generales*), a term that was sometimes applied to what were effectively meetings of the wider royal council without szlachta representatives. Whoever attended, the core of general assemblies before 1493 was formed by the council, comprising the highest lay and ecclesiastical dignitaries: the Catholic bishops, government ministers—in particular the chancellor, vice-chancellor, marshal, and treasurer—and palatines and castellans, the leading royal officials in the provinces, although other dignitaries could attend if invited by the king, and by no means all of those entitled to attend did so.[4]

It was on this as yet ill-defined body that the Polish tradition of consensual politics originally rested. Documents were issued '*de consilio*' or '*de consilio et consensu praelatorum et baronum*'; this phrase usually referred to the council rather than some proto-parliament. Casimir was clear on the council's role, stressing that he had chosen it to advise him above all; its duty to advise the 'country'—that is the community of the realm—was of secondary importance, and he specifically excluded the 'commonality' (*pospólstwo*) from council debates.[5] From around 1400, however, occasions when members of the wider political community were summoned to what were called a 'great' or 'solemn' assembly' (*conventio magna*; *conventio solemna*) a 'general parliament' (*parlamentum generalis*) or simply a 'general assembly' (*conventio generalis*), became more frequent. Although in theory any member of the community of the realm could attend such assemblies—and many did—these were not true parliamentary bodies: decisions were taken by the council and then presented to the assembled masses outside for acclamation, to ensure the maintenance of the public concord and harmony that were so highly prized. They could meet without the king's presence, as in 1423 in Warta, where the assembly agreed the controversial Warta statute, and during Władysław III's minority, his absence in Hungary, and the interregnum after his death. Thirteen general assemblies were held during his short reign; only in 1438 did he attend.[6]

After 1454 when, as a consequence of Nieszawa, sejmiks met more frequently, support grew for the idea that they should send delegates to participate in general

---

[2] Kutrzeba, *Korona*, 117–18. For introductions to the debate see Bardach, 'Początki', 10–13; Wojciech Kriegseisen, *Sejm Rzeczypospolitej szlacheckiej (do 1763 roku)* (Warsaw, 1995), 15–18.
[3] For an alternative view see Bardach, *Historia*, i, 446.
[4] Jerzy Wyrozumski, 'Geneza senatu w Polsce', in Krystyn Matwijowski and Jerzy Pietrzak (eds), *Senat w Polsce* (Warsaw, 1993), 26–8.
[5] Górski, 'Rządy', 102–3.
[6] Wojciech Fałkowski, 'Sejmy bez króla (1440–1446)', in Smołucha et al. (eds), *Historia*, 235–55.

assemblies, who would be accorded a voice in their proceedings. Forced to raise extraordinary taxes for the Thirteen Years' War, Casimir called general assemblies that were in effect meetings of his council, but their decisions were not seen as binding on the districts until ratified by the provincial sejmiks.[7] Although the system emerged without any clear or consistent lead from the government, it developed a logic of its own. In order to avoid endless negotiation with the large numbers of district sejmiks—known as *conventiones particulares*—the lead was increasingly taken by provincial sejmiks; these were also called *conventiones generales*.[8] Wielkopolska's provincial sejmik met at Koło. It comprised delegates from the palatinates of Poznań and Kalisz—which had a joint sejmik held in Środa—of Sieradz and Łęczyca, which had their own sejmiks, and of Inowrocław and Brześć Kujawski—which also had a joint sejmik that met at Brześć, and, in the sixteenth century, at Radziejów. The provincial sejmik was also attended by szlachta from the territory of Dobrzyń. There were no district sejmiks as yet in Małopolska, whose provincial sejmik, for the palatinates of Cracow, Sandomierz, and Lublin, met at Korczyn or Wiślica; it also contained delegates from the district sejmiks of the Ruthenian palatinate, whose separate general assembly sometimes met at Wiszna.[9]

Casimir encouraged the development of provincial sejmiks. He saw them, especially in his early years, as a means of appealing to the ordinary nobility over the heads of the council, which he was struggling to control. He used his powers of appointment to build up a core of royal supporters at the local level, but sejmiks could cause difficulties, as in 1455, when a general assembly—effectively the council—agreed to taxation for the Prussian war that was accepted by the Wielkopolskan provincial sejmik but rejected by its Małopolskan counterpart, which was only persuaded to change its mind after long negotiations. A decision was taken at a general assembly in 1456 to formalize procedure: henceforth extraordinary taxation needed to be explicitly accepted by the community of citizens (*a communitatibus*) as represented in the provincial assemblies at Korczyn and Koło; the demands of the Prussian war meant that this procedure rapidly became institutionalized, and was followed in 1457, 1458, 1459, 1464, 1468, and 1472.[10] As Casimir's control of his council strengthened, however, the sejmiks developed mechanisms to consult and coordinate responses to royal initiatives: in 1489, for example, the Koło sejmik sent fourteen delegates to Korczyn to agree a common position on proposed legislation. Aware of the dangers of separate meetings, which might enable the king to divide and rule, provincial sejmiks began accepting royal proposals on condition that they were agreed by other sejmiks.[11]

---

[7] Knoppek, 'Zmiany', 69–70; Bardach, 'Początki', 37.
[8] National assemblies were termed *conventiones generales totius Regni* to distinguish them from provincial assemblies: Bardach, *Historia*, i, 443.
[9] Bardach, 'Początki', 35; Bardach, *Historia*, i, 447–8; Wacław Uruszczak, 'Sejm w latach 1506–1540', in *Historia sejmu*, i, 67.
[10] Bardach, 'Początki', 37–8.
[11] Knoppek, 'Zmiany', 70; Bardach, 'Początki', 38–9.

As the district and provincial sejmiks developed after 1454, general assemblies, dominated by the council, seemed increasingly anomalous, and szlachta resentment at their effective exclusion from the key debates grew. At a general assembly in Sieradz in 1452, szlachta envoys howled down debate, attacking the council for its tepid conduct of public affairs. Casimir had to continue discussions with eight members of the council behind closed doors.[12] Such tactics might secure the decision he desired, but they were dangerous. Precedents existed for a more formal approach to debate, based on the election of representatives or delegates charged with giving voice to the ordinary nobility. Not all of them were helpful: in 1424 a general assembly at Wiślica summoned two representatives of each heraldic clan, but this harked back to an older form of social organization that was rapidly being supplanted by the idea of the community of citizens that formed the *respublica*, and it was not repeated: delegates from local sejmiks were summoned to the 1434 election assembly after Jagiełło's death.[13] In 1453, at the tense general assembly that sought to persuade Casimir to confirm past privileges and to recognize Lithuania's incorporation, the assembly divided into two chambers to debate 'that which might more easily and in a mature manner lead to the stabilization of the kingdom'.[14] Knoppek sees this as the definitive birth of the bicameral principle in the Polish parliament, but that is to read too much into what was an isolated occurrence. Nevertheless, as the practice of sending delegates to other provincial sejmiks flourished, and as Casimir's control over the council strengthened—thereby enhancing his ability to secure what he desired—the provincial sejmiks increasingly avoided taking separate decisions, preferring to coordinate their stance at a general assembly: in 1468, the general sejmik of Małopolska took no decisions at all, preferring to await discussions at a general assembly in Piotrków, at which two delegates of each district would be present, although it is probably premature to designate the 1468 Piotrków assembly as the first 'formal bicameral sejm', as Knoppek does.[15] As the provincial sejmiks became better at coordinating their response to royal initiatives, Casimir adopted a different strategy, appealing directly to the district sejmiks, where the majesty of the royal name, and the practical direction of the local starosta could often secure the consent he sought. Such meetings of district sejmiks—called *convencio particularis Regiae Majestas* or *convencio particularis regalis*—became regular occurrences after 1470: between 1476 and 1480 they met on eleven occasions in the Łęczyca palatinate alone.[16]

In the peaceful years after 1466 these methods worked well enough. They were to prove insufficient in the years of war after 1492, when the royal government sought high levels of taxation to raise troops for the Ottoman war, and to support Lithuania against Muscovy. It was therefore during the reigns of John Albert and Alexander that the sejm acquired its definitive institutional form. The first general

---

[12] 'quod tepide rempublicam administrarent': *Annales*, xii/i, 136.
[13] Bardach, *Historia*, i, 445; Kriegseisen, *Sejm*, 17.
[14] 'Consilio bipartito, quo facilier maturiorque ederetur pro stabilimento regni in tam difficili eventu provisio': *Annales*, xii, 163.
[15] Knoppek, 'Zmiany' 79, 89–90; for a critique of this view see Górski, 'Rządy', 110.
[16] Bardach, 'Początki', 39.

assembly of John Albert's reign, at Piotrków from 27 February to 3 March 1493, was prepared carefully. The king attended the Małopolskan sejmik at Korczyn, where he received several petitions. At Piotrków he confirmed privileges granted by his predecessors—some of them only for three years—and in return received a substantial grant of taxes.[17] This assembly, however, has passed into history for another reason, as the occasion on which the bicameral sejm became established. It was preceded by meetings of the sejmiks, whose delegates, when they arrived in Piotrków, met and debated separately from the council, in a pattern that rapidly became the norm.

It is only with hindsight that 1493 has been accorded the aura of historical immortality, and too much emphasis is sometimes placed on its significance: general assemblies had occasionally separated into two chambers since the early 1450s, and no legislation was ever passed requiring the calling of a two-chamber assembly, or to define the membership or means of electing the chamber of envoys. There is no sign that the szlachta, or anyone else realized that they had crossed the Rubicon; although the general assemblies of 1496, 1498, 1501, 1503, and 1504 (all in Piotrków), 1502 (in Cracow), and 1503 (in Lublin) were all bicameral assemblies preceded by meetings of the sejmiks, other meetings termed 'general assemblies' in Radom in September 1494 and in Cracow in 1499 were essentially council meetings, while the assembly that elected Alexander in Piotrków in September 1501—managed with such aplomb by Cardinal Frederick—took place according to the traditional procedure, in which the council debated and communicated its decision to the assembled szlachta, who were not delegates of sejmiks.[18] Yet by 1501 such procedures were looking antiquated. At the 1496 Piotrków sejm John Albert, desperate to secure funding for his Moldavian campaign, issued his general privilege consolidating the separate agreements with the various provinces in 1454 into a statute that covered the whole kingdom, thereby strengthening the institutional and legal foundations for the sejm, and for the participation of the ordinary nobility in the political system.[19] Their position was only secured, however, by the political battles surrounding Alexander's election, which opened a new era in Poland's parliamentary history and demonstrated that Lithuania had changed considerably since 1447.

---

[17] Papée, *Jan Olbracht*, 44–6; Andrzej Szymanek (ed.), *Nihil Novi: Z dorobku sejmu radomskiego 1505 roku* (Radom, 2005), 23–4.
[18] Szymanek, *Nihil novi*, 24–8.
[19] Julia Dücker, '*Pro communi reipublicae bona*: König und Reich im jagiellonischen Polen um 1500', in Florian Ardelean, Christopher Nicholson, and Johannes Preiseur-Kappeler (eds), *Between Worlds: The Age of the Jagiellons* (Frankfurt am Main, 2013), 68–9.

26

Shliakhta

At Vytautas's death in 1430 the grand duchy covered 1,000,000 km², with a population of up to 3,500,000. The losses to Muscovy between 1492 and 1514 reduced its territory by just under a third to around 700,000 km². The fall in population by just over a fifth was not so drastic, as these lands were relatively sparsely populated. By 1528 the population was some 2,700,000, reaching 3,500,000 again in 1569.[1] Two long periods of peace between 1435 and 1492, and between 1522 and 1558, broken only by the Muscovite wars between 1533 and 1537, brought rising prosperity. The Order's eclipse opened up the rivers that flowed out of Lithuania into the Baltic just as Europe began its recovery from demographic and economic stagnation. Lithuania was well placed to meet the growing demand—gradual at first but rapidly escalating after 1500—for grain, timber, tar, and other forest products. Colonization took place in the borderlands to the west, depopulated by mutual devastation during the wars against the Order, and in the vast, empty forests that covered so much of Lithuania. As demand from western Europe grew, control and ownership of land became increasingly important for the grand duchy's elites.

The century after the union with Poland saw a fundamental transformation of these elites and a substantial process of social differentiation within them. The Horodło system was formed by Vytautas's vision of a composite state in which Lithuania proper would dominate the grand duchy as a whole, with the most important local offices in the new palatinates of Vilnius and Trakai, and central offices in the chancery limited to Catholics, and therefore overwhelmingly to nobles of Lithuanian origin, while the annexed Ruthenian territories would have substantial control of their own affairs, albeit often under the oversight of Lithuanian Catholic governors. This system came under considerable strain in the 1430s, which saw the crucial concession of social and economic privileges to Ruthenian nobles across the grand duchy. This development, while it left central control firmly in the hands of Lithuanian Catholics, opened the door to the creation of a more coherent Lithuanian-Ruthenian elite that gradually united round the concept of noble liberty enshrined in the privileges of 1387, 1413, and 1434. While this ideal of liberty was strongly influenced by the Polish model, it was adapted to the very

---

[1] Gudavičius, *Lietuvos istorija*, i, 383; Henryk Łowmiański, *Zaludnienie państwa litewskiego w wieku XVI* (Poznań, 1998), 210, 221–2. Niendorf, citing Gudavičius, suggests an area of 500,000–520,000 km² following the losses to Muscovy, although this is not the figure the latter gives, substantially exaggerating the extent of the losses: Niendorf, *Großfürstentum*, 24.

different conditions of the grand duchy, most notably through accommodation of religious diversity: the partial undermining of the grand duchy's composite nature in this period was largely due to the way in which the Ruthenian elites challenged the Horodło system, yet sought a place within it.

Vytautas's policies ensured that this new elite was shaped and differentiated internally by office and service to the grand duke, and by the landed wealth that this service conferred upon those who shouldered its burdens. The first step in its construction was Vytautas's attack on the princely appanages, which marked an assault on the cognatic family structures that had traditionally regulated the inheritance of land and the distribution of political power in both the Lithuanian and Ruthenian traditions. Yet this assault was limited, and did not affect all of the grand duchy's princely class. It was aimed above all at the Gediminid princes, those close family members who might threaten the new order through the Gediminid vision of the grand duchy as the possession of the ruling dynasty as a whole, not of the grand duke alone.

In 1386 there were members of twenty princely families in Jagiełło's retinue, out of some eighty princely families in total. Under Vytautas the princes, almost all of whom were Orthodox, faced increasing pressure on their privileged status.[2] The princes were badly hit in the civil wars. Representatives of 42 princely families supported Švitrigaila, suffering grievous losses in the battle of Šventoji (1435), where 13 princes were killed and 42 captured. Žygimantas targeted Švitrigaila's princely supporters, with families such as the Sangushko, Horodetsky, Pinsky, Polubensky, and Kroshynsky losing their appanages. This heralded a general assault on the remaining privileges attached to appanages, a factor that influenced the princes among the plotters who assassinated Žygimantas in 1440.[3]

Although historians occasionally talk of the princes as a separate estate, the sources reveal no such thing: they were a diverse group, united only by their possession of their inherited titles.[4] There were few privileges extended to them collectively, and the grand duchy's composite nature meant that there were no fora in which they could appear politically as a united group. They varied greatly in the privileges they enjoyed, from the appanage dukes at the top, to the 'service princes' (князя службовіе; князя служилые), who held their land on service tenure from the grand duke or another prince, at the bottom.

Of these 80 princely families, 52 have been identified for Volhynia, the grand duchy's princely heartland, which was markedly different in its social composition to the rest of the Ruthenian lands, let alone to Lithuania proper, where there were few princes.[5] At the top was a small group of wealthy families, mostly of Gediminid or Rurikid descent. Vytautas had not destroyed all the appanages: the duchies of Kobryn (to 1519); Pinsk, Kletsk, and Horodets (to 1524); Mstislau (to 1529); and Slutsk (to 1592) all survived until the families that held them died out in the male

---

[2] Wolff, *Kniaziowie*, 20; Kamieniecki, *Społeczeństwo*, 23, 55, 56.
[3] Яковенко, *Шляхта*, 109; Любавский, *Сеймъ*, 90; Wolff, *Kniaziowie*, xix.
[4] Михаил Кром, *Меж Русью и Литвой*, 2nd edn (Moscow, 2010), 130.
[5] Korczak, *Monarchia*, 60; Кром, *Меж Русью*, 130; Яковенко, *Шляхта*, 90–1.

line, even if in the case of Kletsk, Pinsk, and Horodets, this was only because appanages that had been confiscated by Žygimantas were restored or granted to others by Casimir.[6] These restorations resulted from Casimir's desire to build support in the difficult early years of his reign and only affected a handful of families. The princes did not, collectively, constitute an independent political force.

Casimir's increasing authority is demonstrated by his treatment of Kyiv, the greatest appanage duchy of them all, and the only one with the potential to mount a challenge to rule from Vilnius. It was stripped from Jagiełło's older half-brother Volodymyr in 1394 to be conferred on Skirgaila; after his death it was not returned to Volodymyr, but was granted in 1396 to Ivan Holshansky, one of Vytautas's closest supporters, though as governor, not duke. After Ivan's death in 1401 or shortly thereafter, the governorship was held by his son Mykhailo. Kyiv's faded glamour still hung around the city's decaying walls, however, and the extent to which the Holshansky accepted their position as mere governors is open to question: the marriage of Mykhailo's niece Vasylia to Ivan, Volodymyr's second son, suggests a desire to lay claim to Kyiv's historical legacy; Volodymyr's elder son Olelko married Anastasia, Vasilii I's daughter, in 1417, another equally suggestive match, although it came with Vytautas's approval: if he was wary of granting authority to powerful Gediminid princes, he was willing to pay tribute to their status so long as they remained loyal.[7]

These claims were not forgotten. Both Mykhailo Holshansky and Olelko Volodymyrovych supported Švitrigaila, although Olelko, his brother Ivan, Semen Holshansky, and Fëdor Korybutovych, defected to Žygimantas on the outbreak of civil war. Olelko offered Žygimantas loyal support, which did not save him from being imprisoned shortly before the ungrateful Žygimantas's murder. By opting for Žygimantas, Olelko showed that he was loyal to the wider grand duchy and the union. In 1440, he was one of the first to declare for Casimir. His reward was substantial: shortly thereafter Casimir granted him Kyiv, specifically referring to the return of his patrimony.[8] This was a shrewd gesture to the Ruthenian elites, many of whom had supported Švitrigaila, and some of whom may have supported Olelko as a candidate for grand duke in 1440.[9] Olelko loyally served Casimir until his death in 1454, at which point Kyiv passed to his son, Semën, despite the fact that Semën—who was married to the daughter of Jonas Goštautas, by then leader of the

---

[6] Kamieniecki, *Społeczeństwo*, 51, 52.
[7] Русина, *Україна*, 123; Wolff, *Kniaziowie*, 95–6, 327.
[8] Грушевський, *Історія*, iv, 199, 204, 216, 234–5; Русина, *Україна*, 123. Magocsi—who gives the wrong date for Vytautas's death—mistakenly suggests that all the former Ruthenian principalities were restored 'for a time' in 1440: Paul Magocsi, *A History of Ukraine* (Toronto, 1996), 77–8, 133–4.
[9] The claim is made in Wolff, *Kniaziowie*, 328, and repeated in the entry on Olelko in the Polish biographical dictionary. Wolff cites Stryjkowski's sixteenth-century chronicle in support, but Stryjkowski, though he lists Švitrigaila and Žygimantas's son Mykolas as candidates, does not actually mention Olelko: Maciej Stryjkowski, *O początkach, wywodach, dzielnościach, sprawach rycerskich i domowych sławetnego narodu litewskiego, żemojdzkiego i ruskiego*, ed. Julia Radziszewska (Warsaw, 1978), 422. For Wolff's misreading of the sources for Olelko's life, see Грушевський, *Історія*, iv, 234, n. 3.

Lithuanian opposition to Casimir—was a popular candidate among those urging Casimir to return to the Vytautan model and appoint a separate grand duke.[10]

Too much should not be read into this supposed restoration of the principality of Kyiv. Its return to Olelko and then Semën did not indicate that Casimir was loosening the ties of the annexed lands to the grand duchy. Semën on occasion styled himself 'grand duke of Kyiv' (князем великого князства своего Киевского) and stressed his hereditary rights to the duchy, but if Casimir did not interfere much in its internal affairs, there were distinct limits to its autonomy.[11] The grand duchy may have been a composite state, but it was a state nonetheless, in which Casimir felt free to dispose of its component parts as he wished. The grant of Kyiv to Olelko was for his life only, and although Casimir then bestowed it upon Semën, he prevented him dividing it with his brother Mykhailo in 1455. On Semën's death in 1470 Casimir refused to sanction its inheritance by Mykhailo, who scurried back expectantly from his post as governor of Novgorod. Instead Casimir appointed a Catholic Lithuanian governor, Martynas Goštautas, in 1471. Goštautas may have been Semën's brother-in-law, but the appointment of Kyiv's first Catholic governor gave a clear message. Kyiv was given a new set of privileges to recognize its status and to buy off Olelkovych supporters, but the centre had reasserted its power within the composite state, and the term 'grand duke of Kyiv' began to appear in Casimir's titles.[12] Kyiv was never to return to Olelkovych hands. Semën's widow, his son Vasyl, and his two daughters were granted the duchy of Pinsk, which lacked Kyiv's historic lustre.[13] The treatment of the Olelkovych was consistent with Casimir's general challenge to the collateral system of princely succession: although he was willing to allow inheritance, he did not regard it as automatic, and he assiduously asserted his rights to gather in principalities when families died out in the male line, ignoring the claims of collateral branches, and limiting the rights of their holders.[14] Although there was some discontent when Goštautas arrived in Kyiv to take up his governorship, it soon dissipated and he held the post until 1480.

The lack of serious resistance to the liquidation of the appanage duchies is striking.[15] It is important not to ascribe to Casimir's reign the attitudes of chronicles written later, when some among the Ruthenian elites were projecting their own sense of the past onto the fifteenth century and constructing a narrative of continuity between Kievan Rus' and their own day. There was no chronicler active in fifteenth-century Kyiv, and the contemporary Ruthenian chronicles were composed in Smolensk.[16] There is no contemporary evidence that the Olelkovych

---

[10] Русина, *Україна*, 127–8; Грушевський, *Історія*, iv, 247. Semën's name was again put forward in 1461: Грушевський, *Історія*, iv, 249.
[11] Русина, *Україна*, 128; Korczak, *Monarchia*, 53.
[12] Kamieniecki, *Społeczeństwo*, 20.
[13] Яковенко, *Шляхта*, 105; Pietkiewicz, *Wielkie księstwo*, 103; Wolff, *Kniaziowie*, 330; Łowmiański, *Poliytka*, 232.
[14] Wolff, *Kniaziowie*, xix–xx; Кром, *Меж Русью*, 121–2.
[15] Korczak, *Monarchia*, 57; Грушевський, *Історія*, iv, 268.
[16] Jablonowski, *Westrußland*, 71.

princes were the focus for Ruthenian patriotic feeling, while the absence of any attempt to construct it after their restoration in 1440 suggests that there was little enthusiasm for a challenge to Casimir.

The Kievan tradition revived later, in a very different context, but in the Casimir's reign it was too poorly developed to provide any basis for a challenge to grand ducal power. Kyiv itself had never properly recovered from devastation by the Mongols. Its metropolitans kept the title, but had long departed, and if they did visit Kyiv in the fifteenth century, they mostly resided elsewhere. The southern Ruthenian lands remained relatively sparsely populated. They were far from western European markets, while the onset of regular Tatar raids from the 1480s hampered the weak economic recovery seen earlier in Casimir's reign. There were more congenial parts of the grand duchy for colonists to settle than a region where the dangers of being carted off to the slave markets of Istanbul remained high deep into the seventeenth century.[17]

Thus when, after his failure to secure what he regarded as his patrimony, the disgruntled Mykhailo Olelkovych, together with Fëdor Belsky—another grandson of Volodymyr Olherdovych—and prince Ivan Holshansky hatched a plot to assassinate Casimir during a visit to Lithuania in 1481, it failed dismally. Probably encouraged by Ivan III it was supported largely by Mykhailo's relatives and clients, and by a scattering of disgruntled Lithuanian nobles.[18] Casimir removed Goštautas as governor of Kyiv, appointing him palatine of Trakai, and replacing him with the Orthodox Ruthenian Ivan Khodkevych. Mykhailo had no military force to back up his cack-handed coup, which Khodkevych crushed. The conspirators were tried and condemned to death. Belsky escaped to Moscow; Mykhailo was executed, although his widow was prudently left in place in Slutsk.[19] Khodkevych's actions—and, indeed, his appointment—casts doubt on Hrushevsky's presentation of these events, in which he uncharacteristically follows Długosz and the sixteenth-century Muscovite chronicles uncritically, to back his claim that the Lithuanians now felt able to ignore the Ruthenian element in the grand duchy, and that they sought to rule 'not only without the Ruthenians, but against them'.[20]

Mykhailo Olelkovych's execution marked the end of an era. Švitrigaila had died without issue in 1452; with the re-establishment of direct control over the duchy of Kyiv, there were no serious rivals to the Jagiellons. On Casimir's death in 1492, the only questions were which of Casimir's sons should succeed him as king of Poland, and whether the Vytautan system should be restored, a question answered positively in 1492 with Alexander's elevation, but negatively in 1501, when Alexander declined to allow Sigismund to become grand duke after he ascended the Polish

---

[17] Hrushevsky, *History*, vi, 4–6. [18] Halecki, *Dzieje*, i, 426–7.

[19] Anna Krupska, 'W sprawie genezy tzw. spisku książąt litewskich w 1480–1481 roku. Przyczynek do dziejów walki o *"dominium Russiae"*', *RH*, 48 (1982), 120–46; Кром, *Меж Русью*, 67–8; Halecki, *Dzieje*, i, 429.

[20] Грушевський, *Історія*, iv, 268–73. Hrushevsky makes much of a 1567 letter of Belsky's descendant Ivan to Khodkevych's descendant Jan Chodkiewicz, in which Ivan accuses Khodkevych of betraying Mykhailo, that says more about the 1560s than it does about the 1480s.

throne. A brief flirtation with the idea of granting him Kyiv—Sigismund was understandably keen—came to nothing.

The remaining princes were no political threat. In 1499 Alexander felt secure enough to issue a comprehensive series of privileges regulating the remaining appanage duchies and defining their relationship to the centre. If the privilege for Mstislau granted its 'full rights and lordships' (*со всимъ правомъ и панствомъ*) to its Gediminid prince, Mykhailo Ivanovych Zaslavsky, other grants were less generous. The privileges recognized the *ius ducale* of the princes, which included some judicial powers over local boyars and nobles, but there was no recognition of any wider political claims.[21]

While these privileges were issued against the background of the Muscovite wars and the territorial losses and defections of the 1490s, they display Alexander's confidence that he was not thereby risking Jagiellon power.[22] Apart from a small group at the top, the majority of the princely class had fared badly, not so much because of the actions of Vytautas or his successors, but as a result of the remorseless logic of collateral inheritance. Many families saw their prosperity decline or collapse with the passing of the generations, as uncles and cousins divided, subdivided, and redivided the family patrimony, with each trying to cling on to the social status and title of their father without the means to sustain it. For the more fecund, the decline could be precipitous: such were the Mezetsky in the eastern borderlands, or the Lithuanian Sviriškis, some of whom abandoned their princely titles, as did one branch of the Masalsky which, with the exception of one member, lost its princely status, sinking to the level of service boyars after producing fourteen male descendants in the fourth generation from its protoplast, Sviatoslav Tytovych.[23]

The loss of the loosely attached borderlands has deflected attention away from the substantial consolidation of Jagiellon rule that had taken place by 1500. Alexander could afford his gestures to a handful of the remaining princes because their principalities were small and relatively insignificant, and princely power within the annexed territories was no longer a threat. By 1499 successive grand dukes had proven highly effective at keeping the grand duchy together despite its composite nature. They dealt far more successfully than the rulers of Kievan Rus' or the Piast dynasty in Poland between 1138 and 1320 in overcoming the problems posed by appanages.[24] When Sigismund succeeded Alexander in 1506, Lithuania may still have been a composite state, but the Gediminid dynastic condominium was no more; the Jagiellons had built shrewdly on the foundations laid by Vytautas.

This success was in large part due to the social change that followed the union with Poland, in part stimulated and encouraged by grand ducal policies, but which soon developed a momentum of its own. Gradually a new noble elite emerged that

---

[21] Pietkiewicz, *Wielkie księstwo*, 107–8; Кром, *Меж Русью*, 120–1; Яковенко, *Шляхта*, 65–6.

[22] Backus misunderstands them, arguing that their limited nature was a motive for the flight of border princes into Muscovite service: Oswald Backus, *Motives of West Russian Nobles in Deserting Lithuania for Moscow 1377–1514* (Lawrence, KS, 1957), 18–23; see Pietkiewicz, *Wielkie księstwo*, 107–8.

[23] Кром, *Меж Русью*, 58–9, 61–4; Pietkiewicz, *Wielkie księstwo*, 94–5.

[24] Korczak, *Monarchia*, 55–6.

was a fusion—though by no means a complete one—of the Lithuanian and Ruthenian boyar elites. It was a process in which Polish examples were of considerable influence, and increasingly so after 1492, but it was essentially shaped by social and political developments within the grand duchy. For if Petrauskas is right to emphasize that the elite that came to be socially dominant and to play an increasing role in Lithuania's government in the fifteenth century already existed in 1386, there is no doubt that its nature and position changed dramatically in the century and a half that followed.[25]

The transformation was a complex process. The privileges of 1387 and 1413 did not create the Lithuanian boyar elite, but they did much to shape its development, even if it was a long time before their full effects became clear. By giving legal security of tenure to holders of allodial land, and recognizing in law the rights of landowners to pass on their estates, the privileges launched the process in which the grand duchy's elites ceased to be essentially a military class, required to fight or provide soldiers for the grand duke—or their appanage prince—in return for service tenures on their estates, to a class whose control of the land was based on legally defensible rights of tenure. Although their military obligation remained, many of the duties surrounding it, such as the requirement to maintain castles, were stripped away.

While the legal rights these privileges bestowed were important, their influence should not be overstated. Allodial tenure did not arrive in the grand duchy in 1387. It was known in written Ruthenian law, and therefore the initial failure to extend the privileges to the grand duchy's Ruthenian areas was not as significant as is sometimes suggested. It was also known in the Baltic, Lithuanian tradition, albeit as part of customary, unwritten law, and was by no means a novelty in 1387.[26] Although allodial land existed, it was not yet particularly widespread. The privileges increased the attraction of holding allodial rather than service land, since they gave legal guarantees that it could be passed on to the next generation without interference from the grand duke. The improved legal protection of the right to bequeath land to one's heirs lay behind one of the most significant changes of the fifteenth century: the breaking of the system of cognatic inheritance, which saw estates as the possession of an extended kinship group that had to be consulted over their disposal, in favour of an agnatic system, in which estates descended vertically to the children of their holder. This made it easier for grand dukes to exercise their right to secure the lands of noble families that died out in the male line against the claims of collateral branches.[27] Since the trend towards agnatic inheritance was not accompanied by any move towards primogeniture, subdivision still took place, but its worst effects had, by 1500, been substantially mitigated. The extended kinship groups were, in the absence of written genealogies, relatively loose systems whose

---

[25] Rimvydas Petrauskas, 'Vytauto laikų didikų kilmė', *Lituanistica*, 1/2 (41/42) (2000), 16–31; Łowmiański, *Studia*, 367–8, 386–403. For an English overview of Petrauskas's important arguments, see: Rimvydas Petrauskas 'The Lithuanian nobility in the late fourteenth and fifteenth centuries: Composition and structure', *LHS*, 7 (2002), 1–22.

[26] Łowmiański, *Studia*, 148; Gudavičius, 'Baltų alodo pavbeldėjimas', 100–11.

[27] Łowmiański, *Studia*, 236, 239.

composition tended to reform itself with the passing of the generations. In the fifteenth century, as the landholdings of the leading boyars grew, and as the protection for allods was strengthened, these loose kinship clans were steadily eroded in favour of a more nucleated family structure, except in the Kaunas district and much of Samogitia, where the petty nobility were dominant and, as the 1567 military register demonstrates, petty boyars were still organized in clans for military purposes.[28] Elsewhere, in the decades after 1413, the decay of the clan system and the trend towards agnatic inheritance was emphasized by the gradual adoption of patronymics—in imitation of the Ruthenian tradition—and, towards the end of the century, by the spread of the surnames that made the construction of more accurate genealogies possible.[29]

The greatest beneficiaries were members of a non-princely elite among the newly Catholic, Lithuanian boyars that already existed in 1385, but whose position was strengthened under Vytautas. These were Vytautas's men: the forty-seven Catholic Lithuanian families he selected for the Horodło adoption. Its significance should not be overemphasized: few of the forty-seven fully adopted their new coats of arms with their Latin mottos; others adapted them by replacing the Latin with Ruthenian, while some were to reject them altogether at moments of tension between the grand duchy and Poland in the 1430s and 1450s.[30] Nevertheless, if links with their Polish heraldic clans were initially minimal, the entry of these families into a symbolic, cultural community, with its own name, its own coat of arms, and its own mythological history, gradually formed a new matrix of social relationships in which the importance of kinship was diminished. Between 1413 and 1569 the men who ran Lithuania were almost entirely drawn from these forty-seven families.

Thus if Horodło created neither the Lithuanian boyar estate nor the elite that developed within it, it established a framework for the stratification and diversification of the grand duchy's large boyar class. Under Vytautas, the documents began distinguishing between this group at the top and the boyar masses, using terms such as *baro* or *baronis*; *dominus*, *domini*, 'great boyars' (бояре великіе), and, increasingly, the term 'lord', using a word borrowed from Polish (*пан*; *pan*). In the Horodło adoption the Polish szlachta addressed the Lithuanian 'boyars and nobles' (*barones et nobiles terrarum Lithuaniae*), and the Lithuanians referred to themselves as *nobiles, boyares ac proceres*; the term *pan* and its plural, *pany*, soon became established Lithuanian usage.[31] By Casimir's reign documents referred to 'the princes and lords' ahead of the general nobility; there is much in Jablonowski's suggestion that the gradual integration of the wealthier princes and the lords created a true aristocracy.[32] Documents now used the formula 'We, Casimir, by the grace

---

[28] Łowmiański, *Studia*, 191–210.

[29] Petrauskas, *Diduomenė*, 103–25; Rimvydas Petrauskas, 'XV amžiaus Lietuvos bajorijos struktūra: giminės problema', in Alfredas Bumblauskas and Rimvydas Petrauskas (eds), *Tarp istorijos* (Vilnius, 1999), 123–58.

[30] Petrauskas, *Diduomenė*, 49–50; Banionis, 'Lietuvos bajorai', 189–206.

[31] Jablonowski, *Westrußland*, 37; *AU*, no. 49, 53, 54; no. 50, 58. For Ruthenian usage of the term, see the decrees by Fëdor Lubartovych of 1421, 1428, and 1430: *AZR*, i, no. 30, 42–4, and the decree of 'Pan Stashek of Davydov' of 21 January 1421: *AZR*, i, no. 31, 45.

[32] Jablonowski, *Westrußland*, 37–8.

of God king of Poland and Lithuanian grand duke...with the lords of our council'.[33] These lords filled the new offices created at Horodło—the palatinates and castellans of Vilnius and Trakai—and by the expansion of Vytautas's system of government. It was they who served as governors, starostas, chancellors, and hetmans.

This new elite was not created by Vytautas through office, as Suchocki and other Polish historians have suggested: as Petrauskas convincingly demonstrates, they were drawn from the traditional local elites who had served Vytautas's predecessors, and they were already closely linked by kinship ties.[34] Nevertheless, Vytautas did much to shape the new elite after 1413. In many cases, some of the more local offices remained quasi-hereditary, though there were examples of outsiders who came to dominate local politics through grand ducal patronage, the most prominent being the Kęsgaila family, the descendants of Valimantas, one of Vytautas's earliest supporters, who witnessed the 1398 Salin treaty with the Order, who was possibly killed at the Vorskla, and who was certainly dead by 1412. His son, the Lithuanian marshal of the land, Rumbaudas Valimantaitis, was appointed starosta of Samogitia by Vytautas in 1409, holding the post for about a year; in 1412, his brother, Valimantaitis Kęsgaila succeeded him. Kęsgaila played an active role in Samogitia's christianization, bloodily crushing the 1418 Samogitian rising. Thus began over a century of domination by his descendants, whose rule was initially resented, as the family was not Samogitian, but came from near Ukmergė. Kęsgaila held the position until 1432; there followed a brief hiatus during the civil war, when Kęsgaila, together with Rumbaudas and another brother Jaunutis, palatine of Trakai, initially supported Švitrigaila. After going over to Žygimantas, Jaunutis's secret correspondence with Švitrigaila was intercepted, and he and Rumbaudas were executed. Kęsgaila avoided their fate thanks to Jagiełło's personal intervention, but he was dismissed as starosta, with Mykolas Kantautas appointed in his place. Samogitia, partly because of its resentment at Kęsgaila's rule, and partly because of its historical links with the Kęstutids, supported Žygimantas, and—after his assassination—his son Mykolas. Casimir's reappointment of Kęsgaila as starosta in 1440—probably at the behest of Jonas Goštautas who, along with Kęsgaila, had masterminded the 1440 election—was one of the causes of the 1441 Samogitian revolt. The Samogitians may have secured a new privilege in 1442 giving them the right to elect their starostas and the *tivuny*—the starosta's chief local officials—but Casimir insisted that Kęsgaila—whom he also appointed castellan of Vilnius—returned as starosta in 1443. He held the post until his death in 1450, when Casimir pushed through the succession of his son, Jonas Kęsgaila, despite strong support in Samogitia for Kantautas. This was the true start of Kęsgaila domination. Jonas ignored the 1442 privilege, and its requirement for the election of *tivuny*; he was starosta from 1450 until his death in 1485, when he was succeeded by his son Stanislovas, starosta until his death in 1527, who was succeeded by his son, also

---

[33] 'Казимиръ, Божею милостью король Польскій и великій князь Литовскій...съ паны радою нашою': *AZR*, i, no. 60, 72.
[34] Petrauskas, 'Vytauto laikų', 16–31.

Stanislovas, by which time the family had established itself as the wealthiest and most powerful among the Lithuanian *pany*. Stanislovas the elder was castellan of Trakai (1499–1522) and of Vilnius (1522–7); his son was castellan of Vilnius from 1528/9 until 1532. By this time, however, the Samogitian boyars were again restless, and the younger Stanislovas had to agree to considerable watering-down of the starosta's powers in the spirit of the 1442 privilege. His only son died in infancy, ending the long Kęsgaila control of Samogitia; before his death in 1532 he bequeathed one-third of his vast estates to Sigismund August.[35]

The career of the Kęsgaila was exceptional, but it demonstrates how it was possible for the new class of *pany* to benefit from grand ducal largesse in return for political support, while the fate of Rumbaudas and Jaunutis showed the importance of backing the right horse at the right time. Vytautas and his successors lavishly rewarded their supporters and servants; it was this generosity that underpinned the most dramatic of the many socio-economic changes that affected the grand duchy during the fifteenth century. Successive grand dukes distributed their patrimony on a colossal scale, largely among this narrow elite. While many of the grants, especially under Vytautas, were short-term leases tied to posts such as starosties that were frequently rotated, as time went on lengths of tenure increased, until it became normal to hold starosties for extended periods, and often for life. Important individuals received grand ducal villages and estates as outright gifts to be incorporated into their allodial holdings, either as a reward for long and loyal service, or in order to win their support for contentious measures. As individuals grew richer, grand dukes began to raise loans by mortgaging estates to lords; since they were often unable to repay the loans, many slipped out of their control.[36]

The results were dramatic. Extensive private landed estates were virtually unknown in the Lithuanian heartlands in 1386.[37] By the early sixteenth century a revolution in landholding had taken place. By now there were some 13,000 noble families in the grand duchy, of which around 6,000 (46 per cent) were Lithuanian in origin. In 1386, 80 per cent of the population lived on land directly under the rule of the grand duke; by the time of the great military register drawn up in 1528, this proportion had been reduced to 30 per cent. Five per cent was church land, therefore some 65 per cent of the grand duchy's land was now in noble hands, much of it controlled by the narrow group of families that constituted the new political elite.[38]

The 1528 register was prepared as part of a major transformation of Lithuania's military system. The losses sustained to Muscovy down to the fall of Smolensk in 1514 persuaded the Lithuanian council of the need to match the Muscovite

---

[35] Pietkiewicz, *Kieżgajłowie i ich latyfundium do połowy XVI wieku* (Poznań, 1982), 14, 19–20, 34–9, 42–5; Eugenijus Saviščevas, 'Kęsgailų Žemaitija. Kelios pastabos apie Kęsgailų valdymą Žemaitijoje (1442–1527)', *Lituanistica*, 58/2 (2004), 1–21; Rowell, 'Rusena karas', 5–16.
[36] For a note of caution on the scale of this alienation see Pietkiewicz, *Wielkie księstwo*, 150–1.
[37] Łowmiański, *Studia*, 274–81; Petrauskas, *Diduomenė*, 125.
[38] Łowmiański, *Studia*, 148; Ochmański, *Historia Litwy*, 100–1; Литовськая Метрика: Книги публичныхъ дел. Переписи войска Литовськая, Русская Историческая Библиотека 33 (St Petersburg, 1915).

pomest'e system through comprehensive reform. A 1502 statute stipulated that every noble landholder should raise one armed cavalryman from every ten service units when called upon. Registers were to be drawn up by local starostas or governors to ensure that nobles met their obligations.[39] According to a 1507 statute, each noble was to prepare a list of 'all his people' to be submitted under oath to the starosta or governor, who would determine his obligations. In 1521 Sigismund, concerned that not all had paid what they should in recent tax levies, ordered an inspection of the registers to discover who was in arrears. In a decree of May 1528 the extent of the burden was slightly increased, with one cavalryman to be provided from every eight service units, and commissions were established to investigate the registers drawn up by nobles, and to standardize the service unit (*служба/sluzhba*), an institution modelled on the *Dienste* system used by the Order.[40] The *sluzhba* was formed by grouping together peasant households—normally from two to four—and provided the basis for tax assessments and military service. Nobles had to provide cavalrymen according to the number of service units they held, and had to swear an oath to the accuracy of their declarations in the presence of the local priest.[41] Service was from all landed property, despite Loewe's attempt to show that allodial estates were exempt, which is based on questionable inferences drawn from the composition of the 1528 register and the wording of the 1529 statute rather than empirical research into landholding.[42]

By late 1528 the registers were in Vilnius ready for inspection. The local registers have not survived; what has is the protocol drafted by the chancery based upon them, which contains 19,842 individual names from 13,060 families across the grand duchy, though no data from Kyiv are included for reasons that remain obscure. The register details service obligations expressed in the number of fully equipped cavalrymen nobles were required to bring to musterings of the noble levy, known as the 'service of the land' (*земская служба*). The registers were used as the basis for local tax-collectors to check the declared size of landholdings and estates with the tax paid, to make adjustments for under-declaration, and to prosecute those seeking to avoid paying their taxes.[43]

Musterings were the responsibility of the local ensign (*khoruzhy*), working with the palatine or governor. The register meant that general musterings could now be held, with the first summoned to Minsk in 1534 by the hetman, Jurgis Radvila. General musterings were not always well attended—there was a miserable turnout at Navahrudak in 1538—but the registers meant that hetmans could identify those failing to meet their obligations, for which penalties were severe. General

---

[39] Юрый Бохан, *Вайсковая справа у Вялікім княстве Літоускім у другой палове XIV–канцы XVI ст.* (Мінск, 2008), 306–7; Łowmiański, *Zaludnienie*, 17.

[40] Łowmiański, *Studia*, 435.

[41] Бохан, *Вайсковая справа*, 308–9; Łowmiański, *Zaludnienie*, 15–20; 100; Кром, *Меж Русью*, 124, 127.

[42] Karl von Loewe, 'Military service in early sixteenth-century Lithuania: A new interpretation and its implications', *SR*, 30 (1971), 249–56; *The Lithuanian Statute of 1529*, tr. and ed. Karl von Loewe (Leiden, 1976), 128–39.

[43] Łowmiański, *Zaludnienie*, 22–4; Любавский, *Сеймъ*, 365.

musterings became more common after the outbreak of the Livonian War in 1558. Levies took place at Hanushishki and Krėva in 1561; at Minsk in 1562; and at Rakov in 1565. Muster-lists have only survived for 1565, which produced 8,178 horse, or 40 per cent of the 1528 register. The 1567 muster was more successful: it produced 27,536 horse, 40 per cent more than were listed in 1528. These muster-lists, in contrast to the 1528 register, which listed obligations, recorded those who actually turned up.[44]

These documents and two local registers that do survive—for Volhynia (1545) and Polatsk (1552)—bear testimony to the efficiency of local officials. The 1528 register contains all the council offices, except for those that were vacant, while the Volhynia and Polatsk registers include a high proportion of individuals or families listed in 1528, leading Łowmiański to conclude that the 1528 register represents an accurate listing of the middling nobility.[45] Taken together, they reveal the scale of the internal differentiation that had taken place in the *boiarstvo* since 1386. While a considerable class of middling nobles remained alongside an even larger one of impoverished boyars, many of whom served in person, the registers were dominated by the lords and a few princes, whose extensive landholdings were revealed by the number of horse they were required to raise. Of the 19,842 horse listed in 1528 nearly a third (30 per cent) were provided by this group, although the percentage was smaller in 1567 when it provided 4,890 horse out of 27,776, or under a fifth (18 per cent).[46] Perhaps the ordinary nobility were more assiduous than the magnates in fulfilling their obligations, although the mustering did not include private units raised separately.

By 1528 a handful of families had established considerable landed fortunes. The Kęsgaila were the wealthiest, with the register recording their obligation at 768 cavalrymen, representing no fewer than 6,144 service units, or some 12,288 peasant households; next were the Radvila (Radziwiłł), with 760 (service units; 12,160), and Albertas Goštautas, with 466 (3,728; 7,456), while the Astikaitai— close relatives of the Radvila—were assessed at 337 cavalrymen (2,696; 5,408).[47] These families—all of them among the Horodło 47—owed their wealth to service in the new government institutions established by Vytautas, and the grand ducal council, which was based firmly on this elite. While birth and connections were important, the greatest rewards came to those who had held high government office

---

[44] Łowmiański, *Zaludnienie*, 27–30.   [45] Łowmiański, *Zaludnienie*, 38–45.

[46] Ochmański, *Historia*, 124. There are minor discrepancies in the figures given by historians for the number of horse raised in 1567 in the light of research into the sources. In a more recent estimate, Ianushkevich suggests 27,597: Янушкевіч, *Велікае Княства*, 152.

[47] Ochmański, *Powstanie*, 155; Любавский, *Сеймъ*, 355. Although the service unit was based on the Lithuanian hide, it is difficult to estimate the size of landholdings owing to the varying ways holdings of under one hide were treated: see Łowmiański, *Zaludnienie*, 99–101. The actual numbers of peasant households—hearths (*dymy*) as they were termed—may be higher: Ochmański, on whose figures these are based, uses a multiplier of two to convert service units into hearths, while Łowmiański suggests two to four hearths per unit. Iakovenko uses a multiplier of three, Łowmiański's average, to calculate the number of hearths on the Ostrozky lands. If this multiplier is applied to the Kęsgaila and Radvila families, it produces a figure of 18,432 and 18,240 peasant households. I have, like Ochmański, opted for caution.

in Casimir's reign. Since he was absent for long periods in Poland, government effectively lay in the hands of the chancery and the council. Rewards could be substantial for those who held office at the local level, in particular governors and starostas. It was above all office-holders who received grants of land or rights to particular revenues in their districts, and who benefited from the system.[48]

Council members benefited most. The origins of the council are a matter of some controversy. From 1411, leading Lithuanian politicians increasingly appear in documents as 'councillors'. Article ten of the Horodło treaty, in referring to the forty-seven families adopted into Polish heraldic clans, for the first time delineated a right to be consulted.[49] Gradually, the council became regularized in the form of meetings of the most important officials, most of them with effective life-tenure on their offices. By the 1430s, the formula used by Švitrigaila 'having taken counsel with the princes and lords of our loyal council' (*і мы порадивше съ нашими князи і съ паны съ нашою върную радою*) suggested that the right to give counsel was now held automatically by those of a certain rank and position: hereditary princes and the office-holding lords. Princes could and did hold the offices of governor and starosta of the leading cities that gave them automatic, life-membership of the council and princes were summoned to the wider meetings of the council that came to be known as the sejm (*сеймъ*; *соймъ*), but the new system rested largely on the lords.[50]

This was a consultative, not a consensual system. Although there is copious evidence that grand dukes sought advice there is no indication that they were obliged to take it, and Korczak finds no evidence of any use of the term '*rada*' (council) in an institutional sense until Casimir issued his *Sudebnik* on 29 February 1468, the first attempt at a codification of Lithuanian written law, which contained two clauses (12 and 21) requiring him to pronounce sentence in legal cases in conjunction with his councillors, and established the powers of the council in the grand duke's absence. It formally recognized the need for him to seek council advice, but, although it gave the council certain narrowly defined executive powers, especially with regard to the keeping of the peace, it did not grant it the power of decree.[51]

These measures reflected the problems of government under an absentee grand duke and bore testimony to the practice that had evolved since 1447. Regular council meetings were attended by a narrow core of officials, with broader sessions called to discuss and give public witness to major decisions. The inner council was small, usually comprising the bishop of Vilnius, the chancellor and marshal of the

---

[48] Pietkiewicz, *Wielkie księstwo*, 127.
[49] 'ad consilia nostra admittantur et eis intersint, dum pro bono publico tractatus celebrantur': *AU*, no. 51, 67; Korczak, *Litewska rada wielkoksiążęca w XV wieku* (Cracow, 1998), 18.
[50] *AZR*, i, no. 36, 48; Korczak, *Rada*, 20, 23–49.
[51] И.П. Старостина, 'Судебник Казимира 1468 г.', in *Древние государства на территории СССР (1988–1989)* (Moscow, 1991), 279–312; Korczak, *Rada*, 12–15, 20–4, 32–3, 53. For the debate about the role of witnesses, see Petrauskas, *Diduomenė*, 57–73; Sułkowska-Kurasiowa, 'Doradcy Władysława Jagiełły', in *SPS*, ii (Warsaw, 1982) 188–220, and Klimecka's critical remarks, 'Czy rzeczywiście "doradcy Władysława Jagiełły"?', in *SPS*, iv (Warsaw, 1990) 214–35.

land, and the palatines and castellans of Vilnius and Trakai, whose membership of the council was guaranteed by Horodło. The other Catholic bishops attended rarely; they were prominent in the 1430s, but were not very active under Casimir, possibly because the miserable endowments of their dioceses meant that over forty per cent of bishops were of bourgeois origin. The council was therefore—in contrast to Poland—dominated by secular officer-holders. The tradition, established under Casimir, that the chancellorship—an office first recorded in 1429—was usually combined with that of palatine of Vilnius, and that the marshal of the land was usually palatine of Trakai meant that the inner council was even smaller than it looked.

After 1447 Jonas Goštautas, palatine of Vilnius from 1443, passed into opposition, demanding a return to the Vytautan system and angrily complaining about Polish influence but, as in Poland, Casimir gradually shaped an inner council more to his liking. In Lithuania there was a crucial difference, however: his chancellors were laymen drawn from the elite families, not ecclesiastics, which, given Casimir's long absences after 1454, strengthened the grip of a small group of families over the system. From 1458, he had three chancellors. Mykolas Kęsgaila served from 1444 until his death in 1476; already starosta of Samogitia he was raised to the palatinate of Vilnius in 1458. His successor was Alekna Sudimantaitis, palatine of Vilnius from 1476 until his death in 1491, and chancellor from 1478. He was succeeded by the son of Radvila Astikaitis, Mikolajus Radvilaitis, marshal of the land and castellan of Trakai, who succeeded to both posts in 1491, holding them until 1509, shortly before his death in 1510; to compound the concentration of offices, he was also castellan of Trakai from 1488 to 1492. Casimir's last two marshals Bohdan Sakovych (1480–90), palatine of Trakai 1486–90, and Petras Mantigirdaitis (1491–7), palatine of Trakai 1491–7, held the posts simultaneously, and the tradition continued with Jan Zaberezhynsky, who held both positions between 1498 and 1505, as did Mikalojus Radvila, palatine of Trakai 1505–10; marshal from 1505 to 1509.

Under Casimir's careful and shrewd oversight, the system worked well enough, but however much he was able to shape the council, he had to exercise oversight from afar, and his long absences marked a significant watershed in its operation, as it effectively took decisions on a range of matters, including internal affairs and correspondence with foreign powers, on its own authority.[52] It was after his death that the true breakthrough came. The narrow group of individuals who dominated the inner council were well placed to exact a price for supporting Alexander's election in 1492. The privilege he issued in that year at last provided a proper legal framework for the council's activities, according it significant formal powers. Henceforth the grand duke was obliged not only to seek the council's advice but to secure its agreement on a range of matters, including the despatch of ambassadors, appointment to, and dismissal from, leading offices; the issuing of judgements in important cases; the cancellation of leases on grand ducal land; and, most

---

[52] Korczak, *Rada*, 21.

significantly, over the expenditure of royal revenues. Offices within the palatinates of Vilnius and Trakai had to be filled by those proposed by the palatines.[53] Alexander even promised not to overrule, correct, or express his anger at councillors who opposed his views, although in a series of stipulations often overlooked, Alexander defined areas in which he was still free to exercise his prerogative, in particular with regard to his patrimonial lands.[54]

The 1492 privilege was as significant for Lithuania as the Nieszawa privileges were for Poland. It introduced principles known in Polish law, including a Lithuanian version of *neminem captivabimus nisi iure victum* enshrined in the 1430 Jedlnia privileges, which stipulated that nobody could be imprisoned until convicted of a crime in a court of law.[55] Both sets of privileges considerably limited royal power, but whereas in Poland the Nieszawa privileges helped secure the position of the sejmiks—and therefore the ordinary szlachta—within the political system, the 1492 privileges in Lithuania had the opposite effect, entrenching the power of the new elite of the *pany*, and in particular the narrow group that constituted the inner council. Although meetings of the Lithuanian sejm had become regular, Lithuania was unaffected by the great changes that occurred in the Polish sejm in this period, and these general assemblies, though drawn from across the whole grand duchy, remained bodies in which the council decided and then informed the boyars.

After 1492, the council had the means of holding the grand duke to account, and ensuring that he respected laws passed and decisions made in its presence. The measures concerning international relations seem merely to have formalized what had long been practised. Control over the grand ducal treasury was a major concession, although it remained to be seen what it meant in practice. Perhaps the most significant measures were those concerning appointment to office and tenures on grand ducal land. Alexander had surrendered a considerable degree of control over the political elite: he could only remove individuals from office with their consent, or by advancing them to a more prestigious position; he had to accept the officials bequeathed to him by his father; and had to share control over the appointment of their replacements. The lords of the council now held the keys to the door of their exclusive club.

These changes shaped the course of Lithuanian politics over the next half-century. It was the council, not the sejmiks—which did not yet exist in Lithuania—or the sejm, that had secured control over grand ducal policy in a development that owed much to Casimir's abandonment of the Vytautan system. Its restoration under Alexander was short-lived, and from 1506 the Lithuanian council was again in effective control of day-to-day government. Yet despite the triumph of this new elite of lords the ordinary boyars were not wholly excluded by the new, oligarchic arrangements cemented in 1492, and were to play an increasing political role.

---

[53] *CDP*, i, no. 194, 345–52.
[54] 'quecunque consilia et causas, cum dominiis consiliariis nostris determinabimus et statuemus atque concludemus, ea cum nemine alio immutare, corrigere aut deordinare debebimus. Item quando aliqua consilia et negocia, in consultacione cum dominis nostris tractanda evenerint, et ipsis dominis non placebunt, pro isto super eos commoneri non debemus': *CDP*, i, no. 194, 349–50. Korczak, *Rada*, 52–8; Любавский, *Сеймъ*, 130–1; Pietkiewicz, *Wielkie księstwo*, 68–9.
[55] *CDP*, i, no. 194, 346.

During the fifteenth century the term 'boyar' gradually changed its meaning. The word is of Slavic and military origin: the *boiarstvo* was literally composed of those who fought, and in Kievan Rus' had denoted the greatest landowners at the apex of the social system. After 1387 it gradually lost its primarily military connotations. By the early fifteenth century, a distinction began to be made between 'greater' and 'lesser'—known in the Ruthenian lands as 'younger'— boyars; with the emergence of the new class of lords as a politically dominant and increasingly wealthy elite, the term 'boyar' was used to refer to the mass of the ordinary nobility, who continued to serve in a military capacity when called upon. Other terms were used for the elite as a whole: *shliakhta*, a borrowing from the Polish; *nobiles* in Latin, or *zemianin*, another term that showed clear Polish influence, which was derived from the Slavonic term for land, and marked the development of an elite more firmly based on the ownership and transition of landed property.[56]

It was by no means easy to distinguish just who belonged to the wider *boiarstvo*. The 1387 privileges were issued to Lithuanian boyars who converted to Catholicism, but Horodło merely stirred mud into the water with its designation of an elite encompassed by the adoption, which did nothing to resolve the question of who, precisely, enjoyed the privileges granted since 1387. The extension of most—if not all—privileges to the Ruthenian boyars and to the annexed territories in the 1430s, and in Casimir's general privilege of 1447 clarified little: as Liubavskii observes, every grand duke ritually confirmed the Horodło privilege without offering any suggestion as to who was to be considered a member of the *shliakhta*, or who was to benefit from these generous privileges, which created a strong incentive for individuals to claim noble status.[57]

The problem was that the privileges granted between 1387 and 1434 introduced a distinction between the boyars and the broader class of freemen that was difficult to establish on the ground, especially in areas where there were substantial settlements of military servitors, such as Samogitia or the Kaunas district, which had been in the front line of the war against the Order. While wealthier boyars beyond the Horodło 47 could and did sustain a lifestyle little different from the new elite of lords, and marry into princely and lordly families, it was different at the other end of the scale, where many boyar landholdings were little different from peasant farms, and boyars and their families often lacked dependent peasants and worked the land themselves.[58] Wealthier freemen and peasants could and did percolate into the lower echelons of the *boiarstvo*; this process was aided by the existence of artisans and groups among the upper peasantry with various obligations of a broadly military nature that blurred the dividing-line between them and the lower boyars. These groups were often freed from other obligations, saw themselves as freemen, and resisted the imposition of any measures tying them to the land or suggesting their subservient status. They were hard to distinguish from such groups

---

[56] Jablonowski, *Westrußland*, 38–9; Яковенко, *Шляхта*, 61, 245.
[57] Любавский, *Сеймъ*, 430–1; Kamieniecki, *Społeczeństwo*, 81.
[58] Kamieniecki, *Społeczeństwo*, 94, 97.

as the *putnie* boyars, who undertook various forms of service on the roads, keeping them in repair and assisting grand ducal envoys and servants passing along them. Governors and starostas sometimes issued formal attestations of the noble status of such individuals, with the sources using the striking phrase 'raising a boyar into nobility' (*возведенія в шляхецво бояръ*), an indication of how the term gradually lost its cachet after 1413. By 1500 '*boiarstvo*' and '*shliakhta*' were not necessarily synonyms and there was a substantial group of individuals whose status was legally unclear. Many boyar families, subject to the pressures of subdivision, saw their economic position decline. Struggling to maintain their service obligations, they had to start rendering the dues from which the nobility was now exempt; others obtained peasant land, and had to meet the obligations and dues upon it, while seeking to maintain their status.[59]

Most of the petty boyars had little if any allodial land, and therefore did not benefit from one of the most important elements of the privileges. Their small landholdings were frequently service estates, and the boyars were greatly affected by the reorganization of the *sluzhba* system under Vytautas. Service estates were held at the pleasure of the grand duke who could—and did—confiscate them for many reasons, the most important being the failure to provide service when called upon. There was a market for service estates, and it was not unusual for commoners to buy one in attempts to establish their position as boyars.[60] Boyar families had traditionally supplied a range of services, and it would be naïve to assume that the various privileges meant that a largely petty and illiterate nobility immediately abandoned the customs, traditions, and obligations of previous generations, especially since Vytautas took measures to mitigate the potentially disastrous impact of noble privileges upon the grand duchy's defensive system. As the great latifundia grew in the fifteenth century, boyars could—and increasingly did—secure service tenures from lords and princes, receiving small estates in return for the obligation to turn out when required by their masters. It was these service boyars—some from princely families fallen on hard times—who swelled the retinues and military units of the magnates and wealthier princes.[61]

Even before the 1492 privileges handed such a measure of control over appointments to the *pany*, it was becoming difficult to break into the charmed circle, and there are few examples of individuals rising out of the *boiarstvo* to careers among the elite during the later fifteenth century.[62] Yet the extension of privileges gave even the poorest of boyars a major incentive to retain their status and lay claim to those privileges. By 1500, cases of boyars going to law to defend their *shliakhta* status were common.[63] During the Muscovite wars the government began scrutinizing such claims, and therefore entitlement to exemption from the increasing number of exactions drawn from commoners. The council declared that individuals whose

---

[59] Łowmiański, *Studia*, 183, 205; Любавский, *Сеймъ*, 431–2, 434–7.
[60] Kamieniecki, *Społeczeństwo*, 84, 86–7, 90, 96.
[61] Kamieniecki, *Społeczeństwo*, 93; Mirosława Malczewska, *Latyfundium Radziwiłłów w XV do połowy XVI wieku* (Warsaw, 1985), 62, 64; Pietkiewicz, *Kieżgajłowie*, 74.
[62] Korczak, *Monarchia*, 153.   [63] Любавский, *Сеймъ*, 436–7; Petrauskas, *Diduomenė*, 134.

status was in doubt had to secure the testimony of two neighbours of impeccable noble status to testify that their family were 'boyars and *shliakhta* through the ages' (зъ вѣковъ бояре шляхта); these cases often hinged on such issues as whether or not their grandfathers had cut hay for the grand duke.[64] They were prepared to go to court to defend themselves against demands for services made by lords who sought to treat them as peasants, or against peasants, who accused them of falsely claiming boyar status to avoid the obligations laid upon commoners in their village.[65]

With commissioners despatched into the provinces to examine whether boyars were capable of fulfilling their military obligations, the 1528 military reforms and the general musterings of the noble levy that followed provided boyars with an excellent opportunity publicly to demonstrate their status. Although the register demonstrates the substantial contingents raised by the greatest magnates, it also bears testimony to the thousands of petty boyars who turned out in person in the general musterings that took place over the following decades. Samogitian boyars were particularly well represented, even though they are all but absent from documents recording Alexander's donations of land.[66] For generations after 1528, listings in the register detailing the family and the estate from which service was provided constituted excellent proof of the status of a boyar family's ancestors, and therefore of its claims to a place in the *shliakhta*.

Thus although the fifteenth century saw a substantial economic differentiation within the nobility across the grand duchy, and a growing monopoly of political power on the part of a narrow elite at the top, at the same time a powerful sense of a wider noble estate developed and deepened, in which awareness of the legal privileges of the *shliakhta* played a key role. From the 1430s, if not earlier, this sense of nobility as a privileged group within the grand duchy strengthened in the annexed Ruthenian territories. Apart from the religious differences, there were few cultural barriers to greater integration at the highest level of the nobility. Language was no obstacle as Ruthenian spread steadily across the ethnic Lithuanian territories as the language of law and of written communication. The policy instigated by Jagiełło and Vytautas of granting land to Lithuanian Catholic magnates in Ruthenian lands—at first in the Ruthenian areas of Lithuania proper, and increasingly across the grand duchy—helped bring the elites together, as did intermarriage. This was not a colonial operation in which 'Ruthenian' lands were granted to Lithuanians; it worked the other way as well, particularly during the Muscovite wars, when many loyal Ruthenian nobles were granted lands in Lithuania proper; while most grants were made in substantially Ruthenian areas such as Black Ruthenia, some were made in Lithuanian areas and even in Samogitia, where Ivan Sapieha and Timofei Ivanovych Kapusta received estates.[67]

---

[64] Любавскій, *Сеймъ*, 439. [65] Pietkiewicz, *Wielkie księstwo*, 128, 131.
[66] Pietkiewicz, *Wielkie księstwo*, 133. For examples of petty boyars registered at one horse, see Яковенко, *Шляхта*, 256.
[67] Pietkiewicz, *Wielkie księstwo*, 135.

27

Litva

The emergence of a more integrated Lithuanian-Ruthenian noble elite owed much to the practical toleration of Orthodoxy after 1434, which received its legal definition on 20 March 1499, when Alexander issued an edict confirming the rights of the Orthodox Church in response to a petition from Iozif Bolharynovych, the former Orthodox bishop of Smolensk, recently raised to the metropolitanate of Kyiv in succession to Makary, killed in a Tatar attack in 1497, requesting confirmation of the privileges of the Orthodox Church granted by Iaroslav the Wise.[1] Alexander's edict, the first occasion on which a Lithuanian grand duke had confirmed Iaroslav's privileges, was issued after the 1492–4 war with Muscovy, whose outcome had considerable implications for the Orthodox Church. Under the terms of the 1494 peace Alexander married Helena, daughter of Ivan III, who insisted upon a formal guarantee that she be allowed to continue in the faith of her ancestors, that she should not be harassed by attempts to convert her to Catholicism, and that an Orthodox church be built in the royal castle in Vilnius for her use, although his demand that the wedding be conducted according to the Orthodox rite was rejected. It took place on 15 February 1495 in the cathedral of St Stanisław and St Władysław, conducted by Wojciech Tabor, bishop of Vilnius (see Fig. 10). Metropolitan Makary attended but was not allowed any official role; together with a priest sent from Moscow, he muttered Orthodox prayers *sotto voce*.[2]

Helena was nineteen. Her mother was Sophia Paleologus, niece of Constantine XI, the last Byzantine emperor. She was by all accounts blessed with good looks, and the marriage was happy, although it remained childless. Helena was permitted to worship as she pleased, although she accepted Alexander's request that Catholics be admitted to her retinue. She maintained good relations with Catholic ecclesiastics, showing a particular attachment to the Franciscans. She could not prevent the war of 1500–3 but she was an effective and tactful intermediary between her husband and her father. Although her mother had been a ward of the pope, and had been raised a Catholic in Rome, Helena's refusal to comply with Alexander VI's demand that she recognize the church union provoked a rift with the papacy that was not resolved by the adept diplomat Erazm Ciołek and the pro-union Orthodox magnate Ivan Sapieha, sent to Rome in 1501. She quietly demonstrated her attachment to her church by numerous donations to Orthodox monasteries, and remained in Lithuania after Alexander's death. Although her relations with

---

[1] *AZR*, i, no. 166, 189–91.
[2] Fryderyk Papée, *Aleksander Jagiellończyk*, 2nd edn (Cracow, 1999), 18–20.

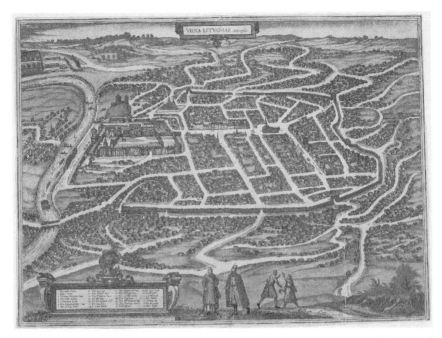

Fig. 10. View of Vilnius in the sixteenth century. With the kind permission of the Zamek Królewski, Warsaw.

Sigismund I deteriorated following the renewal of war with Muscovy in 1512, Crummey's contention that she was imprisoned is unfounded: Sigismund merely prevented her from returning to Muscovy.[3]

Helena was the first Orthodox princess to sit on the grand ducal throne since Jagiełło's mother Juliana. That she could settle so comfortably into life as grand duchess reveals much about the religious and political circumstances of Lithuanian Orthodoxy. There was no need to build an Orthodox church in Vilnius castle for there was already a flourishing Orthodox community in the city, and Helena usually worshipped at the Orthodox church of Our Immaculate Lady.[4] Although, in deference to her father's wishes, she refused openly to support church union, the position of Orthodox believers in Poland as well as Lithuania was crucially influenced by the legacy of the union between the Catholic and Orthodox Churches signed at the Council of Florence on 6 July 1439 and ceremonially proclaimed by Metropolitan Isidore of Kyiv and All Rus' in his cathedral of St Sophia in Kyiv on 5 February 1441. The learned Greek-born Isidore had been appointed metropolitan in 1436 by Joseph II, the pro-union patriarch of Constantinople, in order to secure the participation of the eastern Slavic church in the planned council to discuss a

---

[3] Edward Rutski, *Polskie Królowe*, i (Warsaw, 1990), 157–78; Oskar Halecki, *From Florence to Brest (1439–1596)* (New York, 1958), 100.
[4] Chodynicki, *Kościół*, 77, 79–80.

union that was a desperate bid for help by the Greek church as the Ottomans swept up what was left of the once glorious Byzantine empire and closed in on Constantinople. He was strongly committed to union, willing to accept the Latin interpretation of many of the theological points at issue—including the key controversy over the procession of the Holy Ghost—in order to secure mutual acknowledgement of the sacraments of each church, and the retention of the Orthodox rite.[5]

Isidore arrived in Moscow in April 1437 to solicit support for the union. He travelled to Ferrara, where Eugene IV, who had fled the Council of Basle, had established a rival, papal council that subsequently moved to Florence. Isidore was accompanied by a large entourage of Muscovite clergy, including representatives from Tver, and Avraam, bishop of Suzdal. The Muscovites took an active part in the union discussions, and Isidore and Avraam both signed the union agreement. When Isidore returned to Moscow in March 1441, however, the union was summarily dismissed by Vasilii II, and he was imprisoned, although in September he was allowed to escape after refusing to repudiate the union.

The rejection of the union by the Muscovite church and the abject failure of the Catholic powers to give effective help to Constantinople have helped create a general impression that the Florence union was a complete failure. Viewed from Poland-Lithuania, however, the picture is rather different. For the Florence union created the framework—albeit a loose one—that allowed the Lithuanian Orthodox church and Orthodox society to survive and, in its own modest way, to flourish over the next century or so. This was despite the fact that there was almost no Polish or Lithuanian representation in Florence apart from envoys of the Armenian bishop of Lwów, who signed a separate treaty of union for the Armenian church on 22 November 1439.[6] The conciliarist Polish church broadly supported the Basle council, and the Polish delegates did not follow Eugene to Ferrara and Florence. After the signing of the union, however, Isidore travelled through Poland and Lithuania on his way back to Moscow, energetically promoting the union. Although Oleśnicki, with whom Isidore held discussions, was a supporter of the Council of Basle, he broadly favoured union, and, along with Władysław III, welcomed Isidore warmly enough, allowing him to celebrate mass in Cracow cathedral according to the eastern rite. After Władysław's election to the Hungarian throne, the preparations for his Ottoman campaigns created a favourable political climate for union, especially since the Orthodox church in Moldavia and Wallachia had also signed the union, and on 22 March 1443 Władysław issued a charter guaranteeing the rights and liberties of the Ruthenian church.

For the Jagiellons, church union remained the obvious solution to the grand duchy's religious divide. Yet they faced considerable opposition to the idea not from the Orthodox, but from within the Catholic Church. Oleśnicki might have been sympathetic, but in Lithuania Isidore received a much chillier reception from Motiejus, bishop of Vilnius, a strong supporter of the Basle council, who bluntly refused to recognize the union, Eugene IV, or his representative. This was a

---

[5] Gudziak, *Crisis*, 44–5; Halecki, *Florence*, 49; Chodynicki, *Kościół*, 49–50.
[6] Halecki, *Florence*, 48–9.

foretaste of what was to come: the lack of enthusiasm for union among the Catholic hierarchy was to blight relations between the two churches for generations. The reception from Orthodox bishops, however, was much more positive. As Isidore travelled round Orthodox dioceses, he secured broad support for union.[7]

Despite the repudiation of the Florence union by patriarch Simeon I of Constantinople in 1484, the Orthodox Church in both Poland and Lithuania survived and, despite many problems and difficulties, even flourished down to the mid sixteenth century. While the suggestion that throughout this period theological and theoretical unity between the Ruthenian Orthodox church and Rome survived is unconvincing, unionist sentiment was common among many of the educated hierarchy of the Ruthenian Orthodox church, and informed the approach of the Jagiellons.[8]

The Florence fallout exposed the problems created by the continued jurisdiction of the Moscow-based metropolitan over the Orthodox Church in the grand duchy. After Isidore's escape from Moscow in 1448, Vasilii II raised Jonah, bishop of Riazan, to the metropolitanate; Isidore, now a cardinal, ended his days in exile as the Latin patriarch of Constantinople between 1459 and 1463. Although Casimir had to recognize Jonah's authority over the Orthodox Church in the grand duchy in the peace treaty he signed with Muscovy in 1449, a metropolitan so firmly under Moscow's control was difficult to tolerate. In 1458, in response to Casimir's urgings, Calixtus III agreed to divide the province of Rus' into two. He appointed Gregory, abbot of the Basilian monastery of St Demetrius in Constantinople, a close associate of Isidore, as metropolitan of Kyiv. Gregory was consecrated by the patriarch of Constantinople, Gregory Mammas, then in exile in Rome, and his appointment was confirmed after Calixtus's death by Pius II in 1459. Of the nine Orthodox bishops in the Polish-Lithuanian lands, only two—Briansk and Chernihiv—rejected Gregory, fleeing to Moscow. They were swiftly replaced. The division was permanent.[9]

Although jurisdictional wrangles and battles over titles between the rival metropolitans of Kyiv and All Rus' in Lithuania and Moscow continued after 1458, and although the reestablishment of a patriarch of Constantinople—who claimed jurisdiction over both—in Constantinople under Ottoman scrutiny helped dissipate the pro-union sentiment of the Greek church after 1453, the division of the metropolitanate at last allowed the Ruthenian Orthodox church in Poland-Lithuania to establish its own place within the Jagiellonian political and social system. That it was able to do so, and that the Orthodox elites of Lithuania, despite the frequently expressed view that they were discriminated against and were treated as second-class citizens, were broadly content with their lot was demonstrated by their reaction to the long cycle of wars against Muscovy, when the grand duchy proved

---

[7] Gudziak, *Crisis*, 44–5; Halecki, *Florence*, 54–61; Chodynicki, *Kościół*, 52.

[8] See Ihor Mončak, *Florentine Ecumenism in the Kyivan Church* (Rome, 1987), and Gudziak's review of it: 'The union of Florence in the Kievan Metropolitanate: Did it survive until the times of the union of Brest? (Some reflections on a recent argument)', *HUS*, 17, 1/2 (1993), 138–48.

[9] Halicki, *From Florence*, 85–7; Gudziak, *Crisis*, 45–6.

rather more resilient and its Orthodox, Ruthenian elites less responsive to the blandishments of Moscow than has often been allowed by the nationalist school of Russian history, which glorified Ivan III and Vasilii III and argued teleologically that the absorption of the Ruthenian lands into Russia was a historical inevitability. This version of history was publicized to the English-speaking world by Backus in a study of defections by princes from Lithuania to Muscovy from 1386 until 1569.[10] Backus uses the nineteenth-century Russian nationalist concept of 'West Russia' for the grand duchy's Ruthenian lands, an indication that his study is written firmly within the imperialist Russian historical tradition, whose biases he largely adopts. As Halecki observes with commendable restraint, Backus greatly exaggerates the significance of these 'desertions'.[11]

If such *a priori* nationalist assumptions are laid aside, the evidence points in a different direction. Despite the loss of about a third of the grand duchy's territory by 1514, and despite the defection of many border princes to Moscow in the first two wars, the overwhelming majority of the grand duchy's Orthodox elites remained loyal. Much of the territory lost was only nominally under Lithuanian authority, largely comprising the tiny appanages of the ever-increasing number of border princes in the vast, sparsely populated marchlands, who had accepted Gediminid and Jagiellon overlordship in the long period of Muscovite weakness before 1462, and whose lands had been only loosely integrated into Lithuania's governing structures. Their loyalties were placed under serious pressure in the 1480s through Ivan's policy of border raiding. Following the failure of the Vilnius government to protect them, individual princes began exercising their customary right to leave the service of one lord and join another. There was no mass defection. Before the coming of war in 1492, all defections from among the Upper Oka princes were from the Novosilskii clan—the families of Odoevskii, Vorotynskii, and Belevskii. Casimir protested to Ivan about his acceptance of their service but he did not challenge their right to choose their lord, as the grand dukes of Lithuania had long benefited from movement in the opposite direction: several supporters of Vasilii II fled to Vilnius after his blinding, and were granted hereditary estates. The many defections from Muscovy to Lithuania which took place in the 1430s and 1440s, the 1530s, and the 1560s have often been downplayed or ignored, except for Kurbskii's high-profile flight in 1564. As Rusyna drily observes, westward flights are rarely interpreted as evidence of the political pull of Lithuania by most historians of Russia.[12]

---

[10] Oswald P. Backus, *Motives of West Russian Nobles in Deserting Lithuania for Moscow 1377–1514* (Lawrence, KS, 1957).

[11] Halecki, *Florence*, 122. Particularly striking is Backus's failure to consult Wolff's, *Kniaziowie*, still of great value, but absent from the notes and bibliography. Jablonowski, although he also uses the term *Westrussland*, is far more reliable, while the St Petersburg historian Mikhail Krom's outstanding work on the wars demolishes the Russian nationalist assumptions that Backus uncritically accepts.

[12] Кром, *Меж Русью*, 94; Jablonowski, *Westrußland*, 116–17. Олена Русина, 'Проблеми політичної лояльності населення Велико князівства Литовського у XIV–XVI ст.', *UIZh*, 6 (2003), 3–16. For Kurbskii's defection and the attractions of Lithuania see Inge Auerbach, *Andrej Michajlovič Kurbskij* (Munich, 1985).

Decisions to accept Muscovite rule depended on a range of factors, often reflecting family disputes over the subdivision of lands—as in Odoev in 1492, where the town was divided between the sons of Semën and Ivan Odoevskii, with one half loyal to Lithuania and the other already recognizing Muscovite rule—or because of Alexander's failure to honour his obligation to defend individual princes and their estates.[13] Many waited long before accepting Muscovite rule, and a considerable number of princes and boyars refused, abandoning their estates. They were granted land in other parts of Lithuania in compensation: one such was Ivan Sapieha, who made his career at Helena's court and then in the central administration, surrendering his family estates near Smolensk as the price of loyalty. The migration was so significant that Alexander and Sigismund struggled to find enough land to distribute to princes and boyars who fled westward rather than accept Muscovite rule.[14]

Lithuania's Orthodox hierarchy remained resolutely opposed to the claims of the Muscovite metropolitan, and the outcome of the wars was decided by the conspicuous failure of Ivan and Vasilii to win over the majority of the grand duchy's Orthodox elites.[15] After the easy initial triumphs, in the long war between 1512 and 1522, the only major Muscovite success—admittedly a substantial one—was the capture of Smolensk, which was a military rather than a political triumph. In the opportunistic revanchist wars of 1533–7, launched by Sigismund when Vasilii was succeeded by his three-year-old son Ivan IV (1533–84), Lithuania regained some of the lost territories, including Homel, although it failed to recapture Smolensk.

The important question, therefore, is not why some Ruthenian Orthodox princes accepted Muscovite overlordship, but why the vast majority of Orthodox nobles did not: all but a handful of defectors came from the marchlands. Many Orthodox nobles from other provinces demonstrated their loyalty by fighting for Lithuania.[16] There was little support for the rebellion of Mykhailo Hlynsky (Glinskii) in 1508, who was less the representative of the Ruthenian people as which he has sometimes been presented—he came from a family of Tatar origin and was a Catholic—and more the disappointed courtier, Alexander's marshal of the court, who lost his position as favourite when Alexander died and was replaced by Sigismund. Although Hlynsky did much to ensure Sigismund's smooth succession in Lithuania, his rivals—Lithuanian and Ruthenian—were determined to exclude him from the position he had enjoyed under Alexander. In 1508, when, at the climax of a long and bitter dispute, he murdered his main rival Jan Zaberezhynsky, who had spread the false rumour that Hlynsky was plotting to seize the throne for himself, he was supported by almost nobody apart from his own clientele; like Belsky in 1481, his flight to Moscow was the result of his political failure.[17]

---

[13] Кром, *Меж Русью*, 84–5; Jablonowski, *Westrußland*, 128.
[14] Pietkiewicz, *Wielkie Księstwo*, 130–1, 142, 147; Русина, 'Проблеми', 9–10.
[15] Кром, *Меж Русью*, 138.   [16] Krom, 'Konstituierung', 491–2.
[17] Vladimir Kananović, 'Grand Duchess Elena Ivanovna and Duke Michael Gliński: Aspects of rulership at the Jagiellonian court', in Jacek Wiesiołowski (ed.), *Zamek i dwór w średniowieczu od XI do*

Even when several princes, including Kostiantyn Ostrozky, were captured at the disastrous battle of the Vedrosh river (14 July 1500), most resisted Ivan's blandishments. Ostrozky did swear loyalty to Muscovy in October 1506, three years after Ivan refused to release him under the terms of the 1503 peace, and even led Muscovite troops against the Tatars, but once free from close confinement he escaped, returning to Vilnius by September 1507, where he was appointed hetman, leading the Lithuanian army that crushed the Muscovites at the battle of Orsha (8 September 1514).[18]

The royal response to the Muscovite wars was to extend the privileges of the Orthodox Church. Alexander's 1499 edict affirmed various church immunities, specifically upholding the rights of the church courts and barring attempts by government and local officials from bringing suits against the church in the secular courts. Where Orthodox churches had long existed on estates or in starosties held by Catholics, they were not to be converted into Catholic churches or demolished without the permission of the metropolitan or the local Orthodox bishop.[19] While these stipulations reveal some of the petty discrimination experienced by the Orthodox Church at the hands of Catholic officials and landowners, the position of Orthodoxy was not as bad as is alleged by those who point to a supposed ban on the construction of new Orthodox churches in the grand duchy instituted by Jagiełło, and the ban on Catholic-Orthodox marriages in his privilege for the Lithuanian Catholic church. Neither Jagiełło or any of his successors banned the construction of new Orthodox churches, although a ban on the building of brick or stone Orthodox churches was contained in a 1420 decree on schismatics issued by the synod of the province of Gniezno, which included the Lithuanian bishoprics of Vilnius and Medininkai. Petras of Kustynės, bishop of Vilnius, was present at the synod and it can be assumed that he approved of the measure. Its impact, however, is open to question. It applied only to the archbishopric of Gniezno, which included Lithuania proper and Samogitia, but not to the annexed Ruthenian provinces, where the bulk of the Orthodox population lived, or to the Ruthenian provinces within the kingdom of Poland, which were part of the archdiocese of Lwów. The specification that it applied to churches built of brick or stone indicates that it was intended to control church construction in large towns and cities: the vast majority of Orthodox churches in the countryside and small towns were wooden.[20] In the annexed Ruthenian territories Orthodox nobles were perfectly free, in accordance with local custom and privileges, to build Orthodox churches. By Sigismund I's reign, breaches of this statute were flagrant: Kostiantyn Ostrozky, with Sigismund's permission, began building the magnificent church of the Mother of God in Vilnius in 1511; after his spectacular victory at Orsha he was given

---

XV wieku (Poznań, 2001), 161–5; Кром, *Меж Русью*, 150–1; Pietkiewicz, *Wielkie księstwo*, 113–14; Halecki, *Dzieje*, ii, 40–9; Łowmiański, *Polityka*, 382–5.

[18] *PSB*, xxiv, 486; Wolff, *Kniaziowie*, 347; Zygmunt Wojciechowski, *Zygmunt Stary*, 2nd edn (Warsaw, 1979), 94–5.

[19] *AZR*, i, no. 166, 189–90. [20] Chodynicki, *Kościół*, 77, 79–80.

permission to build two further Orthodox churches in the city, stone-built from the foundations up, dedicated to the Holy Trinity and to St Nicholas.[21]

It was a similar story with regard to the ban on Orthodox-Catholic marriages. This measure sought to protect the many Lithuanian communities scattered across Lithuania proper, where intermarriage between pagan Lithuanians and Orthodox Ruthenians had taken place in pagan times.[22] Even in Lithuania proper the Catholic Church, outside the core Lithuanian territory of Aukštaitija, was not particularly strong, while in Samogitia, its weakness meant that paganism proved difficult to root out entirely. Elsewhere, despite the generous early foundations by Jagiełło and Vytautas, the Catholic church remained poorly endowed, with a sparse network of parishes and a mere five bishoprics covering the whole grand duchy, of which the see of Smolensk was of little consequence and was occupied by Muscovy in 1514. The Catholic church struggled to establish more than a token presence even in some of the Ruthenian territories of Lithuania proper, let alone in the annexed lands where—outside the main cities—it was barely present at all until deep into the sixteenth century. It was certainly not powerful enough to enforce laws against intermarriage or church building, or to mount any serious challenge to Orthodox domination.

The Orthodox were therefore left largely undisturbed to worship as they wished, while the increasing social and political integration at the apex of noble society gradually extended to the council and other political institutions. Although the Horodło ban on the most important offices remained in force, Orthodox Ruthenians were by no means excluded from the wider grand ducal council after the 1430s. Orthodox Ruthenians of princely and non-princely backgrounds penetrated the new office-holding elite. As early as the reign of Vytautas, Prince Vasyl Krasny Ostrozky and Prince Mykhailo Holshansky—of Lithuanian descent, but from a family that had embraced Orthodoxy—had been appointed governors of Vitsebsk, and Kyiv respectively. Ruthenians were appointed in substantial numbers to Švitrigaila's council, but even the reaction after his fall did not lead to wholesale exclusion, and numbers rose steadily during Casimir's reign. Some Ruthenians, such as Prince Semën Pronsky, did convert to Catholicism, but this was by no means necessary to secure office, though most of those favoured were at least nominal supporters of church union. Over the century, the percentage of Orthodox Ruthenians among the elite of princes and lords that Suchocki terms the political nation grew from two families out of fifty-nine (3.4 per cent) between 1387 and 1413, to eleven out of fifty-six (19.6 per cent) between 1413 and 1447, to twenty out of fifty-four (37 per cent) by 1492; of the sixty individuals designated 'councillor' in the sources—excluding the reign of Švitrigaila—listed by Korczak for the fifteenth century, seven (10.6 per cent) were Orthodox Ruthenians: Khodko Iurevych, governor of Polatsk; his son Ivan Khodkovych († 1483), starosta of Lutsk and successively governor of Lida, Minsk, and Kyiv; Ivashko Hoitsevych, governor of Navahrudak until his death after April 1456; Ivan Ilnych, governor of Vitsebsk; Ivashko Ivanovych Iursha,

---

[21] Chodynicki, *Kościół*, 80–1.
[22] Ochmański, *Granica*, 79–80; Chodynicki, *Kościół*, 78.

governor of Bratslav, starosta of Lutsk, and governor of Kyiv; Prince Olelko Volodymyrovych, duke of Kyiv; and Soltan Aleksandrovych, governor of Slonim and then Navahrudak. Two of these—Ivashko Iursha (1488–9) and Soltan Aleksandrovych (1482–93) held the office of marshal hospodarski, a senior court official, with the latter also serving as court treasurer.[23]

Evidence that old barriers were crumbling came in 1511, when Sigismund I, in breach of Horodło, appointed Ostrozky to the position of castellan of Vilnius in recognition of his military and political services; in 1522, he was elevated to the palatinate of Trakai in succession to Albertas Goštautas. Ostrozky was one of the wealthiest landowners in the grand duchy. The 1528 register estimated his contribution to the noble levy at 426 cavalrymen: a total of 3,408 service units, or some 6,816 hearths.[24] That placed him fifth in the table, behind only the Kęsgailas, the Radvilas, Albertas Goštautas, and Iury Olelkovych, duke of Slutsk and son of Olelko Volodymyrovych, who was assessed marginally ahead of Ostrozky at 433 cavalrymen. The presence of Orthodox Ruthenians on the council from the 1430s, and the appointment of Ostrozky as hetman, castellan of Vilnius and then palatine of Trakai indicate that by the early sixteenth century a political nation was emerging in the grand duchy that transcended its composite nature, although, as the reaction to Ostrozky's appointment to the palatinate of Trakai was to show, there were distinct limits to that integration.[25] Given the problems of using the term 'nation' in this context, it might be better to term it a Lithuanian community of the realm: during the long cycle of wars between 1492 and 1537 the whole grand duchy was regularly referred to as *Litva*— the Ruthenian for Lithuania—by both its Orthodox Ruthenian subjects and their Orthodox Muscovite enemies.

As in Poland, this was a political community defined by the privileges on which it was based, with a developing idea of citizenship and a conception of politics that owed much to the Polish example. For Polish cultural influence in the grand duchy had been strong over the century and a half since Krewo. Much of that influence was channelled through the Catholic church, many of whose clergy were Poles, either from Poland itself, or, increasingly, Poles settled in the grand duchy: of 123 known canons of Vilnius cathedral down to the mid sixteenth century, only just over half (66) were Lithuanians; most of the non-Lithuanians were of Polish background.[26]

The substantial involvement of Poles in the Lithuanian Catholic church ensured that Polish influences spread through the new educational institutions established after 1387. A cathedral school was founded in Vilnius in 1397 and parish schools were established by Vytautas in Trakai in 1409. The Franciscans opened a convent

---

[23] Suchocki, 'Formowanie', 66, 73–4; Korczak, *Rada*, 49–50, 78–102.
[24] Iakovenko, using a multiplier of three hearths per service unit, suggests some 10,500 hearths, with a population of *c.*60,000 peasants: Яковенко, *Шляхта*, 95; Krom also uses a multiplier of 2–4: Кром, *Меж Русью*, 127. I have preferred Ochmański's more cautious multiplier of two, which would mean a peasant population on Ostrozky's estates of 34,000–41,000, using Iakovenko's estimate of 5–6 individuals per hearth, still an impressive figure.
[25] See Ch. 33, 422.
[26] Rita Trimonienė, 'Polonizacija', in Vytautas Ališauskas et al. (eds), *Lietuvos Didžiosios Kunigaikštijos Kultūra* (Vilnius, 2001), 498.

school in Vilnius in 1426, and several schools were founded in Samogitia in the first third of the century. By 1550 there were 11 schools in the Samogitian diocese and 85 in the Vilnius diocese.[27] There were no institutions of higher education in Lithuania, and many wealthy nobles from the grand duchy attended Cracow University. In 1409 a bursary was established by Jan Isner, professor of theology, to enable students from across the grand duchy to study in Cracow. Only five attended before 1430, but between that year and 1560, 366 Lithuanian students matriculated. Although some were commoners, they were overwhelmingly from the elite of lords and princes that dominated Lithuanian politics. The majority—100— came from Vilnius, with 34 from Kaunas and 11 from Trakai. Ruthenians also attended: fifty came from Podlasie and the Ruthenian lands. Vytautas's nephew Jan Waydut (Jonas Vaidutis), a canon of Cracow, was the second rector of the refounded university in 1402; the first Lithuanian graduated with a bachelor's degree in 1410, and in the 1420s and early 1430s Hermanas Giedraitis, who took his bachelor and master's degrees in Cracow, taught at the university. In 1488 Prince Andrius Svyriškis (BA 1478, MA 1488) lectured on Aristotle, while Andrius Gaškavičius, bishop of Vilnius (1481–91) was awarded his doctorate in Cracow, where many Vilnius canons also studied.[28]

These developments encouraged the gradual spread of the Polish language among the Lithuanian Catholic clergy, and in society more generally. In 1528 the Vilnius diocese decreed that morals, the basis of the faith, the gospels, and the letters of St Paul should be taught in both Polish and Lithuanian. Schools also taught Ruthenian and occasionally German, but Polish was increasingly dominant: its closeness to Ruthenian meant that there were few barriers to its adoption by members of the Lithuanian elite.[29] Polish, with its sophisticated political vocabulary, strongly influenced by Latin and western European ideas, was a more flexible vehicle for the expression of the new concepts and political forms that spread and developed in the grand duchy after 1387, while Ruthenian suffered from the position of Church Slavonic as a liturgical language. In the relatively few Orthodox schools, the clergy taught Church Slavonic, a formal, ecclesiastical language, rather than literary Ruthenian.[30] Ruthenian was the language of the law, and of the chronicles, which showed more openness to vernacular forms, but Polish had a distinct educational advantage.

Vytautas's reign brought a great deal more activity in Ruthenian—far more legal documents survive for his reign than for earlier periods—and the formation of a chancery that issued a steadily increasing flood of documents in Ruthenian was important for the establishment of the distinct western Ruthenian dialects from

---

[27] Gudavičius, *Lietuvos istorija*, i, 447; Jerzy Ochmański, 'Najdawniejsze szkoły na Litwie od końca XIV do połowy XVI w.', in Ochmański, *Dawna Litwa*, 116–19.

[28] Suchocki, 'Formowanie', 61; Gudavičius, *Lietuvos istorija*, i, 451, 464; Maria Topolska, *Społeczeństwo i kultura w Wielkim Księstwie Litewskim od XV do XVIII wieku* (Poznań, 2002), 62–3; Trimonienė, 'Polonizacija', 499.

[29] Topolska, *Społeczeństwo*, 63.

[30] Antoine Martel, *La langue polonaise dans les pays ruthènes, Ukraine et Russie Blanche, 1569–1667* (Lille, 1938), 12.

which modern Belarusian and Ukrainian emerged. It could not compete with Polish as a language of high culture, however, during the great flowering of vernacular literature that began as Renaissance influences coursed powerfully through Poland from the late fifteenth century. By 1550 it was far easier, as Martel observes, making an analogy with the rapid spread of French across Europe after 1700, for Lithuanians and Ruthenians to adopt a living literary language than to scrabble around constructing their own from myriad local dialects. Thus not only did Polish spread among the elites, but hundreds of Polish loan words—of which *shliakhta* was but one—entered Ruthenian.[31] The Lithuanians themselves had no particular attachment to Ruthenian. Lithuanian itself only became a written language in the later sixteenth century—with the main impetus coming from Protestant Königsberg rather than Lithuania itself—and was in no position to compete with Polish. There were, therefore, few barriers to the increasingly rapid spread of Polish as the language of educated discourse. Although its triumph among ordinary nobles was to come in the century after 1569, its progress among the magnate elite was rapid after 1500.

The church was by no means the only institution that exposed the grand duchy's elites to Polish ideas and Polish institutions. Of great importance was the royal or grand ducal court, largely based in Cracow. While there were grand ducal courts under Vytautas, Švitrigaila, Žygimantas, Alexander, and during Casimir's rule in Vilnius between 1440 and 1447, no separate Lithuanian court was maintained on a permanent basis between 1447 and 1492, or after 1496, except for the period 1544 to 1548, when Sigismund August ruled in Vilnius as grand duke during the last four years of his father's reign. These courts, as royal households and centres of royal power, drew individuals from across the Jagiellonian lands, and acted as important centres for cultural exchange.

The Polish presence at the grand ducal court was always significant. From the outset, several of the secretaries employed by Vytautas in his embryonic chancery were Poles, and the union opened the way for Poles to elbow Germans aside as Latin secretaries, just as Polish religious orders replaced their German counterparts after 1387.[32] The Polish influence should not be overstressed. When Vytautas, as part of his lifelong campaign to display his power and status, refashioned his court, he looked not just to Poland for inspiration, but to the many other foreigners, from Bohemia, the German lands—especially Prussia—and in particular from the Silesian and Mazovian duchies, who visited or took up residence at his court.[33] Yet the Polish influence was undoubtedly strong. The Mazovians were Polish-speakers and both they and the Silesians came from areas strongly linked to Poland and its political model. Among the Poles mentioned in the sources as courtiers or familiars of Vytautas were Stanisław Ciołek, who took temporary refuge with

---

[31] C.S. Stang, *Die westrussische Kanzleisprache des Großfürstentums Litauen* (Oslo, 1935), 1–2; Martel, *Langue*, 12–13.
[32] Kosman, 'Kancelaria' 104–12.
[33] Rimvydas Petrauskas, 'Didžiojo Kunigaikščio institucinio dvaro susiformavimas Lietuvoje (XIV a. pabaigoje– XV a. viduryje)', *LIM*, 1 (2005), 9.

Vytautas after writing a sharp satire on Jagiełło's marriage to Elizabeth Granowska, until he returned to favour to become vice-chancellor of Poland in 1423 after her death. Another prominent individual was Jan of Czyżów, later palatine and castellan of Cracow, who served Vytautas between 1426 and 1430.[34]

The Lithuanian court had traditionally been run by the *hospodarski* marshals, several of whom operated at any one time. Alongside them, Vytautas established new court offices on the Polish model, including master of the horse (first mentioned in 1398), cupbearer (1409), kitchen-master (1409), deputy cupbearer (1410), standard-bearer (1413), chamberlain (1428), and treasurer (1429).[35] These offices were not always filled, and it was not until Casimir's reign that a hierarchy began to appear, including several new offices: steward (1447), deputy steward (1475), and carver (1481), and it was not until the sixteenth century that they were permanently filled.[36]

Even if Lithuanian court offices were only sporadically filled, their holders enjoyed prestige, while only having to perform their duties on Casimir's irregular visits to the grand duchy, and the ceremonial regalia associated with their offices for the most part lay tarnishing in the treasury.[37] The Cracow court was largely run by Poles; when Casimir and his sons travelled to Lithuania, much of it came with them. The court was not, however, a purely Polish institution. Throughout the Jagiellonian period, the Cracow court drew Lithuanians to it in various capacities, and proved an important arena in which members of the Lithaunian elite came into contact with Polish culture, Polish institutions, Polish political ideas, and—most significantly—the Polish language. For the language of the royal court after 1447 was increasingly Polish. Casimir was the last grand duke to know Lithuanian, and while his grandson, Sigismund August spoke excellent Ruthenian, he corresponded with the Lithuanian elite in Polish since—as he confessed to Mikołaj Radziwiłł Rudy in 1549—he did not know the Cyrillic alphabet.[38] Latin was not an option: as Radziwiłł admitted he himself 'hardly knew *est est, non non'*.[39] Power in the union now spoke Polish and it was important that the Lithuanian elite understood.

The Lithuanian presence at the royal court was considerable. One of the conditions upon which Casimir insisted in 1447 was that he would have the right to have Lithuanians at his court, and the court accounts reveal many Lithuanian and Ruthenian names, indicating that a considerable number of court personnel and servants were from the grand duchy. Many were of lowly status, mostly coachmen, falconers, huntsmen, and stablemen—as had been the case under Jagiełło—and there were Lithuanians and Lithuanian Tatars in the royal

---

[34] Petrauskas, 'Didžiojo Kunigaikščio', 28, 29; *PSB*, iv, 83.
[35] Petrauskas, 'Didžiojo Kunigaikščio', 12.
[36] *UWXL*, i, 33, 57–8, 142–3, 149–50, 163–4, 186–7; Krzysztof Pietkiewicz, 'Dwór litewski wielkiego księcia Aleksandra Jagiellończyka (1492–1506)', in Kiaupa and Mickevičius (eds), *Lietuvos valstybė*, 75–6.
[37] Marek Ferenc, *Mikołaj Radziwiłł 'Rudy' (ok. 1515–1584)* (Cracow, 2008), 49; Marek Ferenc, 'Uwagi o dworze litewskim Zygmunta Augusta w latach 1548–1572', in Kras et al. (eds), *Ecclesia*, 537–48.
[38] Sigismund August to Mikołaj Radziwiłł Rudy, Cracow, 23 October 1549: *Listy króla Zygmunta Augusta do Radziwiłłów*, ed. Irena Kaniewska (Cracow, 1997), no. 64, 134; Łowmiański, *Polityka*, 215.
[39] Quoted by Ferenc, *Rudy*, 24.

guard. Yet Lithuanian magnates and politicians visited the court, and sent their children to Cracow to learn the ways of the union state, and to learn Polish; many served as gentlemen of the bedchamber, including Alekna Sudimantaitis, Bohdan Sakovych, Jonas Kučukaitis, Stanislovas Kostevičius, Levko Bohovitynovych, and Jonas Radvila, son of Mikalojus Radvilaitis. Several young nobles from Casimir's Lithuanian entourage, including Sudimantaitis, were captured by the Order at Konitz in 1454.[40] The Lithuanian presence in Cracow in the early years of Casimir's reign was so substantial that Oleśnicki, in his public attack on Casimir in Cracow in June 1452, condemned Lithuanian courtiers for enriching themselves, mawkishly claiming that the king was deaf to the pleas of Polish widows and orphans. He complained that all gentlemen of the bedchamber were Lithuanians, who controlled access to the king and his family, excluding Poles and favouring their own countrymen.[41]

Oleśnicki's bilious outpourings parallel the fuss in London over the Scots brought south by James I after 1603. Yet for all the inevitable conflicts, royal courts provided an ideal environment for networking and establishing political and social alliances in union states, while their rituals and ceremonials allowed for the defusing of conflict through the establishment of norms of display for all parts of the composite realms. This unifying function was displayed by the Lithuanian court, for all its intermittent existence after 1447. The registers of payments to courtiers drawn up during Casimir's stays in Lithuania in 1483 and 1488 contain the names of almost all the young men who were later to dominate Lithuanian politics, from the Radvila, Zaberezhynsky, Mantautaitis, Hlebovych, Sakovych, Davaina, and Nemirych families, alongside the Ruthenian princely families of Zaslavsky and Hlynsky. Courtiers were drawn from across the grand duchy and the whole spectrum of the nobility. Among the 350 Lithuanians and Ruthenians in the accounts there were 33 individuals from Smolensk and 8 from Vitsebsk. Young magnates brought their own retinues to court, and Casimir's court comprised some 1,000 individuals during his visits to Lithuania, though the figures for Sigismund's 1509 visit were lower.[42]

Presence or service at court was the normal route to royal favour. The most spectacular case was that of Alekna Sudimantaitis, a favourite from Casimir's days in Vilnius, who, after service as deputy cupbearer, rose from humble boyar origins to be governor of Polatsk (1466–1476/7), palatine of Vilnius (1477–91) and chancellor (1478–91). After 1447, the newly wealthy Lithuanian magnate families turned out with magnificent retinues to major court occasions; even Długosz was impressed. At the wedding of Casimir's daughter Jadwiga to Georg von Wittelsbach in Landshut in 1475, Jadwiga's entourage consisted of Polish nobles dressed in white

---

[40] Petrauskas, *Diduomenė*, 141; Biskup, 'Spisy jeńców polskich z bitwy pod Chojnicami', *PH*, 56 (1965), 25.
[41] *Annales*, xii, 130; Stephen C. Rowell, 'Trumpos akimirkos iš Kazimiero Jogailaičio dvaro: neeilinė kasdienybė tarnauja valstybei', *LIM*, 1 (2004), 27–8, 47–8.
[42] Rowell, 'Trumpos', 27, 47–8; Pietkiewicz, 'Dwór', 79–80, 105–25.

and Lithuanian nobles dressed in red in a vivid visual tableau of union that is still celebrated annually by the city.[43]

The wealth and ostentation of the leading Lithuanian and Ruthenian magnates was in stark contrast to the hordes of impoverished Scottish lairds who flocked south with James I. By the end of the fifteenth century, the fortunes of the grand duchy's wealthiest lords at least equalled and often surpassed those of their Polish counterparts. This wealth and the status it brought opened the way to what was to become an important trend in the sixteenth century: marriages between members of the magnate elites of Poland and Lithuania. The first such alliance was forged in 1478, between Mikołaj Tęczyński, sword-bearer of Cracow and scion of one of the wealthiest and most influential Małopolskan magnate families, to the daughter of Alekna Sudimantaitis.[44] By 1492 the practice had become common enough for it to raise concerns among the Lithuanian elites about the possibility of Poles using marriage to secure property in the grand duchy. Alexander's privilege of that year contained a clause insisting that Lithuanian noblewomen marrying a Pole or a Mazovian could bring no property into the marriage, but had to distribute any they owned to their relations. If the intention was to prevent such unions, the measure failed, and its repetition in the codifications of Lithuanian law in 1529 and 1566 suggests that it was ineffectual: Tęczyński sold his wife's Lithuanian properties after 1492 to prevent their loss; others challenged or ignored the law. It did not prevent a steady increase in intermarriage. Marriages were entered into by members of the Ruthenian princely families of Khodkevych, Zaslavsky, Zbarazky, and Olelkovych, and were contracted by the Polish families of Tęczyński, Szydłowiecki, Tarnowski, Sieniawski, Dębiński, Uchański, Zborowski, Trzebuchowski, and Działyński. Three families from the grand duchy contracted more than one marriage. The Sapiehas, Catholic converts from Orthodoxy, married three daughters to Poles before 1569, while both the sons of Kostiantyn Ostrozky, Ruthenia's leading Orthodox magnate, married Poles. It was the Radvila family, however, that entered the Polish marriage market in greatest force. Elżbieta Katarzyna, daughter of Jonas Radvila, Lithuanian cupbearer († 1542) married Hieronim Sieniawski, castellan of Kamianets; Stanislovas Radvila († 1531), son of Mikalojus, grand chancellor and palatine of Vilnius, married Magdalena Bonerówna; his sister Anna married Konrad III, duke of Mazovia, in 1497, while the second wife of hetman Jurgis Radvila († 1541), was Barbara Kolanka, from a Polish family long established in Podolia.[45] Jurgis Radvila's son by Barbara was Mikołaj Radziwiłł Rudy (the Red) (Mikalojus Radvila Rudasis, c.1515–84); he too was to marry a Pole, Katarzyna Tomicka, daughter of Jan Tomicki, chamberlain of Kalisz, while his cousin, Mikołaj

---

[43] Rowell, 'Trumpos', 29–30, 33, 44; Włodzimierz Jarmolik, 'Kariery polityczne dworzan litewskich Kazimierza Jagiellończyka', in Zbigniew Karpus et al. (eds), *Europa orientalis: Polska i jej sąsiedzi od średniowiecza po współczesność* (Toruń, 1996), 93–101.

[44] Halecki, *Dzieje*, i, 430–1; Petrauskas, *Diduomenė*, 141–2.

[45] Ewa Dubas-Urwanowicz, 'Uwarunkowania prawne i konsekwencje małżeństw polsko-litewskich przed unią lubelską', in Krzysztof Mikulski and Agnieszka Zielińska-Nowicka (eds), *Między Zachodem a Wschodem: Etniczne, kulturowe i religijne pogranicza Rzeczypospolitej w XVI–XVIII wieku* (Toruń, 2006), 67–73; Ferenc, *Rudy*, 13–14; Marceli Antoniewicz, *Protoplaści książąt Radziwiłłów* (Warsaw, 2011), 33, 49–50.

Radziwiłł Czarny (the Black) (Mikalojus Radvila Juodasis, 1515–65), son of Jonas and brother of Elżbieta Katarzyna, married Elżbieta Szydłowiecka, daughter of Krzysztof, Polish grand chancellor from 1515 to 1532.

Thus Czarny and Rudy, who dominated Lithuanian politics in the 1550s and 1560s and led the resistance to closer union, both had Polish wives, and Rudy was himself half Polish. Their careers demonstrate that the adoption of the Polish language and the attractions of Polish culture, did not lead to the Polonization of the grand duchy's elites in terms of consciousness or identity. Casimir's long reign had frozen the disputes over union, but the issues had not gone away. When the long cycle of wars against Muscovy broke out after his death, the question of the nature and future of the union once again entered the political arena. Some among the grand duchy's elites were now attracted to the idea of closer union; others resisted the increasing pressure from Poland for acceptance by the Lithuanians of the Polish view of an accessory union. The Lithuanian elites were far more sophisticated than they had been at the time of the coronation tempest, and were now capable of engaging the Poles on their own terms. When the two Radziwiłł cousins emerged from the 1540s as the dominant force on the Lithuanian council, they defended their Lithuanian identity and the loose union constructed by their forebears in perfectly modulated Polish. The problem for them was that greater exposure to Polish politics and Polish culture had increased the attraction of closer union among many in the Lithuanian and Ruthenian elites whose command of the Polish language was not nearly so impressive. By the first half of the sixteenth century, the loose, composite, patrimonial Gediminid state had been transformed into a more coherent entity known as *Litva*. The union had spread the vision of a political community of citizens that was open, at least in theory, to Orthodox nobles. Litva had, to a considerable extent, managed to encompass its religious diversity and create, at the level of the wealthiest nobility at least, an elite in which Orthodox Ruthenians could find a place. It was a vision which ensured that most of them rejected the siren call of Muscovy, Europe's only remaining independent Orthodox state after 1453. From the 1520s, however, the fragile unity of this new political nation faced a serious challenge, as Poles once again began to assert their vision of an accessory union in which, so they claimed, Litva had been incorporated into Poland. This challenge provoked rapid change within Lithuania, before the controversy over the union reached its dramatic climax in Lublin in 1569.

PART VI

REFORM

28
Mielnik

Casimir IV died in Hrodna on 7 June 1492 (see Fig. 11). With regard to the succession, the ground had been well prepared, and there was to be no repeat of the dramas of 1430 and 1440. Casimir had secured an oath from his Lithuanian councillors in Brest in 1478 to obey whichever of his sons he designated as his successor as grand duke.[1] He had been absent from Lithuania for most of the previous decade, and there had been pressure for the revival of the Vytautan system. Although he rejected the proposal, after the 1481 assassination plot he made it clear that he intended one of his sons to be grand duke on his death. When his son Casimir died in 1484, Casimir decided that John Albert should succeed him in Poland, and that Alexander should become grand duke of Lithuania. He began preparing both for their future roles. Neither was entrusted with much responsibility, but each spent time at Casimir's side during the last decade of his reign, to gain experience of government.[2]

Thus when Casimir formally nominated Alexander on his deathbed, it came as no surprise. Historians have made much of the fact that Alexander's election on 30 July was in technical breach of the union treaties; the absence of any protest from the Poles suggests that Liubavskii is wrong to see it as provocative.[3] They had long been informed of Casimir's intentions and the embassy sent to Lithuania after his death raised not a squawk of protest, in stark contrast to 1430 and 1440. There was no need to protest: agreement had already been reached, and the Poles, in accordance with the treaties, invited a Lithuanian delegation to attend their own royal election, which pushed for the fulfilment of Casimir's last wishes and opposed the other candidates: Władysław, who wished rather to register his own claims as Casimir's eldest son than to make a serious bid for the throne, and Janusz II, duke of Mazovia, who was supported by Zbigniew Oleśnicki the younger. Cardinal Frederick's dramatic intervention to secure the throne for John Albert was entirely in line with Lithuanian wishes; far from wanting to break the union, the Lithuanians were determined to sustain it and were perfectly happy when John I Albert was elected on 27 August.[4]

It is therefore hard to see why Łowmiański terms the period 1492–8 'the union's greatest crisis'.[5] The rapid completion of the formalities owed much to the

---

[1] Kolankowski, *Dzieje*, i, 398.
[2] Halecki, *Dzieje*, i, 421–2; Papée, *Jan Olbracht*, 17–18; Pietkiewicz, 'Spór', 17.
[3] Любавский, *Сеймъ*, 134–5.   [4] Halecki, *Dzieje*, i, 437–8, 440.
[5] Łowmiański, *Polityka*, 370.

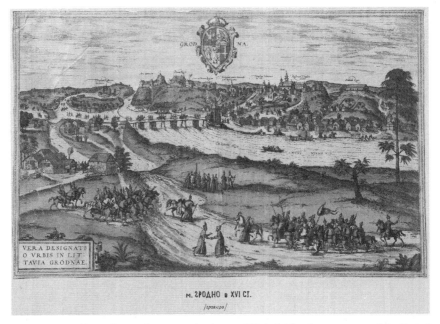

Fig. 11. View of Hrodna in the sixteenth century. With the kind permission of the Zamek Królewski, Warsaw.

realization that Ivan III was already preparing the attack he launched immediately after Casimir's death. The largely harmonious cooperation of the two brothers during John Albert's reign bears testimony to Casimir's careful preparation, and the acceptance of the situation not just by his sons, but by both councils. Alexander spent his childhood in Poland, where he learned Latin and German, his mother's language, but did not visit Lithuania until he was eighteen. He was the first grand duke not to speak Lithuanian, although it did not cause him any problems: the Lithuanian community of the realm defended its republic in Ruthenian or Polish. The new members of the council, schooled by Casimir, did not question the union, and the revival of the Vytautan system accorded with their vision of how the union might best work after his death.[6]

Objections to Casimir's testament came from within the dynasty, but they proved ineffectual. It is usually asserted that the grand duchy was the Jagiellons' hereditary patrimony, but the dynasty's refusal to endorse male primogeniture meant that the succession was never clear, even when a grand duke designated his successor. The tradition of acclamation of the dynasty's choice by the boyars took on a new light after 1413, when Horodło introduced the idea of election on the Polish model, the idea that was taken up so enthusiastically in 1430 and 1440,

---

[6] Pietkiewicz, 'Spór', 17; Jūratė Kiaupienė and Rimvydas Petrauskas, *Lietuvos Istorija*, iv (Vilnius, 2009), 420; Papée, *Aleksander*, 10; Bues, *Jagiellonen*, 118.

and was endorsed by the dynasty with Žygimantas's election in 1432. Casimir may have designated Alexander as grand duke, and the Lithuanians may have accepted his decision, but they still held a formal election. Papée argues that this was a simple enthronement or an acclamation by the assembled boyars, and that there can be no question of a free election, while Kolankowski claims that Alexander was *de facto* grand duke from the moment of his father's death.[7] There is no evidence that the Lithuanians saw matters in this way. Papée's inferences from the absence of the term 'election' in privileges Alexander issued on 6 August 1492, which talked of him as the 'true and rightful heir and natural lord' (*verum et legittimum heredem ac dominum naturalem*) are unconvincing.[8] The concept of natural rights to the throne did not preclude the idea of election and if it was half a century since the last grand ducal election the principle had not been forgotten: the joint summonses from the council and Alexander named him not grand duke, but simply 'The most gracious and beloved prince, by the grace of God son of Casimir, king of Poland and grand duke of Lithuania and Ruthenia' (Наяснѣйшое княжа, Божею милостью Александръ, сынъ Казимера короля Польского и великого князя Литовского и Руского). There is no doubt that this was conceived as an election:

> For we do not wish to elect (*выбирати*) our lord without you, our dearest brothers, but to choose (him) having agreed together with you.[9]

This was not the traditional language of acclamation. It bears eloquent testimony to the development of the idea of the Lithuanian republic or commonwealth.[10] The 1492 election was the first general assembly to which representatives of all the grand duchy's territories were formally invited. The summons spoke of the importance of the election diet for the common good.[11] According to Liubavskii there was good reason to invite Ruthenians from the annexed territories, as there were concerns that they might separately elect Prince Semën Mykhailovych Olelkovych, son of Mykhailo Olelkovych, who had been executed in 1481. Stryjkowski's chronicle, written a century later, tells how Olelkovych arrived with a retinue of 500, and cast his vote for himself, although Papée with good reason doubts the story, pointing to his consistent loyalty to Alexander and Sigismund, most notably during the 1508 Hlynsky rising.[12]

Alexander's enthronement ceremony made clear that he was no absolute, divinely appointed monarch. Grand dukes were not crowned, but he was blessed by Wojciech Tabor, bishop of Vilnius, and handed the sword and sceptre by Petras

---

[7] Papée, *Aleksander*, 11–13; *PSB*, i, 58; Kolankowski, *Dzieje*, i, 399–40. Cf. Gitana Zujienė, 'Lietuvos didžiojo kunigaikščio Aleksandro pakėlimo ceremonialo susiformavimas', in Petrauskas (ed.), *Alexandras*, 56–9.

[8] *CDP*, i, no. 194, 345; Papée, *Aleksander*, 13.   [9] *AZR*, i, no. 100, 115–16.

[10] See Darius Kuolys, *Res Lituania kunigaikštystės bendrija*, i: *Respublikos steigimas* (Vilnius, 2009), 63–89.

[11] 'для доброго и посполитого земьского': *AZR*, i, no. 100, 116.

[12] Любавский, *Сеймъ*, 135; Stryjkowski, *O początkach*, 541–2; Papée, *Aleksander*, 11–12. The story is generally disbelieved: Грушевський, *Історія*, iv, 254; Halecki, *Dzieje*, i, 437.

Mantigirdaitis, palatine of Trakai and marshal of the land, who enjoined him to rule Lithuania according to its traditions and customs and the example of Vytautas, and not by the laws of the Italians, Bohemians, or Germans.[13] This enthronement harangue suggests that the Lithuanian community of the realm no longer regarded their grand dukes as patrimonial autocrats. The privilege granted by Alexander on 6 August made this clear: it extended boyar rights over allodial land and limited grand ducal powers to act without council consent.[14] The Lithuanian republic was dismantling its patrimonial monarchy in another indication that acceptance of the dynasty's wishes on the succession was by no means guaranteed, even if John Albert revived the title of supreme duke to underline the Jagiellonian claim that if the election of grand dukes was permissable, the dynasty maintained its hereditary right to its Lithuanian patrimony. That it was John Albert, rather than the eldest brother Władysław, who claimed the title could be justified by the Gediminid practice of dynastic designation.[15]

Alexander's election brought the question of the nature of the union out of cold storage. When the Lithuanians requested aid against Muscovy in 1493 the Polish envoy Jan Lubrański stated baldly that the Poles were unwilling to become involved in the Muscovite war, and would only send aid if the Lithuanians opened negotiations over renewal of the union. It seemed that the needle was slipping back into the 1450s groove: the Poles urged that the union be confirmed on the basis of the old agreements, while the Lithuanians retorted that they could only confirm it if these agreements were amended. They did not take kindly to the plan presented to them in Vilnius in 1495 by the queen mother and Cardinal Frederick for Sigismund to be granted Kyiv as his appanage.[16]

The dynasty was already concerned about the future. Casimir's sons were all in their thirties; none had yet produced an heir. Alexander had only just married, and his marriage was to prove childless. Władysław had serious marital problems. He followed a disastrous first marriage to Barbara, daughter of Albert Achilles, margrave of Brandenburg, by marrying Beatrice of Aragon, the widow of Matthias Corvinus, in 1490, despite not having divorced Barbara. His second marriage was no more successful, but he managed to secure annulments of both marriages in 1500 and his third wife, Anna de Foix Grailly, gave birth to a son, Louis, in 1506. John Albert never married. At least Sigismund proved his fertility, siring an illegitimate son and two illegitimate daughters by his Moravian mistress, Kateřina Telničanka. It was not until the birth of his son Sigismund August in 1520 that the line of the Polish Jagiellons was secure.[17]

Halecki saw the notion of granting Kyiv to Sigismund as an opportunity to bestow greater status upon the annexed Ruthenian territories within the union by opening the way to the creation of a grand duchy of Ruthenia that might be capable

---

[13] Любавский, *Сеймъ*, 135–6; Stryjkowski mistakenly claims that the ceremony was performed by Ivan Khreptovich, who was marshal hospodarski, as does Zujienė, 'Lietuvos', 58: Papée, *Aleksander*, 12.

[14] Любавский, *Сеймъ*, 130–1. See Ch. 26, 304–5.   [15] Wojciechowski, *Zygmunt*, 82–3.

[16] Halecki, *Dzieje*, i, 442–4.   [17] Wojciechowski, *Zygmunt*, 81.

of providing a more effective defence of Lithuania's frontiers.[18] There is no evidence to suggest contemporaries saw the matter in this way. For Władysław and Sigismund the justification was dynastic: it would solve the temporary problem of a junior prince without visible means of support. Alexander and the Lithuanian council saw things differently, arguing that the grand duchy was indivisible. Land could not be carved out of it to be granted to Sigismund, and Lithuania could not have two lords. The Lithuanian sejm in Brest in March 1496 rejected the idea outright.[19] If anybody realized that the Lithuanians were deploying the same arguments the Poles had used during the coronation tempest, nobody had a sufficient sense of irony to point it out.

Uncertainty over the succession brought the problem of the union into focus. There were other reasons for considering the issue. Ivan III's disapproval of the Kyiv scheme was another reminder that the 1494 'eternal peace' was unlikely to last, as Ivan had no intention of abandoning his claim to be *gosudar'* of all Rus'. The feelers put out by John Albert during discussions of the Kyiv plan were calculated to leave Lithuanian feathers unruffled. As the Lithuanian reply made clear in 1496, the Lithuanian council, with whom, Alexander stressed, he had discussed the matter, appreciated the gesture:

> Your highness ordained... in these matters, that with regard to the agreements and documents between our lands and realms, and the subjects of the councils of both realms, that is the crown of Poland and the grand duchy of Lithuania, they should be presented according to right and agreed custom, without offence to the honour or detriment of either realm.[20]

This document reveals that there was a new set of concepts available to discuss the question of union. Written in Ruthenian, though in the Latin alphabet, it uses the term '*panstwo*' to designate the parties to the union. *Państwo* was the direct Polish translation of the Latin *dominium*, or lordship. By the late fifteenth century it was being used in its modern sense to designate the state as an abstract entity separate from the person of the ruler. Whereas the documents of union from the days of Jagiełło and Vytautas had used *dominium* in its older sense, speaking the language of lordship, those of Alexander and John Albert used *dominium* differently, speaking of the relationship between the various 'states' or 'realms' that they ruled. Where Jagiełło had referred to himself at Krewo as 'grand duke, lord, and natural heir of the Lithuanians and of Ruthenia' (*dux magnus Litwanorum Rusiaeque dominus et haeres naturalis*), Alexander, who styled himself 'Lithuanian, Ruthenian, Samogitian and (of other realms) grand duke' (*вєликій князъ Литовскій, Руский, Жомоитский и иныхъ*), conceptualized his rule rather differently. In his 1499 privilege for the Orthodox church he stated that it was issued to Iosif Bolharynovych, as metropolitan of Kyiv, and to all (Orthodox) bishops 'in our patrimony of the grand duchy of Lithuania, and in our Ruthenian realms (*въ панствахъ нашихъ*

---

[18] Halecki, *Dzieje*, i, 443.
[19] *AZR*, i, no. 135, 156–61; Rowell, 'Dynastic bluff?', 14–15; Halecki, *Dzieje*, i, 444.
[20] *CESXV*, iii, no. 421, 436.

Рускихъ)'.[21] This language, with its view of the relationship within the union as one between abstract political entities conceptualized as 'realms', with the grand duchy itself seen as a composite polity, composed of Lithuania proper and the annexed Ruthenian 'realms', represented an implicit challenge to the Polish incorporationist view of the union.

This conceptual shift made it possible to discuss the union in a new way. The Poles took the hint immediately, sending a high level embassy to the Lithuanian sejm in Vilnius in the summer of 1496, one of whose members was Mikołaj Tęczyński, son-in-law of the late Lithuanian chancellor, Alekna Sudimantaitis. While its main purpose was to secure Lithuanian support for the Ottoman war, it brought with it the Horodło document of 2 October 1413 in which the Lithuanian boyars had sworn loyalty to Jagiełło, Vytautas, and the *corona regni Poloniae*. It was a good choice, for this document made no reference to the incorporation so pedantically insisted upon in the document issued by Jagiełło and Vytautas. The Lithuanians responded positively, agreeing that there was nothing problematic in the document, which they agreed to confirm, and sent an embassy of their own, with their own project for a renewal of the union.[22]

According to Halecki, these discussions were 'only formally' conducted on the basis of the old agreements. Yet if both sides adopted a new attitude towards the agreements drawn up by their forebears, the significance of the old treaties was substantial: the long stalemate over the union had not been over the principle of union, but over the interpretation of what the documents meant. The negotiations were expressly conducted on the basis of the Horodło agreement, with the Lithuanians responding positively to the olive branch offered by the Poles through the tacit abandonment—for the moment at least—of the sternly incorporationist position they had maintained for so long.

The Lithuanian project, drawn up not in Alexander's name, but on behalf of the 'prelates, barons, nobles, and all the inhabitants' of the grand duchy, talked approvingly of the agreements made by their predecessors that had established the alliances, peace, concord, and friendship between the two realms, singling out Horodło for particular praise and stating that they remained fully in force (*in hec usque tempore inviolate servarentur*). It expressly renewed and confirmed the agreements. Referring to the circumstances surrounding the elections of John Albert and Alexander according to the wishes of Casimir, which it recognized as an 'innovation', the project advanced the sensible position that the treaties should not be treated rigidly, but as a flexible framework under which particular contingencies as ordained by God could be taken into account.[23]

There were still disagreements. The Lithuanian suggestion that the arrangements established at Horodło for royal elections in Poland should only be instigated if the Jagiellons died out in the male line proved unacceptable to the Polish envoys, who refused to accept the document. While it would have preserved the union, it would have denied the Poles the fruits of the hard-won victory over Jagiełło by which they

---

[21] *AZR*, i, no. 166, 190.   [22] Halecki, *Dzieje*, i, 445–6.   [23] *CESXV*, iii, no. 422, 418.

established a fully elective monarchy.²⁴ The Poles might in practice favour the natural rights that the Jagiellons claimed to possess, and they might always vote for a candidate who would preserve the union, but they would not surrender the right to choose.

The pressing Polish need for aid against the Ottomans had nevertheless softened the Polish position, suggesting that a compromise might be possible. The Lithuanians were determined to exploit the opportunity to reach agreement on the union's nature. When a 1498 Polish embassy again sought help against the Ottomans, Alexander replied that the Lithuanian council had discussed the matter, and that while in principle it was willing, it could offer no assistance until the question of equality within the union was addressed. This was no simple rebuff, however, for the Lithuanians immediately sent Martin Lintfari, bishop of Samogitia, and Jan Zaberezhynsky, castellan and palatine of Trakai, and a supporter of closer relations with Poland, to John Albert in January 1499.²⁵ That the Lithuanians were serious is demonstrated by the grant of plenipotentiary powers to agree a new union, on behalf of Alexander and 'our whole republic' (*nostris et totiae Reipublicae*).²⁶ The council instructions put matters more bluntly. They laid down what the envoys were to say, observing that previous documents of union in which the grand duchy was not treated equally with Poland 'as is usual between all Christian kings and princes', had never been passed over in silence by their forebears, who had in many embassies and on many occasions informed the Poles that they had never upheld these treaties, and had never wanted to uphold them. Horodło, at least in the Lithuanian boyars' version, was not such a treaty. The embassy was to raise two complaints. One concerned the frequent border incidents between western Podolia, under Polish control, and the Lithuanian-held provinces of eastern Podolia and Volhynia; the other touched on nomination to Lithuanian bishoprics, in which confirmation from the papacy was frequently sent to the king of Poland and not the grand duke.²⁷

The Lithuanians were in a good position after the Moldavian debacle to reopen this issue, discussions of which had stalled in 1453. It was probably at this point that the Lithuanian chancery prepared a document that survives in Book 25 (the book of inscriptions) in the Lithuanian Metryka, the chancery archive, which comprises copies of privileges issued by Lithuanian grand dukes and was compiled in 1541 on the orders of the queen, Bona Sforza.²⁸ The document is a reworking of Horodło that removes all hints of subservience to the kingdom of Poland. While it is possible that it was prepared in the 1440s or 1450s, it is more likely, since Horodło was central to the discussions in 1496 and 1499, that it was drafted in connection with these discussions.²⁹ It is highly revealing of Lithuanian concepts of

---

²⁴ Halecki, *Dzieje*, i, 447. ²⁵ Любавский, *Сеймъ*, 141.
²⁶ *AU*, no. 71, 119–20. ²⁷ *CESXV*, iii, no. 443, 461–2; no. 444, 462–3.
²⁸ It is published in *Lietuvos Metrika* Knyga Nr. 25 *(1387–1546)*, ed. Darius Antanavičius and Algirdas Baliulis (Vilnius, 1998), 44–6 and, with Lithuanian and Polish translations, in *Horodlės aktai*, 281–8. The original does not survive; neither does the 1541 copy, which was recopied in 1598: Baliulis, 'Preface', in *Lietuvos Metrika* Knyga Nr. 25, xiii.
²⁹ For a detailed analysis that does not commit itself with regard to dating see Kuolys, *Res Lituania*, 63–89.

union. Kuolys talks of it as a forgery, but it seems better to regard it as a genuine attempt, in the context of the 1490s discussions, to draft a version of Horodło that would be acceptable to the Lithuanian citizen body. It omits entirely the first clause of the joint document issued by Jagiełło and Vytautas, with its litany of incorporationist synonyms, and radically alters the clause allowing for the election of a grand duke, omitting all reference to only electing candidates put forward by the king of Poland, and of the need to consult with the Poles, baldly stating that the Lithuanians had the right to elect whomsoever they chose as their grand duke.[30]

This confirms Lithuanian attachment to the principle of election, and their awareness that its legal basis rested upon Horodło. The rest of the document details the rights and privileges granted to the Lithuanian nobility in 1413, stressing in almost every case that these were to be enjoyed as they were in Poland (*iuxta consuetudinem Regni Poloniae*), casting doubt on Kuolys's contention that Horodło lost its force after the election of Casimir as grand duke in 1440, and the idea that the Lithuanians took little interest in Horodło. The Lithuanian community of the realm was well aware that its freedoms and liberties depended on the acts of union, and in particular on Horodło. Instead it rejected the Polish idea of an accessory union, and sought to secure Polish agreement to changes in the text of the union treaties that would embody the Lithuanian vision of a union *aeque principaliter*.

The Poles would not accept such a radical redrafting of Horodło, but the firm stance of the Lithuanians brought results, with the agreement of what has been called—though the term is disputed—the Vilnius-Cracow union. John Albert and the Polish council ratified the agreement in Cracow on 6 and 14 May 1499, sending with the ratification a copy of the document drawn up for the Polish nobles at Horodło. Alexander summoned a sejm to Vilnius that agreed to reciprocate on 14 July, sending a copy of the Lithuanian redaction of Horodło.[31] The new agreement closely followed the 1496 Lithuanian proposal, and marked the success of the new Lithuanian approach to relations with Poland, which had persuaded the Poles to modify their insistence that Lithuania had been incorporated.[32]

Some historians have seen the 1499 agreements as establishing a confederation, league, or alliance between two otherwise independent states, linked by no institution.[33] Yet this was no mere alliance. The documents presented the relationship as both a union and a league, stating that the unions and alliances entered into by Jagiełło and Vytautas remained in force. It confirmed the Horodło documents prepared for the Polish nobles and the Lithuanian boyars, rather than the document issued by Jagiełło and Vytautas with the incorporation clause.[34] In an implicit

---

[30] 'praelati, barones et nobiles Magni Ducatus Lithuaniae magnum ducum suum sine liberis et successoribus legitimis decedentem magnum ducem Lithuaniae libera electione, quem voluerint, eligent': *Horodlės aktai*, 283.

[31] *AU*, nos. 72–6, 121–30.   [32] Halecki, *Dzieje*, i, 452.

[33] Kutrzeba, 'Charakter', 172–3; Łowmiański, *Polityka*, 372–3. Halecki agrees, but adds the important qualification 'according to modern legal terminology': *Dzieje*, i, 453.

[34] 'quomodo licet uniones et foedera inter haec dominia... inita et constituta hucusque inviolate serventur'. In the parallel Polish text, 'inter dominia' was translated as 'między państwy' (between states): *AU*, no. 76, 128; 'unionum confoederationumque': *AU*, no. 74, 123.

reference to the events of 1430, 1440, and 1492, it was stated that clarity would be brought to the institution of election as established in 1413. The Lithuanians promised that on the death of their grand duke they would not elect a successor without the knowledge and agreement of their Polish brothers: Polish ambassadors would be invited to attend the election. Similarly, the Lithuanians would be invited to attend Polish royal elections, and the Poles agreed not to elect their king without Lithuanian knowledge and consent.[35] The desire for clarity was laudable, although increased clarity was not necessarily the outcome, since the documents gave no indication as to how the elections were to be conducted. The use of '*pariter*', rendered in the Polish translation as '*wespółek*' (together with), suggests that in the light of the principle of unanimity that governed Polish parliamentary procedures, it was intended that the respective ambassadors would have a veto, at least as a bargaining tool to ensure that consensus was reached.

The document confirmed the Horodło privileges, which included the adoption into Polish heraldic clans, thereby reasserting the vision of a common, fraternal union of political communities. The development of the Lithuanian community of the realm, as expressed in the idea of the Lithuanian *respublica* meant that—as had not been the case in 1413—both parties to the union could conceive of the relationship in different terms within what was becoming a common political culture that used a common political language in which the idea of the *respublica* was as important as that of the state, the *państwo*.

These concepts, embedded in the Vilnius-Cracow documents, and the provisions they made, including the selective confirmation of the Horodło treaties, support Błaszczyk's contention that 1499 represented far more than the establishment of a mere alliance between two otherwise independent states, and that therefore it is justifiable to refer to the 'Vilnius-Cracow union'.[36] It is true that it created no formal, common institutions of government, and therefore does not fit the standard idea of what constitutes a real union, but it established—or rather confirmed—a relationship that was far more than a mere personal or dynastic union. Its main innovation was the agreement over royal elections, which marked a significant advance on Horodło, particularly with regard to Lithuania. Horodło allowed for the election of a grand duke after Vytautas's death, but did not require it, and the Lithuanian boyars promised only to elect such a grand duke as was nominated by Jagiełło or one of his successors, and by the 'prelates lords, nobility, and *proceres* of the kingdom of Poland's.[37] While Vilnius-Cracow did not explicitly state that such an election must take place in future, it strongly implied that when a grand duke died, an election would take place: the promises made by the Lithuanians concerned only consultation with the Poles. The most striking feature of the clauses concerning the succession is the absence of the dynasty—in stark contrast to Horodło. It was the political communities of Poland and Lithuania that were to be

---

[35] *AU*, no. 74, 129.
[36] Błaszczyk, *Litwa*, 36–7; Halecki's conclusion is broadly similar: *Dzieje*, i, 453. Lowmiański terms it the 'so-called union of Vilnius': *Polityka*, 371–4,
[37] *AU*, no. 50, 59.

consulted, not the king of Poland (in the event of the death of the grand duke), the grand duke (in the event of the king's death), or the dynasty. John Albert appreciated the significance of this omission, stressing that he ratified the treaty without prejudice to the dignity and rights of himself or Alexander as grand duke of Lithuania.[38] Yet it remained to be seen how far the Jagiellon claim that Lithuania was their patrimony could be sustained against the idea of elective monarchy, especially since John Albert's ratification was issued only to the Poles.[39]

Halecki dubiously asserts that Alexander did not need to issue a similar caveat in Lithuania because nobody there questioned the Jagiellons' hereditary rights, and that in the light of Jagiellonian solidarity, the equality of election rights suggested in the Vilnius-Cracow union was illusory. There is, however, no mention of any 'supreme duke' of Lithuania in the Lithuanian redaction, and no acknowledgement that on the death of a grand duke supreme power over Lithuania was vested in the king or crown of Poland. There is no mention of the practice of nomination by the dynasty, and the redrafted Horodło clause in the document preserved in the Lithuanian Metryka suggests that the Lithuanian community of the realm now saw the right of free election of their grand dukes as the foundation of their Lithuanian republic. For all that the dynasty continued to assert its hereditary rights in Lithuania, and for all that the Lithuanians themselves were in future to appeal to these rights when it suited them, the Vilnius-Cracow union marked an important watershed. While Bues goes too far in suggesting that in 1499 Lithuania became an elective monarchy, the new union reasserted the principle of royal election in Lithuania. It is by no means clear that, as Rowell claims, the rights of the dynasty were protected by confirmation of Horodło, since in the document issued to the Lithuanian boyars in 1413—which is what was confirmed in 1499—the clauses that deal with the succession make no mention of the dynasty's hereditary rights in Lithuania, but establish what was to happen with regard to the Polish throne should Jagiełło or his successors die without an heir.[40] In 1413 the question of Jagiełło's hereditary rights in Poland was unclear to say the least.

Halecki, who saw the whole union as the 'Jagiellonian idea', in assessing the Vilnius-Cracow union from the dynasty's point of view, asserts that it served the union less well than the 1496 proposal would have done, since it failed to preserve anything that was important from Horodło apart from promises of mutual assistance that had proven illusory since 1422. He therefore concluded that it was not a fresh start, but merely the sanctioning of the status quo, adding, in something of a *non sequitur*, that it marked the end of an era, and was therefore an appropriate point at which to end the first volume of his history of the union.[41] Seen, however, as a staging-post in the process by which the political communities of the realms of Poland and Lithuania envisaged a union that was built from below, not above, it

---

[38] 'Per hoc tamen non intendimus neque volumus dignitate et iuri praefati illustrissimi domini magni ducis ac nostro in aliquo derogare.' *AU*, no. 74, 124; Halecki, *Dzieje*, i, 454.
[39] Halecki, *Dzieje*, i, 454.
[40] Bues, *Jagiellonen*, 123; Rowell, 'Dynastic bluff?', 15–16; *AU*, no. 50, 59.
[41] Halecki, *Dzieje*, i, 455; ii, 2.

marked an important step: the first point at which the principle of royal election as an institution binding those communities together was enunciated. As events after John Albert's death in Thorn on 17 June 1501 were to show, the implications of Vilnius-Cracow were considerable.

For the context had changed. A year earlier, on 3 May 1500, war with Muscovy resumed when Ivan III sent his armies across the border. One seized Briansk, leaving Siversk open to the south. The Poles could not help, since they were fully engaged beating off two large Tatar attacks. A hastily assembled Lithuanian army was destroyed on the Vedrosh river near Dorohobuzh on 14 July, after which the Masalskys and Mezetskys deserted Alexander for Ivan; over the next three years, vast tracts of the grand duchy's eastern borderlands fell under Muscovite control.[42] With Emperor Maximilian I seeking an alliance with Ivan while encouraging the Order to believe it might secure imperial support for a revision of the 1466 Thorn peace, the common interests of the union partners were clearer than at any time since 1422. On hearing of John Albert's unexpected death Alexander, aware that Lithuania was incapable of resisting Ivan alone, declared his candidacy for the Polish throne. The Lithuanian council, disoriented by the crushing Muscovite victories and uncertain of the loyalty of the Ruthenian elites, recognized that Ivan could only be defeated with Polish help. Despite Vilnius-Cracow's reaffirmation of the Vytautan system, it backed Alexander's bid.[43]

Alexander's path to the throne was by no means smooth. Władysław took a more active role than in 1492, first advancing Sigismund's claims, and then putting forward his own candidature when it became clear that Sigismund, who had little to bring to the table compared with Alexander, had few supporters in Poland. An embassy from Władysław's supporters travelled to Buda to urge him to stand.[44] According to Miechowita, Władysław announced his succession to Maximilian and Louis XII of France.[45] If he did, the announcement was premature. Frederick for the moment sustained the appearance of neutrality, writing to assure Władysław and Sigismund of his good will, but he quietly promoted Alexander's election, endeavouring to convince Elizabeth Habsburg, who was ill-disposed towards Helena.[46]

Frederick faced a more difficult task in 1501 than in 1492. There was considerable discontent during the last years of his brother's reign. John Albert confiscated the lands of some 2,400 nobles for failing to answer the summons of the levy during the disastrous 1497 Moldavian campaign, while Frederick was attacked for ordering that noblemen be summarily imprisoned in his episcopal court.[47] Chancellor Krzesław Kurozwęcki was outraged when the increasingly authoritarian king confiscated the lands of Krzesław's recently deceased brother Piotr for peculation during his service as vice-chancellor.

---

[42] Кром, *Меж Русью*, 115–17; Любавский, *Сеймъ*, 143.
[43] Łowmiański, *Polityka*, 374.
[44] *AA*, no. 6, 5–6; no. 11, 12; Papée, *Aleksander*, 46–50.
[45] Miechowita, *Chronica*, 361–2; Nowakowska accepts Miechowita's account: *Church*, 52–3.
[46] *AA*, no. 12, 12–13.   [47] Papée, *Jan Olbracht*, 145–6.

With accusations of tyranny in the air, and a potential Muscovite threat to the Ruthenian lands under Polish rule, Frederick was in no position to decide the outcome of the election with the sort of dramatic and decisive action he had taken in 1492. John Albert's many enemies were determined to clip the monarchy's wings, and Frederick's letters during the interregnum adopted the language of Polish constitutionalism, defending the rights of the council lords, warning his brothers that they must respect electoral law, and berating Alexander after hearing rumours of plans to seize the throne by force.[48] Aware of the dangers of a contested election, he bought Krzesław's support with a promise to reverse the confiscation if Alexander was elected.

It was the council, however, not Frederick, that played the central role in negotiating the terms of Alexander's election. Thus it was not merely an excuse when Frederick explained to Władysław—disingenuously, given his support for Alexander—that he had supported Władysław's election, but had been forced to take account of majority opinion on the council.[49] The spectacular Muscovite advance meant that the Lithuanians were in a much weaker position than in 1444–7, or during the negotiations over the union between 1496 and 1499. The changed circumstances persuaded the Poles to abandon the moderate stance they had adopted in the 1490s, and to reassert their vision of an accessory union during the negotiations conducted with Alexander in September, first in Bielsk and then in Mielnik on the river Bug. Alexander was not in a strong position. He granted plenipotentiary powers to the Lithuanian delegation invited by the Poles to participate in the electoral sejm at Piotrków, in accordance with the 1499 treaty. The envoys were all supporters of closer union: Wojciech Tabor, Jan Zaberezhynsky, Aleksander Holshansky, Mikalojus Radvila, and Petr Olekhnovych. In their accreditation documents—one issued by Alexander in Hrodna on 27 August, and another by the council in Bielsk on 9 September—they were not only given powers with regard to the election, but were permitted to negotiate a new union treaty, with the only condition being that it was not prejudicial to either realm.[50]

Aleksander was duly elected, with the participation of the Lithuanian envoys in accordance with the 1499 treaty, most probably on 30 September, although his election decree bore the same date as the new treaty of union agreed by the Lithuanian envoys in Piotrków on 3 October and formally accepted by Alexander and the Lithuanian council in Mielnik on 23 October. Three days later Alexander issued another document testifying that twenty-seven Lithuanian princes, lords, and nobles had sworn to uphold the new union, and promised to ensure that the whole Lithuanian nobility accepted it.[51]

---

[48] *AA*, no. 30, 27; Nowakowska, *Church*, 53–4.   [49] *AA*, no. 30, 27–8.
[50] 'sine praejudicio utriusque dominii': *AU*, no. 77, 130–1, no. 78, 131–4. Papée, *Aleksander*, 50–1; Halecki, *Dzieje*, ii, 9.
[51] *AU*, nos. 79–83, 134–49; Łowmiański, *Polityka*, 376; Halecki, *Dzieje*, ii, 11–12; Ludwik Finkel, *Elekcja Zygmunta I* (Cracow, 1910), 10–11; Błaszczyk, *Litwa*, 38; Jučas, *Unija*, 180. Piotr Szafraniec, starosta of Marienburg, informed the Danzig council on 30 September that the election had already taken place: *AA*, no. 27, 24.

The Mielnik union, as it is known, demonstrated where the advantage lay in the negotiations. The Poles made it clear that, while they were willing to support the Lithuanians against Muscovy, that support depended upon agreement on the nature of the union. As Frederick later told Władysław, the Poles demanded recognition of the incorporationist vision expressed in the document issued at Horodło by Jagiełło and Vytautas, which had not been ratified in 1499. The original was hauled out of the Cracow chapter archive in March 1502, along with Žygimantas's promise, made in Trakai on 20 January 1433, to return the grand duchy to Jagiełło on his death, and the Hrodna union of 27 February 1434. The originals were described in detail, and copies were made and notarized.[52]

This exhumation demonstrates that for all the solemn oaths sworn in October 1501, the meaning of the Mielnik union was controversial. The terms appeared to represent an outright victory for Polish incorporationism. The first clause decreed that the kingdom of Poland and the grand duchy of Lithuania were perpetually united and combined into one indivisible and uniform body, so as to form one *gens*, one *populus*, one brotherhood (*fraternitas*), one common council, and a body with one head: one king and lord who was to be elected in common. It was stipulated that this election would be valid even if some of those eligible to vote were absent.[53] Elections were to be held in Poland, and the Lithuanian electorate was defined narrowly, comprising the Catholic bishops, the palatines, castellans and 'dignitaries': essentially this meant the wider council.[54] Clause three laid down that common counsel was to be taken on affairs that concerned the 'whole body' of the realm. Each party promised not to desert the other in times of need; clause five decreed the establishment of a common currency, to be regulated by the common council. Other clauses stipulated that treaties with foreign powers were to remain in force unless they breached the laws or customs of either party; all officeholders were to swear an oath of loyalty to the king of Poland, and to uphold the mutually agreed treaties of union. The king was to swear to uphold the liberties and rights of his counsellors and dignitaries, and at his coronation was to confirm the rights and privileges of both realms.[55]

It was a radical document. It envisaged a real union based upon the common election of the monarch, a common council that would deliberate on matters that touched the entire union state, and a common currency. For Halecki, it represented a completely new departure, and he explained away the fact that it was negotiated by the same men who agreed the 1499 treaty—which he claimed merely recognized the status quo—by arguing that the circumstances of the Muscovite war forced the

---

[52] *AU*, nos. 84–6, 149–54.

[53] 'quod regnum Poloniae et magnus ducatus Lithwaniae uniantur et conglutinentur in unum et indivisum ac indifferens corpus, ut sit una gens, una populus, una fraternitas et communia consilia eidemque corpori perpetuo unum caput, unus rex unusque dominus in loco et tempore assignatis per praesentes et ad electionem convenientes votis communibus eligatur, quodque absentium obstantia electio non impediatur et decretum electionis in regno semper sit iuxta consuetudines circa illud ex antiquo servatas.' *AU*, no. 79, 137; no. 80, 140; no. 82, 144.

[54] *AU*, no. 82, 144.

[55] *AU*, no. 82, 137–8, 140–1, 144–5, Halecki, *Dzieje*, ii, 12–14; Błaszczyk *Litwa*, 39; Jučas, *Unija*, 180–1.

Lithuanians into extensive concessions, while the childless Alexander agreed to it on account of his personal ambition, since the principle of common election effectively abrogated the dynasty's hereditary rights to Lithuania.[56] Halecki observed that the document did not explicitly mention incorporation, but others have interpreted it as a triumph for Polish incorporationist views.[57] In Buda, Władysław recognized the implicit threat to the Jagiellons' hereditary rights to Lithuania. A Hungarian delegation that arrived in Cracow after Alexander's coronation formally protested at the slight to Władysław's honour, maintaining that he, as the eldest son, possessed prior rights to the thrones of his father and grandfather by primogeniture. Sigismund came to Cracow in person to assert his own rights to a share of the Jagiellon patrimony.[58]

Alexander needed no instruction on Mielnik's implications, and the question of incorporation remained academic, for the treaty never came into effect, despite its ratification by Alexander and the twenty-seven Lithuanian lords, and despite Halecki's unsubstantiated claim that it was implemented 'for a short time'.[59] Alexander was forced to agree to it as the price of his coronation: although he ratified it in October, he was only allowed to use the title *rex electus* until his formal election, which took place in Cracow on 12 December.[60] Nevertheless, he had room for manoeuvre. He had come to Mielnik with several of his councillors and a large group of officials, but the gathering was far short of a full sejm, and representatives of the annexed territories were conspicuously absent.[61] He therefore promised that confirmation would be sought '*per universos praelatos, barones, nobiles et boiaros Lithwaniae*'.[62] Since such confirmation was neither sought nor received, the document remained a dead letter. Rowell suspects that this was because Alexander was fully aware of its implications, and his ratification was a 'Jagiellonian sham to trick the Poles (with Lithuanian noble support)' into accepting him as their king, although he did order copies be made of the document to be sent out to gather the seals of council members not present in Mielnik. Liubavskii argues that Lithuanian concern about ratifying the agreement was principally due to the Muscovite war, which made the calling of a full sejm impossible; moreover, with the Ruthenians absent from Mielnik, to draw formally closer to Catholic Poland was politically risky, since it might provoke more Ruthenian defections to Ivan.[63]

Both arguments are plausible. Alexander, whose playing of the difficult hand he had been dealt bears out Pietkiewicz's positive assessment of his political ability, was well aware of Polish incorporationist attitudes, and of Mielnik's implications for the dynasty, as he pointed out in a sharply phrased defence of his actions to Władysław, who boycotted Alexander's coronation. In declaring his candidature in August, Alexander told the Polish council that Władysław's claims as Casimir's oldest son

---

[56] Halecki, *Dzieje*, ii, 1–2.
[57] Łowmiański argued that even the Lithuanians accepted that Mielnik incorporated the grand duchy into Poland: *Polityka*, 376; cf. Adamus, 'O prawno-państwowym stosunku', 179.
[58] Finkel, *Elekcja*, 12–14.   [59] Halecki, *Dzieje*, ii, 1; cf. Błaszczyk, *Litwa*, 40.
[60] Papée, *Aleksander*, 54.   [61] Любавский, *Сеймъ*, 144–5.
[62] *AU*, no. 79, 137; no. 80, 141; no. 83, 148–9.
[63] Rowell, 'Dynastic bluff?', 16; Любавский, *Сеймъ*, 145.

had been nullified by his abandoning Poland to take up the Bohemian and Hungarian crowns, and by Casimir's decision to designate John Albert as his preferred candidate for the Polish throne.[64] Alexander berated Władysław for condemning his coronation, and sending his envoys to attack him for allowing the incorporation of the grand duchy into Poland without his consent. Alexander replied that he himself was a member of the dynasty, and that he had been elected unanimously by both the Poles and the Lithuanians. He observed sarcastically that Władysław should well know (*non debuit M.V. ignorare*) that this election was nothing new, and it in no way challenged the natural, hereditary rights of either Władysław or Sigismund, continuing, again sarcastically (*scire enim potest S.M.V.*), with a potted history lesson reminding Władysław of the tradition of dynastic designation, and asserting that what had occurred did not breach Horodło.[65]

Alexander's response was, as Rowell observes, self-exculpatory and tendentious.[66] It nevertheless demonstrates that he had inherited a substantial dose of political realism from his father. He remarked that Władysław's attempt to assert the rights of primogeniture was justifiable neither in historic terms nor in the light of the union treaties. Yet if—for obvious reasons—he was opposed to primogeniture, Alexander did care about his dynasty's natural rights in Lithuania, and ensured that Mielnik never came into effect. He was assisted by two circumstances: the treaty's vagueness concerning how it was to operate in practice, and its narrowly oligarchic character.

For if the Poles regarded Mielnik as securing Lithuanian recognition of their incorporation, the treaty gave no hint of what incorporation meant in practice, unlike the 1454 treaty with the Prussians. Lithuania's political structure was fundamentally different from Poland's, and despite the establishment of the palatinates of Vilnius and Trakai at Horodło, the grand duchy lacked the developed system of local courts and sejmiks that formed the basis of the Polish political system. Mielnik represented a compromise between the only two institutions that were roughly equivalent between the two realms: the ruler's councils. It was the councils that were to come together to elect the common ruler, and to deliberate together on matters that affected the whole realm, not the two sejms, for the Lithuanian sejm was as yet a very different body from its Polish counterpart.

It was this narrow concept of the political system that was Mielnik's greatest weakness. It was effectively agreed between the Polish council and a small group of Lithuanian unionist councillors who had made common cause with their counterparts in Poland, possibly because Alexander's rule had reminded them of the benefits of an absentee ruler for their own control in Vilnius. They were vulnerable once Alexander secured his election. By the time that a six-year truce was agreed with Ivan on 28 March 1503, Lithuanian support for the 1501 treaty had cooled considerably. The Poles had failed to produce any substantial military aid, and Lithuania had been forced to make peace on highly disadvantageous terms. Alexander was secure on the Polish throne, and had no interest in pursuing ratification.

[64] *AA*, no. 21, 21.   [65] *AA*, no. 69, 74–9.   [66] Rowell, 'Dynastic bluff?', 17–19.

On his return to Poland in 1503, the Poles pushed him to produce the promised Lithuanian guarantees, urging him to call a joint sejm in Lublin to confirm the union.[67] Although the invitation to the Lithuanians from the Polish embassy to the Lithuanian sejm in Brest in February 1505 dripped with the language of fraternal harmony, it was rejected on the grounds that Mielnik had been been agreed without the consent of the many who had been absent. Only Wojciech Tabor, Jan Zaberezhynsky, and Aleksander Holshansky spoke in its favour. The wind blew cold and hard against them. The rising star of the new royalist party, which fully backed Alexander's new line, was the energetic and talented Mykhailo Hlynsky. The defeated party was excluded from the council. Zaberezhynsky remained marshal of the land, but Alexander stripped him of the palatinate of Trakai, which, on Hlynsky's recommendation, was granted to Mikalojus Radvila, who had helped negotiate Mielnik, but had prudently changed sides.[68]

Although Halecki was wrong to insist that Mielnik was briefly implemented, he was right to suggest that it marked an important watershed in the process of union. Its first clause was clearly a compromise between the Polish and Lithuanian negotiators. Although the Poles entered the talks determined to insist upon incorporation, this clause—indeed the whole treaty—made no mention of it.[69] Instead it stated that Poland and Lithuania were 'united and combined into one indivisible body'. This formula picked up the imagery of the body politic that shot through the act's preamble, which declared that political harmony depended upon God's creation of kingdoms and duchies as bodies politic, in which the limbs responded to the head, and the head regulated the limbs to ensure moderation and prudence.[70] These phrases were conventional pieties, but the preamble's stress on how the old treaties sought to establish conditions under which friendship and alliance might flourish, in order to improve both Poland and Lithuania (*meliorem promoventia Reipublicae, tam regni Poloniae, quam magni ducatus Lithwaniae*), and upon mutual *caritas* within the 'perpetual fraternal connection' between 'these two most noble nations' (*eorundem ac nobilissimarum Poloniae et Litwaniae nationum*) was reflected in this first clause.[71]

Mielnik echoed the fraternal language of earlier treaties, but this formula was new, hinting at the combination of two polities into one 'indivisible and undifferentiated body', to form one *gens* and one *populus*, one fraternity and one (political) community. Thus, while the clause went on to stress that the king was to form the head of this new body politic, the language was of political community, not of statehood, and the stress that the king was to be elected by this new political nation made it clear that his legitimacy ultimately depended upon the express consent of the community of this new realm.

Like all compromise formulae, this clause was open to different interpretations. That many Poles still saw it as incorporationist became abundantly clear in the years that followed. Its failure to confront the problem of statehood was a weakness,

---

[67] *AA*, no. 277, 458–60.
[68] Любавский, *Сеймъ*, 146–7; Pietkiewicz, *Wielkie księstwo*, 206.
[69] Błaszczyk, *Litwa*, 39. [70] *AU*, no. 79, 135. [71] *AU*, no. 79, 136.

although there were hints that this body might contain two realms in union together: clause 5 suggested that each party to the union would continue to be governed by their own laws and customs, and clause 11 spoke of the preservation of the liberties and offices, and the conservation of the security of both realms (*utriusque dominii salva et salvas conservando*).[72] These phrases suggest that Balzer was wrong to stress that Mielnik formally dissolved the separate authority of the grand duke and sought to end Lithuania's separate statehood.[73] The possibility of a separate grand duke in the future was not excluded. Mielnik instead bears witness to the gradual forming of the notion that two realms could, within a union, fuse themselves into an entity that transcended both of them, as Scotland and England were formally to accomplish in 1707. It also prioritized the union of peoples over the union of states. Although Mielnik never came into effect, the vision of union it embodied was not forgotten.

---

[72] *AU*, no. 79, 138.   [73] Balzer, 'Horodło', 174.

29

Nihil Novi

Mielnik's failure became all too apparent after Alexander's death in Vilnius on 19 August 1506. He had been incapacitated for over a year after suffering a stroke in June 1505. He was not quite 44, but over the following months five further strokes paralysed his left side. Although by November he was able to stand unaided and even ride a horse, in May he suffered a relapse. His condition was not helped by a doctor summoned from Cracow, who prescribed frequent baths and the consumption of copious quantities of wine, which no doubt rendered his last days more bearable, but which probably hastened his end.[1]

The dynasty's position had weakened since 1501. Frederick died in March 1503 aged only 35, and Elizabeth Habsburg followed him into the grave in August 1505. In Alexander's testament of 24 July 1506 he left his considerable fortune to Sigismund, whom he designated his 'only heir and successor to him and his patrimony in the kingdom and the grand duchy'.[2] Having scuppered Mielnik, Alexander was asserting on Sigismund's behalf the dynasty's hereditary claims, not just to Lithuania, but also to Poland.

Sigismund's designation allowed the Lithuanians to seize the initiative. Alexander's favourite Mykhailo Hlynsky, his position strengthened by his victory over a Tatar force at Kletsk on 5 August, led the Lithuanian council in a public demonstration that Mielnik was no more. In an act pregnant with symbolism, Alexander was interred not as he wished in Cracow beside his father and brothers, but in Vilnius cathedral; he remains the only king of Poland buried there.[3] Hlynsky did much to clear Sigismund's path to the throne. Sigismund, aware that some Cracow lords favoured Władysław, negotiated with Wielkopolskan politicians, who did not. As soon as he heard of Alexander's death he hurried to Hrodna, where he met Hlynsky, who supported Sigismund in what amounted not to a coup against the union, as Wojciechowski claims, but a rejection of Mielnik.[4] Envoys were summoned to a sejm to elect a new grand duke. The Polish council, while careful to reassure Sigismund that Lithuania was his patrimony, sent Mikołaj Firlej, ensign of Cracow, to Vilnius to protest at the hasty interment, to remind the Lithuanians of the union treaties, and to request them not to act unilaterally.[5] He was bluntly told that on account of the dangers facing Lithuania, both internal and external, they could not delay. On 20 October, Sigismund was declared 'hereditary and natural

---

[1] Papée, *Aleksander*, 107. [2] *PSB*, i, 60. [3] *AT*, i, appendix, no. 6, 20–1.
[4] Wojciechowski, *Zygmunt*, 86–7. [5] *AT*, i, no. 5, 8; no. 7, 9–10.

lord' and grand duke and prince of Lithuania by the 'unanimous will' of princes and lords from all the grand duchy's lands.[6]

There is no doubt that this was an election. It was politically useful, however, for the council to stress that Sigismund was their hereditary and natural lord, and to emphasize Lithuanian tradition against Mielnik. Yet to do so was not a separatist act. There were no rivals within the dynasty. Władysław had ceded his hereditary rights to Lithuania to Sigismund in 1503, and showed no interest in advancing his claims or those of his son, while as contemporary commentators noted, if the Poles might have elected Władysław or Janusz II of Mazovia, the prospect of the former, who would have to rule four realms, was not enticing, while the Mazovian Piasts were no more attractive than they had ever been.[7] It was therefore highly unlikely that the Poles would do anything other than accept the *fait accompli* and elect Sigismund, which they duly did on 8 December 1506, although he was pointedly reminded that he had no hereditary rights to the Polish throne, and that the council had chosen him because of his personal qualities, and because the Poles had a right of free election that they wished to pass on to their descendants.[8]

Once again, Polish incorporationist claims were impossible to uphold, as the Polish acknowledgement that Lithuania constituted Sigismund's patrimony implicitly recognized. The Lithuanians might have rejected Mielnik's stipulation of a common election, but they sent envoys to the Polish election sejm, even if they turned up late.[9] Implicitly, however, they accepted Mielnik's underlying principle. Sigismund was to rule both realms, and there was to be no grand duke in Vilnius. Casimir's long reign, and the increased powers granted to the council by Alexander in 1492 had demonstrated that Lithuania could be governed without a separate grand duke in a system that suited the narrow group of dignitaries who formed the inner council.

The council faced a difficult task. The Muscovite truce was due to expire in 1509, but Sigismund—encouraged by Tatar promises to attack Muscovy—issued a peremptory demand in 1507 for a return to the 1492 borders that sparked a war which may only have lasted a year, but which demonstrated the incapacity of the Lithuanians to recover by force what they had lost, as well as the unreliability of the Tatars, who changed sides halfway through. An 'eternal' peace was signed on 8 October 1508, in which Lithuania regained a sliver of territory around Lubuch, but few expected it to last. The war demonstrated that the council was no united, harmonious body, but was shot through with rivalries. The loss of favour by Hlynsky after 1506—despite his leading role in Sigismund's election—in part because of Sigismund's suspicions over his close relations with Alexander's widow Helena, and in part because of his bitter rivalry with Jan Zaberezhynsky, revealed the tensions. Hlynsky's murder of Zaberezhynsky on 2 February 1508, his failed

---

[6] Stanisław Górski, 'Commentarius rerum gestarum a Sigismundo primo, Rege Polonie, Magno Duce Lituanie', *AT*, i, no. 8, 13; Любавский, *Сеймъ*, 149.
[7] Rowell, 'Dynastic bluff?', 19.   [8] Wojciechowski, *Zygmunt*, 87.
[9] Stanisław Górski, 'Commentarius', *AT*, no. 5, 8; no. 8, 14.

rising, and his flight to Moscow did not, however, resolve them, and divisions remained over attitudes towards the union.

Breaking the union was impossible. Five thousand Polish troops were paid off in 1508, but eternity lasted a mere four years, and war returned with new intensity in 1512. In the ten-year conflict that followed, Lithuania lost Smolensk in July 1514, in Ivan's greatest military triumph. Kostiantyn Ostrozky's victory at Orsha on 8 September restored Lithuanian pride, but it was to be a century before Smolensk was recovered. The council had governed Lithuania without much difficulty during the long, peaceful years of Casimir's reign, but war was different. Large amounts of money were needed to pay the Polish professionals. Neither the inner nor the outer council could hope to impose the necessary taxes without the support of wider noble society. Thus general sejms with representatives from across the grand duchy became ever more frequent.

The demands upon society were considerable. The 1507 Vilnius sejm agreed to the registration of all noble estates for the purposes of defence, and to introduce a new tax, the 'silver tax' (серебщизна/serebshchyzna), to be raised on the basis of inventories of ploughed land at a rate of 6 groszy per horse-plough, and 3 groszy per ox-plough. Those who farmed without possessing a plough also paid 3 groszy.[10] In 1514, in a vain attempt to save Smolensk, the sejm agreed to raise 7,000 Polish troops; in order to pay for them, it levied a poll tax at a rate of 1 grosz from a peasant, 2 groszy for a boyar, and 1 złoty from officeholders, lords, and prominent nobles.[11]

These were not permanent taxes, but had to be agreed on every occasion they were levied. The constant need for money to pay for war helped to institutionalize the embryonic Lithuanian parliamentary system, although as yet it was still dominated by the council. Ad hoc local assemblies did occasionally meet, but there was no institutionalized system comparable to the one that emerged in Poland after 1454, and envoys were nominated by local officials or magnates. Nevertheless, the substantial demands placed upon Lithuanian society in these years, and the increasing frequency of sejms began to create a sense of common interest and political community among the noble masses, especially after the establishment of the new military registers in 1528, and the frequent musterings of the levy that followed.[12]

These developments gradually loosened the grip of the narrow inner-council oligarchy in Lithuania, but it was not until later that their effects became clear. In Poland the process was much quicker following the establishment of the two-chamber sejm after 1493. A sign that times were changing was the failure to ratify the conditions imposed upon Alexander at Mielnik in 1501. For he had not just been presented with a treaty of union. He had also received notification of his election shot through with reminders that it was not by succession, but by free election that kings ascended the Polish throne.[13] It had been accompanied by a

---

[10] Łowmiański, *Zaludnienie*, 17–18; Любавский, *Сеймъ*, 179–80.
[11] Любавский, *Сеймъ*, 198.   [12] Любавский, *Сеймъ*, 151–70.
[13] *AA*, no. 28, 25.

petition that was a barely disguised attack on John Albert's treatment of Piotr Kurozwęcki, and an encomium to the necessity and virtues of counsel. The demands may have been couched as a petition, but were effectively the terms Alexander had to accept to win the throne. On 25 October 1501 he had sworn to uphold the Mielnik articles, as they are most properly known, which were prepared on the basis of the petition.[14] Traditionally, they were termed the privileges of Mielnik, and condemned as an attempt to entrench a narrowly oligarchic political system dominated by the council. Yet the Mielnik articles, together with the union treaty, represent a coherent and rational attempt to give institutional and legal form to late medieval concepts of the mixed form of government that drew its inspiration from the works of Aristotle, Aquinas, John of Salisbury, and Aegidius Romanus. In the preamble Alexander stated—in the words put into his mouth—that it was possible not only to increase public liberty, but also to secure it, so long as he and his successors respected the law and ruled by the statutes agreed by their predecessors.[15] The first article stated bluntly that a good and just prince must rule according to the laws and on the advice of his councillors, and not arbitrarily. Councillors who gave the prince unpalatable advice should not be persecuted—as Piotr Kurozwęcki had been persecuted—for their honesty and public spirit in telling him the truth, rather than what he wished to hear. If a councillor was accused of a crime by the king, the case against him should not be judged by the king and the rabble (*turba malorum*) of the ordinary nobility in the sejm, but by a tribunal of the senior and wisest among the king's councillors, in a formulation that drew on conciliarist and canon law precepts.[16]

The Mielnik articles, while they sought to protect council interests, were far more than the simple oligarchs' charter as which they are often portrayed. They addressed the problem of establishing the conditions under which the monarch might lawfully be resisted and even deprived of his throne should he behave tyrannically.[17] The third clause stated that if the king broke his coronation oath, the community of the realm would be released from the obligation to respect its oaths of loyalty.[18] It upheld the right of individual protest against royal actions and the right of the political community collectively to withdraw obedience to its elected monarch if he should act against the interests of the state and in a manner offensive to the republic in a phrase that reflected the dual conception of the polity as a state and a political community.[19]

---

[14] *VC*, i/i, 109–13. The best account is Ludwik Sobolewski and Wacław Uruszczak, 'Artykuły mielnickie z roku 1501', *CPH*, 42 (1990), 51–80. They talk of nine articles, but base their discussion on the text as published by Bandtkie in his 1831 *Ius Polonicum*. The text in *Volumina Constitutionum*, in which there are fifteen clauses, draws on a fuller version in Jakub Przyłuski's *Leges seu statuta ac privilegia Regni Polonia omnia* (Cracow, 1553): *VC*, i/i, 101. Nowakowska confuses the petition with the articles and overemphasizes their impact, failing to point out they were never implemented: *Church*, 55–6.

[15] *VC*, i/i, 109.   [16] *VC*, i/i, 110; Sobolewski and Uruszczak, 'Artykuły', 54–5, 69.

[17] 'sed ut tirannum et hostem reputent': *VC*, i/i, 110.

[18] 'extunc universum regnum sit liberum a iuramento et fide praestita': *VC*, i/i, 110.

[19] 'contra statum et offensum reipublicae': *VC*, i/i, 110.

Although the articles assumed that the council spoke for that political community, their political vision was broader, despite the evident contempt for mass opinion. Some were certainly informed by council concerns. Clauses five and six sought to ensure that offices and dignities were filled on council advice within two months of the death of the incumbent.[20] Other clauses, however, followed Nieszawa in seeking to limit the judicial powers of the starostas, and of the king himself. Clause four stated that cases in local land courts presided over by the king when passing through individual provinces should have a right of appeal to the sejm court. Since such cases often involved disputes about royal lands in which the starosta was a party, this was an expression of the principle that an individual—here the king—could not act as judge in a case in which he was involved: *nemo iudex idoneus in casa sua*. This represented the first attempt in Poland to regulate the various courts over which the king presided, in particular in his own court (*in curia*), and in the sejm (*in conventione*), and to advance the claims of the sejm court to be a high court of appeal in civil cases. It implicitly challenged the idea of the monarch as the supreme judicial authority, albeit largely on behalf of the council elite: it was only cases between the king and a senator that were automatically to be referred to the sejm court.[21] Similar concerns lay behind clause fourteen, which sought to curb the independence of starostas in judicial matters by insisting that they respect leading officials and dignitaries within their jurisdiction—bishops, palatines, and castellans—and consult them, in particular in cases involving senators.[22]

Thus for all their concern with the role and interests of councillors as the king's constitutionally sanctioned advisers, the Mielnik articles displayed a clear understanding of the distinction between the person of the monarch and the abstract entity of the state.[23] They sought to inter the mouldering bones of patrimonial monarchy by appealing to the idea of the *respublica* as the political community in whose name the state operated: another clause sought to regulate royal control over the minting of coins, to ensure that the king did not manipulate the currency, but upheld the prescribed weights and quality of coins in order to serve the common good.[24] In particular, the articles attacked the idea derived from Roman law that the king, while bound by divine and natural law, was above, and therefore not constrained by, the written law, and was in this sense absolute (*a legibus solutus*).[25]

The Mielnik articles were fully informed by the swirling currents of political theory in contemporary Latin Christendom. They sought to institutionalize a vision of the political community that saw the council as the natural defender of the common good. They were in that sense indeed oligarchic in their implications, an impression confirmed by the clauses that sought to set boundaries to the king's right of appointment to office, one of his most important prerogatives, thereby establishing control of membership of the narrow political elite that—in the absence of any hierarchy of titles—had no inherited right to power and position.

---

[20] *VC*, i/i, 111.
[21] *VC*, i/i, 111; Sobolewski and Uruszczak, 'Artykuły', 60–1.
[22] *VC*, i/i, 112.
[23] Sobolewski and Uruszczak, 'Artykuły', 66.
[24] *VC*, i/i, 112.
[25] Sobolewski and Uruszczak, 'Artykuły', 65–6.

The articles, like the Mielnik union, were never implemented. With their concern that councillors might be judged by the 'rabble' (*turba malorum*), they betrayed council suspicion of the chamber of envoys, and their vision of the political community was unlikely to win support from the szlachta, however well informed it might be by Aquinas and John of Salisbury. Alexander was given room to manoeuvre by the royal secretary who drafted the articles. Jan Łaski (1456–1531) came from a middling szlachta family; throughout his career he fought against the oligarchic practices of the council magnates. When drafting the articles, he inserted a clause at the end by which Alexander agreed to implement them only *after* his coronation. He appended his provisional seal in Mielnik, adding the important reservation that he would publish the articles under the great seal once he had examined all the kingdom's privileges with a view to 'augmenting and moderating them'. They were neither augmented nor moderated; instead Łaski began preparing the digest of Polish law he published in 1506, and the original document languished in the Vilnius chancery archive until it was exhumed in 1564.[26]

This clause launched Łaski's career. A grateful Alexander appointed him principal secretary (1502), and then chancellor, following Krzesław Kurozwęcki's death in 1503. It was a meteoric rise, but Alexander had much to be grateful for: Łaski gave him the opportunity to build a political consensus against the articles. In so doing, Alexander—with Łaski's advice and encouragement—appealed to the broader mass of the community of the realm against the council oligarchs. In what proved to be the last sejm of his reign, which opened in Radom on 30 March 1505 and formally ended on 14 June, a statute was passed that institutionalized the bicameral sejm and established its central role in Polish political life. Known as '*Nihil Novi*', it is worth paying close attention to its meaning, as it has frequently been misrepresented, and blamed for the subsequent problems of the Polish political system. Its wording reflected the way in which that system had developed since 1382:

> Since the common law and public statutes affect not individuals, but the whole people, therefore in this assembly at Radom, with all the prelates, councillors, barons, and envoys of the land, we consider it to be right and reasonable, and have therefore established, that henceforth and in perpetuity, nothing new [*nihil novi*] should be decreed by us or our successors that is to the prejudice and inconvenience of the *Res Publica*, or to the injury or detriment of whatsoever private interest, or that alters the common law or public liberties, without the common agreement of our councillors and envoys of the lands.[27]

---

[26] *VC*, i/i, 113; Papée, *Aleksander*, 53–4; Stanisław Tymosz, 'Szkic historyczno-biograficzny prymasa Jana Łaskiego (1456–1531)', in Tymosz (ed.), *Jan Łaski*, 16–17; Sobolewski and Uruszczak, 'Artykuły', 7.

[27] 'Quoniam iura communia et constitutiones publicae non unum, sed communem populum afficiunt, itaque in hac Radomiensi conventione cum universis Regni nostri praelatis, consiliariis, baronibus et nuntiis terrarum, aequum et rationabile censuimus ac etiam statuimus, ut deinceps, futuris temporibus perpetuis, nihil novi constitui debeat per nos et successores nostros, sine communi consiliarorum et nuntiorum terrestrium consensu, quod fieret in praeiudicium gravamenque Reipublicae, et damnum atque incommodum cuiuslibet privatum, ad innovationemque iuris communis et publicae libertatis': *VC*, i/i, 138.

This statute was itself nothing new. In many respects it gave legal force to the philosophy expressed in the Nieszawa privileges: the principle derived from Roman law of *quod omnes tangit ab omnibus approbari debet* (that which touches all should be approved by all). It did not place as many constraints on royal power as has been argued by those who see the supposed weakness of the Polish monarchy in the early modern period as one of the major reasons for Poland's political decline. *Nihil Novi* was indeed a watershed that marked the establishment of a truly parliamentary monarchy in Poland, but it was not directed against the king's executive or judicial authority; it merely sought to constrain his ability to change public and common law without consent.[28] It was not concerned with the king's sphere of authority in the *regnum*—that is the state—but sought to limit his ability to pass laws on his own authority that affected the public law of the *respublica*, which was the embodiment of the political community. He could no longer make laws affecting the liberties of the citizens, or which introduced changes to the common law (*ius commune* in Latin, *prawo pospolite* in Polish)—considered as the law that applied to the whole community—although he could make new law on his own authority in other spheres, in the realm of particular law codes that were not part of the common law, where the royal prerogative remained unaffected: in matters concerning fiefs of the crown, the royal cities, the Jewish community, peasants on royal estates, and mining. Moreover, the principle left scope for interpretation. It was by no means clear where the boundaries should be drawn, and kings continued to issue decrees and ordinances on many matters affecting the *respublica*, albeit with the advice and agreement of the council. So long as they could be presented as avoiding legislative innovation, they were perfectly legal under *Nihil Novi*, although such decrees did attract criticism, as Sigismund I discovered in 1538. While the definition of what was permissable was increasingly narrowed by appeal to the principle enunciated in 1505, this was a very slow process, and royal authority remained substantial.[29]

Nihil Novi is often presented as a charter for royal impotence. It was not. It established the sejm, not the council, as the primary institutional defender of the *respublica* and the common weal; with the publication of Łaski's statute, Alexander and his chancellor sought further to curb oligarchic inclinations by providing the means to appeal over the heads of the council to the wider citizen body. *Nihil Novi* was not out of line with principles enunciated elsewhere in this period, as was traditionally argued by historians who saw Poland marching in the opposite direction to those parts of Europe where 'New Monarchs' were supposedly constructing the edifice known as absolute monarchy. The philosophy behind it had,

---

[28] For a warning against the common interpretation of *quod omnes tangit* as providing the basis for ideas of popular or citizen sovereignty see Constantin Fasolt, 'Quod omnes tangit ab omnibus approbari debet: the words and their meaning', in Steven Bowman and Blanche Cody (eds), *In iure veritas* (Cincinnati, OH, 1991), 21–55.

[29] Wacław Uruszczak, 'Sejm walny wszystkich państw naszych: Sejm w Radomiu z 1505 roku i konstytucji *Nihil Novi*', *CPH*, 57/1 (2005), 18; Wacław Uruszczak, 'Konstytucja *Nihil Novi* z 1505 roku i jej znaczenie', in Andrzej Ajnenkiel (ed.), *W pięćsetlecie konstytucji Nihil Novi* (Warsaw, 2006), 16–21. For the *ius commune* see Konstanty Grzybowski, *Teoria reprezentacji w Polsce epoki Odrodzenia* (Warsaw, 1959), 245–72.

indeed, more in common than is often admitted with the views on royal power of Jean Bodin, that much misunderstood *parlementaire* and supposed apologist for absolutism, who, while he certainly upheld the monarch's executive authority, formed a view of sovereignty at odds with Polish tradition, and was highly critical of the Polish system, nevertheless stressed the monarch's inability to alter public law without the consent of the community of the realm.[30] The debate in sixteenth-century Europe was not concerned with establishing the unlimited authority of kings, but the areas of public life in which that authority was unlimited, and the areas in which it was not. This debate was by no means resolved in Poland in 1505. As vice-chancellor Piotr Tomicki wrote to Jan Tarnowski in 1533:

> For it is the majesty of the king that by custom establishes the laws. His Majesty, despite this statute [*Nihil Novi*], in this sphere enjoys the exercise of full authority.[31]

As Tomicki hints, there were many who rejected his interpretation, but Bodin himself could not have put it better.

Nihil Novi was never intended to strip the Polish monarchy of its powers. It was part of a wider process in which Alexander and Łaski sought to establish what constituted public law. For if the citizen body was to know what did, and what did not, constitute new law, it was important that it knew what the law was. Łaski conceived *Nihil Novi* together with his comprehensive digest of Polish law, compiled as a result of Alexander's promise to publish all the privileges agreed to by his predecessors, which the king swore to uphold at Radom, and which was published on his orders in 1506.[32] This massive compilation of the written laws that bound the kingdom, known as Łaski's statute, was a collection of laws chronologically ordered rather than a codification, running to over 1,000 pages. Łaski sought to include all written published law; he included Casimir III's statutes, privileges issued by past Polish monarchs, including those for individual provinces, and royal edicts, and appended Latin translations of the *Sachsenspiegel* and the Magdeburg *Weichbild*, which were widely applied in Poland, and ended with a treatise on Roman law, the *Summa Raimundi*.[33]

The printing of Łaski's statue was an important milestone in the development of Poland's consensual, mixed parliamentary monarchy after Alexander ordered its wide distribution, and called for it to be read out in churches across the kingdom.[34] For the first time the ordinary nobility had direct access to the most important statutes on which Polish law and the Polish political system were based. The desire

---

[30] Grzybowski, *Teoria*, 141–6; Uruszczak, *Sejm walny*, 128–33.

[31] 'Maiestas enim regia, quae condere leges solet. Maiestas sua adversus hanc statuti dispositonem plenitudine potestatis suae utitur': Piotr Tomicki to Jan Tarnowski, 20.III.1533, *AT*, xv, no. 152, 214; Grzybowski, *Teoria*, 141.

[32] *Commune incliti Regni Poloniae privilegium constitutionum et indultuum publicitus decretorum approbatoriumque* (Cracow, 1506); *VC*, i/i, 162–72.

[33] Stanisław Tymosz, '*Statut Łaskiego* i jego wpływ na inne zbiory prawa', in Tymosz (ed.), *Jan Łaski* (Lublin, 2007), 87–106; Piotr Tafiłowski, *Jan Łaski (1456–1531)* (Warsaw, 2007), 42–3; Uruszczak, 'Sejm w Radomiu', 20; *PSB*, 18, 230.

[34] Wacław Uruszczak, *Próba kodyfikacji prawa polskiego w pierwszej połowie XVI wieku* (Warsaw, 1979), 72; Łowmiański, *Polityka*, 523.

to limit royal power was far from the driving force behind the statute: Łaski saw better knowledge of the law as a way to improve the operation of the royal government for which he was responsible. His statute was also concerned with the administration of justice, and contained a series of measures, the *processus iuris*, that were accepted at Radom and which laid down the procedure to be followed for the execution of judgements by starostas and others empowered to implement the law.[35] The statute introduced an important limitation on the famous principle of *neminem captivabimus nisi iure victum* enshrined in the 1430 Jedlnia privileges, which stipulated that nobody could be imprisoned until convicted of a crime in a court of law. Łaski introduced the important amendment that this only applied to those of good character: those recorded as criminals or of bad character in local court records could be imprisoned before a formal guilty verdict.[36]

The printing of Łaski's statute together with the passing of *Nihil Novi* put the sejm at the heart of the political system. The establishment between 1493 and 1505 of a bicameral legislature was followed by the fixing of its composition. The upper chamber, initially still known as the council, was referred to in various formulae, as '*praelati spirituales et saeculares*', '*praelati et consiliarii*', or '*praelati et barones consiliarii nostri*'; it was not until 1532 that it was first officially designated as the senate. After 1495, lesser dignitaries including the chamberlain (*podkomorzy*), the ensign (*chorąży*), the steward (*podstoli*) and some royal secretaries and land judges still occasionally attended, but eventually its membership stabilized at 87: 9 Catholic bishops, 14 palatines, 59 castellans, and 5 government ministers—the grand marshal, chancellor, vice-chancellor, treasurer, and marshal of the court, although it increased in size with the incorporation of Mazovia between 1526 and 1529.[37]

Membership of the chamber of envoys was more fluid. Each province adjusted its practices to accommodate the need to hold more frequent sejmiks, as meetings of the sejm became more regular. After 1506 the Ruthenian palatinate ceased to hold separate sejmiks for the districts of Lwów, Sanok, Przemyśl, and Halych, though Chełm continued to hold its own sejmik as, in other parts of the kingdom, did the territories of Dobrzyń, Gostyń, Sochaczew, and Rawa, which, like Chełm, were outwith the palatinate structure. After 1529 there were seven sejmiks in Małopolska (including the Ruthenian palatinate), nine in Wielkopolska, and ten in Mazovia. The number of envoys varied. The palatinates of Cracow and Sandomierz sent six each in the early sixteenth century, whereas in Wielkopolska, it varied between two and seven per sejmik; the Mazovians sent two from each sejmik, twenty in all, though twenty-one turned up in 1531. A 1520 statute set the upper limit at six per sejmik; in 1531 75 attended: 26 Małopolskans, 28 Wielkopolskans, and 21 Mazovians. This was considerably more than the 45 who had attended in 1504.[38] The senate was not usually so well attended: many of the minor castellans, whose voices counted for less in council debates, attended sporadically if at all,

---

[35] *VC*, i/i, 165–70.
[36] 'De suspectis in crimine, qui bonae fame sunt censendi, et de non captivandis bonae famae nobilibus': *VC*, i/i, 138; Uruszczak, 'Sejm w Radomiu', 19; Uruszczak, 'Konstytucja', 23–4.
[37] Wyrozumski, 'Geneza', 30–1. See Ch. 31, 374–80.   [38] Uruszczak, 'Sejm w latach', 67, 69.

unless they were ambitious; it was not uncommon for minor castellans to be elected as envoys by sejmiks, sitting in the chamber of envoys, where their opinions were more likely to count.

The sejm flourished after 1505 as the apex of a political system that gave institutional form to the ideal of the community of the realm. Local sejmiks were well attended: although the reports of 500 turning up to a sejmik of the Płock palatinate in Raciąż in 1528 was exceptional, attendances of 100–200 were common.[39] Most were middling noblemen, the backbone of the local community, although poorer nobles also participated, especially in Mazovia. Senators could, and did, turn up to sejmik sessions, emphasizing their participation in that community, but the ordinary nobility formed its core.

Nihil Novi and Łaski's statute completed the transformation of the Polish political system through the establishment of the sejm as a parliament in which each chamber played an equal role, together with the king, in the approval of new laws. The days of Oleśnicki, when a small group of aristocrats could dominate government, were over. Henceforth the noble masses could no longer be ignored. Kings and aristocratic politicians had to build consensus in the chamber to secure their aims. This afforded the monarchy opportunities to strengthen its authority through appealing to the chamber over the heads of their councillors if necessary. These new political realities were recognized by Alexander's successor, Sigismund I (1506–48), who called a sejm virtually every year. This ensured that its procedures rapidly became institutionalized and its members developed a unique parliamentary culture, powerfully informed by the example of the Roman republic. As the szlachta drank deeply at the well of Renaissance humanism, the monarchy used its considerable authority to secure important reforms. Above all, the sejm's emergence was to be crucial for the achievement of closer union in 1569.[40]

---

[39] Uruszczak, 'Sejm w latach', 68.
[40] Uruszczak, 'Sejm w Radomiu', 18–19. For the influence of classical legal concepts on the text of *Nihil Novi*, see Jerzy Wójtczak-Szyszkowski, 'Terminologia prawnicza konstytucji *Nihil Novi*', in Ajnenkiel (ed.), *W pięćsetlecie*, 27–31.

30
Parliamentary Government

Throughout his career Łaski promoted the idea of the monarchy working through the sejm to achieve its ends. Sigismund, however, turned away from the course set by Alexander and Łaski to base his rule largely on the council. Łaski was removed from the chancery in 1510, when he was raised to the archbishopric of Gniezno, which left him free to adopt a role as tribune of the szlachta. Nevertheless, after *Nihil Novi* and the printing of his statute it was no longer so easy for the council to carry on its business far from prying eyes. Thirst for knowledge of the law grew, and growing awareness of the law lent szlachta politics a sharper edge. The government now had to explain itelf and its policies if it wished to secure its aims. From the 1520s statutes and tax edicts were regularly printed and distributed on the initiative of Piotr Tomicki, vice-chancellor from 1515 to his death in 1535. Tomicki began publishing the letters drawn up in the chancery addressed to the szlachta, sejmiks, and senators, in which the king summoned individual sejms, outlined his legislative programme, and sought support.[1] His aim was to ensure that the chancery controlled the wording of statutes, but he could not control the interpretations that were put upon them. While it is only from the reign of Sigismund August that diaries of sejm sessions survive, reports of sejms were made by envoys to their sejmiks, while certain interested parties, such as the Danzig council, started sending observers who kept verbatim accounts of sejm debates, although before 1569 they concerned themselves largely with Prussian affairs.[2]

As sejms grew more frequent and reports of their activities circulated more widely, political activists and sejmiks began scrutinizing the actions of the king, his ministers, and his councillors in the light of the written law to which they were subject. Yet this development afforded considerable opportunities to the king not simply to escape the chains with which his councillors sought to bind him, but to secure a radical solution to the monarchy's chronic fiscal problems. The disastrous 1497 Moldavian campaign, which confirmed that the noble levy was worthless, forced politicians to confront the problem of raising and paying professional units to aid the Lithuanians against Muscovy, and to provide more effective defence against Tatar raids. It was to combat the latter that a permanent, if small, professional army known as the common defence force (*obrona potoczna*) was established

---

[1] Anna Odrzywolska-Kidawa, *Podkanclerzy Piotr Tomicki (1515–1535)* (Warsaw, 2005), 79–80.
[2] Uruszczak, *Sejm walny koronny w latach 1506–1540* (Warsaw, 1981), 9.

in 1499, although it only became properly institutionalized after 1520.³ Its numbers remained small: from as few as 400 to a maximum of just over 3,000; it numbered on average 1,000–2,000 between 1548 and 1563. Although a 1525 statute assigned much of the responsibility and the costs to the front-line palatinates, in the dangerous years after Mohács 3,364 cavalrymen were recruited in 1528 and 4,452 were raised for the 1531 Obertyn campaign. The rich starosties of the Ruthenian palatinate could not cope, and the burden had to be spread across the kingdom, which required regular taxes and therefore regular meetings of the sejm.⁴

As the expanding European economy began to experience price inflation, public finances were ill equipped to face the challenges. Casimir was less munificent than his elder brother, but despite his parsimonious reputation by 1492 over half the massive royal domain—some 25–30 per cent of Poland's land—had been alienated, and a considerable proportion of royal income diverted to pay off creditors.⁵ John Albert signed 131 mortgages on royal lands in his short reign; at nearly fourteen per annum this was a rate fifty percent higher than that of his father. He left debts of 28,000 florins to seventeen creditors, of whom the largest was the Cracow banker Johann Boner, owed the colossal sum of 15,000 florins, which did not include the debts of Casimir and Frederick. Alexander paid off 46,500 marks between 1502 and 1504, but if this relieved the immediate pressure, it did nothing to confront the structural problems.⁶

These were serious, but not insurmountable. The Jagiellons are often accused of profligacy, and of blindly alienating royal land. Yet given that the royal government was served by no extensive bureaucracy, the system was more rational and effective than is often allowed. Far from thoughtlessly alienating royal estates, Casimir and his sons acted in a hard-headed manner, deriving the best terms they could for the myriad complex loans they raised. Royal properties bestowed as collateral for loans, or to provide payment or reward for services rendered, were disposed of with considerable attention to detail. Grants were made according to three broad categories: life tenures (*gołe dożywocia*); tenures for service or reward (*ad fideles manus*; *do wiernych rąk*, literally 'to faithful hands'), and mortgages (*zastawy*). Within these categories, there were considerable variations, which the chancery watched carefully. Life tenures in which recipients received all the estate's revenues were relatively rare before 1492, and were used sparingly, since the monarchy sought to avoid losing control of estates for an uncertain period, and since it could be difficult to prevent holders passing on tenancies: some royal estates, particularly in the Ruthenian palatinate, were all but hereditary, although in these cases the

---

³ It was referred to in the diploma granting the starosty of Lwów to Piotr Myszkowski in that year: *VC*, i/i, 91.

⁴ Sucheni-Grabowska, *Odbudowa*, 63; Marek Plewczyński, *Żołnierz jazdy obrony potocznej za panowania Zygmunta Augusta* (Warsaw, 1985), 9, 61; Marek Plewczyński, 'Liczebność wojska polskiego za ostatnich Jagiellonów (1506–1572)',1, *SMHW*, 31 (1988), 28–9.

⁵ The Catholic church held some 15%, with the rest almost entirely in the hands of the nobility: Sucheni-Grabowska, *Zygmunt August: Król polski i wielki książę litewski*, 2nd edn (Cracow, 2010), 33–4.

⁶ Sucheni-Grabowska, *Odbudowa*, 60; Jan Rutkowski, 'Skarbowość polska za Aleksandra Jagiellończyka', *KH*, 23 (1909), 57–8.

holders were obliged to maintain castles and other defensive structures, and to raise troops in time of need. If whole starosties, estates, or villages were occasionally granted to favoured recipients as life tenures it was far more common for grants to be of portions of a village, and sometimes even of as little as a single hide of land; these were usually made not for life but for an indefinite period 'at the king's pleasure'.[7]

Grants 'to faithful hands' were more common. In their simplest form, a contract was drawn up in which the income to be drawn by the holder was specified, as were his obligations to the treasury in rent: contracts often included detailed registers, village by village, listing all the inhabitants and the rents in cash and kind they were to pay; provision was often made for the holder to bear the costs of administration, and to provide for the king on any visits he made to his estates. If in principle such contracts were in the king's interests, the difficulty of administering them ensured that they were still relatively rare, and grants declined after 1500.[8]

The majority of leases were granted in return for loans. The problem was that although some mortgage contracts provided for the amortization of the debt (*zastaw do wytrzymania/do wydzierżenia*) to ensure the estate returned to treasury control when the debt was paid off, most were granted for use 'until redemption' (*zastaw użytkowy/zastaw do wykupienia*). Given that the treasury lacked the resources to buy out its creditors, the latter were difficult to redeem. Amortized mortgages were far more favourable to the treasury, especially since amortization rates were relatively high—from 3.3 to as much as 11.8 per cent, which meant that the debts were paid off relatively rapidly, within five to ten years. The government lacked the administrative resources to monitor them, however, and they were initially used sparingly—only one such contract is known for Małopolska before 1450—although they became more common: under Alexander amortized contracts were issued to a value of 18,957 marks, compared with contracts until redemption worth 88,165 marks. While this represented an encouraging 18 per cent of mortgages, only six such contracts are known to have been issued under Sigismund.[9]

By 1506 many of the monarchy's most lucrative sources of income, including the salt mines of Wieliczka and Ruthenia, had been alienated. The system had reached its limits as inflation ate into the income the monarchy derived from the fixed terms on which its lands were leased. Piecemeal audits were occasionally carried out, but rarely revealed the extent to which leaseholders were profiting. By the 1480s, Casimir's income from the royal lands had sunk to an exiguous 6,600 Hungarian ducats per annum despite the incorporation of Royal Prussia, when the monarchy acquired the Order's estates, which constituted some fifty per cent of the province's land. The royal treasury was drawing rents almost exclusively from the newly acquired Mazovian palatinates of Rawa and Płock, since all but a tiny

---

[7] Rutkowski, 'Skarbowość', 13–14; Sucheni-Grabowska, *Monarchia*, 67–9; Luciński, *Rozwój*, 31.
[8] Rutkowski, 'Skarbowość', 12–13; Sucheni-Grabowska, *Monarchia*, 74–82; Luciński, *Rozwój*, 25–6.
[9] Rutkowski, 'Skarbowość', 16–17; Sucheni-Grabowska, *Odbudowa*, 71; Luciński, *Rozwój*, 32.

handful of its estates in Wielkopolska and Małopolska had been alienated: in 1506 the king had direct control of a mere nineteen complexes of estates. When treasurer Andrzej Kościelecki took office in 1509 he found the princely sum of 61 złoties in the royal coffers.[10]

A solution had to be found, and it was through the sejm that Alexander and Sigismund sought it. For the sejm could approve extraordinary taxation to meet the costs of Poland's increasing military obligations and provide the means by which the monarchy might regain control over the royal domain. Given the szlachta's reluctance to agree to annual musterings of the noble levy, the king was able to raise extraordinary taxes that partly fell upon the szlachta, exempt from ordinary taxes since 1374, apart from the *poradlne*, the value of which was waning partly because of inflation, and partly because of under-declaration owing to the lack of effective means for registering land values in a volatile market. Apart from the *poradlne*, the principal ordinary taxes consisted of customs dues (*cła*), from which the szlachta were exempt, the *stacyjne*, raised from towns and some monasteries, the 'Jewish rent' (*czynsz żydowski*), 200 złoties per annum raised from Jewish communities across the kingdom, and annual sums paid by Danzig (2,000 florins), Thorn, and Elbing (400 florins each).[11]

The szlachta responded. Of thirty-five sejms that met between 1506 and 1540, twenty-seven agreed taxes. Only five called for the noble levy, reflecting a general preference for taxation rather than the levy, which involved nobles in the direct costs of mustering, while the burden of taxation fell substantially on other social groups.[12] Yet the notion that the szlachta paid no tax—still common in general works—is a travesty. Nobles indeed wished to limit the taxes they paid, on the basis that they were obliged to defend the realm in wartime. Since the costs of turning out in the levy were substantial, the szlachta were in principle willing to replace in any individual year the obligation to serve with the payment of taxes in lieu, although the 1514 sejm rejected Sigismund's plan for a *relucja*, in which the obligation to serve would be abolished in return for a permanent tax to support a professional army. A similar scheme proposed by Łaski in 1529, the *mons pietatis*, which envisaged a permanent tax on royal, noble, and ecclesiastical estates, was also rejected. This was only partly because the obligation to serve in the levy was still closely bound up with szlachta identity and was a useful argument in favour of noble tax exemptions. The szlachta was willing to pay extraordinary taxes in time of need; it was suspicious, however, of any permanent, ordinary tax that could be raised without sejm agreement. The citizens were not about to surrender their hard-won right to be consulted.

The principal tax agreed at all of Alexander's sejms and most of Sigismund's was the hide tax (*łanowy*), raised on hides of cultivated land on the same basis as the *poradlne*, which was still collected in years the hide tax was levied. Between 1507 and 1543 the hide tax was collected at various rates, from a lowest tariff of 6 groszy per hide in 1508 and 1511 to a highest of 24 groszy in 1520 and 1538. Rates of 8

[10] Sucheni-Grabowska, *Odbudowa*, 59, 274; Wojciechowski, *Zygmunt*, 181.
[11] Rutkowski, 'Skarbowość', 26–8.
[12] Uruszczak, *Sejm*, 216; cf. table 1 in Sucheni-Grabowska, *Monarchia*, 23–6.

groszy were levied by three sejms; 10 groszy by one; 12 groszy—the most common rate—on thirteen occasions; 14 groszy on one occasion; 16 groszy on two occasions; 18 groszy on four occasions; and 20 groszy on two occasions. Although the hide tax was usually paid by tenant farmers, on six occasions (1520, 1525, 1526, 1527, 1531, and 1532) payment was shared equally between tenants and their noble landlords. The tax was paid in full by the *szlachta zagrodowa*—nobles who farmed their land directly without dependent peasants.[13]

Taxes were agreed on six of the seven occasions in Sigismund's reign when the sejm met in the king's absence (1514, 1517, 1529, 1534, 1535, 1542).[14] They were usually supplemented by other extraordinary taxes, including the *szos*, a property tax levied on towns at 4 per cent and occasionally higher; the excise (*czopowe*) on beer and wine, and extraordinary customs duties. A 1507 council edict—confirmed by the 1509 sejm—introduced a 'new duty' (*nowe cło*), a permanent tax on the export of oxen, hides, wax, honey, fish, and horses, that brought in far more than the 'old duty' (*stare cło*), regularly yielding a quarter and more of the treasury's annual income. Although the szlachta had been exempt since 1496 from the *szos*, the excise, and from duties on products produced on their manors, they were increasingly involved as middlemen in the rapidly developing cattle trade, and were liable for the new duty on all animals not raised on their manors, which were overwhelmingly devoted to arable, not pastoral farming.[15]

In the light of the rates paid in the hide tax, and the regularity with which the sejm levied it on the lands that they owned or farmed directly, the szlachta cannot be accused of avoiding tax, even if they sought to minimize their exposure and used their dominance of the legislature to shift as much of the burden as possible onto other estates. Although the hide tax was largely paid by their tenants, sejm control meant that the taxation burden on farmers was kept relatively low. In 1504, in addition to a hide tax at a rate of 12 groszy, the sejm agreed a levy of customs duty that suspended all exemptions, and imposed a rental tax (*czynszowy*) that was paid by all social orders. It was levied at ten per cent on the lands of the king and the royal family, and on royal estates held by any individual on whatever basis, and at a rate of five per cent on hereditary noble and clerical estates. A similar tax of one quarter of the rental value, and one eighth of the tithe, was levied at Sigismund's coronation sejm in 1507.[16] In 1520, when the sejm met at Bydgoszcz in the presence of the levy, summoned to fight in the 1519–21 war against the Order, it agreed a poll tax, to be paid by all inhabitants of the kingdom, ecclesiastics and laymen; commoners and nobles, at rates that took account of social position and property holdings: the primate paid 300 złoties; other Polish bishops paid 100; Ruthenian bishops paid 50; the castellan of Cracow paid 60—plus 20 as hetman and 10 as starosta of Kazimierz—palatines paid 50 złoties, castellans 10; payment

---

[13] Sucheni-Grabowska, *Monarchia,* 24–6; Rutkowski, 'Skarbowość', 38–9.
[14] Uruszczak, *Sejm*; Sucheni-Grabowska, *Monarchia,* 24–6.
[15] *VC*, i/i, 214–15; Uruszczak, *Sejm*, 200; Wojciechowski, *Zygmunt*, 357–8.
[16] *VC*, i/i, 133, 199; Papée, *Aleksander* 83; Rutkowski, 'Skarbowość', 41–2; Uruszczak, 'Sejm w latach', 98.

by the nobility was determined by the extent of their landholdings and the number of their peasants. Wealthier nobles paid half a złoty; tenant farmers paid 1 grosz; smallholders and cottagers paid half a grosz.[17]

The extent of extraordinary taxes agreed after 1500, however, encouraged support for the idea that the king should not have to turn every year to the sejm for money when he possessed such a large and lucrative domain. The price for the substantial taxes and the suspension of szlachta immunities agreed by the 1504 sejm was the acceptance of limitations on the free disposal of the royal domain and support for its revindication. Previous efforts had failed, thanks to fierce resistance from dignitaries and council members, the system's main beneficiaries. This was not the first attempt to place limits on the royal prerogative with regard to the domain. Jagiełło promised in privileges issued in Cracow (1386) and Piotrków (1388) not to appoint foreigners or members of the royal family to judicial starosties. In 1440, as part of the struggle between Oleśnicki's faction and its opponents, a statute was issued banning the alienation of those royal estates and revenues reserved to the Cracow procurators (*wielkorządcy*) for the upkeep of the royal court and household, or lands granted to Jagiełło's widow Sonka.[18] The Nieszawa privileges banned the mortgaging of judicial starosties or the revenues assigned to their incumbents. In 1460 Casimir confirmed the 1440 edict concerning the Cracow procurators, extending the principle to cover the territory of Bełz on its 1462 incorporation into the kingdom, and to the palatinate of Sandomierz in 1478.[19] He raised a tax at the 1447 sejm to liquidate the mortgages on several royal estates, a ploy used again in 1453 to repurchase Kamianets from the Buczackis, and in 1465, to recover estates from the Odrowąż, whose domination of the Ruthenian palatinate had provoked discontent among the local szlachta.[20]

Such purchases were rare, but they revealed szlachta support for revindication of the domain. Casimir told the 1459 Piotrków sejm that if he had full control of all mortgaged royal estates, he would be able to cover all the realm's needs, including defence.[21] Despite his parsimony he was never able to restore the royal domain, and in Alexander's brief reign royal estates were mortgaged to the value of 171,395 złoties to meet the Muscovite and Tatar threats; this represented no less than a quarter of all sums mortgaged before 1504, and mortgages were contracted at a far faster rate than before 1501.[22]

The 1504 statute *de modo bonorum regalium inscribendorum* reflected general concern at the catastrophic state of the domain. It extended the principles established at Nieszawa and in the edicts of 1440, 1460, 1462, and 1478 to the whole royal domain, in an attempt to render it capable of sustaining the royal court and household, and of meeting the needs of government. It was henceforth illegal for the king to alienate or mortgage royal estates or his income from his regalian rights

---

[17] *VC*, i/i, 356–66.
[18] *VL*, i, 64–5; Jacek Matuszewski, 'Statut Władysława Warneńczyka z 1440 r.: W procesie ograniczania królewskiego prawa dyspozycji domeną ziemską w Polsce', *CPH*, 37/2 (1985), 101–20.
[19] *VL*, i, 91; 106–7.   [20] Sucheni-Grabowska, *Odbudowa*, 47, 54–5.
[21] *Annales*, xii/i, 332; Sucheni-Grabowska, *Odbudowa*, 52.
[22] Rutkowski, 'Skarbowość', 16–17.

without sejm consent, and he could do so only if it was vital for the commonwealth.²³ The statute was almost certainly drafted by Łaski. The thinking behind it was revealed in 1507 by one of his protégés, Stanisław Zaborowski, a middling noble from the Sieradz palatinate, in his *Treatise... on the Nature of the Laws and the Royal Domain, and on the Reform of the Kingdom and the Government of the Commonwealth*.²⁴ Zaborowski probably served as a soldier in his youth, and then entered the church. He was a secretary in the royal treasury in 1505, before rising to be keeper of the treasury in 1512 or 1513, an office he held until his death; he was also a tax-collector in the Cracow palatinate in 1505.²⁵

It seems that Zaborowski took no active part in drafting the 1504 statute; nevertheless, as a treasury official he would have worked closely with Łaski, and it seems reasonable to suppose that his treatise echoes Łaski's ideas. It was a radical document which both reflected and helped form ideas about the nature of the commonwealth. That Łaski and Zaborowski were clerics at a time when the church was coming under considerable pressure to make its own financial contribution to the realm explains to some extent the treatise's nature, although Łaski throughout his career supported the taxation of clerical revenues, a position that angered his fellow clerics.

The treatise's arguments are resolutely secular. It opens by stating that its author was moved to write by the tears and complaints of the poor brought on by high taxes and the devastation of the kingdom, which caused the author to ask whether the alienation of royal lands and regalian rights, whose consequences had visited ruin upon the kingdom, were legal.²⁶ The answer was blunt:

> Neither kings, nor princes, nor anyone else possesses the authority to alienate or assign in any form whatsoever any properties belonging to the kingdom or attached to any of its offices... and if they have acted in breach of this principle, they must revoke the grant, regardless of any oath or agreement that they would not withdraw it.²⁷

Zaborowski drew on authorities from Plato, Aristotle, the Bible, and canon law, to the church fathers and modern writers, including Baldus de Ubaldis and Bartolus de Saxoferrato.²⁸ He advanced a contractual vision of the state, in which the king held his authority in trust for the wider political community: he was the *administrator regni*, the *tutor, conservator, rector, mediator*, and *praepositus* of the kingdom, not its proprietor. All authority was established by God to serve the common good. Thus royal lands were not the dynasty's private property, but belonged to the community of the realm, and should be used by the king for the common good: to support the royal household, to uphold justice, and to defend the realm. ²⁹

---

²³ *VC*, i/i, 130; Sucheni-Grabowska, *Odbudowa*, 67–8; Papée, *Aleksander*, 84.
²⁴ Stanisław Zaborowski, *Tractatus Quadrifidus de Natura Iurium et Bonorum Regis et de Reformatione Regni ac eius Reipublicae Regimine incipit Feliciter* (Cracow, 1507). References are to the modern edition: *Traktat o naturze praw i dóbr królewskich*, ed. Henryk Litwin (Cracow, 2005).
²⁵ Henryk Litwin, 'Stanisława Zaborowskiego życie, sylwetka i traktat', in Zaborowski, *Traktat*, v–x.
²⁶ Zaborowski, *Traktat*, 2.   ²⁷ Zaborowski, *Traktat*, 2.
²⁸ For his sources, see Zaborowski, *Traktat*, 329–41.
²⁹ Litwin, 'Życie', xliv–xlv; Sucheni-Grabowska, *Odbudowa*, 85–8.

These ideas were the common currency of contemporary republican thought. Their peculiar resonance in Poland resulted from the elective nature of its monarchy. Although the community of the realm respected the dynasty's natural rights, kings became kings in Poland by election, and could not be crowned without swearing to uphold the laws, rights, and privileges of the realm. Zaborowski's treatise eloquently demonstrates that ideas of patrimonial, hereditary kingship based on divine right had little purchase in Poland, where the republican ideal of a limited, constitutional monarchy bound by written as well as divine and natural law was securely established by 1500.

The Jagiellons, naturally, did not accept such notions, and Zaborowski's treatise, however convenient its recommendations, reflected the sentiments not of the king, but of Łaski and a group within the royal administration that sought to develop a programme of political reform to release the government from the fiscal morass in which it was floundering. It is a measure of the political intelligence of Alexander and Sigismund that they recognized the political advantages the monarchy could derive from following the reform programme, while rejecting the premises upon which it was based. Thus Alexander consented to the 1504 statute on the royal domain and to *Nihil Novi* in 1505, and accepted Łaski's statute, whose frontispiece was a vivid depiction of the proposition that the monarchy was bound by the law, and subject to the will of the community of the realm as gathered in the sejm (see Fig. 12).

Sigismund's reputation has risen considerably in recent years. Previously, he was dismissed as the poorest of kings, whose nickname, 'Sigismund the Old' reflected the creeping senility and lack of energy he displayed towards the end of his long reign: he was 40 when he was crowned in January 1507, and 81 at his death in April 1548. Szujski, while acknowledging a certain competence in the early years, accused Sigismund of losing his way, and scolded him for allowing himself to become enthralled by the evil genius of his second wife, Bona Sforza (1494–1557), whom he married in 1518. Bobrzyński entitled the relevant chapter of his history of Poland: '[Sigismund's] feeble and short-sighted policy ruins the nation's historic mission and generates anarchy'. Wojciechowski broadly accepts this negative assessment, condemning him as a senatorial king, in thrall to the magnates and his council, who abandoned Alexander's alliance with the ordinary nobility and who, despite his taste for Renaissance architecture, remained essentially medieval in his political outlook.[30]

This picture is still influential, especially outside Poland.[31] In reality Sigismund, while relying on and working through his council, was by no means its prisoner: Ambrosius Storm, secretary of the Danzig council who attended his election,

---

[30] Józef Szujski, *Historyi polskiej treściwie opowiedzianej ksiąg dwanaście* (1880; Poznań, 2005), 167–82; Michał Bobrzyński, *Dzieje Polski w zarysie* (1879; Warsaw, 1974), 235; Wojciechowski, *Zygmunt*, 403–16.

[31] Davies, while recognizing his 'style and energy' in the early years, presents Sigismund as a cautious, conservative king: *God's Playground*, i, 113. For a more positive assessment which nevertheless echoes some of these criticisms, see Jerzy Besala, *Zygmunt Stary i Bona Sforza* (Poznań, 2012), 630–8.

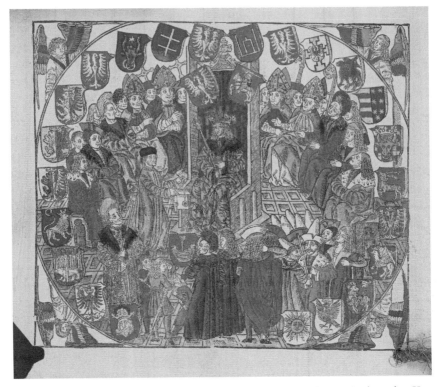

Fig. 12. The estates of the Sejm. Frontispiece, *Statute of Jan Łaski*, 1506. Alexander, King of Poland and Grand Duke of Lithuania surrounded by senators and envoys. Woodcut in Jan Łaski, *Commune incliti Poloniae Regni priuilegium constitutionum et indultuum publicitus decretorum, approbatorumque cum nonnullis iuribus tam divinis quam humanis* (Cracow, 1506), Archiwum Główne Akt Dawnych, Zbiór Dokumentów Pergaminowych, sygn. 5632. By kind permission of the Archiwum Główne Akt Dawnych, Warsaw.

reported that now decisions were taken by the king himself, instead of by the lords of the council, as in Alexander's reign; another Prussian observer noted that he 'listened well and spoke little'.[32] He steered a careful and consistent course throughout his reign. While utilizing the considerable scope afforded him by the royal prerogative, he exploited the profound political divisions among the council elite, cautiously using the sejm to mount a determined assault on the greatest problem facing the royal government by tackling the problem of the royal domain.

Although Sigismund frequently flouted its provisions, the 1504 constitution helped him considerably. It showed no interest in past alienations; its principal concern was to prevent them in the future. Nevertheless, in the climate it created, helped by Zaborowski's view that all alienations of the royal domain were illegal,

---

[32] Quoted by Karol Górski, *Łukasz Watzenrode. Życie i działalność polityczna (1447–1512)* (Wrocław, 1973), 64, 88.

Sigismund put pressure on holders of royal land to reach compromise agreements in which the monarchy bought back mortgaged estates and regalian rights, and renegotiated leases. His approach was practical, sensible, and piecemeal. The 1507 coronation sejm supported revindication of royal lands, passing an act requiring those holding mortgaged royal estates or regalian revenues to present the documents in which they had been granted for scrutiny by the council; those who held them fraudulently were to be punished and would lose their holdings.[33] This declaration of intent was backed with action. Sigismund raised the funds necessary to recover the most lucrative sources of revenue, including the Wieliczka and Ruthenian salt mines, and the customs duties levied in Thorn and Elbing, by turning to wealthy bankers, in particular Boner, who was happy to extend credit in order to restore royal finances, and to the merchants of Cracow, Danzig, Thorn, and Elbing. Creditors were prepared to invest in return for appropriate rewards: the loan advanced by St Catherine's convent in Kazimierz to repurchase the town of Sącz, for example, was repaid at 4 per cent from the proceeds of the Wieliczka salt mine. Using such means, Sigismund embarked on a sustained campaign to revindicate or renegotiate mortgage agreements and repurchase alienated estates and revenues. The aim was to liquidate grants from which the treasury derived no benefit: lifetime leases and contracts in which the holder was allowed to draw all income from the estates held, thereby earning far more than the sum originally lent. Repurchases were paid in instalments, based on the amount of the original loan. Where it was impossible to buy out such grants, the treasury concentrated on converting them into amortized agreements which—at the high rate of 10–20 per cent that was normally applied—ensured that the loan was repaid rapidly and the property redeemed.[34]

Although the Muscovite war of 1512–22, the last war against the Order of 1519–21, endemic Tatar raids, and the intermittent Ottoman threat all required money, and led to further alienations, many of which breached the 1504 statute, Sigismund did much to restore the royal domain: according to the first comprehensive survey of royal property carried out between 1660 and 1670, in the Cracow palatinate, 23 per cent of royal villages from the period 1350–1410 had passed into private hands, whereas only 5 per cent of royal villages known from the period 1470–80 had been lost.[35]

Reforms sought to ensure more efficient administration of the domain. There were two basic forms under which estates were granted: administration (*zarząd*) and lease (*arenda*). In the former, contracts were issued to administrators, who had to produce annual accounts; the division of income between them and the treasury was stipulated, with leaseholders receiving a salary, and the income from specified properties such as manors or mills within the complex. The remaining revenues were designated for the treasury. The treasury's ability to monitor such contracts was, however, limited, and in many cases a straight lease (*arenda*) was preferred, in which the treasury set a cash rent it was to receive from the estate. This tended to

---

[33] *VC*, i/i, 190, 191.   [34] Sucheni-Grabowska, *Odbudowa*, 70, 88–90, 99.
[35] Luciński, *Rozwój*, 54, 58.

favour leaseholders, since they did not have to produce accounts, and since inflation ate into the treasury's income over long leases, but was easier to administer.[36]

Within the limits of what was possible for early modern administrations, Sigismund's reforms were effective enough. On average, under Mikołaj Szydłowiecki the treasury received 39 per cent of the income from estates administered according to the new principles between 1515 and 1532.[37] While this meant that leases on royal land were still lucrative for their holders it represented a substantial improvement on the situation before 1504, when the treasury received little or no income from many alienated estates. Szydłowiecki's administration of the treasury was not as effective or free from corruption as might have been desired, and after his death further reforms, in which the centralization of administrative control over the domain was extended under the more capable control of Jan Spytek Tarnowski, treasurer from 1532 until 1550. With the windfall of the numerous royal estates in Mazovia following the province's incorporation in 1529, the return of amortized estates and estates repurchased in instalments, royal income grew considerably. Inflation ate away at the value of fixed cash rents, but its effects were offset by an expansion of the domain in the great agricultural boom after 1500. If in 1470–80, royal holdings in Małopolska amounted to 349 villages in the palatinates of Cracow (199), Sandomierz (127) and Lublin (23), by 1576–81 the crown held 51 towns and 470 villages—a 36 per cent increase—in the Cracow palatinate alone.[38]

The agricultural boom increased the profitability of royal land. Under Szydłowiecki, the treasury's average annual income from 33 estates in Wielkopolksa, Małopolska, Red Ruthenia, and the Silesian territories of Zator and Oświęcim, was 22,591 złoties; Tarnowski increased this to an average of 39,106 złoties from 41 estates in these provinces, a rise of 73 per cent. The proportion of the net income of estates paid directly to the treasury rose from 39 per cent under Szydłowiecki to 76 per cent under Tarnowski. The income from estates administered directly by the treasury rose fourfold in the same period, from 5,653 to 22,270 złoties. Overall, the income from the royal estates—excluding Mazovia—rose from an annual average of 28,392 złoties between 1515 and 1531 to 49,756 złoties between 1540 and 1548.[39] The trend continued after 1548, when the treasury benefited from the income on the Mazovian estates which returned to its control on Bona's death in 1557: they produced income of 15,180 złoties per annum in the 1540s, and an estimated 30,000 per annum between 1556 and 1566. In these years, although the income from estates in Małopolska, Wielkopolska, Royal Prussia, and the palatinate of Rawa dropped as compared with the 1540s, income from the Ruthenian territories rose from 13,966 to 26,037 złoties per annum, an increase of over 86 per cent. Including the Mazovian estates, income from the royal domain on average in

---

[36] Sucheni-Grabowska, *Odbudowa*, 206–17.
[37] Sucheni-Grabowska, *Odbudowa*, table 10, 222.
[38] Calculations based on figures in Luciński, *Rozwój*, 126–7.
[39] Sucheni-Grabowska, *Odbudowa*, 228–9; Sucheni-Grabowska, *Monarchia*, table 11, 95, a slightly higher figure for the income from Royal Prussia (10,650) as compared with 9,628 in table 30 in *Obudowa*, 270.

these years was 89,585 złoties, which marked an increase of 215.5 per cent since the 1520s.[40]

Taken together with the taxes levied by the sejm, this achievement represents a considerable consolidation of royal and central state power. The royal administration grew steadily. Although the clergy still dominated, the proportion of lay secretaries rose steadily, from 4 per cent before 1506 to 24 per cent in 1548. The figure for secretaries from the middling nobility rose from 30 to 68 per cent under Sigismund; all these trends continued after his death. That this was turning into an established bureaucratic structure is demonstrated by the proportion of secretaries who rose into the royal council and the great offices of state, which climbed steadily.[41]

Sigismund's ministers had a broad and cosmopolitan education. Most studied at Cracow University, which flourished in the early sixteenth century, drawing students from across central and eastern Europe, before the flow of foreign students diminished considerably after the Reformation.[42] While it seems that Łaski, who came from a humble szlachta background, did not attend university, he was a renowned scholar, a correspondent of Erasmus, a famed rhetorician, and patron of the arts. Piotr Tomicki took his bachelor's degree in Cracow, where he was a contemporary of Nicholas Copernicus and his brother Andreas; like them Tomicki also studied in Bologna, where he was taught by the famed rhetorician Filippo Beroaldo and the canon lawyer Antonio da Burgos, taking his doctorate in canon and civil law in 1500; he later established the Cracow chairs of Hebrew and Greek. Jan Chojeński, bishop of Cracow and chancellor (1537–8), studied in Cracow and Siena, where he completed a doctorate in canon and civil law; Samuel Maciejowski, vice-chancellor (1539–47), bishop of Płock (1542–5), bishop of Cracow (1545–50), and chancellor (1547–50) studied philosophy and rhetoric in Padua and Bologna.[43] Poland was governed by men whose political ideals were formed through wide reading in the works of European humanism.

Sigismund, like his father, sought to place his own stamp on government. Just as he had turned away from Alexander's favourite Mykhailo Hlynsky in Lithuania, so he removed Łaski from the centre of power, replacing him as chancellor in 1510 by vice-chancellor Maciej Drzewicki, and appointing his childhood friend Krzysztof Szydłowiecki to the vice-chancellorship. When Szydłowiecki became chancellor in 1515, his brother Mikołaj was appointed treasurer and the vice-chancellorship went to his brother-in-law Tomicki. Control of the council, however, was not enough. Polish politics had become considerably more complex. The szlachta's growing prosperity meant that the wealthy elite of magnates had grown in size, and the

---

[40] Calculations based on table 30 in Sucheni-Grabowska, *Odbudowa*, 270 and table 11 in Sucheni-Grabowska, *Monarchia*, 95.

[41] Andrzej Wyczański, *Między kulturą a polityką. Sekretarze królewscy Zygmunta Starego (1506–1548)* (Warsaw, 1990), 239–41.

[42] Between 1501 and 1510, 1,714 foreigners and 1,501 Poles studied in Cracow: Wojciechowski, *Zygmunt*, 143.

[43] Tafiłowski, *Łaski*, 20–1; Odrzywolska-Kidawa, *Tomicki*, 61–2; Anna Kamler, *Od szkoły do senatu. Wykształcenie senatorów w Koronie w latach 1501–1586* (Warsaw, 2006), 130, 136.

monarchy did not have enough offices, grants of land, and favours to satisfy everyone, particularly in the light of the campaign to restore the domain, which brought confrontation with individuals and families who found their comfortable incomes from royal estates challenged, bought out, or simply revindicated.

The government was not the only power centre. The royal court's political significance grew as Bona used her considerable private fortune to buy up and revindicate estates on her own account, partly as a means of increasing her political influence, and partly to strengthen the dynasty. By the 1540s, without taking into account her extensive Lithuanian holdings, Bona controlled 15 royal towns and 191 villages, including Sambor, then the richest royal property in Poland, with 2 towns and 80 villages. Her estates in the Cracow palatinate alone—1 town and 17 villages—yielded estimated annual revenues of 1,800 złoties. To this was added her enormous 1545 dower settlement, by which she acquired control of the whole royal domain in Mazovia: 35 towns, 258 villages, 98 manors, and 230 mills, with no fewer than 12 judicial starosties, including Warsaw. Her average revenues from Mazovia alone amounted to 10,000–11,000 złoties per annum.[44]

This colossal accumulation of land by the queen did not, however, do as much as it might have for Sigismund's authority. Although Bona had considerable influence over Sigismund, especially in his later years, they by no means always agreed on politics or on patronage, which turned the court into a centre of rivalry and intrigue. Sigismund's trusted ministers, Tomicki and the Szydłowieckis, were lifelong enemies of Łaski who, if he had been removed from the chancellorship, still enjoyed substantial influence as primate. Łaski was close to Bona because of his opposition to the pro-Habsburg, pro-Hohenzollern policies of Sigismund, Tomicki, Szydłowiecki, and the hetman Jan Tarnowski, who saw good relations with the Habsburgs as vital for defence of Poland's southern borders. Bona's wealth enabled her to construct a significant clientele, which included Piotr Kmita (1477–1553), a cultured and educated man who rose to be grand marshal and palatine of Cracow, who had served the Habsburgs in his youth, but who subsequently turned against them. Bona's main protégé was Piotr Gamrat (1487–1545), bishop of Cracow (1538–41) and archbishop of Gniezno (1541–5), whose taste for debauchery accompanied a keen political sense. As Sigismund aged, Bona's influence over appointments grew, and she was able to advance the careers of several of her acolytes.[45]

The divisions within the magnate elite were played out in the sejm. Sigismund appreciated the need for szlachta support, and was able to use it to secure some, at least, of his aims. He was no prisoner of his council: he never granted it authority to govern during his absences in Lithuania as Alexander had done, and, although he was required to take its advice, there was no requirement to follow it on anything other than matters to do with the currency under the privileges of 1422, in contrast to the supposedly patrimonial system in Lithuania, where Alexander's 1492 privilege constrained him more closely. He did, however, rule mostly through his

---

[44] Sucheni-Grabowska, *Odbudowa*, 149–50, 154, 183–4.
[45] Maria Bogucka, *Bona Sforza* (Warsaw, 1989), 108–30.

council, and in particular the small inner council: what the contemporary chronicler Bernard Wapowski termed the *conventus optimatum*. Although he was dependent throughout his reign upon its consent to taxation, Sigismund showed no great regard for the sejm, or appreciation of the possibilities of managing it to achieve his aims. Occasionally he showed open contempt, using the royal prerogative to overrule or ignore sejm decisions: in 1523 he ordered the collection of the excise after it had been rejected by the sejm, and in 1537, on council authority, he ordered the collection of the excise after a turbulent sejm in Cracow refused to agree taxes.[46]

As the battles over government finance grew in scale and bitterness, and as the printing of laws and statutes increased political awareness among the szlachta, Sigismund's style of government came under attack, encouraged by council members who felt excluded by his reliance on his favourites. Bona may have had little time for the sejm, but some of her supporters, including Łaski and Kmita, were willing to turn to the chamber of envoys, and did not treat it with the contempt of Sigismund's coterie of ministers, such as Tomicki, who referred in his correspondence to the ordinary nobility as commoners and plebs.[47]

Early in his reign, Sigismund exploited the fact that the chamber had not yet developed a strong sense of corporate identity. For all the talk of the community of the realm, it remained a gathering of delegates from the individual provinces and territories that constituted that realm; it was conceived as a *conventum generalem omnium terrarum*, and envoys were *nuntii terrarum*, or *nuntii terrestres*. Provincial loyalties remained strong. Envoys from Wielkopolska, Małopolska, and the Ruthenian territories submitted separate petitions, and the sejm frequently agreed separate laws for different provinces, palatinates, and territories. Sigismund could therefore pursue a strategy of divide and rule, seeking to isolate envoys from sejmiks that opposed individual policies.[48]

In the battles over taxation and the royal domain, however, the provincial barriers began to dissolve, and a growing sense of common purpose emerged. For, despite his strenuous efforts to reconstitute and rebuild the royal domain, Sigismund blatantly ignored both the 1504 statute, mortgaging and granting estates without sejm approval, and the various laws that sought to delineate the responsibilities and regulate the holding of major offices of state. These decreed that one of the two chancellors should always be an ecclesiastic, and banned appointments to either office of holders of the most lucrative bishoprics: the archbishopric of Gniezno and the bishoprics of Cracow, Cujavia, Poznań, Ermland, and Płock. The chancellorship and vice-chancellorship were declared incompatible with the offices of palatine and castellan. Sigismund also flouted the Nieszawa ban on the holding of judicial starosties by palatines and castellans.[49] Maciej Drzewicki, chancellor between 1511 and 1515, advanced in 1513 from the bishopric of Przemyśl, which he was allowed to hold, to Płock, which he was not. Krzysztof Szydłowiecki, Drzewicki's successor as vice-chancellor (1511–15) and chancellor

---

[46] Uruszczak, *Sejm*, 21, 26–8; Uruszczak, 'Sejm w latach', 64; Bogucka, *Bona*, 133.
[47] Uruszczak, *Sejm*, 56.   [48] Uruszczak, *Sejm*, 38–9.   [49] *VC*, i/i, 62, 128–30.

(1515–32), retained the castellany of Sandomierz and was promoted to the palatinate (1515) and castellany (1527) of Cracow. Vice-chancellor Tomicki (1515–35) became bishop of Poznań (1520) and then Cracow (1524).

None of this passed unnoticed. The almost annual sejm sessions forced upon Sigismund by his need for taxation provided a regular forum for protest. The many wealthy nobles who felt excluded from Sigismund's inner circle, both those who held office and those who did not, were happy to make common cause with the middling nobility in the sejm. Before his marriage to Bona, Sigismund had managed the sejm reasonably effectively. With his council, he still had a considerable influence over the chamber's composition. It was customary for half the envoys to be elected by office-holders, and half by sejmiks. This meant that royal supporters were able to ensure a good number of envoys were bound in some way to the government, as courtiers, colonels, royal envoys, or tax-collectors: such men constituted 49 per cent of the 102 known envoys from Małopolska in this period, of whom 12 per cent were courtiers, and 44 per cent of 118 envoys from Wielkopolska, of whom 6 per cent were courtiers.[50] Yet opposition to this state of affairs was growing. In 1520, during the last war with the Order, the levy was called out, and a sejm summoned to Bydgoszcz. It demanded the institution of 'sejms for justice'; these were to be preceded by sejmiks in all districts, which were to elect their own envoys, in an attempt to avoid the influence of senators at the provincial sejmiks. The chancery ignored these demands when summoning sejms. While the noble opposition occasionally sought over the next twenty years to exclude senators from envoy elections, their efforts failed, as, on the whole, did attempts to make senators elect envoys separately, as happened at the Wielkopolskan sejmik in Środa (1525) and at the 1538 Cracow sejmik.[51]

Despite this influence over the chamber's composition, Sigismund found the sejm increasingly difficult to manage. Many envoys were local officials, mostly legal officials, who had a good knowledge of the law, and were responsible for upholding and enforcing it. As taxation was levied year after year, envoys expressed increasing concern with the state of the royal domain. The sejms of 1524–5 and 1527, after agreeing to the high rate of 18 groszy for the hide tax, to be paid half by tenant farmers, and half by noble proprietors, voted for a tax on income from repurchase agreements (*wyderkafy*), income from the farming of customs duties, leases on taverns and other rental income, and ordered an assessment of all landed estates for the purpose. This measure was aimed directly at wealthy office-holders, and was opposed by many senators, who did not wish to reveal the true extent of their incomes from royal land. Since they were responsible for overseeing the tax, very little came of it.[52]

Thus the law—and Sigismund's taste for ignoring it—increasingly exercised the chamber. By the 1520s, there were calls not so much for a codification of the law— envoys were reluctant to place responsibility for codification in the hands of the chancery, suspecting it would use the opportunity to rewrite the law—as for its

---

[50] Uruszczak, *Sejm*, 119–20.   [51] Uruszczak, *Sejm*, 110–15.
[52] *VC*, i/i, 432–5; *VC* i/ii, 14; Uruszczak, 'Sejm w latach', 100; Uruszczak, *Sejm*, 204.

'improvement and correction'. Commissions were appointed by the sejm to this end in 1511, 1519–20, 1526–7, and 1532. Although they failed to enact major reform, they built on Łaski's work, informed legislation, and fed into the continuing process by which Polish law was published and made available to the citizen body.[53]

Knowledge of the law stimulated concern at its functioning. Since Cracow University only trained canon lawyers before the establishment of a chair in Roman law in 1533, there was as yet no substantial body of professional civil lawyers, and nobles involved in lawsuits mostly acted for themselves. There was, however, considerable suspicion among the szlachta about Roman law, with its emphasis on the king's role in the legal process, and claims that he was not bound by written law. Calls for correction and improvement of the law grew, and there was a marked preference for publications in the vernacular rather than in Latin, knowledge of which was widespread among the wealthier nobility.[54] Codification found support in the royal government, which desired a greater uniformity of law: Casimir III's statutes had promulgated separate laws for Wielkopolska and Małopolska, but there was growing support for the process begun by the 1496 statute that had codified the separate privileges issued in the 1450s, and a desire to harmonize Mazovian law with the rest of the kingdom after the province's incorporation.[55] Tomicki sought to control the process by preparing a collection of statutes from 1507 to 1523, the *Formula Processus*, which aimed at establishing court procedure, though it was based on Małopolskan procedures, and was only accepted by the Małopolska nobility at the 1523 sejm: the Wielkopolskans initially rejected it, suspicious that senators close to the court had corrupted it, but accepted it in 1553.[56]

A similar fate met the work of the commissions established by Sigismund in 1520 in response to pressure from the szlachta. Opposition from Sigismund and the council at the 1521 sejm meant that little was achieved, although commissions met in 1526 and 1532, as the government took control. Tomicki did not sit on the commissions, but played a large part in their nomination and in guiding their work. They produced the *correctio iurium* in 1532, a collection of 930 articles concerning Polish litigation law and some public law. This was put before the sejm in January 1534, but as the sejmiks had not had time properly to assess it, it was referred to the next sejm, which met in late 1535. Sigismund was in Lithuania and attended neither; concern was expressed at the problems faced by the judicial system in the king's absence. The majority of the envoys, led by the Wielkopolskans, therefore rejected the *correctura* despite Tomicki's efforts, on the grounds that, far from correcting the law, it sought to introduce new law, but principally because it did not represent a true execution of the law: it failed to take account of concern about the operation of the law, downgraded the status of the

---

[53] Uruszczak, *Próba*, 78–81; Uruszczak, 'Sejm w latach', 89.
[54] Uruszczak, *Próba*, 50–1; James Miller, 'The Polish nobility and the Renaissance Monarchy: The "Execution of the Laws" Movement', i, *PER*, 3/3 (1983), 76.
[55] Uruszczak, *Próba*, 56.
[56] Uruszczak, *Próba*, 105–6; Uruszczak, 'Sejm w latach', 103; Odrzywolska-Kidawa, *Tomicki*, 101.

szlachta-controlled land courts, and largely ignored the ecclesiastical and castle courts.[57]

The envoys were right to be suspicious. In publishing the text of *Nihil Novi* the *correctura* introduced subtle but important changes. The king was named supreme judge, and the term 'envoys' (*nuntii terrestres*) was replaced with *proceres*. Although '*proceres*' could refer to office-holders or to the szlachta gathered in the sejm, it was suspected that it was intended to refer to a narrow group high officials, given Sigismund's known preference for working through the council, and in the light of suggestions such as that by hetman Jan Tarnowski in 1530 that some sejm debates should take place without the envoys. If new law could be introduced by the king with the consent of 'leading men' rather than the chamber of envoys, and if the king were to be the supreme judge in consultation with senators, the door would be open to the firm royal government that Sigismund desired and the szlachta feared. In the absence of Sigismund and Tomicki, the proposal failed. For the chamber activists, the law required not innovation but restoration and the removal of faults that had accumulated over the years. Its publication was merely a means to an end: the execution of the common law of the realm.[58]

Gradually, as envoys from the various provinces discovered a common purpose, and as the frequent sejm sessions taught them much about parliamentary strategy, 'execution of the law' (*executio iurium* in Latin, *egzekucja praw* in Polish) became both a slogan and a programme that formed a rallying point for many nobles and not a few disgruntled magnates. It encapsulated the concerns that had been growing since 1506. Sigismund's authoritarian character, his preference for rule through a small coterie of ministers, his tendency to exercise his prerogative to evade and ignore sejm statutes had all caused concern, as had Bona's aggressive repurchase of alienated royal estates. While Bona was associated with politicians such as Łaski and Kmita, who looked to the ordinary szlachta for support, and—to an extent—championed its causes, her aggressive pursuit of border disputes with private estates, and desire to recover individual properties and fields that had slipped out of the royal domain into private hands did not endear her to many among the szlachta, since poorer nobles were less able to defend themselves against her agents. The impression that revindication of the royal domain was designed to enrich the royal family rather than solve the government's financial problems brought magnates and ordinary nobles together in an alliance against what could be presented not as the execution of the law, but as the arbitrary exercise of royal power.[59]

The szlachta became fractious during Sigismund's long absences in Lithuania fighting the 1530s Muscovite wars. Sejmiks were increasingly reluctant to grant sejm envoys plenipotentiary powers, and the practice of furnishing them with instructions was growing. There is evidence of sejmiks insisting that their envoys

---

[57] *VC*, i/ii, 122–3, 129; Uruszczak, 'Sejm w latach', 103; Odrzywolska-Kidawa, *Tomicki*, 100–5; Miller, 'Execution', i, 77.

[58] Uruszczak, *Próba*, 80–3; 187–251.

[59] Sucheni-Grabowska, *Odbudowa*, 166–9. For the origins of the execution movement see Miller, 'Execution', i, 65–87.

were bound by their instructions in 1530, 1533, 1534, 1536–7, and 1538.[60] Divisions were sharpening. The Piotrków sejm that opened on 25 November 1535, the second of two to meet in Sigismund's absence, was so turbulent that primate Andrzej Krzycki called it an 'asiatic diet'. In December it passed the first pieces of legislation calling for the 'execution of privileges' according to the laws of the realm. During the debates, inspection of privileges issued to the church, to cities, and to Royal Prussia was urged to ensure that they were in accordance with the law.[61]

In 1537 matters came to a head. Sigismund had returned to Cracow for a sejm called for 1 November 1536, which assembled eleven days late. The mood in the chamber was ugly. The sixteen-year-old Sigismund August was to swear an oath to uphold the privileges accorded to the realm by his predecessors, following his election as king *vivente rege* (in the lifetime of the king) in 1529.[62] The envoys were determined to secure redress before supply, presenting a string of complaints about the 'new duty', Bona's purchasing of royal estates, the appointment of foreigners to public office, and burghers owning landed estates. They demanded formal recognition of the elective nature of the throne, the freeing of the szlachta from all duties, and not just for goods produced on their estates. As the wind from Wittenberg blew in an easterly direction it amplified the szlachta's traditional anticlericalism, and intensified demands that the church contribute on an equal basis to the defence of the realm: clerics should contribute to the noble levy, from which their village headmen should no longer be exempt; secular lands that had been placed under ecclesiastical law since 1382 should be resecularized; appeals to Rome should be abolished; annates should be used for the defence of the realm, and high church office should be reserved to those of noble birth. These proposals were far too radical for Sigismund. When he made it clear that he had no intention of appointing Gamrat chancellor the envoys—encouraged by Bona's protégés Kmita and Krzycki—refused to take any further part in the sejm, leaving Cracow in a collective huff on 2 February and forcing Sigismund August to take his oath in the presence only of his father and the council.[63]

Sigismund decided on confrontation, ordering the collection of the excise on council authority in March, and summoning the levy to gather at Trembowla near Lwów in early July for an expedition against Peter IV, hospodar of Moldavia, who had been at war with Poland since 1530. The policy backfired spectacularly. Mikołaj Taszycki, the Cracow land judge, called an assembly of the szlachta at Sokolniki near Lwów, which opened on 22 August and declared itself to be a *rokosz*, an allusion to Rákos, the location of the mass assemblies of nobles in Hungary that developed under Jagiellonian rule.[64] The assembly was regarded as a legal act of defiance by the citizen body to a king acting in breach of his oath. The *rokosz* could not force its programme on Sigismund, but despite the energetic scavenging of the

---

[60] Grzybowski, *Teoria*, 76.
[61] VC, i/ii, 136–40; Tadeusz Szulc, *Z badań nad egzekucją praw. Podstawy ustawodawcze egzekucji dóbr, ich interpretacja i nowelizacja na sejmach za panowania Zygmunta II Augusta* (Łódź, 2000), 35–7.
[62] See Ch. 33, 405–6.   [63] VC, i/ii, 122–3; Wojciechowski, *Zygmunt*, 357–61.
[64] Martyn Rady, 'Rethinking Jagiełło Hungary (1490–1526)', *Central Europe*, 3/1 (2005), 10.

large numbers of nobles seeking to feed themselves that earned the episode the dismissive title of the hens' war (*wojna kokosza*) from royal supporters, this was not the anarchic episode that is so frequently portrayed. Its supporters, roused by the circulation of the—probably apocryphal—*Rady Kallimacha*, which purported to be Machiavellian advice given to John Albert by Kallimach, put their demands to Sigismund in an orderly manner, following the normal procedure for sejm debates.[65] They focused on Bona's actions and the boundary judgements they regarded as unjust, made 'without a summons, without a court, and outwith the law', as Taszycki put it.[66] Sigismund defended Bona robustly, while Kmita vacillated between playing to the szlachta gallery and supporting the court. The *rokosz* demanded that judgements concerning the execution of the law on royal properties no longer be made solely on the basis of the chancery archives, but that documents registered in the castle, municipal, and consistorial courts should be taken into account, along with documents sworn before a notary.[67]

For all that, Sigismund was willing to take the assembly seriously, treating it as a camp sejm, and seeking to persuade it—unsuccessfully—to agree taxes, he had not summoned it, and it was therefore technically illegal, as its leaders effectively admitted when they sought to downplay its significance at their trial for *lèse-majesté* in 1538.[68] Although they were found guilty, they were not punished, merely being bound over on oath to serve the king.[69] Thus despite the offers of help against his recalcitrant subjects from a glittering array of European monarchs, including Charles V, Ferdinand I, and Suleyman the Magnificent, Sigismund astutely lowered the temperature. The sejm that opened in Piotrków in January 1538 was stormy. Calls for Sigismund's deposition circulated in Wielkopolska, and with the szlachta and senators at loggerheads, Sigismund defused the situation by accepting the main szlachta demands. He admitted that he had breached the law and promised that he and his successors would not do so again. He accepted the elective nature of the monarchy in a statute that outlawed elections *vivente rege*, and stated that elections should take place at an election sejm with the participation of senators and szlachta. The principle of *Nihil Novi* was reaffirmed, stressing the need for the chamber of envoys to consent to new law.[70] His concessions, including more minor measures from the *rokosz* programme meant that despite its tense beginning the sejm agreed the hide tax at the generous rate of 24 złoties, the highest level of his reign.[71]

With further concessions at the sejms of 1539 and 1540, the envoys secured their first parliamentary triumph, and the campaign for the execution of the laws gained considerable momentum. It was by no means a complete victory, however, and it remained to be seen if Sigismund and his successors would honour their promises. The atmosphere remained tense, as Sigismund's physical and mental

---

[65] Uruszczak, *Sejm*, 222; Władysław Pociecha, *Królowa Bona*, 4 vols, (Poznań, 1949–58), ii, 379–81.
[66] Quoted by Sucheni-Grabowska, *Odbudowa*, 170.   [67] Wojciechowski, *Zygmunt*, 363–4.
[68] Uruszczak, *Sejm*, 222.   [69] Wojciechowski, *Zygmunt*, 367–8.   [70] *VC*, i/ii, 170.
[71] Sucheni-Grabowska, *Monarchia*, 25; Uruszczak, *Sejm*, 213; Wojciechowski, *Zygmunt*, 368.

decline quickened, and Bona secured a considerable measure of influence over the royal government with the elevation of Gamrat to the archbishopric of Gniezno, and the promotion of her protégé Paweł Wolski from vice-chancellor to chancellor in 1538. The new vice-chancellor was another member of her clientele, Samuel Maciejowski. Her triumph was short-lived, however, as a storm of criticism greeted Sigismund's grant of her generous Mazovian dower in 1545. By now, with Bona's activities in Lithuania as well as Mazovia causing concern, the issue of the union began to exercise the attention of supporters of execution of the laws.

31

Mazovia

In 1506 Poland-Lithuania constituted the largest composite polity in Europe. As elsewhere, forces of integration and unification were strengthening. In much of Europe the pressure for closer integration and for institutional centralization came largely from above, with kings and their ministers the driving forces; in Poland-Lithuania, however, much of the impetus came from below, from the ordinary nobility in all parts of the Jagiellonian realms. After 1506 pressure came from the chamber of envoys for changes in the relationship between Poland, Mazovia, and Prussia, although it was applied in different ways with regard to Mazovia and Prussia, thereby changing the context for relations between Poland and Lithuania.

Mazovia's Piast dukes proudly defended their independent status after 1138, exploiting the duchy's geographical position to manoeuvre between Poland, Lithuania, and the Order, playing them off against each other. The flirtation with Bohemia in the 1320s, when homage was sworn to John of Luxembourg, ended in 1352–3 when Siemowit III (c.1313–81) and his brother Casimir I (c.1314–55), swore homage not to the kingdom of Poland but to Casimir III personally, while Charles IV of Bohemia renounced his claims in return for concessions from Casimir over Silesia.[1] When Casimir died in 1370 without an heir, however, the formal link with the Polish crown was broken, and Płock, which had been left to Casimir on the death of Bolesław III, its last, childless duke, in 1351, was restored to Mazovia, reuniting the whole duchy under Siemowit.[2]

Siemowit publicly demonstrated his independence by failing to attend Louis of Anjou's coronation in Cracow. Although his relations with Louis were, on the whole, friendly and he subsequently renewed his 1355 oaths, the Mazovian Piasts showed little desire to tighten their links with the Polish monarchy before or after Krewo. All of Siemowit's sons married Lithuanians: the eldest, Janusz I († 1429), married Danutė (Anna) daughter of Kęstutis; his second son Siemowit IV († 1426) married Algirdas's daughter Alexandra—Jagiełło's favourite sister—in 1387, and the third son, Henryk, married Kęstutis's daughter Ryngailė following his embassy to the Order in 1391–2 to negotiate with Vytautas.[3]

Mazovian unity did not outlast Siemowit III's death in 1381. The duchy was first divided between Janusz I and Siemowit IV, and then parcelled out among their

---

[1] Though the personal nature of feudal ties meant that this did not end residual claims by kings of Bohemia of suzerainty over Mazovia: thus in 1460, during his alliance with Casimir IV, George Podiebrad also renounced his claims: Piotr Węcowski, *Mazowsze w Koronie* (Cracow, 2004), 47.

[2] *Dzieje Mazowsza*, i, 260–3; Bardach (ed.), *Historia*, i, 561.   [3] See Ch. 8, 81.

descendants on their deaths: Janusz had one son, but Siemowit had five, only one of whom—Alexander—entered the church.[4] Further disintegration was prevented by the failure of that generation to proliferate: only one of Siemowit IV's sons, Władysław I († 1455), produced male heirs—Siemowit VI (1446–62) and Władysław II († 1462)—and although Janusz's grandson Bolesław IV († 1454) had four sons, only one of them, Konrad III († 1503) produced male heirs.

Siemowit IV's relations with Jagiełło were complicated by his candidacy for the Polish throne. Although his bid failed, and he attended Jagiełło's baptism and coronation, it is not clear that he swore homage to Jadwiga and Jagiełło, as Janusz I certainly did. He probably did so, however, in 1387 as the price of his marriage to Alexandra. Thereafter Siemowit and Alexandra frequently visited Cracow, and Siemowit's son Siemowit V spent much of his youth at the Polish court.[5] Despite a certain reluctance on account of their fear of potential reprisals, Siemowit and Janusz broadly supported Jagiełło during the war of 1409–11 with the Order, although Siemowit, unlike Janusz, failed to turn up for the Tannenberg campaign, only sending a token force, and maintained links with Sigismund of Luxembourg, who paid him a pension until 1412. Jagiełło accused Siemowit of involvement in a plot to forge money and kill him in 1421, though relations were soon restored.[6] Siemowit V and Casimir II confirmed Mazovia's feudal dependence on Poland in 1425 on behalf of their sick father, but if Siemowit V, Trojden II, and Władysław I all swore homage in 1426, Casimir II, encouraged by Vytautas, did not, while the archdeacon of Płock caused a rumpus by stating during the negotiations that Mazovia was an independent duchy with no ties to the Polish crown. Siemowit V supported Jagiełło against Švitrigaila, but Bolesław IV occupied Lithuanian territory in 1440 with Žygimantas's permission, which provoked a brief war with Casimir in 1444. Bolesław's candidature for the Polish throne in 1446–7 did not help relations, and although both he and Władysław I attended Casimir IV's coronation, there was an unseemly incident over precedence; it is probable that neither of them ever swore homage to him. Władysław I of Płock contested the return of certain Ruthenian holdings of Siemowit V to Poland after his death, while the Lithuanians claimed parts of the territory of Bełz—including Horodło—in a dispute that rumbled on into the 1450s. Although they were both sympathetic to calls from the Order for support against the Bund, Bolesław died in 1454 and Władysław a year later. In the absence of any adult duke, pressure from the Poles ensured that the Mazovians did not support the Order during the war, although many were recruited into the Order's army and a 1459 truce with the Order irritated the Poles considerably. Bolesław's holdings were divided among his four young sons, and were not reunited until the deaths of the three younger brothers between 1480 and

---

[4] There were sixteen separate territories: Czersk, Liw, Warsaw, Nur, Łomża, Ciechanów, Różan, Zakroczym, Wyszogród, Wizna, Płock, Płońsk, Zawkrze, Rawa, Gostyń, and Sochaczew. For the way in which they were parcelled out between 1374 and 1526, see the table in *Dzieje Mazowsza*, 277.
[5] Węcowski, *Mazowsze*, 34; *Dzieje Mazowsza*, i, 287, 291.
[6] Węcłowski, *Mazowsze*, 34; Krzyżaniakowa and Ochmański, *Jagiełło*, 307–8.

1495 left them in the hands of the eldest, Konrad III. Władysław I was succeeded by his infant sons Siemowit VI and Władysław II.[7]

Siemowit VI's death on 1 January 1462, followed rapidly by that of Władysław II, the last male descendant of the junior branch of the Mazovian Piasts, on 27 February, began the slow process by which Mazovia's feudal relationship with Poland was transformed into closer union. Siemowit VI and Władysław II were dukes of Płock, Wizna, Zawkrze, Sochaczew, Gostyń, and Bełz. Various claimants to their duchies emerged, among whom Catherine, daughter of Siemowit IV and widow of Mykolas Żygimantaitis, and Margaret, duchess of Oleśnica, pursued their claims energetically. Casimir moved quickly. The starosta of Rawa, supported by the local nobility, opted for incorporation into Poland, beating off an attack on the castle by forces supporting Catherine. Terms were agreed at the Piotrków assembly in November, and Casimir travelled to Rawa and Gostyń, incorporating them on 7 and 17 December respectively; Bełz, where support for incorporation was also strong, soon followed.[8]

Thus some Mazovians at least were prepared to support Polish rule, though Casimir's efforts to incorporate other territories failed. He occupied Płock castle and bullied some of the local szlachta into swearing oaths of loyalty, but the local elites and the cathedral chapter declared for Catherine, and then Konrad III. The imbroglio required Bohemian mediation and took until 1465 to sort out. In the end, Casimir spent 20,000 red złoties—a considerable sum in time of war—buying off the claims of the children of Konrad V, duke of Oleśnica. In 1476 Casimir persuaded Konrad's daughter Anna to cede her duchy of Sochaczew in return for granting her lifelong tenure of several properties. Initial resistance was bought off by the concession of the full rights of the Polish nobility. Similar tactics finally overcame resistance in Płock: in 1494, John Albert granted Rawa Polish law; when Janusz II died a year later without issue, he incorporated his duchy of Płock into Poland. Konrad III tried to claim all Janusz's lands, but John Albert flexed his muscles, upholding his right to the territories on the basis of judgements of 1462 and 1468 when neither Konrad nor Catherine answered four summonses to appear before tribunals appointed by Casimir to hear the case at general assemblies. When agreement was reached in 1496 Konrad was left with Wyszogród, while only Czersk was recognized as his hereditary possession; his other Mazovian holdings were granted for life only. Although Alexander, on Łaski's advice, was more generous, allowing all Konrad's lands to be passed on to his heirs after his death, John Albert had won an important victory and Alexander secured much-needed money in return for his concession.[9]

Casimir and John Albert's claims stemmed from the terms of the oaths of homage sworn by the Mazovian Piasts concerning the eventual extinction of

---

[7] *Dzieje Mazowsza*, i, 313; Węcowski, *Mazowsze*, 36–47.
[8] *Annales*, xii/ii, 27–30; *Dzieje Mazowsza*, i, 315; Węcowski, *Mazowsze*, 47–51.
[9] *Dzieje Mazowsza*, i, 316–17; Węcowski, *Mazowsze*, 52–63; 71–3, 84–93; Jan Dzięgielewski, 'Mazowsze wobec procesu włączenia do królestwa polskiego', in Dzięgielewski (ed.), *Mazowsze w procesach integracyjnych i dezintegracyjnych w Rzeczypospolitej XVI–XVII wieku* (Warsaw, 2010), 18–19; Papée, *Jan Olbracht*, 88–97.

ducal families in the male line and, in the case of Płock, the 1351 treaty following the death of Bolesław III. Mazovia was regarded by Casimir and the Polish szlachta as an integral part of the historic *corona regni*. Calls for its complete incorporation grew more frequent after the 1503 death of Konrad III, who left two infant sons, Stanisław, born in 1500, and Janusz III, born in 1502. Their mother, Anna, daughter of Mikalojus Radvilaitis, became regent, chairing the ducal council on their behalf, and continued to rule *de facto* after they reached their majorities, until her death in 1522. Her sons did not long survive her. Renowned for their debauched lifestyles, Stanisław died in August 1524; Janusz in March 1526. Their deaths were surrounded by scandal: rumours circulated that they had both been poisoned, with fingers pointed at Bona Sforza and Katarzyna Radziejowska, wife of the palatine of Rawa. They were given substance by the abrupt disappearance from Warsaw of the apothecary Jan Alantzee, and Sigismund was forced to call a commission of enquiry which failed to dispel them, although when their bones were exhumed in 1953 tests proved inconclusive. Few scholars now believe the story, and tuberculosis is the most probable cause of death.[10]

Incorporation was by no means inevitable while the Piasts survived. Poles might regard Mazovia as part of the *corona regni*, but Mazovians had been separated from the kingdom for nearly four centuries. They had their own unique social structure, with a far higher proportion of nobles than in the other Polish lands, and a far lower proportion of wealthy nobles. They had their own political institutions, their own traditions, and spoke their own dialect of Polish. Historical tradition and a substantial Polish-speaking population were not sufficient to secure reunification. Yet there were important differences between Mazovia and Silesia or Prussia. The Mazovian Piasts had not become Germanized like their Silesian cousins, Mazovia was never part of the Empire, and there had been no great influx of German settlers. Mazovian institutions owed much to Polish models: Siemowit III introduced starostas in the fourteenth century, and ducal power remained strong, even after Mazovia developed a parliamentary culture, with assemblies meeting regularly after 1454 in the various duchies, although essentially they were meetings of the ducal councils and office-holders, with the participation on occasion of all nobles who cared to turn up, though their active part in debates was limited.[11] The Mazovian church lay within the archbishopric of Gniezno, and although it defended its autonomy fiercely—Casimir's attempt to persuade the Płock chapter to elect his candidates in 1463 was rejected—nevertheless the monarchy's influence over church patronage became dominant after the incorporation of Płock in 1495: in 1497, when the diocese fell vacant Cardinal Frederick turned up to browbeat the local chapter and its candidate, Canon Mikołaj Bartnicki. He persuaded Bartnicki to assign him his votes, and then renounced the bishopric in favour of his protégé

---

[10] Bogucka, *Bona*, 215–16; Dzięgielewski, 'Mazowsze wobec', 27.
[11] 138 such assemblies took place between 1455 and 1526: see the table in *Dzieje Mazowsza*, i, 334–8; Kaczmarczyk and Leśnodorski (eds), *Historia*, ii, 164–5; Wojciechowski, *Zygmunt*, 260.

Jan Lubrański. Henceforth the bishops of Płock favoured Mazovia's integration into Poland.[12]

Factors favouring integration now began operating strongly. The most powerful were economic and social. The incorporation of Royal Prussia opened up trade down the Vistula through Danzig and Elbing; since the Vistula flowed through Mazovia and Warsaw, Mazovia was firmly integrated into the developing Polish-Lithuanian economy long before 1526. It benefited from its strategic location between Poland and Lithuania, as the transit trade to Silesia and beyond began to develop, particularly in cattle, raised in the great lowlands round the Vistula, Bug, and Narew, and driven through Mazovia to the Prussian and Silesian markets. Salt flowed down the Vistula from Wieliczka, Bochnia, and Ruthenia. Rawa and Płock, incorporated in 1462 and 1495, benefited from receiving the liberties accorded to towns under Polish law, and demonstrated its advantages to the rest of Mazovia.[13]

The same process took place among the Rawa and Płock nobility who, on their incorporation into Poland, came under Polish law and were accorded the rights and liberties of their Polish counterparts, including freedom from ordinary taxes. This made a difference, since the Mazovian szlachta were not protected by the Koszyce privileges, and paid a ducal rent—an ordinary tax equivalent to the *poradlne*—at rates of up to 12 groszy: around 1500 its average annual rate was 4.7 groszy.[14] The acquisition of Polish-style privileges was therefore a substantial incentive, as was the Polish system of local government, in which more authority lay in the hands of the local nobility. Rawa, Płock, and Bełz were established as palatinates after their incorporation. Rawa and Płock were joined to Wielkopolska; Bełz to Małopolska, and the whole panoply of local offices on the Polish pattern was opened up to the local nobility. Intermarriage meant that Mazovian noble families had ever closer connections to families across the border, and a growing minority owned property in Poland. Substantial numbers of impoverished Mazovian nobles sought employment in Poland: many served on the disastrous 1497 campaign, and some were rewarded for their loyalty with grants of land taken from Poles who failed to turn up for the levy.[15]

Thus when the extinction of the dynasty removed the main focus for the maintenance of a separate identity, the incorporation and integration of Mazovia into the *corona regni* proved a relatively uncontroversial and smooth process that was, on the whole, accepted by the Mazovian elites. On 13 September 1526, six months after Janusz III's death, Sigismund accepted oaths of loyalty from his new subjects in Warsaw. It was unclear, however, on what basis Mazovia had returned under the crown. The Polish szlachta regarded it as an integral part of the *corona regni* that should formally be reincorporated, but Sigismund and Bona were tempted by the prospect of establishing it as a base for Jagiellon power, in which

---

[12] Nowakowska, *Church*, 49–50.   [13] *Dzieje Mazowsza*, i, 348–9.
[14] Zientara, 'Społeczeństwo', 155–6; Kaczmarczyk and Leśnodorski (eds), *Historia*, ii, 165.
[15] Dzięgielewski, 'Mazowsze wobec', 18.

royal authority was not as limited as it was in the rest of Poland, a notion supported by some members of the Lithuanian council.[16]

These were pipedreams. There were other claimants, most worryingly Albrecht von Hohenzollern, duke of Prussia, and considerable support among the Mazovian szlachta for the full incorporation that would bring them the rights and liberties of their Polish brethren. There were also many Mazovian opponents of incorporation, and strong support for preservation of elements of the Mazovian system, since the Poles were keen for the Mazovians to share the burdens of taxation, which had risen so considerably in recent years. This issue was aired at the 1527 Cracow sejm. The chamber rejected the idea that Mazovia should remain a feudal dependency of the crown, demanding a written confirmation from Sigismund that it had been incorporated into the kingdom. For Mazovia to take a full part in the sejm would require the establishment of Polish-style sejmiks: it was only Mazovian dignitaries who were summoned to the 1527 sejm.[17]

Mazovian envoys were invited to the 1527–8 sejm, which refused to debate supply until Mazovia's position was clarified, but this proved impossible as the Mazovians wrangled over the terms of incorporation. It was agreed that a sejm should be summoned to Warsaw in January 1529 to allow for full discussion. It opened on 6 January; after tough negotiations lasting a month, Mazovian concerns were sufficiently accommodated for formal incorporation on 11 February. The sejm defined the meaning of Sigismund's 1526 privilege, stating that Mazovia was thereby united and incorporated into the kingdom.[18] Mazovian nobles were freed from all burdens laid upon them by their dukes, and granted the liberties of the Polish szlachta, although their traditional laws and customs were to remain in force insofar as they did not breach Polish law. They were to pay the *poradlne* at two groszy per hide; all other impositions, taxes, and levies could only be raised with their consent. Offices were to be filled by local nobles.[19] Mazovia was constituted as a palatinate; its palatine and seven castellans were to join the senate. It was divided into ten districts, each of which had a sejmik that sent two envoys to the sejm. A separate Mazovian sejm continued to exist until 1540, when it was abolished along with the former central offices of the grand ducal government.[20] The office of governor formally remained until 1577, though its powers were minimal. A commission was established to investigate the differences between Mazovian and Polish law; various problems were cleared up in a new codex of Mazovian law, approved at the 1540 sejm, after which there were relatively few differences between the two. From 1536–7, Mazovians were summoned to the

---

[16] Wojciechowski, *Zygmunt*, 259; Rowell, 'Dynastic bluff?' 13.
[17] Uruszczak, *Sejm*, 74, 209; Dzięgielewski, 'Mazowsze wobec', 29; *VC*, i/ii, 11, 31.
[18] 'et statum huius ducatus in eo ordine et fine statueremus, subiicientes se ipse et alios omnes istius ducatus incolas ad unionem et incorporationem regni ac ad omnem eius defensionem . . . absque quavis contradictione actessuros, cum primum privilegium Maiestatis Regiae': *VC*, i/ii, 51; Uruszczak, *Sejm*, 209.
[19] *VC*, i/ii, 51–2; Dzięgielewski, 'Mazowsze w czasach ostatnich Jagiellonów', in Dzięgielewski (ed.), *Mazowsze*, 32.
[20] Kaczmarczyk and Leśnodorski, *Historia*, ii, 166. The seven castellanies were Warsaw, Ciechanów Czersk, Liw, Wizna, Wyszogród, and Zakroczym.

sejm in the same manner as the rest of the kingdom.[21] Mazovia formally adopted Polish law in 1577, with a few elements of Mazovian customary law embodied in the *Excepta mazowieckie*. The province's integration into the kingdom following incorporation had been rapid, but Mazovia's unique social structure meant that its politics remained distinct from those of Wielkopolska and Małopolska until the partitions.

[21] Dzięgielewski, 'Mazowsze Jagiellonów', 33; Uruszczak, *Sejm*, 75.

32
Prussia and the Union

The relatively smooth incorporation of Mazovia after 1526 and the rapidity of its integration into the Polish system completed a process of unification that had started long before 1526, and owed much to the well-established links of the Mazovian szlachta with their counterparts in Poland that were made easier by a common—albeit distant—history, and commonalities of language and culture. The process was not so smooth in Royal Prussia, where there was no dynastic link to Poland, where German was the language of government, and where incorporation into Poland between 1454 and 1466 was effected by treaties whose meaning—as in Lithuania—was contested. Yet if powerful groups among the Prussian elites proved resistant to forces of integration and unification, seeking to institutionalize and guard their autonomy after 1466, views on the relationship to Poland were by no means monolithic among the complex mosaic of social groups that made up these elites, and forces tending towards unification and closer integration with Poland were strengthened after 1500 by the continuing existence of the truncated *Ordensstaat*, whose grand masters still dreamt of recovering Royal Prussia.

That Royal Prussia had been incorporated into the Polish kingdom in the period 1454–66 was indisputable; as in the case of Lithuania, however, there was considerable disagreement over the nature of that incorporation. The Bund's leaders, who now constituted the province's governing elite, stood firmly on the measures in the union treaties that institutionalized the many differences between Royal Prussia and the rest of the kingdom. Autonomy was embodied in Prussia's own currency minted in Danzig and Thorn—coins had to be issued bearing the king's likeness after 1454, but that was the only common feature—its own coat-of-arms and seal, and its own governor.[1] Government was exercised by the Prussian council (*Landesrat*), which emerged from the Bund's secret council and was given form by the replacement of the Order's governing structure, based on the *Komturei*, by the three palatinates of Pomerelia, Culm/Chełmno, and Marienburg/Malbork, in 1467. Originally it comprised the palatines, castellans, and chamberlains of the three palatinates, and representatives of Danzig, Thorn, and Elbing. The bishops were originally excluded as potential agents of the king or—in the case of Ermland—the Order, but when Casimir began appointing Prussian nobles to the bishoprics, and

---

[1] Małłek, 'Stany', 71; *Historia Pomorza*, ii/i, ed. Gerard Labuda (Poznań, 1976), 45–6; Stanisław Kubiak, *Monety i stosunki monetarne w Prusach Królewskich w 2 połowie XV wieku* (Wrocław, 1986), 24–30; *Urzędnicy Prus Królewskich*, 15–16.

won his battle for control of Ermland, they were admitted in 1479 (Ermland) and 1482 (Culm). With the cities sending two representatives each, membership was stabilized at seventeen in 1526.[2]

It is difficult to distinguish Prussian council meetings from meetings of the estates. The union treaties stipulated that the council could not impose taxation without agreement with the commons, the *gemeyne stete und gemeyne lande*; thus assemblies of the Royal Prussian estates, known originally as *Ständetage* and later, as their form and procedures became regularized, the *Landtag*, became frequent: *Ständetage* met on 111 occasions between 1466 and 1492. While this emergence of parliamentary government paralleled developments in Poland, Lithuania, and Mazovia, the peculiar nature of Prussian society, with the prominent economic position enjoyed by its cities, in particular Danzig, Thorn, and Elbing, meant that the Prussian *Landtag* developed differently to the sejm. After 1466, meetings of the estates comprised members of the council and representatives of the nobility and the cities. Initially the form of its deliberations was not rigidly established and it is hard to determine the extent to which ordinary nobles and envoys from the smaller cities participated in them: the attendance of representatives from the 27 lesser cities—of which Dirschau, Stargard, Konitz, and Marienburg were the most prominent—can be confirmed for only 25 out of those 111 assemblies. The fact that when urban representatives were absent it was noticed and discussed, however, suggests that they probably attended more frequently than these figures suggest. Before 1526 the estates model of western Europe prevailed, in which—apart from the council—representatives of the nobility and the cities debated separately, although an attempt in 1488 to establish a separate chamber for the clergy foundered on the opposition of the other estates: memories of ecclesiastical rule were too fresh and too painful.[3] Attempts by Casimir in 1471 and by Sigismund in 1513 to insist that authority to summon the estates lay solely with the king—as it did in Poland—stimulated fierce resistance, and could not be sustained. Although they accepted that their incorporation into the *regnum* meant that they could not conduct a separate foreign policy, Prussians only participated with great reluctance in the kingdom's institutions: they refused to attend meetings of the royal council, and although Prussians were invited to the royal elections of 1492, 1501, and 1506 on the same basis as Polish nobles, only council members turned up: in 1492 they ostentatiously sent one envoy to vote on behalf of the whole province; in 1506 they sent two palatines and a castellan.[4]

---

[2] Janusz Małłek, 'Ze studiów nad dwuizbowym systemem reprezentacji w Prusach Zakonnych, Prusach Królewskich i Prusach Książęcych od XV do XVIII wieku', *CPH*, 44/1–2 (1992), 237–8; *Historia Gdańska*, ii, *1454–1655*, ed. Edmund Cieślak (Gdańsk, 1982), 262; Karin Friedrich, *The Other Prussia: Royal Prussia, Poland and Liberty, 1569–1772* (Cambridge, 2000), 24–5.

[3] Janosz-Biskupowa, 'Chronologia zjazdów stanów Prus Królewskich w latach 1466–1492', *AUNC, Historia*, 9 (1973), 58, 113; Małłek, 'Dwuizbowy system', 238; Janusz Małłek, 'From the rebellion of the Prussian League to the autonomy of Royal Prussia: The estates of Prussia and Poland in the years 1454–1526', *PER*, 14/1 (1994), 21; Turowski, *Innenpolitische*, 58; Zbigniew Naworski, 'Status Prus Królewskich w Rzeczypospolitej Obojga Narodów: evenement czy reguła?', in Tomasz Ciesielski and Anna Filipczak-Kocur (eds), *Rzeczpospolita państwem wielu narodowości i wyznań* (Warsaw, 2008), 63–4.

[4] *ASPK*, v/i, no. 8, 10; Małłek, 'Stany', 71–2; *Historia Pomorza*, 74; Turowski, *Innenpolitische*, 49.

The council tenaciously defended Prussia's autonomy and institutional structure against the views of Casimir and the Polish council concerning the nature of incorporation, and attempts to exercise control from Cracow. The first major clash came over the office of governor, established by Casimir on 9 March 1454 for Hans von Baysen. The governor was not, however, to be the obedient executor of royal policy: he was elected by the estates and confirmed by the king. The implications were not so evident during the war, when Baysen and his younger brother Stibor, elected following Hans's death in 1459, on the whole cooperated closely with Casimir's government. The governor had wide powers, including the disposal of leases on royal estates. Stibor proved sensitive on matters of honour and status, and his elevation was against Casimir's better instincts. After 1466, when he began to act more as the representative of the council and the estates than the loyal lieutenant for which Casimir had hoped, the king had second thoughts. In March 1467 he abolished the office, appointing Stibor palatine of Marienburg instead, and attempted to govern Prussia through ad hoc commissioners and with the support of Wincenty Kiełbasa, the royalist bishop of Culm. In 1472, facing growing resistance to this policy, Casimir tried to bring the province's administration more in line with Polish norms by appointing Stibor starosta general—an official not dependent upon the estates, who could be dismissed at the king's pleasure—but the estates refused to accept the nomination. Stibor rejected the title, styling himself governor of Prussia until his death in 1480. His son, Nicholaus, was appointed palatine of Marienburg, but Casimir did not grant him the title of governor, or the starosty of Marienburg, naming him instead administrator (*Anwalde*) of Prussia.[5]

This was a meaningless post, and Nicholaus conspicuously refused to act as Casimir's loyal lieutenant, becoming instead a malcontent focus for opposition in both council and estates, which called regularly for the king to appoint a proper leader: a *Haupt des Landes*. At a meeting of the estates in Thorn in 1485 Nicholaus resigned his office and refused to take the oath as a royal councillor. When Casimir proposed a grant of taxation for the Ottoman war, a cause remote from Prussian concerns, he led the estates in forming a brief confederation, complaining about breaches of Prussian privileges, most notably the appointment of non-Prussians as starostas and the taking of decisions concerning Prussia without consulting the Prussian council.[6]

Although the estates demanded an end to the appointment of Poles to Prussian starosties, the confederates could not force Casimir to accept their petitions. He rejected Nicholaus's resignation, but Nicholaus still refused to take the oath, and Casimir abandoned for the moment the attempt to find an amenable local politician to act as governor. He granted all the palatines, bishops, and the three great cities the title of *Anwalde*, which merely recognized its emptiness, and strengthened the role of the starosta of Marienburg as his representative in Prussia. Since 1457 he had appointed outsiders to the post: Ścibor Chełmski, the starosta general of

---

[5] Górski, 'Prussian estates', 45; Górski, *Starostowie malborscy w latach 1457–1510* (Toruń, 1960), 33–4, 74; *Urzędnicy Prus Królewskich*, 11.

[6] Górski, 'Prussian estates', 49–50; Małłek, 'Estates', 23–4.

Wielkopolska (1457–9), Jan Kościelecki, palatine of Inowrocław (1459–75), Kościelecki's brother Mikołaj, palatine of Brześć (1475–8), Piotr Dunin (1478–84), and Paweł Jasieński (1484–5). After Nicholaus's posturing in 1485, Casimir appointed his favourite, Zbigniew Tęczyński, a Małopolskan magnate and political heavyweight.[7]

Tęczyński ran the starosty astutely until 1496, but he was in a difficult position. He did not sit on the council, and his judicial powers were formally limited to his own starosty, the seventeen starosties held by non-Prussians—thirteen were in the hands of native Prussians—and to the villages of the free peasantry, *die freien Bauerndörfer*. It was an unsatisfactory solution to an intractable problem. In Prussia it was the palatines, not the starostas, as in Poland, who exercised jurisdiction over the castle courts. The attempt to establish a dual system of administration risked entrenching division and highlighting the role of the council and the estates in defending Prussian autonomy. The palatines may have been responsible for criminal justice, but there were problems with its administration: since the starostas controlled the royal castles, the courts of the palatines, although known as 'castle courts' had no permanent locations, and the starostas encroached on the powers of the palatines with royal encouragement, using their garrisons to chase bandits and arrest and imprison criminals. The abolition of the governorship left a vacuum at the head of the judicial system, since the governor, presiding over the Prussian council, had heard appeals on the king's behalf from the lower courts. At the estates of 1467 and 1474 bitter complaints were raised against the starostas, while Casimir's attempts to establish a new appeal court in 1468 presided over by the bishops of Culm, Ermland, and Cujavia was first revised by the estates to exclude all non-Prussians and finally rejected in 1472 in the presence of Casimir himself; this left appeals *de facto* in the hands of the Prussian council.[8]

Exerting influence over the council was difficult, however, since Casimir did not enjoy the same measure of control over the episcopate he had secured in Poland, and bishops were excluded from it until 1479. While Casimir established influence over the bishopric of Culm, it was a different matter with regard to Ermland, a 4,250 km^2 wedge of land that thrust deep into the *Ordensstaat* from its narrow connection to Royal Prussia along the Frische Haff near Elbing. The Ermland estates supported the Bund in 1454, withdrawing their obedience to their bishop, Franz Kuhschmalz, but Ermland was not incorporated in 1454, and was only placed under Polish protection in 1464 when its bishop, Paul Legendorf, who vacillated between the two sides during the war, finally opted for Poland.[9] The 1466 Thorn treaty did not regulate Ermland's position, however, and on Legendorf's death in 1467 the chapter provocatively elected one of its members, Nicholaus von Tüngen, instead of Kiełbasa, Casimir's preferred candidate. Tüngen

---

[7] Górski, *Starostowie*, 11, 19, 36, 57–62.

[8] Zbigniew Naworski, *Szlachecki wymiar sprawiedliwości w Prusach Królewskich (1454–1772)* (Toruń, 2004), 44–5, 208; Janina Bielecka, 'Organizacja i działalność sądów grodzkich w Prusach Królewskich od wieku XV do XVIII włącznie', *Archeion*, 65 (1977), 157–8; Bogucka, *Kazimierz*, 126–7; Górski, *Starostowie*, 61–2.

[9] Stanisław Achremczyk, *Historia Warmii i Mazur* (Olsztyn, 1997), 69.

maintained that Ermland was not subject to Polish rule, but was an ecclesiastical principality recognizing no superior but the pope. On this issue, Casimir was supported by the Prussian council, concerned that Ermland might fall under the Order. In 1470 Polish garrisons in the castles beat off Tüngen's attempt to seize them; in 1472, with the Order's support, Tüngen occupied most of the main towns, and although the Royal Prussian estates sought to mediate, Tüngen, encouraged by Matthias Corvinus and the Order, took most of the rest in 1474. Tüngen travelled to Rome to secure papal approval, and in 1477, assured of the Order's military support, formally withdrew his obedience to Casimir. In the brief 'priests' war' that broke out in 1478, Royal Prussia—and Danzig in particular—rallied behind Casimir. The pope had no divisions; Corvinus, despite his fine words, was far away; and the Order's forces were no match for the Poles. Tüngen, facing disaster, was only rescued by Corvinus, who brokered a settlement in 1479. Ermland was explicitly incorporated into Poland, Tüngen swore an oath of loyalty to the crown and was granted a seat on the Prussian council, while his subjects were given the right of appeal to the king, to whom they had to swear oaths of loyalty. Tüngen remained unreconciled to Polish rule until his death in 1489, and Casimir failed in his attempt to have him succeeded by Cardinal Frederick, that notable collector of bishoprics. The candidate elected by the chapter and supported by the papacy and the Prussian estates, was Tüngen's ally on the Ermland chapter, Lucas Watzenrode, son of a Thorn burgher and Copernicus's uncle. Watzenrode, educated in Cologne and Bologna, had begun his career in court service, where he came under the influence of Zbigniew Oleśnicki the younger when he was moving into opposition to Casimir.[10]

As in the case of Lithuania, it was the nature of the union with Poland that was contested after 1466, not the union itself. Despite the vigorous defence of Prussia's privileges and autonomy there were many forces gently pushing it towards closer dependence upon, and cooperation with, Poland, and little desire to challenge the incorporation treaty upon which Prussian liberties rested. As in Lithuania, there were various interest groups that frequently clashed, and were perfectly willing to seek allies in Poland—whether the king or the sejm—to help settle Prussian conflicts. There was much about the Polish system that was attractive, particularly to ordinary nobles who had fought the Order, and who did not feel they had reaped their due reward.

The emergence of the council as the dominant force after 1466 signalled the increasing control of a small group of wealthy noble families, in a sometimes tense alliance with the great cities, who were the true victors of the Thirteen Years War. Many of these families were emigrés from the lands that formed the new *Ordensstaat* after 1466, including the Baysens, the Pfeildorfs, the Mortangens, the Feldens, the Legendorfs, the Cygenbergs, and the Dameraws.[11] Their influence

---

[10] *Historia Pomorza*, ii/i, 49–51, 76–9; Górski, *Watzenrode*, 8–12, 17–21; Achremczyk, *Historia*, 70–1.
[11] Jolanta Dworaczkowa-Essmanowska, 'Ruch szlachecki w Prusach Królewskich w pierwszej połowie XVI wieku', Unpublished Masters dissertation, University of Poznań, 1951; Górski, 'Pierwsze czterdziestolecie Prus Królewskich, 1466–1506', *RG*, 11 (1938), 33–4.

eclipsed that of the ordinary nobles who had fought the Order, whose voice was still heard in the estates, but who were in no position to challenge the council elite. In several respects the council families were more powerful even than in Małopolska, since the Order's legacy ensured that there was a greater proportion of royal land to be granted by the king as starosties: 50.9 per cent of the land after 1466, as compared with 33 per cent in Małopolska; 33 per cent in the palatinates of Ruthenia, Podolia, and Bełz; 15 per cent in Wielkopolska; and 14 per cent in Mazovia. Since the royal lands contained many uncultivated wildernesses and forests, the proportion of cultivated land held by the crown was 38.9 per cent overall, although in the palatinate of Marienburg, royal land comprised 56.7 per cent of all land, and no less than 60.3 per cent of the cultivated land, reflecting the Order's domination of what had been its heartland.[12] Even if Casimir granted more than half the Prussian starosties to Polish outsiders, leases on the rest were controlled by this small elite which—thanks to the principle of *indygenat* guaranteed in 1454–66—dominated high office: the Baysens provided four out of six palatines of Marienburg between 1454 and 1569, one palatine of Culm, one castellan of Danzig, two castellans of Elbing, and frequently held the most significant starosties, including Stuhm (four holders), Mewe, Christburg (three), Tolkemit (three), Golub, and Schönsee. The Zehmen provided two palatines of Marienburg, one of Culm, one of Pomerelia, two castellans of Danzig, and held the starosties of Christburg (two holders), Mewe (two), Stargard (two) and Stuhm.[13]

The tight grip of this small group of families on leaseholds on royal land that were proving ever more lucrative as Prussia's economy began to boom caused much resentment among the wider nobility. Support for closer links with Poland grew among ordinary nobles, many of whom—especially in the Culm palatinate—were Polish or of Polish descent. After 1466 the Prussian elites, whether of Polish or German background, were increasingly drawn to the University of Cracow as it entered its greatest period of intellectual distinction. Between 1466 and 1525, 495 Royal Prussian students matriculated in Cracow, among them Copernicus, who studied there between 1491 and 1495, and his brother Andreas. Matriculations in Cracow substantially exceeded those in Leipzig, the next most popular destination, with 363 between 1471 and 1525. Over half were German-speaking burghers from Danzig, Thorn, and Elbing, including Johann von Höfen or Flachsbinder (1485–1548), from a German emigré family of noble origin that lost its property during the Thirteen Years War and settled in Danzig, where Johann's father made a fortune brewing beer. Johann studied at Greifswald and Cracow, before entering service at John Albert's court and making his reputation as a Humanist and Latin poet. Starting as a secretary under Łaski, he became a trusted diplomat and acquired the name under which he became known in humanist circles across Europe: Joannes Dantiscus, Jan Dantyszek in Polish. He served under Tomicki, and

---

[12] *Historia Pomorza*, ii/i, 201. The figures for Poland are from Sucheni-Grabowska, 'Królewszczyzny', in *Encyklopedia historii gospodarczej Polski do 1945 r.*, ii (Warsaw, 1981), 390.
[13] Górski, *Starostowie*, 73; *Urzędnicy Prus Królewskich*, 194–5; 198–9.

enjoyed a distinguished diplomatic career, undertaking missions to Vienna, Rome, the Netherlands, and London, where he met Thomas Wolsey and Thomas More—he was later to befriend Thomas Cranmer in Regensburg—before ending his career in Prussia, becoming a canon of Ermland (1529), bishop of Culm (1530), and Ermland (1537).[14]

Copernicus and Dantyszek were exceptional, but their careers demonstrate the extent to which the 1454–66 union opened up opportunities in Poland for Prussian nobles and burghers. The path they followed was not unusual, and was one way in which loyalty to the king and the wider union state grew, and spread through various institutions, including the church, where the number of canons on the Culm and Ermland chapters who were either Poles or had been educated in Poland grew. Kings used their power of appointment to introduce royal supporters onto the council, such as Jan Bajerski, created palatine of Pomerelia in 1483.[15] Even as a common Prussian identity developed, based not on nationality but on a shared past, common institutions, and the memory of the struggle against the Order—the subject of a rash of historical works—the growing contacts with Poland created opportunities for the strengthening of royal influence, and there was in consequence a gradual growth of support for the process of unification.

Casimir's death in 1492 opened a new chapter in Prussia's relationship to Poland. His appointment of Zbigniew Tęczyński had hardened opposition to attempts to rule the province directly through the starostas, and he ended his life in a bitter dispute with Watzenrode that looked like it might even end in war when John Albert was ordered to summon the Prussian levy to enforce Casimir's will in Ermland. Yet Watzenrode was no Tüngen, and much of Casimir's hostility to him was artificially sustained by members of the Polish council. Watzenrode may have angered John Albert by attending his coronation and whispering '*et terrarum Prussarum*' after the primate—his former mentor Oleśnicki—had intoned the section of the coronation oath in which the new monarch swore to respect Polish liberties, but the new reign was marked by a change of atmosphere. Watzenrode distanced himself from Oleśnicki's opposition to John Albert and after a dispute with the Order that flared up in 1493 he instigated a rapprochement. When John Albert visited Thorn in October 1494, Watzenrode begged his pardon, and remained at his side throughout his eight-month Prussian stay, becoming one of his closest advisors.[16]

Watzenrode had ambitions to become the dominant politician in Prussia, and perhaps even governor, a prospect that opened up in 1496, when John Albert dismissed Tęczyński. The election of Frederick, younger son of the elector of Saxony, as grand master of the Order in 1498 gave Watzenrode another reason for looking to Poland: Frederick's election was a reaction against the previous grand master, Johann von Tiefen, who, despite initially refusing to take his oath of loyalty after his election in 1489, finally did so in 1493, and thereafter favoured good relations with Poland: he died leading a contingent of troops during the 1497 Moldavian

---

[14] *PSB*, iv, 424–30; *Historia Pomorza*, ii/i, 109–10.   [15] Małłek, 'Estates', 23.
[16] Górski, *Watzenrode*, 48, 70.

campaign. A powerful group within the Order sought to use Frederick's connections to the Empire to reopen the question of its territorial losses in 1466, and his election opened a period of tense relations that lasted until 1525.

The move helped cement better relations between Poland, Ermland—all but surrounded by the *Ordensstaat*—and the Royal Prussian estates. While Watzenrode had defended Prussian autonomy before 1494, thereafter he gradually moved in a more integrationist direction, even supporting the levying of taxes in Prussia to support the Ottoman war. Without consulting the Prussian council or estates, Watzenrode and Nicholaus von Baysen began attending meetings of the royal council, and in 1499 Watzenrode appended his seal to the 1498 peace treaty with Moldavia. At the 1509 Piotrków sejm he broke with precedent by taking a seat in the senate.[17] He continued to defend Prussian autonomy, in 1501 demanding a separate oath from Alexander to uphold Prussian rights against the Polish claim that since Prussia had been incorporated and therefore formed one body with Poland, there was no need. Watzenrode responded that although they were one body, a body has limbs with different functions, an argument that Sigismund August later appropriated with regard to Lithuania. Watzenrode argued that Royal Prussia was a separate country with separate laws, in respect of which it should swear a separate oath of allegiance, as did the Lithuanians, which, Watzenrode suggested, should be to the king alone. Yet his support for Prussian autonomy was broader in theory than in practice. Despite Alexander's failure to appoint him governor, and his surprise nomination of Ambroży Pampowski, palatine of Sieradz, another Pole, as starosta of Marienburg in 1504, Pampowski was subordinated to the council, which Watzenrode saw, under his own guidance, as the key institution in the province. Despite Pampowski's appointment, and despite occasional opposition to individual measures, Watzenrode supported many of the king's centralizing policies, and was keen that he be followed as bishop by a Pole.[18]

Pampowski's appointment did not mark a return to the days of Tęczyński. It came as a direct result of a request from the Prussian estates for a *Haupt des Landes* during Alexander's visit to Marienburg in May 1504, during which he swore to respect the province's privileges and received oaths of loyalty from his Prussian subjects.[19] The request stemmed in large part from the estates' desire for a more effective legal system, and above all for a system of appeal from the lower courts. The failure of Casimir's attempt to establish an appeal court in 1472 left appeals in the hands of the council; since the palatinates also controlled the castle courts, the ordinary nobles—and members of other estates—had little faith in their ability to win any appeal.

Pampowski's appointment did little to solve the problem, and the experiment ended in 1510 when Sigismund removed him as starosta of Marienburg and *Haupt des Landes*. His six years in Prussia, however, marked a distinct change of tone in the relations between the province and the rest of the kingdom. With Pampowski's appointment, Alexander achieved what his father had singularly failed to, since he

---

[17] Górski, *Watzenrode*, 70; Turowski, *Innenpolitische*, 75–6.
[18] Górski, *Watzenrode*, 73–7.   [19] Górski, *Starostowie*, 127.

was accepted on the council despite his lack of *indygenat* status. Despite his precedence disputes with Watzenrode—who had not welcomed the appointment—Pampowski's easy manner gradually won over many among the Prussian elites, and he initiated a process of reform that, while it respected the province's traditions, was much influenced by Polish models.

Watzenrode worked with Pampowski—initially with some reluctance—and other members of the Prussian council on a new Prussian statute, influenced by Łaski's efforts in Poland, that was intended to combat the mounting anarchy that so disturbed the estates: local nobles were often at loggerheads with the towns over trade, disputes were common, and the fragmented nature of the court system meant that few emerged satisfied, and an increasing number sought recourse in violence. The situation was exacerbated by Danzig's robust defence of its privileges, which provoked much resentment not just among the nobility, but among other towns and even its own burghers, excluded from power by the narrow patrician group that ran the city. The state affairs had reached was symbolized by the private war waged by the Materna family of small merchants between 1493 and 1517, which received considerable support from impoverished Cashubian nobles.[20]

Watzenrode, who had urged the establishment of a court of appeal at the 1503 Prussian estates in Elbing, secured the nomination of a royal commission in September 1506 which, in addition to himself and Pampowski, contained two Poles: the archbishop of Gniezno, Andrzej Boryszewski, and the bishop of Cujavia, Wincenty Przerębski. The statute presented to the estates by the commission on 18 September 1506 displayed many Polish influences in its regulation of the judicial system, including the reorganization of the land courts along Polish lines, and its arrangements for the calling of the levy, although much local practice was retained: thus regular musterings were established on the Polish pattern, although they were to be the responsibility not of the palatines and castellans as in Poland, but of local commissions. The powers of starostas over the nobility were reduced, although they retained responsibility for implementing land court verdicts. There was to be a high court of appeal, convened by the starosta of Marienburg, comprising three representatives of the nobility, three of the great cities, and two canon lawyers representing the bishops of Culm and Ermland, appointed by the Prussian council, not the king. The most significant measure was the establishment of a central Prussian treasury, run by a Prussian treasurer, who was to present accounts to the starosta of Marienburg and a commission of the council.[21]

Alexander died before the statute could be enacted, and it foundered on the powerful opposition of Danzig, which refused to recognize the right of the proposed court to hear cases judged in its own courts, and of Elbing, which insisted that because it still operated on Lübeck law, appeals from its courts could only be heard in Lübeck. Sigismund, who proved less accommodating to Watzenrode than

---

[20] *Historia Gdańska*, ii, 270–1.
[21] 'Constitutiones terrarum Prussiae', *CIP*, iii, no.2, 2–10; Zbigniew Naworski, 'Sejmik generalny Prus Królewskich jako trybunał apelacyjny prowincji', *AUNC*, Prawo 30 (Toruń, 1990), 131–2; Górski, *Starostowie*, 140–50; Górski, *Watzenrode*, 78–83.

his elder brothers, struggled for four years to rescue the legislation, but some measures did come into effect, including the establishment of the new Prussian treasury under its first treasurer, Jan Konopacki. Sigismund's attempt to appoint Watzenrode as supreme judge in Prussia, and Pampowski to the position of starosta general to enforce his verdicts failed at the 1509 estates, although Watzenrode took most of the flak, while the astute Pampowski secured his own recognition as supreme judge and his consequent admission to the Prussian council. Pampowski began hearing appeals but the solution was seen as temporary, and was only possible because of Pampowski's political skills: his death at the end of 1510 left Sigismund with no plausible candidate to succeed him, and the long attempt to rule through a Polish starosta general was abandoned.[22] Nevertheless, the acceptance of the first non-native Prussian on the council was a significant moment, and demonstrates that the problems of the judicial system resulted from internal Prussian conflicts rather than any clash between Polish integrationism and Prussian separatism: the 1506 statute was characterized by a sensible spirit of cooperation, in which the common aims of improving the operation of the judicial system combined ideas taken from Polish practice with local Prussian structures and customs.

In 1511 Sigismund sent Łaski to try again. Łaski was no friend of Watzenrode, and favoured Danzig, but he brokered a compromise in a meeting of the estates held in the city in June. The Danzig courts and Danzig citizens—except for individuals who owned landed estates—would not be subject to appeals to the high court, which would only judge appeals from the land courts. This was a partial defeat for the king, as was the clause that overturned the 1506 stipulation that Danzig's representatives on the Prussian council would be selected by the king from four names nominated by the city council, but the 1511 reforms nevertheless marked an important stage in the establishment of a new relationship between Royal Prussia and the rest of the kingdom.[23]

Łaski's astute negotiations revealed much about the complexity of Prussian politics. Watzenrode, who was in dispute with Danzig and had hoped to use ecclesiastical law to settle the dispute in his favour was astonished to see that, with Łaski's encouragement, Danzig was perfectly willing to have its case heard by the sejm, although it was not so happy when Dantyszek—himself born in Danzig—appealed a case to the royal court from the city court in 1512, which was returned to the Prussian council, effectively annulling the Danzig court's verdict.[24]

If even Danzig was willing on occasion to use the institutions of the union state to secure its aims, this was even more true of other groups in society, most notably ordinary nobles, who increasingly saw in Polish law and Polish institutions means to advance their own cause. After the successful implementation of the 1511 statutes, unificatory trends gathered pace. This did not mean that Prussians accepted Polish views of the nature of the incorporation, or that they wished to end their distinctiveness and surrender their autonomy; it meant that Prussians

---

[22] Naworski, 'Sejmik', 132–3; Górski, *Starostowie*, 169–70.
[23] 'Constitutiones terrarum Prussiae', *CIP*, iii, no. 79, 171–84; Naworski, 'Sejmik', 133.
[24] Górski, *Watzenrode*, 93; Naworski, 'Sejmik', 133.

were increasingly ready and willing to adopt or adapt Polish models to suit their local circumstances, and to play an increasing role within the union state. As in Lithuania, there was a broad spectrum of opinion; while there were fierce arguments, their use by nationalist historians to portray the relationship as one of entrenched hostility is greatly overdrawn.

National and ethnic loyalties played little or no role. The greatest impetus for change came from ordinary nobles, who had most to gain from the adoption of Polish-style institutions and Polish noble privileges which, in a province in which urban-dwellers constituted over a third of the population and the three great cities were an integral part of the ruling oligarchy, proved increasingly attractive. From the outset, ordinary nobles had shown an interest in Polish institutions: in 1454, the Prussian estates called for the introduction of local offices on the Polish pattern.[25] In 1488 there were the first signs of support for royal policies from among the nobility—especially the Culm nobility—at the estates, when they accepted most of the royal proposals.[26] Nobles were particularly supportive of royal attempts to reform the Prussian legal and monetary systems: from the early sixteenth century, calls for a currency union with Poland intensified as Prussia suffered from the circulation of poor-quality coins. Nobles were increasingly dissatisfied with some of the features of Culm law, established as the sole law code in Royal Prussia in 1476. Other systems of law previously in operation, such as Polish and Magdeburg law, were no longer recognized, although Ermland was not covered by the decree, and the handful of cities—notably Elbing—that used Lübeck law—were exempted.

Culm law, a mixture of Flemish, Saxon, Magdeburg, and Polish law, had been introduced by the Order and developed to aid its drive to colonize the Prussian lands. The lack of any modern codification of the law, however, caused problems, as did certain of its provisions, most notably with regard to inheritance law. Unlike Magdeburg law, which privileged inheritance in the male line, or Polish law, which stipulated the division of property among all children, Culm law safeguarded inheritance in the female line in a provision of Flemish origin under which daughters could claim up to half of their father's property.[27] This suited the urban environment, but it caused serious problems for ordinary nobles, owing to the peculiar conditions of Royal Prussia following the dismantling of the Order's power. Although this put an end to the Order's control of the land market through the stipulation that it had to approve all sales of land, nobles owned only around one third of the land, while the nature of Culm law meant that they did not enjoy full allodial rights. The protection of daughters' rights in a province where the availability of cultivated land was limited; where—unlike in Poland—there was no

---

[25] 36.7 percent of the inhabitants of Royal Prussia, excluding Ermland, lived in towns—43.1 percent in the palatinate of Marienburg: *Historia Pomorza*, ii/i, 258.

[26] *Historia Pomorza*, ii/i, 75.

[27] Friedrich, *Other Prussia*, 41; Janusz Małłek, 'Prawo chełmińskie w Prusach Krzyżackich (1466–1525) i Prusach Książęcych (1525–1620)', in Zbigniew Zdrójkowski (ed.), *Księga Pamiątkowa 750-lecia prawa chełmińskiego*, ii (Toruń, 1988), 137–9; Janina Bielecka, 'Organizacja i działalność sądów ziemskich w Prusach Królewskich od wieku XV do XVIII włącznie', *Archeion*, 63 (1975), 148.

ban on burghers purchasing landed properties; and where the great cities controlled substantial landed estates, Culm law over the generations promoted subdivision of estates. With leases on royal land in the hands of Poles or members of the narrow group of Prussian council families, there was little chance of securing the capital from that source to mitigate the effects of subdivision. Consequently, by 1570, of 1,232 known noble properties in Royal Prussia three proprietors (0.24 per cent) owned over 100 hides (1,670–1,750 hectares) of farmland; twenty (1.6 per cent) owned more than 60 hides (1,002–1,050 hectares), eighty-four (6.8 per cent) owned more than 20 hides (334–350 hectares). Only 455 (36 per cent) had tenant farmers at all: among the numerous petty nobility the average holding was a mere 3 hides (50.1–52.5 hectares), with 407 estates over 3 hides, but without tenants.[28]

The effects of subdivision were particularly galling as the boom in agricultural products brought ever greater profits to owners of large estates. The lesser Prussian nobility began looking enviously at their Polish counterparts: Polish inheritance law did not support primogeniture, but its weaker protection for the rights of daughters left noble families with more options to counteract property leaving the family by marriage. The Prussian political system, dominated as it was by a narrow group of families, and by the great cities, gave ordinary nobles little hope of effecting any change in the law, as Danzig's blocking of legal reform in 1506 and 1511 demonstrated.

Thus if the Prussians defended the principle of *indygenat*, and opposed Poles acquiring estates and offices in the province, they were by no means hostile to the adoption of Polish institutions and Polish law. Loyalty to the union was strengthened by the renewal of conflict with the Order following the election of the energetic twenty-four-year-old Frederick, younger son of Albrecht, duke of Meissen, as grand master in 1498, and in particular after he was succeeded in 1511 by Albrecht von Hohenzollern, from the Franconian branch of the family, the third son of Frederick I of Ansbach-Bayreuth and his wife, Sophia, Sigismund I's older sister.[29] Albrecht's election opened the last phase of Poland's wars against the Order. Encouraged by Maximilian I, Albrecht adopted a hostile attitude towards his uncle; for the next fourteen years he pursued a revanchist policy, hoping for support from the Empire to overturn the 1466 Thorn treaty.

Albrecht's hopes were soon dashed. Maximilian did pursue a broadly anti-Polish policy and indulged in grand gestures, such as summoning Danzig to the Reichstag in 1495 and placing it under an imperial ban in 1497 for refusing to pay imperial taxes, but he was more interested in advancing Habsburg interests in the Jagiellon kingdoms of Bohemia and Hungary. His hostility was strongest in the years after Sigismund's marriage to his first wife Barbara, daughter of Stefan Zápolya, palatine of Transylvania, but was reduced considerably in July 1515, when he reached agreement with Sigismund in Vienna over the betrothals of Anna, daughter of Sigismund's brother Władysław, to one of his grandsons, Charles or Ferdinand, and

---

[28] Antoni Mączak, 'Prusy w dobie rozkwitu gospodarczego i w okresie walk o zjednoczenie z Koroną', in *Historia Pomorza*, ii/i, ed. Gerard Labuda (Poznań, 1976)', 202–3.
[29] Jacek Wijaczka, *Albrecht von Brandenburg-Ansbach (1490–1568)* (Olsztyn, 2010), 12–13, 38–9.

of his granddaughter Maria to Władysław's son Louis. The marriages did not take place until 1521, when Anna married Ferdinand, and 1522, when Maria married Louis; until they did, Maximilian, and then Charles, who succeeded him as Emperor in 1519, while not entirely friendly towards Poland, at least offered Albrecht no support.

Albrecht, however, encouraged by Vasilii III, who was delighted at the prospect of a war that would distract Sigismund, did not back down. In 1519, as he sought the support of German princes, and of Christian II of Denmark, and as reports came in of his attempts to raise 10,000 men in the Empire, Sigismund decided to act, supported by the Prussian estates and Danzig, which ordered a blockade of the Order's ports. In December 1519 Sigismund launched Poland's last war against the Order. It was a messy affair. Albrecht was unable to secure substantive aid from the many princes he courted, but he raised enough of an army to prove an obstinate foe. Although the Polish forces were larger and superior in the field, Albrecht's imaginative campaigning and seizure of key strongpoints, including Braunsberg and Allenstein in Ermland, meant that the Poles, deficient in infantry and siege guns, had to adopt a strategy of laying waste to the countryside to try and force a settlement. After two years of often desultory fighting, peace was made in April 1521, mediated by Hungary and the Empire.[30]

Despite Albrecht's plucky resistance, the Order's days were numbered. With widespread reports of debauchery among the brothers and a recruitment crisis as the currents of the Reformation coursed across northern Germany, the disadvantages of electing a German prince grand master became apparent. Albrecht was a canny politician; aware that he had little chance of winning another war with Poland, he turned his mind to a possibility that he had long considered: to secularize the Order's lands and turn the *Ordensstaat* into a secular principality. Encouraged by Martin Luther, with whom he entered into a lively correspondence—it was difficult to have a dull correspondence with Luther—Albrecht turned to Sigismund, aware that Charles V, who was executing heretics in the Netherlands with conspicuous enthusiasm, was unlikely to prove sympathetic. Sigismund, unconvinced that the sejm would agree the means necessary to crush the Order, was prepared to listen. On 10 April 1525, in a magnificent ceremony on Cracow market square, Albrecht knelt before Sigismund to swear homage. The *Ordensstaat* was secularized, becoming a fief of the Polish crown, to be held by Albrecht and his heirs. The Poles insisted that they were to be known as dukes in—not of—Prussia; should the dynasty become extinct in the direct male lines of Albrecht and his three brothers, the duchy would revert to Poland.[31]

---

[30] See Marian Biskup, '*Wojna Pruska*': *Czyli walka Polski z Zakonem Krzyżackim z lat 1519–1521* (Olsztyn, 1991); Jan Tyszkiewicz, *Ostatnia wojna z Zakonem Krzyżackim 1519–1521* (Warsaw, 1991).
[31] *Die Staatsverträge des Herzogtums Preussen. Teil I: Polen und Litauen. Verträge und Belehnungsurkunden 1525–1657/58*, ed. Stephan Dolezel and Heidrun Dolezel (Berlin, 1971), nos. 1–9, 12–56. The classic accounts are by Adam Vetulani, *Lenno pruskie od traktatu krakowskiego do śmierci księcia Albrechta 1525–1568* (Cracow, 1930), 1–123, and Stephan Dolezel, *Das preussisch-polnische Lehnsverhältniss unter Herzog Albrecht von Preussen, 1525–1568* (Berlin, 1967).

Generations of Polish historians, with the dubious benefit of hindsight, have castigated Sigismund for his failure to crush Albrecht and the *Ordensstaat*, although Halecki and Vetulani rightly argued that the Cracow treaty should not be judged on account of its unforeseen consequences. There were certainly contemporary politicians, including Dantyszek and the bishop of Ermland, Moritz Ferber, who criticized Sigismund for his niggardly caution and stressed that he need not have been so generous.[32] Whatever the consequences of Sigismund's decision to settle— and he was aware of the dangers of establishing a Hohenzollern duke in Prussia—he had little reason to suppose that it would be easy to crush Albrecht. His Polish and Prussian subjects showed no appetite for voting funds on the necessary scale, while there were good reasons to fear that attempts to do so would galvanize Charles V and Denmark. Relations with Muscovy remained tense; with the Ottoman threat building in the south, it would have been rash to overcommit himself.

Moreover, although the Royal Prussians had proven perfectly loyal during the war, the rapid spread of Lutheran ideas across Prussia in the early 1520s introduced a new note of uncertainty. Sigismund may have acted as midwife for the first Lutheran state in Europe in 1525, but he responded quickly and decisively to stem the spread of Lutheranism in Danzig, which had been torn by political strife since the collapse of the city's finances in 1517, as a consequence of the policies of the narrow patriciate that dominated the city. With tension rising, and demands for reform emerging from the commonality, the spread of Lutheran ideas created a volatile situation. It was by no means clear after 1521 that Danzig would support a new war against Albrecht. It was therefore sensible for Sigismund to settle with Albrecht before dealing with Danzig, where an attempt by the patriciate to reassert its authority in January 1525 backfired badly, provoking riots. In April 1526 Sigismund entered Danzig with 3,000 men to restore order and the Catholic religion. He executed ringleaders of the popular movement and restructured the city's government to take account of the demands of the commonality, while ensuring that the new council of the 100 was dependent on the patrician elite.[33]

Whatever the long-term consequences, the Prussian homage of 1525, as it came to be known, marked Poland's complete victory over the Order, and opened a long period of political stability on the southern Baltic coast which allowed Danzig and Royal Prussia to flourish. Good relations were restored between both parts of Prussia, whose elites still saw themselves as belonging to one country divided into two parts, each enjoying a different relationship to Poland. Since they still shared a common currency and, in Culm law, a common law code, envoys from both parts of Prussia regularly attended meetings of the estates in the other part, to negotiate on matters of common interest: between 1466 and 1488, envoys from the *Ordensstaat* attended the Royal Prussian estates on seventeen occasions, and the relationship resumed after 1525, despite the fact that the Royal Prussians were not pleased at the Cracow treaty, since they had hoped for the reunification of Prussia, or at least the annexation of the diocese of Pomezania.[34]

---

[32] For the debate see Wijaczka, *Albrecht*, 106–15. [33] *Historia Gdańska*, ii, 233–48.
[34] Małłek, 'Estates', 28.

Albrecht retained a close interest in Royal Prussian and Polish politics, but despite his best efforts, ties between Royal Prussia and Poland had strengthened considerably by his death in 1568. The province's social and political divisions were not resolved; indeed they were deepened by the rapid spread of Lutheranism in the cities: Sigismund may have successfully remodelled Danzig's constitution, but his attempt to turn the Protestant tide was a failure. In 1526, Danzig definitively adopted the Reformation; Thorn and Elbing rapidly followed. Catholicism remained strong in the countryside, however, and the victory of Protestantism in Ducal Prussia and the Royal Prussian towns ensured that the bishops of Culm and Ermland looked more eagerly than ever to Poland for support.[35]

The attraction was particularly strong among ordinary nobles, whose experience of Prussian autonomy was rather different to that of the council oligarchy. Although the Prussian council and the Prussian estates continued to conduct their business in German after 1466, the Polish language made rapid inroads among Prussian nobles of German descent from the 1510s and 1520s. It was only in the seventeenth century that Polish became the normal language of debate in the Prussian *Landtag*, but by 1527 there were already complaints from representatives of the great cities that some council members were using Polish at meetings, even though they spoke good German. In 1555 a speech by Wysocki, a Gniezno canon, to the Prussian estates no longer had to be translated into German; by now royal decrees and ordinances to the province were circulated in Polish, and debates in the estates frequently took place in Polish: two protests from the nobility at the *Landtag* in 1563 and 1565 concerning breaches of the province's privileges were written in Polish. The council families were already polonizing their names: the Baysen emerged as the Bażyński; the Zehmen became the Cema; the Dameraw became the Działyńskis, and the Mortangen became the Mortęskis. They polonized the names of their estates, so Paulsdorf became Pawłowo; Witramsdorff emerged as Wytramowice, and Kunzendorff became Conczewicze. The Kleinfelds from 1531 styled themselves Krupocki, taking the name from their estate of Krupoczyn. Some families abandoned their traditional coats-of-arms and sought to attach themselves to Polish heraldic clans: thus the Golststein, originally from the lower Rhine, adopted the Jelita coat-of-arms; the Zieh adopted the Ogończyk crest, and the Hacke attached themselves to the Lubicz.[36]

None of this meant that these families had forgotten their roots, or thought of themselves as Poles. The spread of the Polish language among the nobility ran parallel to the development of a strong sense of Prussian identity that was bilingual and bicultural, as the concept of a *natio Prussica* was consolidated. From 1525 historians based in Royal Prussia, in particular Simon Grunau (*c.*1470–1531) and Caspar Schütz (1540–94), drawing on the work of Erasmus Stella (*c.*1460–1521) and Prussian chroniclers hostile to the order such as Posilge discerned the origins of the Prussian nation in a past that was neither Polish nor German, but derived from

---

[35] The impact of the Reformation in Poland-Lithuania and Royal Prussia will be fully analysed in volume 2 of this study.
[36] Turowski, *Innenpolitische*, 89–91.

the Baltic *Pruzzen*, from whom a handful of noble families such as the Raba and the Machwitz (Machwicz) could claim descent. Bilingualism embedded itself, and individuals would use the Polish or German form of their family name depending on the context.[37]

Identity was not exclusive, as nineteenth-century nationalists urged that it should be, but multi-layered, and it was by no means clear even to contemporaries, what constituted a true native Prussian, an *indygena*. At the 1533 Graudenz *Landtag*, there was a bitter dispute between Jan Dantyszek/Johann Flachsbinder and Stanisław Kostka (1487–1555), appointed Prussian treasurer in 1531, over the estate of a deceased priest in Dantyszek's Culm diocese. Kostka had been born in Prussia, but his father was an immigrant from Mazovia. As a young man Kostka served at Władysław Jagiellon's Buda court, then became a loyal servant of Sigismund. He inherited an estate in Cujavia and was granted several starosties as he rose in royal service, including Golub and Dirschau in Prussia. Despite his Prussian birth he was regarded as an outsider. His appointment as treasurer was not welcome to the council, on which he did not sit. Under attack from Dantyszek and other envoys at the 1533 *Landtag*, he stamped out of the chamber to complain to Sigismund, denouncing his tormentors as anti-Polish. Dantyszek retorted that he and his fellow councillors were no less Poles in their loyalties than Kostka, who had been born among them.[38]

The two sides buried the hatchet at the 1536 *Landtag*. Kostka subsequently worked amicably with Dantyszek and the council, but the exchange reveals the complex web of loyalty and identity that characterized Royal Prussia. Patriotism was multifocal: depending on context, Prussians could claim to be Germans, Prussians or loyal Poles, and their acceptance of individuals as Prussians depended on the acceptance of certain attitudes and norms of behaviour. Awareness among the ordinary nobility of the potential advantages of closer involvement in the politics of the wider union state was growing. The 1511 statute had by no means brought the legal system into a satisfactory state as far as ordinary nobles were concerned, and demands for further reform to Culm law continued. With the council refusing to listen to noble demands they began to look for other channels through which they could press their case. In December 1519 the sejm met in Thorn, where Sigismund had travelled to organize the war against Albrecht. Some Prussian nobles attended, observing the way in which the sejm operated. It was not long before they took to heart the lessons they learnt there. At sejms held in Thorn, and in nearby Bydgoszcz a year later, labour rent in Poland was standardized at one day per week; demands for a similar law in Prussia, where ordinary nobles were just as affected by the ability of wealthy landowners to lure away their tenants, began to be heard. A delegation of Prussian nobles appeared at the 1521 Piotrków sejm with complaints about Danzig. At the next Prussian *Landtag* in Graudenz in March 1522

---

[37] Friedrich, *Other Prussia*, 83–5; *Historia Pomorza*, ii/i, 120; Bömelburg, 'Das Landesbewußtsein im Preußen königlich polnischen Anteils in der Frühen Neuzeit', in Sabine Beckmann (ed.), *Kulturgeschichte Preußens königlich polnischen Anteils in der Frühen Neuzeit* (Tübingen, 2005), 47.

[38] Lengnich, *Geschichte*, document 61, 144.

the nobility presented their *gravamina* and proposals, which included demands for reform of inheritance law, a ban on burghers purchasing landed estates, and better regulation of urban guilds, all of which drew explicitly on Polish models. There was a powerful sting in the tail, for the nobility also demanded that they be free to send one envoy from each palatinate to attend the Polish sejm so that they could secure the same privileges enjoyed by their Polish counterparts, a proposal that was strongly opposed by the council, which defended the separate nature of the Polish and Prussian estates.[39]

The threat was clear: if the council refused to take their demands seriously, then nobles knew an institution that might. The threat did not go unnoticed, and political and judicial reform returned to the agenda. The Prussian estates were already evolving. From around 1512, a lower house on the Polish model was taking shape, albeit in a Prussian form, as the lesser nobility and representatives of the smaller cities began to debate together and coordinate their demands. In 1517 a request was put to the palatines that they respect the Polish principle of summoning envoys from the nobility, but also from the lesser cities, while in 1521 it was laid down that local assemblies—sejmiks to use the Polish term—should meet at least twice a year.[40]

The decisive breakthrough came in the summer of 1526 when Sigismund summoned the *Landtag* to Danzig. He was accompanied by several Polish politicians, including Krzysztof Szydłowiecki, who had taken part in the *Landtag* debates, while the absence of representatives from Danzig and Elbing, in the throes of the Reformation crisis, gave the noble envoys an excellent opportunity to realize their reform programme. The outcome was a new *Landesordnung*, agreed by the estates on 17 July.[41] The document reveals much about the complex process by which unificatory tendencies were melded with respect for local tradition. Sigismund promised only to appoint native Prussians to offices, dignities, and starosties, and ordered that henceforth every palatine should carry with him a copy of Royal Prussia's privileges, to ensure that his judgements were compatible with the law. A commission was appointed to codify and reform Culm law, which was to contain, in addition to Tidemann Giese and Achacius Freunt, both canons of Ermland, two Danzig lawyers, Franz Soldau and Philipp Holkner, but also Łaski's protégé Maciej Śliwnicki, a Gniezno canon, who had helped prepare Łaski's digest of Polish law.[42]

Measures were taken to reform the provision of justice by regulating the land courts, and by establishing that the *Landtag*, not the council, would henceforth hear appeals from the land and urban courts, with a right to appeal against its verdicts within one year to the king. The *Landtag* was to meet biannually, in Dirschau and then in Graudenz, to hear these appeals; its protocols were to be kept

---

[39] Essmanowska-Dworzaczkowa, 'Ruch', 22; Małłek, 'Estates', 28; *Historia Pomorza*, ii/i, 84.
[40] *CIP*, iii, no. 247, 619–21; Małłek, 'Dwuizbowy system', 241.
[41] 'Constitutiones terrarum Prussiae', *CIP*, iv/i, no. 78, 232–9; Essmanowska-Dworzaczkowa, 'Ruch', 31.
[42] *CIP*, iv/i, no. 78, 234; Essmanowska-Dworzaczkowa, 'Ruch', 31–2.

by a competent judge selected from one of the land courts by the council.[43] The most significant measure, however, was the establishment of a system of local assemblies—sejmiks—on the Polish model. These were to meet in the districts of each palatinate in order to elect envoys to the *Landtag*. This measure definitively established the Prussian *Landtag* as a bicameral body—the only provincial sejmik in the union to have this form, with the Prussian council forming the upper chamber—or senate, as it became known—whose composition was fixed at seventeen members. The lower chamber was formed by envoys from the district sejmiks, and by representatives from the councils of the twenty-seven smaller cities. Although they were summoned separately—noble sejmiks were summoned by the palatine, while the summonses for urban envoys were issued by the royal chancery—noble and urban envoys appear to have deliberated together. Urban envoys attended the *Landtag* far more frequently than they had before the reforms: while sessions were sometimes thinly attended, there were only four sessions between 1548 and 1562 at which their absence was noted.[44]

None of these developments heralded any dilution of Prussian determination to protect the province's interests against Polish incursions. Dantyszek, who had argued with Kostka in 1533 over who was the better Pole, threatened to return his diocese to loyalty to the archbishopric of Riga in 1535 during one of his many arguments with the Polish church, while the Prussian clergy adamantly refused to attend Polish synods. Ordinary nobles might look for support to the sejm, but obdurately maintained that although the kings of Poland had committed themselves to defend Prussia, the Prussians had never agreed to similar obligations with regard to Poland.[45]

The establishment of the bicameral *Landtag* opened a new phase in the relationship between Royal Prussia and Poland, which saw the gradual strengthening of integrationist forces, despite frequent rancorous disputes. The most important manifestation of such forces was the establishment of the currency union agreed in the 1526 statute.[46] This was a considerable achievement. A common currency for Poland, Prussia, and Lithuania was proposed by the 1510 Piotrków sejm, but the Prussian estates, while supporting monetary reform, were not generally in favour of currency union. The great cities, keen to defend their profitable minting rights, were hostile. The dispute stimulated the preparation by Copernicus of three versions of his treatise on coins, presented to the *Landtag* in 1517, 1522, and 1526.[47] The promise by Albrecht to abandon the separate minting of coins in the 1525 Cracow treaty, and the absence of envoys from Danzig and Elbing at the 1526 *Landtag*, however, enabled a compromise to be reached. Presented with a *fait*

---

[43] *CIP*, iv/i, no. 78, 235–6; Essmanowska-Dworzaczkowa, 'Ruch', 32; Naworski, 'Sejmik', 134–5; *Historia Pomorza*, ii/i, 355.
[44] *CIP*, iv/i, no. 78, 236; Witold Szczuczko, 'Izba niższa sejmiku generalnego Prus Królewskich 1548–1562. Struktura i tok obrad', in Zenon Nowak (ed.), *W kręgu stanowych i kulturowych przeobrażeń Europy północnej w XIV–XVIII w.* (Toruń, 1988), 142.
[45] Essmanowska-Dworzaczkowa, 'Ruch', 64, 93.   [46] *CIP*, iv/i, no. 78, 239.
[47] Nicholas Copernicus, *Meditata de aestimatione monetae* (1517); *Modus cudendi monetam* (1522); *Monete cudende ratio* (1526).

accompli, the great cities grumbled, but the argument was over details, not the principle of currency union, and a compromise was finally reached in 1529. Henceforth Poland and both parts of Prussia shared a common coinage, although the cities retained their minting rights.[48]

The currency union was a major step in the unification process, and ensured that Prussians would have to take a closer interest in the sejm. This was officially encouraged: from 1537, when, after demands from the szlachta for Royal Prussia to bear its share of defence costs during the Lwów *rokosz*, all royal summonses to the sejm were sent to the Royal Prussian sejmiks. The council may steadfastly have refused to accept Polish invitations to attend the senate, but the appearance of ordinary Prussian nobles at sejms became increasingly common, despite the increasingly sharp tone of demands from the chamber that the Prussians produce the privileges on which they claimed exemption from paying their share of defence costs. The Prussian council insisted that they were not senators, and that ordinary nobles had no right to participate in sejm debates. Sigismund's death in 1548, however, when the council was anxious to obtain a confirmation of Prussia's privileges from Sigismund August, and when the council and the ordinary nobility found common cause in opposition to certain appointments of non-Prussians—several inspired by Bona—to starosties and offices in Prussia, marked the first occasion on which a full delegation from both chambers of the *Landtag* appeared at the sejm.[49]

It was an important moment. While Prussian nobles attended the sejm in growing numbers before 1548, they took no official part in it, merely observing debates and making private representations on matters that concerned them. It was becoming increasingly difficult, however, for the Prussians to ignore the sejm and its decisions, which inevitably bore consequences for Prussia, while Polish demands that the Prussians, whom the Poles were obliged to defend, should bear their share of the common burdens of the union state were put with increasing force. In 1530 Łaski raised the issue in a speech to Sigismund August's coronation sejm. Echoing arguments put by the Poles at Constance a century earlier, he stated that the Prussian and Pomerelian lands belonged to Poland, as was demonstrated by local place-names derived from the 'Polish mother-tongue'. That many of them were now inhabited by Germans was the result of the Order's illegal seizure of these lands, and their expulsion of the Polish population, who were replaced by the Order's German compatriots. These lands had now been restored to Poland. Łaski echoed Oleśnicki's arguments with regard to Lithuania during the coronation tempest, citing the terms '*reunivimus*', '*reincorporimus*', and '*reintegramus*' used in the incorporation privilege as they had been used in Horodło. It therefore followed, Łaski argued, that Poles and Prussians 'form one body; the inhabitants [of both countries] are the subjects of one lord, and constitute one people and one brotherhood'.[50] He challenged the Prussian interpretation of *indygenat*, claiming that

---

[48] Essmanowska-Dworzaczkowa, 'Ruch', 37–8.
[49] Essmanowska-Dworzaczkowa, 'Ruch', 82, 92, 106, 108; *Historia Pomorza*, ii/i, 362.
[50] 'Folgete also daß Polen und Preussen einen Cörper, beyder Einwohner eines Herrn Unterthanen, ein Volck, und eine Brüderschafft ausmachten': quoted by Lengnich, *Geschichte*, 88–9; the original is

because of the nature of the incorporation, Poles could be appointed to any office in Prussia, just as Prussians could be appointed to any office in Poland: a Pole was an *indygena* in Prussia, just as a Prussian was an *indigenatus* in Poland. It was therefore just that the Prussians should contribute to general taxes, and bear the burdens of military campaigns and whatever was necessary to protect the security of the realm, just as the Poles had sacrificed their lives and property to liberate Prussia from the Order's tyranny.[51]

The members of the Prussian council present prepared a written response in which they attacked Łaski's interpretation of the incorporation privilege and grumbled that they had simply come to Cracow to attend the coronation; they therefore had no powers from the *Landtag* to negotiate on matters that touched the whole realm. Łaski's speech may have reflected the views of many Poles, but it achieved little apart from upsetting the Prussians. It was subsequently alleged that Sigismund had made a secret, written undertaking to the szlachta in 1529—the year of Mazovia's successful incorporation—to secure their support for his son's election, in which he promised that when Sigismund August took over the government, he would end the separate status of Royal Prussia, Lithuania, and the Silesian duchies of Oświęcim and Zator, purchased by Casimir IV in 1457. Even if this is true, it seems unlikely that Sigismund, given his tense relations with Łaski, would have encouraged his intervention; indeed he chided him through Tomicki for it, although he had to consume a large slice of humble pie for having failed to invite the Prussians to Sigismund August's election. The Prussians pored over the document he gave them to make amends, in which he confirmed and strengthened Prussia's rights to participate in royal elections, and the Prussians forced him to acknowledge certain council interpretations of the incorporation privilege.[52]

Łaski's speech was the opening shot in a battle that lasted until 1569 over the nature of the relationship between Royal Prussia and Poland. It demonstrates the consistency of Polish views of union and its nature, and highlights the extent to which the szlachta had adopted the interpretation of union that Oleśnicki had outlined a century earlier. As the execution movement gathered strength during the 1540s, calls from the chamber for the Prussians to take their place in the sejm in accordance with the Polish interpretation of the 1454 incorporation grew in strength and frequency. Yet the context was different to that of Lithuania. While Lithuania still faced the unresolved Muscovite threat throughout this period, the Order's defeat and the creation of Ducal Prussia in 1525 had transformed Royal Prussia's situation. Łaski might huff and puff about the sacrifices the Poles had made to liberate it, but that was now ancient history; after 1521 there were, for the moment, no serious threats to Prussian liberty.

---

in BPGdańsk, 300/29, no. 9, f. 414v. Włodkowicz argued at Constance that the Culm lands were naturally part of the Polish kingdom on account of the fact that their inhabitants spoke Polish: Stanislaus Belch, *Paulus Vladimiri*, i (The Hague, 1965), 280 n. 16.

[51] Lengnich, *Geschichte*, 89.

[52] Lengnich, *Geschichte*, 82–3, 89; Małłek sensibly suggests that, if Sigismund did make such a promise to secure support for the election, he had no intention of implementing it: *Dwie części Prus*, 74.

Yet the Poles could not take Royal Prussian loyalty for granted. Albrecht von Hohenzollern, that supple politician, took a close interest in Royal Prussia. He played on the historic unity of Prussia, encouraged family links across the border, and promoted the idea of a general Prussian *indegenat*. He cultivated leading Royal Prussian politicians, including Johann von Werden, the mayor of Danzig ennobled for his part in putting down the troubles in 1525–6, Georg von Baysen, palatine of Marienburg, and Achacius von Zehmen, chamberlain of Pomerelia then castellan of Danzig, and Baysen's successor as palatine of Marienburg. Despite his Lutheranism, he maintained a regular correspondence with the bishops of Culm and Ermland, establishing particularly close relations with Dantyszek.[53] His closest correspondent on the council was Achacius von Zehmen: 320 letters have survived to Zehmen from Albrecht, and 51 replies. These men looked to Albrecht for support during Baltic conflicts, such as the war between Lübeck and Christian II of Denmark (1535–7), and in disputes with Poland. Albrecht supported the council's defence of Prussian autonomy, was happy to encourage the loosening of ties to Poland, and supported council opposition to the programme of the Royal Prussian nobility.[54]

Albrecht's attitude to Poland was ambivalent. He was just as well connected to leading Polish politicians, including Szydłowiecki and Tomicki, and had a wide range of contacts, with 315 correspondents in Poland and 404 in Lithuania between 1525 and 1548.[55] The Cracow treaty had granted him a place in the senate, yet Sigismund refused to summon him to its meetings and failed to invite him to the 1529 royal election. Albrecht protested to no avail when he turned up to the coronation sejm: Sigismund may have humoured the Royal Prussians but he conceded nothing to Albrecht, who received various excuses over the years, but was never admitted to the senate.[56] He did, however, use his extensive network of correspondents to seek support for his main aims, which included Polish recognition for the succession of the Brandenburg Hohenzollerns should his branch fail—a distinct possibility after all his brothers died childless—and more ambitiously, the possibility of the election of his son, Albrecht Friedrich, to the Polish throne should Sigismund August die without a male heir. His support for the council meant that his influence over the Royal Prussian nobility was limited. By April 1537—when Zehmen and Werden travelled to Königsberg to attend a secret council with Albrecht and the ducal Prussian council—the nobility of Culm and Pomerelia were becoming militant, sending a separate delegation to Sigismund for the first time to complain at council policies; throughout the 1540s and 1550s, groups of Prussian nobles attended sejm sessions, while complaining at their local sejmiks about council policy.[57] Yet ordinary Prussian nobles also defended Prussia's status

---

[53] For Albrecht's correspondance with Stanisław Hozjusz, bishop of Ermland, and with officials of the bishopric see *Herzog Albrecht von Preußen und das Bistum Ermland (1550–1568)*, ed. Stefan Hartmann (Cologne, 1993).
[54] For this relationship, see Janusz Małłek, *Prusy Książęce a Prusy Królewskie w latach 1525–1548* (Warsaw, 1976).
[55] Wijaczka, *Albrecht*, 169.   [56] Wijaczka, *Albrecht*, 178–84.
[57] Małłek, *Dwie części Prus*, 75; Małłek, *Prusy Książęce*, 144–5.

and position within the union. Despite their opposition to many of the council's policies, there was no strong support for overturning the Prussian interpretation of the incorporation documents. This meant that as the execution movement stepped up its pressure for closer union with both Lithuania and Prussia in the 1560s, it was the relationship between Poland and Lithuania that took centre stage. Nevertheless, when the showdown came at Lublin in 1569, it did not catch the Prussians unprepared.

PART VII
UNION ACCOMPLISHED

33

Æque Principaliter

On 17 December 1529 Sigismund August was elected king of Poland in Piotrków. He was nine years old. There were several surprising features about his election: firstly, his father was still very much alive; secondly, the election took place at an ordinary sejm and not a specially summoned election sejm; and finally—as a bemused Sigismund told his wife—there was no opposition to what was destined to be the only successful election *vivente rege* in Polish history.[1] The sejm had been called to consider the defence of the realm; there was no mention of the election in the pre-sejm material circulated by the chancery; and the proposal was sprung on a startled senate by Tomicki. The Lithuanians had neither been consulted nor invited; neither had Albrecht von Hohenzollern, who was pressing for recognition of his right to participate in royal elections following his designation as Poland's first senator in the 1525 Cracow treaty.

The ground had been well prepared. The sixty-two-year-old Sigismund fell gravely ill in September 1528; when he developed a raging temperature the following May, the chancery spread rumours that he was likely to die.[2] Sigismund was nevertheless astonished when, responding to Tomicki's proposal, senators and envoys pressed him to effect it as soon as possible. The senate's formal agreement was unanimously approved by the chamber.[3] Contemporaries seemed not to have shared the view of Silnicki and Kolankowski that the procedural irregularities rendered the election illegal.[4] Sigismund August was crowned in Cracow on 20 February 1530 by Łaski, assisted by nine bishops and two suffragans. This time Albrecht was present, although the only Lithuanian who turned up was Mikołaj Wieżgajło, bishop of Kyiv. Sigismund and Bona promised that their son would swear an oath to uphold the privileges conferred by his forebears as soon as he attained his majority.[5]

Not everyone was happy. Concern was expressed at the coronation sejm, not about the election's validity—which nobody challenged—but about the way it had been conducted. Although Łaski had been consulted in 1528, and agreed to perform the coronation, he was caught by surprise by the timing of the election. He accepted the *fait accompli* but protested furiously in private. While the coronation

---

[1] Sigismund to Bona, Piotrków, 21 December 1529, *AT*, xi, no. 429, 316–17.
[2] Pociecha, *Bona*, iii, 83–4.
[3] *AT*, xi, no. 440, 328; Kolankowski, 'Elekcja Zygmunta Augusta', *KH*, 19 (1905), 552.
[4] Silnicki, *Prawo*, 43–50; Kolankowski, 'Elekcja'; Wojciechowski, *Zygmunt*, 272; Uruszczak, *Sejm*, 176, 219–20.
[5] *AT*, xii, no. 48, 56–7; Sucheni-Grabowska, *Zygmunt August*, 19–20; Bogucka, *Bona*, 208–11.

passed off without incident, the coronation sejm did not. Concern that the election would constitute a precedent forced Sigismund to declare on 16 March that future elections could only take place after the king's death.[6] As political opposition to Bona grew, culminating in the 1537 Lwów *rokosz*, condemnation of the election, now seen as an example of her malign influence, became strident, and the 1530 declaration was confirmed at the 1538 Piotrków sejm in a statute that declared elections *vivente rege* to be illegal.[7]

Bona was indeed the driving force behind the election. Sigismund was fifty-three when his son was born. The birth was a surprise, since astrologers had declared that Sigismund would have no male heirs. Bona had already had one daughter, Isabella, in 1519, to add to Jadwiga, born in 1513 of Sigismund's first marriage; three more were to follow: Sophia (1522), Anna (1523), and Catherine (1526). The astrologers seem not to have apologized for misreading the heavenly signs, but they could console themselves that they had been nearly right: the royal couple's only other son, Albert, died on the day of his birth in 1527. After the death of Sigismund's nephew Louis at Mohács in 1526, the male line of the Jagiellons rested on Sigismund August's fragile shoulders.

Bona fought to secure her son's future from the moment of his birth. She looked first to Lithuania, where the Jagiellons' natural rights to the throne had long been exploited by the dynasty and the leading council families. It was a good moment. The death in 1521 of Mikalojus Radvila, chancellor and palatine of Vilnius, brought the prospect of ending the factional rivalry that had raged for years on the Lithuanian council between the Radvila family and the followers of Albertas Goštautas. Goštautas had helped crush the Hlynsky revolt, but was arrested on suspicion of complicity in January 1509.[8] The arrest was encouraged by chancellor Mikalojus Radvilaitis, and his eldest son Mikalojus Radvila, who had supported Hlynsky under Alexander, but who trimmed his sails adeptly when the wind abruptly shifted under Sigismund. As a reward, in January 1509 he was granted Hlynsky's extensive estates of Goniądz and Rajgród in Podlasie, and appointed chancellor and palatine of Vilnius in June 1510 following his father's death.

The council was now dominated by the Radvila brothers. Mikalojus's control of the chancery was buttressed by Jonas (marshal of the land, 1514–15, castellan of Trakai 1522) and Iurgis, court hetman and governor of Kyiv (1511–14), then Hrodna (from 1514). Jonas had married Goštautas's sister Elžbieta. She died in 1503, but despite a dispute over her dowry, Jonas remained close to his brother-in-law, who was staying with him when Hlynsky launched his revolt. He pressed for Goštautas's release, travelling twice to Cracow to lobby Sigismund, and his pleas helped save Goštautas from execution.[9] After Goštautas's release in 1510 there was a staged reconciliation with Mikalojus at the 1511 Brest sejm, and Goštautas was appointed governor of Navahrudak at the 1513–14 Vilnius sejm. Both men

---

[6] *AT*, xii, no. 68, 81–2.   [7] *VC*, i/ii, 76, 163–4.
[8] Marja Kuźmińska, 'Olbracht Marcinowicz Gasztołd: działalność Olbrachta Gasztołda 1503–1522', *AW*, 4 (1927), 360–1.
[9] Marceli Antoniewicz, *Protoplaści książąt Radziwiłłów: Dzieje mitu i meandry historiografii* (Warsaw, 2011), 24–7, 39–40; *PSB*, vii, 300; xxx, 317.

were part of Sigismund's entourage when he travelled to Pozsony and Vienna to negotiate with Maximilian I in 1515. Relations remained poor, however, and were not improved when Mikalojus, having established a rapport with Maximilian, was granted the imperial title of duke of Goniądz and Medele.[10]

This rubbed salt into Goštautas's open wounds. Mikalojus's unconcealed ambition that should Sigismund die without a male heir the succession might devolve upon the dukes of Mazovia, sons of his sister Anna, was calculated neither to improve relations nor reassure Sigismund. The Mazovian marriage was a remarkable step for the Radvila family. Neither they nor the Goštautas were of princely descent; both families owed their position to royal patronage. Grand Radvila claims that they were descended from the Gediminid Narimantas were almost certainly spurious. None of these considerations dulled the ambitions of either family. The acceptance of a title from Maximilian for lands that lay in Podlasie was a direct challenge to Jagiellon claims that the Emperor had no jurisdiction over their territories and marked a new departure for the *pany*, the lords who had come to prominence in the fifteenth century, since neither the Polish nor the Lithuanian nobility used titles apart from that of prince/duke (*kniaz* in Ruthenian, *książę* in Polish), accorded to descendants of Gediminas and Rurik. The Radvila family did not flaunt their title initially, but later used it to blur the distinction and buttress their artfully constructed genealogy. Goštautas eventually secured the papal title of count from Clement VII in 1530, but it was not as prestigious as the Radvila dukedom. It did not help that Goniądz and Medele bordered Goštautas's seat of Tykocin: from 1513 the rivals were involved in bitter and frequently violent boundary disputes.[11]

Sigismund sought to maintain a balance on the council, but his appointment of Goštautas as palatine of Trakai in 1519 increased the tension: during the Muscovite invasion later that year Goštautas stood with his forces at Krėva, but Radvila refused to summon the levy and the Muscovites penetrated to within fourteen kilometres of Vilnius. Radvila arrested several servants of Goštautas who, he claimed, planned to burn down Goniądz castle. Retaliating in advance, his retainers burned Tykocin castle, from which Goštautas barely escaped with his life.[12]

It was no way to run a war. The bitter dispute highlighted Lithuania's dysfunctional system of government. Absentee monarchy and the concentration of government office in so few hands raised the political stakes and generated considerable and often violent rivalry among the handful of families whose wealth had raised them so spectacularly above the boyar masses. Radvila's death opened the way to a resolution, and Sigismund travelled to Lithuania in the summer of 1521 to broker peace. Goštautas now dominated the council, and Sigismund had little choice but to appoint him chancellor and palatine of Vilnius. Sigismund insisted that Bona stay in Cracow to look after the children, but she was already in contact with Goštautas through her confidant Wawrzyniec Międzyleski, bishop of Kamianets, sent to Vilnius in 1519 to mediate.[13]

---

[10] The family later changed it to Goniądz and Rajgród.
[11] Pociecha, *Bona*, iii, 45.   [12] *PSB*, vii, 300–1.
[13] Wojciechowski, *Zygmunt*, 269–70; Kolankowski, 'Elekcja', 536.

Bona had known Goštautas since 1518 when, during a long stay at court, he participated in her entry to Cracow and her coronation. She soon won his support over the succession. The matter was discussed at the second Lithuanian sejm of 1521, which opened in Vilnius in May. It deliberated until Sigismund left Lithuania in early December, mostly regarding taxation: despite the five-year truce agreed with Muscovy on 9 November, the need to maintain defences against the Tatars meant that the burden could not be lightened. Goštautas supported Bona's plan but it did not enjoy an easy passage. Kostiantyn Ostrozky objected, worried at the reaction a unilateral Lithuanian decision would provoke in Poland. Ostrozky had been hetman since 1507; as a Ruthenian prince with extensive estates in Volhynia, he was more concerned about the Tatars than the Muscovites. Since the Tatars raided across all the Ruthenian lands, the needs of defence had stimulated considerable cooperation between Polish and Lithuanian forces, which Ostrozky had encouraged. He fought the Tatars alongside Poles in 1512, winning the battle of Vyshnevets (28 April). He won Sigismund's trust, as was demonstrated by his appointment as castellan of Vilnius in 1511. Ostrozky maintained good relations with both Goštautas and Radvila, and Sigismund asked him to mediate between them. Apart from being an excellent soldier, Ostrozky was an astute politician, and a living example of the way in which the wealthiest and most powerful Ruthenian boyars and princes had integrated into the union state's elite. He was a frequent visitor to the royal court, corresponded with Sigismund in Polish, and was well connected among Polish magnates.[14]

The Orthodox Ostrozky had a rather different view of the relationship with Poland from that of the Catholic lords who dominated the Lithuanian council. He was aware how unpopular unilateral Lithuanian action on the succession would be in Poland. His opposition was frustrating for Sigismund, who did not hide his anger after Ostrozky, during the crucial debate, dramatically fell to his knees, along with several of his supporters, begging him to abandon the plan.[15] Sigismund issued a sharp public rebuke and, if Ostrozky finally accepted the proposal, his stance rallied opposition. It was only when Sigismund agreed to appoint a commission to codify Lithuanian law, a long-running demand of many Lithuanian boyars, that the Lithuanian sejm finally agreed that in the event of Sigismund's death Lithuania would seek no other grand duke but Sigismund August.[16]

This declaration fell short of a formal election. That Sigismund and Bona thought one necessary casts doubt on the claim that the Jagiellons enjoyed an uncontested hereditary right to the grand ducal throne. The Lithuanian promise indicated that there would be a formal election on Sigismund's death. Even to obtain this promise Sigismund had to make concessions, and for the moment that is where the matter rested: Sigismund left Lithuania, and did not return until 1528.

---

[14] *PSB*, 24, 486–7; Kuźmińska, 'Gasztołd', 369; Halecki, *Dzieje*, ii, 82; Tomasz Kempa, *Konstany Wasyl Ostrogski (ok. 1524/1525–1608)* (Toruń, 1997), 18–19; Tomasz Kempa, 'Książęta Ostrogscy a kwestia unii polsko-litewskiej w XVI wieku', *Wrocławskie Studia Wschodnie* 8 (2004), 47–54.

[15] Goštautas to Bona, 31 May 1525, *AT*, vii, no. 36, 259.

[16] Wojciechowski, *Zygmunt*, 270; Любавский, *Сеймъ*, 231; Грушевський, *Історія*, iv, 346; Halecki, *Dzieje*, ii, 76–7; Łowmiański, *Polityka*, 391–2.

Neither the concessions nor the 1522 appointment of the Orthodox Ostrozky as palatine of Trakai brought internal peace. Sigismund's elevation of Ostrozky, who had finally accepted the election plan, was designed to ensure that Goštautas, as chancellor and palatine of Vilnius, could not dominate as the Radvila family had done, but the granting to Ostrozky of precedence in the council was a provocative move that did nothing to promote harmony. Ostrozky's relations with Goštautas had soured, and Goštautas protested vigorously at this breach of Horodło. The breach became permanent when Goštautas pursued Mikalojus Radvila's widow and her sons for compensation for the burning of Tykocin with such zeal that they sought royal protection and attracted Ostrozky's support.

These rivalries made it difficult for the council to restore order. The empty treasury meant that the professional soldiers could not be paid off, while the council could neither defend the southern borders against the Tatars, nor the eastern borders against frequent Muscovite incursions that took place despite the 1522 truce. Lithuania's institutions were all but paralysed: in 1524 Ostrozky arrived at a sejm summoned to Navahrudak, but Goštautas called a separate assembly to Vilnius. Sejms, without the king's mediating presence, failed to agree the necessary taxes, and the council's divisions had serious implications for the provision of justice. Councillors begged Sigismund to return to sort things out, but he was detained by the Prussian negotiations and the Ottoman threat.[17]

As the Lithuanian sejm met more frequently, the council was increasingly challenged. This was not the clash between 'magnates' and 'ordinary nobles' as which it is often portrayed; it was far more complex. The Lithuanian elite had expanded considerably since 1386, and there were plenty of families excluded from high office. The weakness of the Catholic church, which had few bishoprics—and was therefore short of canonries and other plum ecclesiastical posts—closed off an important route for advancement to ambitious outsiders: only Vilnius was tolerably endowed—although it bore no comparison to the wealthiest bishoprics in Poland—and it was only the bishop of Vilnius who played any serious political role. From 1519 until 1536, when, after years of lobbying, he was translated to the far more lucrative bishopric of Poznań, Vilnius was held not by a Lithuanian, but by Sigismund's illegitimate son Jan Zygmuntowicz.[18]

The internal conflicts on the council exacerbated the problems of the legal system. Nobles had been granted substantial privileges since 1387, but were often unable to secure legal protection for their properties in Lithuania's chaotic court system. It did not help that grand dukes, in order to win support, were happy to grant council members extensive judicial privileges. A 1517 decree removed Mikalojus Radvila's lands in Podlasie from the jurisdiction of the common law, placing them under the judicial control of the council and the chancery—held by Radvila himself. Together with the 1513 privilege granting Goniądz and Rajgród to Radvila, which made him the feudal superior of nobles settled in these lands, this

---

[17] Любавский, *Сеймъ*, 232–4; Halecki, *Dzieje*, ii, 77; *PSB*, vii, 301.
[18] Marceli Kosman, 'Polacy w Wielkim Księstwie Litewskim. Z badań nad mobilnością społeczeństwa w dobie unii Jagiellońskiej 1386–1569', *SPS*, i (Warsaw, 1981), 351.

decree turned Radvila's noble tenants into his subjects, a category that expanded through the policy, pursued by several magnate families, of settling nobles on their lands on service tenures.[19] Podlasie therefore became a centre of opposition to arbitrary magnate power. It had briefly fallen under Mazovian rule in the late fourteenth century and again in the 1440s, and was subject to influence from Mazovia and Poland. By 1538 the immigration of Mazovians and Poles, mostly petty and middling nobles, was substantial enough for concern to be expressed at an assembly in Navahrudak.[20] These migrants brought with them Polish ideas and Polish attitudes. By 1500 Polish money was the normal medium of exchange in Podlasie. Podlasian nobles clamoured for the introduction of Polish-style land courts with elected judges. Polish migrants in Drohichyn county secured the right to use Polish law—within certain limits—in a 1444 privilege; these rights were extended in 1492, and in 1516 the Polish system of land courts was introduced. Bielsk county secured certain rights to use Polish law in 1501.[21]

Calls for codification of Lithuanian law were therefore not unwelcome to the council magnates, who could expect to shape the process and ensure that it did not result in a radical shift in power away from the council on Polish lines. A draft codification was already in preparation in 1522, but since it had been drawn up under Mikalojus Radvila, Goštautas rejected it.[22] As chancellor, he now had the opportunity to use codification to institutionalize his own vision for the grand duchy. For Goštautas had a vision. He is frequently depicted as a radical Lithuanian separatist and an anti-Polish defender of Lithuanian sovereignty and independence.[23] Yet if Goštautas certainly advocated and defended Lithuanian autonomy, his vision was more complex. To challenge the union directly would have been to challenge the dynasty, which was committed to union, and had long defended the Lithuanian conception of union against Polish incorporationism. No Lithuanian politician could really contemplate breaking the union, since this would have left the grand duchy, deprived of Polish financial and military support, helpless against Muscovy. Goštautas knew all of this. Rather than defending Lithuanian sovereignty and statehood in the modern sense, he mounted the most coherent intellectual case yet made in favour of the Lithuanian vision of a union of equals—*aeque principaliter*—in which he sought to exploit the royal desire to secure the succession for Sigismund August to achieve recognition of the grand duchy's equal status with Poland within the union.[24]

Goštautas was a sophisticated cosmopolitan aristocrat. He was the grandson of Jonas Goštautas († 1458), one of the Horodło 47, who was adopted into the

---

[19] *PSB*, xxx, 318.
[20] Dorota Michaluk, 'Wymiana rodów na pograniczu koronno-litewskim w XVI–XVII wieku na przykładzie południowego Podlasia', in Jacek Staszewski et al. (eds), *Między zachodem a wschodem: Studia z dziejów Rzeczypospolitej w epoce nowożytnej* (Toruń, 2002), 250, 257.
[21] Błaszczyk, *Litwa*, 117.
[22] Станиславас Лазутка [Stanislovas Lazutka], 'Историческая роль Альбертаса Гоштаутаса в кодификации Первого Литовского Статута', in Irena Valikonytė and Lirija Steponavičienė (eds), *Pirmasis Lietuvos Statutas ir epocha* (Vilnius, 2005), 16–17.
[23] See e.g. Pociecha's view in *PSB*, vii, 301.   [24] Cf. Błaszczyk, *Litwa*, 107.

Awdaniec clan. Jonas supported Švitrigaila, but changed sides in 1432, signing the Hrodna union. He masterminded Casimir's election in 1440, and was created palatine of Trakai (1440) and Vilnius (1443) as a reward. After 1447 he moved into opposition, leading the 1450s campaign to remove from the union treaties all phrases implying that Lithuania was not an equal partner in the union. Albertas's father Martynas († 1483) chose a different path, supporting Casimir and ending his career as palatine of Trakai and a wealthy man. Albertas was his only son; he had one sister, and so inherited most of Martynas's considerable estate, to which he added throughout his life: in 1528, he was assessed at the highest tariff of any individual (466 horses) in the military register. He travelled in his youth, and was probably one of the young men from the Goštautas family seat of Gieraniony who, circa 1492, were students at Cracow University, of which his grandfather had been a benefactor.[25] He learned excellent Polish and Latin, and visited the imperial court in 1501. He was a cultivated man whose political and cultural world extended far beyond Vilnius: a list of some 90 of his books survives: 37 titles (40 per cent) were in Ruthenian; 47 (52 per cent) in Latin; several in Polish, three in Czech, and one in Serbian.[26] He was well-connected at the Cracow court, a regular correspondent of leading Polish politicians, and enjoyed good relations with Albrecht von Hohenzollern.

The 1522 deal gave Goštautas the opportunity to chart his own political course and secure not just the council's authority within Lithuania, but also the position of Lithuania within the union. The succession issue gave him considerable leverage, that was increased by the 1525 Prussian homage and the death of the last two Mazovian dukes in 1526, which raised the question of the relationship of the various parts of the composite Jagiellonian state to each other. In 1526, supported by the Radvila family and bishop Jan Zygmuntowicz, Goštautas told Sigismund that when a papal envoy passed through Vilnius en route to Moscow to discuss a permanent peace treaty between Lithuania and Muscovy, he had informed the council that his mission was to persuade Vasilii III to convert to Catholicism, with the promise that if he did, the pope would offer him a crown.[27] To ensure that the status of his patrimony was maintained, Sigismund August should, so the council suggested, be crowned hereditary king of Lithuania, with the crown supposedly seized by the Poles from Sigismund of Luxembourg's envoys a century earlier.[28]

Halecki sees this embassy as evidence that Goštautas was an advocate of 'extreme particularism', claiming that Bona was behind the idea.[29] Although Bona saw the advantages of the plan, it is unlikely she was its initiator: her brief honeymoon with Goštautas did not long survive 1522. The queen's interest in Lithuania grew in the

---

[25] This was questioned by Fijałek, but it is now seen as probable: see Kuźmińska, 'Gasztołd', 352.
[26] Лазутка, 'Историческая роль', 15–16; *PSB*, vii, 300; Arvydas Pacevičius, 'Bibliotekos', in Ališauskas et al. (eds), *Kultūra*, 107; Jan Jurkiewicz, *Od Palemona do Giedymina*, i: *W kręgu latopisów litewskich* (Poznań, 2012), 53.
[27] The envoy was Sigismund Herberstein, sent by Charles V rather than the pope.
[28] *AZR*, ii, no. 144, 171–6; Любавский, *Сеймъ*, 241–2.
[29] Halecki, *Dzieje*, ii, 77–8; cf. Kolankowski, *Zygmunt August wielki książę Litwy do roku 1548* (Lwów, 1913), 16–17. For a more sceptical view see Błaszczyk, *Litwa*, 106.

1520s, but her support of Ostrozky, and her closeness to Łaski, with whom she shared a deep hostility to Albrecht von Hohenzollern and Sigismund's pro-Habsburg policy, meant that she thought along very different lines to Goštautas, who was pro-Habsburg and close to Albrecht; Goštautas therefore established links to Bona's leading critics, Tomicki and Szydłowiecki.[30]

When in 1529 Bona suggested that the Polish system of land courts should be introduced in Lithuania, Goštautas responded with a carefully constructed argument that constituted an invitation and a warning. After claiming that he was writing neither in his official capacity, nor as a private individual, but in the interests of the common good, Goštautas warned of the consequences of the introduction of Polish law and the Polish court system by discussing his personal circumstances: although he had only one son, he was concerned that should his son have children, and the generations should thereafter multiply, subdivision might take place, reducing the great Goštautas clan to the ranks of the ordinary nobility. After this none-too-subtle warning that his family interests were primary, Goštautas brought up the succession, pointing out that while Poles enjoyed the right of free election, and could choose anyone they wished to be their king, Lithuania was the common patrimony of all the king's sons.[31]

Goštautas was not simply endorsing the idea that Lithuania was a hereditary monarchy: as he stressed, it was the patrimony of the dynasty, not the king's eldest son. The selection of a successor therefore depended on the consent of the Lithuanian sejm, and in practice on the council, whose central role he stressed in a reminder to Bona of how useful the maintenance of Lithuania's distinctive political system was to the Jagiellons. After discussing the external threats faced by the union state, he observed that if in Poland noble envoys had to agree to taxes and the making of laws, in Lithuania matters were differently ordered: nobles were summoned to the sejm simply to be told to do what the king and council had decided. He pointed out that every country had a different way of conducting their parliaments; this was the case in Rome, Venice, Florence, Germany, Spain, France, and—closer to home—Bohemia, Hungary, Prussia, and Mazovia. Given the king's long absences from Lithuania, members of the council were his experts and his eyes. The council could summon the nobles to war, and tell them what to do. Goštautas argued that Lithuanians should therefore be ruled according to Lithuanian custom. He concluded by praising Sigismund's father for respecting Lithuanian customs, and for not trying to reform the grand duchy; instead he permitted it to retain a system that had successfully resisted all its enemies from the time of Attila.[32]

The critical reader might suggest that the system had not proven so effective against less mythical enemies, but the reference to Attila reveals another aspect of Goštautas's vision: the construction of a historical justification for Lithuania's existence as a separate realm, distinct from its neighbours and from Poland, though

---

[30] Bogucka, *Bona*, 118.
[31] 'Rationes Alberti Gastoldi cur judices ex equestri ordine non sint in Lithuania instar regni Poloniae constituendi', *AT*, xi, no. 214, 163–5.
[32] *AT*, xi, no. 214, 164–5.

united with it. Goštautas was closely involved in the rewriting of the grand duchy's history as presented in the contemporary redactions of the Lithuanian chronicles. These drew on the first redaction, composed under Vytautas's influence in the 1420s, and largely based on his *Sache*, which recounted his conflict with Jagiełło and Skirgaila in the 1390s.[33] The Vytautan chronicles were expanded and rewritten in Smolensk in the 1440s. The fullest version of the first redaction, completed around 1446 presented a Lithuanian version of the grand duchy's past, while challenging the Muscovite view of Ruthenian history. The second redaction, the *Chronicle of the Grand Duchy of Lithuania and Samogitia*, was probably compiled between 1510 and 1517.[34] There is evidence that Goštautas was involved in this redaction, but he was the driving force behind the third redaction, the so-called Bychowiec chronicle, which reveals most about his political aims.

The Bychowiec chronicle was a rather different text to the first two redactions, and there is much less consensus concerning the date of its preparation and final compilation. It was first published by Teodor Narbutt in 1846. Narbutt was not altogether trustworthy with regard to his sources, and the subsequent disappearance of the manuscript on which it was based inclined some to regard it as a forgery.[35] There is enough internal and external evidence, however, to accept it as genuine. While the final version was probably compiled between 1538 and the early 1560s, there is much to suggest that it was first assembled, as Jasas suggests, under Goštautas's direction between 1519, the date of the first edition of Miechowita's chronicle, on which it draws, and Goštautas's death in 1539, with most of it completed by 1525.[36]

Whenever the final version was compiled, there is much in the Bychowiec chronicle to suggest that Goštautas was behind it. It has frequently been used as evidence of his supposed separatist aims. Jasas observes that the text does not use the word union once, and ignores many important episodes in the union story. It glorifies the Lithuanian nobility in general and the Goštautas family in particular, mounting a staunch defence of the council after 1440.[37] Although the Bychowiec

---

[33] See Ch. 8, 79.

[34] There are seven versions of the second redaction, which appears under varieties of the same title: *Лѣтописецъ Великого Княжства Литовского и Жомойцького* or *Кроники Вьликаго Княжства Литовскаго и Жомойцького*. One, the Olszewski redaction, appears in heavily polonized Ruthenian in the Latin alphabet: *Wielkiego Księstwa Litewskiego i Żmodzkiego kronika*: Rowell, *Lithuania*, 41; Mečislovas Jučas, *Lietuvos metraščiai ir kronikos* (Vilnius, 2002), 44–85; Jurkiewicz, *Od Palemona*, 47–9, 77–83.

[35] For example Kazimierz Chodynicki, 'Ze studiów nad dziejopisarstwem rusko-litewskiem: t.z. Rękopis Raudański', *AW*, 3 (1925–1927), 387–401.

[36] Jurkiewicz, *Od Palemona*, 77–83; Rimantas Jasas, 'Bychovco kronika ir jos kilmė', in *Lietuvos metraštis: Bychovco kronika*, ed. Rimantas Jasas (Vilnius, 1971), 8–38; Ochmański, 'Nad kroniką Bychowca', *SŹ*, 12 (1967), 155–63. Others, notably Jučas, have argued that the final version was compiled later, in the Olelkovych duchy of Slutsk, or under the guidance of Paweł Holszański, bishop of Vilnius from 1537 to 1555: *Lietuvos metraščiai*, 86–126. Gudavičius and Lazukta use internal evidence to support Jasas's dating and Goštautas's involvement: Edvardas Gudavičius and Stanislovas Lazutka, 'Albertas Goštautas ir Lietuvos istoriografia', *LIS*, 24 (2009), 195–201.

[37] Jasas, 'Bychovco kronika', 22–3, 30.

chronicle, like the second redaction, constructs a history of the Lithuanian people designed to establish their ancient lineage, and presents the grand duchy as a distinct political entity with its own history and traditions, its attitude towards the union, and towards relations with Poland, is rather more complex.

The suggestion that the bulk of the chronicle was compiled in the 1520s is supported by the extent to which it is a direct response to the view of the Lithuanian past promulgated by Miechowita. The need to respond to Miechowita would explain not only why a third redaction was necessary so soon after the second had been compiled, but also why so much of the text differed from the second redaction, and would confirm Jasas's view that the second redaction was compiled between 1514 and 1517, rather than Ochmański's dating of 1522–7.[38]

There was much in Miechowita to reply to, most of it concerning the union. The first redaction, reflecting its origins in Vytautas's entourage, was a tale of princes, largely devoted to the fraught relations between Kęstutis, Jagiełło, and Vytautas, and—reflecting the influence of Herasym and the Smolensk circles that compiled the final version—was concerned with combating the view of the Lithuanian past peddled in the Muscovite chronicles. Little attention is paid to relations with Poland apart from the struggle for control of Podolia and Volhynia: Jagiełło's accession to the Polish throne and the christianization of Lithuania is mentioned merely in passing, while the story of Vytautas's reign focuses almost entirely on his relations with Skirgaila and the Gediminids, and his interactions with Muscovy and the Tatars.

The second redaction is aristocratic in tone. Although it drew heavily on the first redaction, it constructed a completely new account of the origins of the Lithuanians aimed at countering claims in the fifteenth-century Muscovite chronicles that the Rurikids were descended from Prus, a relative of Octavian. This hijacking of the legacy of Rome had to be combated, as did the historical account designed to justify Rurikid claims to be the legitimate rulers of all Rus', and Polish allegations concerning the barbarous nature of the Lithuanians before christianization. The second redaction contains an elaborate account of the legendary origins of the Lithuanians, claiming that they were descended from Prince Palemon, a relative of Nero. The point of this story becomes clear with the construction of lineages that not only defend the honour of the Gediminids against Muscovite claims that Gediminas was grand duke Vytenis's master of the horse rather than his brother, but also assert the ancient and noble descent of several leading families, among them the Goštautas, the Holshanskys, and the Giedraitis, whose descent from the Roman nobles who accompanied Palemon is asserted: the Goštautas from the Colonna, and the Holshanskys and Giedraitis from the Centaurs (Kentauros).[39] The Radvila family are conspicuously absent.

Miechowita required a different response. He drew substantially on Długosz's unpublished *Annals*, echoing much of Długosz's negative attitude to Lithuanians and presenting a view of the union that owed much to Oleśnicki's incorporationist

---

[38] Jasas, 'Bychovco kronika', 19, 30; Ochmański, 'Nad kroniką', 159.
[39] Jurkiewicz, *Od Palemona*, 96–106; 238–9, 251–4.

ideas. He baldly states that with Jagiełło's coronation Lithuania was 'perpetually inscribed and incorporated' into Poland; Horodło was presented in similar terms.[40] Although Miechowita, following Długosz, wrote of the Italian origins of the Lithuanians, he depicted them as barbarous and uncivilized before 1386, dwelling on polygamy and other immoral practices of the Samogitians. The Lithuanians had fallen under the domination of the Ruthenians, by whom they were regarded with contempt, and from whom they were liberated by Vytenis. It was only at Horodło that some Lithuanians received a veneer of civilization through their acceptance into Polish heraldic clans.[41]

The Bychowiec chronicle directly challenges this picture. Although it drew on the earlier redactions it had a very different approach to Lithuanian history. While it retained an account of the Roman origins of the Lithuanians, the story was moved forward to the fifth century. Palemon disappeared, to be replaced by the Roman prince Apolonus and 500 noble families he led out of Italy to escape Attila's depredations after the siege of Aquilea, which had the advantage of considerably reducing the number of generations required for Lithuanian noble genealogies.[42]

This shift sought to bolster the story's historical veracity, but the principal changes concerned Lithuania's relations with Poland, in a direct challenge to Miechowita's version of the union's history. The narrative broadly followed the first redaction in portraying Vytautas as inheriting his grand-ducal title from Kęstutis, and although it dealt extensively with Jagiełło's accession to the Polish throne, it made no mention of Krewo or his agreements with Vytautas. It does, however, mention Horodło, as the second redaction does not. Horodło is presented as a succession pact between Jagiełło and Vytautas, in which the Poles and Lithuanians agree to treat each other as equals, swearing mutual oaths that should Jagiełło die without heirs, the Poles would elect nobody but one of Vytautas's sons, while if Vytautas should die without heirs, the Lithuanians would elect one of Jagiełło's sons.[43]

Thus the union was explicitly endorsed, with a stress on the elective nature of the grand ducal office and the provision that in the event of Jagiełło dying without heirs, Vytautas's sons would rule over both Poland and Lithuania. There is no mention of incorporation or the Horodło adoption, which is shunted forward into the account of the coronation tempest. This had featured in the second redaction, but after describing how Vytautas decided he wanted a crown, and how 'his Polish enemies' had prevented him securing it, the second redaction used the Lutsk assembly of 1429 simply as a means of glorifying Vytautas by dwelling on the magnificence of the occasion and drooling over the guest-list.[44] The Bychowiec chronicle repeats a version of this section but in its creative remoulding of the story it was Jagiełło, concerned at his advanced age ('*ja czełowik letny*'), who proposes that Vytautas should be crowned, and suggests that permission should be sought from Sigismund and the pope. At Lutsk Sigismund is won over, promising to send his

---

[40] Miechowita, *Chronica*, 269, 282.   [41] Miechowita, *Chronica*, 271, 282.
[42] *PSRL*, xvii, cols 473–4; Jurkiewicz, *Od Palemona*, 63–4.
[43] *PSRL*, xvii, cols 508–10, 523–4.   [44] *PSRL*, xvii, cols. 333–5, 394–5, 458–60.

envoy to secure papal agreement. Sigismund then suggests to Jagiełło that he should persuade Vytautas to unite the nobilities of Poland and Lithuania through adoption, to prevent bloodshed and to promote friendship and brotherhood between them, as in the past the Poles had been adopted by the Bohemians, and had assumed their coats of arms.[45]

With Sigismund's endorsement, the Lithuanian nobles assert their status. They reject the proposed adoption by claiming that while the Poles had been commoners until the Bohemian adoption, the Lithuanians, in contrast, were nobles of Roman lineage, who needed no other coats of arms but the ancient ones inherited from their illustrious forebears. Sigismund and Vytautas duly recognize the ancient nature of the Lithuanian nobility, while Vytautas pleads with the nobles to accept the adoption to promote brotherhood with the Poles, and to secure the crown for him and for Lithuania.[46]

The aristocratic nature of this vision of the past is shown by the next passage, in which Vytautas tells Sigismund that he cannot agree until he has consulted his councillors. It is here that the point of the relocation of the story becomes clear, and the brilliance of this exercise in aristocratic one-upmanship can be appreciated in all its sophisticated glory. The way that the Bychowiec chronicler—and through him Goštautas—tells the story, the Lithuanians graciously accept the invitation to lower themselves by accepting the adoption, while providing an explicit justification for the continued use by many Lithuanian families of their old crests. By doing so, they were endorsing the vision of a fraternal, brotherly union proposed at Horodło and confirmed at Mielnik, a vision of union that the Lithuanians had never rejected, and which reflected the actual social relationships and political alliances that had recently been established between the great Polish and Lithuanian magnate families. Linking this tendentious and unhistorical version of the adoption story to the issue of the crown offered to Vytautas by Sigismund enabled the chronicler to accuse the Poles of breaking the fraternal bond by blocking Vytautas's coronation and refusing to recognize Lithuania's equal status in the union.

The Bychowiec chronicle is no anti-union tract, but a radical challenge to the Polish incorporationist interpretation, and the idea of a Polish civilizing mission. Although it was not published until the nineteenth century, it influenced subsequent Lithuanian historians, including Stryjkowski and Kojałowicz. At its heart lay the ideal of a union built round the dynasty and its alliance with the narrow group of families whose genealogy the chronicle presented. Most important were the Goštautas—the only family whose descent was, like the Gediminids, drawn from the Colonnas, which suggests that the Bychowiec chronicle was partly an attempt to place the Goštautas family in the frame as possible successors to the Jagiellons at a time when Sigismund August was an infant.

---

[45] *PSRL*, xvii, col. 526.

[46] 'Lachowe ne była szlachta, ale byli ludy prostyi, ani meli herbow swoich, y welikimi dary toho dochodyli w Czechow... ale my szlachta staraja Rymskaja, kotoryi predki naszy, z tymi herby swoimi zaszli do tych państw... a czerez nich ne potrebujem żadnych innych herbow nowich, ale sie derżym starych swoich, szto nam predki naszy zostawili': *PSRL*, xvii, col. 528.

It was in the context of this redraft of Lithuanian history that the 1526 proposal for elevating Lithuania to the status of a kingdom was made. The pretext was flimsy. It was unlikely that Vasilii would convert to Catholicism or, if he did, that the Muscovite Orthodox church could be persuaded to follow his lead at a time when it was in a much stronger position than during the council of Florence. The embassy brought with it a long, carefully constructed document that reflects the vision of the union embodied in the Bychowiec chronicle and draws heavily on the political language of union. Written like the Bychowiec chronicle in a Ruthenian replete with Polonisms—this time in Cyrillic—it opposed the incorporationist view of the union and presented the Lithuanian case for recognizing that the grand duchy's relationship with Poland constituted a union *aeque principaliter*. It urged Sigismund to support the proposal:

> for the benefit of Your Majesty's descendants: for it will always be better and of greater profit for them if this, Your Majesty's realm and fatherland, retains its titles and laws separate from the kingdom of Poland.[47]

This was not a statement of Lithuania's independence, but a particular view of the union: like Royal Prussia, which also retained its own laws, Lithuania constituted a separate realm within the union. The document observed that the Lithuanians had freely and willingly elected Sigismund August grand duke in 1522—a statement that was not, strictly speaking, accurate—which the Poles had, up to now, refused to do. This would not have been possible had Lithuania been incorporated into Poland. After requesting that Sigismund August be crowned with Vytautas's crown, the Lithuanians stated that if Lithuania were raised to the status of a kingdom, it could not be incorporated into Poland (втѣлено имъ къ корунѣ; привлащоно къ корунѣ Польской), *since no kingdom can contain another kingdom* (бо коруна въ коруну втѣлена быть не може).[48]

This was no call to end the union; neither was it a statement of 'extreme separatism', whatever that might be. It was a restatement of the Lithuanian view of the union as a fraternal relationship between equal partners. It suggested that the Poles should cease thirsting for the humiliation of the grand duchy through incorporation, but allow it to stand as an equal in fraternity and friendship, and in unity against every enemy. If the Poles refused to return the crown, then the envoys were to urge Sigismund to ask pope and emperor to provide a new one for Sigismund August's coronation.[49] The document concluded by proposing that instead of incorporating Mazovia into Poland, Sigismund should grant it as a fief to his son. This would give the Poles a double incentive to elect him king on Sigismund's death, since otherwise Mazovia would be attached to Lithuania rather than Poland.[50]

This was no unilateral declaration of independence. It was a plea for Sigismund to resist unitary visions of his composite realm and to institutionalize the Lithuanian concept of a union of noble citizens whose various realms would be governed separately, as they had been since 1386. Each would retain its own laws and

---

[47] *AZR*, ii, no. 144, 175.   [48] *AZR*, ii, no. 144, 175.
[49] *AZR*, ii, no. 144, 175–6.   [50] *AZR*, ii, no. 144, 176.

customs, and would share a common ruler—or rulers—from within the dynasty, as they had since 1386. Goštautas and the council were aware that the Poles would oppose any such plan, as they had during the coronation tempest; it was therefore important that the Lithuanians defend their equal status and that the Jagiellons should exploit the Polish desire to maintain the union and ward off pressure for closer union by presenting the Poles with *faits accomplis* through the election of a grand duke, as the Lithuanians had in 1430, 1440, 1492, and 1501, thus implicitly endorsing the Lithuanian vision of the union.

Sigismund had no intention of accepting the Lithuanian proposal; it is unlikely that Goštautas believed he would, or was particularly disappointed at its rejection: there was to be no rerun of the coronation tempest when Sigismund returned to Lithuania in 1528, this time accompanied by Bona, for a two-year stay that transformed Lithuanian politics. He summoned a sejm to Vilnius at the end of April that, because of the importance of the issues and the bitter divisions within Lithuanian politics, lasted almost a year, until February 1529.[51] One of its first acts, on 1 May, decreed the preparation of the 1528 military register.[52] The sejm discussed taxation, although it was only with difficulty that Sigismund obtained a new grant of the *serebshchyzna* in July. As in Poland, regular taxation to fund the Muscovite wars provoked serious discontent among ordinary nobles, who not only had to bear the burden of the noble levy but were paying tax rates that had risen steeply since 1492. As in Poland with regard to the royal domain, voices were raised against the large-scale alienation of grand ducal land, mortgaged to a handful of magnates, often on lifelong leases, and with considerable tax exemptions.[53]

The main purpose, however, was to complete the bargain negotiated in 1522. On 18 October 1529, the nine-year-old Sigismund August was enthroned as grand duke of Lithuania after swearing an oath—along with his father—to respect the privileges granted by his predecessors. Once again the Lithuanians had stolen a march on the Poles. With Sigismund August installed as grand duke, no viable alternative in sight following the extinction of the Mazovian Piasts—those persistent if perennially unsuccessful candidates for the throne of their ancestors—and no reason to postpone the decision, the Polish sejm was startled into its election *vivente rege*, which Sigismund hurried back to Piotrków to secure.

In his absence, Goštautas piloted through the codification of the law which was the price for Sigismund August's election. Discussions over its final form extended the sejm until February, when what is known as the First Lithuanian Statute was agreed. It came into force on St Michael's Day (29 September 1529). Written in the chancery Ruthenian that had been the grand duchy's language of government since the fourteenth century, it soon appeared in Latin (1530) and Polish (1532) translations.[54] The Lithuanian success in agreeing a codification contrasted starkly

---

[51] Любавский, *Сеймъ*, 246–7.   [52] *AZR*, ii, no. 152, 187–8.
[53] Любавский, *Сеймъ*, 248–9.
[54] For the original text together with the Latin and Polish translations see *Pirmasis Lietuvos Statutas/ Первый Литовский Статут*, ed. Stanislovas Lazutka et al., iii (Vilnius, 1991). For a good, generally sound English translation, see *The Lithuanian Statute of 1529*, tr. and ed. Karl von Loewe (Leiden, 1976).

with the problems Sigismund faced in Poland, where, after the process foundered in the early 1530s, no successful codification of the law ever took place.

The statute was a considerable achievement. While there is no proof that Goštautas was its author it is certain that he played a substantial role in its preparation, and in steering it through the sejm.[55] With 233 articles divided into thirteen sections, it was a proper codification; not a compilation of previous laws and privileges like Łaski's 1506 digest, but a new legislative code that replaced much previous law, although it did not affect the noble privileges that Sigismund August and his father swore to uphold shortly after its promulgation.[56] It covered a wide range of matters, from the laws regulating military service that underpinned the 1528 register (section II), to violence, homicide, and theft (sections VII and XIII), and included a range of laws regulating Lithuania's agricultural economy on matters such as the value of bees and trees (section IX/14)—an issue of considerable importance in the grand duchy—and the legal remedies for an attack by an untethered dog (section XII/13).[57]

In theory the statute went a long way towards meeting the demands of ordinary nobles, not least because of its extensive provisions with regard to the conduct of the courts, both civil and criminal, and in its articles concerning property, which at last gave some legal shape to the principles enunciated in the various privileges granted since 1387. It clarified inheritance law and devoted one whole section (IV) to the law concerning female inheritance rights and the principles under which women were given in marriage. These provisions provided the basis for the considerable legal rights of noblewomen under Lithuanian law: dowers were protected, as was the right of a widow to live on her portion until her death. The provision was generous—widows could be granted up to a third of their husband's estate as their dower—and provision was made for widows whose husbands had failed to make provision for them. While women could not marry without their family's consent, women of princely families could not be forced to marry against their will.[58]

The statute bears eloquent testimony to the consolidation that had taken place since 1387 within the union state as a whole, and within the grand duchy in particular. While it drew heavily on Ruthenian law, whose roots lay in the *Pravda Russkaia* of Kievan Rus', it enshrined much customary practice within Lithuanian common law, and was influenced by both Polish and Roman law.[59] Knowledge of Polish law had spread widely after Ruthenian translations of the statutes of Casimir III and Jagiełło's land laws were published between 1423 and 1434.[60] By confirming it, Sigismund explicitly endorsed Goštautas's vision of a union *aeque principaliter*, in which the parties to the union were of equal status, and preserved and

---

[55] Лазутка, 'Историческая роль', 14–20.
[56] Juliusz Bardach, 'Statuty litewskie w ich kręgu prawno-kulturowym', in Bardach, *O dawnej i niedawnej Litwie* (Poznań, 1988), 19.
[57] *Lithuanian Statute*, 29–35, 71–80, 96, 111.   [58] *Lithuanian Statute*, 41–7.
[59] *Lithuanian Statute*, 2–12; Bardach, *Statuty litewskie a prawo rzymskie* (Warsaw, 1999).
[60] Stanisław Roman and Adam Vetulani, *Ruski przekład polskich statutów ziemskich z rękopisu moskiewskiego* (Wrocław, 1959), 30.

administered their own laws. In section III/i, which concerned the liberties of the nobility and the grand duchy's territory, Sigismund swore that if God granted to him 'another realm or kingdom' he would not allow Lithuania or its council to be derided or mocked, but would protect them from 'defamation and degradation', as his father had done.[61] Since the kingdom of Poland was the most likely realm that God might bestow on him, this clause sought to enlist Sigismund and his successors in the defence of the grand duchy's status within the union.

While the statute confirmed the privileges of the nobility and met many of their demands for the improvement of judicial procedure, it did much to underpin the oligarchic system. The grand duke was to protect and preserve the position of the council and its chief officials and shield them from denigration. The council's role as an appellate court was enshrined in law. Most importantly, in a clear echo of *Nihil Novi*, the grand duke was to preserve all old privileges and customs; while new law could only be made with the 'knowledge, counsel, and consent' of the council (III/vi).[62] There was no mention of the sejm, and the pleas of the ordinary nobility, supported by Bona, for the introduction of Polish-style elected land courts fell on the deafest of ears.

With Sigismund August's election and the statute's promulgation, Goštautas and his council allies sought to buttress their vision of the union and the relationship with Poland, and to institutionalize the council's dominant position against those calling for a greater role for the nobility. The fact that the statute's eminently sound articles did little to improve the quality of justice actually delivered in the courts, however, meant that the voices of ordinary nobles were not stilled. Grumbling only increased after the failure of the last in the long cycle of Lithuanian-Muscovite wars, launched by an optimistic council in 1534 to exploit the apparent political weakness of Moscow following the 1533 accession of the infant Ivan IV. Despite the 1528 military reforms and the agreement of considerable levels of taxation by the sejm, the Lithuanians failed to win any serious victories, or to recover territory lost between 1492 and 1514 apart from Homel, returned in the five-year truce signed in 1537.

As the clamour grew, the council elite closed ranks. Around 1533 Goštautas buried the hatchet with the Radvila family. In 1536 he married his only son Stanislovas to Barbara, daughter of Jurgis Radvila, castellan of Vilnius, who had been created hetman on Ostrozky's death in 1530. Goštautas was already an old man, however. He died in December 1539; his only son Stanislovas followed him into the grave three years later. The Goštautas were no more, and the door was opened to a long period of Radvila dominance. Barbara was to play a brief, if spectacular, part in that story, as the system that her father-in-law had defended so tenaciously came under increasing pressure.

Goštautas's legacy lived on, however. His ideas formed the basis of council resistance to the campaign for closer union launched by the execution movement

---

[61] *Pirmasis Lietuvos Statutas*, iii, 108; *Lithuanian Statute*, 36. Here, as elsewhere, I have preferred my own translation of certain terms to Loewe's formulations.
[62] *Pirmasis Lietuvos Statutas*, iii, 110–11; *Lithuanian Statute*, 36–7.

in Poland in the 1540s. Yet there were serious contradictions at the heart of his vision. For the enthusiasm of the council elite for composite monarchy and local self-government did not extend to the grand duchy itself, where they stood squarely behind Vytautas's integrationist policy. The Bychowiec chronicle relates an unvarnished tale of Lithuanian conquest of the Rus'ian lands, baldly telling how the cruelties inflicted by Narimantas upon the Poles and the Ruthenians were said by the Ruthenian chronicles to be greater than those of 'Syrian Antioch, Herod, and Nero himself'.[63] It is a story of dynastic and martial expansion, not of cultural transfer and peaceful interaction. Kyiv is conquered by Gediminas, and if the achievements of the Gediminids at the head of joint Lithuanian and Ruthenian armies are lauded, the main emphasis during the narrative of Vytautas's reign is placed upon the struggle with Skirgaila and the subjugation of the appanage princes. The 1430s civil wars are depicted as a clash between Lithuanians and Poles on one side, and Ruthenians, led by Švitrigaila, on the other. Even Žygimantas is accused of favouring Ruthenians over Lithuanians to justify his overthrow.[64]

The Goštautas family had benefited from Vytautas's centralizing policies, and Albertas's father Martynas had served as governor of Kyiv after Casimir's removal of the duchy from the Olelkovych. Goštautas's attitude to Ruthenians was ambivalent, however, as emerged from his clash with Ostrozky in 1522 and the bitterness he showed to him thereafter. In June 1525 he wrote to Bona complaining of Ostrozky's behaviour and revealing his commitment to Vytautas's vision of a system ruled from Vilnius by Lithuanian Catholics. After reminding Bona of the role he had played in 1522, Goštautas launched a sour attack on Ostrozky who had opposed the deal, and on the Radvila family for allying with him. Goštautas complains about their pretensions and the slights and injustices he had suffered at their hands, moans about their title, and accuses them of paying the astrologers who forecast that Sigismund would have no male heir.[65]

The letter's main target is Ostrozky, however. He is sneeringly referred to as 'that wee Ruthenian princeling' (*ruthenus ducaculus*), and condemned as a *parvenu*, born into an insignificant and impoverished family. Ostrozky's sins are rehearsed at length, his military competence questioned, and his malign influence upon Sigismund deplored. Goštautas reserves considerable bile for the Ruthenians, whom, he makes clear, he does not regard as worthy of a place within the republic of citizens to which he frequently refers. They are characterized as 'that perverse people' (*illius perverse gentis*), while the many faults that Goštautas finds in Ostrozky are presented as typical of the Ruthenian character: he is accused of pride, typical 'Ruthenian cunning', and 'Ruthenian duplicity and perfidy'. Goštautas contrasts Ostrozky's career with his own: he had risen through service, 'not through tongue and deceitful gesture in the sycophantic Ruthenian manner'. The letter ends with a passionate denunciation of Ostrosky's elevation to the palatinate of Trakai and a warning that he was in treasonable league with Semën Olelkovych, duke of Slutsk: '*Ruthenus cum Rutheno, ducaculus cum ducaculo ligam iniit*'.[66]

[63] *PSRL*, xvii, col. 487. [64] *PSRL*, xvii, cols 528, 531.
[65] *AT*, vii, no. 36, 259–60. [66] *AT*, vii, no. 36, 263–8.

It is hard to know whether Goštautas's intemperate diatribe merely reflected his annoyance at Ostrozky's behaviour. Relations were cordial before 1522, and there were Ruthenians in the chancery and among Goštautas's entourage. The vehemence of the slurs against Ruthenians, however, suggests something more deep-seated: the Olelkovych were hardly 'wee princelings', despite the loss of their Kyivan patrimony, and the sour epithets, while not for public consumption, reveal that Ruthenians were still regarded with condescension and suspicion by many Catholic Lithuanian aristocrats, at least if, like Ostrozky, they remained Orthodox. While Ruthenian families that converted to Catholicism, such as the Sapieha or Khodkevych/Chodkiewicz, were gradually accepted, those like Ostrozky who remained Orthodox were treated with suspicion and, occasionally, contempt. Nearly a century after they were supposedly accorded the same rights as their Lithuanian Catholic counterparts, Ruthenians were still regarded as second-class citizens by many among the Vilnius elite.

This emerged starkly in the furore over Ostrozky's elevation in 1522. He had already served as governor of Bratslav and Vinnitsa (1497–1500; 1507–16; 1518–30), marshal of Volhynia (1507–22), and hetman (1497–1500; 1507–30).[67] His cordial relations with Radvila and Goštautas meant that there appears to have been no reaction to his appointment to the castellany of Vilnius in 1511, despite the fact that it was one of the offices limited to Catholics at Horodło in 1413.[68] His elevation in 1522 to a position of precedence within the council, however, was a step too far. The subsequent protests demonstrated the extent to which the dominance of the Catholic council elite depended on the union. For it was to Horodło that Goštautas turned. At a stormy sejm in Hrodna he orchestrated loud protests against Sigismund, who was forced to issue a declaration on 23 February 1522 confirming the eleventh article of Horodło. It stated that Ostrozky's elevation was due to his exceptional services, and did not constitute a precedent, noting that Goštautas had agreed to accept Ostrozky's precedence out of his particular esteem and respect for him, and with the council's agreement. Sigismund repeated the promise in confirming Lithuania's privileges in October 1529, as did Sigismund August in November 1551, although the Horodło ban was not included in the Lithuanian statute, and it continued to be honoured in the breach. The Orthodox Ivan Hornostai, a client of Bona who had spent long years in Poland as an agent of the Lithuanian chancery, appointed treasurer in 1519, remained in post.[69]

Yet for all the wealth of some Orthodox nobles, the identification of many with the republican ideals of the grand duchy's developing political culture, and the dynasty's willingness to promote Orthodox integration into the political elite, their religion constituted an important barrier. Goštautas's 1525 letter to Bona and his 1529 memorial against the introduction of land courts on the Polish model demonstrate that, despite his republican rhetoric, his vision of the Lithuanian

---

[67] Яковенко, *Шляхта*, 307.   [68] Kuźmińska, 'Gasztołd', 353, 371.
[69] Czermak, 'Sprawa', 385–93; Chodynicki, *Kościół*, 86–7; Krom, 'Konstituierung', 486; Pociecha, *Bona*, iii, 67–8.

republic he wished to keep distinct from its Polish counterpart was a narrow one: government might be based on consent, but that consent was limited to a small group of magnate families. This constituted its most vital weakness: as his 1525 letter reveals, rivalry was intense, and these families could not even settle disputes among themselves without frequent recourse to violence. It was a republic that held out the benefits of a consensual, republican view to a large number of nobles, yet sought to withhold its full benefits from many, including Orthodox Ruthenians and the dependent nobles given service leases on magnate estates. In a grand duchy undergoing rapid social change, however, it was to prove increasingly difficult to sustain this narrow vision of the republic.

34

Transformation

In 1522 Goštautas formed an alliance with the dynasty over the succession, but despite agreement that the grand duchy formed the patrimony of the Jagiellons, the rapprochement was brief. Bona was no natural ally of the council magnates in either Poland or Lithuania. In Poland, influenced by Łaski, she criticized breaches of the principle of incompatibility through the illegal accumulation of high office in the hands of figures like Tomicki and Szydłowiecki.[1] Nevertheless, despite her association with Łaski, her enthusiasm for the introduction of Polish-style land courts in Lithuania, and her support of individual nobles in disputes with magnates, she was no champion of szlachta democracy. She was, however, a natural and determined reformer. From the late 1520s she began a sustained campaign to improve the agricultural economy on her Lithuanian estates, launching a radical transformation of the grand ducal domain, and eventually of the rural economy across the grand duchy. It brought conflict with members of the council elite, and in particular the Goštautas and Radvila families.

Bona first acquired land in Lithuania in 1519, when Sigismund granted her the duchies of Pinsk and Kobryn. She realized that the most effective way of establishing a firm power-base for her son in Lithuania was to strengthen and restore the grand ducal domain, which was in a pitiful state. The domination of the council families and long periods of absentee rule had meant that no sustained campaign of restoration of the kind undertaken in Poland after 1504 had been attempted. In 1514 Sigismund wrote to all leaseholders of grand ducal manors in the palatinates of Vilnius and Trakai stating that he received no income whatsoever from his properties, and that all the revenues were used to their, and not his benefit.[2] This was an exaggeration, but grand ducal income had suffered considerably from years of neglect. The poor state of central records and the lack of any desire to investigate or reform the domain on the part of those who held so much of it meant that Bona faced formidable obstacles.

Sigismund had already begun experimenting on estates in Samogitia. Decrees issued in 1514, 1527, and 1529 initiated audits, and began removing estates from the hands of the *tivuny*, their traditional administrators.[3] Bona, however, provided

---

[1] Bogucka, *Bona*, 206.
[2] Ludwik Kolankowski, 'Pomiara włóczna', *AW*, 4/13 (1927), 236.
[3] Kolankowski, 'Pomiara', 236–7; Jerzy Ochmański, 'Reforma włóczna w dobrach magnackich i kościelnych w Wielkim Księstwie Litewskim w drugiej połowie XVI wieku', in Ochmański, *Dawna Litwa*, 176; Zofia Drozd, 'Miernicy w pomiarze włócznej w Wielkim Księstwie Litewskim w drugiej połowie XVI wieku', *LSP*, 13 (2008), 40.

the driving force after 1529, bringing to the task considerable administrative skill and an excellent head for business. Using her private wealth, and the gradually increasing revenues from her estates, she began accumulating property. In 1533 she bought the wealthy starosties of Kaunas and Brest from Jurgis Radvila and several Podlasian estates from Goštautas. Three years later Sigismund gave her permission to purchase mortgaged grand ducal land. By the 1540s her holdings extended across the grand duchy, from the starosties of Kremenets and Kovel in Volhynia to Platelė in Samogitia and Palanga on the Baltic coast. She controlled a huge strip of wilderness, 240 kilometres long, from the upper reaches of the Narew to the Niemen at Kaunas. With her holdings in Poland and Mazovia, the proceeds made her wealthy indeed.[4]

Bona was not content simply to own property. From July 1533 she spent three years in Lithuania, with a two-month break in 1535, returning for long stays thereafter. She ran her estates with consummate efficiency, sending auditors to inspect her holdings, investing in them, and energetically litigating in boundary disputes. She standardized rents and obligations, converting the often bewildering array of payments in kind into a consolidated cash rent or, where she established manors, labour rent. She was shocked by the extent to which lesser nobles were oppressed by wealthy magnates, and she decided to break the grip of the Goštautas and Radvila families. She bought out grand ducal estates in their possession and litigated against them. In a 1536 case, the fraudulent behaviour of Mikalojus Radvila concerning a 1515 privilege issued by Sigismund confirming his possession of lands abstracted from the royal domain was revealed. A commission under Piotr Chwalczewski ordered the return of a strip 69 kilometres long and from 12 to 24 kilometres wide that constituted half the Goniądz and Rajgród estates.[5] She did not thereby endear herself to the oligarchs, but won respect from many lesser nobles, who appreciated the fair way in which she approached audits of royal estates: if wealthier nobles saw their holdings confiscated when they could not produce documentary proof they were entitled to them, poorer nobles were often allowed to continue in possession of their tiny holdings.[6]

Her robust approach outraged the oligarchs, who sought support from her opponents in Poland and attacked her for supporting the introduction of Polish-style land courts. Goštautas argued in 1529 that the introduction of Polish law would not work, since in contrast to the consolidated villages with clearly delineated boundaries found in Poland, Lithuanian villages were dispersed, and peasants farmed amid a confusion of homesteads, fields, pastures, and meadows.[7] It was not a particularly coherent argument in favour of Lithuanian custom, and Bona ignored it. Rents were based on the *sluzhba*, which was not on a measure of land, but a group of households. They comprised various levies, most commonly the *diaklo*, a payment in kind, or the *prisevok*, the harvest on a portion of the land held by a

---

[4] Bogucka, *Bona*, 225–6; Sucheni-Grabowska, *Zygmunt August*, 88–9.
[5] Pociecha, *Bona*, iii, 163–7; Sucheni-Grabowska, *Zygmunt August*, 96.
[6] For a detailed analysis see Pociecha, *Bona*, iii, 109–44.
[7] *AT*, vii, no. 214, 164.

leaseholder. The system was neither very remunerative for the lord, producing around 30 groszy per *sluzhba* in the early sixteenth century, nor very satisfactory for the villagers who saw the commercial value of the produce they surrendered rising sharply.[8]

There was an alternative. Polish and Mazovian settlers in Podlasie introduced the hide system (*system włóczny*), based on the Polish *łan* or, as it was known in Mazovia and Lithuania, the *włoka* (*voloka*). The Radvila family appreciated its benefits, and were already introducing it on their Podlasian estates. Bona followed suit. After experimenting in Podlasie, from 1533 she started converting villages to the hide system across her Lithuanian holdings, sending in surveyors to measure the land and reorganize villages along Polish lines. The surveyors established fields in hides of 21.3 hectares, divided into 30 morgs. Units of one hide were divided into three fields of 10 morgs each; lands outside the designated fields, known as *zastenki* (*zaścianki*)—literally 'beyond the wall', referring to the baulks that marked their boundaries—could be rented by peasants for additional payments, although occasionally they were distributed free of charge. The surveyors also marked the boundaries of the common lands used for pasture and haymaking.

Reorganization of village farmland into three fields facilitated the introduction of proper crop rotation. Villagers were required to sow one field with grain, one with winter grain, and leave one fallow every year. The fields were divided up between peasant households. In principle this was done on an equal basis, with each household assigned one hide, but the actual distribution depended on the wealth and capacity of individual households. Some lacked the labour or inventory to farm this much land, and surveyors were flexible, assigning land according to the capacity to farm it. The wealthiest might receive as much as 2–3 hides (43–64 hectares), although the average holding was 0.75 of a hide (16 hectares). Some households were allowed to pool their resources to farm one hide together.[9]

Bona's reforms were systematized in a 1549 decree.[10] By now their benefits were obvious. In 1547 Sigismund August followed Bona's lead, preparing the way for comprehensive reform of the grand ducal domain by ordering an audit of castles and starosties across much of Lithuania proper, Podlasie, and Samogitia. In 1556 he established a commission chaired by chancellor Mikołaj Radziwiłł Czarny that examined audits undertaken since 1547. Finally, on 1 April 1557 he issued his hide decree (*ustawa na włoki*) which, together with four supplementary decrees (20 October 1557, 20 May, 20 June, and 20 October 1558), constituted one of the most radical pieces of reforming legislation in Lithuania's history.[11] He ordered the

---

[8] Drozd, 'Miernicy', 39.

[9] В.И. Пичета, 'Волочная устава королевы Боны и устава на волоки', in Пичета, *Белоруссия и Литва XV–XVI вв* (Moscow, 1961), 23–4; Jerzy Ochmański, 'Reforma włóczna na Litwie i Białorusi w XVI wieku', in Ochmański, *Dawna Litwa*, 166–7; Drozd, 'Miernicy', 47.

[10] 'Устава Королевое её милости на волоки в имениях её милости у Великом князтве литовскомъ мераные а напередъ на волоки цыншовые', published by Kolankowski, 'Pomiara', 238–9.

[11] *Литовская метрика*, *RIB*, xxx, 543–8; Ochmański, 'Reforma włóczna na Litwie'; Drozd, 'Miernicy', 41.

conversion of all grand ducal estates to the hide system, stipulating a hide of 33 morgs (23.5 hectares), slightly larger than that used in Bona's reforms, which meant that farmland was divided into three fields of 11 morgs each (7.8 hectares), although the decree allowed use of the smaller hide or a larger hide of 36 morgs to suit local conditions.[12]

The reforms were based on a growing Polish literature on the principles of agricultural improvement, including Andrzej of Łęczyca's 1555 treatise, now lost, on the science of measurement, and were carried out on a massive scale.[13] Under the direction of Piotr Chwalczewski, brother of Jerzy, bishop of Lutsk, surveyors were despatched with their measuring equipment—little more than primitive cruciform surveying instruments, marked wooden measuring poles, and fathoms of oiled rope—across the grand duchy. Of 64 known surveyors, 35 were local Lithuanians or Ruthenians, five were local Jews, and the rest were Poles or Mazovians—or at least of Polish or Mazovian descent.[14]

The transformation of the countryside was dramatic. The dispersed hamlets defended by Goštautas all but disappeared, replaced by orderly villages at the heart of the field system, with cottages along one side of a central street opposite the farm buildings, to minimize the danger of fires spreading from wooden homesteads to wooden byres full of hay and straw.[15] The surveyors nominated one of the wealthier and more respectable villagers as headman (*wójt*) to oversee payment of rent and taxes, to inspect and maintain external and internal field boundaries, and keep order. In return he received two hides free of all obligations and the right to lease another hide if he so wished. Two to three hides were assigned to the parish church, whether Catholic or Orthodox. Grand ducal servitors such as the *boiare putni*—service boyars who carried letters and messages—received 1–2 hides rent free, while artisans, including millers, smiths, and beekeepers, received various amounts of land or relief from rent: smiths received two hides rent free, while *bobrovniki* (beaver-hunters) received one hide, which was rent-free during the hunting season.[16]

The hide reform was a massive undertaking that casts a favourable light on the capacity of the grand ducal administration. Between 1547 and 1566 almost all the domain in central and western Lithuania proper was reorganized. A cadastre classified land according to four categories: good, medium, poor, and very poor. In Samogitia and the palatinates of Vilnius and Trakai alone, 57,636 hides and 9 morgs were surveyed and reorganized: between 1,227,646 and 1,354,446 hectares. This exceeded cultivated land in Małopolska and Wielkopolska put together (59,350 hides), given that the Polish *łan* was smaller than the Lithuanian *voloka*.[17]

---

[12] Пичета, 'Волочная устава', 23; Kolankowski, 'Pomiara', 241.
[13] Andrzej z Łęczycy, *O nauce mierniczej* (1555); Kolankowski, 'Pomiara', 241.
[14] Drozd, 'Miernicy', 52–68; *PSB*, iv, 2–3.
[15] For a visual representation of the transformation see the maps in Ochmański, *Historia*, 122–3.
[16] Drozd, 'Miernicy', 44, 46, 49; Kolankowski, 'Pomiara', 247; Пичета, 'Волочная устава', 32–3.
[17] Kolankowski, 'Pomiara', 249.

It was not until the end of the century that the reforms were introduced in the annexed territories, but the treasury, whose income from the grand ducal domain had been under 20,000 kop groszy before 1547, soon saw the benefits. By 1588 its revenue from reorganized villages in Samogitia, Podlasie, Volhynia, part of Ruthenia, and the palatinates of Vilnius and Trakai had risen fourfold to just under 82,000 kop groszy per annum, some 200,000 Polish złoties.[18] These spectacular results encouraged private landowners to follow suit. One of the earliest was Radziwiłł Czarny, who, along with Piotr Chwalczewski and the Ruthenian Ostafi Wołłowicz, formed the commission that prepared the 1557 decree. Czarny quarrelled with his fellow commissioners over details of the reform, but from the early 1560s he reorganized his estates along the lines established in 1557. Others followed suit, as did the Catholic Church, after Walerian Protasewicz, bishop of Vilnius (1556–79) initiated the process in his diocese.[19]

It was long argued that the hide reform worsened the position of the peasantry, by depriving peasants of their plots and granting them smaller plots or worse land; by spreading manorial farming and introducing serfdom and labour rent; and by raising rents. The position of the rural population certainly changed dramatically after 1557, but the comprehensive nature of the reform, the way it was conducted, and the rapidity with which it was completed, cast doubt on this simplistic picture. The negative view of the manorial economy formed in later centuries was not shared by contemporary observers, while the replacement of straggling, dispersed hamlets by orderly, consolidated villages attracted approving comment: a Spanish traveller through central Lithuania in 1570 observed that the fields were just as well-cultivated as in Mazovia, and divided up in the same way.[20]

This impression is confirmed by the most remarkable feature of the reforms: they took place without substantial or organized peasant resistance, in stark contrast to the experience of south-western Germany or Ducal Prussia earlier in the century. Picheta even claimed that the reforms were anti-noble in nature, rather than anti-peasant.[21] The surveyors were not accompanied by troops, and the flexibility with which they approached their task suggests that the changes were achieved largely through negotiation and compromise, not force. Drozd claims that the peasants mostly came off worst, being deprived of 'well-cultivated land' which was incorporated into manors, in exchange for lower quality or even fallow land, but offers no evidence to support her generalization, or explanation as to why, if this was so, and if peasant interests really were damaged by the introduction of labour rent, the reform was achieved so quickly and with so little resistance, which in itself is remarkable considering how many of the surveyors were Polish or Mazovian outsiders.[22] Drozd herself quotes one of the surveyors, Jakub Łaszkowski, who claimed that the aim of the reorganization of villages was to produce a more just

---

[18] Kolankowski, 249–50. Kolankowski suggests an income of 10,000 before the reform, but Ochmański shows that his estimate was based on a poor year, and that between 1512 and 1514, the treasury's income from the domain was 18,500 kop groszy: Ochmański, 'Reforma włóczna na Litwie', 169.
[19] Ochmański, 'Reforma włóczna w dobrach magnackich', 177–8, 187–8.
[20] Quoted by Ochmański, *Historia*, 124.   [21] Ochmański, 'Reforma włóczna na Litwie', 159.
[22] Drozd, 'Miernicy', 50.

measurement and apportioning of the land within the village; each was to receive land according to 'what he rightly holds in accordance with justice and the law'.[23]

There is much to suggest that this claim was no idle boast. Four amendments to the decree within a year demonstrate that the government took account of the experience of their surveyors, and adjusted the legislation accordingly: thus the original allocation of one hide of land rent-free for the *wójt* was increased to two hides on Chwalczewski's recommendation, on the grounds that one was insufficient to persuade villagers to take up the burdens of the post.[24] This flexibility and concern for a just settlement was evident in other ways. The decree laid down that the land in the new fields should be apportioned equally; this underlying assumption of equality undoubtedly appealed to peasants, even if in practice they received plots of different sizes according to their capacity. The sharing of strips in a common field was often an improvement over a situation in which, with scattered settlement, some peasants had a monopoly on better land. The assignation of land to individual households took account of the categorization into four classes achieved in the cadastre. Cash and labour rents were calibrated according to the quality of the land: Bona's 1549 decree set rents at 80 groszy per annum for good land, 55 for medium-quality land, and 40 for poor land, with nothing charged for very poor land; these levels were raised in 1557 to 106, 97, and 83 groszy respectively, with a rent of 66 groszy introduced for very poor land. The equivalent figures for labour service were 40 days, 30 days, and 22 days in 1549, and 54, 45, and 31 in 1557; labour rent was not levied for very poor land under either decree. Even in 1557, the labour rent demanded for good land was just over one day per week.[25] Peasants had the right to buy themselves out of labour service, and paid cash rents for part of their holdings, the expansion of labour rent to a standard level of two days in the first period after the reforms probably indicates that peasants preferred labour rent at a time of rising agricultural prices.

The sources do not reveal how division of the fields among peasant households was achieved, but they do reveal how exchanges of land were carried out with nobles to consolidate the domain by regulating boundaries and removing noble holdings from the heart of grand ducal estates. In the Liakhovitsky district, Jan Shenevsky exchanged 10 morgs 22 pruts of land divided into three sections, one of 2 morgs 10 pruts of bad land, and two of medium land (6 morgs 6½ pruts and 2 morgs 2½ pruts respectively) for 9 morgs 22 pruts of medium land. Nikolai Trofym Vasylevych exchanged a hayfield and 10 hides 26 morgs and 27 pruts of scattered land rated bad, for a consolidated block of 3 hides 1 morg and 27 pruts, most classed as medium-quality.[26]

Nobles had to evaluate the quality of the land they currently farmed, its location, and the merits of the exchange on offer. It is clear that bargaining went on before a satisfactory conclusion was reached. Such exchanges suited both sides: it was not

---

[23] Drozd, 'Miernicy', 42; for the full quotation see Kolankowski, 'Pomiara', 244–5.
[24] Drozd, 'Miernicy', 44.
[25] Ochmański, 'Reforma włóczna na Litwie', table 1, 168.
[26] Пичета, 'Волочная устава', 25–6.

just the grand duke who was inconvenienced by the confused pattern of landholding, while for individual nobles, as in Vasylevych's case, the reforms enabled them to mitigate the consequences of a system of partible inheritance that could leave them with scattered strips of little value, or large holdings of poor land. The exchange of land with the domain enabled them to trade off a large but scattered holding for a smaller, consolidated plot that was easier to farm and, if of lower quality, had a lower rental value.[27]

It is likely that similar advantages were apparent to peasants: the size and configuration of their plots, the quality of the land, its location, and its rental value had to be taken into account. Bona, Sigismund, and Sigismund August were aware that their prosperity ultimately depended on peasant productivity, and they by no means always supported nobles against them. Bona's reputation encouraged complaints from peasants against mistreatment, as in the 1532 petition from peasants on the estate of Borysovska in the Vilnius palatinate concerning the behaviour of the leaseholder, none other than Albertas Goštautas.[28] While it would be foolish to assume that all peasants benefited from the reforms, or to doubt that nobles mostly held the upper hand in negotiations, it is by no means evident that the reforms had generally negative consequences for peasant farmers.

They did to an extent encourage the development of the manorial economy, although they were by no means the primary catalyst for its expansion, which had been underway since the late fifteenth century. The spread of manors, however, was mainly confined to the river basins linked to the Baltic in central and western Lithuania proper. Even where manorial farming spread, it by no means pushed out other forms of cultivation, and in practice systems based on cash rent, or—as the 1557 decree—on mixed rental systems—survived across the grand duchy, where the manorial economy was never as widespread as it became in Poland. Manorial farms for the most part constituted a smaller proportion of the hides in the grand ducal domain than hides subject to cash rent: apart from the starosty of Knyszyn, where they constituted 66 per cent of the hides, they made up 43.4 per cent in Sarazh, 41.3 per cent in Hrodna, 31.4 per cent in Kletsk, 30.7 per cent in Kobryn, 20.5 per cent in Brest, and 18.4 per cent in Lyngmiany.[29] The point of the hide reform was to increase agricultural production and grand ducal revenues, not to introduce the manorial system, and surveyors took account of local conditions in reorganizing villages according to the system that best suited them. Where they were introduced, they may well have suited the interests of the peasantry as much as the lord. The decree laid down that the ratio of hides measured where manorial farming was introduced should be one hide of manorial land for every seven hides assigned to the peasants, which meant that peasants, far from suddenly being made 'land poor' as Hrushevsky maintains, had plenty of farmland available to them to benefit from the rising prices for agricultural produce: he assumes, without producing any evidence, that since some land was taken from the peasants, they must

---

[27] Пичета, 'Волочная устава', 26.   [28] Pociecha, *Bona*, iii, 108.
[29] Ochmański, 'Reforma włóczna na Litwie', table 3, 170.

have been left with 'barely a third' of their old holdings. This is to ignore the redistributive tenor of the reforms, which sought not to deprive peasants of land, but to redistribute and reorganize peasant holdings.[30] It is true that where the manorial system was introduced, as in Poland, a new class of cottars with small plots of land was created to provide the labour service on the manor, but this did not mean that wealthy peasants were impoverished to create this class: cottars were either immigrants, impoverished peasants who had little land anyway, or former slaves: one of the results of the reforms was the end of slavery in Lithuania.

The transformation of the structure of peasant rents from a system largely based on obligations in kind to a mixed system of rents in cash and kind, or labour service, means that is difficult to compare the situation before and after the reforms, and attempts to demonstrate that the peasantry were impoverished by substantial rises in rent are dubious. Hrushevsky, for example, determined to show the negative impact of the manorial economy in the south, uses the lower rents in kind demanded of peasant households after the reform to claim that peasant productivity had suffered, an unwarranted assumption, since the reform had radically altered the structure of the rent paid, and lower rents in kind were offset by the introduction of other forms of rent, and in no way reflect the productivity of peasant farms.[31] It is true that rents rose, and that the grand ducal treasury's revenues increased substantially: the estate of Telšė in Samogitia, which in 1547 paid 478 kop groszy to the treasury, by 1588 was producing 1,136, an increase of 138 per cent. Yet simply to use the percentage increase of rent to conclude that peasants were thereby impoverished is unwarranted: if burdens rose by 20 per cent, the increased revenue to the treasury came largely from the surge in agricultural productivity that was the main aim of the reforms, not higher rents. Peasants, as well as lords, benefited from increased productivity, and rent increases did not reflect the increase in agricultural prices, which they were in a better position to exploit after 1557: the price of a barrel of rye in Lithuania rose by 140 per cent between 1529 and 1588.[32] Many peasants prospered. The wealthy tenant in Zantolepce who owned 15 horses, 6 oxen, 7 cows, 200 sheep, 4 goats, and 8 pigs was not unusual.[33] As in Poland, such tenants were in demand, and incidents of peasant flight did not necessarily indicate an inherently oppressive system. Landlords offered good terms to encourage settlement and the establishment of new villages. The two families who absconded from an estate in the Trakai palatinate in 1585 took with them 2 horses, 3 oxen, 4 bullocks, 12 mature sheep, 18 young sheep, 3 goats, 6 mature pigs, 12 suckling pigs, 20 piglets, 6 geese, 24 goslings, 20 hens, 4 barrels of rye, 6 of barley, 12 of milled rye, plus seedcorn, cloth, and 20 carts of hay. They must have prepared their move carefully; they would not have been hard to track down en route to their new home.[34]

Thus, as in Poland, it should not be assumed that because of the undoubted problems of the rural economy from the mid seventeenth century, the manorial

---

[30] Hrushevsky, *History*, vi, 159.
[31] Hrushevsky, *History*, vi, 159.
[32] Ochmański, *Historia*, 121.
[33] Drozd, 'Miernicy', 47.
[34] Śreniowski, *Zbiegostwo*, 26.

system was flawed from the outset, and that its introduction marked a sharp deterioration in the condition of the peasantry. The introduction of manorial farming was not the point of the hide reforms, and it did not triumph as a consequence of them. The transformation of the rural economy took place at a time of buoyant demand for agricultural products, and this is the main reason why it was achieved in such a short period, in contrast to the slower change in the Polish system, which began in a period of agricultural depression a century earlier. The reforms helped complete the process by which the Lithuanian nobility defined itself. As rural society became more stratified, a large group of poor and service boyars found themselves in limbo, with their social status unclear; some were simply excluded from the nobility, emerging as part of the upper stratum of the village. It was they who often served as headmen, but their decline in status was indicated by the fact that the term 'boyar' by 1600—in sharp contrast to its use in Muscovy—no longer denoted a nobleman. Lithuanian nobles thought of themselves as *shliakhta*. Despite the exclusion of many boyars, it remained a numerous class whose voice was soon to make itself heard.

35

Execution Proposed

At some point between 28 July and the end of the first week of August 1547 Sigismund August underwent a clandestine marriage ceremony in Vilnius. His bride was Barbara Radziwiłłówna, widow of Stanislovas, the last of the Goštautai, who died unlamented in 1542. Sigismund August had already benefited from this stroke of fortune. The Lithuanian council, thanks to Bona's influence, was now dominated by her clients, who were hostile to the Goštautas and Radvila families. They were led by Jan Hlebowicz, palatine of Vilnius since 1542, and the Orthodox treasurer, Ivan Hornostai, who had administered the chancery since Albertas Goštautas's death, but whom Sigismund had not dared appoint chancellor after the fuss generated over Ostrozky twenty years earlier. The council insisted on applying the full rigour of Lithuanian law, by which the vast Goštautas estates were escheated to the crown on the family's extinction in the male line. Stanislovas left no testament; although under the 1529 statute Barbara could be granted up to a third of her husband's property, her father Mikołaj Radziwiłł Rudy (the Red), had to write to Bona asking that Barbara's rights be respected; while he received assurances that royal favour would be extended to the young widow, Bona's appointment of Hlebowicz and Hornostai as commissioners suggested that it was unlikely to be extensive. Barbara retained the lands assigned to her in her dowry, but Rudy had to fight even to secure this, and his daughter was effectively living at the grand duke's pleasure.[1]

In more ways than one, as it turned out. At some point after the autumn of 1543 Sigismund August fell for Barbara and began a relationship that had considerable political ramifications. He had come to Vilnius to escape his new wife and the cloying attention of his mother. In May he had married Elizabeth Habsburg, daughter of Ferdinand I, king of Bohemia and Hungary, and Anna Jagiellonka, daughter of Sigismund August's uncle Władysław. The couple had been engaged since 1538, but the marriage did not prosper. The sexually experienced Sigismund August did not take to his timid cousin, who—although she was by all accounts good-looking—was six years his junior and not yet fully matured. After she froze with fright on their wedding night he largely ignored her. Her anxiety was not thereby diminished, and the epileptic seizures that plagued her from childhood grew more frequent. Her doting father expressed his concern at her treatment, and it was no doubt with some relief that Sigismund August left for Lithuania in

---

[1] Ferenc, *Rudy*, 42, 56–8; Zbigniew Kuchowicz, *Barbara Radziwiłłówna* (Łódź, 1976), 77–8. Jerzy Besala, *Barbara Radziwiłłówna i Zygmunt August* (Warsaw, 2007), 50–1.

the autumn for an extended stay, during which he hunted with conspicuous enthusiasm.

Quite when he fell for Barbara is unclear. Five months younger than the twenty-three-year-old grand duke she was very different from Elizabeth. Renowned for her beauty she was already attracting gossip. She showed little grief for Stanislovas, did not long wear mourning, and took pleasure in male company, although not as much as was subsequently insinuated. It is unlikely that—as tradition maintains—the affair began in the autumn of 1543, when Sigismund August visited Podlasie to take possession of the Goštautas estates, despite Kuchowicz's willingness to present Barbara, on the basis of scurrilous material that circulated after the marriage became public, as a sexually liberated woman who seduced Sigismund August during a romantic visit to Gieraniony castle.[2] By the summer of 1544 Elizabeth was herself in Vilnius, sent by Sigismund and Habsburg supporters on the Polish council, alarmed at the damage being done to relations with Ferdinand. Sigismund August was urged to treat her with more respect and he responded, displaying a little more grace and even some affection for his nervous cousin. By this time he had resumed his acquaintance with Barbara, who was living with her mother in Rudy's palace adjacent to the royal castle, and while it is possible that he had already fallen under her spell, the chronicles that touch on the matter—apart from a poisonous account by Stanisław Górski—suggest that the affair only began after Elizabeth's unexpected death in 1545.[3] For the Radziwiłłs the installation of Barbara as a royal mistress could only have harmed the family's reputation; far from encouraging an affair, they probably supported the idea of bringing Elizabeth to Vilnius to ensure that Sigismund August took up residence there.[4]

For the Radziwiłłs saw in the young monarch, already king and grand duke, the ideal means of breaking Bona's influence, which had shattered the Radziwiłł and Goštautas dominance of the council after the deaths of Albertas Goštautas (1539), Czarny's father Jonas Radvila (1522), Rudy's father Jurgis Radvila (1541), and Mikalojus Radvila's son Jonas, starosta of Samogitia (1542). With Jonas's death, the Goniądz and Rajgród Radziwiłłs died out in the male line, although it was not to be until the death of his daughter Anna in 1571 that their estates were escheated to Sigismund August.[5] With the Goštautas removed from the scene, Bona could mould a new council and freeze out the next generation of Radziwiłłs. In 1543 neither Rudy nor Czarny held any significant office, they had not been granted any starosties, and the council was dominated by their opponents, the Chodkiewicz, Zasławski, and Wirszyłła, led by Hlebowicz and Hornostai. While both men were only sons who had been bequeathed substantial property by their fathers—Rudy, Jurgis's son, inherited twenty-six separate estates—their economic position was by no means secure, especially in the light of Bona's drive to restore the grand ducal

---

[2] For example Kuchowicz, *Barbara*, 80–98; Besala, *Barbara*, 50–5.
[3] *Pamiętniki o królowej Barbarze żonie Zygmunta Augusta*, in Michał Baliński (ed.), *Pisma historyczne*, i (Warsaw, 1843), 21.
[4] Sucheni-Grabowska, *Zygmunt August*, 98–101; Ferenc, *Rudy*, 45–6.
[5] *PSB*, xxx, 195.

domain. Excluded from favour, the cousins would have no access to grants of grand ducal land that would enable them to stabilize their fortunes. The reality of their position, in which Rudy was forced to raise loans to keep financially afloat while he settled his father's debts, brought a brief rapprochement with Bona in 1541, in which he and his mother ceded several properties, or parts of properties, but no advancement was secured, and Radziwiłł resentment at her political dominance festered deep.[6]

Czarny and Rudy saw their chance to outflank Bona through the formation of a reversionary interest The orphaned Czarny, five years older than Sigismund August, had been brought up at the Cracow court between 1529 and 1533, where he formed a friendly relationship with the child-king. When Sigismund August took up residence in Vilnius in 1543 he had every intention of moving out of his mother's shadow, and favoured the Radziwiłłs, and families associated with them: the Kishkas, the Dowojnas, the Holshanskys, and the Kęsgailas.

The time was right for striking a blow against Bona's influence. At a sejm hastily assembled in Brest in the summer of 1544, when Sigismund proved too ill to travel to Vilnius—though Bona came—the Lithuanian estates presented Sigismund August with a document containing twenty-five articles complaining at the terrible state of affairs, the way in which taxation registers had been compiled, and the injustice of decisions over estate boundaries made during Bona's reforms. The Radziwiłłs launched a bitter attack on Hlebowicz's conduct of the government, proposing that Sigismund August should take over, which Bona passionately opposed. The plan was acclaimed by the sejm and confirmed by Sigismund on 6 October. Sigismund August was to use the title grand duke, while Sigismund revived the title of supreme duke. Bona blocked the Radziwiłł suggestion that Sigismund August should inherit the grand ducal estates in her possession, and he had to content himself with the revenues from the extensive complex of estates round Hrodna purchased by Bona from Jurgis Radvila ten years earlier. Sigismund retained control of the treasury, but Sigismund August was to receive 18,000 kop groszy per annum.[7]

Bona's attempts to limit the damage could not prevent a significant change of direction in Lithuanian politics, not least because the split with her son proved irrevocable. The restoration of the Radziwiłłs to the centre of power began immediately, with Czarny's appointment as marshal of the land during the sejm. The cousins were then presented with an unexpected opportunity. The sickly Elizabeth fell seriously ill in April 1545; in May she seemed to have recovered, and Sigismund August set off for Cracow to collect her dowry, which had finally arrived from Vienna. In his absence Elizabeth's condition rapidly deteriorated: on 11 June she

---

[6] Ferenc, *Rudy*, 34–5; Sucheni-Grabowska, *Zygmunt August*, 92; Raimonda Ragauskienė, *Lietuvos Didžiosius Kunigaikštystės kancleris Mikalojus Radvila Rudasis (apie 1515–1584)* (Vilnius, 2002), 203–44.

[7] Sucheni-Grabowska, *Zygmunt August*, 93, 106–19; Ferenc, *Rudy*, 47–8; *PSB*, xxx, 336.

suffered fifteen epileptic fits; four days later she was dead, twenty days short of her nineteenth birthday.⁸

The Radziwiłłs were now in a position to exploit Sigismund August's attraction to Barbara. Czarny had no high opinion of his niece, complaining to Rudy that she had the manners of a peasant and criticizing the morals of her entourage, but he appreciated her political value once Sigismund August's roving eye settled upon her.⁹ Rudy now had regular access to Sigismund August, having been appointed Lithuanian cupbearer in 1544, and even more so when he was created master of the hunt in 1546, a significant position given Sigismund August's passion for the chase. Exactly when Sigismund August's relationship with Barbara became physical is unknown, but by early 1547 the affair, which he took no pains to hide, was common knowledge, with rumours circulating that a special staircase and entrance to Rudy's palace had been constructed for discreet nocturnal trysts. While tales that the Radziwiłłs forced his hand by catching the couple *in flagrante* with a priest conveniently in tow are fanciful, there is no doubt that the seriousness of Sigismund August's attachment gave them the opportunity to insist that he save the family's reputation by legitimizing the relationship.¹⁰

The marriage was bound to be controversial. The dynasty's status had risen considerably since Jagiełło had married two commoners in succession (see Fig. 13). After Elizabeth's death there was talk of another prestigious dynastic marriage and the advantages such a match would bring. Sigismund August delayed informing his parents of his new status until December 1547, when he travelled to the Polish sejm at Piotrków. They did not take the news well. Bona's fury was spectacular, if it had to be reined in to preserve decorum and to limit the political damage when the senate was officially informed in January 1548.¹¹

Bona's influence was substantially weakened, however, by the death of her 81-year-old husband on 1 April 1548. Sigismund August immediately made clear that he was not disposed to indulge his mother's taste for power. Bona departed, raging at filial ingratitude, to take up residence in Warsaw, whence she stirred up her clients and carped biliously from the sidelines. Her umbrage was so great that she established an alliance with her old enemy Albrecht von Hohenzollern, who had hoped that his daughter Anna Sophia might marry Sigismund August after Elizabeth's death.¹² Bona's day was past, however. Frustrated by the failure to re-establish cordial relations with her son she left Poland in early 1556, returning to her duchy of Bari, where she died on 19 November 1557, only at the last minute restoring Sigismund August to her testament. He thus secured the return of her estates in Poland and Lithuania, although her death opened a legal struggle with Charles V over the revenues from her extensive Italian lands—the 'Neapolitan sums'—that lasted generations.¹³

---

⁸ *PSB*, vi, 257.
⁹ Ewa Dubas-Urwanowicz, 'Dwaj ostatni Jagiellonowie i Radziwiłłowie: między współpracą a opozycją', in Markiewicz and Skowron (eds), *Faworyci*, 144.
¹⁰ *Pamiętniki o królowej*, 23–4; Ferenc, *Rudy*, 56–8.   ¹¹ Ferenc, *Rudy*, 66–7.
¹² Sucheni-Grabowska, *Zygmunt August*, 174.   ¹³ Bogucka, *Bona*, 250–2.

Fig. 13. Tapestry showing the arms of the Kingdom of Poland (white eagle) and of the Grand Duchy of Lithuania (the rider known as Vytis in Lithuanian, Pogoń in Polish, and Погоня in Ruthenian). By kind permission of the Zamek Królewski na Wawelu, Cracow.

Her ill-starred daughter-in-law was already dead. Sigismund August's idyll did not last long. Around the time of the wedding Barbara began to show the first symptoms of an illness that sources refer to as 'internal stones'. In November 1547 she had what was seen as a miscarriage, but which was almost certainly bleeding from a ruptured abscess. By February 1549 the disease, despite periods of remission, had taken hold. Rumours that she was poisoned by Bona's agents can be dismissed, while the claim that she was suffering from syphilis—anxiously addressed by Rudy—owe more to her lurid reputation than medical evidence. The most likely explanation is that she developed cervical or ovarian cancer.[14] Whatever the cause, she suffered severely. By December 1550 she was largely bedridden, plagued by internal abscesses. At the climax of the tragedy, before her agonizing death on 8 May 1551, the stench of putrefaction was so strong that she dismissed her attendants and only her devoted husband could bear to spend long at her side.

Barbara may not have been queen long, but the consequences of the marriage were considerable. In Lithuania it drew Sigismund August firmly into the Radziwiłł camp, as Czarny and Rudy had planned. With his father dead and Bona safely—if noisily—sidelined, Sigismund August placed considerable power in their hands. Czarny, already marshal, was nominated hetman in December 1549, but refused the offer; instead the post was granted to Rudy in March 1550. Czarny had his eyes on political, not military authority, and in December 1550 he was appointed chancellor in succession to Hlebowicz, who had died in April. Perhaps with an

---

[14] Witold Ziembicki, 'Barbara Radziwiłłówna w oświetleniu lekarskim', *Pamiętnik VI Powszechnego Zjazdu*, i (Lwów, 1935), 144–62, but cf. Ferenc, *Rudy*, 67, and Sucheni-Grabowska, *Zygmunt August*, 341–4, 356–7.

eye to propriety, Sigismund August did not immediately make him palatine of Vilnius, instead appointing the Orthodox Hornostai as administrator; it was only in June 1551 that he felt confident enough to nominate Czarny. Apart from the hetmanship, Rudy was appointed administrator of the Trakai palatinate in 1549, and made palatine a year later, once the storm over the marriage had abated.[15]

Never had one family enjoyed such dominance over the Lithuanian government. Barbara's death made little difference to Sigismund August's relationship with the cousins, with whom he corresponded regularly.[16] Lithuanian politics were defined by the Radziwiłłs for a generation. The reformist currents that Bona had encouraged were stemmed or diverted to ensure that change did not affect the interests of the Radziwiłłs or their associates, while Czarny used the unique concentration of power in his hands and his closeness to the king to ensure that his clients were appointed to offices across Lithuania.[17] The council returned to the model of politics approved by the Radziwiłłs and Goštautas since 1501, in which the inner council played the leading role, and demands from the Lithuanian nobility for greater freedoms on the Polish model were brushed aside. The change was symbolized by Czarny's direction of the commission preparing the 1557 hide reform. The restructuring of the Lithuanian countryside that followed was not allowed to challenge the interests of the great council families. There was, nonetheless, much resentment at their dominance, and their pretentions, especially after Czarny secured the grant of imperial titles from Charles V during a 1547 mission to Augsburg. Following the extinction of the Radziwiłł line of Goniądz and Rajgród, Charles created the titles of duke of Nieśwież and Ołyka for Czarny and his descendants, and duke of Birże and Dubinki for Rudy's line.[18] The titles were recognized by Sigismund August in January 1549, but raised serious concern in both Poland and Lithuania.

With Sigismund August backing the Radziwiłłs so strongly there was little their opponents could achieve for the moment, although it remained to be seen if the political dissatisfaction that had grown steadily during Sigismund's reign could long be contained. In Poland Radziwiłł influence over the king was regarded with deep suspicion, and strengthened the clamour for fundamental political reform. Initially, reaction to the marriage in Poland did not seem particularly alarming. There was little time for the 1547–8 Piotrków sejm to absorb the news and formulate a response, but over the spring and summer many among the szlachta, already nervous at the accession of a king who had already been crowned, began to voice their outrage. In Wielkopolska the opposition was led by Andrzej Górka, castellan of Poznań who, as starosta general, had considerable influence over the provincial sejmik. In Małopolska, the leader was Bona's associate Piotr Kmita, now grand

---

[15] The hetmanship was not yet a permanent position: Rudy served in 1550 and 1553. He was reappointed in 1556, as the stormclouds gathered in Livonia, serving until 1566; he was hetman again in 1577 and between 1584 and his death in 1589: *PSB*, xxx, 321–35.
[16] *Listy orygynalne Zygmunta Augusta do Mikołaja Radziwiłła Czarnego*, ed. S.A. Łachowicz (Vilnius, 1842).
[17] Józef Jasnowski, *Mikołaj Czarny Radziwiłł (1515–1565)* (Warsaw, 1939), 343.
[18] Ferenc, *Rudy*, 65.

marshal and starosta and palatine of Cracow. With Bona and Albrecht von Hohenzollern whipping up their supporters, the opposition was determined to prevent Barbara's coronation, since it would render more difficult their aim of securing the king's renunciation of the marriage, or a papal annulment.

The frenzy dominated the first year of the new reign. Sigismund August planned to hold his first sejm in August, but the Wielkopolskans, pleading various excuses, secured its postponement until October, to give opposition time to coalesce. Feelings ran high. There were calls for a *rokosz* and dethronement from the hotter heads. Sigismund August won the support of Samuel Maciejowski, chancellor and bishop of Cracow, and Jan Tarnowski, hetman and castellan of Cracow, who was on friendly terms with the Radziwiłłs, and for whom Czarny had astutely secured an imperial title from Charles V in 1547, but felt it necessary to send 3,000 troops to ensure their safety at the sejmik of the Cracow palatinate in Proszowice.[19] When the sejm assembled in Piotrków on 31 October, a tidal wave of attacks on the marriage threatened to overwhelm all other business. Most bishops backed the king, except for the primate, Bona's client Mikołaj Dzierzgowski, but Sigismund August was forced to listen to speech after speech that would have earned their makers a short trip to the scaffold in other realms. He complained bitterly to Albrecht von Hohenzollern at how his 'subjects' believed that they could say anything they liked.[20] His subjects, however, believed themselves to be citizens, and that they had a perfect right to criticize royal actions in breach of the law.[21] Never had Stanisław Orzechowski's observation that 'we speak freely with our king, as with any other man' seemed so apt.[22] Andrzej Górka, speaking on behalf of the two chambers on 22 November, reminded Sigismund August that he was an elected monarch who was the servant of freedom, not its master, and was therefore subject to the laws and the dignity of the estates of the realm. He could not, in consequence, choose a wife without senate advice. Górka recalled that Casimir IV had not wished to marry another Elizabeth Habsburg on the grounds that she was ugly, but that he had accepted senate advice. The marriage had therefore been blessed by God, producing four kings and a cardinal.[23]

Sigismund August bore the attacks with some equanimity, publicly at least, defending Barbara's honour where he could and successfully resisting calls to renounce her. His patience paid off. After the flurry of angry opposition in 1548, tempers began to cool. Barbara sat out the Radom sejm, and Sigismund August installed her in Cracow, where his obstinate refusal to break his marriage vows gradually brought a level of grudging acceptance that was sufficient for him to

---

[19] Sucheni-Grabowska, *Zygmunt August*, 178; *PSB*, i, 296.
[20] Sucheni-Grabowska, *Zygmunt August*, 174–5, 184.
[21] Stanisław Orzechowski, *Annales Stanislai Orichovii*, ed. Theodor Działyński (Poznań, 1844), 20–2.
[22] Stanisław Orzechowski, 'Rozmowa albo dyjalog pierwszy około egzekucyjej polskiej korony', in *Stanisława Orzechowskiego polskie dialogi polityczne*, ed. Jan Łos (Cracow, 1919), 78.
[23] *Dyariusze sejmów koronnych 1548, 1553 i 1570 r.*, ed. Józef Szujski, *SRP*, i (Cracow, 1872), 217–23.

secure his aim of having her crowned queen in December 1550, five months before her death.

The episode scarred the king deeply and drove him into even greater dependence upon the Radziwiłłs, who were only too happy to indulge his outrage at his treatment. Thereafter he performed his dynastic obligations, if with a conspicuous lack of enthusiasm. In 1553 he married Catherine Habsburg, Elizabeth's younger sister. The match proved wildly popular, but the couple were never close. Catherine was a widow after a four-month marriage to Francesco III Gonzaga of Mantua. She was thirteen years younger than Sigismund August, but unlike Elizabeth was not blessed with good looks. As the king later confessed, he had never particularly wanted the marriage, and there was no 'attraction of the blood'. Catherine knew of her sister's difficulties; fear that history would repeat itself made her nervous. She suffered fainting fits, which Sigismund claimed were due to epilepsy, although this was fiercely denied by her family. Relations cooled significantly after Catherine, in her only pregnancy, suffered a miscarriage in 1554; thereafter it was public knowledge that the king had abandoned physical relations with her. He was still relatively young, and had several mistresses, but Catherine, spared the dangers of pregnancy, showed no inclination to die. Packed off to her family by her ungracious spouse, she lived on until 1572.[24]

Sigismund August's closeness to the Radziwiłłs ensured that the question of the succession and therefore of the union was a matter for concern long before it became clear he was likely to be the last of the Jagiellons. It was implicit in the storm over Barbara, which strengthened concern among the szlachta over his 1529 election. His accession had been eagerly anticipated during his father's decline into senescence, since it would remove the widely hated Bona from the power she had exercised for so long, and would bring a new, energetic monarch to the throne who might, so it was hoped, listen more sympathetically to the calls for reform that echoed through the sejms of his father's declining years.

His four years in Vilnius, however, raised suspicions that he would not be the monarch for whom the reformers had hoped. Górka's speech at the 1548 sejm, while ostensibly designed to persuade the king to renounce Barbara, was a clear statement of the nature of the Polish system, and the monarchy's place within it. He recalled the shredding of the 1425 agreement on the succession at the 1426 Łęczyca sejm, stating that whatever the king was able to do in 'another of his realms', where he was hereditary lord, and where he could, in consequence, command his unfortunate and unfree people as he saw fit, in this republican kingdom matters were different. A free people could not be ruled by absolute power.[25]

Górka's speech reveals that more lay behind the opposition to the royal marriage than might at first meet the eye. His veiled remarks indicate that the Poles had not forgotten that once again in 1529 they had been forced to accept a royal election in breach of the law after unilateral action by the Lithuanian oligarchs; it is revealing

---

[24] Sucheni-Grabowska, *Zygmunt August*, 416–27.   [25] *Dyariusze*, 221.

that Kmita's first demand in his *votum* at the start of the 1548 sejm was not for the annulment of the marriage, but for the calling of a common sejm to effect closer union with Lithuania.[26]

Thus if the storm over the wedding blew itself out, the 1550s were a turbulent decade, in which Sigismund August's reliance upon the Radziwiłłs and his attachment to Lithuania did little to allay Polish concerns. For, unlike his predecessors, Sigismund August demonstrated his preference for life in the grand duchy. Between 1548 and 1555 he spent just over half his time in Lithuania; the figure rose to 68.5 per cent between 1556 and 1558, and to 81 per cent between 1559 and 1562.[27] He returned to Vilnius as soon as he could after the end of the Polish sejms which he called reluctantly, and which he endured with barely disguised distaste.

His behaviour seemed to confirm Górka's suspicion that patrimonial kingship might appeal more to him than rule over free citizens, a suspicion reinforced by Czarny's role as *eminence grise*. Czarny may have been a fierce opponent of the closer union called for by Kmita, but he defended what he took to be Lithuania's interests through direct engagement in Polish politics. Although—unlike Rudy—Czarny's mother was a Lithuanian, Anna Kiszka, the early death of his parents and his upbringing in Poland meant that he had established links with many leading Polish politicians at an early age. His native language was Polish. His father had written his testament in Latin rather than Ruthenian, but Czarny's grasp of Latin was poor, and although he knew enough Ruthenian to carry out his duties as chancellor, he did not use the language in his correspondence. He had no knowledge of Lithuanian.[28] He persuaded Tarnowski and Maciejowski to support Sigismund August's marriage to Barbara, and in February 1547 he married Elżbieta Szydłowiecka, youngest daughter of Krzysztof, chancellor until 1532. Between August 1547 and December 1550, he spent half his time in Poland. He was present throughout the 1548 sejm; returning to Lithuania in early 1549 once Barbara was installed in Cracow. In 1550 he attended the Piotrków sejm, and Barbara's coronation. He was pro-Habsburg, and after Barbara's death he led the embassy to Vienna to negotiate the marriage with Catherine.[29]

The king's dependence on Czarny, and his consultations with the Radziwiłłs over Polish appointments did not go unnoticed.[30] Neither did his propensity for ignoring the statutes that bound his actions. Between 1548 and 1550 he distributed, without permission from council or sejm, leases on the domain in Prussia on a large scale and on generous terms: assignations of lifetime leases were common, and rents were low. Between 1549 and 1562 Sigismund August raised nearly half a million złoties in loans by mortgaging royal estates in blatant disregard of the law: the treasury lost direct control of 58 towns and 661 villages, almost half

---

[26] *Dyariusze*, 168–9.   [27] Sucheni-Grabowska, *Zygmunt August*, 387.
[28] Jasnowski, *Czarny*, 376, 379, 403.
[29] Calculation based on the itinerary in Jasnowski, *Czarny*, 405–6.
[30] Jasnowski, *Czarny*, 343; Miller, 'Execution', 83.

the royal domain.³¹ Nothing could be more provocative, or demonstrate more effectively that the problem lay not in the law itself, but in its enforcement. If the supreme judge himself—supported by senators and councillors who stood to lose most if the law were to be applied—showed such open contempt for the law, it is hardly surprising that he experienced turbulence in the sejms he had to call regularly to raise taxes to supplement his dwindling income.

The battle over execution of the laws therefore dominated Polish politics throughout the 1550s. At its heart was a struggle between two different political concepts. For the executionists, the king, while accorded respect, and while seen as the fount of justice, was subordinate to the law, and was charged with ensuring that it was upheld and enforced after it had been enacted by the sejm. For Sigismund August, whose sole experience of government had been in Lithuania, where the royal prerogative was far more extensive, the call for execution of the law, and in particular the demands for control over disposal of the domain, represented an intolerable challenge to his authority. He regarded the domain as his patrimony, which he was entitled to distribute as he saw fit. To admit that he was unable to issue privileges setting aside the demands of the law would be to surrender a crucial component of his prerogative. Yet he faced an increasingly confident political class that considered that its rights and liberties were natural and rested not on royal privileges, but on the bedrock of statute law, agreed by the citizens in the sejm.

The turmoil engendered by the clash of these opposing visions was complicated by the rapid spread of the Reformation after 1545. Sigismund I's swift action in Danzig in 1526 had failed to stem the Lutheran tide for long in the Prussian cities, but in the absence of support from the prince, Lutheranism was unable to establish itself in Poland apart from among a few German-speaking communities in cities like Poznań and Cracow. In 1548 there were relatively few Lutheran congregations outside Prussia. There was a lively interest in the new religious ideas in Polish intellectual circles, however, and the position changed suddenly and dramatically from the mid 1540s. The tradition among the szlachta of challenging the special privileges of the clergy meant that many were receptive to Calvinism and other forms of Protestantism whose congregationalist ecclesiology meant that churches could be established without the prince's sanction. Calvinism spread rapidly among the szlachta, while expulsions of Protestants by Ferdinand I in 1548 saw the establishment of congregations of Bohemian Brethren in Małopolska and Wielkopolska. Calls for reform of the Polish church grew stronger. Sigismund August issued a sharply worded edict against heresy in December 1550, but it was too late. By the late 1550s there were 265 Protestant congregations in Małopolska and 120 in Wielkopolska. By 1567, of 73 lay senators, 38 were Protestant.³²

---

³¹ Sucheni-Grabowska, *Monarchia*, 64, Sucheni-Grabowska, *Zygmunt August*, 454–5.
³² Gottfried Schramm, *Der polnische Adel und die Reformation 1548–1607* (Wiesbaden, 1965), 27; Christoph Schmidt, *Auf Felsen gesät: Die Reformation in Polen und Livland* (Göttingen, 2000), 54; Wojciech Kriegseisen, *Stosunki wyznaniowe w relacjach państwo-kościół między reformacją a oświeceniem* (Warsaw, 2010), 443–52. The impact of the Reformation in Poland-Lithuania will be fully analysed in volume 2 of this study.

Many leading executionists were Protestant. Andrzej Górka, encouraged by Albrecht von Hohenzollern, protected Lutherans and propagated Lutheran ideas from the mid 1540s, while Jan Łaski the younger, his namesake's nephew, was one of the earliest Polish intellectuals openly to espouse Protestantism when he resigned his office as provost of Gniezno in 1542. Rafał Leszczyński (c.1526–92), an early Protestant sympathizer, secured his popularity among the szlachta by flamboyantly resigning his office as palatine of Brześć in 1550 since it was incompatible with the starosty of Radziejów under the Nieszawa privileges. He abandoned the senate for the chamber, where he openly embraced Protestantism and put his sense of theatre and oratorical talent to good effect: at the mass opening the 1552 sejm he ostentatiously remained standing and failed to remove his hat at the elevation of the host.[33] Other prominent Protestant executionists included Marcin Zborowski and Mikołaj Sienicki, marshal of the chamber in 1555.

Between 1550 and the conclusion of the council of Trent in 1563 Sigismund August refused to commit himself. He had shown an interest in reformed ideas in his youth, while the adoption of a harsh line was difficult when the Polish clergy itself was divided: the energetic polemicist Stanisław Orzechowski, grandson of an Orthodox priest and a canon of Przemyśl who became a powerful opponent of the executionists, studied briefly in Wittenberg and strongly advocated the abolition of clerical celibacy. In 1551 he plunged the Przemyśl diocese into a scandalous controversy when he married in a Calvinist church. He challenged the inevitable sentence of the episcopal court in the 1552 sejm, where he attracted much support, ensuring that he was eventually allowed to remain a Catholic priest under special dispensation. This was enough to secure his loyalty; after 1563 he vigorously defended the post-Tridentine church.[34] Sigismund August's strongest supporters were not immune to Geneva's siren call: Czarny, after long sympathizing with Calvinism, publicly converted in 1553. Rudy was more circumspect, but by 1562 did not hide his sympathies.

Protestantism's spread strengthened the anti-clerical elements of the reformist programme. These had concentrated on two issues: the jurisdiction of ecclesiastical courts, and the demand that the clergy should share the burden of defence. At the 1536–7 Cracow sejm envoys demanded the abolition of annates and the secularization of all land donated to the church since Louis of Anjou's reign. The articles presented to the king at the 1550 sejm called for a national synod to settle differences between the clergy and the laity, and to outlaw the summoning of nobles before church courts, which had caused protests at the sejms of 1510, 1519, and 1532.[35]

All these demands could be subsumed under the general call for execution of the law. By the 1540s attention was concentrating ever more on the royal domain. At Sigismund I's last sejm in 1547–8, two of the chamber's fifty-three demands requested that the domain should only be distributed in accordance with the law.[36] The slogan 'execution' covered a multitude of royal sins, but although

---

[33] *PSB*, xvii, 132–3.   [34] *PSB*, xxiv, 287–90.
[35] *Dyariusze*, 41; Kreigseisen, *Stosunki*, 445–8.   [36] Szulc, *Z badań*, 37–9.

only one of twenty-three demands put by the chamber to the king at the 1552 sejm mentioned the domain, Sigismund Augustus's flagrant disregard for the law in the distribution of his favours raised the political temperature.[37] For the ordinary nobility, the issue encapsulated much of their concern about the royal government. It was wealthy nobles, senators, and royal officials who gained from the king's flouting of the law; it was these men who were responsible for the administration of justice in the castle courts and as judges in the senate, which heard appeals with the king during sejms. They enjoyed their illegal rewards for running a system in which ordinary nobles were losing faith: at the 1556–7 sejm it was claimed that 12,000 murderers were still at large.[38]

As the executionist demands grew more insistent there was no shortage of opposition to them among senators and wealthy nobles, many of whom stood to lose a great deal if the programme in its most radical form were to be implemented. Few were prepared to tread the populist path followed by Rafał Leszczyński. Some made gestures to appease the demands, but they were limited. Samuel Maciejowski resigned as chancellor in 1550, shortly before his death, and Jan Tarnowski surrendered his life tenure on the starosty of Sandomierz to demonstrate respect for the principle of incompatibility, but few followed their lead, and Tarnowski's resignation meant little: although he surrendered his life tenure, he continued to hold the starosty, and even managed to pass it on to his son.[39]

There were perfectly respectable arguments to be made against the executionists, or at least against the comprehensive revindication of the royal domain. Salaries for office-holders were minimal or non-existent, and were in no way commensurable with the burdens of office, or with the expenses that office-holders incurred in the course of their duties. The many who had lent money to the crown protested that contracts should be honoured. Yet the executionists, as Sienicki made clear, were not opposed to donations to those who served the realm per se, recognizing that state service should be rewarded and loans repaid. Such arrangements, however, were subject to the law, which required that mortgages should only be issued with proper extenuation and amortization of the loan, so that royal creditors were not rewarded by revenues that vastly exceeded the value of the original loan.[40]

By the mid 1550s the executionists were calling for inspection of all documents relating to elements of the royal domain in private hands to ensure that they were held in accordance with the law. Matters came to a head at the 1558–9 sejm. The 1555 sejm had broken up without achieving anything, but the envoys backed a proposal that execution with regard to the royal domain should be achieved according to the statutes of 1440, 1454, and 1504.[41] At the 1556–7 sejm Sigismund August assuaged anger at his failure to honour the promise he had made in 1555 to call a common sejm with the Lithuanians and Prussians to discuss closer union by agreeing to call one to enact execution. When the sejm gathered on 5 December 1558, however, neither the Lithuanians nor the Prussians were

---

[37] 'Articuli od wszego rycerstwa KJMci podane koronne', *Dyariusze*, 38–43; Szulc, *Z badań*, 42.
[38] Miller, 'Execution', i, 86.   [39] Szulc, *Z badań*, 45.   [40] Szulc, *Z badań*, 53.
[41] *VC*, ii/i, 67–71; Szulc, *Z badań*, 55–69.

present. Sigismund August promised to support 'root and branch execution', but it became clear that he was again lining up behind the senators, who called for execution but argued that nobody should actually have to surrender any land. On 3 February, after interminable debates, Jan Kietliński, a Sandomierz envoy, dramatically sought to break the deadlock by tossing at the king's feet his own lease on a royal estate that was contrary to the law. His example was followed by others. As documents piled up up on benches and tables, and overflowed onto the floor around the throne, the treasurer and castellan of Zawichost, Stanisław Tarnowski—who came under heavy attack—urged senators to follow suit. When they did not, Sigismund August optimistically suggested that now that trust had been restored, the sejm could move on to vote taxes, and execution could be postponed to the next sejm. A committee was established under Jan Tarnowski to scrutinize the relevant legislation, but it reached no conclusions, and the sejm broke up in acrimony.[42]

Sigismund August spent the next three and a half years in Lithuania avoiding the issue. Nevertheless, despite its failure, the 1558–9 sejm marked a watershed. The executionists had turned their vague slogans into a concrete programme of action, and Kietliński's *coup de théatre* had demonstrated that the only way in which reform could be achieved was through audits of all royal donations, not through pointless committee discussions on the nature of the law. When Sigismund August returned from Lithuania to open the next sejm on 30 November 1562, the executionists were ready to push their case with renewed determination. The outcome was not what they had expected. This time, much to their surprise, the king was on their side.

---

[42] Szulc, *Z badań*, 72–8; Sucheni-Grabowska, *Zygmunt August*, 470; Miller, 'Execution', i, 87.

36

Execution Achieved

In the autumn of 1562 the politics of union changed forever. It was the Lithuanians, not the Poles, who changed them, although it was through the very Polish mechanism of a confederation formed by members of the ordinary nobility gathered in a military camp near Vitsebsk. Sigismund August had summoned the levy to repel an expected Muscovite invasion. War with Muscovy had resumed in 1558 after Sigismund August's intervention in the complex politics of Livonia. From 1552, encouraged by Albrecht von Hohenzollern, he took the initiative as the decayed Livonian Order, left stranded by the establishment of Ducal Prussia in 1525, entered its death throes. Wracked by internal problems and the conversion of increasing numbers of brothers to Lutheranism, it became involved in bitter disputes with Albrecht's brother Wilhelm, archbishop of Riga from 1539, and the Livonian estates.[1] In 1554 Albrecht suggested that the Order's lands be secularized as a fief under Wilhelm on the Prussian model, and that Livonia should join the union. Sigismund August, aware of growing Muscovite interest in Livonia, and that Charles V regarded it as subject to the Empire, was initially cautious. With encouragement from the Lithuanian council, however, he acted. In 1557 he mobilized a large Polish-Lithuanian army that sat on the border in Pozwol, threatening invasion and forcing grand master Wilhelm von Fürstenberg to end his disputes with Wilhelm von Hohenzollern and Riga.

Czarny urged Sigismund August to incorporate Livonia into Lithuania. The opportunity came in early 1558 when Ivan IV, angered at Dorpat's failure to pay him tribute under a 1502 treaty, invaded, seizing Dorpat and Narva. The Livonian estates appealed to Sigismund August for aid. Over the next three years, as Ivan's forces raided Livonia, annihilating the Order's army at Ermes in 1560 and imprisoning Fürstenberg, Sigismund August sought to mediate. In 1561 the seizure of Reval by Erik XIV of Sweden ended hopes of a peaceful settlement. On 28 November 1561 Sigismund August signed a treaty with the Order and the archbishopric of Riga, by which the Livonian estates recognized him as their overlord. All Livonia, apart from Ösel, which was controlled by Denmark, swore loyalty to Sigismund August as king of Poland and grand duke of Lithuania; he promised to secure sejm agreement for its incorporation into Poland. Czarny proposed that it be incorporated into both Poland and Lithuania, but the Livonians felt they would enjoy

---

[1] The Order ruled 59 per cent of Livonia; the rest was under the control of the archbishopric of Riga (16 per cent) and the bishoprics of Dorpat, Reval, Ösel, and Courland, and of the city of Riga: Sucheni-Grabowska, *Zygmunt August*, 485.

greater security as part of Poland alone. The archbishopric of Riga was confirmed in all its privileges; the Order was secularized; the rights of Lutherans were guaranteed; and it was promised that Livonia would continue to be administered by Germans, with German as the language of government. Gotthard Kettler, Fürstenberg's successor, was appointed governor in Riga. He was granted a wedge of territory along the left bank of the Düna river as duke of Courland and Semgallen, which became a Polish fief. Sigismund August pledged to secure recognition from Ferdinand I, who had succeeded Charles V as Emperor, of the severing of the link to the Empire, but must have realized that this promise might be difficult to honour. The city of Riga initially refused to accept the incorporation treaty, but when Ferdinand failed to send aid it accepted the union.[2]

It was not Ferdinand whom Sigismund August had to fear, but Ivan and Erik. Erik occupied much of northern Livonia, taking Pernau in June 1562, but Ivan was the main threat. Fresh from the conquest of Kazan and Astrakhan, he was disinclined to accept Sigismund August's unilateral action, or surrender the bishopric of Dorpat. His strategy was inspired. While sending forces into Livonia to harry and burn, he launched his main assault on Lithuania, reviving the struggle for control of all Rus'. His military reforms meant that the large armies he deployed, accompanied by a considerable train of siege guns and toughened by the campaigns in the south, were far more formidable forces than those of his father or grandfather. In February 1563 the Muscovites seized Polatsk after a brief siege, opening up central Lithuania and threatening Vilnius itself.[3]

Sigismund August and Czarny lacked the military muscle to back their ambitious Livonian policy. Polatsk had not yet fallen in September 1562 when the Lithuanian levy reluctantly gathered at Vitsebsk, but it was apparent that the size, energy, and ruthlessness of the Muscovite forces meant that Lithuania could not hope to defend itself alone. Sigismund August, who had not called a Polish sejm since 1559, had no money and precious few Polish troops to stiffen the Lithuanian army. Since there was no time to summon a full Lithuanian sejm to Vilnius he decided to treat the levy summoned to Vitsebsk as a camp sejm. He proposed that it vote new taxes, including the *serebshchyzna*, and ordered that it should not disperse until they were agreed. Rudy, as hetman, was supposed to deliver both the taxes and an effective force to counter the Muscovites, but the nobles would only agree taxes at a level far below what was required.

They did not, however, restrict their discussions to taxation. Discontent ran high, and the assembly sent an embassy led by Prince Łukasz Bolko Świrski to the king complaining about the shortage of provisions and asking for the army's dispersal. When Sigismund August refused, a second embassy was sent, under the young steward of Lithuania, Jan Chodkiewicz, son of Hieronim, castellan of

---

[2] Christoph Schiemann, *Rußland, Polen und Livland bis ins 17. Jahrhundert*, ii (Berlin, 1887), 208–309; Knud Rasmussen, *Die livländische Krise 1554–1561* (Copenhagen, 1973), 208–25; Андрей Янушкевіч [Andrei Ianushkevich], *Вялікае княства Літоўскае і Інфлянцкая вайна 1558–1579 гг.* (Мінск, 2007), 21–53; Sucheni-Grabowska, *Zygmunt August*, 490–516; Jasnowski, *Czarny*, 286–91.

[3] Ferenc, *Rudy*, 252–3.

Vilnius, to demand a full sejm to discuss the defence of the realm. When this request was again dismissed the Vitsebsk camp was ready. The levy had not been idle, undertaking a raid on Velizh, which had to be abandoned owing to a lack of supplies. When Rudy left the camp discussions took a new turn.[4]

The envoys were sent back with a petition, drawn up on Sunday 13 September 1562, that radically altered the political landscape. It began with an explosive demand:

> That His Majesty call a common sejm with the Polish lords and that a union be formed in the closest of unity for two reasons: to choose a common ruler, and for common defence; and that there be one common sejm and one common law.[5]

The nobles were in no mood for compromise. If this request was refused, they would empower envoys to negotiate directly with the Poles for closer union. Despite their previous request, they stressed that they would not allow any separate Lithuanian sejm to meet, even if it were summoned to discuss long-standing noble demands, including corrections to the 1529 statute. Nothing was to distract them from their demand for a common sejm with the Poles. Should these requests not be granted within three weeks, the petitioners would advance on Vilnius en masse, would refuse to pay taxes, would not answer summonses of the levy, and would refuse to discuss defence or any other matter. They stated that they were sending envoys to their brothers in Samogitia, and in other districts not represented in the camp to secure their support.[6]

The original petition has not survived. A brief account was published by Działyński in his edition of the diary of the 1562–3 Polish sejm, and two Polish translations were unearthed by Halecki in the Czartoryski library.[7] The uncertain provenance of these documents led Kiaupienė to question the standard interpretation of the Vitsebsk events, most fully developed by Halecki, that the petition demonstrated strong support from the Lithuanian noble masses for closer union, motivated by a desire to throw off the oligarchic rule of the council lords in general, and of the Radziwiłłs in particular.[8] Kiaupienė challenges Halecki's assertion that

---

[4] 'Poselstwo Riczerstwa kxiestwa wielkiego Litewskiego ku kroliowy Je Mczi do Wilna zobozu', in *XVI amžiaus Lietuvos ir Lenkijos politinės kultūros šaltiniai (1562 metų tekstai)*, ed. Jūratė Kiaupienė (Vilnius, 2008), 74, 79; Oskar Halecki, 'Sejm obozowy szlachty litewskiej pod Witebskiem 1562 r. i jego petycya o unię z Polską', *PH*, 18 (1914), 322–6; Ferenc, *Rudy*, 242–3.

[5] 'Aby ye kro mscz zlozicz raczil sziem spolny spany poliaky y vnią aby byly wiedinostwie naywieczey dlya dwv prziczin Dlia iednego pana obranya y dlia yedney obrony aby spolnie szeimowały y prawa yednego vziwały': 'Poselstwo', 74.

[6] 'Poselstwo', 74–5; Halecki, 'Sejm', 326. The nobles did not, as Dembkowski suggests, carry out their threat: Harry Dembkowski, *The Union of Lublin* (Boulder, CO, 1982), 77.

[7] *ŽDU*, ii/i, 157, 367–8; BCzart. 1604 III, 1, 55–74; BCzart. 2208, IV, 1, 267–88. Kiaupienė's edition of the Czartoryski sources contains a partial facsimile reproduction of the version in BCzart. 1604, and a full facsimile of the version in BCzart. 2208: *XVI amžiaus*, 75, 77, 84–5, 89–110.

[8] Jūratė Kiaupienė, *'Mes Lietuva': Lietuvos Didžiosios Kunigaikštystės bajorija XVI a. (viešasis ir privatus gyvenimas)* (Vilnius, 2003), 101–7; Jūratė Kiaupienė, 'Litewskie cechy kultury politycznej szlachty Wielkiego Księstwa Litewskiego w XVI wieku', in Jerzy Wyrozumski (ed.), *Kultura Litwy i Polski w dziejach* (Cracow, 2000), 67–78; and Jūratė Kiaupienė, 'The Grand Duchy and the Grand Dukes of Lithuania in the sixteenth century: Reflections on the Lithuanian political nation and the Union of Lublin', in Richard Butterwick (ed.), *The Polish-Lithuanian Monarchy in European Context*,

the petition represented the emergence of the Lithuanian nobility as an independent political force, and Hrushevsky's contention that the nobles at Vitsebsk acted against the will of the magnates. She argues that Lithuanian politics was determined entirely by clientage relations, and that the events at Vitsebsk were the result of magnate intrigues against the Radziwiłłs led by Chodkiewicz, himself a magnate whose support for closer union was purely instrumental. Far from opposing the magnates, the Lithuanian nobility formed with them a united political nation with a common vision of Lithuanian statehood and nationhood. Clientage links ensured that ordinary nobles failed to develop any independent programme, and the magnates retained political leadership.[9]

Ianushkevich also criticizes the view that the Vitsebsk petition represented an attack by the ordinary nobility on the magnates. He is more willing than Kiaupienė to recognize the nobles as an independent political force, but suggests that the introduction to the petition in the Polish copy, in which the magnates are attacked for attempting to blacken the Poles in the eyes of the ordinary nobles, and for sitting at home enriching themselves while the nobles were called out to fight, was a tendentious interpolation by the unknown Małopolskan translator. Chodkiewicz's involvement and the fact that nobody on the council saw the Vitsebsk events as an anti-magnate attack means it would be wrong to see them in such a light. Ianushkevich argues that support for union was not deep-rooted: the issue was used instrumentally to put pressure on Sigsimund August and the council to accept their demands on other matters, such as taxation.[10]

These arguments have proven influential.[11] Yet if Halecki was undoubtedly too keen to see in the Vitsebsk events mass support from the Lithuanian nobility for his Jagiellonian idea, Kiaupienė's attempt to deny ordinary nobles any political initiative and to reduce them to obedient pawns in the hands of magnate faction-leaders is unconvincing. The division of the Lithuanian elites into 'magnates' and 'szlachta' is a construct of historians which, as Ianushkevich stresses, is not echoed in the sources. Yet if it is possible that the Polish translator put an executionist gloss on the petition's preamble, it is unlikely that he made up the attacks on the Lithuanian council, and on the Radziwiłłs. Ianushkevich does not explain why the copyist should invent the passage. He hints that the executionists wished to stir up Lithuanian nobles against the council, but does not explain how this document might achieve that end, written as it was in Polish, and clearly intended to inform Poles of events in Lithuania. He does not explain his observation that the

c.1500–1795 (Basingstoke, 2001), 82–92. Cf. Halecki, 'Sejm', 350–2; Halecki, *Dzieje*, ii, 153–5; Любавскій, *Сеймъ*, 635–6; Грушевьскій, *Історія*, iv, 361–3; Jasnowski, *Czarny*, 347–8; Stanisław Cynarski, *Zygmunt August*, 2nd edn (Wrocław, 1997), 107–8; Dembkowski, *Union*, 76–8.

[9] Kiaupienė, 'Litewskie cechy', 75; Kiaupienė, 'The Grand Duchy', 87–8. For a fuller treatment of Lithuanian clientage see Kiaupienė, '*Mes Lietuva*', 137–64.

[10] Andrej Januškevič [Андрей Янушкевіч], 'Między królem a Radziwiłłami: kształtowanie kariery politycznej Jana Chodkiewicza w przededniu unii lubelskiej 1569', in Markiewicz and Skowron (eds), *Faworyci*, 167–79; Янушкевіч, *Велікае княства*, 292–7; and Янушкевіч, 'Унія з коронаі ва ўнутранаі палітыцe ВКЛ перад люблінскім соймам 1569 г.', *БГА*, 10 (2003), 29–36.

[11] For example Ferenc, *Rudy*, 242–4.

introductory passage 'did not reflect objective reality'.¹² His suggestion that Chodkiewicz seized the opportunity at Vitsebsk to secure noble support is plausible; Kiaupienė's assumption that the idea of pushing for closer union was foisted upon ordinary nobles as part of a magnate faction struggle is not.

The role of Chodkiewicz and other magnates in the 1562 events is not to be doubted. Although it will never be clear who drafted the petition, it is entirely possible that Chodkiewicz played a key role. Jučas infers that since Chodkiewicz later joined the Radziwiłł in opposing closer union, he may not have been involved. Yet his later opposition to the terms on offer does not mean that he opposed the principle, while the Radziwiłł attitude to union was far more complex than is often allowed.¹³ The widespread resentment at the Radziwiłł stranglehold on power means there is every reason to suppose that the gist of the preamble was indeed composed by ordinary Lithuanian nobles, and that Chodkiewicz, who had every reason to resent Radziwiłł power, jumped on a bandwagon that was already trundling. There were many reasons for resentment of the Radziwiłł grip on power, and of the privileged position of the lords and princes by ordinary nobles, not least the fact that most provided military service separately from the rest of the nobility, did not have to serve under the ensigns who led the local military units, and were not subject to the local courts. The remark about lords sitting at home enriching themselves while others served reflected Lithuanian, not Polish, concerns, and was unlikely to be inserted by a magnate like Chodkiewicz.¹⁴

The ordinary nobility did not burst unexpectedly on the political scene in the Vitsebsk camp. There had been no shortage of complaints and demands for reform before 1562. Political activism grew steadily during Sigismund's reign, expressing itself at the increasingly frequent Lithuanian sejms. Their form and procedure, however, meant that ordinary nobles could do little more than submit petitions to the grand duke, who consulted with the council and replied to them, often simply dismissing them without explanation. Even if the nobles attending the sejm were not elected by local sejmiks—which did not yet exist—in the Polish way, but were nominated by powerful local figures—usually the palatine or governor—the content of those petitions reveals much about noble concerns.

Thus at the 1544 Brest sejm, when Sigismund August and the council formulated a decree on military service without consultation, the nobility protested. The regular military gatherings and local assemblies at which envoys to the sejm were nominated gave nobles the opportunity to formulate their demands. Such assemblies by no means always accepted grand ducal decisions on matters such as the appointment of local officials, and protests became common.¹⁵ In 1547 various issues were raised, including demands that copies of local privileges be made more readily available so that local nobles might better know their rights; that 'corrections' be made to the 1529 statute; that the *serebshchyzna* revenues should be

---

¹² Januškevič, 'Między królem', 170. Jasnowski has no doubts concerning the petition's anti-Radziwiłł tenor: *Czarny*, 348.
¹³ Jučas, *Unija*, 245.   ¹⁴ Любавский, *Сеймъ*, 496.
¹⁵ For examples, see Любавский, *Сеймъ*, 496–508.

examined by auditors; and that reports on its collection should be submitted to the sejm instead of simply being deposited in the treasury.[16]

This assertiveness was encouraged by increasing awareness of the nature of Polish institutions and of Polish law. Kiaupienė downplays this factor, arguing that the ordinary nobility did not know Polish, and could not communicate with Poles.[17] Yet there were many who did understand Polish, while the large number of Polish political and legal terms entering Ruthenian in this period suggests that communication was not unduly hampered by linguistic problems. While the Polish written by Lithuanians was not always entirely clear—as Sigismund August complained to Rudy in 1548—Ruthenian and Polish were mutually intelligible to a considerable degree. There were many Polish Ruthenians among the soldiers, courtiers, and administrators who spent time in the grand duchy, while most of the Calvinist preachers employed by Czarny after his conversion were Poles.[18] Although the practice of sending regular Lithuanian delegations to the Polish sejm ended in 1518—to the pained surprise of the Poles—it revived after 1529 as the pressing need for common defence returned.[19] These delegations may have been irregular, but they enabled Lithuanians to observe the operation of the Polish sejm, and of Polish politics. While this may only have encouraged the council lords to resist egalitarian Polish ways and the restructuring of the Lithuanian sejm along Polish lines, different conclusions could be drawn by those excluded from power.

The opportunities for Lithuanians to assimilate Polish ideas were manifold. There were large numbers of Poles in Lithuania during Sigismund August's reign. Apart from the almost continuous presence of Polish troops from the 1550s, there was always a considerable number of Poles in the royal entourage, which became significant thanks to Sigismund August's long periods of residence in Vilnius. Despite a request at the 1551 Lithuanian sejm that he establish a separate Lithuanian court, Sigismund August did not do so, even when he governed Lithuania as grand duke between 1544 and 1548, although he appointed Lithuanian court dignitaries who served him when resident in the grand duchy.[20] His court was substantial, numbering some 750 individuals, not counting Barbara's separate court.[21] Although the majority of the king's courtiers were Poles, many Lithuanians served him, in Poland as well as Lithuania; several were later appointed to high office, including Havrylo Hornostai (palatine of Minsk then Brest); Mikołaj Dorohostajski (palatine of Polatsk); Jerzy Ościk (palatine of Mstislav then Smolensk); Stanisław Pac (palatine of Vitsebsk); Andrzej Sapieha (castellan of Minsk then palatine of Polatsk and Smolensk); Mikołaj Talwosz (successively castellan of Minsk, Samogitia, and Trakai); Hryhory Volovych (palatine of Smolensk), and Paweł Sapieha, who was already palatine of Podlasie before he became a courtier. Although there were many Germans at the courts of Elizabeth and Catherine Habsburg, Poles dominated the courts of all Sigismund August's

---

[16] Любавский, *Сеймъ*, 519–23.   [17] Kiaupienė, 'Grand duchy', 87.
[18] Sigismund August to Rudy, Cracow, 2 June 1548: *Listy króla*, no. 11, 53; Jasnowski, *Czarny*, 403. For Poles in the chancery under Czarny, see Jasnowski, *Czarny*, 377.
[19] Błaszczyk, *Litwa*, 102.   [20] *AZR*, iii, no. 11, 25.   [21] Ferenc, *Rudy*, 51.

queens, though Lithuanians and Ruthenians also served.²² Lithuanians frequently came to Cracow during the grand duke's long absences in Poland: Czarny was by no means an exception. Lithuanian chancery officials resided at court for long periods, and individuals attended court events, or came to pursue private matters.²³

Thus many more Lithuanians from all levels of the nobility had the opportunity to interact with Poles than a century earlier. There was every opportunity for Lithuanians to learn of the advantages of Polish ways, especially since Poles showed no aversion to boasting about them. The Lithuanian sejm began to sound ever more like its Polish counterpart. At the 1554 Vilnius sejm the nobility petitioned Sigismund August to confirm the privileges, liberties, and freedoms granted by his predecessors, and requested that the 1529 statute be written into them 'word for word'. They asked that land courts be established in every district with elected judges 'according to the custom in the Podlasian land'. Sigismund August was reminded that the 1529 statute had decreed that all were to be judged by the same law, and that every estate should be equal before the law: it was therefore requested that council members and other wealthy and powerful magnates should be placed under the jurisdiction of elected local land courts.²⁴ Ordinary nobles were perfectly capable of grasping the Polish concept of noble equality before the law, and vigorously demanded it long before 1562.²⁵

The Vitsebsk petition represented the culmination of a long process in which ordinary nobles conceived and formulated a range of political demands that were by no means mere instruments in magnate faction-struggles. The demand for one common law was nothing new; neither was the request for closer union. Ever since Mielnik there had been supporters of closer union among the Lithuanian elite. One such was Kostiantyn Ostrozky; another was Jan Zaberezhynsky the younger; yet another was Czarny's own brother, Jan Radziwiłł, who supported Sigismund August's establishment as grand duke in Vilnius in 1544, but who fell out with Czarny in a property dispute. An early Lutheran convert, while in Cracow in 1549–50 he associated with leading Polish executionists including Hieronim Ossoliński, Stanisław Łaski, and Krzysztof Gnojeński. At a banquet he blurted out his support for closer union in the king's presence, stating that he wanted both realms to be subject to the same law, claiming the backing of 'all Lithuania'.²⁶ He died in 1551, but if his claim that 'all Lithuania' supported closer union was fanciful, and if there must be more than a suspicion that his support for closer union owed much to his dispute with Czarny, there was undoubtedly growing support for a reappraisal of the union, and an appreciation among a significant

---

²² Marek Ferenc, *Dwór Zygmunta Augusta* (Cracow, 1998), 55; Agnieszka Marchwińska, *Królewskie dwory żon Zygmunta Augusta* (Toruń, 2008), 160.

²³ For example the document of 4 October 1519 in which Sigismund I granted Bona the duchy of Pinsk was drawn up in Cracow and witnessed by three Lithuanians: Iury Ilnich, marshal of the court, Bohush Bohovitynovych, and Vasyl Vasylevych Kopot: Pociecha, *Bona*, ii, 415.

²⁴ *AZR*, iii, no. 13, 50–1; Любавский, *Сеймъ*, 579–80.

²⁵ Fifty-eight names of those who attended the 1554 sejm are known; though many were wealthier nobles and council lords, middling and lesser nobles were also present: Любавский, *Сеймъ*, 495.

²⁶ Sigismund August to Rudy, Cracow, 6 January 1550, *Listy króla*, no. 68, 142–3.

number of Lithuanians, excluded from power by the Czarny–Rudy axis, of the benefits of Polish law and the advantages of Polish institutions. Such figures undoubtedly encouraged support for closer union among their clients and associates, but ordinary nobles were perfectly capable of seeing the advantages for themselves.

If the Vitsebsk petition was not particularly novel in its demands, Sigismund August's reaction to it transformed the politics of union. Twelve years earlier, at the banquet where he had questioned Jan Radziwiłł's judgement, Barbara was still alive, and Czarny and Rudy were his trusted agents. By 1562, the circumstances were very different. He was only forty-two, over thirty years younger than Jagiełło had been when he unexpectedly produced an heir, but he was locked into a marriage that was likely to remain childless. As the years passed, his relations with Czarny soured. For a decade and more they had been close, personally and politically, and Czarny played a central role in Sigismund August's Livonian adventure. By 1560, however, the consequences of placing so much power in Radziwiłł hands were becoming clear, and discontent was growing among those excluded from influence at both central and local levels by the inexorable amassing of office by Radziwiłł clients and associates. Sigismund August began to realize that the man in whom he had placed so much trust was pursuing policies that were more to the benefit of the Radziwiłłs than to him.[27] There was an unpleasant clash over Sigismund August's support for the marriage of Halshka, heiress to vast Ostrozky estates, to the Polish magnate Łukasz Górka, when Czarny did all he could to thwart the king's wishes and prevent Ostrozky estates falling into Polish hands. The main issues, however, were political. With no prospect of an heir, the question of the future of the union after his death pressed upon the kings's conscience. By 1560 he was reconsidering his position. In May 1562 he replied favourably to a petition from the Małopolskan nobility asking him to summon a joint sejm of all his realms to consider the matter.[28] Although he remained silent on the question in the only surviving response to the Vitsebsk petition, dated 24 September 1562, his later actions suggest that the strong support for union expressed by the Vitsebsk confederation provided him with a welcome opportunity.[29]

He pursued it with remarkable vigour. Although he was known as 'king tomorrow' (*król dojutrek*), thanks to his penchant for procrastination and his guarded style of speaking on controversial matters, Sigismund August announced his Damascene conversion at the Polish sejm summoned in late 1562—after a gap of over three and a half years—in the most dramatic fashion. He had been a senatorial king, placing his trust in both Poland and Lithuania in a small group of royal councillors. He had done little to hide his contempt for the ordinary szlachta, which was only

---

[27] Jasnowski, *Czarny*, 341–3.
[28] 'Posselstwo ku krolowy Je Maczi od slyachty mnieyszy Polsky z nowego miasta': *XVI amžiaus*, 40; 'Responsu Regia Maiestatis nunciis a nobilitate Minoris Poloniae', 26 May 1562: *XVI amžiaus*, 65–6.
[29] In his reply, dated 24 September, he responded only to the request to allow the levy to disperse on account of the shortage of supplies: 'Отпис до Панов Рад от его к(о)р(олевское) м(и)л(о)сти Жикгимонт', Vilnius, 24 September 1562: *XVI amžiaus*, 111–12.

increased by his rough handling at the 1548 sejm over his marriage to Barbara. Despite the rift with Bona from the late 1540s, he was much influenced by her concept of a powerful, personal monarchy and her reform ideas. A highly intelligent, educated, and sophisticated man, he had all his life dressed in the Italian style of his mother's court, and drenched himself in the Italian Renaissance culture she had encouraged in Cracow. His concept of a powerful monarchy based on close cooperation with a small group of loyal councillors had failed, however. In Poland he faced fractious sejms that demanded political reform before they would agree to the taxation he so desperately needed; in Lithuania, where his powers were so much greater, he had failed to create a system capable of effective defence.[30]

Travelling to Piotrków he cast off his Italian finery, pointedly donning the *kontusz*, the simple tunic that was becoming the symbol of the ordinary Polish nobleman, who eschewed the foreign fashions almost uniformly sported by the senatorial elite. He ordered his entourage to follow suit; henceforth he always appeared in Polish dress. Instead of staying in Piotrków castle he based himself in the small wooden manor at Bugaj that was much more like the residences of the ordinary nobility.[31] It was a flamboyant way to signal a radical change in policy. When the sejm assembled on 30 November Rafał Leszczyński, the executionist speaker, welcomed the king by reminding him that he did not rule over Poles by the sword, or by hereditary right, but through election, challenging him to implement the promises he had so often made. Demanding action not words, he ended by imploring God to put fire in the king's heart.[32]

Leszczyński probably did not expect quite so much fire. In the royal proposals Sigismund August publicly endorsed the executionist programme. He stated that decrees had gone out to sejmiks expressing his intention to implement execution, and that holders of royal lands were to produce documents proving that they held them lawfully.[33] As excitement mounted, envoys ripped their own documents to shreds and cast them at the king's feet; others observed that 'it is not the documents but we who are guilty, and our greed, from which the commonwealth never gains any benefit'.[34]

The move had been well prepared.[35] With royal support for execution, the 1562–3 sejm, in stark contrast to its predecessors, passed a range of statutes concerning the royal domain. The constitutions of 1440, 1454, and 1504 were confirmed, and measures taken to implement them. Proof of the right to hold royal land was to be ascertained by compulsory inspection of all relevant documents; lands held in breach of the law were to be returned to treasury control. Mortgages on lands issued before 1504 were to be honoured, as were loans raised with council consent to finance the Prussian war in 1520; all others were subject to revindication, apart from those issued in Mazovia before 1529. Detailed clauses dealt with

---

[30] Sucheni-Grabowska, *Monarchia*, 182.
[31] Marcin Bielski, *Kronika Polska*, Zbiór Pisarzów Polskich, vi/xvii (Warsaw, 1832), 144–5; Cynarski, *Zygmunt August*, 97, 101.
[32] *ŹDU*, ii/i, 6–7.   [33] *ŹDU*, ii/i, 8.
[34] Bielski, *Kronika*, 145.   [35] Sucheni-Grabowska, *Monarchia*, 182.

the various types of leases on royal lands, and clear principles were laid down, such as the stipulation that lifelong leases were to be for one life only. One quarter of the revenue from all royal lands was to be paid to the treasury for defence of the realm. Audits were to be undertaken of all royal estates to establish the size of their revenues. Legislation against incompatibilities in office-holding was reasserted.[36]

The 1562–3 executionist legislation was followed up at the sejms of 1563–4, 1565, 1566, and 1567, despite considerable resistance from those who stood to lose out, and from nobles from Ruthenia, where many held royal land on military tenures designed to encourage szlachta colonization of the south-eastern borderlands to provide defence against the Tatars, which had created a bewildering patchwork in which royal and szlachta holdings were jumbled together, and there were many estates whose exact legal status was unclear.[37] The Ruthenian Orzechowski emerged as an eloquent opponent of execution, attacking the 'demagogues' who, he claimed, were evidence of the sejm's decline.[38]

The complexity of the task was revealed by the audit of royal estates undertaken between 1562 and 1564, and by inspection of the bewildering array of contracts, gifts, and leases, which continued until 1569. Holders of royal land had considerable room for manoeuvre. Particularly troublesome were *frymarki*—exchanges of pieces of land usually carried out to consolidate holdings—since it often came to light that royal land had been swapped for noble land that itself turned out to be royal land. Nevertheless, the legal situation was generally clarified, if only on paper, and important advances were made. The quarter (*kwarta*) levied on royal estates and paid into a quarter treasury established at Rawa in 1569 became institutionalized, although Sigismund August was careful to insist that this was his free gift, and that therefore the monarch was not obliged by law to sanction its payment from royal estates. At the 1567 sejm, after furious lobbying from office-holders, the king was allowed to assign lands as a reward for good service. In order to establish the principles that were henceforth to govern distribution of the royal domain, revenues were divided into five. The quarter was converted into one fifth—though it was still called the quarter—one fifth was to be paid to the leaseholder, and the treasury was to receive the remaining three-fifths.[39] An important battle had been won.

---

[36] *VC*, ii/i, 94–119; Szulc, *Z badań*, 92–100.
[37] Władysław Pałucki, *Drogi i bezdroża skarbowości polskiej XVI i pierwszej połowy XVII wieku* (Wrocław, 1974), 9; Anna Dembińska, *Polityczna walka o egzekucję dóbr królewskich w latach 1559/64* (Warsaw, 1935), 126–37.
[38] Stanisław Orzechowski, *Quincunx*, in *Dialogi polityczne*, 147, 159.
[39] *VC*, ii/i, 198; Pałucki, *Drogi*, 203.

37

Failure

The legislative achievement of the execution sejms was substantial, although it remained to be seen if their statutes were any more enforceable than those of 1440, 1454, and 1504. That was a problem for the future. The szlachta had other matters to consider. For Sigismund August's embrace of the executionist programme was not confined to revindication of the domain. As his response to the Małopolskan szlachta in May 1562 and his instructions for the 1562 sejm demonstrated, he had also changed his position over the union. He discussed the matter with the Lithuanian council before leaving for Piotrków, securing its agreement that the issue should be placed on the sejm agenda.[1] His conversion to the idea did not, however, mean that he was abandoning the Radziwiłłs. Although a delegation from the Vitsebsk camp, led by Jan Chodkiewicz, fulfilled its promise to come to Piotrków if their desire for a joint sejm was rejected, Sigismund August refused to receive it, and it was restricted to private meetings with Polish envoys. Despite the tensions that had arisen between them, Sigismund August had no wish to break with the Radziwiłłs; indeed he intended them to take a leading role in the negotiations.[2] On 6 December 1562 he wrote to Czarny from Piotrków stating his intention to summon a joint sejm of all his realms to discuss 'effective realization of this union'.[3]

The declaration was received with great enthusiasm by the sejm, but the question of the royal domain absorbed so much attention that consideration of the issue was postponed; indeed the envoys showed more interest in the question of closer union with Royal Prussia and the Silesian duchies of Oświęcim and Zator, since there the execution programme with regard to the royal domain was a live issue. Negotiations took place during the sejm, and the Silesians agreed to incorporation subject to certain conditions. The Prussian case was more complex, and no settlement was reached.[4]

A sense of urgency was injected by news of the fall of Polatsk, which reached Piotrków on 25 February 1563. Sigismund August, deeply shaken, opened a debate on how to rescue Lithuania. The Poles responded generously, agreeing to the calling of the levy, an offer that the king tactfully declined, and voting substantial rates of taxation to raise professional troops.[5] The Polish commitment was, however, conditional upon the calling of a common sejm to discuss closer union. Summoned in August 1563 to gather in Łomża, it opened on 11 November in

---

[1] Halecki, *Dzieje*, ii, 155–6; Jasnowski, *Czarny*, 348.   [2] Halecki, *Dzieje*, ii, 158–9.
[3] *Listy króla*, no. 244, 410.   [4] Halecki, *Dzieje*, ii, 157–8; Jasnowski, *Czarny*, 348–9.
[5] *VC*, ii/i, 112–19; Halecki, *Dzieje*, ii/i, 162.

Warsaw, where the accommodation was more suitable, to meet the Lithuanian request that it take place nearer the border. The Lithuanian delegation arrived on 14 December; deliberations continued until early April 1564.

It was preceded by a meeting of the Lithuanian sejm in Vilnius in May and June, which focused on the disastrous military situation following the fall of Polatsk, blame for which was ascribed to the levy. By January 1563 Rudy had a mere 100 horse from the levy at his disposal. Facing a Muscovite army of up to 32,000 with 150–200 siege guns, he could not save Polatsk, whose garrison numbered no more than 2,000 men, including 500 Polish infantry and 30–40 guns. Rudy had only 2,000 Lithuanians under his command, and 1,300–1,400 Polish professionals; after these were joined by forces sent by Czarny, the Lithuanian contingent may have reached 5,000.[6] The 1528 military reforms had not provided Lithuania with an army capable of resisting the Muscovites, and the envoys petitioned for the levy's reform, demanding that starostas and all holding leases on domain land should serve in the district companies, not separately as was then the case. Twenty out of thirty-eight demands concerned defence, and the tenor was notably hostile to the council elite. The programme was not implemented in full, but the sejm did undertake substantial revisions of military obligations. All were to serve from their hereditary estates, raising one man in ten as decreed by the 1544 Brest sejm. Those who failed to respond were to have their estates confiscated, with the grand duke receiving two-thirds of the land and the rest assigned to those who had brought the failure to his attention in what was an informer's charter.[7]

Although the petition did not mention closer union, the extent of noble support for it was clear, allowing Sigismund August to take the initiative. A delegation of twenty-eight was appointed. Led by Czarny it included leading councillors and individuals 'from the estate of lords and princes': Walerian Protasewicz, bishop of Vilnius, Mikołaj Pac, bishop nominate of Kyiv, Rudy's elder son Mikołaj, and Hieronim Chodkiewiz, castellan of Vilnius. There was one noble envoy from each district, and the urban estate was represented by two Vilnius burgomasters.[8] The delegation's composition was a compromise between the council lords and the nobility. The lords had for the first time agreed to the presence of noble representatives, but their hand had been forced by the Polish demand for a common sejm. When the delegation reached Warsaw the Poles complained at its small size, but were told that in the desperate situation faced by Lithuania, defence of the realm was the main priority, and no more men could be spared.[9]

The instructions reveal much about Lithuanian thinking. They envisaged a union *aeque principaliter*, in which Lithuania's dignity and separate status were to be preserved, but in which there were to be common institutions in what was a

---

[6] Ferenc, *Rudy*, 250–1; Янушкевіч, *Вялікае княства*, 61–2.

[7] Andrej Januškevič, 'Początek przełomu: Sejm wileński 1563 r. na tle wojny inflanckiej i reform ustrojowych w Wielkim Księstwie Litewskim', in Ciesielski and Filipczak-Kocur (eds), *Rzeczpospolita*, 81–8; Любавский, *Сеймъ*, 639–42.

[8] *AU*, no. 87, 156; Любавский, *Сеймъ*, приложенія, no. 47, 131–3.

[9] Halecki, *Dzieje*, ii, 166.

blueprint for a real, if limited, institutional union.[10] The Lithuanians insisted that they were based on previous union treaties. The conceptual framework was largely provided by Mielnik, with its concept of two peoples joined into one body, with one common head:

> We wish that in perpetuity there should be one prince, one king, one duke, one lord in the kingdom of Poland as in the grand duchy of Lithuania, under whom it were as if, under one head, each political community formed one body and one people.[11]

The instructions exist in several versions. Kutrzeba and Semkowicz print two Latin versions and a Polish translation, published by Działyński. The parallel Polish translation—which may be Działyński's own, since Kutrzeba and Semkowicz could find neither the original nor the copy he cited—translates *uterque populus* as 'the people of both states' (*lud obojego państwa*) and *gens* as 'nation' (*naród*). These are dubious translations. The Latin text does not here use the term *dominium*, usually translated in sixteenth-century Polish as *państwo*, although it appears elsewhere in the document. The texts are striking, since although they closely echo the formulations of the Mielnik treaty, the way they use the Latin terms is subtly different. According to Mielnik, Poland and Lithuania were to be united '*in unum et indivisum ac indifferens corpus, ut sit una gens, una populus, una fraternitas et communia consilia eidemque corpori perpetuo unum caput, unus rex unusque dominus*'.[12] The 1563 instructions maintain this idea, but stress that this one body should be formed by two separate 'political communities', the best translation of the Latin '*populus*'.

Thus if the instructions accepted the nebulous metaphor of one body politic under one lord elected in common, which would meet regularly in common sejms to discuss matters of common interest, they rejected the idea of one political community, insisting not on Lithuanian statehood, but on the continued existence of a separate Lithuanian political community, a Lithuanian republic. Should Sigismund August produce an heir, the instructions proposed that he be elected *vivente rege*; historians have suggested that this was designed to allow a return to the Vytautan system, but it seems more likely that it was simply an attempt to give the Lithuanians the initiative in the election of a successor, as they had done with Sigismund August himself, in a measure that may have appealed to him as a means of avoiding the dangers of an interregnum.[13] Since the Poles were unlikely to accept the proposal, it may simply have been a bargaining counter.

The instructions made clear the extent to which the Lithuanians were willing to compromise on the road to closer union. The main stress was on the common election of one ruler, who was to embody Lithuania's distinct status. He was to be crowned king in Cracow, but there was to be a separate coronation as grand duke in

---

[10] *AU*, no. 88, 158–70, no. 89, 170–6; *ŹDU*, ii/i, 172–8.

[11] 'Volumus enim, ut in perpetuum sit unus princeps, unus rex, unus dux, unus dominus tam regni Poloniae, quam magni ducatus Lituaniae, sub quo tanquam uno capite uterque populus sit unum corpus unaque gens . . . fuerit': *AU*, no. 88, 162. There are a few minor differences in the second Latin text: *ŹDU*, ii/i, 172.

[12] *AU*, no. 79, 137.   [13] For example Halecki, *Dzieje*, ii, 167.

Vilnius, and the title of grand duke was to be preserved.[14] There was no echo, however, of the plans of the 1420s and 1520s for Lithuania to be raised to the status of a kingdom. It was to remain a separate realm, however, with a separate treasury, separate offices of state, its own laws and court system, and its own army. The principle of closer union was embodied in the acceptance of a common currency, a common foreign policy, and common defence: wars were only to be fought with the agreement of each realm. In a major concession, the Lithuanians agreed that Poles could acquire and hold landed estates in Lithuania in return for similar arrangements in Poland.

It is usually suggested that these instructions marked the hijacking of the Vitsebsk programme by the magnates and the king.[15] While it is true that there were differences between the two documents, they should not be exaggerated. The Vitsebsk petition demanded a common sejm for all matters, but the Vilnius instructions suggested that common sejms be held only for important matters of mutual concern. In practice, if both war and foreign policy were to be conducted in common, and since the need for taxation to pay for war was the most common reason for calling a sejm, it was likely that sejms would, more often than not, have to be common. The Lithuanians had good reason to be wary about the institution of a common sejm on all matters, however. The union state was huge, and Lithuanians would have to travel vast distances to attend sejms, at considerable expense: the instructions therefore warned of the dangers of calling sejms for trivial reasons.[16] In any case, as Halecki observes, separate sejms did not breach the terms of previous treaties of union. In most other respects, the Vilnius instructions were broadly in line with the Vitsebsk petition.

Support for closer union among ordinary Lithuanian nobles did not mean that they accepted the Polish incorporationist programme as outlined by the executionists, who believed that all that was required was for the union treaties to be executed. Although the Vitsebsk petition stressed the need for one sejm and one law, it clearly envisaged the continuation of a separate Lithuanian realm, for which it used the term *państwo*. As in the Vilnius instructions, separate Lithuanian offices were to be maintained, including government offices, from which Poles were to be excluded, as was a separate army under its own hetman. The 1529 Lithuanian statute was to be preserved, albeit amended and improved to include certain liberties and privileges granted under Polish law.[17]

Thus although the Vitsebsk petition was more radical than the Vilnius instructions, enough common ground was found to present a united front to the Poles in support of a union *aeque principaliter*. The envoys were to ensure that Lithuania

---

[14] *AU*, no. 88, 163–4.
[15] For example Halecki, *Dzieje*, ii, 167 and, following him, Dembkowski, *Union*, 85–6.
[16] *AU*, no. 88, 165–6.
[17] 'A obawithelie tego panstwa tutecznego maią te dostoienstwa zaszadzacz i vrzędi swemi sprawowacz zlaski Jego KM iem danemi a nye panowie poliaczi Takze i okolo obroni panistw obvdwuch...za spolnem zezwoleniem woysk koronnego i Lithewskiego kozde znich woisko pod swoią chorągwią y sprawą wielkiego Hethmana thegosz panstwa po dawnemu będą sprawowacz', 'Poszelstwo': *XVI amžiaus*, 87.

retained its dignity, territorial integrity, and, crucially, its legal autonomy and power of government (*dignitas, amplitudo et iuridicio imperiumque*). Its ancient privileges were to be preserved. In the common parliament Lithuanians were to be seated on equal terms, according to their status, and were not to be regarded as inferior to their Polish counterparts; similar demands were made with regard to the army. Poles were not to command campaigns in Lithuania, just as Lithuanians should not in Poland.[18] Lithuania was to be regarded as equal in every respect to Poland, and this equality was to be carefully preserved: thus Vilnius was to have the same status as Cracow.[19]

The 1563–4 negotiations in Warsaw were not about *whether* union, but about the union's nature and the practical arrangements by which it should be institutionalized. After the fall of Polatsk, the Lithuanians could not afford to push the Poles too far. Yet although historians frequently present the matter as a discussion between Poles and Lithuanians, neither side was united in its views. There were radicals and moderates on both sides. Between them was an astute and resourceful monarch who had served his political apprenticeship and was not afraid of dramatic action, or of challenging entrenched tradition.

One such challenge was a decree issued in Vilnius on 7 June 1563, in which Sigismund August unilaterally and perpetually annulled clause eleven of the Horodło treaty, which limited office to Catholic nobles.[20] This was no impetuous act, but had been carefully prepared. The confirmation of Horodło during the fuss over Ostrozky's appointment as palatine of Trakai in 1522 had highlighted the second-class status of Orthodox nobles, who made clear their disapproval, and joined the wider campaign for a revision of noble privileges and amendments to the 1529 statute at the 1544 Brest sejm. Sigismund I claimed that such corrections were unnecessary, but had been forced to promise to appoint a commission of five Catholic and five Orthodox nobles to consider amendments to the statute.[21] It never met. Sigismund August replied, when reminded of the matter at the 1551 sejm, that the nobles had not chosen its members as he had suggested in 1547. This time, however, the commission was established, and began its work.

By 1563 Sigismund August was ready to accept its findings. His decree removed the restrictions on Orthodox nobles being appointed to office, and allowed their entry into Polish heraldic clans.[22] He thereby completed the process, begun in 1432 and 1434, of granting full rights and complete equality to Orthodox nobles. Despite the fuss caused by the appointments of Orthodox nobles to high office in 1522 and 1551, grand dukes had quietly ignored clause eleven for many years. It

---

[18] *AU*, no. 88, 167.

[19] 'Ac ne quid sit reliquum utque per omnia magnus ducatus Lithuaniae regno Poloniae exaequetur, aequum et consentaneum iustitiae, quae aequalitate constat': *AU*, no. 88, 169.

[20] 'Жалованная грамота Литовскому и Русскому дворянству и рыцарству православной вѣры': *AZR*, iii, no. 32, 118–21.

[21] *AZR*, iii, no. 4, 5–6; Любавский, *Сеймъ*, 290–2, 520; Иван Лаппо, *Великое княжество Литовское во второй половине XVI столетия* (Юрьев, 1911), 19; Czermak, 'Sprawa', 393–4; Darius Vilimas, *Lietuvos Didžiosios Kunigaikštystės žemės teismo sistemos formavimasis (1564–1588)* (Vilnius, 2006), 56.

[22] 'Жалованая грамота', 119.

was the Lithuanian council lords who clung to Horodło, not the Jagiellons, who were well aware of the dangers of excluding the Orthodox from power. At a time when they were being asked to contribute on the same basis as Catholics to the war against an Orthodox foe, and when the sejm was decreeing that the Orthodox clergy should pay taxes on the same basis as their Catholic counterparts, it was sensible and just to remove the last remnants of discrimination.

Yet was the context of the war the only motivating factor, as Ianushkevich claims? It was undoubtedly important: as he points out, the concession was made at a sejm called exclusively to deal with the problems of defence after the fall of Polatsk.[23] It opened after Sigismund August's dramatic public conversion to the executionist cause in Piotrków, where the instructions for the Lithuanian delegation to the Warsaw sejm were drafted. It is unlikely, therefore, that the question of the union played no part in the decision. The 1568 confirmation of the 1563 privilege stressed that one reason for the concession was to win Ruthenian support for closer union, although Ruthenians probably did not need much persuasion: Ruthenian nobles had been prominent among those pressing for reform since the 1520s. Orthodox nobles had been present at Vitsebsk, and one of their number, Havrylo Bokei, was a member of the second and third delegations sent with the 1562 petition to Sigismund August.[24] This enthusiasm for reform sounded a warning to the Lithuanian council, which realized that it was not just Muscovy that was angling for Orthodox support. The 1563 privilege was therefore signed by the Lithuanian council, including Czarny and Rudy, and the Catholic bishops. Czarny's conversion to Calvinism had in any case altered his perspective, and opened the way to a different approach to the Orthodox issue.

The Ruthenian question was to play a central role in the drama that lay ahead, but after the end of the Vilnius sejm in July 1563, attention focused on the negotiations that began in Warsaw in early December. The sejm opened on 12 November, bickering its way impatiently through piles of documents thrown up by the execution process. As at Piotrków a year earlier, attendance was high, with 95 envoys present, although the senators proved less assiduous, and many delayed their arrival. The speaker, Mikołaj Sienicki, was an accomplished and experienced politician, an envoy from the Chełm district at every sejm since 1550, who had already served as speaker on three occasions.[25] The Lithuanians were formally welcomed by the senate on 14 December; their letters of accreditation were read on 19 December, but it was not until 7 January that the Poles began discussing the union—although the 1432 Hrodna union had been read out on

---

[23] Янушкевіч, *Вялікае княства*, 274–5; Januškevič, 'Początek' 87.

[24] Januškevič, 'Początek', 275. Cf. Halecki, *Dzieje*, ii, 229–30; Chodynicki, *Kościół*, 87–8. Jaroslaw Pelenski, 'The incorporation of the Ukrainian lands of old Rus' into Crown Poland (1569)', in Anna Cienciala (ed.), *American Contributions to the Seventh International Congress of Slavists, Warsaw, August 21–27, 1973*, iii (The Hague, 1973), 48; Halecki, 'Sejm', 325.

[25] Halecki, *Dzieje*, ii, 171; Anna Dembińska, *Polityczna walka o egzekucję dóbr królewskich w latach 1559/64* (Warsaw, 1935), 106–7; *PSB*, xxxvii, 155. Dembkowski claims he also served in 1550 and 1553, but this is not confirmed in the sources, and it would be unusual for an envoy to be elected speaker before he had established his reputation in the chamber: *Union*, 83, 299, 138–9.

27 November—despite the desire of many senators to start as soon as possible in order to escape the relentless execution process.[26]

The Poles began the debate alone. To their disappointment, the Lithuanian delegation was small and the sejm did not take the form of a common parliament. The Lithuanians for the most part debated separately, although the Poles claimed that the Lithuanian envoys wished to sit among them but were prevented by the council lords.[27] The opening ceremonies on 14 and 19 November were only attended by Czarny, Protasewicz, and Prince Władysław Zbarazky, representing the council, and Rudy's son Mikołaj, representing the 'lords and others from the knightly estate'.[28] Mikołaj was an unconvincing representative of the Vitsebsk petitioners, but he did not in any case have the opportunity to state his views: throughout the discussions, which lasted a month, only Czarny spoke on Lithuania's behalf. He spoke frequently, eloquently, and at length, but this hardly constituted the joint parliament the Poles had so long desired, to their evident frustration.

That Czarny exercised a dominant influence over the Lithuanian delegation is certain. He was closely involved in its nomination, and it contained none of the envoys from the Vitsebsk camp. He controlled what was said in the chamber, and what was reported back to the Lithuanian envoys, although there are occasional hints of dissent, suggesting that the delegation was not united as Jasnowski claims.[29] Czarny has, therefore, been widely blamed for the failure of the negotiations. He is accused of wanting only 'the loosest form of union', and the continuation of the status quo.[30] Only the two large Muscovite armies that invaded Lithuania in January 1563, potentially threatening Vilnius itself, had forced him to compromise, and to contemplate the settlement towards which he was inching, with agreement reached in principle on a number of contentious issues. The situation changed dramatically, however, on 1 February when news arrived of a stunning victory by the Lithuanian army, led by Rudy, over a much larger Muscovite force at Chashniki on the Ula river on 26 January, which enabled Czarny to adopt a much harder line.[31]

The influence of Chashniki on the Warsaw negotiations should not be exaggerated. While it undoubtedly stiffened Czarny's resolve and gave him an excellent propaganda opportunity, the widespread assumption that agreement was close, with only 'a few disputed points' to be settled is optimistic.[32] Nothing had been formally accepted by the Lithuanians before 1 February. There was no agreement on the fundamental issues of the continued existence of separate Lithuanian offices, the preservation of the title of grand duke, and a separate coronation.[33] Although

---

[26] Halecki, *Dzieje*, ii, 171–2.   [27] *ŻDU*, ii/i, 314, 316.   [28] Halecki, *Dzieje*, ii, 172.
[29] Jasnowski, *Czarny*, 352; cf. Halecki, *Dzieje*, ii, 183.   [30] Dembkowski, *Union*, 102.
[31] Rudy had at his disposal 6,000–10,000 men, of whom only about 1,000 were professionals; the Muscovite force numbered 17,000–20,000: Янушкевіч, *Вялікае Княства*, 74–90; Ferenc, *Rudy*, 263–5.
[32] Dembkowski, *Union*, 91, closely following Halecki, *Dzieje*, ii, 179–81.
[33] Although Dembkowski includes this in his list of agreed points: *Union*, 91. Cf. Zujienė, 'Pastangos išsaugoti Lietuvos didžiojo kunigaikščio titulą i pakėlimo ceremonialą', in Liudas Glemža and Ramunė Šmigelskytė-Stukienė (eds), *Liublino unija: Idėja ir jos tęstinumas* (Vilnius, 2011), 66–7.

various compromises had been suggested, none had proven acceptable, and in late January it was agreed that disputed points should be postponed to another joint sejm, a point included in the draft Polish terms presented on 2 February, which suggests that agreement was proving rather more difficult than is usually assumed.[34]

The Warsaw discussions revealed that the two sides were separated by more than differences on practical arrangments. Moreover, if Czarny proved a tough and fearless negotiator, bargaining fiercely and alone in long speeches in a frequently hostile chamber, it was the Poles who were principally to blame for the stalemate. Despite their willingess to concede on minor points concerning practical arrangements, they proved utterly inflexible with regard to the union's nature. This rigidity was signalled on 7 January, when the senate and the chamber debated the union without any Lithuanian presence. Treasurer Walenty Dembiński set the tone, presenting an incorporationist vision of which Oleśnicki would have been proud. He stated bluntly that while it was necessary to strengthen the union, in its essence it had already been achieved. Everything was laid out in the old acts of union; all that needed to be done was to ensure that they were enforced, so that there would, in future, be one single election, as they decreed, and no more separate elections by the Lithuanians. As to the nature of the union, the parties to it formed, in his view, a unitary state. He showed some sensitivity to the Lithuanian desire to retain the grand duchy's name by proposing that although the union state was to have a common name, the title 'grand duchy' might be used for Lithuania as a province alongside Małopolska and Wielkopolska. His proposed name for it—New Poland—showed rather less sensitivity.[35]

Thus Lithuania was to be reduced to the level of a Polish province. There was to be one prince—the king of Poland, who was no longer to bear the title grand duke of Lithuania—one state seal, one marshal's staff—by which Dembiński meant no separate Lithuanian offices—and one legal system. He stated that 'if there is to be a union, let the grand duchy's territories be regarded as lands of the [Polish] crown'. He airily dismissed the issues raised by the Lithuanians in their instructions, saying merely that they could be sorted out.[36] Dembiński set the tone. Bishop Filip Padniewski of Cracow drily observed that when Jagiełło came chasing after Jadwiga's hand he had been told that if he did not wish to accept the terms on offer, which included incorporation, there were plenty of other suitors. Jagiełło had accepted, and the union was effected. While Vytautas and others had ruled Lithuania, they had done so as vassals and lifetime administrators. Suzerainty had always remained with the Polish crown, to which starostas in Lithuania swore their oaths.[37]

The notion that the union was done and that all that was required was some light dusting was even more eagerly propagated in the chamber. For the executionists, the laws had been passed; the treaties agreed; they simply needed to be executed. The Lithuanians were cast as the villains who had ignored the law, and little concern was shown for Lithuanian sensibilities. Yet the matter was by no means

[34] Halecki, *Dzieje*, ii, 180.   [35] *ŹDU*, ii/i, 272.
[36] *ŹDU*, ii/i, 272.   [37] *ŹDU*, ii/i 272–3.

straightforward. Challenged by Czarny, Sienicki had to admit that the crown archives were in such a state of disorder that the Poles could not even find some of the old acts—including the original of the crucial Mielnik treaty—despite the registers recently drawn up by Marcin Kromer, who had quoted them in his great chronicle, published a decade earlier. Fourteen crates of documents were hastily ordered up from Cracow in the hope that the Poles might find the '*spisy*' in which they placed so much store.[38] This slight embarrassment did not, however, prevent speaker after speaker from pontificating about the meaning of the *spisy*. Jagiełło, it was suggested, had tied an indissoluble knot, and the full panoply of Horodło synonyms was trotted out: the Lithuanians were told that they had been incorporated, invisceratered, annexed, and appropriated. Their instructions were in breach of the old agreements, and therefore could not be countenanced. Their sins against the union were paraded before them. They were upbraided for pre-empting royal elections by their separate elevations of successive grand dukes, which was not a 'brotherly act', and told that the union, by incorporating Lithuania, had in eternity 'established not a league or association of political communities, but from two states had formed one state, one people, one council, and one republic, under one lord: the king of Poland'.[39] It was therefore impossible and, indeed, illogical, that Lithuania should continue to have its own title, symbols of its separate status, and offices. Lithuanians, like Małopolskans or Wielkopolskans could of course serve in Polish office under the crown, but many speakers were unable to hide the fact that they regarded Lithuanians as inferior. The primate, Jakub Uchański, observed with studied vagueness that kingdoms always had something in them that was superior to mere provinces or duchies.[40] It was clear where power would lie in this great Polish vision: while the Poles were willing to countenance a Lithuanian as field hetman of the common army, overall command would always lie with a Polish grand hetman.[41]

The Polish vision of union propounded at Warsaw took the metaphor of the body politic alluded to in the Mielnik treaty and used it to promote the idea of a unitary state.[42] From their point of view Mielnik had been agreed with the Lithuanians, even if they had subsequently refused to ratify it. Yet in their insistence that the metaphor of the body politic could only admit one interpretation, and that the union state had therefore to be unitary in nature, they went far beyond Mielnik. There was nothing in its terms about Lithuania's relegation to the status of a province; indeed its second clause specified that bishops, palatines, and dignitaries '*in ipso Ducatu*' would participate in royal elections. Lithuania was regarded throughout as a separate realm, and clause twelve promised to uphold the laws,

---

[38] *ŹDU*, ii/i 291–2, 296–7. Nobody cited the Krewo act, which languished forgotten in the Cracow cathedral chapter archive: Halecki, *Dzieje*, ii, 174.
[39] 'aby był zawżdy nie jako foederatus aut consociatus populus, ale ze dwu Państw jedno Państwa, jeden lud, jedna Rada, jedna Respublica, pod jednym Panem i Królem Polskim': *ŹDU*, ii/i, 293, 294.
[40] *ŹDU*, ii/i, 300.   [41] *ŹDU*, ii/i, 285.
[42] 'aby discrepantia in uno corpore ni w czem nie było': *ŹDU*, ii/i, 294; 'A jeśli jedno ciało i jedna Rada być ma, tedyć to już jedno nie może być roztargnione, ani consilia mogą być rozdwojone, ale zawżdy jedne i spólne': *ŹDU*, ii/i, 358–9.

jurisdictions, customs, prerogatives, liberties, and statutes in each realm (*utriusque dominii*).⁴³

Thus despite the confident Polish claim that the Lithuanian instructions did not accord with the old agreements that they were unable to find, in fact they were very much in the spirit of Mielnik. They accepted its central elements: a common monarch, a common election, a common sejm, and a common currency. On one or two points they did go beyond the Mielnik terms—in the proposal that in certain circumstances there might be separate elections, and in the proposal for a separate coronation—and there was no mention of a common council, which had been proposed at Mielnik. Mielnik, however, had made no attempt to outline the practical implications of its stipulations. In two important respects the Lithuanian instructions went beyond Mielnik, in accepting a common foreign policy, and in the clause allowing Poles to own land in the grand duchy.

These were substantial concessions, and the instructions provided a perfectly workable model for a union *aeque principaliter*. The Poles, as the opening speeches of the sejm demonstrated, were considerably less generous and, in their insistence on the unitary nature of the union state, had themselves moved considerably beyond Mielnik. It is therefore doubtful if there was any great division within the Lithuanian delegation concerning the Polish terms, which showed that they were unwilling to countenance the Lithuanian vision of a union of equal partners.

Czarny defended the Lithuanian position with consummate skill. He listened to the Polish speeches with considerable equanimity and replied with even greater aplomb, demonstrating that he was far from being an opponent of union. What he was not prepared to accept was incorporation. He stressed that the Lithuanians desired closer union regardless of their difficult position, and that they had come to Warsaw to agree it.⁴⁴ Throughout, he highlighted the fraternal relations between the two peoples fostered by the union. He used himself as an example of its benefits, admitting that he called himself a Pole and pointing out that he had married a Pole, was in the process of marrying his daughter to a Pole, and hoped that he might marry all his daughters to Poles—a wish that was fulfilled, albeit after his death.⁴⁵ His appeal was not just to the heart. He opposed the rigid Polish concept of an accessory union that had, supposedly, already created a unitary state with the most coherent defence of the union as a relationship *aeque principaliter* yet mounted, and outlined a viable framework for institutionalizing it that formed the basis for the final compromise at Lublin five years later.

He fought the Poles on their own terms. At the welcoming ceremony, he reminded Sigismund August of his hereditary status—and his lack of heirs—stating that the Lithuanians had come to secure unification, and to establish an effective union. This union, however, should be a union of equals, founded on the

---

⁴³ *AU*, no. 79, 137–8.   ⁴⁴ *AU*, no. 79, 301.
⁴⁵ 'A zatem zwałem się Polakiem': *AU*, no. 79, 351–2. Of his daughters, Elżbieta married Mikołaj Mielecki; Zofia married Achacy Czema—a Prussian; Anna married Mikołaj Tworowski, and Krystyna, Jan Zamoyski.

law, and on equal liberties.⁴⁶ The key issue was the nature of that union, and Czarny was careful in the terms he used: on 18 January he talked of coming to complete 'this holy league'; he also talked of 'this union or confederation'.⁴⁷ He confronted the problem of the union's legal basis by challenging the Polish interpretation of the treaties. As the fourteen crates of documents lumbered up from Cracow, he denied that they had effected Lithuania's incorporation. He observed that Mielnik, on which the Poles placed such store, had never come into effect, and that the Lithuanian copy of Horodło lacked the clause with all the incorporationist synonyms that the Poles paraded before him. It was a disingenuous claim, although not strictly inaccurate, since the document to which he referred contained the oaths of loyalty sworn by the Lithuanian boyars on 2 October 1413, which indeed omitted the relevant clause that was present, however, in the other two versions of Horodło.⁴⁸

He emphasized that 'our copy' of Horodło, while saying nothing about incorporation, emphasized brotherhood and friendship, and maintained that his Lithuanian ancestors had challenged 'those stern words in the old documents that were so hard to accept: *subici, obedire et servire*'.⁴⁹ The vision of union he presented was a stark contrast to the Polish view based on rigid adherence to past agreements, even when they contradicted one another. As he stressed, circumstances had changed since Horodło, and the relationship he described was an organic one, a process of development and growth which could not and should not be determined by literal adherence to outmoded agreements; at one point he compared the relationship to a marriage, and accused the Poles, with considerable justification, of introducing new terms, 'unheard of by our ancestors', despite their veneration for the old documents.⁵⁰ The union should take account of the different nature of what he insisted were the two separate republics that formed it, and respect their separate laws, customs, and traditions, as Mielnik had done. Thus when Padniewski objected that the other copies of Horodło clearly stressed incorporation, and the relevant clause was read out, Czarny responded that the document required long consideration. It was as Padniewski stated, but not without reason the Lithuanians could not praise this privilege issued by Jagiełło, 'since we were neither bought by Poland, nor taken by violence'. In consequence 'our ancestors amended this confederation, which seems hard and unworthy of a Christian people'.⁵¹ Likening the relationship established by the clause to 'the yoke of servitude', Czarny argued that amendments to the treaties had secured the liberty 'that you wish for us'. The Lithuanians, he assured them, would not abandon 'our league with you', but like their ancestors they insisted on removing from the treaties 'those words that sting and vex us'.⁵²

---

⁴⁶ 'gotowi jesteśmy zjednoczenie a skuteczną uczynić Unią': ŹDU, ii/i, 238.
⁴⁷ ŹDU, ii/i, 304.
⁴⁸ ŹDU, ii/i, 304–5, 361; cf. AU, no. 50, 55–9. He was probably referring to the redrafting of Horodło copied into the Lithuanian Metryka on Bona's orders in 1541: see Ch. 28, 333–4.
⁴⁹ ŹDU, ii/i, 301, 305.   ⁵⁰ ŹDU, ii/i 312, 337.
⁵¹ As the reworked copy of Horodło in the Metryka demonstrates.
⁵² ŹDU, ii/i, 307.

Thus Czarny restated the case made by Jonas Goštautas in the 1450s, but in a more constructive and challenging manner. Throughout he appealed to the principles on which the Polish political system was based. Stressing the Horodło adoption, he argued that the union could only be based on this fraternal model. He stressed that the Lithuanians had come here of their own free will, not because they had been ordered to by king or sejm, maintaining that there were certain clauses in the union treaties which ensured that closer union could not come into force.[53]

His audience was not persuaded. His arguments were met with indifference and the occasional sneer: having heard the Poles speak at length about the military aid they had sent to the Lithuanians over the years Czarny mentioned the Lithuanian contribution at Tannenberg and allowed himself a rare flash of anger when Marcin Zborowski, castellan of Cracow, muttered that they had run away.[54] Despite moving far beyond Mielnik, the Poles refused to concede. Their proposals of 19 January 1564 stated bluntly that Lithuania had been definitively incorporated into Poland, 'on which point we stand with determination and will continue to stand'. Despite their call for common sejms, elections were to be carried out by the Polish sejm and members of the Lithuanian council, to the apparent exclusion of the Lithuanian nobility. The proposal stressed at length the unitary nature of the union state. There was to be one treasury—situated, naturally, in Poland—one council, one seal, one hetman, and one marshal—which meant that there were to be no separate Lithuanian government offices, although there were to be local offices on the Polish pattern. All border disputes, of which there were many, were to be decided according to Polish law.[55]

The Poles did take some account of Lithuanian sensibilities by agreeing to remove phrases from the old acts that the Lithuanians found offensive, replacing them with phrases of brotherly love, but in the light of the general tenor of the Polish offer, it is hardly surprising that Czarny and the Lithuanians regarded this as cosmetic tinkering to disguise the harsh incorporationist reality: Czarny remarked that 'you do not want to depart from the old treaties, well then, you are making us into your servants'.[56] The Poles found this perplexing. Uchański remarked that 'they say they will be subjected to us, but we see them as brothers, not servants', wholly unable to see why the unitary Polish model upset the Lithuanians. Padniewski seemed to have no sense of irony when he called the union 'an unbreakable chain'.[57]

Irony was in short supply. As Czarny pointed out, the Poles, by insisting that incorporation had already taken place, and that its nature could not be changed, were denying Lithuanian citizens the free choice that underpinned the Polish system. His explicit appeal to the principle of *quod omnes tangit* was ignored. Once the Lithuanians hardened their stance after the news of Chashniki, the Poles were reduced to begging the king, who had remained largely silent, to impose

---

[53] *ŻDU*, ii/i, 338.   [54] *ŻDU*, ii/i, 302.   [55] *ŻDU*, ii/i, 308–10.
[56] *ŻDU*, ii/i, 311, 312.   [57] *ŻDU*, ii/i, 355, 356.

a settlement: Dembiński openly confessed that he believed the Lithuanians had no choice: 'Where can they go? To the Muscovite tyrant?'[58]

Some Poles did understand. Stanisław Myszkowski, castellan of Sandomierz, argued that it would be a shame to allow the union to founder on the issue of offices and begged the king to intervene. On 12 February Sigismund August finally did, suggesting that the issue of separate offices was not as significant as the Poles supposed, invoking the metaphor of the body politic and pointing out that the arms of a body act separately without compromising its unity. The plea fell into the void, however. The most the Poles were prepared to concede was that if Lithuanian offices were to survive, they should be designated 'crown offices for Lithuania' (*koronne per Lithuaniam*).[59]

The proposal completely missed the point. As Czarny sadly observed in his closing speech, the Lithuanians had a different interpretation of the nature of the union from the Poles: 'you defend your republic; ... do not take it badly if we defend ours'.[60] The issues between them, even before Chashniki, were not minor. As Czarny observed, it was unlikely that the process of union, which had developed over 160 years, could be brought to a conclusion at one sejm; he closed with an appeal to one of the basic principles of the Polish political system: 'we are not here without the mandates and instructions of our brothers, against which we can decide nothing; now we must bring this matter back to our brothers, and there, at our sejm, undertake serious discussions to reach a conclusion'.[61]

The Poles had only themselves to blame. It is entirely possible that agreement could have been reached in Warsaw if they had paid closer attention to the actual terms of Mielnik, to which they appealed so frequently, and had allowed the Lithuanians to retain their offices and the symbols of their separate identity. By the time the two sides reconvened at Lublin five years later, the balance of forces had changed significantly, and the outcome was very different to that which might, with more flexibility from the Poles, have been achieved at Warsaw. As Czarny gently implied more than once, the Poles had failed to respect the basic principles of their own political system.

---

[58] *ŹDU*, ii/i, 359, 362.   [59] *ŹDU*, ii/i, 359, 365.
[60] *ŹDU*, ii/i, 378.   [61] *ŹDU*, ii/i, 377, 378.

38

Interlude

The outlook seemed bleak. Once it became clear that the Lithuanians would reject the Polish terms, the king declared his hand. On 13 March he issued two documents: a 'declaration on the union' and a 'recess of the 1563 Warsaw sejm concerning the Lithuanian union'.[1] In the latter he reviewed the negotiations, summarizing in fifteen clauses what he understood had been agreed, and the outstanding issues to be settled at a future common sejm: Lithuanian offices; the location of future sejms; the establishment of sejmiks in Lithuania; and the question of the grand duchy's title.[2] He publicly endorsed the Polish view of the union. In the declaration he declared baldly and inaccurately that both sides had accepted the old acts of union, showing that the two realms already formed one commonwealth under one ruler. He stated that the agreements made by his forebears had joined both realms into one body, adding with a considerable degree of wishful thinking that they thereby formed one soul (*animus*), one common ideal, one harmonious concord, and one mutual friendship that could not be divided. He stated that one, indivisible commonwealth had been formed out of these two nations; thus two separate commonwealths could not exist.[3] This vision was exactly repeated in the recess.[4] It was the declaration, however, that changed the whole context of the debate. In it the king, lamenting that God had not blessed him with heirs and ignoring the claims of his four surviving sisters and their heirs, renounced in perpetuity his hereditary rights to the Lithuanian throne, vesting them in the *corona regni Poloniae*, asking only that any heirs he might subsequently father should be provided for.[5]

It was a bold move. For three generations the dynasty had formed a common front with the Lithuanians over its hereditary claims to the grand duchy as a means of securing election to the Polish throne. Now Sigismund August was endorsing the Polish vision of incorporation. Halecki suggests that by renouncing his hereditary status Sigismund August felled a tree standing on the path to union.[6] Yet for all their defence of the right to elect their own grand dukes, the Lithuanians had always upheld the Jagiellons' natural and hereditary rights to the grand duchy, which played a vital role in the construction of their vision of a glorious Lithuanian past,

---

[1] *VC*, ii/i, 127–8 and *AU*, no. 90, 179–80; *VC*, ii/i, 128–32 and *AU*, no. 91, 181–5.
[2] *VC*, ii/i, 131; *AU*, no. 91, 184. Kutrzeba and Semkowicz rationalized the numbering of the fifteen clauses; the text in *VC* reproduces the numbering in *Volumina Legum*, which leaps from 5 to 16: *VL*, ii, 30–2. These clauses appear as 19–21 in *VC* and *VL*, and as 9–11 in *AU*.
[3] *AC*, ii/i, 127; *AU*, no. 90, 179–80.   [4] *AC*, ii/i, 129; *AU*, no. 91, 181.
[5] *VC*, ii/i, 128; *AU*, no. 90, 180.   [6] Halecki, *Dzieje*, ii, 190.

and were central to the idea of Lithuania as a separate realm within the union. The act demonstrated that Czarny had been right to warn of the dangers of attempting to coerce the Lithuanians into closer union through an appeal to the king's absolute authority; they were therefore likely to challenge Sigismund August's right to vest the dynasty's hereditary rights in the *corona regni* into which they did not accept they had been incorporated.

The stakes were high. As negotiations with the Prussians at the Warsaw sejm demonstrated, the implications of accepting the incorporationist vision of union were considerable. Despite the guarantee issued in the 1454–66 incorporation treaties that Prussian law would continue to operate, the executionists demanded that the Prussians take their seats in the common sejm, stressing that they considered that the Polish statutes of 1454 and 1504 concerning offices and the disposal of the royal domain also applied to Prussia. Since the royal domain in Prussia was so extensive, this demand was fiercely resisted by the Prussian elite, which had substantial holdings of royal land, and the great cities, which owned considerable landed estates in contravention of Polish laws confining land ownership to the szlachta. To the consternation of the Prussian grandees, however, there was growing support for the executionist programme among the smaller cities—which did not own land—and the increasingly polonized szlachta of the Culm palatinate, most of whom held no royal land.[7]

The Prussian magnates successfully blocked these attempts to force full integration into the Polish sejm and the execution of the Prussian domain; the dangers were demonstrated, however, by the incorporation of the duchies of Oświęcim and Zator. Here the issue of the royal domain was not of burning concern, and the Silesians accepted the extension of the Polish system, albeit with guarantees of their rights and privileges.[8] The question of whether Lithuania would be subject to the execution of the Polish statutes on the royal domain was of great significance for the council lords, whose fortunes were substantially dependent upon their holdings of grand ducal land.

Sigismund August's public endorsement of the incorporationist view did not, therefore, bring union nearer; quite the contrary. Its uncompromising nature was counterproductive. Czarny had reached out substantially to the Poles in terms of the practical concessions he was prepared to accept, but he was not inclined to compromise over the nature of the union. After leaving Warsaw he at first refused to attend the Lithuanian sejm that Sigismund August called to Bielsk in May in the hope of advancing the union cause, encouraging Rudy to stay away. Sigismund August sought to persuade them by denying that the union he was proposing constituted servitude, as Czarny had claimed in Warsaw, but it was probably the suggestion that others might take his absence amiss that brought Czarny hurrying to Bielsk in case the king arranged matters behind his back with Lithuanian unionists.[9]

---

[7] For the debates, see *ŹDU*, ii/i, 252–70. [8] *VC*, ii/i, 134–44.
[9] Sigismund August to Czarny, Bielsk, 31 May 1564, *Listy króla*, no. 275, 460; Jasnowski, *Czarny*, 357.

Although Sigismund August continued to correspond regularly with Czarny, and their private relations remained cordial enough, their alliance was over. When Czarny and Rudy finally appeared in Bielsk they were accompanied by a substantial armed retinue.[10] A Polish delegation attended, led by Uchański and Dembiński, hoping to settle the outstanding matters in the recess and to prepare for a common sejm in Parczew. Despite Dembiński's call for the establishment of 'New Poland' a few months earlier, the Poles were conciliatory. Sensing that many of the ordinary nobles in Bielsk were more favourably disposed to closer union than Czarny or Rudy, they conceded on the main points that had scuppered negotiations in February. In return for the Lithuanians accepting that one commonwealth be created on the basis of the Mielnik treaty—which had been found—they agreed that Lithuania was to preserve its title and a separate hierarchy of offices, open only to Lithuanians or Poles resident in the second generation. Joint sejms were to take place alternately in Poland and Lithuania, and the Lithuanians were to be allowed to hold their own sejms on minor matters that only affected the grand duchy. Finally, in a recognition of Lithuanian concerns about incorporation, it was agreed that the execution would not be extended to Lithuania.[11]

Had these concessions been made three months earlier they might have secured agreement. Now, however, the Radziwiłłs were energetically coordinating opposition, and if they could not prevent the proposal being returned to the Polish sejm in Parczew in June, they and their supporters refused to allow it to become a joint sejm. Instead the Poles, who had patiently waited a month in Parczew for the Bielsk sejm to finish, were fobbed off with a small delegation that lacked powers to negotiate. This did not go down well. Despite the failure to conclude the union the Warsaw sejm had agreed 228,000 złoties in taxes, of which over two-thirds were to support the Lithuanian war against Muscovy. The Poles were understandably outraged, and rejected the Bielsk terms as incompatible with the old treaties; the Lithuanians retorted that they would not depart from them in any way, at which point negotiations collapsed amid mutual recriminations and accusations of bad faith.[12]

The atmosphere was soured by published polemics. The Lithuanians had already complained at the insulting tone of Polish pamphlets before the 1564 publication of Orzechowski's *Quincunx*, in which he scornfully rejected the Lithuanian model of a union *aeque principaliter*, scratching off the large scab that had formed over the wound inflicted at Lutsk in 1429. He breezily asserted that Jagiełło had incorporated Lithuania into Poland, adding that Lithuanians, under the hereditary rule of their grand dukes were, like Muscovites, subject to despotism. It was therefore necessary for their grand duke to abandon his hereditary powers; until he did, Lithuania could not be joined to Poland, as one could no more mix the unfree with the free than one could mix fire with water. A Lithuanian, born in a duchy, was in no way equal to a Pole, born in a kingdom. He praised the principle of equality underpinning Polish ideas of nobility, scoffing at the Lithuanians for their

---

[10] Halecki, *Dzieje*, ii, 194.   [11] Halecki, *Dzieje*, ii, 196.
[12] Halecki, *Dzieje*, ii, 192, 198.

subordination to their magnates and implying they were not true nobles. Lithuanians were therefore equal to Poles in nothing at all.[13]

Orzechowski's sharp tone and dismissive treatment of Lithuanians, which probably owed something to his Ruthenian origins, unleashed a storm. The incandescent Czarny commissioned a reply, almost certainly written by the Polish intellectual Augustus Rotundus, born Augustyn Mieleski in 1520 and educated in Wittenberg. Rotundus served in the Polish chancery before moving to Lithuania, where he became one of Czarny's trusted associates and *wójt* of Vilnius. In his *Conversation of a Pole with a Lithuanian*, published anonymously in Polish in 1565 or 1566, he mounted a frontal assault on Orzechowski, attacking his coarse language and pointing out that not all kingdoms were free, or duchies unfree. He briskly surveyed Polish history, lingering on points at which the Poles had behaved badly or shown themselves to be unfree. He castigated them for oppressing the poor, both noble and non-noble, although these words may have been greeted with a hollow laugh by those Lithuanians who had fallen foul of the Radziwiłłs. He condemned the Poles for their lack of order and their failure to obey their kings, asking pointedly why they had not preserved Podolia from Tatar attacks, and mischievously accusing them of oligarchic tendencies.[14]

With regard to union, the Lithuanian rejected the view that his countrymen were too stupid to appreciate the necessity and benefits of unity, stressing that they were reluctant to enter union with such an anarchic people. Quoting Machiavelli's *Prince*, he argued that a hereditary ruler was better than an elected outsider, praised the Jagiellons, and rehearsed the story of the Lithuanians' Roman ancestry, before recounting the magnificent—and largely legendary—genealogy of the Radziwiłłs. While praising unity, the Lithuanian stressed that in unity there should be diversity, stating that he did not see how the Parczew sejm, 'where you are murdering us' could bring about that desired state.[15]

These polemics did not help the union cause, although Sigismund August was able to reduce Radziwiłł power considerably following Czarny's death, aged fifty, in May 1565, which left leadership of the opposition to closer union in the hands of Rudy, a far less able politician. Although Rudy was eventually appointed chancellor and palatine of Vilnius in March 1566, he was deprived of the hetmanship, which was granted to Hrehory Chodkiewicz, long a rival. Jan Chodkiewicz, Hrehory's nephew, was appointed marshal and governor of Livonia, both offices formerly held by Czarny. The power and influence of the chancellor was reduced by Sigismund August's decision to create, on the Polish model, a new post of vice-chancellor. Despite the name, the vice-chancellor, as in Poland, was not subordinate to the grand chancellor, simply taking over responsibility for part of the chancery's burgeoning workload. Sigismund August was careful not to paralyse the operation of the Lithuanian government by appointing a rival to Radziwiłł, nominating

---

[13] Orzechowski, *Quincunx*, 227–37.
[14] *Rozmowa Polaka z Litwinem: 1564*, ed. Józef Korzeniowski (Cracow, 1890), 3, 10–11, 36–7, 41–3.
[15] *Rozmowa Polaka*, 44, 62, 66–8, 77, 80.

Interlude 473

Ostafi Wołłowicz, an associate of Czarny, but the reduction of the chancellor's influence was of considerable importance in the long term.[16]

For all that there remained substantial support for the Bielsk terms, the peremptory Polish rejection of them at Parczew demonstrated that the senate was more conciliatory than the chamber, dominated by executionists, and recalled the arrogant refusal to compromise displayed in Warsaw. No Lithuanians attended the 1565 Piotrków sejm, which continued the work of execution, and was divided by bitter disputes between Catholics and the growing Protestant lobby. A common sejm promised later in the year was postponed, although the Poles again voted generous financial assistance for Lithuania, amounting to some 483,000 złoties, on the promise that a joint sejm would meet at Lublin before Easter 1566. A Polish sejm was duly summoned to Lublin to assemble the day after Easter, but although a Lithuanian sejm was called to Brest, just across the border, it showed no sign of joining the Poles. A small Lithuanian delegation reached Lublin in June, but it was led by Mikołaj Naruszewicz, a Radziwiłł supporter, and its instructions represented a substantial retreat from the Bielsk terms, envisioning only a common election, a common monarch, a common foreign policy, and common sejms only insofar as they dealt with any of the above matters. The Poles were angered at the Lithuanian intransigence; when the 1567 Piotrków sejm passed without any hint of progress on the union, it seemed as if hopes were dying.

Yet if the cause of closer union seemed moribund, the process of unification continued. Although the Radziwiłłs blocked attempts to implement the Bielsk deal in the summer of 1564, they could not prevent the transformation of the grand duchy's institutional structure along broadly Polish lines. In June 1564 the Bielsk sejm discussed amendments to the 1529 Statute. It was well attended by noble representatives, and debate was heated, ensuring that the session lasted much longer than planned.[17] As discussion of the terms of union continued with the Polish delegation, the Radziwiłłs realized that they would have to concede on structural reform to avoid supporters of closer union making it more difficult for them to resist the Polish offer, while Sigismund August saw concessions on the statute as a means to advance the union cause. On 1 July an act was passed establishing local sejmiks and land courts on the Polish model across the grand duchy.[18] Thus began a process of institutional reform that was completed at the Vilnius sejm of 1565–6. The grand duchy ceased in administrative terms to be a composite state, as the old division between Lithuania proper and the annexed Ruthenian territories was swept away in favour of a consolidated and relatively uniform structure.

The 1564 Bielsk statute stripped grand ducal officials of their judicial powers over most civil and property cases, which were to be vested in the new land courts, controlled by elected local officials. They also lost their judicial privileges, which had removed them from the jurisdiction of the local courts. Henceforth, as in Poland, they were to be subject to the land courts on the same basis as other nobles. Sigismund August issued a privilege on 1 June confirming the new statute, which

---

[16] Ferenc, *Rudy*, 291–3.   [17] Любавский, *Сеймъ*, 676.
[18] Любавский, *Сеймъ*, приложенія, no. 48, 133–40.

Table 1. Palatinates and their Districts in the Grand Duchy of Lithuania following the reforms of 1565–6.

Palatinate	Districts		
	Lithuanian	Ruthenian	Polish
Vilnius	Vilnius	Вильна	Wilno
	Ašmena	Ашмена	Oszmiany
	Lida	Лида	Lida
	Ukmergė	Вилькомерж	Wiłkomierz
		Браслав	Brasław
Trakai	Trakai	Троки	Troki
	Gardinas	Гродна (Hrodna)	Grodno
	Kaunas	Ковно	Kowno
	Upytė	Упита	Upita
Volhynia		Луцк (Lutsk)	Łuck
		Володимир (Volodymyr)	Włodzimierz
		Кремянец	Krzemieniec
Navahrudak	Naugardukas	Навагрудак (Navahrudak)	Nowogródek
	Slanimas	Слоним	Słonim
	Volkovysk	Вольковыски	Wołkowysk
Podlasie	Dorohičinas	Дорогичин	Dorohiczyn
	Melnikas	Мельник	Mielnik
	Bielskas	Бельск	Bielsk
Brest	Brestas	Бресть	Brześć Litewski
	Pinskas	Пииск	Pińsk
Kyiv	Kijevas	Київ	Kijów
		Мозир	Mozyr[1]
Vitsebsk	Vitebskas	Вицебск	Witebsk
	Orša	Орша	Orsza
Minsk	Minskas	Миньск	Mińsk
		Речиця	Rzeczyca
Samogitia	Žemaitija	Жмудь	Żmudź
Polatsk	Polockas	Полацк	Połock
Mstislav	Mstislavlis	Мстислаў	Mścisław
Bratslav		Брацлав	Bratsław

[1] Mozyr district was not included in the 1569 incorporation of the Kyiv palatinate. It remained in the grand duchy and was attached to the Minsk palatinate. See Ch. 39, 491.

was to come into force on 11 November, after the new courts were established (see Table 1).[19]

The reforms could not be implemented quite so rapidly, however, as the territorial jurisdiction of the new courts was unclear due to the uneven nature of the traditional administrative structure.[20] It was not until the commission reviewing the 1529 Statute completed its work at the 1565–6 Vilnius sejm with the Second Lithuanian Statute, a more comprehensive codification of Lithuanian law that placed far more stress on the equality of all nobles before the law, that the new

[19] Любавский, Сеймъ, 677–9; Vilimas, *Lietuvos*, 59–62.   [20] Vilimas, *Lietuvos*, 62.

courts could finally begin their operations. The grand duchy was divided into thirteen palatinates and thirty districts, taking account of traditional administrative divisions, but making adjustments to ensure a more uniform structure. All palatinates henceforth had a palatine and a castellan, although Samogitia, protected by its 1440s privileges, gained a castellan, but was not formally converted into a palatinate, with its starosta exercising the equivalent powers.

Each palatinate was divided into between one and five districts according to its size. Every district had a land court, elected by the local nobility. Of the thirteen palatinates, eight had existed before 1565, as had the starosty of Samogitia; the other four—Brest, Bratslav, Minsk, and Mstislav, were created in 1565–6. To establish a more uniform structure, some palatinates and territories were divided. The Brest palatinate was carved out of the southern lands of the palatinate of Trakai, while those of Minsk and Mstislav were formed from the eastern territories of the Vilnius palatinate. The palatinates of Bratslav and Volhynia, were established from the former territories of eastern Podolia and Volhynia (see Table 1).[21]

The reforms transformed Lithuanian politics. The creation of five new palatinates, together with the establishment of the vice-chancellorship, expanded the council considerably, making it harder for one individual or family to dominate. Although the custom of linking the chancellorship with the palatinate of Vilnius continued, the reduction in size of the palatinate, and its division into five districts—with the consequent increase in the number of elected local officials—considerably reduced the palatine's authority. There were similar consequences for the palatinate of Trakai. While the power of the great families was far from broken, politics opened up dramatically. With more offices, there were more potential political patrons available. Magnate politicians had to compete more assertively to win the support of local nobles, and they had to compete politically as well as socially. The creation of three new palatinates in the annexed Ruthenian territories substantially increased the representation of the Ruthenian lands within the grand duchy's administrative structures, thereby consolidating the 1563 grant of full political rights.

The 1566 Statute, which embodied these changes, came into operation on 25 April. It took time for the new administrative structure to bed in: one of the aims of increasing the number of districts was to ensure more efficient deployment of the noble levy, but the merging of the old districts into the new, and the establishment of new borders and new officials brought confusion, and nobles turned out for musterings in lower numbers than usual. Boundary and jurisdictional squabbles were still being aired at the 1568 Hrodna sejm: the Vilnius district was unhappy at its small size, while the Trakai district wanted to annexe part of the Lida district. There were many such disputes, which took time to resolve.[22]

Certain effects of the reforms were immediately apparent. The first sejm to meet under the new statute assembled in Brest on 28 April 1566 and sat for two months. Sigismund August intended it to prepare the way for union, but the new sejmiks

---

[21] Лаппо, *Великое княжество*, 58.
[22] Лаппо, *Великое Княжество*, 62–4, 68–9; Любавский, *Сеймъ*, 805–5.

were only summoned for 10 April, instead of four weeks beforehand, as was supposed to happen. Discussions focused entirely on taxation, the military situation, the consequences of the reforms, and the problems that had arisen in their aftermath. There was no time to speak of the union. Nevertheless, for the first time a Lithuanian sejm had assembled on the Polish model, with the grand duke issuing his programme for discussion at the sejmiks. Envoys were furnished with instructions on the Polish pattern, instead of learning of the grand duke's proposals only on arrival at the sejm, and the preparation of instructions in advance increased the coherence of debates.[23]

A small delegation was sent to Lublin, where the Polish sejm was waiting. The Poles were annoyed at the delegation's instructions, which agreed to common sejms and common elections, but insisted on the maintenance of separate Lithuanian offices, and demanded that the grand duchy's dignity be preserved.[24] If this suggested that no progress had been made since Bielsk, the context was again changing. 1567 passed under the shadow of increased Muscovite military activity, and saw the failure of a plan to attack Muscovy in order to exploit the political chaos unleashed when Ivan IV launched his bloody *Oprichnina*. The Lithuanian levy gathered in June near Radoshkoviche, north of Minsk, to mount an invasion of Muscovy intended to exploit its internal turmoil and recover lands lost between 1492 and 1514. 27,597 men were registered, supplemented by 6,500 professionals, but the nobles answered the summons slowly, and were still drifting in to the camp in early January 1568. Sigismund August did not turn up until late September, while the passivity of the Lithuanian commanders and problems with paying the professionals meant that the force sat at Radoshkoviche inactive for months. In January, with desertion rife, it was disbanded.[25]

The Radoshkoviche fiasco demonstrated that even in the most favourable of circumstances the Lithuanians were incapable of fighting Muscovy alone, and left Rudy in a weak position when Sigismund August returned to the issue of union with renewed vigour in 1568. He summoned a Lithuanian sejm to Hrodna in May 1568, urging the Lithuanians to attend a common sejm in Lublin. The Lithuanians replied that they wanted closer union, but would only enter it as free men, without coercion.[26] Sigismund August refused to give up. On 20 October he summoned the Lithuanian sejmiks for 11 November. After their discussions, they were to assemble on the border before proceeding to Lublin, where the joint sejm was to open on 23 December.[27] This time the invitation was accepted. Radoshkoviche had persuaded Rudy that new talks on the union were necessary to ensure continuing Polish aid. Sejmiks met across Lithuania to discuss the royal proposals. This time, the Lithuanians turned up. When the sejm closed on 12 August 1569, the union had been transformed.

[23] Любавский, *Сеймъ*, 732–3, 738–45.   [24] Любавский, *Сеймъ*, 745–6.
[25] Kazimierz Piwarski, 'Niedoszła wyprawa t zw. radoszkowicka Zygmunta Augusta na Moskwę w r. 1567-8' *AW*, 4 (1927) 252–86; 5 (1928), 85–119; Stanisław Bodniak, 'Z wyprawy radoszkowickiej na Moskwę w roku 1567/8', *AW*, 7 (1930); Ferenc, *Rudy*, 309–15; Янушкевіч, *Вялікае княства*, 104, 147–53.
[26] Любавский, *Сеймъ*, 795.   [27] Любавский, *Сеймъ*, 815.

39

Lublin

The prospects did not seem good when the Poles gathered in Lublin on the appointed day of 23 December 1568. The Lithuanian sejm assembled in Hrodna before moving to the border town of Wohyń. It only agreed to travel to Lublin after Sigismund August issued a safe-conduct, on Rudy's insistence, on 21 December. It was necessary, since some Lithuanian sejmiks had issued their envoys with instructions forbidding them to attend a sejm outside Lithuania's borders. Sigismund August stated that the common sejm would nevertheless be legal, pledging that no union would be finalized without the agreement of both parties, that Lithuania's laws, privileges, and liberties would be honoured, and that the Lithuanians would be free to return home if union were not agreed.[1]

Rudy had no intention of renouncing the view of the union defended so tenaciously by Czarny at the Warsaw sejm. The Lithuanians arrived in Lublin on 31 December, demonstrating their sense of purpose by refusing to enter negotiations until Sigismund August confirmed the 1566 statute, which he politely refused to do, since it contained a clause banning Poles from owning land or appointment to office in the grand duchy, a point conceded at Warsaw and, if not so generously, at Bielsk. The Polish sejm formally opened on 10 January with the election of the experienced executionist Stanisław Czarnkowski as speaker, but the Poles were frustrated by the Lithuanian insistence that the two sejms should meet separately and negotiations should take place between deputations. Thus although there were occasional joint sessions, there was no truly common sejm. The early discussions did not bode well. Whereas at Warsaw the Lithuanians had accepted Mielnik as a basis for negotiation, they now stated that they no longer wished to return to any of the previous treaties of union, but wanted to start negotiations from scratch. Rudy rejected the Warsaw recess, and when Padniewski complained that the clause in the new Lithuanian statute banning Poles from owning land in Lithuania was in breach of previous agreements, he replied that 'one body' should not preclude the continued existence of 'two commonwealths', urging that a wholly new union treaty be prepared (see Figs 14 and 15).[2]

Having learned from the failure to reach agreement in 1564, Polish senators were inclined to moderation. Proposals drawn up by the senate on 3 February 1569 accepted separate Lithuanian offices, a common sejm only for discussion of

---

[1] *AU*, no. 95, 189–92. Halecki, *Dzieje*, ii, 255; Ferenc, *Rudy*, 329–30. Dembkowski, misreading the place of its issue, misleadingly calls it the 'Volhynian charter': *Union*, 137–8.
[2] Halecki, *Dzieje*, ii, 258–9; Ferenc, *Rudy*, 331–3.

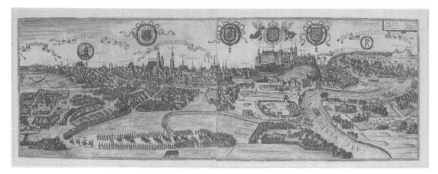

Fig 14. View of Cracow from the north-west by Abraham Hogenberg, c.1603–5. With the kind permission of the Muzeum Historii Polski.

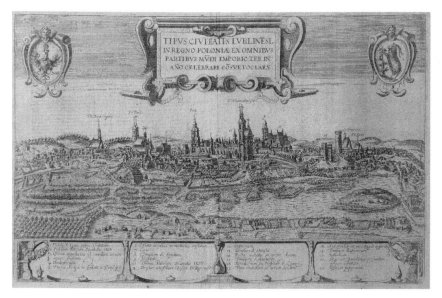

Fig 15. View of Lublin in the sixteenth century. With the kind permission of the Zamek Królewski, Warsaw.

common matters and foreign affairs, the preservation of the title of grand duke, and the redrafting of Sigismund August's 1564 declaration on the union so that his cession of his hereditary rights would be made to the commonwealth of both nations, instead of to the *corona regni Poloniae*. In return, the only concession requested was the repeal of the ban on Poles holding land and office in Lithuania.[3]

The chamber was less accommodating. Although some were inclined to moderation, radicals, led by the Cracow envoys, argued that union had already been

---

[3] Halecki, *Dzieje*, ii, 261–2.

agreed; all that was required was for it to be executed on the basis of the old acts. The chamber's refusal to allow any hint of a separate grand duchy destroyed chances of early agreement. The reluctant Padniewski was forced to defend this hard-line position. In an erudite speech on 12 February he gently criticized the Lithuanians for abandoning Mielnik, which they had accepted as a basis for negotiation in 1564.[4] Despite his willingness to accommodate many Lithuanian demands, he conceded nothing with regard to the nature of the union. He argued that neither side could break the union without the agreement of the other party, maintaining that Jagiełło and Vytautas had incorporated Lithuania into the *corona regni*: 'so that it was already not a *foederatus populus*, but one realm, one people, one council, under one lord'. As a sign of this unity Jagiełło had granted full rights and freedoms to the Lithuanian nobles to ensure that all were equal before the law and enjoyed equal liberty so that, being part of one body, there were no discrepancies.[5] Padniewski could offer the Lithuanians little in the proposals, which began by quoting the clause in Mielnik stating that Poland and Lithuania constituted one uniform, indivisible body according to the act of incorporation. No divisions were to be allowed within this body politic. Elections were to be common, there was to be no separate coronation of the grand duke, and no separate name for the grand duchy. Separate Lithuanian offices were to be allowed, but they were to be open to Poles, who were also to be allowed to acquire land in Lithuania. Otherwise, all signs of duality were to be effaced.[6]

Unsurprisingly, Jan Chodkiewicz rejected the proposals on 15 February. He stated that the Lithuanians did not conceive the union as broadly as the Poles, suggesting that it should be seen as one of allies and friends. He stressed the need for equality between the two peoples, and said that the insistence on incorporation was not a sign of love or fraternity.[7] The Lithuanian proposals maintained all the symbols of Lithuania's status as a separate realm: the continuation of the title of grand duke, separate coronations, a separate seal, and separate offices to which only Lithuanians would have access. They offered rather more than a simple personal union and alliance, which is how Halecki presented them, but they retreated from the position adopted at Warsaw, and were flatly rejected.[8]

Thereafter negotiations became bogged down. In interminable sessions documents were read out and speaker after speaker rambled on with his own views about what they signified. Potted history lessons were proffered and contested; at one point the anonymous diarist wrote wearily that he had not recorded all the speeches of the senators '*propter prolixitatem*'.[9] On 20 February Sigismund August intervened, frustrated by the lack of progress and aware that his intervention in

---

[4] Дневник Люблинского сейма 1569 года: Соединение Великаго Княжества Литовского с Королевством Польским, изд. М. Коялович (St Petersburg, 1869), 56–66 [*Dnevnik*].
[5] *Dnevnik*, 58, 63.
[6] 'Script uniei, ktori podano panom Litewskim, wedlie ządoscи ich od senatu i od poslow koronnich, przez xiedza biskupa Krakowskiego spysany, a przez posli scorigowany': *Dnevnik*, 68–73; Halecki, *Dzieje*, ii, 264–6.
[7] *Dnevnik*, 74–8; Halecki, *Dzieje*, ii, 266. [8] *Dnevnik*, 79–88; Halecki, *Dzieje*, ii, 266–7.
[9] *Dnevnik*, 52.

1564 had come too late. He met the Lithuanians in secret sessions, and when he failed to secure acceptance of the Polish terms, secretly promised the Polish envoys on Saturday 26 February that he would order a joint session of both sejms on the Monday.

No such session took place. After news of the Saturday session leaked out, Rudy and Chodkiewicz demanded that the Lithuanians be permitted to debate separately. When Sigismund August refused, ordering them to attend a joint session on Tuesday morning, Rudy, fearing that the moment that Czarny had predicted had arrived and that the king would enforce concessions, decided he had heard enough. That night, led by Rudy, most Lithuanians hurried from Lublin, leaving behind vice-chancellor Ostafi Wołłowicz and treasurer Mikołaj Naruszewicz as observers.[10]

The chasm between the two sides seemed unbridgeable. Rudy told Roman Sangushko that he wished to preserve the grand duchy, and did not want to see it incorporated into Poland, adding that Sigismund August had decided to give Lithuania to Poland, and was treating the Lithuanians like slaves.[11] Rudy's exasperation is understandable, but he had only himself to blame. The two sides had teetered on the brink of an agreement in 1564, but the optimism generated by Chashniki had long since evaporated. As the Radoshkoviche fiasco confirmed, Lithuania desperately needed Polish aid, and it was clear that the Poles were not willing to offer it without agreement on the union. They had a point. Between 1561 and 1570 the Polish treasury contributed over 2,000,000 złoties to sustain the Lithuanian war against Muscovy, raising 300 companies of professional soldiers. The professional army of 3,500 cavalry and 3,910 infantry sent to aid Lithuania in the autumn and winter of 1563–4 had cost in pay alone 159,365 złoties, or seventy-two per cent of the revenues from the taxes voted by the 1562–3 sejm. With a great effort the Lithuanians raised 6,500 professional soldiers of their own, but the revenues of the Lithuanian treasury between 1561 and 1566 amounted to 2,631,505 Polish złoties, or around 550,000 złoties per annum. Arrears of pay amounted to 161,648 złoties, $3^{1}/_{2}$ groszy. The Poles were aware of the problems the Lithuanians had in paying their professional troops, as many disgruntled and unpaid officers turned up in Lublin to complain and lobby for their pay.[12]

It was not unreasonable for the Poles to seek closer union to ensure that greater control could be exercised over the Lithuanian council, whose decision it had been to declare war. Yet Rudy decided that the Lithuanians could return to first principles and renegotiate the union from scratch, ignoring all previous agreements. It is difficult to imagine that the politically astute Czarny, for all that he shared his cousin's aversion to union on Polish terms, would have adopted such an unrealistic strategy. Czarny had proved himself an adroit parliamentarian; Rudy, accustomed

---

[10] Halecki, *Dzieje*, ii, 272–4.   [11] Ferenc, *Rudy*, 336–7.
[12] Henryk Lulewicz, *Gniewów o unię ciąg dalszy: Stosunki polsko-litewskie w latach 1569–1588* (Warsaw, 2002), 31–2; Kazimierz Pułaski, 'Sprawa o zapłatę zaległego żołdu rotom zaciężnym za Zygmunta Augusta', in Pułaski, *Szkice i poszukiwania historyczne*, serya iii (Cracow, 1906), 200–7; Jerzy Urwanowicz, *Wojskowe 'sejmiki': Koła w wojsku Rzeczypospolitej XVI–XVII wieku* (Białystok, 1996), 75.

to the deferential proceedings of the Lithuanian sejm, was unprepared for the rumbustious cut-and-thrust of Polish parliamentary debate, and had no idea how to finesse the wretched hand he held. A letter from Wołłowicz to Sangushko suggests that the withdrawal was under consideration from early February, shortly after negotiations had begun, which suggests that Rudy was already short of ideas.[13]

The midnight flit backfired spectacularly. Sigismund August was furious. The clandestine departure, without taking formal leave of the king, was construed as disrespectful by king and sejm alike.[14] Yet for all the outrage, it was not unexpected. The Lithuanians had unilaterally withdrawn from negotiations in 1564 when in a much stronger negotiating position; it had taken them five years to return to the table. Neither Sigismund August nor the Poles could wait any longer. The king was in poor health throughout the Lublin sejm, constantly taking medicine and at times confined to his quarters and unable to take part in the proceedings on account of 'stones'.[15] Time might be short, and the rapid Polish response to the Lithuanian departure suggests that strategies had been prepared for just such an eventuality.

By withdrawing, Rudy risked unilateral Polish action. For the majority in the chamber, the union had already been agreed; all that remained was for it to be executed, and execution of the union was precisely what the radicals demanded: as Stanisław Sobek, castellan of Sandomierz, put it, the king should ensure that the union existed in fact, and not just on paper.[16] The hotheads claimed that in defying royal authority the Lithuanians were rebels, and deserved to be treated *in contumaciam*. Those that had departed should be punished, the 1566 statute should be annulled, and some called for the use of force.[17]

Moderate voices prevailed, however. Instead of embarking on an execution of the accessory union that might have unleashed civil war, the senators and the king targeted the Lithuanians' weakest point. Responding to demands made from the floor of the chamber, they revived an issue placed in cold storage in the 1450s: the Polish claims to Podlasie and Volhynia. So long as the Poles had sought to persuade the Lithuanians to accept their concept of accessory union they had not been inclined to raise the matter, since Podlasie and Volhynia, like the rest of the grand duchy, were regarded as an integral part of the unitary union state. Now that the Lithuanians had again rejected an accessory union, calls for their annexation were embodied in the fifteen action points drawn up by the senate on the evening of 1 March. They declared that the Lithuanians had committed a rebellious and contumacious act, and that clauses in the 1566 statute conflicting with the acts of union should be repealed. Podlasie and Volhynia, on the basis of old privileges, belonged to the Polish crown, and all office-holders and citizens in the two provinces were to take an oath of loyalty to it. A guarantee was issued that the execution of the royal domain was not to be effected in either province. The king immediately confirmed the proposals. Stating that 'in every commonwealth the

---

[13] Halecki, *Dzieje*, ii, 274; Halecki, *Przyłączenie Podlasia, Wołynia i Kijowszczyzny do Korony w roku 1569* (Cracow, 1915), 10.
[14] *Dnevnik*, 123; Halecki, *Przyłączenie*, 11–12.   [15] *Dnevnik*, 502.
[16] *ŻDU*, iii, 66.   [17] *Dnevnik*, 122–3.

most vital consideration is to ensure that we never adopt the most extreme of remedies', he declared his support for the immediate annexation of Podlasie and Volhynia by the Polish crown. It was approved on 3 March after a stormy debate, in which radicals called for the incorporation of the whole grand duchy. Separate privileges of incorporation for Podlasie and Volhynia were promulgated two days later. The annexation of Volhynia also covered the palatinate of Bratslav, formed from what had been eastern Podolia in 1564–5.[18]

It was a shrewd strategy. As the Poles were aware, despite the common front presented by Rudy and the Lithuanian lords before their departure from Lublin, there were serious divisions below the surface. Most of the Lithuanians left with Rudy, but the withdrawal was controversial. Although Chodkiewicz had loyally supported Rudy in the sejm's early phases, as he headed away from Lublin through Wołyń, he wrote to Sigismund August blaming Rudy for the departure. Wołłowicz, who remained in Lublin, wrote of his unease to Czarny's son Mikołaj Krzysztof 'Sierotka' (the Orphan), and continued to talk to both king and sejm.[19]

It was now that the significance of the 1564–6 reforms became clear. The establishment of sejmiks across the grand duchy provided a new forum for political activity at the local level. The Vitsebsk petition had revealed considerable support among the ordinary nobility for closer union, while even if the Lithuanian envoys in Lublin had remained largely passive before the departure, some had been furnished with instructions which suggest that the ordinary nobility did not all support Rudy's position. The instructions from Samogitia—where there was a sizeable and voluble population of middling and lesser nobles—and from Volhynia and Podlasie granted their envoys plenipotentiary powers, commanding them not to return until union was complete.[20]

The generally favourable attitude of the Volhynian and, particularly, the Podlasian szlachta towards closer union was well known. The Podlasians had long been inclined to a closer relationship. Polish law had extended its influence over the province since the 1440s, and there had been frequent requests from the local nobility that official documents be drawn up in Polish, since so few could read Ruthenian in the elaborate chancery Cyrillic in which they were written. Podlasian envoys at the 1565–6 Lithuanian sejm had urged Sigismund August to call a common sejm. When Rudy ordered the Lithuanians to leave Lublin, only two of the Podlasian envoys—both supporters of closer union—did so; the other four remained in accordance with their instructions.[21]

Thus the prospects for Podlasie accepting incorporation were good. The decision to incorporate Volhynia was more risky, since it raised the issue of the position of

---

[18] *Dnevnik*, 124–30; *ŻDU*, iii, 62–7; *AU*, no. 96, 193–6; no. 97, 196–207; *VC*, ii/i, 216–26; Halecki, *Przyłączenie*, 26–31, 57–8; Karol Mazur, 'Szlachta wołyńska wobec unii jagiellońskiej w dobie sejmu lubelskiego 1569 r.', *PH*, 95/1 (2004), 38.
[19] Halecki, *Dzieje*, ii, 274–5.
[20] Lulewicz, *Gniewów ciąg dalszy*, 19.
[21] Dorota Michaluk, 'Inkorporacja Podlasia do Korony Królestwa Polskiego w 1569 r.', in Glemža and Šmigelskytė-Stukienė (eds), *Liublino unija*, 147; Halecki, *Przyłączenie*, 32.

the Ruthenian annexed territories within the grand duchy. There were signs, however, that the risk might be worth taking, not least because of the attitude of the leading Volhynian princes, who enjoyed considerable prestige and authority. The wealthiest and most powerful was Kostiantyn Vasyl Ostrozky (1524/5–1608), son of the victor of Orsha. Ostrozky sought to mediate between the Lithuanians and the Poles in the early exchanges at Lublin, and his favourable attitude was noted by the Poles. He remained in Lublin after the Lithuanian departure together with another Volhynian prince, Stefan Zbarazky, palatine of Trakai. Although his ostensible reason for staying was to pursue a private case concerning his claim, through his wife Zofia Tarnowska, to the Polish city of Tarnów, his refusal to leave was significant. He kept his distance, turning down an invitation to meet the king on 3 March on the grounds of illness, and leaving Lublin the day after the promulgation of the incorporation edict, but he did not return to Lithuania, remaining in Tarnów, not far from Lublin, and staying in contact with his friend Sebastian Mielecki, castellan of Cracow. On 29 March he wrote to Sigismund August denying rumours that he was negotiating with the Lithuanians.[22]

On 8 March Sigismund August promulgated decrees ordering Podlasian and Volhynian envoys and office-holders to take their seats in the Polish sejm, and commanding all holders of royal land in both palatinates to swear oaths of loyalty to him and to the Polish crown: the Podlasians were to swear by 27 March; the Volhynians were given until April 3.[23] The critical point had been reached. For these decrees, while directed to the nobility of both provinces, also affected many Lithuanian magnates who held royal lands there, particularly in Podlasie, including Rudy himself, his nephew Sierotka, and Wołłowicz. Sigismund August and the Poles were testing the extent of support for closer union among the ordinary nobility, and the solidarity of the council elite.

The challenge revealed that Rudy had no alternative strategy, and that his support was far from solid. That the Polish reaction took him by surprise merely demonstrates his political naïvety.[24] Encouraged by the initial failure of the Podlasians and Volhynians to obey the king's orders, he summoned leading Lithuanian politicians to Vilnius around 20 March, including Chodkiewicz, Wołłowicz, Wiktoryn Wierzbicki, bishop of Lutsk, Paweł Sapieha, palatine of Navahrudak, Havrylo Hornostai, palatine of Minsk, and Hrehory Wołłowicz, castellan of Navahrudak. Rudy hoped they would support resistance to the annexations; instead he was blamed for the Polish response to the withdrawal. Chodkiewicz, backed by Protasiewicz, who had been too ill to travel to Lublin, criticized the move, urging a more moderate approach. Rudy was defeated. It was agreed that Chodkiewicz should lead a new delegation to Lublin to reopen talks. Rudy's strategy was abandoned; instead the delegation would accept the old treaties as a basis for discussion and revive the old policy of attempting to remove from them

---

[22] Kempa, *Ostrogski*, 46–7; Tomasz Kempa, 'Możnowładztwo i szlachta z Wołynia wobec unii lubelskiej (1569)', in Glemža and Šmigelskytė-Stukienė (eds), *Liublino Unija*, 178; Halecki, *Przyłączenie*, 44–7.
[23] *AU*, no. 98; no. 99, 207–9.   [24] Ferenc, *Rudy*, 337.

phrases deemed disrespectful to Lithuania. The instructions resumed the language of Mielnik, endorsing the idea of the union forming 'one indivisible body' but sought to preserve a separate identity for the grand duchy. They were permeated by a sense of realism. In many points they agreed with the moderate Polish proposals prepared by the senate in February. Lithuania's separate identity was to be preserved by various means. Although the instructions accepted a common election and one coronation, the king was to swear to maintain the privileges of both realms in a document to which both the Polish and Lithuanian seals were to be attached. The only major point of difference was the insistence upon the continuation of separate Lithuanian sejms for matters other than royal elections, defence, and foreign policy. Rudy refused to sign the instructions, but he had nothing left to offer. Sierotka was to be one of the envoys, to ensure that Radziwiłł interests would be defended, but Rudy was isolated and defeated.[25]

The envoys, Chodkiewicz, Sierotka, and Paweł Pac, castellan of Vitsebsk, did not, however, hurry back to Lublin, thereby losing any chance of regaining the initiative. It was probably too late in any case. Although the deadlines for recognizing the annexations had passed without any mass taking of the oaths, three Podlasian deputies—Adam Kosiński and Mikołaj Bujno, both of Mazovian descent, and Kasper Irzykowicz, from a family of well-connected Lithuanian lords—swore as early as 8 March, although Irzykowicz did so reluctantly, fearful of the threat of confiscation; another, Aleksander Hincza, swore two days later. Mikołaj Kiszka, starosta of Drohiczyn, from a magnate family was another supporter of annexation, while deputations from the Podlasian towns of Bielsk and Brańsk—who had not been summonsed—appeared unexpectedly to swear on 29 March.[26]

The Volhynian response was more cautious. As yet all that had arrived from Volhynia were stacks of letters excusing the failure of various officials to swear the oaths, most pleading illness.[27] The incorporation decree reached Volhynia on 16 March, and the initial response came in a petition drafted in Lutsk on 29 March. It expressed surprise that the annexation decree was written in Polish and sent under the crown, not the Lithuanian, seal. It stressed that Volhynia had never belonged to Poland and that the Volhynian nobility had always sworn loyalty to Sigismund August and his predecessors as grand dukes of Lithuania. While the signatories had nothing against brotherly love with the Poles, they stressed that they could not obey the king without the permission of all estates and citizens of Volhynia, and asked him to summon a sejmik 'of this realm of Volhynia' (*тохож панства . . . земли волинской*). As honest men, equal in their rights, they rejected unity with the Polish szlachta on the basis of a decree, and asked the king to act as guardian of their honour and reputation. There was a similar reaction from Bratslav nobles, who wrote to their palatine, Roman Sangushko, on 28 March expressing their concern

---

[25] Halecki, *Dzieje*, 294–5; Halecki, *Przyłączenie*, 94–110; Ferenc, *Rudy*, 342–3.
[26] *AU*, nos. 116–7, 227–8; Michaluk, 'Inkorporacja', 151; Halecki, *Przyłączenie*, 47–8.
[27] Halecki, 117.

at the decree, and asking that he bring troops to defend them, since they feared Polish attacks.[28]

The letter expressed a certain dislike and distrust of Poles, and it, together with the Volhynian petition, has been used to challenge the assumption of Halecki—who did not know the petition—and other Polish historians that the ordinary Ruthenian nobility supported closer union. While Halecki certainly exaggerates the extent of support for the annexation, Kiaupienė's assertion that the Volhynian petition and the Bratslav letter prove that 'the political nation of the grand duchy' opposed the partition of its territory is even more of an over-statement.[29] These sources demonstrate that the initial reaction to the Polish decrees in Volhynia was cautious. Yet it is by no means clear how representative the documents are. The letter from Bratslav was signed by four local officials, and the seals of several other nobles were attached to it, but it is impossible to determine the extent to which it reflected wider attitudes, and Kiaupienė's attempt to use the petition to dismiss Halecki's evidence that royal officials testified to a rapturous reception in Volhynia to the incorporation is unconvincing.[30] It is unlikely that royal officials would have deliberately misrepresented the situation when the stakes were so high. Some were undoubtedly more enthusiastic than others, but the overall reaction was one of caution rather than outright acceptance or rejection. As for the petition, Mazur suggests that it was drawn up at 'some kind of sejmik', but sejmiks could only be summoned by the king, and it is likely that it was a less formal meeting, probably called by Aleksander Chortorysky, palatine of Volhynia, while the traditional formula that it was drawn up in the name of the 'palatine, princes, lords, starostas, officials and the whole knightly estate of the palatinate of Volhynia' is no guarantee that it was truly representative.[31] In 2004, Mazur suggested that the petition showed that 'the nobility of Volhynia or at least a significant part of it' rejected the annexation and was closely linked to the Lithuanian opposition to union, but was later more cautious, arguing that the petition showed that 'the Volhynian nobles, like the Volhynian princes, were playing for time, not wishing to break either with the king or with the Lithuanians'.[32]

This suggestion is far more convincing. The princes remained politically significant in Volhynia, and the petition was taken to Lublin by three clients of Ostrozky, whose attitude was crucial, since he controlled just under a third of the land in Volhynia.[33] Initially the Volhynian princes adopted a studied neutrality. Ostrozky

---

[28] Karol Mazur, 'Nieznana petycja szlachty wołyńskiej do króla w dobie sejmu lubelskiego 1569 r.', in *Соціум. Альманах соціальної історії*, вип 2 (Kyiv, 2003), 41–56. The surviving copy was probably the version sent to Sanguszko: Mazur, 'Nieznana', 43, 50; Mazur, 'Szlachta wołyńska', 41–2, 46–7. The letter of the Bratslav nobles was published in Zygmunt Radzimiński, *Xiążę Roman Federowicz Sanguszko wobec unii lubelskiej 1569 r.* (Lwów, 1911), 11.
[29] Jūratė Kiaupienė, 'Lietuvos Didžiosios Kunigaikštystės teritorinio vientisumo suardymo 1569 m.', in Glemža and Šmigelskytė-Stukienė (eds), *Liublino Unija*, 110–11.
[30] Kiaupienė, 'Lietuvos Didžiosios Kunigaikštystės', 102–13; cf. Halecki, *Przyłączenie*, 87–8.
[31] Kempa, 'Możnowładztwo', 179–80.
[32] Mazur, 'Szlachta', 42–3; Karol Mazur, *W stronę integracji z Koroną. Sejmiki Wołynia i Ukrainy w latach 1569–1648* (Warsaw, 2006), 34.
[33] Яковенко, *Шляхта*, 66; Kempa, 'Możnowładztwo', 181; Mazur, 'Nieznana', 45–6.

did not travel to Vilnius in March, but he and other princes kept in touch with the Lithuanians, and sought to coordinate their actions with the delegation from Vilnius, which returned to Lublin on 4 April, only to find the Poles standing firm.[34] The Bratslav letter suggests that local nobles were reluctant to take a position until they knew the attitude of the princes. In a rapidly developing political crisis it would have been rash to commit to one side or the other until the options were clear. Although the princes remained in touch with the Lithuanians, the petition's demand that the king call a separate sejm in which the Poles would meet with the Volhynians on the border suggests a willingness to negotiate with the Poles directly. Volhynians had sworn oaths to the grand duchy, to which they had a residual loyalty, but they had also sworn oaths to the king. They intended to make up their own minds.[35]

It was not just Podlasians and Volhynians who had to choose. After the Lithuanian departure the sejm, with wind in its sails and time on its hands, confronted another long-standing concern, taking decisive action to execute the 1454 incorporation of Prussia. As in previous years, a healthy number of Prussians, both senators and ordinary nobles, were in Lublin, to observe the sejm and ensure that Prussian interests were not compromised. On 16 March Sigismund August ordered them to take their seats in the sejm, although representatives of the cities were denied places, and Georg Kleefeldt, the mayor of Danzig was arrested on a charge of *lèse-majesté* in a long-running dispute over Sigismund August's desire to establish a privateer fleet on the Baltic. Remarkably, it was the Prussian senators who accepted the invitation without complaint, and it was the representatives of the ordinary nobility who protested, although in the light of the attitude of the Prussian senators, there was little that they could do. Since the 1520s the creation of a common currency and the convergence of Royal Prussian interests in trade and international relations since the outbreak of the Livonian War had sapped resistance to formally joining the sejm, where matters concerning Royal Prussia were frequently discussed. Jan Kostka, the Lutheran castellan of Danzig, was a particularly eager supporter of political integration; once the Prussians took up their seats he spoke frequently in the debates on the Lithuanian union, urging the Lithuanians to follow the Prussian example.[36]

The Prussians joined those Podlasians who had sworn the oath in the chamber of envoys, and the pressure on the Lithuanians grew. The dispute over the incorporation of Podlasie and Volhynia was holding up progress on the wider union, and it was increasingly unclear if Sigismund August's bold gamble would pay off. The deadlines for the swearing of oaths was extended, to 24 April for the Podlasians and to 14 May for the Volhynians, but with no significant response. Sigismund August was forced to issue a third decree to the Podlasians on 23 April, a day before the

---

[34] Mazur, 'Nieznana', 49.   [35] Kempa, 'Możnowładztwo', 179–80.
[36] Małłek, 'Stany', 77; Karin Friedrich, 'Citizenship in the periphery: Royal Prussia and the union of Lublin 1569', in Karin Friedrich and Barbara Pendzich (eds), *Citizenship and Identity in a Multinational Commonwealth, 1550–1772* (Leiden, 2009), 58–9.

deadline expired.³⁷ He was under pressure from the envoys, who insisted that all who failed to swear should be punished without exception, singling out Sierotka, as Wołłowicz wrote to Rudy. The king therefore applied some carefully targeted pressure. On 2 May, *pour encourager les autres* he deprived Vasily Tyshkevych and Hryhory Tryzna, respectively palatine and castellan of Podlasie, of their offices, appointing Mikołaj Kiszka and Adam Kosiński, both of whom had taken the oath, in their place. It was a clever move. Tyshkevych and Tryzna were opponents of closer union, both were of Lithuanian-Ruthenian descent, and neither were natives of Podlasie. They were unpopular among the local nobility, and their removal was widely applauded. Their demotion demonstrated that the king was serious.³⁸

Having made his point, Sigismund August called fresh Lithuanian sejmiks for 10 May and extended the deadline to 22 May. Commissioners were sent to Podlasie and Volhynia to collect oaths on the spot, with considerable success. A stream of Podlasians began arriving in Lublin to take the oath, and a large number of Volhynians appeared on 23 May, a day after the deadline, having secured assurances that they would be treated as equals. The dismissals of Tyshkevych and Tryzna had had the desired effect. The first to appear were Piotr Zbarazky, son of the palatine of Trakai, Vasily Zahorovsky, and Wiktoryn Wierzbicki, bishop of Lutsk, who, despite being a Pole, made a point by replying to Sigismund August's decree in Ruthenian.³⁹ The mass appearance of the Volhynians on 23 May was due to the fact that Ostrozky had finally made up his mind; after due consideration, he chose union with Poland. He arrived in Lublin on 23 May together with three other princes: Aleksander Chortorysky, Kostiantyn Vyshnevetsky, and Bohush Koretsky. The next day he apologized for his late arrival, and swore loyalty to the king and the *corona regni*. Koretsky apologized for the convenient illnesses that had prevented so many from coming earlier and publicly accepted the Polish view that 'the realms (*państwa*) of Podlasie and Volhynia' belonged legally to Poland. Chortorysky asked that the dignity and status of the princely families be maintained, as did Vyshnevetsky, who asserted that the Ruthenian nation was equal in nobility to all others. They all swore after receiving assurances concerning the equality of the Volhynian nobles with their Polish counterparts and a promise that the execution of the royal domain would not apply to Volhynia.⁴⁰

Podlasian consent to incorporation was not altogether surprising, but the Volhynian acceptance of incorporation was quite another matter. Volhynia was the most developed and most populous province in the southern Ruthenian lands. It was here, rather than in Kyiv, that Orthodox Ruthenian culture had thrived, and the princely families had done much to keep the flame burning. Ostrozky, like his father, had long been loyal to Lithuania, but he was a Ruthenian, and he regarded Rus' as his *patria*. Like his father, he had close links to the royal court in Cracow;

---

³⁷ Halecki, *Dzieje*, ii, 304.
³⁸ *Dnevnik*, 335; Halecki, *Dzieje*, ii, 305–7. After a decent interval the unfortunate victims were appointed palatine and castellan of Smolensk, which was under Muscovite occupation, but which at least restored them to the senate.
³⁹ Kempa, 'Możnowładztwo', 181; Halecki, *Dzieje*, ii, 307.
⁴⁰ *Dnevnik*, 377–85; Kempa, 'Możnowładztwo', 181.

like his father he spoke and corresponded in Polish. His wife, Zofia Tarnowska, was from one of the most powerful Polish magnate families; her father was Jan Tarnowski, with whom Ostrozky's father had defended Rus' against the Tatars. Like his father, Ostrozky had spent his life poised between Poland and Lithuania. In the end Lithuania could not command enough of his loyalty. Orthodox Ruthenians had been granted equality before the law in 1434, but they had only secured full political rights in 1563 through an exercise of the royal prerogative, not an act of the Lithuanian sejm. The Catholic Lithuanian elite had been prepared to tolerate them and even extend the hand of friendship, but an invisible web of prejudice and condescension had confined all but the greatest princely families to the margins of power outside Volhynia itself. Incorporation into Poland would efface the political borders that had divided the southern Ruthenian lands since the fourteenth century. In 1569 Ostrozky kept his distance from both sides, but when forced to decide, he opted for Poland. When Ostrozky chose, the Volhynians followed *en masse*.[41]

The dam broke. As the Podlasians and Volhynians voted with their feet, Lithuanians with property in the two provinces rushed to avoid the fate of Tyshkevych and Tryzna. On 26 May Ostafi Wołłowicz, who had defended the grand duchy skilfully, tenaciously, and almost single-handedly after Rudy's departure, capitulated. Sigismund August raised him to the palatinate of Trakai, but he was defiant to the last. In a speech to the sejm he stressed that he had remained loyal to the decisions taken by the Lithuanian council, and stated that he was swearing the oath only with regard to his properties in Podlasie and Volhynia, and not 'on the side of the grand duchy of Lithuania'.[42]

Where Wołłowicz led, others followed. One by one, the great Lithuanian lords, preserved their Podlasian and Volhynian property by taking the oath. Sierotka swore on 1 June.[43] Rudy refused to come to Lublin, but Sigismund August knew better than to punish him. The Lithuanian sejmiks had been summoned for 10 May, and the envoys were supposed to reach Lublin by Whitsun, although by early June only Jan Chodkiewicz and a few others had arrived. They faced a nasty shock. For the annexations were not over. On Saturday 28 May Czarnkowski, marshal of the chamber, presented evidence that 'Kyiv and its whole realm' had always belonged to the Polish crown; the king should therefore require the palatine of Kyiv—Kostiantyn Ostrozky—to take his seat in the senate.[44] The request came not from the Poles, but from the Volhynian and Bratslav envoys, who took their seats around May 27. The idea of annexing Kyiv along with Volhynia and Podolia had appeared in a document drawn up by vice chancellor Franciszek Krasiński on 24 March, but he later scrawled in the margin the comment 'not necessary'.[45] The matter had not been raised in the chamber, although there had been an isolated request on 12 May that Ostrozky should take the oath of loyalty to the crown in his capacity as palatine of Kyiv. Having opted for Poland, however, the Volhynians,

---

[41] *Dnevnik*, 379–82; Kempa, *Ostrogski*, 44–9.   [42] *Dnevnik*, 386–7.
[43] *Dnevnik*, 392.   [44] *Dnevnik*, 387–8; Pelenski, 'Incorporation', 38.
[45] Halecki, *Przyłączenie*, 112–13.

undoubtedly with Ostrozky's encouragement, embarked on a campaign to unite all the lands of southern Ruthenia, securing support from the envoys of the Polish palatinate of Ruthenia. On 1 June Walenty Orzechowski, land judge of Przemyśl asked that the historic claims of Poland to Kyiv and Bratslav be presented, and requested that Ostrozky should take the oath as palatine of Kyiv. On 2 June the Volhynians stated that without Kyiv, Volhynia would be in a 'miserable condition', and raised the issue of Muscovite complaints concerning Lithuanian rule over the Kyiv metropolitanate. The most eager advocate was Havrylo Bokei, land judge of Lutsk and one of the envoys who had brought the Vitsebsk petition to Sigismund August, who demanded the annexation not just of Kyiv, but also of the Brest palatinate, which had a large Orthodox population, but which had formed part of the palatinate of Trakai until 1565.[46]

Some senators were reluctant to approve Kyiv's annexation, on the prescient grounds that it would increase the burden on Poland, which would have to defend this vast and sparsely populated territory from Tatars and Muscovites. The envoys, however, supported the Volhynians, as did Sigismund August. On 6 June 1569 he issued a proclamation in Latin and Polish 'reintegrating and restoring' Kyiv to the *corona regni*. Among the signatories were Ostrozky, who took his oath as palatine of Kyiv the same day, and Sangushko, who had initially resisted the incorporation of his Bratslav palatinate along with Volhynia, but who understood that it must remain with Kyiv.[47] Great care was devoted by professional lawyers to the historical claims to Kyiv in the proclamation, but they were flimsy, and several senators doubted the annexation's legality.[48] Yet the historical justifications were not the most significant considerations, despite the fact that they have exercised generations of historians. The incorporation's success depended on the hard bargaining undertaken in June by envoys from Kyiv, Volhynia, and Bratslav over its final form. It was not until after 24 June that the incorporation privileges for Volhynia and Kyiv were ready. Although the Volhynian privilege was dated 26 May it was probably not finalized until late June. Its terms were significant, and marked a shift in Polish thinking that was to be crucial in the negotiations with the Lithuanians. Written in Polish, not Ruthenian, it stated that 'the Volhynian lands'—defined as the palatinates of Volhynia and Bratslav—had always belonged to the Polish crown, and were now returning to it (see Map 6).

It revoked the loyalty of their citizens to the grand duchy of Lithuania and spoke of their return to Poland 'as equals to equals'. It used the metaphor of the body politic, talking of the return of Volhynia to 'one indifferent and indivisible body', but there was no talk of invisceration, and the vision embodied in the privilege was not of incorporation, but of the union of two realms equal in status. Volhynia was to preserve its rights and privileges, the dignity and position of the princes were to be respected, and guarantees were given concerning the rights and liberties of the

---

[46] *Dnevnik*, 393, 401; Halecki, *Przyłączenie*, 174–7.
[47] *AU*, no. 138, 308–18; *VC*, ii/i, 226–32.
[48] Halecki, *Przyłączenie*, 174; Pelenski, 'Incorporation', 31.

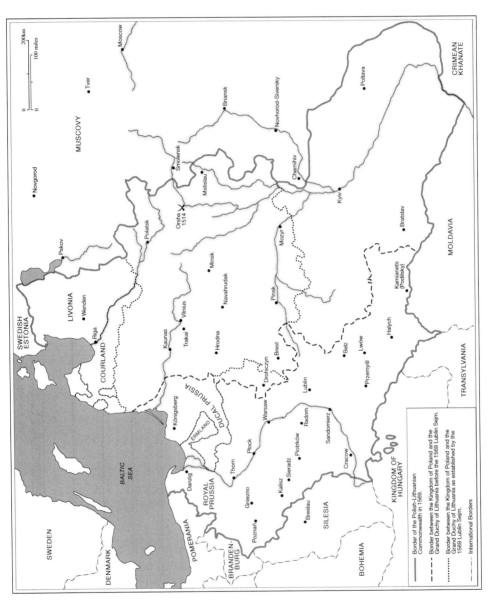

Map 6. The Commonwealth of Poland-Lithuania in 1569.

Orthodox Church. Finally, Volhynia did not adopt Polish law; instead it continued to be governed under the 1566 Lithuanian statute.[49]

This was no accessory union. It recognized the Ruthenian territories of Volhynia and Bratslav as equal partners in a single commonwealth, but allowed them to maintain a separate legal system. With regard to Kyiv, the terms were almost identical. The privilege was backdated to 5 June, the day before Ostrozky took his oath of loyalty as palatine, and declared that the 'land and principality of Kyiv' was returning to the rule of the crown whose rights to it were asserted.[50] This incorporation was not complete, however. Mozyr, one of the palatinate's two principal districts, was excluded, although the Ovruch district, which had participated in the Mozyr sejmik, remained with Kyiv. The fact that Rudy was starosta of Mozyr almost certainly explains this apparently anomalous outcome although it is not clear whether it was Rudy's influence over the local nobility or the king's reluctance to force a showdown at a delicate moment in the negotiations with Lithuania that lay behind the decision. Mozyr was eventually attached to the Minsk palatinate, although border disputes caused problems down to 1641 and beyond.[51]

Thus Dembkowski's claim that if the Lithuanians had returned to Lublin a little earlier 'it is quite possible indeed likely that... they would not have lost the Ukraine' is misguided.[52] The negotiations over the final form of the incorporation took place during June, when the Lithuanians were back in Lublin, but they could do nothing to stop the process. There was no hint after Sangushko's speech on 1 June that the Ruthenians considered remaining with the grand duchy, which had little to offer them compared with the terms agreed by the Poles. Although the Lithuanians protested long and loud after their return, and sought to reverse the incorporations, they were unsuccessful. This was not due to Polish intransigence, but to the choices made by the nobility of the southern Ruthenian lands. By late June the Volhynian envoys were lining up with the hard-line Cracovians over the terms of union with the grand duchy they had left behind.[53] The Lithuanian council lords had only themselves to blame.

There was nothing that Chodkiewicz and his fellow negotiators could do but salvage as much as they could from the political wreckage. The Poles insisted on negotiating on the basis of the royal declaration of 24 March, known as the decree on the union *in contumaciam*, drawn up in response to the Lithuanian departure. Despite its threatening title, it was a surprisingly moderate document. It began by stating the executionist position that the many acts of union had not been fully implemented, although it immediately contradicted itself by stating that the unions

---

[49] *VC*, ii/i, 221–6; *AU*, no. 136, 300–8; Kempa, 'Możnowładztwo', 183; Halecki, *Przyłączenie*, 170–2. The version in *AU* bears the date 27 May, which is accepted by Halecki.

[50] *VC*, ii/i, 226–32; *AU*, no. 138, 308–19.

[51] Henryk Litwin, 'Kijowszczyzna, Wołyń i Bracławszczyzna w 1569. Między unią a inkorporacją', in С.Ф. Сокал and Андрэй Янушкевіч (eds), *Праблемы інтэграцыі і інкорпорацыі ў развіцці Цэнтральнай і Усходняй Еўропы ў перыяд раннага Новага часу* (Minsk, 2009), 197–9; Henryk Litwin, *Równi do równych: Kijowska reprezentacja sejmowa 1569–1648* (Warsaw, 2009), 13–15; Микола Крикун, *Адміністративно-територіальний устрій правобережної України в XV–XVIII ст. Кордон воєводств у світлі джерел* (Kyiv, 1993), 140–4.

[52] Dembkowski, *Union*, 162. [53] *Dnevnik*, 447–8; Mazur, 'Nieznana', 52.

made by Jagiełło and Vytautas had always been sufficiently and thoroughly established. It rehearsed the history of recent negotiations, observing that agreement had almost been reached in 1564, but that the Lithuanians had come to Lublin demanding that the old treaties be ignored and that a completely new agreement be drafted, despite accepting Mielnik in 1564 as a basis for negotiation. It quoted the formula agreed at Mielnik stating that the Polish crown and the grand duchy formed 'one indivisible and uniform body' that was not dual, but 'one commonwealth (*rzeczpospolita*) formed from two nations who had joined and combined into one people (*lud*)'. Thereafter it eschewed all talk of incorporation, closely following the proposals prepared by the senate in January. There was to be one election and one coronation in Cracow, with no separate ceremony in Vilnius, and privileges were to be confirmed in one document. There was to be a common currency, and sejms were always to be common, but the document quoted the metaphor used by Sigismund August in Warsaw, that one body had different members, and it approved separate laws, a separate legal system, and separate offices. The clause in the 1566 statute banning Poles from holding land or office in the grand duchy was to be repealed.[54]

Negotiations began on 9 June, and were completed relatively quickly. The Lithuanians were not in a strong position, and were able to secure few of the demands in the proposal they put to the common sejm on 15 June, based on the instructions drawn up in Vilnius in March. The Poles did omit references to the Lithuanians' escape from Lublin in the historical section at the start of the final treaty, but the Lithuanian desire to have the king's coronation oath issued under the Lithuanian as well as the Polish seal was rejected, as was the request that the wording of Sigismund August's bequest of his hereditary rights to the Polish *corona regni* in 1564 should be altered by adding 'and the grand duchy of Lithuania', which the Polish senate had been prepared to concede in January. Despite Chodkiewicz's opposition, Livonia was formally confirmed as a joint possession of the new commonwealth.[55] There was much debate on details of wording, but the Poles conceded little of substance. The negotiations were complete by the end of June. On 1 July the two sejms met separately to agree the union treaty; after these formalities were complete, they processed together to the Franciscan church to sing *Te Deum Laudamus*. Three days later, on 4 July, Sigismund August formally promulgated the union, and the new commonwealth was born (see Fig. 16). Rudy, sulking back in Lithuania, refused to confirm it, as did Paweł Sapieha and Mikołaj Pac, the castellan and bishop of Kyiv respectively, but they were Lithuanians and the Kyiv palatinate had already decided. Their opposition was of no consequence.

Despite all the trauma of 1569, in one crucial sense the Lithuanians had won. For the Lublin treaty embodied the concept of union for which they had fought

---

[54] *VC*, ii/i, 232–8; *AU*, no. 115, 220–7.

[55] Dembkowski gives the misleading impression that Lithuania after 1569 could not use its own seals: *Union*, 164–5. The issue in June 1569 was whether the Lithuanian seal should be attached to the oath that the king took to uphold the rights and privileges of the commonwealth at his coronation. The Poles objected to this, as it implied the existence of two commonwealths. After 1569, the Lithuanian chancery continued to use its own seals.

Fig. 16. The Union of Lublin (1569). The lords of the council and the envoys of the Grand Duchy of Lithuania renew their union with the Kingdom of Poland at the general sejm in Lublin, 1 July 1569. Polish, parchment, 720 mm × 450 mm. 77 seals attached. Archiwum Główne Akt Dawnych, Warsaw, Zbiór Dokumentów Pergaminowych, sygn. 5627. By kind permission of the Archiwum Główne Akt Dawnych.

since 1429. The brief historical survey with which it began omitted all mention of Jagiełło, Vytautas, and the 'old treaties' of union. The only old treaty mentioned was Mielnik, upon which the Lublin union was explicitly based. As in Mielnik, the language of incorporation was abandoned, and there was no iteration of inviscerating synonyms. The crucial clause describing the nature of the union was based on the formula agreed at Mielnik, but with one key difference. Where Mielnik had talked of Poland and Lithuania being united in one indivisible and uniform body that formed one people, one political community, one brotherhood, and a common council, the Lublin treaty, written in Polish, not Latin, translated the first phrase literally, but added that it 'also formed one uniform and common republic which has already joined and united two states and two nations in one political community'.[56] The use of the term '*już*' (already) reflected the Polish view that the union already existed, and only had to be executed, but it also represented an

---

[56] 'Iż już Krolestwo polskie i Wielgie Księstwo litewskie jest jedno nierozdzielne i nierożne ciało, a także nierożna a jedna a spolna Rzeczpospolita, ktora się z dwu państw i narodow w jeden lud zniosła i spoiła': *AU*, no. 149, 358.

explicit acceptance of the Lithuanian view that the union had always been one between two separate realms. It was, however, the introduction of the term *rzeczpospolita*, 'republic' or 'commonwealth', that was the key that unlocked the door to agreement. The Lithuanians had long defended the separate existence of their own republic, but now accepted the idea of one, common republic in return for the explicit recognition that they constituted a separate nation, and that the grand duchy constituted a separate realm or state within the unitary commonwealth. Thus they agreed to form a common political nation or political community with the Poles—a *lud*, which was the direct translation of the Latin *populus* from the Mielnik treaty—that shared a common currency, a common parliament, and a common king, elected together with the Poles. In return, the Poles recognized the separate and equal status of the grand duchy, preserved in its name, its separate offices, its separate army, and its separate legal system. This was sufficient for the Lithuanians, like the Volhynians, to consider that this constituted the union of equals—*aeque principaliter*—that they had long maintained was the nature of the relationship they had freely entered into with the Poles. In practice, the institution of the idea of common council and the incorporation of the Lithuanian council into the new joint Polish-Lithuanian-Prussian senate meant that it is difficult to speak of a separate Lithuanian government, as opposed to a separate Lithuanian administration, but it was sufficient recognition of the dignity of the grand duchy for the Lithuanians to accept it.

Lublin did not, however, feel like a victory. Lithuanian anger over the loss of the southern Ruthenian palatinates soured the mood considerably. It was two decades and more before the council lords abandoned attempts to reverse it. Thus while the Poles greeted the union with an outpouring of joy, the Lithuanians sang the *Te Deum Laudamus* with heavier hearts. It was by no means clear how the union would work in practice, or how the new commonwealth would cope with the impending death of the last Jagiellon in the male line, but the mixed feelings with which the accomplishment of the union was greeted should not disguise the momentous nature of the achievement. For all that the two realms had come together in pursuit of common interests, and for all that material and self-interest had played a large part in the deal-making that formed the union, it ultimately reached fruition on account of the idea not of a union of realms or states, but of a fraternal union of peoples, a community of the realms. The germ of this idea was present in the Horodło treaty, but it was the Lithuanians, not the Poles, who developed it in the years after 1429. It was this idea that made possible the Union of Lublin and underpinned the new union state. That was to be its greatest strength and its greatest weakness.

Bibliography

Works in Ukrainian, Belarusian, and Russian are given separately below, owing to the different order of the Cyrillic alphabet. Abbreviations in square brackets are in the *List of Abbreviations*.

PRINTED PRIMARY SOURCES

1385 m. rugpjūčio Krėvos Aktas, ed. Jūratė Kiaupienė (Vilnius, 2002). [*KA*]
1413 m. Horodlės aktai, ed. Jūratė Kiaupienė and Lidia Korczak (Vilnius and Cracow, 2013). [*Horodlės aktai*]
XVI amžiaus Lietuvos ir Lenkijos politinės kultūros šaltiniai (1562 metų tekstai), ed. Jūratė Kiaupienė (Vilnius, 2008).
Acta Tomiciana, 18 vols (Poznań and Kórnik, 1852–1999). [*AT*]
Acten der Ständetage Preussens unter der Herrschaft des Deutschen Ordens, ed. Max Toeppen, 5 vols (Leipzig, 1874–86). [*ASP*]
Akta Aleksandra króla polskiego, Wielkiego księcia litewskiego itd. (1501–1506), ed. Fryderyk Papée (Cracow, 1927). [*AA*]
Akta Stanów Prus Królewskich, 8 vols (Toruń, 1955–93). [*ASPK*]
Akta Unji Polski z Litwą 1385–1791, ed. Stanisław Kutrzeba and Władysław Semkowicz (Cracow, 1932). [*AU*]
Bielski, Marcin, *Kronika Polska*, Zbiór Pisarzów Polskich, cz. vi, tom xvii (Warsaw, 1832).
Bodin, Jean, *On Sovereignty*, ed. and tr. Julian Franklin (Cambridge, 1992).
Codex diplomaticus Maioris Polonia documenta, et iam typis descripta, et adhuc inedita complectens, annum 1400 attingentia, iii: *(1350–1399)* (Poznań, 1879). [*CDMP*]
Codex diplomaticus Poloniae quo continentur privilegia regum Poloniae, magnorum ducum Lituaniae, bullae pontificium nec non jura a privatis data... ab antiquissimis inde temporibus usque ad annum 1506, i, ed. Leon Rzyszczewski (Warsaw, 1847). [*CDP*]
Codex diplomaticus Prussicus: Urkunden-Sammlung zur ältern Geschichte Preussens aus dem Königl. Geheimen Archiv zu Königsberg, ed. Johannes Voigt, 6 vols (Königsberg, 1836–61). [*CDPr*]
Codex epistolaris saeculi decimi quinti, i/i: *1384–1444*, ed. Józef Szujski (Cracow, 1876). [*CESXV*]
Codex epistolaris saeculi decimi quinti, i/ii: *1444–1492*, ed. Józef Szujski (Cracow, 1876).
Codex epistolaris saeculi decimi quinti, ii: *1382–1445*, ed. Anatol Lewicki (Cracow, 1891).
Codex epistolaris saeculi decimi quinti, iii: *1392–1501*, ed. Anatol Lewicki (Cracow, 1894).
Corpus iuris polonici, Sectiones primae: Privilegia, statuta, constitutiones decreta mandata regnum Poloniae spectantia comprehendentis, iii: *Annos 1506–1522 continens*, ed. Oswald Balzer (Cracow, 1906). [*CIP*]
Czarnkow, Johannes de, [Janko of Czarnków], *Chronicon Polonorum*, ed. Jan Szlachtowski, *MPH*, ii (Lwów, 1872), 601–756.
Die aeltere Hochmeisterchronik, in *SRPr*, iii, ed. Hirsch, Töppen, and Strehlke (Leipzig, 1866), 519–719.
Długosz, Jan, *Annales seu cronicae incliti Regni Poloniae*, x, *1370–1405* (Warsaw, 1985). [*Annales*]

Długosz, Jan, *Annales seu cronicae incliti Regni Poloniae*, x/xi: *1406–1413* (Warsaw, 1997).
Długosz, Jan, *Annales seu cronicae incliti Regni Poloniae*, xi: *1413–1430* (Warsaw, 2000).
Długosz, Jan, *Annales seu cronicae incliti Regni Poloniae*, xi/xii: *1431–1444* (Warsaw, 2001).
Długosz, Jan, *Annales seu cronicae incliti Regni Poloniae* xii/i: *1445–1461* (Warsaw, 2003).
Długosz, Jan, *Annales seu cronicae incliti Regni Poloniae* xii/ii: *1462–1480* (Warsaw, 2005).
Długosz, Jan, *Roczniki czyli kroniki sławnego Królestwa Polskiego*, x: *1370–1405* (Warsaw, 2009). [*Roczniki*]
Długosz, Jan, *Roczniki czyli kroniki sławnego Królestwa Polskiego*, x/xi: *1406–1413* (Warsaw, 2009).
Długosz, Jan, *Roczniki czyli kroniki sławnego Królestwa Polskiego*, xi: *1413–1430* (Warsaw, 2009).
Długosz, Jan, *Roczniki czyli kroniki sławnego Królestwa Polskiego*, xi/xii: *1431–1444* (Warsaw, 2009).
Długosz, Jan, *Roczniki czyli kroniki sławnego Królestwa Polskiego*, xii/i: *1445–1461* (Warsaw, 2009).
Długosz, Jan, *Roczniki czyli kroniki sławnego Królestwa Polskiego*, xii/ii: *1462–1480* (Warsaw, 2009).
Długosz, Jan, *The Annals of Jan Długosz: A History of Eastern Europe from A.D. 965 to A.D. 1480*, tr. Maurice Michael (Chichester, 1997).
Dusburg, Peter von, *Chronica terrae Prussiae*, in *SRPr*, i, eds Hirsch, Töppen, and Strehlke (Leipzig, 1861), 24–219.
Dyariusze sejmów koronnych 1548, 1553 i 1570 r., ed. Józef Szujski, in *SRP*, i (Cracow, 1872).
Ehrlich, Ludwik (ed.), *Polski wykład prawa wojny* (Warsaw, 1955).
Falkenberg, Johann, *Liber de doctrina potestatis papae et imperatoris editus contra Paulum Vladimiri Polonum in Sacro Constantiensi Consilio*, in *Rerum publicarum*, 196–232.
Górski, Karol (ed.), *Związek pruski a poddanie się Prus Polsce: Zbiór tekstów źródłowych* (Poznań, 1949).
Górski, Stanisław, 'Commentarius rerum gestarum a Sigismundo primo, Rege Polonie, Magno Duce Lituanie', *AT*, i, no. 8, 13.
Herzog Albrecht von Preußen und das Bistum Ermland (1550–1568): Regesten aus dem Herzoglichen Briefarchiv und den Ostpreußischen Folianten, ed. Stefan Hartmann (Cologne, 1993).
Ius Polonicum: Codicibus veteribus manuscriptum et editionibus quibusque collatis, ed. Wincenty Bandtkie Stężyński (Warsaw, 1831). [*Ius Polonicum*]
Lengnich, Gottfried, *Geschichte der Preussischen Lande: Königlich-Polnischen Antheils seit dem Jahr 1526 biß auf dem Todt Königes Sigismundi I* (Danzig, 1722).
Liber cancellariae Stanislai Ciołek, ed. Jacob Caro (Vienna, 1874).
Lietuvos metraštis: Bychovco kronika, ed. Rimantas Jasas (Vilnius, 1971).
Lietuvos Metrika Knyga Nr. 25 (*1387–1546*), eds Darius Antanavičius and Algirdas Baliulis (Vilnius, 1998).
Listy króla Zygmunta Augusta do Radziwiłłów, ed. Irena Kaniewska (Cracow, 1997).
Listy oryginalne Zygmunta Augusta do Mikołaja Radziwiłła Czarnego, ed. S.A. Łachowicz (Vilnius, 1842).
Materiały do dziejów dyplomacji polskiej z lat 1486–1516 (kodeks zagrzebski), ed. Józef Garbacik (Wrocław, 1966).
Miechowita, Maciej, *Chronica Polonorum* (Cracow, 1519; 2nd edn, 1521).
Oeuvres de Ghillebert de Lannoy, Voyageur, Diplomate et Moraliste, ed. Charles Potvin (Louvain, 1878).

Orzechowski, Stanisław, *Annales Stanislai Orichovii*, ed. Theodor Działyński (Poznań, 1844).
Orzechowski, Stanisław, *Rozmowa albo dyjalog pierwszy około egzekucyjej polskiej korony*, in *Stanisława Orzechowskiego polskie dialogi polityczne (Rozmowa około egzykucyjej oraz Quincunx) 1563–1564*, ed. Jan Łos (Cracow, 1919).
Ostroróg, Jan, *Memoriał w sprawie uporządkowania Rzeczypospolitej*, ed. and tr. Andrzej Obrębski (Łódź, 1994).
Ostroróg, Jan, *Monumentum pro comitiis generalibus regni sub rege Casimiro pro Reipublicae ordinatione* (n. d.; Warsaw, 1884).
'Pamiętniki o królowej Barbarze żonie Zygmunta Augusta', in *Pisma historyczne*, i, ed. Michał Baliński (Warsaw, 1843).
Pirmas Lietuvos Statutas/Перевый Литовский Статут, iii, ed. Stanislovas Lazutka, Irena Valikonytė, and Edvardas Gudavičius (Vilnius, 1991).
The Lithuanian Statute of 1529, tr. and ed. Karl von Loewe (Leiden, 1976).
The Political Works of James I, ed. Charles Howard McIlwain (Cambridge, MA, 1918).
Posilge, Johann von, *Chronik des Landes Preussen*, in *SRPr*, iii, eds Hirsch, Töppen, and Strehlke (Leipzig, 1866), 79–388.
'Poszelstwo Riczerstwa kxiestwa wielkiego Litewskiego ku kroliowy Je Mczi do Wilna zobozu', in *XVI amžiaus*, 76–87.
'Projekt unji polsko-litewskiej z r. 1446', ed. Bolesław Ulanowski, *Archiwum Komisji Prawniczej*, 6 (1926), 235–9.
Przyłuski, Jakub, *Leges seu statuta ac privilegia Regni Polonia omnia* (Cracow, 1553).
Regesta historico-diplomatica Ordinis S. Mariae Theutonicorum, i: *Regesten zum Ordensbriefarchiv*, ed. Walther Hubatsch (Göttingen, 1948–50).
Rerum publicarum scientiae quae saeculo XV in Polonia viguit monumenta litteraria, ed. Michał Bobrzyński (Cracow, 1878).
Rozmowa Polaka z Litwinem: 1564, ed. Józef Korzeniowski (Cracow, 1890).
Schütz, Kasper, *Historia rerum prussicarum* (Leipzig, 1599).
Scriptores Rerum Prussicarum: Die Geschichtsquellen der Preussischen Vorzeit bis zum Untergange der Ordensherrschaft, ed. Theodor Hirsch, Max Töppen, and Ernst Strehlke, 5 vols (Leipzig, 1861–74). [*SRPr*]
Skarbiec dyplomatów papieżkich, cesarskich, królewskich, książęcych, uchwał narodowych, postanowień różnych władz i urzędów posługujących do krytycznego wyjaśnienia dziejów Litwy: Rusi Litewskiej i ościennych im krajów, ed. Ignacy Daniłowicz, 2 vols (Wilno, 1860–2). [*Skarbiec*]
Die Staatsverträge des Deutschen Ordens in Preussen im 15. Jh., ed. Erich Weise (Marburg, 1970).
Die Staatsvertäge des Herzogtums Preussen, Teil I: Polen und Litauen: Verträge und Belehnungsurkunden 1525–1657/58, eds Stephan Dolezel and Heidrun Dolezel (Berlin, 1971).
Stanisław of Skarbimierz, 'De bellis justis', in Ehrlich (ed.), *Polski wykład*, 90–144.
Stryjkowski, Maciej, *O początkach, wywodach, dzielnościach, sprawach rycerskich i domowych sławetnego narodu litewskiego, żemojdzkiego i ruskiego*, ed. Julia Radziszewska (Warsaw, 1978).
Volumina Constitutionum, 2 vols (Warsaw, 1996–2008). [*VC*]
Volumina Legum: Leges, statuta, constitutiones et privilegia Regni Poloniae, Magni Ducatus Lithuaniae omnumque provinciarum annexarum, a Comitiis Visliciae anno 1347 celebratis usque ad ultima regni comitia, 8 vols (repr. Warsaw, 1980). [*VL*]

Wigand von Marburg, *Chronik*, in *SRPr*, ed. Hirsch, Töppen, and Strehlke, ii (Leipzig, 1863), 429–662.

Włodkowic, Paweł [Paulus Vladimiri], *Tractatus de Ordine Cruciferorum et de bello Polonorum contra dictos fratres ad confutanda scripta Johannis de Bamberga (Johannis Fal[k]enberg) in sacro Constantiensi Generali Concilio*, in *Rerum publicarum*, 233–96.

Włodkowic, Paweł [Paulus Vladimiri], *Tractatus de potestate papae et imperatoris respectu infidelium* in *Rerum publicarum*, 161–94.

Zbiór praw litewskich, ed. A.T. Działyński (Poznań, 1841). [*ZPL*]

Zaborowski, Stanisław, *Tractatus Quadrifidus de Natura Iurium et Bonorum Regis et de Reformatione Regni ac eius Reipublicae Regimine incipit Feliciter* (Cracow, 1507).

Zaborowski, Stanisław, *Traktat o naturze praw i dóbr królewskich*, ed. Henryk Litwin (Cracow, 2005).

Žemaitijos žemės privilegijos XV–XVII a, ed. Darius Antanavičius and Eugenijus Saviščevas (Vilnius, 2010).

Źródłopisma do dziejów unii Korony Polskiej i W.X. Litewskiego, ed. A.T. Działyński (Poznań, 1861).

Акты относящіеся къ исторіи Западной Россіи: Собранные и изданные Археографическою Коммиссіею, 5 vols (St Petersburg, 1846–53; repr., ed. C.H. van Schooneveld, the Hague, 1970–1).

Дневник Люблинского сейма 1569 года: Соединение Великаго Княжества Литовского с Королеством Польским, изд. М. Кояловичъ [ed. Michael Koialovich] (St Petersburg, 1869). [*Dnevnik*]

Литовская Метрика: Книги публичных дел. Переписи войска Литовская, Русская Историческая Библиотека, 33 (St Petersburg, 1915). [*RIB*]

Полное Собрание Русских Летописей, xvii: *Западноруские летописи*, eds С.Л. Пташицкий and А.А. Шахматовий (St Petersburg, 1907). [*PSRL*]

Полное Собрание Русских Летописей, xxxii: *Летописи белорусско-литовские*, ed. Б.А. Рыбаков (Moscow, 1975). [*PSRL*]

Полное Собрание Русских Летописей, xxxiii: *Холмогорская летопись, Двинской летописец* (Leningrad, 1977). [*PSRL*]

Полное Собрание Русских Летописей, xxxv: *Летописи белорусско-литовские*, ed. Б.А. Рыбаков (Moscow, 1980). [*PSRL*]

SECONDARY SOURCES

Achremczyk, Stanisław, *Historia Warmii i Mazur* (Olsztyn, 1997).

Adamus, Jan, 'O prawno-państwowym stosunku Litwy do Polski', in *Pamiętnik VI Zjazdu Powszechnego Historyków Polskich w Wilnie 17–20 września 1935 r.*, i: *Referaty* (Lwów, 1935), 174–80.

Adamus, Jan, 'Państwo litewskie w latach 1386–1398', in Stefan Ehrenkreutz (ed.), *Księga pamiątkowa ku uczczenia 400. rocznicy wydania I Statutu Litewskiego* (Wilno, 1935), 15–48.

Ajnenkiel, Andrzej (ed.), *W pięćsetlecie konstytucji Nihil Novi: Z dziejów stanowienia prawa w Polsce* (Warsaw, 2006).

Ališauskas, Vytautas, Jovaiša, Liudas, Paknys, Mindaugas, Petrauskas, Rimvydas, and Raila, Eligijus (eds), *Lietuvos Didžiosios Kunigaikštijos Kultūra* (Vilnius, 2001).

Alter, Peter, *Nationalism* (London, 1989).

Antoniewicz, Marceli, *Protoplaści książąt Radziwiłłów: Dzieje mitu i meandry historiografii* (Warsaw, 2011).
Arieta, Jon and Elliott, J.H. (eds), *Forms of Union: The British and Spanish Monarchies in the Seventeenth and Eighteenth Centuries* (Donostia, 2009).
Auerbach, Inge, *Andrej Michajlovič Kurbskij: Leben in osteuropäischen Adelsgesellschaft des 16. Jahrhunderts* (Munich, 1985).
Avižonis, Konstantinas, *Die Entstehung und Entwicklung des Litauischen Adels bis zur litauisch-polnischen Union 1385* (Berlin, 1932).
Backus, Oswald P., *Motives of West Russian Nobles in Deserting Lithuania for Moscow 1377–1514* (Lawrence, KS, 1957).
Baczkowski, Krzysztof, *Walka o Węgry w latach 1490–1492* (Cracow, 1995).
Baczkowski, Krzysztof, 'Zbigniew Oleśnicki wobec II unii polsko-węgierskiej 1440–1444', in Kiryk and Noga (eds), *Oleśnicki*, 53–71.
Bahlcke, Joachim, 'Unionsstrukturen und Föderationsmodelle im Osten des ständischen Europa: Anmerkungen zu vergleichenden Ansätzen über das frühneuzeitliche Ostmitteleuropa', *Comparativ*, 5 (1998), 57–73.
Balzer, Oswald, *Genealogia Piastów* (1895; 2nd edn, Cracow, 2005).
Balzer, Oswald, *Królestwo Polskie 1295–1370* (1919–20; 2nd edn, Cracow, 2005).
Balzer, Oswald, *Tradycja dziejowa unii polsko-litewskiej* (Lwów, 1919).
Balzer, Oswald, 'Unia horodelska', *RAU* (1912/1913), 146–77.
Banaszak, Marian, 'Chrzest Żmudzi i jego reperkusje w Konstancji', in Marek Zahajkiewicz (ed.), *Chrzest Litwy: Geneza, przebieg, konsekwencje* (Lublin, 1990), 57–76.
Banionis, Egidijus, 'Lietuvos bajorai 1413 m. Horodlėje', in Čaipitė and Nikžentaitis (eds), *Žalgirio*, 189–206.
Barański, Marek, *Dynastia Piastów w Polsce* (Warsaw, 2005).
Bardach, Juliusz, 'Krewo i Lublin: Z problemów unii polsko-litewskiej', in Bardach, *Studia*, 11–67.
Bardach, Juliusz, 'Początki sejmu', in *Historia sejmu*, i, 6–62.
Bardach, Juliusz, *Statuty litewskie a prawo rzymskie* (Warsaw, 1999).
Bardach, Juliusz, 'Statuty litewskie w ich kręgu prawno-kulturowym', in Bardach, *O dawnej i niedawnej Litwie* (Poznań, 1988), 9–71.
Bardach, Juliusz, *Studia z ustroju i prawa Wielkiego Księstwa Litewskiego XIV–XVII w.* (Warsaw, 1970).
Bardach, Juliusz (ed.), *Historia państwa i prawa Polski*, i: *Do połowy XV wieku* (Warsaw, 1964).
Baronas, Darius, Dubonis, Artūras, and Petrauskas, Rimvydas, *Lietuvos Istorija*, iii: *XIII a.–1385 m.* (Vilnius, 2011).
Baszkiewicz, Jan, *Odnowienie królestwa polskiego 1295–1320* (Poznań, 2008).
Belch, Stanislaus, *Paulus Vladimiri and his Doctrine concerning International Law and Politics*, 2 vols (The Hague, 1965).
Besala, Jerzy, *Barbara Radziwiłłówna i Zygmunt August* (Warsaw, 2007).
Besala, Jerzy, *Zygmunt Stary i Bona Sforza* (Poznań, 2012).
Bielecka, Janina, 'Organizacja i działalność sądów ziemskich w Prusach Królewskich od wieku XV do XVIII włącznie', *Archeion*, 63 (1975), 145–64.
Bielecka, Janina, 'Organizacja i działalność sądów grodzkich w Prusach Królewskich od wieku XV do XVIII włącznie', *Archeion*, 65 (1977), 154–74.
Biskup, Marian, 'Do genezy inkorporacji Prus', *PZ*, 7/8 (1954).

Biskup, Marian, 'Dyplomacja polska w czasach Casimira Jagiellończyka' i: W kręgu wielkiego konfliktu zbrojnego z Zakonem Krzyżackim (1454–1466)', in Biskup and Górski (eds), *Kazimierz Jagiellończyk*, 173–229.

Biskup, Marian, 'Spisy jeńców polskich z bitwy pod Chojnicami', *PH*, 56/1 (1965), 88–103.

Biskup, Marian, *Trzynastoletnia wojna z Zakonem Krzyżackim 1454–1466* (Warsaw, 1967).

Biskup, Marian, *'Wojna Pruska', czyli walka Polski z Zakonem Krzyżackim z lat 1519–1521* (Olsztyn, 1991).

Biskup, Marian, *Wojny polskie z zakonem krzyżackim 1308–1521* (Gdańsk, 1993).

Biskup, Marian, 'Z zagadnień wojskowości polskiej okresu wojny trzynastoletniej', in Biskup and Górski (eds), *Kazimierz Jagiellończyk*, 141–72.

Biskup, Marian and Górski, Karol (eds), *Kazimierz Jagiellończyk: Zbiór studiów o Polsce drugiej połowy XV wieku* (Warsaw, 1987).

Biskup, Marian and Labuda, Gerard, *Dzieje Zakonu Krzyżackiego w Prusach* (Gdańsk, 1986).

Błaszczyk Grzegorz, *Burza koronacyjna: Polska-Litwa 1429–1430: Dramatyczny fragment stosunków polsko-litewskich w XV wieku* (Poznań, 1998).

Błaszczyk Grzegorz, 'Czy była unia krewska?', *KH*, 110/4 (2003), 83–96.

Błaszczyk Grzegorz, *Dzieje stosunków polsko-litewskich*, ii/i: *Od Krewa do Lublina* (Poznań, 2007).

Błaszczyk Grzegorz, *Dzieje stosunków polsko-litewskich od czasów najdawniejszych do współczesności*, i: *Trudne początki* (Poznań, 1998).

Błaszczyk Grzegorz, *Litwa na przełomie średniowiecza i nowożytności 1492–1569* (Poznań, 2002).

Blum, Jerome, 'The rise of serfdom in eastern Europe', *AHR*, 62/4 (1957), 807–36.

Bobrzyński, Michał, *Dzieje Polski w zarysie* (1879; Warsaw, 1974).

Bobrzyński, Michał, *Jan Ostroróg: Studyum z literatury politycznej XV wieku* (Cracow, 1884).

Bobrzyński, Michał, *O ustawodawstwie nieszawskim Kazimierza Jagiellończyka* (1873; 2nd edn, Cracow, 1973).

Bodniak, Stanisław, 'Z wyprawy radoszkowickiej na Moskwę w roku 1567/8', *AW*, 7 (1930), 799–808.

Bogucka, Maria, *Bona Sforza* (Warsaw, 1989).

Bogucka, Maria, *Kazimierz Jagiellończyk i jego czasy* (Warsaw, 1981).

Bömelburg, Hans-Jürgen, 'Das Landesbewußtsein im Preußen königlich polnischen Anteils in der Frühen Neuzeit', in Sabine Beckmann (ed.), *Kulturgeschichte Preußens königlich polnischen Anteils in der Frühen Neuzeit* (Tübingen, 2005), 39–60.

Bömelburg, Hans-Jürgen, *Frühneuzeitliche Nationen im östlichen Europa: Das polnische Geschichtsdenken und die Reichweite einer humanistischen Nationalgeschichte (1500–1700)* (Wiesbaden, 2006).

Boockmann, Hartmut, *Johannes Falkenberg, der Deutsche Orden und die polnische Politik: Untersuchungen zur politischen Theorie des späten Mittelalters* (Göttingen, 1975).

Borkowska, Urszula, 'Edukacja Jagiellonów', *RH*, 71 (2005), 99–119.

Bostel, Ferdynand, 'Zakaz Miechowity', *Przewodnik Naukowy i Literacki*, xii (1884), 438–51, 540–62, 637–52.

Bradshaw, Brendan, 'The Tudor Reformation and Revolution in Wales and Ireland: The origins of the British Problem', in Bradshaw and Morrill (eds), *The British Problem*, 39–65.

Bradshaw, Brendan and Morrill, John (eds), *The British Problem, c.1534–1707: State Formation in the Atlantic Archipelago* (Basingstoke, 1996).

Brenner, Robert, 'The agrarian roots of European capitalism', in T.H. Aston and C.H.E. Philpin (eds), *The Brenner Debate: Agrarian Class Structure and Economic Development in Pre-Industrial Europe* (Cambridge, 1985), 213–328.

Bues, Almut, *Die Jagiellonen: Herrscher zwischen Ostsee und Adria* (Stuttgart, 2010).
Bumblauskas, Alfredas, and Petrauskas, Rimvydas (eds), *Tarp istorijos ir būtovės: Studijos prof. Edvardo Gudavičiaus 70-mečiui* (Vilnius, 1999).
Burleigh, Michael, *Prussian Society and the German Order: An Aristocratic Corporation in Crisis c.1410–1466* (Cambridge, 1984).
Bush, Michael, 'Serfdom in medieval and modern Europe: A comparison', in Bush (ed.), *Serfdom*, 199–224.
Bush, Michael (ed.), *Serfdom and Slavery: Studies in Legal Bondage* (Harlow, 1996).
Butterwick, Richard (ed.), *The Polish-Lithuanian Monarchy in European Context, c.1500–1795* (Basingstoke, 2001).
Bylina, Stanisław, 'Oddźwięki husytyzmu w królestwie polskim', in Stanisław Bylina, *Hussitica: Studia* (Warsaw, 2007), 163–79.
Bylina, Stanisław, Kiersnowski, Ryszard, Kuczyński, Stefan K., Samsonowicz, Henryk Szymański, Józef, and Zaremska, Hanna (eds), *Kościół—Kultura—Społeczeństwo: Studia z dziejów średniowiecza i czasów nowożytnych* (Warsaw, 2000).
Čapaitė, Rūta and Nikžentaitis, Alvydas (eds), *Žalgirio laikų: Lietuva ir jos kaimynai* (Vilnius, 1993).
Cerman, Markus, 'Social structure and land markets in late medieval central and east-central Europe', *Continuity and Change*, 23/1 (2008), 55–100.
Cerman, Markus, *Villagers and Lords in Eastern Europe, 1300–1800* (Basingstoke, 2012).
Chodynicki, Kazimierz, *Kościół prawosławny a Rzeczpospolita polska 1370–1632* (Warsaw, 1932).
Chodynicki, Kazimierz, 'Ze studiów nad dziejopisarstwem rusko-litewskiem. T.z. Rękopis Raudański', *AW*, 3 (1925–7), 387–401.
Chorążyczewski, Waldemar, 'Początki kancelarii pokojowej za Jagiellonów', in Waldemar Chorążyczewski and Wojciech Krawczyk (eds), *Polska kancelaria królewska między władzą a społeczeństwem*, iii (Warsaw, 2008), 37–46.
Chorążyczewski, Waldemar, *Przemiany organizacyjne polskiej kancelarii królewskiej u progu czasów nowożytnych* (Toruń, 2007).
Christensen, Aksel, *Kalmarunionen og nordisk politik 1319–1439* (Copenhagen, 1980).
Ciesielski, Tomasz and Filipczak-Kocur, Anna (eds), *Rzeczpospolita państwem wielu narodowości i wyznań* (Warsaw-Opole, 2008).
Colley, Linda, *Britons: Forging the Nation 1707–1837*, 2nd edn (New Haven, CT, 2005).
Conrad, Klaus, Neitmann, Klaus, Wermter, Ernst, and Arnold, Udo (eds), *Ordensherrschaft, Stände und Stadtpolitik: Zur Entwicklung des Preußenlandes im 14. und 15. Jahrhundert* (Lüneburg, 1985).
Cowan, Edward J., *For Freedom Alone: The Declaration of Arbroath, 1320*, 2nd edn (Edinburgh, 2008).
Creveld, Martin van, *The Rise and Decline of the State* (Cambridge, 1999).
Crummey, Robert, *The Formation of Muscovy 1304–1613* (London, 1987).
Cynarski, Stanisław, *Zygmunt August*, 2nd edn (Wrocław, 1997).
Czaja, Roman, 'Der Handel des Deutschen Ordens und der preußischen Städte: Wirtschaft zwischen Zusammenarbeit und Rivalität', in Nowak (ed.), *Ritterorden*, 111–23.
Czaja, Roman, 'Związki gospodarcze wielkich szafarzy zakonu krzyżackiego z miastami pruskimi na początku XV wieku', in Nowak (ed.), *Zakon*, 9–33.
Czapiuk, Alina, 'O plonach zbóż w Polsce i w Wielkim Księstwie Litewskim w XVI i XVII wieku', in Cezary Kuklo (ed.), *Między polityką a kulturą* (Białystok, 1999), 233–47.
Czermak, Wiktor, 'Sprawa równouprawnienia katolików i schizmatyków na Litwie (1432–1563)', *RAUWHF*, serya ii, 19 (1903), 348–405.

Czwojdrak, Bożena, 'Jan Hincza z Rogowa: Rycerz królowej Zofii', in Markiewicz and Skowron (eds), *Faworyci*, 61–6.
Czwojdrak, Bożena, 'Kilka uwag o konfederacji Spytka z Melsztyna z 1439 roku', in Panic and Sperka (eds), *Średniowiecze*, 197–211.
Czwojdrak, Bożena, 'Królowa Zofia Holszańska a biskup krakowski Zbigniew Oleśnicki: Konflikt, współpraca czy rywalizacja', in Kiryk and Noga (eds), *Oleśnicki*, 143–55.
Czwojdrak, Bożena, *Zofia Holszańska: Studium o dworze i roli królowej w późnośredniowiecznej Polsce* (Warsaw, 2012).
Dąbrowski, Jan, 'Die Krone des polnischen Königtums im 14. Jahrhundert: Eine Studie aus der Geschichte der Entwicklung der polnischen ständischen Monarchie', in Hellmann (ed.), *Corona Regni*, 399–548.
Dąbrowski, Jan, *Korona Królestwa Polskiego* (Wrocław, 1956; repr. Cracow, 2010).
Dąbrowski, Jan, *Ostatnie lata Ludwika Wielkiego 1370–1382* (1918; 2nd edn, Cracow, 2009).
Dąbrowski, Jan, *Władysław I Jagiellończyk na Węgrzech (1440–1444)* (Warsaw, 1922).
Dainauskas, Jonas, 'Kriavo akto autentiškumas', *Lituanistikos instituto 1975 metų suvažiavimo darbai* (1976), 51–71.
Dainauskas, Jonas, 'Autentyczność aktu krewskiego', *LSP*, 2 (1987), 125–42.
Davies, Norman, *God's Playground: A History of Poland*, 2 vols, 2nd edn (Oxford, 2005).
Davis, S. Rufus, *The Federal Principle: A Journey through Time in Quest of a Meaning* (Berkeley, CA, 1978).
Dėdinas, V., 'Vytauto vidaus ir užsienio politika ligi Žalgirio mūsio', in Šležas (ed.), *Vytautas*, 45–68.
Dembińska, Anna, *Polityczna walka o egzekucję dóbr królewskich w latach 1559/64* (Warsaw, 1935).
Dembkowski, Harry, *The Union of Lublin: Polish Federalism in the Golden Age* (Boulder, CO, 1982).
Deuerlein, Ernst, *Die historischen und philosophischen Grundlagen des föderativen Prinzips* (Munich, 1972).
Deveikė, Jonė, 'The Lithuanian diarchies', *SEER*, 28 (1950), 392–405.
Dolezel, Stephan, *Das preussisch-polnische Lehnsverhältniss unter Herzog Albrecht von Preussen, 1525–1568* (Berlin, 1967).
Drozd, Zofia, 'Miernicy w pomiarze włócznej w Wielkim Księstwie Litewskim w drugiej połowie XVI wieku', *LSP*, 13 (2008), 35–68.
Dubas-Urwanowicz, Ewa, 'Dwaj ostatni Jagiellonowie i Radziwiłłowie: Między współpracą a opozycją', in Markiewicz and Skowroń (eds), *Faworyci*, 135–48.
Dubas-Urwanowicz, Ewa, 'Uwarunkowania prawne i konsekwencje małżeństw polsko-litewskich przed unią lubelską', in Krzysztof Mikulski and Agnieszka Zielińska-Nowicka (eds), *Między Zachodem a Wschodem: Etniczne, kulturowe i religijne pogranicza Rzeczypospolitej w XVI–XVIII wieku* (Toruń, 2006), 67–73.
Duchhardt, Heinz, *Der Herrscher in der Doppelpflicht: Europäische Fürsten und ihre beiden Throne* (Mainz, 1997).
Dücker, Julia, '*Pro communi reipublicae bona*: König und Reich im jagiellonischen Polen um 1500', in Florian Ardelean, Christopher Nicholson, and Johannes Preiseur-Kappeler (eds), *Between Worlds: The Age of the Jagiellons* (Frankfurt am Main, 2013), 61–78.
Dundulis, Bronius, *Lietuvos kova dėl valstybinio savarankiškumo XV amžiuje*, 2nd edn (Vilnius, 1993).
Dyskant, Józef, *Zatoka Świeża 1463* (Warsaw, 1987).

Dzięgielewski, Jan, 'Mazowsze w czasach ostatnich Jagiellonów', in Dzięgielewski (ed.), *Mazowsze*, 31–53.
Dzięgielewski, Jan, 'Mazowsze wobec procesu włączenia do królestwa polskiego', in Dzięgielewski (ed.), *Mazowsze*, 11–29.
Dzięgielewski, Jan (ed.), *Mazowsze w procesach integracyjnych i dezintegracyjnych w Rzeczypospolitej XVI–XVII wieku* (Warsaw, 2010).
Dzieje Mazowsza, i, ed. Henryk Samsonowicz (Pułtusk, 2006).
Dzieje Wielkopolski, i, ed. Jerzy Topolski (Poznań, 1969).
Dziubiński, Andrzej, *Stosunki dyplomatyczne polsko-tureckie w latach 1500–1572 w kontekscie międzynarodowym* (Wrocław, 2005).
Ekdahl, Sven, *Die 'Banderia Prutenorum' des Jan Długosz: Eine Quelle zur Schlacht bei Tannenberg 1410* (Göttingen, 1976).
Ekdahl, Sven, 'Die Flucht der Litauer in der Schlacht bei Tannenberg 1410', *ZO*, 12 (1963), 11–19.
Ekdahl, Sven, *Die Schlacht bei Tannenberg 1410: Quellenkritische Untersuchungen*, i: *Einführung und Quellenlage* (Berlin, 1982).
Ekdahl, Sven, 'Die Söldnerwerbungen des Deutschen Ordens für einen geplanten Angriff auf Polen am 1. Juni 1410: Ein Beitrag zur Vorgeschichte der Schlacht bei Tannenberg', in Bernhart Jähnig (ed.), *Beiträge zur Militärgeschichte des Preussenlandes von der Ordenszeit bis zum Zeitalter der Weltkriege* (Marburg, 2010), 89–102.
Ekdahl, Sven, 'Žalgirio mūsis ir jo reikšmė Ordino gyvenimui', in Čapaitė and Nikžentaitis (eds), *Žalgirio laikų*, 3–33.
Elazar, Daniel J., *Exploring Federalism* (Tuscaloosa, AL, 1987).
Elliott, J.H., 'A Europe of composite monarchies,' *P&P*, 137 (1992), 48–71.
Elliott, J.H., *Imperial Spain* (London, 1963).
Enemark, Poul, 'Motiver for nordisk aristokratisk unionspolitik: Overvejeler omkring kildegrundlag og tilgangsvinkler i unionsforskningen', in Ingesman and Jensen (eds), *Danmark*, 166–81.
Fałkowski, Wojciech, *Elita władzy w Polsce za panowania Kazimierza Jagiellończyka (1447–1492)* (Warsaw, 1992).
Fałkowski, Wojciech, 'Idea monarchii w Polsce za pierwszych Jagiellonów', in Fałkowski (ed.), *Polska około roku 1400*, 195–218.
Fałkowski, Wojciech, 'Król i biskup: Spór o rację stanu królestwa Polskiego w latach 1424–1426', in Kiryk and Noga (eds), *Oleśnicki*, 123–42.
Fałkowski, Wojciech, 'Polsko-litewskie negocjacje w 1446 roku', in Kras et al. (eds), *Ecclesia*, 465–76.
Fałkowski, Wojciech, 'Rok trzech sejmów', in Manikowska et al. (eds), *Aetas media*, 425–38.
Fałkowski, Wojciech, 'Sejmy bez króla (1440–1446)', in Smołucha et al. (eds), *Historia*, 235–55.
Fałkowski, Wojciech (ed.), *Polska około roku 1400: Państwo, społeczeństwo, kultura* (Warsaw, 2001).
Fasolt, Constantin, 'Quod omnes tangit ab omnibus approbari debet: The words and their meaning', in Steven Bowman and Blanche Cody (eds), *In iure veritas: Studies in Canon Law in Memory of Schafer Williams* (Cincinnati, OH, 1991), 21–55.
Ferenc, Marek, *Dwór Zygmunta Augusta* (Cracow, 1998).
Ferenc, Marek, *Mikołaj Radziwiłł 'Rudy' (ok. 1515–1584): Działalność polityczna i wojskowa* (Cracow, 2008).

Ferenc, Marek, 'Uwagi o dworze litewskim Zygmunta Augusta w latach 1548–1572', in Kras et al. (eds), *Ecclesia*, 537–48.

Fijałek, Jan, 'Kościół rzymskokatolicki na Litwie: Uchrześcijanienie Litwy przez Polskę i zachowanie w niej języka ludu po koniec Rzeczypospolitej', in Kłoczowski (ed.), *Chrystianizacja*, 129–318.

Finkel, Ludwik, *Elekcja Zygmunta I. Sprawy dynastii jagiellońskiej i unii polsko-litewskiej* (Cracow, 1910).

Forstreuter, Kurt, *Das Preußische Staatsarchiv in Königsberg: Ein geschichtlicher Rückblick mit einer Übersicht über seine Bestände* (Göttingen, 1955).

Forsyth, Murray, *Unions of States: The Theory and Practice of Confederation* (Leicester, 1981).

Freedman, Paul, and Bourin, Monique (eds), *Forms of Servitude in Northern and Central Europe: Decline, Resistance, and Expansion* (Turnhout, 2005).

Friedberg, Jan, 'Zatarg Polski z Rzymem podczas wojny 13-letniej', *KH*, 24 (1910), 422–67.

Friedrich, Carl Joachim, *Trends of Federalism in Theory and Practice* (London, 1968).

Friedrich, Karin, 'Citizenship in the periphery: Royal Prussia and the union of Lublin 1569', in Karin Friedrich and Barbara Pendzich (eds), *Citizenship and Identity in a Multinational Commonwealth: Poland-Lithuania in Context, 1550–1772* (Leiden, 2009), 49–69.

Friedrich, Karin, *The Other Prussia: Royal Prussia, Poland and Liberty, 1569–1772* (Cambridge, 2000).

Fröschl, Thomas (ed.), *Föderationsmodelle und Unionsstrukturen: Über Staantenverbindungen in der frühen Neuzeit vom 15. zum 18. Jahrhundert* (Vienna, 1994).

Frost, Robert, 'Ordering the Kaleidoscope: Nation and State Power in the lands of Poland-Lithuania since 1569', in Oliver Zimmer and Len Scales (eds), *Power and the Nation in History* (Cambridge, 2005), 212–31.

Frost, Robert, *The Northern Wars: War, State and Society in Northeastern Europe 1558–1721* (Harlow, 2000).

Frost, Robert 'Unmaking the Polish-Lithuanian Commonwealth: Mykhailo Hrushev'skyi and the making of the Cossacks', *HUS*, 27 (2004–5), 313–33.

Gąsiorowski, Antoni, *Itinerarium króla Władysława Jagiełły 1386–1434* (Warsaw, 1972).

Gawęda, Stanisław, 'Ocena niektórych problemów historii ojczystej w "Rocznikach" Jana Długosza', in Stanisław Gawęda (ed.), *Długossiana: Studia historyczne w pięćsetlecie śmierci Jana Długosza* (Warsaw, 1980), 181–203.

Gawlas, Sławomir, 'Dlaczego nie było w Polsce feudalizmu lennego?', *RDSG*, 58 (1998), 101–23.

Giedroyć, Michał, 'The arrival of Christianity in Lithuania: Early contacts (thirteenth century)', *OSP*, NS 18 (1985), 1–30.

Glemža, Liudas and Šmigelskytė-Stukienė, Ramunė (eds), *Liublino unija: Idėja ir jos tęstinumas* (Vilnius, 2011).

Górczak, Zbyszko, *Podstawy gospodarcze działalności Zbigniewa Oleśnickiego biskupa krakowskiego* (Cracow, 1999).

Górecki, Piotr, *Economy, Society and Lordship in Medieval Poland, 1100–1250* (New York, 1992).

Górski, Karol, *Łukasz Watzenrode: Życie i działalność polityczna (1447–1512)* (Wrocław 1973).

Górski, Karol, 'Młodość Kazimierza i rządy na Litwie (1440–1454)', in Biskup and Górski (eds), *Kazimierz Jagiellończyk*, 9–17.

Górski, Karol, *Państwo krzyżackie w Prusach* (Gdańsk/Bydgoszcz, 1946).

Górski, Karol, 'Pierwsze czterdziestolecie Prus Królewskich, 1466–1506', *RG*, 11 (1937), 17–66.

Górski, Karol, 'Rządy wewnętrzne Kazimierza Jagiellończyka w Koronie', in Biskup and Górski (eds), *Kazimierz Jagiellończyk*, 82–127.

Górski, Karol, *Starostowie malborscy w latach 1457–1510* (Toruń, 1960).

Górski, Karol, 'The Royal Prussian estates in the second half of the 15th century and their relation to the Crown of Poland', in Górski, *Communitas, princeps, corona regni: Studia selecta* (Warsaw, 1976), 42–56.

Górski, Karol, 'Wojna trzynastoletnia (1454–1466)', *PZ*, 10 (1954), 331–52.

Górski, Karol, *Z dziejów walki o pokój i sprawiedliwość międzynarodową: Ostatnie słowo Pawła Włodkowica o Zakonie Krzyżackim* (Toruń, 1964).

Goyski, Maryan, 'Sprawa zastawu ziemi dobrzyńskiej przez Władysława Opolczyka i pierwsze lata sporu (1391–1399)', *PH*, 3 (1906), 22–51, 174–98, 333–50.

Graff, Tomasz, *Episkopat monarchii jagiellońskiej w dobie soborów powszechnych XV wieku* (Cracow, 2008).

Graff, Tomasz, *Kościół w Polsce wobec konfliktu z zakonem krzyżackim w XV wieku* (Cracow, 2010).

Graff, Tomasz, 'Zbigniew Oleśnicki i polski episkopat wobec unii personalnej z królestwem Węgier w latach 1440–1444', in Smołucha et al. (eds), *Historia*, 349–64.

Grygiel, Jerzy, *Życie i działalność Zygmunta Korybutowicza: Studium z dziejów stosunków polsko-czeskich w pierwszej połowie XV wieku* (Cracow, 1988).

Grzybowski, Konstanty, *Teoria reprezentacji w Polsce epoki Odrodzenia* (Warsaw, 1959).

Gudavičius, Edvardas, 'Baltų alodo pavbeldėjimas ir disponavimas juo', in Gudavičius, *Lietuvos Europėjimo keliais*, 100–11.

Gudavičius, Edvardas, 'Baltų alodo raida', in Gudavičius, *Lietuvos Europėjimo keliais*, 87–99.

Gudavičius, Edvardas, *Lietuvos Istorija*, i (Vilnius, 2001).

Gudavičius, Edvardas, 'Vytautas kaip Europos dinastas', in V. Merkys (ed.), *Lietuvos europėjimo keliais: Istorinės studijos* (Vilnius, 2002), 263–9.

Gudavičius, Edvardas and Lazutka, Stanislovas, 'Albertas Goštautas ir Lietuvos istoriografija', *LIS*, 24 (2009), 195–201.

Gudavičius, Edvardas (ed.), *Lietuvos Europėjimo keliais* (Vilnius, 2002).

Gudziak, Borys A., *Crisis and Reform: The Kyivan Metropolitanate, the Patriarch of Constantinople, and the Genesis of the Union of Brest* (Cambridge, MA, 1998).

Gudziak, Borys A., 'The union of Florence in the Kievan Metropolitanate: Did it survive until the times of the union of Brest? (Some reflections on a recent argument)', review of Ihor Mončak, *Florentine Ecumenism in the Kyivan Church* (Rome, 1987), in *HUS*, 17, 1/2 (1993), 138–48.

Guzowski, Piotr, *Chłopi i pieniądz na przełomie średniowiecza i czasów nowożytnych* (Cracow, 2008).

Guzowski, Piotr, 'System dziedziczenia chłopów na przełomie średniowiecza i czasów nowożytnych w świetle sądowych ksiąg wiejskich', in Cezary Kuklo (ed.), *Rodzina i gospodarstwo domowe na ziemiach polskich w XV–XX wieku: Struktury demograficzne, społeczne i gospodarcze* (Warsaw, 2008), 29–48.

Guzowski, Piotr, 'Sytuacja ekonomiczna chłopów polskich w XV i XVI w. na tle europejskim', in Wijaczka (ed.), *Między zachodem a wschodem*, 5–35.

Gzella, Jacek, *Małopolska elita władzy w okresie rządów Ludwika Węgierskiego w latach 1370–1382* (Toruń, 1994).
Hagen, William, *Ordinary Prussians: Brandenburg, Junkers and Villagers, 1500–1840* (Cambridge, 2002).
Hagen, William, 'Subject farmers in Brandenburg-Prussia and Poland: Village life and fortunes under manorialism in early modern Central Europe', in Bush (ed.), *Serfdom*, 296–310.
Halecki, Oskar, *Dzieje unii jagiellońskiej*, 2 vols (Cracow, 1919–20).
Halecki, Oskar, *From Florence to Brest (1439–1596)* (New York, 1958).
Halecki, Oskar, *Jadwiga of Anjou and the Rise of East Central Europe* (Boulder, CO, 1991).
Halecki, Oskar, 'Litwa, Ruś i Żmudź jako części składowe Wielkiego Księstwa Litewskiego' *RAUWHF*, serya ii, 34 (1916), 214–54.
Halecki, Oskar, *Ostatnie lata Świdrygiełły i sprawa wołyńska za Kazimierza Jagiellończyka* (Cracow, 1915).
Halecki, Oskar, *Przyłączenie Podlasia, Wołynia i Kijowszczyzny do Korony w roku 1569* (Cracow, 1915).
Halecki, Oskar, 'Sejm obozowy szlachty litewskiej pod Witebskiem 1562 r. i jego petycya o unię z Polską', *PH*, 18 (1914), 320–52.
Halecki, Oskar, 'Unia Polski z Litwą a unia kalmarska', in *Studia historyczne ku czci Stanisława Kutrzeby*, i, 217–32.
Halecki, Oskar, 'Wcielenie i wznowienie państwa litewskiego przez Polskę (1386–1401)', *PH*, 21 (1917–18), 1–77.
Halperin, Charles, *Russia and the Golden Horde: The Mongol Impact on Russian History* (Bloomington, 1987).
Hartung, Fritz, 'Die Krone als Symbol der monarchischen Herrschaft im ausgehenden Mittelalter', in Hellmann (ed.), *Corona Regni*, 1–69.
Hayton, D.W., Kelly, James, and Bergin, John (eds), *The Eighteenth Century Composite State: Representative Institutions in Ireland and Europe, 1689–1800* (Basingstoke, 2010).
Hejnosz, Wojciech, 'Prawnopaństwowy stosunek Prus do korony w świetle aktu inkorporacyjnego z r. 1454', *PZ*, 10 (1954), 307–30.
Hejnosz, Wojciech, 'Przywileje nieszawsko-radzyńskie dla ziem ruskich', in *Studia historyczne ku czci Stanisława Kutrzeby*, i, 233–46.
Hellmann, Manfred (ed.), *Corona Regni: Studien über die Krone als Symbol des Staates im späteren Mittelalter* (Darmstadt, 1961).
Historia Gdańska, ii: *1454–1655*, ed. Edmund Cieślak (Gdańsk, 1982).
Historia Pomorza, ii/i, ed. Gerard Labuda (Poznań, 1976).
Historia sejmu polskiego, i: *Do schyłku szlacheckiego Rzeczypospolitej*, ed. Jerzy Michalski (Warsaw, 1984).
Historia Śląska, ed. Marek Czapliński (Wrocław, 2002).
Hoensch, Jörg, *Kaiser Sigismund: Herrscher an der Schwelle der Neuzeit 1368–1437* (Munich, 1996).
Hoensch, Jörg, 'König/Kaiser Sigismund, der Deutsche Orden und Polen-Litauen' *ZOF*, NF 46 (1997), 1–44.
Hrushevsky, Mikhailo, *History of Ukraine-Rus'*, i, ed. Andrzej Poppe and Frank Sysyn (Edmonton, Alberta, 1997).
Hrushevsky, Mikhailo, *History of Ukraine-Rus'*, vi: *Economic, Cultural, and National Life in the 14th to 17th Centuries*, ed. Myron Kapral and Frank Sysyn (Edmonton, Alberta, 2012).

Hughes, Christopher, *Confederacies: An Inaugural Lecture delivered in the University of Leicester 8 November 1962* (Leicester, 1963).
Ihnatowicz, Ireniusz, Mączak, Antoni, Zientara, Benedykt, and Żarnowski, Janusz (eds), *Społeczeństwo polskie od X do XX w.* (Warsaw, 1979; 1988).
Ingesman, Per and Jensen, Jens Villiam (eds), *Danmark i senmiddelalderen* (Aarhus, 1994).
Inglot, Stefan, *Z dziejów wsi polskiej i rolnictwa*, 2nd edn (Warsaw, 1986).
Ivinskis, Zenonas, 'Jogaila valstybininkas ir žmogus', in Šapoka (ed.), *Jogaila*, 309–28.
Ivinskis, Zenonas, 'Jogailos santykiai su Kęstučiu ir Vytautu iki 1392 metų', in Šapoka (ed.), *Jogaila*, 45–79.
Ivinskis, Zenonas, 'Litwa w dobie chrztu i unii z Polską', in Kłoczowski (ed.), *Chrystianizacja*, 15–126.
Ivinskis, Zenonas, 'Vytauto jaunystė ir jo veikimas iki 1392 m.', in Šležas (ed.), *Vytautas*, 1–44.
Izydorczyk-Kamler, Anna, 'Praca najemna na wsi małopolskiej w XVI i pierwszej połowie XVII wieku', *KH*, 97/1–2 (1990), 3–31.
Jablonowski, Horst, *Westrußland zwischen Wilna und Moskau: Die politische Stellung und die politischen Tendenzen der russischen Bevölkerung des Großfürstentums Litauen im 15. Jh.* (Leiden, 1961).
Janosz-Biskupowa, Irena, *Chronologia zjazdów stanów Prus Królewskich w latach 1466–1492* (Toruń, 1973).
Januškevič, Andrej [Янушкевіч, Андрэй], 'Między królem a Radziwiłłami: Kształtowanie kariery politycznej Jana Chodkiewicza w przededniu unii lubelskiej 1569', in Markiewicz and Skowron (eds), *Faworyci*, 167–79.
Januškevič, Andrej [Янушкевіч, Андрэй], 'Początek przełomu: Sejm wileński 1563 r. na tle wojny inflanckiej i reform ustrojowych w Wielkim Księstwie Litewskim', in Ciesielski and Filipczak-Kocur (eds), *Rzeczpospolita*, 81–8.
Jarmolik, Włodzimierz, 'Kariery polityczne dworzan litewskich Kazimierza Jagiellończyka', in Zbigniew Karpus, Tomasz Kempa, Dorota Michaluk, and Stanisław Alexandrowicz (eds), *Europa orientalis: Polska i jej sąsiedzi od średniowiecza po współczesność* (Toruń, 1996), 93–101.
Jasas, Rimantas, 'Bychovco kronika ir jos kilmė', in *Lietuvos metraštis: Bychovco kronika*, ed. Jasas (Vilnius, 1971), 8–38.
Jasnowski, Józef, *Mikołaj Czarny Radziwiłł (1515–1565)* (Warsaw, 1939).
Jawor, Grzegorz, *Ludność chłopska i społeczności wiejskie w województwie lubelskim w późnym średniowieczu (schyłek XI–początek XVI wieku)* (Lublin, 1991).
Jellinek, Georg, *Die Lehre von Staatenverbindungen* (Berlin, 1882).
Jóźwiak, Sławomir, Kwiatkowski, Krzystof, Szweda, Adam, and Szybkowski, Sobiesław, *Wojna Polski i Litwy z Zakonem Krzyżackim w latach 1409–1411* (Malbork, 2010).
Jučas, Mečislovas, *Lietuvos ir Lenkijos unija (XIV a. vid.–XIX a. pr.)* (Vilnius, 2000).
Jučas, Mečislovas, *Lietuvos metraščiai ir kronikos*, 2nd edn (Vilnius, 2002).
Jučas, Mečislovas, 'Nejvykęs Vytauto vainikavimas', in *Vytautas Didysis ir Lietuva*, 54–65.
Jučas, Mečislovas, 'Vytautas ir Čeku husitai', in *Vytautas Didysis ir Lietuva*, 43–53.
Jurkiewicz, Jan, *Od Palemona do Giedymina: Wczesnonowożytne wyobrażenia o początkach Litwy*, i: *W kręgu latopisów litewskich* (Poznań, 2012).
Kaczmarczyk, Zdzisław and Leśniodorski, Bogusław (eds), *Historia państwa i prawa Polski*, ii: *Od połowy XV wieku do r. 1795*, 2nd edn (Warsaw, 1966).
Kamieniecki, Witold, *Społeczeństwo litewskie w XV wieku* (Warsaw, 1947).
Kamiński, Andrzej, 'Neo-serfdom in Poland-Lithuania', *SR*, 34 (1975), 253–68.

Kamler, Anna, *Chłopi jako pracownicy najemni na wsi małopolskiej w XVI i pierwszej połowie XVII wieku* (Warsaw, 2005).
Kamler, Anna, *Od szkoły do senatu: Wykształcenie senatorów w Koronie w latach 1501–1586* (Warsaw, 2006).
Kananović, Vladimir, 'Grand Duchess Elena Ivanovna and Duke Michael Gliński: Aspects of rulership at the Jagiellonian court', in Jacek Wiesiołowski (ed.), *Zamek i dwór w średniowieczu od XI do XV wieku* (Poznań, 2001), 161–5.
Kantorowicz, Ernst H., *The King's Two Bodies: A Study in Medieval Political Theology* (Princeton, NJ, 1918).
Karpat, Josef, 'Zur Geschichte des Begriffes Corona Regni in Frankreich und England', in Hellmann (ed.), *Corona Regni*, 70–155.
Kempa, Tomasz, *Konstany Wasyl Ostrogski (ok. 1524/1525–1608): Wojewoda kijowski i marszałek ziemi wołyńskiej* (Toruń, 1997).
Kempa, Tomasz, 'Książęta Ostrogscy a kwestia unii polsko-litewskiej w XVI wieku', *Wrocławskie Studia Wschodnie*, 8 (2004), 47–54.
Kempa, Tomasz, 'Możnowładztwo i szlachta z Wołynia wobec unii lubelskiej (1569)', in Glemža and Šmygielskytė-Stukienė (eds), *Liublino Unija*, 172–87.
Kętrzyński, Stanisław, *Zarys nauki o dokumencie polskim wieków średnich*, 2nd edn (Poznań, 2008).
Kiaupa, Zigimantas, *The History of Lithuania* (Vilnius, 2002).
Kiaupa, Zigimantas, *Lietuvos valstybės istorija* (Vilnius, 2006).
Kiaupa, Zigimantas and Mickevičius, Arturas (eds), *Lietuvos valstybė XII–XVIII a.* (Vilnius, 1997).
Kiaupienė, Jūratė, '1385 m. rugpjūčio 14 d. aktas Lietuvos-Lenkijos unijų istoriografiojoje (problemos formulavimas)', in Kiaupa and Mickevičius (eds), *Lietuvos valstybė*, 247–67.
Kiaupienė, Jūratė, '1413 m. Horodlės dokumentų "gyvenimai" ', in *Horodlės aktai*, 255–80.
Kiaupienė, Jūratė, 'Akt krewski z 14 sierpnia 1385 r.: Gdzie kryje się problem: W dokumentacie czy w jego interpretacjach?', *KH*, 108/4 (2001), 47–61.
Kiaupienė, Jūratė, 'Lietuvos Didžiosios Kunigaikštystės teritorinio vientisumo suardymo 1569 m.: Problema Liublino Unijos istoriografijos kontekste: Tradicijų ir naujų interpretacijų erdvė', in Glemža and Šmygielskytė-Stukienė (eds), *Liublino Unija*, 102–13.
Kiaupienė, Jūratė, 'Litewskie cechy kultury politycznej szlachty Wielkiego Księstwa Litewskiego w XVI wieku', in Jerzy Wyrozumski (ed.), *Kultura Litwy i Polski w dziejach: Tożsamość, i współistnienie* (Cracow, 2000), 67–78.
Kiaupienė, Jūratė, *'Mes Lietuva': Lietuvos Didžiosios Kunigaikštystės bajorija XVI a. (viešasis ir privatus gyvenimas)* (Vilnius, 2003).
Kiaupienė, Jūratė, 'The Grand Duchy and the Grand Dukes of Lithuania in the sixteenth century: Reflections on the Lithuanian political nation and the Union of Lublin', in Butterwick (ed.), *The Polish-Lithuanian Monarchy*, 82–92.
Kiaupienė, Jūratė, 'W związku z polemiką Grzegorza Błaszczyka w sprawie unii krewskiej', *KH*, 110/3 (2003), 97–8.
Kiaupienė, Jūratė and Petrauskas, Rimvydas, *Lietuvos Istorija*, iv: *Nauji horizontai: Dinastija, visuomenė, valstybė: Lietuvos Didžioji Kunigaikštystė 1386–1529 m.* (Vilnius, 2009).
Kidd, Colin, *Unions and Unionism: Political Thought in Scotland, 1500–2000* (Cambridge, 2008).
Kiryk, Feliks and Noga, Zdzisław (eds), *Zbigniew Oleśnicki książę kościoła i mąż stanu* (Cracow, 2006).

Klimecka, G., 'Czy rzeczywiście "doradcy Władysława Jagiełły"?', in *SPS*, iv (Warsaw, 1990) 214–35.
Kłoczowski, Jerzy (ed.), *Chrystianizacja Litwy* (Cracow, 1987).
Kłodziński, Abdon, 'W sprawie przywilejów nieszawskich z r. 1454', in *Studya historyczne wydane ku czci prof. Wincentego Zakrzewskiego* (Cracow, 1908), 241–73.
Knoll, Paul, 'Louis the Great and Casimir of Poland', in S.B. Vardy, Géza Grosschmid, and Leslie S. Domonkos (eds), *Louis the Great, King of Hungary and Poland* (New York, 1986), 105–27.
Knoll, Paul, *The Rise of the Polish Monarchy: Piast Poland in East Central Europe, 1320–1370* (Chicago, 1972).
Knoppek, Witold, 'Zmiany w układzie sił politycznych w Polsce w drugiej połowie XV w. i ich związek z genezą dwuizbowego sejmu', *CPH*, 7/2 (1955), 55–95.
Koczerska, Maria, 'Autentyczność dokumentu unii krewskiej 1385 roku', *KH*, 99 (1992) 59–78.
Koenigsberger, H.G., '*Dominium Regale* or *Dominium Politicum et Regale*: Monarchies and parliaments in early modern Europe', in Koenigsberger, *Politicians and Virtuosi: Essays in Early Modern History* (London, 1986), 1–25.
Kołacz, Małgorzata, 'Powinności chłopskie w ziemi chełmskiej w XV–XVI wieku', in Wijaczka (ed.), *Między zachodem a wschodem*, 36–47.
Kolankowski, Ludwik, *Dzieje Wielkiego Księstwa Litewskiego za Jagiellonów*, i (Warsaw, 1930).
Kolankowski, Ludwik, 'Elekcja Zygmunta Augusta', *KH*, 19 (1905), 531–57.
Kolankowski, Ludwik, 'O litewską koronę.' *KH*, 40 (1926), 386–99.
Kolankowski, Ludwik, *Polska Jagiellonów* (Lwów, 1936).
Kolankowski, Ludwik, 'Pomiara włóczna', *AW*, 4 (1927), 235–52.
Kolankowski, Ludwik, *Zygmunt August wielki książę Litwy do roku 1548* (Lwów, 1913).
Kollmann, Nancy Shields, 'Collateral succession in Kievan Rus'', *HUS*, 14/3–4 (1990), 377–87.
Kollmann, Nancy Shields, *Kinship and Politics: The Making of the Muscovite Political System, 1345–1547* (Stanford, CA, 1987).
Kołodziejczyk, Dariusz, *Ottoman-Polish Diplomatic Relations (15th–18th century)* (Leiden, 2000).
Kołodziejczyk, Dariusz, *The Crimean Khanate and Poland-Lithuania: International Diplomacy on the European Periphery (15th–18th century)* (Leiden, 2011).
Koneczny, Feliks, *Jagiełło i Witold* (Lwów, 1893).
Korczak, Lidia, 'Horodło: Na drodze ku dziedzicznej monarchii jagiellońskiej', in *Horodlės aktai*, 57–69.
Korczak, Lidia, *Litewska rada wielkoksiążęca w XV wieku* (Cracow, 1998).
Korczak, Lidia, *Monarchia i poddani: System władzy w Wielkim Księstwem Litewskim w okresie wczesnojagiellońskim* (Cracow, 2008).
Korczak, Lidia, 'O akcie krewskim raz jeszcze (na marginesie rozprawy J. Dainauskasa)', *SH*, 34 (1991), 473–9.
Korczak, Lidia, 'Wielki książę litewski Świdrygiełło wobec soboru bazylejskiego i papieża Eugeniusza IV', in Smołucha et al. (eds), *Historia*, 339–48.
Kosman, Marceli, *Drogi zaniku pogaństwa u Bałtów* (Wrocław, 1976).
Kosman, Marceli, 'Kancelaria Wielkiego Księcia Witolda', in Kosman, *Orzeł i pogoń: Z dziejów polsko-litewskich XIV–XV w.* (Warsaw, 1992), 102–42.
Kosman, Marceli, 'Polacy w Wielkim Księstwie Litewskim: Z badań nad mobilnością społeceństwa w dobie unii Jagiellońskiej 1386–1569', in *SPS*, i (Warsaw, 1981), 347–78.

Kras, Paweł, Januszek, Agnieszka, Nalewajek, Agnieszka, and Polak, Wojciech (eds), *Ecclesia Cultura Potestas: Studia z dziejów kultury i społeczeństwa* (Cracow, 2006).
Kriegseisen, Wojciech, *Sejm Rzeczypospolitej szlacheckiej (do 1763 roku)* (Warsaw, 1995).
Kriegseisen, Wojciech, *Stosunki wyznaniowe w relacjach państwo-kościół między reformacją a oświeceniem* (Warsaw, 2010).
Krom, Mikhail [Кром, Михаил], 'Die Konstituierung der Szlachta als Stand und das Problem staatlicher Einheit im Großfürstentum Litauens (15./16. Jahrhundert)', *JGO*, 42 (1994), 481–92.
Krupska, Anna, 'W sprawie genezy tzw. spisku książąt litewskich w 1480–1481 roku: Przyczynek do dziejów walki o "*dominium Russiae*"', *RH*, 48 (1982), 120–46.
Krzyżaniakowa, Jadwiga, 'Portret niedokończony: Kazimierz Jagiellończyk w *Annales* Jana Długosza', in Kras et al. (eds), *Ecclesia*, 465–76.
Krzyżaniakowa, Jadwiga, 'Rok 1413', in Karol Olejnik (ed.), *Pax et bellum* (Poznań, 1993), 75–85.
Krzyżaniakowa, Jadwiga and Ochmański, Jerzy, *Władysław II Jagiełło* (1990; 2nd edn, Wrocław, 2006).
Kubiak, Stanisław, *Monety i stosunki monetarne w Prusach Królewskich w 2 połowie XV wieku* (Wrocław, 1986).
Kuchowicz, Zbigniew, *Barbara Radziwiłłówna* (Łódź, 1976).
Kuczyński, Stefan, *Wielka wojna z zakonem krzyżackim w latach 1409–1411* (Warsaw, 1955).
Kuklo, Cezary, *Demografia Rzeczypospolitej przedrozbiorowej* (Warsaw, 2009).
Kula, Witold, *An Economic Theory of the Feudal System* (London, 1976).
Kula, Witold, *Teoria ekonomiczna ustroju feudalnego*, 2nd edn (Warsaw, 1983).
Kuolys, Darius, *Res Lituania kunigaikštystės bendrija*, i: *Respublikos steigimas* (Vilnius, 2009).
Kurtyka, Janusz, *Latyfundium tęczyńskie: Dobra i właściciele (XIV–XVII wiek)* (Cracow, 1999).
Kurtyka, Janusz, *Podole w czasach jagiellońskich* (Cracow, 2011).
Kurtyka, Janusz, 'Podole w średniowieczu', in Kurtyka, *Podole*, 91–160.
Kurtyka, Janusz, 'Posiadłość, dziedziczność i prestiż: Badania nad późnośredniowieczną i wczesnonowożytną wielką własnością możnowładczą w Polsce XIV–XVII wieku', *RH*, 65 (1999), 161–94.
Kurtyka, Janusz, *Tęczyńscy: Studium z dziejów polskiej elity możnowładczej w średniowieczu* (Cracow, 1997).
Kurtyka, Janusz, 'Wierność i zdrada na pograniczu: Walki o Bracław w latach 1430–1437', in Kurtyka, *Podole*, 217–56.
Kurtyka, Janusz, 'Z dziejów walki szlachty ruskiej o równouprawnienie: Represje lat 1426–1427 i sejmiki roku 1439', in Kurtyka, *Podole*, 25–66.
Kutrzeba, Stanisław, 'Charakter prawny związku Litwy z Polską 1385–1569', in *Pamiętnik VI Powszechnego Zjazdu*, i, 165–73.
Kutrzeba, Stanisław, *Historia ustroju Polski*, ii: *Litwa*, 2nd edn (Lwów, 1921).
Kutrzeba, Stanisław, *Historia ustroju Polski: Korona* (updated repr. based on 8th edn, Poznań, 2001).
Kutrzeba, Stanisław, 'Przywilej jedlneński z 1430 r. i nadanie prawa polskiego Rusi', in *Księga pamiątkowa ku czci Bolesława Ulanowskiego* (Cracow, 1911), 271–301.
Kutrzeba, Stanisław, 'Unia Polski z Litwą', in *Polska i Litwa w dziejowym stosunku* (Cracow, 1914), 447–658.
Kuźmińska, Marja, 'Olbracht Marcinowicz Gasztołd: Działalność Olbrachta Gasztołda 1503–1522', *AW*, 4 (1927), 348–91.
Lassere, David, *Étapes du féderalisme* (Lausanne, 1954).

Lewicki, Anatol, *Powstanie Świdrygiełły: Ustep z dziejów unii Litwy z Koroną* (Cracow, 1892).
Lewicki, Anatol, 'Sprawa unii kościelnej za Jagiełły', *KH*, 11 (1897), 310–37.
Lewicki, Anatol, 'Über das staatsrechtliche Verhältnis Littauens zu Polen unter Jagiełło und Witold', *Altpreussische Monatsschrift*, 31 (1894), 1–94.
Lewicki, Anatol, 'Wstąpienie na tron polski Kazimierza Jagiellończyka', *RSAU*, 20 (1887), 1–40.
Leinz, Josef, 'Die Ursachen des Abfalls Danzigs vom Deutschen Orden: Unter Besonderer Berücksichtigung der Nationalen Frage', *Jahrbuch der Geschichte Ost- und Mitteldeutschlands*, 13–14 (1965), 1–59.
Litwin, Henryk, 'Kijowszczyzna, Wołyń i Bracławszczyzna w 1569: Między unią a inkorporacją', in С.Ф. Сокал and Андрей Янушкевіч (eds), *Праблемы інтэграцыі і інкорпорацыі ў развіцці Цэнтральнай і Усходняй Еўропы ў перыяд раннага Новага часу* (Minsk, 2009), 186–203.
Litwin, Henryk, *Równi do równych: Kijowska reprezentacja sejmowa 1569–1648* (Warsaw, 2009).
Loewe, Karl von, 'Military service in early sixteenth-century Lithuania: A new interpretation and its implications', *SR*, 30 (1971), 249–56.
Lönnroth, Erik, *Sverige och Kalmarunionen 1397–1457*, 2nd edn (Gothenburg, 1969).
Łowmiański, Henryk, *Polityka Jagiellonów* (Poznań, 1999).
Łowmiański, Henryk, *Studia nad dziejami Wielkiego Księstwa Litewskiego* (Poznań, 1983).
Łowmiański, Henryk, 'Wcielenie Litwy do Polski w 1386 r.', in Marceli Kosman (ed.), *Prusy—Litwa—Krzyżacy* (Warsaw, 1989), 294–402; first published in *AW*, 12 (1937) 36–145.
Łowmiański, Henryk, *Zaludnienie państwa litewskiego w wieku XVI* (Poznań, 1998).
Luciński, Jerzy, *Rozwój królewszczyzn w Koronie od schyłku XIV wieku do XVII wieku* (Poznań, 1970).
Lückerath, Carl, *Paul von Rusdorf, Hochmeister des Deutschen Ordens 1422–1441* (Bad Godesberg, 1969).
Lüdicke, Edith, 'Der Rechtkampf des Deutschen Ordens gegen den Bund der preussischen Stände', *AF*, 12 (1935), 1–43, 173–217.
Lukowski, Jerzy and Zawadzki, Hubert, *A Concise History of Poland* (Cambridge, 2001).
Lulewicz, Henryk, *Gniewów o unię ciąg dalszy: Stosunki polsko-litewskie w latach 1569–1588* (Warsaw, 2002).
Maciejewska, Wanda, 'Dzieje ziemi połockiej (1385–1430)', *AW*, 8 (1931–2), 3–13.
Mačiukas, Žydrūnas, 'Teisinis Vytauto karūnacijos ginčas', in Kiaupa and Mickevičius (eds), *Lietuvos valstybė*, 271–83.
Mačiukas, Žydrūnas, 'Zigmanto Liuksemburgiečio veiksnys Lietuvos santykiuose su Vokiečių ordninu 1411–1418 m.', in Bumblauskas and Petrauskas (eds), *Tarp istorijos*, 159–76.
Magocsi, Paul, *A History of Ukraine* (Toronto, 1996).
Malczewska, Mirosława, *Latyfundium Radziwiłłów w XV do połowy XVI wieku* (Warsaw, 1985).
Maleczyńska, Ewa, *Rola polityczna królowej Zofii Holszańskiej na tle walki stronnictw w Polsce w latach 1422–1434* (Lwów, 1936).
Małłek, Janusz, *Dwie części Prus: Studia z dziejów Prus Książęcych i Prus Królewskich w XVI i XVII wieku* (Olsztyn, 1987).

Małłek, Janusz, 'From the rebellion of the Prussian League to the autonomy of Royal Prussia: The estates of Prussia and Poland in the years 1454–1526', *PER*, 14/1 (1994), 19–29.
Małłek, Janusz, 'Powstanie poczucia krajowej odrębności w Prusach i jej rozwój w XV I XVI wieku', in Małłek, *Dwie części Prus*, 9–17.
Małłek, Janusz, 'Prawo chełmińskie w Prusach Krzyżackich (1466–1525) i Prusach Książęcych (1525–1620)', in Zbigniew Zdrójkowski (ed.), *Księga Pamiątkowa 750-lecia prawa chełmińskiego*, ii (Toruń, 1988), 131–47.
Małłek, Janusz, *Prusy Książęce a Prusy Królewskie w latach 1525–1548* (Warsaw, 1976).
Małłek, Janusz, 'Stany Prus Królewskich a Rzeczpospolita Polska w latach 1526–1660', in Małłek, *Dwie części Prus*, 67–81.
Małłek, Janusz, 'Ze studiów nad dwuizbowym systemem reprezentacji w Prusach Zakonnych, Prusach Królewskich i Prusach Książęcych od XV do XVIII wieku', *CPH*, 44/1–2 (1992), 231–43.
Małowist, Marian, 'Poland, Russia and western trade in the 15th and 16th centuries', *P&P*, 13 (1958), 26–39.
Małowist, Marian, 'The economic and social development of the Baltic countries from the 15th to the 17th centuries', *EcHR*, 2nd ser., 12/2 (1959), 177–89.
Małowist, Marian, 'The problem of the inequality of economic development in Europe in the later Middle Ages', *EcHR*, 2nd ser., 19/1 (1966), 15–28.
Manikowska, Halina, Bartoszewicz, Agnieszka, and Fałkowski, Wojciech (eds), *Aetas media, aetas moderna: Studia ofiarowane profesorowi Henrykowi Samsonowiczowi w siedemdziesiątą rocznicę urodzin* (Warsaw, 2000).
Marchwińska, Agnieszka, *Królewskie dwory żon Zygmunta Augusta* (Toruń, 2008).
Markiewicz, Mariusz and Skowron, Ryszard (eds), *Faworyci a opozycjoniści: Król a elity polityczne w Rzeczypospolitej XV–XVIII wieku* (Cracow, 2006).
Martel, Antoine, *La langue polonaise dans les pays ruthènes, Ukraine et Russie Blanche, 1569–1667* (Lille, 1938).
Mason, Roger, 'Imagining Scotland: Scottish political thought and the problem of Britain 1560–1660', in Mason (ed.), *Scots and Britons: Scottish Political Thought and the Union of 1603* (Cambridge, 1994), 3–13.
Mason, Roger, 'Scotching the Brut: Politics, history and national myth in sixteenth-century Britain', in Mason (ed.), *Scotland and England 1286–1815* (Edinburgh, 1987), 60–83.
Matusas, Jonas, *Švitrigaila Lietuvos didysis kunigaikštis* (1938; 2nd edn, Vilnius, 1991).
Matuszewski, Jacek, *Przywileje i polityka podatkowa Ludwika Węgierskiego w Polsce* (Łódź, 1983).
Matuszewski, Jacek, 'Statut Władysława Warneńczyka z 1440 r.: W procesie ograniczania królewskiego prawa dyspozycji domeną ziemską w Polsce', *CPH*, 37/2 (1985), 101–20.
Mazur, Karol, 'Nieznana petycja szlachty wołyńskiej do króla w dobie sejmu lubelskiego 1569 r.', in *Соціум. Альманах соціальної історії*, вип, 2 (Kyiv, 2003), 41–56.
Mazur, Karol, 'Szlachta wołyńska wobec unii jagiellońskiej w dobie sejmu lubelskiego 1569 r.', *PH*, 95/1 (2004), 37–52.
Mazur, Karol, *W stronę integracji z Koroną: Sejmiki Wołynia i Ukrainy w latach 1569–1648* (Warsaw, 2006).
Michaluk, Dorota, 'Inkorporacja Podlasia do Korony Królestwa Polskiego w 1569 r.', in Glemża and Šmigelskytė-Stukienė (eds), *Liublino unija*, 142–56.
Michaluk, Dorota, 'Wymiana rodów na pograniczu koronno-litewskim w XVI–XVII wieku na przykładzie południowego Podlasia', in Jacek Staszewski, Krzysztof Mikulski, and Jarosław Dumanowski (eds), *Między zachodem a wschodem: Studia z dziejów Rzeczypospolitej w epoce nowożytnej* (Toruń, 2002), 250–62.

Mikulski, Krzysztof and Wroniszewski, Jan, 'Folwark i zmiany koniunktury gospodarczej w Polsce XIV–XVII wieku', *Klio*, 4 (2003), 25–40.
Miller, James, 'The Polish nobility and the Renaissance Monarchy: The "Execution of the Laws" Movement', i, *PER*, 3/3 (1983), 65–87; ii, *PER*, 4/1 (1984), 1–24.
Mončak, Ihor, *Florentine Ecumenism in the Kyivan Church* (Rome, 1987).
Moszczeńska, Wanda, 'Rola polityczna rycerstwa wielkopolskiego w czasie bezkrólewia po Ludwiku Wielkiego', *PH*, 25 (1925), 33–159.
Nadolski, Andrzej, *Grunwald 1410* (Warsaw, 2010).
Nalewajek, Agnieszka, *Dokument w Rocznikach Jana Długosza* (Lublin, 2006).
Narbutt, Teodor, *Dzieje starożytne narodu litewskiego*, 10 vols (Vilnius, 1835–41).
Naworski, Zbigniew, 'Status Prus Królewskich w Rzeczypospolitej Obojga Narodów: Evenement czy reguła?', in Ciesielski and Filipczak-Kocur (eds), *Rzeczpospolita*, 61–80.
Naworski, Zbigniew, *Szlachecki wymiar sprawiedliwości w Prusach Królewskich (1454–1772): Organizacja i funkcjonowanie* (Toruń, 2004).
Neitmann, Klaus, 'Die preussischen Stände und die Aussenpolitik des Deutschen Ordens vom I. Thorner Frieden bis zum Abfall des Preussischen Bundes (1411–1454)', in Conrad et al. (eds), *Ordensherrschaft*, 27–79.
Niendorf, Matthias, *Das Großfürstentum Litauen: Studien zur Nationsbildung in der Frühen Neuzeit (1569–1795)* (Wiesbaden, 2006).
Niendorf, Matthias, 'Die Beziehungen zwischen Polen und Litauen im historischen Wandel: Rechtliche und politische Aspekte in Mittelalter und Früher Neuzeit', in Dietmar Willoweit and Hans Lemberg (eds), *Reiche und Territorien in Ostmitteleuropa: Historische Beziehungen und politische Herrschaftslegitimation* (Munich, 2006), 129–62.
Nikodem, Jarosław, 'Akt krewski i jego znaczenie', in Z. Wojtkowiak (ed.), *Poznań-Wilno: Studia historyczne w roku tysiąćlecia Państwa Litewskiego* (Poznań, 2010), 111–43.
Nikodem, Jarosław, 'Charakter rządów Skiergiełły i Witolda na Litwie w latach 1392–1394', *LSP*, 11 (2005), 153–63.
Nikodem, Jarosław, 'Data urodzenia Jagiełły: Uwagi o starszeństwie synów Olgierda i Julianny', *Genealogia*, 12 (2000), 23–49.
Nikodem, Jarosław, 'Gniewosz-Jadwiga-Wilhelm: Krytyka przekazu "Annales" Jana Długosza', *PH*, 98 (2007), 175–96.
Nikodem, Jarosław, *Jadwiga, król Polski* (Wrocław, 2009).
Nikodem, Jarosław, 'Jedynowładztwo czy diarchia? Przyczynek do dziejów ustroju W. Ks. Litewskiego do końca XIV w.', *ZH*, 68 (2003), 7–30.
Nikodem, Jarosław, 'Kaributo maištas', *LIM* (2007), 1, 5–20.
Nikodem, Jarosław, 'Objęcie władzy przez Jagiełło w 1377 r.', *PH*, 92/4 (2001), 451–60.
Nikodem, Jarosław, *Polska i Litwa wobec husyckich Czech w latach 1420–1433: Studium o polityce dynastycznej Władysława Jagiełły i Witolda Kiejstutowicza* (Poznań, 2004).
Nikodem, Jarosław, 'Ponownie o dacie urodzenia Jagiełły', *Genealogia*, 16 (2004), 143–58.
Nikodem, Jarosław, 'Problem legitymizacji władcy Władysława Jagiełły w 1399 r.', in *Nihil superfluum esse: Prace z dziejów średniowiecza ofiarowane profesor Jadwidze Krzyżaniakowej* (Poznań, 2000), 393–401.
Nikodem, Jarosław, 'Przyczyny zamordowania Zygmunta Kiejstutowicza', *BZH*, 17 (2002), 5–33.
Nikodem, Jarosław, 'Rola Skirgiełły na Litwie do r. 1394', *Scripta Minora*, 2 (1998), 83–129.
Nikodem, Jarosław, 'Spory o koronację Wielkiego Księcia Litwy Witolda w latach 1429–1430, i: "Burza koronacyjna" w relacji Jana Długosza', *LSP*, 6 (1994), 55–75.
Nikodem, Jarosław, 'Uwagi o genezie niedoszłego przymierza Zygmunta Kiejstutowicza z Albertem II', *Docendo discimus* (Poznań, 2000), 335–56.

Nikodem, Jarosław, *Witold Wielki Książę Litewski (1354 lub 1355–27 października 1430)* (Cracow, 2013).
Nikodem, Jarosław, 'Wyniesienie Świdrigiełły na Wielkie Księstwo Litewskie', *Białoruskie Zeszyty Historyczne*, 19 (2003), 5–31.
Nikodem, Jarosław, *Zbigniew Oleśnicki w historiografii polskiej* (Cracow, 2001).
Nikodem, Jarosław, 'Zbigniew Oleśnicki wobec unii polsko-litewskiej, i: Do śmierci Jagiełły', *NP*, 91 (1999), 101–51.
Nikodem, Jarosław, 'Zbigniew Oleśnicki wobec unii polsko-litewskiej, ii: W latach 1434–1453', *NP*, 92 (1999), 85–135.
Nikžentaitis, Alvydas, 'Litauen unter den Grossfürsten Gedimin (1316–1341) und Olgerd (1345–1377)', in Marc Löwener (ed.), *Die 'Blüte' der Staaten des östlichen Europa im 14. Jahrhundert* (Wiesbaden, 2004), 65–75.
Nikžentaitis, Alvydas, *Witold i Jagiełło: Polacy i Litwini w wzajemnym stereotypie* (Poznań, 2000).
Nowak, Przemysław, 'Dokumenty pokoju w Raciążku z 1404r.', *SŹ*, 40 (2002), 57–77.
Nowak, Tadeusz, 'Walki obronne z agresją Brandenburgii i Zakonu Krzyżackiego w latach 1308–1521', in Janusz Sikorski (ed.), *Polskie tradycje wojskowe*, i: *Tradycje walk obronnych z najazdami Niemców, Krzyżaków, Szwedów, Turków, i Tatarów, X–XVII w.* (Warsaw, 1990), 43–135.
Nowak, Tadeusz and Wimmer, Jan, *Dzieje oręża polskiego, 963–1795* (Warsaw, 1981).
Nowak, Zenon, 'Krewo i Kalmar: Dwie unie późnego średniowiecza', in Nowak (ed.), *W kręgu stanowych i kulturowych przeobrażeń Europy Północnej w XIV–XVIII w.* (Toruń, 1988), 57–75.
Nowak, Zenon, 'Materiały źródłowe do sprawy wyroku wrocławskiego Zygmunta Luksemburskiego w procesie polsko-krzyżackim z 1420 r.', *ZH*, 41/3 (1976), 149–65.
Nowak, Zenon, *Współpraca polityczna państw unii polsko-litewskiej i unii kalmarskiej w latach 1411–1425* (Toruń, 1996).
Nowak, Zenon (ed.), *Ritterorden und Region: Politische, soziale und wirtschaftliche Verbindungen im Mittelalter* (Toruń, 1995).
Nowak, Zenon (ed.), *Zakon krzyżacki a społeczeństwo państwa w Prusach*, Roczniki Towarzystwa Naukowego w Toruniu, 86/3 (Toruń, 1995).
Nowakowska, Natalia, *Church, State and Dynasty in Renaissance Poland: The Career of Cardinal Fryderyk Jagiellon (1468–1503)* (Aldershot, 2007).
Ochmański, Jerzy, *Dawna Litwa: Studia Historyczne* (Olsztyn, 1986).
Ochmański, Jerzy, *Historia Litwy*, 3rd edn (Wrocław, 1990).
Ochmański, Jerzy, *Litewska granica etniczna na wschodzie od epoki plemiennej do XVI wieku* (Poznań, 1981).
Ochmański, Jerzy, 'Nad kroniką Bychowca', *SŹ*, 12 (1967), 155–63.
Ochmański, Jerzy, 'Najdawniejsze szkoły na Litwie od końca XIV do połowy XVI w.', in Ochmański, *Dawna Litwa*, 116–19.
Ochmański, Jerzy, *Powstanie i rozwój latyfundium biskupstwa wileńskiego (1387–1550)* (Poznań, 1963).
Ochmański, Jerzy, 'Reforma włóczna na Litwie i Białorusi w XVI wieku', in Ochmański, *Dawna Litwa*, 158–74.
Ochmański, Jerzy, 'Reforma włóczna w dobrach magnackich i kościelnych w Wielkim Księstwie Litewskim w drugiej połowie XVI wieku', in Ochmański, *Dawna Litwa*, 175–97.
Odrzywolska-Kidawa, Anna, *Podkanclerzy Piotr Tomicki (1515–1535)* (Warsaw, 2005).
Olejnik Karol, *Władysław III Warneńczyk (1424–1444)*, 2nd edn (Cracow, 2007).

Olesen, Jens, 'Erik af Pommern og Kalmarunionen: Regeringssystemets udformning, 1389–1439', in Ingesman and Jensen (eds), *Danmark*, 143–65.

Ó Siochrú, Micheál and Mackillop, Andrew (eds), *Forging the State: European State Formation and the Anglo-Scottish Union of 1707* (Dundee, 2009).

Pacevičius, Arvydas, 'Bibliotekos', in Ališauskas et al. (eds), *Kultūra*, 94–108.

Pałucki, Władysław, *Drogi i bezdroża skarbowości polskiej XVI i pierwszej połowy XVII wieku* (Wrocław, 1974).

Pamiętnik VI Powszechnego Zjazdu Historyków Polskich w Wilnie 17–20 września 1935 r., 2 vols (Lwów, 1935).

Panic, Idzi and Sperka, Jerzy (eds), *Średniowiecze polskie i powszechne* (Katowice, 2002).

Papée, Fryderyk, *Aleksander Jagiellończyk* (1949; 2nd edn, Cracow, 1999).

Papée, Fryderyk, *Jan Olbracht* (1936; 2nd edn, Cracow, 1999).

Paszkiewicz, Henryk, *O genezie i wartości Krewa* (Warsaw, 1938).

Pelenski, Jaroslaw, 'The contest between Lithuania and the Golden Horde in the fourteenth century for supremacy over eastern Europe', in Pelenski, *The Contest for the Legacy of Kievan Rus'* (New York, 1998), 131–50.

Pelenski, Jaroslaw, 'The incorporation of the Ukrainian lands of old Rus' into Crown Poland (1569)', in Anna Cienciala (ed.), *American Contributions to the Seventh International Congress of Slavists, Warsaw, August 21–27, 1973*, iii (the Hague, 1973), 19–52.

Petrauskas, Rimvydas, 'XV amžiaus Lietuvos bajorijos struktūra: Giminės problema', in Bumblauskas and Petrauskas (eds), *Tarp istorijos*, 123–58.

Petrauskas, Rimvydas, 'Der litauische Blick auf den polnisch-litauischen Staatsverband: "Verlust der Staatlichkeit" oder Bewahrung der Parität', *Zeitschrift für Ostmitteleuropaforschung*, 53 (2004), 363–72.

Petrauskas, Rimvydas, 'Didžiojo Kunigaikščio institucinio dvaro susiformavimas Lietuvoje (XIV a. pabaigoje–XV a. viduryje)', *LIM*, 1 (2005), 5–38.

Petrauskas, Rimvydas, *Lietuvos diduomenė XIV a. pabaigoje–XV a.* (Vilnius, 2003).

Petrauskas, Rimvydas, 'The Lithuanian nobility in the late fourteenth and fifteenth centuries: Composition and structure', *LHS*, 7 (2002), 1–22.

Petrauskas, Rimvydas, 'Vytauto laikų didikų kilmė', *Lituanistica*, 1/2 (41/42) (2000), 16–31.

Petrauskas, Rimvydas (ed.), *Lietuvos didysis kunigaikštis Aleksandras ir jo epocha* (Vilnius, 2007).

Piekosiński, Franciszek, 'Czy Władysław Jagiełło był za życia królowej Jadwigi królem Polski czy tylko mężem królowej?', *RAUWHF*, serya ii, 35 (1897), 287–9.

Pietkiewicz, Krzysztof, 'Dwór litewski wielkiego księcia Aleksandra Jagiellończyka (1492–1506)', in Kiaupa and Mickevičius (eds), *Lietuvos valstybė*, 75–131.

Pietkiewicz, Krzysztof, *Kieżgajłowie i ich latyfundium do połowy XVI wieku* (Poznań, 1982).

Pietkiewicz, Krzysztof, 'Spór wokół Aleksandra Jagiellończyka (1461–1506)', in Petrauskas (ed.), *Aleksandras*, 16–34.

Pietkiewicz, Krzysztof, *Wielkie Księstwo Litewskie pod rządami Aleksandra Jagiellończyka: Studia nad dziejami państwa i społeczeństwa na przełomie XV i XVI wieku* (Poznań, 1995).

Piwarski, Kazimierz, 'Niedoszła wyprawa t zw. radoszkowicka Zygmunta Augusta na Moskwę w r. 1567–8', *AW*, 4 (1927), 252–86; 5 (1928), 85–119.

Plewczyński, Marek, *Wojny Jagiellonów z wschodnimi i południowymi sąsiadami królestwa polskiego w XV wieku* (Siedlce, 2002).

Plewczyński, Marek, *Żołnierz jazdy obrony potocznej za panowania Zygmunta Augusta: Studium nad zawodem wojskowym w XVIw.* (Warsaw, 1985).

Plokhy, Serhii, *The Origins of the Slavic Nations: Premodern Identities in Russia, Ukraine, and Belarus* (Cambridge, 2006).
Pociecha, Władysław, *Królowa Bona*, 4 vols (Poznań, 1949–58).
Pocock, J.G.A., 'British History: A plea for a new subject', *JMH*, 47 (1975), 601–21.
Pocock, J.G.A., 'The limits and divisions of British History: In search of the unknown subject', *AHR*, 97 (1982).
Polska i Litwa w dziejowym stosunku (Cracow, 1914).
Potkowski, Edward, *Warna 1444* (Warsaw, 1990).
Prochaska, Antoni, *Król Władysław Jagiełło*, 2 vols (Cracow, 1908).
Prochaska, Antoni, 'O rzekomej unii z 1446', *KH*, 18 (1904), 24–31.
Pułaski, Kazimierz, 'Sprawa o zapłatę zaległego żołdu rotom zaciężnym za Zygmunta Augusta', in Pułaski, *Szkice i poszukiwania historyczne*, serya iii (Cracow, 1906), 197–212.
Rabiej, Piotr, 'Dokumenty unii horodelskiej', in *Horodlės aktai*, 83–117.
Rachuba, Andrzej, Kiaupienė, Jūratė, and Kiaupa, Zigmantas, *Historia Litwy: Dwugłos polsko-litewski* (Warsaw, 2009).
Rady, Martyn, 'Rethinking Jagiełło Hungary (1490–1526)', *Central Europe*, 3/1 (2005), 3–18.
Radzimiński, Zygmunt, *Xiążę Roman Federowicz Sanguszko wobec unii lubelskiej 1569 r.* (Lwów, 1911).
Ragauskienė, Raimonda, *Lietuvos Didžiosius Kunigaikštystės kancleris Mikalojus Radvila Rudasis (apie 1515–1584)* (Vilnius, 2002).
Rembowski, Aleksander, *Konfederacja i rokosz*, ed. Jola Choińska-Mika (1895; 2nd edn, Cracow, 2010).
Reynolds, Susan, *Kingdoms and Communities in Western Europe 900–1300*, 2nd edn (Oxford, 1997).
Rhode, Gotthold, *Die Ostgrenze Polens: Politische Entwicklung, kulterelle Bedeutung und geistige Auswirkung*, i (Cologne, 1955).
Roberts, Peter, 'The English Crown, the Principality of Wales and the Council of the Marches, 1534–1641', in Bradshaw and Morrill (eds), *The British Problem*, 118–47.
Robertson, John, *A Union for Empire: Political Thought and the British Union of 1707* (Cambridge, 1995).
Roman, Stanisław, 'Konflikt prawno-polityczny 1425–1430 r. a przywilej brzeski', *CPH*, 14/2 (1962), 63–92.
Roman, Stanisław, *Przywileje nieszawskie* (Wrocław, 1957).
Roman, Stanisław, 'Zagadnienie prawomocności przywileju czerwińskiego z 1422 r.', *CPH*, 11/2 (1959), 73–93.
Roman, Stanisław and Vetulani, Adam, *Ruski przekład polskich statutów ziemskich z rękopisu moskiewskiego* (Wrocław, 1959).
Rösener, Werner, *The Peasantry of Europe* (Oxford, 1994).
Rowell, Stephen C., '1386: The marriage of Jogaila and Jadwiga embodies the union of Poland and Lithuania', *LHS*, 11 (2006), 137–44.
Rowell, Stephen C., '1446 and all that', in Valikonytė (ed.), *Lietuva ir jos kaimynai*, 188–277.
Rowell, Stephen C., 'Bears and traitors, or, Political tensions in the Grand Duchy ca. 1440–1481', *LHS*, 2 (1997), 28–55.
Rowell, Stephen C., 'Casimir Jagiellończyk and the Polish gamble', *LHS*, 4 (1999), 7–39.
Rowell, Stephen C., 'Dynastic bluff? The road to Mielnik, 1385–1501', *LHS*, 6 (2001), 1–22.

Rowell, Stephen C., 'Forging a Union? Some reflections on the early Jagiellonian monarchy', *LHS*, 1 (1996), 6–21.
Rowell, Stephen C., 'Krėvos aktas: Diplomatijos ir diplomatikos apžvalga', in *KA*, 69–78.
Rowell, Stephen C., *Lithuania Ascending: A Pagan Empire within East Central Europe, 1295–1345* (Cambridge, 1994).
Rowell, Stephen C., 'Pious princesses or the daughters of Belial: Pagan Lithuanian dynastic diplomacy 1279–1423', *Medieval Prosopography*, 15/1 (1994), 3–75.
Rowell, Stephen C., 'Pomirtinis Vladislovo Varniečio gyvenimas: Vidurio Europos Karalius Artūras iš Lietuvos', *LIM* (2006/2), 5–30.
Rowell, Stephen C., 'Rusena karas žemaičiuose: Keletas pastabų apie 1442 m. privilegijos genezės', *Žemaičių Praetitis*, 8 (1998), 5–28.
Rowell, Stephen C., 'Trumpos akimirkos iš Kazimiero Jogailaičio dvaro: Neeilinė kasdienybė tarnauja valstybei', *LIM* (2004/1), 25–55.
Russell, Conrad, 'Composite monarchies in early modern Europe: The British and Irish example', in Alexander Grant and Keith Stringer (eds), *Uniting the Kingdom: The Making of British History* (London, New York, 1995), 133–46.
Russell, Frederick, 'Paulus Vladimiri's attack on the Just War: A case study in legal polemics', in Brian Tierney and Peter Linehan (eds), *Studies on Medieval Law and Government presented to Walter Ullmann* (Cambridge, 1980), 237–54.
Rutkowski, Jan, 'Skarbowość polska za Aleksandra Jagiellończyka', *KH*, 23 (1909), 1–78.
Rutski, Edward, *Polskie Królowe*, 2 vols (Warsaw, 1990).
Sahanowicz, Henadź [Саганович, Генадзь], 'Źródła pamięci historycznej współczesnej Białorusi: Powrót zachodniorusizmu', in Jerzy Kłoczowski and Andrzej Gil (eds), *Analizy Instytutu Europy Środkowo-Wschodniej*, 14 (Lublin, 2006), 5–29.
Samsonowicz, Henryk, 'Der Deutsche Orden in seinem Verhältniss zur Gesellschaft Polens unter kultur- und verwaltungsgeschichtlichen Aspekten', in Nowak (ed.), *Ritterorden*, 99–110.
Šapoka, Adolfas, 'Valstybiniai Lietuvos Lenkijos santykiai Jogailos laikais', in Šapoka (ed.), *Jogaila*, 185–266.
Šapoka, Adolfas (ed.), *Jogaila* (Kaunas, 1935; repr. 1991).
Sarnowsky, Jürgen, *Die Wirtschaftsführung des Deutschen Ordens in Preußen (1382–1454)* (Cologne, 1993).
Sarnowsky, Jürgen, 'Zölle und Steuern im Ordensland Preußen (1403–1454)', in Nowak (ed.), *Ritterorden*, 68–72.
Saviščevas, Eugenijus, 'Kęsgailų Žemaitija: Kelios pastabos apie Kęsgailų valdyma Žemaitijoje (1442–1527)', *Lituanistica*, 58/2 (2004), 1–21.
Sawyer, G.F. *Modern Federalism* (London, 1969).
Schiemann, Christoph, *Rußland, Polen und Livland bis ins 17. Jahrhundert*, 2 vols (Berlin, 1887).
Schmidt, Christoph, *Auf Felsen gesät: Die Reformation in Polen und Livland* (Göttingen, 2000).
Schmidt, Christoph, *Leibeigenschaft im Ostseeraum: Versuch einer Typologie* (Cologne, 1997).
Schramm, Gottfried, *Der polnische Adel und die Reformation 1548–1607* (Wiesbaden, 1965).
Scott, Tom, 'Economic landscapes', in Robert Scribner (ed.), *Germany: A New Social and Economic History* (London, 1996), 1–31.
Semkowicz, Władysław, 'Braterstwo szlachty polskiej z boyarstwem litewskim w unii horodolskiej 1413 roku', in *Polska i Litwa w dziejowym stosunku*, 393–446.

Semkowicz, Władysław, 'O litewskich rodach boyarskich zbratanych ze szlachtą polską w Horodle w 1413 r.', *LSP*, 3 (1913; repr. 1989), 3–139.

Sepiał, Marcin, 'Zastaw na dobrach ziemskich i dochodach królewskich w okresie panowania Władysława III Warneńczyka na Węgrzech (1440–1444)', *ZNUJPH*, 125 (1998), 35–49.

Sikora, Franciszek, 'Uroczystości koronacyjne królowej Zofii w 1424 r.', in Bylina et al. (eds), *Kościół—Kultura—Społeczeństwo*, 161–79.

Sikora, Franciszek, 'W sprawie małżeństwa Władysława Jagiełły z Anną Cylejską', in Janusz Bieniak, Ryszard Kabaciński, Jan Pakulski, and Stanisław Trawkowski (eds), *Personae—Colligationes—Facta* (Toruń, 1991), 93–103.

Silnicki, Tadeusz, *Prawo elekcji królów w dobie jagiellońskiej* (Cracow, 1919).

Skurvydaitė, Loreta, 'Lietuvos valdovo titulas ir valdžia XIV a. pab.–XV a. viduryje', *LIS*, 7 (1999), 18–27.

Skurvydaitė, Loreta 'Lietuvos valdovo titulatūra: Kada Vytautas ima tituluotis Didžiojo kunigaikščiu?', *LIS*, 8 (2000), 9–19.

Šležas, Paulius (ed.), *Vytautas Didysis, 1350–1430* (Kaunas, 1930; repr. Vilnius, 1988).

Śliwiński, Józef, *Powiązania dynastyczne Kazimierza Wielkiego a sukcesja tronu w Polsce* (Olsztyn, 2000).

Smołucha, Janusz, Waśko, Anna, Graff, Tomasz, and Nowakowski, Paweł (eds), *Historia vero testis temporum: Księga jubileuszowa poświęcona Profesorowi Krzysztofowi Baczkowskiemu w 70. Rocznicę urodzin* (Cracow, 2008).

Sobolewski, Ludwik and Uruszczak, Wacław, 'Artykuły mielnickie z roku 1501', *CPH*, 42 (1990), 51–80.

Sochacka, Anna, *Jan z Czyżowa, namiestnik Władysława Warneńczyka* (Lublin, 1993).

Sperka, Jerzy, 'Biskup krakowski Zbigniew Oleśnicki a ugrupowanie dworskie w okresie panowania Władysława Jagiełły i w pierwszych latach Władysława III', in Kiryk and Noga (eds), *Oleśnicki*, 107–22.

Sperka, Jerzy, 'Faworyci Władysława Jagiełły', in Markiewicz and Skowron (eds), *Faworyci*, 41–59.

Sperka, Jerzy, *Szafrańcowie herbu stary koń: Z dziejów kariery i awansu w późnośredniowiecznej Polsce* (Katowice, 2001).

Sperka, Jerzy, 'Zmiany na arcybiskupstwie gnieźnieńskim, biskupstwie krakowskim i urzędach kancelaryjnych na przełomie lat 1422 i 1423', *TK*, 5 (1997), 139–46.

Społeczeństwo Polski Średniowiecznej. Zbiór studiów (Warsaw, 1981–). [*SPS*]

Śreniowski, Stanisław, *Zbiegostwo chłopów w dawnej Polsce jako zagadnienie ustroju społecznego* (1948; 2nd edn, Łódź, 1997).

Stang, C.S., *Die westrussische Kanzleisprache des Großfürstentums Litauen* (Oslo, 1935).

Steiger, Heinhard, *Staatlichkeit und Überstaatlichkeit: Eine Untersuchung zur rechtlichen und politischen Stellung der Europäischen Gemeinschaften*, Schriften zum Öffentlichen Recht, Bd 31 (Berlin, 1966).

Stone, Daniel, *The Polish-Lithuanian State, 1386–1795* (Seattle, WA, 2001).

Strayer, Joseph, *On the Medieval Origins of the Modern State* (Princeton, NJ, 1970).

Studia historyczne ku czci Stanisława Kutrzeby, 2 vols (Cracow, 1938).

Sucheni-Grabowska, Anna, 'Królewszczyzny', in *Encyklopedia historii gospodarczej Polski do 1945 r.*, ii (Warsaw, 1981), 389–91.

Sucheni-Grabowska, Anna, *Monarchia dwu ostatnich Jagiellonów a ruch egzekucyjny* (Wrocław, 1974).

Sucheni-Grabowska, Anna, *Odbudowa domeny królewskiej w Polsce 1504–1548*, 2nd edn (Warsaw, 2007).

Sucheni-Grabowska, Anna, *Zygmunt August: Król polski i wielki książę litewski*, 2nd edn (Cracow, 2010).
Suchocki, Jerzy, 'Formowanie się i skład narodu politycznego w Wielkim Księstwie Litewskim późnego średniowiecza', *ZH*, 48/1–2 (1983), 31–78.
Sułkowska-Kurasiowa, Irena, 'Doradcy Władysława Jagiełły', in *SPS*, ii (Warsaw, 1982), 188–220.
Sułkowska-Kurasiowa, Irena, *Polska kancelaria królewska w l. 1447–1506* (Wrocław, 1967).
Sužiedėlis, Simas, 'Lietuva ir Gediminaičiai sėdant Jogailai į didžiojo kunigaikščio sostą', in Šapoka (ed.), *Jogaila*, 11–44.
Szczuczko, Witold, 'Izba niższa sejmiku generalnego Prus Królewskich 1548–1562. Struktura i tok obrad', in Zenon Nowak (ed.), *W kręgu stanowych i kulturowych przeobrażeń Europy północnej w XIV–XVIII w.* (Toruń, 1988), 137–48.
Szczur, Stanisław, 'W sprawie sukcesji andegaweńskiej w Polsce', *RH*, 75 (2009), 61–104.
Szujski, Józef, *Historyi polskiej treściwie opowiedzianej ksiąg dwanaście* (1880; Poznań, 2005).
Szulc, Tadeusz, *Z badań nad egzekucją praw: Podstawy ustawodawcze egzekucji dóbr, ich interpretacja i nowelizacja na sejmach za panowania Zygmunta II Augusta* (Łódź, 2000).
Szymanek, Andrzej (ed.), *Nihil Novi: Z dorobku sejmu radomskiego 1505 roku* (Radom, 2005).
Tafiłowski, Piotr, *Jan Łaski (1456–1531): Kanclerz koronny i prymas Polski* (Warsaw, 2007).
Tęgowski, Jan, 'Data urodzenia Jagiełły oraz data chrztu prawosławnego jego starszych braci', *Genealogia*, 15 (2003), 137–44.
Tęgowski, Jan, 'Kilka uwag do genealogii Gedyminowiczów', *SŹ* 36 (1997), 113–6.
Tęgowski, Jan, 'O następstwie tronu na Litwie po śmierci Olgierda', *PH*, 84 (1993), 127–34.
Tęgowski, Jan, *Pierwsze pokolenia Giedyminowiczów* (Poznań and Wrocław, 1999).
Tęgowski, Jan, 'Wprowadzenie w życiu postanowień aktu krewskiego w l. 1385–1399', *Studia z dziejów państwa i prawa polskiego*, 9 (2006), 77–91.
Tęgowski, Jan, 'Zagadnienie władzy w Wielkim Księstwie Litewskim w okresie między unią krewską a zgonem Skirgiełły (1385–1394)', *ZH*, 66/4 (2001), 7–18.
Topolska, Maria, *Społeczeństwo i kultura w Wielkim Księstwie Litewskim od XV do XVIII wieku* (Poznań, 2002).
Topolski, Jerzy, *Gospodarstwo wiejskie w dobrach arcybiskupstwa gnieźnieńskiego od XVI do XVIII wieku* (Poznań, 1958).
Topolski, Jerzy, *Przełom gospodarczy w Polsce XVI wieku i jego następstwa* (Poznań, 2000).
Trajdos, Tadeusz, *Kościół katolicki na ziemiach ruskich Korony i Litwy za panowania Władysława II Jagiełły (1386–1434)*, i (Wrocław, 1985).
Trencsényi, Balász and Zászkaliczky, Márton (eds), *Whose Love of Which Country? Composite States, National Histories and Patriotic Discourses in Early Modern East-Central Europe* (Leiden, 2010).
Trimonienė, Rita, 'Polonizacija', in Ališauskas et al. (eds), *Kultūra*, 492–507.
Turowski, Ernst, *Die innenpolitische Entwicklung Polnisch-Preußens und seine staatsrechtliche Stellung zu Polen vom 2. Thorner Frieden bis zum Reichstag von Lublin (1466–1569)* (Berlin, 1937).
Tymieniecki, Kazimierz, 'Wpływy ustroju feudalnego w Polsce średniowiecznej', *RDSG*, 3 (1934), 77–112.
Tymosz, Stanisław, 'Statut Łaskiego i jego wpływ na inne zbiory prawa', in Tymosz (ed.), *Łaski*, 87–106.
Tymosz, Stanisław, 'Szkic historyczno-biograficzny prymasa Jana Łaskiego (1456–1531)', in Tymosz (ed.), *Łaski*, 13–47.

Tymosz, Stanisław (ed.), *Arcybiskup Jan Łaski, reformator prawa* (Lublin, 2007).
Tyszkiewicz, Jan, *Ostatnia wojna z Zakonem Krzyżackim 1519–1521* (Warsaw, 1991).
Uluntaitis, V.P., *Lenkų įvykdytas lieutuvių tautos genocidas* (Chicago, 1989).
Uruszczak, Wacław, *Historia państwa i prawa polskiego*, i: *966–1795* (Warsaw, 2010).
Uruszczak, Wacław, 'Konstytucja *Nihil Novi* z 1505 roku i jej znaczenie', in Ajnenkiel (ed.), *W pięćsetlecie*, 16–21.
Uruszczak, Wacław, *Próba kodyfikacji prawa polskiego w pierwszej połowie XVI wieku* (Warsaw, 1979).
Uruszczak, Wacław, *Sejm walny koronny w latach 1506–1540* (Warsaw, 1981).
Uruszczak, Wacław, 'Sejm walny wszystkich państw naszych: Sejm w Radomiu z 1505 roku i konstytucji *Nihil Novi*', *CPH*, 57/1 (2005), 11–24.
Uruszczak, Wacław, 'Sejm w latach 1506–1540', in *Historia sejmu*, i, 63–113.
Urwanowicz, Jerzy, *Wojskowe 'sejmiki': Koła w wojsku Rzeczypospolitej XVI–XVII wieku* (Białystok, 1996).
Urzędnicy centralni i dostojnicy Wielkiego Księstwa Litewskiego XIV–XVIII wieku: Spisy, eds Andrzej Rachuba and Henryk Lulewicz (Kórnik, 1994). [*UWXL*]
Urzędnicy Prus Królewskich XV–XVIII wieku: Spisy, ed. Krzysztof Mikulski (Wrocław, 1990). [*UPK*]
Valikonytė, Irena (ed.), *Lietuva ir jos kaimynai: Nuo normanų iki Napoleono: Prof. Broniaus Dundulio atminimui* (Vilnius, 2001).
Vetulani, Adam, *Lenno pruskie od traktatu krakowskiego do śmierci księcia Albrechta 1525–1568: Studjum historyczno-prawne* (Cracow, 1930).
Vetulani, Adam, 'Rokowanie krakowskie z r. 1454 i zjednoczenie ziem pruskich z Polską', *PH*, 45 (1954), 188–236.
Vilimas, Darius, *Lietuvos Didžiosios Kunigaikštystės žemės teismo sistemos formavimasis (1564–1588)* (Vilnius, 2006).
Voigt, Johannes, *Geschichte Preussens von den ältesten Zeiten bis zum Untergange der Herrschaft des Deutschen Ordens*, 9 vols (Königsberg, 1827–39).
Vries, Jan de, *The Economy of Europe in an Age of Crisis, 1600–1750* (Cambridge, 1976).
Vytautas Didysis ir Lietuva, ed. Brigita Balčtienė (Vilnius, 1996).
Wallerstein, Immanuel, *The Modern World System*, i: *Capitalist Agriculture and the Origins of the European World-Economy in the Sixteenth Century* (New York, 1974).
Wasilewski, Tadeusz, 'Daty urodzin Jagiełły i Witolda: Przyczynek do genealogii Giedyminowiczów', *PW*, 1 (1991), 15–34.
Wawrzyńczyk, Alina, *Gospodarstwo chłopskie na Mazowszu w XVI w.* (Warsaw, 1962).
Wawrzyńczyk, Alina, *Studia nad wydajnością produkcji rolnej dóbr królewskich w drugiej połowie XVI w.* (Wrocław, 1974).
Wawrzyńczyk, Alina, 'W sprawie gospodarstwa chłopskiego na Mazowszu w XVI w.', *ZH*, 29/4 (1964), 39–44.
Węcowski, Piotr, *Mazowsze w Koronie: Propaganda i legitymacja władzy Kazimierza Jagiellończyka na Mazowszu* (Cracow, 2004).
Weise, Erich, 'Zur Kritik des Vertrages zwischen dem Preußischen Bund und dem König von Polen vom 6. März 1454', *AF*, 18 (1941), 231–61.
Wermter, Ernst Manfred, 'Die Bildung des Danziger Stadtterritoriums in den politischen Zielvorstellungen des Rates der Stadt Danzig im späten Mittelalter und in der frühen Neuzeit: Bemerkungen und Fragen zur städtischen Verfassungsgeschichte', in Conrad et al. (eds), *Ordensherrschaft*, 81–123.
Wijaczka, Jacek, *Albrecht von Brandenburg-Ansbach (1490–1568)* (Olsztyn, 2010).

Wijaczka, Jacek (ed.), *Między zachodem a wschodem*, iv: *Życie gospodarcze Rzeczypospolitej w XVI–XVIII wieku* (Toruń, 1997).
Williamson, Arthur, *Scottish National Consciousness in the Age of James VI* (Edinburgh, 1979).
Wimmer, Jan, *Historia piechoty polskiej do roku 1864* (Warsaw, 1978).
Wiskont, Antoni [Viskantas, Antanas], 'Wielki książę litewski Witold a unia horodelska', *AW*, 7 (1930), 469–93.
Wojciechowski, Zygmunt, *Zygmunt Stary* (1946; 2nd edn, Warsaw, 1979).
Wolff, Józef, *Kniaziowie litewsko-ruscy* (Warsaw, 1895).
Wróbel, Dariusz, 'Zbigniew Oleśnicki a kwestia pruska i krzyżacka', in Kiryk and Noga (eds), *Oleśnicki*, 85–101.
Wroniszewski, Jan, *Szlachta ziemi sandomierskiej w średniowieczu: Zagadnienia społeczne i gospodarcze* (Poznań, 2001).
Wünsch, Thomas, *Konziliarismus und Polen: Personen, Politik und Programme aus Polen zur Verfassungsfrage der Kirche in der Zeit der mittelalterlichen Reformkonzilien* (Paderborn, 1998).
Wyczański, Andrzej, 'Czy chłopu było źle w Polsce XVI wieku?', *KH*, 85 (1978), 627–41.
Wyczański, Andrzej, *Między kulturą a polityką: Sekretarze królewscy Zygmunta Starego (1506–1548)* (Warsaw, 1990).
Wyczański, Andrzej, 'O folwarku szlacheckim w Polsce XVI stulecia', *KH*, 61/4 (1954), 169–91.
Wyczański, Andrzej, *Studia nad folwarkiem szlacheckim w Polsce w latach 1500–1800* (Warsaw, 1960).
Wyczański, Andrzej, 'Uwagi o utowarowieniu gospodarki chłopskiej w dawnej Polski', in Stefan Kuczyński (ed.), *Nummus et historia: Pieniądz Europy Środkowej* (Warsaw, 1985), 303–7.
Wyrozumski, Jerzy, 'Czy późnośredniowieczny kryzys feudalizmu dotknął Polskę?', in Tomasz Jasiński, Jan Jurek, and Jan Piskorski (eds), *Homines et societas: Czasy Piastów i Jagiellonów: Studia historyczne ofiarowane Antoniemu Gąsiorewskiemu w sześćdziesiątą piątą rocznicę urodzin* (Poznań, 1997), 104–13.
Wyrozumski, Jerzy, 'Formowanie się politycznej i ustrojowej wspólnoty polsko-litewskiej w latach 1385–1501', *CPH*, 45/1–2 (1993), 445–55.
Wyrozumski, Jerzy, 'Geneza senatu w Polsce', in Krystyn Matwijowski and Jerzy Pietrzak (eds), *Senat w Polsce: Dzieje i teraźniejszość* (Warsaw, 1993), 21–34.
Wyrozumski, Jerzy, 'Kmieć czy chłop w Polsce średniowiecznej?', in Manikowska et al. (eds), *Aetas media*, 356–62.
Wyrozumski, Jerzy, *Królowa Jadwiga: Między epoka piastowską i jagiellońską*, 2nd edn (Cracow, 2006).
Żabiński, Zbigniew, *Systemy pieniężne na ziemiach polskich* (Wrocław, 1981).
Zajączkowski, Stanisław, 'Przymierze polsko-litewskie 1325 r.', *KH*, 40 (1926), 567–617.
Zakrzewski, Stanisław, 'W pięćsetną rocznicę: Bitwa nad Świętą inaczej pod Wiłkomierzem 1 września 1435 r.', in *Pamiętnik VI Powszechnego Zjazdu*, i (Lwów, 1935), 551–8.
Zawitkowska, Wioletta, *W służbie pierwszych Jagiellonów: Życie i działalność kanclerza Jana Taszki Koniecpolskiego* (Cracow, 2005).
Ziembicki, Witołd, 'Barbara Radziwiłłówna w oświetleniu lekarskim', in *Pamiętnik VI Powszechnego Zjazdu*, i (Lwów, 1935), 144–62.
Zientara, Benedykt, *'Melioratio terrae*: The thirteenth-century breakthrough in Polish History', in J.K. Federowicz (ed.), *A Republic of Nobles: Studies in Polish History to 1864* (Cambridge, 1982), 37–42.

Zientara, Benedykt, 'Społeczeństwo polskie XIII–XV wieku', in Ihnatowicz et al. (eds), *Społeczeństwo polskie*, 91–210.

Zujienė, Gitana, 'Lietuvos didžiojo kunigaikščio Aleksandro pakėlimo ceremonialo susiformavimas', in Petrauskas (ed.), *Aleksandras*, 56–67.

Zujienė, Gitana, 'Pastangos išsaugoti Lietuvos didžiojo kunigaikščio titulą i pakėlimo ceremonialą', in Glemža and Šmigelskytė-Stukienė (eds), *Liublino unija*, 64–71.

Żytkowicz, Leonid, 'Badania nad gospodarką chłopska w królewszczynach mazowieckich XVI i początkach XVII w.', *ZH*, 29/4 (1964), 28–37.

Żytkowicz, Leonid, 'Grain yields in Poland, Bohemia, Hungary and Slovakia in the 16th to 18th centuries', *APH*, 24 (1971), 51–72.

Żytkowicz, Leonid, 'Ze studiów nad wysokością plonów w Polsce od XVI do XVIII w.', *Kwartalnik Historii Kultury Materialnej*, 14/3 (1966), 457–90.

Бохан, Юрый [Bokhan, Iurii], *Вайсковая справа у Вялікім княстве Літоускім у другой палове XIV–канцы XVI ст.* (Minsk, 2008).

Войтович, Леонтій [Voitovich, Leontii], *Геналогія династій Рюриковичів і Гедиміновичів* (Kyiv, 1992).

Войтович, Леонтій [Voitovich, Leontii], *Княжа доба на Русі: Портрети еліти* (Bila Tserkva, 2006).

Войтович, Леонтій [Voitovich, Leontii], *Удільні князівства Рюриковичів і Гедиміновичів у XII–XIV ст.* (L'viv, 1996).

Грушевський, Михайло [Hrushevsky, Mykhailo], *Історія України-Руси*, 10 vols (repr. Kyiv, 1993).

Крикун, Микола [Krykun, Mykola], *Адміністративно-територіальний устрій правобережної України в XV–XVIII ст.: Кордон воеводств у світлі джерел* (Kyiv, 1993).

Кром, Михаил [Krom, Mikhail], *Меж Русью и Литвой: Пограничные земли в системе русско-литовских отношений конца XV–первой трети XVI в.*, 2nd edn (Moscow, 2010).

Кром, Михаил [Krom, Mikhail], '"Старина" как категория средневекового менталитета (по материалам Великого княжества Литовського XIV–начала XVII вв.)', *Mediaevalia Ucrainica*, 3 (1994), 68–85.

Лаппо, Иван [Lappo, Ivan], *Великое княжество Литовское во второй половине XVI столетия: Литовско-Русскій повѣтъ и его сеймикъ* (Iur'ev, 1911).

Лазутка, Станисловас [Lazutka, Stanislovas], 'Историческая роль Альбертаса Гоштаутаса в кодификации Первого Литовского Статута', in Irena Valikonytė and Lirija Steponavičienė (eds), *Pirmasis Lietuvos Statutas ir epocha* (Vilnius, 2005), 14–20.

Любавский, Матвей [Liubavskii, Matvei], *Литовско-Русскій Сеймъ: Опытъ по исторіи учрежденія въ связи съ внутреннимъ строемъ и внѣшнею государства* (Moscow, 1900).

Любавский, Матвей [Liubavskii, Matvei], *Областное деление и местное управление Литовско-Русского государства ко времени издания первого Литовского статута* (Moscow, 1892).

Любавский, Матвей [Liubavskii, Matvei], *Очерк историй литовско-русского государства до Люблинской унии включительно* (1910; citations from 2nd edn, St Petersburg, 2004).

Максимейко, Николай [Maksimeiko, Nikolai], *Сеймы литовско-русскаго государства до люблинской уній 1569 г.* (Khar'kov, 1902).

Пичета, Владимир И [Vladimir I. Picheta], 'Волочная устава королевы Боны и устава на волоки', in Пичета, *Белоруссия и Литва XV–XVI вв* (Moscow, 1961), 21–42.

Русина, Олена, [Rusyna, Olena], 'Проблеми політичної лояльности населення Велико князівства Литовського у XIV–XVI ст.', *UIZh*, 6 (2003), 3–16.

Русина, Олена [Rusyna, Olena], *Україна під Татарами і Литвою* (Kyiv, 1998).

Сагановіч, Генадзь [Sahanovich, Henadz], *Нарыс гісторіі Беларусі ад старажытнасці да канца XVIII стагоддзя* (Minsk, 2001).

Скочиляс, Ігор [Skochylias, Igor], *Галицька (Львівська) єпархія XII–XVIII ст.* (L'viv, 2010).

Старостина, И.П. [Starostina, I.P.], 'Судебник Казимира 1468 г.', in *Древние государства на территории СССР (1988–1989)* (Moscow, 1991), 279–312.

Шабульдо, Феликс [Shabul'do, Feliks], *Земли юго-западной Руси в составе Великого княжества Литовского* (Kyiv, 1987).

Янушкевіч, Андрей [Ianushkevich, Andrei], *Вялікае княства Літоўскае і Інфлянцкая вайна 1558–1579 гг.* (Minsk, 2007).

Яковенко, Наталя [Iakovenko, Natalia], *Українська шляхта з кінця XIV до середини XVII ст. (Волинь і Центральна Україна)*, 2nd edn (Kyiv, 2008).

Янушкевіч, Андрей [Ianushkevich, Andrei], 'Унія з коронаі ва ўнутранаі палітыце ВКЛ перад люблінскім соймам 1569 г.', *Беларускі Гістарычны Агляд*, 10 (2003), 29–36.

UNPUBLISHED DISSERTATION

Dworzaczkowa-Essmanowska, Jolanta, 'Ruch szlachecki w Prusach Królewskich w pierwszej połowie XVI wieku', unpublished Masters dissertation, University of Poznań, 1951: Instytut Historii, Uniwersytet Mikołaja Kopernika, Toruń, Diss. maszynopis, no. 78.

Glossary

Unless otherwise indicated, terms are Polish.

Annexed territories Lands of Kievan Rus′ annexed by the Gediminids and not absorbed into Lithuania Proper: the duchies of Vilnius and Trakai. See Chapter 6, 67.

Boyar (Ruth. *боярь*; Lith. *bajoras*) Noble. The term boyar is originally Slavic, derived from the word for warrior.

Camp sejm (*sejm obozowy*) Also 'horseback sejm'. A sejm formed after the assembly of the noble levy. A form of confederation, camp sejms were regarded as particularly representative by the szlachta.

Castellan Originally the keeper of a royal castle. Castellans were below palatines in the local hierarchy of office, apart from in Cracow—and later in Vilnius. *Ex officio* members of the royal council, when the Polish sejm was institutionalized after 1493 castellans became members of the senate. In Poland there was a distinction between major castellans (one or sometimes two per palatinate) and minor castellans in less important towns. There were no minor castellans in Lithuania.

Castle court (*sąd grodzki*) The main royal court in the localities, presided over by the starosta.

Chałupnik Cottar. A poor peasant.

Confederation The principle of confederation emerged in the fourteenth century to provide a legal basis for associations formed for specific aims. Its political merits became apparent to the nobility after 1352, the first noble confederation. The confederations of 1382 and 1384 that settled the succession embedded the principle within Polish political practice. A formal pact or *foedus* was drawn up, and oaths were taken to uphold it.

Gosudar′ (Russ.) Literally 'lord', *gosudar′* denoted independent authority. The term was used by Vytautas and was borrowed by the grand dukes of Muscovy in the fifteenth century, who used it in their official titles to claim authority over all the Ruthenian lands from the reign of Ivan III (*Государь всея Русию*).

Hetman The commander of the army.

Hide (*łan*) The main measure of land in Poland, known as the *włoka* in Mazovia and Lithuania. Two main systems were used: the Flemish hide (16.7 to 17.5 hectares), and the Franconian hide (22.6 to 25.36 hectares).

Indygenat (Lat. *indigenus*) The principle of indigeneity, by which only those born in an individual province could hold office there and enjoy all the provincial privilege. The principle of indigeneity was granted to Royal Prussia in the incorporation acts of 1454 and 1466.

Kmieć (pl. *kmiecie*) The non-noble tenant farmers at the apex of village society. The *kmiecie* were the main tenants of noble landowners, farming the lands designated as farmland for tax purposes.

Komornik A landless rural labourer who received board and lodging from lords or wealthier peasants in return for his labour.

Land court (*sąd ziemski*) The principal local civil court for cases involving landed property and a wide range of other civil matters. It was presided over by elected judges. The system was extended to Lithuania by the Second Lithuanian Statute in 1566.

Lithuania proper (Lat. *Lithuania propria*) The heartland territories of Aukštaitija formed by the core Lithuanian duchies of Vilnius and Trakai.

Metryka The main chancery archive.

Palatine (*wojewoda*) The principal provincial office-holder. Responsible for organizing the local noble levy in time of war and for the defence of his palatinate. A member *ex officio* of the royal council and, after the establishment of the sejm, of the senate.

Pan (pl. *pany*) Lord. Originally the term referred to members of the elite of the nobility; over time it became the standard form of address for all the szlachta.

Pańszczyzna Labour service (literally 'that which is owed to the lord').

Poddaństwo Subject status. Peasants were subject to the baronial courts of their landlords, and could not, after the early sixteenth century, appeal against their verdicts in the royal courts. In this sense they were the subjects of their lord, although in Poland-Lithuania they were never his possessions.

Pomest'e (Russ.) The basis of the military service system in Muscovy after the 1470s. *Pomest'e* estates were allocated in return for military service.

Poradlne The main, permanent land tax paid by the Polish szlachta. From 1374 it was levied at a rate of 2 groszy per hide.

Prawo rycerskie (Lat. *ius militaris*) 'Military Law'. Lands were granted under military law to nobles in Poland in frontier provinces, in particular in the Ruthenian palatinate, in return for which they had to perform various specified military services.

Rokosz A form of confederation, a *rokosz* was a formal act of rebellion against a monarch considered to be acting in breach of his coronation oath. It derived its name from Rákos in Hungary, where Hungarian nobles gathered to protest against their kings.

Sejm Diet or parliament.

Sejmik Dietine. The sejmiks were parliamentary bodies at the local level, attended by the noble citizens. Their position in the Polish system was established by the 1454 Nieszawa privileges.

Serebshchyzna (Ruth.) 'The silver tax'. Introduced by the 1507 Lithuanian sejm, the silver tax was levied on land on several occasions thereafter.

Shliakhta (Ruth.) See szlachta.

Sluzhba (Ruth.) 'Service unit'. In Lithuania a *sluzhba* was formed by grouping households in order to determine the level of military service owed by individual nobles

Starosta, Starosty (lit. elder). Starostas were the chief royal administrative officials, who also had judicial powers, being responsible for the castle court in the local *gród* (castle). The term starosty was used to denote complexes of royal estates leased out or mortgaged to individual nobles, but without judicial or administrative powers. Their holders were known as 'non-judicial starostas' (*starostowie niegrodowi*). See Chapter 23, 275–6.

Starosta General The provinces of Wielkopolska and Małopolska had general starostas. In the fourteenth and fifteenth centuries these officials had considerable power and prestige among the local nobles, and took a leading role in the provincial sejmiks.

Szlachta (Ruth. *Шляхma/Shliakhta*) Nobility. Derived from the German *Geschlecht* (family). The privileges granted by monarchs between 1374 and 1454 established the szlachta as the dominant political estate.

Tivun (Ruth.) (*ciwuń*) A local royal official in Lithuania. Roughly equivalent to a Polish starosta, but without judicial powers: the main responsibility was to administer the royal domain and collect taxes.

Vivente rege (Lat.) An election held in the lifetime of the king.

Włoka (Ruth. *Voloka*) See hide.

Wójt Headman. Under German law, the *wójt* (*Vogt*) was the headman of the village; in a town, the mayor.

Zagrodnik (pl. *zagrodnicy*) A peasant granted a small plot of land (literally a garden). The *zagrodnicy* formed the labour force for the noble manor. They were often hired by tenant farmers to provide the labour-rent owed on their plots.

Gazetteer

The first column gives the form used in the book; the remaining columns give the equivalents in other languages: Cz. = Czech; Hun. = Hungarian; Lat. = Latin; Slk. = Slovakian; Sln. = Slovenian; Ro. = Romanian; Russ. = Russian.

Place names in Polish

Polish	German	Lithuanian	Ukrainian	Belarusian	Other
Bełz			Belts		
Bydgoszcz	Bromberg				
Chełm			Kholm		
Dobrzyń	Dobrin				
Drezdenko	Driesen				
Drwęca	Drewenz	Druvinčia			
Koszyce					Košice (Slk.) Kassa (Hun.)
Koźmin			Valia Kuz'mina		Valea Cosminului (Ro.)
Lubicz	Lübitsch				
Lubowla					Lubovňa (Slk.) Ólubló (Hun.)
Lwów	Lemberg		L'viv		Leopolis (Lat.) Lvov (Russ.)
Melno	Meldensee				
Oświęcim	Auschwitz				
Spisz	Zips				Spiš (Slk.) Szepes (Hun.)

Place names in Lithuanian

Lithuanian	Polish	German	Ukrainian	Belarusian	Other
Ašmena	Oszmiana			Ashmiany	
Astrovas	Ostrawa				
Eišiškės	Ejszyszki			Eishishki	
Kaunas	Kowno			Kovno	
Krėva	Krewo			Kreva	
Medininkai	Miedniki				
Palanga	Połąga	Polangen			
Trakai	Troki	Tracken			
Ukmergė	Wiłkomierz				
Vilnius	Wilno	Wilna		Вільня/Vil'nia	

Place names in German

German	Polish	Lithuanian	Ukrainian	Belarusian	Other
Allenstein	Olsztyn				
Beuthen	Bytom				
Braunsberg	Braniewo				
Bütow	Bytów				
Christburg	Dzieżgoń / Dzierzgon				
Christmemel	Skirstymoń	Skirsnemunė			
Culm	Chełmno				
Dirschau	Tczew				
Ehlau	Iława				
Ermland	Warmia				
Frauenburg	Frombork				
Gilgenburg	Dąbrówno				
Konitz	Chojnice				
Marienburg	Malbork				
Marienwerder	Kwidzyń				
Memel	Kłajpeda	Klaipėda			
Mewe	Gniew				
Oppeln	Opole				
Osterode	Ostróda				
Ragnit	Ragneta	Ragainė			Neman (Russ.)
Ratibor	Racibórz				
Sagan	Żagań				Zaháň (Cz.)
Salin (Salinwerder)	Salin				
Schönsee	Kowalewo				
Schwetz	Świecie				
Schwetzin	Świecino				
Stolp	Słuck				
Stuhm	Sztum				
Tannenberg[1]	Grunwald	Žalgiris			
Tolkemit	Tolkmicko				

[1] The Polish name for the village of Tannenberg is Stębark, which is where the Teutonic Knights were positioned. The Poles derived the name 'Grunwald' from Grünfeld, another village on the battlefield. The Lithuanian Žalgiris is a direct translation of Grunwald.

Place names in Ukrainian

Ukrainian	Polish	Lithuanian	German	Belarusian	Other
Chortorysk	Czartorysk				
Halych	Halicz				
Kamianets Podilsky	Kamienec Podolski				
Kyiv	Kijów				Kiev (Russ.)
Novhorod-Siversky	Nowogród Siewierski			Nouharad Seversky	
Volodymyr	Włodzimierz				

Place names in Belarusian

Belarusian	Polish	Lithuanian	German	Ukrainian	Other
Brest	Brześć Litewski	Brestas			
Hrodna	Grodno	Gardinas	Garthen/Garten		
Mahiliou	Mohylew				Mogilev (Russ.)
Mstislaŭ	Mscisław				Mstislavl' (Russ.)
Navahrudak	Nowogródek	Naugardukas			
Polatsk	Połock				Polotsk (Russ.)
Vaukavysk	Wołkowyski	Volkovyskas			
Vitsebsk	Witebsk				

Place names in other languages

Other	Polish	Lithuanian	Ukrainian	Latin	Turkish
Celje (Sln.)					
Cetatea Alba (Ro.)[1]	Białogród		Bilhorod	Castrum Album	Akkerman
Samogitia (Lat.)	Żmudź	Žemaitija			

[1] This was the ancient Phoenecian settlement, then the Genoese colony of Montecastro; ruled by Moldavia from 1359, it was renamed Akkerman by its Turkish conquerors.

Index

The children of Gediminas and Algirdas are given their patronymics to identify them. The former are designated Gediminaitis (males) or Gediminaitė (females); the latter are designated Algirdaitis or Algirdaitė for those who were pagan and then Catholic; Olherdovych for those who converted to Orthodoxy. The children of Kęstutis are designated Kęstutaitis and Kęstutaitė. The offices given are the most prestigious held in the individual's career.

Acre 27
Adamus, Jan 50, 96
Adelheid of Hesse (1324–71), queen of Poland 7
Adwaniec clan 411
Aegidius Romanus (Giles of Rome) (c.1243–1316) theologian, archbishop of Bourges 347
Alantzee, Jan, apothecary 377
Albert III Achilles (1414–86), elector of Brandenburg 330
Albert II (Albrecht V von Habsburg) (1397–1439), king of Hungary and Bohemia; king of the Romans 179, 180, 182–3, 186, 212, 277, 278
Albrecht von Hohenzollern (1490–1568), grand master of the Teutonic Order, duke of Prussia 379, 392–4, 396, 405, 412, 436, 443, 446
  and Lithuania 411
  and Poland 401, 405, 439
  and Royal Prussia 395, 398, 401
Albrecht Friedrich von Hohenzollern (1553–1618), duke of Prussia 401
Albrecht III of Saxony (1443–1500), duke of Meissen 392
Aldona (Anna) Gediminaitė († 1339), queen of Poland 7, 28
Aleksandrovych, Soltan († before 1498), treasurer of Lithuania 317
Alexandra Algirdaitė († 1434), duchess of Mazovia 132, 374, 375
Alexander (1461–1506), grand duke of Lithuania, king of Poland 296, 334, 353–4, 365, 376, 388, 406
  childhood and education 265–6, 328
  character and reputation 265–7, 289
  political abilities 267, 361
  death of 314, 344, 389
  election and enthronement as grand duke of Lithuania (1492) 285, 304, 327–30, 335, 341
  election as king of Poland (1501) 274, 290, 337–8, 341, 346, 382
  and the government of Lithuania 305, 308, 314, 319, 327–8
  and the Lithuanian council 333

privilege for the Lithuanian nobility (1492) 304–5, 307, 322, 329–30, 366
privilege for the appanage princes (1499) 296
and the Orthodox church 309, 315, 332
and the government of Poland 346–9, 350, 357, 366
and the sejm 350–1, 354
and the royal domain 356
and the union 330, 333–4, 336, 338–43
Alexander of Mazovia (1400–44), bishop of Trent 375
Alexander I († 1432), hospodar of Moldavia 142
Alexander V (c.1339–1417), antipope 123
Alexander VI (1431–1503), pope 274, 309
Alexius († 1378), metropolitan of Moscow 164
Alfonso V (1432–81), king of Portugal 51
Algirdas Gedimimaitis (c.1300–77), grand duke of Lithuania 3, 20–1, 25–6, 28–30, 53, 74, 75, 77, 79, 82, 84, 86, 152, 154–5, 160, 163, 188, 195
Algirdičiai dynasty 83–4, 85
Allenstein 225, 393
Allodial landholding
  in Lithuania 68, 115, 297, 300, 307, 330
  in Poland 64, 244, 254
  in Prussia 391
Alšėniškai family *see* Holshansky, family of
Alter, Peter 36
Anastasia Vasileevna († 1470), daughter of Vasilii I 293
Ancient Greek city states, leagues of 36
Andrei Olherdovych (Algirdaitis) († 1399), duke of Polatsk 24, 29–31, 77, 86, 87
Andrzej of Łęczyca, writer on agriculture 427
Angevin dynasty 6, 10–14, 16, 50–1, 277
Anna of Celje (1380/1–1416), queen of Poland 92, 96, 119, 132, 138
Anna Jagiellon (1503–47), queen of Bohemia and Hungary, queen of the Romans 392, 433
Anna Jagiellonka (1523–96), queen of Poland, grand duchess of Lithuania 406
Anna of Oleśnica († 1481), duchess of Sochaczew 376

Anna (Ona Sudimantaitė-Vytautienė) († 1418), grand duchess of Lithuania 79, 94, 134
Anna Sophia Ivanova of Tver, grand duchess of Lithuania 157, 170
Anna Sophia von Hohenzollern (1527–91), duchess of Mecklenburg 436
Anne de Foix Grailly (1484–1506), queen of Bohemia and Hungary 330
Antioch 421
Antonius IV († 1397), patriarch of Constantinople 164
Aquinas, Thomas (1225–74), theologian 347, 349
Aragon, kingdom of 51–2, 56, 124
Arbroath, declaration of (1320) 11
Aristotle (384–322 BCE), philosopher 318, 347, 360
Armenian Orthodox church 311
Árpád dynasty 6
Ašmena 71–2, 170
Ašmena, battle of (1432) 173
Astikas, Kristinas (1363–1442/3), castellan of Vilnius 170, 185, 187
Astrava agreement (1392) 81–3, 87, 92
Astrakhan, khanate of 282, 447
Attila († 453) ruler of the Huns 412
Aukštaitija 27, 69, 71, 72, 101, 125, 163, 316
Austria 33
Avraam († 1452), bishop of Suzdal 311

Backus, Oswald P. 296, 313
Bajerski, Jan († 1484), palatine of Pomerelia 387
Bakshty 163
Baldo de Ubaldis (1327–1400), jurist 360
Baltic Sea 25, 126, 230–1, 291, 394, 401, 429, 486
Balzer, Oswald 47, 93, 343
Barbara of Celje (1392–1451), queen of Hungary, queen of the Romans 142
Barbara Radziwiłłówna, (1520/3–51), queen of Poland, grand duchess of Lithuania 420, 433–9, 441
Barbara von Hohenzollern (1464–1515), queen of Bohemia 330
Barbara Zápolya (1495–1515), queen of Poland, grand duchess of Lithuania 392
Bardach, Juliusz 89
Bari, duchy of 436
Bartnicki, Mikołaj (*c.*1450–1516), canon of Płock 377
Bartolus de Saxoferrato (1313–57), jurist 360
Basilian Order 165
Basle, council of (1431–45) 177, 272, 311
Bauernkrieg (Peasants' War) (1525) 253
Baysen, von (Bażyński) family 385, 386, 395
Baysen, Gabriel von († 1474), palatine of Culm 214

Baysen, Georg von (1469–1546), palatine of Marienburg 401
Baysen, Hans von (*c.*1390–1459), governor of Prussia 213–16, 219, 383
Baysen, Nicholaus von († 1503), palatine of Marienburg, *Anwalde* of Royal Prussia 383, 388
Baysen, Stibor von († 1480), palatine of Marienburg, governor of Royal Prussia 383
Beatrice of Aragon (1457–1508), queen of Bohemia and Hungary 278, 330
Belarus, republic of 3
Belarusian language 319
modern nation of 44, 45, 165
Belevskii family 313
Belsky, prince Fëdor Ivanovych († *c.*1506) 283, 295, 314
Belts, duchy of 29; *see also* Bełz: territory of
Bely, duchy of 285
Bełz 13, 82
territory of 358, 375, 376
palatinate of 378, 386
Bełżyce 193
Benedictine Order 72, 163
Berezina, river 67
Bernard von Falkenberg († 1455), duke of Oppeln 131
Beroaldo, Filippo (1453–1505), scholar and rhetorician 365
Bessarabia 175
Biecz 168
Bielsk 338, 470–1, 473, 476, 477
Birken, Rutger von († 1474), mayor of Thorn 214
Birutė of Palanga († 1382), grand duchess of Lithuania 29, 79, 160
Birże and Dubinki, imperial duchy of 438
Bitschin, Konrad (*c.*1400–64), Prussian chronicler 74–5
Black Death 210, 231–2
Black Ruthenia 13, 20, 67, 163, 165, 308
Black Sea 25, 85, 184, 280
Błaszczyk, Grzegorz 49, 53, 81, 83, 89, 92, 95, 114, 122, 144, 151, 155–6, 159, 172, 186, 199, 335
Blue Horde 30
Blue Waters, battle of (1362) 21
Bniński, Andrzej (1396–1479), bishop of Poznań 273
Bobrzyński, Michał 217, 237, 361
Bochnia 378
Bodin, Jean (1530–96), political thinker 38, 44, 351
Bodzęta (Bodzanta) (1320–88), archbishop of Gniezno 4, 14, 15, 252
Bogisław V (1317/18–74), duke of Pomerania 7

Bogislaw VIII (1363/4–1418), duke of Stolp 104
Bohemia, kingdom of 4, 11, 12, 16–17, 33, 51, 53, 136–7, 140, 179, 182–3, 211, 213, 266, 277–8, 280–1, 283, 319, 341, 374, 376, 392, 412, 416
Bohemian brethren 442
Bohovitynovych, Bohusz († 1530), Lithuanian marshal hospodarsky 452
Bohovitynovych, Levko († after 1505), grand ducal secretary 321
Bokei, Havrylo († 1577), land judge of Lutsk 461, 489
Bolesław I (967–1025), king of Poland 5
Boleslaw I († 1431), duke of Teschen 131
Bolesław II († 1313), duke of Mazovia 28, 377
Bolesław II 'the Bold' (1042–81), king of Poland 5
Bolesław III Krzywousty (the Wrymouth) (1086–1138), duke of Poland 5
testament of 5, 8
Bolesław III (c.1320–51), duke of Płock 6, 374
Bolesław IV (c.1421–54), duke of Warsaw 186, 188, 190, 193–5, 200, 232, 375
Bolesław V († 1488), duke of Warsaw 228
Bolesław/Iurii (1310–40), duke of Mazovia, prince of Halych-Volhynia 13, 28
Bolharynovych, Iosif († 1501), metropolitan of Kyiv and All Rus′ 309
Bologna 123, 365, 385
Bona Sforza (1494–1557), queen of Poland, grand duchess of Lithuania 333, 466
family of 407
and Lithuania 406, 408, 411–12, 418, 420, 421
and the Lithuanian council 433–5
as reformer of grand ducal domain 424–6, 429, 434–5, 452
and Mazovia 364, 366, 373, 377
and Polish politics 367, 378, 405, 412, 424, 439
and the ordinary nobility 424–5
patronage and clientele of 366, 371, 373, 422, 433, 436, 439
and the royal domain 366, 370–1, 373
reputation and unpopularity of 361, 372, 406, 437, 440
and Royal Prussia 399
Boner, Johann (1462–1523), Cracow banker 355, 363
Boniface IX (c.1350–1404), pope 89, 90, 123
Boris Aleksandrovich (1399–1461), grand duke of Tver 142
Boryszewski, Andrzej (1435–1510), archbishop of Lwów then archbishop of Gniezno 273, 389
Bosnia 184
Bosphorus 13

Brandenburg, margravate of 5, 16, 28, 33, 213, 261
Bratslav 84
palatinate of 475, 484
annexation of by Poland (1569) 482, 485–6, 488–9, 491
Braudel, Fernand 242
Breslau 134–5, 141, 179
duchy of 261
Briansk 205
duchy of 29, 77
Orthodox diocese of 312
Brest (Brześć Litewski) 4, 105, 170, 194, 199, 327, 331, 342, 406, 429, 435, 450, 460, 475
palatinate of 475, 489
starosty of 424
Brześć (Kujawski) 138, 214
assembly in (1425) 138, 140–1, 150, 167, 440
palatinate of 288
peace of (1435) 174, 178, 211, 212
Buczacki family 359
Buda 6, 110, 337, 340, 396
treaty of (1369) 7
Bues, Almut 336
Bug, river 110, 132, 338, 378
Bugaj 454
Bujno, Mikołaj, ensign of Drohiczyn 484
Bukovina 281
Buonaccorsi, Filippo (Callimachus, Kallimach) (1437–98), humanist and writer 280, 372
Burgos, Antonio da, canon lawyer 365
Burgundy, duchy of 184
Burleigh, Michael 210
Bydgoszcz 104, 105, 251
sejm session in (1520) 251, 358, 368, 396
Bystrytsa 71, 72
Byzantine empire 163, 184, 283, 311

Calixtus III (1378–58), pope 223–4, 312
Calvinism 442
Ćambor, Višel († 1393), Bohemian-Moravian nobleman 132
Canon law 39, 94–5, 117, 147, 164, 172, 203–4, 212–15, 347, 360, 365, 369, 390
Carinthia 280
Caro, Jacob 217
Cashubia 389
Casimir I (c.1211–67), duke of Cujavia 6
Casimir I (c.1314–1355), duke of Czersk 6, 374
Casimir I (c.1396–1433/4), duke of Oświęcim 131
Casimir II († 1442), duke of Mazovia 131, 186
Casimir III (1310–70), king of Poland 6, 8, 11–14, 28, 54, 63, 77, 92, 163, 231, 286, 374, 375, 377

Casimir III (1448/9–80), duke of Płock 228
Casimir III, statutes of 64, 254, 351, 369, 419
   translation into Ruthenian 419
Casimir IV Jagiellończyk (1427–92), grand duke of Lithuania, king of Poland 400
   birth and childhood 153–4
   and the Bohemian throne 179
   character and education 265–6
      political skills 188, 191, 207, 266–7, 286
   court of 194, 195, 266, 319, 320
   death and the succession 280, 295, 327–8, 332, 340–1, 387
   as a dynastic politician 205, 277–8, 280–2, 285
   election as grand duke of Lithuania (1440) 185–6, 187–8, 190, 194, 199, 203, 222, 327, 334, 335, 411, 418
   as grand duke of Lithuania 188–9, 190, 195, 280, 299, 303–6, 345, 412
      accused of favouring Lithuania 201, 267
      and the Lithuanian council 191, 346
      relations with Muscovy 189, 312–13
      and the union with Poland 189, 201, 204, 323
      and the Ruthenian lands 189–90, 193, 195, 201, 207, 293–5, 421
         assassination plot against (1481) 295
      and the Orthodox church 312
   marriage and family 277–8, 280, 330
   negotiations over Polish throne (1444–7) 191–5, 200, 267
   and Polish politics 232, 235–41, 269–76, 287–9, 375
      finances and the royal domain 267, 355–6, 359
      and Mazovia 374, 376
      use of patronage 268–9, 272–3, 299
   and Prussia 214, 216, 219–20, 222–4, 227, 382–6, 388
Casimir Jagiellon (1458–84) 280, 283, 327
Casimir of Stolp *see* Kaźko of Pomerania
Castellan, office of 352–3
Castiglione, Branda da (1350–1443), cardinal 131
Castile, kingdom of 51–2, 55, 124, 149
Catherine Habsburg (1533–72), queen of Poland, grand duchess of Lithuania 440–1, 451
Catherine Jagiellonka (1526–83), queen of Sweden 406
Catherine of Anjou (1370–8) 8
Catherine of Mazovia († 1479/80) 376
Catholic church 100, 109, 117, 121, 165; *see also* Church union
   schism of 109, 123, 165, 272
Cebulka, Mikołaj (*c*.1389–after 1456), secretary to Vytautas 122
Centaur (Kentauros) family 414

Cerekwica 223, 232, 234, 235–7
Cerekwica, privileges of (1454) 223, 224, 239
Cervera, treaty of (1469) 51–2, 55
Červonka, Oldřich († 1465), Bohemian mercenary 226
Cesarini, Julian (1398–1444), cardinal 131
Cetatea Alba 280–1
Charles I (1600–49), king of Great Britain and Ireland 41
Charles IV Luxembourg (1316–78), king of Bohemia, Holy Roman Emperor 7, 8, 11, 374
Charles V (1500–58), king of Castile and Aragon, Holy Roman Emperor, etc 51, 282, 372, 392–4, 411, 436, 438–9, 446–7
Charles VII (1403–61), king of France 51
Charles Robert of Anjou (1288–1342), king of Hungary 7
Charles Valois (1446–72), duke of Normandy and Acquitaine 51
Chartorysk 168
Chashniki, battle of (1564) 462, 467, 480
Chełm 13, 240, 251–2, 352, 461
Chełmski, Ścibor († 1469), starosta general of Wielkopolska, starosta of Marienburg 383–4
Chernihiv 165
   Orthodox diocese of 312
Chernihiv-Siversky, duchy of 67
Chodkiewicz, Hieronim (*c*.1515–61), starosta of Samogitia 447, 457
Chodkiewicz, Hrehory (1513–72), grand hetman of Lithuania, castellan of Vilnius 472
Chodkiewicz, Jan (1537–79), castellan of Vilnius 295, 447, 449–50, 456, 472, 479, 482–4, 488, 491–2
Chojeński, Jan (1486–1538), grand chancellor of Poland, bishop of Cracow 365
Chojnice, battle of *see* Konitz: battle of
Chorny Horod 85
Chortorysky (Czartoryski) family 208
Chortorysky, prince Aleksander († after 1477) 180, 185–6, 188
Chortorysky, prince Aleksander Fëdorovych (1517–71), palatine of Volhynia 485, 487
Chortorysky, prince Ivan († *c*.1460) 180, 185–6, 188
Christburg 212, 224, 386
Christian II (1481–1559), king of Denmark and Norway 393
Christmemel, treaty of (1431) 157, 168, 169, 208
Christmemel, treaty of (1432), 169
Chronicles 165, 318
   Bychowiec chronicle 143–4, 413–15, 420
   and Rus' 421

and the union 416
Halych chronicle 165
Lithuanian chronicles
 first redaction 189, 413, 415
 second redaction 413–14
 third redaction *see* Chronicles: Bychowiec chronicle
 and the union 414
Muscovite chronicles 295, 413–14
Nikiforovskaia chronicle 188
Ruthenian chronicles 25, 74, 143, 294, 421
Chrząstowski, Piotr (*c*.1389–1452), bishop of Przemyśl 272
Church Slavonic 318
Church union 163–5, 309–12, 316
 union of Armenian church with Rome 311
Chwalczewski, Jerzy († 1549), bishop of Lutsk 425, 427
Chwalczewski, Piotr († 1566), castellan of Biechowo 427–9
Ciechanów, duchy then territory of 16, 375
Ciołek, Erazm (1474–1522), bishop of Płock 280, 309
Ciołek, Stanisław (1382–1437), vice-chancellor of Poland, bishop of Poznań 319–20
Clement VII (1342–94), antipope 11
Clement VII (1478–1534), pope 407, 411
Collateral succession 5, 20, 21, 87, 234
Cologne 385
Colonna family 414, 416
Community of the realm 11, 14–16, 118–19, 184, 203, 360
Conciliarism 123, 272–3, 347
Confederation, legal principle of 14, 117, 127
 confederations, individual
 of Małopolska and Wielkopolska (1382) 118
 of Spytek of Melsztyn the younger (1439) 182, 268–9
 Vitsebsk (1562) 446
 rokosz 371, 439
 Lwów *rokosz* (1537) 372, 399, 406
Constantine XI (1405–53), Byzantine emperor 309
Constantinople 25, 26, 184, 224, 278, 311
 patriarchate of 163–4, 312
Constance, council of (1414–18) 109–10, 113, 116, 121–7, 136, 175, 399
Copenhagen 54
Copernicus, Andreas (*c*.1465–before 1518) 365, 386
Copernicus, Nicholas (1473–1543), astronomer, canon of Frauenburg 365, 386–7, 398–9
Corona regni Poloniae 11–12, 14–15, 17
Coronation tempest (1429) 142–51, 153, 155, 169, 173, 186, 188, 200, 323, 331, 399, 415, 418

Courland, diocese of 446
Courland and Semgallen, duchy of 447
Cracow 4, 6, 8, 34, 54, 72, 76–7, 80, 83–4, 89, 92, 132, 139, 141, 150, 152, 167, 171, 178, 183, 192, 194, 199, 214–15, 290, 321, 334, 339, 340, 344, 355, 359, 363, 367, 371, 374, 379, 383, 386, 393, 400, 405–8, 435, 439, 442, 452, 454, 458, 460, 464, 466, 478, 487, 492
 cathedral of St Stanisław in 3–4, 131, 183, 309, 311
 diocese of 141, 248, 265, 269, 272–4, 367, 464
 castellany of 368
 duchy of 5–6, 28, 64
 palatinate of 64, 137, 239, 256, 268, 288, 352, 356, 363–4, 366, 368
 sejmik of 368
 treaty of (1525) 393–4, 398, 401, 405
 university of 101, 117, 123–4, 125, 318, 365, 369, 375, 386, 411
Cracow lords 88, 89, 91, 92, 235, 344; *see also* Małopolskan lords
Cracow procurators (*wielkorządcy*) 359
Cranmer, Thomas (1489–1556), archbishop of Canterbury 387
Creveld, Martin van 52–3
Crimean Tatars *see* Tatars: Crimean
Cromwell, Oliver (1599–1658), lord protector of England 43
Crown of Poland *see Corona regni Poloniae*
Crummey, Robert 310
Cujavia
 diocese of 102, 177, 367, 384
 duchy of 10
 palatinate of 214, 396
Culm (Chełmno) 107–8, 212, 214, 216, 228
 diocese of 102, 107, 228, 381–2, 384, 387, 395, 396
 palatinate of 218, 381, 386, 401
Culm law 210, 212, 216, 219, 231, 391, 394
 inheritance law 391, 397
 Landesordnung (1526) and reform of 397
Curonians 18, 20
Cygenberg family 385
Cyprian (*c*.1336–1406), metropolitan of Kyiv, Rus', and Lithuania 74, 164, 165
Czarnkowski, Stanisław (1526–1602), marshal of the Lublin sejm (1569) 477, 488
Czarny *see* Radziwiłł, Mikołaj Czarny (the Black)
Czech language 411
Czema, Achacy (Achacius von Zehmen the younger) († 1576) 465
Czersk, duchy then territory of 16, 375, 376
Czerwińsk 105, 140, 232, 234
 privileges of (1422) 140, 167

Dąbrowski, Jan 56
Dainauskas, Jonas 49
Dameraw (Działyński) family 385
Dantyszek, Jan (Joannes Dantiscus, Johann von Höfen, Johann von Flachsbinder) (1485–1548), bishop of Ermland, humanist scholar and diplomat 386–7, 390, 394, 396, 398, 401
Danube, river 142, 167, 280
Danutė (Anna) (1362–1448), duchess of Mazovia 374
Danutė (Elizabeth) († 1364), duchess of Płock 28
Danzig 107, 210, 213, 216–17, 224, 225–8, 231, 338, 354, 357, 361, 363, 377, 381–2, 385–6, 390, 392–3, 396–7
  Lutheranism in 394–5, 397, 442
  minting rights of 398–9
  privileges of 224, 389
  remodelling of constitution (1526) 394, 395
Dardenelles 184
Daugirdas, Jonas († 1443), palatine of Vilnius 180, 185
Daumantas of Nalšia († 1299) 26
Daumantas, pagan starosta of Samogitia 188
Davaina (Dowojna) family 321
Davis, S. Rufus 37
Dębiński (Dembiński) family 322
Dėdinas, V. 81, 88
Dembiński, Walenty († 1584), treasurer then grand chancellor of Poland 463, 468, 471
Dembkowski, Harry 448, 461–2, 491–2
Denmark, kingdom of 51, 394, 446
Derby, earl of *see* Henry IV, earl of Derby, king of England
Dijon 10
Dirschau 224–8, 382, 396, 397
Divine law 124, 140, 219
Długosz, Jan (1415–80), historian, archbishop of Lwów 34, 67, 71–2, 74–5, 80–2, 88, 90–2, 103, 119, 125, 133–4, 137, 139, 143–5, 149, 153, 171, 176, 180, 182–3, 185, 187, 190, 192, 194, 215–6, 224, 228, 232, 235–7, 239, 248, 256, 268–9, 295, 321, 415
  and Casimir IV 201, 265–7, 272–3, 280
  composition of the *Annals* 141–2
  diplomatic and political activities of 201, 230
  dislike of Lithuanians 75, 414
  negative view of Jagiełło and the Jagiellons 75, 107–8, 131–2, 175, 177, 265–6
  and the union 114, 215
  and Zbigniew Oleśnicki 141–2, 144, 178, 265
Długosz, Janusz († 1482), burgrave of Cracow 228
Dmitrii Donskoi (1350–89), grand duke of Muscovy 28–29, 31, 34, 77, 80, 282

Dmitrii Shemeika († 1453) 282
Dmitry Olherdovych (Algirdaitis) († 1399), duke of Briansk 24, 29, 31, 77–8, 84, 86–7, 131
Dnieper, river 152, 163
Dniester, river 85, 280
Dobrotwór 132
Dobrzyń 104, 105
  territory of 12, 80, 99, 100, 102, 108, 238, 288, 352
Dodukov, battle of (1392) 84
Dominican Order 72, 126, 163
Don, river 85
Domarat of Pierzchna († 1399/1400), starosta general of Wielkopolska 12, 14
Donelaitis, Kristijonas (1714–80), Prussian-Lithuanian poet and philologist 44
Dorohobuzh 337
Dorohostajski, Mikołaj († 1597), palatine of Polatsk 451
Dorpat (Tartu) 446
  diocese of 446, 447
Dowojna family 435
Dresdenko 102
Drohiczyn 72, 188, 410
Drozd, Zofia 428
Drwęca, river 135
Drzewicki, Maciej (1467–1535), grand chancellor of Poland, archbishop of Gniezno 365, 367
Dubissa river 31, 125
Dubissa, treaty of (31 October/1 November 1382) 31, 34
Duchhardt, Heinz 42
Düna river 447
Dunin, Piotr (*c.*1415–84), palatine of Brześć, starosta of Marienburg 227–8, 384
Durad Branković (1377–1456), despot of Serbia 182
Dutch republic 36
Dyneburg 18
Działyński family *see* Dameraw family 322
Działyński, Theodor 448, 458
Dzierzgowski, Mikołaj (1490–1559), archbishop of Gniezno 439

Edigü Mangit (1352–1419), emir of the Golden Horde 86
Ehlau 226, 227
Ekdahl, Sven 106
Eišiškės 146
Elazar, Daniel 37
Elbing 107, 131, 212–13, 225, 227, 231, 357, 363, 377, 381–2, 384, 386, 389, 391, 395, 397–8
  palatinate of 218
  treaty of (1464) 228
Elizabeth I (1533–1603), queen of England 51
Elizabeth Habsburg (1436–1505), queen of Poland, grand duchess of

Lithuania 266, 277–8, 280, 330, 337, 344, 439
Elizabeth Habsburg (1526–45), queen of Poland, grand duchess of Lithuania 433–4, 435–6, 439, 451
Elizabeth Łokietkówna (1305–80), queen of Hungary 7, 10, 12
Elizabeth of Bosnia (1339/40–1387), queen of Hungary 4, 10, 15–16, 34, 50, 52, 56, 183
Elizabeth of Luxembourg (1409–42), queen of Bohemia, Hungary, and the Romans 136, 179, 182–4
Elizabeth of Pomerania (1346/7–93), queen of Bohemia 7
Elizabeth Pilecka-Granowska (c.1372–1420), queen of Poland, grand duchess of Lithuania 132, 148, 271, 320
Elliott, J.H. 40–3, 51
Engels, Friedrich (1820–95) 242
England, kingdom of 39, 41–3, 51, 53, 61, 258, 261
Erasmus, Desiderius (1466–1536) 365
Erik II († 1474), duke of Stolp 228
Erik XIV (1533–77), king of Sweden 446, 447
Erik of Pomerania (1381/2–1459), king of Denmark, Norway, and Sweden 54–5, 131, 142, 154, 213
Erlichshausen, Konrad von († 1449), grand master of the Teutonic Order 212–13
Erlichshausen, Ludwig von (1410–67), grand master of the Teutonic Order 213–14, 216, 226–8
Ermes, battle of (1560) 446
Ermland (Warmia), diocese of 107, 212, 214, 223, 225, 228, 230, 367, 381–2, 384, 387, 391, 393
 relationship to kingdom of Poland 384–5, 388, 395, 398
Eufemia Gediminaitė († 1341), princess of Halych-Volhynia 28
Eugene IV (1383–1447), pope 154, 269, 311
European Union 36
Execution of the laws, movement for (kingdom of Poland) 369, 370, 372–3, 420–1, 442–5, 473
 calls for common sejm to effect closer union 441, 444, 476–7
 execution sejms and legislation (1562, 1563–4, 1565, 1566, 1567) 454–5, 456
 incorporationist interpretation of union 459
 and the grand ducal domain 470, 487
 and pressure for execution of the union with Lithuania 373, 400, 441, 453, 463, 479
 and the royal domain 442–4, 454–5, 456
 exemptions for Volhynia and Lithuania 487
 and Royal Prussia 470, 486

Falkenberg, Johannes († c.1435), Dominican theologian and polemicist 126
Fałkowski, Wojciech 202
Fëdor, Orthodox, bishop and metropolitan of Halych 163
Fëdor Koriatovych († 1414), duke of Podolia 84, 166
Fëdor Korybutovych (c.1380–1442), duke of Podolia 170, 293
Fëdor Lubartovych (c.1351–1431), duke of Lutsk and Siversk 84, 87, 298
Fëdor Olherdovych (Algirdaitis) († 1400), duke of Ratno 24, 29, 84, 87
Fëdor Vesna († 1392), governor of Vitsebsk 84
Felden, family of 385
Ferrara 311
Flachsbinder, Johann von *see* Dantyszek, Jan
Foedosius, Orthodox bishop of Polatsk 164
Felix V (1383–1451), antipope 269
Ferdinand I (1503–64), king of Bohemia and Hungary, king of the Romans, Holy Roman Emperor 282, 372, 392–3, 433, 434, 447
Ferdinand II (1452–1516), king of Aragon and Castile 51–2, 55
Feuchtwangen, Siegried von († 1311), grand master of the Teutonic Order 27
Feudalism 62, 67, 205, 234
Fijałek, Jan 411
Firlej, Mikołaj († 1526), grand hetman of Poland, castellan of Cracow 344
Florence 412
 council of (1431–49) 310–11, 417
 union of 310, 312
Forsyth, Murray 36
Fotius († 1431), metropolitan of Moscow 154–5
France, kingdom of 42, 66, 412
Francesco III Gonzaga (1533–50), duke of Mantua 440
Franciscan Order 27, 72–3, 309, 317–18, 492
Franklin, Julian 38
Frauenburg 228
Frederick I von Hohenzollern (1371–1440), elector of Brandenburg 138
Frederick I von Hohenzollern (1460–1536), margrave of Ansbach-Bayreuth 392
Frederick II von Hohenzollern (1413–71), elector of Brandenburg 138, 193, 223
Frederick II (1412–64), elector of Saxony 277
Frederick III (1415–93), Holy Roman Emperor 213–14, 220, 224, 277, 278, 280
Frederick Jagiellon (1468–1503), bishop of Cracow, archbishop of Gniezno, cardinal 267, 273–4, 281, 290, 327–8, 330, 337–9, 355, 377, 385
Frederick of Saxony (1473–1510), grand master of the Teutonic Order 387–8, 392

French language 319
Freunt, Achacius, canon of Ermland 397
Frische Haff 384
Fürstenberg, Wilhelm von (1500–68), grand master of the Livonian Order 446

Galicia and Lodomeria, kingdom of 13
Gamrat, Piotr (1487–1545), archbishop of Gniezno 366, 371, 373
Gaškavičius, Andrius, bishop of Vilnius (1481–91) 318
Gaudemantė (Sophia) Traidenytė († 1288), duchess of Mazovia 28
Gedgaudas, Jurgis († 1435), palatine of Vilnius 170, 175
Gediminas (c.1275–1341), grand duke of Lithuania 3, 20–1, 24–7, 29, 68, 163, 407, 414, 421
Gediminid dynasty 3, 20, 24, 26, 28–9, 31, 34, 50, 53, 56, 67, 73–4, 76, 78, 82, 86, 97, 100, 109, 117, 127, 132, 137, 151, 154–5, 158–9, 161–2, 170, 180, 189, 194, 204, 205, 222, 283, 292–3, 313, 323, 330, 407, 414, 416, 421
   claim to rule All Rus' 26
Geneva 443
Genocide 45, 48, 126
Genoa 184, 280
German language 318, 328, 381, 395, 447
German law 63, 231–2, 247, 248, 254
Germany 53, 209, 319, 412, 428
Giedraitis family 414
Giedraitis, Hermanas († c.1439) 318
Gierianiony 411, 434
Giese, Tidemann (1480–1550), bishop of Ermland 397
Gilgenburg 105
Giray dynasty (Crimea) 283
Giżycki, Paweł (c. 1400–63), bishop of Płock 193
Glinskii, Mykhail see Hlynsky, Mykhailo
Glogau, duchy of 281
Gniewkowo, duchy of 10, 11, 99
Gniezno 13
   archdiocese of 11, 102, 141, 149, 228, 230, 252, 257, 269, 274, 315, 354, 367, 377
   cathedral 13
Gnojeński, Krzysztof († after 1599), executionist politician 452
Golden Horde 28, 31, 85, 282–3
Golub 126, 386
Golubac, battle of (1428) 142
Goniądz 406–7
Goniądz and Medele see Goniądz and Rajgród
Goniądz and Rajgród, imperial ducal title of 406, 409, 425, 434, 438
Górecki, Piotr 246

Górka family 214
Górka, Andrzej (1500–51), castellan of Poznań, starosta general of Wielkopolska 438–41, 443
Górka, Łukasz († 1475), palatine of Poznań 224, 268
Górka, Łukasz (1533–73), palatine of Poznań 453
Górski, Karol 215–17
Górski, Stanisław († 1572), canon of Cracow, historian 434
Goštautaitė, Elžbieta († 1503) 406
Goštautas, family of 407, 410–11, 413–14, 424–5, 433, 438
Goštautas, Albertas (1480–1539), grand chancellor of Lithuania, palatine of Vilnius 302, 317, 429, 433–4
   and Bona Sforza 408, 412, 424–5, 427
   character 410–11
   and the history of the grand duchy 412–13
   rivalry with the Radvila family 406–7, 420
   separatist reputation 410
   vision of union 410–12, 418–20, 422–3
Goštautas, Andrius (1342–1408) 79, 80
Goštautas, Jonas (c.1383–1458), chancellor of the grand duchy of Lithuania 170, 185–6, 200, 293, 299, 304, 410–11, 467
Goštautas, Martynas (1428–c.1481), governor of Kyiv, palatine of Trakai 294–5, 411, 421
Goštautas, Stanislovas (c.1507–42), 420, 433–4
Gostyń, duchy then territory of 16, 352, 375, 376
Granowski, Wincenty (c.1370–1410), castellan of Nakło 132
Graudenz 396, 397
Great Horde 282–3
Gregory II († 1474), metropolitan of Kyiv and All Rus' 312
Gregory III Mammas († 1459), patriarch of Constantinople 312
Gregory XI (1336–78), pope 7, 10
Gregory XII (c.1326–1417), pope 123
Greifswald 386
Grotniki, battle of (1439) 182
Grunau, Simon (c. 1470–1531), historian of Prussia 395
Grunwald (Grünfelde), battle of see Tannenberg: battle of
Gruszczyński, Jan (1405–73), grand chancellor of Poland, bishop of Cujavia, archbishop of Gniezno 214, 271–3
Grzymalita family 12
Gudavičius, Edvardas 67, 81, 413
Gutsherrschaft 242, 245–6
Gutswirtschaft 242, 245–6, 261
Guzowski, Piotr 259

Index

Habsburg dynasty 17, 34, 205, 366, 392, 412, 434, 441
Hagen, William 245–6
Haina 71
Halecki, Oskar 33–4, 47, 68, 79, 81–3, 96, 137, 155, 170, 186, 188, 199, 313, 330, 332, 336, 339–40, 342, 394, 411, 448, 449, 459, 469, 479, 485
Halych 13, 167, 240, 352
Halych-Volhynia, principality of 13, 20–1, 28, 33, 165, 166
Hamilton, Alexander (*c*.1755–1804), president of the United States of America 45
Hanover, electorate then kingdom of 38, 42
Hanseatic league 210
Hedwig of Sagan (1350–90), queen of Poland 7
Hejnosz, Wojciech 218
Helena Ivanovna (1476–1513), grand duchess of Lithuania, queen of Poland 309–10, 314, 337, 345
Henry (Heinrich von Porwalle) († 1350), bishop of Kyiv 163
Henry IV (1425–74), king of Castile 51
Henry IV (1367–1413), earl of Derby, king of England 80, 105
Henry V (*c*.1319–69), duke of Sagan 7
Henryk of Mazovia (1368/70–1392/3), bishop nominate of Płock 81, 374
Hens' War (*wojna kokosza*) (1537) 372; *see also* Confederation: *rokosz*
Herasym († 1435), metropolitan of Kyiv and All Rus′ 185, 414
Herberstein, Sigismund (1486–1566) 3, 411
Hetmanate, Cossack (seventeenth century) 160
Hincza, Aleksander, Podlasian envoy 484
Hincza of Rogów, Jan (*c*.1400–74), treasurer of Poland 178, 268
Hlebovych (Hlebowicz) family 321
Hlebowicz Jan (1480–1549), grand chancellor of Lithuania, palatine of Vilnius 433–5, 437
Hlynsky family 321
Hlynsky, Mykhailo (*c*.1470–1535) 314, 342, 344, 365, 406
 rising of (1507) 314, 329, 345–6, 406
Hobbes, Thomas (1588–1679), political philosopher 52
Hohenzollern dynasty 366, 393, 394, 401
Hoitsevych, Ivashko († after 1456), governor of Navahrudak 316
Holkner, Philipp, Danzig lawyer 397
Holszański, Paweł (*c*.1485–1555), bishop of Vilnius 413
Holshansky (Alšėniškai, Holszański), family of 53, 84, 414, 435
Holshansky, Aleksander (*c*.1440–1511), castellan of Vilnius 338, 342
Holshansky, Iury (*c*.1410–after 1457) 200

Holshansky, Ivan († *c*.1402), governor of Kyiv 76, 84, 131, 293, 295
Holshansky, Mykhailo († 1448) 293, 316
Holshansky, Semën († 1433) 170
Holy Roman Empire 24, 27, 33, 38, 66, 100, 102, 109, 126, 147, 182, 212, 222, 224–5, 277, 377, 392, 393, 446–7
Holy Trinity, church of (Vilnius) 316
Homel 314, 420
Hornostai, Havrylo († 1587), palatine of Minsk 451
Hornostai, Ivan (*c*.1480–1551), treasurer of the grand duchy of Lithuania, palatine of Navahrudak 422, 433–4, 438
Horodets, duchy of 292–3
Horodetsky family 292
Horodło 110, 115, 168, 375
 adoption of Lithuanian boyars by Polish heraldic clans 115–16, 119–20, 143, 151, 160, 174, 176, 298, 302–3, 335, 415–16, 467
 ambiguity and lack of clarity of 127, 152, 156, 161–2, 204
 as basis of Lithuanian noble liberties 119, 206, 334, 460–1
 and bilateral assemblies 187, 200
 conflicting interpretations of 119–20, 152
 and election of grand duke 112, 114, 118–19, 138, 152, 155–6, 173, 186–7, 192–3, 199, 200, 203, 328, 334–5
 exclusion of Orthodox Ruthenian boyars 120–1, 158–9, 160, 162–3, 168–9, 174, 176, 200, 292, 316–17, 409, 422
 repeal of (1563) 460, 475, 488
 and the government of Lithuania 113, 155, 172, 200–1, 299, 304, 306, 341
 impact of 151, 292
 and the incorporation of Lithuania 110–13, 119, 121, 127, 143, 171, 194, 199, 201, 204, 206, 332, 339, 399, 464, 466
 Jagiełło and 113, 116, 117, 217, 415
 role in later union negotiations 332–6
 and the succession 127, 138, 203, 341, 415
 union of (1413) 50, 56, 110–21, 147, 150, 159, 217, 219
 and vision of a community of citizens 122, 127, 202, 494
 Vytautas and 118–19, 151, 217, 291, 415
Hrodna 21, 67, 79, 80, 92, 171, 192, 327, 338, 422, 429, 435, 475, 476, 477
 privileges of (1432) 174–5
 treaty of (1398) 85, 86, 89
 'union' of (1432) 170–3, 178–9, 185–7, 199, 201, 339, 461
 renewals of 173, 174
Hrubieszów 111

Hrushevsky, Mykhailo 21, 44, 45, 96, 113, 153, 156, 159, 164, 168, 171, 174, 295, 429, 430, 449
Hughes, Christopher 38
Hungary, kingdom of 4, 6, 13, 16, 17, 21, 24, 28, 51, 53, 84, 88, 109, 133, 142, 182–6, 188–9, 191, 235, 268, 277–8, 280–1, 283, 287, 311, 341, 371, 392, 393, 412
Hunyadi, János (c.1406–56), voivode of Transylvania 184, 278
Hus, Jan 123, 136
Hussites 136–7, 140, 142, 177, 179, 182, 278

Iakovenko, Natalia 302, 317
Ianushkevich, Andrei 449, 461
Iaroslav the Wise (c.978–1054), grand prince of Rus′ 20, 309
Ihumen 163
Île-de-France 96, 261
Ilnych, Iury († 1526), Lithuanian marshal of the court 452
Ilnych, Ivan, governor of Vitsebsk 316
Innocent IV (1195–1254), pope 25
Innocent VII (1339–1406), pope 123
Innocent VIII (1432–92), pope 273
Inowrocław 214
  palatinate of 288
International law *see Ius gentium*
Ireland, kingdom of 39, 42
Irzykowicz, Kasper, chamberlain of Mielnik 484
Isabella Jagiellonka (1519–59), queen of Hungary 406
Isabella I (1451–1504), queen of Castile and Aragon 51–2
Isabeau of Bavaria (c.1370–1435), queen of France 131
Isaiah († 1334), patriarch of Constantinople 163
Isidore (1384–1463), metropolitan of Kyiv and All Rus′ 310–12
Isner, Jan (1345–1411), theologian 318
Istanbul 283, 295
Iurii I (1252–1308), prince of Halych-Volhynia 26
Iurii Sviatoslavich († 1407), duke of Smolensk 78, 100
Iurii of Galich (1374–1434) 282
Iursha, Ivashko Ivanovych, governor of Bratslav 169, 316–17
Iury, duke of Pinsk 100
Iury Lengvinevich, Gediminid prince 88, 189, 200, 204
Iury Narimuntovich († after 1398), duke of Belts 29
Ius gentium 122, 124
Ivan III (1440–1505), grand duke of Muscovy 283, 295, 309, 313–15, 327, 331, 337, 341, 447
Ivan IV (1530–1584), grand duke of Muscovy 3, 314, 320, 446, 447, 468, 476

Ivan Volodymyrovych (Belsky) († c. 1452), duke of Bely, governor of Novgorod 170–1, 193, 293
Ivinskis, Zenonas 81, 119

Jablonowski, Horst 298
Jadwiga (Hedwig) Jagiellonka (1457–1503), duchess of Bavaria-Landshut 278, 321
Jadwiga Jagiellonka (1408–31) 119, 122, 138–9, 193, 223
Jadwiga Jagiellonka (1513–73), electoress of Brandenburg 406
Jadwiga of Anjou (1374–1399), queen of Poland
  breakdown of relations with Jagiełło 88, 89
  claim to Polish throne 52
  court and clientele 88, 89, 102
  election and coronation 4, 12–13, 15–16, 17, 33–4, 78
  engagement to William von Habsburg 8, 10, 17, 34, 47
  and Lithuania 77–8, 82, 89, 91
  marriage to Jagiełło 4, 13, 33, 49, 52, 56, 143, 463
  pregnancy and death 34, 57, 91, 92
  as queen regnant of Poland 17, 77, 88–90, 95–6, 375
Jagiełło, Władysław (c.1351–1434), grand duke of Lithuania, king of Poland
  birth, education, and early life 29, 74–5, 160
  conversion and baptism 4, 33, 50, 53, 109, 121, 375
  patrimony 50, 118
  and the Catholic church 4, 33, 71–3, 125, 127, 163–4, 175, 272, 308, 316
  character and reputation 47–8, 75, 154, 177, 188, 202, 265–6, 320, 413, 414
  love of hunting 75, 131, 133, 235
  court of 88, 320
  death of 75, 97, 119, 138, 139, 168, 172–3, 176–8, 289
  as dynastic politician 29–30, 97, 118, 122, 134, 137–41, 143, 145–6, 152–4, 187, 232, 293
  defence of hereditary rights of his sons to the Polish throne 123, 137, 139–41, 143, 145–6, 153–4, 191, 232, 332, 336
  family and marriages 3–4, 33, 49, 50, 56, 131–3, 143, 160, 177, 193, 266, 271, 274, 277, 293, 310, 320, 374, 436, 453, 463; *see also* Jadwiga of Anjou; Anna of Celje; Elizabeth Pilecka-Granowska; Sophia (Sonka) Holshanska
  foreign policy 109–10, 142
    relations with Muscovy 31
    relations with Prussia and the Teutonic Order 31, 33–4, 99–108, 110, 164, 209, 211, 265, 375

and the government of Lithuania 50, 57,
  67, 76, 83, 151–7, 169–72, 299,
  415–6
 as absentee grand duke 76, 83, 155–6
 conflict with Kęstutis 3, 30–1, 414
 regalian rights in Lithuania 92
 relations with Ruthenia and
  Ruthenians 69, 120, 160, 163–9,
  174–6, 308
 as supreme duke of Lithuania 93, 118,
  154–6, 172, 178, 292
 as king of Poland 127, 138–41, 177, 191,
  215, 232, 235, 254, 274, 419
 basing of rule on Małopolska 235
 clientele 99, 102, 178, 271, 274
 coronation 3, 12, 50, 53, 55–7, 77,
  375, 415
 finances and the royal domain 225,
  232–3, 359
 and Mazovia 375
 and the Orthodox church 31, 163–5,
  174, 315
 and paganism 31, 71–2, 121
 and the Polish throne 17, 33–4, 88, 92, 123,
  202, 336, 414
 political aims of 87, 92, 127, 137
 political skills of 75, 76, 175, 188, 191
 relations with Vytautas 30–1, 34–5, 74–90,
  92, 97–8, 100, 110–11, 127,
  131–2, 134–8, 142–50, 178, 180,
  205, 413–16
 and the union 33–4, 45, 47, 53, 56–7, 61,
  67–8, 110–13, 115–21, 151, 160,
  178, 183, 205, 217, 265, 331–2,
  334–6, 339, 415, 453, 464, 466,
  471, 479, 492, 493
Jagiellonian dynasty 50, 83, 140, 182, 184,
  205, 232, 265–7, 285, 295–6,
  311–13, 320, 328, 330, 332, 335,
  341, 344–5, 355, 361, 366, 371,
  374, 378, 407, 410, 416, 436, 440
 hereditary rights in Lithuania 147–8, 153,
  191, 193, 199–200, 328, 330,
  340–1, 344–5, 408, 411, 424, 440,
  465, 469
 loyalty to 186–7, 193
 natural rights to Polish throne 147, 150, 199,
  333, 344, 361
Jagiellonian Europe 277–85
Jagiellonian idea, the 47, 336, 449
Jakub of Dębno (1427–90), grand chancellor of
  Poland, castellan of Cracow 271,
  274–6
Jakub of Korzkiew (c.1350–1425), bishop of
  Płock 101, 123
Jakub of Sienno (1413–80), bishop of Cracow,
  archbishop of Gniezno 272
James VI and I (1567–1625), king of Scotland,
  king of England and Ireland, king of
  Great Britain 41, 50, 321, 322

Jan of Czyżów (1373–1459), castellan of
  Cracow 186, 200, 268–9, 271, 276
Jan of Rzeszów (1345–1436), archbishop of
  Lwów 132
Jan Zygmuntowicz (Jagiellon) (Jan z książąt
  litewskich) (1499–1538), bishop of
  Vilnius, bishop of Poznań 274,
  409, 411
Jane, Johann von, palatine of Pomerelia 224
Janisław († 1341), archbishop of Gniezno 12
Janko of Czarnków (c.1320–86/7), vice-
  chancellor of Poland, chronicler 7
János Corvinus (1473–1504) 278, 281
Janusz I (c.1346–1429), duke of Mazovia 16,
  104, 142, 188, 374, 375
Janusz II (1455–95), duke of Mazovia 228, 273,
  327, 345, 376
Janusz III (1502–26), duke of Mazovia 377,
  378, 407, 411
Janusz Suchywilk (c.1310–82), archbishop of
  Gniezno, chancellor of Poland 7
Jarosław 281
Jasas, Rimantas 413, 414
Jaśko of Oleśnica († 1413), starosta of Vilnius 80
Jasnowski, Jerzy 450, 462
Jastrzębiec, Andrzej († 1398), bishop of
  Vilnius 72
Jastrzębiec, Wojciech (c.1362–1436), chancellor
  of Poland, archbishop of
  Gniezno 97, 101, 123, 131, 141,
  143, 268, 274
Jaunutis Gediminaitis († 1366), grand duke of
  Lithuania 21, 155
Jedlnia 119, 153
 privileges of (1430) 150, 167, 174, 352
Jelita clan 395
Jellinek, Georg 37–9, 42–3, 50, 203–6
Jeňcik of Hičina († 1395), Moravian
  nobleman 132
Jewish community in Poland 124, 350, 357
Joanna (1462–1530), queen of Portugal 51
Joanna (1479–1555), queen of Castile and
  Aragon 51–2
Jobst I (1351–1411), margrave of Moravia, king
  of the Romans 104
Jogaila *see* Jagiełło, Władysław
Johann II (after 1365–1424), duke of
  Ratibor 131
Johann IV († by 1497), duke of Oświęcim 214
John I Albert (Jan I Olbracht) (1459–1501), king
  of Poland, supreme duke of
  Lithuania 200, 386, 387
 character and reputation 265–7
 death of 337
 early career 283, 327–8
 and the Hungarian throne 280–1
 election to the Polish throne 273–4, 285,
  327, 335, 341, 382, 418
 as king of Poland 333, 337–8, 347, 372
 and Mazovia 376

John I Albert (Jan I Olbracht) (1459–1501), king of Poland, supreme duke of Lithuania (*cont.*)
    privilege of (1496) 240
    and the royal domain 355
    and the sejm 289–90
    as supreme duke of Lithuania 330
    and the union 331, 333–4, 336
John VIII Palaelogus (1392–1448), Byzantine emperor 131, 142
John XXII (1249–1334), pope 6, 27
John XXIII (c.1370–1419), antipope 123, 141
John of Luxembourg (1296–1346), king of Bohemia 6, 27, 374
John of Salisbury (1120–80), theologian, bishop of Chartres 347, 349
Jonah († 1461), metropolitan of Moscow 312
Jordan, Wilhelm († 1461 or after), Danzig councillor 213, 216
Joseph II (1360–1439), patriarch of Constantinople 310–11
Jučas Miečislovas 137, 144, 413, 450
Juliana Holshanska († c.1448), grand duchess of Lithuania 134
Juliana of Tver (c.1325–92), grand duchess of Lithuania 25, 29, 31, 74–6, 160, 310
Jungingen, Konrad von (c.1355–1407), grand master of the Teutonic Order 90
Jungingen, Ulrich von (1360–1410), grand master of the Teutonic Order 103–4, 106

Kalisz
    palatinate of 288
    peace of (1343) 7, 89, 100, 122, 135, 209
Kallimach *see* Buonaccorsi, Filippo
Kalmar 51, 53
Kamianets (Podilsky) 100, 163, 167, 207, 280, 359
    Catholic diocese of 167
Kamieniecki, Witold 68
Kantautas, Mykolas, starosta of Samogitia (1434/5–c.1440) 299
Kapusta, Timofy Ivanovych († 1515), Ruthenian boyar 308
Karamzin, Nikolai (1766–1826) historian of Russia 74
Kaributas Algirdaitis († after 1404) 3, 29, 30, 50, 79, 82–4, 87
Karigaila Algirdaitis († 1390) 4, 29, 80
Karijotas Gediminaitis († 1365), duke of Navahrudad 24
Kauernik 105
Kaunas 33, 34, 72, 110, 173, 298, 306, 318
    starosty of 425
    treaty of (1404) 100
Kazan, khanate of 282, 447
Kazimierz 363

Kaźko of Pomerania (1351–77), duke of Stolp 7, 11, 12
Kesdorf, Frank von († 1435), grand master of the Livonian Order 173
Kęsgaila family 189, 299–300, 302, 317, 435
    and Samogitia 189
Kęsgaila, Jonas (c.1405–85), starosta of Samogitia 299
Kęsgaila, Mykolas Valimantaitis († c.1450), castellan of Vilnius 170, 187, 299, 304
Kęsgaila, Stanislovas Jonavičius (c.1451–1527), starosta of Samogitia, castellan of Vilnius 299
Kęsgaila, Stanislovas Stanislovaitis (1505–32), starosta of Samogitia 299–300
Kęstutid dynasty 31, 76, 83, 134, 172, 190, 205, 299
Kęstutis Gediminaitis († 1382), grand duke of Lithuania 3, 21, 25, 29–31, 69, 74, 76, 79, 82, 86, 122, 155, 163, 172, 374, 414, 415
Kettler, Gotthard (1517–87), grand master of the Livonian Order, duke of Courland 447
Kežmarok 137
Khodkevych (Chodkiewicz) family 322, 422, 434
Khodkevych, Ivan (c.1420–84), governor of Kyiv 295, 316
Khodko Iurevich († after 1447), Ruthenian boyar 169, 175, 316
Kiaupienė, Jūratė 114, 449–50, 451, 485
Kidd, Colin 43–4
Kiełbasa, Wincenty (Wincenty 'Kiełbasa' Gosławski) (c.1425–78), bishop of Culm 230, 383, 385
Kierdej, Jan Hryćko († 1462), palatine of Podolia 186
Kietliński, Jan, executionist activist 445
Kiev *see* Kyiv
Kievan Rus' 13, 18, 20–1, 28, 53, 159–60, 165, 189, 285, 294, 306, 419
Kilia 280, 281
Kishka (Kiszka) family 435
Kiszka, Anna, mother of Mikołaj Radziwiłł Czarny 441
Kiszka, Mikołaj (1524–87), starosta of Drohiczyn, palatine of Podlasie 484, 487
Kleefeld, Georg (1522–76), mayor of Danzig 486
Kleinfeld (Krupocki) family 395
Klemens of Moskorzew († 1408), vice chancellor of Poland 79–80
Kletsk
    battle of (1515) 344
    duchy of 292–3, 429
Kmita, Piotr (1477–1553), grand marshal of Poland, palatine of Cracow 366–7, 370, 372, 438, 441

Kniprode, Winfried von (c.1310–82), grand master of the Teutonic Order 28
Knoppek, Witold 289
Kobryn, duchy of 292, 424, 429
Koczerska, Maria 49
Koenigsberger, H.G. 40
Koialovich, Mikhail (1828–90), historian of the Russian empire 44
Kojałowicz, Wojciech Wijuk (1609–77), historian 416
Kökeritz, Dypold von, German knight 141
Kolanka, Barbara († 1550), wife of Jurgis Radvila 322, 434, 435
Kolankowski, Ludwik 113, 143–4, 328, 405
Koło 194, 288
Königsberg 107, 225, 227, 319
Königsberg, palatinate of 218
Koneczny, Feliks 47, 81
Koniecpolski family 232
Koniecpolski, Jan Taszka († 1455), grand chancellor of Poland 177, 178, 214, 268, 269, 270–1
Koniecpolski, Przedbór († c.1458), castellan sandomierski 268, 269
Konitz 225, 226, 227, 228, 382
  battle of (1454) 223–4, 226, 239, 268, 271, 321
Konopacki, Jan († 1430), treasurer of Royal Prussia 390
Konrad I (1187/8–1247), duke of Mazovia 6, 27
Konrad III (1447/8–1503), duke of Mazovia 228, 375, 376, 377
Konrad V († 1439), duke of Oleśnica 376
Konrad IX 'the Black' (c.1415–71), duke of Oels-Kosel 131
Konrad X 'the White' (1420–92), duke of Beuthen-Kosel 131
Kopot, Vasyl Vasylevych († 1530), Lithuanian marshal hospodarsky 452
Kopyl, duchy of 84
Koprzywnica, Cistersian monastery of 92
Korczak, Lidia 49, 303, 316
Korczyn 182, 241, 288–9
Korczyn privileges (1456) 241
Koretsky, Bohush (1510–76) 487
Koronowo, battle of (1410) 107
Kościelecki, Andrzej (1455–1515), treasurer of Poland 357
Kościelecki, Jan († 1498), palatine of Inowrocław 384
Kościelecki, Mikołaj († 1510), palatine of Brześć 384
Košice *see* Koszyce
Kosiński, Adam († 1573), castellan of Podlasie 484, 487
Kosman, Marceli 77
Kostevičius, Stanislovas, Lithuanian boyar 321

Kostka, Jan (1529–81), treasure of Royal Prussia, castellan of Danzig 486
Kostka, Stanisław (1487–1555), treasurer of Royal Prussia 396, 398
Koszyce 8, 12
  privileges of (1374) 8, 12, 65–6, 167, 236–7, 247, 357, 378
Kot, Wincenty (c.1395–1448), vice-chancellor of Poland, archbishop of Gniezno 177, 192, 193, 195, 200, 269
Kovel, starosty of 425
Kozelsk, duchy of 285
Kozłowski, Mikołaj († 1443), professor at Cracow University 72
Koźmin, battle of (1497) 281
Krasiński, Franciszek (1525–77), vice-chancellor of Poland, bishop of Cracow 488
Kremenets, starosty of 425
Krėva (Kreva, Krewo) 3–4, 30–1, 34, 50, 56, 71, 117, 147, 407, 415
Krewo Act (1385) 3–4, 5, 47–57, 75, 77, 81–2, 87, 91, 94, 102, 121, 160, 162, 172, 183, 317, 331, 374, 464
  authenticity of 49
  consequences of 217
  nature of 47–9, 50, 55–6, 61, 68, 88–9, 111, 114, 116, 119, 121, 204
  origins of 5, 28, 33, 34
  as prenuptial agreement 49, 52, 92
  Vytautas and Krewo 76, 149
Krom, Mikhail 313, 318
Kropidło, Jan (c.1360–1421), bishop of Cujavia 101, 123
Kroshynsky family 292
Krzycki, Andrzej (1482–1537), archbishop of Gniezno 371
Krzywousty *see* Bolesław III Krzywousty
Krzyżaniakowa, Jadwiga 171
Krzyżanowski family 271
Küchmeister, Michael († 1423), grand master of the Teutonic Order 102–3, 110, 211
Kučukaitis, Jonas, Lithuanian boyar 321
Kuczyński, Stefan 106
Kuchowicz, Zbigniew 434
Kuhschmalz, Franz († 1457), bishop of Ermland 213, 214, 384
Kula, Witold 242, 244–5
Kulko, Cezary 231
Kulikovo Field, battle of (1380) 28, 30–1
Kuolys, Darius 334
Kurbskii, Andrei (1528–83) 3, 313
Kurowski, Mikołaj († 1411), archbishop of Gniezno 101, 103
Kurowski, Piotr († 1463), castellan of Lublin 133, 193–4
Kurozwęcki family 232

Kurozwęcki, Krzesław († 1459), castellan of Lublin, starosta general of Wielkopolska 235
Kurozwęcki, Krzesław (c.1440–1503), grand chancellor of Poland, bishop of Cujavia 337, 338, 349
Kurozwęcki, Piotr († 1499), vice-chancellor of Poland 337, 347
Kurtyka, Janusz 92, 244
Kustinitza, battle of (1443) 184
Kutná Hora, battle of (1428) 137
Kutrzeba, Stanisław 47, 67, 95–6, 113, 202, 251, 286–7, 458, 469
Kyiv 20, 21, 82–3, 163, 164–5, 171, 178, 205, 280, 293, 295, 301, 316, 330, 406, 421, 487
  Catholic diocese of 163
  duchy of 29, 67, 84, 87, 170, 189, 293–4, 296, 422
  palatinate of 474
    annexation of by Poland (1569) 488–9, 491–2

Labour service 99, 115
Łabuński, Mikołaj († 1467), bishop of Kamianets 272
Landshut 321
Languedoc 261
Lannoy, Ghillebert de (1386–1462), Burgundian diplomat 18
Łaskarz, Andrzej (1362–1426), bishop of Poznań 123
Łaski, Jan (1456–1531), grand chancellor of Poland, archbishop of Gniezno 236, 267, 274, 354, 357, 360–1, 365–7, 370, 376, 386, 390, 397, 399, 400, 405, 412, 424
  as tribune of the szlachta 349, 350, 351, 354
Łaski, Jan, the younger (1499–1560), Protestant theologian and reformer 443
Łaski, Stanisław (1491–1550), castellan of Sieradz 452
Łaski's statute (1506) 236, 349–54, 361, 397, 419
Lasocki, Mikołaj (c.1389–1450), bishop nominate of Cujavia 272
Łaszkowski, Jakub, (c.1532–after 1596), royal secretary 428–9
László I (Ladislas I) (c.1040–95), king of Hungary and Croatia 71
László the Posthumous (1440–57), king of Hungary and Bohemia 183, 191, 278
Latin 266–7, 271, 298, 318, 320, 328, 410, 418, 441, 458
Latvian language 18
Lazar Branković (c.1421–58), despot of Serbia 182
Lazutka, Stanislovas 413

Łęczyca 15, 102, 136, 173, 238
  assembly in (1426) 140, 142, 145, 150, 165, 440
  duchy of 12
  palatinate of 240, 288
Legendorf, family of 385
Legendorf, Paul von († 1467), bishop of Ermland 228, 384
Leipzig 386
Lélius, Petras, palatine of Trakai 180, 185
Lengnich, Gottfried (1689–1774), historian of Royal Prussia 216–17
Lengvenis Algirdaitis († 1431) 3, 29, 50, 79, 83, 100, 152
Leopold III von Habsburg (1351–86) 8, 34
Leopold IV von Habsburg (1371–1411), duke of Further Austria 109
Lessen 225
Leszczyński, Rafał (1526–92), palatine of Brześć 443–4, 454
Letzkau, Konrad († 1411), mayor of Danzig 211
Lewicki, Anatol 47, 171, 174–5, 192, 202
Lida 71, 72, 76, 85, 163, 475
Lintfari, Martin († 1515), bishop of Samogitia 333
Lithuania, grand duchy of 4, 18–35, 266, 270, 281, 309–23, 369, 385, 399
  origins and expansion of 20, 24–5, 159
  raids on neighbours 18, 20, 27–8, 33, 99
  relations with Poland to 1385 17, 27, 28, 33
  economy of 291, 295
    population of 159, 291
    rural economy 306, 424–32
    grand ducal domain 300, 308, 418
      alienation of 418
      hide reform in 425–32, 438
    hide system (*system włóczny*), introduction of 426–32
      effects on peasantry 428–32
    landholding in 68, 85, 292, 297, 300
      inheritance custom and inheritance law 68, 292, 294, 297, 419
      question of Poles owning land in Lithuania 465, 477–8
    manorial system and labour rent 428–32
    village structure 425–6
  education in 317–18
  government and political system of 26, 77, 92, 94, 119, 127, 160, 169, 291, 341, 407, 472
    absentee monarchy, effects of 407, 412, 424
    administrative structure of 151, 200, 218
    as a consensual political system 154, 199, 303
    chancery of 291, 303, 318–19, 333, 421–2, 452
      Lithuanian Metryka (chancery archive) 333, 336, 349

Index

community of the realm in 95, 127, 151, 199, 317, 323, 328, 334, 336, 346
as a composite realm 53, 66–7, 88, 121, 158–9, 189, 291, 292, 294, 296, 317, 323, 473
as a dynastic patrimony 53–4, 66, 68, 91, 118, 151, 203, 205–6, 323, 330, 336, 345, 366, 412
elective principle in 200, 334, 336, 334–5, 412
grand ducal council 146, 285, 287–9, 299–300, 302–5, 316–17, 345–6, 379, 411, 413, 420, 475
  divisions on 409, 418
  Radziwiłł domination of (1540s and 1550s) 323, 409, 435
grand ducal court 319–20, 451–2
grand duke, office and title of 116, 118, 152, 201, 459, 462–3, 478–9
Lithuania and the union 69, 118
  autonomy of 134, 151, 169, 410
  influence of Polish culture upon 317–23, 453; *see also* Lithuania: nobility in: Polish cultural influence
  plans to secure royal status 86, 89–90, 143–4, 146, 172, 416, 459
  relations with Poland after 1386 72, 135, 146–8, 151, 185, 415
    exploitation of grand ducal elections for political advantage 345, 405, 411–12
  resistance to closer union 420
  separatism and separatists 83, 86, 146–7, 154–5, 186–7, 202–3, 345, 410, 417
  statehood and independence 93, 96–7, 113–14, 121, 134, 146, 151, 155–6, 166, 171, 186–7, 202, 342–3, 417, 449, 458
  status of within union 186, 190, 270, 417
  unionism and unionists 186–7, 323, 333, 338, 341, 448–50, 452, 470–1
as a republic 120, 328, 329, 330, 333, 335–6, 421–3, 458, 466, 468
role of Poles in Lithuanian government 97, 319
Sejm 303, 305, 341, 346, 412, 451, 452
  origins of 192, 200, 201, 329
  domination of by council 412, 420, 450
  increasing frequency of sessions 409, 450
  transformation of (1566) 476
succession in 5, 119, 127, 134, 150–5, 203, 408
supreme duke, title and office of 116, 190, 199, 336, 435
taxes and financial system 346, 408, 409, 418, 449

silver tax (*serebshchyzna*) 346, 418, 447, 450
Vytautan system 155, 170, 180, 185, 189, 195, 291, 294–5, 299, 304–5, 327–8, 337, 421
foreign relations *see also* Wars
  relations with Muscovy 25, 200, 282–5, 394, 400, 407, 408, 411
  territorial losses to Muscovy 285, 291, 300, 313, 337, 345
  relations with the Teutonic Order 27–8, 95, 99, 394
  relations with the Ottomans 281, 283
law and legal system 297, 408–10, 418
  demands for the introduction of the Polish court system 412, 420, 424–5, 452
  establishment of Polish-style sejmiks and elective courts (1566) 473–5, 482, 485
  First Lithuanian Statute (1529) 322, 418–20, 422, 448, 450, 452, 459, 473–4
  Polish law, influence of 190, 419, 451
  Ruthenian law, influence of (*Ruskaia pravda*) 419
  Second Lithuanian Statute (1566) 322, 473–6, 477, 481, 491
  Sudebnik of Casimir IV (1468) 303
military system of 300–2, 307–8, 371, 450
  inability of Lithuanians to sustain war without Polish support 345–6, 451, 457, 476, 480
  military servitors 306–7
  noble levy 308, 446–7, 457, 475
  Polish military and financial support for 101, 136, 289, 337, 339, 341, 346, 354, 410, 456, 473
  reforms and register of (1528) 300–2, 308, 346, 411, 418–19, 457
  register of (1567) 298, 302
  sluzhba (service unit) 301, 307, 425–6
nobility in 53–4, 68, 115, 291–308
  emergence of Lithuania-Ruthenian elite 291–309, 408
  impact of union upon 187, 452
  kinship 68, 297, 298
  magnates 298–9, 302, 321, 361, 409, 424
    clientage and ordinary nobles 449
    council oligarchs 425, 438, 440–1, 461, 491
    divisions among 409, 482
    intermarriage with Polish nobility 322–3, 434–5, 441, 465
  judicial privileges of 409
  as a military class 297, 306
  ordinary nobles 302, 305, 346, 361, 407, 409, 419
    as independent political force 449

Lithuania, grand duchy of (*cont.*)
  demands for reform 420, 422, 438, 450
  resistance to council magnates 448, 452
  origins of 414–15
  pany (lords) 85, 298–300, 305–7, 318, 407
  partible inheritance, effects of 429
  petty and impoverished boyars 302, 307–8, 432
  dependent and service boyars 297, 409–10, 426, 432, 455
  Polish cultural influence and 'Polonization' of 116, 318–20, 323, 452, 465
  political role of 95, 152, 200, 346
  princes 84–5, 88, 292–6, 318
    appanage duchies 67, 84–5, 87, 160, 162, 166, 188–9, 292–4, 296, 313, 330, 421
    privileges of 127, 151, 291, 297, 306–8, 318, 420, 422, 450, 452
    role of Vytautas's men; the Horodło families 158, 170–2, 186, 298–9, 302, 306, 410
    service to grand duke 292, 297, 307
    stratification and diversification of 298–308
  office-holding in 299, 302–3, 409, 421
    edict removing restrictions (1563) 460
    office restricted to Catholics 120–1, 160, 166–7, 176, 200, 316
    question of Poles holding Lithuanian office 477, 478
  religion in
    Catholic church in 149, 164, 316, 409, 428
      Catholic political domination 84, 87, 96, 120, 158, 166, 200, 291, 408, 421–3, 488
      competition with Orthodox church 73
      episcopate of 304, 409
      establishment of 71–3
      Polish clergy in 317, 318
      privileges of 73, 115, 158, 371
      conversion and Christianization of 33, 50, 53, 68, 71–3, 101, 111, 143
    Orthodox church 24, 31, 121, 163–5, 292, 309–12
      discrimination against 73, 31–6, 422, 423
      rights and privileges of 309, 315, 489, 491
      toleration of 163, 174–6, 309
    paganism 24–5, 27, 104, 109, 121, 163, 316
      destruction of temples and sacred groves 71–3, 125
      and the Gedimind dynasty 4, 26, 27, 28, 31
      increasingly difficult position of 29, 31
      relations between pagan and Orthodox populations 24, 25, 31, 73
    relations with Catholic church 2
    rights of pagans, infidels, and schismatics 124–5
  religious diversity of 291, 308
  Ruthenian territories of 29, 31, 53, 66–7, 111, 121, 147, 158–9, 165, 267, 285, 292, 475
    annexed Ruthenian territories 66–7, 78, 121, 160, 162, 166, 171, 173–6, 189, 291, 294, 296, 306, 308, 315–16, 329–31, 428, 473, 475, 483, 489
    relations between Lithuanian and Ruthenian inhabitants 20, 24–5, 66–7, 186–7, 189, 295, 422
    Ruthenian influence on 159–60
    Ruthenian loyalty to 190, 285, 293, 337, 487–8, 491
    Ruthenians as second-class citizens 422–3, 488
Lithuania proper 67, 121, 160, 163, 165, 169, 170, 174–6, 291, 293, 308, 315, 332, 426–7, 429, 473
Lithuanian language 18, 67, 71, 73, 145, 160, 266, 319, 328, 441
Lithuanians 159, 444
  identity of 158, 160
  legendary origins of 414–15
  modern nation of 44, 45, 158
Liubartas Gediminaitis († 1384), duke of Lutsk and Volodymyr 29, 84
Liubavskii, Matvei K. 47, 67, 81, 113, 306, 327, 329, 340
Livonia 20, 27, 77, 225, 438, 446, 447, 453; *see also* Unions: of Poland-Lithuania and Livonia
Livonian Order (Knights of the Sword) 26, 30, 77, 104–5, 107, 126, 142, 149, 173–4, 209, 228, 446
Livs 18
Liw, duchy then territory of 16, 375
Lizard League (*Eidechsengesellschaft*) 211
Loewe, Karl von 301
Łokietek *see* Władysław I Łokietek
Łomża 456
  duchy then territory of 375
Łomżyński, Mateusz († 1505), bishop of Kamianets 273
London 321, 387
Lordship 86, 113, 118, 147, 156, 161, 165, 205, 331
Louis II Jagiellon (1506–26), king of Bohemia, king of Hungary 282, 330, 406
Louis XII (1462–1515), king of France 337
Louis of Anjou (1326–82), king of Hungary and Poland 4, 6–8, 10, 12–14, 16, 28–9, 54, 65–6, 80, 156, 231, 374, 443
Lower Austria 280

Łowicz 11
Łowmiański, Henryk 50, 53–5, 68, 81, 89, 96, 113, 159, 169, 185–6, 302, 327, 340
Lübeck 389
Lübeck law 216, 389, 391
Lubicz clan 395
Lübitsch mill 135
Lublin 4, 49, 54, 79, 100, 115, 247, 290, 342, 473, 476–7, 480, 482, 484–6, 487–8, 492
  palatinate of 239, 268, 288, 364
  sejm (1569) 402, 468, 477–94
    withdrawal of Lithuanians 480–1
  union of (1569) 323, 492–4
Lubovňa 109
Lubowla (Lubovňa), treaty of (1412) 109, 137
Lubrański, Jan (1456–1520), bishop of Poznań 330, 378
Lubuch 345
Ludwig VII (c.1368–1447), duke of Bavaria 131
Lusatia 278
Luther, Martin (1483–1546), theologian and church reformer 393
Lutkowic, Jan (c.1405–71), vice-chancellor of Poland 272, 273
Lutsk 142, 143, 144, 168, 174, 187, 193, 207, 208, 280, 415, 484
  duchy of 76, 81–3, 87; see also Volhynia
Luxembourg dynasty 6, 10, 16, 33, 104, 109, 136, 184, 205
Lwów 13, 82, 91, 174, 240, 280, 352, 371
  archdiocese of 265, 315

Mably, Gabriel Bonnot de (1709–85), philosopher 45–6
Machiavelli, Nicolò (1469–1527) 472
Machwitz (Machwicz) family 396
Maciejowski, Samuel (1499–1550), grand chancellor of Poland, bishop of Cracow 365, 373, 439, 441, 444
Magdeburg law 210, 219, 231, 351, 391
Magnus Eriksson (1316–74), king of Sweden and Norway 51
Mahiliou 67
Maišiagala 71
Makary (Chort) († 1497), metropolitan of Kyiv and All Rus' 309
Małopolska, province of 6, 14–15, 94, 96, 119, 194, 207, 231, 240–1, 268, 275, 356, 367, 369, 378–9, 386, 438, 453, 456, 463
  eclipse of Wielkopolska 12–13
  economy of 248, 250, 259, 427
  magnate power in 64, 141, 234; see also Małopolskan lords
  nobility in 64, 65
  noble levy of 224–5, 227, 236, 239, 240, 281
  political divisions in 193

  political domination of Poland by 12–13, 54, 64, 235
  political structure of 238–9, 241, 288, 352
  Reformation in 442
  royal domain in 357, 364
  and the sejm 368
Małopolskan lords 12, 33, 54, 79, 99, 141, 177–8, 193, 207, 214, 232–4, 237, 270, 271, 272; see also Cracow lords
Małowist, Marian 242
Malski, Wojciech († 1454), palatine of Łęczyca, governor of Wielkopolska 235, 268
Mamai (1335–80), khan of the Blue Horde 30, 85
Mantautaitis family 321
Mantigirdaitis, Petras († 1459), marshal of Lithuania 170, 185, 187
Mantigirdaitis, Petras († c.1497), marshal of Lithuania, palatine of Trakai 304, 329–30
Manvydaitis, Jonas (c.1395–1458), palatine of Vilnius 185, 200
Marburg 213
Margaret, duchess of Oleśnica († 1466) 376
Margaret I (1353–1412), queen of Denmark, Norway, and Sweden 51, 55
Marienburg (Malbork) 27, 75, 103, 105, 107, 213–14, 222, 224, 226–7, 382
  palatinate of 381, 386
Marienwerder 212, 224
Maria/Anna of Vitsebsk († before 1349), grand duchess of Lithuania 24
Markist Order 72
Marsiglio of Padua (c.1275–c.1342), political philosopher 126–7
Martel, Antoine 319
Martin V (1369–1431), pope 126, 131, 136, 165
Mary of Anjou (1371–95), queen of Hungary 8, 10, 88, 96
Mary of Hungary (1505–58), queen of Bohemia and Hungary 393
Masalsky, princely family of 296, 337
Masalsky, Sviatoslav Tytovych Karachevsky († after 1365), Ruthenian prince 296
Materna family, private war against Danzig 389
Matthias Corvinus (1443–90), king of Hungary 230, 278, 280–1, 330, 385
Matusas, Jonas 186
Maximilian I (1459–1519), Holy Roman Emperor 337, 392–3, 407
Maximos († 1305), metropolitan of Kyiv and All Rus', 163
Mazovia, duchy then palatinate of 6, 16, 62, 190, 231, 247–8, 249, 258, 281, 319, 353, 374–80, 369, 396, 410, 412

Mazovia, duchy then palatinate of (*cont.*)
    cultural links to Poland 377, 381
    economy of 250, 378, 428
    as fief of the Polish crown 6, 375
    incorporation and integration of 352, 376, 377–9, 381, 400, 417
    nobility of 64, 377–9
    parliamentary culture of 377
    political structure of after 1529 352, 379–80
    royal domain in 357, 364, 366, 373, 386, 425, 454
Mazur, Karol 485
Medele 407
Medininkai 71, 72
Medininkai, diocese of *see* Samogitia: diocese of
Medyka 250
Melno, peace of (1422) 126, 127, 134–5, 211
Memel 99
Mewe 225, 228, 386
Mezetsky, princely family of 296, 337
Michelow 216, 228
Miechowita, Maciej (1457–1523), historian and chronicler 266–7, 274, 277, 337, 413–14
Międzyleski, Wawrzyniec († 1529), bishop of Kamianets 407
Mielecki, Mikołaj (1540–85), grand hetman of Poland, palatine of Podolia 465
Mielecki, Sebastian (*c.*1500–74), castellan of Cracow 483
Mielnik 188, 338, 340
    articles of (1501) 346–9
    petition of (1501) 346–7
    union of (1501) 339–45, 416, 452, 458, 464–8, 471, 477, 479, 484, 492–4
    and Horodło 341
Mikhail Javnutovich, duke of Zaslav 84
Mikołaj of Blaschewitz (*c.*1405–74), bishop of Przemyśl 272
Mindaugas (*c.*1203–63), grand duke and king of Lithuania 18, 20, 25–7, 53, 68, 72, 155
Minsk 67, 71, 301, 476
Minsk, palatinate of 475, 491
Modrzew 252
Mohács, battle of 282, 355, 406
Moldavia, principality of 109, 188, 280, 281, 290, 333, 354, 371, 378, 387–8
Monarchy
    absolute monarchy 348, 350–1, 440
    composite monarchy 40, 86, 151, 321, 421
    elective monarchy 51, 88, 199, 203, 205, 268, 277
    hereditary monarchy 51, 199, 205, 361
    multiple monarchy 40–2
Mongols 13, 18, 20–1, 163, 165, 282, 295
Monvidaitis, Ivaško, Lithuanian nobleman 170
Moravia, margravate of 278

More, Sir Thomas (1478–1535), lord chancellor of England 387
Mortangen (Mortęski) family 385
Moscow 3, 25, 31, 74, 77–8, 100, 138, 163–4, 205, 283, 311–12, 314
    metropolitanate of 312
Mosiński, Maciej of Bnin († 1493), palatine of Poznań, starosta general of Wielkopolska 276
Mother of God, Orthodox church of (Vilnius) 315
Motiejus of Trakai (*c.*1370–1453), bishop of Vilnius 185, 187, 200, 201–2, 206, 311
    defence of Lithuanian conception of union 202
Mozyr, district of 474, 491
Mstislau 77, 152, 189
    battle of (1386) 77–8
    duchy of 292, 296
    palatinate of 475
Muscovy, grand duchy of 25, 28, 33, 85, 101, 107, 138, 164, 209, 261, 282, 286, 289, 291, 310, 312, 316, 323, 345, 408, 410–11, 414, 457, 461, 489
    attraction of for Orthodox Ruthenians 29, 283, 313–15
    claim to rule All Rus′ 285, 331, 447
    Orthodox church in 311–12, 417
Muslims 124
Mykhailo Zygmuntovych († 1435), son of Zygmunt Korybutovych 173
Mykolas Žygimantaitis († 1452) 79, 138, 171–2, 179, 180, 185, 188, 190, 192, 193, 204–5, 207, 299, 376
Myszkowski, Piotr, starosta of Lwów 355

Nadolski, Andrzej 106
Nakło 168
Narbutt, Teodor (1784–1864), historian of Lithuania 44, 413
Narew, river 378
Narimantas Gediminaitis († 1348), duke of Hrodna, Polatsk, and Pinsk 24, 80, 407, 421
Naruszewicz, Mikołaj († 1575), treasurer of Lithuania 473, 480
Narva 425
National history, writing of 39, 168, 313
Nationalism and political unions 36, 48, 390, 396
Natural law 122, 124
Navahrudak 21, 26, 67, 85, 102, 131, 164, 301, 406, 409
Nemenčinė 71
Neminem captivabimus nisi iure victum, legal principle of 352
Nemirych family 321
Neopolitan sums 436

Nero (37 CE–68 CE), emperor of Rome 414, 421
Netherlands 51, 258, 387, 393
Netimer (fl. 1009), ruler of Lithuania 18
Neu-Marienwerder, castle of 35
Neumark 80, 102, 135, 223
New World 231, 243
Nicholas V (1397–1455), pope 213, 269, 272
Niemen, river 20, 33, 85, 96, 125, 165, 425
Nieśwież and Ołyka, imperial duchy of 438
Niendorf, Matthias 67
Niepołomice 111, 115, 136
Nieszawa 126, 214, 236, 271
   privileges of (1454) 224–5, 236–41, 248, 276, 286–7, 305, 348, 350, 359, 367, 443
Nihil Novi, statute of (1505) 349–51, 353–4, 361, 370–1, 420
Nikodem, Jarosław 74, 81–3, 92, 96, 97, 134–5, 137–8, 144, 152, 171, 177, 180, 186, 188
Normandy 261
Norway, kingdom of 51
Noteć, river 102
Novgorod 74, 85, 100, 135–6, 138, 145, 209, 282–3, 294
   duchy of 24, 25
Novhorod-Siversky 205
   duchy of 20, 29, 84, 152
Novosilskii clan 313
Nowa Góra 233
Nur, duchy then territory of 375
Nuremberg 147

Obertyn, battle of (1531) 355
Oboltsy 71, 72
Ochmański, Jerzy 75, 302, 318, 413
Octavian (Augustus) (64 BCE–14 CE), emperor of Rome 414
Odessa 85
Odoev 314
   duchy of 285,
Odoevskii family 313
Odoevskii, Ivan († c.1470) 314
Odoevskii, Semën († 1473) 314
Odrowąż family 232, 271, 359
Ogończyk clan 395
Oka river 85, 283, 313
Oleg Ivanovich, duke of Riansk 100
Olekhnovych, Petr († 1516), Lithuanian master of the kitchen 338
Olelko Volodymyrovych († 1455), prince of Kyiv 170–1, 189, 193, 293–4, 317
Olelkovych family 322, 421–2
Olelkovych, Iury (c.149–1542), duke of Slutsk 317
Olelkovych, Mykhailo († 1481/2), duke of Slutsk, governor of Novgorod 294–5

Olelkovych, Semën (c.1420–70), duke of Slutsk and Kyiv 293–4, 421
Olelkovych, Semën Mykhailovych († 1505), duke of Kopyl and Slutsk 329
Olesko 207
Oleśnicka, Dorota, wife of Jan Taszka Koniecpolski 178, 270
Oleśnicki, Dobiesław († 1440), palatine of Sandomierz 186
Oleśnicki, Jan Głowacz (c.1400–60), marshal of the kingdom of Poland, palatine of Sandomierz 64, 178, 268, 270
Oleśnicki, Zbigniew (1389–1455), bishop of Cracow, cardinal 75, 133, 153, 157, 169, 171, 179, 192–3, 200, 205, 270–4, 311, 353, 359
   and Casimir IV 191, 194, 235, 265, 267–70, 321
   foreign and dynastic policy 278
   and Jagiełło 75, 103, 139–43, 145, 149–50, 177
   opposition to Prussian war 214, 223–4, 270
   and the reign of Władysław III 177–8, 183
   and the union with Lithuania 142, 146, 153–4, 156, 175, 201–2, 463
   and the union with Hungary 184
   and the union with Prussia 399, 400, 414–15
Oleśnicki, Zbigniew, the younger (1430–93), archbishop of Gniezno 273, 274, 275, 327, 385, 387
Olivares, Gaspar de Guzmán, Count duke of (1587–1645) 41
Opatów 256, 281
Opoki 236, 239
Oporowski family 214
Oporowski, Władysław (1395–1453), vice-chancellor of Poland, archbishop of Gniezno 146, 147, 149, 171, 177, 214, 235, 269–70, 272–3
Oprichnina 476
Orda, Napoleon (1807–83), artist 3
Ordensstaat see Teutonic Order
Orsha 71
Orsha, battle of (1514) 315, 346, 483
Orthodox Church *see also* Church union
   divisions within 163
   metropolitanate of Halych-Volhynia 163
   metropolitanate of Kyiv and All Rus′ 25, 26, 295, 489
   metropolitanate of Lithuania 26
Orzechowski, Stanisław (1513–66), political writer 439, 443, 455, 471–2
Orzechowski, Walenty (1527–88), land judge of Przemyśl 489
Ościk, Jerzy (1530–79), palatine of Mstislav then Smolensk 451
Ösel 446
Ösel, diocese of 446
Osieck 247, 249

Ossoliński, Hieronim († 1575/6), castellan of Sącz 452
Osterode 210, 212, 224
Ostrih 158
Ostroróg, Jan (1436–1501), palatine of Poznań 273
Ostrozky, princely family of 302
Ostrozka, Halshka (Elżbieta) (1539–82) 453
Ostrozky, Dashko (Danilo) Federovych († after 1420), 158
Ostrozky, Ilia (1510–39) 322
Ostrozky, Kostiantyn (c.1460–1530), grand hetman of Lithuania, palatine of Trakai 315, 322, 346, 408, 412, 420–2, 433, 452, 483, 488
  appointment to office in breach of Horodło 317, 409, 422, 433, 460
  and Poland 408
Ostrozky, Kostiantyn Vasyl (1526–1608), palatine of Kyiv 322, 483, 485–9, 491
Ostrozky, Vasyl Federovych Krasny († after 1461) 193, 200, 316
Oświęcim and Zator, duchies of 364, 400
  incorporation into Poland (1563–4) 456, 470
Ottoman empire 13, 167, 282, 286, 312
  conquest of the Balkans and Constantinople 277, 280, 311
  threat to Europe 109, 182–4, 190, 224, 278, 280, 363, 409
Our Immaculate Lady, Orthodox church of (Vilnius) 310
Ovruch, district of 491

Pac, Mikołaj (1527–85), bishop of Kyiv 457, 492
Pac, Paweł (1527–95), castellan of Vitsebsk then Vilnius 484
Pac, Stanisław († 1588), palatine of Vitsebsk 451
Padniewski, Filip (1510–72), bishop of Cracow 463, 466, 477, 479
Padua 123, 365
Palanga 126, 135, 425
Palatio, Andrea da, papal legate 142
Palemon, legendary protoplast of the Lithuanians 414–15
Palestine 27
Pampowski, Ambroży (c.1450–1510), starosta general of Wielkopolska, starosta of Marienburg 388–90
Papée, Fryderyk 266–7, 328
Parczew 115, 190, 194, 200–2, 204–7, 471–3
Partitions of Poland-Lithuania 44, 65, 286
Paszkiewicz, Henryk 54
Paweł of Bojańczyce († 1453), bishop of Kamianets 167
Perekop Tatars *see* Tatars: Perekop
Peremyshl, duchy of 283

Perez, Louis, bishop of Silves 213
Pernau 447
Peter († 1326), metropolitan of Kyiv and All Rus' 163
Peter IV (c.1487–1546), hospodar of Moldavia 371
Peter of Dusburg († after 1326), German chronicler 26
Petras of Kustynės († 1422), bishop of Vilnius 315
Petrauskas, Rimvydas 54, 297, 299
Pfeildorff, family of 385
Pfudnzoll 210, 212, 219
Philip the Fair (1478–1506), king of Castile, duke of Burgundy 52
Philotheos († 1379), patriarch of Constantinople 164
Piast dynasty 4, 5, 8, 10, 12, 14, 16, 51, 96, 139, 234, 247, 296
Piasts
  Mazovian 13, 131, 195, 345, 374–8, 418
  Silesian 6, 12, 17, 104, 123, 131, 195, 223
Picheta, Vladimir 428
Piccolomini, Enea Sylvio *see* Pius II
Pietkiewicz, Krzysztof 66, 267, 340
Pilecki, Jan (c. 1405–76), castellan of Cracow 193–4, 271, 274–5
Pińczów 268, 273
Pinsk 24
Pinsk, duchy of 292, 424, 452
Pinsky family 292
Piotrków 190–4, 226–7, 235, 269–71, 274, 289–90, 338, 359, 371–2, 376, 388, 396, 398, 405–6, 418, 436, 438–9, 441, 454, 456, 461, 473
Pius II (1405–64), pope 223, 272–3, 312
Platelė 425
Plato 360
Plauen, Heinrich von (c.1370–1429), grand master of the Teutonic Order 107, 109–10, 210–11
Plauen, Heinrich von († c.1441), komtur of Danzig 211
Plauen, Heinrich Reuß von († 1470), grand master of the Teutonic Order 213, 224
Plichta, Jakub († 1407), bishop of Vilnius 72, 92
Płock
  diocese of 273, 367, 375, 377–8
  duchy of 16, 374–7
  incorporation into Poland of (1495) 378
  palatinate of 353, 356, 378
Plokhy, Serhii 159
Płońsk, duchy then territory of 16, 375
Pniewski, Jan, archdeacon of Cracow 273
Pocock, J.G.A. 39
Podiebrad, George (1420–71), king of Bohemia 278

Podlasie 28, 30, 67, 188, 251, 318, 406–7, 409–10, 434, 452, 481, 487
  annexation of (1569) 482–4, 486
  immigration into from Poland and Mazovia 410, 426
  introduction of Polish law and legal system 410, 482
  privilege (1444) 410
  rural economy in 425–6, 428
Podolia, duchy of 24, 29, 80, 87–8, 100, 153, 166–9, 172, 178, 183, 185, 194, 200–1, 207, 230, 237, 240, 268, 270, 280, 472
Podolia, eastern 166, 178, 207, 333, 475
Podolia, western 97, 152, 156, 157, 166, 207, 333, 386
Poland, kingdom of 4, 12, 24, 53, 172, 216, 278, 281, 374, 378
  economy and society of 231–3; *see also* Poland, kingdom of: rural economy
    cities, privileges of 378
    currency, devaluation of 247
    German settlers in 231–2
    internal market 232, 251
    population 231–3, 247
    specie, shortage of 232, 247
    stagnation of (fifteenth century) 231
  foreign policy
    relations with Mazovia 374–80
    relations with Muscovy 44
    relations with the Ottomans 281, 283, 363
    relations with the Teutonic Order 7, 28, 33, 89, 99, 100, 102–3, 109, 122, 135, 209–30, 385, 387–8, 392–3, 399, 400
      propaganda battle with 102, 104–5, 110, 116, 121–2, 126
  law in 190, 210, 216, 219, 233, 254, 349–52, 379
    codification of 368–9, 419; *see also* Łaski's statute
    knowledge of the law 354, 367, 369
    local elective courts 176, 200, 341
      castle courts 244, 275–6, 370, 372, 444
      land courts 244, 276, 348, 370, 412
  military system of 234, 286, 371
    common defence force (*obrona potoczna*) 354
    during Thirteen Years War 222, 224–5
    noble levy 223, 234, 241, 276, 337–8, 357, 368, 371, 378
  office-holding 275, 348, 367, 379
    incompatibility, legal principle of (1504) 367, 424, 443, 454
  politics and government
    as a composite, decentralized polity 62, 95, 190, 200, 267
    community of the realm 49, 51–3, 94, 96, 127, 138–40, 150, 191, 194, 199, 201–2, 286, 347, 348
    as a consensual system 66, 94, 199, 200, 287, 350, 357
    government of 94, 274–5, 355, 365
      chancery 269, 274–5, 354, 355
    monarchy of
      corona regni Poloniae 47, 50, 52, 56–7, 61, 65, 81–2, 94–6, 100, 116–17, 122, 127, 147, 166–7, 172, 177, 219–20, 236, 274, 332, 336, 377–8, 463, 469, 478–9, 481, 487, 489, 491–2
      elective monarchy in 51–2, 88, 92, 119, 140–1, 199, 268, 333, 361, 371, 372, 439
      election *vivente rege* 405, 406, 458
      judicial and prerogative powers 268, 348, 350, 358, 362, 441, 442
      limited monarchy in 53, 95, 139, 305, 361
      regnum Poloniae 52, 56–7, 94, 116–17, 147, 148, 206, 219, 350
      royal patronage and powers of appointment 268, 269, 288
      royal domain 225, 232–5, 244, 248, 257, 348, 350, 355–7
        alienation of 232, 356, 358, 360, 362–3
        as the property of the community of the realm 360
        reform of under Sigismund I 362–4, 366–7, 370
        statute on the royal domain (1504) 359–62, 367
      succession law and succession 7, 8, 14, 52, 94–5, 97, 138, 145, 148, 150, 268, 286
      royal finances 225–6, 232, 238, 267, 348, 354–6, 367
      royal power 242–3, 267, 270, 350, 352–3, 365–6
    parliamentary system 207, 226, 286–90, 350
      chamber of envoys 287, 289, 349, 352, 367, 370, 372, 374, 478, 481
      composition and procedure 287–8, 352, 367, 368
      frequency of 368, 370
      instructions and powers of envoys 370–1
      noble domination of 241–3, 261
      sejm, camp (horseback) 227, 272
      sejmiks 200, 238–41, 256, 286–9, 305, 341, 352–3, 354
      senate 287, 352, 399, 444, 477, 481, 484, 492, 494
      bicameralism 286, 289–90, 346, 349, 352, 353
      as the heart of the political system 352, 354–5
      origins 236, 238, 286–7

Poland, kingdom of (*cont.*)
    royal council (senate council) 268, 274, 286, 304, 338, 347–50, 362, 365, 366, 439
    sejm 220, 305, 347, 350, 354, 362, 382, 393
    political thought and political culture 123, 126–7, 190, 215, 347
    as a republic/commonwealth 347–8, 350, 361, 440, 466, 468
  reconstitution of (1320) 6, 238, 267
  religion
    Catholic church 136, 175
      appointment of bishops 272
      ecclesiastical courts 443
      and union with Lithuania 77, 143
      and union with Prussia 220
    Reformation 442–3
  rural economy 242–61
    area of cultivation 247, 249
    grain trade 231, 242–4, 257
    labour rent 245–8, 252, 253–7, 260–1, 396
    labour service 242, 245, 249–51
    manorial farming 242–60
    market forces and 246, 248, 255–7, 260
    pastoral farming 257–8
    peasants
      access to royal courts 251
      burdens on 261
      cottagers and day labourers 249, 250
      mobility and flight of 243, 251, 253–6
      resistance of 244–5
      royal peasants 350
      sale of land 253–4
      as subjects of their lords 245
      tenant farmers (*kmiecie*) 245, 247, 249, 250, 253–5, 261
      zagrodnicy 249–50, 253
    productivity of 258–61
    rents in cash and kind 246–8, 252–4, 257
  szlachta 64, 233, 351
    anti-clericalism among 235, 371, 443
    egalitarianism 64–5, 298, 407, 451–2, 471
    heraldic clans 62, 64, 115, 160, 174, 289, 303, 395, 415
    landholdng 62, 64, 233–4
      partible inheritance, practice of 62, 233, 247, 306
    and the law 352, 354
    magnates 62, 233–5, 253, 319, 365–6, 370, 424
      opposition to reform of the royal domain 442, 444
      and Polish culture 319, 323
      and the szlachta 236, 367
    middling szlachta 233–4, 236, 243, 253–4, 270–1, 288–90, 347, 353, 368, 370

ordinary nobility *see* Poland: rural economy: szlachta: middling szlachta
poor nobles 233, 249, 353, 358, 370
privileges and liberties of 4, 65, 68, 140, 165–6, 219, 235, 270, 289, 376, 379, 391, 442
  right of resistance (*de non praestando oboedientia*) 150, 215, 234, 235, 347
scartabellat (cadet nobility) 65
seigneurial courts 247, 251
taxation and the nobility 65–6, 357–9
titles, opposition to 407
as warrior class 223, 234
Ruthenian population of 166–7, 189
Ruthenian territories of 240–1, 252, 275, 338, 367
  annexation of Ukrainian palatinates (1569) 482, 484–5, 488–9, 491
taxation system 65–6, 102, 238, 261, 288, 355, 357–9, 365, 379
  excise (*czopowe*) 358, 367, 371
  hide tax (*łanowy*) 357–8, 368
  land tax (*poradlne*) 65–6 , 102, 165, 238, 247, 267, 270, 357, 378, 379
  new duty (*nowe cło*) 358, 371
  poll tax (1520) 358–9
vassal duchies of 205, 350
Polatsk 21, 24, 30, 79, 189, 302, 447
  capture by Muscovy (1563) 456–7, 460, 461
Polatsk, duchy of 29–30, 67, 77–8 , 84
Polesie 67
Polish, language 266, 318, 320, 323, 328, 377, 381, 395, 399, 408, 410, 418, 441, 451, 458, 484
Polish People's Republic 45, 231, 242, 243, 244
Polubensky family 292
Pomerania, duchy of 104
Pomerelia 6, 102, 108–9, 122, 212, 214, 216, 219, 227–9, 399
  palatinate of 218, 381, 386, 387, 401
Pomestle system 283, 300–1
Pomezania, diocese of 107, 230, 394
Poradlne see Poland, kingdom of: taxation system: land tax
Posilge, Johann von (c.1340–1405), Prussian chronicler 82, 86, 395
Poznań 177, 266, 442
  diocese of 367, 409
  palatinate of 288
Pozsony (Bratislava) 407
Pozwol 446
Prague 6, 7, 136–7
Prague, university of 123–4
Přemyslid dynasty 6
Pronsky, Semën (1510–55), palatine of Kyiv 316
Proszowice 439

Index

Protasiewicz, Walerjan (c.1505–79), bishop of Vilnius 428, 457, 462, 483
Prussia 6, 7, 27, 33, 81, 105, 126, 152, 214, 224, 236, 319, 399; *see also* Unions: individual, of Poland and Prussia
  administrative structure of 218
  duchy of (from 1525) 393–4, 395, 400, 428, 446
    relations with Royal Prussia 394–5
  as hereditary possession of the Polish crown 216–18
  influence of Polish political, administrative and judicial culture upon 218, 297, 304
  privileges of 215, 218–19, 225
  Prussian law 216, 219
  rebellion of (1454) 213–16
  Royal 216, 230–1, 265, 275, 374, 377, 417
    autonomy of 381, 383, 388, 395, 401
    Catholic church in 394, 398
    council of (*Landesrat*) 381–2, 385, 388, 390, 400
    council elite of 386, 395–6, 470
      refusal to participate in Polish institutions 382, 397, 399
    court system of 384, 388–90
    culture of 381, 395
      bilingualism 396
      German language 381, 395
      Polish language 395, 399, 400
      Prussian identity 395–6
    and defence of the union state 399, 400
    economy of 259, 377, 386, 392, 486
      convergence of trade interests with Poland 486
      currency of 381, 394
      currency union with Poland (1526) 391, 398–9, 486
    estates of (*Landtag*) 382, 388–9, 391, 393–5, 412
      establishment of bicameral structure 397, 398
      establishment of sejmiks 397, 398, 401
    free peasantry in 384
    incorporation treaties (1454, 1466) 381–2, 470, 486
      disputes over nature of incorporation 381–2, 385, 388, 390, 399–400, 402
      incorporation (1569) 486
    indygenat (native) status, principle of 389, 392, 396, 399–400, 401
    influence of Polish models 389, 390–1, 397
    institutional structure of 383, 384
      Anwalde (administrator) of 383
      governorship of 381, 383, 384
      Landesordnung (1526) 397
      starosta general of 383
    law in 389, 470
    1511 statute 390, 396
    loyalty to union state 387, 392, 394, 401
    Lutheranism in 394, 395, 397
    nobility of
      attendance at Polish sejms 396–9
      attraction of Polish system for 390–1
      ordinary nobility 385–6
      petty nobility 392
      and Polish heraldic clans 395
      subdivision of estates 392
      support for closer ties to Poland 395–6
      office-holding in 386, 391–2, 397, 399, 400; *see also* Prussia: Royal: *indygenat*
    privileges of 371, 383, 388, 395, 397, 399
    political reform, desire for 397, 438
    process of integration into kingdom of Poland 381–402
      forces favouring closer integration 381, 385, 388, 390, 394, 398–9
      pressure for closer union 456, 470
    relations with Ducal Prussia 394–5
    royal domain in 356, 364, 386, 470
    social structure of 382
      cities and landowning 470
      role of the cities 382, 391–2
    taxation in 382, 383, 400
    treasury 389–90
Prussian Bund (union) 210, 213–16, 219–20, 222–7, 237, 375, 381, 384
  act of submission to Poland (1454) 216
  justification for rebellion against the Order 216, 219, 220
Prussian estates 210, 2
Prussian homage (*Hołd pruski*) (1525) 253, 393–4, 411
Prussian, language 18
Prussians (*Pruzzen*) (pagan Baltic tribe) 18, 26–7, 62, 124, 396
Przemyśl 13, 240, 250, 352
Przemyśl, diocese of 357, 443
Przemysł II (1257–96), king of Poland 5, 6, 12
Przerębski, Wincenty (c.1450–1513), vice-chancellor of Poland, bishop of Cujavia 389
Przeworsk 281
Pskov 79, 100–1, 135–6, 138, 145, 209, 282, 283
Pskov, grand duchy of 30
Pulkau, Johann von, member of the Lizard League 211
Putzig 228

Quarter treasury and quarter tax 455
Quod omnes tangit, principle of 350, 467

Raba family 396
Rabiej, Piotr 114
Raciążek, peace of (1404) 99–101, 110

Raciąż 353
Radlica, Jan († 1392), chancellor of Poland 12
Radom 92, 239, 439
  sejm (1505) 349
Radomsk 13–15, 290
Radoshkoviche military camp (1567) 476, 480
Radvila (Radziwiłł) family 302, 317, 321–2, 406, 411, 414, 420–1, 424–6, 433, 434, 439, 472, 484
  domination of the Lithuanian council 434, 438, 448, 453
  rivalry with the Goštautas family 406–7
  use of clientage and clients 453
Radvila Astikaitis (1384–1477), castellan of Vilnius 170, 175, 304
Radvila, Jonas (1474–1522), grand marshal of Lithuania, castellan of Trakai 321, 323, 406, 434,
Radvila, Jonas († 1542), starosta of Samogitia 322, 434
Radvila, Jurgis (1481–1541), grand hetman of Lithuania, castellan of Vilnius 301, 322, 406, 420, 434, 435
Radvila, Mikalojus (1470–1521), grand chancellor of Lithuania, palatine of Vilnius 304, 338, 342, 406, 408, 409, 410, 425, 434
Radvilaitė, Anna (Ona) (1475/6–1522), duchess of Mazovia 322, 407
Radvilaitis, Mikolajus (after 1450–1509), grand chancellor of Lithuania, palatine of Vilnius 304, 321, 377, 406
Radvila, Stanislovas († 1531) 322
Radziejów 288, 443
Radziejowska, Katarzyna 377
Radziwiłł, Jan (1516–51), carver of Lithuania 452, 453
Radziwiłł, Mikołaj Czarny (the Black) (Mikalojus Radvila Juodasis) (1515–65), grand chancellor of Lithuania, palatine of Vilnius 322–3, 436–9, 441, 446, 453, 456–7, 472–3, 477, 479
  as a Calvinist 443, 451, 461
  and the hide reform 426, 428
  links to Polish magnates 435, 441, 452
  and Polish politics 441
  political talents 480
  and the union 462–8, 470–1
Radziwiłł, Mikołaj Rudy (the Red) (Mikalojus Radvila Rudasis) (c.1515–84), grand hetman and grand chancellor of Lithuania, palatine of Trakai 322–3, 433–7, 447–8, 451, 453, 461–2, 477, 480–1, 484, 487
  as a Calvinist 443
  poor political judgement 480–1, 483
  and the union 471, 488, 491, 492
Radziwiłł, Mikołaj (1546–89), palatine of Navahrudak 457, 462
Radziwiłł, Mikołaj 'Sierotka' (1549–1610), palatine of Vilnius 482–4, 487–8

Radziwiłłówna, Anna (1476–1522), duchess of Mazovia 322, 377
Radziwiłłówna, Anna († 1571) 434
Radziwiłłówna (Tworowska), Anna Magdalena (1553–90) 465
Radziwiłłówna, Elżbieta Katarzyna (1520–65), 322
Radziwiłłówna (Mielecka), Elżbieta (1550–91) 465
Radziwiłłówna (Zamoyska), Krystyna (1560–80) 465
Radziwiłłówna (Czema), Zofia Agnieszka (1522–after 1599) 465
Radzyń 240
Rákos 371
Ragnit 102
Rajgród 406
Ratno 207
  duchy of 29
Rawa 455
  duchy of 16, 375, 376
  incorporation into kingdom of Poland (1462) 376, 378
  palatinate of 356, 364, 378
Red Ruthenia, 13, 56, 64, 84, 109, 166–7, 174, 183, 189, 207–8, 231–2, 281, 364, 378, 455
Reformation 365, 371, 393, 395
Regensburg 222
Rembowski, Aleksander 14
Renaissance culture 265, 278, 319, 353, 361, 365, 454
Reval, diocese of 446
Reynes, Nikolaus von (1360–1411) 211
Reynolds, Susan 11, 14, 16, 53
Rėza, Liudvikas (Ludwig Rhesa) (1776–1840), Prussian-Lithuanian philologist 44
Rhode, Gotthold 88, 92
Riazan 20
Riga 446–7
  archdiocese of 398
Robert I (1274–1329), king of Scotland 11
Robertson, John 39
Rokičana, Krystyna 7
Rokosz see Confederation: *rokosz*
Roman law 348, 350–1, 369, 419
Roman, Stanisław 237, 240–1
Rome 27, 78, 123, 164–5, 213, 267, 272–3, 309, 312, 371, 385, 387, 412, 414
  Roman republic 353
Rotundus, Augustus (Augustyn Mielecki) (c.1520–82), writer and polemicist 472
Rowell, Stephen 55–6, 113, 117, 122, 159, 190, 202, 336, 340, 341
Różan, duchy then territory of 375
Rudau, battle of (1370) 74
Rudy *see* Radziwiłł, Mikołaj Rudy (the Red)
Rudolf († 1454), duke of Sagan 223

Rupert I (1352–1410), king of the Romans 104
Rurik (830–79), Varangian chieftain 407
Rurikid dynasty 13, 21, 165, 283, 285,
    292, 414
Rus' (Ruthenia) 26, 91, 158–76, 189, 217, 280,
    408; *see also* Lithuania, grand duchy
    of: Ruthenian territories; Poland,
    kingdom of: Ruthenian territories
  identity and culture 158, 165, 166,
    294–5, 487
  law 159, 165, 167, 297
  nobility 68, 87–8, 165, 292, 293, 313
    adoption of Ruthenian boyars by Polish
      heraldic clans 174, 176, 460
    and closer union 461, 485
    influence of Polish culture on 318
    privileges of 162–3, 167, 174–6, 189–90,
      291, 306
  Ruthenian language 73, 77, 145, 159, 166,
      266, 298, 318, 320, 328, 331, 410,
      417, 441, 451
    as language of government and the law in
      Lithuania 160, 166, 308, 318, 482
Rusdorf, Paul von (c.1385–1441), grand master
  of the Teutonic Order 131, 135,
  144, 154, 155, 157, 168, 179–80,
  211, 212
Russell, Conrad 40
Russia 44, 165
Rusyna, Olena 313
Ruthenia *see also* Rus'
  palatinate of 288, 352, 354, 356, 359,
    363, 386
Ryngailė Kęstutaitė († by 1430) 79, 81, 374
Rytwiański, Dziersław (1414–78), castellan of
  Cracow 178–9, 268–9, 275
Rytwiański, Jan (1422–78/9), grand marshal
  of Poland, palatine of
  Cracow 271, 275

Sachsenspiegel 351
Sącz 363
Sakovych (Sakavičius, Sakowicz) family 321
Sakovych, Bohdan († 1491), palatine of
  Trakai 304, 321
Salic Law 38
Salin island 85, 86, 89, 91, 188
  treaty of (1398) 85, 86, 90, 99, 101, 110,
    208, 299
Salomea († 1144), queen of Poland 5
Sambor 281
Samogitia 25, 27–9, 69, 108, 114, 122, 126,
    162, 185, 225, 298–300, 306, 308,
    315, 448, 475, 482
  conversion and christianization of 125,
    299, 316
  diocese of 125, 315, 318
  grand ducal domain in 424, 426–8, 430
  as heartland of petty boyars 308
  immoral practices of 415
  as pagan stronghold 27, 72, 101, 110, 124,
    188, 316
  privilege of (1442) 299, 475
  relationship to Lithuania proper 67, 68, 110,
    121, 125, 135, 160
  risings against Lithuanian rule (1418,
    1441) 299
  risings against the Teutonic Order (1405,
    1409) 102–3, 104
  special status of 188–9, 299–300
Samogitian language 125
  and the Teutonic Order 28, 30, 33, 86, 89,
    99–100, 102, 110, 122,
    134, 135
Sandomierz 17, 157, 165, 168, 214, 269,
    281, 444
  castellany of 367
  palatinate of 63, 239, 248, 256, 268, 270,
    288, 352, 358, 364
Sangaila, Jonas († after 1433), castellan of
  Vilnius 170
Sangushko family 208, 292
Sangushko, Roman (c.1537–71), field hetman of
  Lithuania, palatine of
  Bratslav 480–1, 484, 489, 491
Sanok 132, 240, 352
Santok 102
Sapieha family 322
Sapieha, Andrzej (1539–1621), palatine of
  Polatsk then Smolensk 451
Sapieha, Ivan (c.1431–c.1517), palatine of
  Vitsebsk 308, 309, 314
Sapieha, Paweł († 1579), palatine of Navahrudak
  then Podlasie 451, 483, 492
Šapoka, Adolfas 48
Saxony, electorate of 213
Scandinavia 51
Schönsee 211, 386
Schütz, Caspar (1540–94), historian of
  Prussia 215–16, 395
Schwetzin, battle of (1462) 227–8
Scotland, kingdom of 11, 41–4, 51, 149
Segovia, treaty of (1475) 51
Semën Andreevich († 1386), son of Andrei
  Olherdovych (Algirdaitis) 78
Semkowicz, Władysław 458, 469
Sepieński, Mikołaj, Vytautas's secretary 143,
    145
Serbia 142, 182, 184
  Serbian language 411
Seren, duchy of 285
Siberia, khanate of 282
Sicily, kingdom of 149
Siemowit III (c.1313–81), duke of Mazovia 16,
    81, 374, 377
Siemowit IV (c.1352–1426), duke of
  Mazovia 4, 10, 11, 104, 374, 376
  as candidate for Polish throne 15–16, 193

556 *Index*

Siemowit V (c.1389–1442), duke of
    Mazovia 104, 131, 177, 375
Siemowit VI (1442–61/2), duke of
    Mazovia 375–6
Siena 365
Sienawski family 322
Sieniawski, Hieronim († 1582), castellan of
    Kamianets 322
Sienicki, Mikołaj (c.1521–82), executionist
    leader 443–4, 461, 464
Sieradz 13, 15–16, 168, 170, 177, 191–2, 237,
    268, 289
  duchy of 12
  palatinate of 240, 250, 288
Sierotka *see* Radziwiłł, Mikołaj 'Sierotka'
Sigismund Korybutovych (c.1395–1435), duke
    of Novhorod-Siversky 137, 173
Sigismund of Luxemburg (1368–1437), king of
    Hungary, king of the Romans, Holy
    Roman Emperor 8, 10, 33, 56,
    80, 102, 105, 131–2, 136, 140,
    153, 167, 179, 182–3, 222, 277,
    375, 411
  and the coronation tempest 142–50, 415–16
  and the Teutonic Order 88, 99, 104, 109–10,
    126, 136, 137, 157
  hostility to Poland-Lithuania 88, 99, 109, 134
Sigismund I 'the Old' (1467–1548), king of
    Poland, grand duke of
    Lithuania 251, 252, 274, 341, 438
  character and reputation 265, 361–2,
    366, 370
  political abilities of 361, 366
  death of 361, 399, 436, 437
  early career 295–6, 331
  election as grand duke of Lithuania 314, 344–5
  election as king of Poland 345, 382
  family 309–10, 330, 392–3, 406, 421, 434
    and Bona Sforza 366, 424, 425
  and foreign policy 281
  as grand duke of Lithuania 329, 422, 450
    and the council families 407–8, 411,
      420, 433
    and the grand ducal domain 424
    and the Orthodox church 315–16,
      317, 460
    and taxation 301, 408
  health and senility of 361, 366, 372–3,
    435, 443
  and Polish politics
    and the royal court 319, 366, 396
    and the royal domain 356, 357, 362–4,
      366–7, 370, 373, 452
    and the royal prerogative 367, 370
    and the sejm 353, 357, 367, 369, 371,
      393, 443
    as a senatorial king 354, 361, 365–6,
      369, 370
    and the succession 405–6

  and the szlachta 350, 371–2, 400
  and Royal Prussia 382, 389, 393–5, 397, 401
  and the union 417
Sigismund II August (1520–72), king of Poland,
    grand duke of Lithuania 354, 401
  birth and childhood 330, 406, 416
  character and reputation 265, 453–4
  court of 319, 451–2
  election and enthronement as grand duke of
    Lithuania (1528) 406, 408,
    410–11, 417–18, 420
  election *vivente rege* as king of Poland
    (1529) 371, 400, 401, 405, 418, 440
    controversy over legality of 405–6
  coronation (1530) 399–400
  estrangement from Bona Sforza 435, 454
  as grand duke of Lithuania 449, 450, 476
    alliance with the Radziwiłłs 433–41,
      456, 471
    and the grand ducal domain 300, 426
    and the Lithuanian nobility 449, 452
    and the Orthodox church 460
    preference for life in Lithuania 441, 451
    refusal to confirm 1566 statute 477
    rejection of Vytautan system 345
    renunciation of dynasty's hereditary rights
      in Lithuania 469, 492
    rule in Vilnius (1544–48) 319, 440, 442
  health of 481
  as king of Poland
    and the execution movement 444–5,
      453–6, 461
    and the ordinary nobility 453
    privilege of (1551) 175
    and the royal domain 441–2, 444, 456
    and the royal prerogative 441–2, 444,
      454, 488
    and the succession 440, 453, 465
  and Livonia 446–7
  marriages
    Elizabeth Habsburg (1544) 433–4, 435–6
    Barbara Radziwiłłówna
      (1547) 433–41, 453
      opposition to 438–40, 454
    Catherine Habsburg (1553) 440
  and the union 388, 440, 453–5, 467–9,
    475–6, 481–2, 484, 486–7, 492
    'Declaration on the Union' and 'Recess . . .
      concerning the Lithuanian Union'
      (1564) 469, 477–8
    endorsement of Polish incorporationist view
      (1564) 469, 470
Silnicki, Tadeusz 405
Silesia 6, 136, 179, 231, 273, 278, 281, 319,
    364, 374, 377–8, 456
  Polish claims to 7, 12; *see also* Piasts: Silesian
Simeon I of Trebizond († after 1486), patriarch
    of Constantinople 312
Siversk, duchy of 84, 337

Skalski, Mikulas of Valdštejn, Bohemian
    mercenary 214
Skirgaila Algirdaitis († 1394), duke of Polatsk
    and Trakai 3, 50, 76, 80, 87,
    414, 421
  character of 78, 83
  death of 83, 293
  as governor of Lithuania 77–8
  loyalty to Jagiełło 29–30, 87
  paganism and conversion to
    Orthodoxy 29–30, 78, 83
  political role of 4, 31, 34, 79, 81–3
  relations with Vytautas 77–9, 83–4
Słabomierz 257
Slavery 68–9, 295, 430
Śliwnicki, Maciej († 1551/2), canon of
    Gniezno 397
Slonim 21
Slutsk, duchy of 292–3, 295, 317, 413
Smolensk 25, 67, 85, 100, 106, 152, 171, 294,
    314, 321, 346, 413, 414
  diocese of 316
  duchy of 77–8, 188–9
Smotrych, siege of (1431) 168
Sobek, Stanisław († 1569), treasurer of Poland,
    castellan of Sandomierz 481
Sochaczew, duchy then territory of 16, 352,
    375–6
Sochaczew, starosty of 247
Sofia 184
Soldau, Franz, Danzig lawyer 397
Solórzano Pereira, Juan de (1575–1655), Spanish
    jurist 41
Sonka see Sophia (Sonka) Holshanska
Sophia (Sonka) Holshanska (c.1405–61), queen
    of Poland, grand duchess of
    Lithuania 131–4, 138, 170,
    178–9, 187, 191, 359
  political activities of 182, 192–4, 214,
    268, 269
  Vytautas and 131–4, 137
  Zbigniew Oleśnicki and 177
Sophia Jagiellon (1464–1512), margravine of
    Ansbach-Bayreuth 392
Sophia Jagiellonka (1522–75), duchess of
    Brunswick-Wolfenbüttel 406
Sophia (Ofka) of Bavaria (1376–1425), queen of
    Bohemia 132, 136
Sophia of Lithuania (1371–1458), grand duchess
    of Muscovy 80, 122
Sophia Palaelogus (1453–1505), grand duchess
    of Muscovy 283, 309
Sovereignty 37, 83, 93, 147, 151, 203–5
  indivisibility of 38–9, 41–2, 44, 203
  Landeshoheit 38
  national sovereignty 44, 54, 86, 205
Soviet Union 45, 48
Spain 412
Sperka, Jerzy 92

Spisz 183
Sprowski, Jan (of Odrowąż) († 1464), archbishop
    of Gniezno 235, 272
Spytek of Melsztyn (1364–99), castellan of
    Cracow, duke of Podolia 86–8, 90,
    97, 166
Spytek of Melsztyn the younger
    (1398–1439) 177–9, 182
Środa 238, 240, 288, 368
Stanisław I (1500–24), duke of Mazovia 377,
    407, 411
Stanisław of Ostroróg (c.1400–76), palatine of
    Poznań, starosta general of
    Wielkopolska 235
Stanisław of Skarbimierz (c.1365–1421), rector
    of Cracow University 124
Stanisław of Szczepanów (1030–79), bishop of
    Cracow 5, 71, 142
Stargard 382, 386
Starina 88, 159, 162, 163
Starodub 205
Stębark *see* Tannenberg
Stefan III (1433–1504), hospodar of
    Moldavia 228, 281
Stela, Erasmus (Johannes Stüler) (c.1460–1521),
    historian of Prussia 395
St Catherine's convent, Cracow 363
St Florian's Church, Cracow 141
St Mark's Church, Cracow 71
St Nicholas's Church, Vilnius 27
St Nicholas's Orthodox Church, Vilnius 316
St Sophia's Cathedral, Kyiv 310
Starosta, office of 12, 140, 167, 232, 237, 239,
    275–6, 348, 358, 367, 377
State, nature of 36, 38, 54, 118, 203
  composite state 40, 42, 87–8
  contractual basis of 360
  state sovereignty 40, 117, 205
  unitary state 37, 38, 41, 43, 86, 94, 161,
    203–4, 206, 219
Storm, Ambrosius, secretary of Danzig
    council 361
Steiger, Heinhard 36
Strayer, Joseph 40, 42
Streshevska 163
Stryjkowski, Maciej (1547–93), historian and
    chronicler 329, 416
Strzempiński, Tomasz (1398–1460), bishop of
    Cracow 272
Stuhm 214, 224, 386
Styria 280
Suchocki, Jerzy 316
Sudimantaitis, Alekna († 1491), grand chancellor
    of Lithuania, palatine of
    Vilnius 304, 320, 332
Suleyman the Magnificent (1494–1566), Sultan
    of the Ottoman Empire 372
Suzdal, battle of (1445) 282
Sužiedelis, Simas 45

Šventoji river, battle of (1435) 173, 178, 292
Sviatoslav II Ivanovich (c. 1318–86), duke of Smolensk 77
Sviriškis (Świrski), princely Lithuanian family 296
Sviriškis, Andrius, Lithuanian prince 318
Švitrigaila Algirdaitis (c. 1373–1452), grand duke of Lithuania 4, 29, 172, 178, 189, 375
    career after his fall 190, 193, 201, 204
    Catholicism of 4, 83, 152, 158, 169
    character 84, 152, 153, 168
    death of 188, 195, 207, 237, 295
    election of 154–6, 157, 176, 199, 203, 327, 335, 418
    as grand duke 152–7, 168–9, 173–4, 176, 206, 303, 319
    foreign policy 156, 158, 168, 173
    opposition to and overthrow of 169, 170, 173–5, 180
    relations with Jagiełło 87, 97, 99, 153–5, 167–8, 170
    relations with Teutonic Order 99–101, 152, 157, 168, 179, 211, 216
    relations with Vytautas 153
    supporters of 101, 154, 158, 166, 168–9, 171, 292–3, 299, 411
        Ruthenian support 158, 170–1, 173, 175, 177, 180, 185–9, 316, 421
    and the union 155, 158, 188
Swantibor III (c.1351–1413), duke of Stettin 104
Sweden, kingdom of 51
Świrski, Łukasz Bolko (c.1535–93), Lithuanian prince 447
Swiss confederation 36
Szafraniec, Jan (1363–1433), grand chancellor of Poland, bishop of Cujavia 136, 137, 141, 178
Szafraniec, Piotr († 1437), palatine of Cracow 136, 137, 172
Szafraniec, Piotr († 1508), castellan of Wiślica, starosta of Marienburg 338
Szarlejski family 214
Szarlejski, Mikołaj (c.1400–57), palatine of Brześć 214, 223–4
Székesfehérvár 184
Szécsi, Dénes (c.1410–65), archbishop of Esztergom 184
Szujski, József 361
Szydłowiecki family 322
Szydłowiecka, Elżbieta (1533–62), wife of Mikołaj Radziwiłł Czarny 323, 441
Szydłowiecki, Krzysztof (1467–1532), grand chancellor of Poland, castellan of Cracow 323, 365–7, 397, 401, 412, 424

Szydłowiecki, Mikołaj (1480–1532), treasurer of Poland, castellan of Sandomierz 364–6

Tabor, Wojciech (c.1453–1507), bishop of Vilnius 309, 329, 338
Talwosz, Mikołaj († 1598), castellan of Trakai 451
Tannenberg 105
    battle of (1410) 74, 105–7, 109–10, 116, 127, 141, 155, 183, 209, 211, 223–4, 265, 375, 467
Tarnów 483
Tarnowski family 178, 322
Tarnowska, Zofia (1534–70), wife of Kostiantyn Vasyl Ostrozky 483, 488
Tarnowski, Jan (1367–1433), palatine of Cracow 141, 143
Tarnowski, Jan Amor († 1500), castellan of Cracow 271
Tarnowski, Jan Amor (1488–1561), grand hetman of Poland, castellan of Cracow 351, 366, 370, 439, 441, 444–5
Tarnowski, Jan Spytek (1484–1553), treasurer of Poland, castellan of Radom 364
Tarnowski, Stanisław (1514–68), treasurer of Poland, palatine of Sandomierz 445
Taszycki, Mikołaj († 1545), land judge of Cracow 371, 372
Tatars, 85, 101, 414; *see also* Blue Horde; Golden Horde
    Crimean 280–3, 286, 315, 344–5, 359, 408–9, 455, 488–9
    raids on Poland-Lithuania 205, 295, 309, 337, 354, 363, 471
    Lithuanian 320–1
    Perekop 3, 142
Tautvilas Kęstutaitis († 1390) 80, 93
Tęczyński family 178, 233, 322
Tęczyński, Andrzej (1412/13–61), castellan of Wojnicz 233
Tęczyński, Jan († 1405), castellan of Cracow 102, 233
Tęczyński, Jan († 1470), palatine of Cracow 200, 233, 234, 268, 271
Tęczyński, Mikołaj (c.1464–98), sword-bearer of Cracow, palatine of Ruthenia 322, 332
Tęczyński, Nawój (1380–1425) 233
Tęczyński, Zbigniew (1450–98), starosta general of Royal Prussia 384, 387–8
Telničanka, Kataŕyna, mistress of Sigismund I (c.1480–1528) 330
Templars (Order of the Knights Templar) 27
Temür Kutlugh (c.1370–99), khan of the Golden Horde 85–6
Teognost († 1353), metropolitan of Kyiv and All Rus' 163

Terek river, battle of (1395) 85
Teutonic Order 75–6, 89, 144, 154, 164, 176, 322, 358
  acquisition of the Prussian lands 6, 7, 27, 215, 399
  crusade against pagans 18, 25, 26, 27, 125
  decline of the Order after 1410 168, 209–12, 226, 286, 291, 393
    Prussian opposition to 208, 210–12, 385–6, 387, 400
  hostility to the Polish-Lithuanian union 79, 101–2, 113, 123, 155
  and anti-union coalitions 80, 109, 126, 157, 186, 385, 387–8
  the *Ordensstaat* and the government of Prussia 27, 102, 105, 135, 209–13, 216, 218, 228, 253, 301, 356, 381, 386, 391, 400
  the *Ordensstaat* after 1466 228, 381, 384–5, 393, 394; see also Prussia: duchy of
  relations with Lithuania 27, 28, 30–1, 33–4, 57, 80, 89–90, 95, 97, 104, 108–9, 142, 149, 168–9, 179, 195, 200, 205, 291, 299, 306, 321, 374
  and the conversion of Lithuania 27, 33, 124
  raids on Lithuania 33–4, 85, 99, 104, 109
  and Samogitia 27–8, 30, 33, 79, 86, 89, 99–102, 108, 110, 122, 124–5, 134
  and Vytautas 76, 79–80, 85, 89–90, 99–101, 135, 142, 145, 149, 153
  relations with Poland 7, 10, 16, 89, 99–102, 104, 108, 110, 113, 122, 126, 135, 142, 168, 173, 209, 238, 363, 368, 374–5, 388, 392, 394; see also Wars
  relations with Royal Prussia after 1466 385, 388, 392–3, 400
Thorn 99, 107, 131, 135, 211, 213–16, 224–6, 337, 357, 363, 381–2, 385–7, 395–6
  sejm meeting in (1519) 251, 396
  peace of (1411) 108–11, 126, 134, 211, 213, 392
  peace of (1466) 228, 230, 337, 384
Tiefen, Johann von (c.1440–97), grand master of the Teutonic Order 387
Timur (Tamurlane) (1336–1405), Tatar amir 85
Tokhtamysh (Tohtamış) († 1406), khan of the Golden Horde 31, 85
Tomicka, Katarzyna († 1551), wife of Mikołaj Radziwiłł Rudy 322
Tomicki, Jan († 1549), chamberlain of Kalisz 322
Tomicki, Piotr (1464–1535), vice-chancellor of Poland, bishop of Poznań 351, 354, 365, 366–70, 386, 400–1, 405, 412, 424

Trąba, Mikołaj (1358–1422), vice-chancellor of Poland, archbishop of Gniezno 101, 105, 123, 132–3
Traidenis († 1282), grand duke of Lithuania 28
Trakai 30, 33, 149, 154, 171, 180, 188, 317, 318, 339
  duchy of 29, 31, 67, 76, 78–9, 82, 87, 122, 172, 185, 204–5
  palatinate of 113, 118, 120–1, 160, 200, 291, 305, 341, 407, 421, 424, 427–8, 430, 438, 475, 489
  privilege of (1434) 175–6
Trembowla 371
Treniota (c.1210–64), grand duke of Lithuania 26
Trent, council of 443
Trojden II († 1427), duke of Mazovia 131, 375
Tryzna, Hryhory, castellan of Podlasie, then Smolensk 487, 488
Trzebuchowski family 322
Tsamblak, Grigorii (c.1365–1420), metropolitan of Kyiv and All Rus' 164–5
Tüngen, Nicholaus von († 1489), bishop of Ermland 384–5, 387
Turo 252
Tver 85, 282, 311
  duchy of 25
Tworowski, Mikołaj († 1595) 465
Tykocin 407
Tyniec, abbey of 72
Tyshkevych, Vasyl (1492–1571), palatine of Podlasie, then Smolensk 487–8

Uborch 163
Uchański family 322
Uchański, Jakub (1502–81), archbishop of Gniezno 464, 467, 471
Ugra river 283
Ukmergė 71, 173
Ukraine 44
  Ukrainian language 319
  modern nation of 44–5, 165
Ula river 462
Ulanowski, Bolesław 202
Ulrich II (1406–56) count of Celje 277
Ulug-Mehmet († 1445), khan of the Golden Horde 282
Unions
  types of 36–46, 203–4
    accessory unions 41–2, 88, 95, 119, 147, 151, 323; see also Unions: types of: incorporating unions
    confederal unions 36, 46, 334
    dynastic unions 37, 42
    federal unions 36, 37, 38, 39
    foundation treaties 39, 43, 61, 206
    historical-political unions 38, 204
    incorporating unions 36, 61, 95; see also Unions: types of: accessory union

Unions (*cont.*)
- juridical unions 37, 204
- leagues of states 38
- personal unions 37, 41–3, 51
- real unions 37–8, 43, 51, 204–6, 335
- *Staatenstaat* 38
- unions *aeque principaliter* 42, 151, 204
- union as process 40, 43, 61
  - cultural and political assimilation within unions 61
- individual
  - heptarchy, Ango-Saxon 41
  - of Aragon and Castile (1469) 51–2, 66
  - of Austria and Hungary (1867) 43
  - of Britain and Hanover (1715–1837) 38, 42
  - of Britain and Ireland (1801) 39
  - of England and Scotland
    - (1603) 41–2, 50, 51
    - (1652) 43
    - (1707) 38–9, 42, 343
  - of Kalmar (1397–1523) 51, 54
  - of Norway and Sweden (1319–43;1362–4) 55
  - of the Picts and Scots 41
  - of Poland and Bohemia (1300–6) 4
  - of Poland and Hungary
    - (1370–82) 4, 5, 8, 10, 33, 42, 51, 57
    - (1440–4) 42, 183–4
  - union of Poland and Lithuania 4, 33, 42, 91–2, 94, 110, 114, 116–17, 126, 166, 172, 178, 183–4, 199–208, 339, 374, 460
    - as an accessory union 199, 341–2, 465, 481, 491
    - as a body politic 342–3, 399, 464, 468, 484, 492–3
    - citizenship in 176, 206, 289, 334, 439
    - common council and parliament, calls for 339, 460, 462, 465, 473
    - common defence and foreign policy 95, 100, 151, 286, 337, 459, 473
    - common election, Polish desire for 339, 345, 458, 463, 476, 479
      - Lithuanian opposition to 465
    - as a composite state 110, 161–2, 374, 411
    - as a confederal union 334, 466
    - as a consensual system 95–6, 117, 122, 127, 188, 190, 199, 207
    - crisis of 127, 154–5
    - currency union 339, 398, 492, 494
    - as a dynastic union 50, 113–14, 119, 199, 203, 285, 335
    - as an elective monarchy 95–6, 199, 203, 335–7
    - as a feudal relationship 96, 463
    - as a fraternal relationship 171, 188, 194, 199, 202–3, 339, 342, 416, 417, 465–7, 493, 494
    - international status of 98, 107
    - issue of separate offices in Lithuania 462–3, 471, 476
    - joint council meetings and assemblies 115, 120, 151, 156, 187, 200
      - Lublin (1389) 79
      - Horodło (1413) 109–21
      - Parczew (1441) 190
      - Lublin (1448) 200–1, 206
      - Parczew (1451) 200–2, 205–6
      - Parczew (1453) 200, 202, 204, 206
      - Brest (1454) 200, 209
      - Warsaw (1563–4) 461–8, 477, 479
      - Lublin (1569) 477–94
    - as a league of independent states 334, 335, 479
    - Lithuanian conception of 61, 114, 204, 323, 333–4
    - Lithuanian projects of union (1451/3, 1496) 202–3, 332–4
    - loyalty to 293
    - nationalist hostility to 45–6, 49
    - ordinary nobility and pressure for closer union 374, 457, 459, 471
    - as a personal union 48, 50, 95, 113, 114, 119, 199, 203, 204, 205, 335, 479
    - Polish incorporationist interpretation of 47–8, 49–50, 56–7, 68, 79, 81, 88–9, 91, 94–6, 112, 114, 117–19, 143, 146–7, 150–1, 153, 156, 175, 187, 192, 199–200, 206–7, 270, 323, 331–2, 334, 338–40, 345, 410, 416, 463, 467
      - desire to create unitary state 463–4, 467
      - view of Lithuania as a province of Poland 201, 463
    - process of union 61, 114, 120, 127, 205, 285, 342
      - cultural convergence 116, 318–20, 323, 452, 465
      - emergence of pan-union elite 322–3
      - growth of a common political culture 323, 335
      - institutional convergence 113, 118, 120, 341, 473–4
      - royal court, role of 319–22, 451
    - as a real union 119, 205–6, 335, 339
    - as a union of equals (*aeque principaliter*) 147, 151, 202, 204, 206, 333–4, 410–13, 415, 417–19, 457, 459, 465, 471, 479, 492–4
    - as a union of peoples 114, 115, 119–20, 147, 342
    - as a union of political communities or republics 147, 323, 335, 342–3, 417, 466, 471, 493–4
    - as a union of states 343

Index 561

union treaties
  as foundation of political liberty in Lithuania 200, 206
  Lithuanian campaign to amend 172, 200–1, 204, 207, 330, 467
  role of in discussions over union 154, 173, 187, 191, 199–200, 206, 327, 332, 333–4, 411, 459, 463, 479, 483, 492, 493
  as a unitary commonwealth 494
  of Poland and Prussia (1454, 1466) 215–21; *see also* Prussia: Royal
    as accessory union 217, 338
    act of incorporation (1454) 215, 216, 217, 218, 341, 399
    autonomy of Prussia within 219, 220–1
    citizenship in 220
    consensual basis of 217–20, 335
    as dynastic union 217
    extension of Polish privileges to 219, 220
    as a fraternal union 399
    as league of two separate states 217
    as incorporating union *minus plena* 219
    participation of Prussians in Polish assemblies 220
    as personal union 217–18, 220
    as real union 218
    as reunification 217, 219
    ius indigenatus in 219
    negotiations for union (1454) 214–15
  of Poland and Saxony (1697–1763) 42
  of Poland-Lithuania and Livonia
    discussions over incorporation into Lithuania 446
    discussions over incorporation into Poland 446–7
    incorporation into both Poland and Lithuania 446, 492
  of Sweden and Norway (1815–1905) 43
United Kingdom 37, 42
United States of America 38, 45
Urban V (1310–70), pope 7
Urban VI (*c.*1318–89), pope 123

Vaidotas Kęstutaitis († after 1401) 93
Vaidutis, Jonas *see* Wajdut, Jan
Vaišvilkas (1223–67), grand duke of Lithuania 26
Valimantas (*c.*1345–99/1412), Lithuanian boyar 299
Valimantaitis, Jaunutis († 1432), palatine of Trakai 180, 299, 300
Valimantaitis, Kęsgaila *see* Kęsgaila, Mykolas Valimantaitis
Valimantaitis, Rumbaudas († 1432), marshal of the grand duchy of Lithuania 170, 180, 299, 300
Valdemar IV Atterdag (*c.*1320–75), king of Denmark 51

Varna, battle of (1444) 184, 191, 277, 278
Vasilii I (1371–1425), grand duke of Muscovy 80, 84–5, 100, 135, 282, 293
Vasilii II (1415–62), grand duke of Muscovy 135, 138, 142, 205, 282–3, 311–13
Vasilii III (1479–1533), grand duke of Muscovy 283, 313–14, 393, 411, 417, 447
Vasilii Kosoi (1421–48), prince of Zvenigorod 282
Vasyl Drutsky-Krasny 169
Vasyl Mykhailovych Narymuntovych, duke of Pinsk 50
Vasyl Semënovych, duke of Pinsk 294
Vaukavysk 4, 21, 49–50, 52, 67
Vedrosh river, battle of (1500) 315, 337
Velizh 448
Venice 27, 109, 184, 412
Vetulani, Adam 215, 394
Victoria (1819–1901), queen of Great Britain and Ireland 278
Vienna 213, 280, 387, 392, 407, 435, 441
Vilnius 4, 18, 27, 30, 33, 71–2, 77–8, 80, 85, 88, 92, 97, 99, 121, 148–9, 153–5, 160, 169, 171, 180, 185–6, 192, 199, 201, 282–3, 293, 301, 309–10, 313, 317–19, 321, 330–1, 334, 341, 344–5, 406–8, 418, 422, 434–5, 440–1, 447–8, 451–2, 457, 459–61, 486, 492
  cathedral of 71, 317, 344
  diocese of 71, 163, 315, 318, 409, 428
  duchy of 29, 50, 67, 78, 82, 172
  palatinate of 113, 118, 120–1, 160, 200, 291, 305, 341, 424, 427–9, 438, 475
Vilnius-Cracow union (1499) 334–7
Vilnius-Radom, treaty of (1401) 91–8, 111–12, 114–17, 122, 147, 152
Vinnitsa 84
Vistula, river 96, 99, 105, 224–5, 228, 377
Vitsebsk 21, 30, 72, 77, 84, 87, 169, 171, 189, 316, 321, 447
  confederation of (1562) 446–9, 453, 456, 459, 461
  petition calling for closer union 448–50, 452–3, 482, 489
  duchy of 29, 67, 84
Vladimir-Suzdal′ 25
  duchy of 20
Vladimiri, Paulus *see* Włodkowic, Paweł
Vogelsang, Heinrich von (*c.*1360–1415), bishop of Ermland 107
Voigt, Johannes (1786–1863), Prussian archivist and historian 144
Volhynia 13, 67, 84, 88, 165–9, 172–4, 176, 178, 189, 195, 200–1, 207–8, 214, 237, 268, 270, 280, 293, 302, 333, 408, 425, 428, 481, 489

Volhynia (cont.)
  as centre of Orthodox culture 487
  palatinate of 475, 484, 486, 487
    annexation of (1569) 482, 484–5,
      488–9, 491
  privilege of (1452) 207
Volodymyr 13, 84
Volodymyr II Monomakh (1053–1125), grand
  prince of Rus′ 20
Volodymyr Olherdovych (Algirdaitis) († c.1399),
  duke of Kyiv 24, 29, 82–4, 189,
  293, 295
Volodymyr the Great (958–1015), grand prince
  of Kyiv 20
Vorotynsk, duchy of 285
Vorotynsky family 313
Vorotynsky, prince Ivan († 1535) 285
Vorskla river, battle of (1399) 86, 90–1, 97,
  99, 166
Vygantas Algirdaitis († 1392) 4, 29, 50
Vysegrád 7
Vyshnevets, battle of (1512) 408
Vyshnevetsky, Kostiantyn († 1574) 487
Vytautas Kęstutaitis (1352/3–1430), grand duke
  of Lithuania 74–90, 106, 158–9,
  172, 179
  birth and early career 3, 29, 74–5
  baptisms 4, 50, 76
  and the Catholic church 83, 125, 163, 316–17
  character and reputation 75–6, 144–5,
    186, 202
  death 113, 134, 148–50, 153, 166, 282, 291
  family of 79, 80, 93–4, 122, 134, 142, 282,
    318, 376, 415
    patrimony of 79, 82, 93, 122–3
  foreign policy 85–6, 97, 100–1, 280, 414
    relations with Muscovy 85, 99, 100–1,
      107, 145, 282, 394, 414
    relations with the Teutonic Order 31,
      99–100, 105, 109, 110
    flights to Prussia (1382, 1390) 31, 76,
      79, 374
  and the government of Lithuania 84–5, 87,
    93, 161–2, 189, 192, 201, 207,
    291, 292, 302, 307, 319, 330, 421,
    463; see also Lithuania, grand duchy
    of: government and political system;
    Lithuania and the union: the
    Vytautan system
  and the Lithuanian noble elite 76, 80, 83,
    91, 127, 148, 201, 292, 296,
    298–9, 302, 332, 416, 421
    clientele 85, 119, 148, 180, 186, 187,
      292, 299, 300
  and plans to raise Lithuania to royal
    status 86, 89–91, 102, 143–5,
    148, 188, 411, 415–16, 417
  and Ruthenia 84–5, 160, 162, 292, 308,
    316, 318
  legacy of 151, 189, 291, 292
  and the Lithuanian chronicles 413–14
  and the Orthodox church 163, 164
  and Poland 149, 268, 375
    and Polish politicians 97, 319–20
    and the Polish throne 97
  political aims of 86, 88, 91, 97, 282, 29
    as dynastic politician 80, 97, 122, 134,
      137, 282, 415, 421
    relations with Jagiełło 30–1, 34–5, 74–90,
      92, 97, 100, 134–50, 148, 172,
      180, 202, 205, 217, 414, 415
  succession to 134, 151–4, 415
  titles and status of 86, 93, 111, 113, 154,
    415, 463
  and the union 111, 113, 115–16, 118–20,
    127, 134, 151, 205, 331, 332,
    334–5, 339, 415, 479, 492, 493
Vytenis (c.1260–1315/16), grand duke of
  Lithuania 20, 26, 414–15

Wacław (c.1293–1336), duke of Płock 28
Wajdut, Jan (1365–1402), rector of Cracow
  University 318
Wales, principality of 39, 42, 61
  act of incorporation into England (1536) 61
Wallachia, principality of 174
Wallenrode, Friedrich von († 1410) marshal of
  the Teutonic Order 103, 106
Wallerstein, Immanuel 243
Wapowski, Bernard (1450–1535), historian and
  cartographer 366
Wars
  Golub war: Poland-Lithuania against the
    Teutonic Order (1419) 126
  Great Northern War (1700–21) 217
  Great war: Poland-Lithuania against the
    Teutonic Order
    (1409–11) 99–108
  Hunger war: Poland-Lithuania against the
    Teutonic Order (1414) 126
  Livonian War (1558–83) 302, 446, 447, 456,
    457, 461, 462, 471, 480
  Lutsk war between Poland and Lithuania
    (1431) 166, 168–9
  Lithuanian civil war (1432–7) 170, 177, 185,
    188, 280, 285, 421
  Lithuanian-Mazovian war (1441–4) 189–90,
    193
  Lithuanian-Muscovite wars (1492–1537) 285,
    291, 296, 307–10, 315, 323, 330,
    337–8, 340, 345–6, 359, 363, 370,
    407, 418, 420
  Polish war against the Ottoman Empire
    (1497) 289, 332–3, 337, 354, 378,
    383, 397–8
  Polish war against the Teutonic Order
    (1519–21) 368, 393–4, 396,
    400, 454

Index

Priests' war: Poland against the Teutonic
 Order (1478–9) 230, 385
Thirteen Years War (1454–66), 222–30,
 237, 240, 268, 271–2, 288,
 385, 386
 financial problems of Order 226–7, 228
 Lithuania and 222, 225, 230
 papal support for Order in 222–3
 resilience of Order 222, 225
 war against the Teutonic Order (1422) 140
 war against the Teutonic Order (1431) 168
 war of retreat: Poland-Lithuania against the
  Teutonic Order (1419) 126
Warsaw 105, 366, 377, 378, 379, 457, 460,
 471, 492
 duchy of 16, 375
 sejm (1563–4) 461–8
Warta
 river 102
 statute of (1423) 140, 254, 287
Wartislaw VIII (1373–1415), duke of
 Wolgast 104
Wasilewski, Tadeusz 74–5
Watzenrode, Lucas (1447–1512), bishop of
 Ermland 385, 387–90
Wawrzyniec of Kalinowa († 1453), royal
 marshal 133
Wawrzynczyk, Alina 258–9
Wayknecht, Peter († after 1507), abbot of
 Sagan, Silesian chronicler 74
Wenzel († 1488), duke of Sagan 131
Wenzel of Luxembourg (1361–1419), king of
 Bohemia, king of the Romans 33,
 80, 104, 132, 136
Werden, Johann von (1495–1554), mayor of
 Danzig 401
Western Ruthenianism, doctrine of 44–5
White Ruthenia 21
Wieliczka 267, 356, 363, 378
Wielkopolska
 duchy of 5
 province of 6, 10, 79, 94, 96, 102, 119, 178,
  194, 231, 240, 268–9, 275, 344,
  367, 369, 378–9, 386, 438,
  439, 463
 economy of 248–9, 250, 259, 427
 nobility of 64, 65, 235, 241
  as heartland of middling szlachta 64, 234
 noble levy of 223, 225, 234, 236,
  239, 281
 political structure of 238, 288, 341, 352
 opposition to Angevin rule 11–14
 opposition to domination of
  Małopolska 12–13, 177, 207
 and the sejm 368
 royal domain in 356
 and Prussia 214, 235
 Reformation in 442
Wieluń 251

edict of (1424) 140
Wierzbicki, Wiktoryn († 1588), bishop of
 Lutsk 483, 487
Wieżgajło, Mikołaj († 1533), bishop of
 Kyiv 405
Wilhelm von Hohenzollern (1493–1568),
 archbishop of Riga 446
William von Habsburg (1370–1406) 8, 10, 17,
 34, 35, 47, 50, 109
Wilson, Woodrow (1856–1924), president of
 the United States of America 44
Wirszyłła family 434
Wiskont, Antoni (Viskantas, Antanas) 118
Wiślica 14, 239, 288–9
Wiśliczka, Mikołaj, tutor to Jadwiga
 Jagiellon 122
Wiszna 288
Wittenberg 371, 443
Wittelsbach, Georg von (1455–1503), duke of
 Bavaria-Landshut 321
Wizna, duchy then territory of 16, 375, 376
Wladislaus of Oppeln (1225–81), duke of
 Oppeln 8, 12, 80, 99
Władysław I († 1455), duke of Płock 131, 195,
 375
Władysław I Łokietek (1260/1261–1333), king
 of Poland 4, 11, 12, 28, 62, 286
Władysław II († 1462), duke of
 Mazovia 375, 376
Władysław II (Ulászló II) (1456–1516), king of
 Bohemia, king of Hungary 273,
 278, 280–2, 327–8, 330–1,
 337–41, 344–5, 396, 433
Władysław III Laskonogi (Spindleshanks)
 († 1231), duke of Wielkopolska,
 duke of 27
Władysław III (1424–44), king of Poland and
 Hungary, supreme duke of
 Lithuania 132–3, 137–40, 143,
 153–4, 191, 193, 200, 213, 235,
 268, 274, 277–8, 311, 355,
 375, 392
 and alienations of royal land 225, 232, 267
 crisis of government in Poland under 182,
  184–5, 190
 election as king of Poland 177–8, 199
 as king of Hungary 182–5, 187
 and Lithaunia 178–9, 185–90
 minority of 178, 287
Władysław the White († 1388), duke of
 Gniewkowo 10, 11
Włodkowic, Paweł (Paulus Vladimiri)
 (c.1370–1435), rector of Cracow
 University 117, 123–6, 175, 176
Woda of Szczekocin, Piotr († 1454), vice-
 chancellor of Poland 224, 268,
 269, 271
Wohyń 477
Wojciechowski, Zygmunt 344, 361

Wolff, Józef 313
Wolfram, Piotr († *c.*1415), procurator of the diocese of Cracow 123
Wołłowicz, Hrehory († 1577), palatine of Smolensk 451, 483
Wołłowicz, Ostafi († 1587), treasurer and vice-chancellor of Lithuania, palatine of Vilnius 428, 480, 481, 483, 487, 488
Wolsey, Thomas (1473–1530), archbishop of York, cardinal 387
Wolski, Paweł (1487–1546), grand chancellor of Poland, bishop of Poznań 373
Wyczański, Andrzej 244–5, 250, 251, 261
Wysz, Piotr (1354–1414), bishop of Cracow 101
Wyszogród, duchy then territory of 16, 375–6

Zaberezhynsky family 321
Zaberezhynsky, Jan († 1508), marshal of Lithuania, palatine of Trakai 304, 314, 333, 338, 342, 345
Zaberezhynsky, Jan Janovych († 1538), palatine of Navahrudak 452
Zaborowski, Stanisław († 1529) 360–3
Zahorovsky, Vasyl († 1580) 487
Zakroczym, duchy then territory of 16, 375
Žalgiris, battle of *see* Tannenberg: battle of
Zaremba, Wawrzyniec († after 1433), castellan of Sieradz 170
Zaslav, duchy of 84
Zaslavsky/Zasławski family 321–2, 434
Zaslavsky, Mykhailo Ivanovych (*c.*1450–1529), duke of Msitslau 296
Zator *see* Oświęcim and Zator, duchies of
Zawisza the Black (*c.*1379–1428), Polish knight 136–7
Zawkrze, duchy then territory of 375–6

Zbarazky family 322
Zbarazky, Piotr (1548–1603/4) 487
Zbarazky, Stefan (*c.*1518–85), palatine of Trakai 483, 487
Zbarazky, Władysław (1540–82) 462
Zborowski family 322
Zborowski, Marcin (1492–1565), castellan of Cracow 443, 467
Zehmen (Czema) family 386
Zehmen, Achacius von (*c.*1485–1565), palatine of Marienburg 401, 465
Zhydachiv 84
Zinnenberg, Bernard von († 1470), Moravian mercenary 223, 227
Žižka, Jan (*c.*1360–1424), radical Hussite leader 137
Złotoryja castle 10, 99
Zöllner von Rottenstein, Konrad (*c.*1325–90), grand master of the Teutonic Order 10, 31, 79
Zólyom 10
Žygimantas Kęstutaitis (1365–1440), grand duke of Lithuania 50, 79, 192, 199, 205, 206
  assassination of 172–3, 180–2, 185–6, 188, 192, 201, 292, 421
  character of 180–1, 187, 293
  as heir to Vytautas 93, 134, 138, 152
  as grand duke of Lithuania 173–4, 179–80, 205, 292–3, 299, 319
  foreign policy of 173, 375
  Lithuanian opposition to 180, 185–7, 292, 421
  and Poland 173–4, 178–80, 186, 205, 339
  relations with Ruthenians 170, 173–6, 180, 293, 421
  seizure of power 170–2, 199, 293, 329
  supporters of 180, 185, 293, 299

Printed and bound by CPI Group (UK) Ltd, Croydon, CR0 4YY